Acclaim for BENITA EISLER's

Byron

"[Byron's story] has never been so well handled as it is now by Benita Eisler. . . . The tale itself is always fascinating, occasionally astonishing, and intermittently horrific; the telling is uniformly shrewd, confident and non-judgmental."
—Andrew Motion, *Financial Times*

"A thrilling, enthralling, and sensitively detailed account of the life of one of England's most talented and troubled artists."
—*The Atlanta Journal-Constitution*

"The strength of Eisler's masterful biography lies in her rare insight into how the embattled poet distilled from his life of scandal and betrayal a literary art of soaring power. . . . The many readers still attracted to this complex and multi-faceted poet will find no truer portrait." —*Booklist*

"Insightful . . . an admirably full and well-balanced account of an extraordinarily crowded and dramatic life."
—*The Boston Globe*

"Perceptive . . . readable and richly documented."
—*The Economist*

"Lively . . . a page-turner. . . . [Byron's] seesawing moods and volatile allegiances . . . are reported with sensitive understanding."
—*The New York Times Book Review*

ALSO BY BENITA EISLER

O'Keeffe and Stieglitz: An American Romance

BENITA EISLER

Byron

Benita Eisler is the author of *O'Keeffe and Stieglitz: An American Romance*. She lives in New York City.

Byron

Byron

Child of Passion, Fool of Fame

BENITA EISLER

VINTAGE BOOKS

A DIVISION OF RANDOM HOUSE, INC.

NEW YORK

FIRST VINTAGE BOOKS EDITION, MAY 2000

Copyright © 1999 by Benita Eisler

All rights reserved under International and Pan-American Copyright Conventions.
Published in the United States by Vintage Books, a division of Random House,
Inc., New York, and simultaneously in Canada by Random House of Canada
Limited, Toronto. Originally published in hardcover in the United States by
Alfred A. Knopf, a division of Random House, Inc., New York, in 1999.

Vintage and colophon are registered trademarks of Random House, Inc.

Owing to limitations of space, all acknowledgments for permission to reprint
previously published and unpublished material may be found following the index.

The Library of Congress has cataloged the Knopf edition as follows:
Eisler, Benita.
Byron—child of passion, fool of fame / Benita Eisler. — 1st ed.
p.   cm.
Includes bibliographical references and index.
ISBN 0-679-41299-9 (alk. paper)
1. Byron, George Gordon Byron, Baron, 1788–1824.
2. Poets, English—19th century—Biography. I. Title.
PR4381.E37 1999
821'.7—dc21
[B]   98-35261
CIP

Vintage ISBN: 0-679-74085-6

Book design by Dorothy S. Baker

www.vintagebooks.com

Printed in the United States of America
10 9 8 7 6 5 4 3 2 1

FOR GLORIA LOOMIS

Censure no more shall brand my humble name
The child of passion and the fool of fame

Cancelled lines from

"Childish Recollections" (1806)

Contents

PART THREE: EXILE INTO HERO

Photographic sections follow pages 208 and 432

Illustrations

William and Caroline Lamb in bed with Augustus hovering above, sketch by Lady Caroline Lamb from her notebooks (Reproduced by permission of Hertfordshire Archives and Local Studies. Ref D/ELB F67)

Augusta Leigh, drawing by Sir George Hayter (Fotomas Index)

Gold gimbal ring belonging to Lord Byron, c. 1813 (The Pierpont Morgan Library, New York. MA56. Photograph: Joseph Zehavi)

Photographic section following page 432

Annabella Milbanke, 1812, engraving after miniature by Sir George Hayter (Fotomas Index)

Lady Melbourne, oil on canvas by Sir Thomas Lawrence (Melbourne Hall. Photograph: Derbyshire Countryside Ltd.)

Jane Elizabeth, Countess of Oxford, 1797, oil on wood by John Hoppner (Tate Gallery, London, 1999)

Annabella Milbanke, Lady Byron, oval miniature on ivory, mounted in gold as a brooch, by unknown artist (Reproduced by permission of the Keepers and Governors of Harrow School. Photograph: National Portrait Gallery, London)

George Gordon, Lord Byron, 1817, detail from original plaster sculpture by Bertel Thorvaldsen (Thorvaldsens Museum, Copenhagen. Photograph: Ole Woldbye)

Villa Diodati, engraving by Edward Finden after drawing by William Purser from *Illustrations of the Life and Works of Lord Byron*, by Edward and William Finden, John Murray, 1833 (City of Nottingham Museums; Newstead Abbey)

Percy Bysshe Shelley, wooden bust attributed to Marianne Leigh Hunt (Reproduced by permission of the Provost and Fellows of Eton College)

Claire Clairmont, 1819, oil on canvas by Amelia Curran (City of Nottingham Museums; Newstead Abbey)

Allegra, Venice, 1818, unknown artist (John Murray Collection)

Countess Teresa Guiccioli, engraving by T. A. Dean after painting by W. Brockedon (Mary Evans Picture Library)

Letter from Allegra to Lord Byron, Bagnacavallo, Italy, 28 September 1821, recto and verso (The Pierpont Morgan Library, New York [MA52])

Missolonghi, c. 1824, engraving by Edward Finden after drawing by William Purser from *Illustrations of the Life and Works of Lord Byron*, Edward and William Finden, John Murray, 1833 (Fotomas Index)

Byron wearing Greek helmet, lithograph by Bouvier (City of Nottingham Museums; Newstead Abbey)

George Gordon Noel, Lord Byron, 6th Baron, 1822, oil on canvas by William Edward West (Scottish National Portrait Gallery)

Letter following page 839

Letter from Byron to Annabella, 23 November 1814 (Earl of Lytton, MS. Dep. Lovelace Byron 39, fols. 148r–149v. Photograph: Bodleian Library, Oxford)

PART ONE

Becoming Byron

CHAPTER I

"Shades of the Dead! Have I Not Heard Your Voices?"

O N MONDAY, May 17, 1824, near noon, six men gathered in the high-ceilinged drawing room at 50 Albemarle Street, off Piccadilly, in a house that served as both home and office to the publisher John Murray. For days the group had been quarreling among themselves. Alliances shifted. Messages flew back and forth, and meetings between pairs continued through the morning. Once they were finally assembled, an argument flared between two of their number, John Cam Hobhouse, a rising young parliamentarian from a wealthy Bristol family, and Thomas Moore, a Dublin-born poet and grocer's son. Angry words threatened to turn into physical violence. Finally, the decision of the host prevailed, and calm was restored. Murray then asked his sixteen-year-old son to join them. Introduced as heir to his father's business, the boy was invited to witness a momentous event. A servant appeared, carrying two bound manuscript volumes. While the group drew closer to the fire blazing in the grate, two others, Wilmot Horton and Colonel Doyle, took the books and, tearing them apart, fed the pages, covered with handwriting familiar to all those present, to the crackling flames. Within minutes, the memoirs of George Gordon, sixth Lord Byron, were reduced to a mound of ashes.

Byron had been dead for one month to the day. The ship carrying the poet's embalmed body (vital organs removed and packed separately) had taken four weeks to sail from Greece to England. In the interval, furious debates had exposed enmities old and new among those who were to be present at the burning of the manuscript. Quarreling had flared over the ownership of the manuscript, intensifying with arguments about potential damage to the poet's already seamy reputation and the pain his unexpurgated memories would cause his former wife, their daughter, and his half sister. Each of the six men had his own stake in the dispute. John Cam Hobhouse, a Whig M.P. and Byron's executor and oldest friend, wanted only to sanitize the poet's name for posterity. In the last years of his life, Byron had given his memoirs to his fellow poet Tom Moore. The needy Moore had, with Byron's approval, promptly sold the copyright to Murray. Then, at the burning, he tried to save the manuscript. But it was too late. Finally, Horton and Doyle, the two responsible for the actual destruction of the volumes, represented the interests of Lady Byron, the poet's estranged wife and the mother of his child, and his half sister, Augusta Leigh, respectively.

"The most timid of God's booksellers,"[1] Byron had once called Murray, his publisher and now enthusiastic host of the auto-da-fé. Still, the decision to destroy the most personal words of his best-selling author (which, in the event, Murray had not even read), weighed against the enormous profit potential of publishing the memoirs, underlines the fear that the known facts of Byron's life inspired in those who loved him—and their horror of revelations yet unknown.

BYRON'S FAME as a poet and his notoriety as a man were one; the scandals of his life—whoring, marriage, adultery, incest, sodomy—became the text or subtext of his poems, made more shocking by the poet's cynicism shading into blasphemy. The heroes of the poems might be pirates or princes, but Byron's voice—the passionate sorrowing youth turned world-weary libertine—made his works instant bestsellers. Editions of his first advertisement for himself, *Childe Harold's Pilgrimage,* sold out within three days. And this was not even the most frankly autobiographical of Byron's works. Penned from self-imposed exile in Italy, published in eagerly awaited installments, *Don Juan* delighted London gossipmongers with plentiful allusions to the scandal surrounding the poet's divorce from his young wife of one year and his subsequent flight from English "hypocrisy and cant." In the few years left to him, Byron added the glamour of revolutionary politics to his erotic and literary engagements. In exile, he joined the underground secret society called the Carbonari in the struggle to rid Italy of the Austrians, before dying at Missolonghi, bled to death by his doctors, while training troops for the liberation of Greece. Mourned throughout the world, the poet would not have shared the belief that his end was untimely. He had lived so hard and fast, he said, that before his death at age thirty-six, he felt himself to be an old man.

Indeed, the brief arc of his life spanned an era whose turbulence mirrored the poet's own stormy existence. In 1788, the year of Byron's birth, George III succumbed to the first attack of madness, the violent symptoms of which required the appointment of his oldest son, the Prince of Wales, as Regent. The King regained his reason the following year and resumed power, but already the high living "Prinnie" and his dissolute friends had changed the tone of the court. Twenty years before he was officially declared Prince Regent, George Frederick Augustus of Hanover's indulgences in food, drink, gambling, and women, along with more durable interests in architecture and decor, ushered in the glittering froth of brilliance, luxury, and vice we know as the Regency. Its sensibility—at once restless, sensual, melancholy, and exuberant— might be characterized by a term invented a hundred years later to describe a strangely similar spirit: *fin-de-siècle*.

In 1789, the year after Byron was born, the French Revolution fired the dreams—and fueled the nightmares—of all Europe. Its bloody overthrow of the old order was the crucial event that continued to haunt Byron's generation, shaping his choice of heroes and villains among his elders. Charles James Fox, the leader of the radical Whig opposition and the idol of Byron's youth, had declared the fall of the Bastille "the greatest and best event in the history of the world." For the Tory government, however, in power for most of Byron's lifetime, the French Revolution gave legitimacy to the politics of reaction. The excesses of the Terror turned fiery young republican sympathizers among the first generation of Romantic poets, notably Wordsworth and Southey, into middle-aged monarchists, reviled by Byron as turncoat opportunists.

Fear of revolutionary contagion provided the excuse for repressive measures; in 1794 habeas corpus was suspended, the first in a series of acts amputating the civil rights of Englishmen. Censorship and spying became the order of the day; any form of association, especially among the dispossessed, could be prosecuted as a crime. Starting in 1793, when the Girondist government declared war on England, patriotism was invoked to justify further curtailing of individual freedoms. The political reality that permitted the Regency to waltz on unafraid was that England had become a police state. Byron, the newly crowned king of London drawing rooms in 1814, saw clearly that as a poet who was also a satirist and social critic, as a peer who spoke out for the rights of starving weavers or Irish Catholics, he would not long be indulged for his youth, talent, and title.

War with France began when Byron was five years old; it would continue until 1815, when he was twenty-seven. Like that of other ardent youths throughout Europe, the poet's political consciousness was shaped by an idealized image of Napoleon as the personification of heroic conquest in the name of republican principles. Besides, for the adolescent rebel, Tory England's demonized enemy was a natural ally.

Less consciously, Byron absorbed another Napoleonic lesson: The little corporal who declared himself Emperor was the herald of a new era, the age of the self-made man.

In England, too, this new breed was increasingly prominent. The war with France had galvanized a sluggish economy, ushering in the first phase of the Industrial Revolution, which would change the face of England. The first of England's dark satanic mills helped to float the Regency extravaganza. While the poor suffered more, a new class of entrepreneur-inventors—ironmasters and coal barons, pottery manufacturers and bankers—rode to dazzling fortunes. Their sons, like the two brilliant Peel brothers (one of whom became Prime Minister), were among Lord Byron's few commoner classmates at Harrow. And there would be more. Great landowning grandees were still the most visible stars on the brilliant stage of the Regency, but new money and talent were joining the featured players.

It was a febrile age. Social, political, and cultural certainties were shifting, like tectonic plates, under the feet of young men starting out in life. Mobility, then as now, had its price. The pressures of public life destroyed individuals as never before. Between 1790 and 1820, nineteen members of Parliament committed suicide and twenty others went mad; two of those who took their own lives, Sir Samuel Romilly and Sir Samuel Whitbread, were closely associated with Byron. "In every class there is the same taut neurotic quality," the historian J. H. Plumb observed, "the fantastic gambling and drinking, the riots, brutality and violence, and everywhere and always a constant sense of death."[2]

BYRON WAS a child of his age and subject to all its fissures. The great Regency portraitist Sir Thomas Lawrence met the poet only once, but where others found simply beauty, the painter saw all the conflicts of Byron's character: "its keen and rapid genius, its pale intelligence, its profligacy, and its bitterness; its original symmetry distorted by the passions, his laugh of mingled merriment and scorn; the forehead clear and open, the brow boldly prominent, the eyes bright and dissimilar, the nose finely cut, and the nostril acutely formed; the mouth well made, but wide and contemptuous even in its smile, falling singularly at the corners, and its vindictive and disdainful expression heightened by the massive firmness of the chin, which springs at once from the centre of the full under-lip; the hair dark and curling but irregular in its growth; all this presents to you the poet and the man; and the general effect is heightened by a thin spare form, and, as you may have heard, by a deformity of limb."[3]

Heir to instability, Byron clung to the certainty of inherited land

and ancient title, even as he vowed to seize the rewards of talent and energy.

"The way to *riches*, to *Greatness*, lies before me," Byron wrote to his mother at age fifteen. "I can, I will cut myself a path through the world or perish."[4]

Heroic words proclaimed by a poor scion of the peerage, they resonate like a battle cry. Throughout a dispossessed childhood, his blood thrilled to tales of the first Byrons, Radulfus (Ralph) de Burun and his brother, reputed to have arrived in Britain as liegemen of William the Conqueror:

> Erneis, Radulphus—eight-and-forty manors
>
> . . . .
>
> Were their reward for following Billy's banners;[5]

he wrote of his ancestors, inventing the imposing number of residences out of whole cloth; no one knows precisely where the brothers settled. For their loyalty in the service of William I, they were, however, rewarded with landholdings in the north of England substantial enough to warrant mention in the Domesday Book. By the time of Henry II, the spelling of the family name had become for all time Byron, and with the reign of Henry VIII, the Byron settlement in Nottingham was recorded. That monarch's largesse accounted for the establishment of the first Lord Byron at Newstead Abbey, the site associated with the Byrons from then on.

Newstead Abbey had been founded four hundred years earlier by Henry II, the murderer of Thomas à Becket, for the Order of Canons Regular, known as the "black canons" after the color of their robes. In the course of the following centuries, the order had erected an elegant Gothic church of the soft, gray local granite, along with an adjoining priory, whose handsome cloister flanked an open court with a central fountain. At the time of the dissolution of the monasteries, Henry VIII sold the lands to John Byron of Colewyke for £810. Sir John, the first Byron proprietor, lost no time in transforming the cloistral into the baronial. He seems to have been in the vanguard of the later Romantic taste for ruins; he retained the southern side of the nave as one wall of his own residence, and using only what he needed of the church and priory to repair his buildings, he allowed the remains to fall into picturesque disrepair.

The same Sir John continued his sacrilegious ways by getting with child a neighbor's wife. His illegitimate son from this union could only inherit Newstead by deed of gift, but the seigneur did what was needed to wipe the bar sinister from his heir's coat of arms by marrying the boy's mother. Three years after the lands had passed to his son, in 1576, the new owner was knighted by Elizabeth I. As the second Lord Byron, he was also the first to be immortalized—as "Little Sir John of the Great Beard."

The fourth lord married three times. His third wife was Frances Berkeley, the poet's great-grandmother. Lord Byron and Lady Frances's second-born, John, the poet's grandfather, joined the navy, rising from commodore to vice-admiral. He survived a shipwreck off Patagonia, and in his *Narrative*,[6] published years later, he described the horrifying experience of being forced to eat the skin and paws of a favorite dog. Byron pillaged this last gruesome episode for the shipwreck scene in *Don Juan*. He predeceased his older brother, William, the granduncle of the poet, who became the fifth Lord Byron at the age of fourteen. William too joined the navy, but, after being rescued from a vessel that foundered with all other hands on board lost, he resigned his commission. Remaining on land, William soon acquired a less heroic reputation and sobriquet: the Wicked Lord. During his tenure at Newstead Abbey it became known as Folly Castle, after the model château he built on the lake, alleged to be the scene of licentious *fêtes champêtres*.

In his middle forties, the Wicked Lord added the notoriety of being a murderer to his reputation as a whoremaster. On January 26, 1765, in the course of a dinner in London at a tavern in Pall Mall, the Wicked Lord fell into a dispute with a neighbor and kinsman, Viscount Chaworth of Annesley Hall. Where the fault lay remains uncertain, but it is a matter of record that in an empty upper room of the tavern, lit by a single candle, Lord Byron ran his shortened sword through his opponent's belly.

From a brooding sense of guilt and grievance, the fifth lord descended into episodic madness. Dark tales were told in Nottinghamshire: how his lordship shot his coachman dead over a trifle, then, heaving the corpse into the carriage with his wife, took the lucklesss servant's place on the box and drove off. Other rumors claimed that, when displeased, he would throw Lady Byron into the pond.

When he sank into debt, he stripped what was left of the forests for salable timber. Then, in an illegal act that would cast a long shadow over his grand-nephew's life, he leased the most valuable property in the Byron family holdings, twenty thousand acres of coal mines in Rochdale in Lancashire, for £60 annual rent.

John Byron, the first of the vice-admiral's nine children and the father of the poet, was born in 1756. Known as "Mad Jack," he seemed, from an early age, destined to turn his own father's strengths into weaknesses, and the elder's weaknesses into vices. When a few terms at Westminster proved him to be no scholar, he was sent to a military school near Paris; there he acquired the extravagant tastes that would keep him in lifelong debt. Heartless and swaggeringly handsome in his Guardsman's uniform, armed with elegant French and boundless sexual appetite and unburdened by scruples of any sort, he seduced chambermaids and countesses. Since his parents were no longer able or willing to pay his gambling debts, it was said that he turned his sexual prowess to good account, charging the better-off of his lovers for services rendered.[7] This proved an uncertain way to finance his needs. It was time to find a rich and well-connected wife.

In the summer of 1778 the twenty-two-year old captain of the Guards met his match in one of the reigning beauties of the London salons. The Marchioness of Carmarthen, wife of the Marquess (later fifth Duke of Leeds), was born Amelia d'Arcy, Baroness Conyers, and Countess of Mertola. A *coup de foudre* struck Amelia when she first saw the alluring Jack Byron. Lunch in the country was followed by overnight flight, with the outraged Marquess in pursuit. When the lovers eluded him, he locked his wife out of their house in town.

Now that disgrace had made Amelia his responsibility, it might have been expected that Captain Byron's ardor would have cooled. His mistress, however, had attractions beyond the erotic. Only months before their first meeting, the death of her father, the Earl of Holderness, had left his only child an heiress with a lifetime income of £4,000 a year. As soon as Captain Byron found lodgings for them, the Marchioness sent for her clothes and jewels, requesting in the note to her husband that he include the new vis-à-vis he had recently given her; no gentleman would deprive even an errant wife of her carriage. After ordering his coachmaker to paint out his coat of arms, the vehicle was duly delivered along with Amelia's other belongings. The lovers settled in France, dividing their time between Chantilly and Paris, where they were married in 1779.

Of the three children born to Amelia and Jack Byron, only the last, Augusta, the poet's half sister, born in 1783, survived infancy. Shortly after her birth, her mother died, at the age of twenty-nine. Both the cause and even the place of Amelia's death remain mysterious.* She is variously held to have died of consumption, of a fever contracted from going hunting too soon after childbirth, and, more ominously, of "illusage" at the hands of her husband.[8]

---

*Some reports have her dying in Paris, but her death certificate gives London.

Byron later defended his father, then long dead, against lingering rumors that his "brutal conduct" had been the cause of his first wife's death: "It is not by 'brutality' that a young Officer in the Guards seduces and carries off a Marchioness, and marries two heiresses. It is true that he was a very handsome man, which goes a great way," his son said knowingly.[9]

The widower may have been grieved by the untimely loss of his wife and the mother of his daughter, then less than a year old. More certainly, he mourned the loss of Amelia's £4,000 income, which ceased immediately on her death. Disinherited by his father and accustomed now to grand living, his most pressing task was to land another heiress. Every fortune hunter knew where the pickings were best. In the spring of 1785 the expatriate returned to England and went to Bath.

Catherine Gordon of Gight, near Aberdeen, had been orphaned for three years. She came to Bath that spring at the invitation of her uncle, Admiral Robert Duff, and his wife, who had a house there. Now twenty, Catherine's corpulence made her look much older and gave her the rolling gait that some were unkind enough to describe as a waddle. Her education was even sketchier than that deemed necesary for most girls, and she was as socially awkward as she was plain. But as the thirteenth Laird of Gight, Catherine was the sole heir to a fortune worth close to £30,000 in Aberdeen bank shares, salmon-fishing rights, and lands, including a castle of her own.

From its primitive past to the sixteenth century, the history of the Gordons of Gight is drenched in bloodshed. By the eighteenth century, the violence of the males of the family seemed to have turned inward, becoming black depression. In January 1760 Catherine Gordon's maternal grandfather had drowned himself in the icy waters of the Ythan River rushing just below the castle walls. Thirteen months after the death of Catherine's middle sister, Abercromby, in 1777, her father's body was found in the Bath Canal. A year later in 1780, Margaret, the youngest, too, was dead. The deaths of her two sisters were so painful that Catherine Byron never told her son of their existence. Byron always believed his mother to have been an only child. Then, in 1782, two years after little Margaret's death, Catherine's mother died. Within five years she had lost her entire family. Admiral Duff's invitation to Bath early in 1785 seemed a timely one.

A few months after her arrival, on May 13, 1785, Catherine Gordon and John Byron were married by the rector of St. Michael's Church, Bath. Before their deaths, the bride's parents had included a clause in their wills stipulating that in the event of female succession to the Gight estates, their daughter must either marry a Gordon or her husband

must take the Gordon name. Jack Byron might now be John Byron
Gordon, but he was, as ever, broke and hounded by creditors. For the
moment, his wife could not withdraw from her inheritance the large
sums needed by her husband to pay his debts. He tried dunning his
father's bankers, to no avail; the vice-admiral, who was to die a few
months later, had been in earnest when he disinherited his wastrel son.

Catherine's troubles were just beginning. Without a marriage settlement, her husband's debts had now become her responsibility. Lacking
ready cash, she had no choice but to pay the most pressing of Jack's
creditors by selling off part of the lands of Gight. One farm was sold;
forests were cut down and their timber marketed. Shares in the
Aberdeen Banking Company and the salmon fisheries went next; then
another £8,000 mortgage was taken out on the estate. Jack Byron still
harbored delusions of being a local grandee, attempting to influence district politics; as the final humiliation, in the parliamentary election of
1786 his vote was disallowed.

In March the following notice appeared in the *Aberdeen Journal*:

> To be Selt
> The Mains of Gight
> Enquiries to Mr. Byron Gordon, Gight

Later that spring, possibly in April, the Byrons left for England.

As soon as Jack surfaced in London, he was seized for debt and
hauled off to King's Bench prison, from which he was bailed out for
£176 by his tailor. In August, the couple rented a house in South
Warnborough, Hampshire, where Catherine remained with her maid
while Jack kept moving to stay ahead of the bailiffs while attempting to
pry money from his mother's family. The following year, the earl of
Aberdeen bought the castle of Gight and all its lands for £17,850.
But a relative of Catherine's reported that "Every penny of the purchase price . . . except £1,222.10 and £3,000 reserved for Mrs. B's own
use, and put out at mortgage, was swallowed up by Capt. Byron's
creditors."[10]

Fear of her husband seeps through Catherine's letters. "I should not
wish [that] Mr. Byron should know that I wrote or spoke to anybody on
this subject, because if he did he would never forgive me."[11]

Soon she had further reason to be anxious. In April 1787 Catherine
was pregnant. By July 18, the couple had settled in a house in Cowes,
on the Isle of Wight. True to form, Captain Byron did not linger in his
new home; in July he set off for Paris. Before leaving, he had managed
to pry from Catherine £700 out of £1,000 she had just received from

her estate. Eight weeks later he had spent it all, leaving a new trail of debts in his wake.

Within months, the enormously pregnant woman journeyed to Chantilly to join her husband. Captain Byron may have welcomed his wife as a bearer of fresh supplies of cash. He also needed a stepmother for Augusta, his daughter by Amelia. And Chantilly was conveniently near Paris, making it an easy matter to leave for nightly diversions in town.

As her time drew near, Catherine, accompanied by her maid and Augusta, made her way slowly back to England. Still in danger of arrest, Jack Byron remained in France. Arriving in London, she delivered the four-year-old girl to her grandmother, the dowager Countess of Holderness—the first of a series of grand foster homes for Augusta, motherless and with a fugitive father.

Catherine Byron had no rich relations to welcome her and her unborn child. In mid-December, six weeks before her baby was born, she moved into a furnished first-floor back drawing room, above a per-fumer's shop at 16 Holles Street, Cavendish Square. Knowing no one in London, Catherine only had her maid as company, and her condition, along with lack of space, made any prospect of social life unlikely. New Year's Day 1788, however, brought a surprise visitor, John Leslie. Describing himself as "a very near relation" (probably a first cousin), Leslie had just been appointed by the Edinburgh commissioners of the Gight estate to supply the Byrons with the minimum funds needed for their expenses, while a trust was being established to prevent further erosion of the principal. The commissioners also asked Leslie to report on the welfare of the twenty-two-year-old mother-to-be, whose finances, like the rest of her life, seemed to be in chaos. Catherine's state moved her visitor to immediate action: "She tells me that she expects to be brought to bed in two or three weeks & wished for some Money. I gave her a draft on my Banker for Twenty Guineas on your acct, . . ." Leslie reported to Edinburgh, adding a skeptical postscript, "She tells me she expects Mr. Byron in London every day—and that he goes to Scotland on business with you."[12] The next day Catherine herself wrote to the commissioners' London agent to assure but also to warn him: "I don't want much and if there was to be large sums, it would only be thrown away as it was before."[13] The passive fatalism of her tone reveals that Jack Byron was back.

Just before the baby's birth, a family friend from Aberdeen intro-duced Catherine to a London lawyer. Her association with John Hanson, a solicitor practicing at 6 Chancery Lane, was to cast a long shadow over her unborn son's life.

On Tuesday, January 22, Catherine Byron was delivered of a son, named for her father, George Gordon. Her labor was long and difficult. The baby was born with a caul* and a malformed right foot.

For Byron, his deformed foot became the crucial catastrophe of his life. He saw it as the mark of satanic connection, referring to himself as *le diable boiteux*, the lame devil. At the same time, he persisted in blaming his mother for the abnormality, citing her "excess of delicacy"[14] during the period immediately preceding the delivery. This phrase has been taken to refer either to Catherine's insistence on wearing corsets in the last stages of pregnancy or to her modesty during the final obstetrical examinations. Byron's accusation seized on the most damning charge he could find to describe the damage inflicted upon him by his mother: She had cursed, crippled, and symbolically castrated her son. Physically painful in his early years, making him an object of mockery or pity in childhood and adolescence, Byron's deformity would cause him emotional injury beyond any other psychic wound he would ever sustain. Turned inward, his rage became depression, but also something more insidious: the sense that he had a special dispensation from the moral sanctions imposed upon others and a lifelong entitlement to the forbidden.

SINCE THE BABY was not born on the sabbath, with its debtors' amnesty, his father did not risk an appearance. But Jack Byron kept in close touch with Holles Street. Four days after his son's birth, he fired off a letter to the Edinburgh agent for his wife's estate: "Notwithstanding your writing to Mr. Leslie to furnish Mrs. Byron with money, he has not done it, and she has not any to go on with. . . . She was brought to bed of a Son on Monday last & is far from well. . . ."[15]

He might have gotten the day of his son's birth wrong, but where money was concerned, Captain Byron was ever the uxorious husband. In this instance, Catherine may have shrewdly neglected to tell him of a recent draft of £50; if Jack had gotten wind of it, there would have been nothing left to pay the midwife and doctors.

Once again, the commissioners dispatched John Leslie to Holles Street. Catherine was too weak to see him, Leslie reported to Edinburgh, but he noted that mother and son were doing well, making

---

*In every culture, the caul, the transparent birth sac that shrouds the newborn's upper extremities if the amniotic fluid leaked earlier, has been held to be a lucky charm. Many believed that a caul conferred second sight. After Byron's delivery, Mrs. Mills, the nurse, sold it to John Hanson, to insure the safety of his brother, a naval officer. It did not prove effective, as two years later the young man was lost at sea.

no mention of the infant's malformed foot. He left Catherine a message that he had from 10 to 20 guineas for her if she would send her maid to his office. For a few days he heard nothing, then word came from the maid that Mrs. Byron needed 100 guineas. Leslie forwarded her request to the Edinburgh executors who agreed, at the same time warning her against all further expenditures not deemed absolutely essential, and demanding an itemized list of Jack Byron's debts.

Catherine replied, in her rambling style with its uncertain grammar: "I shall make Mr. Becket [another lawyer] give you an account of all Mr. Byron's debts that we know of as soon as possible, but I hope the money wont [sic] be given to him but to have somebody to pay them for he will only pay what he is obliged to pay and there will be still more debts coming in & more demands for money. I am sorry he is getting a new carriage."16

Jack Byron, for his part, never let poverty inhibit his spending habits. A fine new carriage was a necessity for him—just as it would later be for his son. Meanwhile, Catherine promised to give Watson an itemized list of her needs for the next two months—the period of time she planned to remain in London. Believing she had to leave Holles Street within days, she had found other lodgings, while anxiously waiting for her errant spouse to come for her: "I will not go to Bath nor will I leave this till Mr. Byron gets a house & is fixed for I am tired of so many journeys," she wrote to Edinburgh. "I hope by the time my little boy is able to travel Mr. Byron will have got a house in some cheap country whether Wales or the north of England."17

None of her hopes was to materialize. Plans for the new quarters, at 2 Baker Street, Portland Square, fell through. Nor was Jack Byron ever to assume the responsibilities of a husband, father, or head of household. They never again lived together for more than a few months, and his only role in Catherine's life would be to continue badgering her for money.

ON FEBRUARY 29, 1788, George Gordon Byron, then five weeks old, was christened at Marylebone Parish Chapel, at the top of Marylebone High Street. Seven years earlier, Hogarth had used the interior as the setting for the fifth scene of *The Rake's Progress*, in which the ruined spendthrift marries a rich old maid. If the rake of a father was present now, he did not emerge from hiding to risk arrest. The infant's sponsors (seemingly in absentia) were the Duke of Gordon and Catherine's cousin, Colonel Robert Duff of Fetteresso. The only official record of the event was inaccurate: The parish clerk forgot that 1788 was a leap year, noting the date as March 1 in the register.

By the middle of April, mother and son were still in the back draw-ing room at Holles Street, where Jack Byron appeared for furtive visits. At two and a half months, baby "Geordie"—in the broad Scots twang of his mother—would now be taken out on a fine day for a turn in Cavendish Square. Just around the corner on Oxford Street was a shop window whose beguiling display of children's and dolls' shoes could only have summoned his mother's most melancholy thoughts. The doc-tor had said that before her son began to walk he would require special boots.* Where would the money be found to pay for such expensive articles?

Still, even the most rigorous demands of frugality couldn't dampen Catherine's pride in her baby. On April 19, she ordered nine yards of white lutestring, a thin, satiny fabric, from Roach and Coy, Pall Mall, silk weavers to Their Majesties, followed by an order for one yard of blue taffeta; the color and quantity of both suggest the traditional out-fits of well-born young children of both sexes.

Shortly afterward the household left Holles Street, destination unknown. For the next year there is no trace of them. Then, in early August 1789, Jack Byron reappears in a rented house on the grounds of Sandgate castle, in Folkestone, Kent. From there he made brief trips to the coast of France. A longer junket across the Channel proved ill-advised; no sooner had Jack set foot on French soil than he came close to being imprisoned for debt. By 1790 he was established in Aberdeen; whether he came there just before or after the arrival of his wife and baby son is uncertain. For a few brief unhappy months, they were a family.

---

*John Hunter, the famous surgeon and anatomist, was the doctor who examined Byron's foot a few days after his birth. Unfortunately, he left no record of the exami-nation or of his opinion. We have only Catherine Byron's word for the doctor's re-assuring remarks that her son's foot would "be very well in time" with the prompt use of an orthopedic boot.[18]

CHAPTER 2

"A Verra Takkin' Laddie"

*T*HE BYRONS' new lodgings at 10 Queen Street in Aberdeen were above a perfumer's shop (like those on Holles Street) and across from the Greyfriars Church, the only remaining pre-Reformation church in the city. It was on Queen Street that Jack Byron reentered, briefly, the lives of his wife and son.

Unhappy as the newlyweds had been in the castle at Gight, their quarrels worsened in cramped quarters shared with a two-year-old and his stern, Scripture-quoting nursemaid, Agnes Gray. That Jack Byron stuck it out for even a short time attests to his desperate need for the pocket money grudgingly doled out by Catherine, and followed by scoldings and tantrums when the coins swiftly disappeared. As the atmosphere turned stormier, Jack moved out, taking rooms at the other end of the street. A cautious entente was established; neighbors even recalled the captain taking tea with his wife. Meeting Agnes Gray on the road without her charge, he inquired tenderly after his little son: Could the boy stay with him for a while? he asked the nurse. Catherine agreed to the request coldly, but Agnes promised her mistress that the captain would not keep the boy for long; he was such an uncontrollable little terror. She had recently scolded Geordie for soiling a new frock, and the toddler—he had gotten into one of his "silent rages" (as the poet later described them)—seized the garment with both chubby hands and tore it from top to bottom, staring at her the while with sullen defiance.[1]

After one night spent with his father down the street, he was returned to Catherine.

In his stubbornness and fierce temper, alternating with rushes of tenderness and affection, the son was an emotional mirror image of his mother—one reason for the violence of their relations. Catherine Byron, too, was given to tearing her clothes when she flew into a rage. What the small boy observed of his mother's behavior—terrifying outbursts of fury followed by the most abject expressions of love and remorse, accompanied by showers of kisses—he would emulate in his own. The difference was one of control: Byron's anger could be silent or thunderous, as he chose. When his behavior aroused his mother's rage, she would call him a "damn'd lame brat"[2] and castigate him savagely for being all Byron, just like his miserable father. Then, her wrath discharged, he would be smothered in her ample embrace. His earliest attachment, then, convinced him of the unreliability of women, just as his first memories of marriage were of its miseries.

Jack remained in Aberdeen and in Catherine's good graces just long enough to cajole £300 out of her, which she had to borrow at 15 percent interest per annum on the capital, from the legacy she was to receive on the death of her grandmother. Even while living at opposite ends of Queen Street, their final hours of harmony ran out with the money. At the last, Catherine seems to have refused to see him, as Jack was reduced to writing her to beg for a guinea.

His sister, Frances Leigh, was proving an easier mark. The expatriate general's wife had regularly supplemented Catherine's handouts with her own pin money. Then, in September 1790, with the money he had wheedled from his wife, Jack Byron left Britain for good, joining his sister Fanny in France.

The Leigh household in Valenciennes could not have been more congenial to the errant brother. The general having departed, his lady consoled herself with assorted gallants found in the circles of whores and actresses at the local theater. Wine and brandy flowed constantly, as one amorous adventure merged with the next. Brother and sister were soon comparing notes on conquests and on the sexual tastes and endurance of their partners. Between assignations with others, Jack Byron and his sister Fanny became lovers.

Then, in November, only two months after Jack's arrival, their mother, Sophia, died in Bath. Promising to look after her brother's interests along with her own, Frances speedily made for England and the settlement of their parent's estate. Jack, left behind in Valenciennes, hoped that Fanny might still wrest something for him from the complex tangle of wills and trusts. But he soon became desperate without her, and knowing all too well his sister's sexual energy and need for variety, began to fear he had been forgotten. After a note from her at Dover on her arrival, he received a letter from Fanny in London with the news that she had installed herself in 30 Brompton Road, Knightsbridge, for what appeared to be an extended stay. He began to bombard her with lachrymose notes, alternating pleas for money and protestations of undying passion with reports of his sexual encounters in an attempt to pique her jealousy: "I declare I can find no woman as handsome as you. I have tried several, but when I do anything *extraordinary* I always think of you," he told her gallantly. "The Marigny slept with me two nights running but she is the worst piece I ever met with & we are at present brouillé as I have no money & she want [sic] some."[3]

At first, Jack's only visitor had been one of Fanny's old lovers. But soon the pace of his sexual activity resumed: "I have more on my hands than I can do," he wrote Fanny, "as La Henry who does the Business well is always after me & I love to oblige her, Da Mio, now and then. . . . She told me that I did it so well she always *spent* twice every time, I know this will make you laugh but she is the best piece I ever f——. I was in bed with her here," he confessed.

Even the most mercenary local belle, Mlle. Marigny, was induced to forget about money with him. For Jack, however, this was an affair of principle rather than pleasure, he assured Fanny, since the lady revealed herself to be "as wide as a church door."

But with Fanny gone, the tradesmen now demanded payment in cash, and he began to sell off his sister's possessions: The silver was pawned, the harpsichord went next. But her beloved little bird was well, Jack assured her.

As the house was emptied of its furnishings, chaos filled the void. Relations between Jack and the one remaining servant turned violent: "Josephine is in the best of order as she gets no money and plenty of abuse. It is the only way to treat her," Jack wrote Fanny at the beginning of his stay. But now Josephine, like her master, was usually drunk. On Christmas Day, "due to her insolence, I was obliged to kick her downstairs."

He was soon reduced to begging Fanny, like Catherine, for small sums. He also asked her for news of Augusta. The girl's grandmother, Lady Holderness, and her uncle, the Earl of Carlisle, with whom Augusta was now staying at Castle Howard, detested Jack Byron so much that he dared not write to his daughter directly. He feared that earlier letters sent care of her maid had been intercepted.

Then, on December 29, Jack wrote to Fanny to say that he had been very ill "& spitting blood these three days." Fearing that he was near death, he asked his sister to be his heir, but shrewdly, Frances Leigh declined the honor: She knew she would inherit nothing but debts.

. . .

MEANWHILE, the family left behind in Aberdeen had moved again. After Jack's departure, Catherine left Queen Street for larger quarters around the corner at 64 Broad Street. Once again the Byron household—mother, son, and maid—was to live above a shop, but now, at least, they had an entire first floor.

Obliged to furnish her own lodgings for the first time since her marriage, Catherine had taken out further loans on her small income. On January 21, in desperation, she wrote to Frances Leigh, the sister-in-law she had never met, who was now living in London: "Though I have not the pleasure of being personally known to you, I hope you will forgive this trouble." She had written to her husband "some time ago," she explained, begging him to ask his sister for the loan of £30 or £40. He had replied loftily that he would not dream of troubling Fanny, when she had been so good to him already, but that he would write to another person—unnamed—who would come to her aid. But no help was forthcoming. Reminding Fanny that it was her brother's extravagance that had led to her predicament, she added, "I only say this to let you know in what situation I am in, and that me nor my child have not at present a farthing nor know where to get one."[4]

Fanny does not seem to have answered the cry for help. Eight days later she merely wrote to Jack with word of Catherine's note from Scotland, without apparently mentioning its imploring message. Even hearing of his wife's letter was enough to convince him that he was being calumnied: "What can the correspondence of Mrs. Byron be?" he wrote to Fanny on February 4. "I hope not for money as she has had quite enough and never would give me a farthing."[5]

By February 19, Jack's letters to London had become hysterical. "For God's sake, send me some [money] as I have a great deal to pay. With regard to Mrs. Byron . . . she is very amiable at a distance but I defy you and all the other apostles to live with her for two months for, if any body could live with her it would be me. . . . For my son, I am happy to hear he is well; but for his walking, 'tis impossible, for he is clubfooted."[6]

This is the first reference in writing by anyone to Byron's deformity and the first time he is mentioned by his father at all.

Eyed enviously only a few months earlier for the immaculate elegance of his dress, the handsome Jack Byron had now become a filthy drunk; the pawnshops had claimed even a change of clothing: "I hope you will bring me a Coat as I have not one on my back—with some Linen," he begged Fanny on March 30.[7]

But Fanny could not have come without risk. She would be liable for her brother's debts, and if she returned to France, Jack admitted, her carriage and person could be seized at Boulogne.

The bailiffs were about to take all the furniture, including his bed. The silver having long since gone, they took pity on him, lending him cutlery to eat whatever scraps he could afford. He was down to his last three pairs of stockings "and these full of holes—Shoes I have none that can be called so."[8]

At this low point in her brother's life, Frances Leigh seems to have had an inspired idea; sick of Jack's pleas of poverty and complaints of illness, his excuses for turning her home into a brothel and for pawning all her possessions, she decided on a surrogate nurse and housekeeper. She invited Catherine and her nephew George to Valenciennes for an indefinite stay.

Catherine declined. Her circumstances would not permit her to leave Scotland for some time, she wrote to her sister-in-law. In the meantime she had another favor to ask of her. As Fanny was still in London, she enclosed a letter to Mr. Hunter, whose address she had lost, asking her to give it personally to the surgeon. Shortly after George's birth, Catherine explained, Hunter had written to an Aberdeen colleague, giving him directions for making a corrective shoe for the young child, "but it was never right made, or it would have answered better, and as Mr. Hunter saw George when he was born I am in hopes he will be able to give you directions for a proper shoe to be made without seeing it [*sic*] again."[9]

When this was done, could Fanny please advance payment to the maker of the orthopedic shoe and mail it to Aberdeen? Catherine would pay the subsequent bill as directed to her. There is no record of how Frances Leigh received this complicated request from the sister-in-law she would never meet.

By midsummer Jack Byron knew he was dying—either because he planned to end his own life or because he recognized the inexorable final stages of tuberculosis. In his last letter to Fanny, on June 8, he implored her forgiveness for everything. She was the only person, he told her, he had ever really loved. This time Fanny rushed home to his bedside in Valenciennes. On July 21, in the presence of two notaries, he dictated his will. He named Fanny his executrix, leaving her the £500 he still believed he would inherit from his mother. To his wife he bequeathed nothing, but to his three-year-old son, George Gordon, he left the responsibility of paying off his debts and the expenses of his funeral. Captain John Byron died on August 2, 1791, aged thirty-six.

Frances Leigh relayed the news of her brother's death to his widow. When her letter reached Aberdeen, Catherine's screams were heard, it was said, the length of Broad Street. She had always loved Jack; his behavior aroused her fury but left her passion undiminished. She proved worthy of the Gordon motto, *Je ne change qu'en mourant* ("Loyal unto death"), and she was outraged by her sister-in-law's assumption that any wife must be relieved to be rid of such a husband. Catherine replied frostily to the letter from Valenciennes: "My dear Madam. You wrong me very much when you suppose I do not lament Mr. Byron's death. It has made me very miserable. . . . Necessity not inclination parted us at least on my part and I flatter myself that it was the same with him and notwithstanding all his foibles for they deserve no worse name I most sincerely loved him."[10]

As Catherine had not been able to afford the trip to Valenciennes for herself and son, Fanny now offered to take George for a while. But his mother, despite a lingering illness, refused to part with him—even for a visit: "I shall be happy to let him be with you sometime but at present he is my only comfort and the only thing that makes me wish to live."[11]

Alone and friendless, estranged from her own family, Catherine then asked her sister-in-law to act as George's unofficial guardian: "I hope if anything happens to me you will take care of him."[12]

In a sentimental early verse, Byron idealized the absent father—and killed off his mother:

> Stern death forbade my orphan youth to share
> The tender guidance of a father's care
> Can rank or even a guardian's name supply
> The love that glistens in a father's eye?[13]

Years later, he acknowledged that memories of his father were inextricably linked with witnessing the savage battles between his parents: "I was not so young when my father died but that I perfectly remember him; and had very early a horror of domestic broils." Byron's last words on his father shudder with prophecy: "He seemed born for his own ruin and that of the other sex."[14]

At three, George was eager to explore the world beyond "domestic broils" and unprepared for the indifferent cruelty of strangers. Accosted by a neighbor who announced, "What a pity that such a handsome little lad should be lame," he struck at her with his toy whip: "Dinna ye speak of it," he ordered.[15]

In revenge, he developed a special agility for mischief and a fierce aversion to authority.

"A verra takkin' laddie, but ill to guide" was the view of his Duff relations in Banff.[16] His "taking" qualities—the shyness that would suddenly eclipse his imperial manner; his warm nature, high spirits, and yearning to be loved; above all the irresistible charm that was a Byron birthright—made it impossible to be severe with him. Catherine Byron's own failure in self-control made her an inconsistent disciplinarian. Lacking a father's guidance, her son, she decided, needed masters as soon as they could be found.

Thus, in the autumn of 1792, when Byron was four and a half years old, his mother took him around the corner to Long Acre, where a "mixed school of good esteem though small pretensions," costing a guinea a year, was run by a Mr. Bowers.[17] Catherine Byron was clear about what she expected for her son: "I have sent George to you that he may be kept in about," she is reported to have told Mr. Bowers, using the local expression for keeping a child in line, physically and morally.[18] As dispiriting as the one-room school must have been, it left memories of warmth and care that also point to a decidedly populist beginning to Byron's education: "The dialect was the broadest, the tone of the school the roughest . . . and yet at the bottom there was genuine kindness and humanity," a schoolmate remembered.[19]

Byron himself only recalled the limitations of his first classroom, in particular Bowers's method of catechism: "I learned little there—except to repeat by rote the first lesson of Monosyllables—'God made man— let us love him'—by hearing it often repeated—without acquiring a letter. Whenever proof was made of my progress at home—I repeated these words with the most rapid fluency, but on turning over a new leaf—I continued to repeat them—so that the narrow boundaries of my first year's accomplishments were detected—my ears boxed—(which they did not deserve—seeing it was by *ear* only that I had acquired my letters)—and my intellects consigned to a new preceptor."[20]

His new teacher was John Ross, who kept a school in an old dancing hall at the south end of Drum's Lane, an unpaved throroughfare off the north end of Upperkirkgate, and a hard walk from Broad Street for the little boy with a limp.

Byron recalled Ross as "a very decent—clever—little Clergyman," adding that under his tutelage "I made an astonishing progress—and I recollect to this day his mild manners & good-natured painstaking." In only a few months, the five-year-old read fluently. "The moment I could read—my grand passion was *history*," Byron remembered, "and why, I know not, but I was particularly taken with the battle near Lake Regillus in the Roman History, put into my hands the first."[21]

He quickly moved beyond what Ross's school could teach him.

Now, to prepare her son for Aberdeen's selective grammar school, Catherine Byron engaged "a very serious—saturnine—but kind young man named Paterson for a tutor—he was the son of my Shoemaker," Byron recalled, "but a good Scholar as is common with the Scotch—He was a rigid Presbyterian also."[22]

Catherine Byron's involvement with her son's lessons did not end with boxing his ears for pretending to read while reciting by rote. One day, John Paterson's illness led to the substitution of his older brother Joseph as tutor. The six-year-old was translating Horace's verse about death knocking at the palaces of kings and the huts of the poor. When he had finished he looked up in Mr. Joseph Paterson's face and asked, "Mr. Paterson, will I die?"

The tutor replied that "certainly he would, and was proceeding to add something, when Byron's mother started up, rushed forward, drew off the boy, and having emphatically contradicted the statement made, assured her son again and again that he would never die, and ended by dismissing the temporary tutor with distinct intimations that if his brother could not find another substitute she would."[23]

Despite this strangely un-Christian denial of death, Catherine Byron attended church faithfully with her son. Perhaps she felt that the restlessness of a small boy would protect him from any warnings of death and damnation that might issue from the pulpit. Indeed, a parishioner who occupied the same pew recalled George's favorite form of distraction during the long sermons: He would stick pins into his mother's plump arms.

With Jack Byron dead, his widow and son were welcomed back into the Duff and Gordon folds and they were now frequent guests of Catherine's grandmother, Margaret Duff Gordon, Lady Gight, and her sister, Miss Abercromby, who lived together in Banff. There, playing one day with the pastor's son, George fell from a tree, suffering cuts and bruises. The local doctor was sent for, Byron later recalled, "who insisted on bleeding me in spite of screams and tears which I had at command; for I was a complete spoiled child. . . . At last he produced the lancets, of which I had a great horror, having seen them used to bleed my nurse and I declared that if he touched me I would pull his nose. This, it seems, was a tender point with the doctor, and he gave the bleeding up."[24]

He would not always be so lucky.

Time spent with his mother's family, where he was the only male, reinforced the small tyrant's belief in divine right: "Having thrown a stone at a bird and missed and accidentally injured a little girl," an early biographer records, "he remained at first impenitent and treated the child's angry nurse with amazing if un-convincing arrogance saying, 'Do you know I'm Byron's son?' An hour later he enquired . . . about his victim & presented a bag of sweets as a peace offering."25 Here, certainly, is the insufferable lordling daring anyone—and a servant, no less—to object to *his* behavior and then buying off with a pack of sweets. Lurking behind the boy-emperor, though, is the worried fatherless child: *Do you know I'm Byron's son?* This was a rhetorical question loaded with irony: In Duff country being "Byron's son" was a stigma, better left forgotten.

In late summer 1794 Catherine received news that would dispel any taint still attached to Geordie's name. Jack Byron's nephew, William, grandson of the Wicked Lord, was dead, killed by a cannonball at the Battle of Calvi in Corsica on July 31. Her son, George Gordon Byron, six and a half, was now heir presumptive to the title and the estates of the fifth Lord Byron, who was living out his last reclusive years in Newstead Abbey.

It was crucial that George, as a future peer, receive a proper education. Thus, in January 1795, still some days before his seventh birthday, "George Bayron Gordon" (the misspelling of his name as it first appeared in the school register reflected local pronunciation) entered the second form at the Aberdeen grammar school.

George now exchanged his red jacket and black nankeen trousers for his first school uniform: a short-tailed coat of blue cloth with yellow cuffs and facings, corduroy knee breeches, and—a delight to any seven-year-old—a waistcoat with full gilt brass buttons. The elegance of the pupils' turnout notwithstanding, the grammar school, with its low fees, was as democratic as any such academically rigorous institution of the period could be.

Low fees, however, made for a no-frills education. The school, one of the poet's classmates noted later, "was a little like Byron himself—it had a long pedigree but a short purse."26 To supplement the bare curriculum, Catherine Byron, like most other parents, paid an extra 6 shillings and sixpence per quarter for her son to attend a writing school kept by a Mr. Duncan on St. Nicolas Street. Here Byron learned to form the swooping diagonals of the capital Ns and Ws seen in his first letters.

As in every boys' school, games and physical prowess were the measures of acceptance. Byron's lameness ruled out sports requiring speed, but he soon became popular for other skills: He was an ace at marbles and handy with his fists. His willingness to engage any challenger—"fearless, and always more ready to give a blow than to take one," as a schoolmate described him27—was an impulse that is still explained by the boy's strong sense of honor and fair play, his hatred of bullies, and his desire to defend their victims. But large elements of pride, aggression, and the need to compensate for his lameness seem also to lie behind a reflexive physical response to anger or slight.

At the grammar school, even more than at most such institutions, two different cultures were represented by life within and without the grim stone building: "The work of the School was conducted in English, the work of the playground in broad Scotch."[28] Byron moved easily between the two, with a social fluidity that would always be his special pride. Perhaps from a desire to fit in with the less bookish, more popular boys, the keen pupil became an uneven student; from one quarter to the next of his last three years at the school,* his place in class fluctuated wildly, ranging from a high of sixth to a low of twenty-third in a form whose average size was thirty-two pupils. He was never one of the outstanding fifty pupils to be honored on Visitation Day in October, when members of the town council bestowed prize books on the best scholars.

After school and on holidays, he was allowed to roam the city with his new friends. Now that he had won social acceptance, he became less defensive about his lameness; he could even joke about it—at least when accompanied by another boy with a similar disability: "Come and see the twa laddies with the twa clubfeet going up the Broad Street," he announced one day as he set off with his friend.[29] He had learned how to ward off mockery with self-mockery—a bitter lesson, but also a step toward mastering pain.

INEVITABLY Byron became his mother's escort, regularly attending spectacles where few children of his age were to be seen. On February 28, 1797, he accompanied Catherine Byron to a "one night only" performance at the Theatre Aberdeen of selected scenes from Shakespeare, including "the farce of CATHERINE AND PETRUCHIO." Thus began, at age nine, Byron's lifelong passion for the stage. His involvement in the proceedings suggests a prior reading of the play. At the moment when Petruchio says "Nay, then, I swear it is the blessed sun," the youngest member of the audience leaped from his seat and shouted, "But I say it is the moon, Sir."[30]

Besides sharing a fondness for the theater and a tendency to indulge in histrionics at home, mother and son were both avid readers. Catherine Byron had always devoured newspapers and periodicals, and

---

*School records from his first year at the grammar school have been lost.

she kept up with the political issues of the day, forming independent and loudly aired opinions. She shocked High Church Tory acquaintances by her passionate espousal of the French revolutionary cause; Byron literally learned his republican sympathies at his mother's knee.

Catherine's well-documented fondness for novels makes it likely that she was a subscriber to one of the city's two lending libraries. Her son later calculated that he had read four thousand works of fiction, his favorites being *Don Quixote* and the works of Smollett (especially *Roderick Random*) and of Scott. From the first, though, he preferred travel and history; his happiest hours of reading combined all three. During Aberdeen's freezing, wind-lashed winters, the *Arabian Nights* offered escape into desert tents and palace harems. At the very end of his life he remembered Knolles's *Turkish History* as "one of the first books that gave me pleasure as a child; and I believe it had much influence on my subsequent wishes to visit the Levant, and gave, perhaps, the oriental coloring which is observed in my poetry." Besides these two well-worn volumes, he recalled devouring "Cantemir, De Tott, Lady M. W. Montague, Hawkin's Translation from Mignot's History of the Turks . . . all travels or histories or books upon the East I could meet with . . . before I was *ten years old.*"[31]

Otherwise, his imagination was fired by accounts of naval action, and he remained "passionate for the Roman history." More surprising was this pronounced aversion: "When a boy I could never bear to read any Poetry whatever without disgust and reluctance," he said.[32]

He might tease his mother in church, but his Presbyterian tutors, along with a succession of Scripture-reading nurses, including Agnes Gray and her sister May, made sure he had read most of the books of the Bible "through and through before I was eight years old," he later told his publisher, John Murray, "that is to say, the *Old* Testament, for the New struck me as a task, but the other as a pleasure."[33]

For one story especially, the conflict of Cain and Abel, he felt the ambiguous thrill of identity: He could elevate his own deformity to the grandeur of a curse—the mirror image of a sense of election. The belief that he was predestined to evil continued to haunt him, not without pride. In the preface to his own drama *Cain*, he noted: "Gessner's 'Death of Abel' I have never read since I was eight years of age, at Aberdeen. The general impression of my recollection is delight."[34]

Among other books he read at this time, one in particular deepened his romance with the "fascination of the abomination." John Moore's *Zeluco* was a popular gothic novel with an antihero condemned to commit crimes by dark forces beyond his control and whose first victim is his mother. Like Byron's, Zeluco's father had died when he was very young and, as Byron told the story, "Very soon after his death, he indulged, without control, every humour and caprice. . . . His temper became more and more ungovernable, and at length seemed as inflammable as gunpowder, bursting into flashes of rage at the slightest provocation."[35]

Catherine allowed that her own failings, along with the absence of sisters, had deprived her son of a civilizing influence. Dancing school, she decided, might be one means of providing the social polish needed by a future peer. He was enrolled in classes held by a Mr. Francis Peacock of Peacock's Close. The dancing master's talents had left him poor, and his house was surrounded by slums where drunken prostitutes amused themselves by emptying chamber pots on the heads of passing policemen. Byron's trip to and from Peacock's classes would have offered the boy a dizzying contrast of experiences: He learned the courtly manners and dances of the aristocracy next to the city's most brutalized inhabitants.

It was in Mr. Peacock's dancing school that Byron, not yet eight, met and fell in love with his distant cousin Mary Duff. Twenty years later, he still pondered the precocity of his obsession: "How very odd that I should have been so utterly, devotedly fond of that girl, at an age when I could neither feel passion nor know the meaning of the word. . . . Now what could this be? . . . We were both the merest children. I had and have been attached fifty times since that period; yet I recollect all we said to each other, all our caresses, her features, my restlessness, sleeplessness, my tormenting my mother's maid to write for me to her, which she at last did, to quiet me. Poor Nancy thought I was wild, and, as I could not write for myself, became my secretary. I remember, too, our walks, and the happiness of sitting by Mary, in the children's apartment, at their house, not far from the Plainstones at Aberdeen, while her lesser sister Helen played with the doll, and we sat gravely making love in our own way."

In his twenties when he wrote this, he could still summon the precise image of his beloved's face, her dark-brown hair and hazel eyes, and he continued to ponder the intensity of erotic feeling he experienced long before puberty: "How the deuce did all this occur so early? Where could it originate? I certainly had no sexual ideas for years afterwards, and yet my misery, my love for that girl were so violent, that I sometimes doubt if I have ever been really attached since."[36]

Eight years later, Catherine Byron, not without malice, told her sixteen-year-old son that she had just received a letter from Edinburgh with news that "your old sweetheart Mary Duff is married to a Mr. Coe [actually Mr. Cockburn, a wine merchant]."

"And what was my answer? I really cannot explain or account for my feelings at that moment; but they nearly threw me into convulsions, and alarmed my mother so much, that after I grew better, she generally avoided the subject—to me—and contented herself with telling it to all her acquaintance."[37]

In important ways, our first love remains the only one. Byron's passionate attachment to an older female relative*—at once a mother, sister, and twin soul—was a primal scenario that would play itself out again.

When he was about eighteen, Byron wrote a series of what he called "memory poems." In one of these he summons both the wonder and the urgency of his feelings for Mary. He is Adam, experiencing love before the Fall, his passion undefiled by knowledge, sexuality, terror, or ambition; his entire world was then bounded by one immensity of feeling:

> Untutor'd by science, a stranger to fear,
>   And rude as the rocks, where my infancy grew,
> No feeling, save one, to my bosom was dear,
>   Need I say, my sweet Mary, 'twas centred in you?
>
> Yet it could not be Love, for I knew not the name,
>   What passion can dwell in the heart of a child?
> But, still, I perceive an emotion the same
>   As I felt, when a boy, on the crag-cover'd wild:
> One image, alone, on my bosom imprest,
>   I lov'd my bleak regions, nor panted for new,
> And few were my wants, for my wishes were blest,
>   And pure were my thoughts, for my soul was with you.[38]

Besides being lovesick, the eight-year-old boy caught scarlet fever. When he did not seem to be making a full recovery, his mother decided he must be moved from the dark back bedroom of Broad Street. As it was summer, she took rooms in a farmhouse belonging to a Mr. James Robertson, on the Deeside at Ballerich, forty miles from Aberdeen, where the convalescent drank goat's milk to bring back his strength. It was here that Byron began another love affair—with Dee Valley and its highlands.

On foot, if the terrain was not too rough, or on horseback, Byron,

---

*Interestingly, Mary Duff appears to have been born in 1788, making her exactly Byron's age. But he always referred to her as being at least three, and on one occasion six, years his senior.

dressed in the blue and green Gordon tartan, roamed the rugged countryside, where each rise unfolded a view of the river's silver meander. His health returned, along with his spirits. Accompanied by a gillie, he insisted on climbing the steep banks of the Linn of Dee, a gorge where the river suddenly narrows to rush between high limestone banks and crash over outcroppings of rock.

His most intense feelings of union with nature as part of his own past were reserved for the mountains; they were his birthright, and he now laid claim to far-off Morven and, closer to home, the summit of dark Loch na Garr, rising from a ring of clouds.

In *Lachin Y Gair*, written when he was nineteen, Byron mourns the lost innocence of childhood—a conventional enough topos. But for the young poet, then living in England, the mountain also symbolized exile from heroic possibility. He has been banished from the manly northern virtues of his Scottish heritage, to be corrupted by the degenerate softness of the South:

> Away, ye gay landscapes! ye gardens of roses!
>   In you let the minions of luxury rove;
> Restore me the rocks, where the snow-flake reposes,
>   Though still they are sacred to freedom and love:
> Yet, Caledonia! belov'd are thy mountains,
>   Round their white summits though elements war,
> Though cataracts foam, 'stead of smooth flowing fountains,
>   I sigh for the valley of dark Loch na Garr.
>
> .   .   .   .
>
> Years have roll'd on, Loch na Garr, since I left you,
>   Years must elapse, e'er I tread you again;
> Nature of verdure and flowers has bereft you,
>   Yet still are you dearer than Albion's plain:
> England! thy beauties are tame and domestic,
>   To one, who has rov'd on the mountains afar;
> Oh! for the crags that are wild and majestic,
>   The steep, frowning glories of dark Loch na Garr.[39]

Late in the winter of 1797 Catherine Byron received word from Newstead: Old Lord Byron was gravely ill and not expected to recover. At this eagerly awaited news she sprang into action. Her first concern was to salvage the dying man's few remaining assets before they disappeared.

Finally, on May 21, at one o'clock in the morning, the fifth Lord Byron expired, aged sixty-five. The nine-year-old boy was now the sixth Baron Byron of Rochdale, heir of the granduncle he had never seen, whose estates included the lands of Newstead and Rochdale in Lancashire, along with property in Norfolk.

Catherine Byron's fears were more than justified. At his death the Wicked Lord—duelist, collector, creator of follies—was so poor that no money could be found for a proper funeral; his remains moldered for almost a month at Newstead Abbey until credit could be arranged for expenses. The bills were sent to Catherine, who apparently paid them without a murmur.

She was learning that the privilege of being mother to a lord could be ruinous. Catherine now had to put her furniture, excluding linen and plate, up for sale. The money she received enabled her to meet the funeral expenses, but there was not enough left to cover the coach fare for mother and son to Newstead. She was unable, therefore, to follow the counsel of her London advisers and establish herself and the new Lord Byron at Newstead immediately. Recalling his helpfulness to her in the hard days at Holles Street, she instead engaged John Hanson, of Hanson and Birch, to represent her interests in Nottinghamshire. It was the first and only time that this particular solicitor would act with dispatch. Hanson, accompanied by his wife, installed himself at Newstead, where he proceeded to examine the condition of his new client's property. The next pressing matter was the appointment of a nobleman to act as guardian to the fatherless young lord.

Most probably Catherine Byron was the first to tell her son of his new estate. On the momentous day of the old lord's death, he is supposed to have run to his mother and asked her whether "she perceived any difference in him since he had been made a lord as he perceived none himself."[40] But it was at the democratic grammar school that he learned of the difference between a commoner and a peer. At morning roll call, when his name was read out as "Georgius Dominus de Byron," he stood up to reply "adsum" when suddenly, overcome with embarrassment at the silent stares of his schoolmates, he burst into tears. Later the same day he was given his first taste, literally, of the privileges of rank. The master sent for him and, instead of the awful consequences that usually followed upon this summons, he was offered cake and wine. As Byron later recalled to his friend Hobhouse, it was the master's deference toward him, more than the treat, that impressed upon him the awe a barony inspired.

Even without the additional expenses, her son's elevation to the peerage found his mother poorer than ever. Catherine's Aberdeen attorney, Mr. Crombie, laid out her finances to the London agent to see if the boy's inheritance might not ease her circumstances. After noting his client's desire "to have a Nobleman joined with her as Guardian to her son," he urged:[41] "I wish you would consult Mr. Hanson whether Mrs. Byron would be entitled on application to the Chancellor to a certain allowance out of her son's Estate beside for her maintenance." Given all that she owed and the small income she could expect—about £150 a year—he concluded, "All this will not be sufficient for enabling her to live in that respectable state she is entitled to from the rank of her Son."[42]

Thus began for mother and son the process of mortgaging a future that would always appear rosier than it turned out to be. For the present, the immediate requirement of selling her furniture also forced Catherine to give up the Broad Street rooms. With no money for the trip south, the two appear to have spent part of the summer in a cottage called Honey Brae on the outskirts of Aberdeen. We next hear of the young lord (whether alone or accompanied by his mother is unknown) boarding with his old nurse, Agnes Gray, now married with two children of her own and living at 177 Barron Street, Woodside, a working-class suburb of Aberdeen. There, in one of the first of many lordly gestures, he is said to have presented a gold watch to Agnes Gray Melvin's firstborn, named after her charge, George Gordon.

By the end of August Catherine had scraped together enough cash for the journey to Newstead. She and Geordie said their farewells to friends and family and, accompanied by May Gray, who had replaced her sister as George's nurse, set out by coach from Aberdeen, crossing the Dee River, south toward England.

For Byron, the humdrum existence of a provincial schoolboy had ended. The journey south, he later said, was "a change from a shabby Scotch flat to a palace." A new life beckoned, promising to restore him to his rightful place in a procession of heroic knights, loyal vassals, and lords of vast domains. The changeling orphan of his imagination had been rescued and revealed to be a prince.

CHAPTER 3

A Peer's Progress

*T*WO DAYS LATER, a coach carrying the weary trio turned off the Great Northern Road twelve miles south of Nottingham and four miles from Mansfield. Rattling up to the Newstead tollgate, the carriage stopped long enough for the tollmistress to have a good look at the passengers; she saw a woman whose girth and slovenly dress made her look far older than her thirty-three years and a young nursemaid holding on her lap a boy of about ten. The plumpness of her charge made clear his relation to the larger lady and strengthened the impression that he was far too big to be seated where he was.

For Catherine Byron the journey was a royal progress, the triumphal return of an exiled monarch. Their proletarian life had been a testing and a disguise. Mother and son could now reveal themselves as Queen Regent and princeling. The fairy-tale sequence of events leading to their arrival provided Catherine, an avid reader of romantic novels, with her script. Pretending to know little of the place where she now found herself, she asked the tollmistress who might be the noble owner of the seat.

"It was Lord Byron's, but he is dead," was the answer.

"And who is the heir now?" Catherine asked, prolonging with feigned ignorance this delicious prelude to a happy ending when all her past sufferings would be redeemed.

"They say," replied the tollkeeper, "it is a little boy who lives at Aberdeen."

"And this is him, God bless him!" burst out the proud May Gray, stealing her mistress's moment of glory and possessively kissing the lordling seated in her lap.[1]

Two miles farther along, the sandy road curved around a hill and suddenly, like a mirage across the lake, rose the granite walls of Newstead Abbey. When the coach pulled into the courtyard and the three travelers descended, they were greeted by another trio: old Joe Murray, the fifth lord's faithful retainer, accompanied by John Hanson, the tall, elegantly dressed solicitor, and his wife, who had arrived from London a few days earlier to welcome the new Lord Byron and his mother.

In a larger sense, too, the journey from Aberdeen to Newstead Abbey represented both a reversal of fortune and a restoration. With the 377 miles he had just traveled, little Geordie, with his Aberdeen accent, became a Briton as well as a peer. The English, called "Sassenachs" derisively by the Scots, for their part were even more contemptuous of their neighbors to the north. Remembered bitterly as traitors for the insurrectionary disloyalty of Jacobites to the Crown, Scots were seen as provincial primitives, either warring tribesmen or small-time shopkeepers. In England, to be a Scot by birth was a lifelong obstacle to preferment in public life.[2] Small wonder that Byron would always be torn between nostalgia for the Eden of his childhood, with its romantic trappings of "Scotch plaids, Scotch snoods, the blue hills and clear streams,"[3] and the fear that trace elements of his early years would taint his complete acceptance as a gentleman among the Regency *ton*. Thomas Moore, Byron's friend and first biographer, tells of the poet flying into a rage—only partly humorous—when a young woman told him she still heard echoes of the Scots accent in his speech: "Great God, I hope not!" he is supposed to have exclaimed. "I'm sure I haven't. I would rather the whole d——d country was sunk in the sea—I the Scotch accent!"[4] But the artless girl was not the only one to notice the lingering burr; others were simply more discreet.

Scotland was also his mother's country. On the threshold of adolescence, he was just beginning the struggle to separate from his only living parent, the mother whose uninhibited passions terrified even as they bound him to her. Catherine Gordon Byron, ignorant and impoverished, object of pity or scorn, embodied the country he was leaving behind with regret and relief.

On moving to England, the nine-year-old Byron assumed his father's legacy. Disgraced black sheep that he was, Captain Jack Byron, related by blood or marriage to some of the grandest families in England, had provided his son with a fixed position in society in Britain and on the Continent, one that would always mean more to him than talent. He was a peer of the realm, and no one would ever be allowed to forget it.

Before leaving school, Byron had already tasted the nominal privileges of rank. But while enjoying the deference due a peer, he had still been living in cramped, furnished rooms above a shop. Now, as he stepped from the public coach onto the sandy soil of the abbey courtyard, he ascended, actually and symbolically, to a splendid estate. He had become a member of the landed aristocracy and the ruling class.

SEEN FOR the first time, Newstead appeared as romantic as any illustrated fairy tale, a vision of history fused with fantasy: from the splashing fountain in the center of the courtyard (moved from the cloisters by earlier lords) to the Gothic stone tracery remaining on the abbey facade to the pair of shimmering lakes bridged by a waterfall and guarded by twin model forts to, finally, in the same strange scale between life and doll size, Folly Castle.

Even with the great oaks gone, the park was still verdant with spruce and maple. It was the end of August, and the dilapidated state of the farms, with their run-down buildings, was hidden by the lush greenery. Among the harsh realities it softened were the estate's encumbered finances. Although it had been valued at £90,000 and found to yield an annual revenue of between £1,200 and £1,500, the combination of the late lord's debts and Catherine Byron's small income made needed repairs an impossible undertaking. Catherine was quick to decide that the forty-odd tenant farmers should be paying much higher rent. A competent estate manager was clearly the first order of business. To save expenses, Hanson retired old Joe Murray from active service and hired a local man, Owen Mealey, as overseer. Cash was still tight, however, and spending it on servants was seen as an extravagance. On taking the job, Mealey had been promised a bed for the overseer's lodge. But now, he was told, there was no money to buy one.

Initially Hanson had been horrified by the idea of the young lord and his mother camping in the few habitable rooms left in the ruined abbey, where rain poured into the roofless refectory and wind howled through damp galleries and cavernous reception rooms. He wrote to James Farquar, an Edinburgh lawyer who had befriended Catherine. Expressing his disapproval of her plans by getting her name wrong, Hanson reported, "I have seen Mrs. Gordon and I find she has a great wish to live at Newstead—I doubt very much the prudence of it at least at first, it strikes me it would be better for her to take a House or Lodgings in or near London till the Affairs are arranged and it is known what she is to have allowed her." He added, "The Young Lord is a fine sharp Boy not a little spoilt by Indulgence but that is scarcely to be wondered at."[5]

· · ·

A BRILLIANT August slid into a warm September. A few days before he left, on the fourth of the month, Hanson took Byron to meet his nearest neighbors at Annesley Hall. There he was introduced to his young kinswoman, Mary Ann Chaworth; her mother, Mrs. Ann Clarke; and her stepfather, the Reverend William Clarke. Home from her London boarding school, Mary Ann, at twelve, was a romantic-looking girl, small and spritelike, with dark, soulful eyes and curling tendrils of silky chestnut hair.

On their first meeting, Byron was less interested in Mary Ann herself than in their intriguing bond of murder. Twenty years earlier, the Wicked Lord had run his cousin William Chaworth, Mary Ann's great-uncle, through the belly with a short sword. Along with other ancestors, a portrait of the murdered man hung in the great hall at Annesley. Their likenesses filled the ten-year-old with terror; they all stared down at him with looks of hatred, he insisted, stalking him in his nightmares.

While summer weather still held the discomforts of Newstead at bay, Mrs. Byron invited the Clarkes and Mary Ann over for a return visit. Before the family appeared, Hanson teased the boy about the charming visitor: "Here is a pretty young lady—You had better marry her," he joked. But there was wishful thinking as well as humor in the lawyer's remarks. An only child, Mary Ann would soon be a woman of considerable property. With her well-farmed family estates adjoining Newstead, a union would be the saving of his client's land-poor status.

Byron, though, saw only the crime that divided them: "What, Mr. Hanson, *the Capulets and the Montagues* intermarry?"[6] Casting Mary Ann as Juliet and himself as Romeo would soon give his growing passion for the young woman a romantically tragic model, along with providing him with an essential escape hatch. They were doomed to love and to separate.

Hanson, meanwhile, had relented; mother and son could remain at Newstead through the fall. Making the most of an Indian summer, Byron reveled in the freedom of the outdoors. His forebear's fantasies made a perfect playground for a ten-year-old boy. Folly Castle and the two forts, together with the model boats on the lake, provided endless occasions for military and naval engagements. Indoors there was the Wicked Lord's arsenal, including the actual sword that had killed his cousin William Chaworth, listed in the inventory as "of Iron and Steel, of the Value of Five Shillings."[7] Most fascinating of all to Byron was his great-uncle's collection of firearms. He no longer had to make do with pretending.

A large wolf dog named Wooly had become Byron's special pet. One day the animal angered his new master, either by biting or perhaps merely disobeying him. Hanson recalled to his son, Newton, that Byron's "countenance suddenly became pale, he rushed into the Abbey, seized a loaded gun or pistol of the Keeper's with which he hurried back to the Dog in the Garden, seized hold of him and threw him on his back, exclaiming, Wooly you have done so & so, you shall *die* Wooly."[8]

Far from being alarmed at this display of violent behavior in a child, Hanson saw only lordly resolve, tempered finally by Christian mercy. His son's memoirs further confirm the lawyer's belief that his young client could do no wrong: "My father used to say the decision of character displayed, his action and expression, & the emphasis with which he uttered the determination, the reflexion in the midst of his passion were so finely depicted that he should never forget it as long as he lived. He did not slay the Dog, arresting as it were his fixed resolve on the very verge of its destructive execution."[9]

Theatricality, quickness to take offense, violent impulses followed by forgiving, even contrite, behavior—these were not examples of childish self-indulgence but fixed elements of the Byronic character. Firearms, too, became as essential to him as they had been to his great-uncle; throughout his adult life, Byron carried small loaded pistols in his waist-coat pocket, and the weapons remained within reach at night. Indoors and out he practiced shooting.

Less threateningly, he now planted a young oak in the park, on the lawn sloping down to the lower lake. He could see the oak from the long windows of the old refectory, used as the main drawing room by his forebears, before the fifth lord had allowed it to fall into ruin. The decayed setting gives added poignancy to Byron's identification with the seedling: "He had an idea that as *it* flourished, so should *he*," recalled Tom Moore.[10]

Nearby in Nottingham, there were relatives to be visited: Byron's great-aunt, the fifth lord's brother's widow, the Honorable Mrs. Frances Byron, lived with her sister, Mrs. Ann Parkyns, also widowed, and the latter's two daughters, in a house in Gridlesmith Gate (now Pelham Street). Another aunt, Mad Jack's sister, Charlotte Augusta Byron Parker, also lived nearby, with her husband, son, and two delicately pretty girls. Introduced by their Nottingham relations, the young lord and his mother were soon welcome additions to social life among the local gentry.

As THE YOUNGEST of two males in the female-dominated Byron-Parker-Parkyns family, Byron was made much of. His Great-aunt Frances sent him a pony, a thoughtful as well as generous gift, to make a lame boy's explorations of Newstead less tiring. But Byron was big for his age and overweight as well, and it soon became apparent that the rider was too large for the small steed.

In the first letter he ever wrote (suprisingly late, for a bookish boy of nearly eleven), Byron thanked his great-aunt for the present. Using his best copybook hand he strikes the attitude of a gracious gentleman farmer:

> Dear Madam,—My Mamma being unable to write herself desires I will let you know that the potatoes are now ready and you are welcome to them whenever you please—
>
> She begs you will ask Mrs. Parkyns if she would wish the poney to go round by Nottingham or go home the nearest way as it is now quite well but too small to carry me—
>
> I have sent a young Rabbit which I beg Miss Frances wil accept off and which I promised to send before—My Mamma desires her best compliments to you all in which I join—I am
>
> Dear Aunt Yours Sincerely
>
> BYRON
>
> I hope you will excuse all blunders as it is the first letter I ever wrote[11]

Soon Newstead's new owners were driven indoors by the cold, there to suffer the bone-chilling damp of the abbey in winter. In late November, mother and son moved to Nottingham, taking lodgings first with a Mr. Gill in St. James Lane, near the castle, before moving to Park Row. Then, in the winter of 1798–99, Catherine Byron installed her son, in the care of his nurse, May Gray, with his Parkyns relatives, while she moved back and forth between Newstead and London.

The reasons for their separation are unclear; in the dead of winter there was little that could be done (and no money to do it with) to improve Newstead. Hanson's choice of overseer, Owen Mealey, was already installed in the lodge, from which he would thenceforth act as spy, reporting to the solicitor on the new owners, their tenants, and visitors—never to their advantage.

Looking into ways to improve his client's financial prospects, Hanson had approached the Earl of Carlisle, Captain Byron's cousin, who agreed—reluctantly—to act as the boy's guardian in an "advisory" capacity. Hanson was hoping that the peer would use his influence at court to obtain an allowance from the King's Civil List, and he provided Catherine with appropriate draft letters to Carlisle and to another noble connection, the Duke of Portland. Catherine may have decided that visits to Hanson's office in Chancery Lane were essential to ensure the distracted solicitor's continuing efforts on her behalf.

Then there was the matter of Byron's lame foot, now in the care of a Nottingham quack named Lavender. Fourteen years later, Lavender was to list himself in the *Nottingham Directory* as "surgeon," but in 1799 and earlier he was still "trussmaker to the general hospital." Catherine does not seem to have inquired very closely into his credentials before entrusting her son to his care. Lavender's prescribed course of treatment consisted of rubbing the afflicted foot with hot oil; it was then twisted into a "normal" position and forced into a sort of wooden cast, designed to hold it rigidly in place. Lavender's therapy was not only torture, but also proved to be without any benefit whatsoever. Typically, Byron was stoical about the excruciating pain of these sessions; what he could not tolerate was Lavender's ignorance and pretensions in other matters. In later life Byron gleefully described how on one occasion he had taken revenge on his tormentor. Assembling random letters of the alphabet to suggest words and sentences, he had asked Lavender what tongue this text might be: "Italian," declared the pompous quack—an answer greeted by roars of laughter from his patient.[12]

Words became an early weapon in Byron's arsenal, one especially useful for exposing the pretensions of his elders. In language he discovered a powerful instrument of both defense and attack. The first poem attributed to him, four lines of doggerel, is pure aggression:

> In Nottingham county there lives at Swine Green,
> As curst an old lady as ever was seen;
> And when she does die, which I hope will be soon
> She firmly believes she will go to the moon.[13]

The object of the ten-year-old's malediction was his great-aunt, who seems never to have had any but the kindliest impulses toward her grandnephew.

Along with his advanced verbal skills, the young lord showed a sophisticated grasp of culture as status, accompanied by shame at his own lack of education. Most boys his age would have rejoiced in freedom from schooling and the liberty to explore Nottingham, with its medieval market square and famous fairs. But his experience as a poorer pupil at the elite Aberdeen grammar school made him acutely sensitive to the links of knowledge, power, and social position, and he felt himself losing ground in all three areas. From his Aunt Parkyns's house he wrote to his mother at Newstead, noting that his cousins had a tutor. Could he not receive instruction before or after the girls had their lesson? Catherine refused; either she saw no merit in the request, or feared private lessons would be unaffordable. Her son persisted: "Mr. Rogers could attend me every night at a separate hour from the Miss Parkyns's & I am astonished you do not acquiesce in this scheme," he wrote, "which would keep me in mind of what I have almost entirely forgot, I recommend this to you because if some plan of this kind is not adopted I shall be called or rather branded with the name of a dunce which you know I could never bear. I beg you will consider this plan seriously & I will lend it all the assistance in my power." Then, in an imperious postcript, he concluded, "Pray let me know when you are to send the horses to go to Newstead. May Desires her duty & I also expect an answer By the miller."[14]

Never able to refuse her son anything for long, Catherine relented, and for several months, in the spring of 1799, Dummer Rogers tutored Byron; together he and his pupil read Virgil and Cicero. During these sessions at home with his cousins, Byron's foot was screwed into its wooden contraption. The tutor could feel the boy's suffering. On one of his visits Rogers said, "My lord, I don't feel comfortable at having you sitting opposite me there, in such pain as you must be." To this Byron replied, "Never mind, Mr. Rogers, you shall not see any signs of it in me."[15]

DURING THE late winter and early spring of 1799 Byron lodged alone with May Gray. It was during this period that the nursemaid began regularly taking the boy into her bed and masturbating him.[16] Gray also had adventures with young men her own age. She brought coach drivers home with her and, after getting drunk with her new companions, beat the child she had earlier initiated into sexual activity. The beatings were the only behavior that Byron reported to his mother. In their cramped lodgings it seems inevitable that Byron would also have witnessed the couplings of the drunken May and her chaise boys. Mrs. Parkyns lost no time in writing to Hanson in London that Gray's drinking and lewdness were the scandal of Nottingham. Catherine Byron, twelve miles away at Newstead, where she was visited by her son and other guests from town, must have been told of her servant's conduct.

Gray's unchecked abuse of the boy, the torment of the quack Lavender's mistreatment of his foot, and his desultory lessons with Dummer Rogers all convinced Hanson that Byron must be removed from Nottingham promptly. But not promptly enough, if Byron is to be believed. Before he left, the nurse had doubled her punishments as revenge.

Shortly after their arrival at Hanson's house in Earls Court, the lawyer wrote to Catherine Byron. "I assure you Madam," he began judiciously, "I should not have taken the liberty to interfere in your domestic Arrangments, had I not thought it absolutely necessary to aprize you of the procedings of your Servant, Mrs. Gray; her conduct towards your son while at Nottingham was shocking. . . . My honorable little companion tho' disposed to retain his feelings, could not refrain, from the harsh usage he had received at her hands, from complaining to me, and such is his dread of the Woman that I really believe he would forego the satisfaction of seeing you if he thought he was to meet her again. He told me she was perpetually beating him, and that his bones sometimes ached from it . . . but Madam this is not all, she has even—traduced yourself."[17]

Here, Hanson's lawyerly discretion prevented his detailing further— at least in writing—what he also knew. It remained for Byron's lifelong friend, John Cam Hobhouse, to write down what Hanson had told him in conversation, just after the poet's death in 1824: "When [Byron] was nine years old at his mother's house a free Scotch girl used to come to bed to him & play tricks with his person—Hanson found it out & asked Lord B—who owned the fact—the girl was sent off."[18]

But not immediately. Regardless of what she may have heard, Catherine was in no hurry to dismiss her countrywoman, whose family had been so good to her and her son. When May was sent back to Aberdeen, the Grays persisted in believing that their daughter had been calumnied and made the victim of a nasty little boy's revenge on a strict caregiver. They could produce proof, moreover, that her charge repented of his tales: the present to May of the handsome gold watch, the first timepiece Byron ever owned, along with a portrait of him holding a bow and arrow.

Byron's reports of May brutalizing him and his determination to have her fired point to shame at his complicity, as well as a desire for revenge; the rage of a boy, between latency and adolescence, whose first lover and surrogate mother tortures him with her infidelities.

In the journal he kept for a few months in Pisa in 1821–22 and to which he gave the name "Detached Thoughts," Byron reflected guardedly on the relationship between his lifelong attacks of depression and his premature induction into the darkness of sexual obsession: "My passions were developed very early—so early—that few would believe me—if I were to state the period—and the facts which accompanied it— Perhaps this was one of the reasons which caused the anticipated melancholy of my thoughts—having anticipated life."[19]

The consequences of this tortured episode bled into his entire life.

The "anticipated melancholy" he would always experience was accompanied by another, related impulse—to cut off (or dilute with others) an exclusive attachment to one woman before he could be humiliated or rejected. May Gray had taught him the Bible, along with the forbidden knowledge called biblical. He would always associate orthodox Christianity with cant and hypocrisy, even while he was constantly drawn to conventionally devout women—to their everlasting regret and his own.

WITH EVIDENT RELIEF, Hanson took off for London with his "little friend" in the second week of July.[20] Catherine sent May Gray ahead to accompany Byron's belongings; the bandages and contraption for his foot required considerable room. It was the last duty Gray would discharge for her employer.

On July 12, 1799, Hanson's carriage rumbled through Brompton Village to his house in Earls Court, then a semirural retreat. Byron himself would not have remembered the city he had left as an infant, but his ties with the neighborhood were more than those of a visitor. Only a few years earlier, Hanson had purchased the grand house of the great surgeon and anatomist John Hunter, who had crossed London to examine the newborn Byron's malformed foot. Before his death in 1793, the house had accommodated Hunter's examining rooms, laboratory, and anatomical museum along with a menagerie of wild animals whose bodies he dissected at their deaths. Hunter's zoo had been replaced by the young Hanson family, consisting of three boys—Hargreaves, two months younger than Byron; Newton, three years the junior of their guest, and Charles, the youngest—as well as two girls. The elder, Mary Ann, was of marriageable age, but it was her younger sister, Laura, at seven the baby of the family, who pronounced on the new arrival. With the children all assembled, Byron was led into the room, holding their father's hand. After formal introductions, the little girl came closer to the object of so much curiosity and examined him from head to foot. Mindful of what must not be mentioned, she turned to the others and "exclaimed with great gravity and emphasis, 'Well he is a pretty Boy however!' "[21]

The day after their arrival, Hanson called on Lord Carlisle to discuss plans for his ward's education and conferred with Dr. Matthew Baillie on the best course of treatment for Byron's foot. The physician suggested that the boy be brought to his house at St. Bartholomew's Close for a thorough examination of the deformity. Baillie also agreed to be present on July 15, when Hanson took Byron to meet his official guardian.

Frederick Howard, fifth Earl of Carlisle, was then fifty. In his youth, he and his close friend as well as gambling and drinking companion, Charles James Fox, were known as the two best-dressed men in London. Like Fox, Carlisle soon turned his attention to the serious game of politics, serving in the American colonies and then as an immensely popular and humane Lord Lieutenant of Ireland. Subsequently he held the post of Lord Privy Seal and, moving ever further to the right, upheld the bill suspending habeas corpus. A knowledgeable collector of art, Carlisle was also an amateur poet and playwright of talent whose literary efforts had been praised by Samuel Johnson and Horace Walpole. Byron's orphaned half sister, Augusta, often stayed with her Howard cousins as they moved between the splendors of Castle Howard in Yorkshire and the grandeur of Grosvenor House in town.

It was to Grosvenor House that Hanson brought his young client on July 15. The meeting was not a success. Despite his usual confidence of winning over every adult, Byron had been unhappy at the prospect of the presentation. The grandness of the connection may have frightened him, or he may have anticipated—quite rightly—that the presence of Dr. Baillie ensured the humiliating experience of hearing his foot openly discussed. All efforts of his guardian to put him at ease were rebuffed. In a breathtaking breach of manners on the part of a child, Byron turned, after a short time, to Hanson and said, "Let us go."[22]

In contrast, Byron's delight in the warmth of family life, his natural good spirits, and his affectionate nature allowed him to fit in easily with the Hansons young and old. The Hanson boys accepted their guest's preference for mornings spent reading on the divan, attributing this otherwise suspicious trait to his lameness. Soon Byron exonerated himself by his keenness to rush out of doors at about one o'clock for games, at which he excelled.

Two days after his unhappy visit to Grosvenor House, Hanson took Byron to see Dr. Baillie at 6 St. Bartholomew's Close. Baillie did not seem to have been informed of the quack Lavender's painful device to which the boy had been subjected through the late winter and spring. After carefully examining the foot, Baillie assumed that nothing had been done in the way of treatment, proof—if such were needed—that his new patient's torment had been for nothing. The eminent specialist confirmed that "if the proper means had been taken at the first in Infancy [as Baillie's uncle and mentor, Dr. Hunter, had earlier proposed] the malformation might have been brought round. The right foot was inverted and contracted as it were in a heap and of course did not go fully and flatly to the ground. But as it grew, if it had at first been forced into a frame by constant and gradual pressure on the inside to the right side and also pressed down on the instep much if not the whole of the Evil might have been cured. But little could be done after the lapse of ten or eleven years."23

This bleak prognosis notwithstanding, Baillie was not planning to give up the case. He recommended the services of a Mr. Laurie to design yet another device in the form of an adjustable brace worn on the foot and ankle, to be made by a Mr. Sheldrake in the Strand. Baillie's description of the deformation contradicted Catherine Byron's hopeful claim of an improvement in her son's disability. As recently as April 15, she had written to a cousin in Fetteresso that "Lord Byron has felt no bad effects from the turning of his foot and it is now almost quite well, so like his other foot that strangers have asked which foot it was."24 Writing to Lord Carlisle three months later to thank him for his help, she noted of his ward: "Since I have brought him to England I have had him under the care of a Person here who is successful in curing Persons of deformity and I think his foot is much improved."25 Meanwhile, swallowing her pride and staunch Whig loyalties, on July 23, 1799, Catherine Byron sent off a letter of appeal to the Duke of Portland, the Tory leader of the House of Lords, seeking His Grace's help in obtaining a pension to maintain herself and her son.

Portland lost no time in speaking to the King, and a month later he was able to report to Mrs. Byron that the Prime Minister, Mr. Pitt himself, had been ordered to pay her £300 a year out of the Civil List "to commence forthwith."26 Portland's intervention was certainly motivated by self-interest, as much as by desire to help an impoverished young fellow peer and his mother; he owed the Byron estate the substantial interest of £1,000 on a complex mortgage transaction. This timely favor was excellent insurance against being sued for the debt when Byron came of age.

The royal rescue came not a moment too soon. Before her request was granted, Catherine Byron's income from her capital had shrunk to £122 per annum. Besides the new and higher medical expenses, there would now be bills for Byron's schooling. In the same letter to her cousin Mrs. Duff, Catherine Byron had noted loftily that "Lord C. is very partial to a public Education."27 But clearly the boy's sketchy and erratic studies might have made enrollment in Eton (Lord Carlisle's alma mater) or Harrow difficult. Accordingly, in consultation with Byron's guardian, Hanson decided upon a small school in the peaceful London suburb of Dulwich, maintained by a Dr. Glennie in his home on Lordship Lane.

An Anglicized Scot, Dr. Glennie and his wife boarded the boys in their house, a stately Georgian building in a rural setting (the land now belongs to Dulwich College), and on August 22, Hanson accompanied Byron to Dulwich. The boy was wearing his new leg iron, and the visible disability, joined with his rank and grand connections, prompted Glennie to offer the new pupil his own study, making him the only boy in the school to have a private room.

A week later Hanson wrote to Catherine Byron. In the same letter in which he reported May Gray's seduction of her son, he also relayed some good news: "I left my entertaining companion with Mr. Glennie last Thursday week and I have since learned from him that he is very comfortable and likes the situation. His schoolfellows are very fine youths, and their deportment does very great credit to their Preceptor. I succeeded in getting Lord Byron a separate room, and I am persuaded the greatest attention will be paid him."[28]

Despite his privileged status, Byron described the school to his younger cousin as "a damned place."[29] But that may have been the requisite complaint intended to cast the writer as a man of the world, chafing at schoolboy constraints.

In fact, Byron seems to have reasonably enjoyed his two years in Dulwich, where, as the only peer, he was certainly the big fish in Dr. Glennie's pond. Although he had to repeat, using the English grammar, most of the Latin learned in Aberdeen and since forgotten, studies with Glennie (the only master) were not arduous. All the boys were given the run of books in the doctor's study, but by far the most popular work there was a pamphlet written by the brother of one of Glennie's friends describing the shipwreck of the *Juno* off Arracan in 1795. Like the narrative written by Byron's grandfather, "Foul Weather Jack," describing the hardships he had survived off the coast of Chile, this account found its way into *Don Juan*. In these verses Byron contrasts the responses of two fathers among the crew to their sons' deaths: The parent who, informed of his loss, carries on with his work high on the mizzenmast is the survivor. The father who attempts, with tender ministrations, to revive his son dies of grief as the boy's body is lowered overboard.[30]

> There were two fathers in this ghastly crew,
>   And with them their two sons, of whom the one
> Was more robust and hardy to the view,
>   But he died early; and when he was gone,
> His nearest messmate told his sire, who threw
>   One glance on him, and said, "Heaven's will be done!
> I can do nothing," and he saw him thrown
> Into the deep without a tear or groan.

The lesson Byron seems to have taken from this drama was that a father's connection with his son is maintained at the parent's peril. Seen in this forgiving light, Captain Byron did not decide to abandon, then to forget, his only child; disengagement was the price of his survival.

AT DULWICH, Dr. Glennie encouraged Byron's determination to excel at games, "an ambition," noted Glennie judiciously, "which I have remarked to prevail in general in young persons laboring under similar defects of nature."[31] Now, in a gesture of liberation and defiance, Byron threw his leg iron into a nearby pond.

The most exciting games married physical agility with imaginative play. At the end of the eighteenth century, highwaymen and footpads still took cover in Dulwich Wood, between attacks on travelers passing nearby Sydenham Hill. Byron and his schoolmates loved to play brigand, ordering terrified strangers to "stand and deliver." While Byron was a student, the unsolved murder of Old Matthews, a hermit who had lived peacefully for thirty years in a cave in the woods, shocked the school. The hermit's death and other unsettling incidents caused rumors to circulate that the school, or those connected with it, were marked for the next attack. With a perfect excuse for nocturnal forays (including the use of firearms), Byron apparently organized his fellow students into a vigilante posse, with himself as commander, to patrol the local lanes.

FREEDOM TO PLAY highwaymen and police with real guns, kindly discipline from above, and the leadership role he was granted by his peers channeled some of the aggression that had made Byron's first stay with the Hansons a mixed blessing for his hosts. In July, after first breaking rules by going "below stairs" at Earls Court, he had mercilessly teased the elderly cook until she flew at him, screaming, "You a Lord indeed! I wonder who the d——l ever made you a Lord!" When she pursued him upstairs in her rage, Byron is supposed to have seized a gun from the wall in the entrance hall and started firing bullets into the old woman's high starched hat, until he was restrained. Even without firearms, he was a loose cannon. On a subsequent visit to the Hansons, Lord Portsmouth, another volatile young nobleman, had teased Byron by pulling his ear. "There happened to be some large shells laying near to Byron," Newton Hanson recalled, "and he instantly seized one of them and threw it with all his might at the Earl. Fortunately it missed him."[32]

Now, after fewer than three months of school, Byron wrote to Hanson in November with a lofty message on the news of the Earl's recent nuptials: "I congratulate myself on Lord Portsmouth's marriage hoping his lady when he and I meet next will keep him in a little better order."[33] The letter, written to Hanson at Newstead, also reveals more than a little homesickness for his adopted family; he reproached the lawyer for not visiting him at school, making it plain that he was expecting an invitation for the Christmas holidays, three weeks away.

Byron did indeed spend the winter vacation at Earls Court but without the older Hansons; leaving their London establishment and brood in charge of Mrs. Hanson's sister, the lawyer and his wife spent most of the holidays at Newstead, trying to get affairs there in order.

When the Hansons returned to Earls Court in January they brought Catherine Byron with them for a few days' visit. The family now had ample occasion to witness the mother's violent alternations of humor toward her son. As Newton Hanson recalled, "Byron had a sad trick of biting his Nails which sometimes used to call forth from his mother sudden and violent Ejaculations of Disgust accompanied by a Box on the ear or Hands."[34] It was no coincidence that this obvious expression of anxiety was most remarked on during his mother's visit.

After her son's return to school, Catherine remained in London, taking lodgings in Sloane Terrace, about two miles from Earls Court. Her new rooms must have brought back unhappy memories of Holles Street. Although her real income had improved, her expenses had increased alarmingly. She lived frugally, denying herself everything but the barest necessities to give Byron all the advantages of a rich young peer. Nothing was too good or too expensive for her son. With her £300 pension already reduced by taxes and Hanson's fees, she was now paying the exorbitant tuition charged by Dr. Glennie—£43 5s 6p per year. On top of this, she insisted that Byron enjoy a generous allowance, which included outfitting him at his father's fashionable tailor, the same Mr. Milne who had bailed Jack Byron out of the King's Bench Prison.

Reasons for her indulgence are not lacking. With adolescent rebellion gathering force, Catherine wanted to tie her son to her through dependence on her generosity. There was the vicarious pleasure of the marginalized woman whose socially sought-after child redeems her own position of outcast. Finally, Catherine's complicated feelings about Byron's lameness—feelings that included shame, guilt, and anger—were relieved by compensation; Byron had arrived at school shackled with a leg iron. She determined that he would shine by other measures.

What his mother did not realize was that she herself was a source of shame to her son, second only to his lameness. Finding London unbearably lonely, she paid frequent—and unwelcome—visits to Dulwich. Dr.

Glennie in particular, a snobbish Anglicized Aberdonian, loathed Mrs. Byron as representing everything he had left behind.

Catherine would bring Byron back to town for long weekends—times when he was supposed to be studying hard to catch up. Often she kept him in town for the entire following week. Dr. Glennie harbored suspicions that during these furloughs Mrs. Byron was busy corrupting her son, "collect[ing] around him a numerous circle of young acquaintances, without exercizing, as may be supposed, much discrimination in her choice."[35]

She was also without inhibitions; she did not hesitate to make scenes, when her angry voice, drowning Dr. Glennie's genteel tones, could be heard throughout the school. Following an especially loud outburst one of her son's friends said to him, "Byron, your mother is a fool."

Torn between shame and loyalty he replied, "I know it, but you shan't say so."[36]

As if this wasn't enough, scandalous rumors began to fly between Earls Court and Dulwich. According to John Hanson, Catherine had fallen in love! And with a French dancing master, a M. de Louis encountered in Brompton. Hanson further maintained that Mrs. Byron had even "laid a plan for carrying B. to France. The Frenchman called at Dulwich to take him away but the Master would not let him go."[37]

At thirty-six, there was nothing unseemly about Catherine Byron's forming an attachment to a man. But it would be highly unlikely that she had made plans to emigrate. England was at war with France, a country still in the aftermath of the Terror: "Milord" would not have received an aristocrat's welcome, and his mother would most certainly have lost her royal pension. Whether affair or infatuation, there is no further mention of the dancing master M. de Louis.

In the summer of 1800 Byron stayed for the last time in Nottingham, probably in rooms his mother had rented in Park Row. He also fell in love. Once again, the object was a slightly older female relation. But this time his emotional upheaval found new expression: "My first dash into poetry," Byron recalled, "was the ebullition of a passion for my first Cousin Margaret Parker one of the most beautiful of Evanescent beings—I have long forgotten the verses—but it would be difficult for me to forget her—Her dark eyes—her long eye-lashes!—her completely Greek cast of face and figure! . . . I do not recollect scarcely anything equal to the *transparent* beauty of my cousin—or to the sweetness of her temper—during the short period of our intimacy—she looked as though she had been made out of a rainbow—all beauty and peace."[38]

Nottingham, then, was the setting for Byron's first experiences of sacred and profane love: the torment of living with May Gray, with its alternation of sexual games, guilt, humiliation, and probable physical abuse, and his idealized love for the undefiled beauty of Margaret Parker.

Now he was buffeted between two other poles of joy and suffering: the rapture he experienced in his cousin's presence and his agony during the twelve hours of night that he and Margaret must be apart. Living for the bliss of reunion with the beloved, Byron would scarcely have focused on the upheavals racking the city of Nottingham that summer. The rising price of bread combined with the depressed wages of the weavers ignited two days of rioting at the end of August. Starving mobs raided granaries and bakeries. Their number and frenzy were such that the locally raised militia could do nothing to quell the rioters; they may have been reluctant to fire on their fellow citizens. It took thunderstorms of extraordinary violence to disperse the crowds.

Catherine Byron, if not her son, was happy to leave the city. Byron unenthusiastically returned to Dulwich, to brood about Margaret, while his mother, in London, tried to chivy Hanson into settling her financial affairs; she wanted to know what could be done to make Newstead a paying and livable property.

That past January she had had her first audience with Lord Carlisle, which seems to have been an uneventful discussion of his ward's future. In October, however, reports of her behavior from Hanson and Dr. Glennie, including an account of the French dancing master's visit to the school, produced an outraged summons to Grosvenor House. A stormy scene took place, following which Catherine was forbidden to see her son. His guardian was a powerful man. Carlisle now informed Glennie, "I can have nothing more to do with Mrs. Byron—you must now manage her as best you can."[39]

Once again, Byron spent the Christmas holidays in London with the Hansons, but this year his mother stayed in Nottingham; it was preferable to attend the theater alone there than to be snubbed by her son, his guardian, and his lawyer.

Hanson, meanwhile, had secured Carlisle's agreement that it was time for a proper public school to take over Byron's education. Although Carlisle was an Etonian, Hanson's son Hargreaves was at Harrow, and the lawyer's acquaintance with the head, Dr. Joseph Drury, would help persuade him that Byron's erratic schooling should be no obstacle to admission. Following a second audience with Carlisle, the decision was made. Dr. Glennie was asked to make a special effort to prepare the boy for the Harrow spring term, which began after Easter.

Moping over his beloved Margaret, Byron was no more assiduous a scholar than before. But now the boredom of Dulwich was tempered by the knowledge that it would not be for long: "I am going to leave this damned place at Easter and am going to Harrow," Byron loftily wrote to his cousin, George Anson Byron, in February.[40]

"To Harrow he went," Glennie reported, "as little prepared as it is natural to suppose from two years of elementary instruction, thwarted by every art that could estrange the mind of youth from preceptor, from school, and from all serious study."[41]

CHAPTER 4

"A Home, a World, a Paradise to Me"

*H*ARROW WAS prepared for the problem student. After Hanson's visit to Dr. Joseph Drury early in the year, the headmaster summoned Byron for a private audience: "I took my young disciple into my study and endeavoured to bring him forward by enquiries into his former amusements, employments and associates, but with little or no effect;—and I soon found that a wild mountain colt had been submitted to my management."[1]

Used to the defenses of adolescent boys, Drury saw straight through the mulish behavior as a symptom of Byron's excruciating self-consciousness about his deformity, his inadequate preparation, the disparity between his grand relations and a childhood lived on the fringes of respectability. Soon Drury, like everyone else, had fallen under the spell of Byron's charming awkwardness and feminine beauty: the large gray eyes fringed with long black lashes that stared intently from the pale face framed in auburn curls.

For Byron, his lameness would always qualify his good looks, making both harder to bear, but the physical flaw encouraged others to drop their guard; sympathy and protectiveness completed the seduction of beauty and charm. His quicksilver intelligence, too, delighted his elders: "There was mind to his eye," Drury observed, adding, "His manner and temper soon convinced me that he might be led by a silken string to a point, rather than by a cable."[2] By the same token, the good doctor realized that disaster would follow if Byron, big for his age but far behind his peers in scholarship, were placed with younger boys. Thus, before the term began, Drury had assured him that he would board privately with his tutor, the headmaster's son, until he had caught up sufficiently to join the form appropriate to his age.

When Byron arrived at Harrow in April 1801, the school looked physically much the same as it had in 1615, the year its first and at that time only building, the School House, was finished. The only additions were lodgings: The Headmaster's House and a random assortment of boarding and so-called Dame Houses for the younger boys were the entire school.

Until the seventeenth century, a thorough classical education for a young aristocrat was the exception in England. One Tudor nobleman is reported to have said he would rather his son should "hang than be learned."[3] Gradually, however, literary cultivation came to count among the attributes of a gentleman. By the middle of the eighteenth century, five years spent among one's peers at one of the great public schools—Winchester, Eton, Westminster, and Harrow—had become basic training for the ruling class. By the time Byron entered, the free day pupils (for whom the school had been founded) were almost entirely gone, replaced by fee-paying boarders drawn from among the sons of the nobility and of the growing entrepreneurial and professional classes.

A visit to the Fourth Form Room never failed to impress upon the new boy a sobering sense of the tradition of which he was now a part. Its oak walls, divided into bays and blackened by time, were carved with the names of departed graduates. At one end of the room were the flogging stools, and in the closet to the right of the large fireplace freshly cut birch rods were kept. Once admitted, the older pupil's day began here at 6:00 a.m., when he filed in to take his place at one of the graded benches, prepared—well or badly—to be heard in the first recitation, his Greek text, which was illuminated only by thin coils of tallow; the master alone had the right to a candleholder.

Henry Drury, Byron's private tutor and housemaster, was twenty-three years old and just down from Cambridge when the difficult thirteen-year-old was placed in his charge. "A big stalwart man, genial but terrible" was one old boy's memory of the master,[4] but other descriptions of the younger Drury suggested that he and his new pupil were made for each other. The tutor was a brilliant classicist, but his real genius lay in the ability to inspire fear; although "often idle and capricious himself, he had the art of constantly keeping his boys in terror of his vigilance & of managing a whole class while his attention was necessarily fixed on one at a time."[5]

Living and studying alone under his tutor's infamous all-seeing gaze, Byron passed a thoroughly miserable first term. "A degree of shyness hung about him for some time," the senior Drury observed, which had little occasion to dissipate, segregated as he was from the other students.[6]

As the school's youngest master, Henry Drury was unsure of his own authority and clearly took Byron's resistance to discipline personally. Adding fuel to the younger Drury's resentment was his father's soft spot for the spoiled young peer and the special treatment he had been ordered to give him. Byron's efforts to become part of school life were less than successful. "I was a most unpopular boy," he later noted, a judgment confirmed by the frequency of occasions where he had to defend himself.[7] Even in a culture where most quarrels were settled with fists and feet, the number of fights to which Byron was party seems to have surpassed the norm. The cruelty and violence of adolescents toward the stigmatized makes it certain, moreover, that these fights were caused in part by taunts about his deformity. When later he talked about his lameness to the poet Leigh Hunt, Byron said Harrow "made him feel it bitterly," most often, as the butt of crude jokes.[8] On one occasion, he awoke to find his leg in a tub of water. That he acquitted himself well in the frequent scrapes (tacitly encouraged by school authorities), despite his handicap, was a matter of great pride: "At Harrow I fought my way very fairly," he recalled, adding that he believed he had lost only one fight out of seven; even this defeat, he insisted, was due solely to the fact that his entire boardinghouse conspired to take on Byron in turn, while he pounded away without even a second.[9]

Byron's Harrow contemporaries are divided as to whether he played the role of aggressor or defender in these combats. His first roommate, Sir Thomas Bernard, remembered him as a bully, and he may well have appeared in this light at the period when he was most thin-skinned.[10] Generally, though, he was recalled as the champion of other younger, smaller victims, particularly if, like himself, they were handicapped. William Harness, lamed from an accident in early childhood, never forgot Byron's protective role: "Harness, if any fellow bullies you, tell me and I'll thrash him if I can," he had told the frightened ten-year-old.[11] Byron himself gave less lofty motives for a thrashing he administered to Lord Herbert for his supposed bullying of another boy: "I like licking a Lord's son," he announced at the moment of victory.[12]

As his new concern with status and scorekeeping suggests, Harrow unleashed Byron's competitive streak. For the first time he found himself outclassed on several fronts. The only peer among commoners at Dulwich, he was now outranked by lordlings, like the Duke of Dorset, from the grandest titled families along with scions of mercantile fortunes such as the Peel brothers, Robert (the future Prime Minister) and William. In sports he had to accept that he could never be more than an alternate on the new playing field, where cricket had recently displaced archery as the Harrow game of choice. More galling still, he now found himself among academic stars. Even when he had caught up in his studies, he was still upstaged by dazzling scholars among his fellow students. Twenty years later, Byron would record every calibration of who outshone whom at what: "Peel, the Orator and statesman . . . was my form fellow, & we were both at the top of our remove. . . . As a Scholar—he was greatly my superior—as a declaimer & actor—I was reckoned at least his equal—As a school boy *out* of school—I was always *in* scrapes—and *he never*—and *in school*—he *always* knew his lesson— and I rarely—but *when* I knew it—I knew it nearly as well—In general information—history, etc., etc.—I think I was *his* superior—as also of most boys of my standing."[13]

Not for Byron the tedious swot of daily lessons, with their fixed numbers of Greek and Latin lines to be parsed, memorized, or translated. He sidestepped the competition by assuming the posture of the brilliant, erratic idler, describing himself as being "capable of great sudden exertions—(such as thirty or forty Greek Hexameters—of course with such prosody as it pleased God) but of few continuous drudgeries."[14]

Possibly the infrequency of his efforts made the results appear the more brilliant. By the end of June he was not only placed in the Fourth Form, but also at the top of the remove. Taking the measure of others' gifts, he would show what he could do—and with less effort. If for him the race was literally handicapped, that, too, would become an asset, goading him to outstrip the rest. In the verse drama *The Deformed Transformed*, written nearly twenty years later, Byron fixed clearly the connection between his lameness and his ferocious determination to greatness:

> Deformity is daring.
> It is its essence to o'ertake mankind
> By heart and soul, and make itself the equal—
> Aye, the superior of the rest. There is
> A spur in its halt movements, to become
> All that the others cannot.[15]

In the jungle of a great public school, he now learned that cooperation more than competition shielded individual vulnerability. Another prodigy among his classmates, George Sinclair, was such an effortless versifier that he did the translations and themes for half the school. "He . . . used at times to beg me to let him do my exercize," Byron recalled, "a request always most readily granted upon a pinch, or when I wanted to do something else, which was usually once an hour. On the other hand, he was pacific and I savage; so I fought for him, or thrashed others for him, or thrashed himself to make him thrash others when it was necessary, as a point of honour and stature, that he should so chastise."[16]

His closest friendships offered a haven from the need to prove himself. Edward Noel Long, a commoner, had entered at the same time as Byron. The bond of being new boys, together with Long's accepting, matter-of-fact affection, inspired a rare trust; he was neither awed, like Byron's younger acolytes, or determined, like the established school leaders, to knock the chip off Byron's shoulder. Forged at Harrow, their friendship matured with them.

BY THE TIME the summer holidays arrived in June, Byron knew he had survived the worst of school. He was more than ready to enjoy London, where his mother had taken rooms at 16 Piccadilly. Mrs. Massingberd, Catherine Byron's landlady, was a widow from a good Derbyshire family who had fallen on lean times. Her lodger's broad Scots accent and unfashionable dress would scarcely have prepared her for the handsome, imperious young lord, with his newly acquired Harrow drawl, who now appeared with his mother. Both Mrs. Massingberd and her daughter promptly fell under the Byron spell, all the more enthralling since *Lord* Byron (as Catherine emphatically referred to her son) rarely appeared at 16 Piccadilly, even while he was in London, spending most of his vacation with the Hansons in Earls Court.

It was to the Massingberds', however, that Dr. Baillie and his associate Mr. Laurie, at Hanson's behest, came on August 4 to examine Byron's foot. In time for his departure for Harrow the previous spring, Laurie had devised a boot fitted inside with a brace around the ankle, a welcome change from the highly visible iron contraption shackling his lame foot from ankle to shin that he had worn to Dulwich and tossed away. Now, however, the foot was supposed to be kept bandaged at all times—a great deal to ask of a new boy at a public school. This would have been the first occasion Dr. Baillie and his associate would have to observe Byron's progress. There was no visible improvement as yet, but the doctors remained optimistic—*if* their patient was faithful to boot and bandage, keeping the whole dry and properly laced.

BOTH MOTHER and son clearly needed a holiday, and at the end of summer they repaired to Cheltenham. Following the discovery of mineral springs in 1716 and the construction of a pump room in 1738, Cheltenham had become, after Bath, *the* fashionable spa. As Catherine had begun to suffer from bouts of a mysterious illness (whose symptoms she never specified), the curative waters could be said to justify the expense. Sedately strolling the town's tree-lined avenues was not, however, an exciting diversion for a schoolboy and it may have been in response to her son's boredom that they soon left Cheltenham for the natural beauty of the nearby Malvern Hills. The only sight in England that reminded him "even in miniature, of a mountain,"[17] the Malvern landscape excited Byron's nostalgia for the Scottish highlands.

At the end of September, the long vacation was over. For Byron, the relief of getting away from his mother was offset by the dread of returning to Harrow. As she prepared to set off alone once again, heading this time for Brighton, Catherine wrote to Hanson, asking him whether Byron could spend the night in Earls Court on his way from Cheltenham to school.

The day after she had settled into rooms at 16 Prospect Street, Brighton, Catherine wrote to Dr. Baillie to complain about the size of his bill. As a ward of Chancery, Byron now received a £500 annual allowance. Meanwhile, taxes had reduced his mother's income to £200, and this was doled out to her irregularly. As she maintained no permanent home for her son, she was scrupulous about not spending any of his money on herself and she lived so close to the bone that any unexpected expense threw her into a near-hysterical state: "After looking over your bill I think it comes extremely high at the rate of a hundred and fifty pounds a year, and two guineas a visit to Harrow, I think a great deal of Money," she wrote to Baillie. But always fair, she added: "I am however sensible that Lord Byron certainly walks better than he did therefore you may continue your visits to him at Harrow, but do not go there before Monday the 28th in case anything should prevent my son from being at Harrow before that time."[18]

Ceding to Catherine's need to economize, Baillie does not appear to have visited Byron at school until December 7, when he reported gloomily to Catherine on her son's condition: "I found his foot in a much worse state than when I last saw it,—the shoe, entirely wet through and the brace around the ancle [*sic*] quite loose; I much fear his extreme Inattention will counteract every exertion on my part to make him better. I have only to add that with proper care and bandaging, his foot may still be greatly recovered; but any delay further than the present vacation—would render it folly to undertake it."[19]

Byron's neglect of the deformed foot points to his happier state of mind. He was beginning to make friends and to be included in the informal activities that made up the social life of the school—cricket, and swimming in the pond known as the Duck Puddle, along with nocturnal escapades that involved sneaking out of the boardinghouse after six o'clock lockup to play jack-o'-lantern tag in the dark, marshy meadows. Slowly he found himself appreciated for his generosity and warmheartedness, along with his fierce loyalty to friends. As he became known as a game fellow, his limp was forgotten; he was not going to jeopardize this newly won acceptance by doing anything to call attention to his lameness, such as fussing with bandages or a brace.

At first his circle had consisted exclusively of younger boys who were flattered by his attention and grateful for his protection. The role of noble dispenser of patronage and largesse was one he would always find most congenial. It was no coincidence, either, that his young disciples were drawn from the peerage. A year earlier, the new boy and despised outsider had taken special pleasure in thrashing a lord; now, one of the monitors remembered, when Lord Delawarr was on the list for discipline, Byron tried to intervene on his behalf. "Pray don't lick him," Byron begged. When the monitor asked: "Why not?" he was told, "Why, I don't know—except that he is a brother peer. But pray don't."[20]

Under the system that prevailed at the great public schools, school monitors controlled discipline, including punishment for all offenses not serious enough to come before the masters. This included the de facto right to regulate the tradition of fagging, a form of slavery in which younger boys served the older students. Byron, like every other student, would have had to submit to this apprenticeship in humiliation. Apparently he found it too painful to mention until he himself was in the position of master.

As Christmas approached, Byron set off once again for London. At this term's end, however, he left school without the sense of escaping a prison of sadistic turnkeys and savage inmates. Still homeless, Catherine Byron had rented rooms in Half Moon Street, Piccadilly, to spend some of the holidays with her son. As before, Byron divided his time between his mother and the festive family activities of the Hansons.

It was during this holiday season that Byron seems to have met, for the first time, his half sister, Augusta, now seventeen. Until this year they had been kept apart by the ill feeling that smoldered between their elders; Catherine had always felt snubbed by Lady Holderness, Augusta's Dutch grandmother. The old woman had died in October, and in her letter of condolence to Augusta, Catherine made it clear that the deceased had been the main obstacle to warm relations with the stepdaughter she had not seen in thirteen years. But her haughty tone reveals wounds that rankled still: "As I wish to bury what is past in oblivion I shall avoid all reflections on a Person now no more," Catherine wrote. "My opinion of yourself I have suspended for some years. The time is now arrived when I shall form a very decided one." Thawing slightly, she went on to assure Augusta of the "unalterable regard and friendship of myself and Son. . . . I take it upon myself to answer for him although he knows so little of you, he often mentions you to me in the most affectionate manner, indeed the goodness of his heart and amiable disposition is such that your being his Sister had he never seen you would be sufficient claim upon him and assure you every attention in his power to bestow." She concluded, "Your brother is at Harrow School and if you wish to see him I have now no desire to keep you asunder."[21]

Reestablishing relations with Augusta was probably not unrelated to her stepdaughter's recent inheritance. Perhaps she had gone from being a poor relation, like Catherine herself, to being an heiress? In her disarmingly blunt style, Catherine wrote to Hanson for the answer: "Do you know what Lady Holdnerness has left Augusta? I wish you would find out and let me know. I shall be quite anxious till I hear."[22] Whether Hanson was more forthcoming about others' finances than he proved to be concerning her own is uncertain. But he would probably have known that Augusta's legacy gave her an income of £350 a year—ample for a young woman of average expectations, but a pittance in the glittering circles in which Augusta moved, where marriageable girls, such as her Howard cousins, enjoyed the value added of imposing dowries.

As it happened, Augusta was besotted with her cousin, Charles Leigh, the son of Fanny and her husband, the general. Young Leigh was a guardsman whose only known interests were gambling and horses. His family frowned on the match; it was clear that he would need an heiress to indulge his expensive tastes.

From the first, those who saw Byron and Augusta together were struck by the resemblance between the half sister and brother. In the two likenesses that survive of Augusta, it is hard to see where they look alike. Striking similarities must have emerged in mobile traits—fleeting changes of facial expression, of manner and gesture. They were said to have the same laugh, for example, and both suffered from the excruciating Byron shyness with strangers.

Whatever their appearance had in common, it was all in Byron's favor. There was never any disagreement about his beauty, while no one ever suggested that Augusta was even pretty. Before she was worn by sorrow and seven children, she was, however, thought to be attractive, with a languid, yielding quality enhanced by the family tendency to fleshiness (unlike her half brother, she does not ever seem to have done battle with her genes by dieting). Augusta's schedule was dictated by whichever relation she was visiting at the time; she and Byron saw each other in London during school holidays. But their brief acquaintance called up new emotions for both. Some were familial: The orphaned young woman and fatherless boy were both homeless and rejoiced in the discovery of a sympathetic sibling. Other feelings aroused were more troubling; these would lie dormant until, unbidden, they would ignite like a flash fire, devastating everything in their path.

In February, Byron, accompanied by Hanson's son, went back to school. And for the first time since her marriage, Catherine Byron returned to Bath. Revisiting the scenes of past happiness in the most dismal month of the year could not have provided much cheer. At the end of March she was back in London, in rented rooms at 23 George Street, Portman Square, where Byron joined her for the Easter holidays. Catherine's relative Pryse Lockhart Gordon, who lived nearby, saw something of mother and son during this visit, and years later he remembered the fourteen-year-old Byron as a "fine, lively, restless lad, full of fire and energy, and passionately fond of riding."[23] This was a passion Gordon shared with his young cousin, and he lent him a pony so they could ride together in Hyde Park. When Byron saw Pryse Gordon again, in Brussels fourteen years later, he reminded him of their outing: "I remember your pony was very handsome and a fast galloper, and that we raced and that I beat you, of which I was not a little proud."[24]

Byron had revised most of what actually happened, except his own boastfulness at the time. To deflate his young relative's swelled head, Gordon had demanded slyly: "Do you know the proverb, that there is a great deal of riding in a borrowed horse?" Significantly, Byron had not heard the adage, but when its meaning was explained, "He good humouredly drew in his reins, and acknowledging the rebuke, added: 'If the pony was mine, I would bet you my month's pocket-money that I would be at Kensington Gardens before you.'" Gordon accepted the wager and agreed to race the next day. Byron, however, couldn't resist some crowing at home: "He blabbed [this] to his mother who would on no account permit the course. But the ride was not to be abandoned, and he gave his parole [word] that he would not gallop, and kept religiously to it; for though he was a spoiled child and had too much of his own way, he never did anything intentionally to disoblige or vex her—at least so she has often told me."[25]

Back at school, Byron found Harrow ever more to his liking as he successfully negotiated its complex tribal rites. He now became a close friend, as well as protector, of Harness, and the younger boy rewarded Byron's protective love with total devotion. They soon discovered they had more in common than their lameness. Avid readers of romances and verse, both were starting to write poetry. As a measure of his trust,

Harness made a gift of these first efforts to Byron, who later wrote to him, saying: "How well I recollect the perusal of your *'first flights.'* There is another circumstance you do not know: the *first Lines* I ever attempted at Harrow were addressed to *you.*"[26]

Byron may have muddled the dates or exaggerated somewhat to flatter his friend, since elsewhere he noted that he had attempted a drama, "at thirteen years old, called 'Ulric and Ilvina' which I had sense enough to burn."[27] He also destroyed the poems inspired by Harness.

Now that solitude was no longer imposed upon him, he could choose to be alone, reading—novels, travel narratives, and poetry. But it was writing, he now discovered, that offered an outlet for emotions not easily articulated in schoolboy conversation, while providing at the same time the perfect form to express a rich fantasy life. He had found the ideal place to withdraw with his thoughts: under an elm in Harrow chuchyard, at some distance from the other graves, where a blue limestone slab covered the tomb of John Peachey, Esq., of the island of St. Christopher's. Late that winter his adored cousin Margaret Parker died, apparently of tuberculosis of the spine, following the death of her beautiful younger sister. The fifteen-year-old Byron tried to make sense of senseless loss and waste and to give voice to his affliction. But "On the Death of a Young Woman, Cousin to the Author and Very Dear to Him" emerged stillborn, touching on every clichéd trope from weeping angels to the pitiless King of Terrors who had "seiz'd her as his prey."[28]

By now, the idealized love he had felt for his cousin had been displaced by intense relationships with fellow students. "My school friendships were *with me passions* (for I was always violent)," Byron wrote of these years.[29] Half a century later, Harrow was to become infamous for the flagrancy of its homoerotic relationships. Whether Byron and his friends acted out these passions sexually is uncertain. The histrionics occasioned by their friendships—explosions of jealousy and power plays, mutual accusations of betrayal and pleas for forgiveness—point to issues of threatened possessiveness and sexual exclusivity. Byron's susceptibility to insult seems to have exceeded that of any of those close to him: On one occasion he took offense when a favorite addressed a letter to him as "my dear Byron" instead of "my dearest"; the same correspondent's expression of regret at the departure for Spain of one of their circle, Lord John Russell, incited thunderbursts of outrage. How could the latter's absence be any cause for sorrow, when Byron had just announced his intention to set off in March for a voyage of six years' duration? Many placating words were required to soothe the Byronic ego. "It is quite impossible you can think I am more sorry for John's absence than I shall be for yours," the penitent wrote.[30] It would never be enough for Byron to be loved; he required constant assurance that he was loved *best*. His own fidelity and devotion, he judged, were unwavering; others were fickle or subject to corrupting influences.

If they were sexual, the passionate alliances of Byron and his friends were at least serially monogamous and drenched in romantic feelings and language. But in Harrow's homoerotic underworld, every form of transgressive sexuality, from gang rape to sadomasochistic activities, was openly indulged. In Rendall's, one of the houses, it was later reported that "Every boy of good looks had a female name and was recognized either as a public prostitute or as some bigger fellow's bitch. Bitch was the word in common usage to indicate a boy who yielded his person to another. The talk in the studies and dormitories was incredibly obscene. One could not avoid seeing acts of onanism, mutual masturbation and the sport of naked boys in bed together. . . ." Three students, known as "the Beasts," ruled this jungle; the most genial of their number "was like a good natured bugimands ape, gibbering on his perch and playing ostentatiously with a prodigiously developed phallus. One bitch by the name of Cookson, who had served variously all three Masters, and was known as the *notissima fossa* of the House, fell out of favor." His punishment was clearly meant to serve as an example: "After he had been rolled on the floor, indecently exposed and violated in front of spectators, [the three] took to 'trampling' on Cookson whenever they encountered him; . . . they squirted saliva and what they called 'goby' upon their bitch, cuffed and kicked him at their mercy, shied shoes at him and drove him with curses whimpering into his den."[31]

AT THE BEGINNING of the Christmas holidays in 1802 Byron joined his mother in Bath; Hanson had rented Newstead, and for the time being she was homeless. Together mother and son attended a fancy dress ball given by Lady Riddel at her house at 14 Royal Crescent. Anticipating a lifelong fondness for Eastern costume for himself and his heroes, Byron came dressed as a Turkish boy, a diamond crescent glittering in his brocade turban. Probably paste, the brooch looked real enough to tempt a local footpad. As he was entering the house, a thief tried to wrench it from his headgear before being chased off by a fellow guest.

A month short of his fifteenth birthday, Byron seems to have been a sought-after younger guest among the Bath hostesses, especially those with teenage daughters. Inevitably, Catherine Byron benefited from her son's popularity. Since they were both enjoying themselves, they got along well for a change. Twice Catherine wrote to Owen Mealey asking him to send a basket of game from Newstead to Harrow for Byron's birthday on January 22.

At the end of January, however, Byron was still in Bath. The holiday season, as well as the school vacation, was long over, but still he refused to return to Harrow. Just before the term ended in November, antagonism had once again flared between Byron and his tutor, Henry Drury, who complained of the boy's "Inattention to Business, and his propensity to make others laugh and disregard their Employments as much as himself." Relations were so stormy that Drury senior had been forced to intervene by way of "many serious conversations" with the offender and pleas to his son for greater patience.[32]

Now, after asking Hanson if Byron could have a bed for a night or two on his way back to Harrow from Bath on January 25, Catherine was obliged to write again the next day to cancel the request: "Byron positively refuses to return to Harrow to be Henry Drury's pupil as he says he has been used ill for some time past," she explained. "You may be surprised that I do not force him to return but he is rather old and has too much sense for that."[33]

A loving but authoritarian father, Hanson was unsympathetic to this sort of indulgence, which he may have suspected had more to do with the mother's dependence on her son's companionship. His reply clearly put Catherine on the defensive, but she promptly advanced a common-sensical rationale for letting her son have his way: "I might force him to return to be sure," she wrote to the lawyer on January 19, "but I know he would not remain & I do not choose that he should wander the country as other boys do who have been sent to school against their inclination."[34]

Hanson did not answer this letter, or another anxious communiqué about her son's missed schooling, or further pleas from Catherine to settle the finances at Newstead. On the school front, however, he swung into action. Consulting with Dr. Drury, he received the head's assurance that if Byron returned to Harrow in mid-February he would be tutored by and board with Mr. Evans, a hearty and uncomplicated master. Once again the fond mother wrote to Hanson, requesting a bed for Byron in Earls Court on February 15. She also asked him to advance Byron £10 to pay outstanding bills at Harrow and to provide him with pocket money. She noted that she would then draw £115 instead of the £125 due on his allowance. She concluded by forwarding an ingenuous request from the prodigal pupil himself, along with a stern one from his mother: "Byron wishes you would write to Mr. Evans not to be prejudiced against him by H. Drury. I do not wish him to remain more than one night in London."[35]

Meanwhile, Hanson's negligence had created problems at Newstead. Leaving negotiation of the lease to their mutual friend Lord Grantley, he now discovered that the new tenants, the Launders sisters, were under the impression that they were to have "what accommodation the house will afford until the young Lord had come into his majority," or January 1809. Hanson, however, had been under the impression that the women had only leased the property as a temporary measure, to secure a roof over their heads while they searched for a permanent home in the vicinity. Mealey, the overseer, who could always be counted on to complain about anyone who expected him to do any work, reported to Hanson that the ladies "had bought many articles of new furniture since they come and all their talk is that they mean to stay until my Lord comes of age."[36] The sisters certainly gave every appearance of digging in. Then, noting the misunderstanding about the length of their intended stay, Hanson said that he was perfectly willing to lease the estate to them for the six remaining years of Byron's minority; the Misses Launder passed and Hanson closed with Lord Grey de Ruthyn, who signed the lease in April. Grey, a twenty-three-year-old bachelor and passionate hunter, was to have the manor house and park for £50 a year until Byron came of age.

Returning to Harrow in mid-February, Byron found tensions eased under the tutelage of the more paternal Dr. Evans. But there was a positive reason for the boy's happier state of mind: He had fallen in love.

Eleven-year-old John Fitzgibbon, Earl of Clare, was another in the series of Byron's attachments to younger new boys, but unlike his more transient schoolboy passions, "that with Lord Clare began one of the earliest and lasted longest—being only interrupted by distance—that I know of," Byron recalled eighteen years later. "I never hear the word 'Clare' without a beating of the heart—even *now*, & I write it—with the feelings of 1803-4-5—ad infinitum,"[37] he wrote in 1821. Frozen in time and place, his idealized feelings for the young Anglo-Irish nobleman survived because they were never exhausted by intimacy or repressed through shame. But he also allowed other young acolytes, such as his fag John Wingfield, the son of Lord Powerscourt, to vie for his favor. One of these youthful stalwarts, John Cecil Tattersall, saved Byron's head from being bashed by the butt end of a musket during a fracas with some local youths. In "Childish Recollections" (1806), a Miltonian epic dedicated to his band of intimates, Byron immortalized his young friend's protective heroism:

> High pois'd in air, the massy weapon hung,
> A cry of horror burst from every tongue
> Whilst I, in combat with another foe,
> Fought on, unconscious of th'
> Impending blow;
> Your arm, brave Boy, arrested his career,
> Forward you sprung, insensible to fear;
> Disarm'd, and baffled, by your conquering hand,
> The groveling Savage roll'd upon the sand.[38]

Harrow students were hated locally for their hooliganism and arrogance; their neighbors would have had reason to disagree as to just who were the "Savages" in the frequent altercations between the young gentlemen and their "rustic" adversaries.

Henry Drury was not done with Byron yet. On May 1, Catherine received a letter from her son, explosive with a sense of virtue outraged. His former master "has behaved himself to me in a matter I neither *can* nor *will bear.* . . . Today in church I was talking to a boy who was sitting next me, *that* perhaps was not right, but hear what followed. Taking the other offender off alone, Drury abused me in a most violent manner, called me *blackguard* said he *would* and *could* have me expelled from the School, & bade me thank his *charity* that *prevented* him." What upset Byron most was the possible loss of face Drury's behavior might cause him among his fellow students: "What must the boys think of me to hear such a message ordered to be delivered to me by a *master*," he wrote, adding melodramatically, "better let him take away my Life than ruin my *character*."[39]

Then, with a brilliant thrust of logic, he went to the heart of Drury's troubled feelings: "If I had done anything so *heinous* why should he allow me to stay at the School, why should he himself be so *criminal* as to overlook faults, which merit the *appellation* of a Blackguard." Why, indeed? Concluding his analysis of Drury's impotence, Byron declared triumphantly: "If he had it in his power to have [me] expelled he would long ago have *done* it, as it is, he has done *worse*, if I am treated in this manner, I will not stay at this *school*." Convinced that he could obtain no justice by appealing to the senior Drury, he implored his mother to intervene, begging her to write to the headmaster and ending with a touch of emotional blackmail: "If you love me you will now show it."[40]

When she received Byron's latest outcry, Catherine was back in Nottingham, in lodgings in Park Row. From here she kept an eye on Newstead and looked for an affordable house in the vicinity. Distraught over her son's letter, she sent it on to Hanson with this plea: "For God's sake, see to settle the Business. If he will not return there he must go to some other School. I will not have his education interrupted & I have at present no home or house to receive him." Then, in one of those straight-to-the-point remarks that made her so disliked, she observed: "It is extremely vexatious and very odd that the Doctor cannot make his son behave with Propriety to the Boys."[41] Hanson took the risk of sending Byron's letter on to Dr. Drury, who replied promptly on May 15, apologizing for his son's behavior and adding further praise of Byron's character: "He possesses, as his letter proves, a mind that feels, and that can discriminate reasonably on points in which it conceives himself injured." A further conversation with his aggrieved student calmed matters once again. More than ever convinced of the qualities of Byron's intellect, Drury tactfully moved the discussion back to his failings: "I feel particularly hurt to see him idle, negligent and apparently indifferent," he wrote to Hanson.[42] A firm believer in Byron's potential, the master was startled to find any skeptics. Summoned by Lord Carlisle to be informed of his ward's reduced prospects of inheritance, Drury assured the grandee, "He has talents, my lord, which will *add lustre to his rank.*"

"Indeed!!!!" was the guardian's astonished reply.[43]

A few weeks later, Byron wrote to thank his mother for a recent draft, noting pettishly that he had already written to her "several *times*" asking her to pursue Dr. Sheldrake or Hanson to "make an instrument for my leg immediately as I want one, rather." He added matter-of-factly that he had that very day (June 23) been placed in a higher form and that "Dr. Drury and I go on very well."[44]

He had moved from pariah to star: idolized by his juniors, popular with his peers, the headmaster's pet. Even Henry Drury was coming around. He and Byron were to be great friends; his former tormentor would become the chosen recipient of his spiciest letters from abroad.

Already Byron began to anticipate with dread leaving Harrow. No longer a prison, the school, soon to be immortalized as "Ida," playground of the the gods, had become "A home, a world, a paradise to me."[45]

CHAPTER 5

"Love, Desperate Love"

ITH NEWSTEAD rented for the next five years, Catherine Byron energetically set out to provide a real home for herself and her son. While living in Park Row, Nottingham, she had visited Southwell, about twelve miles to the east, on the banks of the Neet River, and had liked what she saw. The town that had grown up around the glorious Gothic minster was prosperous, tranquil, and cheap.

Burgage Manor, the property she rented from a Dr. Falkland, was (and still is) the most imposing house in Southwell: The handsome, three-story Georgian mansion, built of cream-colored render (brick plastered to resemble stone), dominates the sloping green. After her hopes of settling in Newstead had been disappointed, she was especially pleased, she wrote to Hanson, "that the Manor had a garden and grounds just as I could wish."[1]

More than anything, she wanted to have a home to which her son would return with pleasure and pride. According to her agreement with Lord Grey de Ruthyn, he was entitled to the furnishings at Newstead, excepting the family portraits. These she took with her when she moved to Southwell early in July, accompanied by two female servants. Other household necessities, such as curtains, she purchased herself. The owner of Burgage Manor had left the house well stocked with books, but Catherine, great reader that she was, promptly joined the local circulating library.

Arriving on July 26, Byron and Southwell made poor first impressions each upon the other. With his grand new Harrow friends and taste of high life in London and Bath, the fifteen-year-old was seized with an instant loathing for the unsophisticated provincials who were his mother's new neighbors. The intensity of his animus, though, suggests a defensive mind-set: These rustics would never be able to appreciate the distinction that his Harrow friends discerned in him. He was right. The lordling whose arrival was anticipated with curiosity turned out to be a lame, overweight, painfully shy adolescent whose handsome face was, at the moment, marred by an absurd fringe of hair plastered across his forehead.

Catherine Byron's first effort to provide a home for her son ushered in the stormiest period of their relationship. Too much time alone in the privacy of their own house exacerbated tensions that soon exploded in quarrels. Then there was the unfortunate coincidence that the move to Southwell, where he would be expected to act as his mama's perfect young cavalier, coincided with the beginning of adolescent rebellion, a need to test limits and establish distance. Furthermore, the fifteen-year-old's excruciating self-consciousness was flayed by Catherine's social deficits: Her physical unattractiveness, awkwardness, and insistence upon bluntly speaking her mind—all qualities Byron knew from bitter experience—produced reactions ranging from patronizing sympathy to contempt and outrage. Instant dismissal of the Southwell gentry as "old maids and parsons" was Byron's defense against their rejection of his graceless mother.

Each quarrel left a residue of new bitterness. To a boy hungry for approval, his mother's crudely expressed criticisms eroded his confidence and made him deeply anxious. By the same token, his fundamental generosity and sense of fairness forced Byron to acknowledge that his behavior toward her—expressed in the languidly sneering Harrow tone he had recently acquired—drove Catherine literally wild.

He began writing to Augusta, seeking in her sisterly love and approval a maternal substitute. In his first surviving letter to her, written from Burgage Manor on March 4, 1804, Byron apologizes for failing to reply to several notes she had sent to him at Harrow. She should not attribute his "neglect to a want of affection, but rather to a shyness naturally inherent to my Disposition." For the future, she must consider him "not only as a *Brother* but as your warmest and most affectionate *Friend* and if ever Circumstances should require it as your *protector*. Recollect, My Dearest Sister, that you are *the nearest relation* I have in *the world both by the ties of Blood and Affection*," he wrote.[2] His mother, clearly, did not qualify.

In late summer Byron fled Southwell and returned to Newstead, where he installed himself in the overseer's lodge with a less-than-enthusiastic Owen Mealey. Knowing him to be alone but for the servants, his neighbors the Clarkes promptly invited him to call, and soon he was spending all his time at Annesley Hall. At first the attraction was that of a warm family circle who readily included him. Then he fell in love. Mary Ann Chaworth, his little "Juliet" of two years ago, was now a young woman. To a natural vivacity and the bloom of her eighteen years, a fashionable London boarding school had added the requisite accomplishments of a lady: French, music, and dancing. Proficient in all three, Mary Ann was clever without being bookish, and a superb horse-woman. She and Byron explored the surrounding parks of Newstead and Annesley, returning always to their favorite destination: a hill whose graceful sweep of trees was known locally as the Diadem. There was one obstacle—or, more likely, added attraction—to Byron's passion for his "Morning star of Annesley": Mary Ann was besotted with a local squire, twenty-six-year-old Jack Musters.

Rumored to be the illegitimate son of the Prince Regent, Musters was, in the memory of a contemporary, "as regularly educated for hunt-ing as a churchman for church," and the famed sporting writer Nimrod recalled that the dashing young master of the South Notts Hunt was "known to the country around as being the best rider, the best jumper, the best dancer and the best pugilist the Nottingham region could produce."[3] He was also known as a suave seducer, bedding scullery maids and their titled mistresses with equal energy. His pleasures being unprofitable, however, the land-poor Musters was widely rumored to be seeking an heiress.

The Clarkes, Mary Ann's mother and stepfather, were terrified that he would carry off their daughter and her substantial fortune. As she was underage, the Reverend George Clarke brought a petition before the Lord Chancellor, Lord Eldon, in the name of his wife and himself, to have Mary Ann made a ward of court, citing Musters's threat that "he would have Miss Chaworth" and stating their objections to the marriage.[4] On pain of imprisonment, Musters was forbidden to marry Mary Ann, to see her, or even to write to her without the consent of the Clarkes or the court. Naturally, these attempts to thwart both passion and greed only heightened the lovers' determination: They now had to resort to clandestine meetings and secret letters.

Seeing her lover for only stolen moments left Mary Ann considerable free time. She did not discourage Byron's adoring attention and proba-bly used their excursions on horseback as a convenient cover to com-municate with her suitor. But Byron could hardly have been unaware that Mary Ann was in love with another. Thanks to the hospitality of the Clarkes (who were obviously hoping that their young neighbor would supplant the undesirable Musters), he had found yet another ideal love object: accessible yet unavailable.

At first he spent only his days at Annesley, returning to Newstead for the night: He was afraid, he later told Tom Moore, "of the family pictures of the Chaworths[;] he fancied 'they had taken a grudge to him, on account of the duel and would come down from their frames at night to haunt him.' " But a worse fright drove him to accept Mrs. Clarke's offer of the Blue Room as his own. " 'In going home last night I saw a bogle,' " he told Mary Ann and her cousin Ann Radford, "which Scotch term being wholly unintelligible to the young ladies he explained that he had seen a ghost."[5]

Now that he was in residence at Annesley, he did not have to be on his best behavior; when Mary Ann was too attentive to other friends who called, he sulked, pulling at the corner of his handkerchief (a lifelong nervous habit, along with nail-biting), or, more disruptively, practiced shooting holes with his pistol in the door leading to the terrace. Mary Ann later described Byron as a "rough boy,"[6] not lacking in manners but prone to uncontrollable explosions of temper or manic boastfulness: "I think I'm a good-looking fellow," he would suddenly announce to assembled young ladies, who giggled cruelly behind their hands.[7] His happiest moments were those when he had Mary Ann to himself—or could nurse the illusion that he did. Then she would sing his favorite song, the Welsh air "Mary Anne," accompanying herself on the harpsichord. On a day he would remember in every erotically charged detail, Byron joined the Clarkes on an excursion to Matlock, where they explored the famous Peak Cavern in Castelton. "When I was fifteen years of age," he recalled years later, "it happened that in a Cavern in Derbyshire—I had to cross in a boat—(in which two people only could lie down)—a stream which flows under a rock—with the rock so close upon the water—as to admit the boat only to be pushed on by a ferryman (a sort of Charon) who wades at the stern stooping all the time— The Companion of my transit was M.A.C. with whom I had been long in love and never told it—though *she* had discovered it without—I recollect my sensations—but cannot describe them—and it is as well."[8] Even in this rare instance of words failing him, Byron, significantly, connected the incident of physical closeness and sexual arousal with Charon, the diabolic oarsman rowing the damned to their eternal doom.

Certainly the outcome of that joyous day was punishment in the form of shame and suffering. Teased by her maid about falling in love with their guest, Mary Ann supposedly replied, in Byron's hearing: "What! Do you think I should care anything for that lame boy?"

According to Moore, this remark struck Byron "like a shot through his heart. Though late at night when he heard it, he instantly darted out of the house, and scarcely knowing whither he ran, never stopped until he found himself at Newstead."

Whether Byron overheard the remark himself, or whether it was repeated to him by another, or whether Mary Ann even said it—all of this remains unclear. When Tom Moore asked Mary Ann Chaworth Musters, late in her unhappy life, whether she had said this about Byron, she replied that it was "possible"—a softened admission, it would seem. But in the margin next to this passage in his copy of Moore's *Life*, Byron's friend Hobhouse penciled firmly: "I do not believe this story."[9]

In the event, passion prevailed over outraged pride. When Dr. Clarke rode after Byron to Newstead, the lovelorn boy is said to have returned to Annesley that same night. There he remained, buffeted by alternating currents of hope and despair—the same impulses that would charge Byron's relations with women throughout his life.

Despite entreaties from his mother, he refused to return to Southwell. The fall term began at school, and still he would not leave Newstead. In his letters to Burgage Manor he tried placating Catherine by negotiating with her day by day: "I know it is time to go to Harrow. It will make me *unhappy* but I will *obey*," he wrote to his mother in mid-September. "I only *desire, entreat,* this one day, and on my *honour* I will be over tomorrow. . . . Those that I most Love live in this county, there fore in the name of Mercy, I entreat this one day to take leave."[10]

No stranger to the pain of love, Catherine Byron was able to sympathize with her son's sufferings. More than a month later, he was still shuttling miserably between Annesley and Newstead. On October 30, Catherine wrote to Hanson, enclosing the boy's letter, written six weeks earlier: "You may well be surprised and so may Dr. Drury, that Byron is not returned to Harrow. But the Truth is, I cannot get him to return to school though I have done all in my power for six weeks past. He has no indisposition that I know of, but love, desperate love, the worst of all maladies in my opinion." She went on to explain to Hanson that even if Byron had been of age and "the lady disengaged, it is the last of all connexions I would wish to take place. To prevent all trouble in future, I am determined he shall not come here again until Easter."[11]

Her offer to sacrifice Byron's next visit to Southwell is a measure of Catherine Byron's feelings about the Chaworths. She concluded by asking Hanson to make some other arrangements for her son over the winter holidays. "I don't care what I pay," she declared, promising to visit Newstead the next day and "make a last effort to get him to Town."[12]

Maternal pleadings proved useless. Only the reappearance of Jack
Musters drove home to Byron the hopelessness of his attachment.
Stalking rumors of a rival, Musters apparently invited Byron for a day
of swimming at Colwick Castle, his family seat on the Trent River. After
their swim, Musters spied a ring of Mary Ann's on the pile of Byron's
clothes on the riverbank and defiantly seized it. A furious exchange followed. Musters asserted his claim to both the young woman and her
ring, saying, "I shall keep it." Leaving Byron at Colwick, where he was
spending the night, Musters rode over to Annesley, demanding an explanation from his beloved. Undoubtedly frightened, Mary Ann insisted
that Byron, demanding a keepsake, had taken the ring; she had seen no
harm in letting him keep a valueless trinket. But Musters was now worried, and he used this equivocal incident to exact a promise from Mary
Ann: She must declare herself bound to him and send the cripple packing.[13] Taking no chances, he returned to Colwick, and threatened Byron
with a thrashing if he went near Miss Chaworth again. But Jack and his
family were now alerted: His heiress was vulnerable to other suitors. In
August 1803 the Musterses presented their own petition to Lord Eldon
for a review of the case against their son. The Lord Chancellor agreed,
summoning both parties to his chambers. Despite the Clarkes' testimony that Musters was a "Monster of Profligacy and Depravity," other
witnesses prevailed.[14] Eldon reversed his earlier judgment; the lovers
were allowed to see one another and presumably to enter into an unofficial engagement.

For Byron, the end of hope was the beginning of obsession; he could
not tear himself away from the scene of so much happiness and torment.
In "The Dream," written thirteen years later, the poet evoked the feelings of obliteration that Mary Ann's loss inflicted on him:

> He had no breath, no being, but in hers;
> She was his voice; he did not speak to her,
> But trembled on her words; she was his sight,
> For his eye followed hers, and saw with hers,
> Which coloured all his objects:—he had ceased
> To live within himself; she was his life,
> The ocean to the river of his thoughts,
> Which terminated all: upon a tone,
> A touch of hers, his blood would ebb and flow,
> And his cheek change tempestuously—his heart
> Unknowing of its cause of agony.
> But she in these fond feelings had no share:

Her sighs were not for him; to her he was
Even as a brother—but no more; . . .

. . . .

. . . even *now* she loved another,
And on the summit of that hill she stood
Looking afar if yet her lover's steed
Kept pace with her expectancy, and flew.[15]

When he was feeling wretched, Byron behaved his imperious worst; he had long overstayed his visit at Owen Mealey's lodge, and when he moved on October 10, the overseer wrote complaining to Hanson: "Lord Byron left here yesterday he has been here since the second of August and he talks of coming again next week. . . . My Lord has been a very great hindrance to me since he has been here." He added, "The most of all me time has been taken up waiting of Lord Byron since the 1st of August. When I tell him that you will blame me not to attend to the work he says he [does not] Care that he must be waited on."[16] Byron returned briefly to Southwell, only to be drawn back to Newstead. Then, claiming that the empty abbey was haunted, he spent his nights at Annesley and during the day spied miserably on Mary Ann.

Lord Grey de Ruthyn had gone hunting in Yorkshire immediately after taking possession of the abbey in August. As soon as he had managed to persuade those "Angels of Creation"—as he gallantly termed the Misses Launders—to vacate, he had written to Catherine Byron, saying that her son would be welcome to stay at Newstead but for the lack of plate and other amenities unnecessary to a bachelor but essential for receiving guests. In late October, when Lord Grey returned to the abbey, he repeated his invitation to Byron. Most likely, hearing of the dramas at Annesley and listening to Mealey complain about the young lord's many impositions on him, Lord Grey decided that the absence of silver and crystal would be of no moment to the lovesick youth with nowhere else to go.

On December 29, Byron moved into the abbey and Mealey now reported to Hanson: "Lord Byron is at Newstead with Lord Gray [*sic*] they goe out these moonlight nights and shuit pheasants as they sit at Roost. There is a great deal said about Lord Byron in the neighborhood for staying away from school, and now being tutored by Lord Gray [*sic*] that kills all the game in the Country he has had 16 Hares in the House at one time he says he will turn the gardens into hare warren."[17]

For such a keen sportsman as young Lord Grey, it seems unlikely that his preferred sport would be shooting pheasants at roost and only slightly more plausible that this nobleman, concerned about silver and glass, should plan to turn Newstead's gardens into a rabbit warren. Mealey's malice, however, also included a talent for innuendo; his remark that the older peer was "tutoring" his truant guest was surely not meant to suggest that he was helping Byron make up missed schoolwork.

Whatever took place between Byron and Lord Grey during these wintry weeks ended their friendship; Byron left Newstead precipitously soon after the New Year, staying in Southwell until he returned, finally, to Harrow at the end of January for the new term. In a series of letters to Augusta, written in March from Burgage Manor, and then from school, he raged against Lord Grey's behavior, reiterating his loathing of the young man who had recently been his intimate. Adding to his injured feelings was his mother's insistence that he make up his differences with her tenant:

> I am not reconciled to Lord Grey, *and I never will*. He was once my *Greatest Friend*, my reasons for ceasing that Friendship are such as I cannot explain, not even to you my Dear Sister (although were they to be made known to any body, you would be the first), but they will ever remain hidden in my own breast.—They are Good ones however, for although I am *violent* I am not *capricious* in my *attachments*—My mother disapproves of my quarreling with him, but if she knew the cause (which she never will know), She would reproach me no more. He Has forfeited all *title to my esteem*, but I hold him in too much *contempt* ever [even?] *to hate him*.[18]

The "unmentionable" nature of Lord Grey's crime would have been clear to anyone hearing or reading Byron's account of his flight from Newstead. Lord Grey had made sexual advances to Byron that the younger boy repulsed. Or wished he had. In his copy of Moore's *Life*, next to the passage stating that "an intimacy had sprung up between Byron and his noble tenant," Hobhouse later noted: "And a circumstance occurred during this intimacy which certainly had much effect on his future morals."[19]

Laws attending the punishment of sodomy in Georgian England were murderously harsh. Evidence (frequently acquired through entrapment) leading to conviction could entail sentences ranging from actual execution by hanging, to public pillory—an invitation to the mob to carry out informal lynching. Whether Byron knew of actual cases and their victims' fate, he would certainly have been aware of the criminal significance of sexual relations between men, no longer protected by the anonymity of the school dormitory.

It is in this atmosphere of terror that the hysterical tone of Byron's fulminations against Lord Grey, his compulsive return to the subject, along with his refusal to specify the nature of his host's heinous acts ("I would if I could") must be seen. The intensity of his fear, moreover, points to an earlier complicity, followed by a guilty need to exonerate himself. Byron's homoerotically charged friendships at Harrow make it hard to believe that he could be shocked by Lord Grey's overtures; more likely it was his own response that frightened him.

Four years later, Lord Grey was still in a state of pained perplexity about the cause of the rift. In a letter written in reply to one received from Byron but now lost, he wrote: "With respect to that part of your letter which recalls to my recollection the days of our youth, I can only say it will ever be the farthest from my wish to assume any character to your lordship but that of Friend, but as you seem to suppose me so well acquainted with the cause of your sudden secession from our former friendship, I must beg leave to assure you that much as I have reviewed every circumstance and given to each its most full & weight interest, still I am now at a loss to account for it."[20]

One would have to suppose Lord Grey to have been obtuse, disingenuous, or writing for eyes other than Byron's to conclude that he invented feelings of puzzlement and pain. But he has more telling evidence of Byron's change of heart *subsequent* to his flight from Newstead: "We parted in 1804 the best of friends. . . . Your letters were afterwards most affectionate, nay I have even now a trifling pledge of your esteem which your mother gave me, and therefore under all these events, you cannot wonder at my being somewhat surprised— (you say the break was harmful to yourself, I need not say to you who know I have not the power to command my feelings when deeply wounded what my sensations were)." And he closes by reminding Byron of a blow that "having sunk too deep can never be forgotten."[21]

Both in tone and substance, Lord Grey's words reveal a dignified young man of deep feelings, unlikely to have imposed himself sexually on an unwilling partner. The question remains: Who seduced whom? At fifteen, Byron was already a charmer bent on conquest. At the very least, it seems likely that he led his host on, believing he could be flirtatious and seductive with Lord Grey, as he was with his Harrow friends, while still retaining control. Byron may have never imagined that Lord Grey, a simpler, less sophisticated fellow, took him seriously and assumed, in the romantic solitude of Newstead, that if his guest behaved seductively, he wanted to be seduced.

To complicate matters, Catherine Byron herself had become smitten with Grey de Ruthyn. At first the object of her visits to Newstead had been the protection of her property: If Lord Grey was not a good tenant, "It should at least be put out of his power to be a bad one," Catherine wrote tartly to Hanson.[22] But she soon succumbed to the appeal of the sporting young bachelor. They even held political views in common: Both Grey and Catherine Byron were Whigs in a solidly Tory county. As ever, Mealey was first to report his employer's besotted state and her son's angry reaction: "He [Lord Grey] is very thick with Mrs. Byron and Lord Byron is displaised [sic] at it."[23] Where Byron was concerned, Mealey had understated matters; his rage at his mother's double betrayal knew no bounds: "All our disputes," he wrote Augusta, "have been lately heightened by my one with that object of my cordial, deliberate detestation, Lord Grey de Ruthyn."[24]

Hoping for a reconciliation, or at least some enlightenment as to his wrongdoing, Lord Grey had called at Burgage Manor during the long vacation. When Byron refused to see him, his mother, Byron reported to Augusta, "threatened, stormed, begged me to make it up, he himself loved me and wished it." Adamant, Byron would not stir from his room. Referring to his thirty-nine-year-old mother as "the Dowager," he now made great sport of her infatuation for a man fifteen years her junior. "She has an excellent opinion of her personal attractions," he wrote to Augusta, "sinks her age a good six years, avers that when I was born she was only eighteen, when you my dear Sister as well as I know that she was of age when she married my father, and that I was not born for three years afterward, but vanity is the weakness of *your sex*."[25] Far from returning her affections, Byron told Augusta, Lord Grey behaved as if he disliked his mother. (As he never saw the visitor, Byron does not explain how he was able to observe his behavior so closely.)

Was Grey de Ruthyn using the lonely widow to intervene on his behalf with her son, or did he, in some measure, reciprocate her feelings? Certainly he continued to make Catherine welcome at Newstead. As Mealey reported to Hanson on July 30, "Mrs. Byron and him [Lord Grey] is greater than ever, he has dined with her several times since you left here and whatever he says is right with her." Mealey's surveillance now included opening Lord Grey's mail, as he added, "When he writes to her it is 'My dear Mrs. Byron.' "[26]

Catherine's infatuation—her last—seems to have subsided into friendship. There are no further reports of intimate dinners, but Lord Grey extended to her other kindnesses; he allowed Catherine the use of his franking privileges as a member of the House of Lords, addressing her envelopes himself, including those for payment of Byron's Harrow bills.

AT SOUTHWELL Catherine now turned to cultivating her neighbors, especially those with young people at home who could make Byron's vacations enjoyable, distract him from thoughts of Mary Ann, and provide an alternative to conflict between mother and son. She first called on Margaret Pigot, who lived directly across the green from Burgage Manor in a tidy house with well-tended lawns, gardens of flowers and vegetables, hothouses, and a splendid magnolia tree.

The widow of a Derbyshire doctor, Margaret Becher Pigot had returned to her native Southwell on the death of her husband nine years earlier with four children ranging in age from eleven-year-old Elizabeth to a baby of a few weeks. The Bechers were a prominent local family. Generous and sociable, Mrs. Pigot surely did much to ease Catherine Byron's acceptance in the closed circles of a small town. For the first time in her adult life, Mrs. Gordon Byron (as she now called herself) was a fixture in the rounds of teas, assemblies, and amateur theatricals that formed the social calendar of Southwell. Despite her son's unfortunate introduction to his new home, she felt secure enough to try again.

On April 9, a few days before his return to Harrow for the summer term, Byron wrote to Augusta:

> My mother Gives a *party* to night at which the principal *Southwell Belles* will be present, with one of which although I don't as yet know whom I shall so far *honour having never seen* them, I intend to *fall violently* in love, it will serve as an amusement pour passer le temps and it will at least have the charm of novelty to recommend it, then you know in the course of a few weeks I shall be quite au desespoir, shoot myself and Go out of the world with eclat, and my History will furnish materials for a pretty little Romance which shall be entitled and denominated the loves of Lord B. and the cruel and Inconstant Sigismunda Cunegonda Bridgetina &c&c princess of Terra Incognita.—Don't you think that I have a very Good Knack for *novel writing*?[27]

The truth of this spoof lay in the future; for the present, the host was so agonizingly shy, recalled his neighbor, Elizabeth Pigot, that his mother was forced to send for him three times before he would join their young guests in the drawing room for a round game. More than the company of strangers, Byron may have dreaded the games, in which one player designated as "it" remains outside the circle. Like dancing, circle games drew attention to his lameness.

Failing to launch her son at her soirée, Catherine coaxed him across the green the next morning to call on the Pigot family. The visit promised to be another disaster. Elizabeth Pigot, then twenty-one, found their sixteen-year-old neighbor still "very shy and formal in his manner," she recalled years later. But then she turned the conversation to her guest's recent visit to Cheltenham—where he had stayed, what diversions he had found, including the plays performed during their stay.

"I mentioned I had seen the character of Gabriel Lackbrain very well performed.* His mother, getting up to go, he accompanied her, and I, in allusion to the play, said 'Good-by, Gaby.' Then," Elizabeth remembered, "his countenance lit up, his handsome mouth displayed a broad grin, all his shyness vanished, never to return, and upon his mother saying, 'Come Byron, are you ready?'—no, she might go by herself, he would stay and talk a little longer, and from that moment, he used to come in and go out at all hours as it pleased him, and in our house considered himself perfectly at home."28

Once again Byron had found a surrogate family, with a daughter older than he was, whose heart was given to another (in this case, a young army officer serving in India). Elizabeth Pigot, however, differed in one important respect from the other unattainable sister figures who attracted him. Although a slender, appealing young woman, she aroused neither romantic nor erotic feelings on his part (her own attachment to Byron is more problematic), becoming, instead, one of the two women in his life in whom he confided as a sensible, intelligent, and trustworthy friend.

A small-town professional family, the Pigots were something new in Byron's experience; they could not have been farther from the Chaworth-Clarkes, with their concerns about fortune hunters and good marriages. Like his late father, Henry, the eldest Pigot, was destined for a career in medicine, and had begun his studies at Edinburgh shortly before the Byrons' arrival. Margaret Pigot was a talented gardener, and she and her daughter were both gifted watercolorists. In Byron's first letter to Elizabeth he accepted her offer to design for him a bookplate with the family escutcheon, featuring a mermaid with a curled tail.

Most important, Elizabeth encouraged Byron's poetry writing,

---

*In the play *Life* by Frederick Reynolds (1767–1833?), Gabriel Lackbrain is a country bumpkin whose vanity combined with obtuseness makes him the easy mark of a fortune-hunting scam.

becoming his copyist, editor, and eventually proofreader. In her function of bibliographer she also noted on her copy: "Facsimile of the *first* bit of Poetry Ld B. ever wrote down at Southwell."[29] Penned in the hectic few weeks after his flight from Newstead and Lord Grey, and just before his return to school, the poem titled "To D" pledges undying love to a Harrow friend, Delawarr, whom he would be seeing again in a few weeks:

> And, when the grave restores her dead,
>   When life again to dust is given,
> On *thy dear* breast I'll lay my head,
>   Without *thee*! *where* would be *my Heaven*?[30]

Thanks to the Pigots, and to Elizabeth in particular, Southwell now wore a very different aspect. But as soon as he returned to Harrow, Byron found himself in more trouble than ever. Accused by the headmaster of making his house "a scene of riot and confusion," he was further informed that Dr. Drury, his brother, Mark Drury, and worse, his new housemaster, Dr. Evans, had called him a *Blackguard* to other students; finally, as he complained in a long woeful letter to his mother, the same Mark Drury was "continually reproaching me with the narrowness of my fortune."

Byron never challenged the crass snobbery behind the master's remarks. He accepted the rigid social division of the school; a student was either a scholar (a day pupil and thus beneath consideration) or a gentleman, denoting both means and style. He refuted his accuser on substance: "His manner is disagreeable," he wrote to his mother in tones of pained dignity. "I have as much money, as many Clothes, and in every respect of appearance am equal if not superior to most of my school-fellows, and if my fortune is narrow, it is my misfortune, not my fault." The needling, however, from "this upstart Son of a Button maker" provoked Byron's most grandiose vision of his future: "The way to *riches* to *Greatness* lies before me, I can, I will cut myself a path through the world or perish in the attempt," he declared.[31]

For the present, his heroism would be tested by his spending the long summer vacation at Burgage Manor. With the Pigot house across the green as an escape, however, relations between mother and son even enjoyed moments of harmony. Both were fond of the theater, and a playbill dated August 8, 1804, announced a new production under the patronage of "Mrs. and Lord Byron."

That summer, Byron and Elizabeth Pigot began writing verses

together. After a discussion on the subject of love, Elizabeth had composed the following quatrain:

> Away, Away—your flattering arts
> May now betray some simplet hearts
> And *you* will *smile* at their believing
> And *they* shall weep at your deceiving.

Byron's reply to this verse, later published as "Answer to the Foregoing Address'd to Miss ——.," was written on the flyleaf of Elizabeth's copy of *Letters of an Italian Nun and an English Gentleman. Translated from the French of J. J. Rousseau,* which both had recently read:

> Dear simple girl, those flattering arts,
> From which thou'dst guard frail female hearts,
> Exist but in imagination,
> Mere phantoms of thine own creation;
> For he who views that witching grace,
> That perfect form, that lovely face,
> With eyes admiring, oh! believe me,
> He never wishes to deceive thee:
>
> . . . .
> Then he, who tells thee of thy beauty
> Believe me, only does his duty;
> Ah! fly not from the candid youth,
> It is not flattery, 'tis truth.[32]

Allowing for the persiflage required of this kind of gallantry in verse—somewhere between parlor game and Valentine card—the "candid youth" was also managing to have it both ways: He might lie to other women in his role of cynical seducer; Elizabeth's beauty rendered deceitful praise impossible—the greatest flattery of all!

As her verse suggests, Elizabeth's preferred role of trusted friend and confidante may have been self-protective; she was only too aware of Byron's contempt for the husband-hunting young ladies among her friends. Her own feelings for him were probably more romantic than she dared acknowledge. She marked only one passage in Rousseau's work, declaring the rational love of friendship to be "truer" than passion's uncontrollable rapture: "The sincerity of affection is not proved by wild and incoherent declamation. Pure and solid love is ever accompanied with reason; and though its language may glow with more than common animation, though to common observers, it may sometimes appear to stray from its associate, it never quits in reality, that sober guidance which can alone preserve it from folly, and intemperance."[33]

Ruling out passionate love at age twenty-one suggests fear more than rationality. There was no further mention of the far-off young naval officer (it was said he had died in India), and Elizabeth Pigot never married.

JUST RECOVERING from his obsession with Mary Ann Chaworth, Byron retreated into the safe intimacy of Elizabeth's company. Undoubtedly jealous, Catherine now professed to worry that the new friendship would prove another romantic entanglement. In her direct style, she made known her concern to Margaret Pigot, who was reassuring about her daughter and Byron: "Though Elizabeth regards him very much as a friend, she sees all his faults clearly, and there is not a spark of anything like love."[34]

If Byron had known of this, the fragile entente between mother and son that summer would have been over. As it was, he wrote to Hanson describing his parent as "truly amiable"—a unique phrase of approval not to be repeated in Catherine's lifetime.[35] The Pigots spent late August traveling; from Burgage Manor, Byron wrote to Elizabeth thanking her for the bookplates bearing the Byron seal that she had drawn for him, and he flirtatiously observed that, besides ornamenting his books, they "convince me, that *you* have not entirely *forgot* me."[36] He hoped she would return before he left Southwell for Hampshire, where the Hansons had invited him for a shooting party at their country house. He reminded her of the watch ribbon and purse she was to knit for him, hoping to have it before his departure for school.

The shooting vacation fell through, and Byron apparently remained at Southwell until he returned to Harrow in October. Deprived of a sympathetic feminine presence, he intensified his correspondence with Augusta. His half sister was despondent over the obstacles to her cousin's courtship. General Leigh was not pleased with Augusta's modest income and was making problems about the match.

With the wounds inflicted by Mary Ann still untreated, Byron's advice to the lovelorn Augusta was couched in a savage cynicism that would have justified Elizabeth Pigot's worst fears: While he sympathized with his sister in her distress, he felt "a little inclined to laugh at you, for love in my humble opinion, is utter nonsense, a mere jargon of compliments, romance and deceit; now for my part had I fifty mistresses, I should in the course of a fortnight, forget them all. . . . Can't you drive this Cousin of ours out of your pretty little head, (for as to *hearts* I think they are out of the question)." And he concluded with this

suggestion: "If you are so far gone, why don't you give old L'Harpagon*
(I mean the General) the slip, and take a trip to Scotland, you are now
pretty near the Borders."37

Neither Augusta nor her colonel were prepared to risk the censure
(and worsened financial circumstances) that were sure to follow upon
an elopement. Augusta would always suffer from the poor female relation's fear of displeasing; she begged Byron to burn her letters. He
refused, but promised, not very reassuringly, that they would remain
"invisible."38

Byron himself was far from invisible. In his role of troublemaker
and ringleader, he made Dr. Drury's "house a scene of riot and
Confusion"39—Drury's words—and was accused of undermining discipline throughout the school. On November 2 Byron reported with uncon-
vincing jauntiness to Augusta, "I had a thundering Jobation from our
Good Doctor which deranged my *nervous system* for at least five minutes." Despite his inability to stay out of trouble, he and the head were
"very good friends," Byron insisted, "for there is so much of the
Gentleman, so much of mildness, and nothing of pedantry in his character,
that I cannot help liking him and will remember his instructions with
gratitude as long as I live. He leaves Harrow soon, apropos so do I."40

Buried in this casual-sounding afterthought was news he chose not
to relay. Drury had spoken privately to Byron, informing him that he
could not recommend his return to Harrow in the new term. No specific
misdemeanors were ever named; only the sulfurous whiff of Byron's
unhealthy influence on other boys was invoked. Early in December the
master apparently wrote a tactful account of his decision to Catherine
Byron. As she told Hanson, Drury "thinks highly of my son, but he does
not think it proper he should remain longer at Harrow."41 To Augusta,
Byron continued to be vague: "When I leave Harrow I know not."42 But
his sister had already been informed of the real state of affairs by
Hanson—the only one to whom Drury had written candidly: "During
his last residence at Harrow his conduct gave me much trouble and
uneasiness and, as two of his Associates were to leave me at Christmas,
I certainly suggested to him *my wish* that he might be placed under the
care of some private Tutor previously to his admission to either of the
Universities. This I did with no less a view toward the forming of his
mind and manners, than to my own comfort."43 No further clarification
emerges from any of those involved.

---

*Because of his concern about Augusta's fortune, Byron compares General Leigh to
Molière's miser in the play *L'Avare*.

Augusta and Hanson now agreed that over the Christmas holidays, a family conference must be convened with Lord Carlisle. Byron now had more reason than ever to dread the vacation and the inevitable confrontation with his parent: "I shall do everything I can to avoid a visit to my mother wherever she is," he wrote to Augusta,[44] adding his hopes for an invitation to spend Christmas with the Hansons in London. Augusta needed no further prompting to ensure that he was invited to Earls Court for the holidays, while making certain that Catherine, increasingly hostile to all of her son's other attachments, should never suspect that the invitation had come at Byron's behest.

He had not visited London for two years and the city's diversions made banishment from Harrow seem remote. Byron's theater-loving friends would have envied him one experience in particular: He attended several performances at Covent Garden starring the boy actor William Henry West Betty, known as "The Young Roscius." This December 1804 was his debut season, and the thirteen-year-old's adulatory reception by both the press and the public made him an instant idol. His appearance in *Barbarossa* created a near riot of the crowds surging on the theater, to the point that the militia had to be called to restore order. Nonchalantly, Byron noted to Augusta that he had seen the prodigy several times "at the hazard of my life, from the *affectionate squeezes* of the surrounding crowd," finding him by no means worthy of the "ridiculous praises showered upon him by *John Bull*."[45] Not so the Prime Minister, William Pitt, who adjourned the Commons so members should not miss Master Betty's performance as Hamlet.

On January 22, 1805, Byron turned seventeen. If his mother had hoped to celebrate his birthday with her son, she was disappointed. Nor did he give any sign of later plans to visit Southwell. Catherine Byron never wasted any time on false pride. The next day she wrote to Hanson, pleading, "As soon as there is a tolerable day, I beg you will send Byron down—I shall be quite unhappy till I see him."[46]

Eclipsing all other events of his stay in London was an invitation to dine with his guardian, Lord Carlisle, at Grosvenor House, on January 26. Byron's earlier surliness toward his relation melted in the warmth of his reception by the other Howards: "On further acquaintance, I like them all very much," he declared to Augusta, "I think your friend Lady G[ertrude] is a sweet girl. If your taste in *love*, is as good as it is in *friendship*, I shall think you a *very discerning little Gentlewoman*, His Lordship too improves upon further acquaintanceship,"[47] he concluded patronizingly.

Carlisle's invitation was not motivated by hospitality alone. He had been conferring with Hanson about his ward's departure from Harrow and was obviously trying to get to know him better before intervening with Dr. Drury. His guardian's opinion of Byron had also improved since their last meeting, three years earlier, and he now shared Hanson's sympathetic view of the boy's distress at being asked to leave school. As the lawyer wrote to Catherine about her son, "He seems now to think that his not returning to Harrow . . . after what has been said would amount in the opinion of his Friends to an Expulsion and . . . that idea hurts him very much. . . . [As] he has a great wish to speak in the Summer* he seems bent upon his returning."[48]

Together the lawyer and the powerful peer succeeded in persuading Dr. Drury to change his mind. Byron was allowed to return in February for his final two terms before going to university. He had hoped to be admitted to Oxford, but there were no rooms available at Christ Church, his only choice of college. This, at least, was the reason Byron gave to Augusta. But the real cause of his rejection may have been his uncertain status (tantamount to present-day suspension) at Harrow when he applied.

Byron had not seen his mother since September, and in early April he could no longer defer a visit to Southwell. After less than two weeks together, their clashes were more frequent—and more bitter than ever. Catherine not only tore into her son but also reviled his other attachments, to Augusta and Lord Carlisle, blaming the Byron side of the family for all his failings: "I have never been so *scurrilously* and *violently* abused by any person, as by that woman," he wrote to his sister. "Within one little hour, I have not only [heard] myself, but have heard my *whole family* by the fathers side, *stigmatized* in terms that the *blackest malevolence* would [perhaps] shrink from, and that too in words [you] would be shocked to hear. Such, Augusta, such is my mother; *my mother,* I disclaim her from this time."

By damning her son as a Byron, as genetically stained, Catherine ironically soldered his first powerful bonds with his half sister—bonds of love and acceptance but also of secrecy and shame: "To you Augusta, I must look up, as my nearest relation," he wrote on April 23, "to you I must confide what I cannot mention to others, and I am sure you will pity me, but I entreat you to keep this a secret, nor expose that unhappy failing of this woman which I must bear with patience."[49]

A little more than a week later, Byron was free and back in London. He delayed his return to Harrow by two days to hear "our *Sapient*

---

*At Harrow's final Speech Day, for which Byron had been preparing King Lear's address to the Storm.

and *Noble Legislators* of Both Houses debate on the Catholic Question, as I have no doubt," he wrote to Augusta, "there will be many *nonsensical*, and some *Clever* things said on the occasion."[50] (The petition to relieve the civil, naval, and military disadvantages of the Catholics was roundly defeated in both Lords and Commons.) Of equal interest to Byron as the subject* under debate were the respective skills of the speakers. Since inheriting the title, Byron had visualized himself in the House of Lords, persuading his fellow peers with eloquence and style. More immediately, with Speech Day looming at school, he decided it was more important to pick up some pointers on moving hearts and minds than to attend the first meeting of the incoming head, Dr. Butler.

Byron had been boarding at the headmaster's house before the new head's arrival. His dislike of Butler was such that he now considered a change of residence on his return. Grieved at the possibility, his friend Tattersall wrote to dissuade him: "What the devil do you think I am to do without you, you don't consider what a *vacancy* there will be. Butler will certainly go *raving mad* (when he finds out what sort of fellow you are & I shall go *melancholy mad* for the loss of you)." In his new house, Tattersall warned, they would "only lead your innocent mind from the paths of virtue, in which you & I have walk'd arm & arm together as yet, yea they will lead thee astray, & make straight thy way to *eternal perdition*."[51]

They planned to leave for " 'arrow on the 'ill 'cadamy" together, Tattersall trying to delay his departure "till Friday that you & I may go all to the play together, & mayhap pick up a tidy wench."[52]

His London holiday—including the plays, with or without wenches—had left Byron out of pocket. Immediately upon arriving at school he dispatched an urgent note to Hanson, begging for an immediate draft to pay his tuck shop bills.

Thereafter he busied himself with polishing his selection for the first of two Speech Days, marking the end, respectively, of the spring and summer terms. Several months earlier he had chosen, from Edward Young's† tragedy *The Revenge*, the fiery speech of Zanga over the body of the slain Alonzo.

---

*His second speech in the House of Lords, on April 21, 1812, would be on behalf of the Catholic claims to the full rights of British subjects.

†Author of the more famous *Night Thoughts*. Young's earlier work was a pastiche of Othello, with Zanga modeled on Iago—a role that one critic noted acidly "gave opportunity for effective rant." The part won by Byron was also coveted by several other boys in his form, suggesting that they had seen the play performed over the recent vacation, with the great John Kemble in the starring role.

Byron had been so immersed in preparing his monologue for June 5 that he failed to invite Augusta until it was too late. He apologized on the night of the performance (without giving any indication of how his efforts had been received), promising to extend a more timely invitation for the next—and final—Speech Day a month hence.

Since Byron's departure from Southwell, Augusta, too, had been the target of Catherine's wrath, the poor girl having received a "specimen of one of the dowager's talents for epistles in the *furioso* style," her brother noted sympathetically. "She is as I have before declared certainly mad (to say she was in her senses, would be condemning her as a Criminal), her conduct is a *happy* compound of derangement and Folly," he told his sister.[53] In fact, a disturbing suggestion of persecution mania does characterize Catherine's behavior at this time. In one instance, she tried forbidding Byron to visit the house of Lord Carlisle. On the other hand, so many people disliked her, including her son's guardian, that her feelings of persecution confirm the reflection that even paranoids have enemies.

Byron, meanwhile, was exuberantly engaged in persecuting his newest enemy, Dr. Butler, Drury's successor as head of the school. Instead of moving, he remained in the Headmaster's House, the better to torment the poor man in situ. The resident guerrilla was not, however, prepared to take the consequences of his behavior: "Afterwards . . . when Butler threatened him," Moore reported, "he cried and blubbered like a child."[54] Already he was more comfortable with the pen than with the sword. Satirizing Butler as Pomposus, Byron delighted his fellow seniors with a broadside that also paid homage to his favorite poet, Pope:

> Of narrow brain, yet of a narrower soul,
> Pomposus holds you, in his harsh controul;
> Pomposus, by no social virtue sway'd,
> With florid jargon, and with vain parade;
>
> . . . .
>
> Mistaking pedantry, for learning's laws,
>   He governs, sanction'd but by self applause.[55]

His final insult was to decline the traditional invitation to dine with the headmaster extended to senior boys at the end of term.

Despite his last months of troublemaking, Byron finished the term as monitor, ranking third in his form. Once again he threw himself into preparing for Speech Day on July 4. This time, instead of Young's imitation of Shakespeare, he chose King Lear's searing address to the storm. Two days before the event, he traveled to Cambridge to enroll in person at Trinity College. He also reminded Augusta on this same Tuesday (having given her the date a month earlier): "If you intend doing me the *honour* of attending, I would recommend you not to come without a Gentleman, as I shall be too much engaged all the morning to take care of you, and I should not imagine you would admire *stalking* about by yourself." He concluded this rather ungracious invitation with an equivocal jest: "I *beg Madam* you may make your appearance in one of his Lordships most *dashing* carriages as our Harrow *etiquette* admits of nothing but the most *superb* vehicles, on our Grand *Festivals.*"[56]

Augusta did not appear. Byron, perhaps fearing he would be more vulnerable to stage fright if she were among the audience, had meant to put her off. In the event, he seems to have suffered an attack of nervous exhaustion immediately after his performance and left the room. To his indignation, the Old Harrovian who wrote the account for the London newspapers omitted any mention of his contribution, along with those of his friends Long and Farrer. Byron harbored dark suspicions that he was being taught a lesson.

Still, his last term at Harrow had been the best. Weeks before the final farewells, he experienced a sense of loss and regret—"it broke my very rest for the last quarter—with counting the days that remained," he wrote later in his "Detached Thoughts." "One of the deadliest and heaviest feelings of my life to feel that I was no longer a boy."[57] This was the real source of Byron's sorrow: He mourned the end of youth's privileged absolution. For the moment, this painful vision pushed from his consciousness happier evidence of all Harrow had given him, starting with admiration and love, from juniors, peers, and even masters. Most important for the future, the school's safely patrolled avenues of dissent allowed the adolescent rebel to feel like a revolutionary.

THE HOLIDAYS were beginning. Byron had decided on visiting London and Augusta, when, to his horror, he was informed of his mother's plan to join him. All his defiance evaporated and he wrote to Hanson, pleading with the lawyer to cover for him; he had lied to his mother, telling her that the vacation began a week later.

Already he felt adrift in that limbo between school and university. Painfully nostalgic for the effortless comradeship of Harrow, he tried to prolong its pleasures. On August 2 he played in the cricket match against Eton. He needed a second to run for him, but he batted respectably enough. Still more enthusiastically, he joined in the drunken revels that followed, beginning with a play at the Haymarket Theatre, where meeting up with some Etonians resulted in a row. Peace declared, the seven former combatants crammed amicably into one small box. Now that their noisemaking made it impossible for other theatergoers to hear the performance, a wider fracas threatened, and the schoolboys had to make a speedy exit. "How I got home after the play, God knows," he confessed, "as my brain was so confused by the heat, the row and the wine I drank, that I could not remember in the morning how the deuce I found my way to bed."[58] The next evening at eight o'clock, he set out for Southwell, arriving the following afternoon.

August with his mother in Burgage Manor seemed a life sentence; her "*diabolical* disposition," he wrote to Augusta, "seems to increase with age and to acquire new force with Time. . . . It is a happy thing that she is my mother and not my wife, so that I can rid myself of her when I please."[59] He did not think he could last the month in Southwell, he told his sister. To indulge his spleen so unforgivingly while trying to assert his independence, he had to strip his parent of every redeeming quality, especially the economies she continued to make on his behalf.

"As I am to have a very handsome allowance, which does not deprive her of a sixpence, since there is an addition made from my fortune by the Chancellor for the purpose, I shall be perfectly independent of her,"[60] he informed Augusta grandly. In fact, he was mistaken on all counts. The allowance from Chancery for his education was paid to Catherine Byron in quarterly installments; she would have been more than entitled to deduct some portion of it for her own maintenance. As it was, she gave over the entire amount to Byron on his going to Cambridge in the fall, applying to Chancery for an allowance for herself of £200. Not only was this refused her, but also her pension from the Civil List was reduced from £350 to £200.

Most likely Byron's lofty inaccuracy was informed by the need *not* to know of his financial dependence on his mother, nor of her generosity and sacrifice. Although her son had not invited her to either Speech Day at school, she wrote proudly to Hanson on June 23, "The fame of Byron's oratory has reached Southwell" and instructed him to send the star "a dozen of wine to Harrow, 6 Port 6 Sherry." Catherine Byron would continue to beggar herself to see that her son lived like a lord: Just before he enrolled at Trinity College early in July, she further requested of Hanson to "have everything found him he can possibly want, even his gown that he may begin clear with his five hundred a year."[61]

She found other ways to revenge herself for his rejection.

At the end of August, Mary Ann Chaworth and Jack Musters were married. When Catherine Byron broke the news to her son, another person (probably Elizabeth Pigot) was present who later described their interchange: "His mother said, 'Byron, I have some news for you'—'Well, what is it?'—'Take out your handkerchief first, for you will want it.'— 'Nonsense!'—'Take out your handkerchief, I say.' He did so, to humour her. 'Miss Chaworth is married.' An expression, very peculiar, impossible to describe, passed over his pale face, and he hurried his handkerchief into his pocket, saying, with an affected air of coldness and nonchalance, 'Is that all?'—'Why, I expected you would have been plunged in grief!' He made no reply, and soon began to talk about something else."[62]

He was becoming expert in disguising his deepest feelings, even though swallowed rage was more damaging than explosions of anger between mother and son: "No Captive Negro, or Prisoner of war, ever looked forward to their emancipation, and return to Liberty with more Joy, and with more lingering expectation, than I do my escape from [this] maternal bondage, and this accursed place, . . ." he wrote to Augusta, "I wander about hating every thing I behold."[63]

To ease his sense of imprisonment, he indulged fantasies of a future characterized by lordly hospitality. Writing to a Harrow classmate, Charles Gordon, now "*my* dearest Friend," he promised, "when I have finished my *Classical labours* and my minority is expired, I shall expect you to be a frequent visitor to Newstead Abbey, my seat in the county, which lies about 12 miles from my mothers house where I now am; there I can show you plenty of hunting, shooting, and fishing, and be assured no one will ever be a more welcome Guest than yourself."[64]

Then, a few weeks later, on September 23, he was free, on the way to London, where he would join the Hansons for the deferred visit to Farleigh,* their house near Basingstoke, Hampshire, before going up to Cambridge in October.

In this last year and a half he had changed profoundly; Augusta had been the first to seize on the transformation.

"In the year 1804," Byron remembered, "I recollect meeting my Sister at General Harcourt's in Portland Place—I was then *one thing*, and *as* she had always till then found me. . . . When we met again in 1805—(she told me since) that my temper and disposition were so completely altered, I was hardly to be recognized."[65]

---

*Owned by Hanson's client and future son-in-law, the Earl of Portsmouth, Farleigh appears to have been made available gratis to the lawyer, who passed the property off as his own.

CHAPTER 6

"Fickle as Wind, of Inclinations Wild"

*W*HEN BYRON arrived in Cambridge on October 24, 1805, he had indeed changed—if less dramatically than he believed. He was no longer the adolescent addicted to rebellion for its own sake. He had learned the adult art of concealment; only a trusted few were now privy to his passions and fervent idealism, and he had become still more adroit at disguising the despair whose symptoms would paralyze him periodically throughout his life.

"When I went up to Trinity, in 1805, at the age of seventeen and a half," Byron afterward recalled, "I was miserable and untoward to a degree. I was wretched at leaving Harrow, to which I had become attached during the last two years of my stay there; wretched at going to Cambridge instead of Oxford, wretched from some private domestic circumstances of different kinds, and consequently as unsocial as a wolf taken from the troop."[1]

But the wolf had a thicker hide now, and took positive—sometimes wicked—pleasure in assuming many guises, among them that of the cool and cynical aristocrat who was also a warm host, convivial drinking companion, and favorite of the town's sizable population of whores.

Arriving insouciantly just before lectures began, Byron addressed, first, a matter of much greater urgency: "Dear Sir," he wrote to Hanson in a new tone of lordly command, "I will be obliged to you to order me down 4 Dozen of Wine, Port—Sherry—Claret, & Madeira, one Dozen of Each."[2]

Even without artificial stimulus, his spirits were rising. "I have got part of my furniture in, & begin to *admire* a College Life," he told Hanson.[3] He was always readily distracted by new people, new places, and new clothes—especially fancy dress. Now, to his delight, he discovered that, as a peer, he was expected to distinguish himself from the ordinary scholars in drab cap and gown by donning, for official occasions, a costume allowed only to student nobles, consisting of a robe covered in gold embroidery, worn with a matching hat: "Yesterday my appearance in the Hall in my State Robes was *Superb*," he told Hanson, "but uncomfortable to my *Diffidence*," he added, in an attempt at modesty.[4] He lost no time in commissioning a portrait of himself in this splendid rig from the fashionable painter George Sanders. In a bow toward democratic principles, though, Byron was painted holding the tasseled mortarboard of the rank-and-file student. Other expensive appurtenances of a gentleman were nonetheless required: "You may order the Saddle, & & for Oateater,"* he instructed the lawyer.[5] He also asked the latter's son, Hargreaves, still at Harrow, to immediately send his shirt stocks and the remains of his library, both of which had been left at school.

Four weeks into the term and Byron was a member in good standing of the fast set—rich "gentleman commoners" and young noblemen like himself whose titles accorded them traditional exemptions from lectures and examinations in the unimpeded pursuit of pleasure: "This place is the *Devil*," Byron wrote to Hanson (not without a certain *épater les bourgeois* glee), "or at least his principal residence, they call it the University, but any other appellation would have suited it much better, for Study is the last pursuit of the Society; the Master eats, drinks and Sleeps, the Fellows *drink dispute* and *pun*, the *employments* of the under Graduates you will probably conjecture without my description. I sit down to write with a head confused with dissipation, which though I hate, I cannot avoid. I have only supped at home 3 times since my arrival, and my table is constantly covered with invitations, after all I am the most *steady* man in the College."[6]

Byron did not exaggerate; sober critics of the universities had been lamenting their decline for fifty years. By the middle of the eighteenth century, Oxford and Cambridge had fallen into intellectual and moral decay; the riotous *dolce vita* of their rich and titled students set the tone of both institutions. Since Isaac Newton's genius had shed its luster on Trinity in the 1720s, the college's claim to scholarly eminence had faded. Fellows spent their feeble energies on internecine strife, in pallid imitation of Whig and Tory, High Church or Low conflicts. Poorer students who aspired to the college sinecures of their elders or (if they enjoyed some landed connections) to a parish living outside academe, did as best

---

*A gray, and one of three horses that Byron kept at college.

they could to augment whatever classical learning they had had flogged into them in school with a few principles of theology. Significantly, a once-distinguished Greek scholar of Trinity, Richard Porson, had, by the time of Byron's arrival, become a slovenly drunk, terrifying undergraduates and fellows alike with his outbursts.

If little learning or teaching took place, the beauty of Cambridge, natural and man-made, delighted Byron's aesthetic sense. Trinity College in particular appealed to his love of spaciousness and harmony combined. Now identified with certainty, Byron's rooms were in Nevile's Court, named after Trinity's master builder and polymath patron, who had been responsible for persuading his friend Christopher Wren to design the majestic library on the river side of the court.

The windows of Byron's rooms overlooked Wren's masterpiece, a few footsteps from his door, but he never mentions it or the splendors contained within, which include carvings by Grinling Gibbons and the manuscripts of poems of Milton. But he was well pleased with his own accommodations, exaggerating their opulence to impress Augusta: "I am now most pleasantly situated in *Super*excellent Rooms* flanked on one side by my tutor, on the other by an old Fellow, both of whom are rather checks upon my *vivacity*," he wrote to his sister on November 6. "I am allowed £500 a year, a Servant and Horse, So feel as independent as a German Prince who coins his own Cash, or a Cherokee Chief who coins no Cash at all, but enjoys what is more precious, Liberty."[7]

His sense of liberation, he added, came from having "escaped the Trammels or rather *Fetters* of my domestic Tyrant Mrs. Byron." His sudden rush of independence and wealth, however, was purchased with counterfeit coin, and required a total denial of their source. Enjoying "one of the best allowances in College," he does not credit this to any generosity on his mother's part; quite the reverse: "I need scarcely inform you," he wrote to Augusta, "that I am not in the least obliged to Mrs. B for it, as it comes off of [*sic*] my property, and SHE refused to fit out a single thing for me from her own pocket, my Furniture is paid for & she has moreover a handsome addition made to her own income."[8]

---

*The rooms now accepted to have been Byron's quarters during his two years at Trinity would be considered no more than pleasant and are certainly not large. They are, however, light and airy, with windows looking out on both Nevile's Court and the library, and neighboring St. Johns' College. In the absence of residence records, Byron's suggestion of their splendor added to the problem of determining the actual location.

Once again, he misrepresented the family finances. Writing to Hanson during Byron's last term at Harrow, Catherine explained why her son's forthcoming college expenses made it urgent that the solicitor help obtain a supplement to her pension: "When he does go an additional allowance must be granted (me) as I intend giving up the five hundred a year to him as I believe he cannot live upon less & before he goes it will take two hundred & fifty pounds to fit him for college, a hundred & fifty for Furniture Plate & linen, fifty for his Wardrobe, and he must have a horse, I suppose which will be fifty more.

"I am sorry I cannot make him a present of these things, but I have never been so fortunate as to secure any addition to my pension . . . and I am determined not to run into debt."9

Neither hope nor determination availed. No addition was made to her pension (nor is there any evidence that Hanson ever bestirred himself in the matter), and to pay her son's bills, she was obliged to go into debt herself.

Beyond the sadness of unrecognized sacrifice lies Catherine's fatal weakness: She could never refuse a man—the more extravagant and ungrateful, it would seem, the more readily she was exploited. There is a cruel echo of his father's lie about his wife's meanness—"She would never give me a farthing"—in Byron's baseless complaint to Hanson: "I know Mrs. Byron too well to imagine that She would part with a *Sous.*"10

Deprived materially and emotionally, Catherine derived vicarious satisfaction from seeing her son live like a lord. She never questioned the entitlement of a peer—even a land-poor lordling who was still a student—to establish himself with the proper furniture and silver, along with clothes, horses, and servants. Only the fondest naïveté (the same she had shown toward Jack Byron) could have allowed her to hope that giving Byron his own money to spend would keep him from spending more.

The rich are always expensive companions. Keeping up with his new friends, a circle of young bucks whose pleasures involved the careless squandering of money, Byron, by his own admission, was "carried away by the Tide." Yet, after boasting to Hanson of the "dissipations" attendant upon his frenetic social life, he was enraged by the lawyer's mild suggestion that he live more soberly: "Your *indirect* charge of Dissipation does not affect me, nor do I fear the strictest enquiry into my conduct, neither here nor at *Harrow* have I disgraced myself, the 'Metropolis' & the 'Cloisters' are alike unconscious of my debauchery, and on the plains of *merry Sherwood** I have experienced *Misery* alone; in July I visited them for the *last* Time."[11]

Blaming his mother for all his other sorrows, he ended in a crescendo of self-pity: "Mrs. Byron & myself are now totally separated, injured by her, I sought refuge with Strangers, Too late I see my error, for how was kindness to be expected from *others* when denied by a *parent*."[12]

Hanson had merely pointed out that in ordering furniture for his rooms, Byron had run up bills exceeding the small separate allowance (£100) he was annually accorded by Chancery for this purpose. Byron chose to misunderstand, seeing the lawyer's remarks as evidence of deception. Byron had been promised funds to furnish his rooms; now, he was told, these bills were on his personal account: "I will *never* pay for them out of my allowance, and the Disgrace will not attach to me, but to *those* by whom I have been deceived."[13]

Peace was, finally, restored. Byron was always ready to admit that he had been wrong, and he now allowed that he had misunderstood Hanson's meaning; the lawyer had simply reminded him that he was not entitled to draw upon any additional furniture allowance until after the new year. Hanson might despise Catherine Byron, but he was equally indulgent of her son's spending habits.

As to any hints about debauchery, Byron's indignant denial was close to becoming truth; now that his social acceptance was assured among the *jeunesse dorée*, he could excuse himself from long nights of drinking and whoring. For wholesome pleasures and real companionship he turned to his Harrow classmate Edward Noel Long, also at Trinity, with whom he shared a fondness for riding, reading, and talking, but especially for swimming. Their friendly rivalry took the form of competitive feats of diving: "Though Cam's is not a very 'translucent wave,' " Byron would recall nostalgically, "it was fourteen feet deep, where we used to dive for, and pick up—having thrown them in on purpose—plates, eggs, and even shillings. I remember, in particular, there was the stump of a tree (at least ten or twelve feet deep) in the bed of the river, in a spot where we bathed most commonly, round which I used to cling, and 'wonder how the devil I came there.' "[14]

Evenings were often spent in music making. A talented musician, Long played both flute and violin, often for Byron's private pleasure. In keeping with his new sobriety, their chief beverage was soda water. They rushed to buy the quarto edition of Tom Moore's new collection, *Epistles, Odes and Other Poems*, reading it together in Byron's rooms.

---

*Newstead Abbey adjoined Sherwood Forest.

Soon he had further reason to appreciate such chaste pastimes. In September a series of cautionary letters from another Harrow friend, Tattersall, disclosed the unhappy consequences of nights spent a roving. The first began:

> Hearken, my Lord Beerun, hearken
> To the dismal news I tell,
> How that I am near embarking,
> For the fiery gulph of Hell!!!!

After this jaunty prelude, Tattersall got down to the unlovely details: "Trusting to your secrecy I will to you unfold a secret which will make thine ev'ry individual hair to stand on end, like quills upon the fretful porcupine; you cannot but remember the merry evening we passed with the Etonians, perhaps you may remember also that I left the Theatre very early but do not know that I took a Dulchinsa [*sic*] from thence & attended her home, where we passed half an hour in Amorous Dalliance, but alas she has given me something more than I bargained for, in short Sir! I am *pox'd.*"[15]

Now, in his final year at Harrow, Tattersall mourned Byron's absence but took consolation living in his friend's old room, which he also found "very convenient for dressing my privies without molestation." Unhappily, he had made the mistake of going to the local surgeon to be examined; the latter promptly reported his venereal disease to the school, and he was expelled indefinitely. Whether he would be allowed to return or not "all depends upon how my *Clap* turns out," he wrote to Byron, adding news of three other mutual friends of theirs who had been "lavender'd" for the same cause. While he was at home, Tattersalls's infected genital area was treated by bleeding: "I had six leeches applied to the swelling the day before yesterday who continued at their luscious food some time and diminished the size of the Bubo."*[16]

Neither fear nor Long's peaceful companionship alone could have kept Byron from Cambridge's taverns and brothels. Yoked to a deep emotional hunger, his urgent sexuality required an exclusive object. Looking back on this period in his life, he recalled, "I took my gradations in the vices—with great promptitude—but they were not to my taste—for my early passions though violent in the extreme—were

---

*For the unlucky Tattersall, the wages of sin were early death. He graduated from University College, Oxford, and taking Holy Orders two years later, died, aged twenty-two, "after a week's violent illness and two months of disordered health."

concentrated—and hated division or spreading abroad.—I could have left or lost the world with or for that which I loved—but though my temperament was naturally burning—I could not share in the common place libertinism of the place and time—without disgust.—And yet this very disgust and my heart thrown back upon itself—threw me into excesses perhaps more fatal than those from which I shrunk—as fixing upon one (at a time) the passions which spread amongst many would have hurt only myself."[17]

The one he fixed upon—"with a violent tho' pure passion," he insisted—was a slender fifteen-year-old choirboy with pale-gold hair and dark eyes. John Edleston was a chorister of Trinity Chapel, and it was his glorious singing that captivated Byron: "His *voice* first attracted my notice, his *countenance* fixed it, & his *manners* attached me to him forever," Byron told Elizabeth Pigot, who longed to hear more about his "protégé."[18]

Trinity Chapel's seating plan makes it perfectly possible that Byron had first heard his beloved's silvery voice before he saw the singer's delicate features illumined by candlelight. Unlike the traditional placement of a church choir, in stalls before the altar or above the congregation in the organ loft, college choristers (both men and boys) were seated inward, alongside the section reserved for undergraduates. Thus, at first by accident and later by design, Byron and Edleston could have been seated next to one another, or close enough for the boy's voice to have been heard distinct from the others.

There is another version of Byron's first encounter with Edleston: According to his Harrow friend William Harness, Byron was supposed to have saved the younger boy from drowning in the Cam. Probably apocryphal, this anecdote is symbolically important, emphasizing as it does the inequalities—physical and social—between the two young men: the heavyset young lord whose arm and chest muscles had been powerfully developed by swimming and boxing, rescuing the small, delicately built younger boy, who may not have been able to swim at all. Edleston was far from being Byron's first homoerotic attachment, but he was the first passion outside of Byron's own class to be made known to certain friends and lovingly described to others.[19]

Born in London in 1790, John Edleston (or Edlestone) was "exactly to an hour, two years younger than myself,"[20] Byron noted romantically. He was baptized in St. Martin's-in-the-Fields, a working-class parish where his parents had been married, and was four years old when his family moved back to Cambridge, their place of origin. The Edleston lodgings, close to the open market under New Shire Hall, suggest that his father may have been a butcher or other market trader. Orphaned at age ten, John Edleston probably began singing in the choir of his parish church of St. Mary the Great, where his parents were buried. When he was twelve, he was recruited by Trinity Chapel, whose choir foundation provided schooling, meals, and, for boy singers, a stipend of 1.5 shillings quarterly, paid to parents or guardians. Thus, at fifteen, Edleston would have received an education far beyond that which a butcher or greengrocer's son might normally have acquired. To his natural intelligence, access to the manners and speech of undergraduates, fellows, and choirmasters was added a refinement that, together with his chiseled beauty and sweet voice, made him appear an angelic figure to Byron, a special being whose innocence must be protected:

> The kiss so guiltless and refin'd
> That Love each warmer wish forebore;
> Those eyes proclaim'd so pure a mind,
>   Ev'n passion blush'd to plead for more.[21]

When Byron found Edleston, he also discovered and "rescued" an orphan free of both parental restraints and the embarrassing mannerisms of his class. At the same time, adopting the orphaned younger boy as his protégé established Byron as a father figure, creating sexual complexities as tantalizing as they were doubly forbidden: Incest and sodomy together were sins worthy of the mark of Cain.

Having a boyfriend in the choir seems to have been a tradition among certain Trinity undergraduates. Like the half-starved "ballet rats" of the Paris Opéra during the Second Empire, the choristers' pittance made it inevitable that these youths would be eager to supplement their earnings through the favors of rich young gentlemen. Edward Long left college before Byron, to join the navy. His letters to his friend, inquiring after various choristers and their patrons, leave no doubt that these "couples" enjoyed a semi-official status. Yet Byron felt guilty about Edleston to the point where he became obsessed with the need for secrecy; only Elizabeth Pigot and Ned Long were entrusted with knowledge of the nature and object of his love. Clearly the "pure tho' violent passion" was an explosive situation waiting to ignite. Byron's need to be guardian angel and protector of purity could not long survive his "naturally burning" temperament.

Secrecy is the favorite illusion of lovers, even when, like Byron and Edleston, they are always together. "I certainly *love* him more than any human being," he confided to the sympathetic Elizabeth, noting that Edleston "is perhaps more *attached* to *me*, than even I am in *return*. During the whole of my residence at Cambridge, we met every day, summer and winter, without passing *one tiresome moment*, & separated *each time* with increasing Reluctance."[22] In a notebook Byron kept from his Harrow years on, he entered these prophetic lines from *As You Like It*:

> And wheresoeer we went like Juno's Swans
> Still we went coupled, and inseparable.[23]

Alone together, they swam in a pool of the river a few miles below Grantchester,* walked, read, or rode Byron's horses. In public, the need for discretion intensified desire:

> Ours too the glance none saw beside;
>   The smile none else might understand;
> The whisper'd thought of hearts allied,
>   The pressure of the thrilling hand.[24]

Now, the pleasure Byron took in hearing his beloved sing was mixed with a secret possessive pride. Besides the Trinity choir, there were other musical occasions when Byron would have listened eagerly for his friend's pure notes to soar above the other voices. Trinity shared its choristers with neighboring St. John's College, and for special musical offerings, with St. Mary's as well. In a jocular letter to Elizabeth Pigot, Byron describes an accident that befell him, through his determination not to miss a concert: "Got up in a Window to hear the Oratorio at St. Mary's, popped down in the middle of the *Messiah*, tore a *woeful rent* in the Back of my best black Silk gown, & damaged an *egregious pair* of Breeches, mem.—never tumble from a church window, during Service."[25]

There were also more informal occasions of music making in Cambridge at which choristers moonlighted. But surely his most treasured memories of Edleston's ravishing voice would have been private ones, of songs sung for his pleasure alone. One of Byron's favorites was a popular love song, often performed as a curtain raiser to light theatrical offerings, "Oh, No! My Love, No!," described as "beloved by all classes" and also known as "Parting Moments":

> While I hang on your bosom distracted to leave you,
> High swells my sad heart and fast my tears flow,

---

*Now dammed by a concrete weir, the large, brackish puddle, in a thickly wooded area, is still known as "Byron's Pool."

Yet think not of coldness I seek to accuse you,
Did I ever upbraid you?
Oh, No! My Love, No![26]

One of Byron's first poems addressed to Edleston is titled "Stanzas to Jessy":*

There is a bosom all my own,
  Has pillow'd oft this aching head,
A mouth, which smiles on me alone
  An eye, whose tears with mine are shed.[27]

A year later, from Chatham, where he was training before being shipped out to fight in the Peninsular Wars, Long wrote to Byron: "Memory constitutes my greatest happiness—while we were on parade this morning the band played that song with which you used so often to soothe mother stona at night ('When I hang on your bosom')."[28]

In the months before he left Trinity, Ned Long had gracefully ceded to Edleston some of the pleasures he had earlier enjoyed with Byron: riding, swimming, reading, walking, and listening to music. From being his constant companion, Long now became Byron's chosen confidant in Cambridge to hear the true nature of his feelings for the chorister (a role Elizabeth Pigot played by correspondence from Southwell). Byron believed that his school friend was the only member of their Cambridge circle who was aware of his intense attachment to the younger boy. But if, as he also says, he and the chorister were inseparable from the day they met, his secret would have been an open one in the small world of the university. The rowdy companions of dissipations past would have been particularly curious about the cause of Byron's defection to monogamy.

Byron was especially anxious that none but Long and Elizabeth should know of Edleston's gift to him of a cornelian ring in the shape of a heart. He was planning to spend the Christmas holidays in London, and the present was a keepsake on the occasion of their first separation. The small coral-colored stone, mounted on a thin gold band, is sized to be worn on the little finger, giving the jewel the poignant air of a child's ring.†

---

*As the poem is addressed to Edleston, the dedicatory name in the title suggests a diminutive based on J(ohn) E(dle) S(ton) or JES. Another nickname for Edleston seems to have been "Mother Stona."

†Now in the collection of Byron memorabilia originally owned by the poet's publisher John Murray.

Byron was touched to the point of astonishment by the gift—"the *Hero* of my *Cornelian*,"[29] he christened the donor in a letter to Elizabeth.

"*Pignus Amoris* (The Color of Love)" is one of several poems Byron wrote about the ring and its giver. Referring to the diminutive memento as "this toy of blushing hue," Byron equates the color with Edleston's shame in presenting a gift of small value—perhaps relative to Byron's handsome presents. ("He offered it with downcast look / As *fearful* that I might refuse it.")[30] Threaded through the sequence celebrating the cornelian is the conceit that the modest value of the jewel gives proof of the greater worth of the donor and the inestimable value of his love. Indeed, his friend's poverty relative to his own wealth was never far from Byron's thoughts. It may also be, however, that he exaggerated Edleston's situation to enhance his own need for the boy's total dependence on him, or to justify giving him substantial sums of money, along with expensive gifts.

By November Byron had gone through his entire quarterly allowance; there would be no funds forthcoming to him until the new year. With unpaid debts at Harrow as well as Cambridge, he was desperate. One of the reasons for his visit to London was to see where he could beg or borrow money. On November 9 Byron wrote to Mrs. Massingberd at 16 Piccadilly, where he and his mother had stayed earlier, asking to rent two rooms for himself and a servant, beginning December 18. Massingberd must have had available several types of accommodation, differing in privacy, size, and price, as Byron expressly stated his preference for rooms in the apartment his landlady shared with her daughter, where he would also take his meals.

Hardly had he arrived in town when, through a newspaper advertisement, Byron put himself in touch with the reigning monarch of moneylenders. "Jew" King made his fortune by lending large sums at usurious rates to young rakes made desperate by gambling debts and other follies. He owned an elegant house in Clarges Street, Piccadilly, and drove about London in a splendid yellow carriage. King knew trouble when he saw it and promptly informed his young correspondent that he never transacted business with minors. Byron now realized he must find someone legally of age and willing to cosign his loans as collateral guarantor. His first thought was Augusta.

On Boxing Day, December 26, he wrote to his sister to be sure he could count on seeing her in town at the end of January, "as I have some subjects to discuss with you, which I do not wish to communicate in my Epistle,"[31] he noted. He had thought to flee Cambridge and his creditors there, along with his engulfing passion for Edleston. Neither was left behind. His obsession with the chorister pursued him to "the

Metropolis," while his lack of money was more keenly felt in the city, with all of its temptations to the extravagant.

By the next day, December 27, Byron realized that his situation could not wait on Augusta's plans—always subject to change, in any case—to visit a month hence. He wrote to her again, saying that before he could divulge "the Business I mentioned rather mysteriously in my last [letter]" he must first swear her to "the most inviolable Secrecy." She may refuse the favor he is about to ask, with no ill feelings, but if she repeats it, "all confidence all Friendship between us has concluded," he warned. To secure Augusta's sympathy, Byron blamed his predicament on his mother: "Like all other young men just let loose, and especially one as I am freed from the worse than bondage of my maternal home, I have been extravagant, and consequently am in want of Money." Assuring Augusta that he would never accept any offer of hers were he "in danger of Starvation," he finally comes to the point: "All I expect or wish is that you will be joint Security with me for a few Hundreds a person (one of the money lending tribe) has offered to advance in case I can bring forward any collateral guarantee that he will not be a loser, the reason of this requisition is my being a Minor, and might refuse to discharge a debt contracted in my non age." He then grandly assured his sister that, in view of the property he is soon to inherit—"worth 100 times the sum I am about to raise," half of which would be hers on his death—she could not, in any event, suffer any loss.[32]

As to his prospects for inheritance, Byron's optimism would have been justified had he not been misinformed. Hanson had been jollying his client along (while doing nothing, as usual) about the outcome of their suit to regain the Rochdale property with its valuable collieries, leased by the fifth lord.*[33] Byron's reference, however, to the "few Hundreds" he was trying to borrow was an outright falsehood; the first of several loans he would secure from "those sordid bloodsuckers"[34] began with £3,000 (whose interest, added to the principal, would make the repayment owed on each debt in this amount £5,000).

Acknowledging his own shame and anticipating Augusta's reaction, he admitted to desperation; she was the only one he could trust, from whom refusal did not mean rejection: "I know you will think me foolish if not criminal, but tell me so yourself and do not rehearse my failings to others." He was especially concerned that Lord Carlisle and

---

*The leasor's countersuit dragged through Chancery for fifteen years before being settled in Byron's favor in 1822, two years before his death.

"that chattering puppy Hanson" (who had just given him £50 as a gift) not be told of what he was about to do.

"I am now trying the experiment," he told Augusta, "whether a woman can retain a secret, let me not be deceived."[35]

Augusta did not choose to accept the challenge. Wise to the tightening noose of indebtedness that characterized all dealings with moneylenders, she refused to guarantee security but, instead, offered to lend Byron whatever he needed. His chivalric code of honor did not permit borrowing money from a lady, and he refused. Augusta was now terrified, and fear for her brother overriding her desire to be worthy of his confidence, she told both Carlisle and Hanson of his predicament.

It would be some time before Byron would learn of these conversations. Meanwhile, he was gracious about her refusal and touched by her offer to lend him the funds herself. With her intuitive understanding of him, which Byron would come to value above all else, Augusta guessed at griefs having nothing to do with money. She asked whether he might be suffering from a nervous debility or some other illness, and begged him to tell her how she could help restore his good spirits.

Byron longed to confide in Augusta, but he wanted her admiration even more (another reason why he preferred to pay usurious rates to moneylenders rather than borrow from her). He could confess to the loving, unworldly Elizabeth Pigot the nature of his troubled love for Edleston, but he wanted Augusta, with her grand connections, to see him as a dashing—even cynical—man of the world. He replied with an artful mix of truth and evasion: "Your efforts to reanimate my sinking spirits will, I am afraid, fail in their effect," he wrote on January 7, 1806, "for my melancholy proceeds from a very different cause to that which you assign, as, my nerves were always of the strongest texture. I will not however pretend to say I possess that *Gaieté de Coeur* which formerly distinguished me, but as the diminution of it arises from what you could not alleviate, and might possibly be painful, you will excuse the Disclosure. Suffice it to know, that it cannot spring from Indisposition, as my Health was never more firmly established than now, nor from the subject on which I lately wrote [his need to raise money], as that is in a promising Train, and even were it otherwise, the Failure would not lead to Despair.—You know me too well to think it is *Love*."[36]

The "promising Train" had been furthered by an unexpected ally. As a *table d'hôte* boarder, he had come to know the Massingberds, mother and daughter. Both women were charmed and flattered by the young peer's confidences, which surely included his financial troubles.

Mrs. Massingberd was in a position to sympathize; she was herself in debt. Using her income as collateral, she had borrowed heavily from relatives and now found herself unable to pay the interest. She readily agreed, nonetheless, to stand joint security for her young lodger, inviting another moneylender, a Mr. Howard of Golden Square, to 16 Piccadilly. Byron was asked to remain in another room while Howard and Massingberd drew up the papers—on which the underage borrower's name never appears.

Massingberd's role in Byron's deepening entanglements with the moneylenders remains to this day a subject of dispute. Was his landlady a parasite exploiting a gullible youth or herself a dupe, too ready to believe the seductive young lord's grandiose claims of future fortune? At a distance of almost two hundred years the financial transactions themselves are too tortuous to untangle—a Dickensian nightmare of loans raised on annuities (sometimes, but not always, meaning life insurance) or by mortgaging future income. To complicate matters further, the principal had been raised from a third party to the agreement, as moneylenders rarely put up their own money. The only fact that can be stated with certainty is that Massingberd signed for a series of Byron's loans from the "tribe of Levi" whose terms she appeared sincerely to believe were advantageous to both of them. In her disfavor is the evidence that she took a brokering fee, skimming interest "off the top" for her own immediate use. Massingberd's defense rests on the disastrous consequences to herself and her daughter of her role as go-between. When the notes came due, Byron was safely out of the country, but the Massingberds were en route to debtors' prison.

For the moment, disaster had been averted; the landlady and her young lodger both had cash in hand. Now, however, Byron learned that his exhortations of secrecy to Augusta had been ignored. He was furious, breaking off all communication with his sister. For months her despairing letters—page after page of abject apology—went unanswered, as did her pleas to Hanson to intervene with Byron on her behalf: "I own *I* perfectly despair of my Brother altering his Tone to me—for when one has put oneself very much in the wrong, it is very difficult to get right again," Augusta wrote to Hanson on February 18.[37]

Newly solvent, Byron settled his outstanding Harrow debts and Cambridge bills to the amount of £231, leaving £75 to be paid by Hanson for his furniture. In the flush of feeling himself an independent man of means, he wrote to his mother, in tones of swaggering insolence, of his intention to remain in town: "I happen to have a few hundreds in ready Cash lying by me, so I have paid the accounts, but I find it inconvenient to remain at College, not for the Expence, as I could live on my Allowance (only I am naturally extravagant) however the mode of going on does not suit my constitution, improvement at an English University to a Man of Rank is you know impossible, and the very Idea *ridiculous*." Then, coming to the point of his letter, he announced his plan of passing a couple of years abroad. The Napoleonic Wars had revised the itinerary of the conventional Grand Tour—"Tis true I cannot enter France, but Germany, and the Courts of Berlin, Vienna, and Petersburg, are still open." He would prefer to take his leave with her approval, along with that of Hanson and Lord Carlisle, and to travel accompanied by a tutor of their choosing, but if consent was not forthcoming, he planned to go anyway.

"Let me have your Answer, I intend remaining in Town a month longer, when perhaps I shall bring my Horses and myself down to your residence in that *execrable* Kennel. I hope you have engaged a Man Servant—else it will be impossible for me to visit you, since my Servant must attend chiefly to his horses, at the same Time, you must cut an Indifferent Figure with only maids in your habitation."[38]

Byron's sneering insults hit their mark. Mixed with her outrage, however, were Catherine's fears for her son. Before he had come of age, he was turning into his wastrel father: "That Boy will be the death of me, & drive me mad," she wrote despairingly to Hanson. "I never will consent to his going abroad. Where can he get Hundreds; has he got into the hands of Moneylenders, he has *no feeling, no Heart*. This I have long known; he has behaved as ill as possible to me for years back, this bitter Truth I can no longer conceal, it is wrung from me by *heart rending agony*. . . . God knows what is to be done with him—I much fear he is already ruined; at *eighteen*!!!"[39]

IN FLIGHT FROM imprisoning love—maternal or passionate—Byron plunged into all the pleasures that London offered a titled young man with money to burn. A few blocks from Piccadilly, at 13 Bond Street, were the rooms of the fencing master Henry Angelo. Byron had known Angelo since Harrow, where the swordsman gave private lessons to students. Angelo's partner was "Gentleman" John Jackson, noted pugilist and boxing champion of England from 1798 to 1803. Byron now began to hone his sparring skills, along with taking more interest in the professional side of the sport, with its championship matches, betting, and investments in promising fighters.

Thirteen Bond Street functioned as a combination gym and social club; there was a shooting gallery where Byron could practice with his pistols, spar with professional pugilists, and engage in swordplay with masters of the rapier. The studio also provided a venue less public than Vauxhall Gardens or the masquerades at the Panthéon for the demi-monde and young aristocrats to meet: sporting types and gamblers, actresses and dancers. At least one well-known singer, Madame Catalani, seems to have doubled as procuress, arranging intimate suppers backstage, where she introduced her young protégées to favored clients such as Byron.

Rumored to be lovers as well as partners, Angelo and Jackson would have been discreetly hospitable to those seeking companions among their own sex; the legitimate business of their rooms, with its atmosphere of masculine athleticism, was both an attraction and a cover for any risky business conducted there. And cover was essential. Police raids on establishments rumored to be homosexual meeting places, along with the forced exile of the rich and aristocratic aesthete William Beckford in 1785, had served notice that the sodomy laws were not dead letters.

At 13 Bond Street, an amiable provision for every taste and need was particularly welcome to Byron at this time. Jackson, more than Angelo, seems to have become his intimate: Twice the poet refers to the elegant pugilist as "my old friend & corporeal Pastor & Master"[40]—a tribute that need not have been confined to the boxer's skills in the ring.

In the first weeks of the new year 1807, the weather was too stormy for riding. Kept indoors, Byron brooded. Away from Edleston, his feelings for the boy were more turbulent and confused than ever. How could he accommodate to the reality of life his most passionate attachments if they were also criminal? If he could not live without Edleston, he could not live in the world. He was painfully aware that the perfect love he now experienced had little in common with the institutionalized pairings of adolescent boys at school.

Other doubts, too, had to be dispelled. He had to prove that his lameness did not make him less of a man—but more. Writing of his favorite poet, the hunchback Alexander Pope, Byron noted the "unhappy dispensation of Nature that deformed persons . . . are born with very strong passions. They are condemned to combat, not only against the passions which they feel, but the repugnance they inspire."[41] This mark of Cain also conferred special rights of power over weaker creatures. His spirits quickened with a wild sense of transgression—of crossing boundaries before which others quailed.

Fifteen years later, defending Pope against the moral sanctions of a minor poetaster, Byron was reminded of "a little circumstance which occurred when I was about eighteen years of age. There was then (and there may be still) a famous French entremetteuse who assisted young gentlemen in their youthful pastimes. We had been acquainted for some time, when something occurred in her business more than ordinary, and the refusal was offered to me (and doubtless to many others) probably because I was in cash at the moment, having taken up a decent sum from the Jews, and not having spent much above half of it. The adventure on the tapis, it seems required some caution and circumspection. Whether my venerable friend doubted my politeness I cannot tell; but she sent me a letter couched in such English as a short residence of sixteen years in England had enabled her to acquire. After several precepts and instructions the letter closed. But there was a postscript. It contained these words:—'Remember, Milor, that *delicaci ensure everi succes.*' "

Chilling in its every implication, this incident recalled from Byron's eighteenth year has never been placed in context. Attacking the cant and hypocrisy of Pope's detractors, he compared their "laudable delicacy . . . this crying-out elegance of the day" to the finer sensibility of the procuress. Who can doubt that her "more than ordinary" offer was the provision of very young children for the pleasure of her clients? Nor were her fears for Byron's want of "politeness" to be understood as concern for the cruelty or violence to be inflicted on small bodies. Freedom from all restraint was, after all, what her "young gentlemen" were paying for in large coin. In a civilized society, "caution and circumspection" were essential to avoid scandal, and to permit buyer and seller to continue their mutually profitable and pleasurable transactions.

"The *delicacy* of the day," Byron concluded, "is exactly, in all its circumstances, like that of this respectable foreigner. 'It ensures every succes.' "[42]

WITH THE DISTANCE of time and place, Byron was able to place the more troubling of his youthful pastimes in the moral context of an England whose proto-Victorian puritanism averted its gaze from the traffic in every vice. In a poem written within months of his first season of London debauch, he is unsparing of himself; neither youth nor affliction is summoned to excuse the horrors of which he has been guilty:

> In law an infant, and in years a boy,
> In mind, a slave to every vicious joy,
> From every sense of shame and virtue wean'd,
> In lies an adept, in deceit a fiend;
> Vers'd in hypocrisy while yet a child,
> Fickle as wind, of inclinations wild

Woman his dupe, his heedless friend a tool,
Old in the world, though scarcely broke from school;
Damaetas ran through all the maze of sin
And found the goal, when others just begin;
Ev'n still conflicting passions shake his soul,
And bid him drain the dregs of pleasure's bowl;
But, pall'd with vice, he breaks his former chain,
And, what was once his bliss, appears his bane.[43]

Vice may indeed have begun to pall. But he had also run out of money; London's pleasures did not come cheap. Hints from Hanson that he could lose his allowance if he was no longer a student gave him little choice. Trying moral blackmail, Byron sought to raise a loan from the solicitor himself; if Hanson would only lend him money at the legal rate, he could at least pay off the usurious interest charged by the Jews. (Hanson seems to have remained unmoved by this businesslike proposition.) On April 10 Byron wrote snappishly to the lawyer: "In a few Days I set off for Cambridge and will trouble you for £200 due to me since Lady Day last as that alone delays my departure."[44]

Back in college, he resumed his extravagant style with a vengeance. The reunion with Edleston seems to have inspired a manic spending spree. First there were gifts, most likely showered on his friend: a silver hunting watch, gold chain, gold seal, key, and an engraving. He spent lavishly on decorating his rooms. Perhaps to console himself for the deferred Grand Tour, he looked to the East for inspiration. From the austerity of his Chatham barracks, Ned Long wrote nostalgically, "Nothing could have exceeded the luxury of your little room when filled up with the Ottoman and those lamps à la Grecque."[45] Grand public gestures came next: Byron contributed 30 guineas to the subscription for a statue in memory of Pitt, the Prime Minister who had also been a patron of Trinity.

"He has also bought a Carriage," Catherine wailed to Hanson, "which he says was intended for me which I *refused* to accept of, being in hopes it would stop his having one."[46] Invoking his mother had merely been a way of justifying this latest indulgence. He went on to add horses and harnesses, not forgetting footmen appropriately uniformed.

He moved to new heights of imperious behavior. When his attempt to import Angelo to Cambridge as official fencing master to the university was foiled by the Mayor, Byron's letter of outrage to his swordsman friend has a "mad Pretender" quality—that of a ham actor playing the Prince Regent. Referring to his ally in the affair, Lord Altamont,

Byron promises Angelo: "We will endeavor to bend the O[b]stinacy of the *Upstart* Magistrate. . . . Believe me, we will yet *humble* this *impertinent Bourgeois.*"[47]

On June 16 he wrote meekly to Hanson, asking for that quarter's allowance of £125, which was duly sent by the solicitor on the twenty-eighth. Ten days later he was still in Cambridge—"detained . . . by the painting of my Carriage," he grandly informed Mrs. Massingberd. She, in turn, had been preparing Byron for bad news: Another loan she was trying to raise for him now appeared to have fallen through. Graciously, he assured her that she was not to blame: "Believe me the obligation I feel is equal, as if success had attended our Endeavors. I bear the disappointment with philosophy, notwithstanding the Inconvenience the failure will produce."[48]

The worst inconvenience of all: Poverty now forced him to return to his mother, Burgage Manor, and Southwell.

CHAPTER 7

A Literary Cub

$\mathcal{M}$Y TIME has lately been much occupied with very different pursuits," Byron wrote to his Harrow favorite, the Earl of Clare, from Southwell. "I have been *transporting* a servant, who cheated me,—rather a disagreeable event: performing in private theatricals;—publishing a volume of poems (at the request of my friends, for their perusal);—making *love*—and taking physic. The last two amusements have not had the best effect *in the world*; for my attentions have been divided amongst so many *fair damsels*, and the drugs I swallow are of such variety in their composition, that between Venus and Aesculapius I am harassed to death."[1]

The deities of love and healing were far from his only tormentors. When Byron arrived in Southwell in late July, the first sight of the prodigal emerging from his newly refurbished coach with the Byron coat of arms emblazoned on the side ignited his mother's rage. Forced back to Burgage Manor, out of pocket and burdened with debt, Byron was now hostage to all of Catherine's pent-up wrath and resentment. In this round of hostilities, his mother had the advantage. Not only was the sharp Scotswoman onto his dealings with the moneylenders, she also had sniffed out that Byron's refusal to return to college, coupled with his sudden insistence on going abroad, meant that he had "become inveigled with some woman." (She was mistaken only in the gender of his attachment.) Other grievances had been festering for some time. Earlier in the year, Catherine had heard rumors through her Nottingham connections that Byron's servant Frank Boyce had been making purchases on credit and borrowing money in his master's name all over the county. When she aired her suspicions at the time, Byron had dismissed her for a meddlesome fool. Soon, however, Boyce was revealed to have been guilty of all this and more, including the theft of his employer's belongings from his Trinity rooms. Now, under his mother's triumphant gaze, Byron was forced to institute procedings against his former servant.

As long as she had the upper hand at home, Catherine became Byron's fierce defender when others dared criticize him. She took a haughty tone with Hanson, who had relayed his own complaints: "My son has been with me some time and is to remain till he returns to Cambridge in Octr. I am perfectly satisfied with his conduct indeed I have no reason to be otherwise."[2] In a curious slip, she misdated her July letter "October," as though hastening the day when he would return to college.

Across the green, the Pigot house, a domestic paradise of calm and cheer, stood always ready to welcome him, and Byron now spent most of his time there with his adoptive family. Freed from the burden of courtship, he was as open with Elizabeth as it was possible to be with a respectable young woman. Her humor, intelligence, and undemanding intimacy could always jolly him from rage and gloom. In John Pigot, now home on vacation from his medical studies in Edinburgh, he found a receptive mind and a warm heart. His first friend of scientific bent, John also wrote poetry himself. Byron, however, did not share the future physician's eclectic interests; unlike Shelley, he had little curiosity about the great scientific discoveries of the day. For complete relaxation he could be a small child again, playing games with little Edward, the youngest member of the family. Like Byron, the Pigots were dog lovers; they discussed and compared the virtues of Byron's beloved Boat-swain, the gentle Newfoundland who had been his favorite since he was acquired as a pup four years earlier; his new acquisition, a puppy named Savage; and Elizabeth's woolly dog Wousky. All these creatures delighted in tormenting Mrs. Byron's pug Gilray—perhaps a projection of their owners' hostility.

During Byron's seven-month stay in Southwell—his longest—he also came to know and admire another Pigot relation, the Reverend John Becher, a divine of literary tastes and considerable sophistication. Becher added to the surprising number of Byron's friends to enter Holy Orders; beginning with the ill-fated Tattersall, they came to include William Harness, his lame friend from Harrow, and a new Cambridge intimate, Francis Hodgson. Even allowing for the severely restricted professions permissible for "gentlemen"—the armed services, the law, and the church—he gravitated toward those who would be concerned with the state of his soul. Like the friendships with devout women to whom he felt a deep attraction, his male friendships reveal a yearning for the saving power of love.

As soon as Elizabeth saw Byron, she realized that on this visit he would require more than escape, sympathy, or even diversion; his mind needed "something to fasten on," as he said himself—the stimulus and discipline of intellectual exercise. Elizabeth now took on the role of Byron's amanuensis, acting as secretary and editor, making fair copies in her elegant hand, and reading over recent verses with him. From here, it was a natural next step for her, or the Pigots together, to propose that Byron gather together his best poems with a view to publication. John Ridge, a bookseller and printer whose shop was in the Market Square of nearby Newark, was the obvious choice for a small, privately printed edition. With Elizabeth's help and encouragement Byron undertook to reread and revise all the poetry he had written (and carefully saved) from early adolescence to his latest *vers de circonstance*, anecdotes relating his life and loves in Southwell.

Byron's first published volume, which would be be given the title *Fugitive Pieces*, has much to tell us about the eighteen-year-old beginner and the poet he would become. Thirty-eight in number, most of them juvenilia, the poems selected for this first venture established the crucial element of Byron's literary enterprise: poetry as autobiography.[3] Beginning with the dedication, designed to shield the poet from anticipated criticism, we feel the alternating currents of Byronic defiance and self-protection:

> TO THOSE FRIENDS, at whose Request they were Printed
> for whose
> Amusement or Approbation
> They are
> Solely Intended
> These TRIFLES are respectfully dedicated by the AUTHOR.[4]

Still more self-exculpatory, the Foreword offers the poet's extreme youth as a defense against literary crimes, along with his hope of being awarded a gold star for gentlemanly behavior; he has, after all, refused to expose his work to any but his small circle of intimates: "As these POEMS were never intended to meet the public eye, the apology is necessary for the form in which they now appear. They are printed merely for the perusal of a few friends to whom they are dedicated; who will look upon them with indulgence; and as most of them were composed between the age of 15 and 17, their defects will be pardoned or forgotten, in the youth and inexperience of the WRITER."⁵ Significantly, the writer's name does not appear on the title page. Following these arch disclaimers, the first poem in the volume, "On Leaving N——st——d," is one of the few to be dated precisely, 1803, thereby establishing the precocious talent of the fifteen-year-old author, along with his heroic and ancient lineage:

> Thro' thy battlements, Newstead, the hollow winds whistle;
> Thou, the hall of my fathers, art gone to decay;
> In thy once smiling garden, the hemlock and thistle
> Have choak'd-up the rose, which late bloom'd in the way.⁶

Into this gothic setting of ruins reverting to nature Byron introduces a procession of forebears, piling body upon body in service of king and country: "Paul and Hubert too sleep, in the valley of Cressy, / For the safety of Edward and England they fell."

Along with a gallery of heroic canvases depicting the Byronic presence in Scottish and English history, *Fugitive Pieces* also included schoolboy translations from the classics. These are not arresting: " 'Twas now the hour when Night had driven, / Her car half round yon sable heaven" may be taken as typical.⁷

Romantic lyrics, whether an elegy to his cousin Margaret Parker or tributes to the charms of several Southwell belles and Harrow favorites, offer no more than a reshuffling of current sentimental clichés: "To Mary, on Receiving Her Picture" trots out the hoary trope of Art paralyzed before living Beauty ("Here, I can trace—ah no! that eye, / Whose azure floats in liquid fire, / Must all the painter's art defy, / And bid him from the task retire").⁸

Exceptions are the two poems to Edleston discussed above: the lyric "To E——" inspired earlier (according to the author) by another boy of unequal rank and revised—perhaps for this edition—to contain a double reference. The other is "The Cornelian," with its touching simplicity reminiscent of a popular air:

> Some who can sneer at friendship's ties,
>   Have for my weakness oft reprov'd me,
> Yet still the simple gift I prize,
>   For I am sure, the giver lov'd me.⁹

Early attempts at satire struggle for the sparkle of Pope, only to sputter in verbiage:

> The sons of science, these, who thus repaid,
> Linger in ease, in Granta's sluggish shade;
> Where on Cam's sedgy banks supine they lie,
> Unknown, unhonour'd live,—unwept for, die;[10]

Moreover, Byron's ham-handed ridicule of poor Dr. Butler as "Pomposus" would have been of interest only to other old Harrovians.

Bits of political polemic, however, had already begun to unleash a snarling energy that required only greater control and polish to succeed: "Oh! factious viper! whose envenom'd tooth, / Would mangle still the dead, perverting truth" was the opening salvo in Byron's attack on a writer who had denigrated Charles James Fox, the recently deceased hero of liberal Whigs.[11]

Stealthily a new kind of verse also makes its debut. Born of disillusioned love, its satirical edge, slyly undermining the romantic with the ribald, is spiced with a realism that foreshadows the Byron of *Childe Harold*, "Beppo," and *Don Juan*. The title "To a Lady, Who Presented to the Author a Lock of Hair, Braided with his Own, and Appointed a Night, in December, to Meet him in the Garden" puts the reader on notice. The poet is taking aim at lovers in a cold climate, placed at risk of health by the silliness of young women warmed only by their sentimental readings:

> Why should you weep, like Lydia Languish,
> And fret with self-created anguish?
> Or doom the lover you have chosen,
> On winter nights, to sigh half frozen;
> In leafless shades, to sue for pardon,
> Only because the scene's a garden?
> For gardens seem, by one consent
> Since SHAKESPEARE set the precedent,
> Since Juliet first declar'd her passion,
> To form the place of assignation.
> Oh! would some modern muse inspire,
> And seat her by a sea-coal fire;
> Or had the bard at Christmas written,
> And laid the scene of love in Britain;
> He surely, in commiseration,
> Had chang'd the place of declaration
> In Italy, I've no objection;
> Warm nights are proper for reflection;

But, here, our climate is so rigid,
That love, itself is rather frigid.[12]

One of Byron's favorite jokes also makes its first appearance here; he would always delight in finding a resemblance between the English climate and the sexual response of his countrywomen.

CHEERFUL ABSORPTION in editorial labors across the green soon provoked violent explosions at home, where the noise of Byron and his mother fighting was heard far beyond the walls of Burgage Manor. The local apothecary claimed that each had appeared in his shop to enjoin him not to sell any poisonous substance to the other; both confided to him their fears of the enemy's suicidal intentions, but threats of murder may have also impelled this preventive measure. Finally, on August 8, in the final moments of a battle audible all over Southwell, Catherine Byron hurled the fire tongs at her son, who fled across the green. With help from the Pigots, he smuggled his clothes from the house in small bundles and, in the middle of the night, leaving pistols and servants behind, he made for London.

He had underestimated "Mrs. Byron Furiosa," as he now dubbed his mother.[13] Enraged, Catherine promptly set off in pursuit. Her hired chaise and pair, however, were no match for her son's imperial coach and four; it would be four days before she arrived at 16 Piccadilly.

Byron believed himself safe and his whereabouts a secret. His terror on receiving a note from his "momentous Eve" "has driven the natural Ruby from my Cheeks, & completely *blanched* my woebegone Countenance," he told Elizabeth in the facetious tone that could not disguise real dread.[14] Not even his mother's impending descent caused him to forget the poems he had left, in haste, with Ridge before his retreat from Southwell: "I presume the printer has brought to you, the offspring of my *poetic Mania*," he added in a transparent effort at nonchalance. Then, in his first directive as a soon-to-be-published poet, he instructed Elizabeth, "Remember in the 1st Line to read '*loud* the winds whistle' instead of '*round*,' which that Blockhead Ridge has inserted by mistake & makes nonsense of the whole Stanza.*—Adio! now to encounter my *Hydra*."[15]

---

*This line was from the first poem to appear in the debut volume, *Fugitive Pieces*. In this first collection, the poem was titled "On Leaving N——st——d." In a subsequent edition Byron changed the poem's title to read "On Leaving Newstead Abbey," and the phrase itself to "the hollow winds whistle."

On midnight of the same Sunday, August 10, Byron sent off another mailing addressed to John Pigot, with an enclosed note: "Dear Pigot,—This *astonishing* packet, will doubtless amaze you, but having an idle hour this evening, I wrote the inclosed Stanza's, which I request you to deliver [to] Ridge to be printed *separate* from my other *Compositions*, as you will perceive them to be *improper* for the perusal of Ladies, of course none of the females of your family must see them."[16]

These quarantined verses were stanzas addressed "To Mary." A fever chart of erotic engagement, fulfillment, and betrayal, the fourteen poems move far beyond the sexual strutting of the adolescent male, laying bare the wounds of the displaced lover: shock, sickening humiliation, cold fury; present loss tormented by memories of past happiness:

> Rack'd by the flames of jealous rage,
>   By all her torments deeply curst,
>   Of hell-born passions far the worst
>
> . . . .
>
> No more that bosom heaves for me
>   On it another seeks repose
>   Another riots on its snows,
> Our bonds are broken, both are free
> No more with mutual love we burn,
>   No more the genial couch we press
>   Dissolving in the fond caress;
>   Our love o'erthrown will ne'er return.[17]

"Mary" is no "Corinna" or "Phyllis," those generic constructs who served the metaphysical poets as vehicles of erotic imagery. All the evidence suggests that Byron's uncoy mistress existed in all her slutty inconstancy. Tom Moore describes her as a "young woman of humble, even equivocal, station,"[18] his circumspect way of saying that she was one of London's hundreds of thousands of poor pretty girls who, while their youth and looks lasted, tried to avoid the perilous life of a common prostitute. The most beautiful and ambitious hoped, like Emma Hart, the future Lady Hamilton, to become the consort of a man of title.

Early in the poem, Byron drops a series of hints about the nature of Mary's infidelities. A practiced liar, she has greeted his withdrawn manner with "suspicious tears" and "feign'd alarms" until, "disdaining thy polluted kiss," he flees. Alone with his rage, he strips his language of poetic conceits and moves to direct accusation: "You quickly sought a second lover."[19]

The young woman's faithlessness had little to do with passion and everything to do with poverty—her own and Byron's. If he could not support her, she had to find a lover who could. If she failed, she would be back, older and less desirable, patrolling the foyer of Drury Lane or the paths of Vauxhall Gardens.

Elizabeth Pigot seems to have been the first friend to whom Byron revealed the girl's identity. He showed her a miniature of "Mary" (probably commissioned by the poet) and a lock of her pale yellow hair. Possibly to distinguish her from one of Byron's local belles of the same name, Elizabeth called the less respectable young woman "Naughty Mary." The Pigots may have even glimpsed the golden-haired siren. It was later said that Byron kept a mistress in Southwell, in a cottage in a section of town known as the "Bullpit," to which he would gallop in the dark of night.[20] If true, her sequestered situation may have contributed to Mary's restive impulse.

In the last stanzas of "To Mary" the poet has assimilated his loss; he can revisit images of sexual bliss, his earlier pain muted to pleasurable melancholy:

> Even now I cannot well forget thee,
>   And though no more in folds of pleasure,
>   Kiss follows kiss in countless measure,
> I hope *you* sometimes will regret me
>
> And smile to think how oft we've done,
>   What prudes declare a sin to act is,
>   And never but in darkness practice,
> Fearing to trust the tell-tale sun.

And in a gorgeous stanza with echoes of John Donne, Byron slips into the present to evoke past rapture:

> Now, by my soul, 'tis most delight
>   To view each other panting, dying,
>   In love's *extatic posture* lying,
> Grateful to *feeling*, as to *sight*.[21]

By August 16, Byron had heard from Pigot about his separate mailing. Predictably, his friend had reservations about the poem's frank description of sexual pleasure. With a slight hint of swagger, Byron's defense was the truth of his experience. Agree as he might about the immodest dress of this latest offspring of his Muse, "It was impossible to give it any other *garb*, being *founded* on *Facts*," he declared.[22]

Meanwhile, he could also report to Pigot from London that he had stood his ground and manfully confronted his mother, just now returning to Southwell. But her retreat had followed another battle royal that shook the Massingberd establishment from attic to basement. Byron claimed himself "the Victor" but he did not emerge unscathed: "After an obstinate Engagement of some hours, in which *we* suffered considerable damage, from the quickness of the enemy's Fire, *they* at length retired in Confusion. . . . To speak more intelligibly, Mrs. B. returns immediately, but I with all my *laurels* proceed to Worthing, on the Sussex coast."[23]

Before he left, Byron issued new instructions for Pigot regarding his verses: "Will you desire Ridge to suspend the printing of my poems, till he hears further from me, as I have determined to give them a new form entirely; this prohibition does not extend to the 2 last pieces, I have sent with my letters to you."[24] "To Mary" and the other verses contained in the "*astonishing* packet to Pigot" were, presumably, to be printed—whether as separate broadsheets or folded into the others, whose final selection was just now being revised, is unclear.

Two days later, Byron dispatched another letter, with a more complicated request: Pigot must order Byron's servant Charles and his horses, held hostage by his mother, to proceed immediately to Worthing. In addition, the veterinary surgeon, who was to have treated the horses, had not been paid for an outstanding bill; the miscreant Frank Boyce had clearly pocketed the money intended for this purpose. Would Pigot please send the bill along with Charles? In a postscript, Byron admitted the imposition upon his friend, while adding a few more errands to his list: "I delegate to you, the *unpleasant* Task, of dispatching him [Charles] on his Journey, Mrs. B orders to the contrary, are not to be attended to; he is to proceed 1st to London, & then to Worthing without Delay. Every thing I have left must be sent to London, my *Poetics* you will *pack up* for the Same place & not even reserve a Copy for yourself & Sister, as I am about to give them an *entire new* form, when they are complete you shall have the *1st Fruits*. Mrs. B. on no account is to *see*, or *touch* them."[25]

Having delegated all matters pending to Pigot, Byron set out to join his friend Edward Long at Worthing on the Sussex coast. The devoted Long still enjoyed Byron's intimate confidences, including word of his most recent and wildest plan: to carry off an "inamorietta" from Southwell to Cambridge. Whether his plot involved the lascivious Mary or another is uncertain; he had already found distraction from the pain of her betrayal by flirting with the local "virgins," as he called South-well's marriageable young women.

To Long, Byron confided another piece of news that his friend found astonishing: "I confess I was rather surprised on hearing that you had received a letter from Edleston," Long wrote to Byron, adding, "I dare-say E's letter is very well-written and affectionate."[26] Long's surprise suggests that Byron was the one who had broken with the chorister, while his patronizing speculation about the contents of the letter and writer's style points to the likelihood that Byron had retailed Edleston's "forgiveness," along with samples of the boy's painstaking grammar, for the amusement of his own friends.

Edleston's accusing presence, more than poverty or debt, also explains Byron's refusal to return to Cambridge; as long as he remained a student, he would continue to receive his allowance plus "extras" from Chancery; both sources of funds were placed at risk by his staying in Southwell.

HENRY LONG, Edward's younger brother, was, in the way of small boys, alternately exploited, spoiled, and ignored by his elder sibling and the latter's friends. Still a year away from Harrow, Henry was a keen observer of his elders, and his recollections of Byron's visit that summer, set down years later, retain the younger boy's awe of their noble guest, colored inevitably by his later celebrity.

As it turned out, the Longs were not at Worthing, where Byron had expected to find them: "We all went to Little Hampton and there appeared Lord Byron," Henry recalled. "He made urgent and immedi-ate enqueries after my brother, who was absent somewhere—but they soon met. Byron had with him his horses and his dog Boatswain."[27] Their guest's unexpected arrival, along with his friend's absence, raise the question of whether Byron had in fact been invited to join the Longs on the Sussex coast or whether he had simply appeared. In the event, he did not stay with the family but established himself at the Dolphin Inn. Henry wondered "why he did not take up his quarters at the Beach House Hotel. . . . The Dolphin was but a poor place in a dirty village." (Lack of money was probably the answer.)

The visitor promptly displayed his impressive marksmanship, firing at oyster shells by the pier. Henry had several occasions to witness the competitive element in the friendship between his brother and Byron: "Daily bathing was carried on with great vigour & here Lord Byron was in his element." Henry added, "I had good reason to know his excel-lence in the art of swimming, for he was very fond of carrying me about on his back. There I sat like Orion on the dolphin." Sensing the resentment of the left-out little brother, Byron had gone out of his way to make amends with water games.

Leaving Henry on shore, Byron and Long set off for more adventurous swimming. They had hitched a ride on a collier coming into the tidal port, and arriving back at the pier thoroughly soaked, "They sent a servant to order the bathing man to come down to shore and draw down a machine in which they proposed to have their dry things and dress. Stripping off everything except their drawers and shirts, they jumped from the end of the pier . . . into the river which as it was now nearly low water was rushing out with fearful rapidity. They shot out to sea & were carried to such a distance as I could barely discern their heads, popping up and down like little ducks upon the sea. By making an immense semi-circle . . . they at last arrived in safety at the spot where the machine was prepared to receive them."

Byron's spirits always soared with strenuous physical activity, especially when combined with the excitement of danger. Now he also had real cause for rejoicing. He wrote to John Pigot, "You will probably not be less pleased with this Letter when it informs you, that I am £30,000 richer, than I was at our parting, having just received Intelligence from my Lawyer, that a Cause has been gained at Lancaster assizes, which will be worth that Sum, by the Time I come of Age." *[28] Byron enjoined Pigot to keep his mother ignorant as to the value of his inheritance, while he himself promptly informed Mrs. Massingberd of his dramatic change in fortune.

By the middle of September immediate poverty drove Byron back to Southwell. Within days, however, he escaped the dramas in Burgage Manor to find himself the producer, director, and star of two private theatricals. The double billing, Richard Cumberland's popular comedy *Wheel of Fortune* and Richard Allingham's *Weathercock*, was to be performed in the living room of the Leacrofts, the local banker and his family. Their daughter, Julia, was smitten with Byron, and several poems to her in his first collection suggest that her feelings were, at least briefly, reciprocated. The Leacrofts' offer of their house, along with considerable help in the details of production, point to their encouragement of Julia's interest in the eligible young peer.

He had also agreed to write a prologue to *Wheel of Fortune*, and this new literary labor, together with memorizing his lines, convinced Byron that a retreat was essential. Taking John Pigot with him, he set out for

---

*Hanson's good news was premature—by almost twenty years.

Harrogate in a smart new chaise. His groom had been sent ahead with the two saddle horses, Brighton and Sultana, along with Nelson, Byron's new bull mastiff. With much laughter and barking the group settled into rooms at the Crown Hotel, Low Harrogate.

On this vacation dramatic and literary activities were the order of the day: "How do our theatricals proceed? Lord Byron can say *all* his part, and I *most of mine*. He certainly acts it inimitably," John Pigot wrote to Elizabeth. Byron was also "*poetising*, and since he has been here, has written some very pretty verses."[29] One poem, at least, was inspired by a girl whose chaste loveliness touched him: "To a Beautiful Quaker" celebrated a sober young woman to whom the poet had spoken only once. After the burning humiliation of his treatment by "Mary" and the dangerous depths of his passion for Edleston, he returned with relief to the safe distance of idealized romance.

Ever the most thoughtful of friends, Byron realized that his withdrawal into words—written or spoken—excluded Pigot. He made a point of being more companionable, an effort appreciated: "He is very good in trying to amuse me as much as possible but it is not in my nature to be happy without either female society or study."[30] Deprived of his medical texts, Pigot now joined Byron in versifying, applying the same diligence to this endeavor that he gave to his lecture notes: "Your brother John is seized with a poetic mania," Byron informed Elizabeth, whom he had taken to addressing by her middle name, Bridget, and "is now rhyming away at the rate of three lines *per hour*—so much for *inspiration*."[31] He announced in the same letter that his original selection of poems, being slowly printed on Ridge's hand press, had now almost doubled in number; additions included work he had believed lost, and new ones he was constantly adding.

Pigot's affection for his friend deepened. "Few people understood Byron; but I knew that he had a naturally kind and feeling heart, and that there was not a single spark of malice in his composition," he told Moore. Byron was "naturally shy, *very* shy, which people who did not know him took for pride."[32] And Elizabeth Pigot recalled that whenever Byron saw an unknown person approaching their house, "He would instantly jump out of the window to avoid them."[33] When forced into unwelcome social situations, he manifested his discomfort by the disconcerting habit of counting aloud from one to ten.

All who knew him attest to Byron's excruciating shyness in the presence of strangers, due, in large measure, to sensitivity about his limp. And many had reason to be aware of his spontaneous—even impulsive—acts of kindness and generosity, sometimes involving large sums of money he could ill afford. But it is also true that Byron intensely needed to come first with everyone he loved—or even liked—and would adjust his social persona accordingly. Companions of the most diverse type each believed their friendship with him to be the privileged one, based on shared tastes or distastes, sins or virtues. Observing his friend retire to his Harrogate rooms after dinner without so much as a glass of wine during the meal or afterward, the abstemious Pigot was convinced that Byron "was no more a friend to drinking than myself," a conclusion that would have caused howls among his other cronies.[34]

Between learning his lines and producing new poems, Byron had never gotten around to writing his promised introduction for *Wheel of Fortune*. The piece would have to be written between stage stops on the return trip. Getting into the carriage at Chesterfield, he announced, "Now, Pigot, I'll spin a prologue for our play," and before they reached Mansfield, his friend reported, "he had completed his task,—interrupting, only once, his rhyming reverie, to ask the proper pronunciation of the French word *début* and on being told it, exclaiming, 'Ay, that will do for rhyme to *new*.' "[35]

These lines sounded the theme of the prologue, the indulgence due the actors' age and inexperience, the same "debutant's defense" he would use in the preface to his first volume of poems:

> No COOKE, no KEMBLE, can salute you here,
> No SIDDONS draw the sympathetic tear;
> To night, you throng to witness the debut,
> Of embryo Actors, to the drama new;
> Here, then, our almost unfledg'd wings we try;
> Clip not our pinions, ere the birds can fly.[36]

Byron's debut was a soaring triumph. From the moment he stepped in front of the makeshift curtain and approached the flickering candles that, serving as footlights, separated the stage from the audience in the Leacrofts' drawing room, the evening was his.

After the witty prologue, Byron returned immediately as the moody Penruddock in *Wheel of Fortune*, a role that would come as close to a case of typecasting as any actor ever enjoyed. Described by the playwright as a "gloomy misanthrope, due to his having been cross'd in love in his younger days," the melancholy antihero introduces himself by saying, "I have the mark of Cain, the stamp of cruelty imprinted upon my forehead."[37]

After suffering and sacrifice, Byron was next able to showcase his comic talents. The faithless, changeable Tristram Fickle in Allingham's

The Weathercock was a part that allowed him to borrow from happily recalled performances of his favorite Restoration comedies, along with works by an older fellow Harrovian, soon to become a good friend, Richard Brinsley Sheridan.

As though the prologue and two male leads weren't enough, Byron also had the last word, delivering the epilogue written by his friend the Reverend J. T. Becher. The text, a lampoon of several prominent citizens among the audience, was crafted to display Byron's gifts of "doing" people. On opening night, though, the actor was too subtle; none of the victims caught on. Only when he broadened his mimicry for the following performances were faces observed turning red.

In performing as in writing, Byron found an exhilarating forgetfulness, along with the immediate approval of an audience; together they dispelled his paralyzing self-consciousness. The importance of the event for him, emotionally, did not even permit his usual deprecating remarks about the provinciality of Southwell. Writing to the Earl of Clare in early November, he grandly invokes his star turn in these homemade dramatics as the cause of delaying his return to Cambridge: "I am about to visit College, after having protracted my Residence here, much longer than was my original Intention.—I have been principally detained by some private Theatricals, in which I sustained the first parts."[38]

His triumph enhanced Byron's already considerable aura of glamour in Southwell. Few were the marriageable young women who did not envy Miss Ann Bristoe, the ingenue in both plays. Yet in his own eyes, if not those of his fans, the romantic hero had a fatal flaw: his weight. Byron had inherited his mother's tendency to corpulence, rendering this disposition the more hateful. By the fall of 1806 he weighed in at more than 200 pounds. For a young man of his height—5 feet, 8½ inches—this was more than pleasingly plump. It made no difference to his personal ideal of beauty that thinness, in either sex, was equated with unhealthiness and poverty.

In one of the poems to appear in Byron's first collection, he had ridiculed himself as a "stout" swain. Now he determined to create a new persona: pale and slender, haunted by secret sorrow and wasting loss. In November he undertook what we would call a crash diet, including a regimen of exercise, baths, and medicine as prescribed by a noted physician.

Benjamin Hutchinson was well known in both Southwell and London, where he was a founding member of the Royal College of Surgeons and was attached to Guys Hospital. He had attended Byron since 1804 or 1805 (for ailments unspecified, although not, we can assume, related to his foot). The doctor's report, dated November 19,

1806, began by advising a change in his patient's sleeping habits—no more day / night reversal: "Mr. Hutchinson judges it to be essentially requisite that Lord Byron should arise every morning at 8 o'clock and take a walk of three or four miles and a repetition of Exercize in the Course of the Day would materially conduce to the production of the wished for effect." As for diet, the doctor eliminated all malt liquor and white wine, allowing two glasses of port after dinner (the main meal of the day, taken by the upper classes in the late afternoon). While eating, only water, or water mixed with Imperial Cream of Tartar, was permitted. "Animal food" was allowed only once in the day—presumably at breakfast or dinner—since no supper should be taken "except a biscuit and the Imperial mixed with water." Three times a week Mr. Hutchinson prescribed immersion in a hip bath, along with a medicinal powder (type and function unspecified) mixed in nearly half a pint of water, to be taken three times a day.[39]

That Byron took the new regime seriously is suggested by a pen-and-ink sketch by Elizabeth Pigot, one of a satirical series she titled "Lord Byron and his Dog"; this scene shows the poet in his hip bath. The results, though, were still more revealing of the patient's determination to remake himself: By April he had lost twenty-three pounds.

Like dieters everywhere, Byron became obsessed with his regime and its results. In all of his letters (and, we can assume, conversations) he treated friends to details of his food intake, the exercise he undertook, what he wore during these exertions, and the news of each pound shed: "I wear *seven* Waistcoats, & a great Coat, run & play at Cricket in this Dress, till quite exhausted by excessive perspiration," he wrote to Hanson.[40]

Curiously, Byron made no mention of Hutchinson nor gave any hint that the regimen had been medically prescribed. The physician's role—and Byron's silence about it—raise the question of whether beauty alone was the rationale for these drastic measures. Possibly Byron's excessive weight was placing a dangerous strain on his foot. Certain features of Hutchinson's program, however, point in another direction: Elimination of alcohol, the quantity of water, probably joined with purgatives and the hip baths, were also prescribed treatments for venereal disease. The medicinal powder in question may well have been mercury, just then coming into favor for the treatment of syphilis.

In a letter to the Earl of Clare dated February 6, 1807—approximately six weeks after he had started Hutchinson's regime—Byron wrote: "Though my health is not perfectly re-established, I am out of all danger, and have recovered everything but my spirits, which are subject to depression."[41] Thus Clare, if no one else, was aware that

Byron had been suffering from a fairly serious illness that past fall or early winter. In an undated letter, probably written in early spring or about the time of Byron's most dramatic weight loss, Edward Long wrote: "I hope your Gonnorhea (Virulanta) has by this time entirely disappeared."[42] A severe case of venereal disease, emerging at the peak moment of Byron's conquest of Southwell, would certainly explain why he preferred the rationale of beauty to health in justifying his regime.

BY THE END of November the first copies of *Fugitive Pieces* issued from Ridge's hand press. Throughout the fall Byron had added new verses, and he continued to make changes in the originals. Now he proudly presented copies to the Pigots and their kinsman the Reverend John Thomas Becher, vicar of Rumpton and Midsomer Norton, who was also Byron's literary mentor and father figure. To no one's surprise but the poet's, Becher was scandalized, naming "To Mary" and possibly one of several more obliquely erotic poems addressed "To Caroline" as the offenders. Although Becher couched his criticisms in light verse of his own (now lost), Byron was stung and clearly alarmed. His reply, "Answer to Some Elegant Verses, Sent by A Friend to the Author, complaining that one of his descriptions was rather too warmly drawn," sets the tone for an anxious conciliatory apologia, which begins by alternating flattery and contrition:

> Candour compels me, Becher! to commend,
> The verse which blends the censor with the friend;
> Your strong, yet just, reproof extorts applause,
> From me, the heedless and imprudent cause;

Moving to his own defense, Byron makes a stirring case for passion: The old succumb to its madness; why should the young display more restraint?

> The wise, sometimes, from Wisdom's ways depart;
> Can youth then hush the dictates of the heart?
> Precepts of prudence curb, but can't controul [*sic*],
> The fierce emotions of the flowing soul.
> When Love's delirium haunts the glowing mind,
> Limping Decorum lingers far behind.[43]

In reply to Becher's fears that his words will "taint the virgin's mind," Byron falls back on an old saw that innocence is her best protection, while invoking the pure source of his own song: "My Lyre, the Heart;— my Muse, the simple Truth."

Byron was not persuaded by his own arguments. On the same day— November 26—that he completed his rhymed "reply" to Becher, and without waiting to hear his friend's reaction, Byron called in the copies he had presented to his Southwell circle and burned them all. Only four survive, among them the volume that belonged to the Reverend John Thomas Becher.

From the end of November through the last days of December, Byron worked furiously at choosing a collection of poems to replace *Fugitive Pieces*, ones that would raise no hackles. Then, in early January, he took off for London. His usual state of impoverishment and indebtedness had come to a crisis. Thinking to induce their stubborn young client to return to Cambridge, Hanson's partner Birch had withheld Byron's quarterly allowance. This was definitely the wrong strategy; enraged, Byron wrote a sarcastic letter to Hanson, declaring that if he had entertained thoughts of returning to Trinity, such tactics effectively dissuaded him.

From his rooms at Dorant's Hotel, Albemarle Street, Byron once again, through the dubious offices of Mrs. Massingberd, sought help from the moneylenders. Their terms were worse than before: For £3,000 that Byron would receive now, he must agree to pay £5,000 when he came of age (in two years), or interest on the larger amount six months after it fell due. To this agreement Massingberd added another provision: From the "new" £3,000 he was to pay off the earlier loan for which she had stood security. Now, however, with a lien on Massingberd's property, the moneylenders refused to advance Byron the funds without another adult to stand security for him. Mr. Dorant agreed to sign for his guest, and leaving the hotelier with funds to cover the interest, Byron returned to Southwell, flush with cash and more dangerously in debt than ever.

EARLY IN January 1807, the new collection, *Poems on Various Occasions,* had been printed by S. & J. Ridge of Newark in an edition of about one hundred copies and was ready for distribution. By January 13 of the new year, Byron was able to send John Pigot a copy of the new volume—"*vastly* correct, & miraculously *chaste,*" the author noted with a certain sour irony.[44] Consisting of "all my *Juvenilia,*" the sanitized collection had gained in girth what it had lost in heat: sixty-six poems to the earlier volume's thirty-eight. Still worried about lingering scandal, Byron begged Pigot to destroy the copy still in his possession once he received the new mailing. (Pigot tore out the offending poem "To Mary," but kept the book.) In his nervousness, Byron now issued contradictory assurances: The new collection was "much more complete; that *unlucky* poem to my poor Mary has been the Cause of some Animadversion from *Ladies in years*. I have not printed it in this Collection in Consequence of my being pronounced, *a most profligate Sinner*. . . . I believe in general they have been favourably received, & surely the Age of their Author, will preclude *severe* Criticism," he added worriedly.[45] To further assure—and reassure—friends and potential enemies, Byron had omitted other amorous poems, along with some passages from elsewhere that might offend:

> Though the kisses are sweet,
> Which voluptuously meet,
> Of kissing I ne'er was so fond,
> As to make me forget,
> Though our lips oft have met,
> That still there was *something beyond*.[46]

Deferring to the sensibilities of his clerical friends, he removed the first line of a stanza in another poem "To Caroline" beginning "No jargon of priests o'er our union was muttered." If the cuts tamed Byron's lusty muse, his additions must be seen as regressive—both sexually and poetically. "Childish Recollections" is a 410-line eulogy of Byron's Harrow attachments in which he draws upon every romantic and sentimental cliché, idealizing his intimates with classical names and heroic virtues.

Back in Southwell, with trouble receding on the literary front, the "profligate Sinner" felt free to pursue his courtship of several local belles. Of Anne Houson Byron declared, "She is a *beautiful* Girl, & I *love* her." But his fervor seems to have been confined to having "conversed with rather too much *Vivacity*."[47] His attentions to Julia Leacroft were more problematic. She may have put it about herself that Byron intended to carry her off, but it is also possible that their intimacy had progressed far beyond what was permissible for a marriageable young woman. In response to rumbles from the elder Leacrofts, one of the poems, "To Julia," was rededicated in the new publication to the generic "Lesbia." (To appease Julia's father, the poet added a note in the reprinted version of "To a Lady Who Presented the Author a Lock of Hair," declaring that the line "Since Juliet first declared her passion" did not refer to their daughter but to Shakespeare's heroine.) Still, claiming that Byron had compromised his sister, Captain John Leacroft now hinted at redress with sword or pistol. Byron believed—or chose to believe—that the unchaperoned freedom he had enjoyed with Julia was part of a concerted effort to entrap him; his friend Hobhouse clearly echoed Byron's version when he later remarked of the Leacrofts that they had "winked at an intercourse between him and [one] of the daughters in hopes of entangling him in an unequal marriage."[48] Byron's reply to the captain was a model of diplomatic and wily bluff calling. Commending his erstwhile friend on the "representation which was temperate and gentlemanly" of his family's position, Byron argued that as they were all victims of local gossip, "the only effectual method to crush the animadversions [one of his favorite words] of officious malevolence, is by my declining all future intercourse with those whom my acquaintance has unintentionally injured."[49] Poor Julia!

In Cambridge the new term had begun. Byron's tutor, the Rev. Thomas Jones, wrote to inquire when the Trinity prodigal might return. On February 14, Byron sent a petulant reply; he complained, first, about the university's emphasis on mathematics and metaphysics, noting, "I have other Reasons for not residing at Cambridge, I dislike it; I was originally intended for Oxford; my Guardians determined otherwise. I quitted the Society of my earliest associates, who are all '*Alumni*' of the latter, to drag on a weary term, at a place where I had many acquaintances, but few friends. I therefore can never consider *Granta* as my '*Alma Mater*' but rather as a *Nurse* of no very promising appearance, on whom I have been forced, against *her* Inclination, & contrary to mine."[50]

He did not mention another reason for avoiding Cambridge. Two days earlier, Byron had received a letter from Long, still training for the navy in Chatham. "I hear from my friends that your protégé is to leave the choir at Easter," Long reported.[51] So Edleston would be there for at least another month. To his friend and confidant Byron could freely beg further news of the chorister's plans; in one of his next letters Long promised, "Will enquire the future fate of Edleston for your information."[52] His dismissive remarks to his tutor notwithstanding, Byron was clearly planning to return to Trinity.

"If possible I will pass through Granta, in March, pray keep the subject of my *Cornelian* a *Secret*," he warned Long.[53]

But there is no record of this flying visit—if such took place. Instead, Byron seems to have continued complaining about Southwell, "the *place* I *abhor*," he wrote to Hanson, where he was "condemned to exist, (I cannot say live) at this *Crater* of Dullness, till my Lease of Infancy expires."[54] He bewailed his own poverty and his mother's avarice— "I lent Mrs. B. £60 last year, of this I have never received a *Sou*. & in all probability never shall"—and detailed every stage in his newly attenuated appearance.[55] Many of their acquaintances, he wrote to

Long, "have hardly believed their optics, my visage is lengthened, I appear taller, & somewhat *slim*."[56] Byron had a curious explanation for a still more astonishing change in his appearance: " *'Mirabile dictu,'* my Hair once black or rather very dark brown is turned (I know not how but I presume by perpetual perspiration) to a *light Chesnut*, nearly approaching *yellow*, so that I am metamorphosed not a little," he told Long.[57] The young trainee had now joined the Guards and was waiting to sail for Spain and the Peninsular War. To John Pigot Byron now wrote to congratulate him on qualifying as a physician, assuring his friend that "the Title of *Dr.* will do wonders with the *Damsels*."[58]

On June 11 he reminded Hanson curtly that on the twenty-fifth of the month his quarterly allowance would fall due. By the first week in June, he informed the solicitor, he had also pledged himself to pay more than £350 "to enable me to get rid of Cambridge forever," for which he would need two additional quarters' allowance, "or in all including the legal advance, £375."[59]

Through the spring he had been working furiously on a third volume of poems. Describing it to Long, he noted that "20 of the present pieces, will be cut out, & a number of new things added." Among the additions were new translations and imitations "from Virgil; some Odes from Anacreon, & several original Odes, the whole will cover 170 pages, my last production has been a poem in Imitation of Ossian, which I shall not publish, having enough without it.* Many of the present poems are enlarged and altered, in short you will behold an 'Old friend with a new face,' " he announced.[60]

After promising Long that he would have *"all"*—including recent poems omitted, when they next met, Byron was back to crowing about his slender new self: "On Tuesday I found myself reduced to 12 st. 11 lb. What sayest thou, Ned? do you not envy?"[61]

Hours of Idleness, Byron's first volume to be issued to the public, appeared in the last week of June. On the twenty-seventh, the poet was back in his old rooms in Nevile Court, where Edleston called on him the evening after his arrival. The chorister had seen Byron walking near Trinity twice, but owing to his dramatic loss of weight, *"knew* me not, till pointed out to him, by his Brother or Cousin," Byron reported proudly to both Long and Elizabeth Pigot. As for Edleston, "He is much grown & rather improved."[62] Neither friend would have been taken in by the cool tone. Once again Byron was in thrall to his angelic choirboy.

---

*Oscar of Alva: A Tale was included after all. It was a lifeless minisaga of highland clans suggesting that Byron should have obeyed his first editorial impulse.

CHAPTER 8

"Paper Bullets of the Brain"

UOYANT IN the anonymity of his thinness and his new celebrity as a published poet, Byron savored a triumphal return to Cambridge. With Edleston's first visit to his rooms, their intimacy was reestablished—sweeter, if anything, for the separation. As though to fix forever the intense happiness of the moment, Byron wrote to Elizabeth: " 'The *Hero* of my *Cornelian*' (who is now sitting *vis-à-vis*, reading a volume of my *poetics*,)" Byron reported with modest understatement, had been "very glad to see his former *patron*."[1]

Still, the private joy of their reunion did not keep Byron from plunging into the summer term's social swim. Despite the absence of most of his old friends, he was deluged with invitations; that weekend he managed to attend "3 *Oratorios*, 2 Concerts, a *fair*, a *boxing match* & a *Ball*," while the following week found him "out at different places every day, engaged to more *dinners* &c.&c. than my *stay* would permit me to *fulfil*."[2]

At all these occasions Byron continued to delight in the disbelief that greeted his loss of weight. The shy, overweight boy with a limp had become a pale, romantic figure. He had even grown an inch since his last visit to Cambridge, he told Elizabeth. Gleefully he parried queries about the ill health that could have caused such emaciation. He had only planned to stay for a few days, to settle his bills, but his new role of social lion, together with Edleston's presence, combined to delay Byron's departure.

Their time together was coming to an end. Along with physical growth, Edleston's voice had changed, and he would soon graduate from his role of boy chorister. Either he did not choose to move into men's singing parts (paying barely more than the pittance received by children), or his new, deeper voice was unlovely and he had not been asked to remain in the choir. In the fall he would be moving to London, where, Byron wrote to Elizabeth, he was "to be stationed in a mercantile house of considerable eminence in the Metropolis."[3] This pompously vague description referred to a lowly clerkship in South Sea House, a warren of offices on Lombard Street from which British private and public investments in the Pacific colonies were controlled. Since Byron had boasted to Long and others that he was arranging for his protégé's new career in the City, the humble apprenticeship had to be exalted to a position worthy of the patron.

Edleston's new job was to begin in October. But suddenly Byron once again decided they should not see each other: "At this moment I write with a *bottle* of *Claret* in my *Head & tears* in my *eyes*, for I have just parted from 'my *Cornelian*' who spent the evening with me," Byron wrote to Elizabeth on July 5, a week after his return to Cambridge. "As it was our last Interview, I postponed my engagements to devote the hours of the *Sabbath* to friendship, Edleston & I have separated for the present, & my mind is a *Chaos of hope & Sorrow*."[4]

To soften the blow of dismissing the boy from his life a second time, Byron indulged the fantasy (which he may even have believed) that their separation would be temporary: "We shall probably not meet, till the expiration of my minority." By then Byron would have come into his inheritance from the Rochdale and Norfolk estates, and Edleston would have completed his apprenticeship at the "mercantile house"; "I shall leave to his *decision*, either *entering* as a *Partner* through my Interest, or residing with me altogether. Of course he *would* in his present *frame* of mind prefer the *latter*, but he may alter his opinion previous to that period, however he shall have his choice," Byron concluded.[5]

The choice offered Edleston in this grandiose scenario—being kept by Byron or having his lover purchase a partnership for him—is poignant in its naïveté. Byron was trying to salve both his conscience and dull their shared pain by limning a fantasy of the future, when his wealth would allow them to transcend the criminal consequences of their love and live openly together. In epic enumeration, Byron then compared the two of them to famed—and accepted—same-sex lovers past and present: "We shall put *Lady E. Butler & Miss Ponsonby** to

---

*Two noblewomen who lived together for fifty years (1779–1829) in the Vale of Llangollen, dressing as men and receiving a steady pilgrimage of curious visitors. Byron had seen them at the theater one evening in identical male evening dress, and the couple made a deep impression on him.

the *Blush*, *Pylades & Orestes* out of countenance, & want nothing but a *Catastrophe* like *Nisus & Euryalus*,* to give *Jonathan & David* the 'go by,' " he jauntily informed Elizabeth.[6]

There was no reason now for Edleston to remain in Cambridge until fall; his presence would only prove awkward for both of them. Putting a brave face on the situation, Byron organized a farewell dinner in his friend's honor at the Hoop, a favorite local tavern. Now that their affair was ended, Byron no longer troubled with secrecy. Fourteen other friends were invited to the dinner, during which were consumed twenty-three bottles of wine and some claret cup. The bill of 15 guineas was one of the very few in his life that Byron paid promptly.

With the problem of Edleston solved, Byron changed his plans, deciding to return to Cambridge in October—when the boy with the angelic voice would be safely established in his clerkship. Already he anticipated the coming term: "My Rooms &c. &c. are finished in *great Style*, several old friends *come up* again, & many *new* acquaintances made, consequently my inclination leads me *forward*."[7]

In the meantime he threw himself into ever more frenzied merry-making, marked by a vast intake of spirits and accompanyingly oafish behavior: "Met with another '*accidency*,' upset a *Butter Boat* in the *lap* of a *lady*, looked very *blue*, *spectators* grinned, 'curse 'em' apropos, sorry to say, been *drunk* every day, & not quite *sober yet*. . . . This place is a *Monotony* of *endless variety*," he wrote to Elizabeth, concluding, "Got a Headach [*sic*], must go to bed, up early in the morning to travel, my 'protégé' breakfasts with me, parting spoils my appetite."[8]

Elizabeth's reply (one of only two letters from her to Byron that survive) shows how clearly she understood his passion for the younger boy, along with the confusions of gender aroused by their relationship: "My dear Tristram Fickle et l'Amoureuse," she addressed Byron, "for it would be wrong to omit the *latter title*," she added.[9]

DESPITE "the continued routine of Dissipation" in Cambridge and the strain of breaking with Edleston, Byron still managed to suffer all of a fledgling author's obsession with the fate of his new book. As his public literary debut, *Hours of Idleness* aroused "sundry palpitations," he

---

*When Nisus, beloved of Euryalus, slips and falls in the funeral games, he helps his friend win the prize by tripping the lead runner. Later, fighting the Italians, Nisus sacrifices his life to rescue Euryalus from the enemy. Byron included his version of Virgil's tale (from Book 9 of the *Aeneid*) in *Hours of Idleness*.

told William Bankes. Bankes was the only one of Byron's old Cambridge set who was also a member of the group of intellectuals which now began to look with interest on the poet in their midst. During Byron's season in Southwell, Edward Long had taken the liberty of giving Bankes a copy of his friend's second privately printed volume—a move that distressed the poet considerably. Byron was rarely easy with his intellectual equals, and he correctly anticipated that the brilliant Bankes—classicist, art collector, amateur archaeologist of distinction, and heir to Kingston Lacy and Corfe Castle—would show no special indulgence toward the poet's youth or aristocratic bloodlines. By the same token, Byron knew he could trust Bankes's candor; as he told him, "Your Critique is valuable for many Reasons. . . . It is the only one, in which flattery has borne so slight a part. . . . I am *cloyed* with insipid Compliments, & have a better opinion of your Judgement & Ability than your *Feelings*."[10] Responding in his next letter to changes Bankes had suggested, Byron told him: "I cannot evince greater respect for your alteration, than by immediately adopting, this shall be done in the next Edition."[11] With Elizabeth Pigot Byron could be open in his unlofty concern with sales, publicity, and what his publisher was not doing for him: "Has Ridge sold well? or do the Ancients demur? what Ladies have bought?" he grilled Elizabeth, adding, "All disappointed I dare say nothing *indecent* in the present publication, sorry for it."[12] The last phrase is crossed out.

A week later, July 13, Byron was in London, installed at Gordon's Hotel on Albemarle Street and hovering over Crosby, the London bookseller who acted as agent for Ridge. The latter had sent a number of copies of the volume to Crosby on consignment, for sale in London and elsewhere in England, as Ridge himself lacked any resources for distribution.

In reply to Elizabeth's query, the Newark printer had noted that sales of the new book were slow. Byron was outraged by this news: "What the Devil, would Ridge have? is not 50 in a fortnight before the Advertisements a sufficient sale, I hear many of the London Booksellers have them, & Crosby has sent Copies to the principal watering places. Are they *liked* or *not* in Southwell."[13] As he had not mailed his letter to Elizabeth, by the next day Byron was able to include a report from the reviled printer, now reinstated in the author's good graces: "I heard from Ridge this morning. . . . He says the poems go on as well as can be *wished*, the 75 sent to *Town* are circulated, & a demand for 50 more, complied with, the day he dated his Epistle, though the Advertisements are not yet half published."[14]

Byron personally sent a copy to his guardian Lord Carlisle.*15 Claiming indisposition, his lordship thanked the author before having read his book. As Carlisle himself had had poetry published and plays performed without much notice taken of either, a certain envy may have colored his condescending tone. Telling Byron of his "sincere satisfaction in finding you employ your leisure in such occupations," he then urged him to "persevere, whatever the reception may be, and though the Public may be found very fastidious, you will stand better with the world than those who only pursue their studies in Bond Street or Tatershall's [*sic*]."16

Hearing that Byron was in London, Augusta poured forth her grief at their estrangement to Hanson, pleading with him to act as mediator: "Will you tell me if you think there is the slightest hope of his forgiving me—or the least possibility of my doing anything in the world to obtain his forgiveness? I wd not torment you, but that I am sure you would wish for a reconciliation between us and that I am perfectly wretched in his continuing angry—& you know that there is not anything I wd not do to regain his good opinion & affection, which I trust I don't quite deserve to have lost—for that idea wd greatly augment my distress."17

Augusta was about to wed the man she had been in love with for six years, but her despair over the rift with a half brother she hardly knew suggests that Byron had already stirred feelings that were more than sisterly. On August 17, exactly one month after she had written to Hanson, Augusta Byron, twenty-four, married her thirty-six-year-old cousin Colonel Charles Leigh. The newlyweds moved to Six Mile Bottom, near Newmarket, convenient for the bridegroom's consuming interest in horses and gambling.

For his part, Byron was less unforgiving than indifferent; he had more urgent matters on his mind than Augusta. No sooner had he arrived at Gordon's Hotel than he was claimed by the feverish distractions of London—to whose demimonde he was now well known. Teasing the provincial Elizabeth, he exuberantly catalogued his familiarity with high life and low—"annals of Routs, Riots, Balls & Boxing matches, Dowagers & demireps, Cards & Crim-Con,† Parliamentary

---

*Catherine Byron had sent two copies of the earlier volume, *Poems on Various Occasions,* to Augusta with the expectation that she would forward one to her Uncle Carlisle. Hanson, too, had sent Augusta a copy of the same edition. Thanking the solicitor, Augusta noted that she had liked "some of them very much." But ever cautious, she added that "you will laugh when I tell you that I have never had the courage to shew them to Lord Carlisle for fear of his disapproving others."

†Adulterous relationships.

Discussion, Political Details, Masquerades. Mechanics, Argyle Street Institution* & Aquatic races, Love & Lotteries, Brooks's & Buonaparte, Exhibitions of pictures with Drapery, & *women without*; Statues with more *decent dresses*, than their *originals*, Opera-singers & Orators, Wine, Women, Wax works & Weathercocks." He continued to "*decrease* instead of enlarging," he added, "which is extraordinary as *violent* exercise in London is impracticable, but I attribute the *phenomenon* to our *Evening squeezes*, at public & private parties."[18]

Once again Byron was obliged to chivy Hanson to obtain his quarterly allowance from Chancery; this time the lawyer had another excuse for delay: His client had signed a draft for the sum, using the fictitious name "Hannibal Higgins." Hanson was not amused, warning Byron of the illegal nature of this sort of joke and the unpleasant consequences that could ensue. Realizing the futility of attempts to curb Byron's spendthrift habits, and his dangerously mounting debts, Hanson proposed appointing his mother as his treasurer, a suggestion that should have been made five years earlier. At this, Byron went into high dudgeon, informing the lawyer that "Mrs. Byron has already made more *free* with my *funds* than suits my convenience, & I do not [propose] to expose her to the danger of Temptation,"[19] an allusion, no doubt, to the £60 his mother had drawn on his allowance for the maintenance of horses and servants in Southwell. He did not, of course, factor into his account of his mother's fiscal irresponsibility her most recent efforts to keep him from sinking deeper into the quicksand of usurious debt. Using her own annuities and tiny income from Scotland as collateral, Catherine had guaranteed loans of £1,000 each.

ON THIS VISIT to London, Byron also arrived with a brand-new identity: At age twenty he had become a man of letters, and thus part of a tribe he affected to disdain. For the first time he was buffeted by the author's alternating currents of pride and anxiety. He exulted at the sight of his slender volume, with its blue-green cloth cover, displayed in bookshops, while suffering the suspense of waiting for reviewers' attention and doing everything he could to attract their equivocal gaze.

The first review, in the July 1807 issue of *Monthly Literary Recreations*, was all he could have hoped. "The young and noble author of these poems introduces them with a degree of modesty, which does honour to his feelings as a poet and a lord." The critic added that even

---

*A noted gambling "hell."

"his defects proceed from the warmth of his feelings and the facility with which he writes. . . . His beauties grow on the soil of genius."[20]

Byron professed to be unaware of the identity of the editor, along with the fact that the journal was owned and controlled by Ben Crosby himself, who used the publication shamelessly to puff his books and their authors. In the same issue featuring this notice, Byron reviewed Wordsworth's two volumes of poems, his first work since *Lyrical Ballads*. Although more respectful toward the principal "Laker" (as Byron later dubbed those poets) than he would soon become, the beginner's mixed review of the great first-generation Romantic is a classic instance of youth patronizing age: "The characteristics of Mr. W's muse are simple and flowing, though occasionally inharmonious verse, strong and sometimes irresistible appeals to the feelings, with unexceptionable sentiments. The pieces least worthy of the author are those entitled 'Moods of my own Mind,' we certainly wish these 'Moods' had been less frequent, or not permitted to occupy a place near works, which only make their deformity more obvious."[21]

Byron sent Crosby a poem that appeared anonymously in the same July issue of *Monthly Literary Recreations*. Never acknowledged by Byron or published in any authorized edition of the poet's work during his lifetime, the "Stanzas to Jessy" can only be read as an elegy to his love for Edleston. Their separation, experienced in the first verse as death, has, by the final stanza, become a spiritual impossibility.

> There is a mystic thread of life
>   So dearly wreath'd with mine alone,
> That destiny's relentless knife
>   At once must sever both, or none.
>
> .   .   .   .
>
> There are two souls whose equal flow
>   In gentle stream so calmly run,
> That when they part—they part?—ah no!
>   They cannot part—those souls are one.[22]

In Nottingham, sales remained sluggish, but Byron decided to attribute this to provincial ignorance. In the literary capital, he had received a first respectful review, and the book had been purchased by a titled relation, the Duchess of Gordon, whose son, Byron's cousin, happened to be staying at the same hotel. "Ridge, you tell me does not proceed rapidly in Notts, very possible," Byron wrote Elizabeth. "In Town things wear a most promising aspect & a *Man* whose works are praised by *Reviewers*, admired by *Duchesses* & sold by every Bookseller in the Metropolis, does not dedicate much consideration to *rustic Readers.*"[23]

More encouraging than a copy bought by a distant Scottish connection, however titled, was the news that Crosby "has disposed of his second importation, & has sent to Ridge for a *third* (at least so he says)," to which Byron added, "In every Bookseller's I see my *own name*, & *say nothing*, but enjoy my *fame* in *secret.*"[24]

Working at "intervals of leisure, after 2 in the *Morning*," he had written 380 lines of a new poem, an epic blank verse on Bosworth Field,* the battle fought in 1485 between Richard III and Henry Tudor that placed the Tudor dynasty firmly on the throne of England. Using a newly purchased history of the battle as background, he was planning a work that would consist of eight to ten books, to be completed in a year.

"So much for *Egotism*," he wrote to Elizabeth. "My *Laurels* have turned my Brain, but the *cooling acids* of forthcoming criticisms will probably restore me to *Modesty*"—an unhappily prescient remark.[25]

He continued to revile Southwell's citizens—"Mohawks who inhabit your Kraals"[26]—for lying in wait to ensnare him for their daughters: "I saw the *designs* of all *parties*, while they imagined me *every thing* to be *wished*," he wrote in a bitter outburst.[27] Only Elizabeth was spared his flayed memories: He wanted her to know that he appreciated her superior qualities, in particular the generosity of her affection: "You were my only *rational* companion. . . . You gave yourself more trouble with me & my *manuscripts*, than a thousand *dolls* would have done, believe me, I have not forgotten your good nature, in *this Circle* of *Sin*, & one day I trust shall be able to evince my gratitude."[28]

On August 11 he announced to Elizabeth plans for a Hebridean tour with an unnamed friend; the following week they were to proceed in his carriage to Edinburgh and from there, north toward the coast, with Iceland the final destination. "What would you say to some Stanzas on Mount *Hecla*? they would be written at least with *Fire*."[29] But the voyage never took place; lack of money may have been the reason. Or a change of mind—or heart about his companion. Elizabeth wrote to her brother: "How can you ask if Lord B. is going to visit the Highlands in the summer? Why don't *you* know that he never knows his own mind for ten minutes together?"[30]

Instead, Byron found adventure free and close to home; he swam the Thames, from Lambeth, passing under Westminster and Blackfriars

---

*Lost or destroyed early, the manuscript has never come to light, so there is no way of knowing whether Byron ever completed the poem.

bridges, an estimated distance of three miles. The poet Leigh Hunt, an aquaintance later to become a friend and collaborator, saw Byron in the water, with "Gentleman" John Jackson, his "Professor of Pugilism," waiting on the shore. Hunt came away with the impression that the swim had been undertaken to win a bet.

Byron's movements for the remainder of the summer are unclear. He was in Cambridge on August 20 when he wrote to Lord Clare, alerting him that he would return to Trinity in the fall: "Illness prevented my Residence for the last twelve months."[31] This suggests the tenacity of his "Gonorrhea Virulanta." Wherever he passed the two and a half months between early August and mid-October, Byron arrived at Dorant's Hotel in London on October 19, broke and begging Hanson for his allowance. Either the lawyer obliged with unusual dispatch, or his client found a fresh source of money. Arriving in Cambridge on about the twenty-fourth, he spent his first two days staying up until four in the morning playing hazard, a card game where stakes tended to be high. Informed by the authorities that he could not keep his new bulldog, Smut, in college rooms, he acquired another pet: "I have got a new friend, the finest in the world, a *tame Bear*," he wrote to Elizabeth. "When I brought him here, they asked me what I meant to do with him, and my reply was 'he should *sit* for a *fellowship*.'"[*32] Notwithstanding the legend that still persists of the bear residing in the tower turret above his master, he was more probably quartered in the college stables.

Byron's rooms newly refurbished with the elegant new ottoman and lamps *à la Grecque*, he was ready to play host, as he had in his first term. Now, though, his guests were no longer confined to undergraduate roisterers but represented a sophisticated brew of characters and classes: "We have eternal parties here, and this evening a large assortment of *Jockies*, Gamblers, *Boxers*, *Authors*, *parsons*, and *poets*, sup with me.—A precious Mixture, but they go on well together." Byron sagely attributed the conviviality of his unlikely guests to his own mix of qualities—"I am a *spice* of every thing except a Jockey," he wrote to Elizabeth, adding that he had just been thrown from his horse.[33]

Among the parsons was Francis Hodgson, just appointed resident tutor at King's College. An Etonian, Hodgson was an accomplished classicist whose translation of Juvenal had been published that same year and had been accorded a respectful notice in the *Edinburgh*

---

*This phrase was also the tag line in a favorite university joke in which the slurred speech of the boozy undergraduate inserts an "h" in the appropriate place, further explaining why Byron's answer "delighted them not."

Review. Byron was further awed by Hodgson's literary connections: His father, the vicar of Croydon, was a close friend of William Gifford, the former editor of the *Anti-Jacobin* and later the editor and principal critic of the *Quarterly Review.* The elder Gifford was also the author of two satires of London literary life, the *Maeviad* and the *Baviad,* to both of which Byron rendered the homage of imitating them in his work-in-progress. With Hodgson junior, Byron shared a passion for Pope and Dryden, but he also enjoyed shocking the young divine with accounts of his carnal adventures and dismissal of Christianity. Preferring orthodoxy in others, Byron respected his friend's faith, though Hodgson was no saint himself. Periodically he succumbed to the lure of pretty whores, after which he needed Byron's reassuring words on sins of the flesh.

Two of Hodgson's brilliant Eton friends had preceded him to Cambridge, and both now became part of Byron's expanded circle. The wit, dandy, and compulsive gambler Scrope Berdmore Davies emerges as possessing the character closest to Byron's in its elusive complexity. He was the son of a country parson, and his abilities at Eton had won him a scholarship to King's. But he was more often to be found in London, lounging about the gaming tables at Crockford's or White's, where he occasionally won, but more often lost, large sums of money. A friend of Beau Brummell (whose end in disgrace and exile he would, sadly, repeat), Davies lived his life on the existential edge, linen immaculate, risking more than he would ever possess on a turn of the dice.

The intellectual leader of their group, Charles Skinner Matthews, son of a Hertfordshire M.P., moved effortlessly from one academic set of laurels to another; he was a scholar and prizeman at Trinity when he and Byron met, and within months he would win a highly competitive fellowship at Downing College. He was also the most courageous of the circle, with a moral fearlessness new to Byron, one owing nothing to adolescent heroics. Matthews's atheism and radical politics, openly expressed at a time when seditious political opinions and blasphemy in matters of religion could mean imprisonment, had earned him the nickname "Citizen"—rather like being dubbed "Comrade" in the twentieth century. Less loudly proclaimed but known to all his friends was Matthews's open homosexuality. He seems, moreover, to have accepted his sexual identity completely. While Byron and others of their circle were still grappling anxiously with their own same-sex attachments, Matthews barely bothered to cover his tracks in his pursuit of like-minded or willing youths. He referred to these sexual adventures by the code name *méthode,* from the Greek root of "method," which also denotes "practice." Practicing pederasts now became "Methodists," a joke much enjoyed by his intimates. Matthews inspired admiration but also fear on the part of his friends who were less willing to risk their future for the indulgence of pleasures about which they also felt considerable guilt. Byron had met Matthews the year before, in 1807, introduced by another of the "Methodist" fraternity, the aesthete and collector William Bankes. While Byron was starring in Southwell theatricals, Matthews had taken his rooms in Nevile Court. Byron's tutor, the classicist Thomas Jones, had then warned him, "Mr. Matthews, I recommend to your attention not to damage any of the moveables, for Lord Byron, Sir, is a young man of *tumultuous passions*."[34] Matthews loved this phrase and, mimicking the delivery of the circumspect Reverend Jones, delighted visitors to the rooms by exhorting them to handle the very door with extreme caution.

Matthews's closest friend now become another Byron intimate. John Cam Hobhouse seemed an unlikely associate for either one of the other complicated young men. His constant presence in Byron's life from this time on is usually explained in terms of his being a foil: Conventional, plodding, priggish "Hobby," the steadying anchor, is cast as Sancho Panza among his quixotic and volatile friends. Byron himself liked to recall the initial repulsion Hobhouse had felt toward him, "after hating me for two years, because I wore a *white hat*, and a *grey* coat, and rode a *grey* horse (as he says himself), [he] took me into his good graces because I had written some poetry. I had always lived a good deal, and got drunk occasionally, in their company—but now we became really friends in a morning."[35]

The son of a Whig M.P. for Bristol, Hobhouse came from a Dissenting tradition: Both his mother's family, the Cams, and his stepmother were prominent Unitarians, and the influence of his two wives had prevailed on Hobhouse senior, who converted to send his oldest son to a Nonconformist school. The headmaster was a friend of Coleridge's and Southey's, and would invite the more advanced students to meet these eminent poets. As Hobhouse's father was in London for the parliamentary session, it was decided that the boy should continue his studies at Westminister School before matriculating at Trinity in 1807.

An industrious classical scholar and voracious reader, Hobhouse nurtured ambitions both literary and political. He kept up with Greek and Latin, translating assiduously and laying plans for poetic collaborations with Byron. Terrified by women, he was a "Methodist" more by default than from enthusiasm; he seems, in fact, to have had an aversion to sex in any form.

His real passion was politics. Hobhouse now drew Byron into the Whig Club, whose membership of ten points to the predominantly Tory leanings of aristocratic Cambridge. Here Byron met young peers, sons of Whig grandees, such as Lord Tavistock (his sponsor for club membership), Lord Ellenborough, and the Duke of Devonshire. Another, Douglas Kinnaird, the heir to a Scottish banking fortune, would become a lifelong friend. Less interested in drink and debauch, Byron's new companions were obsessively political and already grooming themselves for public life.

Among parsons, politicos, and gamblers, Byron still found time for literary labors: He had added several hundred more lines to his epic on Bosworth Field and had written 214 pages of a novel and 380 lines of a satire, to be called *British Bards*, which took on the entire literary establishment. (Alternating between prudence and impudence as he often did, Byron had already decided to publish this work anonymously.) Then there were 250 lines of another poem in rhyme, along with half a dozen smaller pieces.

Now that he had published a work under his own name, he had to face reviewers with few reasons to indulge a poet who announced himself "George Gordon, Lord Byron, a Minor." He rejoiced to Elizabeth that "I have been praised to the skies" in the *Critical Review*,[36] which found in *Hours of Idleness* "ample evidence of a correct taste, a warm imagination and a feeling heart." With less success he tried to sound insouciant about attacks that followed, taking the sensible stance that even a scathing review helped sales of the book: "It keeps up controversy and prevents it from being forgotten . . . beside the first men of all ages have had their share, nor do the humblest escape, so I bear it like a philosopher."[37] Those close to the poet knew better than to believe him.

Byron was particularly stung by the personal tone of ridicule heaped on him by one Hewson Clarke, a sizar* of Emmanuel College, Cambridge. Writing in the October issue of *The Satirist*, Clarke, too, assaulted the peer's posturing as "boy poet": "There certainly must be a wonderful charm in the name of *author*, and a prodigious desire in men to see their own work in *print*, or what could have induced 'George Gordon, Lord Byron, a minor' to have favored the world with this collection?" Noting the triple epigraphs from Homer, Horace, and Dryden, Clarke sneered, "Isn't he a Classical Lord?"[38] This first salvo was followed by a lampoon on a certain lord and his bear, and another whose malice included savaging Mrs. Byron as a drunken harridan (inducing her son to consider libel action).

---

*A sizar received a stipend based on need, which explains Clarke's venom toward a young aristocrat with literary pretensions.

This critic was certainly well informed about the most intimate particulars of Byron's life. Reviewing the second edition of *Hours of Idleness* the following year, Clarke alluded to Byron's relationship with Edleston and the shabby way the chorister had been sent packing: "In the paltry volume before us, we think we observe *some* proof that the still small voice of conscience will be heard in the cool of the day. Even now the gay, the gallant, the accomplished bear-leader is not happy, even now the monitory pang is felt, and conscience, cruel inexorable conscience, extorts the fearful avowal:

> "Tho' Pleasure stirs the maddening soul
> The Heart—the heart is lonely still—"

And Clarke concluded, mysteriously: "There is still one beloved and intimate friend left to his lordship besides his bear, one whose counsels, wild, dangerous plunging as they have hitherto been, Lord Byron has never slighted. To that guide of his youth, that inseparable bosom counsellor, we conjure his lordship to attend."[39]

Writing to Elizabeth Pigot in late October, Byron detailed the praise and abuse of reviews that had appeared the same day. This was the last letter he would ever exchange with his Southwell friend and confidante: "Write, Write, Write!!!" he begged her in a postscript,[40] but it does not appear as though either wrote again to the other. With Cambridge life soon to be behind him, Southwell receded to a still more remote past.

Byron spent Christmas at Trinity. Then he left Cambridge for good; he would return only to collect his M.A. degree the following June. But the Cambridge friendships would endure: Scrope Davies, Hodgson, Hobhouse, Kinnaird. There was one exception: As far as we know, Byron never saw John Edleston again.

BY EARLY January 1808 Byron was once again established at Dorant's Hotel. In November, Ridge had urged a new edition of *Hours of Idleness*, and he was still hard at work, omitting some poems and adding others, just as he had done earlier. Taking a cue from the critics, Byron omitted the preface, with its embarrassing pleas to indulge the youthful poet. Residence in the metropolis had also made him more political: The new edition was dedicated to his powerful cousin, Lord Carlisle, "from his obliged ward and affectionate kinsman."[41] Since his cool initial reception of the book, the peer had written to Byron a second, warmer note about the volume, including, along with his words of praise, "a few trifles of my own."[42]

A new professionalism was emerging in Byron's perspective on his work, which now extended to the design and production of the second edition. Visiting from Cambridge earlier, he had made the rounds of bookshops, reporting back to Ridge: "When I was in London, I observed the Booksellers objected to the size, & two or three said, the poems should have been printed in the same size, as Ld. Strangford's & Little's* poems, in this opinion I coincide, & with your leave the next Edition shall be printed & *bound* in the same manner, & in the same coloured Boards as Little. I dont admire the yellow *backs*." Determined to retain as much control as possible over the finished product, he asked Ridge: "You could not have the second Edition printed in London? could you? if it made no difference to you, I should prefer it, as I could superintend the proofs in person." If this proved unfeasible, he would ask his Southwell friend John Becher to supervise correcting the sheets. Like all authors, he tried using the modest success of the first printing to argue for a bigger run this time: "I think our next Edition, should be on *hot press* as the first has gone off well."[43]

During his last weeks in Cambridge, Byron bombarded Ridge with corrections and addenda, along with suggestions for illustrations (Harrow, Newstead, or a portrait of the poet?). Loyally, he tried persuading Crosby, the London bookseller, to publish Hobhouse's satire in imitation of Juvenal; as the work was too short to justify a volume to itself, Byron proposed that a four-hundred-line poem of his be included, a satire "of the same nature, but original . . . the subject the poetry of the present Day."[†44]

Even while the new edition was in the press, negative criticism of the available volume mounted. In the interval, Byron's acquaintances who were also insiders had time to alert him to the slashing he could expect from the *Edinburgh Review*. With exceptional protectiveness (and perhaps to forestall any impulse on her part to humiliate him), Byron now wrote to John Becher asking him to warn Mrs. Byron, cautioning her "not to be out of humour with them [reviewers] and to prepare her mind for the great hostility on their part."[45]

When it finally appeared in January, however, Byron was devas-

---

*Thomas Little was the pseudonym of the Irish poet Thomas Moore, who used the pen name for his more passionate love lyrics, one of the favorite readings of Byron and John Edleston.

†Ridge did not take Hobhouse's work. When it was published by Longman in 1808, in a volume called *Imitations and Translations*, several short poems of Byron's were included, but not his original satire, which was published separately.

tated. The *Edinburgh Review* was the most distinguished and influential journal of the day, where, with prosecutorial logic, Henry Brougham (later Baron Brougham and Vaux and future Lord Chancellor) now demolished Byron on every score: for pleading his minority, his privilege, and worst of all, for lack of talent or originality. It was not enough, Brougham said, for the poet to understand that feet should scan and final syllables rhyme: "We would entreat him to believe that a certain portion of liveliness, somewhat of fancy, is necessary to constitute a poem, and that a poem in the present day, to be read, must contain at least one thought, either in a little degree different from the ideas of former writers or differently expressed." He concluded, "We must take these poems as we find them, and be content, for they are the last we shall ever have from him."[46]

Like the mother tigress she was, Catherine Byron was furious; only she was allowed to utter a word of criticism of her son. She was soon made aware, moreover, of how deeply wounded Byron was by the attacks on his poetry. To Becher he tried to make light of them: "I think *I* could write a more sarcastic critique on *myself* than any yet published."[47] But in March, Catherine wrote to an unknown correspondent (either Becher or Hanson) to note her concern over a recent letter from her son in which "he abuses himself worse than the Edinr Reviewers, he says if I have any regard for him I will never mention his poetry to him more as he wishes to forget it was well enough but as a Man he has done with it for ever.

"He says however that he has been better treated than he deserved to be . . . but that it is not anything that could be said of him that would prevent his writing, but that he has really no opinion of his talents in that way and now has no pleasure in the employment. Now the plain English of all this is that he is really discouraged and depressed and that this odious Review has convinced him that he really has no Talents. I am really grieved to the Heart of all this."[48]

"As an author, I am cut to atoms by the E[dinburgh] Review," Byron wrote to Hobhouse. "It is just out and has completely demolished my little fabric of fame. This is rather scurvy treatment from a Whig Review, but politics and poetry are different things, & I am no adept in either, I therefore submit in Silence."[49]

"This was not the case," Hobhouse said. "He was very near destroying himself."[50]

DESPAIR and humiliation had dashed his literary hopes; guilt and loss were the price of banishing Edleston, whose presence in London would have haunted the wintry streets. Failure bounded the present, driving Byron to seek refuge in an idealized schoolboy past. His old enmity with Henry Drury, which had softened to a truce on leaving Harrow, had warmed into friendship. He made frequent visits back to his old haunts now, sometimes on Drury's invitation and accompanied by other friends, such as William Harness and Edward Long. Byron was elated to find that the students read his poetry and he had become a celebrity among old boys and new. On several occasions he pressed lavish gifts— a gold piece and a £5 note—into the hand of an embarrassed Henry Long, Edward's younger brother, now in his final year. He wrote to James de Bathe, in the same sixth form, inquiring whether he might be interested in accompanying him on a planned voyage to the East. With Drury as mediator, Byron reconsidered his animus toward Dr. Butler, finally enjoining Ridge to suppress in the new edition, "Childish Recollections," with its savage lampoon of the headmaster as "Pomposus." He also saw the futility of a retreat into boyhood in the very year he was to turn twenty-one. Instead, that same January 1808, he found an older man who provided support and sympathy.

Robert Charles Dallas was born in Jamaica, where his father, a physician, had amassed a fortune. The younger Dallas had studied law in London with the intention of returning to the West Indies as an administrator, but the climate proved damaging to his wife's health. He returned to England, where he led the life of a man of letters, churning out moralizing essays, plays, poems, and unreadable three-volume novels. Dallas was also Byron's kinsman; his sister Henrietta had married the poet's uncle George Anson Byron. Byron never ceased to feel the loss of a real family and was always positively disposed toward blood relations, however remote. Dallas was also a flatterer and a sycophant— qualities that often sufficed for Byron, especially at low points in his life, when he was insatiable for approval. The older man had picked the perfect moment to introduce himself with an ecstatic letter of praise for *Hours of Idleness.*

Dallas also entertained fantasies of reform in which he would rescue his errant young relative from a life of sin, leading him back to the fold of orthodox Christianity; this fond hope Byron was honest (or perhaps nervous) enough to quash at the outset. Reminding Dallas that in his short life "I have been already held up as the votary of Licentiousness, and the Disciple of Infidelity," he went on to assure his would-be redeemer that his reputation was well deserved: "In Morality I prefer Confucius to the ten Commandments, and Socrates to St. Paul (though the two latter agree in their opinion of marriage) in Religion, I favour the Catholic emancipation, but do not acknowledge the Pope, and I have refused to take the Sacrament because I do not think eating Bread or drinking wine from the hand of an earthly vicar, will make me an Inheritor of Heaven. . . . I believe Truth the prime attribute of the Deity, and Death an eternal Sleep, at least of the Body.—You have here a brief compendium of the Sentiments of the *wicked* George, Ld. B."[51]

CHAPTER 9

Lord of the Manor

*I*NDEED, BYRON SEEMED deter-
mined to prove that he was *"wicked* George." With the new year of
1809 he plunged frantically into London's pleasures. He saw more of
Scrope Davies, often joining him for games of hazard. In February they
joined the Cocoa Tree Club; "& next week the dice will rattle," Byron
promised Hobhouse.[1] Charles Matthews, "father of all mischiefs,"[2] was
addicted to hazard, and the play of Matthews and his two most amusing friends fizzed with laughter. Happily, Byron's enthusiasm for the
game was short-lived; his debts were mounting steadily even without the
disaster of a night's bad hand. He lacked, moreover, the monomania of
the obsessive gambler.

His passion for boxing, however, intensified. With his friend
"Gentleman" John Jackson, Byron became a familiar sight in the world
of "the Fancy," backing and betting on prizefighters and traveling to
matches in the company of managers, gamblers, and others who shared
this sporting taste. Their speech—the language of the ring, the streets,
and inevitably the criminal underworld—made liberal use of the slang
known as "Flash," and Byron delighted in his mastery of this urban
argot, adding the "gemman from Lunnun" to his repertoire of characters.

But losing himself in sex was the surest means he knew of distraction from failure and self-doubt. Once again he threw himself into
sexual marathons, repeating the pattern that had followed his flight
from Lord Grey de Ruthyn. As before, his London partners were very
young and poor girls whom he rescued—temporarily—from a life of
whoring. He saved news of his exertions for the Rev. John Becher: "To
give you some idea of my late life, I have this moment received a
prescription from Pearson, not for any *complaint* but from *debility*, and

literally *too much love*. . . . In fact, my blue-eyed Caroline, who is only sixteen, has been lately so *charming*, that though we are both in perfect health, we are at present commanded to *repose*, being nearly worn out."[3] The next day, February 26, he relayed the same bulletin less coyly to Hobhouse: "I am buried in an abyss of Sensuality, I have renounced *hazard* however, but I am given to Harlots, and live in a state of Concubinage. I am at this moment under a course of restoration by Pearson's prescription, for a debility occasioned by too frequent Connection.—Pearson sayeth, I have done sufficient with [in?] this last ten days, to undermine my Constitution."[4]

The previous evening, in the company of Lord Altamont (later the Marquess of Sligo), Byron had attended the Opera Masquerade at Covent Garden, where afterward "we supped with seven whores, a *Bawd* and a *Ballet-master* in Madame Catalani's apartment behind the scenes. . . . I have some thoughts of purchasing d'Egville's pupils, they would fill a glorious Harem."[5]

Byron's notion of purchasing the dancing master's young students as a child harem sounds priapic, but on a deeper level, his fantasy reveals a desperate urge to escape. He felt devoured by Caroline—consumed, literally, by her sexual voracity and his own. And he feared, after the faithless Mary, another emotional entanglement threatening to engulf him. The vision of a swarm of androgynous children, available yet undemanding, would continue to beckon him with a promise of safety. "I am at present as miserable in mind and Body, as Literary abuse,* pecuniary embarrassment, and total enervation can make me," he wrote to Hobhouse. "I have tried every kind of pleasure, and it is 'Vanity.' "[6]

A few weeks later, on March 14, Byron was, in fact, ill—probably with a recurrence of venereal disease. Confined to his room at Dorant's, taking laudanum to ease the pain, he may have been exaggerating when he repeated what his surgeon had told him, that "another quarter would have settled my earthly accounts," but it reflected his state of mind.[7]

While he lived, however, he returned to a regime of more of the same, airing plans to reestablish at Newstead the infamous Medmenham Abbey—home to the Hell-Fire Club of fifty years before, whose "monks" were notorious for the orgies staged there—"or some similar temple of Venus, of which I shall be Pontifex Maximus—You have heard of one *nymph*. Rumour has been kind in this respect, for alas! I

---

*The *Edinburgh Review* critique had just appeared, which, in Byron's words, had "cut to atoms" the poet and "demolished his little fabric of fame."

must confess that *two* are my *property*, one under my own immediate custody, as the other will be also when I am recovered."[8]

On March 28 he wrote to Becher, giving Dorant's Hotel on the heading of his letter but telling his friend, "I am still in or rather near town residing with a nymph, who is now on the sofa vis-à-vis, whilst I am scribbling. . . . I have three females (attendants included) in my custody. They accompany me, of course."[9] Two weeks later, Byron had added to his roll call of sexual partners and expanded his activities to include seducing another man's mistress: "I proceed as usual turning the twenty-four hours to the best account, particularly the nocturnal moiety," he wrote Hobhouse. "My Belles would probably differ, were they together, one is *with* me, and the other *for* me—or any body else, I dare say in my absence.—Besides, I amuse myself with the 'chere amie' of a French Painter in Pall Mall, a lively Gaul—and occasionally an Opera Girl from the same Meridian." Not yet recovered from his illness, he had energy and aggression to spare: On his first night out, he went to the theater, where a row with two strangers turned violent. He gave one adversary a black eye. Afterward Byron recovered, along with ten friends, at a "house of Fornication," he told Hobhouse.[10]

Debauch could not break the spell the bewitching Caroline had cast over him. At some point that spring Byron paid 100 guineas to "redeem Miss Cameron" from a Madame D. (perhaps the bawd who appeared with her seven young whores at the Opera supper party).[11] Byron established the girl in rented quarters at Brompton, then a London suburb where few questions were asked about transients.

His new domestic arrangements shocked his friends. To the young men in Byron's set, living openly with a whore was breaking the rules of right-thinking rakes. Tom Wildman, a Harrow classmate, visited the establishment at Brompton and was reportedly astonished to find Miss Cameron invited downstairs to meet him. Before he departed, Wildman nosily observed that Byron and his mistress had separate beds. And Tom Moore, himself an energetic philanderer, noted priggishly, "An amour (if it may be dignified with such a name) of that sort of casual description which less attachable natures would have forgotten, and more prudent ones at least concealed, was by him converted, at this period, and with circumstances of most unnecessary display, into a connection of some continuance,—the object of it not only becoming domesticated with him in lodgings at Brompton, but accompanying him afterwards, disguised in boy's clothes, to Brighton."[12]

Cross-dressing—particularly if combined with crossing class lines— always titillated Byron. When he took Caroline to Brighton in March, she was not only dressed as a boy but also introduced as a close relation. His own explanation of this masquerade is an entire Byronic text on gender, class, and sexuality: "Another of the wild freaks I played during my mother's lifetime, was to dress up Mrs.——— and to pass her off as my brother Gordon, in order that my mother might not hear of my having such a female acquaintance."[13] Lady Perceval was staying in Brighton at the same time, and she often met Byron accompanied by the same young person. Certain suspicions she harbored were confirmed when she addressed his companion: "What a pretty horse that is you are riding!"—"Yes," answered the Cockney rider, "it was *gave* me by my brother!"[14]

News of Byron's besotted state reached Cambridge in rumors that he was planning to marry the sixteen-year-old prostitute, an act of gallantry as well as passion; she was also pregnant. Still in boy's clothes, she returned, unaccompanied, it seems, from Brighton to London. There, in an anonymous contemporary account, "the young gentleman miscarried in a certain family hotel in Bond Street, to the inexpressible horror of the chambermaids and the consternation of all the house."[15]

Caroline's pregnancy terminated (possibly by self-induced abortion), Byron was able to assure the disapproving Hobhouse that marriage with Miss Cameron was not imminent (if, indeed, it had ever been seriously considered). At the end of March, they were back in Brompton—together: "I am still living with my Dalilah, who has only two faults, unpardonable in a woman—she can read and write," he wrote to Hobhouse.[16]

In his vulnerable state, he turned once again to Augusta. Repeating the cause of their estrangement, Byron reopened communications by asking another favor: Would her husband, Colonel Leigh, secure the Prince of Wales's help on behalf of Byron's friend Mr. Wallace? The army officer did not wish to return to his regiment in the East Indies, having served in that insalubrious climate for nine years. Delighted as she was by the renewal of relations with her beloved brother, she was not able to help him this time, either.

Augusta was expecting her first child, and Byron, now back to the teasing, good-natured manner he used with his sister, proposed making the baby his namesake and legatee—*if* it was a boy. "Pray name my nephew after his uncle, it must be a nephew (I *wont* have a *niece*) I will make him my *heir*, for I shall never marry, unless I am ruined, and then his *inheritance* would not be great."[17] (Augusta could not oblige, giving birth to a daughter, Georgiana Augusta, on November 4, 1808.)

Meanwhile, Byron fretted over the question of whether Cambridge would award him an M.A. Nine terms of residence were the requirement for the degree, and Byron had spent only three and a fraction at

Trinity. His debts, compounded by usurious interest, were finally beginning to alarm him—at least when he wasn't borrowing more and spending whatever he had: "*Entre nous,* I am cursedly dipped," he confessed
to Hobhouse. "My debts, *every* thing inclusive, will be nine or ten thousand before I am twenty-one. . . . Newstead I may *sell*—perhaps I will
not."[18] He was waiting for Lord Grey to vacate the abbey at the expiration of his lease in June, when he planned a visit.

Poems Original and Translated, the new, revised edition of *Hours of
Idleness,* appeared at the end of March, but demoralized as he was by
the criticism of the preceding volume, Byron could summon little interest in its publication. He had added five poems, variations on the theme
of regret for lost youth and innocence. Perhaps seeing the new verses
further depressed him, as a commentary on his bleak present life. He
sent one of the very few volumes he distributed to the faithful Becher,
who had hovered over the proofs in Newark, and tried to take the high
ground, reassuring his friend that neither his health nor his spirits had
been damaged by the reception of the earlier edition.

After the savagery of the critics, the boxing world seemed more welcoming than ever; in April Byron himself arranged a match near the
Rubbing House on Epsom Downs between Tom Belcher, the pint-sized
English favorite, and Dan Dogerty, the Irish champion backed by Byron
and Jackson. On May 10, Byron accompanied another pugilist, Tom
Cribb, to a match between John Gully, defending champion of England,
and the challenger, Bob Gregson. Jackson had gradually added the functions of pimp, purchasing agent, and general go-between to his other
roles; Byron now asked him to buy a greyhound and a pony—probably
for Caroline.

Boxers, animals, and "misses two"—as Hobhouse dubbed the
Brompton ménage—were expensive, and on May 12, Byron arranged
another rendezvous with Mrs. Massingberd. On this visit he was
accompanied by Scrope Davies. Six years his friend's senior, Scrope most
probably stood as joint security to guarantee further funds from the
moneylenders, as Byron would not turn twenty-one until January 1809.
On June 4 he planned to attend Speech Day at Harrow, when his protégé, William Harness, was to recite the same passage from *King Lear*
that Byron had chosen three years earlier. Arriving late, Byron missed
his friend's performance: "However I heard your *Fame,* & congratulate
myself on the escape of my *Vanity,*" he told Harness, with a flattering
interpretation of his own ambivalence.[19]

Whether or not his recent efforts to borrow more money had succeeded, on June 15, Byron was begging Hargreaves Hanson to intercede
with his father, the "Baron of Exchequer," for an emergency advance on

his allowance;[20] he was leaving for Brighton the following day, and if he failed to catch the senior Hanson in his office the next morning, funds should be directed to him at the seaside resort.

Byron, joined by Scrope Davies and Hobhouse, remained in Brighton for most of the summer. On July 4 he went down to Cambridge to take his degree. But he took no pleasure in the leniency of the university in bending the rules: "Alma Mater was to me 'injusta Noverca,' "* he wrote sourly to Harness, "and the old Beldam only gave me my M.A. degree because she could not avoid it."[21] Back in Brighton, he indulged his passion for swimming and for sailing, a new enthusiasm. A Cambridge friend, Wedderburn Webster, was struck by "the dextrous manner in which Byron used to get into his boat; for while standing on the beach I once saw him vault into it with the agility of a harlequin, in spite of his lame foot."[22] And Captain Gronow, memoirist and man-about-town, visiting Brighton at this time, recalled Byron as particularly "fond of boating, and was generally accompanied by a lad, who was said to be a girl in Boy's clothes."[23]

Caroline, then, was with him at the beginning of his summer holiday. But all was not well between them, and by July 20, it was over. Byron wrote to Mrs. Massingberd: "I have parted with Miss Cameron, & I beg she may have her Clothes & the trunk containing them."[24] There is no mention of the cause of their breakup. Did Caroline assume that Byron's claims to sexual variety entitled her to the same? Evidence of her hatred for Hobhouse suggests that the misogynist may have used his influence during those weeks to make mischief between the lovers. In November Scrope Davies reported to Byron, "Caroline was at the play on Monday parading the Lobby—she came up to me, and without any ceremony commenced the most violent attack on Hobhouse I ever witnessed—an interview between the two, would be no bad interlude between the play and farce."[25] "Parading the lobby" was only a level removed from walking the streets; if Davies is to be believed, this encounter suggests that Caroline, now seventeen, was thrown back into a life of prostitution.

In two poems written that August, Byron revealed depths of regret and loss that he could never acknowledge in his letters, with their coarse and flippant references to his "Harlots."

In the first he seems to accept blame for ending the affair, suggesting, too, that a general desiccation of feeling is the cause. "And Wilt Thou Weep When I Am Low" asks the poet, in the certainty that he deserves no tears:

---

*An unjust stepmother.

> My heart is sad, my hopes are gone,
>   My blood runs coldly thro' my breast;
>   .   .   .   .
> Sweet lady! once my heart was warm,
>   With every feeling soft as thine,
>   But beauty's self has ceas'd to charm
>   A wretch created to repine.[26]

His present "death of the heart" is made more painful by the memory
of passion shared:

> Remind me not, remind me not,
> Of those belov'd, those vanish'd hours,
>   When all my soul was given to thee;
>   .   .   .   .
> I dreamt last night our love return'd,
>   And sooth to say that very dream
>   Was sweeter in its phantasy
> Than if for other hearts I burn'd,
>   For eyes that ne'er like thine could beam
> In rapture's wild reality.

Feeding on the past, occupying dream and fantasy, memory destroys the
present.

RELIEVED TO have Caroline gone, Hobhouse and Scrope Davies set
about distracting their friend with nights made hazy by drink, sobered
by nocturnal swims. Jackson came often from London, "the expense of
the professor's chaise thither and back being always defrayed by his
noble patron."[27] Possessive and disapproving, Hobhouse penned a
spiteful lampoon on Byron's fondness for the boxer. He was probably
unaware of the many favors Jackson rendered Byron; this summer the
pugilist was kept busy conveying Byron's threats to sue the provider of
the unsatisfactory pony, and placating his Brompton landlord, the aptly
named Mr. Louch, for claims of damaged property; amenities that
Byron had provided for the lodgings were to be sold to raise needed
funds: "Dispose of the bidets, &c. as you best can,"[28] he instructed
Jackson.

Safely back in an all-male circle, Byron turned his interest to a local
tradesman's young son. John Cowell had the same first name as Edleston,
and his father was also a butcher. The boy was intellectually gifted, and

Byron soon announced his intention to help him obtain a scholarship to
Eton. With Henry Drury's support, Cowell was admitted for the winter
term in January. Meanwhile, the lad's parents were dazzled by the
young lord's patronage of their son, and they readily agreed to allow
Byron to take the boy off alone on a trip lasting several days.

In a worldly sense, Byron's role in Cowell's life was a happy one,
redeeming his broken promises to Edleston. His new protégé did so well
at Eton that he was awarded a scholarship to Trinity (probably with
Byron's further sponsorship). Cowell's letters overflow with nostalgia,
along with affection and gratitude; they suggest, in a troubling way,
however, that the younger man's emotional life had come to a premature halt with the end of his summer's intimacy with Byron. Cowell
reads and rereads his patron's occasional letters, and his replies all voice
the fervent hope that Byron will not forget him. There is not a word
about new friends, interests, activities, or plans for the future. Indeed,
Cowell's last surviving letter to his benefactor, written from Trinity
College in 1814, exudes feelings of loss. "It is perhaps of no consequence to you to know," he wrote, "that I always *have* and always *shall*
consider the moment of my introduction to you the most fortunate of
my life [Cowell later qualified this to "one of"] and the recollection of
it and the contemplation of it gives me more delight than any other
event* that I am acquainted with."29

WHILE BYRON was enjoying Brighton, his critics took no holiday. His
principal persecutor, Hewson Clarke, writing in *The Satirist*, published
an anthology of all other attacks on *Hours of Idleness*. Then, in the June
issue of his journal, he produced his own savage lampoon, "Lord B——
to His Bear" (all printed anonymously).30 Reading this in Cambridge in
early July, Byron flew into a rage, writing to Clarke in telegraphic style:
"Report universally attributes to your pen, passages in the Satirist of
this, & *last* month alluding to me [in such?] marked & unjustifiable
manner, that I can no longer delay requiring an explanation.—I shall
expect (if you are not the author) an immediate & unequivocal disavowal.—In case this proposal should not meet your approbation, my
friend Mr. Hobhouse is instructed how to act."31 Unchastened, Clarke
followed with a fresh attack in the August *Satirist*, this time taking on
the new edition of *Hours of Idleness: Poems Original and Translated*.
Dismissing the volume as "This pretty little collection of namby-pamby

---

*Byron encountered Cowell and his fiancée in Hastings in the summer of 1814, so
his protégé did move on to other happy events in his life.

verses," he sneered, "But stay, Ladies, 'tis a truly harmless Lord, now—
he is without his Bear, and is himself muzzled."[32]

ALONG WITH concern about her son's low spirits, Catherine Byron
persisted in her efforts to secure action from Hanson in the matter of the
Rochdale estates, stalled in litigation; the lawyer had promised to visit
the Lancashire property himself at the end of July, calling on Catherine
along the way, but he neither made the trip nor answered her letters
demanding an explanation. Furious, she now wrote to Birch, the junior
associate, noting that Hanson "seems to be a sleeping partner in the
firm."[33] Her anger produced as little effect on her lawyers as upon her
son. Charles Hanson, his father's apprentice, wrote across the letter,
"What impertinence!" Goaded by the lawyers' indifference, Catherine
tried another tack: She found Lancashire connections who reported to
her that the portion of the estate not under litigation (and whose revenues unquestionably belonged to Byron) was yielding a large income—
to others. Now that she had numbers at her disposal, "Mrs. Byron
Furiosa" wrote to Birch again: "If it had been properly managed Lord
Byron ought to have had more than thirty thousand pounds saved
out of that property by the time he came of age. *I will speak the truth*,
why is my Son permitted to be thus plundered by you and Mr. Hanson?
Why don't you prevent it? What reparation can you make to him?"[34]

Catherine's accusing voice, speaking the truth, did nothing to
advance her son's case; it was soon clear that neither Hanson nor his
partner had even troubled himself to learn in which court the Rochdale
lawsuit would be heard—Chancery or King's Bench?

Closer to home, deteriorating conditions at Newstead were a further
source of anxiety, and one reason, at least, why Catherine's "pen-
chant"—as Byron derisively described his mother's affection for Lord
Grey—had ended along with his lease. During the five years of his ten-
ancy, the abbey's worsening squalor had become grist for local gossip:
"I have not seen Newstead myself," Catherine had written to Hanson
during the past winter, "but . . . all the County talks of it and says it is
quite a disgrace for any Person in the character of a Gentleman to keep
a place in such a Beastly state (that was the expression that was used.)"[35]

Among other reported damage, new dining room windows had disappeared, but it was the grounds where the depredations of his lordship,
obsessed with hunting, were said to have done their worst. Young trees
planted to replace the old oaks stripped for timber by the fifth Baron
had been destroyed by the hares and rabbits Lord Grey raised for shooting. He flew into tantrums at the attempt to cut back undergrowth in
the woods, as it provided cover for his game. He forced ponds to run

dry, Owen Mealey reported, and when the overseer objected, Lord Grey told him that he would be glad to pay 1,000 guineas for every fish that could be gotten from them—by what means, he cared not.

For his part, Lord Grey had many complaints about Mealey that he conveyed to Byron, assuring his landlord that it was his wish "to restore this manor to my Lord Byron more plentifully stocked with Game than it was on my taking possession of it."[36]

Byron felt compelled to worry the wounded feelings that hung between him and his tenant. After assuring Lord Grey vaguely that he would look into Mealey's behavior and discussing various other house-keeping matters, Byron wrote: "I cannot conclude without adverting to circumstances, which though now long past, and indeed, difficult for me to touch upon, have not yet ceased to be interesting.—Your Lordship must be perfectly aware of the very peculiar reasons that induced me to adopt a line of conduct, which however painful, and painful to me it certainly was, became unavoidable."

Byron never liked anyone to bear him a grudge, and he had reason enough to feel ashamed of his behavior toward Grey de Ruthyn; in many ways, the self-indulgent Lord Grey was a primitive version of Byron himself. Their correspondence ended with Byron's revealing remarks; although "much intercourse between us must entirely cease . . . I shall always be happy, when we do meet, to meet as friends, and endeavor to forget we have been otherwise."[37]

At the end of August Byron left Brighton. He called on Hanson in Chancery Lane, hoping that a visit would prize his quarterly allowance—late as usual—from the lawyer. Then he set off for Newstead, stopping at Cambridge on the way. From there he wrote to Jackson, asking him to replace his lost swordstick, and to renew his supply of Lamb's Conduit Street Remedy. Byron's reliance on this popular cure for venereal disease suggests a recurrence of earlier symptoms or a new infection.

INSTALLED AT Newstead by September 13, Byron promptly set about renovating the abbey, now "filled with workmen and undergoing a thorough repair," he told Jackson.[38] Indeed, the first bill—£260 from the stonemason—was much too high for him to contemplate settling from his allowance, obliging him to "draw on Mr. Hanson" for payment. In general, the improvements undertaken by Byron during the fall of 1809 and continuing until June 1810 were cosmetic. He wanted elegant yet cozy apartments for himself and his guests, along with a great hall and dining room worthy of the host as master of revels.

He was also concerned with restoring the park for the enjoyment of visitors. But his first project—filling and restocking the ponds drained by Lord Grey—presented legal difficulties. Not yet twenty-one, Byron may be forgiven for failing to act the prudent householder; indeed, where his renovations were concerned, he might well have said, *"Après moi, le déluge."* His "thorough repairs" did not include replacing the most damaged part of the abbey; one later visitor reported that he "permitted so wretched a roof to remain that in about half a dozen years the rain had visited his proudest chambers."[39]

Meanwhile, he was intent on rendering all that showed vibrant with his favorite colors—yellow and scarlet. In early November, he wrote to his mother, "I am now fitting up the *green* drawing room, *the red* (as a bedroom), and the rooms over as sleeping rooms."[40] Located in the abbey part of the building, these, along with the former Prior's Hall, became Byron's private apartment, well separated from the guest quarters. The green drawing room, now redone in red, became his small private dining room, its oriel window provided with a "superb scarlet Morine French curtain . . . and handsome folding draperies richly fringed." His favorite colors were echoed in the dining room's most splendid object, a carved eagle, "richly gilt and standing upon a scarlet and gold stand and gold balls." The adjoining red "State Room," retaining its original color scheme, now became the principal guest bedroom, lavishly furnished with a "lofty bed with japanned and gilt pillars, a 'domed top surmounted by a coronet' . . . and scarlet draperies supported by eagles, richly gilt." Fitted Kidderminster or Brussels carpets were ordered for all the rooms.

In decorating his own smaller bedroom and adjoining dressing room, Byron changed to a yellow color scheme. His "very superb" bed, crowned with a baldachin, boasted "feet posts carved and finished with burnished gold hung with full green silk and yellow draperies, rich silk French fringe, gilt cornice surmounted by a coronet, lines, tassels, etc." He also managed to crowd into this moderate-sized bedroom "six japanned chairs, a japanned dressing chest, a swing dressing glass in a mahogony frame, a mahogony 'chest of drawers night table' and a japanned chiffonier bookcase with brass wire doors and yellow curtains."[41]

Byron's library-study reflected his tastes better than the grand new appointments of the rest of the abbey renovations. Instead of flower pots, two japanned and gilt tripod flower stands supported a "couple of the most perfect and finely polished skulls." Byron delighted in his collection of the remains of the abbey's former residents, found in the crypt. To the horror of more squeamish guests, he liked to quaff wine from one of these relics, mounted in silver. Byron was never fond of art.

As this was a library, however, he suffered the requisite neoclassical busts of Cicero and Milton, while his political hero Charles James Fox was commemorated by both a marble figure and an engraved portrait. Byron's extensive collection of books was accommodated in mahogany-fronted bookcases with seventeen sliding shelves, and his writing was done on a pillar-and-claw library table fitted with drawers and inlaid with satinwood.

Daunted by Newstead's galleries and great dining room (sometimes called the salon), Byron left these as he found them, stripped and derelict. The portraits and prints that once had lined the paneled walls had long been sold off. Its emptiness made the space ideal as an impromptu games room and theater. For his first house party, he planned an all-male production of Edward Young's *The Revenge*. Byron's declamation of the hero's lament over his dead friend's body had been the high point of his first Harrow Speech Day, and he was looking forward to reenacting his moment of stardom, when he would also, for the first time, play host in his ancestral seat to Harrow friends, among others. He issued invitations to Henry Drury, Hodgson, and Hobhouse to join him, promising to invite "Gentleman" Jackson as soon as the workmen should leave. To ensure the most professional production possible, he planned to engage a local carpenter to construct a stage at one end of the hall. As it happened, only Hobhouse was free to visit, but the hall, with a sarcophagus placed at the end where the stage was to have been, came to be used for all sorts of other activities by Byron and his guests, including reading, fencing, single-stick, and shuttlecock. Its length made it an ideal shooting gallery, where visitors enjoyed the host's favorite sport—firing pistols at bottles.

The cost of the renovations was staggering; the bill from the Nottingham upholsterer Brothers alone came to upward of £1,500. (Unpaid, it would bring the bailiffs to the abbey when Byron was on his travels, leaving his mother to deal with the disgrace and debt—for which he had left no provision.) On some level, Byron knew that he was behaving irresponsibly, but with the most disingenuous reasoning, he rationalized this new round of debts by his imminent travels; in his absence the abbey would serve as his mother's residence and, in the event of his death, would belong to her.

For the time being, however, she should resign herself to staying away from Newstead. While he was there, "I shall live in my own manner, and as much alone as possible, when my rooms are ready, I shall be glad to see you, at present, it would be improper, & uncomfortable to both parties."[42] As Catherine was still living in Southwell, her son's refusal to allow even a day's visit was surely a humiliating blow.

Anticipating her reaction, Byron evoked a rosy picture of the future: "You can hardly object to my rendering my mansion habitable, notwithstanding my departure for Persia in March (or May at farthest) since *you* will be the *tenant* till my return, and in case of any accident (for I have already arranged my will to be drawn up the moment I am twenty one) I have taken care you shall have the house & manor for *life*, besides a sufficient income.—So you see my improvements are not entirely selfish."[43]

His desire for solitude did not exclude friends—or festivities. Byron requested from D'Egville, the Covent Garden ballet master whose pupils he had fancied, a pattern for a Turkish costume. For copying the "Rich Masquerade Jacket and Trimmings" and "Full Trimmed Turban," along with other swashbuckling accessories, the local tailor added £11.9s.6d. to Byron's already large outstanding bill.[44]

Hobhouse stayed at Newstead through November. Without mentioning him by name, Byron told his mother that he and a houseguest would be attending the Infirmary Ball in Nottingham on October 12; perhaps they would see her there.

With no one to escort her and little money to spend, it appears unlikely that Catherine Byron attended the dance benefiting Nottingham General Hospital, an annual event that opened the social season for the local gentry. Among those who did, however, was Mary Ann (Chaworth) Musters, a patroness of the ball, and her handsome husband, Master of the South Notts Hunt.

Now the mother of two young children, Mary Ann could only have been astonished at the changes three years had wrought in her admirer. Then, obsessed with Musters and their clandestine romance, she had dismissed an overweight boy, his awkwardness emphasized by a limp, his manner alternately sullen and importuning. She was now introduced to a slender young man, dressed in the height of London fashion. News of his published poems had already made their writer a local celebrity. The head that drew the admiring glances was the face of romanticism itself: pale skin, luminous gray eyes, and glossy auburn curls.

Byron's appearance was not Mary Ann's only surprise. The lovesick schoolboy's hesitant stammer followed by a rush of talk had become the urbane conversation of a man of the world. Mrs. Musters was also the county's leading young hostess; she promptly invited Byron and Hobhouse to a dinner party at Annesley Hall.

Unrequited love is slow to die. Kept alive by remembrance of pain and humiliation, by images of idyllic autumn days, Byron's passion for Mary Ann still smoldered, awaiting only the match of this chance

encounter to flare again. In an agony of anticipation, he waited out the
time before the Musterses' dinner. "Hobhouse hunts &c. I do nothing,"
he told Hodgson.[45] But he took time out from nervous ennui to add
more lines to his satire on the literary establishment, check on the workmen, still putting the finishing touches to curtains and carpets, and
rehearse in his mind the pose he would strike at Annesley.

In the event, nothing went as planned. Overcome by emotion, both
Byron and Mary Ann froze in silence, causing more eyebrows to be
raised than if they had flirted outrageously. Worst of all was the moment
when Mary Ann's eldest child, an enchanting little girl of two, named
after her mother, was brought down from the nursery. Byron was obliged
to look into the same eyes that had haunted his dreams, pick up this
miniature of her mother, and kiss her good night.

Riding back to Newstead with Hobhouse, Byron knew he could
expect no sympathy; he vented his jealousy instead, repeating to his
friend coarse local gossip about the Musterses' marriage. Once safely
alone in the privacy of his apartments, however, Byron poured out his
feelings in a series of poems, which he enclosed, several days later, in a
letter to the sympathetic Hodgson. He could not allow his houseguest
to read the verses: "Hobhouse hates everything of the kind, therefore I
do not show them to him."[46]

The evening had been such a disaster that he could not even summon
his usual mordant humor to dispel its horrors: "You know, laughing is
the sign of a rational animal, so says Dr. Smollett," Byron reminded
Hodgson. "I think so too, but unluckily my spirits dont always keep
pace with my opinions.—I had not so much scope for risibility the other
day as I could have wished, for I was seated near a woman, to whom
when a boy I was as much attached as boys generally are, and more than
a man should be. I knew this before I went, and was determined to be
valiant, and converse with 'sang froid,' but instead I forgot my valour
and my nonchalance, and never opened my lips even to laugh, far less
to speak, & the Lady was almost as absurd as myself, which made both
the object of more observation, than if we had conducted ourselves with
easy indifference—You will think all this great nonsense, if you had seen
it you would have thought it still more ridiculous."[47]

Three years later, the pain of the dinner at Annesley had not dulled:

> I've seen my bride another's bride,—
> Have seen her seated by his side,
> Have seen the infant, which she bore,
> Wear the sweet smile the mother wore,

> When she and I in youth have smiled,
> As fond and faultless as her child;—
> Have seen her eyes, in cold disdain,
> Ask if I felt no secret pain;
> And *I* have acted well my part,
> And made my cheek belie my heart,
> Return'd the freezing glance she gave,
> Yet felt the while *that* woman's slave;—
> Have kiss'd, as if without design,
> The babe which ought to have been mine,
> And show'd, alas! in each caress
> Time had not made me love the less.[48]

When he managed to find his tongue, Byron held forth on his travel plans for the coming spring; from the Greek Isles, he planned to visit Persia and even India. The provincial heiress had never been farther than London. She was awed but also devastated. She had fantasized a second chance. She saw herself galloping to Newstead, turning Byron from lonely moodiness. They would become lovers and he would rescue her from the humiliation of the scorned wife.

She was jolted from her "freezing glance"—in Byron's words—to ask why he would want to leave England. He answered her question in one of two poems to Mary Ann that he enclosed in his letter to Hodgson; both address the impossibility of transforming love into friendship:

> Well! thou art happy, and I feel
> That I should thus be happy too;[49]

he begins, in the conversational style of an intimate letter. He can tolerate her husband's "blest" state, though it cost him "some pangs to view his happier lot." What he cannot bear is the pain inflicted by the sight of their little daughter: "When late I saw thy favourite child / I thought my jealous heart would break." In little Mary Ann, her mother's sexual possession by another man is made flesh.

Hope foreclosed leaves only "the sullen calmness of despair." Distance and motion alone hold out a promise of healing:

> In flight I shall be surely wise,
>   Escaping from temptation's snare;
> I cannot view my Paradise
>   Without the wish of dwelling there.[50]

. . .

WITHOUT HAVING paid a single bill for Newstead's new splendor, Byron was, once again, without funds. From his October visit to the abbey, Hanson had supposedly set off for Rochdale, to see for himself his client's property. He had given no sign of life in the month since his trip north. Byron had grandly—and uncharacteristically—turned down an advance on his allowance when the lawyer had been in Notts; now he was once again desperate for funds. When he finally did hear from Hanson, it was to learn that the solicitor had been ill, which suggested that he had never made the trip to Lancashire after all.

The oddest aspect of the Rochdale case—given the value of the property and its potential income—is the lack of interest of all concerned in seeing it for themselves, or in sending reliable representatives. Byron himself now sounded an indifferent note, assuring Hanson blandly on November 18, "As for my affairs I am sure you will do your best, and though I should be glad to get rid of my Lancashire property for an equivalent in money, I shall not take any steps of that nature without good advice and mature consideration."[51]

If this was guaranteed to dissuade the lawyer from any uncharacteristic impulse to action, Byron's following remarks would have caused a relapse of his recent illness. For the first time he informed Hanson of his plans for travel to the East that spring; the purpose of his trip, as with the conventional Grand Tour, was educational and moral: "I wish to study India and Asiatic policy and manners," after which "my judgment will be more mature, and I shall still be young enough for politics." Surpassing the intangible value of the journey would be its economy. "With regard to expence, travelling through the East is rather inconvenient than expensive: it is not like the tour of Europe, you undergo hardship, but incur little hazard of spending money." Further, it was cheaper than staying at home, since "If I live there I must have my house in town, a separate house for Mrs. Byron; I must keep horses, etc., etc. When I go abroad I place Mrs. Byron at Newstead (there is one great expence saved), I have no horses to keep." After this reassuring news of future economies, Byron let the ax fall: "You honour my debts; they amount to perhaps twelve thousand pounds, and I shall require perhaps three or four thousand at setting out, with credit on a Bengal agent. This you must manage for me."

To his mother, however, Byron tactfully omitted any specific discussion of money, as Catherine certainly would have been astounded to learn that her son was keeping her at Burgage Manor at his own expense. Instead, he wrote simply, "I shall take care of you," before retreating into the pieties of travel as "broadening": "If we see no nation but our own, we do not give mankind a fair chance, it is from *experience* not *Books*, we ought to judge of mankind.—There is nothing like inspection, and trusting to our own senses."[52]

IN THE REMAINING months of his stay, Byron tried to create at Newstead a surrogate family. As parent figures he reinstated two elderly servants: Old Joe Murray, once the Wicked Lord's majordomo, now became the butler, with Nanny Smith installed as head housekeeper. Close to Byron in age, Fletcher, his valet, functioned as a double; soon he would play Leporello to Byron's Don Juan, but now he took on the role of the "good" older brother who replaced the thieving Frank Boyce. The part of the youngest servant, Robert Rushton, was also the most ambiguous. The handsome son of a tenant farmer, the lad was Byron's page and his favorite. He slept in a small room, like a child's, that could only be entered through his master's bedroom.

Christmas was coming, but it was soon apparent that Byron and his family of servants would be the only celebrants at the abbey. Hobhouse was leaving shortly to spend the holidays at home; Jackson regretted that he was unable to leave town at this season. Byron's mother was pointedly not invited: "Mrs. Byron I have shaken off for two years," he wrote to Augusta on November 30, "and I shall not resume her yoke in future, I am afraid my disposition will suffer in your estimation, but I never can forgive that woman, or breathe in comfort under the same roof.—I am a very unlucky fellow, for I think I had naturally not a bad heart, but it has been so bent, twisted, and trampled on, that it is now become as hard as a Highlander's heel-piece."[53]

It seemed as though everyone else's domestic ties had become more binding. Augusta was nursing her first child, Georgiana Augusta, who was born November 4. Then, as though to emphasize the cruel consequence of his own attachments, Boatswain, Byron's huge, gentle Newfoundland, died of fits on November 10. As Moore describes the scene, "Byron was so little aware . . . of the nature of the malady, that he, more than once, with his bare hand, wiped away the slaver from the dog's lips during the paroxysms."[54] Given his familiarity with dogs, however, Byron's behavior reveals not ignorance but his refusal to acknowledge the death throes of the stricken animal.

In the event, he was inconsolable. "Boatswain is dead!" Byron began his letter to Hodgson. "He expired in a state of madness on the 10th, after suffering much, yet retaining all the gentleness of his nature to the last, never attempting to do the least injury to any one near him.—I have lost every thing except Old Murray."[55]

Byron's elegy to Boatswain, intended to be carved on the monument above the dog's grave, went further than the conventional trope of contrasting human failings with the virtues of dumb beasts. In eulogizing his pet, the poet's sorrow turns to self-pity; he *is* Boatswain:

> But the poor dog, in life the firmest friend,
> The first to welcome, foremost to defend,
> Whose honest heart is still his master's own,
> Who labours, fights, lives, breathes for him alone,
> Unhonoured falls, unnoticed all his worth,
> Denied in heaven the soul he held on earth:
>
> . . . .
>
> To mark a friend's remains these stones arise,
> I never knew but one, and here he lies.[56]

This time Byron made the mistake of showing the verses to Hobhouse. Embarrassed by grief, Hobhouse jokingly changed Byron's ending to "here *I* lies," the play on words reflecting his view both of his friend's tendency to exaggeration and his excessive self-love. Hobhouse then produced his own prose epitaph for the dog. Intended as a lampoon of the genre, these lines—universally assumed to be Byron's own—were the ones chiseled on Boatswain's monument in the abbey gardens:

> Near this spot
> Are deposited the Remains of one
> Who possessed Beauty without Vanity
> Strength without Insolence
> Courage without Ferocity,
> And all the Virtues of Man without his Vices.
> This Praise, which would be unmeaning Flattery
> If inscribed over human ashes,
> Is but a just tribute to the Memory of BOATSWAIN, a Dog. . . .

When pastiche proved no help in cheering his host, Hobhouse tried horseplay, with more success. Byron had converted the medieval "slype," a shallow pool in which the monks very occasionally immersed themselves, into a plunge bath. He and his guest decided to test the echo effect caused by the high stone walls with the help of a female bather: "Hobhouse & myself nearly suffocated a person in the Bath yesterday, by way of ascertaining the soundings," Byron wrote to Hodgson, sounding his usual playful self: "I was obliged to jump in, and extricate the Drownee."[57]

Meanwhile, along with efforts to raise money for his journey, Byron set about the organizational tasks essential for travel to places still remote and visited by few Englishmen. In his best imperial style, he went straight to the top, writing to the Duke of Portland, then Tory Prime Minister, for permission to move freely through territories controlled by the East India Company. The "head of his Majesty's Government,"[58] as Byron addressed his lordship, clearly found this communiqué from a twenty-year-old presumptuous in the extreme, and his brusque reply, making clear his disapproval, required Byron to write another, apologetic letter. Taking the hint, he addressed further correspondence to less exalted officials.

Alone over the holidays, Byron's bitter feelings of loss and exclusion put him in the perfect misanthropic humor to hone his new satire. His gloom was never without an angry edge, and few in the literary world would escape his slash-and-burn attacks, among them victims he would have cause to regret attacking. For inspiration he asked Hodgson to find him a copy of a poem by his favorite contemporary satirist, Gifford's "Epistle to Peter Pindar," and he read more deeply in the works of his idol Alexander Pope. To facilitate writing and revising he worked from proofs that he had Ridge run off for him in nearby Newark.

Contemplation of his coming of age—he would turn twenty-one on January 22—depressed him further, and he decided to flee the traditional rural revels required of a landowning noble, for the anonymity of London: He would not even accept Hanson's invitation to celebrate the occasion at a dinner with the solicitor and his family in Chancery Lane. He planned to spend the day alone, he said; if he joined other companions, he did not choose to name them. He asked Hanson to play host at Newstead in his place, permitting the locals to enjoy their merrymaking while seeing that the bacchanal did not get out of hand: "You will be extremely welcome here and your presence will preserve order in my absence, the tenants are to have a good dinner and plenty of Ale & Punch, and the *Rabble* will have an Ox and two Sheep to tear in pieces, with *Ale*, and *Uproar*."[59]

Along with provisions for a lordly feast to celebrate the attainment of his majority, Byron also left his Newstead entourage with another traditional reminder of *droit du seigneur*. Writing to Hobhouse on January 16, Byron noted, in his typically throwaway style, "Nothing of moment has occurred . . . except that Lucinda is pregnant and Robert [Rushton] has recovered of the Cowpox, with which it pleased me to afflict him."[60] On the eve of his departure for London, Byron wrote to Hanson with instructions about household expenses. He was to see that Owen Mealey paid the workmen. As for the servants: "You will discharge my Cook, & Laundry Maid, the other two I shall retain to take care of the house, more especially as the youngest is pregnant (I need not tell you by whom) and I cannot have the girl on the parish."[61] Byron's pride, along with his sense of honor, was offended by the common practice of turning out pregnant maidservants. He knew the fate of country girls who bore illegitimate children: surviving on the pittance provided by parish poor rates, the dreaded workhouse, or making their way to the nearest city and pursuing a life of prostitution. Along with keeping Lucy employed, Byron made provision—exceptionally generous by the standards of the day—for her and their child in his will: Lucy was to have an annuity of £100 (later reduced to £50); the other £50 was to go to the child.

In his poem "To My Son," Byron addresses his natural child, challenging the convention that would withhold from his "little *il*legitimate" a father's loving concern, along with any claim to social position:

> Why, let the world unfeeling frown,
> Must I fond Nature's claim disown?
> Ah, no—though moralists reprove,
> I hail thee, dearest child of love,
> Fair cherub, pledge of youth and joy—
> A Father guards thy birth, my Boy![62]

The poem itself has left a legacy of questions. Dated 1807 by Moore, Lucy's pregnancy did not take place until early 1809. But even if Moore misread the date, the housemaid did not die the early death of the young mother eulogized by the poet whose "lowly grave the turf has prest." According to the housekeeper, Nanny Smith, Lucy got over the "high and mighty airs she gave herself as Byron's favorite,"[63] married a local lad, and ran a pub in Warwick. The fate of the child is unknown. Either Byron addressed another illegitimate son, or he changed the scenario to conform to the sentimental moralizing of the period, which required that the fallen woman must pay with her life: "Thy mother's shade shall smile in joy, / And pardon all the past, my Boy!"[64]

Whether or not Lucy's child was the subject of the poem, the baby completed Byron's Newstead "family," giving a sense of rightness to his return. From a ruin he had created a home—part fantasy, part reality. From a carefree student he had become a householder and a provider for servants, tenants, Lucy, and their child—even (on his own terms) for his mother. Too self-conscious to celebrate his majority with manorial tributes and peasant debauch, he was, nonetheless, poised to fulfill the social and political expectations of manhood.

CHAPTER 10

The Great Escape

*J*ANUARY 22, 1809, Byron's twenty-first birthday, fell on a Sunday. He had arrived in London three days earlier, putting up this time at Reddish's Hotel, St. James's. While Newstead, with Hanson as his proxy, celebrated his coming of age with noisy excess, Byron's own modest indulgence took the form of breaking his diet to enjoy a feast of bacon, eggs, and ale—favorites he saved for "jubilees," he said.

He did not relish, after all, the prospect of spending this momentous birthday alone. As soon as he arrived he invited Robert Dallas, his literary kinsman, to call on Sunday morning. Dallas found his young relative "in high spirits," but his description of Byron's manner and "the overflow of his gaiety" point to a manic outpouring punctuated by bursts of anger.[1]

Lord Carlisle was the principal target of Byron's wrath. Earlier, he had reacted bitterly to Carlisle's indifference to his poetry. But now he had fresh fuel to stoke his fury. On coming of age, Byron was entitled to take his seat in the House of Lords. Under the impression (mistaken, as it happened) that presentation by a member was part of protocol, he had written to Carlisle, in the expectation that his guardian would introduce him at the opening session of Parliament, thus eliminating at the same time the need for written bona fides. Instead of the warmly avuncular response he had hoped for, however, the grandee answered with the briefest note, merely informing his young relative of the proper procedures, including the required documentation.

Byron felt humiliated by the perceived rebuff and still more outraged by the necessity of establishing official proof of his legitimacy. (The fact that such proof was required of all new members did nothing to assuage his wrath.) Time being of the essence, he now had to implore Hanson to rush a clerk to Carhais in Cornwall (for which the lawyer would charge him exorbitantly) to locate the marriage license of Byron's grandfather to the poet's grandmother, Sophia Trevanion. According to Dallas, Byron swore revenge on Carlisle with the most effective weapons at his command: "determined to lash his relation with all the gall he could throw into satire."[2]

Feelings of betrayal by this powerful father figure further embittered him toward family in general: "He declaimed against the ties of consanguinity, and abjured even the society of his sister, from which he entirely withdrew himself."

After venting his resentment on this subject, Dallas recalled, "Byron attacked the editor and other writers of the *Edinburgh Review* and then told me that, since I last saw him he had written a Satire on them which he wished me to read."

Dallas left with the loose printed quarto sheets of Byron's new work, titled *The British Bards, a Satire*:

> Laugh when I laugh, I seek no other fame,
> The cry is up, and scribblers are my game[3]

The poet made good on his warning; reading the new work, even the conventional Dallas found himself "surprised and charmed by the nerve it envinced." He wrote to Byron immediately, telling him of the "infinite pleasure the poem had given him." With this letter, Dallas assumed the role he would play in Byron's literary life for the next few years: a combination of editor, agent, and publicist, with occasional attempts at collaboration—attempts that Byron managed to veto with considerable tact. Dallas first suggested that the title of the satire be changed to his own clumsy "The Parish Poor of Parnassus." Then, after blandly informing the author that he had made "a few other alterations of passages, straws on the surface, which you would make yourself were you to correct the press," Dallas announced that he was enclosing "some two dozen lines" of his own, which "if they neither offend your ear nor your judgment, I wish you would adopt."[4]

Byron's reply was masterful: "My only reason for not adopting your lines is because they are *your* lines. You will recollect what Lady Wortley Montague [*sic*] said to Pope: 'No touching, for the good will be given to you, and the bad attributed to me.' "[5]

Diplomacy was all the more important as Byron now asked Dallas to find a publisher for the satire, a task made the more delicate as he wished the work to appear anonymously. There was good reason to take cover.

Then, after all of Byron's threats to destroy Carlisle in print, Dallas was startled to find himself in possession of an earlier version of the work, in which the poet introduces his noble relation with a "panegyric":

> On one alone Apollo deigns to smile
> And crowns a new Roscommon in Carlisle.[6]

Dallas correctly assumed that Byron had inserted the flattering couplet in London at the moment of soliciting Carlisle's sponsorship in the House of Lords. Now, when Dallas pointed out that the poem's assault on every contributor to the *Edinburgh Review* would point to him as the author, Byron saw the chance to "revise" his earlier flattery of the peer and protect his own anonymity:

> Roscommon! Sheffield!* with your spirits fled,
> No future laurels deck a noble head;
> Nor e'en a hackney'd Muse will deign to smile
> On minor Byron, or mature Carlisle.[7]

This diversionary tactic may have made the poet's identity harder to guess, but his delight in naming names caused Longman, Dallas's publisher, to reject the work in late January, citing the author's excessive "asperity."

As a lament for a past Golden Age of English Letters in the degenerate present, Byron's satire rang few changes on a familiar trope; indeed, both subject and style—the sparkle of heroic couplets—owed everything to Byron's emulation of Pope:

> Then, in this happy Isle, a POPE's pure strain
> Sought the rapt soul to charm, nor sought in vain;
> Like him great DRYDEN poured the tide of song,
> In stream less smooth indeed, yet doubly strong.

---

*Like the Earl of Roscommon, John Sheffield, third Earl of Mulgrave, later first Duke of Buckingham and Normanby, was a seventeenth-century noble who was also a poet, translator, and, in Sheffield's case, patron and friend of both Pope and Dryden.

> Then CONGREVE's scene could cheer, or OTWAY's melt;
> For Nature then an English audience felt—[8]

Byron's use of nostalgia to savage his elders was at this point still more callow than clever; included among his victims were Wordsworth and Coleridge, hardly poets guilty of denatured artifice. As for his most despised enemies, there was no crime of which they they were not accused:

> A man must serve his time to every trade
> Save Censure: Critics all are ready made
>
> . . . .
>
> Fear not to lie, 'twill seem a sharper hit,
> Shrink not from blasphemy, 'twill pass for wit;
> Care not for feeling—pass your proper jest,
> And stand a Critic hated, yet caress'd.[9]

Dallas now submitted the satire, newly entitled *English Bards and Scotch Reviewers*, to another publisher. James Cawthorn agreed to publish the work, shrewdly deciding that the anonymous poet's mix of invective and gossip might even sell. He was right. The first edition, published in March 1809, had to be reissued immediately, with more printings to follow.*

As soon as his poem was accepted, Byron bombarded Dallas with corrections and changes, including numerous additions, to be forwarded to the publisher: "Print soon or I shall overflow with more rhyme," he warned in a postscript.[10]

Now the poet felt completely free to "indulge the malice of his Muse," in Dallas's words.[11] While the poem was still in press, he added sixteen more lines attacking his guardian:

> No Muse will cheer with renovating smile,
> The paralytic puling of CARLISLE;
>
> . . . .
>
> So dull in youth, so drivelling in his age,
> His scenes alone had damned our sinking stage;[12]

English Bards went into five editions until, in 1816, a more mature Byron, repudiating his juvenile malice, decided to suppress further reprints. At this point Cawthorn went on to pirate several more editions.

When the poem appeared in March, the author was accused of lampooning the aged peer, who suffered from a degenerative nervous disorder. Shame drove Byron from anonymity. He had been completely unaware of Carlisle's illness, he insisted, and, given his own disability, he would be the last to mock a fellow sufferer. Neither claim seems convincing. His guardian had betrayed him; Byron could forgive his own father, but not those who failed to replace him.

Dallas did his best to step into the breach. On March 13, only days before his satire was to appear, Byron took his seat in the House of Lords. By odd coincidence, Dallas happened to be passing Byron's rooms in St. James's that morning, and seeing his friend's coach, decided to call. Dallas's description of what followed leaves no doubt as to his role in fanning the flames of Byron's bitter feelings to his own advantage.

> His countenance, paler than usual, showed that his mind was agitated, and that he was thinking of the nobleman to whom he had once looked for a hand and countenance in his introduction to the House. He said to me:—"I am glad you happened to come in; I am going to take my seat and perhaps you will go with me." I expressed my readiness to attend him; while at the same time I concealed the shock I felt on thinking that this young man, who, by birth, fortune and talent, stood high in life, should have lived so unconnected and neglected by persons of his own rank, that there was not a single member of the senate to which he belonged, to whom he could or would apply to introduce him in a manner becoming his birth. I saw that he felt the situation and I fully partook his indignation.[13]

Byron sulked through the ceremony with ill-concealed anger. He was greeted on arrival by officers of the House, with whom he settled the required fees, and who then informed the Lord Chancellor, Lord Eldon, of the new member's presence. Attendance was sparse that day, calling more attention to the pallid young man who strode defiantly into the chamber and past the "woolsack," the upholstered bench where the Lord Chancellor sat, without so much as a glance. Advancing to the presiding officer who administered the oaths, Byron was duly sworn in. Immediately, Lord Eldon left his seat and, extending his hand, approached the new member with warm words of greeting. Byron responded with a stiff bow and the insulting gesture of touching only his fingertips to Lord Eldon's palm. The Lord Chancellor, Dallas observed, "did not press a welcome so received, but resumed his seat; while Lord Byron carelessly seated himself for a few minutes on one of the empty benches to the left of the throne, usually occupied by the Lords in Opposition."[14]

Byron had a political explanation for his rudeness to Lord Eldon: "If I had shaken hands heartily," he told Dallas, "he would have set me down for one of his party—but I will have nothing to do with any of them, on either side; I have taken my seat, and now I will go abroad."[15]

Whether or not this constituted Byron's real reason for his outrageous behavior, it is certainly true that the new parliamentarian was determined to avoid commitment to either Whig or Tory: "I cannot say that my opinion is strongly in favor of either party," he wrote to Hanson earlier in the year. "On the one side we have the late underlings of Pitt, possessing all his ill Fortune, without his Talents, this may render their failure more excusable, but will not diminish the public contempt; on the other hand we have the ill assorted fragments of a worn out minority." Then, in the very same letter, the desire to have an effective voice caused him to change his mind: "I shall stand aloof, speak what I think, but not often, nor too soon, I will preserve my independence, if possible, but if involved with a party, I will take care not to be the *last* or *least* in the Ranks.—As to *patriotism* the word is obsolete, perhaps improperly so, for all men in this country are patriots, knowing that their own existence must stand or fall with the Constitution, yet every body thinks he could alter it for the better, & govern a people, who are in fact easily governed but always claim the privilege of grumbling.—So much for Politics, of which I at present know little, & care less, by and bye, I shall use the Senatorial privilege of talking, and indeed in such times, and in such a crew, it must be difficult to hold one's tongue."[16]

Meanwhile, Byron's plans to go abroad immediately after taking his seat in the House ran afoul of the usual obstacle: lack of money. As the Rochdale case suffered new deferrals, he was forced to abandon the hope that a settlement of his Lancashire estates would finance his travels. But the law's delay was far from the worst of his problems. While still at Newstead, he had correctly anticipated that news of his return to London would have the moneylenders and Mrs. Massingberd knocking at his door, and he delegated to Hanson the job of appeasing his creditors. Byron's only signs of regret for his extravagance was to complain about tradesmen's charges: "You will easily perceive several most enormous impositions in the prices," Byron wrote in a note to Hanson that accompanied a bill from a Nottingham silversmith, "more particularly a charge of £17.17s.0D.!!! for mounting a cup [the famous skull]— £3.3s.0 D.!! for a Mustard pot and sundry other articles in the same proportion. . . . I will never pay the bill in its present state, and I doubt not your opinion will coincide with mine as to the enormity of the attempt to defraud."[17]

In February he had written in desperation to Hanson: "I am *dunned* from Morn till Twilight, money I must have or quit the country, and if I do not obtain my seat immediately, I shall sail with Ld. Falkland in the Desiree Frigate for Sicily.—I have a considerable sum to pay tomorrow morning and not five pounds in my purse."[18]

Captain John Cary, Lord Falkland, was a naval officer, man-about-town, and drinking companion of Byron's. Late one night, following a drunken quarrel with another of their party, Falkland was killed in a duel; he left a pregnant wife and three young children. After the birth of the baby, who was also his godchild, Byron called on the widow. Before leaving, he discreetly tucked a folded £500 note in a teacup. The worse Byron's financial situation, the more irresistible he found the grand gesture. (In this case, his generosity was misunderstood: Lady Falkland took the gift to mean that Byron was in love with her, and for years afterward harassed the poet with letters and declarations of passion.)

Then, in early March, Byron made the first of several cash gifts to Francis Hodgson, who, like Byron, was constantly in debt. To spare his friend's feelings, these were called "loans," but unlike his financial transactions with Scrope Davies, no notes or IOUs ever changed hands. His first gift to Hodgson was clearly substantial; in the accompanying letter, Byron wrote that he was sending a draft "as notes are *bulky*."[19]

Attaining his majority, taking his seat in the House of Lords, along with the prospect of a long absence from England—all intensified Byron's nostalgia for lost youth and scattered friends. He visited Harrow often now. Writing to William Harness, Byron asked him to sit for his portrait, one of a gallery of likenesses he was commissioning: "I am going abroad if possible in the spring," he wrote to the younger man, "and before I depart, I am collecting the pictures of my most intimate Schoolfellows. . . . I have employed one of the first miniature painters of the day to take them, of course at my own expense. . . ."[20]

With the refurbishment of Newstead, Byron's spending had assumed an imperial style. Now that he was an adult, however, he was legally liable for debts; with a large unpaid principal and mounting interest, he could no longer go to the moneylenders. Until now he had given little thought to a much safer source of credit: marriage to an heiress whose family would view his title as fair exchange for her fortune. He played with the possibility, but without enthusiasm: "I suppose it will end in my marrying a *Golden Dolly* or blowing my brains out," he told Hanson, "it does not much matter which, the Remedies are nearly alike."[21] Standard practice among the impoverished peerage, this solution offended Byron's sense of the chivalric honor he attached to his title. His mother, the practical Scotswoman, had no such qualms: In late January Catherine had told Hanson how much she wished her son would look to his fortune "in the old and usual way by marrying a Woman with two or three thousand pounds [a year]."22 Two months later, she sounded a more desperate note: "I wish to God he would exert himself and retrieve his affairs. He must marry a Woman of *fortune* this spring," wrote Catherine, herself a victim of just such a union. "Love matches is all nonsense."23

Returning to Newstead at the beginning of April, probably to escape his London creditors, Byron busied himself trying to raise money for his journey; he had already booked a passage on the Malta packet for May, and would forfeit both the fare and his luggage, which had been sent ahead, if he failed to leave. He flogged Hanson to pursue the expedient of raising a mortgage on the abbey, and begged him to chivy the Duke of Portland for £1,000 owed to the estate. Meanwhile, he had other crushing news: His dear friend Edward Long had been drowned. On his way to Lisbon, where he was to join the Peninsular war forces, Long's transport had collided in the dark with another vessel, and all aboard were lost. In reply to a plea from the grieving family, Byron agreed to write his friend's epitaph. But the task proved too painful and had to be abandoned.

Hanson was not happy about his client's travel plans. Added to the difficulties of raising a loan when Byron was already close to £12,000 in debt, his trip would give the appearance of his skipping the country to flee his creditors, with the prospect of debtors' prison waiting on his return. He wrote to Byron, arguing strongly against a prolonged stay abroad. The response was swift and adamant: "If the consequences of my leaving England, were ten times as ruinous as you describe, I have no alternative, there are circumstances which render it absolutely indispensible, and quit the country I must immediately."24

What circumstances these were that compelled Byron's urgent departure have never been revealed. If he or his intimates wrote of them, their letters have not survived. We know that his flight had nothing to do with embarrassments related to money or women: Like all young men of his class, he was open, when not actually boastful, about excess in both. He seemed to have gotten over Mary Ann Musters. And certainly he had no fear of enraged reactions from those he attacked in his satire: The roar of the baited bull was the point of the game.

Byron cloaked only his homosexual attachments with fearful discretion. Stigmatized as a capital crime by the larger society, his relations with men, until this point, could be rationalized into familial models: schoolboy brothers or working-class sons. When passion threatened these categories, Byron knew it was time to flee.

Early in March, after what appears to have been a long silence, he had heard from John Edleston. Dated "Old South Sea House, Old Broad Street," the boy's letter suggests that his clerkship was proving a disappointment, as he wrote to ask whether Byron could be of any help in obtaining another position. Byron, however, read the letter as a request for money. In Edleston's reply—his only words to survive—the stilted phrases sweat pain and humiliation:

> My Lord,
>   I had this day the honour of receiving your Lordship's letter of yesterday's date, and feel, most gratefully feel, the additional obligation which your Lordship generously offers to confer upon me by pecuniary assistance to form some permanent means of subsistence; at the same time that I am incapable of describing my sensations on the occasion, I feel it my duty to explain the meaning of my former letter which has been entirely misunderstood by your Lordship; I had not the most distant intention of soliciting any pecuniary aid from your Lordship, in my present circumstances, my only wish being to be favored with your personal influence and patronage to assist me in obtaining employment in some respectable occupation, where my services might meet with such remuneration as would maintain me without being burthensome to anyone as I have no prospect, at the present, of any Business in which I could establish myself on my own account.

Should such an opportunity present itself, he might consider seeking Byron's support, Edleston wrote, but as he viewed such good fortune as "entirely beyond my hopes, I must beg again to acknowledge the deep and grateful sense I have of the honour conferred upon me by your Lordship's parental kindness; of which I shall cherish an everlasting remembrance."[25]

Surely, the poignance of a nineteen-year-old orphan thanking a twenty-one-year-old for his "parental kindness" was not lost on Byron.

After nearly two years of silence, Edleston's letter would have summoned emotions his lover thought were safely dead and buried. How much easier, then, to read the boy's plea for Byron's "personal influence and patronage" as a cry for financial help.

Vulnerable still to the snare of his love for the former chorister, Byron, now legally an adult, faced a greater risk of suffering its consequences of disgrace, imprisonment, or death. On the eve of the Regency—the most licentious period in English history—the "love that dare not speak its name" was more unmentionable than in Oscar Wilde's time. To any contemporary of Byron's, the urgency of his flight would have held no mystery.

In Edleston's absence, Byron had found a safer replacement. "Like me, a friendless animal" was the way he described his young page, Robert Rushton.[26] When he returned to London from Newstead at the end of April, Byron brought with him Rushton and Byron's valet, William Fletcher, who was to look after the boy when he was not with his master. Now, when Byron discovered that Fletcher had taken Rushton along on a visit to a whore, he exploded with rage: "I have detected Fletcher in a connection with prostitutes, and of taking to a woman of the town the very boy whom I had committed to his charge," he wrote to his mother, "which lad he sent home with a lie in his mouth to screen them both, after the most strict injunctions on my part to watch over his *morals*, & keep him from the *temptations* of this *accursed place.* . . . Did you ever hear any thing so diabolical?" Byron went on, "He did not even deny it, for I found the address of the strumpet *written in his own hand.*"[27] Knowing her son's precocious patronage of whores, Catherine Byron must have been startled to read such hysterical moralizing.

During this same visit to London Byron had his will drawn up—"I should like to sign it while I have anything to leave," he wrote to Hanson.[28] He bequeathed £25 a year for life to Rushton.

The page is one of two intimates with whom Byron chose to be painted (the other is Countess Teresa Guiccioli, his "last attachment"). In 1807 George Sanders, the same artist commissioned to paint miniatures of the poet's friends, began work on the famous painting of Byron landing from a boat (see illustration in first insert). In this composition, Rushton stands behind his master, holding the skiff.

Having sent Rushton back to Newstead in the more reliable custody of old Joe Murray, Byron soon followed. He had decided on a farewell visit to the abbey, but, unlike his solitary stay at Christmas, this descent was planned to be house party and spring bacchanal. From London he had first invited Hodgson, who, perhaps mercifully, was unable to come, and another Cambridge crony, James Wedderburn Webster. Hobhouse, Matthews, and Scrope Davies completed the party.

Although later reports conflated all of Byron's Newstead visits into one continuous orgy, this particular gathering seems to have consisted of endless rounds of schoolboy horseplay; scary "haunted house" pranks and dress-up were the amusements of choice, with copious quantities of drink the most serious form of debauch: "We went down to Newstead together, where I had got a famous cellar, and *Monks'* dresses from a masquerade warehouse," Byron later recalled. "We were a company of some seven or eight, with an occasional neighbor or so for visitors, and used to sit up late in our friar's dresses, drinking burgundy, claret, champagne, and what not, out of the *skull-cup*, and all sorts of glasses, and buffooning all around the house, in our conventual garments."[29] Matthews had been ill when he received Byron's invitation. Barely convalescent when he arrived at Newstead, he appeared daily before noon, which marked him as a monster of heartiness in this decadent crowd: "Our average hour of rising was one," Matthews wrote his sister. " I, who generally got up between eleven and twelve, was always—even when an invalid—the first of the party, and was esteemed a prodigy of early rising. It was frequently past two before the breakfast party broke up. Then, for the amusements of the morning, there was reading, fencing, single-stick, or shuttlecock, in the great room, practising with pistols in the hall; walking, riding—cricket—sailing on the lake, playing with the bear, or teasing the wolf." The main meal, served at about four, was followed by the host's favorite ritual: "I must not omit the custom of handing round, after dinner, on the removal of the cloth, a human skull filled with burgundy. Then, after revelling on choice viands, and the finest wines of France, we adjourned to tea, where we amused ourselves with reading, or improving conversation . . . and after sandwiches, etc. retired to rest. A set of monkish dresses, which had been provided, with all the proper apparatus of crosses, beads, tonsures, etc. often gave a variety to our appearance, and to our pursuits. Between seven and eight we dined; and our evening lasted from that time till one, two, or three in the morning. The evening diversions may be easily conceived."[30]

Byron's images of Newstead revels hinted at scenes of sacrilege. In *Childe Harold* he teased readers with suggestions of sex and blasphemy:

> Monastic dome! condemn'd to uses vile!
> Where Superstition once had made her den
> Now Paphian girls were known to sing and smile;
> And monks might deem their time was come agen,
> If ancient tales say true, nor wrong these holy men.[31]

"Paphian girls"—a classical euphemism for prostitutes—seems an unmistakable allusion to Byron's "harlots two," who were possibly treated to a trip to the country, but he may also have recast the buxom country girls who were Newstead's household servants as votaries of Venus—a more alluring image of female sexuality than young chambermaids, seduced and left with child by their master. As for the fleshly pleasures of this particular party, neither Hobhouse nor Matthews would have rejoiced to find women among the "choice viands" provided by their host. This was a party summoned by Byron to re-create that "paradise of boys"—William Beckford's phrase—he was about to leave.

Dissension was already darkening the playing fields of Eden. Matthews, as temperamental as Byron, threatened to throw Hobhouse out of a window after an argument. Not wishing to take sides, the host tried to make light of the incident, assuring "Hobby" that the window was low and the ground grassy. Hobhouse decided that the only gentlemanly course was for him to leave, which he did—accompanied by the offending Matthews! They had decided to walk to London together, passing and repassing each other in injured silence. The party was over.

Along with his farewell celebration, Byron's other purpose at Newstead was to say good-bye to his mother and to arrange for her move from Burgage Manor to the abbey on his departure. Now that his friends had left, he had no excuse to postpone seeing her. Their hours at Newstead—the last they would ever spend together—were worse than Byron's most dreaded anticipation.

Early in April, Catherine had heard of her son's plans—now definite—to go abroad in May, leaving his debts without security. She had also been ill; consulting expensive doctors in Nottingham for "Medicle advice" increased her worries about money. "Byron is now at Newstead," she wrote to Hanson on April 9, "and talks of going abroad on 6th May next, for God['s] sake see to get him to give security for the one thousand pounds I am bound for." Exceptional for her class, Catherine Byron also worried about the suppliers, who were, inevitably, the last to see any money—if, indeed, they were ever paid at all: "There is some tradespeople at Nottingham that will be completely ruined if he does not pay them which I could not have happen for the whole World. . . . The grief I feel at my son's going abroad and the addition of his leaving his affairs in so unsettled a state . . . I think altogether it will kill me."[32] Unable to insist on sharing power of attorney with Hanson in her son's absence or to resist Byron's demand that she give up comfortable Burgage Manor for Newstead, Catherine now took out her frustration in tantrums and insults.

Two years later, in Greece, Byron recalled to Lord Sligo the terrible final scene with his mother: "Even a few days before we parted, for the last time, on my leaving England, she, in one of her fits of passion, uttered an imprecation upon me, praying that I might prove as ill-formed in mind as I am in body."[33]

FROM BATT'S HOTEL in Jermyn Street, where he was now staying, Byron completed the final arrangements for the trip. To his chagrin, Hanson was out of town. His allowance from Chancery was three months late. Temporary rescue arrived at last in the form of a £6,000 loan negotiated by Hanson's partner Birch from his friend, a Mr. Saw-bridge. Only £2,000 of the agreed amount was available to Byron before he left England, but he was able to arrange for interest on past loans to be paid from this installment and for letters of credit to be sent ahead through Hammersley, the international bankers with agents in Malta and Constantinople. Finally, this fresh infusion of cash and credit allowed him to choose his travel companion. To the delighted Hobhouse, who had picked this inconvenient time to fall out with his rich father, Byron advanced the funds necessary to join him on his grand tour.

Before leaving for points east, Byron deleted verses Hobhouse had contributed to the first edition of *English Bards and Scotch Reviewers*, which was to go into a second printing in May. Announcing the "era-sure" to his readers, he took the occasion to plug Hobhouse's first book of poems, to be called *Imitations and Translations* (including several by Byron). In a new preface to his own satire, Byron explained the change as reflecting the desire to defend the work as entirely his own. He had resolved no longer to take shelter in anonymity; the new edition, more robust by some 354 lines, was published under his own name.

Their literary enterprises well launched, the two friends made for Falmouth and the Malta packet on about June 19. Besides Hob-house, Byron's entourage now included Joe Murray, the old Newstead butler; his valet, William Fletcher, forgiven for his corruption of inno-cence; Robert Rushton; and Friese, a Prussian servant who had previ-ously been employed in Persia.

After a flurry of farewells, they arrived at Wynn's Hotel in Falmouth, only to learn they had missed the packet; they would now have to await the departure of the Lisbon mail boat, which was delayed by the weather—for several weeks, as it turned out.

Happily, the picturesque Cornwall port was to prove more diverting than Byron anticipated; its attractions had been foreshadowed in a curi-ous near encounter on the road from London to Falmouth. Their party changed horses on Hertford Bridge, at an inn where "the great Apostle of Paederasty Beckford! sojourned for the night," Byron wrote to Hodgson. "We tried in vain to see the Martyr of Prejudice, but could not." Even more "singular," Byron reported, Beckford's former lover, Lord Courtenay, had "travelled the same night on the *same road* only one stage *behind* him."[34] The coincidence—if such it was—was singular indeed; years earlier, Beckford's alleged seduction of the adolescent Courtenay had detonated the scandal that caused the older man's flight and exile.

In 1809, Falmouth was a relatively new port; its explosion from a fishing village to a bustling center of shipping and commerce was due largely to the General Post Office, which had chosen the port in 1788 as a station for its newly established Spanish mail boats, the packets that took passengers like Byron and his retinue to Malta, Lisbon, Brazil, or the West Indies. The Napoleonic Wars had led to the crowding of the city and its harbor still further: Two squadrons of frigates were permanently moored there, with ships of the line and smaller vessels of war constantly coming and going, along with prize warships taken hostage from the French enemy. All this maritime activity provided the town with a population of brilliantly uniformed boys and young men, clad, as one resident recalled, "in dashing marine trim"; the crews of the mail packets, in particular, were handpicked to be particularly "well dressed and generally young and handsome."[35]

A day or so after their arrival in Falmouth, Byron added an ecstatic "wish-you-were-here" postscript to Hobhouse's letter to their friend "Citizen" Matthews: "My dear Mathieu, I take up the pen which our friend has for a moment laid down merely to express a vain wish that you were with us in this delectable region, as I do not think Georgia* itself can emulate in capabilities or incitements to the 'Plen. and optabil.—Coit.' the port of Falmouth & parts adjacent. We are surrounded by Hyacinths and other flowers of the most fragrant nature, & I have some intention of culling a handsome Bouquet to compare with the exotics we expect to meet in Asia.—One specimen I shall certainly carry off, but of this hereafter."[36]

Written in a quasi-private code, the friends' allusions, in the form of classical references, are nonetheless more accessible than Matthews's pedantic play on *la méthode*. Byron has abbreviated a quotation from *The Satyricon*—"*coitum plenum and optabilem*," or "complete intercourse to one's heart's desire"—used by the narrator in Petronius's satire to describe a sexual conquest.

His correspondent was delighted by the news from Falmouth and congratulated Byron on the "splendid success of your first efforts in the

---

*Georgia, home of the Circassians, famous for their beauty.

mysterious, that style in which more is meant than meets the eye." Hobhouse, however, was warned to be more careful; putting dashes under his code words, Matthews cautioned, "would go near to letting the cat out of the bag, should the tabellarians [i.e., mailmen] be inclined to peep." In scholarly camp, Matthews now entered into "the language of flowers":

> As to your Botanical pursuits, I take it that the flowers you will be most desirous of culling will be of the class polyandria and not monogynia but *nogynia*.* However so as you do not cut them it will all do very well. A word or two about hyacinths. Hyacinth, you may remember, was killed by a Coit, but not that "full and to-be-wished-for Coit." Have a care your Abbey [*sic*] Hyacinth be not injured by either sort of coit. If you should find anything remarkable in the botanical line, pray send me word of it, who take an extreme interest in your anthology; and specify the class and if possible the name of each production. . . .
>
> Adieu my dear Lord; I wish you, not as Dr. Johnson wished Mr. Burke, all the success which an honest man can or ought to wish you, but as grand founder and arch-Patriarch of the Methode I give your undertaking my benediction, and wish you, Byron of Byzantium, and you, Cam of Constantinople, jointly and severally, all the success which in your most methodistical fantasies, you can wish yourselves.[37]

FROM EARLY YOUTH Byron had been adroit in presenting himself differently to different friends and lovers, adjusting to the needs of each; each one, in turn, would believe that he or she was the privileged kindred spirit. This skill, often observed in the narcissist, with his insatiable need to be loved, is nowhere more evident than in the way Byron adjusted the account of his Falmouth stay to the particular tastes of the correspondent: "Citizen" Matthews was, of course, privileged with a tiltillating report that also flattered the scholar's classical erudition; with his former Harrow tutor and now friend, Henry Drury, who may not have been unacquainted with the forbidden pleasures of homoerotic relations, Byron was open, in an unspecific way, about the feasts of boy love they anticipated in the East.

---

*Polyandrous flowers have male stamens; monogynia describes the class of flowers with female stamens, while "*nogynia*" is Matthews's coinage to mean without female characteristics.

"Hobhouse has made woundy preparations for a book at his return, 100 pens two gallons Japan Ink, and several vols best blank is no bad provision for a discerning Public.—I have laid down my pen, but have promised to contribute a chapter on the state of morals, and a further treatise on the same to be entitled, 'Sodomy simplified or Paederasty proved to be praiseworthy from ancient authors and modern practice.' "[38]

To a sober friend like the young reform politician Edward Ellice, Byron played the conventional tourist, careful to include both genders in his praise of Falmouth's youth: "The Inhabitants both female & male, at least the young ones, are remarkably handsome, and how the devil they came to be so, is the marvel! For the place is apparently not favourable to Beauty."[39]

Writing to the cleric Francis Hodgson, Byron could indulge his misogyny, but without alluding to any bouquets of hyacinths: "The Town contains many Quakers and salt-fish, the oysters have a taste of copper owing to the soil of a mining country, the women (blessed be the Corporation therefore!) are flogged at the cart's tail when they pick and steal, as happened to one of the fair sex yesterday noon."[40]

By June 25 Captain Kidd and his crew of the Lisbon packet were still waiting on favorable winds. They boarded on June 30, but the wind dropping once again, the vessel remained riding at anchor in Falmouth Roads. Five days later they were still becalmed. Meanwhile, Byron wrote to Hanson to acknowledge receipt of a letter of credit. At the same time he refused Scrope Davies's request for a bond protecting him from Byron's creditors in case of his friend's death, Scrope having guaranteed another loan from the moneylenders. Honesty, however, compelled Byron to admit he was reneging on an earlier agreement: "It is true I offered to sign any satisfactory instrument for Mr. Davies, but I think the codicil sufficient, without a Bond of indemnity which shifts the responsibility completely."[41] In his letter to Hodgson a few days earlier, Byron had written: "I leave England without regret, I shall return to it without pleasure.—I am like Adam the first convict sentenced to transportation, but I have no Eve and have eaten no apple but was sour as a crab."[42]

Finally it dawned on him that, within hours, creditors, debts, and dangerous attachments would be left behind. His spirits lifted before the anchor was weighed, and he burst into doggerel for a rollicking farewell for Hodgson and England:

> Huzza! Hodgson, we are going,
> Our embargo's off at last,

> Favourable Breezes blowing
> Bend the canvass o'er the mast;
>   . . . .
> Hobhouse muttering fearful curses
> As the hatchway down he rolls
> Now his breakfast, now his verses
> Vomits forth and damns our souls,
>   Here's a stanza
>   On Braganza;
> Help!—a couplet—no, a cup
> Of warm water—
> What's the matter?
> Zounds! my liver's coming up.
> I shall not survive the racket
> Of this brutal Lisbon Packet.[43]

Finally, on Sunday, July 2, a light wind swelled the ship's sails, carrying her from Falmouth Roads to the mouth of the Tagus River in an astonishing four and a half days. The "nineteen souls in all," including Byron and his motley party, did indeed survive the Lisbon packet. But the first discomforts were nothing compared to the sufferings of the trip: "I have been sea sick and sick of the sea," Byron groaned with relief as his torment was ending.[44] Hobhouse, who suffered a broken wrist along with nausea, merely noted the "rough passage." To physical woes, old Joe Murray (taken along at the last moment instead of the Prussian servant), Fletcher, and Robert Rushton added acute homesickness. With the first sight of landfall on July 7, however, bleak memories of the voyage were crowded out by brilliant light and color; port officials steered them through the narrow, eight-mile Tagus channel, lushly green on both banks.

Soon the channel opened into Lisbon's inner bay and the city rose on steeply sloped hills reflected in the water:

> Her image floating on that noble tide,
> Which poets vainly pave with sands of gold.[45]

Byron's adventures were beginning. He was now the hero of his own life.

CHAPTER II

"The Foe, the Victim, and the Fond Ally"

*L*ISBON'S REFLECTION in the bay was, in fact, far from serene; the waters heaved with the massed presence of the British fleet:

> . . . a thousand keels did ride
> Of Mighty strength, since Albion was allied,
> And to the Lusians did her aid afford. . . .[1]

Written months later, Byron's lines acknowledged his country's timely intervention at this most troubled period for Portugal. During his first weeks there, however, it was the picturesque rather than the political that engaged him. Initially he seems to have missed the reality behind the reassuring sight of English naval power: Britannia might rule the waves, but it was Napoleon who dominated the face of Europe.

More than a year before Byron sailed up the Tagus, Britain's war against France had shifted to the Iberian Peninsula. Portugal was the weak link in Napoleon's Continental System, the closing of Europe's market to British goods. In November 1807 Napoleon conquered Portugal by using Spain as a staging area for troops and supplies. When reality dawned, the royal Portuguese House of Braganza, with fifteen thousand loyalists, fled to Brazil, and without firing a shot the French took control of Lisbon. Napoleon then turned on his allies; fresh troops poured into Spain.

The Spanish now revolted, forcing the abdication of Charles IV in favor of his son Ferdinand. Refusing to recognize the new sovereign, Napoleon declared his brother Joseph Bonaparte King of Spain. On May 2, 1808, the people of Madrid rose up and, with bare hands or armed only with knives, attacked Napoleon's elite Mamelukes. Rebellions erupted throughout the country, and one by one the occupied Spanish provinces rid themselves of the Napoleonic troops. Envoys from the newly formed juntas were sent to England, where they received a tumultuous welcome.

Two months after the envoys' return from Britain, the Tory government sent money, arms, and, most crucial, an army to Spain: Ten thousand men under the command of Sir Arthur Wellesley, future Duke of Wellington, set sail from Cork for the Peninsula. By August 1808 Wellesley was in the final stage of defeating the French forces under Jumot at Vimiera, near Lisbon. Then, in one of the most bizarre episodes in modern military history, before the triumphant general could secure his victory, he was replaced. To ratify letting victory slip away, Whitehall convened the Convention of Cintra, in which the defeated French troops, with all their artillery, were provided safe conduct home in British warships. To complete the debacle, Sir John Moore, the fourth general to follow Wellesley, was dispatched to Spain to divert Napoleon; this he managed to do, but at the cost of his own life as his army was driven home from the port of Corunna.

As the 1809 new year dawned, England had never looked more feeble in her effort to halt the Napoleonic juggernaut. But within six months, the tide had turned. Wellesley was returned to command the Peninsular forces. In mid-May he entered Spain for the first time and on Sunday, July 7, 1809, the day Byron landed in Lisbon, His Majesty's armies were approaching the town of Talavera, within striking distance of Madrid.[2]

Two young gentlemen with their servants and luggage disembarking for the grand tour in the midst of one of the bloodiest wars of the Napoleonic era—the scenario suggests an opera buffa of Byron's contemporary Rossini, starring Byron and Hobhouse in the roles of "accidental tourists."

Byron's route through Portugal and Spain was decided by chance: England's war with France had ruled out the conventional tour through Europe, dictating, instead, an Eastern itinerary. Days before his departure, his plan had been to proceed directly to Gibraltar, and on to Constantinople via Malta. Arriving in Falmouth, he had learned that the Malta packet would not be sailing for some time. Still, even an unplanned detour doesn't quite explain Byron's seeming oblivion to the war. Part of the answer may lie in his resolutely apolitical stance. His dismissal of both Whigs and Tories was part of a lofty indifference to history as it was happening, including Britain's war against Napoleon. Unlike other young Englishmen of liberal persuasion and quick sympathies, Byron had not yet taken the Spanish cause to his heart. Such views

as he held before sailing up the Tagus were confined to the negative reports of Portugal and her citizens repeated by every English
traveler.

No greater contrast could have assaulted the senses than that
between the chimerical city rising from the water and the squalid
reality of her streets and citizens:

> But whoso entereth within this town,
> That, sheening far, celestial seems to be,
> Disconsolate will wander up and down,
> 'Mid many things unsightly to strange ee;
> For hut and palace show like filthily. . . .[3]

In the interests of decorum, the poet had sanitized his first impressions;
his original lines read:

> Mid many things that grieve both nose and ee;
> For hut and palace smelleth filthily.[4]

The sights and smells had worsened by the time of Byron's arrival.
Before decamping, the French forces had slaughtered ten thousand
dogs, the city's only form of garbage disposal.[5]

Byron and Hobhouse had barely settled into rooms at the Buenos
Ayres Hotel in the upper town when they fell prey to the favorite form
of fleecing tourists. Captain Kidd, of the Lisbon packet, brought them
to a local merchant, a Mr. Bulkeley, who charged 13 percent for changing their money, Hobhouse reported, while another fellow Briton, J. W.
Ward (later first Earl of Dudley), would boast that meeting Byron and
finding him a "person of no common mind . . . by no means prevented
me from cheating him extremely."[6]

They were now ready to saddle up and visit the "marvelous sights"
in the area, as Byron described them to Hodgson.[7] But the distinctive
marine motifs of Manueline architecture impressed the two visitors less
than the ignorance of the local monks; one friar pointed to a picture of
soldiers using firearms, explaining to a shocked Hobhouse that the
scene was that of an ancient Roman battle! Byron, for his part, was
delighted to discover that his Harrow Latin was closely related to the
language spoken by his learned hosts.

Travel soon exacerbated the differences between the two friends,
along with a sea change experienced by each. Infamous since Cambridge
days for his dislike of bathing and clean linen, Hobhouse now bid fair
to become the caricature Englishman abroad, bewailing the lack of

hygiene and the natives' filthy ways. He shuddered as they passed a man "pulling lice and fleas, chiefly lice, from his bosom and breeches, and cracking them by the tens on the step. The women who are the ugliest race of animals, really frightful, are as nasty." There were no bookstores, "only stalls with a few dirty books."

Their hotel may have been as squalid as the others, but at least it was run by an Englishman, a Mr. Barnewell, and was "situated on a hill where the English used to reside," Hobhouse noted wistfully.[8]

Byron, on the other hand, as immaculate as any dandy, took a tolerant view of the customs of the country. He let himself be carried along by local life; his passive good humor caused him to relax into a kind of baby talk. "I am very happy here," he wrote Hodgson, "because I loves oranges, and talk bad Latin to the monks, who understand it, as it is like their own,—and I goes into society (with my pocket-pistols), and I swims in the Tagus all across at once, and I rides on an ass or a mule, and swears Portuguese, and have got a diarrhoea and bites from the mosquitoes. But what of that? Comfort must not be expected by folks that go a pleasuring."[9]

Freed from the constraints of home and in high spirits, Byron seems to have missed the signals that permissiveness and puritanism were here attached to different kinds of behavior than in England. In this Catholic country, Hobhouse was shocked to see mixed audiences go wild watching Iberian dances "of a lascivious character."[10] Accompanied by new friends, a racy crowd of young English staff officers posted in Lisbon, Byron became an addict of the Italian opera, whose erotic appeal he had earlier denounced when its highly paid stars visited London. His lighthearted remark about pistols needed for forays into society was grounded in reality; he later claimed to have been held up at gunpoint one evening on his way to the theater. He related the incident to an undeclared war on foreigners: "It is a well-known fact that in the year 1809, the assassinations in the streets of Lisbon and its vicinity were not confined by the Portuguese to their countrymen; but that Englishmen were daily butchered: and so far from redress being obtained, we were requested not to interfere if we perceived any compatriot defending himself against his allies."[11] Other accounts, however, suggest that Byron's would-be assailant was the husband of a lady with whom he had flirted openly at the opera.[12]

According to the *Reminiscences* of Captain Gronow, one of the dashing officers later to enjoy a career as a Regency dandy and diarist, Byron immediately "became the idol of the women, and the lionizing he underwent [in Lisbon] might have made him exceedingly vain, for he was admired wherever he went."[13]

Escaping from feminine adulation and its attendant risks, Byron sought safer challenges. Only a few days after their arrival, he swam the Tagus from Old Lisbon to Belém Castle downstream and, "having to contend with a tide and countercurrent, the wind blowing freshly, was but little less than two hours in crossing the river," Hobhouse noted, whose pride in his friend's achievements was often a way of deflecting envy.[14] This was a far more arduous feat than swimming the Hellespont, which he would do the following spring, but the earlier record has never acquired the mythic status of the Turkish crossing, perhaps because the Tagus never produced legendary lovers such as Hero and Leander to welcome Byron into the pantheon of romantic swimmers.

Lisbon's pleasures were soon exhausted, and on July 12, Byron and Hobhouse were glad to escape the squalor of the city, baking in the summer heat, for the journey through the mountains to Sintra, fifteen miles from the capital.

Nothing prepares the traveler for the mirage of Sintra. Perched on the northern slope of the Serro do Cintra, the town, ringed in sea mist, rises from a mountain mass covered with pine, mimosa, cedar, and eucalyptus trees, while just above, gray and jagged rocks pierce the sky. Describing "Cintra's glorious Eden," Byron captured its magic quality, like the fantastic terraced landscape in a Book of Hours:

> The horrid crags, by toppling convent crown'd,
> The cork-trees hoar that clothe the shaggy steep,
> The mountain-moss by scorching skies imbrown'd
> The sunken glen, whose sunless shrubs must weep,
> The tender azure of the unruffled deep,
> The orange tints that gild the greenest bough,
> The torrents that from cliff to valley leap,
> The vine on high, the willow branch below,
> Mix'd in one mighty scene, with varied beauty glow.[15]

Sintra's drama was the more dazzling as it allied "beauties of every description, natural & artificial, Palaces and gardens rising in the midst of rocks, cataracts and precipices," Byron wrote to his mother.[16] The "artificial" was a mountainside version of the Brighton Pavilion; hugging one of the peaks, the Palacio da Pena, completed just before Byron's visit, is a fantastic pastiche, part adaptation of a sixteenth-century monastery, part imitation of a medieval fortress. From another summit rose the Castelo dos Mouros, a vast Moorish fortification, while in the center of town the twelfth-to-fifteenth-century royal palace combined Moorish, debased Gothic, and elements of pure fantasy, with its

riot of blue-tiled rooms and two huge conical chimneys. Byron may
have spent only one day and a night in Sintra, but its impact on his
imagination has been ignored. Sintra and its dizzying mélange of styles
and forms was his first experience of the East, his dream of the *Arabian
Nights* made visible.

Before leaving his new paradise, Byron insisted on making a long-
planned pilgrimage: "The first and sweetest spot in this kingdom is
Montserrat, lately the seat of the great Beckford," Byron wrote to
Hodgson.[17] Driven from England in 1785, the author of *Vathek* had
made Quinta da Montserrat, a Moorish palace just outside the town,
into a private fantasy of lakes, vistas, and gardens of tropical luxu-
riance. After spending vast sums, he had lived there for only two years.
When Byron saw his idol's coach on the road from Falmouth, the exile
had been back in England for more than a decade. Visiting Montserrat
now, Byron and Hobhouse found it deserted and empty of furniture, its
famous gardens grown to weeds. The picturesque ruin inspired some
conventional verses on the transience of earthly splendors; Byron had
decided to suppress more personal reflections on Beckford. But the
deleted words and phrases left in parentheses point to the indecision
caused by a subject too close for comfort:

> Unhappy Vathek! in an evil hour
> (By one fair form) Gainst Nature's voice seduced to deed accurst,
> Once Fortune's minion, now thou feel'st her Power!
> Wrath's vials on thy lofty head have burst,
>
> . . . .
>
> How wondrous bright thy blooming morn arose
> But thou wert smitten with unhallowed thirst
> Of nameless crime, and (round thee twining close) thy sad day
>   must close
> (Scorn, Exile,) To scorn, and Solitude unsought—the worst of woes.[18]

The hill town had also given its name to the Convention of Cintra, mentioned earlier, and for the long work that would become *Childe Harold's
Pilgrimage*, Byron produced six Spenserian stanzas lamenting the ignoble event.* In their original version, the poet maintained the aggressive
spirit of *English Bards and Scotch Reviewers*, with savage attacks on the

---

*In England, outrage over the sellout inspired Wordsworth to a pallid imitation of
Milton in his pamphlet *Concerning the Convention of Cintra* (1809).

generals responsible, in his view, for the disgrace, starting with Sir Arthur Wellesley, future Duke of Wellington:

> Dull Victors! baffled by a vanquished foe,
> Wheedled by conynge tongues of laurels due,
> Stand, worthy of each other in a row—
> Sirs Arthur, Harry, and the dizzard Hew
> Dalrymple, seely wight, sore dupe of t'other tew.*[19]

BEFORE SETTING OFF on the four-hundred-mile trek to Gibraltar, Byron abandoned Hobhouse for the day to visit the Monastery of Mafra, ten miles north along the coast. An ocher-colored mass plainly visible from Sintra's heights, Mafra's eight-hundred-foot facade, longer than the main streets of many towns, housed a palace, church, and monastery. Byron was duly impressed by the sheer scale of the structure, which somehow manages to make beauty irrelevant: "the boast of Portugal, as it might be of any country, in point of magnificence without elegance."[20] Admiring the monastery's splendid library with its rococo decorations in grisaille, Byron was startled to be asked by one of the monks whether the English had books in *their* country.

As the French had retreated before reaching southern Spain, Byron and Hobhouse now decided on the more dramatic overland route to Gibraltar. Keeping Robert Rushton with them, Byron sent Fletcher and old Joe Murray ahead by boat with the bulk of the baggage. To complete their entourage he hired a Portuguese servant and guide named Sanguinetti, who was probably familiar with the route.

On July 21 the four left Lisbon, crossing the Tagus to the town of Aldea Gallega on the opposite bank, where they bought mosquito netting and hired five horses before spending the night at a local inn. At four o'clock the following morning they set off in a southeasterly direction, passing through the vineyards of Estremadura and the mysterious cork forests of the Alentejo. On either side, the road that led to Montemor and the Spanish frontier was "bordered by a vast number of crosses—signs of the murders which from time immemorial had taken place along its track," Hobhouse confided melodramatically to the

---

*More politic after his grand tour, Byron omitted for publication the three stanzas naming names. He was thus spared historical inaccuracy, as Wellesley was shown to have actively opposed the agreement, but as the youngest commanding officer present was overriden by his seniors.

detailed journal he kept of the trip.[21] In fact, the crosses were probably just the devotional souvenirs of pious travelers. In any event, the safety of their group was vouchsafed by Byron's traveling outfit, consisting of a staff officer's uniform (always to remain his favorite costume) and by the government orders he carried with him. Along with protection, extra comfort came with the epaulets; he enjoyed "every possible accommodation on the road, as an English nobleman in an English uniform is a very respectable personage in Spain at present," he wrote to his mother.[22] The fine roads and excellent horses allowed a record-breaking pace of seventy miles a day. Along the way they were sustained by the bare necessities, "eggs and wine and hard beds . . . in such torrid weather, quite enough."[23]

In Montemor they admired the splendid views from the ruined Moorish fortifications that give the settlement its name, before proceding on to Elvas, the frontier fortress that stands on the border overlooking the vast reaches of southern Spain. They arrived just before the gates were shut for the night, and despite the late hour, the governor insisted on the weary travelers' presenting themselves in a formal ceremony. The following afternoon, Hobhouse and Byron, bowing to local tradition, bathed in the Caia, the narrow river separating Portugal from Spain.

Passing Badajoz, the first town on the Spanish side of the border, they pushed on to Albuena before stopping for the night. Now they were confronted by evidence of a country at war: "Spain is all in arms, and the French have every thing to do over again, the barbarities on both sides are shocking," Byron reported to Hanson.[24] Their little group suffered only an attempted requisition: In Albuera, the authorities of the junta tried—without success—to seize their horses. Two years later, when the tiny village had become the scene of one of the bloodiest battles of the war, Byron immortalized the site retroactively, along with the Battle of Talavera, which was fought on July 27 and 28, just days after Byron would arrive in Seville. "You have heard of the battle near Madrid," Byron wrote to his mother from Gibraltar. "In England they will call it a victory, a pretty victory! two hundred officers and 5000 men killed all English, and the French in as great force as ever," adding somewhat guiltily, "I should have joined the army but we have no time to lose before we get up the Mediterranean & Archipelago."[25] He might don the becoming scarlet uniform for safe conduct, but he despised England too much to seriously consider dying for king and country.

Approaching the town of Monasterio, they passed two French prisoners and a seventy-year-old Spanish spy being taken to Seville to be hanged. Two thousand patriot troops were garrisoned in the town itself.

Even in a region where civilians would suffer the ravages of war continuously, life, including its impromptu moments of gaiety, went on.

Hobhouse, inhibited and self-conscious, marveled at the Spanish capacity for spontaneous pleasure. They were eating a meal of boiled chicken in the house of a courier who had given them lodgings, when "a large woman bolted into the room & began to dance when Sanguinetti played his flute to a Fandango tune," he noted in his journal.[26] All writers on Byron have lamented that the pedestrian "Hobby" kept the travel diary and not the poet—a considered division of labor: "I have forborn writing," Byron told his mother.[27] And his letters are few for the two years he spent abroad. He hated travel writing, in any case: "Damn description, it is always disgusting," he wrote to Hodgson.[28]

But he had not given up all writing—even in these months of intense activity. In an intimate journal begun earlier, he continued to sift the past, examining experiences and feelings too raw—or too dangerous—to divulge. Other immediate impressions—of people and events seen, along with battles unseen—were left to steep, awaiting their literary transformation. When he came to write *Childe Harold* three months later, he would change the chronology, and even geography, of the journey through Portugal and Spain, as he shaped the material to become a moral indictment of war.[29]

In the process the poet, too, changed. The young aristocrat, "infinitely amused" by the novelty and excitement of otherness and, most intoxicating of all, by his distance from England, delighting in his "most superb uniform . . . indispensable in traveling,"[30] had not disappeared; he had spun off a new poetic persona. In place of the petulant author of *English Bards and Scotch Reviewers*, settling literary scores and sneering at his elders, the poet invents a narrator for the new work who husbands his savagery to condemn the suffering and waste of war.

Crossing the rugged mountain range that rises between the northern plains and the province of Andalusia, Byron finally saw the grim evidence of preparations for killing: "The Sierra Morena was fortified in every defile through which I passed on my way to Seville."[31] In *Childe Harold*, the traveler's observation quickens into the drumbeat of a call to arms:

> At every turn Morena's dusky height
> Sustains aloft the battery's iron load;
> And, far as mortal eye can compass sight,
> The mountain-howitzer, the broken road,
> The bristling palisade, the fosse-o'er-flow'd,

> The station'd bands, the never-vacant watch,
> The magazine in rocky durance stow'd,
> The holster'd steed beneath the shed of thatch,
> The ball-pil'd pyramid, the ever-blazing match,
> Portend the deeds to come. . . .[32]

Conflating the Battles of Talavera and Albuera into one "glorious field of grief,"* Byron's imagination re-created the sounds and sights of carnage and compacted them into scenes that have come to stand for all war:

> Hark!—heard you not those hoofs of dreadful note?
> Sounds not the clang of conflict on the heath?
> Saw ye not whom the reeking sabre smote;
> Nor sav'd your brethren ere they sank beneath
> Tyrants and tyrant's slaves?—the fires of death,
> The bale-fires flash on high:—from rock to rock
> Each volley tells that thousands cease to breathe;
> Death rides upon the sulphury Siroc,
> Red Battle stamps his foot, and nations feel the shock.

Presiding over the slaughter, a Goya-esque deity battens on human sacrifice:

> Lo! where the Giant on the mountain stands,
> His blood-red tresses deep'ning in the sun,
> With death-shot glowing in his fiery hands,
> And eye that scorcheth all it glares upon
> Restless it rolls, now fix'd, and now anon
> Flashing afar,—and at his iron feet
> Destruction cowers to mark what deeds are done;
> For on this morn three potent nations meet,
> To shed before his shrine the blood he deems most sweet.
>
> By Heaven! it is a splendid sight to see
> (For one who hath no friend, no brother there)

---

*The first took place a week after they had left Portugal for Spain; the Battle of Albuera was fought on May 16, 1811, when Byron was in Malta awaiting return passage to England. He added this description later to his original passage on Talavera.[33]

Their rival scarfs of mix'd embroidery,
Their various arms that glitter in the air!
What gallant war-hounds rouse them from their lair,
And gnash their fangs, loud yelling for the prey!
All join the chase, but few the triumph share;
The Grave shall bear the chieftest prize away,
And Havoc scarce for joy can number their array.[34]

Without ever having seen a battle, Byron became the first major poet of modern warfare; with the Industrial Revolution well under way, the "mountain howitzer" and "bristling palisade" were ever improving their capacity for killing on a massive scale. In the wars Byron would memorialize there were no winners:

The foe, the victim, and the fond ally
That fights for all, but ever fights in vain,
Are met—as if at home they could not die—
To feed the crow on Talavera's plain,
And fertilize the field that each pretends to gain.[35]

The worst hardship suffered by Byron was the difficulty of finding a hotel room in Seville. Headquarters of the grand junta, the Spanish rebel government allied with England, the city of thirty thousand had exploded in months to a city of a hundred thousand residents. Both inns favored by the English were fully booked, but thanks to the British consul, Mr. Wiseman, lodgings were found for the travelers in a house (one of six) owned by "two unmarried ladies in the Calle de las Cruzes No. 19—Josepha Beltram & sister," Hobhouse recorded. "Went supperless & dinnerless to Bed all 4 in one little Room."[36]

The next day, Byron and Hobhouse called on the English ambassador, John Hookham Frere. Recently recalled in disgrace for dismissing Wellesley and dispatching Moore on the disastrous Corunna campaign, the scapegoated Frere had now been reinstated, as he was a great favorite of the junta. A man of parts, the ambassador was a jurist, poet, translator, and founding editor of the *Anti-Jacobin Review*. Under his pen name, "Whistlecraft," Frere would later inspire Byron's most radical shift in style. On this afternoon, as His Excellency was at dinner, the visitors left their cards, but there is no evidence the ambassador ever received them. They then visited the cathedral that Byron later decided he preferred "to St. Paul's, St. Sophia's and any religious building I have ever seen."[37] Once inside the church, he felt nothing but distaste for the paintings by Velázquez and Murillo but, feeling this required some explaining, added in a letter written later to his publisher John Murray: "You must recollect however—that I know nothing of painting—& that I detest it—unless it reminds me of something I have seen, or think it possible to see—for which [reason] I spit upon & abhor all the saints & subjects of one half the impostures I see in the churches and palaces."[38] Byron's repugnance toward religious painting points to the residual anti-Catholicism of a Calvinist childhood, but as he would soon express the same loathing for the "realistic" sculpture of the Parthenon, there were clearly elements of the plastic artist's ordering of visual experience that either eluded him or aroused a form of unaccountable anxiety.

He was much happier out of doors, admiring the architectural harmony of the city, and, especially after Lisbon, the absence of dirt: "Seville is a beautiful town, though the streets are narrow they are clean," he told his mother. Fatigued from the exertions of sightseeing, they returned to their crowded lodgings and went to bed "after tunes from Sanguinetti and the two ladies."[39] Neither the Portuguese servant's music making nor young Rushton's services filled Byron's need for a valet. To replace Fletcher, still waiting in Lisbon for a passage to Gibraltar, Byron hired a lieutenant in the Spanish army.

In Seville Byron also seems to have engaged the services of a guide, one Antonio Bailly, who, retracing the poet's itinerary with later foreign visitors, told the following story. He had taken Byron up the tower of the cathedral to admire the panoramic view of the city. Inspired by the sight, the poet removed a gold pencil from its case, but, as he was about to write on the wall of the parapet (whether a verse or merely his name was unclear), a small dog that had followed them began snuffling at the poet's lame foot. "This put Byron into a towering rage, and imprecating curses on the little dog which he kicked away in his rage, he threw the gold pencil far away on the roof of the cathedral below."[40]

Byron's high spirits had been sustained by the traveler's illusion that he has left his griefs and burdens behind. The sudden realization that his lameness was apparent to any stray dog, the explosion of anger that followed—both seem completely in character. His former Harrow master and friend Henry Drury had given the poet a gold pen as a going-away present—not a detail, therefore, that Bailly had invented.

Another Englishman visiting Seville called on Byron and Hobhouse during their stay. Sir John Carr was such a prolific writer of travel books that he was known as "Jaunting Carr," churning out volumes whose titles—*The Stranger in France* and *The Stranger in Holland*—suggest he may have been father of the guide series.*

Carr refrained from mentioning Byron in his Spanish guide, but another tourist attraction of Seville was duly noted by both writers: the legendary Augustina, "Maid of Saragoza," who single-handedly had loaded and fired the guns of her native city when the artillerymen were killed by the enemy. Now she "walked daily on the Prado, decorated with medals and orders, by command of the Junta," Byron noted.[41] He was entranced by the equally celebrated soft and feminine side of this legendary woman warrior—a mix he found to be typically Spanish:

> Yet are Spain's maids no race of Amazons,
> But form'd for all the witching arts of love:
> Though thus in arms they emulate her sons,
> And in the horrid phalanx dare to move,
> 'Tis but the tender fierceness of the dove
> Pecking the hand that hovers o'er her mate.[42]

Meanwhile, the tunes sung earlier by their landladies had turned into love songs. Byron was taken aback by the frank sexual overtures of one of the "women of character," as Byron described the two sisters to his mother, before detailing their looks and mounting infatuation for him: "The eldest a fine woman, the youngest pretty but not so good a figure as Donna Josepha, the freedom of women which is general here astonished me not a little, and in the course of further observation I find that reserve is not the characteristic of Spanish belles, who are in general very handsome with large black eyes, and very fine forms. The eldest honoured your *unworthy* son with very particular attention, embracing him with great tenderness at parting (I was there but 3 days) after cutting off a lock of his hair, & presenting him with one of her own, about three feet in length, which I send, and beg you will retain till my return.† Her last words were, Adio, tu hermosa! Me gusto mucho.

---

*Byron satirized the author and his book on Spain in three stanzas of *Childe Harold's Pilgrimage*, which, along with other verses mocking well-known figures, he later suppressed.

†Donna Josepha's long "fall" of black hair, along with a pale-gold lock of Edelston's, are now preserved in the collection of Byron memorabilia originally owned by the poet's publisher John Murray.

'Adieu, you pretty fellow! You please me much.' She offered a share of her apartment, which my *virtue* induced me to decline she laughed and said I had some English Amante (lover) and added that she was going to be married to an officer in the Spanish army."[43]

Donna Josepha became even more uninhibited; when their guests left, "after kissing our hostess and sister," Hobhouse noted, "one of the women asked Ld. B. why he had not come to bed to her at 2 o'clock according to invitation."[44]

It was a two-day journey through dramatic country to Cadiz. The group traveled in two carriages with four horses, making an agreeable stopover in Xeres, center of sherry manufacture. There Byron was able to report to his mother, proud of her heritage, that they had "met a great merchant, a Mr. Gordon of Scotland, who was extremely polite and favoured me with the Inspection of his vaults & cellars, so that I quaffed at the Fountain head."[45] They arrived at Cadiz at seven-thirty on Saturday, July 29, and instantly Sintra and Seville were forgotten: "Cadiz, sweet Cadiz! is the most delightful town I ever beheld, very different from our English cities in every respect except cleanliness (and it is as clean as London) but still beautiful and full of the finest women in Spain, the Cadiz belles being the Lancashire witches of their land."[46]

While her son was abroad, Catherine Byron was the only recipient of regular correspondence from him. Long, newsy, and even personal, these letters are often triumphant accounts of conquests and compliments; their tone alternates between mere swagger and the assumption that a parent's pride allows us to dispense with the seemly modesty demanded by society. On a deeper level, however, Byron's letters to his mother confirm the irreplaceable intimacy of their attachment, including the pain that both were adept at inflicting on the other. He knew how lonely she was, just as he knew that her cruel words on parting expressed the intensity of her love and her grief at separation.

In Cadiz, the British consul was more forthcoming than the literary ambassador in Seville; the day after they arrived, Byron and Hobhouse were invited to Sunday dinner, where their fellow guests were Lord Jocelyn and Mr. Wellesley Pole, the Duke of Wellington's nephew. After the meal, the party crossed the bay to Puerta Santa Maria, where the only bullfight still permitted by the grand junta was to take place.

The *corrida*, with its elements of blood sport and religious ritual, made as profound an impression on Byron as it has on every other literary visitor. He devoted eleven stanzas of *Childe Harold* to the sabbath rite of "death in the afternoon," its savagery made more naked by splendid costumes and richly caparisoned horses. Byron found the blood lust

of the spectators more shocking than the disemboweling of young men
and splendid beasts:

> Hark! heard you not the forest-monarch's roar?
> Crashing the lance, he snuffs the spouting gore
> Of man and steed, o'erthrown beneath his horn;
> The throng'd Arena shakes with shouts for more;
> Yells the mad crowd o'er entrails freshly torn
> Nor shrinks the female eye, nor ev'n affects to mourn.[47]

Seated in the governor's box in the center of the amphitheater, Byron
and Hobhouse were well positioned to observe the frenzied excitement
the killing aroused in men and women, grandee and peasant. This communal experience, embracing the majesty of ritual slaughter, confirmed
for Byron the superiority of the ordinary Spaniard over his English
counterpart, whose paltry Sunday pleasures Byron was now moved to
satirize:

> Then thy spruce citizen, wash'd artizan,
> And smug apprentice gulp their weekly air:
> Thy coach of Hackney, whiskey, one-horse chair,
> And humblest gig through sundry suburbs whirl. . . .[48]

The bull's dance of death and the "wild plunging of the tortur'd horse"
become, in Byron's great stanzas, both epic and *Liebestod*:

> On foams the bull, but not unscath'd he goes;
> Streams from his flank the crimson torrent clear:
> He flies, he wheels, distracted with his throes;
> Dart follows art; lance, lance; loud bellowings speak his woes.
>
> .   .   .   .
>
> One gallant steed is stretch'd a mangled corse;
> Another, hideous sight! unseam'd appears,
> His gory chest unveils life's panting source,
> Tho' death-struck still his feeble frame he rears[49]

Hobhouse remained convinced that Byron had left the arena as revolted
by the brutal spectacle as he was himself. They had both taken their
leave early: "The death of one or two horses completely satisfied [our]
curiosity." He was unable to resist a dig at Byron's selective squeamish-
ness: His friend was ready to cheer on the brutality of boxing, but was
repelled by the cruelty of the *corrida*—"An Englishman who can be

much pleased with seeing two men beat themselves to pieces cannot
bear to look at a horse galloping around an arena with his bowels trail-
ing on the ground."⁵⁰

Returning to Cadiz at nine that evening, they were more than ready
for an undemanding evening at the theater. When the performance
ended, the two young men paid a visit to a bordello, one of many such
establishments in town. In contrast to staid and "proud Seville," Cadiz

> Calls forth a sweeter, though ignoble praise.
> Ah, Vice! how soft are thy voluptuous ways!
> While boyish blood is mantling who can 'scape
> The fascination of thy magic gaze?⁵¹

Driven from Paphos, where she had been the ruling deity, Venus had
happily settled in Cadiz

> And fix'd her shrine within these walls of white:
> Though not to one dome circumscribeth she
> Her worship, but, devoted to her rite
> A thousand altars rise, for ever blazing bright.⁵²

Byron and Hobhouse were woken before dawn the next day,
August 1, by the rumbling of cannons. They strolled out in time to see
a celebration honoring General Cuesta for the victory at Talavera,
which included a salute in honor of the landing of Lord Wellesley. The
visitors were lukewarm in their cheers: British forces under Wellesley
had wrested what might be considered a victory from Napoleon, yet
Spanish reports credited General Cuesta and his token backup with
winning the day.

Standing on the quai, they watched the ambassador and his entourage disembark. According to an elaborately planned ritual, the enemy
flag had been so placed on the ground that Wellesley's first act on
Spanish soil was to trample the French standard. Byron had only sneers
for the arriving envoy "charioteering over the French flag" and even less
patience for the interminable "speech of a patriotic cobbler of Cadiz."⁵³
In the early evening they returned to the Alameda, where they met
Wellesley Pole and a Cambridge friend of Byron's, Gally Knight.

The next day Byron and Hobhouse were rowed out to the *Atlas* for
dinner. While on board, their host, Admiral Purvis, arranged for their
passage to Gibraltar on the frigate *Hyperion*, leaving the following day.

Byron regretted his imminent departure: "Just as I was introduced and began to like the grandees I was forced to leave," he lamented to his mother.[54] On his last evening, he enjoyed a glittering performance at the opera. There he discovered that the "Paphian girls" who had entertained him the previous night were not the only votaries of Venus in Cadiz. As a guest of Admiral Cordova, commander of the Spanish fleet, Byron was standing behind the ladies in the closed candlelit box, when his host's daughter made it clear that she was smitten with him. The attraction was mutual. Byron, as Hobhouse noted of his friend that evening, was "a little mad & apt to fall in love,"[55] and in Señorita Cordova he found the perfect example of the Spanish beauty: "long black hair, dark languishing eyes, *clear* olive complexions, and forms more graceful in motion than can be conceived by an Englishman used to the drowsy listless air of his countrywomen," he wrote to his mother.[56]

Señorita Cordova, like other unmarried young women, was not shy; as Byron remarked with some astonishment, "If you make a proposal which in England would bring a box on the ear from the meekest of virgins, to a Spanish girl, she thanks you for the honour you intend her, and replies 'wait till I am married & I shall be too happy.' " In her determination to sit next to him, "this fair Spaniard dispossessed an old woman (a[n] aunt or a duenna) of her chair and commanded me to be seated next herself, at a tolerable distance from her mamma." Observing Byron's inadequate Spanish, "she proposed to become my preceptress in that language; I could only reply by a low bow, and express my regret that I quitted Cadiz too soon to permit me to make the progress which would doubtless attend my studies under so charming a directness." But the admiral's daughter did not give up: "I have an invitation on my return to Cadiz which I shall accept, if I repass through the country on my way from Asia."[57]

Before leaving Spain, Byron celebrated in verse the archetypal Spanish seductress. "The Girl of Cadiz," with its elastic rhymes, is more limerick than love poem:

> Oh, never talk again to me
>   Of Northern charms and British ladies;
> It has not been your lot to see,
>   Like me, the lovely Girl of Cadiz.

Inflating the rhetoric only makes matters worse; his hymn to the sexuality of Spanish women turns into a feeble echo of Pope's "Rape of the Lock":

Prometheus-like, from heaven she stole
   The fire, that through those silken lashes
In darkest glances seem to roll
   From eyes that cannot hide their flashes:
And as along her bosom steal,
   In lengthen'd flow her raven tresses,
You'd swear each clustering lock could feel,
   And curl'd to give her neck caresses.[58]

Byron at his worst, though, is still revealing; he allows us to see the process through which the dangerously erotic is tamed into the decorously romantic. Burned by the disapproval that greeted the stanzas to Mary and Caroline, the poet seems determined to avoid any exaltation of sexual pleasure as provided by the señoritas of the "Seraglio" (Hobhouse's euphemism for the local brothel). The unavailable "Girl of Cadiz" falls, dead doggerel on the page.*

AFTER THE beauty of Spanish women, cities, and landscape and the thrilling savagery of the bullfight, Byron sank into a depression the moment he arrived in Gibraltar, "the dirtiest most detestable spot in existence."[59] This was not unrelated to the Englishness of the settlement, where they were trapped for two weeks, awaiting the arrival of servants, luggage, and the departure of the Malta packet. The days were the worst: The August heat combined with the suffocating sirocco turned the only excursion, exploring the fortifications, into an endurance test.

Driven indoors, Byron was browsing through the garrison library when he encountered another literary countryman. Nine years Byron's senior, John Galt was a Scot employed as a representative of Scottish merchants to sell (and probably smuggle) goods into Spain and the East. Galt's commercial activities subsidized the man of letters; he produced a steady stream of novels, travel books, essays, a biography of Cardinal Wolsey, and, inevitably, a life of Byron. Risen from the workhouse, Galt had a fine-tuned sense of class distinction, and he was immediately struck by Byron's studied, understated elegance: "His dress indicated a Londoner of some fashion . . . with just so much of a peculiarity of style as served to show, that although he belonged to the order of metropolitan beaux, he was not altogether a common one."[60] Observing his

---

*Byron himself recognized the failure of "The Girl of Cadiz." He pulled the stanzas from the Cadiz section of *Childe Harold* before publication, and the poem remained unpublished until after his death.

neighbor at the library table, Galt sensed that certain of Byron's mannerisms were first adopted for effect, but had since become reflexive, in particular an exaggerated and theatrical frown, at which "his brows lowered and gathered; a habit, as I then thought, with a degree of affectation in it."[61]

Byron's frown was more in evidence when he boarded the packet *Townshend* on Saturday evening, August 19, bound for Malta. He had just sent Robert Rushton, in the care of old Joe Murray, home to England. A few days before they left, Byron had given Murray one of his longest letters to his mother, written from Gibraltar, in which he was guardedly frank about the reason for sending Rushton home: "Show the lad any kindness as he is my great favourite, I would have taken him on but you *know boys* are not *safe* amongst the Turks." Byron then crossed out this last phrase, substituting these instructions: "Say this to his father, who may otherwise think he has behaved ill."[62]

Byron's reasons for sending Rushton home were probably tangled. Their shipboard intimacy in close quarters may have raised eyebrows among their fellow Britons on the voyage out. Turkish and Greek acceptance of homosexuality was well known; with his announced intention to cull as many "hyacinths" as possible in the East, Byron could have seen a danger to Rushton in the assumption that he was available to others besides his master. Planning to indulge himself with local boys, Byron was in no position to protect his page.

Galt was a fellow passenger on the Malta packet, and he had installed himself on board before Byron and Hobhouse arrived at the quai. Byron, with his famous scowl, impressed Galt as a young man much concerned that no one forget his rank: "In the little bustle and process of embarking their luggage, his Lordship affected, as it seemed to me, more aristocracy than befitted his years, or the occasion. . . . Hobhouse with more of the commoner, made himself one of the passengers at once; but Byron held himself aloof, and sat on the rail, leaning on the mizzen shrouds, inhaling, as it were, poetical sympathy from the gloomy rock, then dark and stern by the twilight."[63] Galt's picture of the brooding Byron, against the background of Gibraltar's looming hulk, is also a generic portrait of the romantic poet. When the lights were lit and the other passengers gathered in the main cabin, he "made himself a man forbid." It seemed to Galt that Byron's figure was not merely shrouded in darkness but also wrapped in the "sackcloth of penitence," and he was reminded of "him who shot the albatros [*sic*], the Ancient Mariner himself."

When Byron emerged from his gloom, it was to erupt into irritability: "He spoke petulantly to Fletcher, his valet; and was evidently ill at ease with himself and fretful towards others," Galt recalled. Three days out, however, Byron had tired of his own bad temper. The passage to Sardinia was slowed by dropping winds, and once he could seize the spotlight by organizing amusements to while away the hours, "he became playful." He suggested shooting at bottles, providing all the pistols needed for his fellow passengers. With the calm seas, the skiff was lowered, and Byron, in company with the captain, caught two turtles and a shark, which proved a disappointment when served for breakfast. Landing in Cagliari, Byron and the captain rode out into the countryside, while Hobhouse explored the town. When the *Townshend*'s passengers were invited to dinner by the British ambassador, Byron and Hobhouse both donned the uniform of aides-de-camp. Hobhouse was in great form, making himself agreeable to all and entertaining his fellow passengers with jokes and stories, some of these fairly scatalogical—"more after the manner and matter of Swift than of Addison," Galt noted delicately. Galt was himself suffering from what he described as a "nervous dejection," and he was aware that the thoughtful Hobhouse was making special efforts to cheer him.

Where Byron's spirits were concerned, the devoted Hobby had his work cut out for him. After dinner at the embassy, host and guests went on to the opera. The first part of the evening went well; the royal family was in the audience, and, after depositing most of his party in a loge where they would have a good view of the bejeweled crowned heads, the ambassador led Byron to his private box, thereby making plain to all those present that he was accompanied by a Briton of rank. Byron's delight in this mark of distinction was boundless—and, in fact, seems to have overflowed the bounds of gentlemanly restraint. Making his farewells to their host, who had accompanied the party to the gate of the upper town, Byron thanked the envoy with a flowery speech, delivered "with more elocution than was precisely requisite," as Galt put it with dry Scots irony. This performance amused Hobhouse mightily, and once their host had gone he began imitating his friend. Sharp words ensued, with the poet becoming "petulant" and Hobhouse walking on, leaving him behind. Byron's lameness, the rough pavement, the dark, Hobhouse's humiliation of him—all combined to flay his sense of vulnerability: He now took hold of Galt's arm, "appealing to me if he could have said less, after the kind and hospitable treatment we had all received." Galt lied: "His Lordship's comfort at the moment seemed in some degree dependent on being confirmed in the good opinion he was desirous to entertain of his own courtesy."

Byron's behavior that evening toward Galt and Hobhouse points again to the conflicting impulses governing his choice of friends. Lytton

Strachey, debunker not only of eminent Victorians but also of their pre-decessors, claimed of Byron that "indeed, he was probably incapable of friendship. There was no give and take about his nature; and his vanity was such that he preferred to be flattered by an insignificant mind, like [Tom] Moore's to being treated as an equal by a noble one, like Shelley's."[64] Certainly, Galt and Dallas must be added to the list of lesser spirits. But Byron was the first to recognize his own insatiable need for admiration and attention, to make up the unconditional parental love he had never enjoyed. He once said that he would have liked less frankness and more flattery from Hobhouse, for example, even as he acknowledged that honesty was the true measure of Hobby's love and respect.

THE NEXT MORNING Byron claimed ill health, keeping to his cabin for the day. From an exchange with Hobhouse, Galt surmised that their friend was ashamed of his behavior of the night before, and needed Hobhouse to "forgive" him before he would emerge: "It was necessary to humour him like a child," Hobhouse explained.[65] Having over-indulged himself at the ambassador's table, Byron now returned to his diet, eating only the smallest servings of bread and vegetables, with an occasional half glass of wine mixed with water.

As they sailed along the sun-dappled Sicilian coast, his mood lightened and his conversation, "overflowing with glee," sparkled. The watered wine was forgotten. Champagne was uncorked and pro-nounced "in the finest condition." His bubbling spirits were soon flat-tened, however. Approaching the harbor of Valletta, Malta's capital, Byron requested that word of their arrival be sent ahead to the island's governor, Sir Alexander Ball. Long after the other passengers had dis-embarked, Byron still waited on board with Hobhouse for the salute from the batteries he felt was due his rank. But the cannons remained silent, and at twilight the two travelers, "unnoticed and unknown," were rowed to port.[66]

CHAPTER 12

"Places Without a Name, and Rivers
Not Laid Down in Maps"

*A*RRIVING AT nightfall on August 31, the two stragglers explored the hilly city but, finding no lodgings, returned to sleep on board ship. The next day, Friday, they went into Valletta again, visiting the Church of St. John, the shrine of the Knights of Malta. Returning to the *Townshend*, they found an invitation from the governor to dine with his family. In hopes of further hospitality, Byron and Hobhouse now left the ship with all their belongings and proceeded to the palace. From there the governor and his guests were driven by carriage to his country house in San Antonio. Dinner should have been a warning that the envoy and his lady were not forthcoming; the meal consisted of only one course, "with lectures on temperance and commendation of our abstinence," Hobhouse noted drily.[1] Far from inviting them to stay, Sir Alexander suggested that the two travelers book passage on the brig *Wizard*, leaving for Smyrna that Sunday. They were then driven back to town and left to fend for themselves.

That evening, Galt was among the guests at supper with a Mr. Chabot, one of Valletta's leading merchants. There was a knock at the door, and Byron appeared accompanied by Hobhouse. The uninvited visitors seem to have agreed on a script: Hobhouse recited a litany of slammed doors and "full up" notices at the local inns, by way of apology for begging food and a bed for the night. Byron, meanwhile, punctuated his friend's recitation with sardonic laughs, "not altogether without spleen—a kind of malicious satisfaction," Galt recalled, at the absurdity of "personages so consequential wandering destitute in the streets."[2] Chabot accommodated the two for the night, and the next day they returned to the governor's palace to ask further help in finding a place to stay. Ball gave them short shrift, but his secretary found them a pleasant house in the higher part of Valletta, at No. 3 Strada di Forni.

As soon as they were settled, Byron purchased an Arabic grammar and began lessons with a monk who worked in the town library. Clearly, he still planned to travel to the East. Meanwhile, he slipped happily into the enjoyable round of summer life in a colonial capital. After his morning lesson, he would visit the public baths; in the afternoons he usually sailed to the beach at La Pietà for a swim. Then came dinner with his new friends, often folllowed by the opera. He enjoyed the extended hospitality of Mr. Chabot, at whose house he met everyone of importance passing through Malta; he was particularly drawn to Spiridion Forresti, a cosmopolitan raconteur, whose connections to diplomatic and political circles in the Levant provided Byron with the stories he loved; he bet Mr. Wherry, the British consul in Smyrna, 20 guineas that he could infiltrate the female slave market in Constantinople. He also met Commissioner Fraser and his charming wife, Susan. One of Malta's assiduous hostesses, Mrs. Fraser promptly invited the visitors to call, at which time they were introduced to her dear friend and houseguest, Constance Spencer Smith. Instantly, Byron fell in love.

A "tall pretty woman with fat arms well made" is how Hobhouse described "*la célèbre* Mrs. Spencer Smith."[3] Local gossip had assured that her fame—spiced with a touch of notoriety—preceded her. Other, more alluring descriptions are confirmed by an engraving after her portrait. She was ravishingly beautiful, with skin so fine it appeared translucent, golden hair, and brilliant blue eyes, always modestly downcast. The latter was probably the giveaway: Mrs. Spencer Smith was a lady with a past.

When Byron met the seductive Constance she was twenty-six. (She told her new, younger admirer she was not yet twenty-five.) Born in Constantinople, where her father, Baron Herbert, had been Austrian ambassador to the Sublime Porte, she had been married in her teens to a British diplomat, Charles Spencer Smith. Claiming delicate health, she had left her husband and two young sons and was taking the waters at the fashionable spa of Valdagno, near Vicenza, when Napoleonic troops overran northern Italy. Mrs. Spencer Smith took refuge with her sister in Venice, where, shortly after her arrival, she was arrested (charges unclear) on the orders of Napoleon himself. Under armed guard, she was to be taken to France and delivered to the infamous prison of Valenciennes. Meanwhile, Mrs. Spencer Smith had aroused the passion of another visitor to Venice, a twenty-two-year-old Sicilian nobleman, the Marquis de Salvo. In a daring escape plan, he followed the prisoner to Brescia on the shore of Lake Garda, where, with the aid of a rope ladder, boy's costume, carriages, and two waiting boats, he carried her to the safety of her family in Graz.

The Sicilian marquis had disappeared from the scene, and she now claimed to be on the way home to her husband in England. Byron, at least, believed her; he wrote a fulsome description of his new love in a letter he entrusted to Mrs. Spencer Smith, which she was to deliver to Catherine Byron at Newstead. In it Byron assured his mother that "this very extraordinary woman . . . married unhappily yet has never been impeached in point of character."4

At twenty-two, Byron's experience of women had been limited to teenage whores, servant girls, and provincial virgins. He had never met anyone remotely like Constance: a woman of the world, with all the advantages of beauty, breeding, and culture who was at ease in the courts, salons, and watering places of Europe and had the added glamour of being on Napoleon's "wanted" list. In Byron she encountered a young poet of patrician beauty, brilliance, and charm, just emerging from the chrysalis of adolescence. Malta gossip remained divided on the question of who was the more besotted.

Their first meeting at the Frasers' was followed by a second—that same evening. From then on, they were constantly together. "Since my arrival here," Byron wrote to his mother, "I have had scarcely any other companion. I have found her very pretty, very accomplished, and extremely eccentric."5 His cool tone and the subsequent cooling of his passion led some to believe that this was a mere flirtation. Hobhouse, however, generally prone to underplay his friend's attachments, confirmed that Byron was in love with the Austrian charmer. Galt disagreed, insisting that Byron "affected a passion for her; but it was only Platonic," a view hard to reconcile with Galt's following remark: that she "beguiled him of his valuable yellow diamond ring."6 (Mrs. Spencer Smith was taking no chances.) Byron himself was unequivocal about his feelings for his "new calypso," as he later confided to Lady Melbourne, the one friend with whom he was reliably frank: "In the autumn of 1809 in the Mediterranean I was seized with an *everlasting* passion, considerably more violent on my part than this has ever been—every thing was settled—& *we* . . . were to set off for the Friuli;* but lo! the

---

*Constance's mother, Baroness Herbert, lived in Trieste, Friuli's largest city. Unless this was a serious attachment, it seems unlikely that Byron would have chosen to go with Constance to the region where her only surviving parent happened to live. The Friuli was part of the Austrian empire until the Treaty of Vienna, in 1809, when it was ceded to Napoleon.

Peace spoilt every thing, by putting this in possession of the French, &
some particular occurrences in the interim determined me to go on to
Constantinople—However we were to meet next year at a certain time,
though I told my amica there was no time like the present, & that I
could not answer for the future.—She trusted to her power, & I at the
moment had certainly much greater doubts of her than myself."[7]

At Constance's request, Byron wrote a poem in her album. Allowing
her discretion—an album was intended to be shown to others—the lines
strike a strangely elegiac note for a lover urging his mistress to fly with
him. Comparing his signature on the page to the name carved on "cold
sepulchral stone," he invited her to "reflect on me as on the dead."[8]
Before leaving Malta, Byron, renaming his muse, addressed a second
poem, of forty-four lines, "To Florence." If Constance read the tribute
carefully, she may have found cause to doubt that there would be a
reunion: "Though Time restore me to my home, / I ne'er shall bend my
eyes on thee," he predicted.[9]

As it happened, there were no ships leaving Malta bound for
"Stamboul's Oriental Halls" or even for Athens.[10] By now, Byron
was used to chance deciding their itinerary; the two travelers happily
accepted the governor's offer to arrange passage for them on the *Spider*,
a brig escorting a convoy of British merchant ships to Patras and
Prevesa. From September 14 she waited at anchor for the wind to
change. Two days later, expecting to be parted at any moment, Byron
and his beloved made their plans to meet in Malta the following year.
But the winds remained unfavorable, keeping passengers on shore for
two more days. Then, at 11:00 p.m. on the eighteenth, after dinner with
the Frasers, Byron announced to Hobhouse that he had challenged a
Captain Cary, aide-de-camp to General Oakes, to a duel. He had met
the young officer at a dinner with Oakes soon after their arrival. During
the course of the meal, a heated discussion of politics, accompanied by
Oakes's sneering reception of his remarks, had led Byron to consider
calling him out then. Now, however, he was impelled to action by a
recent insult: "I [was] informed that you have since mentioned my name
in a public company with comments not to be tolerated," Byron told
Cary.[11] A gentleman could not spell out a lady's name in such a communiqué, but it was clear that Cary's offending comments had linked
Byron sexually with Mrs. Spencer Smith. Although he was due to sail
the next day, Byron suggested 6:00 a.m. as the time for the duel, his
opponent to choose the place.

Before the *Spider* weighed anchor at noon on September 19,
messages flew back and forth among Byron, the "warlike Captain,"
and several intermediaries, including the brig's commanding officer.

Finally, a long letter from Cary in which he disclaimed any intention to offend was accepted. Honor had been satisfied. Billowing sails now carried Byron toward Homer's wine-dark Ionian Sea.

On board the *Spider*, passengers were constantly reminded that a brig-of-war serving as convoy ship made for a very different voyage than a mail packet; two months later Byron would write, in the cadence of a sea chantey, of "the gallant Frigate tight" whose "convoy spread like wild swans in their flight." Belowdecks, the massed guns and ammunition created a "little warlike world within." Less exciting, the ship's escort role required that she adjust speed to the slower merchant ships,

> Then must the pennant-bearer slacken sail
> That lagging barks may make their lazy way.[12]

FOUR DAYS out of Malta Byron had his first sight of Greece from the channel between Cephalonia and Zante. Before them, to the east, rose the mountains of the Peloponnese and, beyond, the looming Pindus range of Albania. Hobhouse, especially, rejoiced in the varied scenery of the Ionian Islands, "peculiarly agreeable to our eyes, which had been so long fatigued with the white waste of Malta."[13] For Byron, the most moving sight was "Sappho's Leap," at the southeasternmost point of Ithaca, from where the poet, martyr to betrayed passion, is supposed to have flung herself into the sea. Passing that "last resort of fruitless love," Byron reflected on the cruel paradox:

> Dark Sappho! could not verse immortal save
> That breast imbued with such immortal fire?
> Could she not live who life eternal gave?[14]

He contrasts the feelings inspired by these rocks, sacred to the artist's sufferings—"a spot he longed to see, nor cared to leave"—with his hero's distaste for the shrines of war:

> Actium, Lepanto, fatal Trafalgar;
> Mark them unmov'd, for he would not delight
> (Born beneath some remote inglorious star)
> In themes of bloody fray, or gallant fight,
> But loath'd the bravo's trade, and laugh'd at martial wight.[15]

The Ionian Islands were then in the possession of the French, and as soon as the *Spider* entered the Gulf of Corinth, on the twenty-fourth, she was in enemy waters. She took the offensive, chasing and capturing a ship used to transport currants. The seized vessel was swiftly outfitted from the brig's arsenal as a privateer: Muskets, cutlasses, and a small cannon were lowered into the prize boat, along with nine volunteers from the *Spider* to serve as crew, including Hobhouse and the ship's surgeon. While Byron remained on board the brig, his delighted friend plunged into the thick of an exciting—if small-scale—naval battle. For the next day and a half they cruised the islands in their makeshift man-of-war, capturing a seventy-ton Turkish brig that had fired on them. Her crew surrendered at once, and the victorious Britons brought her into Patras the next morning.*

They approached the town just as dawn was breaking over the mountains. Patras itself nestled at the foot of a hill verdant with gardens, groves of orange and lemon trees, and fields of currant bushes that, when seen from a distance, reminded Hobhouse of the bright green of an English meadow. Drawing closer to port, they also saw, for the first time, evidence of Greece's status as a province of the Ottoman Empire in "the minarets of the Turkish mosques . . . glittering in the first rays of the sun."[16]

Byron ardently wished to walk on Greek soil, so he and Hobhouse strolled the fields north of town until a signal from the brig brought them back to the ship at noon.

The *Spider* now set her course for Prevesa, the southernmost port of Albania. That evening there was another naval engagement, when the little brig seized a boat from Ithaca and a Turkish ship from Dulcigno. This time Byron boarded the captured vessel, rummaging in her armory. But instead of booty for his gun collection, he discovered only outmoded and worthless arms.

Disembarking at Prevesa on September 29, the travelers found themselves in a region whose shoreline was in sight of Italy, yet, as the historian Gibbon had noted, was less known to Englishmen than the interior of North America. In 1809 Albania might have stood for uncharted "foreignness" itself. Geographically the country had no fixed boundaries; the name referred roughly to a region that, embracing ancient Epirus and Illyria, stretched along the Adriatic from the northernmost part of western Greece to Montenegro, then from the coast

---

*Byron never mentions the episode at all; Hobhouse omits the naval engagement in the first edition of his *Journey*, published in 1813, but includes a detailed account in his memoirs, *Recollections of a Long Life,* published when he was sixty-five. It has been suggested that the ongoing war would have placed the incident in the "censored" category. But Byron may also have felt a certain shame about sitting out the engagement.

east to Macedonia and Thessaly, whose rugged mountains formed a natural border.

For centuries its fierce mountain tribesmen had fought back successive onslaughts by Greeks, Romans, and Slavs. They were no match, though, for the Turkish juggernaut. By 1478 Albania was part of the Ottoman Empire.

Throughout the seventeenth and eighteenth centuries Turkish power steadily declined. Far from the Sublime Porte, Albania was left to its own warring factions. Then, at the very end of the eighteenth century, a former robber chieftain, the brilliant and ruthless Ali Pasha, took command of the region. He became known as Vizier of the Three Tails and exercised the power of a total despot, governing with a combination of terror and efficiency. The sultans left him unchallenged, while the French and English, intent on furthering their own ambitions in the East, both shamelessly wooed the ex-bandit. For his part, Ali Pasha played the two European powers off against each other, as it suited his interests at the moment. Not for nothing was he called the "Mahometan Buonaparte."

Happily for Byron, 1809 was the year of the British. In his southern capital where he was known as "the Lion of Jannina," the ruler now prepared to greet the two young travelers with all the flattering hospitality due distinguished emissaries of a friendly nation.

Both Ali Pasha and his fiefdom had captured Byron's imagination before he reached her shores. "Land of Albania! Let me bend mine eyes / On thee, thou rugged nurse of savage men!" he had written and he waxed lyrical about the dangers he hoped to meet:

> Here roams the wolf, the eagle whets his beak,
> Birds, beasts of prey, and wilder men appear,
> And gathering storms around convulse the closing year.[17]

Such expectations did little to prepare the visitors for the squalor of Prevesa, a straggling settlement of miserable dwellings and filthy alleyways. They arrived in a downpour, causing Hobhouse to note mournfully that "few places will bear being visited on a rainy day, least of all a Turk town. . . . Never afterwards, during our whole journey, did we feel so disheartened, and inclined to turn back, as at this instant."[18] Their first night, spent at "Consul Signior Commiate's" house, required the sodden travelers to deal with the challenge of Turkish plumbing.

"The Privy at the consul's," Hobhouse noted, was of a "peculiar construction." Located in a chamber off the sitting room and reached by a flight of steps, it provided, in place of a toilet seat, a board reach-

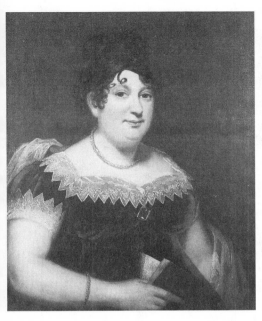

Catherine Byron, the poet's mother, had neither beauty, grace, nor charm, but she brought a considerable fortune to the marriage for her wastrel husband to spend.

64 Broad Street, Aberdeen (second building from right), where Byron, his mother, and his nursemaid, Agnes Gray, lived from 1791 to 1798 in rooms above the perfumer's shop on the ground floor.

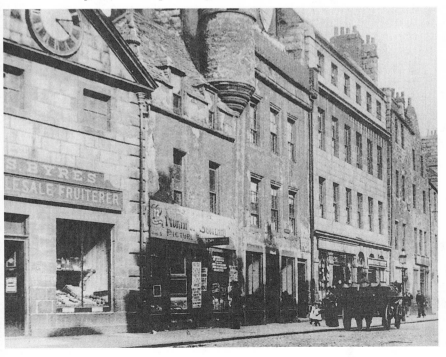

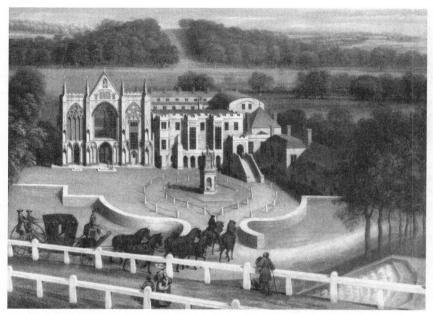

Newstead Abbey, Nottinghamshire, the seat of the Byron family from the time of Henry VIII until its sale by the poet in 1817.

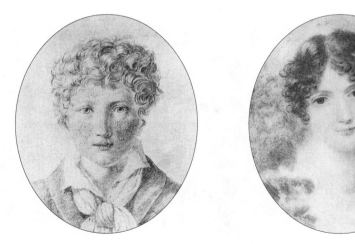

LEFT: Byron at Harrow, looking much younger than the twelve-year-old who entered the school in April 1801. By the time he left three years later, Byron was a star to his fellow students and a feared troublemaker to those in authority.

RIGHT: Mary Ann Chaworth, three years older than Byron, was his first great but unrequited love. Heiress to Annesley Hall, the property adjoining Newstead Abbey, the pretty young woman treated the overweight sixteen-year-old like a younger brother. Unhappily married to a local rake, Mary Ann tried without success to rekindle Byron's early feelings for her.

This portrait miniature of Byron, attributed to Prepiani and painted in Venice in 1819, was entrusted by him to Polidori to be delivered to John Murray, with instructions for the publisher to have it set as a locket for his half sister, Augusta. On the reverse of the 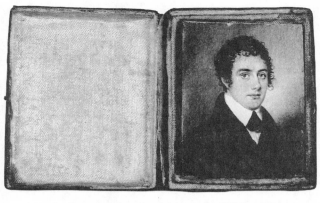 portrait is an inscription written in Augusta's hand, which reads: "This miniature of my 'poor' brother was the best taken and given to me on my birthday."

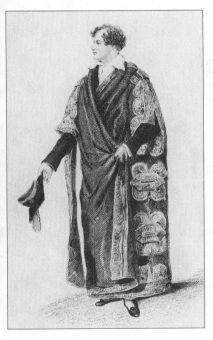

Although Byron commissioned this portrait of himself in academic gown at Cambridge, he does not wear the traditional nobleman's hat by which aristocrats distinguished themselves from commoners, but instead is shown democratically holding a mortarboard.

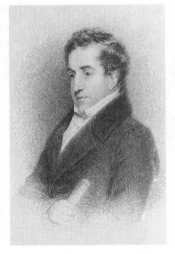

John Cam Hobhouse was Byron's loyal friend, traveling companion, and defender from their Cambridge days. He stood by the poet in the dark days of his marriage, separation, and flight from England. The poet dedicated Canto IV of *Childe Harold's Pilgrimage* to Hobhouse, "a friend often tried and never found wanting."

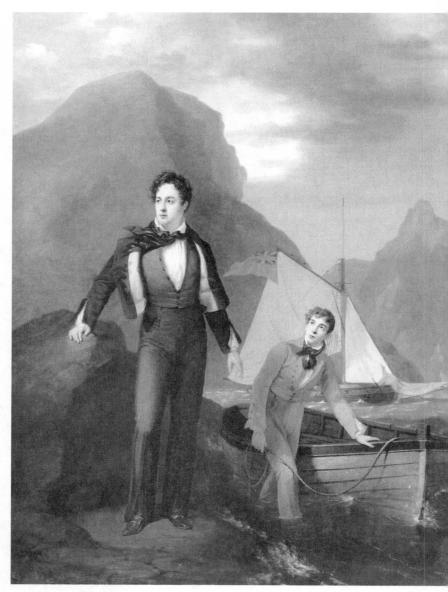

In this portrait by George Sanders, begun in 1807, Byron is depicted with his page, Robert Rushton. According to Caroline Lamb, Byron confessed that Rushton was one of the boys he had seduced as a young man. Along with its possible sexual iconography, the painting seems to predict Byron's literary identity as the Romantic wanderer of *Childe Harold's Pilgrimage* and other poems.

The original of this much-copied portrait by Thomas Phillips of Byron in Albanian dress hangs in the British Embassy in Athens. The poet bought the "very magnifique" costume on his trip to Greece in 1809.

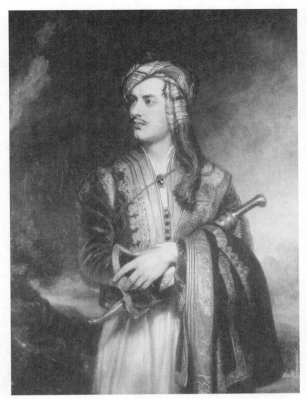

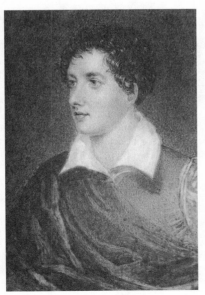

This miniature by James Holmes was commissioned for Scrope Davies. When the poet wrote to Holmes to order a print for Augusta, he said: "I prefer that likeness to any which has been done of me by any artist whatever."

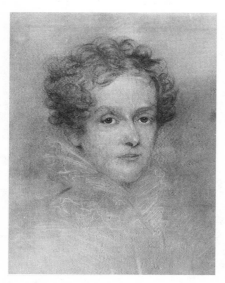

A portrait by Sir Thomas Lawrence of Byron's most famous lover, Lady Caroline Ponsonby, who became Lady Caroline Lamb, wife of the second Viscount Melbourne.

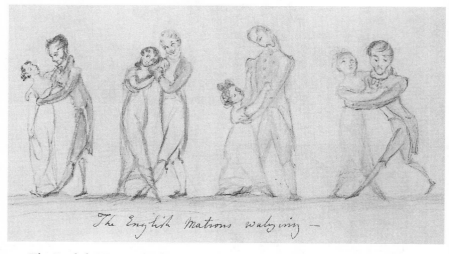

The English Matrons Walzing [sic], by Lady Caroline Lamb, from drawings found in her private notebooks. Her brilliance and talent—in conversation, writing, and personal style—were much admired by her contemporaries.

OPPOSITE BOTTOM: In this strange, visionary drawing, Augustus hovers above his parents as they lie together in bed. Caroline's fearful expression and firm grip on the child seem to prefigure Augustus's early death in his twenties.

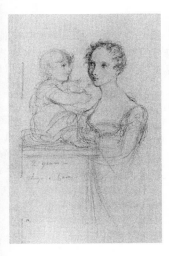

Caroline Lamb with her son Augustus, age two. The only child of Caroline and William Lamb to survive infancy, Augustus was mildly retarded and suffered from physical disabilities that worsened with time. The composition underlines the tenderness that Caroline would always feel toward her son.

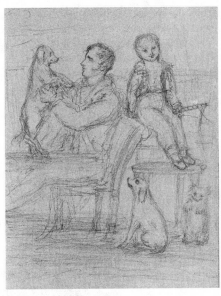

In contrast to Caroline's self-portrait with Augustus, William Lamb is shown here playing with his dogs but apparently ignoring his son.

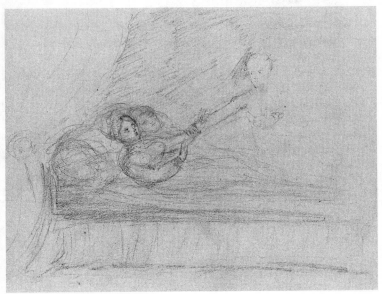

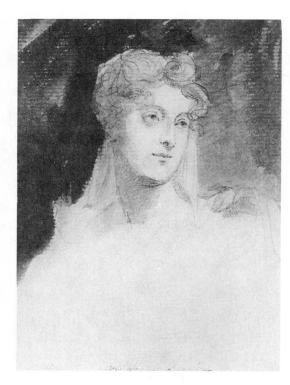

This portrait of Augusta Leigh by Sir George Hayter is the only authenticated likeness to survive of Byron's half sister and lover, for whom his "perverse passion" threatened to bring ruin to them both. The artist has captured her languid sensuality, recalled by the poet in his description of Dudú the slave girl in *Don Juan*—"A kind of sleepy Venus," whose body suggests "a soft Landscape of mild Earth."

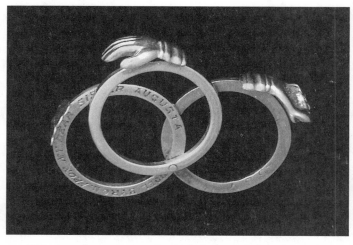

This ingenious three-part gimbal ring, designed on the swivel principle of a sextant, is a marvel of concealment. Closed, the clasped hands are a traditional friendship ring; opened, the hidden inner ring reveals two hearts, along with the engraved inscription: *Noel Byron from My Dear Sister Augusta.*

ing from one side of the room to the other, placed over a triangular opening in the wooden floor . . . into which the discharge falls with no unpleasant noise," Hobhouse noted precisely. However, "if you be not precisely instructed you may not be aware how to take advantage of the said bench but do as my friend Ld B did, i.e. sit down on the margin of the triangle itself with your knees to your nose in a most distressing position."[19] Hobhouse did not connect his friend's avoidance of the benchboard with his lame foot.

Their introduction to Albania left the travelers in such low spirits that even the morning's bright skies did little to cheer them. The best they could manage was "to feel more resigned to our misery," Hobhouse recalled.[20] They now moved into their own primitive house provided for them on Ali Pasha's orders and called on the governor, who lived in a new military compound near the harbor, recently built by the vizier. Expecting a splendid setting worthy of a leader whom many deemed more powerful than any sultan, they were shocked to be shown into a barracklike room "naked" of furniture. The governor himself was as unkempt as his boisterous Albanian guards, who guffawed throughout the interview. But they were hospitably received with the traditional tiny cups of syrupy coffee followed by long-stemmed pipes.

As a measure of Britain's current "favored nation" status, Prevesa boasted two English vice-consuls, one of whom was assigned to Lord Byron and his companion—a provision certainly related to "Milord's" title. The ex-robber Ali Pasha was highly sensitive to rank; he himself was addressed as "Most High, Most Powerful, and Most Illustrious Prince" by the English ambassador to Constantinople. Other official titles were simply misleading. The "English Vice Consul" was an Italian-speaking Greek who neither spoke nor read English. He prided himself, nonetheless, on his knowledge of the British character, including the crucial importance of breakfast. When Byron and Hobhouse asked to visit the ruins of Nicopolis, requesting an early-morning departure for the day's excursion, their host smiled knowingly and promised that whatever time they chose to set out would be *dopo la collazione*," after breakfast.

Nicopolis, the "city of victory," had been built by Emperor Augustus to celebrate his triumph over Antony and Cleopatra in the naval battle of Actium. The site was less than an hour's easy ride across plains and through olive groves. The ruins themselves offered ample reflection on transient monuments to pride: Stretching across the isthmus separating the Ionian Sea from the Ambracian Gulf, Augustus's city was now scarcely more than rubble.

Byron's recent experiences in Spain were still vivid in his mind; he had seen the sufferings imposed by imperial ambition and he now applauded time's leveling of despotic display:

> Look where the second Caesar's trophies rose!
> Now, like the hands that reared them, withering:
> Imperial Anarchs, doubling human woes!
>   GOD! was thy globe ordained for such to win and lose?[21]

Beyond the moral lesson they proposed, the ruins also stirred the romantic sensibilities of both young men, formed as much by "Gothick" taste as by classical education. Even Hobhouse forgot to be the serious antiquarian and waxed lyrical at the "melancholy grandeur" of this vast, once-populous site, its "sole tenant" a solitary shepherd, while the "bleating of the sheep, the tinkling of their bells, and the croaking of the frogs were the only sounds to be heard."[22]

They returned to Prevesa just long enough to make the necessary arrangments for the arduous trek inland, over the mountains to Jannina. Byron had hired a Greek named George to serve as dragoman for their journey through Albania. Arguably the most essential requirement for any foreign traveler to these parts, the dragoman functioned as translator and travel agent; he arranged for food, lodgings, and horses and had responsibility for paying the local providers. He was expected to impress the Turks with the dignity of his employers, while exploiting the Greeks to their advantage. George's servile behavior toward all Turks revealed to Byron that a subjugated people would inevitably behave like slaves. This would become the source of painful conflict in his championship of the Greek cause. Though sympathetic to the humiliations of the conquered, he was repelled by the symptoms of their abject state: the "cringing submissive tone," the constant lies and thievery.[23] Indeed, George was most skillful in the exercise of his profession's principal perk: robbing his employers blind. But he was also bustling, cheerful, and, in the main, efficient. In his present service, one of his duties would have daunted any lesser man: seeing to the luggage and its transportation. Together, Byron, Hobhouse, and Fletcher, the only remaining English servant, traveled with four large leather trunks weighing each about eighty pounds when full, three smaller trunks, a canteen, three beds with bedding, and two light wooden bedsteads.[24] All of these were ultimately destined to be carried on horses and required special sacks, each large enough to hold a bed, a large trunk, and one or two smaller articles. As the travelers had arrived in Albania at the start of the rainy season, they were relieved to find sacks that came in three layers—of waxed canvas, horsehair, and leather—which, combined, kept the contents dry. With the addition of four English saddles and bridles, all the baggage was now loaded into a large boat in Prevesa, to be taken along with its owners down the gulf to Salora. They arrived in Salora, consisting of one house, the Albanian troops' barracks, and a pier, to find that only four horses were available; they needed ten, and would have to spend one night at the very least awaiting reinforcements.

Byron would have reason to be glad for the delay. The two nights he spent in the barracks of Salora provided him with his first direct experience of ordinary Albanian life. (Its domestic side would remain firmly closed, since wives and daughters were shielded from the outsider's gaze.) The Albanian mountain men were like the Highlanders of his boyhood memory. Their commander, Captain Elmas, was no cleaner than his guards, but they were warm hosts. Out came the inevitable tiny cups of coffee and the pipes, after which the guests were installed in one of the barracks' empty rooms and left to a private dinner of fish, bread, and wine, along with an invitation to join the captain later in his apartment.

Always fascinated by natural authority, Byron was impressed with the way Captain Elmas could be open and familiar with his men while retaining complete control over them. Both his guests were intrigued by the curious strutting walk of the captain and his troops: chests thrust out, heads thrown back, they advanced while swaying slowly from side to side. The captain's strut was even more exaggerated than his men's, causing the poet to marvel at "the magisterial and superlatively dignified air of a man with great holes in his elbows, and looking altogether, as to his garments, like what we call a bull-beggar."[25] By the second evening, the two visitors had become part of barracks life; they sat cross-legged on the floor with their hosts, eating grapes, smoking, and, with the aid of an interpreter, joking and satisfying their curiosity about one another. The Albanian soldiers were enamored of the visitors' gold watch chains, while the captain cast covetous eyes on Byron's superb Manton gun, intended as an offering to the vizier. Lusty singing ended the evening. Sung in both Albanian and Romaic (modern Greek), songs were begun by a lead singer who chanted a recitative in a nasal monotone. The entire group then joined in for the chorus, of which the last note was held as long as breath allowed. The songs celebrated the courage and daring of the Albanians, including their more spectacular feats of rape, robbery, and kidnapping. Hobhouse noted that "there was scarcely one of them in which the name of Ali Pasha was not roared out with peculiar energy."[26] Byron later included in *Childe Harold* his own

free translation of an Albanian love song whose first words—
"Tambourgi! Tambourgi!"—conveyed something of the "wild howl"*
of the original, along with the traditional tribute to their leader: "I talk
not of mercy, I talk not of fear; / He neither must know who would
serve the Vizier."27

Byron later radically revised one of his original verses, in which the
trophies of conquest had included both girls and boys. In an early version of the stanza the singer boasts:

> I ask not the pleasures that riches supply,
> My sabre shall win what the feeble must buy;
> Shall win the young minions with long flowing hair
> And many a maid from her mother shall tear.

The poet changed "minions" to read "bride."28

Nights of easy, all-male companionship were the times when Byron
would always feel happiest, because he felt most freely himself.
Inevitably, the high spirits, crude jokes, songs, and unself-conscious
camaraderie summoned memories of Harrow, Cambridge, and his companions in the sporting life. Acceptance by these rough mountaineer
soldiers flattered him more than invitations from duchesses. He was
aware, too, of the freedom to be enjoyed in a country where sexual relations between men, who might also be husbands and fathers, were neither criminal nor even especially remarkable. His Albanian hosts
claimed the right to take "maids" and "minions" as they desired. In a
long letter to his mother, Byron wrote that he had "never found soldiers
so tolerable";29 he would soon return to the Salora barracks for a longer
visit.

Setting out northward across marshy country, their caravan now
consisted of six horses with their riders: Hobhouse, Fletcher, George the
dragoman, Byron himself, and two Albanian soldiers they had hired in
Salora to serve as guards. The luggage was piled on four other horses.
They stopped for the night in Arta, a picturesque town in a loop of the
wide Arakhthos River. Before leaving the next day, they took on four
additional Albanian soldiers who were armed with sabers and long
guns; the mountains between Arta and Jannina were rife with bandits,

---

*Of Byron's rendition of an Albanian song, shouted over the elements during a
storm on Lake Geneva in the summer of 1816, Shelley noted: "It was a strange wild
howl that he gave forth, but such as, he declared, was an exact imitation of the
Albanian mode."

and they were taking no chances. There was a two-hour delay while George wrangled with the peasant owners of the horses, each objecting to the weight his beast was expected to carry. Then no rope could be found to secure such items as bedsteads to the horses' backs. It was noon before they left.

Climbing a narrow pass through the immense stony mountains that lie between Arta and Jannina, they were alarmed to hear the sound of musket shots. In seconds, a "gigantic fellow" who had fired the gun was joined by two even more ferocious-looking ruffians and a pack of large, howling dogs. Each of the men carried pistols and sported a large knife stuck in his belt. Their heads were covered and faces shadowed by the peaked hoods of their shaggy capotes. Leaning on their long guns, they stared fixedly at the Englishmen. This sinister group's members were not robbers, after all; they were shepherds, more alarmed by the strange sight of men on horseback carrying open umbrellas than the travelers had been by the descent of huge, hirsute brutes from the mountains.

That night, the rain still pouring down steadily, they stopped at a han, one of the hostels for traders that dotted even remote regions of the Ottoman Empire. At the han of St. Demetre, their party of seven found they were to share one room with four Albanian Turks and a priest—the only one of their fellow guests who did not sleep with a pistol by his head. The English travelers passed a restless night.

Rain continued into the next morning while they picked their way across another range of mountains followed by an endless plain. Then, as a gentle rise prepared them for still another climb, a gleam of sun broke through the clouds, illuminating the city of Jannina, curving along the shore of a crystalline lake. Hobhouse recalled the ecstatic vision of that moment: "The houses, domes and minarets, glittering through gardens of oranges and lemon trees, and from groves of cypress—the lake spreading its smooth expanse at the foot of the city—the mountains rising abruptly from the banks of the lake—all these burst at once upon us, and we wanted nothing to increase our delight, but the persuasion that we were in sight of the Acherusian lake, of Pindus and the Elysian Fields."[30]

As their caravan approached the city, the shimmering mirage yielded to gory reality. Swinging from a tree across from a butcher shop was a man's arm, still attached to the side that had been torn from his body. The remains of a prisoner who had been beheaded five days before, this piece hung from a bit of string tied around one of the corpse's fingers. "Lord B and myself a little sick,"[31] Hobhouse noted in his diary.

The vizier himself was not in the city; he had been called away, his secretary explained to the visitors, to wage *"une petite guerre"* against Ibrahim Pasha, near Ali's birthplace in the northern capital of Tepelene; he hoped to receive the distinguished travelers there soon. Meanwhile, Byron found the ruler's attention to be the more flattering in his absence: "He had heard that an Englishman of rank was in his dominions," Byron reported proudly to his mother, "& had left orders in Yanina with the Commandant to provide a house & supply me with every kind of necessary, *gratis,* & though I have been allowed to make presents to the slaves &c, I have not been permitted to pay for a single article of household consumption."[32] The latter gesture of hospitality was especially welcome as there had been no word—nor money—from Hanson since Byron's departure, and the poet's imploring letters went unanswered.

From their spacious quarters in the mansion of a Greek merchant, Nicolo Argyri, Byron and Hobhouse set out each day on horses provided by the vizier to explore Jannina and the surrounding country. Escorted by the English resident, Captain Leake, they admired the splendid city with its bustling main thoroughfare and elegant houses. The population, numbering nearly thirty thousand, was predominantly Greek, and their many schools supported the community's claim to overshadow Athens as a center of culture in the midst of barbarian ignorance. On meeting the local schoolmaster, Athanasius Psallida, a leading Greek scholar, Byron was shown the only library he was to see outside of Constantinople, while the purity of the language spoken by this cultivated man, and passed on to his students, persuaded him that "Joannina in Epirus is universally allowed . . . to be superior in the wealth, refinement, learning and dialect of its inhabitants."[33]

To the English visitors the doctor spoke Latin, in which tongue he confirmed that "pederasty which here was openly practised, was to be found more or less in every large body of men living without females, who, said he, with the utmost coolness," Hobhouse noted, decorously retaining the learned doctor's original phrase, " *'aut puerii aut mastupratione utuntur'* "—must either use boys or masturbate.

"The Dr himself looked a little rogueish," Hobhouse decided.[34] Visits to Ali Pasha's young grandsons—each in his separate palace—took the visitors a world away from the self-conscious culture of the Greek colony. Byron found ten-year-old Hussein Bey, son of Mouctar Pasha, the vizier's eldest; his cousin Mahmout, already a pasha at twelve; and the latter's seven-year-old brother "totally unlike our lads," with "painted complexions like rouged dowagers." Hobhouse carefully avoided all mention of the youths' cosmetically enhanced looks, but Byron could not resist dancing to the edge of a dangerous subject, describing the seductive boys to his mother as "the prettiest little animals I ever saw."[35]

The vizier was famously addicted to young boys; a visiting French military envoy observed of the ruler that "he is almost exclusively given up to Socratic pleasures, and for this purpose keeps up a seraglio of youths, from among whom he selects his confidants and even his principal officers." Veli Pasha, Ali's oldest son and Mahmout's father, "was still more notorious for these appetites,"[36] along with a reputation for cruelty far exceeding his parent's. It seems likely that the cousins' rouged faces alluded to a dynastic practice of pedophilia that began with the pashas' own sons.

Hussein Bey received his guests with great poise. Byron was attired in his splendid staff uniform, complete with a "very magnificent sabre," but his young host restrained a natural childish impulse to touch. Hobhouse did not behave with similar decorum; after admiring the Bey's watch, he reached for a silver box in the shape of a heart hanging from the boy's neck, at which point the lad drew away, saying, "No! No!" His bearded tutor then explained that this was a sacred amulet. Hobhouse's uncharacteristically free gesture was clearly in response to others' manner toward the princeling; he was "surprised to see one of the ill dress'd looking ruffians who attended the young Boy go up to him when he left his room & kiss him most tenderly," while the lad behaved in a way "peculiarly intimate with Sig Nicolo," their host.[37]

When his guests asked to see the rest of the palace, Hussein ordered all rooms cleared of women. Now, for the first time in Albania, Byron saw chambers sumptuously furnished with Turkish carpets, sofas upholstered in figured silks, and Venetian glass in all the windows. In one room they admired a recessed marble bath with a playing fountain. Hobhouse supposed this to be a bedchamber, and he was startled to learn from their grave young guide that all rooms were used "indiscriminately" for sleeping.

Twelve-year-old Mahmout was said to have inherited his grandfather's genius; he received in the vizier's palace, having already inherited a pashalik. This lad, the eldest, now invited them to meet his little brother, installed in a palace of his own. The seven-year-old was troubled by the youth of his English visitors: Wasn't Byron very young, he inquired of the poet "with all the gravity of three score, to be wandering about the world without any body to take care of me?" The Albanians had no notion, Byron explained to his mother, of traveling for pleasure.[38]

Invited to accompany the young nobles on a visit across the city, Byron and Hobhouse were awed by the combination of pomp and reverence attending their progress; a messenger preceded them through the streets, followed by officers of the various palaces waving wands and silver batons. Next came the English visitors, the adolescent pasha, his little brother and cousin, all astride horses caparisoned in gold. As the youthful bey passed, merchants emerged from their shops; those who were walking stood stock still. Then every subject paid homage to the royal heirs with the traditional reverence of bending bodies very low, touching the ground with their right hand, then bringing it up to their mouths and foreheads, "for the *adoration* of the great is, in its primitive and literal sense, still preserved among the Orientals," Hobhouse noted.[39] Byron was still more impressed by the dignity with which Mahmout, his favorite, received the obeisance of his subjects.

On horses provided by Ali Pasha, Byron and Hobhouse, attended by Fletcher and George, set off to enjoy the neighboring sights, beginning with the magnificent views of the city itself. From the hilly suburbs they had a sweeping panorama of the Pindus Mountains cradling the twelve-mile expanse of Lake Pamvotis, with its two woody islands. The larger was home to a village founded in the sixteenth century by refugees from the Peloponnese, along with five monasteries. (In one of these Ali Pasha, fleeing from the Turks, would die in 1822.)

Directly opposite the smaller island was a triangular promontory jutting out from the city; this was the moated fortress protecting Ali Pasha's palace. A Topkapi in miniature, the vizier's domain was a self-contained town boasting a splendid mosque, a harem said to house three hundred young girls, and stables and outbuildings for military and domestic use. On the outskirts of Jannina they were shown the ruler's summer residence, a one-story pavilion in the French style set in the midst of a wild, luxuriant garden. The feature that most impressed the visitors was a fountain placed in the center of the main octagonal hall; from its basin rose a marble model of a fortress mounted on small brass cannons that, at a signal, spouted forth jets of water, accompanied by an organ in a recess of the room playing popular Italian tunes.

Despite these diversions and marvels, Byron often seemed withdrawn. At thirty-two Captain Leake, the English resident, was close enough in age to the travelers to become a friend as well as adviser and guide. He observed that on a number of occasions Byron "turned aside from the contemplation of nearer objects and from the conversation of those about him to gaze with an air distrait and dreamy upon the distant mountains."[40]

Some of the talk around him contributed to his withdrawal. Hobhouse's reaction to their surroundings took the form of a litany of complaints: He hated the local wine, *retsina,* and was outraged to discover "there was no one who could mend an umbrella in the whole place."[41] Increasingly, Byron became irritated by these displays of English provincialism. The continuous laments of Fletcher about the food, cold, vermin and how much he missed England, Newstead, his wife, and his farm provoked much Byronic mockery. But the homesick valet was also a taunting reminder to Byron that he had no real home or loving family; he wrote to his mother, "I have no one to be remembered to in England, & wish to hear nothing from it, but that you are well."[42] Catherine Byron was far from well, but she did not choose to burden her son with news of her illness.

Before leaving Jannina, they made an excursion to a famous classical site in the vicinity. Near a village named Chercovista were the remains of Homer's "wintry Dodona," a vast complex that had boasted an oracle of Zeus, famed from earliest preclassical times, and one of the most splendid amphitheaters in the ancient world. When Byron and Hobhouse visited the ruins, however, the identity of the site was still problematic and the theater required an imaginative effort at reconstruction, being then a vast scattering of stones on a hauntingly beautiful hillside. "Oh! where, Dodona! is thine aged grove / Prophetic fount, and oracle divine?"[43] Byron later asked, but he was aware of the importance of what he had seen and, like most tourists, was excited by the thought of being among the "first" foreigners to have seen it.

Leaving Jannina on October 11, they headed over the mountains toward Tepelene and the first meeting with their mysterious host, Ali Pasha:

> He pass'd bleak Pindus, Acherusia's lake,
> And left the primal city of the land,
> And onwards did his further journey take
> To greet Albania's chief, whose dread command
> Is lawless law; for with a bloody hand
> He sways a nation, turbulent and bold.[44]

The first stage of the trip proved a turbulent prelude indeed to their audience with the vizier. Just as night fell in the mountains near Zitza, the heavens opened. In the darkness, made darker by torrential rains, the group was separated. Byron, with George the Greek dragoman, a priest, and the querulous Fletcher, fell behind, while the prudent Hobhouse rushed ahead with the others to reach the village. The "lost" party had much to contend with besides the weather. A pair of their horses stumbled and fell; two of the guides, terrified, ran off, while George, powerless to stop them, "stamped swore cried and fired off his pistols, which manoeuvre being performed without due notice alarmed the 'valet' into fears of his life from robbers . . . the whole situation becoming so serious that Ld B laughed,"[45] Hobhouse was later to recount. But nine hours later, with no sign of his friend, Hobhouse was not laughing. In a state of near panic, he ordered flares lit and guns fired to point the lost travelers in the direction of town. In the meantime, Byron and his group were waiting out the storm patiently—only an hour's ride away. In the shelter of some Turkish tombstones, by the banks of a stream swollen by torrents and illuminated by flashes of lightning, the poet, under his thick, woolen capote, was dry enough to compose a poem of eighteen stanzas."* The savagery of nature and the terrors just survived are the preludes to a love poem: "One thought has still the power / To keep my bosom warm," the image of "Sweet Florence."[46]

The alluring adventuress was a universe away from the Albanian women, who, Byron observed, and not altogether disapprovingly, "are treated like slaves, *beaten* & in short complete beasts of burden, they plough, dig & sow, I found them carrying wood & actually repairing the highways." While the men occupied themselves solely with killing— making war and hunting—"the women are the labourers, which after all is no great hardship in so delightful a climate," he noted airily, for- getting the less than delightful climate he had just experienced.[47] Look- ing more closely at these happy Amazons, Hobhouse observed women carrying water long distances from fountains to villages "looking very faint under the weight of their large pitchers, one of which they carry on the head, the other in the hand."[48]

The hardships of women as beasts of burden would have been most visible in their day's stopover at Zitza, a tiny hillside village "clinging to its rocky summit like a mountain goat," Byron noted, adding, to his mother, that "always excepting Cintra in Portugal," Zitza was "the most beautiful Situation . . . I ever beheld."[49] Here they stopped to dry out, refit luggage and animals, and recover from the "fatigues and disas- ters of the night."[50] Byron was so captivated by this enchanted aerie that he decided then to include a stay in the white-walled Greek monastery just above the village on his return south.

Leaving Zitza on October 13, they struggled north through the

---

*The full title of the poem is "Stanzas Composed October 11th 1809, During the Night; In a Thunderstorm, When the Guides Had Lost the Road to Zitza, Near the Range of Mountains Formerly Called Pindus, in Albania." The subtitle is one of the longest in the history of poetry.

mountains toward Tepelene, impeded by more torrential rains and roads washed out by earlier storms. Accommodations, too, became rougher; shelter no longer meant sharing a han with other wayfarers, but of evicting the animals from sty or stable.

Byron delighted in roughing it. His, however, was not the romantic encounter with nature uncontaminated by fallen humanity, but the keen, competitive edge of a young man testing his mettle and coming out ahead—of his less fit, less adventurous companions. Unlike Hobhouse, who never stopped complaining "of hard beds and sharp insects,"[51] or Fletcher, with his "perpetual lamentations after beef and beer,"[52] Byron had no quarrel with their unvarying diet of eggs, fowl, and grapes, priding himself that he "could sleep where none but a *brute* could, and certainly where *brutes did* for often have the *Cows* turned out of their apartment *butted* at the door all night extremely disappointed with their unaccountable ejectment."[53] Troubled by sexual ambivalence, by evidence of the feminine in his character, Byron's triumph over nature served to confirm his manhood.

FINALLY, on October 19, just as the sun was setting, Byron looked across the steep banks of the Vijosë River and "saw, like meteors in the sky / The glittering minarets of Tepalen."[54] The sights and sounds in the courtyard within the fortress walls that rose straight from the riverbanks excited his poetic imagination but also his memories of boyhood reading; Walter Scott's descriptions of feudal border castles in his *Lays* came to his mind, suggested also by the change in the native garb. Instead of the loose, dun-colored woolen garments worn by the Greek population in the south, Byron was now dazzled by a scene of Oriental splendor. Writing to his mother, he summoned the "new and delightful spectacle" that burst upon him as he rode through the gateway in the grim fortress walls: "The Albanians in their dresses (the most magnificent in the world, consisting of a long *white kilt*, gold worked cloak, crimson velvet gold laced jacket & waistcoat, silver mounted pistols & daggers), the Tartars with their high caps, the Turks in their vast pelises & turbans, the soldiers & black slaves with the horses, the former stretched in groups in an immense open gallery in front of the palace, the latter placed in a kind of cloister below it, two hundred steeds ready caparisoned to move in a moment, couriers entering or passing out with dispatches, the kettle drums beating, boys calling the hour from the minaret of the mosque, altogether, with the singular appearance of the building itself."[55]

In rapid-fire journalistic prose, Byron conveys the sights, sounds, and movement of the brilliant scene; within weeks he would shape these jottings into poetry. His fidelity to the material of his impressions allows us to watch the process of this transformation:

> The wild Albanian kirtled to his knee,
>> With shawl-girt head and ornamented gun,
>> And gold-embroider'd garments, fair to see;
>> The crimson-scarfed men of Macedon;
>> The Delhi with his cap of terror on,
>> And crooked glaive—the lively supple Greek
>> And swarthy Nubia's mutilated son;
>> The bearded Turk that rarely deigns to speak,
> Master of all around, too potent to be meek.[56]

One presence is notably missing from the "motley scene": "Here woman's voice is never heard," as "Tam'd to her cage" she remains invisible, limited to procreation and nurture. "Blest cares!" Byron calls her role, exalting the division of the maternal and sexual: "Herself more sweetly rears the babe she bears, / Who never quits the breast, no meaner passion shares."[57] With the Muslim madonnas out of the way, Byron was daringly frank about their replacements as objects of the "meaner passion":

> For boyish minions of unhallowed love
> The shameless torch of wild desire is lit,
> Caressed, preferred even to woman's self above.*[58]

That night their sleep was sporadic, interrupted by constant carousal in the long open gallery outside their apartment ("like an English inn," Hobhouse described their quarters). When they managed to drop off despite the racket, they were startled into wakefulness, like present-day visitors to Muslim lands, by the piercing wail of the muezzin calling the faithful to prayer.

Happily, their long-awaited audience with Ali Pasha didn't take place until noon. Shortly before the hour, the vizier's secretary arrived; their escort wore his shabbiest cloak, lest he appear too rich and a fit subject for extortion, he confided to the visitors—an insight into their host that might well have given pause. But whatever trepidations they may have

---

*Byron had second thoughts and canceled this verse before *Childe Harold's Pilgrimage* was published in 1812.

felt evaporated with their first sight of the vizier. It was almost impossible to connect the terrifying tales of rape and mass murder with the genial, roly-poly sixty-two-year-old with round blue eyes and a long, curling white beard who now greeted them. Always vulnerable to flattery, Byron was instantly won over by the vizier's posture as he entered the marble-paved room: "He received me *standing*," he told his mother, "a wonderful compliment from a Mussulman, & made me sit down on his right hand." Captain Leake had smoothed the way for his young countryman, alerting the ruler that Byron was "of a great family." The vizier then "desired his respects to my mother, which I now in the name of Ali Pacha present to you," Byron wrote to Catherine proudly. The poet's good looks confirmed his vaunted pedigree: "He said he was certain I was a man of birth because I had small ears, curling hair, & little white hands, and expressed himself pleased with my appearance & garb. I was dressed in a full suit of Staff uniform with a very magnificent sabre & He told me to consider him as a father whilst I was in Turkey, & said he looked on me as his son—Indeed he treated me like a child, sending me almonds & sugared sherbet, fruit & sweetmeats 20 times a day.—He begged me to visit him often, and at night when he was more at leisure."[59] Byron accepted the pasha's invitation, visiting him three times during his stay, but he does not give the hour or any details of their meetings.[60]

Given his preference for very young boys and girls, it may be that Ali Pasha's seduction always began with the treats craved by children. A shrewd judge of human nature, the vizier would also have sensed that the fatherless Byron was vulnerable to the attentions of a doting sugar daddy. For his part, Byron was always fascinated by duality—in himself and others—and he kept returning, in letters and, later, in verse to the contrast between Ali Pasha the warm father figure with twinkling blue eyes and white beard, and Ali the bloodthirsty despot: "He has the appearance of anything but his real character," Byron wrote his mother, "for he is a remorseless tyrant, guilty of the most horrible cruelties."[61]

Like Napoleon, it was Ali as a superman, placing himself above all natural and human law, that excited Byron's "fascination of the abomination," in Joseph Conrad's phrase, along with a lingering envy. Unburdened by Christian conscience and possessing absolute power, Ali indulged every excess without shame or guilt. No vice, however, had left its imprint on him. Certain that his own lameness was the mark of Cain, Byron was obsessed with the pasha's appearance; far from acquiring the face he deserved, the despot's had remained innnocent of sin or sorrow:

ALI reclin'd, a man of war and woes;
Yet in his lineaments ye cannot trace,
While Gentleness her milder radiance throws
Along that venerable aged face,
The deeds that lurk beneath, and stain him with disgrace.[62]

As a parting gift, Ali allowed Byron to keep with him the Albanian soldier named Vassily he had provided during his visit. But this legacy, too, was a reminder of the pasha's darkest self. Of all his bloody acts, none was as infamous as the vizier's murder of Phrosyne, a beautiful seventeen-year-old girl, along with all of her friends. In one of several versions of the tale, which Byron had heard "in many a Romaic and Arnout ditty," Ali's daughter-in-law, Mouctar's wife, had complained to the ruler of her husband's straying affections, naming the lovely young woman as the cause. Although Phrosyne was guiltless, Ali ordered her, along with sixteen of her companions, to be sewn into sacks and thrown from the fortress walls into the lake below. Vassily, Byron's new servant, was one of the soldiers who had executed the murders.

Their return to Jannina, in good weather, took four days—half the time of the tortuous trip to Tepelene. On the way back they spent the night with the monks in the monastery at Zitza. In deference to his distinguished guests, the abbot assured them that the excellent wine they now enjoyed had been pressed by hand, not by the bare feet of local peasants. Now, looking out from the white-walled cloister, Byron celebrated, with pantheistic fervor, the glory of nature:

Monastic Zitza! from thy shady brow,
Thou small, but favoured spot of holy ground!
Where'er we gaze, around, above, below,
What rainbow tints, what magic charms are found!
Rock, river, forest, mountain all abound,
And bluest skies that harmonize the whole.[63]

Arriving in Jannina on October 26, they returned to their quarters in Nicolo Argyri's house. Their host had become enamored of Fletcher, Byron's valet, and tried to kiss him, Hobhouse noted. But his disapproval of this impulsive gesture points more to the Englishman's feelings about class and decorum than to worry about homosexuality. After almost two months in Albania, Hobhouse took pederasty for granted, but the public embrace of a servant was quite another matter. Fletcher left no record of his reaction to Eastern sexual mores, but he renewed his war against local vermin: "He has been lousing all day with great success especially in my lord's shirt," Hobhouse reported.[64]

During their last week in the city, they sailed on the lake, visited the bazaar, and watched a Greek wedding wind through the streets. Under her high cap studded with gold coins, the bride's face was covered thickly with red and white paint, reminding Hobhouse of the wax effigy of Elizabeth I in Westminster Abbey. They also attended a puppet show, one of the most popular entertainments of Ramadan. Performed in a corner of a dirty coffeehouse by an itinerant Jewish puppeteer, the story played by shadow puppets, cutouts made of greased paper, featured a hero possessing an enormous penis supported by a piece of string hung from his neck. The action that most delighted the young male audience was the finale, when the protagonist "held a solil[o]quy addressed to the appendage alluded to, which he snubbed most soundly with his fist . . . a prelude to the devil descending & removing this engine from before & affixing it to his posterior." Hobhouse was duly horrified: "Nothing could be more beastly," he confided to his diary, along with a detailed description of each obscene gesture. Byron, however, assured his friend that he had seen puppet shows in England just as bad, and "worse" performances by the morris dancers of Nottinghamshire.[65]

During their last week in Jannina, Byron sent the splendid Manton rifle to Ali Pasha and bought for himself two "very 'magnifique' Albanian dresses the only expensive articles in this country they cost 50 guineas each & have so much gold they would cost in England two hundred," he wrote to his mother.[66] Of all his fancy dress uniforms, Byron took special delight in this costume; thus turbaned and brocaded, he sat for his famous portrait by the painter Thomas Phillips. While he was wearing the gorgeous robes, questions of gender were blurred. In his fantasy Byron now became what he beheld: an Oriental potentate, powerful and free, to whom nothing was forbidden.

SINCE LEAVING England, Byron had written few letters. Usually a pleasurable outpouring of what was most immediately on his mind, correspondence was now an irksome chore. "Indeed the farther I go the more my laziness increases, and my aversion to letter writing becomes more confirmed," he wrote to his mother, who was the only recipient of her son's occasional long communiqués. As for the expected record of their grand tour, he left that to the methodical Hobhouse, who "scribbles incessantly."

"I keep no journal," he told Catherine.[67]

In fact, Byron did keep a journal, "a very exact journal of every circumstance of his life, and many of his thoughts while young," he later
told a friend. While they were traveling in Albania, he had shown the
journal to Hobhouse, who, disturbed by what he read, begged Byron to
burn the manuscript. After much pleading, he agreed. But in a strange
foreshadowing of a later memoir burning, it seems to have been
Hobhouse who "destroyed the manuscript" after all.[68] It would not be
unlike Byron to recognize the risk of having his intimate journal seen by
others, while knowing himself unequal to the task of reducing to ashes
the only record of his early life.

Five days after their return to Jannina, between the time Hobhouse
would have read the journal and received his friend's permission to burn
it, he reported that Byron was "engaged in writing a long poem in the
Spenserian stanza."[69]

Childe Harold's Pilgrimage, the new poem, replaces, in both real and
symbolic senses, the "missing" journal. There is a sense of momentous-
ness in the way Byron records its precise dates of composition. On the
cover of Cantos I and II, composed largely while he was in the East, are
these words: *Byron—Joannina in Albania Begun Oct. 31, 1809 Concluded Canto 2nd March 28, 1810. Byron*. The suggestion of a dateline
is telling. The first cantos of *Childe Harold* introduce the twenty-
two-year-old poet as engaged reporter, recording all he observes and
experiences—battles, bullfights, love affairs—as they happen.

"A fictitious character," Byron calls Harold, "introduced for the
sake of giving some connection to the piece," which, indeed, consists of
a series of disconnected incidents roughly following the poet's itinerary
through Portugal, Spain, and the Levant. And again, in the same preface, "Harold is the child of imagination," he says.[70] Of course, he insists
too much. And he knows that we know. But playing hide-and-seek with
his creator's autobiography is only one of Childe Harold's functions. A
Byronic double, Harold is also the author's Frankenstein monster,
allowing him to externalize cynicism, coldheartedness, moral paralysis,
and, finally, the sin of despair. This particular pilgrim's progress is not
from darkness to light, but from one confusing encounter to another
with history in all its squalor and grandeur: the bloodshed and waste of
the Peninsular War, along with its excitement and heroism; the butchery
of the bullfight with its mesmerizing catharsis of ritual and ceremony;
Ali Pasha and his court, a feast of the senses sustained by mass slaughter, rape, and robbery; the tragedy of Greece, trampled by Turks,
despoiled by Britons, and inhabited by thieving, sniveling Greeks, who
deserved to be slaves.

Harold himself is no innocent: "Childe," an archaic title denoting the scion of a noble house, takes irony as its premise—and promise. A youth still, he has vices that further darkened a tainted heritage: "Few earthly things found favour in his sight / Save concubines and carnal companie." Now he suffers from the libertine's ultimate punishment:

> Worse than adversity the Childe befell;
> He felt the fulness of satiety;
> Then loath'd he in his native land to dwell,
> Which seem'd to him more lone than Eremite's sad cell.[71]

Following his jaunty mock-epic opening, Byron's canvas darkens. Like the poet himself, the dissipated young noble will be wrenched from his immoral complacency. The rake's progress turns into a painful voyage of self-discovery on the "downward path to wisdom."

This is the drama that draws us into the poem, not its wealth of "colorful" incident and exotic settings. A cipher himself, Harold, like his alter ego, the poet-narrator, is the antihero of an existential serial; what moral sense will he make (if any) of the barrage of contradictory impressions and of his own shifting reaction to tyrants and peasants, heroes and cowards, femmes (and hommes) fatales? How will our uncandid Candide play the hand he is dealt? A faceless wanderer when first we meet him, spiced up with a past of commonplace sins, Harold will gradually acheve tragic stature by becoming—God help him—an intellectual! Victim, now and forever, of "Consciousness, awaking to her woes," there will be no escape possible for him ever again.

Byron had been away from England for nearly six months—months overflowing with high adventure, danger, and undreamed-of sexual freedom. Yet he was still a prisoner "dragging on his chain":

> What Exile from himself can flee?
> To Zones, though more and more remote,
> Still, still pursues, where-e'er I be,
> The blight of life—the demon, Thought.[72]

CHAPTER 13

Civilization and Its Discontents

*I*T WAS A sizable troupe—Byron, Hobhouse, Fletcher, George the Greek dragoman, and Vassily the Albanian officer, along with baggage and horses—that now made its way back toward Arta and the coast. After a raucous reunion with their friends in the barracks of Salora they hired a galley to row them down the Ambracian Gulf to Prevesa.

Once on the water, Hobhouse and Byron realized, with astonishment, the diminutive scale of the location of the most famous sea battle of antiquity. Each used the identical phrase to express his surprise: "Today I saw the remains of the town of *Actium*, near which Anthony lost the world in a small bay where two frigates could hardly manouvre [*sic*]," Byron wrote to his mother,[1] and Hobhouse noted in his journal that the gulf was "not big enough for the manoeuvres of two of our modern frigates."[2] Byron was so pleased with his own phrase describing the scene where "Anthony lost the world," that he used it again—twice—in one poem: "Stanzas Written in Passing the Ambracian Gulph" celebrates the site where "For Egypt's Queen / the Ancient World was won and lost," and summons memories of his own "Sweet Florence":

> Though Fate forbids such things to be,
> Yet, by thine eyes and ringlets curl'd!
> I cannot lose a world for thee,
> But would not lose thee for a world![3]

As Byron's verse makes all too clear, however, the poet and his mistress are not Antony and Cleopatra; passion has dwindled into persiflage.

South of Arta, in Acarnania, warring tribes were murdering each other, and Byron's thoughts of traveling overland to the Gulf of Lepanto were deemed ill-advised. As it turned out, Ali Pasha's solicitude toward his handsome visitor extended to the outermost borders of his territory: On orders from the vizier himself, the governor of Prevesa prepared an armed galliot for their trip to Patras. She came with a crew of forty, of whom four were Greek. On weighing anchor, it was alarmingly apparent that the Turkish majority were no navigators; they ran aground while trying to clear the harbor and, with freshening winds, had still greater difficulties trying to round Cape Doukato. As the ship rolled violently, the crew's terror exceeded the passengers' fears. Santa Maura (the Italian name for Leukas) had been annexed by Napoleon, and the Turks, in dread of being taken prisoner, now fled below. Byron gleefully recalled his own calm amid the pandemonium: "Fletcher yelled after his wife, the Greeks called on all the Saints, the Mussulmen on Alla, the Captain burst into tears & ran below deck telling us to call on God, the sails were split, the main-yard shivered . . . & all our chance was to make Corfu which is in possession of the French, or (as Fletcher *pathetically* termed it) 'a *watery* grave.'—I did what I could to console Fletcher but finding him incorrigible wrapped myself up in my Albanian capote (an immense cloak) & lay down on deck to wait the worst, I have learnt to philosophize on my travels, & if I had not, complaint was useless."[4]

In a last-minute attempt to avert shipwreck, Byron and Hobhouse begged the captain to give up command of the ship to the Greeks; he would gladly give it up to anybody, was the reply. By rigging up two small staysails and taking down the yards, they managed to regain the Albanian mainland many miles north of Prevesa at about 1:00 a.m. The next morning the ship dropped anchor in the Bay of Phanari, where a group of Suliote tribesmen led the weary passengers to their village. The following day their host, the Albanian primate, would not allow them to leave without a guard of his own men to accompany them as far as Prevesa. When Byron tried offering him money for accommodating their large company, the chief refused: "I want you to love me, not to pay me," he said.[5]

Byron was deeply moved by the pride, generosity, and goodwill shown them by the fierce Suliotes, Greek Albanians who might have been expected to make quick work of the shipwrecked Turks and their foreign passengers. Simple, rugged tribesmen, hospitable to strangers, they became, in Byron's memory, an elite warrior class. He saw them as a strike force of freedom, helping to transform a country of greedy warlords and their followers into an independent nation. The Suliots only lacked a leader.

A fragment of manuscript preserved in the Beinecke Library at Yale contains a discarded version of stanza 73 of *Childe Harold*. Addressing "Fair Greece! Sad relic of departed worth / Immortal, though no more! though fallen, great!" the poet asks: "Who now shall call thy scatter'd children forth?"[6]

In this earliest version of the poem, the rhetorical question of who will lead the Greeks from bondage to freedom is repeated, with biblical variations, no fewer than five times. Five times, the answer—never published—was scrawled between the lines, in the poet's unmistakable hand: *Byron*. The manuscript fragment has been recently dated by the editor of Byron's complete poems to 1809. Thus, before he had seen Athens, the heart of Greece's glorious past, Byron had cast himself in the role of her future savior.

RETURNING to Prevesa, Byron had come full circle. His sympathy for the country and its people seemed reflected by the change of climate between their arrival and their departure. They had landed in Prevesa in a chill, steady rain; now, on November 12, it was warm enough for Byron to swim in the sea. Water was his element; wherever the sun shone and Byron could swim became, at that moment, home.

The wild, romantic region he had passed through encouraged heroic rehearsals of his future. Now, however, he had to confront an uncertain present. Trying to sound purposeful, he told his mother (in a long letter from Prevesa) that his immediate plan was to proceed to Athens, where he intended to "study modern Greek" and spend a year exploring the country before setting out for Asia.[7] On one subject, however, he was adamant: "I never will revisit England if I can avoid it," he wrote to Hanson; "It is no country for me.—Why I say this is best known to myself." Five lines later, he declared again, "I never will live in England if I can avoid it, *why* must remain a secret."[8] Like a mantra, he would repeat these two phrases.

His insistence on remaining abroad forced Byron to a change of heart on another issue. Earlier, he had been unequivocal that nothing would ever induce him to sell Newstead. Now, determined that he would never return to England, he realized that he would soon need a dependable income more than ancestral halls, and he told Hanson, "I have only one subject to write upon, which is the old one of remittances, if none have been already made I expect some to be forwarded immediately,— The sale of the copyholds & the remainder of the £6,000 must have furnished a tolerable floating sum, for my purpose, till the Lancashire business can be arranged and sold, & if that is insufficient much as I regret it, Newstead must follow the rest, & the produce be laid out either in mortgage or well secured annuities for my own life."

With his claim to the Rochdale collieries still dragging through the courts, Byron's need for cash collided with his chosen role of benevolent landlord: "I wish you would order the rents of Newstead to be raised, or at least regularly paid," he told Hanson. "However I don't wish to oppress the rascals, but 'I must live' as the saying is."[9]

ACCOMPANIED BY thirty-seven Albanian soldiers provided by the governor, they now traveled south on horseback and arrived without incident at the Gulf of Arta. Crossing at Vonitsa, they landed the following day at Utraikee, where Byron and his party spent their first night on Greek soil. Another small garrison and customs port, Utraikee had been attacked only five days earlier by a band of robbers who had murdered a Greek and a Turk. His luck in missing bloody encounters still held.

That night, Byron and Hobhouse joined the Albanian guards seated around roaring fires lit along the pebbly beach. With their hosts they ate roasted goat to the sound of water lapping on the sands. Then, when "the feast was done . . . the red wine circling fast . . . the native revels of the troop began:

> Each Palikar his sabre from him cast,
> And bounding hand in hand, man link'd to man,
> Yelling their uncouth dirge, long daunc'd the kirtled clan.[10]

The music, "half sang, half scream'd," the wine, the dancing, the heat—transformed the "uncouth" soldiers into Dionysian celebrants, divinely animal:

> . . . as the flames along their faces gleam'd,
> Their gestures nimble, dark eyes flashing free,
> The long wild locks that to their girdles stream'd.[11]

For Byron, the attraction of the "barbarous" dancers, whirling and screaming, was enhanced by the revelation of their criminality: To a man they were robbers only recently turned soldiers; the verses of their longest song, lasting more than an hour, detailed the acts of theft and murder executed by their band of sixty, with the refrain

> Robbers all at Parga!
> Robbers all at Parga![12]

Warriors, criminals, lovers of boys; pagans with more instinctive charity than professing Christians—Byron's experience of these men was a glimpse of life before the Fall, an Eden without hypocrisy, repression, and guilt. No Rousseau, nor even Shelley, he would never propose living outside society, and he had no real interest in reform; he wanted to break laws, not change them. His weeks in Albania allowed him to examine this conflict, whose drama became *Childe Harold*; from now on Byron would voice in his poetry and accept in himself that duality was destiny.

AFTER SIX more days on horseback through forests and uninhabited plains, they reached the coast, spending one night in Natolico, a village rising on stilts out of the water of a salt marsh stretching inland from the Bay of Lepanto. The town had to be approached in punts; water flowed through most of the wooden streets. A governor presided over this watery hamlet, but he proved indifferent to the visitors: The influence of Ali Pasha faded with the distance from Albania. The exhausted travelers were all the more grateful for the hospitality of a Jewish physician, who told them "he was honored of our partaking of his little misery," Hobhouse noted.[13] The phrase lingered in the visitors' minds.

The next day, November 20, Byron and his retinue proceded by land to "a town called Messalonge," as Hobhouse spelled it. Here Byron took care to dress in his splendid regimentals, causing the Greek gentleman who bore the imposing title "Vice Consul for the English Nation" to mistake him for Britain's ambassador. Even when proven wrong, he extended the courtesies of his house to the visitors for their stay of two days. A town of some five thousand Turks and Greeks, Missolonghi prospered from fish and its by-products: red mullet, *bourtarago* (a kind of roe sausage), and caviar were the local cash products. Scattered among the many small boats, rows of stakes extended from the shore for several miles into the deeper water, and wicker fishermen's huts stood on poles in the marshy bay. Especially on a sunny day, the approach to the town from the shallow blue-green water still suggests a miniature Venice rising from the lagoon.

Before leaving, Byron dismissed their military escort, giving each man a sequin; he kept one Turkish Albanian, Dervish Tasheere, to join the honest and devoted Vassily, George the dragoman, and the querulous Fletcher, reducing his personal suite to four attendants. Their company now numbered six as they boarded a small decked vessel, called a *terbaculo*, bound for Patras. Hobhouse was struck by the emotional farewell exchanged by Dervish and his fellow soldiers: "At parting with him, all his companions embraced him, and accompanying him to our boat, fired off their guns as a last salute to the whole party." A squall came up as they left the shallow waters; on this rainy afternoon, the huts on their spindly poles now appeared "wretched to us, the waves washing over them at every gust of wind."[14]

Patras was a welcome vision in the bright sunshine. Unfolding across a mountain slope down to the sea, the most prosperous town in southern Greece was "one blooming garden of orange and lemon plantations, of olive groves and vineyards." Now the two representatives of nations at war (who also happened to be first cousins), Samuel Strané, the Greek-born English consul, and Mr. Paul, the Austrian consul, outdid one another in providing entertainments for the visitors. Hobhouse hardly dared express—even to his diary—the joy he felt in seeing the simplest amenities of civilization: "After long disuse of tables and chairs, we were much pleased by these novelties."[15] For his part, Byron was always drawn to the concrete symbolism of Roman Catholic worship. He was fascinated by a local legend claiming that Patras was the site of the crucifixion of St. Andrew, and that the strange chasm running from top to bottom of the mountain opposite the city was said to have been created when the mountain was rent at the moment of the saint's martyrdom.

During the week and a half they spent in Patras, Byron dismissed George, their thieving dragoman, and hired in his place Andreas, a Greek who had lived in Constantinople and who spoke Turkish, French, Italian, and a bastard Latin learned as a choirboy in Rome. Vostitza was a two-day journey along a shore scented with orange and lemon, making up for the poor roads. Nearing their destination, Byron had his first thrilling sight of snowcapped Mount Parnassus, soaring above lesser peaks across the brilliant blue Bay of Corinth.

His excitement demanded immediate expression. In the middle of the first canto of *Childe Harold*, Byron interrupted his tribute to "Spain's dark-glancing daughters" to render homage to a place that he had until now known only from myth:

> Oh, thou Parnassus! whom I now survey,
> Not in the phrenzy of a dreamer's eye,
> Not in the fabled landscape of a lay,
> But soaring snow-clad through thy native sky,
> In the wild pomp of mountain majesty![16]

In his five stanzas celebrating Parnassus, Byron speaks of himself only to voice his sense of unworthiness: Compared to the immortal poets who once dwelled on her heights, he is the "humblest of thy pilgrims passing by":

> When I recount thy worshippers of yore
> I tremble, and can only bend the knee;
> Nor raise my voice, nor vainly dare to soar.[17]

But the lines to Parnassus reveal Byron's ambition to be crowned with the laurel wreath of poetic genius:

> Yield me one leaf of Daphne's deathless plant,
> Nor let thy votary's hope be deem'd an idle vaunt.[18]

SITUATED ON a small peninsula in the Gulf of Corinth, Vostitza proved unexpectedly diverting, and the travelers lingered for nine days. The region, including the town of several thousand inhabitants, was ruled by a Greek "coda-bashee," or elder, appointed by the Turks.

The son of Veli Pasha's chief minister, the "elder," Andreas Londos, was not yet twenty years old and less than five feet tall. His size and youth notwithstanding, it was immediately clear to the visitors that Signor Londos wielded great power. Observing the stream of "visitants, claimants, and complainants" seeking his favor, the Englishmen were impressed by "the singular spectacle of a Greek in authority—"a sight which we had never before seen in Turkey," Hobhouse noted.[19]

More astonishing, they discovered that Londos, Ali Pasha's young satrap, was also an ardent Greek patriot—the first Byron had encountered. Londos told the poet about his hero, Constantine Rhigas, the first martyr in the struggle for Greek independence. A poet and nationalist whose efforts to organize a revolution against the Turks twenty years earlier had led to his murder in Vienna in 1798, Rhigas's radical organization, the Hetaira, had been disbanded, but his heroic legacy had survived in the form of patriotic songs written in Romaic. One evening during their visit, Londos and the local doctor were playing chess when the name of Rhigas was spoken. Londos "jumped suddenly from the sofa, threw over the board, and clasping his hands, repeated the name of the patriot with a thousand passionate exclamations, the tears streaming down his cheeks," Hobhouse reported. He then sang, with fervor, Rhigas's famous revolutionary anthem. This stirring scene, evidence of poetry acting as the bellows of revolt, keeping its dying embers alive, made a deep impression on Byron. The living connection between the dead leader and his impassioned young follower was sustained by verse. As soon as he had learned sufficient Romaic, Byron rendered in English the patriotic hymn first heard that evening in Vostitza. It began:

> Sons of the Greeks, arise
> The glorious hour's gone forth.[20]

Londos would prove a worthy follower of Rhigas, becoming, in turn, a leader in the Greek war of independence.

Meanwhile, he was the perfect host, arranging expeditions, including shooting parties, in the surrounding countryside. Five years later, the painful image of one of these outings inexplicably resurged in Byron's memory: "The last bird I ever fired at was an *eaglet*, on the shore of the Gulf of Lepanto, near Vostitza. It was only wounded, and I tried to save it, the eye was so bright; but it pined and died in a few days; and I never did since, and never will, attempt the death of another bird."[21]

Before leaving Vostitza, Byron tried without success to take with him a living souvenir of his stay. He had become smitten with another youth—one younger and more frivolous than his host. Eustatius Georgiou was a foot-stamping beauty who was well aware that his girlish good looks made him a prized commodity in the sexual marketplace; he carried a parasol to shield his complexion from the sun and was clever (and probably experienced) enough to play his English pursuer, amorous one day and rejecting all overtures the next. Byron thought he had arranged to have the boy sent ahead to Athens, like an exotic pet, but in a letter that reached him three weeks later, Georgiou bowed out.

Now, crossing to the port of Salona on December 14, they spent the night in a miserable one-room han filled to the ceiling with onions! Riding toward Chrisso on horses brought from that town, they discovered, to Byron's delight, that they were approaching the very roots of Parnassus. From there a guide conducted them to Castri, the modern town on the site of Delphi. While climbing the flank of Mount Parnassus, Byron spotted a flight of six eagles; it was the number, "not the species—which is common enough—that excited my attention."[*][22] The day before he had written his stanzas to the summit of poetic inspiration. A believer in portents, Byron now "seized the Omen," voicing "a hope that—Apollo had accepted my homage."[23]

---

*In his journal of 1814, Byron recorded having seen six eagles. Seven years later, the number had doubled, to twelve.

Castri, a squalid village, had been built over the ruins of ancient Delphi. Until 1891—when France purchased the entire site, moved the inhabitants, and sent teams of archaeologists to reveal the great amphitheater, the foundations of the Temple of Apollo, and the exquisite Treasury of the Athenians—travelers had to use their imagination to reconstruct the ancient city. Still, Byron and Hobhouse wandered happily among evocative scraps of the past: a shaft of column lying on the ground, sections of crumbling wall, rows of seats reaching up the slope that were clearly the remains of the Pythian stadium. For Byron, the prophetic pilgrimage was the climb up an "immense cleft rending the mountain from the clouds to our feet."[24] As they ascended, they found themselves "sprinkled with the spray from the immortal Castalian spring, sacred to Apollo and the muses as source of poetic inspiration." Byron took the importance of its water seriously: He drank from half a dozen streams. At the spot where they drank was a hut sheltering the shafts of two marble columns; on one was scratched "Aberdeen, 1803," and in another place "H. P. Hope 1799". Having been away from home so long, Hobhouse found "something agreeable in meeting even with the name of a countryman," and he and Byron then added their inscriptions to the record of earlier visitors.

They spent the next night in Arakhova, once the most considerable town in Livadia. From here they looked down at what they first took to be the sea, but which turned out to be the plain of Thebes. Three hours' ride over flat plains brought them to the "Schist Crossroads," the ominous junction of the ancient roads from Thebes, Delphi, Daulis, and Ambrossos. Hobhouse was so moved by the dark association of the place that he wanted to cry out, "Here, Laius was killed by Oedipus."[25] It's curious that Byron, identifying as he did with other "cursed" heroes, showed no special interest in Oedipus, whose malign beginnings would have suggested parallels with his own: When Laius is told that his son will murder him, he nails the infant's feet together with an iron and abandons the baby in the mountain fastness. The peasants who rescue the lame foundling name him Oedipus, meaning "swollen foot."

Livadia, the Roman Achaea, was now part of Greece proper, and home to the wealthiest Greeks. Among these was the archon, Logotheti;* as guests in his grand house, Byron and Hobhouse had occasion to observe his pashalike way of life, including fifty attendants—servants,

---

*The local, Turkish-appointed administrator, the archon, was usually Greek and often an ecclesiastical authority, who would add to his wealth by doubling the taxes levied by the Porte.

priests, secretaries, and a personal physician. With his own fondness for a lavish suite, Byron could only have envied the low cost of living in Greece—the archon spent annually on his entire household the equivalent of £1,142, he reported.

In further homage to history, unmixed with myth, they made a detour north to Caperna, site of ancient Chaeronea, where two of the principal battles of the ancient world were fought: Here the Athenians and the Thebans were defeated by the forces of Philip II and Alexander of Macedon; and in 86 B.C. Sulla defeated the army of Mithridates. Hobhouse was awed by the flatness of the site—there was "not even a molehill to impede the manoeuvres of hostile armies and . . . space sufficient for a slaughter ten times more considerable than that of the myriads who fell before the Macedonian and Roman conquerors."[26] Byron, as ever, was more engaged by human encounters and local mores; he was amused by a bishop who made it clear he thought religion was only for peasants and by a lovely peasant girl in a miserable mountain village whose hair, hanging down to her feet, was plaited with her entire dowry in coins. This was an essential advertisement, their Albanian servant Vassily explained, to the few eligible males of the region, and even though the girl and her mother were near starvation, neither would dream of stripping a single *para* of her portion money, "so much does their hope of future good overcome their feelings of present suffering," Hobhouse noted approvingly.[27]

Thebes in the pouring rain drove Byron indoors. While the indefatigable Hobby set off, umbrella unfurled, to investigate the remains of the ancient city, Byron returned to *Childe Harold*, escaping the weather and the dismal town and shaping memories of the brilliant colors and blood lust of the Spanish bullfight into verse.

Delays in obtaining horses gave Byron the chance for a swim—a pleasure never to be missed. Then, on the twenty-fourth of December, their troupe set off again. They did not make Athens by nightfall and stopped in the "miserable and half-deserted village of Scourta,"[28] where they spent Christmas Eve in a hovel adjoining—a manger! Cows and pigs occupied the lower part of the stable, while the pilgrims made do with a loft above. Sleep was impossible, as smoke from the fire next door almost suffocated them; the roof of the stable having no opening, flakes of soot rained down on them throughout the night.

At two-thirty the next day, after a ride of more than four hours, they reached the summit of a mountain. On their right, Hobhouse identified the ancient ruins of Fort Phyle, guarding one of the passes from Boeotia into Attica. Looking down across a vast plain, they could see a town rising around an outcropping on which some buildings were visible;

beyond, they could just make out the sea. Descending, they rode through olive groves and cultivated fields, still green in late December, then crossed the bridge over the Cephissus River. An hour later they arrived at the city walls of Athens. It was eight-thirty on Christmas Day 1809.

Disappointment mingled with disbelief colored their first stroll the next morning. The Athens of antiquity, whose marble splendors, illustrated in schoolbooks and engraved in handsome folio albums, Byron had pored over since childhood, had all but disappeared. Centuries of looting and sacking had reduced the *polis* of Pericles and Phidias to a squalid village of narrow, crooked streets huddled at the northern and eastern bases of the Acropolis. To his amazement, Hobhouse found that a brisk walk of forty-seven minutes took him around the walls of the entire town. Inside, her ten thousand inhabitants—Turks, Albanians, Greeks, and Jews—lived mostly in ramshackle houses and were taxed 30,000 crowns annual tribute for the protective custody of the Kislar Aga in Constantinople. The town itself—only forty-third in size and importance in the Ottoman Empire—was ruled by his local representatives.

In Athens, Byron and Hobhouse were no longer the exotic English travelers they had been in Albania. For three quarters of a century, the intense British interest in classical art, architecture, and archaeology that had created the Georgian style had also encouraged swarms of amateurs, artists, and scholars to visit the sites of the ancient world. A group of youthful aristocrats had returned home in 1732 to found the Society of Dilettanti, whose purpose was to support the collection, exhibition, and publication of antiquarian discoveries. Recently, the ranks of these visitors had been increased by the Napoleonic Wars, which changed the intinerary of a wealthy young man's grand tour from Rome to Athens. Female travelers, too, had followed the intrepid Lady Mary Wortley Montagu to include Greece on their tour through the East; a few weeks after their arrival in Athens, Byron and Hobhouse were amazed to discover that "several of our fair countrywomen have ascended the rocks of the Acropolis."[29]

Despite the influx of foreigners, the town still had no hotel or inn; rumors of a tavern were bruited from time to time, but none had yet appeared. In the absence of public accommodation, three or four leading families took in guests; there was no official charge, but visitors were expected to make a contribution to the household. Byron and Hobhouse now found rooms in the house of Tarsia Macri, widow of the Greek-born English consul. Her property, notable for a tall flagpole that still flew the Union Jack, consisted of two houses separated by a garden wall where the travelers were installed, each in his separate apartment.

Breaking through the wall shortly after their arrival, Byron and Hobhouse could enjoy the easy access to one another to which they had become accustomed, along with a common courtyard filled with lemon trees. They picked the fruit to flavor the "pilaff [*sic*] and other national dishes served at our frugal table," Hobhouse noted, sounding hungry.[30] The widow Macri clearly depended on the contributions of her boarders; she had three young daughters, who would soon require dowries.

On their first day, Byron and Hobhouse received a call from Spiridion Logotheti, the British vice-consul, and explored the city. One of the few ancient structures surviving in the lower town, the handsome Temple of Theseus, was a five-minute walk from the Macri house. As they discovered, the classical "ruins" were the only sturdy buildings in Athens; as such, they were still in use. The Theseum was a church; the octagonal Tower of the Winds was now the headquarters of the Dervishes, whose whirling worship Hobhouse learned, to his delight, was open to the public every Friday. The fourth-century Monument of Lysicrates, popularly known as the Lantern of Demosthenes, now served as the library for the padre of the French Capuchin convent, whose buildings had mushroomed around it.

Then, on the following day, December 27, they received the visit of one Giovanni Battista Lusieri. Known to all Athens as Don Tita, the Neapolitan Lusieri had been a landscape painter in his native city when Sir William Hamilton, British envoy in Naples, husband of the legendary Emma, and antiquarian collector, hired him to make topographical drawings in Greece. In 1799, as he was nearing the end of his labors for Hamilton, Lusieri had been engaged by Lord Elgin, the British ambassador in Constantinople, for a similar project: to make detailed drawings of all surviving antiquities in the Attic region. He reported to Elgin on both the extraordinary quality of the marble sculpture on the Acropolis and on its deteriorating condition. It was then decided to extend his work to include making plaster molds. Three-dimensional copies, Elgin decided, would further the object of his enterprise: to inspire young English artists by examples of genius.[31]

Written permission from the Ottoman bureaucracy in the form of *firmans* allowed the efficient Lusieri to supervise the erection of scaffolding on those structures of the Acropolis that had withstood centuries of depredation. Elgin now decided to extend his request to the removal of the endangered works to England. Permission—undoubtedly expedited by the bribery essential to doing any business in the Ottoman Empire—was granted, but in terms so vague as to perpetuate arguments up to the present about what activities were authorized. Still, the only formal objection raised by Turk or Greek at the time of Elgin's project concerned the use of scaffolding; the Turkish military garrison installed on the Acropolis feared that Lusieri's workmen would peer into their harem.

Over a ten-year period, then, beginning in 1800 and ending just before Byron's arrival in Athens, Lusieri had overseen an army of draftsmen, artisans, and laborers; for the first four years he had supervised the inventory of antiquities and the making of drawings and plaster casts; then, beginning in 1804, he assumed the role of agent in what is still considered one of the most controversial acts in modern cultural history: the removal and shipment of sculpture, soon to be known as the Elgin marbles, from the Parthenon to London.*

Before Lusieri's final shipment reached its destination, his patron, Lord Elgin, on his way back to England, was arrested by Napoleon and imprisoned in France for three years. On his release and return home, he failed to interest His Majesty's government in housing his treasures. Elgin then rented a house at the corner of Park Lane and Piccadilly, on the grounds of which he constructed a shed to exhibit the marbles. From the summer of 1807, select groups of visitors flocked to see the eccentric Scottish peer's treasures. The artists Benjamin Haydon, John Flaxman, Benjamin West, and the great sculptor Antonio Canova himself were rapturous; the world of fashion, dandies, and dilettanti reacted with disdain.

Byron was among those who later came and sneered. By his own admission, he had little feeling for art and readily echoed the opinion of his contemporaries who equated beauty with the smooth, neoclassical look of Greco-Roman or Hellenistic sculpture (which, not coincidentally, many of them collected). These arbiters found the realism of the Parthenon sculpture, roughened by centuries of exposure and ill treatment, barbaric. In *English Bards and Scotch Reviewers*, Byron immortalized their views:

> Let ABERDEEN and ELGIN still pursue
> The shade of fame through regions of Virtu;
> Waste useless thousands on their Phidian freaks,
> Mis-shapen monuments and maimed antiques;

---

*If anything, controversy has intensified in recent years. Questions of how to redress past sins of cultural colonialism, along with a new international commitment to police thefts at archaelogical sites, have reopened debate on every issue raised by the removal of the Parthenon sculpture, from Elgin's real motives to demands for the return of the marbles to Greece.

And make their grand saloons a general mart
For all the multilated blocks of art.[32]

Lest any reader should miss his point in verse, Byron added a note to this stanza, pointing out, "Lord Elgin would fain persuade us that all the figures, with and without noses, in his stoneshop, are the work of Phidias! Credat Judaeus!"[33]

Elgin was scarcely the first British emissary to recognize the genius of classical art and to set about securing choice examples for royal collections. In 1628 Sir Kenelm Digby had delighted Charles I with a treasury of "old Greek marbles-bases, columns and altars,"[34] brought back from a mission to the Mediterranean, and from 1621 to 1628, one of Elgin's predecessors, Sir Thomas Roe, British ambassador to Constantinople, acted as agent for two of the greatest collectors, the Duke of Buckingham and the Earl of Arundel.

Now, playing out the hostilities between France and England in the appropriation of art, Napoleon's ambassador to Constantinople, M. Gouffier-Choiseul, in hot pursuit of the same antiquities as Elgin, employed an agent in Athens with credentials remarkably similar to Lusieri's.

Trained as an artist, Louis François Sebastien Fauvel was also a talented classical scholar who had essentially ghostwritten two imposing illustrated volumes on antiquities for his patron. Duly rewarded for his labors, Fauvel had been appointed French consul in Athens, making him the leader of local Frank or European society. He had been about to edge out Lusieri for the last and largest shipment of the Parthenon marbles, along with other important works, when Franco-Turkish hostilities erupted and Fauvel was imprisoned. Released just before the arrival of Byron and Hobhouse, Fauvel was trying to recoup his losses, the most important asset being a specially constructed cart and winch indispensable for the removal and transportation of the enormous marbles to the port of Piraeus.

All Athens was now divided in loyalty as "a war more than civil," Hobhouse noted, "was raging on the subject of my Lord Elgin's pursuits in Greece, and had enlisted all the Frank settlers and the principal Greeks on one side or the other of the controversy," to which he added an important observation: "To retain them themselves never is, I believe, an object of their wishes."[35]

Given his scornful view of the "Phidian freaks" as Elgin's folly, Byron initially took an Olympian view of the fierce rivalry between Fauvel and Lusieri; soon he and Hobhouse were enjoying the friendship and admiring the private collection of antiquities of both these charming and cultivated men. On the same day that he called on the English visitors, Lusieri escorted them to see the *waiwode*, an essential preliminary—along with a gift of tea and sugar—for obtaining permission to visit the Acropolis. Meanwhile, Byron appreciated his hospitality, his small but choice collection of marbles, along with Lusieri's own "beautiful" drawings, and eagerly welcomed his companionship as knowledgeable guide to Athens and later, on excursions to Sunium. Receiving Fauvel's visit shortly after Lusieri's prompt call, Byron praised the Frenchman as one "to whose talents as an artist, and manners as a gentleman, none who have known him can refuse their testimony." *36

Thus we are startled to read in Byron's notes dated January 3, 1810, which would accompany the first two cantos of *Childe Harold's Pilgrimage*, that he savages both his new friends, lamenting, "How are the mighty fallen, when two painters contest the privilege of plundering the Parthenon." (Byron, it should be added, had not yet visited the Acropolis himself when he wrote this, permission having been delayed.) With a Hydriot vessel waiting in the harbor "to receive every portable relic," Byron conjured up a Lord Elgin who "boast[s] of having ruined Athens," while "an Italian painter of the first eminence, named Lusieri, is the agent of devastation," adding, "Between this artist and the French Consul Fauvel, who wishes to rescue the remains for his own government, there is now a violent dispute concerning a car employed in their conveyance, the wheel of which—I wish they were both broken upon it—has been locked up by the Consul."37

On January 5, Christmas Day according to the Julian calendar still observed in Athens, Byron dined with the "agent of devastation" himself, in his house at the foot of the Acropolis. Three days later the poet, accompanied by Lusieri and Hobhouse, finally climbed the steep rocks of the sacred site. He had already chosen his enemy and battleground; once he saw the ruins themselves, he had all the ammunition needed to fire into poetry.

To appreciate the sense of sacrilege that assailed Byron on reaching the summit, we have to imagine the Acropolis, the heart of Periclean Athens, as it was in 1810. Used as a fortress for centuries, the crumbling walls still held gun emplacements; the same barricades filled the porch

---

*As a measure of the self-contained society that was Athens, it is interesting to note that the Napoleonic Wars in no way chilled the warmth of the highest-ranking French official toward English visitors.

of the Erectheum and the gates of the Propylea. Any unoccupied ground had been covered with the "mean whitewashed houses" of the resident garrison, Hobhouse reported sadly.[38] Rebuilt as a mosque, the Parthenon had been turned into a magazine by the Turks in the seventeenth century; during the siege of Athens in 1657 by Venetian forces under General Morosini, a well-placed shot had ignited the gunpowder, blowing off the roof. Byron and Hobhouse were shown the large hole in the ground blasted by the shell.

Byron begins Canto II of *Childe Harold's Pilgrimage* with a lament for the desecration of the Parthenon:

> Goddess of Wisdom! here thy temple was,
> And is, despite of war and wasting fire,
> And years, that bade thy worship to expire. . . .[39]

After the battlefields of Spain, the desolation of her people, and the slaughter of young heroes, the poet confronts another tragedy: the decay and loss of the most brilliant civilization that man, blessed by banished gods, would ever create.

> Look on its broken arch, its ruin'd wall,
> Its chambers desolate, and portals foul:
> Yes, this was once Ambition's airy hall,
> The dome of Thought, the palace of the Soul:
> Behold through each lack-lustre, eyeless hole,
> The gay recess of Wisdom and of Wit
> And Passion's host, that never brook'd control:
> Can all, saint, sage, or sophist ever writ,
> People this lonely tower, this tenement refit?[40]

Yet, even as he concedes the indifference of present-day Athenians to the despoiling of past glory—"Unmov'd the Moslem sits, the light Greek carols by"[41]—Byron readies his attack on the real adversary:

> . . . worse than steel, and flame, and ages slow
> Is the dread sceptre and dominion dire
> Of men who never felt the sacred glow

Vilest of these insensate "plunderers" is Lord Elgin: "The last, the worst, dull spoiler" whose Scottish blood seems to have predestined him to commit this crime:

Cold as the crags upon his native coast,
His mind as barren and his heart as hard.
Is he whose head conceiv'd, whose hand prepar'd,
Aught to displace Athena's poor remains.[42]

Using Elgin as straw man allowed Byron to move *Childe Harold* from romantic melancholy at the sight of ruins to righteous wrath at the rape of Greece.

Demonizing his fellow Scot now became Byron's obsession; he was not going to be swayed by mere fact—even when it was seen or heard firsthand. On their second visit, Byron and Hobhouse queried a laborer whose house on the Acropolis Lusieri had purchased to search its foundations for sculptural remains; the fellow had laughed at their questions, recalling that the statuary and columns he had found on the site had been burned into lime, which he used to build his dwelling! After noting that in the two weeks between his first and second visit to the Acropolis "two large pieces of the Parthenon"[43] had fallen to the ground, Hobhouse predicted: "If the progress of decay should continue to be as rapid as it has been for more than a century past, there will, in a few years, be not one marble standing upon another on the site of the Parthenon."*[44]

For Byron's part, the more he saw of what the painter Turner later called Elgin's "rescue from barbarism" of the surviving marbles,[45] the more barbaric was his treatment of the Scottish peer and career civil servant.

There was no suffering in the life of Thomas Bruce, seventh Earl of Elgin, that Byron failed to mock in print: His first allusion to the "Phidian freaks" in Park Lane "with and without noses" points to the disease that ate away the lower part of Elgin's nose—scurrilously and falsely whispered to be syphilis. Another stanza (later suppressed) in *Childe Harold* caricatures his victim as a "man distinguished by some monstrous sign" and compares him to Attila the Hun as being "surely horned."[46] This was no very subtle allusion to the cuckold's attribute placed on her lord's head by Lady Elgin, whose adultery with a Scottish neighbor while her husband was imprisoned in France delighted gossips

---

*History provides ample evidence of continued destruction of the remaining marbles. The Acropolis was twice bombarded by the Turks during the Greek war of independence (1821–1826); its ruins were severely damaged by an earthquake in 1894 and were used as a Nazi stronghold during World War II.

on both sides of the Channel. Finally, an entire poem, *The Curse of Minerva,* written just before Byron would leave Greece the following year, was conceived, in the poet's own words, to "immolate" Elgin "with gusto."[47]

In this new poem, the goddess's malediction begins with Scotland itself, "a land of meanness, sophistry and mist" from which Minerva "sent a Pict to play the felon" in Greece.[48] As Elgin's oldest son was epileptic, Byron could conveniently extend the goddess's curse to all his issue: "Without one spark of intellectual fire, / Be all the sons as senseless as the sire."[49] For tolerating Elgin's villainy, England herself will be blighted. Giving full reign to his apocalyptic fantasies of revenge on his own country, Byron prophesies nothing less than her total devastation. Abroad, Britain's armies will be defeated, her empire will crumble; at home, invading forces, followed by anarchy and famine, will devastate the land.

Beginning with *English Bards,* Byron had used satire for revenge. But nothing in his writing approaches the malice and hysteria of his persecution of Elgin.

This personal vendetta toward a man he had never met, who bore him no ill will whatsoever and whose activities were defended by many of those Byron most respected, has perplexed writers on the poet for more than a century; labeling his behavior "perverse" and "childish," however, fails to explain his campaign of vilification.

The principal clue lies in Byron's own word "immolation": He knows he is engaged in the sacrifice of an innocent man; the ritual murder has nothing to do with the actions of the victim. As His Majesty's minister to the Sublime Porte, the ambassador was emissary to the Ottoman oppressor of Greece; thus, both generally and specifically, Elgin represented hated patriarchal authority. As a Scot, it was also his misfortune to personify the maternal adversary; he was Catherine Byron's countryman, bearing the genes Byron repudiated—if somewhat ambivalently—within himself. (In *The Curse,* Byron takes pains to exempt himself, as one of the "letter'd and the brave," from the taint of his fellow Scots.[50])

A homely man to start with, the ambassador's disfiguring disease became the counterpart of Byron's lameness: Crushing Elgin erased his own "mark of Cain." Finally, by casting the diplomat as the Antichrist, Byron found the perfect villain for his "mental theatre" (the term he later used to describe his verse plays). In the struggle for the salvation of Greece, the poet now stands ready to be privileged as savior.

All fantasies are dress rehearsals; the name scrawled on the manuscript page of the stanzas of *Childe Harold* in answer to the question of who will save Greece prepares us for the arrival of a hero to quicken glory long extinguished:

> Ancient of days! august Athena! where,
> Where are thy men of might? thy grand in soul?
> Gone—glimmering through the dream of things that were.[51]

In his study of Orientalism, defined as the scientific, intellectual, or artistic appropriation of the Eastern culture, Edward Said has identified a revivalist mission: the belief that the writer "speaks for" a people understood as silent, without a collective consciousness, and hence, in political and historical senses, dead. Robbed even of her relics by Elgin the predator, Greece, land of the gods and cradle of human genius, of statesmen, artists, and philosophers, is a mute blankness.

It was Greece, Byron said, that made him a poet; in return, he would punish her enemies and give voice to her silenced people. If he could not redeem her plundered past, he would awaken the conscience of Europe to her rightful future.[52]

CHAPTER 14

"That Seeming Marble-Heart"

YRON'S TEN WEEKS in Athens were among the happiest he had ever known. If these months lacked the intensity of periods colored by passionate attachments, they offered other pleasures and satisfactions.

Elgin's removal of the Parthenon marbles had provided a moral cause, allowing Byron to objectify his hatred of England, Scotland, power, and authority, all personified in one gratifying enemy, while he cast himself as hero in the tragedy of a country he had grown to love. Still, in coming to know his Athenian neighbors, he was less given to idealizing them as a people; collectively they were "the hopeless warriors of a willing doom,"[1] but inevitably, as Byron became attached to individuals, he grew fond even of their failings: "I like the Greeks, who are plausible rascals, with all the Turkish vices without their courage."[2]

Socially he basked in the role of lionized visitor: The handsome English *milordi* who made such endearing efforts to learn Romaic, together with his more diffident friend, was plied with invitations. Their arrival coincided with the holiday season, and Frank society celebrated with balls, parties, and masquerades—the last, with their opportunity for appearing in costume, being Byron's favorite.

January 12—New Year's Day in Greece—found Byron and Hobhouse celebrating at home, where dinner was served by the three Macri girls. Unlike their invisible Turkish or Albanian counterparts, young women from the Europeanized Greek families were allowed, within the home, to mingle freely with foreigners. Besides waiting at table, the Macri daughters played, sang, and danced for their guests. Since leaving Smyrna Byron had enjoyed no feminine companionship, and here were three adorable—and adoring—nymphets waiting on his pleasure. A few weeks later, from the safety of the Dardanelles, Byron described his delightful predicament to Henry Drury: "I almost forgot to tell you that I am dying for love of three Greek Girls at Athens, sisters, two of whom have promised to accompany me to England, I lived in the same house, Teresa, Mariana, and Kattinka, are the names of these divinities all of them under 15."[3] Teresa, the youngest, was then only twelve, but already "nubila," Hobhouse noted appreciatively. Much too shy to flirt with respectable young women, Hobby had become the regular client of the local prostitutes. Inhibited even in his diary, he says nothing about the women or the experiences, recording only money spent and climaxes achieved (the latter indicated by numerical symbols). At the same time, both men continued to explore the sexual freedom of the East, with its disregard for gender. Returning from an excursion along the Bay of Phalareum, Hobhouse noted: "Din'd—to bed—after Byron dressing up in female apparel & dancing with Demetrius."[4]

In Tom Moore's somewhat vague recollections of a conversation with the poet, Byron is recalled as saying that in paying homage to one of the Macri sisters, he "had recourse to an act of courtship often practised in that country—namely, giving himself a wound across the breast with his dagger."[5] This gesture may have been taken as customary gallantry, but other evidence of Byronic extravagance was not. John Galt reappeared in Athens at this same time and spent many companionable hours with his fellow Britons. His claim that Byron's feelings for the twelve-year-old Teresa were "innocent and poetical, though he spoke of buying her from her mother" seems contradictory, to say the least.[6] Madame Macri apparently decided to accept the tender offer, but, to Byron's horror, chose to see the transaction in the most respectable light: "The old woman Teresa's mother was mad enough to imagine I was going to marry the girl," Byron later reported to Hobhouse.[7]

Fury at what he saw as an attempt to entrap him did not tarnish happier memories. Before leaving Greece he immortalized Teresa in one of the worst—and most famous—lyrics he ever wrote:

> Maid of Athens, ere we part,
> Give, oh, give me back my heart!
> Or, since that has left my breast,
> Keep it now, and take the rest![8]

The provincial pleasures of Athenian society were eclipsed by the lure of the outdoors. In the last three weeks of January, the mornings and evenings were frosty, but noon found "the sun shining hotly," Hobhouse noted. With the mild weather and excellent roads, "scarcely a day elapsed without our riding to some distance from the city."[9]

In the mornings Byron slept or worked at home: He was writing the Albanian section in Canto II of *Childe Harold*, while Hobhouse puttered about nearby sites, measuring the drums of surviving columns (an activity Byron loved to mock). Then, in the afternoons, they "topographized Attica," Byron reported, riding past gardens and olive groves toward Piraeus.

On this first excursion to the famous port city for Athens, they had planned to visit the two-hundred-ton Hydriot merchant vessel anchored in the harbor with the last shipment of the Elgin marbles in her hold. But before they could go on board, they were "insulted by a renegado Spaniard," according to Hobhouse. They promptly brought a complaint against the man, a slave laborer in the port, to the local *waiwode*, who ordered him "bastinadoed," which consisted of flinging the victim on his back while his feet, bound together to a stake fixed in the ground, were lashed with a bundle of sticks. In his agonized rage, the prisoner managed to fling his shoes in a bystander's face, after which he "roar'd most abundantly and shit his breeches."[10] As a reward, Byron and Hobhouse invited the captain who administered the sentence home to their apartments, where he was offered a pipe and a handsome tip.

It's tempting to dismiss Hobhouse's gusto in retailing each detail of the flogging (reported by Fletcher) as evidence of the "vice Anglais." But the incident is troubling for other reasons. It suggests, on Byron's part, a vindictiveness that, far from lashing out only at the powerful, like Lords Carlisle or Elgin, pursued, with far crueler consequences, the most powerless of the lower orders—in this case, a slave.

Piraeus itself was disappointing, with hardly a trace of ancient magnificence to be seen. But their swing around the Munychian Peninsula more than compensated. The rumble of the waves washing over the pebbly beach at Phaleron inspired Byron to speculate that Demosthenes might well have practiced declaiming on that very spot, to get used to the clamor of a large, noisy audience.

Returning to town in early evening, they were overwhelmed by the beauty of the sight that rose before them. As they approached the Acropolis from the west, the columns of the Parthenon appeared perfectly aligned against the sunset sky; with the devastated parts of the temple invisible and the silhouette of the Theseum in sight, they could imagine themselves galloping toward ancient Athens.

The wreckage of mankind's most glorious monuments aroused Byron to melancholy or wrath, but nature in Greece was paradise before the Fall, "one vast realm of wonder," he said. No poetry he would ever write breathes more sensuous pleasure than the marvelously observed specificity of sound, sight, and smell seized from his wanderings in the countryside around Athens:

> Sweet are thy groves, and verdant are thy fields,
> Thine olive ripe as when Minerva smil'd,
> And still his honied wealth Hymettus yields;
> There the blithe bee his fragrant fortress builds,
> The freeborn wanderer of thy mountain-air.[11]

Byron's tribute to the fragrance of Attic air and that of the famed local honey were no figures of speech; both were perfumed by the wild thyme, then in bloom everywhere.

Along with rides to the summit of Hymettus, they made a rough three-hour journey to Mount Pentelicus. From the side of the mountain had been quarried most of the marble used in the construction of ancient Athens. John Galt, who accompanied his friends, found the vast excavation itself less interesting than the enormous "drapery of wood-bine" festooning the mouth of the cavern. They dined on olives and fried eggs in the monastery at the foot of the mountain, where several of the brothers made clear to Byron that he should come again— alone—an invitation he would soon accept.

Visiting Eleusis, Byron and Hobhouse were offered a twelve-year-old, "brought here to be deflowr'd—but B would not," Hobhouse confided to his diary.[12] The gender of the new recruit is unspecified, but the child's age was the same as that of Teresa Macri, whom Byron had offered to buy from her mother. So it would not seem to be the physical act or the commercial nature of the transaction, but something distasteful in the particular circumstances that caused Byron to decline.

BY JANUARY 19, the springlike weather favored a longer excursion, and they set off, accompanied by the faithful Vassily, and the Greek servant Demetrius, along with baggage and horses, in the direction of Cape Sunium and what they thought to be the Temple of Minerva.* The southernmost point of Attica, Sunium (officially Cape Colonna) is a

---

*Byron believed, with all his contemporaries, that the temple at Sunium was dedicated to Minerva. Only in 1898 was the sanctuary correctly identified as dedicated to Poseidon by an inscription found at the site.

rocky promontory reaching like a gaunt arm into the Aegean Sea. From Athens, the three-day trip was far from the simple drive along the "Apollo coast" of today's pilgrim. Delayed by two days of rain in the village of Keratea, they emerged into sunshine only to plunge into darkness once again as they decided to explore the caves of nearby Mount Parne. Accompanied by a local guide who claimed to know the cavern well, they confidently penetrated its black depths that were illuminated only by the flickering lights of their pine torches. Hours later, they were still wandering, directionless, from chamber to chamber, when the guide confessed he was completely lost and as disoriented as the visitors. By now the pine torches were beginning to burn down; once the light failed, they would never escape. Hobhouse voiced the unspoken dread of all: "The mind cannot easily picture to itself any 'slow sudden' death more terrible than that of him who should be buried in these subterranean solitudes."[13] Then, just as the last torch burned out, a faint light appeared ahead. It was the mouth of the cavern; they had come full circle.

This time, punishment of the offender was not entrusted to others. Hobhouse himself took charge of beating the guide, an old man who had claimed to know the caves well but, as it turned out, had visited them only once as a child. Byron loved repeating the story of their narrow escape and his own fear. In the retelling, he would relive his feelings of panic, John Galt recalled, and work himself into a state of hysteria, "a species of excitement and titillation which moved him to laughter."

On January 23 they rounded the last curve in the coastal road, and the narrow spit of Sunium came into view. All past dangers were forgotten at the sight of the temple's sixteen remaining columns, seeming from a distance to float above the sea.

Sunium immediately claimed a privileged place in Byron's imagination. Other temples had disappeared: If not ravaged by Elgin and his ilk, then they had been

> Broke by the share of every rustic plough:
> So perish monuments of mortal birth,
>
> . . . .
>
> Save where Tritonia's airy shrine adorns
> Colonna's cliff, and gleams along the wave;[15]

Boyhood reading had prepared Byron for the drama of the site: A favorite poem, "The Shipwreck" (1762), by William Falconer, was set in the stormy sea below Cape Colonna. Now, as they came to the temple from the land side, what had appeared from a distance as a single line of columns was revealed as the ruins of a vast monument covering the whole of the flat promontory.

Unlike the copper-tinged marble of the Acropolis, the pearly sheen of the remains of the Temple of Poseidon seemed to glow against the brilliant sky, dark rocks, and rolling water. Although much of the monument that Byron saw survived only in fragments scattered on the ground, their dazzling whiteness, along with the isolation of the setting, still suggested to him an unravaged sanctuary whose perfection had been so gently eroded by time as to become part of nature. Reclaimed by the gods, the site came to stand for "The Isles of Greece" as they had been, and in his famous poem of that name, Byron in a real sense reconsecrates the temple with a challenge: To become his final resting place, the monument—and Greece herself—must prove worthy of the poet as hero:

> Place me on Sunium's marbled steep,
> Where nothing, save the waves and I,
> May hear our mutual murmurs sweep;
> There, swan-like, let me sing and die;
> A land of slaves shall ne'er be mine—[16]

The next day they continued north, toward Marathon. Here, reliance on history remembered, along with the poet's imagination, had to do the work of more visually evocative ruins; arriving at dusk, Byron and Hobhouse rode past the barrow raised over the bodies of the 192 Athenian heroes of the victory over the Persians without realizing that this was the sight they had come to see. But the following day, as they paced off the historic plain, whose name for centuries had been synonymous with legendary valor, Byron found Marathon's past surprisingly present for him: "Age shakes Athena's tower, but spares gray Marathon." The very emptiness of the place acted as a stimulus to his own powers of evocation: "The flying Mede, his shaftless broken bow / The fiery Greek, his red pursuing spear."[17] There was something more poignant in so much stillness: "What then must be our feelings when standing on the tumulus of the two hundred [Greeks] who fell on Marathon?"[18] Nursing his own hunger for fame, he was fascinated by the paradox of anonymous immortality; of the deed that survived the most unknown of soldiers:

> . . . the vanish'd Hero's lofty mound;
> Far on the solitary shore he sleeps.[19]

Historical ironies multiplied: "The Battle-field, where Persia's victim horde / First bowed beneath the brunt of Hellas' sword"[20] was offered to him for sale, Byron reported, for the equivalent of about £900, causing him to ask, "Was the dust of Militiades worth no more? It could scarcely have fetched less if sold by *weight*?"[21] Whether by Greek or Turk, whether the Parthenon marbles or the plain of Marathon, all of Greece was for sale. And in a more honest recess of his being, Byron understood this. Like Sunium, Marathon, as a reminder of past glory, could serve to transform shame into hope. Implicit in Byron's most famous lines is the assumption that he will be part of the great promise fulfilled, a resurgent Greece:

> The mountains look on Marathon—
>   And Marathon looks on the sea;
> And musing there an hour alone,
>   I dream'd that Greece might still be free;
> For standing on the Persian's grave,
> I could not deem myself a slave.[22]

Now, for the first time since they had set out together from Falmouth more than six months earlier, the two friends separated. On February 8 Hobhouse went off alone to tour the Negroponte, while Byron, he wrote, "was detained" in Athens. In fact, the poet may have seized this opportunity to escape from the occasionally suffocating busyness of this most thorough of tourists. Without Byron, however, Hobhouse found less pleasure in what he saw. In his account of this part of his travels he pays tribute to his friend's character as well as brilliance, acknowledging his dependence on both: "You will attribute any additional defects in the narration of this short tour, to the absence of a companion, who, to quickness of observation and ingenuity of remark, united that gay good humour which keeps alive the attention under the pressure of fatigue and softens the aspect of every difficulty and danger."[23]

For the next two weeks Byron worked steadily, finishing the second canto of *Childe Harold* and diverting himself with his new Franco-Greek friends, including the Macri women. Hobhouse returned to Athens on February 13 during a spell of humid tropical weather. Two days later, at 11:30 p.m., the two friends were reading together in Byron's rooms when "the branches of the lemon trees, in the court yard 'shook without a wind' the door of our chamber swung open, and the whole building began to totter; it was an earthquake, but only of the mildest."[24]

. . .

THEN, on March 4, Captain Ferguson of the *Pylades*, the sloop holding the Elgin marbles they had been unable to visit in Piraeus, offered them passage to Smyrna—leaving the next day. With his growing attachment to Athens, Byron accepted with mixed feelings. Smyrna was the port of call before Constantinople, the next stop on his improvised itinerary; he could not refuse a free passage. They spent their last evening in Athens, and the following day they galloped toward the port "at a quick pace, in order to rid ourselves, by the hurry, of the pain of parting."[25]

Boarding the *Pylades*, Byron and Hobhouse joined two other British passengers: A young physician, Dr. Francis Darwin, and a friend were returning to Smyrna after cruising with the sloop for several weeks, including a stop in Malta to unload a shipment of Lord Elgin's treasures bound for England.

After a swift crossing of the Aegean, unfavorable winds caused the ship to spend more than thirty hours in the narrow Gulf of Smyrna. When they finally dropped anchor on March 6, Byron and Hobhouse were rowed to dine on board the *Salsette*. From there they moved, with servants and baggage, into the mansion of the British consul, Mr. Francis Wherry, where they would remain for their five weeks in the city.

After the austerity of the Macri household, the Wherrys' lavish table delighted the ever-hungry Hobhouse and tested Byron's willpower: There was every variety of fish, including nine kinds of oysters; woodcock, snipe, and boar, not to forget excellent mutton to gladden the heart of homesick guests; nearby vineyards provided sweet wine from muscat grapes and a dry white, while the local gardens offered an abundance of fresh fruit, including the famous local figs. Tropical temperatures made the visitors grateful for the sherbet shops in every little street, which turned fruit juice into cooling ices. The same heat also encouraged periodic epidemics of the plague, from which well-off families—foreign and Turkish—escaped to country houses; the Wherrys took their guests with them to their villa, "a mansion fitted up in English style, with excellent gardens and vineyard attached," Hobhouse noted approvingly.[26] On another Sunday, while Europeans and Greeks were enjoying the nearby beaches, Byron and Hobhouse joined the Turkish spectators to watch their national game, *djerid,* a form of polo played on horseback by every skilled rider from the governor to the lowliest cavalryman.

Smyrna in 1810 was the principal city of Asia Minor and the commercial heart of the Ottoman Empire. Since the middle of the eighteenth century, British and European banking and insurance firms and merchants purveying every product from pianofortes and Pinaud talc to Pear's soap had given Smyrna's French quarter the name of *Petit Paris*. Social life had been more glittering before the Napoleonic Wars had riven the colony into opposing camps. But the casino still held weekly balls, and the daytime visitor found there a reading room stocked with all the British and European journals.

When provincial society palled, other diversions were readily available. Two weeks after they arrived, Hobhouse called on the local pimp, a Mr. Frank. Young boys were the offering of choice, and Byron was relieved that he had removed his handsome page, Robert Rushton, from the danger of others' desires; he wrote unambiguously to his mother: "Pray take care of Murray and Robert and tell the boy it is the most fortunate thing for him that he did not accompany me to *Turkey*."[27] A visit to the ruins of Ephesus was the only excursion that took Byron and Hobhouse out of the city for several days. Once past the garden suburbs and pastureland, they found themselves at nightfall in a marshy area inhabited by armies of loudly croaking frogs. After a night spent at a "filthy han," Hobhouse recalled, they awoke to still more desolate scenery—a vast plain where the rest stops were a few squalid coffeehouses and whose only evidence of human habitation was melancholy clusters of Turkish tombstones. They slept the second night at Aiasaluk, the straggling village nearest the ruins of Ephesus, and the following morning crossed the Menderes River, to the site of the largest ancient city of Asia Minor.

As disappointing as the scattered stones of Nicopolis, Dodona, and Delphi had seemed, their situations, at least, provided the settings of former glory. The remains of Ephesus* offered no images, natural or man-made, to quicken the poetic imagination. Its great harbor was now a silted-up river valley; all that survived of the huge amphitheater were a few steep steps climbing crazily into the void. The teeming population of early Christians had long since been replaced by thousands of jackals, who howled among the ruins.

It was the desolate region between Smyrna and Ephesus that continued to haunt Byron. In two works, both written six years later, he used the journey from the city to the ruins to mark the stages of a crucial quest. In "The Dream," an unmistakably autobiographical poem, this unlikely spot offers to the poet, wandering in limbo, a vision of paradise:

---

*The splendid reconstruction of Ephesus—its avenues, great library, baths, and brothel—is the achievement of modern archaeology.

> . . . he was not
> Himself like what he had been; on the sea
> And on the shore he was a wanderer;
> There was a mass of many images
> Crowded like waves upon me, but he was
> A part of all; and in the last he lay
> Reposing from the noon-tide sultriness
> Couched among fallen columns, in the shade
> Of ruin'd walls that had survived the names
> Of those who rear'd them;

While he sleeps, the rightful tenants of the land guard him, their horses
and camels grazing near a fountain; a man

> Clad in a flowing garb did watch the while,
> While many of his tribe slumber'd around:
> And they were canopied by the blue sky,
> So cloudless, clear, and purely beautiful,
> That God alone was to be seen in Heaven.[28]

A week before Byron and Hobhouse were to leave Smyrna, John
Galt appeared. He had seen a good deal of Byron in Athens and he was
now struck by his friend's "much altered" state. In "that short space"
of a few weeks, "something changed and not with improvement."
Byron was not only "less cordial" to everyone; he was also irritable
to the point of truculence in conversation, unable to tolerate any disagreement with his views. Galt recognized that Byron's hostility and
arrogance defended a paralyzing indecision: "He seemed to be actuated
by no purpose. He spoke no more of passing 'beyond Aurora and the
Ganges,' but seemed disposed to let the current of chance carry him as
it might."[29]

Galt attributed Byron's depressed state to anxiety about money and
fear of being reduced to dependence on others. In fact, Byron had
received no answers to his letters to Hanson pleading for funds. But this
was an old story. He had never before been known to allow lack of
money to depress him.

He had, however, depleted his creative energy in writing *Childe
Harold*, along with his intense feelings for Constance Spencer Smith.
Now, in place of passion, he was consumed by a sense of betrayal cou-
pled with emptiness.

By the middle of January Byron announced, in verse more triumphant than elegiac:

The spell is broke, the charm is flown!
Thus is it with life's fitful fever.[30]

His thralldom to Constance was over and he was ready to celebrate his narrow escape. Had "Fair Florence" dared imagine he could be one of her many trophies of love? Instead, she

. . . found, in sooth with some amaze,
One who, 'twas said, still sigh'd to all he saw,
Withstand, unmov'd, the lustre of her gaze[31]

A self-help manual follows: "Disguise ev'n tenderness if thou art wise; / Brisk confidence still best with woman copes."[32]

Bracing advice has clearly come too late. In the final stanza of a sequence of six charting the course of his passion for "Florence," the poet explodes in a burst of bitterness:

'Tis an old lesson; Time approves it true,
And those who know it best, deplore it most;
When all is won that all desire to woo,
The paltry prize is hardly worth the cost:
Youth wasted, minds degraded, honour lost,
These are thy fruits, successful Passion! these![33]

Neither the passage of time nor the diversions of pashas and Greek boys tames the savagery of Byron's epitaph to his love for Constance Spencer Smith. From the tender opening of the sequence to the final wounded howl, a crucial betrayal of love has taken place. Two years later, writing to his new confidante, Lady Melbourne, Byron recalled "[Of] this most ambrosial amour, which made me on one occasion risk my life, & on another almost drove me mad" nothing was left but a few letters and "certain baubles which I dare swear by this time have decorated the hands of half Hungary, & all Bohemia.—Cosi finiva la Musica."[34]

Whatever gossip Byron had heard about the inaptly named Constance, its source was undoubtedly the Wherrys, his hosts in Smyrna who had also been visiting Malta at the same time. The revelation that he had, indeed, been one lover among a "whining crew," and other unsavory reports, would account, in part, for Byron's depressed state during his weeks in Smyrna. Along with the mementos that survived this amour was a melancholy legacy of disillusion:

If kindly cruel, early Hope is crost
Still to the last it rankles, a disease
Not to be cur'd when Love itself forgets to please.[35]

He finished the first draft of *Childe Harold* on March 28, dating the manuscript himself. Two weeks later, he and Hobhouse embarked on the *Salsette*, bound for Constantinople. In the midst of farewells on the pier, just before being rowed to the frigate, Mrs. Wherry, the consul's wife, clipped a lock of Byron's hair, tears streaming down her face. Hobhouse, at twenty-three, decided to be indulgent: "Pretty well for fifty-six years at least," he noted in his diary.[36]

Byron's spirits rose with the *Salsette*'s sails. The "shadowy restlessness" that had dogged him for nearly five weeks was only dissipated by motion itself, and at sunset on the second day out they had just dropped anchor when a violent storm came up. Byron's exultation as the heavens opened was more than delight in the romantic turbulence of sea and sky. We hear his own spirit set free by nature's anarchy: the sea, "short, dashing and dangerous, and the navigation intricate and broken by the isles and currents."[37] Surveying the drama from the pitching, rolling deck, he felt a new godlike purchase on life and death.

Elemental rage dispelled his sense of entropy, rushing in to fill the vacuum left by the end of love and the completion of *Childe Harold*. Now his resurgent energy was unaffected by calm and unexpected delay. Permission to enter the Dardanelles required an imperial order from Constantinople; for the next two weeks, the *Salsette* was obliged to ride at anchor, waiting on the bureaucracy to bestir itself. Meanwhile, Byron, accompanied by Hobhouse and officers from the ship, enthusiastically explored the legendary northwestern promontory of Asia Minor known as the Troad. Since Heinrich Schliemann's excavations in the early 1880s established the modern Hissarlik as the site of ancient Troy, that haunting rise of land, separated from the sea by a windswept plain, has yielded further layers of Trojan settlement. At the beginning of the nineteenth century, however, polite arguments among antiquarians and scholars about the exact location of Homer's Ilium had burst into heated debate, fueled by one book. Jacob Bryant's *Dissertation Concerning the War of Troy and the Expeditions of the Grecians, as Described by Homer; Showing That No Such Expedition Was Ever Undertaken, and That No Such City of Phrygia Existed*, published in 1796, was the work that turned every classically educated Englishman into a partisan expert on the question.

Controversy always aroused Byron. To prepare himself for the debate and, if possible, to have the last word, he read not only "that blackguard Bryant," as Byron called him, but even a twelve-volume rebuttal! "Hobhouse and others bored me with their learned localities and I love quizzing," he said.[38]

Characteristically, Hobby had carefully examined and analyzed the arguments on both sides of the issue, adding his own observations to the travel journals he planned on publishing. Just as characteristically, Byron trusted only his intuition, the feelings that overwhelmed him on that hallowed ground: "I have stood on that plain *daily*, for more than a month in 1810," he later declared, with only some exaggeration, and despite the efforts of pedants to persuade him otherwise, "I still venerated the grand original as the truth of *history* (in the material *facts*) and of *place*. Otherwise it would have given me no delight. Who will persuade me, when I reclined upon a mighty tomb, that it did not contain a hero? —Its very magnitude proved this. Men do not labor over the ignoble and petty dead—and why should not the dead be Homer's dead?"[39]

Why not, indeed! Seventy years later, Byron's intuition would be confirmed. A few miles inland, beyond the huge barrow known as the "Tomb of Antilochus," the historical Troy emerged.

Justifying his own privileged knowledge of history as instinctive, Byron now defended another poet's translation of Homer as true to nature and to place: Lesser minds, such as Wordsworth and the "Cockney poet" Leigh Hunt had faulted his idol Pope's rendering of the *Iliad* for liberties taken with the original. Unlike these "home-keeping bards," as Byron called them, he had been there; standing on the site of ancient Troy, his *Iliad* open to the moonrise scene at the close of Book 8, he could bear witness as a poet and reporter to Pope's genius: "I have read it on the spot; there is a burst, and a brightness, and a glow about the night in the Troad, which makes the 'Planets vivid' and the 'pole glowing.' The moon is—at least the sky is—clearness itself; and I know no more appropriate expression for the expansion of such a heaven— o'er the scene—the plain—the sky—Ida—the Hellespont-Simois— Scamander—and the Isles—than that of a 'flood of glory.' "[40]

ON MAY 1, just as the *Salsette* finally received permission to proceed, the wind dropped; for ten more days they remained at anchor off the Asian shore of the narrow straits, bordered by the pine-covered hills of Gallipoli. Two days later, Byron successfully swam the Hellespont, a feat that, as much as anything he wrote, assured him fame through his lifetime and immortality thereafter. Nothing would have pleased him more. "I plume myself on this achievement more than I could possibly do on any kind of glory, political, poetical, or rhetorical."[41]

At this point, the distance between the two shores was little more than a mile wide; a few months before, Byron swam the Tagus from Old Lisbon to Belém Castle, a longer, rougher swim—but, as far as the poet was concerned, that feat counted for nothing. Swimming the Hellespont, was, first, to measure himself against a heroic lover who died for passion. "Nor adverse winds, nor raging seas can ever make him stay, whom Love commands," Ovid says of Leander. More important, Ovid's hero was both myth and literary invention, fitting models for a poet.

Byron had made one earlier attempt at the crossing, with Hobhouse. But after an hour of swimming they were still only in the middle of the strait, whose waters were chilled by streams of melted ice descending from the Mount Ida range. At this point, exhausted and numb with cold, the swimmers were taken back into the boat.

Three weeks later, the straits had warmed sufficiently for them to try again. In the meantime, Byron had studied the currents carefully. He now knew to avoid crossing at the likeliest-looking place—between the two closest points of land. There the waters flowing down from the Black Sea, channeled by shores only a mile apart, create a current twice as strong as that farther up the strait.

Shortly after ten on the morning of May 3, Byron and Lieutenant Ekenhead of the *Salsette* plunged into the the water about two miles above Roumelia Castle on the European side; even here, the current forced them to swim downstream about two miles farther than the distance straight across: They emerged at a point approximately a mile and a half below the anchorage of the *Salsette*. Ekenhead's time was one hour and five minutes; Byron took five minutes more. Three weeks later, Byron added a note to Hobhouse's journal entry describing the feat: "The whole distance Ekenhead and myself swam was more than four miles. The current very strong and cold. Some large fish near us when half across. We were not fatigued, but a little chilled. Did it with little difficulty."[42]

As a gentleman athlete, Byron felt compelled to treat the achievement with modesty and a light touch. In both verse and letters, he bows to good form. But later, when he came to describe the swimming skills of Don Juan, his own achievement had been elevated—albeit humorously—to the benchmark of legendary performances:

> A better swimmer you could scarce see ever,
> He could, perhaps have pass'd the Hellespont,
> As once (a feat on which ourselves we prided)
> Leander, Mr. Ekenhead, and I did.[43]

Since boyhood, swimming had been the sport where Byron's lameness was temporarily obscured. The waters offered freedom to a body more fettered than others and liberated his mind from the deadweight of frequent depression: "I delight in it [the sea]" he told a friend, "and come out with a buoyancy of spirits I never feel on any other occasion."[44]

From Harrow's Duck Puddle to the Cam's pool where he claimed to have rescued Edleston from drowning, swimming was also the activity he shared with his closest friends:* Edward Long, Charles Matthews, Scrope Davies, along with younger favorites from Harrow to Athens.

Now, crossing the Hellespont helped dissipate any anxiety that his sexual adventures in the East had effeminized him. Unlike boxing, swimming was never a traditionally "manly" sport, but as a champion swimmer, Byron acquired the star athlete's aura of triumphant masculinity. Months after the event, he mentioned the achievement in every letter—sometimes twice to the same recipient. To his mother, he wrote of the feat three times; Catherine Byron's "damn lame'd brat" had foiled her curse by physical prowess, daring, and skill. He would not let her forget it.

THREE WEEKS of delay off the Dardanelles, punctuated by the drama of his swim, had allowed Byron the leisure for reflection and letter writing: "I am like the jolly miller caring for nobody and not cared for. . . . I smoke and stare at mountains, and twirl my mustachios very independently," he told Henry Drury. Literary vendettas seemed more remote the longer he remained away from England: "The Mediterranean and the Atlantic roll between me and Criticism, and the thunders of the Hyberborean Review† are deafened by the roar of the Hellespont."[45]

Recalling the diversity of those he had met in his *Wanderjahre*, he came easily to the cosmopolitan's worldview; Albanian or Turk, Greek or Briton, men were simply human: "I see not much difference between ourselves & the Turks, save that we have foreskins and they none, that they have long dresses and we short, and that we talk much and they little.—In England the vices in fashion are whoring & drinking, in Turkey, Sodomy & smoking, we prefer a girl and a bottle, they a pipe and pathic."[46]

Leveling sexual preference to unimportant differences of custom

---

*Hobhouse was the exception. His dislike of swimming was undoubtedly related to his horror of washing.

†The *Edinburgh Review*, which had demolished *Hours of Idleness*.

made it easier for Byron to avoid resolving the conflict within himself; if hashish, whores, or sodomy were matters of "fashion" only, these practices were safely removed from considerations of morality.

Still, his recent sexual experiences in the tolerant Levant engulfed him in self-disgust along with a resolve to change: "I hope you will find me an altered personage," he wrote soberly to Francis Hodgson on May 5. "I do not mean in body, but in manner, for I begin to find out that nothing but virtue will do in this damned world. I am tolerably sick of vice, which I have tried in its agreeable varieties, and mean on my return to cut all dissolute acquaintance, leave off wine and carnal company, and betake myself to politics and Decorum."[47]

CHAPTER 15

"The Vices in Fashion"

*O*N SUNDAY MORNING, May 13, Byron and Hobhouse, along with their fellow passengers, crowded the deck of the *Salsette*, straining for the first view of Constantinople. As the ship entered the Golden Horn, Constantinople's famed harbor, the weather turned hazy, obscuring the shores, but gradually, object after object emerged from the mist, until, at last, "unfolding before us was the prospect of a vast capital, rising from forests of cypresses, and overtopped with innumerable domes and slender spires," Hobhouse recalled. As they coasted under the "gloomy walls of the Eastern Caesars," an eerie silence seemed to transform the fabled metropolis into a city of the dead, where "no distant hum or murmur was heard within and not a human being could be seen without their solitary circuit."[1]

At sunset the frigate anchored just below Seraglio Point; now the silence was shrouded in a darkness so enveloping that "we might have believed ourselves moored in the lonely cove of some desert island and not at the foot of a city whose vast extent and teeming population made it known proudly by its rulers as the 'Refuge of the World.' "

Where foreigners were concerned, their initial impression of Constantinople as a desert island would prove all too apt. If Smyrna's *Petit Paris* had isolated resident Europeans, in the capital of the Ottoman Empire Westerners were restricted by law to the Pera district, then a suburb across the harbor from Stamboul, the old city. On the heights above the Galata district, where banks and commercial establishments, along with wine houses and brothels, climbed from the waterfront, the elegant Avenue de Pera was lined with the mansions, consulates, and churches of the Western nations. Visitors wishing to cross the Golden Horn to the old city, where all the antiquities and bazaars were to be found, had to engage the protection of a Janissary, one of the elite, educated officers who acted as guards, guides, and, unofficially, as spies.

The next morning, Byron and Hobhouse boarded the captain's boat for shore. The north wind was blowing so hard they had to be towed for almost a mile before they could cross the harbor. When they looked up at the cypresses rising above them, they saw, in a crumbling niche of the seraglio wall, two dogs gnawing on a dead body, a sight that six years later would find its way into Byron's poem *The Siege of Corinth*. Finally they were able to land at the foot of the steep stairs, where horses awaited them for the long climb. The streets were narrower than those of Jannina and much dirtier; every crossing was marked by heaps of refuse, little diminished by packs of gaunt scavenger dogs. In Constantinople, it was forbidden by law to mistreat these animals; the Turks believed dogs to have souls, Hobhouse explained. Reaching the Avenue de Pera, the travelers were delighted to find that their inn, owned by a Frenchman, M. Marchand, provided the most comfortable public accommodation they had enjoyed in their year abroad. The large billiard salon in the many-roomed mansion was the gathering place for all the idle young men of the quarter. Byron and Hobhouse rhapsodized over butter from nearby Belgrade, the best London porter, and every kind of wine, except port. Shrinking funds, however, made it imperative that they find cheaper lodgings, and after three days they rented a house nearby on the avenue, facing a small convent and the lane leading to the residence of the French embassy. Exploring the quarter, they found a fairground opposite the nearby artillery barracks featuring wrestling matches that competed with *djerid*, an equestrian form of darts, as the favorite Turkish sport; the wrestlers wore tight leather drawers and, with heavily oiled bodies and shaved heads, lunged at each other from a squatting position, like Japanese sumo wrestlers.

Below Pera, the streets of Galata throbbed with music drifting from the *tabagies*, coffeehouses that also sold wine, ostensibly to foreigners only; typically, a *tabagie* was a large room with a tiled floor, a fountain in the center, and a gallery for guests that ran around the four walls. The principal attraction of certain wine shops was the *yemakis*, or dancing boys. Jews or Greeks (but never Turks), the youths' specialty was a form of "dirty dancing" of an explicitness that Hobhouse, in the published version of his journal, assures readers loftily, "no Englishman would patiently contemplate for a moment"; his unpublished diaries, however, note that he and Byron paid several visits to one of these "buggery shops." For regular patrons, the performance was a prelude; as soon as the dancers were finished, "de Turk take & bugger dem," their Janissary explained.[2]

In all places offering refreshment, guests were provided with water pipes, but Byron and Hobhouse also visited the coffeehouses of the *teriakis*, or opium eaters. In these coffeehouses, located in the Armenian quarter near the mosque of Suleiman, addicts would swallow three or four lozenges at a time, each stamped with the words *mash Allah*, "the work of God."

Passing on the official visitors' tour of the mosques, they explored those open to foreigners on their own. Byron found the mosque of Suleiman to be the most beautiful, but he confessed to a preference for the Gothic cathedral of Seville and even "St. P[aul']s," noting of his abbreviation, "I speak like a *cockney*."[3]

They joined one official tour of the arsenal followed by an inspection of the Turkish fleet. The Capudan Pasha, or High Admiral, boasted a reputation for ferocity: "He cuts off heads every day, and a Frenchman's ears; the last is a serious affair," Byron reported to Hodgson.[4] A grim reminder of the Russo-Turkish War then being fought was the sight of two or three hundred Russian prisoners in leg chains, marching to their forced labor in the dockyards.

Byron missed his page, Robert Rushton. He wrote to the captain of the *Salsette*, explaining that as he did not wish to be "entirely without an Englishman, I venture to beg of you (if my request is not improper) to permit me to take a youngster from your ship as a substitute." There is no record of the captain's reply. Writing to his mother, Byron begged her to "take some notice of Robert who will miss his master, poor boy." Learning that Rushton's sister had become pregnant by a young tenant farmer, Byron was insistent that they marry. "I will have no gay deceivers on my Estate," he declared with paternalistic firmness, "and I shall not allow my tenants a privilege I do not permit myself, viz *that,* of debauching each other's daughters." Then, recalling at least one past incident that would contradict this self-righteous posture, he qualified: "God knows, I have been guilty of many excesses, but as I have laid down a resolution to reform, and *lately* kept it, I expect this Lothario to follow the example and begin by restoring this girl to society."[5]

WITH HIS usual intensity, Byron plunged into his immediate surroundings, wandering with Hobhouse through the maze of the old city. He visited the covered bazaar, where he bought his mother some attar of roses. They both submitted to the rough pleasure of the Turkish baths, returning several times. Of the famous sights of antiquity, they marveled at the largest of the underground cisterns, *yere-batan,* with its thousand and one huge pillars, the workplace of numberless "half naked pallid wretches employed in twisting silk through the long corridors by the glare of torches."[6] For Byron, the most evocative experience was riding on horseback inland along the ramparts of the fifth-century Theodosian land walls: "Imagine, four miles of immense triple battlements covered with *Ivy*," he wrote to his mother, "surmounted with 218 towers, and on the other side of the road Turkish burying grounds (the loveliest spots on earth) full of enormous cypresses, I have seen the ruins of Athens, of Ephesus, and Delphi, I have traversed great parts of Turkey, and many other parts of Europe and some of Asia, but I never beheld a work of Nature or Art, which yielded an impression like the prospect on each side, from the Seven Towers to the end of the Golden Horn."[7]

They rode out to the poetically named Valley of Sweet Waters, a favorite picnic spot, where Byron swam in the Lycus River. In the ambassador's barge he sailed as far as the Cyanean Symplegades, the rocky outcrop marking the point where the Black Sea flows into the Bosporus. Jason was supposed to have sailed past the rocks on his quest for the Golden Fleece; now Byron "scrambled" to their height at "as great a risk as ever the Argonauts escaped in their hoy," he wrote.[8] Besides his torn trousers and scraped behind, the result was also some classical doggerel, in the form of a very free translation of the nurse's dole from the *Medea* of Euripides:

> Oh how I wish that an embargo
> Had kept in port the good ship Argo!
> Who, still unlaunch'd from Grecian docks,
> Had never pass'd the Azure rocks;
> But now I fear her trip will be a
> Damn'd business for my Miss Medea, &c. &c.[9]

Exhausted by the rigors of rock climbing, the returning sightseers gladly abandoned themselves to passive pleasure as their barge glided along the shore: "Each villa on the Bosphorus looks a screen / New painted, or a pretty opera-scene,"[10] Don Juan would later observe.

SINCE THEIR ARRIVAL, Byron and Hobhouse had dined every evening with the ambassador, Sir Robert Adair. After their chilly reception in Malta, the embassy's hospitality here seems to have renewed Byron's confidence in the privileges of rank. Early on the morning of May 28 the entire British colony—residents and visitors—assembled, as was the custom, to accompany their ambassador to the first of his leave-taking audiences at the Sublime Porte; in failing health, Adair was returning home on the *Salsette*, ordered from Malta for his journey to England. Byron appeared at the embassy dressed in his scarlet regimentals, heavy with gold epaulettes, and wearing a lavishly feathered cocked hat. He promptly made known to Adair his expectation of a leading place in the procession, ahead of the next ranking official, Sir Stratford Canning. The ambassador explained that their Turkish hosts only recognized precedence for embassy officials; other guests would have to follow along as "rank and file." Byron exploded with wrath and fumed off "with that look of scornful indignation which so well became his imperious features."[11]

After three days of sulking, he was sufficiently ashamed of himself to write to the ambassador. But his apology to Adair is marked by the archness of tone of an adolescent forced to appear contrite: "On all occasions of this kind one of the parties must be wrong, at present it has fallen to my lot, your authorities (particularly the *German*) are too many for me—I shall therefore make what atonement I can by cheerfully following not only your excellency but your servant or your maid your ox or your ass, or anything that is yours."

Blame for his rudeness was not to be laid to pique at being denied precedence, Byron insisted, but the reverse, his antisocial nature: "The fact is that I am never very well adapted for or very happy in society, and I happen at this time from some particular circumstances to be even less so than usual. Your excellency will I trust attribute my omissions to the *right* cause rather than disrespect."[12]

In Byron all contradictions converged: Hypersensitivity to status, yearning to be loved for himself alone, the "craving void" he described within himself, which made him require constant diversion, and the strains he felt playing a social role—all were aspects of the same troubled sense of identity. As his ties to England loosened, moreover, these divisions seemed to deepen.

One longtime English resident of Constantinople recalled a revealing series of encounters with the poet. Shortly after hearing of Byron's arrival, this gentleman entered a tobacco shop, where he saw a handsome young man with auburn curls, brilliant blue eyes, and a very noticeable limp. Persuaded that the shopper having difficulties making himself understood was indeed Byron, he helped him with his purchase in Turkish. Byron appeared both grateful and delighted to meet a compatriot: "When His Lordship thus discovered me to be an Englishman, he shook me cordially by the hand, and assured me, with some warmth in his manner, that he always felt great pleasure when he met with a countryman abroad." The two then strolled the streets of the old city, his new guide pointing out sights a visitor might otherwise have missed. The chance meeting and long walk gave Byron's companion the sense of having "established between us in one day a certain degree of intimacy which two or three years frequenting each others' company in England would most likely not have accomplished." Later that week, however, the same Englishman met Byron at the ambassador's residence. When he asked to be formally introduced to his sightseeing companion of a few days before, he was shocked and humiliated by the response: With a few frosty words, Byron turned his back on him.

But there was a third act of *Childe Byron*. A few days afterward, the perplexed gentleman saw the poet approaching him in the street "with a smile of good nature in his countenance. He accosted me in a familiar manner; and, offering me his hand, said, 'I am an enemy to English etiquette, especially out of England; and I always make my own acquaintances without the formality of an introduction. If you have nothing to do and are disposed for another ramble, I shall be glad of your company.' "13

The new invitation was eagerly accepted. And the anonymous Briton tells us why: "There was that irresistible attraction in his manner, of which those who have had the good luck to be admitted into his intimacy, can alone have felt the power."14 There is no better account of Byron's extraordinary magnetism. He was, quite simply, irresistible.

His periods of ill humor, however, were becoming more noticeable, requiring more of his charming apologies. John Galt remarked on Byron's lengthening spells of moodiness, and on the fact that other foreign residents of Pera reportedly found his manner so bizarre as to pronounce him insane.

On July 10 the departing ambassador, accompanied once more by the entire British colony, was to have a final audience with the Sultan. This time Byron was on his best behavior. He appeared again in his dazzling regimentals, but now he had decided to give a star performance in the role of simple British subject, honored to attend his ambassador and "delighting those who were nearest him," as the young Stratford Canning recalled, "by his well-bred cheerfulness and good humoured wit."15 Both proved essential in surviving the rigors of the day.

Promptly at 4:30 a.m. the British residents convened and proceeded from the ambassador's mansion to Tophana, the landing stage of Pera; as the sun rose over the hills of Asia, dun-colored smoke issued from the *Salsette*'s cannon as a salute to the imperial barge was fired. The report was a signal for the ambassador's guests to mount the horses that had been sent from the royal stables. The entire entourage was then rowed across the harbor, arriving at the palace just in time to witness four thousand Janissaries making a run for their meal of pilaf, set out in little copper pots on the ground of a huge courtyard. Finally, at ten o'clock, the exhausted visitors were served a twenty-two-course banquet, but many of the dishes were whisked from the table before they could be tasted; Byron and Hobhouse were among the lucky ones who managed to find seats.

Fifteen or twenty of the ambassador's party, including Byron and Hobhouse, who had been chosen to witness the Sultan's audience, were then issued fur-lined robes. Pushing and jostling, they followed Adair into a small chamber, where Sultan Mahmoud II received them, seated on a low four-poster bed made of pearl-encrusted silver and studded with precious gems. Small, with velvety black eyes, brows, and beard, the Sultan had ascended the throne only two years before. He appeared much older than his twenty-five years: Diamonds blazed from the breast of his yellow satin robe and covered the hilt of his dagger, and on the front of his high turban, a huge triple sprig of diamonds held a plume of bird of paradise feathers.

After an exchange of letters, gifts, and compliments, the entire embassy and suite of guests rode back to the first Courtyard of Health, where, still robed in their fur-lined cloaks, they were obliged to remain astride their horses in the broiling July sun until past noon.

Mahmoud II seems to have made little impression on Byron. His only reference to the event and its host is a laconic mention of having met the Sultan. Mahmoud found Byron unforgettable: "His youthful and striking appearance and the splendour of his dress, visible as it was by the looseness of the pelisse over it, attracted greatly the Sultan's attention, and seemed to have excited his curiosity," a witness recorded. His Imperial Majesty's fascination with the poet has a curious explanation: Fourteen years later, Mahmoud persisted in the belief that the handsome English lord whom he saw in 1810 was not Byron at all but a woman dressed in man's clothes.[16]

Four days later Byron and Hobhouse were on board the *Salsette* once again, bound for England with the returning ambassador. Hobhouse, too, had been recalled home, but unlike his friend, he was ready to return. Byron's funds were insufficient to allow him to realize his earlier project of pushing on to Persia and the Far East. His low spirits seem to have taken complete possession of him, leaving no energy for travel, and although he had planned on continuing *Childe Harold* in the

Troad and Constantinople, he found himself unable to write. With no more alluring—or affordable—options, he now decided on another stay in Greece. Thus, three days after the *Salsette* sailed down the Bosporus, arriving at the island of Zea, the two friends said good-bye. Hobhouse was unabashedly emotional at the parting: "Took leave, *non sine lacrymis,* of this singular young person, on a little stone terrace at the end of the bay, dividing with him a little nosegay of flowers, the last thing perhaps I shall ever divide with him."[17]

Byron was glad to be alone, at least for the moment. As he wrote—twice—to Catherine Byron, "I am . . . woefully sick of travelling companions after a years experience of Mr. Hobhouse."[18] Tom Moore, in his *Life* of the poet, rhapsodized on Byron's need for solitude: "So enamoured . . . had he become of these lonely musings, that even the society of his fellow traveller, though with pursuits so congenial to his own, grew at last to be a chain and a burthen on him; and it was not till he stood, companionless, on the shore of the little island in the Aegean, that he found his spirit breathe freely."[19]

Age and experience found Hobhouse grown less sentimental. In the margin of his copy of Moore's *Life* he underscored these maunderings, and we can fairly hear him snort as he scrawls in the margin: "On what authority does Tom say this? He has not the remotest grasp of the real reason which induced Lord B to prefer having no Englishman immediately [or] constantly near him."[20]

That Hobhouse knew the "real reason" may be inferred from a poem Byron had written for him a month before they went their separate ways: "Farewell Petition to J[ohn] C[am] H[obhouse] Esq." is a humorous list of commissions in verse that he wished his friend to discharge for him on returning to England. Among these is a coded message for Charles Skinner Matthews, their prophet of pederasty:

> All hail to Matthews! wash his reverend feet,
> And in my name the man of Method greet,
> Tell him, my guide, Philosopher, and Friend,
> Who cannot love me, and who will not mend,
> Tell him that not in vain I shall essay
> To tread and trace our "old Horatian way,"
> And be (with prose supply my dearth of rhymes)
> What better men have been in better times.[21]

There is no mistaking the sexual agenda outlined in Byron's greeting to the "man of Method": His verse is nothing less than a vow to "keep the faith" of their little group as votaries of "Greek love," the reference to "our old Horatian way," a reminder of the moral superiority of men who cast women from their lives.*

Without the inhibiting presence of Hobhouse, Byron was free to consecrate the next months to an erotic pilgrimage. Word spread quickly that the handsome young lord's traveling companion had returned home and that he was alone. When Byron arrived in Athens on July 14 he found a welcoming committee in the person of Lord Sligo and his motley entourage. Dubbed "the Marchesa" by Byron, Howe Peter Browne, Marquess of Sligo (formerly Lord Altamont), had been on the fringes of Byron's Cambridge set. A Wildean figure, the young Anglo-Irish peer's extravagance, his mannered homosexuality combined with an anarchic propensity for creating chaos wherever he went had earlier made Byron wary of his overtures.

But the next day Byron received calls from three other English travelers, who made him look more favorably on Sligo's eccentricity; Frederick North (later fifth Earl of Guilford) he pronounced "the most illustrious humbug of his age and country."22 Henry Gally Knight, who would earn distinction for his architectural writings, earned only Byron's scorn for daring to pen Eastern romances—soon to be seized as the poet's exclusive turf: "I despise the middling Mountebank's mediocrity,"23 he declared. For his third visitor, Byron's contempt may be readily imagined: John Nicholas Fazakerly, a noted classical scholar, was a star witness on behalf of Lord Elgin who had testified to the government's Select Committee as to the danger of allowing any great works of antiquity to remain in Greece.

Byron now readily succumbed to Sligo's pleadings that they travel together to the Peloponnese. He was already beginning to miss Hobhouse, and the lavishness of the Marchesa's travel arrangements promised diversion from the low spirits that continued to dog him: "Sligo has a brig with 50 men who wont work, 12 guns that refuse to go off, and sails that have cut every wind except a contrary one, and then they are as willing as may be," he wrote to Hobhouse. Having paid for the tub and its crew for six months, Sligo was understandably reluctant to abandon his "precious Ark," as Byron called the vessel.24 Finally, though, he was persuaded to cut his losses, and the two young peers prepared to make the trip overland.

Byron did not travel light; his retinue rarely numbered fewer than six, with beasts and baggage to match. But he had more than met

---

*The Horatii were brothers sworn to protect Rome against the Curatii. When their sister fell in love with the enemy chieftain, they unhesitatingly murdered her.

his match now. Sligo had " 'en suite' a painter, a captain, a Gentlemen misinterpreter (who boxes with the painter) besides sundry idle English Varlets.—We were obliged to have 29 horses in all," he reported to Hobhouse in some awe.[25]

The day before their departure, the temperature in Athens had climbed to 125 degrees: "You Northern Gentry can have no conception of a Greek summer," Byron told his mother.[26] The corpulent Sligo was no horseman: "You may . . . suppose that a man of the Marchesa's kidney was not very easy in his seat."[27] But Sligo would make no concessions to the tropical heat; all his servants were clad in leather breeches.

The shared discomforts of the trip drew Byron and Sligo together; their new intimacy soon extended to the exchange of confidences—in the Marchesa's case, confessions too dangerous to be committed to paper: "Sligo has told me some things, that ought to set you and me by the ears, but they shan't, and as proof of it, I wont tell you what they are till we meet," Byron wrote to Hobhouse.[28] In return, Byron vented his rage toward his mother. Bathing together in the Gulf of Lepanto, Byron explained his "aversion"—in Sligo's word—by pointing to his naked leg and exclaiming, "Look there!—It is to her false delicacy at my birth I owe that deformity; and yet, as long as I can remember, she has never ceased to taunt and reproach me with it." And he concluded his indictment by telling Sligo, "Even a few days before we parted, for the last time, on my leaving England, she, in one of her fits of passion, uttered an imprecation upon me, praying that I might prove as ill-formed in mind as I am in body!"[29]

The double wound—maimed at birth by his mother's false modesty and cursed by her afterward for its consequences—has the mark of Byronic invention; its extreme of cruelty combined with injustice validated his hatred. And with Sligo as the chosen audience, his myth of maternal castration and torment also justified turning away from women, returning to the "old Horatian way."

By the time they reached Corinth, Byron had tired of the Marchesa: "He has all the indecision of your humble servant, without the relish for the ridiculous which makes my life supportable," he told Hobhouse, adding, "I wish you were here to partake of a number of waggeries which you can hardly find in the Gunroom or in Grubstreet."[30] Declining Sligo's offer of a cooling sea voyage, Byron took his leave and headed for Patras. The good-natured Marchesa was amiable about the defection; he himself was bound for Tripolitza. They planned to meet again in Argos in late summer, when Byron would be on his way back to Athens, a place Sligo needed, for the moment, to avoid, as he was "in some apprehension of a scrape with the Navy concerning certain mariners of the King's ships," Byron reported.*31

There was a brief detour to Vostitza, where Byron enjoyed a passionate reunion with his "dearly beloved Eustatius," he of the green parasol and seductive sulks. The lad was now ready to follow his patron "not only to England, but to Terra Incognita," Byron announced proudly to Hobhouse. Four days later poet and protégé set off together, "the dear soul on horseback clothed very sprucely in Greek garments, with those ambrosial curls hanging down his amiable back." In Patras the happy pair stayed once again with Mr. Strané, the British consul, now installed in a grand new house, but the idyll was not to last. A serious quarrel erupted; the boy resumed his pettish ways. Predictably, the more Byron tried to please him, the more impossible he became. Finally it was agreed he should return to his father. "Our *parting* was vastly pathetic," Byron reported with his familiar ironic deflection, "as many kisses as would have sufficed for a boarding school, and embraces enough to have ruined the character of a county in England, besides tears (not on *my* part) and expressions of 'Tenerezza' to a vast amount. All this and the warmth of the weather has quite overcome me," he wrote. He now spent his time "alone very much to my satisfaction, riding, bathing, sweating, hearing Mr. Paul's musical clock, looking at his red breeches."

The lovers soon made up. All contrition, the prima donna of the parasol called on Byron three times in one day, even giving up his offending accessory for a green eyeshade: "We have *redintegrated* (a new *word* for you) our affections at a great rate," Byron told Hobhouse, adding, "Now is not all this very ridiculous? [P]ray tell Matthews it would do his heart good to see me traveling with my Tartar, Albanians, Buffo, Fletcher and this amiable παιδη [boy] prancing by my side."32

It was early August when Byron and his raffish entourage set off for Tripolitza, where, armed with a letter of introduction from Ali Pasha, he was to call on the latter's son Veli, sultan of the Morea (the present Pelopponese). Although his host was busily preparing to join forces with his father against the Russians, he received his guest with still

---

*This was no mere scrape. Sligo was tried and convicted on charges of abducting twelve to fourteen of His Majesty's sailors from the brig *Pylades*: He served at least four months in Newgate and was fined £5,000. His rank and fortune would certainly go far in explaining the light sentence, as does his choice of lads of low estate; unlike Beckford or Wilde, Sligo did not carry off scions of the peerage.

greater splendor than had been offered at the paternal court. Soon Veli, too, had fallen under Byron's spell, presenting him with a "pretty stallion" along with displays of affection that might have been more pleasing were they not so public: "He honored me with the appellations of his *friend* and *brother*, and hoped that we should be on good terms not for a few days but for Life.—All this is very well," Byron confided to Hobhouse. "But he has an awkward manner of throwing his arm around one's waist, and squeezing one's hand in *public* [which] very much embarrasses *ingenuous youth*," Byron added rather disingenuously. In the presence of Mr. Strané, the British consul, the smitten vizier asked Byron "if I did not think it very proper that as *young* men (he has a *beard* down to his middle) we should live together. He said he wished all the old men . . . to go to his father, but the young ones to come to him, to use his own expression, 'vecchio con vecchio, Giovane con Giovane.' " And he invited Byron to visit him at Larissa when he should be less distracted by military matters—an invitation, as Byron made plain to Hobhouse, he fully intended to accept. Veli Pasha's "squeezes and speeches," public and otherwise, helped cool Byron's passion for his young companion. He sent Eustatius home: "He plagued my soul out with his whims, and is besides subject to *epileptic* fits," adding, "tell M[atthews this]." Then, with a clear reference to the boy's sexual talents, Byron conceded that ". . . in *other* matters he was very tolerable, I mean as to his *learning*, being well versed in the Ellenics.—Give my *compliments* to *Matthews* from whom I expect a congratulatory letter."[33]

By August 23, after a brief reunion with the Marchesa in Argos, Byron was back in Athens. He did not return to the Macri establishment; the widow's expectations for her daughter had made that impossible. But in Byron's absence, his friends—Sligo and Dr. Francis Darwin among them—had covered the walls of his apartment there with graffiti, some of them clearly obscene. To Byron's name, followed by the honorific "B.A." penned earlier by Hobhouse, one of the band added "A.S.S."; among other messages were "compliments" from Jackson the boxer; d'Egville the dancing master-procurer; and Miss Cameron, Byron's teenage lover now turned streetwalker.

Wisely, Byron removed to a resolutely undomestic setting. The Capuchin convent at the foot of the Acropolis housed a boarding school for the sons of Europeanized Athenian families together with a hostelry for visiting foreign gentlemen. Little if any instruction seems to have taken place within its walls. The abbot was in his cups most of the time, leaving his guest free to enjoy the pleasures of a deer park populated by a playful group of six dark-eyed "Sylphs," as Byron called them, including Nicolo Giraud, Lusieri's young brother-in-law and already Byron's designated "favourite," all vying for the attentions of their honored visitor. This was a "paradise of boys" such as only Beckford could have dreamed of, and Byron took full advantage of his privileged status. He was given the Lantern tower* for reading and study, but there is little reason to suppose it was used much for this purpose: "We have nothing but riot from noon til night," he told Hobhouse; he was "vastly happy and childish." Lest Hobby have any doubts as to the innocence of their games, he promised "a world of anecdotes for you and the Citoyen."[34]

With Nicolo Byron studied Italian, making enough progress to translate an ode from Horace. The boy's attachment to him was serious, and while Byron was evasive about his own feelings, he never failed to record the passion he aroused in others: "I am his 'Padrone' and his 'amico' and the Lord knows what besides."[35]

August 24 was an idyllic day. Despite the heat, Byron swam, as usual, across Piraeus harbor, this time with Nicolo for company. The Greek boy was no swimmer, Byron told Hobhouse, but he made up for it by wearing no drawers. (Byron still could not bring himself to swim naked.) He had spent the better part of the day, he wrote archly, conjugating the Greek verb, to embrace or kiss "(which word being Ellenic as well as Romaic may find a place in the *Citoyen*'s Lexicon)." But there were still barriers to be overcome. Perhaps Nicolo was reluctant to perform certain acts, as Byron had not yet attained that state of total and complete satisfaction expressed by their old code—"pl & opt C. [complete intercourse to one's heart's desire]," he complained.[36] Meanwhile, he promised Matthews a letter signaling his conquest of the boy's remaining inhibitions.

Fearing the Capuchin idyll was "too good to last," Byron decided on another tour of the Morea. He had planned to go with Lusieri; intimacy with his young relation Nicolo now turned Elgin's agent into a "new ally." Of course, the boy insisted on accompanying them. But in the middle of September it was only Byron and Nicolo, along with two Albanian servants, who set out for Olympia and Patras.

This time Byron did not escape the region's dread fever. He lay in bed shaking and sweating while he was purged with enemas and emetics. After three days the fever subsided, but he suffered a still more serious relapse. Against all odds he survived, and within a few days he was

---

*Established by the French in the seventeenth century, the convent was built around the famed Monument of Lysicrates, popularly known as the Lantern of Demosthenes; unlike the newer building, it still survives.

well enough to write to Hobhouse with an account of his treatment by two local doctors, which eerily foreshadows his fatal illness fourteen years later: "When I was seized with my disorder, I protested against both these assassins, but what can a helpless, feverish, toasted and watered poor wretch do? in spite of my teeth & tongue, the English Consul, my Tartar, Albanians, Dragoman forced a physician upon me, and in three days vomited and glystered me to the last gasp."[37]

No sooner had Byron recovered than "poor Nicolo, who had waited on me day and night," was stricken, he wrote to Hobhouse on October 2. Nursing his patron had not been the only means of contagion. Fever had long been thought to act as an aphrodisiac, and, as Byron later confided to Lady Melbourne, "it is perfectly true." The combination of a dangerously high temperature and sexual passion had all but caused him to die at the moment of ejaculation. "No *petite mort*, this!—."[38] Two days later, on October 4, Byron wrote to Hobhouse triumphantly, asking him to "tell M that I have obtained above two hundred pl & opt C's and am almost tired of them."[39] Whether this surfeit of erotic fulfillment involved only Nicolo as partner, he does not say. He was still fond enough of the boy, but his sexual obsession, with its attendant scorekeeping, seems to have run its course.

They returned to Athens and the Capuchin convent on October 13. But now Byron threw himself into the social life of the town—not as the lionized visitor he had been on his arrival, but as a distinguished resident member of the English colony. He saw more of Lord Sligo and spent several evenings getting to know and dislike that legendary eccentric, Lady Hester Stanhope. Niece of former Prime Minister William Pitt the Elder, Lady Hester, now thirty-four, was traveling about the Levant with an entourage that included her physician and a handsome young lover. They had first seen Byron swimming in Piraeus harbor, just before his departure with Nicolo for the Morea. Byron's loathing for learned and articulate women (unless their brilliance was softened by flattering attentions toward him) found a perfect target in Lady Hester, who clearly terrified him; indeed, it has been suggested that she was the reason for his hasty departure: "I saw the Lady Hester Stanhope in Athens," he recalled, "and do not admire 'that dangerous thing a female wit.' . . . She evinced a similar disposition to argufy with me, which I avoided by either laughing, or yielding, I despise the sex too much to squabble with them."[40]

Byron's dislike of Lady Hester was reciprocated. She found him a tiresome poseur. Famed as a mimic, Lady Hester kept drawing rooms in gales of laughter with her Byron imitation: She "did" the poet giving orders to his servants in a peculiarly affected French-accented Romaic. She even refused to find him handsome: "He had a great deal of vice in his looks—his eyes set close together, and a contracted brow."[41] More sympathetic, her physician, Dr. Meryon, noted Byron's "singular mode" of entering a room, when "he would wheel round from chair to chair, until he reached the one where he proposed sitting, as if anxious to conceal his lameness as much as possible."*[42]

It was Michael Bruce, Lady Hester's lover, who now fell under Byron's spell. The night Bruce was to leave for Constantinople, he embarrassed the poet by making a passionate "profession of Friendship, . . . the only one I ever received in my life, and certainly very unexpected," Byron assured Hobhouse, "for I had done nothing to deserve it." Friendship was a euphemism; "I am too old for a Friend, at least a new one,"[43] he bade Hobhouse tell Matthews.

His own adventure in the "romantic & chivalrous" would involve the rescue of a slave girl, but its consequences were safely literary: The incident gave Byron the idea for *The Giaour*. Returning one afternoon from Piraeus, Byron encountered a procession heading in the direction of the water. Its purpose was grimly evident. A young slave woman, visibly writhing in a sack, was being taken to be tossed into the sea—the classic Turkish punishment for women held to be sexually culpable. As soon as he realized the purpose of the cortege, Byron is supposed to have drawn his pistol, leading the group's chief at gunpoint back to the governor's house in Athens. Pleas, threats, bribery—finally, the poet's eloquence prevailed. On condition that she disappear from Athens, the prisoner was released into Byron's custody, and he had her escorted to Thebes and safety.

Other versions of the story name Byron (or his Turkish servant) as the girl's lover and thus the instrument of her near execution. Byron made sure to raise more questions and answer none: The chapter of the tale that could never be told, he declared, was more bizarre than any adventure of the Giaour; "to describe the *feelings* of *that situation* were impossible—it is *icy* even to recollect them."[44]

There's at least a possibility that the tale was a complete fabrication by the hero of the piece. Sligo's account, which Byron himself allowed as the "official" version, was, indeed, based on what he heard in Athenian drawing rooms and coffeehouses. But a curious question of

---

*From Meryon's description, Byron's way of making an entrance would seem to call attention to, rather than disguise, his limp.

what actually happened emerges in a letter to Byron, then back in England, from Sligo, still in Athens. Sligo's letter, dated October 1811,[45] was written in response to a request from Byron to tell him the story then making the rounds in Athens. If the poet was, indeed, both an eyewitness and a principal player in the events, why would he solicit second- and third-hand accounts? Unless, of course, he had "planted" the incident and was anxiously awaiting news as to how his seedling had grown.

The next months in Athens were enjoyably busy, with Byron ever more involved in the life of the expatriate community. On two occasions he threw himself into the controversy that simmered around the issue of commemorative stones for two traveling Englishmen who had died in Greece. John Twedell, an antiquarian, had expired eleven years earlier, but the issue of his burial in the Theseum, the choice of tablet and accompanying inscription, had become heated due to an unused verse by Lord Elgin composed in 1803, followed by a competing epitaph in Greek penned by a local divine, the Rev. Robert Walpole. For Byron this was a happy opportunity to enter the lists in the anti-Elgin faction. After much intrigue, including the nocturnal theft of one marble tablet and its replacement by another, Byron and the Walpole faction prevailed. Flushed with this triumph, Byron leaped into a similar tug-of-war ten days later over the stone of another compatriot, George Watson, who had been buried in the Theseum the year before. This time Byron may have felt a decided kinship with the deceased; he wrote the Latin epitaph himself, explaining to Hobhouse, "I knew him not, but I am told that the surgeon of Lord Sligo's brig slew him with an improper potion, and a cold bath."[46]

As the warm fall imperceptibly turned into the mild Attic winter, English visitors proliferated. In November Byron saw something of a pair who would both make their names as distinguished architects: Charles Robert Cockerell, also to become famous as the discoverer of the Aegina marbles, and John Foster of Liverpool. More of a revelation, however, was his introduction to a delightful and spirited group of young Europeans: "I am on good terms with five Teutones & Cimbri, Danes and Germans," he wrote to Hodgson in the middle of November.[47]

Well-born, passionately interested in the arts, curious about modern as well as classical Greece, Byron's new friends seemed to him free of the provincialism and moral earnestness that he always disdained in his countrymen—especially the traveling kind. Among them were architects, archaeologists, and a painter. Professionals *and* gentlemen, cosmopolitan without being bohemian, these contemporaries from the Continent confounded Byron's snobbery on every front. That he also paid homage to one Dane—"as pretty a philosopher as you'd wish to see"—makes clear that personal attractions were not lacking in his new companions.

In early December Byron made another visit to his beloved Sunium with a group of friends. Unbeknownst to them, the party narrowly missed abduction by Mainote pirates, who had taken refuge in caves hidden in the cliffs below the temple. Only the loud voices of Byron's Albanian servants—a race much feared locally for its ferocity—had dissuaded the robbers from attacking the group above.

For the rest of the month, Athenian social life was enlivened by the seasonal round of balls and parties given by the English colony. Byron's life had taken on the settled quality of routine—enjoyable enough, but with little of the unexpected. By now, even the "scamperings . . . peltings and playings" of his acolytes at the convent had begun to pall; he often retreated now to his study, where he worked on the copious notes that would be appended to the first two cantos of *Childe Harold*. Making sense of the material he had collected on Albanian and Romaic language and culture was made easier by lessons in the latter. His tutor, M. Marmaratouri, was not only a writer and translator himself, but also a leader of the Greek patriots. Besides helping Byron render Rhigas's famous war song, along with two popular ballads, into English, Marmaratouri very likely enlightened his pupil about the Greek underground resistance to Ottoman rule. From exile and in clandestine activities at home, he and his fellow patriots were working to rouse their countrymen from the torpor of a subject people. Meanwhile, Byron's perspective on his hosts had shifted gradually but dramatically. From his early contemptuous dismissal of the Greeks as "hopeless warriors of a willing doom," he had moved, first, to patronizing pedagogy:

> Hereditary bondsmen! know ye not
> Who would be free themselves must strike the blow?[48]

Now, after living among them for the better part of two years, he saw a different people. Betrayed by those who should have delivered her, victim of European indifference or rapine, pawn in the shifting alliances of the Napoleonic Wars, Greece had in vain sought help from the Russians, the French, and now the English: "But whoever shall appear with arms in their hands will be welcome; and when that day arrives, heaven have mercy on the Ottomans, they cannot expect it from the Giaours."[49]

Although Byron did not cover this manuscript page with his name, we can have no doubt that on some level, he had already assigned himself this heroic role.

IN JANUARY Byron wrote to his mother that he was "done with authorship"; within weeks, however, he would be writing furiously. At the same time, he told Hodgson of his plans to push farther east than Constantinople, but allowed, in his charmingly evasive style, "I am sure of nothing so little as my own intentions."[50]

Any notions he harbored of remaining abroad indefinitely were subject to new pressures to return home. Funds were running out, and the only word from Hanson took the form of urging him to sell Newstead. (Hanson's deafness to Byron's entreaties for money may have been designed to persuade him to do so.) More seriously, both his honor and his exalted view of friendship were impugned by reports of the financial straits and emotional stress into which his extended absence had plunged Scrope Davies.

In the spring of 1808, when Byron was still a minor, Davies, with Mrs. Massingberd acting as go-between, had guaranteed a series of loans for his friend in the amount of £4,500. After his departure for the Levant the following June, Byron had given Davies permission to open his will. What he read did nothing to assuage his fears: There was "no mention made either of me or the annuities, unless you include them in the word debts. But how am I to substantiate my claim in the event of your death?" Davies now wrote.[51] Even in Byron's absence, with the loans still unpaid, annuitants or lenders would descend on him. When Hanson informed him that there was no money available to pay even the interest due on Byron's loans, Davies panicked: "Under my present anxiety existence is intolerable—I cannot sleep—and much fear madness," he wrote to his friend.[52] This cry was followed by a humorous effort to arouse Byron's dormant sense of honor. He penned a parodic account of his own suicide, a tragedy that resulted in murder charges against Byron as the cause.

Byron had left England with his financial affairs in total disarray. Writing to Hanson, he admitted not only to irresponsibility but also to a certain complicity in leaving his friend holding the bag. He had, in fact, reneged on his promise to Davies: "It is true I offered to sign any satisfactory instrument for Mr. Davies, but I think the codicil sufficient, without a Bond of indemnity which shifts the responsibility completely, now as there must be a reliance either on my part upon Mr. D. or on Mr. D.'s upon me, I see no reason why it should not stand in its present state."[53]

As Byron's stay abroad lengthened, Davies became ever more desperate. In July he had written to Byron that, happy as he was to have heard from him, he would be happier finally to see him, as "I am not only not relieved from responsibility, but am obliged to pay the Arrears. . . . I can say no more at present but that I am subject to arrest day after day and nothing but your return can relieve me."[54]

Davies's anguish finally got to Byron, for on November 25 he wrote to Hobhouse: "Tell Davies, in a very few months I shall be at home to relieve him from his responsibility which he would never have incurred so long, had I been aware 'of the law's delay' and the (not Insolence) but 'Indolence of office.' "[55] The last remark was an allusion to the habitually dilatory Hanson, who, by failing to answer Byron's letters for more than a year, allowed him to assume that Rochdale and his Norfolk property had both been sold and his debts liquidated, with ample funds to spare.

Now that he was disabused of any notion of solvency, Byron had a new excuse to vacillate about returning to England. He reiterated that he could not come home "without a further supply [of money]."[56] These remarks, to be sure, suggest an attempt at arm twisting more than any statement of intent, and indeed, a few weeks later, he informed the lawyer that, having received a *firman* allowing him to visit Egypt and Syria, "I shall not return to England before I have visited Jerusalem Grand Cairo."[57]

Byron's twenty-third birthday, on January 22, found his contentment undisturbed by money problems—his own or others'. In high spirits, he described to Hodgson his idyllic situation at the Capuchin convent as it might be reported by a Cockney visitor, with "Hymettus before me, the Acropolis behind, the temple of Jove to right, the Stadium in front, the town to the left, eh, Sir, there's a situation, there's your picturesque! nothing like that, Sir, in Lunnun, no not even the Mansion House."

Feasting on woodcocks and red mullet every day and with three horses to ride, he could wish for nothing save a few books, "one's own works for instance, any damned nonsense on a long Evening."[58]

With little to read, Byron was driven back to writing. On March 2 he began *Hints from Horace*. Planned as a sequel to *English Bards*, the new satire was more polished and less shrill: an elegant offering in a well-worn tradition, that of free imitations of Horace's *Art of Poetry*, with liberal borrowings from Byron's favorite, Alexander Pope. Possibly because of its happy association of time and place, Byron would always rank this poem as one of his best—not a view shared by readers or critics since. Along with repeating swipes at his elders: ("Write but like

Wordsworth—live besides a lake / And keep your bushy locks a year from Blake [a Fleet Street barber]"") the new poem also revealed more of the maturing Byron's own ambitions, his conviction that

> . . . Poesy, between the best and worst
> No medium knows,—you must be last or first[59]

Despite some sparkling passages whose verve presages *Don Juan*, *Hints* gives little reason to agree with the author's high estimate, and various plans for publishing it—accompanying a new edition of *English Bards*, or facing Horace's Latin—all fell through. A few weeks later he began another work, *The Curse of Minerva*. Before the poem changed course, continuing the savage attack on Lord Elgin begun in *Childe Harold*, the first stanza explodes on our vision like a Turner, opening with Byron's famous lines on Greece:

> Slow sinks, more lovely ere his race be run,
> Along Morea's hills the setting Sun;
> Not as in Northern climes obscurely bright,
> But one unclouded blaze of living light;
> O'er the hush'd deep the yellow beam he throws,
> Gilds the green wave that trembles as it glows[60]

On March 19 Byron gave a supper for the entire Frank colony. To repay his social debts all at one time hinted of the host's plans to leave Athens shortly. In preparation for his return to England and relations with women, he embarked on a series of casual sexual adventures with the local heterae: "I had a number of Greek and Turkish women, and I believe the rest of the English were equally lucky for we were all *clapped*," he wrote to Hobhouse.[61]

Exactly one month later, he was host at a farewell dinner. Of those he would leave behind in Athens, the most inconsolable was his Albanian servant Dervish; during preparations for his master's departure he wept continuously. Byron was deeply affected by this display of feelings, which, "contrasted with his native ferocity, improved my opinion of the human heart."[62]

On April 22 Cockerell and Foster, along with two German friends, saw Byron, accompanied by Nicolo Giraud and a pair of Greek servants, aboard the transport *Hydra*, bound for Malta. But the next day, as their friend's ship was still at anchor waiting on a favorable wind, they decided on another, musical farewell. Passing under the stern in an open boat, they lustily sang one of Byron's favorite songs. As soon as he came to the porthole, the serenaders were invited on board for a glass of port. Warned that the ship was under sail, they left an hour later. But it was only the following afternoon that they watched the *Hydra* weigh anchor and, sails billowing, round Cape Colonna. It was Byron's last sight of his beloved Sunium.

On board the *Hydra* he had Lusieri to distract him from his gonorrhea combined with a case of hemorrhoids. Supreme irony, his friend was escorting the last of Lord Elgin's marbles to Malta, where, like Byron, they would await passage to England.

In Valletta, meanwhile, Constance Spencer Smith was waiting for Byron's return. True to their parting vows, she had come back to Malta early in the fall of 1810, but the weeks turned into months, with no word or sign of Byron's promised reappearance. Ever more anxiously she dispatched letters to mutual friends and friendly sea captains bound for Athens. Dated November 12, her first letter to Byron that survives gets right to the point: "Conceiving a promise allways [*sic*] to be sacred I never forgot the conversation you had with me last year on the 16th September,"[63] she wrote reproachfully. On March 3 of the new year, 1811, she wrote again. Mentioning her earlier unanswered letters, she voices the hope of all rejected lovers: Perhaps her notes have gone astray. Life had taught Constance to be realistic—whatever Byron's feelings, she must salvage her self-respect: "If your plans and sentiments are changed have the goodness to answer in sending back this letter." Captain Ferguson of the *Pylades* felt sorry for the lovelorn woman; with more compassion than honesty, he told her that Byron "did mean to write"; repeating these consoling words to her lover, she added wistfully: "Malta is rather more brilliant than it was and perhaps you would like it."

Byron arrived on the last day of April, hoping that his silence had discouraged Constance into leaving. "But she *was* there," he recalled later, "& we met—at the Palace & the Governor (ye most accommodating of all possible chief magistrates) was kind enough to leave us to the most diabolical of explanations. It was in the Dog days, during a sirocco (I almost perspire now with the thoughts of it), during the intervals of an intermittent fever (my love had also intermitted with my malady) and I certainly feared the Ague and my Passion would both return in full force. I however got the better of both, & she sailed up the Adriatic & I down the Straits."[64]

THE REALIZATION of Byron's worst fear—being in thrall to a woman—had been averted. But his recurrent sicknesses, the alternating fever of love and ague, caused him to remain in Malta for a month. All the "diabolical explanations" with which he had come prepared had been swept away. The aftermath of both forms of delirium was not a sense of deliverance, but profound depression.

Finally, on June 2, Byron boarded the frigate *Volage* for the six-week voyage to England. The ship set sail in an atmosphere of celebration. A month earlier, along with four sister vessels, she had returned victorious from a defeat of combined French and Italian squadrons at Lissa, off the Dalmatian coast. Hailed as naval heroes, her crew had spent the month feted by all Malta.

Being upstaged did nothing to raise Byron's spirits. The young sailors were reminders that at twenty-three, he was no longer a boy. Just before embarking, he had parted from his own faithful young friend, enrolling Nicolo in a Jesuit school to improve his languages for a business career. What Byron had not been able to do for Edleston perhaps he could provide for Nicolo. As a further gesture of responsibility, he made a handsome provision for him in his will.

A week before leaving Malta, Byron wrote a journal entry in the form of a list, dispiritedly headed "Four or Five Reasons in Favor of a Change." In his present state of mind they were soon extended to seven: "1st At twenty three the best of life is over and its bitters double. 2ndly I have seen mankind in various countries and find them equally despicable, if anything the Balance is rather in favor of the Turks. 3dly I am sick at heart." Quoting Horace, he confessed "Me jam nec *faemina* [Nor maid nor youth delights me now]. 4thly A man who is lame of one leg is in a state of bodily inferiority which increases with years and must render his old age more peevish & intolerable. Besides in another existence I expect to have *two* if not *four* legs by way of compensation. 5thly I grow selfish and misanthropical, something like the 'jolly Miller' I care for nobody no not I and Nobody cares for me. 6thly My affairs at home and abroad are gloomy enough. 7thly I have outlived all my appetites and most of my vanities aye even the vanities of authorship."[65]

He tried to cheer himself by writing a spate of letters full of plans and projects. Then suddenly all his foolery fails him; he can no longer whistle in the engulfing darkness: "Dear Hobby, you must excuse all this facetiousness which I should not have let loose, if I knew what the Devil to do, but I am so out of Spirits, & hopes, & humour, & pocket, & health, that you must bear with my merriment."[66]

Five weeks later, on July 11, he disembarked at Sheerness.

PART TWO

Fame and Infamy

CHAPTER 16

Childe Harold's Homecoming

THE RETURNING traveler arrived with two Greek servants, three live tortoises, four Athenian skulls, and a vial of Attic hemlock. Along with the last shipment of the Elgin treasures, the hold of the *Volage* also contained marbles acquired by Hobhouse and entrusted to Byron. After his attacks on the Scottish peer (the manuscript of his most savage polemic, *The Curse of Minerva,* was in his baggage), we may wonder whether Byron perceived any irony in his first errand on English soil: storing Hobhouse's booty in the customs house at Sheerness.

When he arrived in London on July 14, Byron settled into the familiar comfort of Reddish's Hotel, on St. James's Street. The miasma that had enveloped him during the voyage lifted like the Ushant fogs. Of his recent physical afflictions, "an *Ague,* & a *Clap,* and the *Piles,*" there was no further mention.[1] Bristling with energy, he promptly immersed himself in business—his publications, property, and finances—along with the pleasure of reunions with friends.

His first visitor was Scrope Davies. "[He] came to me *drunk* last night," Byron reported to Hobhouse, "& was very friendly, & has got a new set of Jokes, but to you they are doubtless not new."[2] Byron must have been relieved by his friend's good humor: Scrope's financial woes were largely Byron's fault, and the promptness of his call, along with evidence of hard drinking, suggest that desperation lay behind the jokes. Byron had returned determined to settle his outstanding debts. From shipboard he had written to Hanson, begging £30 or £40; he had debarked without even the cash needed to pay the customs duty and coach from Portsmouth to London. He now insisted that Hanson discharge his debt—"dishonoured" for two years, he confessed—to Miller, his patient bookseller.

His own first appointment was a visit to his publisher, James Cawthorn, on Fleet Street. During his last months of travel Byron had fired off a series of scolding letters to Cawthorn for failing to forward mail, but on finding parcels from the publisher awaiting him in Athens and Malta, he wanted to tender his apologies in person, as well as to toast the good news also contained in Cawthorn's mailing: The fourth edition of *English Bards and Scotch Reviewers* was almost sold out, and the publisher was ready to launch a fifth printing. Byron left his latest work, *Hints from Horace,* a fresh attack on his contemporaries, with Cawthorn, intending it to be published as an appendage to any reissue of *English Bards.*

Byron's alacrity in visiting Cawthorn is another measure of the changes wrought by his grand tour. The aristocratic amateur was gradually shedding his feudal armor, to reveal the ambitious poet, not afraid to take himself seriously. He no longer needed a go-between to mediate dealings with his publishers.

His newfound confidence now gave off sparks in other directions. He wrote to Hobhouse, reminding him of their plan to establish a literary forum of their own—"a periodical paper, something in the Spectator or Observer way. There certainly is no such thing at present.—Why not get one, Tuesdays & Saturdays." Knowing his own work habits and "Citizen" Matthews's dangerous views on freedom of speech, he told Hobhouse: "You must be Editor, as you have more taste and diligence than either Matthews or myself." He proposed that each issue of their biweekly should feature "one or two essays, miscellaneous, according to Circumstances, but now & then politics, and always a piece of poetry of one kind or other." He was familiar enough with London literary life to predict that they would never want for contributors, and with his new practicality, he reasoned "it would be pleasant, and with success, in some degree, profitable."[3]

Byron had written to Dallas with word of his imminent arrival, inviting his kinsman to call on him in London and concluding with the tantalizing news that he had a freshly completed work in hand, "but don't let that deter you," Byron teased, "for I shan't inflict it upon you. You know I never read my rhymes to visitors."[4] Sure enough, Dallas scurried over to Reddish's Hotel immediately on reading these words, only to discover that the traveler had not yet arrived. He left a welcoming note, together with a practical proposal for helping Byron to deal with his tangled finances: "I wish you would allow me to recommend to you a gentleman I have long known . . . one of the best accountants in the kingdom. He would, I am confident, save you a world of trouble and a world of money."[5] Byron ignored the suggestion, one of the most sensible he would ever receive—just as he would later ignore Hobhouse's related pleading to dismiss Hanson and engage a more conscientious lawyer. At some level Byron thrived on confusion in his financial affairs and incompetence on the part of those who were supposed to manage them. Uncertainty absolved him of responsibility, giving him permission to borrow and spend in ignorance.

According to Dallas, when he called again he found Byron too distracted to do more than greet his visitor warmly and pack him off with the manuscript of his Horatian imitation, saying he believed satire to be his forte. They arranged to have a leisurely breakfast the following morning. That night Dallas read the "paraphrase" as Byron described *Hints from Horace.*

"I must say I was grievously disappointed," Dallas recalled of the verses, adding that "a muse much inferior to his might have produced them in the smoky atmosphere of London, whereas he had been roaming under the cloudless skies of Greece, on sites where every step he took might have set such a fancy as his 'in fine phrenzies rolling.'"[6]

On his visit the next day, Dallas was, of course, careful not to be "disparaging" of the poem. He did, however, permit himself to express "some surprise" that Byron had returned with nothing else. Byron confessed that he had occasionally written other short poems, "besides a great many stanzas in Spenser's measure." Opening a small trunk, he took out a sheaf of manuscript pages and gave them to Dallas, noting that they had been read by only one other person, "who had found very little to commend, and much to condemn" in the lines—an opinion that Byron claimed to share.[7]

Dallas is precise in recording his own immediate and overwhelming enthusiasm for the new work: "I could not refrain from writing to him that very evening, the sixteenth of July," he recalled, when he told the poet: "You have written one of the most delightful poems I have ever read. If I wrote this in flattery, I should deserve your contempt rather than your friendship. . . . I have been so fascinated with Childe Harold, that I have not been able to lay it down."

Along with praise, the conventional Dallas freely expressed his misgivings about the poem's polemical stance, urging his friend, in the same letter, to "some alterations and omissions which I think indispensable."

Again, according to Dallas, Byron persisted in rating the work as much inferior to his satire. But finding Dallas's enthusiasm persuasive, he apparently agreed to "curtail and soften" some of the stanzas his friend had deemed offensive, especially those expressing "harsh political reflections on the Government,"[8] and to allow Dallas (now in possession of both the manuscript and the copyright by gift of the author) to oversee *Childe Harold*'s publication while delaying Cawthorn's plans to bring out *Hints from Horace*. Overjoyed, Dallas rushed the scrawled pages to his nephew, who was entrusted with making a fair copy for the printer.

Now the only question that remained to be settled was who would publish *Childe Harold*. Since his return, Byron had heard literary gossip dismissing Cawthorn as second-rate; as he would shortly advise Hobhouse, one could not overstate the importance of the right publisher: "Much depends on him, & if the first men of the profession court your work, why deal with a vendor of lampoons?"[9]

Byron himself was disposed toward William Miller, who, as it happened, was his bookseller. In his version of the story, Dallas now trotted off to deliver the two cantos in person to the publisher's offices on Albemarle Street. But far from courting *Childe Harold* and its author, Miller promptly rejected the work; he, too, was worried by the poet's skeptical posture toward orthodox Christianity and by his jabs at the Tory establishment. More personally, he told Dallas, he could not publish a work that attacked his friend and patron Lord Elgin. Byron's graceful letter to Miller assured the publisher that critical opinion, he had no doubt, would deal with the work still more harshly; meanwhile, he disassociated himself from any conscious blasphemy toward church or state by a double alibi: He was a mere imitator of an earlier poet, as *Childe Harold* "was intended to be a poem on *Ariosto's plan*, that *is* to *say* on *no plan* at all."[10] That Byron recognized this claim to be untrue is revealed by his recourse to the same paradox that would be advanced by the surrealists one hundred years later: His poem was "intended" to have "no plan."

Following Miller's rejection, Byron decided to leave the matter in Dallas's hands and, with the proviso that he not take *Childe Harold* to Cawthorn or Longman,* left him free to place the work where he chose.

True to his resolve to deal promptly with creditors, on July 16, two days after arriving in London, Byron wrote to Mrs. Massingberd expressing "concern . . . for the difficulty you have been under with regard to the annuities." He assured his former landlady that he had "returned to England for the purpose of arranging the business," which,

---

*The publisher was on Byron's enemies list for having rejected *English Bards and Scotch Reviewers*.

he promised, would be settled as soon as he and Hanson returned from a planned trip to the Rochdale collieries. At the same time, however, he gave Massingberd a weapon for keeping the moneylenders at bay: "You are perhaps not aware of the illegality of the transaction, and if I hear that any further difficulty takes place, I shall be under the necessity of bringing the whole before a Court, but if Mr. Howard will remain quiet for a short time, and not compel us to such measures I shall make every effort to discharge you from your responsibility."[11] Byron was suggesting that Massingberd resort to a little blackmail; Mr. Howard had transacted unlawfully with a minor, and if he gave his guarantor any further problems, she should turn him in to the authorities.

The following day Byron set off for a reunion with Hobhouse. To placate his father, Hobby had, improbably, joined the "Cornish Miners," an elite militia regiment training in Dover before being sent to Ireland to keep the peace. But as Byron had no cash for the long coach to the coast, the two friends agreed to meet halfway, in Sittingbourne. For two days they caught up with one another's lives while sightseeing in nearby Canterbury.

The repressive atmosphere of Tory England had already infected Hobhouse, together with his new role as captain in a militia unit training to quell riots and other forms of rebellion. Anxiously he warned Byron against discussing his sexual adventures in the East with anyone, *especially* not their outspoken friend "Citizen" Matthews, and he confided his relief that some unbuttoned letters of his own had apparently been lost at sea. Hobby was undiscouraged by the fate of his first published work. Despite Byron's contributions, Hobhouse's collection, *Imitations and Translations,* had found so few buyers that Scrope Davies was moved to inquire after Hobhouse's "miss-sell-any." Most unfair of all, the erotic whiff of his version of Boccaccio, while failing to help sales, had managed to call down censure. When Hobhouse was on his way home, he had received word from Hodgson that a certain Hudson (probably of Trinity College) had accused the collection of "indecency." Sensibly deciding to devote himself to prose (and thereby also softening the edge of competition with his friend), Hobby was now hard at work on the journal of his travels with Byron through the East.*

A Journey Through Albania and other Provinces of Turkey in Europe and Asia, to Constantinople, During the years 1809 and 1810 was the lively result and the only narrative in which Byron can be said to figure as both hero and muse. The poet reciprocated by assuming the role of agent for his friend, trying, without success, to persuade Miller to publish the work before placing the book with Cawthorn.

A few days after his return from Sittingbourne, Byron visited Henry Drury at Harrow, where his former tutor's household was already enlivened with several young children. More surprising, his Cambridge crony "Bold" Webster, oafish mascot of their group, had taken to himself a beautiful, rich, and well-born young bride, Lady Frances Annesley, daughter of the Earl of Mountnorris and sister of Viscount Valentia. Eager to display his prize, Webster importuned Byron with invitations to visit them in the country, but failing to lure his friend from town, arranged an evening at the theater so his guest could admire Lady Frances's superior sensibilities as she wept through the tragic proceedings onstage. Writing to Hobhouse, Byron made sport of this fresh instance of Webster's idiocy. With the eye of a predator, he had noticed that the young bride already treated her husband with a certain contempt.

When he was not exalting his wife's tender heart, Webster drove a tough bargain. Byron had ordered a vis-à-vis from Goodall, the most fashionable London coachmaker. Realizing the impracticality of a two-seater for his social life, involving, as it often did, parties of friends, he later agreed to exchange this occasional vehicle, plus 200 guineas, for Webster's coach. When the coach arrived with its upholstery and lining in tatters, Byron was outraged. An acrimonious exchange followed; as he now made plain, he would neither accept the carriage with worn fittings nor deliver the vis-à-vis. With a swipe at Webster's aspirations, Byron taunted: "The Coronet will not *grace* the pretty 'Vis' till your tattered lining ceases to dis*grace* it."[12] But Byron soon softened; he never liked anyone to go away with a grudge and, as Webster felt so strongly that he had gotten a bad bargain, Byron sold the smaller chaise back to Goodall, paying Webster a further supplement to renovate his carriage.

In his two-year absence from England, other bachelor acquaintances had succumbed to marriage and domestic life. Byron was reminded of his mother's plea to find a "golden dolly." If he was to continue ordering carriages when he hadn't the fare for the public coach to take him from London to Dover, he must think of selling his own coronet for a sizable settlement.

"Money is the magnet," he wrote to Augusta, whose marriage was already a misery, with a gambling husband and a new baby every year. "As to women, one is as well as another, the older the better, we have than a chance of getting her to Heaven."[13]

As yet, no aging heiress had come to his rescue. In Chancery Lane, however, Hanson, acting with exceptional efficiency, was actually drawing up copyhold* papers for Byron to sign that would legally establish his inherited claim to the Wymondham estates in Norfolk. He wanted the documents in his hands, Byron wrote to his mother on July 23, before he set out for Newstead and the long-overdue tour of the Rochdale collieries.

That same week, Byron discovered that an old enemy, Hewson Clarke of Cambridge, had renewed his attacks, this time widening his target to include Byron's grandfather and both of his parents. In the March 1811 issue of *The Scourge*, a scurrilous scandal sheet published while the poet was still abroad, Clarke had unleashed the full fury of his revenge for the dismissal of his lowly origins in Byron's Postscript to the second edition of *English Bards and Scotch Reviewers* by writing: "It may be reasonably asked whether to be a denizen of Berwick-on-Tweed, be more disgraceful than to be the illegitimate descendant of a murderer, whether to be the offspring of parents whose only crime is their want of title, be not as honorable as to be the son of a profligate father, and a mother whose days and nights are spent in a delirium of drunkenness."[14]

HONOR DEMANDED that Byron seek satisfaction against these slurs on his parents, his legitimacy, and, by extension, his right to a peerage. The last two, he told Hobhouse, were "separate concerns," from the action he planned on behalf of his mother, the personal attack on whom had cut more deeply. Exploring the grounds for a libel suit, he had given the offending issue of *The Scourge* to the attorney general, predicting gleefully that when the matter came before the court, "it will be a long & loud affair."†[15]

Another target of Byron's wrath was still unaware of the persecution to come. On leaving Greece, Lusieri had given Byron a letter to be forwarded to Lord Elgin, which Byron had mailed on his return to England. Anxious to thank the courier in person and to have a first-hand account of his agent's progress, Elgin wrote to Byron several times between July 27 and 31 to request a meeting. Understandably embar-

---

*In practical terms, copyhold rights established the hereditary claims of both the lord and his laborers to the land they cultivated.

†Ultimately, the attorney general, Sir Vicery Gibbs, persuaded Byron against bringing suit; too much time had elapsed between the publication of the article and the response. As the first to attack, moreover, Byron had provoked Clarke's wrath, thereby further weakening his case.

rassed at the prospect of a face-to-face encounter, Byron tried putting
him off, first with a written report on "all I knew about his robberies,"[16]
he told Hobhouse, followed by an evasive letter in which Byron tried to
cast his refusal to meet Elgin in an honorable light: Lest he should later
be accused of "double dealing," he wrote, his lordship should know
that he planned to publish his own views on the marbles.[17]

In the event, both were spared the awkwardness of a confrontation.
On July 31 Byron received word that his mother was dying.

The news, relayed by a Newstead servant, could not have come as a
complete shock. In two letters that reached him on his travels, Catherine
wrote that she had been very ill. Then, shortly after Byron arrived in
London, he apparently received a note from a Nottingham surgeon
advising of his mother's serious condition but assuring him that his
patient did not appear to be in imminent danger. (The surgeon's letter
may also have prompted Byron to write to his mother on July 23, when,
without mentioning her illness, he promised that he would be leaving
London for Newstead as soon as possible.) In itself, however, a letter
from a surgeon to his patient's next of kin could be taken as warning
enough, had Byron chosen to read the message carefully. Indeed, the
doctor's optimistic prognosis proved short-lived; his mother's condition
deteriorated rapidly. Alarmed, the surgeon, Mr. Marsden, now advised
that her son be sent for immediately. A servant was dispatched from
Newstead to London, but before he had reached Nottingham, Robert
Rushton overtook him with the news: Catherine Byron was dead.

On the day of her death, August 1, Byron received another letter
from Newstead with word only that his mother was dying. He rushed
to the Hansons' house, where he learned that the lawyer was not home.
He left a frantic note explaining that, as he had no money for the coach
fare to Nottingham, he had drawn on him for £40. But the following
day, Byron was still in London when the abbey servant arrived with the
mournful news. Setting out immediately, Byron wrote from Newport
Pagnell to John Pigot, now a practicing physician in Chester: "My poor
mother died yesterday! and I am on my way from town to attend her to
the family vault." In this account, Byron suppressed the first letter from
the surgeon informing him of Catherine Byron's condition. "I heard *one*
day of her illness, the *next* of her death," he wrote, quoting the consoling report he had received from those witnesses to her dying: "Thank
God her last moments were most tranquil. I am told she was in little
pain, and not aware of her situation."[18]

There is no record of the cause of Catherine's death at age forty-six.
In the two years she lived at Newstead, she suffered attacks of unspecified illness, when she was attended by two physicians: Dr. Hutchinson

(the same who had prescribed Byron's diet) and Mr. Marsden, the Nottingham surgeon; obesity and the likelihood that there was some truth behind Clarke's remarks about her drunkenness point to renal, liver, circulatory, or heart failure as possibilities.* As the final measure of her unvalued life, local gossip repeated a farcical version of her last moments: She was said to have died "from a fit of rage, brought on . . . by reading over the upholsterer's bills." (Although enormous, her son's £2,100 bill from Brothers had arrived four months before her death, along with the bailiffs who threatened the liquidation of Newstead furnishings, until they were persuaded, probably by Hanson, to defer their claims.)

Byron did not absorb the fact of his mother's death until he saw the corpse laid out in a Newstead bedchamber. Then his state of shock gave way to grief. He knew too well how irreplaceable was the intensity of Catherine Byron's love. Her rage, insults, and mockery, and his own fury and flight, were feeble attempts to escape their need for each other. Astute as ever, John Galt noted from his conversations with Byron that his mother's affection, "so fond and dear," was repaid in the son's most "casual and incidental expressions . . . concerning her." His love for her, Galt observed, "was not at any time even of the ordinary kind."[19]

On the night of Byron's arrival at Newstead, Catherine's maid, passing the room where her mistress lay, heard strange sounds within. The master was sitting in the dark, next to his mother's body. When the servant reproached him for giving way to unmanly grief, he burst into tears, blurting, "Oh, Mrs. By, I had but one friend in the world and she is gone!"[20] Beyond her exclusive love, Byron recognized the unchanged innocence of the country girl, and pursuing his libel suit with renewed zeal, he told Hanson, "I will have no stain on the Memory of my Mother, with a very large portion of foibles & irritability, she was without a *Vice* (& in these days that is much)."[21]

He was unable to accompany Catherine Byron's remains to their final resting place in the family vault at Hucknall Torkard. Paralyzed, Byron stood in the abbey doorway, watching the servant pallbearers and carriage carrying the coffin disappear down the sandy road. Calling for Robert Rushton to bring his boxing gloves for their daily session, he

---

*Her obesity, as well as her chronic and ultimately terminal illness, are often attributed to dropsy, a frequent nineteenth-century description still repeated unquestioningly today. In fact, dropsy or edema—the condition of swelling due to effusion of watery fluid into intercellular spaces of connective tissue—is not a disease, but a symptom of the diseases mentioned above, along with other possible ones.

sparred without speaking, jabbing and pummeling with a violence he had never shown before, the page recalled. Then, abruptly, his master threw down the gloves and left the room.

For her son, the tragedy of Catherine Byron's death was the pain of missed opportunity. Their last meeting before Byron left England remained an unhealed wound. They had missed, by a single day, the redemptive promise of forgiveness and love.

Now, left to wander Newstead's rooms, empty or overfurnished in his manic decorating spree, Byron pondered his mother's failed life and his own confused existence. Then, only days after Catherine Byron was buried, he was dealt another blow: On Friday evening, August 2, he was told, Charles Skinner Matthews had drowned while swimming the River Cam.

Byron received the news in a note from Hobhouse, dated August 3, containing a letter from Scrope Davies, who had been in Cambridge at the time of the tragedy. To add to the shock, the day after Byron learned of the event, he received a letter from Matthews written the day before he died.

With characteristic generosity, Byron felt the loss most keenly for Hobhouse; as he confessed to Dallas, he himself had admired the dead man more than he had loved him. But Matthews had been Hobhouse's closest friend, possibly the only human being to whom the wary Hobby bared his soul. Byron even feared for his friend's sanity.

It was not grief alone that devastated Hobhouse. He was crushed by guilt. He was not alone. Guilt enveloped the nervous mourning of the small circle of Matthews's friends; it flickered through all of their consoling words to one another, in the silence of words they dared not say: Matthews's death was not an accident.

A century earlier, the case had been made that most people found drowned were, in fact, suicides. The pains taken to conceal the act point to the very different view of ending one's own life that prevailed in the eighteenth and well into the nineteenth century, when, as one historian notes, "The degree of animus directed against self-slaughter is hard for the modern mind to grasp."[22] Until our own century, a suicide, it was believed, committed a crime against both his sovereign and his God. The consequences to the suicide's survivors went beyond the ruin of reputation, desecration of memory, or even loss of salvation. The heirs of the dead forfeited their inheritance; the possessions of a suicide became the property of the Crown. Family and friends would do everything possible to ensure that an ambiguous fatality was stamped with the verdict "accidental death."

All the circumstances of Matthews's death were suspicious. He drowned while swimming alone in the early evening, but not in the River Cam itself. Matthews had gone to a bathing spot he knew well, which can be located with some certainty as a canal cut in the river, north of Newnham Mill.* A few days after he had heard the news, Byron, mourning unguardedly to Scrope Davies, noted that Matthews had "drowned in a ditch,"[23] confirming that the distance between the banks was a matter of yards; a few strokes would carry any swimmer from one side to the other, while the branches of trees sweeping the water would provide a natural rope for anyone in difficulty. The weakest piece in the official version of Matthews's death, however, emerges from one of the obituaries: He is supposed to have been caught in the weeds and dragged to his death, yet the newspaper account itself notes that he drowned "in the presence of three gentlemen strolling along the banks."[24]

His friends would not have wondered at the despair driving Matthews to take his own life. His intimate circle had all left Cambridge; there was no one to soften the pitiless reality of his future, which promised only suffering for "Citizen" Matthews, atheist, homosexual, a man determined to speak his mind, with no private means or grand connections to shield him. He had saved discretion for his death. Inquiring after his friend's effects, Byron learned that "not a scrap of paper has been found, at Cambridge, which is singular."[25]

Mourning defined the emotional poles separating Byron and Hobhouse. Byron charged friends of the dead man to recall his brilliance, originality, courage, and wit. "In ability, who was like Matthews? How did we all shrink before him? . . . We will drink to his Memory, which though it cannot reach the dead, will soothe the Survivors."[26] Hobhouse could deaden pain only by obliterating its cause: "We have a right to endeavor to forget all those whom we have lost," he wrote to Byron from Cork on August 25. "There is nothing left for us but an oblivion of all that has passed respecting them. Were we to call to mind the amiable qualities of their heads and hearts—what end would there be to our grief? As to our mutual friend, let us never mention his name more. He is gone forever."[27]

There seemed no end to Byron's losses. In the frenzy of leaving London for Newstead and his dying mother, he had learned, without quite registering the news, that one of his Harrow favorites,

---

*Now part of the Croft Nature Reserve. Unlike a body of water with a natural shoreline, which after 180 years could be subject to dramatic erosion, time has had little opportunity to alter the parallel lines of the canal's man-made banks.

John Wingfield, had died of a fever in Coimbra, Portugal, joining Ned Long in the roll of school friends who had perished in the Peninsular War.

On December 12 he wrote to Catherine Byron's solicitor, Samuel Bolton of Nottingham, enclosing a draft of his will. He left Newstead to his young cousin, George Anson Byron, who as next in line to the title was "heir at law." His other major bequest was £7,000, to be paid to "Nicolo Giraud (resident of Athens and Malta in the year 1810) to receive the above sum on his attaining the age of twenty-one." To his servants Demetrius Zograffo, Joseph Murray, and William Fletcher, he left £50 a year for life, with the additional bequest to Fletcher of the Mill at Newstead, "on the condition that he payeth rent, but not subject to the caprice of the landlord." His page Robert Rushton was to receive this same annual income for life, with a further sum of £1,000 when he came of age. Byron's only other cash bequest was £2,000 to John Hanson, Esq. Byron's library and "furniture of every description" were to be divided between J. C. Hobhouse and S. B. Davies. Regarding his outstanding debts to the latter, Byron was rather vague, stating, "The claims of S. B. Davies to be satisfied on proving the amount of same." In a subsequent note, however, he directed that the stipulation of proof be dropped.[28] This change may have been prompted by Davies's visit to Newstead, when, as Byron reported to Hodgson, their friend's "gaiety (death cannot mar it) has done me service; but after all, ours was a hollow laughter."[29] He had also appointed Davies one of his executors, to which Bolton objected on the grounds that executors were entitled to repay themselves any debts owed them by the deceased without consultation with their co-executors. But Byron insisted that Davies be retained. The solicitor had left blanks for the first names of the others: the Reverend Becher of Southwell and R. C. Dallas. Byron's real feelings about his relative were revealed in a note scribbled in the margin opposite the designated space. "I forget the Christian name of Dallas—cut him out."[30]

Summer was drawing to a close. In the abbey's galleries, for the first time in his life Byron felt solitude as abandonment: "At three and twenty I am left alone, and what more can we be at seventy?" He grieved for the dead as witnesses of his youth: "With whom can I retrace the laughing part of life?" he asked Dallas.[31] Each death further loosed his moorings, until his mood ascended, quite literally, to a state of manic levity: "I am very lonely, & should think myself miserable, were it not for a kind of hysterical merriment, which I can neither account for, or conquer," he confessed to Hobhouse.[32]

Both loneliness and hysteria were eased by writing. From the middle of August on, Byron posted several long letters daily—to Hobhouse, Hodgson, Hanson, Augusta, and Dallas, to whom he explained, "I am writing I know not what to escape from myself."[33]

GRADUALLY his manic state subsided. He acknowledged that the mystery of death confounded his powers of thought; yet even as he declared the uncertainty of his belief, he spoke as a rationalist: "There is to me something so incomprehensible in death, that I can neither think or speak on the subject.—Indeed when I looked on the Mass of Corruption, which was the being from whence I sprang, I doubted within myself whether I *was*, or She was not—I have lost her who gave me Being, & some of those who made that Being a blessing. —I have neither hopes nor fears beyond the Grave, yet if there is within us a 'spark of that Celestial Fire' M[atthews] has already 'mingled with the Gods.' "[34]

Unlike the aggressively atheistic Matthews, Byron always allowed for the possibility of the divine, while his avowed perplexity, together with professions of sinfulness, challenged orthodox friends to work harder for his salvation. His many contradictory statements to his friends on the nature of his religious belief further encouraged their efforts; perhaps they were meant to. He was, in any case, well aware of the differing nature of their concerns: Dallas was concerned with the political rather than with the spiritual consequences of Byron's disbelief. Hodgson, on the eve of ordination, worried about the peril to his friend's soul; he suggested reading lists and advanced lumbering refutations of Byron's airy arguments against religion. Hodgson found especially distressing his rejection of the afterlife: "I will have nothing to do with your immortality; we are miserable enough in this life without the absurdity of speculating upon another," Byron declared.

His recent travels had only reinforced doubt: What kind of faith condemned millions for reasons of their ignorance alone? He demanded a more just measure of who should be saved or damned, arguing, along with Voltaire and other Enlightenment thinkers, for virtue as the only condition of salvation: "As to revealed religion, Christ came to save men; but a good Pagan will go to heaven, and a bad Nazarene to Hell. . . . Why are not all men Christians? or why are any? If mankind may be saved who never heard or dreamt, at Timbuctoo, Otaheite, Terra Incognita, &c., of Gallilee and its Prophet, Christianity is of no avail, if they cannot be saved without, why are not all orthodox? . . . Who will believe that God will damn men for not knowing what they were never taught? I hope I am sincere," he announced, now doubting himself along with orthodoxy. "I was so at least on a bed of sickness in a far distant country, when I had neither friend, nor comforter, nor hope to sustain me. I looked to death as a relief from pain, without a wish for an after-life, but a confidence that the God who punishes in this existence had left that last asylum for the weary."

Describing himself as "born to opposition," Byron could no more embrace established religions than he could profess blind adherence to a political party. He could never be a follower, and his loathing of institutions forced him into a position of aristocratic agnosticism. A moralist who recognized cant and hypocrisy behind any assertion of morality, he saw only the chasm that separated doctrine and practice. Still, refusal to profess Christianity, he wrote to Hodgson, did not make him a pagan: "I am no Platonist, I am nothing at all; but I would sooner be a Paulician, Manichean, Spinozist, Gentile, Pyrrhonian, Zoroastrian, than one of the seventy-two villainous sects who are tearing each other to pieces for the love of the Lord and the hatred of each other. Talk of Galileeism? Show me the effects—are you better, wiser, kinder by your precepts? I will bring you ten Mussulmans shall shame you in all goodwill towards men, prayer to God and duty to their neighbors. And is there a Talapoin* or a Bonze, who is not superior to a fox hunting curate? But I will say no more on this endless theme; let me live, well if possible, and die without pain. The rest is with God, who assuredly, had He *come* or *sent*, would have made Himself manifest to nations, and intelligible to all."[35]

To confirm Byron's dim view of the Anglican clergy, Hodgson himself was soon revealed as the weakest of sinners and, worse in Byron's eyes, a fool for love. Hodgson had been asked to look after the mistress of a friend serving in the navy; predictably, he himself was soon infatuated with the girl. Whether or not she was the "common strumpet" described by Byron, the young woman's sexual favors were easily diverted. When Hodgson's friend returned to find he had been betrayed, the young divine all but collapsed, pouring out his shame and self-loathing in tearful letters to Byron at Newstead.

Byron's response was coldly unsympathetic. Perhaps Hodgson's misery reminded him of his own humiliated passion for the yellow-haired Mary. His devout friend had made a fool of him as well. Without being converted, Byron had admired, perhaps even envied, the young cleric's faith, looking to him as a model for the Christian life. And now

---

*The term, used by Voltaire and other eighteenth-century French writers, describes Buddhist monks of Ceylon and Indochina.

Hodgson was blubbering away like any bumpkin in thrall to the first whore picked up in the Haymarket.

In Byron's most scarring early memory, pious hypocrisy had masked the cruelty and corruption of May Gray, his Scripture-quoting nurse and seducer. The small boy had been punished, driven from childhood, he later said, by the knowledge of heaven and hell as sexual torment. His apprehension of Christianity would remain that of a clever, angry schoolboy scoring off the arrogance and moral vacuity of the established church; in Georgian England, moreover, the vicars of Christ did not often exemplify a Christian vocation. Too intellectually rigorous and class-conscious to consider the evangelical alternative or dissenting sects whose "enthusymusy" he derided, Byron seized for himself the starring role of fallen angel, the outcast branded with the mark of Cain.

SLOWLY HE EMERGED from mourning. In mid-August, when Scrope Davies visited Newstead on his way to Harrogate, his host seemed closer to his old self. By the end of the month Byron was ready to resume negotiations with publishers. He wrote first to Cawthorn, with a ploy for putting off the imminent publication of *Hints from Horace*. Dallas was to have supplied the Latin original as part of the edition, which he had so far failed to do. There the matter stood, requiring further discussion "at some future period," Byron noted vaguely. Now, apologizing for the "domestic calamity" that had prevented his writing earlier,[36] Byron introduced himself in a letter to John Murray II. Although money was not at issue—Dallas owned the copyright, and in any case, gentlemen did not write for pay—Byron sounded every inch the professional. There were certain conditions to which Murray must agree concerning the publication of *Childe Harold*, and the author would give nothing away by appearing pleased by the publisher's interest.

Before leaving London, he had learned from Dallas that Murray planned to show the manuscript to William Gifford, a poet Byron admired whose satires had served as contemporary models for *English Bards and Scotch Reviewers*. As it happened, Gifford served as Murray's literary adviser and was editor of the *Quarterly Review*, published by Murray as the Tory answer to the cultural Whiggery of the *Edinburgh Review*. Thus, nothing would have been more natural than for John Murray to seek Gifford's opinion of *Childe Harold*; the poem was also sufficiently dangerous in its criticism of state and church to warrant a second opinion.

For his part, however, Byron saw this as a shameful acknowledgment that he needed a quasi-paid endorsement, similar to the modern-day blurb. He wrote to Dallas, "It is bad enough to be a scribbler, without having recourse to such shifts to extort praise, or deprecate censure. It is anticipating, it is begging, kneeling, adulating—the devil! the devil! the devil! and all without my wish, and contrary to my desire."[37]

More temperately, he declared to Murray, "Now, though no one would feel more gratified by the chance of obtaining [Gifford's] observations on a work than myself there is in such a proceeding, a kind of petition for praise that neither my pride or—whatever you please to call it—will admit.—Mr. G. is not only the first Satirist of the day, but Editor of one of the principal Reviews.—As such, he is the last man whose censure (however eager to avoid it) I would deprecate by clandestine means.—You will therefore retain the M.S. in your own care, or if it must needs be shown, send it to another.—Though not very patient of Censure, I would fain obtain fairly any little praise my rhymes might deserve, at all events not by extortion & the humble solicitations of a bandied about M.S.—I am sure a little consideration will convince you it would be wrong." He concluded on a more conciliatory note: Should Murray "determine on publication," he had a number of smaller, unpublished poems, along with notes, and a "short dissertation on the Literature of the modern Greeks,"[38] all of which were meant to follow *Childe Harold* in the same volume.

As it happened, his letter was too late: Murray (whom Byron had yet to meet) had already shown Gifford the manuscript of *Childe Harold*, Cantos I and II, weeks before receiving Byron's first comuniqué from Newstead. Gifford's reaction, however, as relayed by the unctuous Dallas, melted Byron's earlier objections: "Of your Satire* he spoke highly, but this Poem he pronounces, not only the best you have written, but equal to any of the present age, allowing however, for its being unfinished, which he regrets."[39] Intoxicated by the praise, Byron now wrote to Dallas, "As Gifford has been ever my 'Magnus Apollo' any approbation such as you mention, would, of course, be more welcome than 'all Bokara's vaunted gold, than all the gems of Samarkand.' "[40]

Gifford's regret at the poem's unfinished state provided reinforcement for Dallas's urgings to complete the work; at the same time Dallas now had Murray on his side in efforts to persuade Byron to delete material that both feared might offend. Astutely, Murray cast his concerns in marketing terms. In his first letter to the poet, he pointed out that certain remarks on Britain's role in Spain and Portugal "do not harmonize with the general feeling" and might work against the popularity of the

---

English Bards and Scotch Reviewers.

poem.⁴¹ Byron's reply was gracious but firm: Thanking Murray for his praise, he declared, "With regard to the political & metaphysical parts, I am afraid I can alter nothing, but I have high authority for my Errors in that point, for even the *Æneid* was a *political* poem & written for a *political* purpose, and as to my unlucky opinions on Subjects of more importance, I am too sincere in them for recantation—On Spanish affairs I have said what I saw, & every day confirms me in that notion of the result formed on the Spot." Then, shifting to Murray's own commercial ground, he added playfully, "As for the 'Orthodox,' let us hope they will buy on purpose to abuse, you will forgive the one if they will do the other."⁴²

On one crucial point, Byron yielded to his publisher. Fearing renewed attacks and anxious that he not be identified with *Childe Harold*, he wanted the poem published anonymously. In the face of Murray's resistance, however, Byron agreed to a compromise form of identity: The title page would read: "By the Author of *English Bards and Scotch Reviewers*." Given the ill feeling aroused by that first satire, however, this designation might have seemed more provocative than the name Lord Byron alone.

He was happy to leave Dallas with the task of seeing the manuscript through the press, chivying him at intervals about changes or the placement of a just-unearthed sheaf of notes to the poem. His other efforts as an author were devoted to soothing the ruffled feelings of Cawthorn, displeased by Byron's stalling on the publication of *Hints* and still angrier to learn that he was not to be the publisher of the other new work.

In the next weeks Byron tried to cheer Augusta, coaxing her, in a series of letters, to visit him at Newstead; to new babies and money worries had now been added the anxiety of scandal. Her husband, Colonel Leigh, equerry to the Prince of Wales, had been found cheating his royal patron on the sale of a horse. The ensuing quarrel put this sinecure at risk and threatened to turn financial difficulties to disaster. Although Byron teased her about his hatred of children, saying, "I abominate the sight of them so much that I have always had the greatest respect for the character of *Herod*," he assured her that even her young would be welcome. They could all convene in Cambridge and he would bring her back to Newstead: "We will travel in my *Vis.*—& can have a cage for the children & a Cart for the nurse.—Or perhaps we can forward them by Canal," he joked.⁴³

The playful invitation to Augusta signaled Byron's emergence from mourning. By the end of September he was ready to think of sexual attractions closer to hand: "I am plucking up my spirits and have begun to gather my little sensual comforts together," he reported to Hodgson. Lucy, the maid who had borne Byron's son, returned from Warwickshire, and was now promoted to "commander . . . of all the makers and unmakers of beds in the household." For this task he engaged a bevy of especially pretty servant girls, dismissing "some very bad faces" hired in his absence. To best display their attractions he decreed a new dress code, explaining to Hodgson, "As I am a great disciplinarian, I have just issued an edict for the abolition of caps; no hair to be cut on any pretext; stays permitted, but not too low before;* full uniform always in the evening."44

On September 25 Byron left Newstead for the long-deferred visit to Rochdale without Hanson, whose affairs kept him in London indefinitely. Either because of Hanson's defection or for other reasons, Byron got as far as Lancashire and extended what was to have been a brief stopover into a lengthy visit to Hopwood Hall, a manor house belonging to Robert Hopwood, a rich local squire. His hostess was the former Cecelia Byng, one of five famously beautiful sisters; two others were visiting at the time. Byron was probably invited at the behest of a fellow guest, Elizabeth Fraser, whom he had met when she was visiting her family in Malta (the same Frasers who were hosts to Constance Spencer Smith). Thus, when he arrived the hall was filled with attractive young women who all made much of him; he found it hard to leave for a solitary inspection tour of his coal mines.

On Byron's first night he refused to come down for dinner, explaining that it was his "starving day." "Every other day he eats only a biscuit, fruit &c and never sits down to meals on those days; he was once, he says, a great size,"45 recalled another guest, Mary Loveday. When she warned him of the dangers of such extreme dieting, and in particular of "the baneful effects of vinegar," which Byron imbibed in quantity, he replied that "he would rather not exist than be large and so he is a pale languid-looking young man who seems as if he could not walk upright from sheer weakness." Reinforcing the impression of feminine fragility, Byron wore long white linen pantaloons (in place of the dark breeches and light silk stockings then in fashion) and a long gold chain around his neck.

At the beginning of his visit, Miss Loveday observed, Byron appeared ill at ease and self-conscious, "always prowling about in the two sitting rooms, taking up many books and reading a little in each; then watching us and seeming inclined to talk." But the poet's "fidget-

---

*The higher-laced stays exposed more breast.

ing manner" made her too nervous to converse with him alone. Byron recognized that his awkwardness needed an explanation; he told Elizabeth Fraser that "what makes him so dislike society and feel so shy is from early ill usage." He did not, apparently, elaborate. He had a less mysterious reason for his discomfort among strangers. "One of his feet is shorter than the other and the high clumping shoe he wears on it sounds bad."

As his stay lengthened, Byron relaxed enough to forget himself, especially when the subject under discussion touched off a passionate reaction—his dim view of humanity, for example. Then, Miss Loveday recalled, "he works himself up in a way quite to shock one; but these are evidently the paroxysms of the moment, for he is afterwards as gentle as a lamb." At other times he was able to confine his disagreement to good-humored disapproval: When a fellow guest read aloud from Mary Brunton's recently published novel *Self-Control*, "he came in very often and smiled at 'the cant of it' as he termed all the serious parts."

He seemed surprised to have his own skeptical remarks taken seriously. Hearing Byron toss off one of his irreligious opinions, the devout Miss Loveday said that she pitied him from the bottom of her heart, to which he reportedly replied, "Do you indeed!" in tones of astonishment and respect. He was always susceptible to the sympathy of a pious young woman.

BYRON RETURNED to Newstead on October 9, where a letter from Ann Edleston awaited him, dated September 26, informing him of her brother's death from consumption four months earlier, on May 16. He was twenty-one.

Edleston's death while Byron was still at sea had a cruel irony. On the long voyage home, beset by sickness, Byron had allowed himself to fantasize an earthly reunion, even as the boy was buried in the crypt of Great St. Mary's Church in Cambridge. With Edleston dead, feelings of guilt and betrayal joined grief and loss.

Tormented into poetry, Byron now revised one stanza of Canto II of *Childe Harold* and added two more. His new version of the ninth stanza was inserted after a meditation on the possibility of eternal life. Only a few months earlier, he had vehemently rejected the Christian belief in the spirit's immortality; now he felt consoled by its promise. If there was "A land of souls beyond that sable shore,"

> How sweet it were in concert to adore
> With those who made our mortal labours light!
> To hear each voice we fear'd to hear no more![46]

The revised verse that followed, Byron explained in a note to Dallas, had been "somewhat altered, to avoid a recurrence in a former stanza:

> There, thou!—whose love and life together fled,
> Have left me here to love and live in vain—
> Twin'd with my heart, and can I deem thee dead,
> When busy Memory flashes on my brain?[47]

Byron regretted having told Dallas of Edleston's death and tried lamely to throw his possessive friend off the scent: "I think it proper to state to you," he wrote at the end of the note accompanying the sheet of revisions, "that this stanza alludes to an event which has taken place since my arrival here, and not to the death of any *male* friend."[48]

In the event that Dallas failed to make the connection between the revised lines and the poet's grieving, two new stanzas followed shortly. "I send you a conclusion to the *whole*," Byron wrote to Dallas about the additional verses, which were to provide a new conclusion to Canto II of *Childe Harold*. Edleston's death had transformed Byron's first major work from picaresque satire to tragedy, a lament for the end of love and the emotional destitution of the poet:

> Thou too art gone, thou lov'd and lovely one!
> Whom youth and youth's affection bound to me;
> Who did for me what none beside have done,
> Nor shrank from one albeit unworthy thee.
> What is my being? thou has ceas'd to be![49]
>
> . . . .
> Oh! ever loving, lovely, and belov'd!
> How selfish Sorrow ponders on the past,
> And clings to thoughts now better far remov'd!
> But Time shall tear thy shadow from me last.
> All thou could'st have of mine, stern Death! thou hast;
> The parent, friend, and now the more than friend:[50]
>
> . . . .
> What is the worst of woes that wait on age?
> What stamps the wrinkle deeper on the brow?
> To view each lov'd one blotted from life's page,
> And be alone on earth, as I am now.[51]

Reassured by the enthusiastic reception of his new stanzas, Byron went off to Cambridge to visit Davies at Kings. This change of scene brought only fresh grief. Drunk to the point of insensibility most of the time,

Davies was hardly the companion to divert his friend from sorrow.
Every sight and sound quickened memories of the chorister—the chapel
and walks of Trinity, but especially the music, which seemed to rise
everywhere:

> The voice that made those sounds more sweet
> Is hush'd, and all their charms are fled;
> And now their softest notes repeat
> A dirge, an anthem o'er the dead![52]

There were places too painful to be visited or even acknowledged: In the
"Thyrza" poems, Byron claimed for his dead love an unknown grave.
But in fact, he knew that Edleston was buried with his family in Great
St. Mary's. Mortally ill, the young clerk had returned from London to
die at home; his death from consumption had followed that of his pub-
lican uncle, only two weeks earlier, from the same disease. Even if
Edleston himself had not shown Byron the site of the family crypt, a
fresh paving stone would have likely marked the spot in the church.

"I am very low spirited," Byron told Hobhouse. "The event I
mentioned in my last has had an effect on me, I am ashamed to think
of. . . . Wherever I turn, particularly in this place, the idea goes with me,
I say all this at the risk of incurring your contempt, but you cannot
despise me more than I do myself.—I am indeed very wretched. . . . I
have been in Lancs, Notts. but all places are alike, I cannot live under
my present feelings."[53]

On the day before he left Cambridge, Byron wrote to Margaret
Pigot, mother of John and Elizabeth, his former confidante: "You may
remember a *cornelian* which some years ago I consigned to Miss Pigot,
indeed gave to her, & now I am going to make the most selfish and rude
of requests." So began an awkward plea to his former neighbor for the
return of the ring. There followed a lurching explanation of Edleston's
death, Byron's want of any other mementos of his friend, and his promise to replace the keepsake with something of his own for Elizabeth.
Along with the writer's embarrassment at the "silly subject" of his
letter,[54] Byron's tortuous phrasing to Mrs. Pigot, who was to act as go-
between, deepens the mystery of why he had broken off communications with her daughter. The only clear fact to emerge from this note is
that the end of his relations with his onetime intimate friend was understood and accepted by her family.

On October 28 Byron arrived in London, moving into rooms at
8 St. James's Street. Three days later he sent Dallas several short
poems, which he described as "a few stanzas on a subject which has

lately occupied much of my thoughts." Then, with another try at throwing Dallas off Edleston's track, Byron explained, "They refer to the death of one to whose name you are a *stranger*, and, consequently, cannot be interested. I mean them to complete the present volume. They relate to the same person I have mentioned in canto 2d, and at the conclusion of the poem."[55]

The poems in question, still entitled simply "Stanzas," conclude the sequence "To Thyrza." In contrast to the elegiac verses that ended *Childe Harold*, which leave the poet alone in the universe, the new series, its male subject veiled with a woman's name, points the mourning lover back to the world to accept its demands for artifice and falsity. His purer self has been buried along with his forbidden love:

> I must not think, I may not gaze
> On what I am, on what I was.[56]

If this was a tragedy, it was also a liberation—from the burdens of transgression and guilt. Edleston's death was the final expression of the boy's selfless love; in dying, he unchained his Promethean lover. Even as he grieved, Byron could not suppress the note of relief:

> One struggle more and I am free
> From pangs that rend my heart in twain;
> One long last sigh to love and thee,
> Then back to busy life again.[57]

CHAPTER 17

"Ambition Was My Idol"

*I*N LONDON, the charmed circles
of Whig society prepared to embrace Byron as one of their own. He was
poised to enter the world of great houses in town and country seats set
amid landscapes that improved on nature. Here, talent, brains, charm,
and good looks mingled with power, ambition, and money—both old
and new.

Whig society was the creation of its hostesses: beautiful, clever,
and seductive women whose power drive found its outlet in political and
sexual machinations, often combined. Alcove and boudoir were their
Parliament. Ladies Melbourne, Holland, and Jersey, called *regnantes* in
the gallicized language of the *ton*, had all been schooled at the feet of the
now dead Georgiana, Duchess of Devonshire. For thirty years Georgiana
had used Devonshire House as a salon to further the political fortunes of
Charles James Fox, the much-lamented tutelary genius who joined revolutionary ideals to an aristocratic love of pleasure. Another star was the
playwright Richard Brinsley Sheridan, the managing director of the
Drury Lane Theatre, member of Parliament, Secretary of the Navy, and
unforgettable wit. Now Fox was dead, and Sheridan, exhausted and
alcoholic, was fading. The Whig salons awaited a new idol.

Byron's entrée into this worldly Parnassus began modestly, at the
house of Samuel Rogers, whose poem "The Pleasure of Memory" he
had long admired. Rogers was an assiduous host and collector of
people; he was perhaps the only male *saloniste* of the day, and he
delighted in introducing brilliance and talent to each other. Invitations
were prized to his small, elegant house on Arlington Street, Piccadilly,
decorated by the artists John Flaxman and Thomas Stothard and filled
with antiquities, engravings, and books.

With Byron's first visit to Arlington Street, in early November 1811, he could—and did—boast that he was now in the company of "the first men of the land." Rogers had never met Byron until the poet appeared at his door that evening; his invitation was advance notice of imminent celebrity. A fellow guest, the poet and singer Tom Moore, also a new star of Whig drawing rooms, had other reasons for wanting an introduction to Byron: Moore had bungled an earlier effort to meet his titled competitor when he had challenged Byron to a duel that never took place.

Rogers had heard of Byron's shyness with strangers and, as a measure of the older man's sensitivity, he first received the unknown alone in the drawing room, asking Moore and Thomas Campbell, another poet admired by Byron, to withdraw for a short while. When the introductions had been made and the company seated at dinner, Rogers was taken aback by his new friend's abstemiousness: "I asked Byron if he would take soup. No, he never took soup.—Would he take some fish? No, he never took fish. Presently I asked him if he would eat some mutton. No, he never ate mutton. I then asked him if he would take a glass of wine. No, he never tasted wine.

"It was now necessary," Rogers recorded, "to inquire what he *did* eat and drink; and the answer was 'Nothing but hard biscuits and soda water.' Unfortunately, neither hard biscuits nor soda water were at hand; and he dined upon potatoes bruised down on his plate and drenched with vinegar."

Some days later Rogers met Hobhouse and took the occasion to ask, "How long will Byron persevere in his present diet?" To which the acerbic Hobby replied, "Just as long as you continue to notice it." Rogers supplies us with a postscript: "I did not then know, what I now know to be a fact,—that Byron, after leaving my house, had gone to a club in St. James's Street, and eaten a hearty meat supper."[1]

Despite the histrionic aspect of his starvation diet and the surreptitious after-hours stuffing, there was no question that Byron was, in fact, emaciated at the start of 1812. While Dallas noted that others attributed the poet's evident depression to insufficient nourishment, Byron himself insisted that his drastic dieting had the opposite effect, that "far from sinking his spirits, he felt himself lighter and livelier for it; and that it had given him a greater command over himself in every other respect."*[2] To assuage his hunger pangs, Dallas reported, Byron con-

---

*Byron's equation of starvation and self-mastery is identical to the testimony of young women suffering from Anorexia nervosa, who perceive a refusal of food as empowering behavior affording them control over their bodies.[3]

stantly chewed mastic, a gum resin distilled from the sap of pine trees. This socially unacceptable habit enlarges the Byronic attributes of rebellious hero, his jaw working a menacing wad of gum.

Byron now dined often, if sparsely, at Arlington Street, a short stroll from his own rooms in St. James's. Rogers's guests, along with the well-appointed setting, gave to his dinners the atmosphere of an exclusive Regency club, an impression furthered by the usually all-male guest list.

For Byron, the absence of women was an added attraction. To at least one of Rogers's invitations he had given a qualified acceptance: He would be delighted to come *if* no females were to be present. His misogyny, never far from the surface, seems to have been exacerbated by recent losses, starting with the sense of abandonment triggered by his mother's death. Yet another strain of his unwilling dependence on the opposite sex was the urgent need to find an heiress: "I must marry— you know how I hate women," he had written to Hobhouse, the friend most likely to sympathize with his plight. Remarking on the success of Anna Seward, a poet known as "the Swan of Litchfield," Byron transformed her literally into an author from hell, "with 6 tomes of the most disgusting trash, sailing over Styx with a Foolscap over her periwig as complacent as can be," and added venomously, "Of all Bitches, dead or alive a scribbling woman is the most canine."[4]

But he was no less biased in judging his male contemporaries. Dismissing Wordsworth and, soon, Keats, he extolled the lifeless verses of Walter Scott as the best of British poetry, followed in close order by that of his friends Samuel Rogers and Thomas Campbell. And immediately below this pantheon came another versifier, soon to become Byron's close friend and future Boswell.

If Richard Sheridan personified the many-faceted brilliance of Whig society, Tom Moore, a Dublin grocer's son, exemplified its new mobility. Neither a gentleman nor much of a poet, Moore managed, through affecting recitations of his verses, to become an honored guest at the grandest houses in London. His noble patrons were legion: The Lords Lansdowne, Moira, Russell, and Holland all provided him with help, ranging from a sinecure in Bermuda to housing at home.

Moore had read law at Trinity College, Dublin, where a flirtation with revolutionary activity had convinced him of the folly of alliance with the wrong side. Shedding dangerous political sympathies along with his Roman Catholicism, Moore thereafter devoted himself to joining, not overthrowing, the ruling class. He set off for London in 1799, ostensibly to continue his law studies; instead, building on an introduction to Lord Moira, he busied himself with collecting subscribers for the publication of his translations of Anacreon. "At once," his biographer tells us, "Moore started out upon a round of visits which, with necessary intervals, he was to continue to make for the next forty years."[5] With a few more machinations in the right quarters, Moore received permission to dedicate the work to the Prince of Wales. This coup did so much for sales of the book that the poet was soon known as "Anacreon" Moore.

His performing talents sealed Moore's triumph. Invited to sing, he accompanied his own lyrics of lost love on the pianoforte. Female tears flowed, and his success was assured. "Dick Whittington did not conquer London with such speed and ease."[6]

As a Cambridge student, Byron had appreciated Moore's earliest appearance in print (which the Irish poet now preferred to forget), cynical, mildly erotic verses published under the name Thomas Little. Since then Moore had been hurt to read, in both a stanza and a note to the second edition of Byron's *English Bards and Scotch Reviewers*, what appeared to be an attack on his manhood.

The real target of Byron's mockery had been Francis Jeffrey, editor of the *Edinburgh Review*, whom the poet believed, wrongly, to have been responsible for the unfavorable anonymous notice of *Hours of Idleness*. Similarly, a poor review had goaded Moore in 1805 to challenge Jeffrey to a duel; the critic accepted, but on reflection both men seem to have had second thoughts. No sooner had the principals and their seconds convened at Chalk Farm, on the outskirts of London, than, mysteriously, the constabulary appeared, putting an end to the illegal engagement. Reading of this *opera buffo* in the newspapers, Byron found the perfect scenario to expose his enemy's cowardice; too bad if Moore's honor had to suffer as well:

> Can none remember that eventful day,
> That ever glorious, almost fatal fray,
> When LITTLE's leadless pistols met his eye
> And Bow-street Myrmidons stood laughing by?[7]

No reader was likely to miss the significance of "Little's leadless pistols" or his "evaporated" balls. Moore was far more humiliated by these aspersions on his manhood than by Jeffrey's dismissal of his verse. Now, reviving the earlier long-forgotten episode, he challenged Byron; perhaps he hoped that one show of courage would expunge any lingering memories of the last failed encounter. On January 1, 1809, while Byron was abroad, Moore sent him a letter noting that in Byron's poem, "*the lie is given* to his own public explanation of the affair" and added, "I trust Your Lordship will not deny me the satisfaction of knowing whether you avow the insult contained in the passage alluded to." Then, with the tortuousness that characterized all of Moore's dealings with his social betters, he concluded, "It is needless to suggest to Your Lordship the propriety of keeping our correspondence secret."[8]

In fact, Byron never saw Moore's first letter. While he was abroad, Hodgson had been entrusted with forwarding his personal mail, but on seeing the Irish poet's pretentious seal, he had sensed trouble and decided to hold the letter. With the catastrophic series of events that followed his return, Byron never got around to opening the elaborately sealed missive. Then, on October 11, 1811, a year and a half after his first letter had gone unanswered, Moore wrote again. In the meantime he had married a seventeen-year-old Anglo-Irish dancer, Bessy Dyke; about to become a father, he hoped to preserve his honor with still less risk to his person. He assured Byron that "notwithstanding the injury of which I complain, the spirit in which I address you is neither revengeful nor ungenerous," and, after many sheets covered with moral hair-splittings, Moore finally revealed the real object of his writing: "It would give me at this moment the most heart-felt pleasure if by any kind, candid and satisfactory explanation, you would enable me to ask for the honour of your intimacy, and let me try to convince you that I am *not exactly* the kind of person, who would set his name to a mean and cowardly falsehood." He could hardly convey to Byron "the feeling which your work excited in me." Should His Lordship "feel inclined to meet my sincere wishes for reconcilement," Moore proposed his "best and most valued friend Mr. Rogers (whose worth and talent Your Lordship seems to appreciate) and I have no doubt that he will be most happy to become a mediator between us."[9]

BYRON BEHAVED with more than his usual circumspection. There was his own honor to consider; he did not wish to be seen as avoiding a challenge. Moore was, after all, the more established poet and the drawing room darling of Whig society, Byron's own potential constituency. He had made sure to leave Moore's original letter, unopened, in Hodgson's possession, taking care to inform Moore of this fact and even, in the most legalistic language, offering to open this first letter in Moore's presence. Though Byron answered each of Moore's many subsequent notes prior to their first meeting in the most courteous tones, he described to Hobhouse, with patronizing amusement, the "Irish Melodist['s]" acrobatic efforts to stand on his dignity while groveling for Byron's favor. Referring to "the Bard's" letter as a *"demi-hostile semi-amicable* epistle (for it began with a complaint & ended with a hope that *we* should be *'intimate'*),"[10] Byron made it clear that he recognized Moore's fawning for what it was: "Tommy loves a Lord," he was to say, long after they had become friends.[11]

Samuel Rogers's peacemaking dinner was a great success. Byron's eating habits may have raised eyebrows, but his manners, easy and deferential at the same time, left the desired impression on the older men. He reciprocated by inviting his host, along with fellow guests Moore and Campbell, to dinner at Dorant's Hotel, asking Hodgson to join him and meet his new literary friends. A recent evening with Hodgson had skirted disaster. The clergyman had gotten so drunk at dinner that he regaled their companions with tales of Byron's homosexual adventures, including an offer to the famous "Abbé Hyacinth" at Falmouth of £200 a year for his services as procurer. Byron's distress on hearing his erotic confidences recited by others seems to have had a sobering effect; he would now exercise more restraint in relating his sexual exploits on his travels to all listeners. No scandal must be attached to his name now. While still abroad, he had been proposed for membership in the Athenian Club, a gathering of aristocratic young men with serious antiquarian interests deepened by Mediterranean travel. Realizing that his attacks on Lord Elgin's collecting zeal, soon to appear in print with the publication of *Childe Harold*, would also apply to many "Athenians," Byron declined the membership. But he was pleased to accept nomination to the Alfred. Although he liked to deprecate the Alfred's high-minded membership as "too sober and literary" and its premises at 23 Albemarle Street as only "a decent resource on a rainy day,"[12] he was, nonetheless, proud of being elected out of 354 candidates for 6 vacancies. And he lost no time in enumerating to acquaintances the roster of distinguished names with whom his own was now associated; beginning with his friend John Cam Hobhouse's father to the Archbishop of Canterbury and Lords Holland and Valentia, to such literary powers as William Gifford, to Byron's Harrow classmate the future Prime Minister Robert Peel.

When not in the depths of depression, Byron was the most convivial of men. He was prompt in reciprocating hospitality and in cultivating those he wanted to know better. In his rooms in St. James's, conveniently close to "clubland," Byron played host to Rogers and to the talented and powerful he now met at Arlington Street or at the Alfred. Among these "new faces and fashionable men," as Dallas called them, would soon be found Lord Holland himself. The adored nephew of Charles James Fox, whose political standard-bearer he remained, Henry Richard Vassall Fox, third Lord Holland, and his wife, the redoubtable hostess of Holland House, had been among those rudely treated by Byron in *English Bards and Scotch Reviewers*. As generous and large-spirited as his uncle, Holland would soon show himself to be forgiving, tendering "pacific overtures" to the young poet.

As the publication of *Childe Harold* drew closer, its author began to fret about offending in the new work others whom he had dismissed in *English Bards*. Much revision took place; sheets of rewritten stanzas flew back and forth between Byron and Dallas, then Dallas and John Murray, publisher of the new work. Now that he was welcome in the select company of those who counted—who were all his seniors by a decade or more—Byron felt ever more anxious to distance himself from the posturing of his literary alter ego. As he announced to Dallas, "I by no means intend to identify with *Harold*, but to *deny* all connexion with him. . . . I would not be such a fellow as I have made my hero for all the world."13

IT IS NOT CLEAR just when Byron first met John Murray II, the man who was to be his publisher and friend for the next decade. It seems likely that Dallas would have introduced them as soon as Byron had returned from Newstead to London in late October. Murray described the poet as first dropping by his shop, accompanied by Hobhouse. Hobby had left with his regiment for Ireland in August 1811 and was not demobilized until early February 1812; during that time his only meeting with Byron was at Sittingbourne. Thus, late February (Hobhouse's first leave began on February 21) was the earliest the two friends could have called on the publisher, then located in Fleet Street. Here Murray's father, a retired half-pay naval officer, newly arrived from Edinburgh in 1768, had purchased a partnership in a stationery and printing shop. The older Murray had died when his son was fifteen, and as soon as he was out of school, John Murray II bought out the partner's son. Ten years Byron's senior, Murray was now thirty-three, and a combination of hard work, business acumen, and literary taste had already propelled him to the forefront of London publishers. In his first coup, he had lured Sir Walter Scott, the most popular and prolific of British poets, to his imprint; he also published the less well known but probably equally profitable Mrs. Rundell's *Domestic Cookery*, the first perennial best-seller among English cookbooks.

Although Byron would later have reason to find him a panderer to the "cant and hypocrisy" of public opinion, Murray, in the decade of his happy professional and personal relations with the poet, was as open-minded and courageous as a publisher could be in a politically repressive era and still stay in business and out of jail. A loyal Tory himself, Murray had arranged in 1805 to become the London publisher of the fiercely iconoclastic showcase of Whig opinion, the *Edinburgh Review*;

three years later, on signing Scott, he also became the publisher of that author's organ, the staunchly Tory *Quarterly Review*.

After this first visit Byron took to the habit of dropping by while the sheets of *Childe Harold* were still in press: "Fresh from the fencing rooms of Angelo and Jackson, using his cane for a sword," Murray recalled, the poet would "amuse himself by renewing his practice of 'Carte et Tierce' [lunging] at the bookshelves while Murray was reading passages of the poem, with occasional ejaculations of admiration at which Byron would say: 'You think that a good idea, do you Murray?' Then he would fence and lunge at some special book which he had picked out on the shelves before him." As Murray afterwards said: "I was often very glad to be rid of him."14

A MONTH IN London had brought home to Byron the truth about his finances and spending habits. He felt perfectly justified in ignoring the former; moving in fashionable social circles required him to spend a great deal more on clothes. As early as January 1812 he began ordering a new wardrobe. From that month through September 1813 he ran up a bill for £900 from his tailor, besides purchasing footwear, headgear, linen, and jewelry from other purveyors, along with swords and pistols. He had a passion for fine white quilted waistcoats; at first he might have worn these for half mourning, the outfit required on emerging from full mourning for his mother. By June 1812, however, he owned more than twenty-four of them. He preferred white trousers of nankeen (fine cotton), silk, or white jean; as these could only be worn once, he felt justified in ordering sometimes two dozen at a time. Byron's most extravagant costume, however, was commissioned for a single occasion that never took place. In June he was presented to the Prince Regent at a party given by a Miss Johnson. The Prince had been so flattering about *Childe Harold*, and so gracious to its author, that Byron decided to pay his respects at a Court levee. That morning Dallas called on Byron in his rooms, where, to his amazement, he found the poet, hair powdered and arrayed in a "superfine olive coat lined through with white silk and adorned with 25 Elegantly Cut & Highly Polished Steel buttons, a very rich Embroidered Court dress Waistcoat," a pair of "rich black silk breeches," and a "rich steel dress sword" with a chain and silk sword belt. Without the requisite buckled shoes and cocked hat, this costume cost £52.15 Only after he was fully dressed and coiffed did Byron learn that the levee had been called off.

Added to the cost of clothing there was the expense of his rooms in St. James's, playing host there or at hotels and coffeehouses, club membership, and a subscription to a box at the Theatre Royal, Covent

Garden. Neither his temperament nor his way of life could admit of pleasures deferred. He had recently heard from several parties independently that Rochdale would be worth £30,000 to £40,000 more *if* he could invest half that amount in improvements. Even were he to lay his hands on such a sum, Byron well knew that it would never end up in capital improvements to his Lancashire estates. He returned to the easiest of unpalatable solutions: marrying wealth.

In late November Byron visited Cambridge once again; perhaps he hoped to exorcise its ghosts. If so, the visit was a mixed success. Besides seeing Hodgson, he enjoyed a reunion with his younger Harrow favorite, the lame William Harness, who, like Hodgson, had recently been ordained. The university town was still a place of suffocating memories. In the past he had found Sundays there less "lemancholy"—Byron's own word—than the silent Sabbath elsewhere. Now, however, the music soaring from the city's churches poisoned the peace: "The organ is a sad remembrancer," he wrote to Hodgson.[16] Byron was glad to leave.

Back in London, diversions proliferated: "Tomorrow, I dine with Rogers & am to hear Coleridge, who is a kind of rage at present," Byron wrote to Harness on December 15.[17] This was his first experience of a major literary occasion: Samuel Taylor Coleridge's series of fifteen lectures on Shakespeare and Milton, given at the London Institution through December and January, was one of those historic events that all two hundred of those present—a mix of the fashionable, political, and cultural worlds—recognized as having more than passing significance. A rising young poet had to be seen there as confirmation that he had arrived. Byron's presence, as he sat muffled dramatically in a great cloak, was duly noted. He made sure that all of his regular correspondents were aware of his attendance, as Rogers's guest, on the evening of December 16. In one of the earlier lectures in the series Coleridge had indirectly attacked Campbell by dismissing his poem "The Pleasures of Hope" with the poet himself in the audience. Thus, even before he heard Coleridge hold forth, Byron was meditating a counterattack, fantasizing a future occasion when Coleridge would denigrate another of his friends and he would be famous enough to take on the older poet in just such a public setting. Dismissing Coleridge, whose early radical zeal had yielded to a middle-aged conservatism, as "this reformed schismatic," Byron declared, "Were I one of these poetical luminaries, or of sufficient consequence to be noticed by the man of lectures, I should not hear him without an answer."[18]

For a theater lover like Byron, the contemporary stage offered a feast of legendary talents: The magnificent Mrs. Siddons and her brother

John Kemble were Shakespearean actors whose electrifying performances were noted by every member of their audience who has left memoirs, and Byron was no exception: "Last night I saw Kemble in Coriolanus, he was glorious and exerted himself wonderfully." In the audience were his old Harrow favorites Lord Clare and Delawarr together. As the thought of Clare would never cease to make Byron's heart beat faster, a certain resentment of Delawarr may have motivated Byron's crowing about the "excellent place" he had found, coming to the theater at the last minute, as compared to his friends whose efforts had been "less fortunate."[19]

The hidden wound of his own blasted love made him intolerant of those whose passions had fixed on unworthy objects. With Edleston dead, the purity of their love had become hallowed and it was obscene to hear Hodgson and another clerical friend, Bland, "deify their common strumpets—Romantic attachments for things marketable at a Dollar!" Byron raged. Both divines had gone to a "stew," the lowest of brothels, from which visit they had now added syphilis to their woes, Byron reported to Harness.

"When I compare myself with these men my Elders & Betters, I really begin to conceive myself a monument of prudence, a walking statue without feeling or failing.—And yet the World in general hath given me a proud preeminence over them in profligacy," he added bitterly. Then, feeling ashamed of his want of sympathy for friends' griefs, however tawdry, he added, "I like the men, & God knows, ought not to condemn their aberrations, but I own I feel provoked when they dignify all this with ye name of love."

Finally, he related his anger to his pain. He had read "Hodgson's epistle . . . full of his petty grievances, and this at the moment when (from circumstances it is not necessary to enter upon) I was bearing up against recollections, to which *his* imaginary sufferings are as a scratch to Cancer. These things combined put me out of humour with him & all mankind." Hovering on the brink of confession to the younger Harness, he admitted: "The latter part of my life has been a perpetual struggle against affections which embittered the earlier portion, & though I flatter myself I have in a great measure conquered them, yet there are moments (and this was one) when I am as foolish as formerly.—I never said so much before, nor had I said this now if I did not suspect myself of having been rather savage in my letter, & wish to inform you thus much of ye cause."

Despite Hodgson's weakness for women and wine, his inability to handle either, and the unfortunate timing of his confessions, Byron still respected his friend's vocation. At Hodgson's insistence he read the volume of letters from Richard Watson, an eighteenth-century Cambridge divine and later bishop, to Edward Gibbon. But Byron remained unpersuaded by the arguments for orthodox belief: "[It] is a gloomy creed," he complained of Christianity, "and I want a better, but there is something Pagan in me that I cannot shake off. In short, I deny nothing, but doubt everything."[20]

As Hodgson and Harness had yet to meet, Byron invited both friends to spend Christmas with him at Newstead; he had hoped that Moore could join them, but between the obligations of fatherhood and the volume of invitations for grand festivities in town, Moore declined. Thus, with his two friends (Hodgson was obliged by his girth to ride outside with the coachman), Byron set off in his coach on December 19 "to be sulky for a fortnight."

Reports of violence raging throughout the Nottingham area were filling the newspapers. The war had closed foreign markets, causing the laying off of workers in the stocking and lace manufacture; a new cost-saving method of cutting stockings from larger pieces of cloth* had thrown thousands out of work, leaving families on the edge of starvation. Desperate weavers, forced to rent their machines usually from middlemen, were smashing what they still saw as the instruments of their suffering before marching off to set fires to the establishments or assault the owners. When the militia was called in, the insurgents were joined by local sympathizers. Children lined the streets jeering at the soldiers. From London Byron kept Hobhouse, still in Ireland, informed: "Riots in Notts, breaking of frames & heads, & outmanoeuvring the military," he wrote with some glee. And two days later, on the eve of his departure for Newstead, he wrote: "Hodgson thinks *his frame* will be broken amongst the rest.—I hope not."[21]

Newstead was too remote for invasion by mobs. Byron continued revising *Childe Harold* and listening to Hodgson and Harness argue theology. He missed Hobhouse's worldly common sense and confessed himself sick of Harrovians. When his guests retired for the night, Byron, wearied by intellectual exertions, escaped—not to his own bedchamber,

---

*Unlike classic Luddite agitation elsewhere, the Nottingham uprisings did not involve new machinery, but a cheaper method of producing hosiery and gloves, using fewer looms and workers. Byron was unaware of the difference, and his ignorance has been taken as evidence that he never troubled to acquire any firsthand knowledge of the local troubles.

but above, to a freezing maid's room on the top floor. There, Susan Vaughan was waiting to warm her master.

He was already besotted with his new favorite, who had displaced Lucy, the mother of his child, and black-eyed Bess, a brief object of his attentions, as sultana of his Newstead seraglio. In an airy apology in verse to "Lucietta," Byron explained:

> There's another, that's slyer,
> Who touches me nigher,—
> A Witch, an intriguer,
> Whose manner and figure
> Now piques me, excites me,
> Torments and delights me—[22]

He had given all three young women gold chains with lockets. Susan told him how much she preferred her gift, containing a lock of his hair, to Lucy's, although, as she coyly confessed, she was unable to open it without her master's help.

On Christmas Day Byron wrote to Hobhouse: "I am at present principally occupied with a fresh face & a very pretty one too . . . a Welsh Girl whom I lately added to the bevy, and of whom I am tolerably enamoured for the present." But he gave the lie to this equivocation by looking forward to his release from the bonds of passion. "I shall most probably be cool enough before you return from Ireland," he wrote to Hobby, more in hope than expectation. Soon enough, he confessed to being "foolishly fond": Susan's singsong accent and cheeky good humor enchanted him, but it was her exuberant sexuality that held him in thrall.[23]

Among her official duties, Susan acted as nursemaid to the young Fletcher boys, the sons of Byron's valet. Soon she would remind Byron of the time he had "come up to our room, when I was in bed—the time you locked the door. You woked [sic] the boys and asked George if he knew you." The oldest Fletcher lad not only knew his lordship but also remembered all he subsequently saw and heard. Byron seems to have intended him to witness, if not participate in, their lovemaking. Susan, however, was uneasy when she learned that George had been telling "storys" about their master's visit.

In her earthy style, with its sly lascivious touches, she reported to Byron on her interrogation of the boy: " 'He looks very earnestly at me and says he: Why, Susan, have you forgot Lord Byron coming to *bed to us*? So I asked him, what about that? Ah, says he, by G——d, if you have forgot it, I have not yet. Don't you remember, Susan, me Lord putting his hand so nicely over your *bosom*? . . . The D[evi]l may have George Fletcher, if he did not *kiss* you besides, and Bessy too.' "[24] Susan tried to convince the lad that it was not Lord Byron at all that he had seen, but young Fletcher was having none of it; there was only one Lord Byron.

Byron had left Newstead for London and the opening of Parliament on January 11. Susan sent this report in one of many letters she wrote to Byron in the weeks following. It is a troubling document. In her account we see Byron orchestrating his sexual encounter with Susan (nicknamed Taffy) as a reenactment of the erotic games indulged with his nurse, May Gray, "coming to bed with him and playing tricks with his person" before he was displaced by her coachboys. Now Byron awakens the boys to make sure they will "know" their master. Then, in a curious postscript, Susan replayed May's punishment of Byron, beating George Fletcher for what he had seen and done. Her hold over Byron, too, was fueled by what May Gray had taught him to require and to exact from women: wounds of humiliation that would never heal.

With the exception of a final pained note, Byron's letters to Susan— three were mailed en route to London alone—have not survived. From her side of the correspondence, however, a vivid self-portrait emerges of a seductive, spirited charmer adept at manipulating Byron's state of jealous agitation and enjoying the envy of her less favored fellow servants. Alas for "Taffy," this was to prove her downfall. A few weeks later the truth of Byron's suspicions was revealed, reported to him with gleeful spite by Robert Rushton, his page and former favorite. After fanning the flames of his master's jealousy, Rushton, with Byron's encouragement, intercepted a letter from Susan to her new lover; he then sent the incriminating document to London. Here was the evidence Byron had dreaded and desired in equal measure. He had been cynically, heartlessly betrayed and, worse, made an object of ridicule in the servants' hall.

When he received the proof of Susan's infidelity, at the end of January, Byron collapsed into a state of rage and grief, combined with self-pity and self-hatred, hardly equaled in his emotional history. Incapable of maintaining even a pretense of pride, his letter to Susan strives feebly for a tone of forbearing dignity, only to collapse into blubbering accusation: "I write to bid you farewell, not to reproach you.— The enclosed papers, *one in your own handwriting,* will explain everything.—I will not deny that I have been attached to you, & am now heartily ashamed of my weakness.—You may also enjoy the satisfaction of having deceived me most completely, & rendered me for the present sufficiently wretched.—From the first I told you that the continuance of our connection depended on your own conduct.—All is over.—I have little to condemn on my own part, but credulity; you threw yourself in my way, I received you, loved you, till you have become worthless, & now I part with you with some regret, & without resentment." After further histrionics in the same vein, Byron, echoing the wronged lover of every novel he had read, orders Susan: "Return to your relations, you shall be furnished with the means, but *him*, who now addresses you for the last time, you will never see again."[25]

With his friends, however, Byron felt no need for pompous deflections of pain; he voluptuously invoked a physical self-loathing, revealing the prophecy that Susan had been chosen to fulfill: "I do not blame her, but my own vanity in fancying that such a thing as I am could ever be beloved,"[26] he wrote to Hodgson.

In his despair Byron wrote three poems, sometimes known as the Susan Vaughan cycle. Of small literary value, they are nonetheless key texts in tracing the poet's roiling emotions, especially when read together with the far more successful "Stanzas," the meditation on Edleston's unmarked grave written at about the same time. The Vaughan poems confirm that the fickle maidservant had only enacted her predetermined role as female flagellant.

"La Revanche," the first of the cycle, suggests that the poet is aware of his own ready-made scenario, in which the lighthearted Susan had been cast to type. Inverting self-knowledge into a rhetorical question, Byron wonders:

> Why did I hold thy love so dear?
> Why shed for such a heart one tear?[27]

Writing to her master in London, Susan had quoted a bit of sentimental verse by way of assuring him of her eternal constancy: "And my true faith can alter never / Though thou art gone perhaps forever." Taking this keepsake-box couplet as its ironic epigraph, "On the Quotation" plays obsessively with the tawdry truth that followed on the young woman's lofty profession of fidelity:

> And thy true faith can alter never?—
> Indeed it lasted for a—week!

Once again, Byron acknowledges that Susan was merely following his script:

> I knew the length of Love's forever,
>   And just expected such a freak.

After only "Seven days and nights of single sorrow" Susan had replaced him with a younger man, one who had the advantages of novelty, youth (read: sexual vigor), and availability. Thanks to Rushton, Byron was certainly aware of the identity of his successor. The image of Susan yielding to one seducer, however, was not sufficient to flay Byron's feverish jealousy, and he fantasized a rapid sequence of her lovers:

> And if each week you change a lover,
>   And so have acted heretofore,
> Before a year or two is over
>   We'll form a very pretty *corps*.[28]

Susan's infidelity provided further confirmation of the vileness of her sex. Confined to his bed two weeks later with a kidney stone, Byron again wrote to Hodgson, the friend likeliest to sympathize: "If the stone had got into my heart instead of my kidneys, it would have been all the better. However, I have quite recovered *that* also, and only wonder at my folly in excepting my own strumpets from the general corruption. . . . I have one request to make, which is, never to mention a woman again in any letter to me, or even allude to the existence of the sex."[29]

In the last known poem of the Susan Vaughan cycle, Byron begins on a note of weepy self-pity:

> Again deceived! again betrayed!
>   In manhood as in youth,
> The dupe of every smiling maid
>   That ever "lied like truth.—"

Unlike the arrested emotions of the first two Vaughan poems, which in their mix of self-absorption and exhibitionism reach back to Byron's adolescent wound inflicted by the yellow-haired "Mary," this last poem moves from its histrionic opening "Again deceived! again betrayed!" toward a larger understanding of the dynamic of sexual passion. The poet is able to confront the infernal chain that makes of each lover alternately victim and executioner:

> In turn deceiving or deceived
>   The wayward Passion roves,
> Beguiled by her we most believed,
>   Or leaving her who loves.[30]

Now he can allow—at least in verse—that it was Vaughan's faithlessness that joins her to him, as they become another pair of riders on that
cruel carousel *"la ronde,"* the circle of unloved lovers whose timing is
always out of sync.

Only death has the power to freeze love as memory, rendering
immutable all that time would destroy. In "Stanzas," John Edleston, the
dead chorister, unlike the vibrant Susan Vaughan, is preserved from
inflicting or suffering pain:

> Yet did I love thee to the last
>   As fervently as thou,
> Who did'st not change through all the past,
>   And can'st not alter now.
> The love where Death has set his seal,
> Nor age can chill, nor rival steal,
>   Nor falsehood disavow:
> And, what were worse, thou can'st not see
> Or wrong, or change, or fault in me.[31]

The year 1812 had begun inauspiciously, with Byron in a "state of
ludicrous tribulation," as he now described himself to Moore. The
author of *Irish Melodies* had written to him, waxing rapturous about
the younger man's poetry: Normally, praise from the more established
literary lion would have buoyed him, "but, now I can think of nothing
but 'damned, deceitful—delightful woman,' " he told Moore.[32]

Fortunately, the parliamentary calendar compelled his attention. His
political career would be launched with his maiden speech to the House
of Lords, and he had yet to choose the subject, a choice determined by
the bills currently in debate. He had to decide between the ongoing
drama of Catholic emancipation and a bill recently introduced to make
the destruction of knitting frames by angry weavers a capital offense,
punishable by death. Byron's speech would be a crucial test of his political ambitions; he must make his mark and brilliantly, causing the Tory
forces of reaction to writhe while rallying the paternal pride and gratitude of new friends and fellow Whigs such as Lord Holland.

"The poet yields to the Orator," Byron declared.[33] Poetry might
engage him, but politics, he now believed, was his destiny. Along with a

career in uniform, statecraft was the only other occupation possible for a young aristocrat with talent and ambition. From the moment he inherited the title and estates of Newstead, his political course had been, in a real sense, predetermined: Harrow, Cambridge (where, despite his protestations of political independence, he had soldered future contacts by joining the highly select Whig Club), his introduction to the House of Lords followed by the required postgraduate preparation for politics: the grand tour.

Byron had always harbored doubts about the worth of versifying. Sexual anxieties would have rekindled earlier fears about the writing of poetry as passive and feminine, as opposed to the vigorous, manly pursuit of orator and parliamentarian. He discarded his early political ideal of nonalignment. Less naïve now, he saw his place in history validated by allegiance to the Whig cause, even as rebelliousness determined his ideological bent. "I was born to opposition," he had said of himself, but he was also born into the Whig tradition of patrician outsiders excluded from power for a quarter century—his entire lifetime. From his earlier fantasy of himself as future liberator of Greece, he could now, more realistically, audition for the role of prophet who would lead the Whigs out of their twenty-five years in the wilderness.

Before leaving for the East, Byron had consciously begun to prepare himself for a parliamentary career. High on his essential reading list were volumes of parliamentary debates from the Whig Revolution of 1688 to 1742. He may even have read them. In 1809, between his introduction to his fellow peers and his departure on the Grand Tour, he had attended the Lords seven times: in March, April, and May.

In the new year, he would manage, despite the distractions of debt, his obsession with Susan Vaughan, and the excitement generated by the publication of *Childe Harold's Pilgrimage* in March, to attend the House of Lords twenty-four times between January and July 1812. He was present for all major debates (including, to be sure, those on subjects that his own three speeches addressed). He participated in sessions of dull committee work as well as those devoted to dramatic issues: Roman Catholic claims and the Orders in Council (by which, using the excuse of war, the Tory government officially sanctioned acts of piracy and kidnapping by the British navy). He even found time to attend a debate on the leather tax.

By February 1 Byron seems to have decided in favor of speaking on Catholic Emancipation. This was the reform measure that had been most ardently—and unsuccessfully—pursued by Charles James Fox and most stubbornly resisted by George III. The claim for full constitutional rights for Britain's Roman Catholics had long been a Whig rallying point. In February of the preceding year, with the King's apparently irreversible madness, the Prince of Wales had become regent. His Whig friends assumed their day had come; reform would prevail. They were wrong; their "Prinnie" promptly stabbed them in the back, assuming a solidly Tory posture.

Also on February 1, Byron wrote to Hodgson of his attendance at Lords the night before. Byron and his old partner in crime, Lord Sligo (now restored to the role of lawmaker after serving a brief prison term for kidnapping sailors), had "paired off" during the session, effectively canceling out each other's votes. The evening had not, however, been wasted. Anxious about his forthcoming debut, Byron was reassured by the undistinguished oratory of his fellow peers: "I did not speak, but I might as well have," he told Hodgson, "for nothing could have been inferior to the Duke of Devonshire, Marquis of Downshire, and the Earl of Fitzwilliam. The Catholic Question comes on this month, and perhaps I may then commence. I must 'screw my courage to the sticking place' and we'll *not* fail,' " he wrote.[34]

Three days later he had changed his mind, deciding instead to test his rhetoric on the more immediate and explosive issue of the Frame Work Bill. Directed at the rioting workers in Nottinghamshire, the measure, if passed, would make the destruction of machinery punishable by death. The greater emotional impact and topicality of the weavers' cause, affecting crucially the district he represented, made the life-or-death debate the more dramatic alternative. Considerations of career and patronage, however, also weighed in his decision. As it happened, Lord Holland, the nephew and political heir of Fox and the leader of the moderate Whig opposition, was also the recorder of Nottingham. For Byron to address an increasingly volatile situation in his home district was also to provide a natural introduction to this influential peer; Holland, he hoped, might be disposed to take him up as a protégé, which would redeem his earlier disappointment with his guardian Lord Carlisle.

Writing to Samuel Rogers on February 4, Byron asked his fellow poet to act as go-between and to introduce him to the Whig leader. Opening his letter to Rogers with "With my best acknowledgments to Lord Holland," Byron proceeded to detail the message he wished conveyed to the peer. If the upper house did not shelve the Frame Work Bill for further discussion, Byron sought "with his Lordship's approbation [to] give notice of a motion for a committee of enquiry—I would also gladly avail myself of his most able advice, & any information in documents with which he might be pleased to entrust me, to bear me out in the statement of facts it may be necessary to submit to the house."

Having thus paid homage to Holland's intelligence, experience, and wisdom, Byron went on to declare his sense of urgency and, indirectly, his own qualifications as observer, justifying his self-appointed role as advocate of the weavers of Nottingham: "From all that fell under my own observation during my Xmas visit to Newstead, I feel convinced that if *conciliatory* measures are not very soon adopted, the most unhappy consequences may be apprehended.—Nightly outrage & daily depradation are at their height, & not only the masters of frames who are obnoxious on account of their occupation, but persons in no degree connected with the malcontents or their oppressors, are liable to insult & pillage."[35]

Holland replied directly to Byron, making plain his willingness to help in any way he could. By way of providing information on the local crisis, he enclosed a letter sent to him in his capacity of recorder, from a Mr. Coldham, town clerk of Nottingham. Coldham found the riots a "cause of serious alarm and permanent danger," but he opposed the government's death penalty bill because it would cut off his information from spies. Byron disagreed: "My view of the question differs in some measure from Mr. Coldham's," he noted in his appreciative reply to Holland. He went on to enumerate what would be the two main thrusts of his speech: "My own motive for opposing ye bill is founded on its palpable injustice & its certain inefficacy."[36]

As the scheduled debate drew near, Byron became increasingly anxious. Instead of relying on a few notes for an extemporaneous delivery, his nervousness led him to write the speech out in its entirety. On several occasions he apparently practiced parts of it, with Dallas as his audience. That gentleman was not favorably impressed, noting that Byron's "delivery changed my opinion of his power as to eloquence, and checked my hope of his success in Parliament. He altered the natural tone of his voice, which was sweet and round, into a formal drawl, and he prepared his features for a part—it was a youth declaiming a task. This was the more perceptible, as in common conversation, he was remarkably easy and natural."[37]

Dallas attributed Byron's artificial style of oratory to "a fault contracted in the studied delivery of speeches from memory, which has been lately so much attended to in the education of boys." And he warned: "It may wear off, and yield to the force of real knowledge and activity, but it does not promise well; and they who fall into it are seldom prominent characters in stations where eloquence is required."[38]

Debates in both houses of Parliament on the Frame Work Bill took place on the evening of February 27, leaving Byron to get through the day and overcome his stage fright as best he could. When it was over,

Dallas was forced to admit that the speech as delivered "produced a considerable effect in the House of Lords, and . . . many compliments from the Opposition Peers."

Unwilling to be excluded from a single second of his friend's moment of glory, Dallas rushed to intercept Byron in the corridor, just as he emerged from the great chamber. Intoxicated by the mixture of relief and triumph, the speaker was "glowing with success and much agitated." Byron was not so transported, however, that he forgot the code governing the manners of gentlemen. As Dallas recalled, "I had an umbrella in my right hand, not expecting that he would put out his hand to me—in my haste to take it when offered, I had advanced my left hand—'What' said he, 'give your friend your left hand on such an occasion?' " Even at this heady moment, however, Byron shrewdly noted that political success would create publicity for the new poem, due to reach the public in two weeks. He concluded this conversation in the corridor, Dallas recalled, "with saying, that he had, by his speech, given me the best advertisement for *Childe Harold's Pilgrimage*."[39] This observation alone places Byron squarely in the modern age. He was honing his genius for orchestrating publicity, making sure that each event built on the other. The shifting images tantalized: Solitary poet, passionate reformer, wounded aristocrat—all were "advertisements for myself."

That evening, Byron was among the dinner guests at Holland House. His first invitation to the "first of Whig tables" announced his arrival on the political scene. Although there was considerable overlap in guest lists, Holland House in Kensington was at the emotional antipodes from the earlier center of Whig influence, Devonshire House in Piccadilly. The dazzling Georgiana's court had reflected its volatile empress, dead now for six years. In her ascendancy, Devonshire House had stood for intrigue, erotic or political, conducted in seductive whisperings exchanged on discreetly placed sofas, or still more intimately in boudoirs. For those who shared their hostess's obsession with gambling, there were gaming rooms where cards snapped and dice rattled until the candles guttered. Freedom, if not license, had been the order of the day and night; guests wagered or danced, flirted or struck political deals over flutes of champagne. Meals were haphazard; the glamorous, powerful, handsome men and women came and went as they pleased.

Lady Holland's days of erotic conquest were over. She had found love with her courtly, adoring husband, whose political power allowed her to stake a claim to intellectual and social dominance. Invitations to her famous round dinner table, seating no more than sixteen, were planned and executed with all the discipline that her idol,

Napoleon Bonaparte, applied to his military campaigns. Guests were invited for their contribution to the sprightly, knowledgeable talk. Regulars such as Samuel Rogers could be counted on to play the conversational equivalent of field marshal, orchestrating his hostess's human symphony.

Many found Holland House and its presiding genius more daunting than pleasurable; a Piccadilly chemist boasted of having invented a pill just to calm the nerves of first-time guests. The hostess may well have enjoyed exacerbating the social insecurities of intellectuals—they might sing more memorably for their supper. At Holland House "alienation was the badge of admission," one acute observer decided.[40]

Byron was unlikely to have been cowed either by the grandeur of the setting or the hauteur of Lady Holland. Immediately following his triumphant debut in the House of Lords, he pulled up to Holland House's lighted portico in his own splendid coach, his coat of arms painted on the side. Upon entering, he was shown into the vast library, which ran the entire length of the west wing on the upper floor. No palace boasted a more splendid one; its coffered ceiling consisted of seven vaulted compartments, each set in oak with a painted blue ground, alternating a skylight and chandelier. A bay window in the middle of the room looked onto the Dutch garden (which may still be seen today) planted by Lord Holland himself.

The poet was more critical of the creature comforts provided by his hosts. Lady Holland's aversion to heat was notorious. The cavernous rooms were kept freezing, and the hostess took umbrage when shivering guests attempted to move the fire screens so they could huddle closer to the flames. Convalescents and women who had recently given birth were advised to decline invitations in the winter months.

As it was now February, the announcement of dinner and the imminent prospect of hot food and excellent wine would have been greeted eagerly. From the library, guests were ushered into the adjoining Gilt Room. There the fifteen or sixteen elect and their hostess were seated (some said tightly packed, the better for Lady Holland to control conversation) at the circular seventeenth-century table, where the sparkling lusters of a great chandelier overhead illumined the brilliance of the Hollands' famous Sèvres porcelain.

Byron's first dinner at Holland House came off brilliantly. In the intimate setting his manner of speaking resumed its natural, unaffected, and playful character; his memorable laugh had ample occasion to punctuate the sallies of his fellow guests: Lord and Lady Lansdowne, Lord Grey, Lord Lauderdale, Lord Cowper, and the Dukes of Devonshire and Bedford. He charmed his prickly, domineering hostess and, if he did not find in Lord Holland the mentor and father figure he hoped for, he now counted the genial peer his friend.

On the days following, compliments continued to pour in, and Byron, like a schoolboy reporting home on his high marks, proudly repeated them all to Hodgson: "I have had many marvelous eulogies repeated to me since in person & by proxy from divers persons *ministerial—yea ministerial!* as well as oppositionists, of them I shall only mention Sir F. Burdetts. *He* says it is the best speech by a *Lord* since the 'Lord knows when' probably from a fellow feeling in ye sentiments.—Ld H[olland] tells me I shall beat them all if I persevere, & Ld. G[renville] remarked that the construction of some of my periods are very like *Burke's*!! And so much for vanity—I spoke very violent sentences with a sort of modest impudence, abused every thing & every body, & put the Ld. Chancellor very much out of humour, & if I may believe what I hear, have not lost any character by the experiment.—As to my delivery, loud & fluent enough, perhaps a little theatrical."[41]

Holland's real views, however, did not echo the praise that had delighted Byron: "His speech was full of fancy, wit, and invective, but not exempt from affectation nor well reasoned, nor at all suited to our common notions of Parliementary [*sic*] eloquence," he noted in his diary. Coming from the peer most positively disposed toward him, Holland's final dismissal of Byron's political ambitions is all the more damning: "His fastidious and artificial taste and his over-irritable temper would, I think, have prevented him from ever excelling in Parliament."[42]

Ultimately, political rhetoric must be judged by its influence on events; by this measure Byron's first speech, along with two later ones, were failures.[43] His stirring words had no effect whatsoever on the issue; the government never troubled to respond. The Frame Work Bill easily passed in the House of Commons that very evening; the majority of Tory peers among those listening to Byron's speech made it a foregone conclusion that it would pass the House of Lords.*

IN HIS HEART, Byron knew that parliamentary rhetoric—the measured civil style of argument required to persuade his fellow peers—was not for him. From the first, he was never able to conquer his stage fright. Then, as he later admitted, the painstaking give and take of negotiation,

---

*Later the crime was quietly reduced from a felony to a misdemeanor, so that executions were avoided while face was saved for the supporters of law and order.

of compromise, of politics defined as "the art of the possible" bored him. Now, after the cheers and compliments, came the inevitable letdown. His stirring phrases had made nothing happen. Byron seems to have known this, too; he could never have trimmed his wrath to the pattern of reasoned eloquence admired by Holland. Even the "violent sentences" in his speech were tame compared with the provocative and politically inflammatory verses on the same issue that he now sent to the *Morning Chronicle*. Going straight for the jugular of his adversaries, Byron's *An Ode to the Framers of the Frame Bill* opens by naming names:

> Oh well done Lord E[ldo]n! and better Lord R[yde]r!
> Britannia must prosper with councils like yours;
> HAWKESBURY, HARROWBY, help you to guide her,
> Whose remedy only must *kill* ere it cures. . . .

After indicting the author of the bill, Lord Liverpool (later Baron Hawkesbury), for demanding summary executions of the accused without benefit of judge or jury, Byron went on to add charges of deliberate class genocide:

> The rascals, perhaps, may betake them to robbing,
> The dogs to be sure have got nothing to eat—
> So if we can hang them for breaking a bobbin,
> 'Twill save all the Government's money and meat. . . .

With a tweak at Malthusian theories of overpopulation, he notes:

> Men are more easily made than machinery—
> Stockings fetch better prices than lives—
> Gibbets on Sherwood will *heighten* the scenery,
> Showing how Commerce, *how* Liberty thrives!

From savage Swiftian irony, Byron ends with a call to action, whose import could not have been misunderstood:

> Some folks for certain have thought it was shocking,
> When Famine appeals, and when Poverty groans,
> That life should be valued at less than a stocking,
> And breaking of frames lead to breaking of bones.
> If it should prove so, I trust by this token,

(And who will refuse to partake in the hope?)
That the frames of the fools may be first to be *broken*,
Who, when asked for a *remedy*, sent down a *rope*.[44]

As always, Byron was torn between theory and action. He had worked himself into a state of righteous wrath, only to be frustrated by the glacial pace of change and the caution of fellow Whigs such as the moderate Holland. Yet he was unwilling to ally himself with fearless advocates of the people, such as the radical Whig M.P. Sir Francis Burdett, or to accept the consequences of inciting others to violence. He insisted that his *Ode* be published anonymously.

As it turned out, his best hope for the consequences of his speech— that it would help publicize the author of *Childe Harold's Pilgrimage*— proved unnecessary. The poem reached the public on the tenth of March. Within three days, the five hundred folio copies sold out, creating frenzied word-of-mouth excitement among the hundreds who left the bookshops disappointed. Byron was in that dazed and dazzled state of an ambitious young man whose fantasies have suddenly come to pass, and he recalled the moment in the most envied words ever attributed to an author. He awoke one day, he supposedly said, to find himself famous.

TOM MOORE is the only source for Byron's remark on the phenomenon of his fame.[45] Whether or not the phrase was his, the image is consistent with the one Byron took pains to cultivate: While he slept in the innocence of obscurity, celebrity was thrust on him.

In fact, the record of Byron's collaboration in his legend is clearer than the origin of this famous disclaimer. From his first privately printed poems, he crafted a persona of romantic extremes: the glamour of privilege, of rank, beauty, and brilliance, with the mystery of privation, of sin and lovelessness, punished by solitude. Now he had orchestrated his political debut to promote *Childe Harold*, whose hide-and-seek with his author had whetted public appetite to a frenzy of curiosity.

And still, celebrity came as a shock. Until this point, his life had been a rehearsal; he could change costume, switch roles and gender; he could even fail. With his sudden thrust onto the public stage, the door of the dressing room closed—forever.

CHAPTER 18

Caro's Waltz

WITH THE publication of *Childe Harold's Pilgrimage*, promise had become fame. The crush of carriages delivering invitations to Byron's rooms in St. James's choked the street; his presence was solicited at routs, assemblies, balls, masquerades, theater parties, and suppers. Those known to be friends of the poet enjoyed a surge in popularity; could they not persuade him to attend? His appearance crowned the efforts of the most ambitious hostesses. The effect of his entrance was electrifying; any lingering awkwardness, the young lion's *féroce* air, only added to Childe Harold's allure. Throughout the spring of 1812 his name sounded a constant buzzing undertone to all conversations.

He accepted as many invitations as could be fitted into the twenty-four hours of the day. Soon, along with the pleasure of being sought after, he was enjoying the festivities themselves. Shedding his self-consciousness in the role of star, he shone amid galaxies of brilliantly gowned and jeweled women. In gilt-framed mirrors he saw his slender, black-garbed figure and pale face multiplied, lit softly by thousands of candles reflected in the lusters of branching chandeliers.

Earlier he had announced to Dallas his distaste for society; he was "resolved never to mix with it." Converting his envy to disapproval, Dallas observed that Byron "not only willingly obeyed the summons of fashion, but became a votary. . . . He talked of the parties he had been at, and of those to which he was invited, and confessed an alteration in his mind; 'I own,' said he, 'I begin to like them.' "[1]

And yet . . . and yet . . . as Byron himself would say, the stacks of gilt-edged cards, promising glamour and gaiety, the flattering sight of heads all craned in his direction, only underlined the emptiness at his heart's core, the chasm between the feast of public adulation and the hunger of a passionate nature with no object of attachment. He had little need of Dallas's moral censure; his felt his own seduction by the crowd as a betrayal of love, the abandonment of one to whom he had pledged lifelong remembrance.

Dated *March 14,* four days after *Childe Harold*'s appearance at the booksellers, Byron wrote one of two final poems in the "Thyrza" cycle. Both are more poignant for being the last known poems to John Edleston. In "Stanzas" the poet pleads the dead youth's forgiveness:

> If sometimes in the haunts of men,
>   Thine image from my breast may fade,
> The lonely hour presents again
>   The semblance of thy gentle shade:
>   . . . .
> Oh, pardon that in crowds awhile,
>   I waste one thought I owe to thee,
> And, self-condemned, appear to smile,
>   Unfaithful to thy Memory![2]

The second poem, two quatrains titled "On a Cornelian Heart Which Was Broken," plays with a conventional topos, the smashed keepsake as emblem of blasted love. But the actuality of the chorister's prized gift allows us, contemporary readers, to move beyond the tired conceit; the modest jewel has acquired a history of its own:

> Yet precious seems each shatter'd part,
>   And every fragment dearer grown.[3]

Death has transformed the sad bits of red stone into holy relics of love. Buried with the unassuming youth, whose life left barely a trace, was a wholeness and purity of love that Byron would never know again. This certitude was the most bitter knowledge he had ever faced. In the glare of celebrity, his public role as the season's prize social catch left Byron more vulnerable to the sense of false self that was always there, lying in wait for him, ready to pounce at moments of greatest triumph. Sometimes this took the form of a resurgence of that sullen conviction that his lameness was his most recognizable attribute. Rogers recalled leaving a grand reception with the poet when one of the link boys*

---

*In an era before gas lamps, young boys carrying torches led visitors to their carriages.

addressed him by name. Rogers asked how the lad happened to know him; Byron replied bitterly: "Know me! All the world knows me! I am deformed!"[4]

He clung to the image of himself as a cripple, even as the limp became less noticeable with the passage of time. His lameness had a function: As moral stigma, it justified his subversive self that required, more than tenderness and affection, the anarchic irrationality of passion. He could not long remain content playing the tame lion of Whig drawing rooms, his "dark underlook" sending delicious shivers down the spines of ladies seeking a safe encounter with danger. Fatality thrust him toward a wilder, more wounded version of himself.

Lasting fewer than five months, Byron's affair with Lady Caroline Lamb is still the best-known episode of his life. Their passion—his brief, hers lifelong—came to define the canon of romantic love: scandalous, destructive, doomed, and inevitable. Reimagined by biographers, novelists, and filmmakers, "the fatal passion" may be the first one in history to be fictionalized by one of the lovers.

Caroline Lamb's novel *Glenarvon*, published in 1816, was written to revenge herself on Byron. A crazy gothic jumble of plots and subplots, castles, kidnappings, and murdered babies, the rambling, three-volume narrative is also a brilliant social satire of Whig society, especially of the women who manipulated its chess board of power. In Calantha, the heroine who is seduced and abandoned by the satanic nobleman of the book's title, the author has left a pitiless self-portrait. She reveals herself as our contemporary in her insistence on the primacy of childhood in determining what we shall become.[5]

It was Caroline/Calantha's "misfortune to meet with too much kindness, or rather too much indulgence from almost all who surrounded her." The qualification here is significant. "The wildest wishes her fancy could invent, were heard with the most scrupulous attention and gratified with the most unbounded compliments."

No self-discipline, then, had ever been expected of the child-woman she became. "Her violence, her caprices, her mad frolics" were all forgiven her. Indulgence is merely another form of neglect; unattended, the author and her creature were fixed in the certainty of their otherness, irredeemably estranged from their fellow human beings.[6]

"I am not like those I see—my education, my habits, my feelings are different," Calantha says. "I am like one uncivilized and savage; and if you place me in society, you will have to blush every hour for the faults I shall involuntarily commit."

Before they met, friends recognized the predestined planetary movement of the two toward one another and assumed their roles, first as messengers, then as chorus, commentators, and confidants of the principal players. Tom Moore and Samuel Rogers, both part of Lady Caroline's court, insisted that they must know each other. For some time, Rogers had served as Caroline's literary mentor, and early in March he gave her a set of proofs of *Childe Harold*, well before the volume appeared in the bookstores. She was instantly enraptured: The mysterious hero, the noble worldling who nurses hidden wounds, his abandonment to whim and impulse were, to her, instinctive attitudes: "Thoughts, swift as lightning, hurried through her brain," she wrote of Calantha, "projects, seducing but visionary crowded upon her view: without a curb she followed the impulse of her feelings; and these feelings varied with every varying interest and impression. Such character is not uncommon, though rarely seen amongst the higher ranks of society."[7] Byron's cantos now confirmed to her the existence of that most romantic article of faith: a twin soul.

WHEN LADY CAROLINE asked Rogers to describe the author of *Childe Harold*, the older poet, yielding perhaps to his famous malice, replied by testing her determination, dismantling the romantic image. Byron, he regretted to say, was afflicted with a clubfoot and bit his nails.

Passion kindled by the written word is deaf to reality; Caroline was in love with the fictive Byron. "If he is as ugly as Aesop, I must know him," she said.[8] In transparent anonymity, she wrote to the poet, asking him to reply care of Hookham's Book Shop. Proposing the expedient of a "drop" before they had even met was in itself a defining gesture: The writer implied that she was a lady, most certainly married, and one acquainted with the etiquette of adulterous relations.

In the spring of 1812 the former Lady Caroline Ponsonby was twenty-seven. At nineteen she had married William Lamb, oldest surviving son and heir of Lord and Lady Melbourne. Eight years later, the "wild, delicate, odd, delightful person, unlike everything,"[9] as the Duchess of Devonshire described her, had become a restless and unhappy wife, her disappointment in marriage symbolized by two miscarriages followed by the birth of a mentally retarded son. Within weeks her life would be transformed.

Their first meetings have the symbolic quality of dance or dream. Byron first saw Lady Caroline Lamb at a reception given by Lady Westmoreland, but when he approached to be introduced to her, the author of the fan letter turned on her heel and stalked off. She had determined that the idol of all London must, from the first, be aware of her singularity; she would not be another in the throng of beauties, blue-stockings, or heiresses vying for his attentions. She was right in one respect: Byron's interest was always piqued by indifference, real or feigned. But he needed no extravagantly rude gesture to distinguish her from the others. He recognized the need to be singular; it was identical to his own. Like him, Caroline was unfinished, incomplete, trying on and taking off masks, personae, genders.

Within days they met at Holland House, where Caroline appeared late one afternoon at the end of a long ride from Piccadilly to Kensington. Still flushed and in riding clothes, she was seated between Tom Moore and Rogers when Lord Holland entered with Byron. Once more she withdrew; this time she insisted on changing her costume before their host could introduce them.

There is a voluptuousness in Caro's insistence on delay; the exquisite frustration of hide-and-seek, the choreography of display and disappearance. Defining herself through dualities, she is first seen in the masculine severity of a black riding habit, setting off the sweaty, disheveled suggestion of intimacy, only to reappear transformed into her feminine public self, the elegant Regency lady, perfectly coiffed and all but naked in a diaphanous gown. With that first meeting she announced to Byron all that would attract and repulse him in the next stormy months, along with a commanding—and irresistible—challenge: Complete me. And in a real sense, he did.

"Ariel," "Sprite," "Fairy Queen," "Savage," "Squirrel": From childhood these had been the pet names bestowed on Caro by adults or her Cavendish cousins. Later, to her Melbourne in-laws, William's sister and brother, she became "the little Beast." All the names describe something not quite human, but feral and untamed. Her appearance underlined the androgynous nature of a being in suspension between child and adult, boy and girl. She was small, unfashionably slender and flat-chested in an age that admired opulent female attributes: splendid, snowy breasts, buttocks, and bellies. Daringly, she had cut her hair, and her short, flaxen curls framed a thin face that large, dark eyes caused to seem even thinner.

Her kind of allure held no appeal for Byron, who shared the taste of his contemporaries. Her figure, "though genteel, was too thin," he complained, "wanting that roundness that grace and elegance would vainly supply."[10] Byron's initial distaste, later savored in all its irony, will echo the musings of Proust's Swann, wondering at his dead passion for Odette: "To think that I've wasted years of my life, that I've longed to die, that I've experienced my greatest love, for a woman who didn't appeal to me, who wasn't even my type!"[11]

As a woman, Caroline Lamb may not have been Byron's type,

but she resembled, to an astonishing degree, the poet's own description of John Edleston. They had the same pale-gold curls, dark eyes, and slender body. The most eerie reminder of the musical youth, however, was Caro's bewitching voice—"soft low caressing, that was as much a beauty and a charm, and worked much of the fascination that was peculiarly hers."[12]

She had always loved to dress as a page. There is a famous painting of her in page's costume where she appears as a graceful blond boy, holding aloft a large tray heaped with grapes. Historically the page signifies sexual ambiguity and figures in countless plots involving cross-dressing, gender disguise, and mistaken identity. By the Regency, however, pages as a category of household servant were no longer in fashion. In taking on Robert Rushton as his personal attendant, Byron revived the title as a means of disguising his intimacy with the boy; significantly, this was the only homosexual relationship he confessed to Caroline.

When as a young bride Caro moved into Melbourne House to live with her in-laws, she had insisted on hiring her own pages to attend her. She designed their sepia and scarlet uniforms, often wearing the same livery herself. On at least one occasion she raised eyebrows by appearing at the opera accompanied only by one of these attendants, who sat beside her in the Melbourne box. She precipitated the final act of her own life through an injury inflicted on a page by hurling an object at his head in a fit of temper. When she rushed out into the street screaming that she had killed the boy, her husband was finally induced to sign the separation papers that had been lying on his desk.

That first evening at Holland House they were joined by William Lamb, who still hoped for a tranquil if not happy marriage. Byron and Lord Melbourne's heir had met only a few weeks before, at one of Lady Holland's bachelor dinners. Byron would already have heard that great things were expected of the clever and handsome graduate of Eton and Trinity, his own Cambridge college.

"William Lamb, a rising young genius, dines here for the first time tonight," Lady Holland had noted in her Dinner Books thirteen years earlier. It would be twenty-two years before Lamb would fulfill his promise and become, as Lord Melbourne, Queen Victoria's first Prime Minister. Meanwhile, he was moving gradually from being a permanently promising youth whose sole occupation was as tutor and consort to his captivating young wife, toward exploring politics. He had also become the husband of a woman with few resources and infinite need.

Boredom and disappointment had led Caroline into the arms of the first man who offered romantic excitement, an affair that ended with Caroline in disgrace, chastised roundly by both her mother-in-law, Lady Melbourne, and by the redoubtable Lady Holland, mother of her erstwhile lover. It was a small world. Caroline's own reaction to the scandal had been alternating outbursts of defiance and contrition. Lamb maintained, as he would often be called on to do, a posture of gentlemanly forbearance or perhaps indifference—with him, it was hard to tell.

Before the dinner at Holland House was over, Caroline had invited Byron to one of her morning receptions, the next day, March 25. As he made his way to Whitehall and Melbourne House, he would have had reason to reflect upon his hostess, whose aura of scandal was known to him, along with its cause. Later he was to say cruelly that he could never stand accused of having ruined Caro; her reputation was in shreds before they met. Now, however, sin only added to the fascination of the lisping, childlike creature of rude manners and grand connections. There was romance in the litany of names and titles to which Lady Caroline Lamb was connected by blood and marriage; their very sounds stirred Byron's heraldic imaginings, beginning with the ducal Devonshire, Carteret, Cavendish, Churchill, Ponsonby, Spencer. The newer Melbourne title had been a reward for the gold of the Lambs. Extravagant behavior and patrician disdain for convention were Caroline's birthright.

Passion is most often based on misprision, and from the outset, Byron misread Caroline Lamb. He mistook the frightened acting out of an abandoned child for the liberating freedom of an aristocratic woman of the world. Writing to the Anglo-Irish novelist Lady Morgan, who befriended her in her last tragic years, Caroline included a brief life history. Her story, as told there, conforms to that of her fictional Calantha in *Glenarvon*. The letter was written in 1821, just after the death of her mother. Separated from William and accompanied only by a maid, she was driven to wander aimlessly around England and France.

> My mother having boys wished ardently for a girl. . . . I who evidently ought to have been a soldier was made a naughty girl, forward & touchy—like Richard the 3rd. I was a trouble not a pleasure all my childhood for which reason after my return from Italy when [*sic*] I was from the age of 4 until 9, I was ordered by the late Dr. Warren neither to learn anything nor see anyone, for fear the violent passions & strange whims they found in me should lead to madness of which however he assured everyone there were no symptoms. I "differ" but the end was that until 15 I learned nothing. My

instincts (for we all have instinctive preferences) was for music, in it I delighted. I cried when it was pathetic. . . . Of course I was not allowed to follow it up. My angel mother's ill health prevented me from living at home. My kind Aunt Devonshire took me & the present Duke loved me better than himself & everyone passed me those compliments which are shown children who are precious to their parents delicate & likely to die. I wrote not. Spelt not. But I made verses which they all thought beautiful. For myself I preferred washing a dog or polishing a piece of Derbyshire spar or breaking in a Horse to any compliment in the world (drawings rooms, shall I say *with*drawing rooms as they now say) looking glass, fussy & dress, Company & form were my abhorrence. I was I am religious. I was courageous but I was & am unlearned.

At twelve, the highly strung tomboy fell violently in love with her future husband, on reading his verses—thus preparing for a later passion conceived via *Childe Harold*. When they met one year later, she found the black-eyed William Lamb "beautiful . . . & the most daring in his opinions & in his love of liberty & independence. . . . I adored him."[13] It was mutual, if perhaps less wholesome, on William's part: Caroline "appealed to his particular taste for little girls."[14] Watching her at play with her cousins on a visit to Brocket, the Melbourne country estate in Hertfordshire, William had chosen her as from a slave market or brothel: "Of all the girls of Devonshire House, this is the one for me."[15]

In the narrative of her life, Caroline Lamb passes over the dissolution of the marriage that had begun with so much love on her part. To her mother-in-law, however, she defended her errant ways with an accusation of her own. Her husband had corrupted her: "The principles with which I came to William merited praise and ought to have been cherished," she told Lady Melbourne. "They were the safeguards to a character like mine, and nobody can tell the almost childlike innocence and inexperience I had preserved till then. All at once this was thrown off. . . . William himself taught me to disregard without horror all the forms and restraints I had laid so much stress on. . . . He called me prudish—said I was strait-laced,—amused himself with instructing me in things, I need never have heard or known, and the disgust I first felt for the world's wickedness I till then had never heard of, in a very short time gave way to a general laxity of principles which, little by little, unperceived of you all, has been undermining the few virtues I have possessed."[16]

Caroline's version of her descent from innocence to immorality may owe something to the eighteenth-century novel, as well as representing an attempt to justify her own behavior through a scenario in which she is the victim. Still, she rarely troubled to lie; she was a moralist to the end. This account of her downfall—written in 1810, two years before she met Byron—may be faulted only in its indictment of William alone. In reality, her corruption took place much earlier, at the hands of those charged with protecting her, and it was too painful for Caroline ever to confront, except by reenacting the behavior of the "bad child," the little girl who was a "trouble not a pleasure for all of my childhood" and who deserved to be punished.

Byron's heritage of madness and suicide was passed through the men in his family. Caroline Lamb's addiction to destructive impulses was a legacy of the Spencer women. Her "Aunt Devonshire," the legendary Duchess Georgiana, was just as helpless in the face of her gambling obsession as was her idol Charles James Fox. By the end of her short life she had accumulated nearly £1 million of debt. Caro's mother, Henrietta, Countess of Bessborough, shared her older sister's weakness for gaming, but in the younger woman this passion was eclipsed by compulsively frenetic sexual activity. Caroline's own grandmother, Lady Spencer, is said to have condemned the Bessborough house in Cavendish Square, as a place unfit to raise a little girl. In a large establishment, where servants supervised children in nurseries well segre-gated from parental life, this says much for the excesses of Henrietta's behavior. Thus it was that the four-year-old was packed off to Italy for five years, with only a maidservant.

During this exile her mother, accompanied by her Aunt Georgiana, visited Caro and the maid, Fanny, in Naples. What might have been a joyful reunion, however, turned out to reopen the wounds of abandonment. As soon as Henrietta arrived, she fell passionately in love with the man who was to torment her for the next seventeen years, Lord Granville Leveson-Gower, a rich young noble thirteen years her junior. If Caroline had imagined rescue was at hand, she now had to face her mother's ever more erratic behavior: elation, despair, whispered secrets. Henrietta would tearfully leave Naples and her sobbing child, only to be drawn back by Granville's magnetic hold over her. Caroline's crazed jealousy was learned when she was in competition with her mother's lover, dreading that each time Henrietta rushed off at his summons, she would never see her adored parent again.

"That beautiful pale face is my fate," Caro famously wrote in her diary the night she met Byron.[17] Before she was an adolescent, Caroline had purchased her mother's precious attention by becoming a consoling parent, privy to every suffering that a man could inflict on a woman. She knew what was waiting for her when she met Byron: "Mad, bad, and dangerous to know"[18]—Caroline's words were Henrietta's legacy to her daughter.

When the French Revolution drove the wanderers home to England, Caroline, now nine, lived briefly with her Grandmother Spencer. Cavendish House and Roehampton, the Bessboroughs' villa outside London, posed more dangers for a girl on the brink of womanhood than they had for a child. Soon, Caroline was turned over to her Devonshire relations, long a ménage à trois: Her Aunt Georgiana, dead at forty-seven, had been replaced by her dearest friend, Lady Elizabeth Foster, mother of two of the Duke's children. No one was in charge of the boys and girls, cousins and half cousins, some of unknown parentage, who ran wild through the grandeur of Devonshire House in Piccadilly or romped the park of Chatsworth. Meals were sporadic, when they appeared at all, but they were served, Caroline recalled, on the best silver. Adult mannerisms were passed on; Caroline now learned the cooing drawl with its lingering, lisping accent on certain syllables, the hallmark of the "Devonshire House set," and adult passions were rehearsed by the young. Caro's cousin, the Marquess of Hartington and future Duke of Devonshire, was in love with her. At the news of her engagement, he went to pieces and the doctor was called. Vowing that he would never take a bride himself, he gave Caro her wedding dress. On the day of her marriage to William Lamb, Caroline was said to have become hysterical, tearing her gown at the altar. The rending of clothes may be an act of contrition or mourning, of grief or guilt.

From this inauspicious beginning, the newlyweds began married life in Melbourne House under the eye of Caroline's mother-in-law. Before he had taken a fancy to Caroline, Lady Melbourne's favorite son had had an affair with her mother, Henrietta Ponsonby; Lady Melbourne made no secret of her hatred for both mother and daughter. On learning of the engagement, she told Henrietta that she "hoped the daughter would turn out better than the mother, or William might have to repent of his choice."[19]

Lady Melbourne was notorious for such bitchery, but she was feared even more for mischief making. It was said of her that she could never see a happy marriage without trying to destroy it. To this end, she gave the newlyweds the first-floor apartment in Melbourne House, the better to prey on the vulnerability of their union; from the floor below, she watched the young Lambs' growing estrangement.

To avoid being alone together, the Lambs maintained open house; their entertaining began at noon—when Caroline and her friends practiced the latest dance craze from Germany, the waltz—and lasted well into the next day.

ON THE MORNING of March 25, Byron mounted the triple parade of steep stairs rising from the rotunda to the reception rooms above. At Caroline's order, a rope grip had been placed along the side to aid his hesitant climb. At the top, Byron emerged into a suite of three interconnected drawing rooms. Strains of music led him to the salon consecrated to dancing, where, from the sidelines, he could observe Lady Caroline in her glory. If he could not make out what she said, he heard the bursts of laughter that greeted her daring and often risqué sallies. More than anything else, it was her physical grace that affected him—almost viscerally. Aware always of his dragging foot, which made him feel nailed to the floor, he was mesmerized by Caro's quicksilver presence; she seemed in constant motion, dematerialized, in her clinging, swirling gown. (Caroline was so thin that, as she once lispingly confided to Byron's friend William Harness, she wore "sixth pair of thick thockings" to give more shape to her legs.)

Like all libertines, Byron was deeply conservative, and his sense of propriety was offended by the new dance. Watching couples in each other's arms, moving as one body to the music, he recognized an erotic public rehearsal for a private act. Amid the lightly waltzing couples, Byron and Caroline affirmed the sexual as dark and forbidden. He was not her first lover, but he was the first to arouse her violent passion and, with it, a sense of sin that spoke to his own. The first act of her fall, Caroline remembered, like Emma Bovary's took place in a closed carriage. When memory became her only solace, she enshrined the moment when all reason was abandoned to feeling, and she was bitter when Byron later sought to dismiss her as a cold schemer: "But was I cold when first you made me yours?" she demanded. "When first you told me in the carriage to kiss your lips and I durst not—and after thinking it such a crime it was more than I could prevent from that moment—you drew me to you like a magnet and I could not indeed I could not have kept away."[20]

For his part, Byron made no attempt to struggle. Writing to Tom Moore on the evening after the first waltz reception, he already sounded the jaunty proprietorial note of a master of revels, understood as sexual conquistador as well: "Know all men by these presents, that you, Thomas Moore, stand indicted—no—invited, by special and particular solicitation, to Lady C L***'s to-morrow even, at half past nine o'clock, where you will meet with a civil reception and decent entertainment."21

Behind the high-ceilinged state rooms, Byron was now directed to another narrow set of stairs with convex iron balustrades. He needed no rope now to aid his climb as he negotiated the ill-lit steps that led to Caroline's apartments on the floor above. From these stairs, Melbourne House stands revealed as a theater of intrigue. Backstage scaffolding, they close the space between public and private lives, while providing a series of observation points, of porous spaces between two worlds. On a landing there is a window; only yards away and directly opposite, there is another in the parallel wall of the H-shaped structure. In her apartment on the ground floor, Lady Melbourne, "the Spider," waited, monitoring all comings and goings; what she did not see would be reported to her.

As he climbed, Byron retraced another erotic passage, marking the ascent from his own imperial bedchamber at Newstead to the chilly reaches of the servants' quarters where Susan Vaughan had waited for him. Now, on the second floor of Melbourne House, the daughter of a countess and niece of a duchess invited him to be her lover.

Caroline's room, like its occupant, was startlingly small. The arched alcove was filled by her bed, and there was space for a writing desk, a love seat, and a chair or two. But her windows opened on the romantic landscape of St. James's Park, where swans floated on the lake.

Most probably it was after this first visit that Byron sent Caroline a fresh rose and carnation accompanied by a challenge: "Your Ladyship, I am told, likes everything that is new and rare, if only for a moment."22 His intuition was accurate with one exception: her passion for him. If we had no other evidence, the flowers, carefully dried, were in her room at Melbourne House at her death in 1828.

Excessive, extravagant, her reply to this courtly persiflage should have served as warning: Byron is the Apollonian god of light and she the humble sunflower that, "having once beheld in its full lustre the bright and unclouded sun that for one moment condescended to shine upon it, never while it exists could think of any lower object worthy of its attention and admiration."23

With his unlovely compulsion to pass around intimate correspondence, Byron showed Tom Moore another letter he received from Caroline; in it she offered to sell her jewels should he need cash. From their earliest conversations, then, he had confided his troubles to her, including worries about money. But he also wrote to Caroline, as often as ten times a day. Dallas observed that on one of his visits, Byron was so immersed in writing to his lover that he could not be interrupted, making his visitor wait while he covered page after page, smiling and sounding the phrases softly to himself.

In the weeks that followed, Byron visited Melbourne House every day. In deference to his lameness and hatred of seeing her in the arms of other men, Caroline canceled her waltz mornings. The reception rooms were silent and dark when he made his now familiar way, climbing the many steps to his destination.

Often Caroline would have six-year-old Augustus brought from his nursery at the summit of the house, adjoining the servants' quarters. The mother's pride in the handsome boy was the more insistent as his abnormalities were becoming more pronounced. Increasingly, he had difficulty running or even holding objects, a condition attributed to a softening of the bones said to be the result of inherited syphilis. Byron's claim to loathe children was a pose; he entered their play with delight, and he most likely made special efforts to engage Augustus with games and affection. In contrast, there is a poignant drawing by Caroline that shows William Lamb seated in a chair, playing with his dogs; his back is turned to his little son, who sits, ignored, on a table.

On every visit Byron brought with him a new book. Along with other unsatisfied desires, Caroline's quick and hungry mind craved sustenance. He had teased her by saying that her notions about love came from reading vulgar novels; now the burden was on him to provide texts to refine her taste. For verse, he brought copies of his own poems, eagerly solicited and read aloud, but we can wonder whether he discouraged her earlier fondness for Wordsworth in favor of the soporific verses of Campbell and Rogers, with their musings on the pleasures of hope and memory, or the lilting stanzas of their friend Tom Moore. With the few hours available, reading more probably served only as an erotic overture. Byron certainly knew Dante's famous prelude to the adulterous love of Paolo and Francesca: "They read no more that day."

If only Caroline could have been satisfied with the freedom that permitted her intimacy without compromise, liberties tacitly accorded women of her class, *provided* that they followed one rule: no public scandal. It was precisely the dissolution of the barrier between public and private, however, that she demanded. Outrage, shame, and disgrace were sacrifices on the altar of love. To this end, she seemed determined to reenact her mother's humiliations at the hands of Lord Granville, only more openly, more abjectly. She hung on Byron at gatherings to which they were both invited; she sulked and chaffed him familiarly if he appeared too engaged by any other woman, insisting on leaving in his carriage. When not invited, she stood outside houses where Byron was a guest, chatting with link boys and coachmen until he emerged. One night, after a reception at Devonshire House to which she had not been asked, Rogers was horrified to recall, "I saw her—yes, saw her,—talking to Byron, with half her body thrust into the carriage which he had just entered." As an older friend of both lovers, Rogers was also called on to play the role of mediator. Often he arrived home to find Caroline pacing back and forth in the garden behind his house; she would tearfully confide her latest quarrel with Byron, begging him to reconcile them.24

There is something breathtaking about Caroline Lamb. In her short reign—a matter of months—she manages to dwarf for posterity Byron's other lovers. An aristocrat, she traffics only in absolutes; pride is for peasants, face-saving calculations for clerks. Her passion for Byron has become a measure of *l'amour fou*: public displays of howling need; operatic scenes of vengeance or solitary suffering; excesses of brandy and laudanum; banishment and exile; and finally, an early, disfiguring death. She is an embarrassment to everyone, including her own biographers. But her grandeur remains inviolable precisely because it is self-defined. Let others be ashamed; she can never be ridiculous in her own eyes.

Self-conscious and insecure, with none of Caro's sovereign indifference to others' opinion, Byron was soon terrified, as much by her as by his own helplessness before this patrician who was also a primitive force of nature—"your heart—my poor Caro, what a little volcano! that pours *lava* through your veins." Then, reaching for what he conceded to be one of his "detestable tropes and figures," he insisted that he would not wish her heart "a bit colder," not like that hardened lava, the *pietra dura* "brought in vases tables &c. from Vesuvius . . . [when hardened] after an eruption."25

But that is exactly what he would have liked, and his metaphor could not have been better chosen. Attracted by this wild creature, "young and of the first connexions," as he later boasted, possessing, too, "an infinite variety of mind,"26 he wanted Caroline to remain a flattering attribute, visible confirmation of his own sexual power; like the *pietra dura* objects so prized by collectors, he wanted Caroline's savage nature frozen into decorative form.

Initially she had fulfilled her function, and Byron cynically recalled, "I was soon congratulated by my friends on the conquest I had made, and did my utmost to show that I was not insensible to the partiality I could not but perceive. I made every effort to be in love, expressed as much ardour as I could muster, and kept feeding the flame with a constant supply of *billets doux* and amatory verses."27

His lies—if such they ever were—became truth as he was swept up in the all-or-nothing game of this daughter and niece of gamblers who "played deep." Byron had never engaged with high rollers before, still less with one who was also a woman of considerable position in society. In sexual wagers, unlike other games of chance, Caroline had everything to lose, and her losses could never be recouped. In a verse dedicated to Caroline, he wrote:

> For the first step of Error none e'er could recall
> And the woman once fallen forever must fall[28]

Byron has often stood accused of the apparent frankness that conceals truth, of swaggering confessions of sin rather than painful admissions of paralyzing conflict. But surely no poet has ever confronted more openly love's thralldom as primal helplessness:

> Ashamed of my weakness however beguiled
> I shall bear like a Man what I feel like a Child.[29]

The more obsessed he became, the more desperately he reached for the mask of Regency rake. His fear was more than the male terror of being unmanned by passion. He was also aware that reviews of *Childe Harold* were being written for all the major journals, including notices by critics who harbored no friendly feelings toward the author; he could ill afford to have his personal life transformed into judgments about the new work.

From the first days of their intimacy, Byron begged Caroline to respect the proprieties. At first she merely defied him, as she had always defied everyone; now, even when it became a question of losing him, she could not control her actions. She agonized over whether they should *both* accept an invitation to Lady Grey's. Byron urged her to go—but only if she could behave: "This same prudence is tiresome enough," he conceded, "but one *must* maintain it, or what can we do to be saved?" he asked, only half-facetiously. And as a further admonition, he scrawled on the outside of his folded letter, "Keep to it."[30]

A futile reminder, where Caro was concerned. Nothing could assuage her fear of losing anything she cared for. In verses written when she was an adolescent, she had lamented the blighting effect of her love:

> Oh! Ever thus, from childhood hour
> I've seen my fondest Hopes decay,
> I've never loved a tree or flower

> But 'twas the first to fade away
> I never nurs'd a dear Gazelle
> To glad me with its soft black eye
> But when it came to know me well,
> And love me, it was sure to die![31]

By anticipating catastrophe, she hastened its arrival. Spying and jealous scenes, ever more shocking displays of public ardor—everything she did seemed calculated to undermine Byron's fragile sense of social acceptance and autonomy, to threaten his need to control relations with women. But he also instigated scenes of his own, triggered by jealousy of William Lamb. Byron had taken the measure of his rival, and what he saw aroused all his feelings of inadequacy. Lamb might be a dilettante, but he was no negligible cuckold, happy to find consolation elsewhere. Byron was humiliated to realize that William was confident that his wife's obsession with Byron, like her earlier infatuation, would soon blow over. Caroline never denied, moreover, her love for and dependence on her husband. Her confessions sent Byron into fits of rage that turned murderous when she declared that William would always occupy a place in her heart that no other man could challenge. When she refused to swear that she loved him better than William, Byron threatened, "My God, you shall pay for this. I'll wring that obstinate little heart."[32]

The public and private realms of his life were hurtling toward collision. His pleas to Caroline for prudence were warnings to himself as well. Circumspect behavior now assumed a pressing political dimension. In the third week in April, Byron was scheduled to deliver his second speech to the House of Lords, on behalf of Catholic Emancipation. Historically the issue most identified with Whig efforts toward reform, the petition to yield to four million Roman Catholics, mainly in Ireland, the rights enjoyed by all other British subjects had been argued and defeated in four other major parliamentary debates between 1805 and 1811. Byron's first address had been a rehearsal. This speech was his appointment with history. He might yet fill the prophetic role of the leader carrying the opposition to victory.

CHAPTER 19

The Spider's Stratagem

O
N THE DAY before the debate was to take place, the Earl of Donoughmore presented "The General Petition of the Roman Catholics of Ireland to the House of Lords." He made the claimants' case in simple, stirring words: "Our object is avowed and direct; earnest, yet natural: it extends to an equal participation of the civil rights of the constitution of our country, equally with our fellow subjects of all other religious persuasions: it extends no further. We would cheerfully concede the enjoyment of civil and religious liberty to all mankind; we ask no more for ourselves. We seek not the possession of offices, but mere eligibility to office, in common with our fellow citizens; not power or ascendancy over any class of people, but the bare permission to rise from our prostrate posture, and to stand erect in the empire."[1]

In contrast, Byron's address seems more a vehicle driven by anger and frustration—personal rather than political. He was still smarting from the betrayal by the Prince of Wales who, upon becoming regent, had become a born-again Tory, sending his Whig friends into retirement. Byron had launched an attack on the royal renegade so scurrilous it could only be published anonymously. Printed in the *Morning Chronicle* of March 7, "Lines to a Lady Weeping" was based on a notorious incident of a month earlier, reported to the poet. At a reception given by the regent at Carlton House, his young daughter, Princess Charlotte, was supposed to have cried on hearing her father openly vilify his Whig supporters:

> Weep, daughter of a royal line,
>   A Sire's disgrace, a realm's decay;

Ah, happy! if each tear of thine
Could wash a father's fault away![2]

Unyielding opposition to Catholic claims seems to have been the only
political principle identified with the pleasure-loving royal heir. Thus the
debate of April 21 provided Byron with a welcome opportunity to move
from anonymous authorship to frontal attack on the Prince's new Tory
allies.

His weapon, however, was literary polemic rather than the political
art of persuasion. Recycling the rhetoric of *English Bards and Scotch
Reviewers* (moderated by parliamentary sanction against personal
attacks on fellow members), Byron continued to score off enemies of
reform rather than propose solutions.

Seizing on a classic refrain of the Crown and its Tory supporters,
that the "time" was not ripe for granting these claims, Byron turned this
temporizing on its head: "It is not the time, say they, or it is an improper
time, or there is time enough yet. In some degree, I concur with those
who say, it is not the time exactly; that time is past."

The Tory argument, he pointed out, translated the silence of the Irish
peasantry—a silence based on illiteracy—into satisfaction with the status quo, and it played on fears of demagoguery by insisting that claims
for reform came only from "agitators." To this, Byron seized on an
analogy bound to shock his listeners. The present condition of the Irish
was worse than that of black slaves: "It might as well be said," he noted,
"that the negroes did not desire to be emancipated, but this is an unfortunate comparison, for you have already delivered them out of the
house of bondage without any Petition on their part, but many from
their taskmasters to a contrary effect; and for myself, when I consider
this, I pity the Catholic peasantry for not having the good fortune to be
born black."[3]

With Hobhouse stationed in Ireland, Byron had the advantage of
an on-the-spot source. In a letter from Enniscothy on March 10,*
Hobhouse had enclosed a communication from the Bishop of Ferns
detailing recent injustices suffered by his countrymen; these ranged from
the locking of barns used as chapels by rural congregations to the
acquittal of a Protestant yeoman who had already been convicted by a
jury of killing a Catholic.

Byron's address was delivered to a full House of Lords on Thursday,
April 21. He was eighth on a roster of eleven speakers. None of his

---

*The letter has not survived.

London literary friends—Moore, Rogers, Campbell—troubled to attend. Only the loyal Hobhouse, home on leave, noted in his diary that he had "staid up all night heard Byron—who kept the House in a roar of laughter."[4]

Unlike his arguments, Byron's jokes, at least, did not go unappreciated. But these were not enough to launch a parliamentary career. The speech dealt a second major blow to his political ambitions. This time, moreover, no compliments followed. The most eloquent testimony of failure comes from Byron himself: There is not a single mention of the speech in any of his journals or letters.

DISTRACTION AS WELL as disappointment explain Byron's strange silence about his parliamentary ambitions. His letters allude repeatedly to his present "scrape," and if anything he underplayed its seriousness. By the middle of May the open scandal of his affair with Caroline Lamb left all other gossip forgotten; no one could remember lovers among the "first rate" who so openly flouted all the rules governing social order.

Suspecting that Byron was in retreat, Caroline now resorted to stalking him. Disguised as one of her own pages, she managed to gain entry to his rooms, where Fletcher found her rifling his master's papers. Soon afterward she burst in on Byron when, in a predictable effort to assert his sexual independence, he was entertaining another lady.

He felt trapped in the role of pariah. Between the nightmare of notoriety and the knowledge that he was still under Caro's spell, he was reduced to desperate pleading, writing to her on May 19: "M[oore] is in great distress about us, & indeed people talk as if there were no other pair of absurdities in London.—It is hard to bear all this without cause, but worse to give cause for it.—Our folly has had the effect of a fault.— I conformed & could conform, if you would lend your aid, but I can't bear to see you look unhappy, & am always on the watch to observe if you are trying to make me so.—We must make an effort, this dream, this delirium of two months must pass away, we in fact do not know one another, a month's absence would make us rational, you do not think so, I know it."[5]

He tried to strip Caro—and himself—of the illusion cherished by lovers who also happen to be survivors of other liaisons: This affair is "different." "We have both had 1000 previous fancies of the same kind & shall get the better of this & be as ashamed of it according to the maxim of Rochefoucault: 'Few are unashamed of having loved, when they love no longer.' " For Byron, the maxim could not have been more apt. They needed time apart, he told Caroline, hoping that

absence would substitute for will in severing his bonds. He was steeled
to test the pledge he had given her in verse, on her gift to him of a fine
gold necklace:

> Ah Caro! do I need the chain?
> Nor dare I struggle to be free,
>   Since gifts returned but pain the giver,
> And the soft band put on by thee,
>   The slightest chain, will last for ever![6]

He would take it upon himself, he announced, to leave London. "Now
dont abuse me, or think me altered," he insisted, "it is because I am not,
cannot alter, that I shall do this, and cease to make fools talk, friends
grieve, and the wise pity."[7] There was more truth than gallantry in his
temporizing. Besides the fascination Caroline continued to exert on him,
he had to struggle against his own passivity. He would often use a fresh
lover to pry himself from a stale affair. Now he found an effective ally
in a new friend.

Not for nothing was Lady Melbourne known as "the Spider." She
had been waiting for Byron to call on her. As he well knew, however, the
enmity between Caroline and her mother-in-law was such that he would
not have been a welcome guest of the older woman while paying daily
visits to his lover. Thus, with Byron's first call on Lady Melbourne he
announced that his trysts upstairs had ended.

Seated on the sofa next to his hostess in her cozy salon, he threw
himself on her mercy. He was counting on her, he explained, to do for
him what he was incapable of doing himself: getting rid of her troublesome daughter-in-law. He wanted managing and would put himself
completely in her power, he told Lady Melbourne: "So far from being
ashamed of being governed . . . I am always but too happy to find one
to regulate or misregulate me."

"Will you undertake me?" he begged.[8] No plea could have
delighted her more.

At sixty-two, Elizabeth Milbanke, Viscountess Melbourne, was no
longer the beauty who had captured a fortune though marriage. She
had, however, kept the more durable attributes of charm, intelligence,
and the qualities—more French than English in her time—of tact and
discretion that had for twenty-five years made her the preferred company and confidante of powerful men. Unlike most women, she herself
confided in no one: "No man is safe with another's secrets, no woman
with her own," she once remarked.

Rumors had long circulated about her liaisons, and their legacy: The handsome and brilliant Lord Egremont, patron and host of Turner at Petworth, was widely held to be the father of William Lamb. (When his legal father refused him the allowance of his late older brother, Peniston, this was taken as official denial of his Lamb paternity.) George, his younger brother, was usually assigned to his namesake, the Prince Regent himself. And there were many more lovers, all chosen from the ranks of privilege, who did not leave issue. Discretion ensured that rumors never gained the currency of fact. As a measure of her good sense, Lady Melbourne stayed on excellent terms with all her lovers, which allowed her to seek advice and favors as needed.

Her only passion was for power. Unlike Georgiana and her feckless sister, Henrietta, Lady Melbourne never lost her head or her heart. Or it may be that her heart had been broken so long ago, it could no longer be lost.

She had been married at sixteen to Sir Peniston Lamb, then twenty, but only months after the wedding her husband took a mistress, and the seventeen-year-old wife learned to swallow every humiliation. What the young Lady Melbourne also learned was "a completely cynical attitude to the world and its ways"[9] and more: an avenging impulse to destroy innocence and happiness wherever it appeared to flourish.

Lady Melbourne inspired "something close to fear" in all who knew her, and the portrait that emerges from her contemporaries confirms Oscar Wilde's view that life copies art. Those who had read *Les Liaisons Dangereuses*, the great epistolary novel by her contemporary Choderlos de Laclos—readers as disparate as her niece Annabella and Lady Holland—unfailingly invoked the character of Mme. de Merteuil, evil genius of intrigue, to describe Lady Melbourne. Yet forewarned was not to be forearmed: The spider of Melbourne House seemed to immobilize her victims.

Byron's growing intimacy with Lady Melbourne while he was still entangled with her daughter-in-law raised eyebrows even among the most tolerant: "Things have come to a pretty pass when they take the mothers as confidantes," the regent grumbled.[10]

Her intuition for men's weaknesses was wedded to an instant grasp of their needs, and she now set about to provide exactly what Byron sought in a woman friend.

"Once you told me you did not understand friendship," she wrote to him after his first tête-à-têtes with her. "I told you I would teach it to you, and so I will, if you do not allow C. to take you quite away."[11]

As part of her lessons, she enveloped him in maternal indulgence distanced by a cool wit. At the same time, she allowed him to reveal himself without having his confessions held against him, encouraging him to shift the weight of his problems to a powerful parental figure who would "make them go away." Reciprocally, Byron knew what the favor of a sought-after young man conferred on a woman past her prime. He reinforced the public prestige of his attentions to Lady Melbourne by a steady stream of intimate letters, in the spirit of an *amitié amoureuse*, assuring his correspondent that she was still an enchantress who "defied Time."

No one can accuse Lady Melbourne of misleading Byron as to the nature of their bargain. But "C." did not, after all, prove so easy to dislodge—not least because of Byron's own ambivalence. After reviling his mistress and bemoaning her behavior to the sympathetic ears of Lady Melbourne or the mysogynistic Hobhouse, Byron would then rush to meet Caro or reassure her in letters of his undying passion.

ON MAY 11 a failed Liverpool merchant, John Bellingham, having decided that the government was to blame for his troubles, walked into the lobby of the House of Commons, where he shot and killed Prime Minister Spencer Perceval. A week later, Byron and two school friends, "Long" Bailly and John Madocks, rented a window opposite the gallows erected in front of Newgate Prison, to observe the assassin's hanging—a spectator event whose popularity placed a premium on such choice viewpoints.

At one with the mob that crowded every alley and window, Byron was swept along by the erotic surge of excitement and release generated by the ritual of public execution. He was already at a high emotional pitch when he visited Caroline on the night Perceval was killed, but on the eve of Bellingham's hanging, she reported, he "came to me, *pale* and exceedingly agitated, and said he must see him die."[12] He left Melbourne House early that night, and when he reappeared the next morning, he seemed "calm and tranquil."

But there was an element missing from the necessary catharsis: "I have seen him suffer," Byron said of the assassin, "and he made *no confession*."[13]

Death's randomness—the assassin's refusal to admit guilt, the awful reckoning of public execution, and the erotic rhythm of the drama—all led him back to Caroline, their passion revealed as *Liebestod*. At the very moment he was about to betray her, he was moved to make a profession of faith—soon to be broken. Six years later, she reminded him of what he had said: "At the time of the death of Perceval, you promised me—do you remember—that whatever might happen, whatever my conduct might be, you would never cease to be my friend."[14]

Byron's three visits to Caro in the days between the murder and the execution assume the symmetry of parable, marking his sense of implication in the tragedy. Their own drama, each of them alternating roles of executioner and victim, was playing out, moving toward its denouement: Byron's delivery of Caroline Lamb into the hands of Lady Melbourne.

Writing to Moore two days after the execution, the poet acknowledged as much. Persuaded by her lover that nothing was changed between them, Caroline had agreed to go with the family to Brocket Hall. Conflating the assassin's corpse and his lover's body, Byron jokingly proposed their common burial: "On Monday, after sitting up all night, I saw Bellingham launched into eternity, and at three the same day, I saw ***L[ady Caroline Lamb] launched into the country."15

Byron's desire to rid himself of Caroline had taken on new urgency. Lady Melbourne had decided that he must marry, and she now settled on her niece, Annabella Milbanke, as the wife who would best suit her purposes.

Anne Isabella, as she had been christened, was the daughter of Lady Melbourne's brother Sir Ralph Milbanke and the former Judith Wentworth of Seaham in County Durham. Sir Ralph's means would have been more than respectable had he not incurred debts in his determination to win a parliamentary seat. On her mother's side, however, was a fortune, and the prospect of a greater legacy to come; Annabella was known to be the heiress of her childless uncle and aunt, Lord and Lady Wentworth.

Both her parents were over forty when she was born, and she was a doted-upon only child. Adored as a prodigy, her taste for learning had been encouraged, especially by her mother, a woman of superior intellectual gifts married to a hearty squire. As a small girl Annabella had awed her elders by a precocious religiosity, along with a most unfeminine gift for mathematics. She had far surpassed her governess, and for some time she had worked on her own, puzzling out geometrical problems with only Euclid as her guide. Removed as she was by interests, upbringing, and geography from the amorality and worldly ambitions of Devonshire and Melbourne houses, the combination of wide reading, social isolation, and fierce intelligence gave her the ironic gaze of a Jane Austen—her favorite novelist.

Now it was her second London season, and Annabella was aware that her parents were investing much to ensure that she make the right marriage. To save money this year, they had closed their London house on Upper Berkeley Street and had remained in the North, entrusting their daughter to her godmother, Lady Tamworth. Thanks to her aunt, however, Annabella soon came to regard Melbourne House as a second home. Her quicksilver cousin Caroline promptly took her up, as did the new Melbourne daughter-in-law, George Lamb's wife, Caroline St. Jules,* the illegitimate daughter of Georgiana's successor as Duchess of Devonshire, Elizabeth Foster.

The country girl was now plunged into the social whirl of the Whig *ton*: balls, routs, rides, receptions, theater parties. She sat for Hayter, one of the most fashionable painters of the day. Annabella could more than hold her own: When the portraitist wanted her to wear her hair down, in the careful disarray of curls favored by Regency belles, his young sitter refused; it was not in the "nature of my character," she told him.[16]

It was on Byron's initiation to Melbourne House at Caroline's waltz morning that Annabella had first seen the lionized poet—"the object of universal attention," she wrote to her parents at Seaham. She also carefully scrutinized Caroline, the planetary center of her own orbit of admirers. If any woman could be described as the antithesis of her febrile cousin, it was Annabella, beginning with her appearance: Miss Milbanke's every feature seemed to partake of roundness: her apple-shaped face, rosy cheeks, and small body, which tended to the buxom.

Exuding a self-confidence bordering on arrogance, Annabella intrigued her worldly relations. Caroline in particular saw her as an exotic pet and showered her with invitations. Caro's reputation, however, was such that Annabella thought it prudent to reassure her parents: The party to which she had just been asked was "not a very dangerous one." At first everything about her glamorous relative fascinated the provincial, not least the whiff of scandal surrounding her. But Annabella's sensitivity—generally ignored in the subsequent condemnation of her as a humorless prig—also responded to Caro's tenderness and generosity. Yearning to be loved herself and suffering the disillusionment of an unhappy marriage, Caro felt for the awkward situation of her young cousin, alone for the first time, dispatched to London to find a husband.

Lady Melbourne, however, was far from pleased by Annabella's friendship with Caroline, and she lost no time in discrediting her daughter-in-law in the eyes of her devout niece. "Lady M. spoke to me about her in a confidential manner," Annabella wrote home. "She says that she has a very good heart but unhappily joined with . . ." (here, a later censor has torn the sheet bearing the Spider's warning). But soon

---

*Known as "Caro-George," to distinguish her from "Caro-William."

enough, her aunt's campaign to poison Annabella's affection for Caro required no help.

When Annabella saw Byron for the first time, she was instantly smitten. Like Caro, she had prepared herself by reading *Childe Harold* a few days earlier, but she was unprepared for her dazzlement at the sight of the poet: "The comet of this year, Lord Byron shone with his customary glory.

"I did not seek an introduction to him," Annabella explained to her mother, "for all the women were absurdly courting him and trying to *deserve* the lash of his satire." In the twinkling of an eye, Caroline had become a rival, and Annabella's venom was now directed toward her cousin, described as so "kind" and "friendly" just a few days earlier: "Lady C has of course seized on him notwithstanding the reluctance he manifests to be shakled [*sic*] by her." She now mocked Caroline's Devonshire House lisp, which she had found charming a few weeks earlier; with its bleating sounds, Lamb speech was all "Bah-bah-Ba-a-a," Annabella reported.

Waltzing was abhorrent to her, and she compared her whirling cousin to a rabid dog who had infected others with her disease: "I really thought Ldy. C had bit half her company and communicated the nonsense mania—waltzing was one of the amusements." Byron's refusal to waltz, in Annabella's interpretation, had nothing to do with his lameness; this was how the poet expressed his disdain for frivolity and corruption. The fierce moralist was in love, and she now recruited the poet of sinful reputation to the side of the righteous: "I saw Lord Byron for the first time," Annabella confided to her diary on March 25. "His mouth continually betrays the acrimony of his spirit. I should judge him sincere and independent—sincere at least in society as far as he can be, whilst dissimulating the violence of his scorn. He very often hides his mouth with his hand when speaking."

Gestures and expressions that to an impartial observer might suggest irritation, impatience, or simply boredom became, for Annabella, revelations of a kindred spirit. "It appeared to me that he tried to control his natural sarcasm and vehemence as much as he could, in order not to offend; but at times his lips thickened with disdain and his eyes rolled impatiently." She had transformed the poet, sulking on the sidelines, into a social critic.

Still, Annabella was forced to observe that the corrupt social whirl, with Caroline at its vortex, had swallowed the real Byron. Cloaking her jealousy in puritan disapproval, Annabella declined to attend a party on the second floor of Melbourne House on the eve of Good Friday, telling her mother, "I neither suit nor will suit myself to the vagaries of these *unnatural naturals*." Lady Melbourne gave every appearance of agreeing with her pious niece: "No person is more just & sensible than she on points of conduct," Annabella innocently reported, "and my own opinion is strengthened by hers."

Lady Melbourne knew perfectly where her daughter-in-law Caroline was headed: into the arms of the sensational new poet. She had also taken the measure of Annabella; her uncommon mix of innocence and strength of character; the ironic intelligence and appealing idealism. With a decent fortune thrown into the bargain she just might do for Byron, thus ending another scandal before it began.

For his part, Byron had not failed to notice Caro's serious clever cousin. Indeed, he had heard of her two years earlier, not, however, in a context designed to pique his interest. A certain Miss Milbanke, Byron noted to Dallas, had become the patroness of one Joseph Blackett, a shoemaker turned poet in County Durham. Byron had only contempt for autodidact versifiers and those who "discovered" them, and he had acerbic words to say about both in *English Bards and Scotch Reviewers*. Now that he had met and talked with Annabella on several occasions at Melbourne House and again at a reception at Lord Glenbervie's, he was forced to admit that something in her grave wit discouraged his usual mockery.

As a measure of his interest, Byron was on his best behavior on these occasions, presenting to the critical young woman his sober, reflective self, the Byron calculated to win her good opinion. Not trusting to her own impressions, however, Annabella made inquiries; claiming to know Lord Byron "intimately," Lord Glenbervie assured her that "this extraordinary man is deeply repentant for the sins of his youth [the poet was then twenty-four] and sincerely desirous to be put in the right way." It would appear that Lady Melbourne had enlisted help in her campaign to bring them together.

On April 19 Annabella was among the guests at a small dinner given by Lady Caroline; the only others present were William Lamb, his brother George, George's Caroline, Samuel Rogers, and Byron. Avoiding "politics or party," the conversation was confined to matters of "taste and literature," Annabella reported, with the group deciding on the thirty best English novels. Following this literary evening, Annabella artlessly entrusted several of her poems to Caroline to show to Byron. Replying to Caro, he was far more admiring of both the poetry and the poet than his jealous mistress could have wished. The poems, Byron wrote, "display fancy, feeling, & a little practice would very soon induce facility of expression." He had shown the manuscript to another poet who was still more unstinting in his praise, calling the poems "beautiful."

"But are these all, has she no others?" he asked Caro, adding, "She certainly is a very extraordinary girl, who would imagine so much strength & variety of thought under that placid countenance." He left it to Caroline's discretion to report as much or as little of his remarks as she saw fit, and he concluded by assuring her, "I have no desire to be better acquainted with Miss Milbank [*sic*], she is too good for a fallen spirit to know or wish to know, & I should like her more if she were less perfect."[17]

Caro could not have been pleased by Byron's praise of her cousin's poems and still less by his remark that Annabella was too good for him, implying that she, Caroline, was not. Thus, on the next occasion when the two women were alone, Caroline seems to have hinted broadly that Byron was her lover and that the younger woman should not waste her time.

Now, with her cousin gone to the country, Annabella basked in the occasions at which she and Byron found themselves fellow guests. On June 1 she confided to her diary: "Lord Byron was there in a gentle mood."

IN THE MIDDLE of June Byron went to Newstead, accompanied by Hobhouse. The property was disintegrating. There was no management, and the tenants, demoralized by rumors of an impending sale, had little incentive to productive farming; some were paying no rent at all. Byron could see the value of the estate diminishing before his eyes, and this melancholy evidence, along with his constant need for cash, pushed him toward the decision he had until now obstinately refused to consider: Newstead must be sold. With no proprietorial concerns to cloud his visit, Hobhouse was having a glorious time. The easygoing Susan had been replaced by other pretty and accommodating maidservants, and the sexual fear that usually froze Hobhouse at home in England dissipated. "A week of delirium" was his happy diary entry.[18]

Two weeks later, a frantic Caroline returned from Hertfordshire. Her condition had provoked a crisis of anxiety in her mother. Seeing her own cycles of despair, hope, and desperation reenacted by her daughter, Lady Bessborough was reduced to near hysteria herself—hardly the state of mind to help her child. Indiscreetly, she detailed her daughter's every lurid scene to her ex-lover, Lord Granville, heedless of the fact that these tales would be grist for the gossip mill of his wife, the homely Harriet Cavendish; she had always hated her cousin Caro and now delighted in giving the widest currency to instances of her crazed behavior.

Lady Bessborough also confided in Hobhouse who, although no admirer of Caro ("the Lamb that taketh not away the sins of this world" being a favorite joke), was Byron's one friend who could be relied on to be discreet and helpful in a crisis, which was not long in coming.

On Caroline's return to town, she was confronted with the humiliating evidence that Byron wanted to be rid of her and that he had enlisted Lady Melbourne's help in this enterprise. Abandoned by her lover and trapped in the house of her enemy, Caroline was desperate. She had heard that Byron was planning a flight to Harrow to avoid her, and on July 29 she appeared in his rooms, disguised in a man's outer clothing.

As it happened, Hobhouse was having dinner with Byron, and he has left a careful record of the bizarre events that followed and his own role in them.

On arriving upstairs, Caroline disappeared with Byron into the bedroom, where, according to Hobhouse, who remained in the sitting room, she pulled off the first layer of her disguise, revealing her page's costume underneath. To reassure his friend that he was merely trying to reason with Caro privately, Byron would emerge every few minutes, "so that nothing could have happened, besides which, both parties were too much agitated to admit a doubt of their conduct at that time," noted Hobhouse judiciously. To further protect Byron's reputation (Caro's being, presumably, beyond saving), Hobhouse took the step of summoning as witness a Mr. Dollman, a neighboring shopkeeper, who further confirmed the necessity of the lady's immediate departure. At this point Caro was alone in the bedroom, refusing to budge. Finally she was prevailed on to don yet another disguise, that of one of Byron's female servants, and to come into the sitting room. However, she still refused to leave the house. Now it was Byron who capitulated: "Then we must go off together," he said wildly. Hobhouse continued to plead with Caroline to leave without her lover—to no avail; instead, she became hysterical, threatening, "There will be blood spilt." Losing patience, Hobhouse retorted, "There will be indeed unless you go away."

Anticipating the drama to come, Hobhouse had earlier ordered a hackney coach, which was now waiting downstairs. He urged Caroline to take it to his lodgings, where she could change back into her own clothes (brought by her in a bundle) and transfer herself in another hackney to her own carriage or to the house of a friend. She would go nowhere, she now insisted, unless Byron accompanied her; she begged Hobhouse to allow them to stay alone in his lodgings. This request he flatly refused, and Byron, no doubt relieved, made plain he had no wish for any such arrangement: "Indeed it would be wrong to expect it of you. I do not expect it," he told Hobhouse.

It was now Caroline's turn to capitulate. What choice did she have? Assured of the forgiveness of all the Lambs, she crept back to Melbourne House.

Hobhouse was clear about his own role in the tragicomedy: His sole concern was Byron's welfare. As he notes legalistically in his diary, "My first wish was that he should give this lady no power over him by consenting to any serious folly, and my next was to prevent a public disclosure and an elopement. This latter event would, as B. assured me and assures me, have certainly taken place but for the part I played in the transactions of yesterday, which I have noted down, twenty-four hours only after they took place, in case it should ever be necessary to defend myself (and Byron) from any misrepresentation."[19]

Hobhouse leaves no doubt that Byron had been prepared to elope with Caroline. Why this never happened remains unclear, along with the circumstances of her return to Whitehall. On some level Caro feared being abandoned by her lover when it really was too late. She had none of the steely determination of a woman prepared to risk everything for passion and to live outside society. At just the moment when she could have claimed Byron, it would seem that her courage, ever fragile, deserted her. For his part, Byron was clearly motivated by far stronger feelings than chivalric notions of honorable behavior: "Is there anything on earth or heaven [which] would have made me so happy as to have made you mine long ago? & not less *now* than *then*, but *more* than ever at this time—you know I would with pleasure give up all here & all beyond the grave for you. . . . I care not who knows this—what use is made of it—it is to *you* & to *you* only that they owe yourself, I was and am *yours*, freely & most entirely, to obey, to honour, love—& fly with you when, where, & how you yourself *might* & *may* determine."[20]

This is not the letter of a man prepared merely to do the "gentlemanly thing" by a woman he has "ruined." Loving Caroline despite himself, it seems likely that Byron welcomed, in his passive way, the force of circumstance deciding matters for him.

Melbourne and Cavendish houses now feared worse to come. Lady Melbourne asked Byron to leave town at the earliest opportunity; Lady Bessborough begged him not to see Caroline under any condition, including the impossible one of avoiding all gatherings where her daughter might be present. Byron despised Henrietta; he dubbed her

Lady Blarney, after the silly society woman in Goldsmith's *Vicar of Wakefield*, but the name is also a swipe at the Ponsonbys' Irish origins. In a contorted feat of reasoning, he blamed Henrietta for his whole imbroglio with Caroline, claiming to Lady Melbourne that Blarney had challenged his vanity by implying that her daughter was merely using him to pique the jealousy of another man, thus inciting him to seduce her.

On August 9 Caroline sent Byron a cutting of her pubic hair with an inscription:

> Caroline Byron—
> next to Thyrsa Dearest
> & most faithful—God bless you
> own love—ricordati di Biondetta
> From your wild Antelope

Her allusion to "Thyrsa" suggests that Byron himself told Caroline of her resemblance to his dead love—without revealing the boy's identity.

Accompanying her gift was a long, rambling letter in which she asked Byron for a cutting in exchange: "I ask you not to send blood but Yet do—because if it means love I like to have it I cut the hair too close & bled much more than you need—do not you the same." But she had other matters on her mind, too: "Byron, tell me why a few conversations with the Queen Mothers always change you."

She grieved at his news of Newstead's impending sale, lingering on what might have been: "Why not have kept it & taken Biondetto there & have lived & died happy. Yet you give us both up no ties can bind but Newstead A[ntelope?] bears your unkindness in sullen silence. I will kneel & be torn from your feet before I will give you up—or sooner be parted with."[21]

Then, on August 12, Lady Bessborough went to Melbourne House to persuade Caroline to accompany her to Roehampton, where they would be joined by William Lamb; from there they would set out together to the Bessborough estates in Ireland for a peaceful family holiday. She found Caroline in a fury, threatening to run off with Byron. Lord Melbourne (by his own admission) lost his temper and shouted, "Go and be damned. He won't have you." At this, Caroline, "without even a hat," tore down the long stairs, past the startled servants, as her father-in-law shouted "Stop her!" to no avail. Lady Bessborough drove up and down Parliament Street, but Caroline had disappeared.

As it happened, Caro did not make good her threat. Together, the "Queen Mothers"—Lady Melbourne and Lady Bessborough—rushed to Byron's rooms, but he knew nothing of her flight or whereabouts. Appearing to Lady Bessborough as "frightened and astonished" as they were, he promised to restore Caroline if he could find her—which he proceeded to do with uncharacteristic efficiency. What he discovered must have surprised him further. Caroline had planned her getaway—as much to escape from him as from her captors at Melbourne House. His servant delivered a letter from the coachman who had taken her from a chemist's shop in Pall Mall. Her letter to Byron repeated the contents of ones delivered to her family. She was leaving England. She had booked a place on the coach to Portsmouth. From there she was planning to embark on the first available vessel; she cared not its destination. Through threats and bribery Byron induced the same hackney coachman to lead him to the surgeon's house in Kensington, near Holland House, where Caroline was hiding. He had to force his way in, as she refused to see him or anyone else. Persuading the surgeon that he was her brother, Byron managed, "almost by force," to drag her into his coach and deliver her to Lady Bessborough at Cavendish House. Henrietta was too hysterical for rational argument; thus, it was left to Byron, largely using the weapon of shame—"How could she cause such suffering to her mother?"—to induce her to return to her husband. After William had promised that he would "receive and forgive" his wife, Caroline entered the house. "The Melbournes, too, were very good, and she seemed much touched by her reception." Thus concluded Lady Bessborough's account to Granville, though she added one further subject of grief: "I think of the bad look to the lackeys employed at Holland House."[22]

The Bessborough women's trials were not over. Before Caroline had been returned, her mother had begun spitting blood. The following day, Henrietta was found senseless on the floor of her carriage, her mouth drawn to one side. Although the stroke proved a mild one, one of the servants saw it as a further punishment for Caroline's sins: "Thank God she is better," a Mrs. Peterson wrote to the prodigal daughter. "Lord Bessborough would not let me send for you he said the sight of you would make her worse. You have for many months taken every means in your power to make your mother miserable and you have perfectly succeeded but do not quite kill her—you will one day or other *fatally* feel the wickedness of your present conduct."

Byron's role in this drama gives further proof of his reluctance to let Caroline get away. He did not want her tormenting him, nor could he allow her to escape. Still, his conscience was not easy at delivering his helpless lover to her enemy. On August 14 he wrote to Lady Melbourne to plead for mercy toward his abandoned mistress: "She never did nor

can deserve a single reproach which must not fall with double justice &
truth upon myself, who am much more to blame in every respect. . . .
No one has a right to interfere with *her* but yourself & Mr. L[amb] . . .
& if she is to be persecuted for my faults—to be reproached with the
consequences of a misplaced affection but too well returned—by any
but *you* & *yours* (who have acted so differently with a kindness which
I did not believe to exist in human nature) I cannot & will not bear it,
without at least taking my own just share of the consequences. In the
meantime, command me—& dear Ly. M. comfort & be kind to her, you
have been, she owns it with the greatest gratitude, in every thing of this
kind the *man* is—& must be most to blame, & I am sure not less so in
this instance than every other."23

He had acted the gentleman—and more. He had not only found and
returned the errant wife, he had also taken responsibility for her behavior. But he had done so with no risk of blame. Lady Melbourne, as
Byron well knew, adored him and loathed Caroline.

Byron could now reassure "Lady M" that only pressing business
prevented him from keeping his promise to her that he would leave
London. Newstead Abbey was to be auctioned at Garroway's Coffee
Shop this very day—August 14. As soon as that melancholy matter was
concluded, he planned to join her and other friends at fashionable
Cheltenham spa.

CHAPTER 20

By the Waters of Cheltenham

YRON HAD planned to leave London for Cheltenham after the sale of Newstead Abbey. At the auction itself, bids had been disappointing, but the following day, Thomas Claughton, a lawyer from Lancashire, offered £140,000, and a few days later his offer was accepted. Byron knew that he had taken the only possible course of action, but he still found it hard to accept the loss of Newstead. The property, more than the title *Lord* Byron, was his tangible patent of nobility, and with his immediate family dead or dispersed, the abbey reassured Byron of his place in a historic continuum that might have reached to his own heirs.

Writing to Hanson, he clutched at the possibility of retaining residual ownership, if only that of a symbolic portion: "When the mortgage is secured on Newstead—I wish to know whether the titled deeds will not remain in *our* hands as is usual in all well secured mortgages *not* in *Register Counties.*"[1]

That done, he was off in the Bristol coach to Cheltenham. He was looking forward to enjoyable company in a new setting. Joining him at the resort were Lady Melbourne; her daughter, Emily, Lady Cowper; Lord Moira, the Irish peer and one of Tom Moore's great patrons; Lord and Lady Jersey; Lord and Lady Holland; and Lady Oxford, the freethinking muse of Whig reformers.

His destination was also imposed by medical urgency. Attacks of kidney stones recurred regularly now. The most recent episode had been the most severe: He was ready to try a concentrated cure. The strong saline waters of the Gloucestershire spa had been found especially effective for dissolving the painful calcium obstructions of his condition.

Instead of proceeding directly to Cheltenham, Byron decided on a detour with his friend Colonel Berkeley, who persuaded him that a stay at Berkeley Castle nearby in Gloucestershire was the ideal prelude to the more salubrious routine of the spa.

Berkeley combined the sporting tastes of Byron's old circle of dissolute Regency bucks with literary interests and public-spirited liberal politics. A hard-riding libertine and master of Cheltenham hounds, he was also a cultivated man with a passion for theater. Another residence, known as German House, was darkly rumored to be used by the colonel for elaborate sexual entertainments. That Berkeley was attacked from every local pulpit did nothing to lower him in Byron's esteem.

When Byron moved from Berkeley Castle to The Plough on Cheltenham High Street he exchanged feudal grandeur for a "Sordid inn," he noted dejectedly to William Bankes. The revels at Berkeley had further reminded him of the loss of Newstead, a scene of similar riot. Cheltenham, last visited at age thirteen, when he rushed to his room to see the sun setting behind the Malvern Hills, summoned the realization—always painful for Byron—that his youth was over.

In the early morning and late afternoon, visitors taking the curative waters crossed the silvery little Chelt River via a picturesque wooden footbridge, to stroll along the Well Walk, an *allée* lined with double rows of elm and lime trees, leading to the Royal Well. Every night the elegant new Assembly Rooms, designed by the busy Henry Holland, rang with music from the ballroom, punctuated by sounds of laughter, shuffling cards, and clicking dice.

Besides taking the waters, Byron put himself under the care of the town's most eminent physician, a French émigré, Dr. Boisragon. His name conjures up a quack in a Molière comedy, but although his treatment was described as a bitter potion worse than the malady, Byron makes no further mention of painful attacks for more than a month. The mineral waters themselves, however, seem to have caused unpleasant, probably diuretic, side effects. Byron wrote to Lord Holland: "The waters have disordered me to my heart's content, you were *right*, as you always are."[2]

Shortly after his arrival Lord and Lady Holland had rescued Byron from The Plough, inviting him to stay in their large rented house near the theater at the fashionable Cambray end of the High Street.* His hosts then returned to London with considerable time left on the new lease—time they appear to have generously donated to their houseguest.

---

*Later divided into three separate houses—the present nos. 38, 40, and 42—to accommodate ground-floor shops.

Byron now had the pleasant villa on the High Street, whose tall rear windows looked over the mill pond and the winding Chelt, to himself.

In this tranquil atmosphere, free of both pain and Caro's accusing scenes, he could catch up on *Childe Harold*'s fortunes. As most of the important journals of cultural opinion were quarterlies, reviews were still coming in. Moreover, the date printed on a given number had little to do with its appearance; thus the February 1812 issue of the crucial *Edinburgh Review* had only appeared in May. At that point Byron had written a brief note to Murray, asking to see the notice as soon as his publisher had a copy, but this being at the height of his affair with Caroline, he makes no mention of his reaction to the review—one to gladden any poet's day.

After the *Edinburgh Review*'s earlier unfavorable notice of his work, Byron had lashed out at the editor, Francis Jeffrey, under the mistaken assumption that he had been the author of the anonymous dismissal. This time, however, Jeffrey himself did indeed sound the first notes in what would be a chorus of praise.

In his admiration for the new work, Jeffrey pointed to a "tone of self-willed independence and originality about the whole composition— a certain plain manliness and strength of manner, which is infinitely refreshing after the sickly affections of so many modern writers." In his view it was precisely the tension between Byron's masculine and feminine selves that distinguished *Childe Harold*: "Those stern and disdainful reflections . . . through which we think we can sometimes discern the struggling of a gentler feeling to which he is afraid to abandon himself."

Tracking the man behind the poet, however, Jeffrey unmasks a certain coldness of heart: "There is much strength, in short, and some impetuous feeling in this poem—but very little softness; some pity for mankind—but very little affection; and no enthusiasm in the cause of any living men or admiration of their talents and virtues."[3]

The *Quarterly Review*, John Murray's house organ, was also the staunchly Tory vehicle of his best-selling author, Sir Walter Scott. Torn between the political and the literary, the reviewer hedged his bets, noting that the "poem exhibits some marks of carelessness, nay of caprice, but many also of sterling genius."[4] Hewing to its Tory line more openly, the *Anti-Jacobin* did not equivocate. Now that Byron had openly identified himself with Whig issues, this journal singled out "the deficient character of the Childe . . . his political prejudices . . . unpatriotic defects [which] add to the irreligious principles of this bastard of the imagination. . . . The sneer at official characters in the last stanza is contemptible and unworthy [of] such a writer as Lord Byron, who must know the falsehood of it and who cannot harbor the monstrous idea that men who are enlisted in the service of the state are less virtuous or less honest than their fellow creatures."[5]

Byron was relieved by what critics did not say. The poet's private life (as opposed to his politics) was not under review. In the next few weeks he cleared the last hurdle when his old adversary the *Satirist* pointedly did not assign the review to Hewson Clarke, who had raised personal spite to new levels in attacking Byron's mother. Far from attacking, the *Satirist*'s anonymous critic placed the final laurels on the poet's brow, saying that "*Childe Harold* contains many passages which would do honor to any poet, of any period, in any country," and declaring of Byron's stanzas on Greece, "This is exquisite poetry."[6]

Now he could add critical triumph to public adulation. These were notices worth saving: "I want all the Reviews, at least the Critiques, quarterly monthly &c. Portuguese & English extracted & bound up in one vol. for my *old age*," he told Murray. In high spirits, he teased his publisher for having recently added Lucien Bonaparte to his list of authors: "Is it not somewhat treasonable in you to have to do with a relative of the 'direful foe' as the Morning Post calls his brother?" And confident in the knowledge that he had surpassed Murray's wildest expectations, he imposed upon him for a short list of commissions: to extract his Greek books from Hobhouse ("He has had them now a long time"), and to send these to Cheltenham, along with "ye. first begotten copy" of Walter Scott's new poem, *Rokeby*.[7] He reminded the publisher to forward his fan mail, along with the latest periodicals, and he repeated an earlier request for the new edition of Adair's *An Essay on Diet and Regimen*. Dr. Boisragon had prescribed a more nourishing regime, including meat and fat.

"Soothed by success," as Dallas described his protégé, Byron was trying to live sensibly while enjoying what Cheltenham had to offer. Socially speaking, this did not include much novelty. The same Whig hostesses who vied to capture the poet in town had established themselves in rented "cottages" to outdo one another in elaborate festivities; the beautiful heiress Sophia, Countess of Jersey, regularly gave enormous parties for one hundred guests or more. Social notices in the newspapers described "elegant gouters" or *"déjeuners après minuits"* featuring "Pandean bands" of wandering musicians and "Fantoccini," or marionette shows. There were theater parties, walks, rides, routs, balls—the same round of engagements transported from London by the same fashionable set on holiday. Byron insisted to friends in town on his efforts to avoid most of this empty frivolity, although rumors of his attentions to Bessy Rawdon, the accomplished and much-traveled daughter of Lord Moira, a frequent host, had reached Whitehall. Quizzed by Lady Melbourne, Byron assured her that although "Miss R has always been a mighty favorite with me . . . she *waltzes*, & is for many reasons the very last woman on earth I should covet (unless she were 'my neighbor's wife' & then the breaking a commandment would go far in her behalf)."[8]

The hated waltz music made him feel haunted by Caro, but now Byron began to find larger metaphors in the rhythms and suggestively merged bodies of the dance. His poem *Waltz*, written in Cheltenham, has some of the savagery of his attack on Lord Elgin. With the new satire, however, Byron's politics appear to have reversed course. In *Childe Harold* and *The Curse of Minerva*,* the poet, fired by republican sympathies, took aim at an England whose envoy was given license to plunder the heritage of a helpless people. Now, in *Waltz*, which demonizes the fashionable dance, we read Byron at his most puritanical and reactionary. The poem's subtitle, "An Apostrophic Hymn," announced his mission: He is the satirist as evangelical scourge of God.

Byron's new poetic persona is a stock figure of innocence, the naïve country squire. Representing the purity of "Old England," he has been set loose in fashionable London to goggle at the imported immorality that threatens to seduce his wife and daughter, starting with the nakedness of the dancers, whose "legs must move to conquer as they fly. / If but thy coats are reasonably high." Comparing the German imports of wine and waltzing, Byron finds the corruption of the dance the more dangerous, leading, as it must, from sexual license to mongrelization of the English race:

> Imperial Waltz! imported from the Rhine,
> (Famed for the growth of pedigrees and wine)
> Long be thine import from all duty free,
> And hock itself be less esteemed than thee;
> In some few qualities alike—for hock
> Improves our cellar—*thou* our living stock.
> The head to hock belongs—thy subtler art
> Intoxicates alone the heedless heart;
> Through the full veins thy gentler poison swims,
> And wakes to wantonness the willing limbs.

Calvinist echoes of the Aberdeen sermons of his boyhood reverberate through this strange polemic. The poem's coarse satirical thrusts suggest

---

*A small edition of the work was to be privately printed and distributed to friends the following year.

that Byron's posture of cosmopolitan worldliness and his relativist view
of morals had been discarded with his return home:

> Waltz—Waltz—alone both arms and legs demands,
> Liberal of feet—and lavish of her hands;
> Hands which may freely range in public sight,
> Where ne'er before—but—pray "put out the light."
> . . . .
> Round all the confines of the yielded waist,
> The strangest hand may wander undisplaced;
> The lady's in return may grasp as much
> As princely paunches offer to her touch.[9]

The Prince Regent was the most ardent practitioner of the waltz; with
such asides about the royal girth, it is hardly surprising that neither
Byron nor Murray was willing to risk probable criminal proceedings if
the poem were to be published. It was brought out anonymously by a
printer in Paternoster Row; the date of issue and the number of copies
printed are unknown.

AS AN ALTERNATIVE to watching others waltz, Byron turned to the
wise conversation of his confidante Lady Melbourne. And indeed, his
friend had serious business to conduct with him: arranging his marriage
to her niece Annabella.

He had told Lady Melbourne that his life was in her hands: "So far
from being ashamed of being governed . . . I am always but too happy
to find one to regulate or misregulate me. . . . Will you undertake me?"
he had asked. With her efforts to rid him of Caroline showing every success, she now turned her energies to seeing him wed.

As the evil genius who brokered one of the most infamously
wretched marriages in history, Lady Melbourne's role in delivering her
niece into Byron's hands has sealed posterity's sinister verdict on her. Yet
Byron's plea that she "undertake" him reveals more than passivity; he
seems to have recognized in her his satanic Other, ceding not only his
life to her but his soul. He had at first tried a double game.

Informing Lady Melbourne of what she most certainly knew
already—that Caroline and her family were "safely deposited in
Ireland"—Byron declared, "I wish this to end, & it shall certainly not
be renewed on my part.

"It is not that I love another, but loving at all is quite out of my
way," he insisted. "I am tired of being a fool, & when I look back on
the waste of time, & the destruction of all my plans last winter by this

romance, I am—what I ought to have been long ago.—It is true from early habit, one must make love mechanically as one swims, I was once very fond of both, but now as I never swim unless I tumble into the water, I don't make love till almost obliged."[10]

Immediately he had blundered into two lies. Despite his promise to end their affair, he was still writing to Caroline. Once cornered, he tried to defend himself: He had continued writing to Caro merely to keep her spirits up and to forestall any angry descents upon him from Ireland. He needed until December to end matters gradually. "In the mean-time, I must & do write the greatest absurdities to keep her 'gay' & the more so because ye. last epistle informed me that '8 guineas a mail & a packet *could* soon bring her to London.' "

Had he told Lady Melbourne that he did not love another?

"I deceived you & myself in saying so, there was & is one whom I wished to marry, had not this affair intervened," he confessed. "As I have said so much I may as well say all—the woman I mean is Miss Milbank [*sic*]—I know nothing of her fortune, & I am told that her father is ruined, but my own will when my Rochdale arrangements are closed, be sufficient for both," he added grandly. Still, he took pains to let Melbourne know that he had small expectations of success. "I know little of her & have not the most distant reason to suppose that I am at all a favorite in that quarter, but I never saw a woman whom I *esteemed* so much."

Caroline remained the principal obstacle; he felt chained by his own code of gentlemanly behavior: "I had made up my mind, to bear ye consequences of my own folly; honour, pity, & a kind of affection all forbade me to shrink, but now if I can *honourably* be off, if *you* are not deceiving me, & if she does not take some accursed step to precipitate her own inevitable fall (if not with me, with some less lucky successor) if these impossibilities can be got over, all will be well."

Lady Melbourne was his only hope, and he was abject in assurances that, from now on, he was completely her creature: "Now, my dear Ly. M. I am completely in your power, I have not deceived you. . . . If through your means, or any means, I can be free, or at least change my fetters, my regard & admiration would not be increased, but my gratitude would[;] in the mean time it is by no means unfelt for what you have already done."[11]

Thus was the bargain struck, the partnership forged. He could lie to others, but in Lady Melbourne he had found the one person to whom lies were unnecessary—because they were unavailing. As long as he could be honest with her, the others did not matter.

Conspiracy now begins to darken the tone of their letters.

"C[aroline] is suspicious about our counter plots, & I am obliged to be treacherous as Talleyrand, but remember *that treachery is truth* to you," Byron wrote.[12] With glee he documented the many lies he now wrote to Caro, placing them, like sacrifices, on Melbourne's altar. In return she sent Byron one of William Lamb's confidential notes to her; he then sent her a letter of Lady Bessborough's.

As a seal of their new alliance, Lady Melbourne decided to endorse Byron's strategy for getting rid of Caroline by degrees, and gave him permission to continue writing to her. Now that he had been officially permitted to "manage" her as he could, Byron panicked.

"*Manage* her," he wrote to Lady Melbourne on September 15, "it is impossible—& as to friendship—no—it must be broken off at once, & all I have left is to take some step which will make her hate me effectually for she must be in extremes."[13]

Only two days after Byron had defended the expediency of keeping Caroline cheerful, he now insisted on breaking with her—and violently. Just in case, however, the Spider gently nudged her prey to see if he still twitched. He had just made confession of his love for her niece, was he sure of himself? she asked.

"You ask 'am *I* sure of myself,' & I answer—no—but *you* are, which I take to be a much better thing," he told her. After this flattering gesture of fealty Byron gave a brisk assurance of good sense regarding the object of his suit: "Miss M. I admire because she is a clever woman, an amiable woman & of high blood, for I still have a few Norman & Scotch inherited prejudices on the last score, were I to marry. As to LOVE, that is done in a week, (provided the Lady has a reasonable share) besides marriage goes on better with esteem & confidence than romance, and she is quite pretty enough to be loved by her husband, without being so glaringly beautiful as to attract too many rivals." He had only one lingering doubt about her niece: "*Does Annabella waltz?*"[14] Her aunt readily dispelled his fears.

ON ANOTHER FRONT, too, Byron now recoiled from competition. Acting on behalf of the Management Committee of the Drury Lane Theatre, Lord Holland invited the poet to enter a contest for a poetical address to be spoken from the stage by the noted actor Robert Elliston at the gala opening of a new theater on October 10.* The winner would receive 20 guineas.

---

*The new theater replaced a building that had burned to the ground three years earlier.

Reluctant to disappoint Lord Holland, Byron made a stab at fulfilling the request, but the confining nature of occasional verse, together with anxiety about competing, froze inspiration. In his "public" poetry he was a polemicist, not a celebrant—a role he left to toadies such as the poet laureate, Robert Southey. Byron liked to think of himself as a "great Hater," a description, borrowed from Samuel Johnson, of the anonymous political journalist who signed his columns "Junius." In the end, Byron destroyed his first, unfinished attempt at the address without showing the lines to Lord Holland—"I have just committed them to a flame more decisive than that of Drury," he wrote, advising his sponsor candidly, "I think you have a chance of something much better, for prologuising is not my forte, & at all events either my pride or my modesty won't let me incur the hazard of having my rhymes buried in next month's magazine: . . . I am still sufficiently interested to wish to know the successful Candidate—& amongst so many—I have no doubt—some will be excellent, particularly in an age when writing verse is the easiest of all attainments."[15]

Little more than a week later, he received word from a desperate Lord Holland: Of the 112 submissions by "all of Grub Street," none was acceptable. He begged Byron to reconsider. With his unworthy competitors off the stage and despite a tight deadline, Byron was pleased to accept the invitation. On September 22 he promised Lord Holland, "In a day or so I will send you something which you will still have the liberty to reject if you dislike it, I should like to have had more time but will do my best, but too happy if I can oblige *you* though I may offend 100 Scribblers & the discerning public." But, in a postscript, he enjoined Lord Holland to "Keep *my name a secret* or I shall be beset by all the rejected."[16]

In the absence of more compelling ideas—"My thermometer is sadly below the poetical point," he had written to Murray—Byron now attacked the address with a will. Drafts flew back and forth between Cheltenham and London. He sent Lord Holland two versions of some lines, inviting him to choose the one he preferred and offering to produce other "versicles" if these failed to suit. Enthusiasm and industry, however, could not compensate for the poor match between poet and project. Despite his determination to avoid clichés inspired by the rebuilding of the theater—sixty-nine of the contestants had used the image of a phoenix rising from the ashes—his own efforts were scarcely more memorable:

In one dread night our city saw and sighed,
Bowed to the dust, the Drama's tower of pride;

In one short hour, behold the blazing fane
Apollo sink, and Shakespeare cease to reign.[17]

Annabella Milbanke was in the opening night audience, and she noted, with characteristic acumen, that Elliston "spoke Lord Byron's address vilely."[18] The Milbankes had taken a villa in Richmond, a fashionable suburban retreat on the Thames, but Annabella was spending most of her time at Melbourne House while her aunt negotiated Byron's proposal of marriage. From Whitehall Annabella wrote to Lady Gosford to say that "Lady M. showed me yesterday all the letters relative to me that she received from Lord Byron."[19] It was from the safer precincts of Richmond, however, that she sent "Lady M." her own thoughts on the subject, including a "Character" of Byron and finally, sometime after October 8, her carefully considered rejection of the poet's offer.

Any other young woman he had met since the launching of *Childe Harold*—including many more desirable than Miss Milbanke—would have been overcome by the flattery of a proposal from Lord Byron. Here was a provincial twenty-two-year-old, of no vast fortune or dazzling looks, not yet engaged at the end of her second London season, who turned him down! Her reasons, as outlined to Lady Melbourne, reveal independence, modesty, and good sense worthy of the Jane Austen heroines she admired. She told her aunt, "I do not give my answer without the serious deliberation which is due to the honorable and disinterested nature of Lord B's sentiments. I am convinced that he considers my happiness not less than his own in the wishes which he has expressed to you and I think of them with the sincerest gratitude."

Yet not even a "decided preference" would have induced her to yield "till my judgment has been strengthened by longer observation." "I should be totally unworthy of Lord B's esteem, if I were not to speak the truth without equivocation. Believing that he never will be the object of that strong affection which could make me happy in domestic life, I should wrong him by any measure that might, even indirectly, confirm his present impressions. From my limited observations of his conduct, I was predisposed to believe your strong testimony in his favor," she assured Lady Melbourne, "and I willingly attribute it more to the defects of my feelings than of his character that I am not inclined to return his attachment."

She would welcome his friendship. Given the pain caused by rejection, she doubted this would be Byron's choice. For herself, however, she noted simply: "I have no reason for withdrawing from an acquaintance that does me honor, and is capable of imparting so much rational pleasure, except the fear of involuntarily deceiving him."

Annabella ended with a dig at Melbourne's mediating role in Byron's suit: "Perhaps the most Satisfactory Method of acquainting him with the contents of this letter would be to let him have it."[20]

Lady Melbourne was furious. This little prig from provincial society (which she herself had escaped at sixteen) coolly rejecting the catch of the season—of any season—and making her look a fool in the bargain! Annabella would pay for this humiliation. Now, however, she did as her niece asked, forwarding her letter of rejection to Byron, along with Annabella's "Character" of the poet not intended for his eyes. But at this time of her waning powers, she needed Byron's devotion too much to abandon her stratagem of "pinning him to her side through her niece." Thus, her covering letter to Byron (now lost) apparently expressed the hope—so maternally protective—that the rejected lover would not seek revenge by cutting Annabella.

"Cut her! my dear Ly M marry—Mahomet forbid!" Byron replied in his characteristic playful tone. "I am sure we shall be better friends than before & if I am not embarrassed by all this I cannot see for the soul of me why *she* should. Assure *her* con tutto rispetto that The subject shall never be renewed in any shape whatever."[21] Because he would not be able to call her *Zia* (Aunt), he teasingly suggested she choose her own name.

Insouciance was always Byron's first line of defense. In fact, his fragile ego was much affected by Annabella's rejection. He had never wanted the marriage in the first place, he wrote, assuring his mother confessor, "were it not for my embarras with C[aroline] I would much rather remain as I am." Further, he could only agree with Miss Milbanke: They scarcely knew each other and thus, despite proposing marriage to her, his deeper feelings, like Annabella's, were never really engaged: "I have had so very little intercourse with the Fair Philosopher that if when we meet I should endeavor to improve our acquaintance, she must not *mistake* me, & I assure her I never shall mistake her.—I *never did* you will allow."

Then, in one of his perverse impulses to tell all before drawing back just in time, he hinted broadly of shameful attachments that he believed marriage alone could cure. While waiting for Annabella's answer, "I felt something very like remorse for sundry reasons not at all connected with C[aroline] nor with any occurrences since I knew you or her or hers; finding I must marry however on *that score* I should have preferred a woman of birth & talents, but such a woman was not at all to blame for not preferring me; my *heart* never had an opportunity of being much in the business, further than that I should have very much liked to be *your relation*."[22]

Aware of the risks of intimacy with Lady Melbourne, Byron was always careful to flatter and placate. His letters to the sixty-two-year-old woman offer more compliments and gallantries than to all of his other female correspondents combined: "I have no very high opinion of your sex," he told her just before his failure with Annabella, "when I do see a woman superior not only to all her own but to most of ours I worship her in proportion as I despise the rest."[23]

He took pains to reassure Lady Melbourne on another sensitive point: Her failure to deliver her niece in no way diminished his appreciation of her labors. Annabella was a problem defying solution: "I thank you again for your efforts with my Princess of Parallelograms," he wrote in his most quoted description of Annabella, "who has puzzled you more than the Hypotenuse. . . . Her proceedings are quite rectangular, or rather we are two parallel lines prolonged to infinity side by side but never to meet."[24]

He would never utter more prophetic words.

BYRON REFUSED to heed his own warning; instead, he urged Lady Melbourne not to give up. Refusal by the Princess of Parallelograms had enhanced her value: "Tell A[nnabella] I am more proud of her rejection than I can ever be of *another's acceptance*."[25] He felt a challenge—this time, a moral one—and he was optimistic that he would prevail.

Meanwhile, the storm warnings from Ireland intensified; Caroline was preparing to lay siege once more. Byron delegated Lady Melbourne to repel this attack and to rid him of Caro by any methods she chose. "Whatever step you take to break off this affair has my full concurrence."[26] Byron was well aware of the brutal tactics that would be used; recently, Lady Melbourne had left a letter he had written to her for Caroline to find—a letter disparaging his former lover in the most humiliating terms. Learning this from a stricken Caro, he had merely teased: "How could you Lady M—how could you 'wear a pocket with a hole [in it]'?"[27] Now, however, Lady M made it clear that he could not delegate all of the dirty work to her; she sent Byron suggestions for a letter of dismissal to Caroline, to be written by him. When he read her words—words that would be taken as coming from his heart—he was sickened with shame and guilt: "*What* you wished me to write would be a little too indifferent and *that* now would be an insult & I am much more unwilling to hurt her feelings now than ever. . . . I have always felt that one who has given up much, has a claim upon *me* (at least—whatever she deserves from others) for every respect, that she may not feel her own degradation, & this is the reason that I have not written at all lately, lest some expression might be misconstrued by her."[28]

Now it was Lady Melbourne's turn to retreat. She did not want to appear the monster, and risk Byron's exalted opinion of her. She had acted only from the most humane motive, she assured him, namely, her fear that he might be killing poor Caro with too much kindness: "Do not . . . mistake me, I would not have you say a harsh sentence to her for the World, and anything that could be deem'd insulting. I had not the least intention of advising you to do it. There is no kindness that I would not have you shew her, but sacrificing yourself to her, would only be romantic and not kind. . . . It must lead to unhappiness and misery. If a little trifling impression of coldness at present would prevent this *finale,* how much more kind to give a little present pain, and avoid her total ruin."[29]

But Byron held to his earlier impulse: He did not write to Caroline at all. He turned instead to the pleasures Cheltenham had to offer.

With his inner circle of friends gone, he was reduced to a "cynical solitude," he wrote to Lord Holland. This Byronic image was far from the reality. In fact, he was busy laying siege to an Italian opera singer, reassuringly—and, it appeared, happily—married. Still more to his liking, she did not know a word of English. Byron loved hearing her speak her native tongue, he told Lady Melbourne. He had spoken Italian with Nicolo Giraud, one of his Greek favorites, and his nostalgia for a period associated with erotic abandon was further aroused by the lady's Mediterranean coloring: "She has black eyes & *not* a very white skin, & reminds me of many in the Archipelago I wished to forget, & makes me forget what I ought to remember." Unhappily, his new love's sensual gusto also embraced the pleasures of the table; like many singers, she enjoyed a prodigious appetite, requiring frequent and ample meals.

Byron was always repelled by the sight of a woman eating. His reaction was in contrast to the mores of the time. The Regency was a period of lavish meals consumed by both sexes; the richer the household, the richer and more copious the fare. A "lady" was not recognized as such because she picked at her food, and it showed, as the girth of both Ladies Holland and Melbourne proved. Although he did not relate his feelings about women and food to his mother's obesity or his own obsessive dieting, Byron recognized his reaction as troubled, and he reached for his usual playful defense: "I only wish she did not swallow so much supper, chicken wings—sweetbreads—custards—peaches & *Port* wine—a woman should never be seen eating or drinking, unless it be *lobster sallad* [sic] & *Champagne.*"[30]

Meanwhile, his go-between was still working on her niece, warning Annabella to "come down from your stilts" or she would find no husband at all. Now, hearing of Byron's latest conquest, she teased him:

"Poor Annabella, her innocent eyes will have to contend with the Black and probably experienced ones of yr. Innamoratta [sic]." Did his new operatic love "pick the chicken bones like Catalani? Do you think you can manage both her and C.?"[31] But the opera singer had departed for a concert engagement in London.

Now Byron began to call regularly on one of the few London hostesses still in residence. Lady Oxford's rented villa, Georgiana Cottage, on Bath Road, was a few minutes' walk from his house on the High Street and was a lively place, filled with visitors and the Oxfords' five children. By mid-October Byron felt so at home that he was writing letters from a corner of the drawing room while other callers lounged and chatted nearby.

He had met Lady Oxford that spring in London, where she entertained lavishly at Mortimer House, the family's residence in town. Byron would have attracted her notice; she was a leading hostess of the radical wing of the Whig party and an intimate of the Princess of Wales, who had been humiliated and cast out by the Prince after one year of marriage. Most probably it was Lady Oxford who proposed Byron for membership in the Hampden Club, which he joined on June 12. There the party's "Genteel reformers," as Byron dubbed them, mingled with "Blackguards" such as Francis Place, advocates of the people who were themselves of working-class origin. It was not a milieu in which Byron would ever feel comfortable. He saw too clearly the ironies inherent in trying to unite divergent class interests under one banner—gentleman radicals helping the lower orders to abolish the privileges of their betters. He would have been all the more intrigued, then, by the Countess as recruiter of the club and its muse. Well before their first meeting, Byron had heard much about Lady Oxford.

She was born Jane Elizabeth Scott in 1772 in Inchin, near Southampton, where her father was vicar and chaplain to the King. As a clergyman's daughter she was more literate than most girls of the period, imbued early with the words and idealism of the French Revolution. At twenty-two Jane Scott had married Edward Harley, fifth Earl of Oxford. She is said to have met her husband, who was one year her senior, through her brother, William, when both young men were contemporaries at Oxford. It was further rumored that she was forced—even sold—into a loveless match. That her brother later turned out to be her blackmailer gives added credibility to the story.

They were an ill-matched pair: the young Countess, brilliant, idealistic, romantic, and—not least—ambitious, and her lord, so innocuous and passive that hardly anyone troubled to describe him, except Byron.

Idealizing his new love, he turned her into a helpless victim, declaring that "she had been sacrificed, almost before she was a woman, to one whose mind and body were equally contemptible in the scale of creation; and on whom she bestowed a numerous family, to which the law gave him the right to be called father."[32] Only the law, however. The Oxfords' five beautiful children, widely believed to have been sired by as many fathers, were known by the *ton* as the "Harleian Miscellany," after the great collection of manuscripts amassed by an earlier Lord Oxford.

Jane may have been sold into marriage, but neither she nor Lord Oxford took his rights of ownership seriously. The Countess confided to the Princess of Wales that she had told her husband the precise circumstances that led to her affair with her first lover, the radical reformer Sir Francis Burdett. When left "for above a week in a house alone in the country with so handsome and enterprising a man" as Sir Francis, inevitably she had yielded the final favors. The Earl "immediately said her candour and frank confession were so amiable that he entirely forgave her."[33]

Sir Francis Burdett's friendship with Byron and his influence on the poet's political ambitions have been largely overlooked. In personal attributes and political importance, the older man was everything Byron wanted to be—but for the company he kept. Byron could not accept the notion that reform might require a gentleman to associate with his social inferiors.

A patrician reformer in the mold of Fox, Burdett was far more radical than his idol. Young Turks worshiped him: "That man is, in my eyes, perfectly fascinating and irresistible," Hobhouse rhapsodized to Byron. Handsome, clever, and charming, at age twenty-three, Burdett had married Sophia Coutts of the banking family, and his wife's fortune, along with his indifference to a peerage or office, strengthened his incorruptibility and made him as hated and feared by the establishment as he was popular with the masses.

Like his lover Lady Oxford, Burdett was honest to a fault. His marriage, like hers, had been unhappy from the start, and although he swiftly took consolation elsewhere, Lady Oxford was his first great passion. Chastised by his father-in-law as a faithless husband, Burdett replied: "The Truth (in my opinion) is, marriage is ill calculated to realize the fleeting dream of happiness, much less those ideas which youthful imagination creates; it is I think the worst bond & has with great truth been call'd the grave of love."[34]

When his affair with Lady Oxford ended, the two remained close friends; her subsequent lovers were recruited from the Burdett circle. She had taken up with two Whig noblemen in turn: Lord Granville and the handsome but deaf Lord Archibald Hamilton. In displacing Hamilton, Byron saw himself anointed as the latest in an apostolic succession of aristocratic reformers.

WHEN IT WAS Byron's turn, in the fall of 1812, to become infatuated with Lady Oxford, she was forty and, in the eyes of most men, at the height of her allure. Eulogizing her "autumnal" loveliness a decade later, Byron recalled that his lover "resembled a landscape by Claude Lorraine [sic] with a setting sun, her beauties enhanced by the knowledge that they were shedding their dying beams."[35]

In her portraits by Hoppner and especially Romney, Lady Oxford appears more adorable, with slightly uptilted nose and rosebud mouth, than beautiful in the grand manner. Her character—spontaneous, warmhearted, and sexually and politically passionate—inspired as it captivated men.

Along with the "kind and gentle" nature that Byron admired in women (compelling even Lady Holland's qualified good opinion), Lady Oxford's liberal views, informed by what the radical ex-clergyman Horne Tooke described as the most brilliant mind in England, were something new in Byron's experience. In a letter to Lord Holland, after the defeat in the Commons of the bill on behalf of Catholic claims, she urged him to renewed effort in the struggle: "I . . . am sincerely sorry the Catholics have succeeded so ill . . . first because it is melancholy to see the majority as the *vide* [sic] of prejudice and illberality (& I might add detestable sycophancy), this pulse of the people has been felt during the struggle of the Passions for simple justice, and if you have a mind to make one last effort to raise a falling Country I really think you may move forward with some effect and a glimmering chance of success."[36]

By strange coincidence, Jane and Caroline Lamb had once been intimates. In dozens of ardent letters, the younger woman had addressed her older friend as "Aspasia," after Socrates' learned mistress. The friendship had horrified Lady Melbourne, who detested Lady Oxford. She had cautioned her daughter-in-law that those who flouted society's rules would pay the consequences. But here was a woman who for nearly twenty years had flouted and triumphed.

Byron's new love demanded to be taken at her own moral measure, and he complied. With all of her adulteries, he would never describe Jane as "fallen" in the way he had conventionally dismissed Caroline. Even when Lady Oxford would prove "inconstant" to him, Byron cast her faithlessness in masculine terms: She was "fickle" but never dishonest. Now, on the brink of passion, he was proud of entering the lists in Lady Oxford's court of love. He wasted no time in informing mutual friends—and hers—of his conquest. To Lord Holland he conveyed the news with a nudging gloss on the psalmist: "By the waters of Cheltenham I sate down & *drank*, when I remembered thee Oh Georgiana Cottage!"[37]

His mistress (for they were already lovers) had returned with her docile lord and children to Eywood, their country house, near Presteign, Herefordshire. In the next weeks Byron was desolate. At the end of October he had seized the challenge, "setting off through detestable roads" to follow his love home.[38]

CHAPTER 21

In Armida's Bower

"$\mathcal{H}$AVE WE NOT passed our last month like the Gods of Lucretius?" Lady Oxford asked Byron,[1] and for once he could agree with his whole heart. He spent four months out of the next six—from November of 1812 to June of the following year—at Eywood. During this period he made short visits elsewhere: to London, back to Cheltenham, a few days with Lord and Lady Jersey at Middleton, their estate in Oxfordshire; a brief stop at Harrow and possibly Farleigh, John Hanson's borrowed property in Hampshire. But with one exception—a trip to London accompanied by Lady Oxford—Byron left Eywood each time with regret and returned with relief to "Circe's Palace."

Eywood was architecturally undistinguished, but the romantically landscaped setting, enlivened by his hostess and her children, created the idyllic retreat of which Byron had always dreamed: an arcadia in which he was both oldest son and younger lover. The twenty-five acres of pleasure gardens with their artificial lakes had been laid out by Capability Brown, and when Byron arrived on November 24, the weather was still mild enough for him to spend much of his time outdoors, "on the water, scrambling and splashing about with the children or by myself."[2]

ABOVE THE MARBLE fireplace in Byron's rooms there hung a print of Rinaldo and Armida, principals in one of the poet's favorite works, Tasso's *Jerusalem Liberated*, an epic poem celebrating Godfrey of Boulogne's crusade to liberate the Holy Sepulcher. Now, in his letters from Eywood, Byron repeatedly cast himself as Rinaldo, the young crusader, abducted, seduced, and effeminized by Armida, the pagan princess. Lady Oxford is now his "Enchantress," Tasso's other name for the golden-haired siren. Armida is able to work her magic because her feminine beauty and sexuality disguise a cold masculine intelligence—"a manly mind and thoughts nature conceal." She persuades the guileless Rinaldo to abandon any principle but that of pleasure; instead of pursuing valor and glory, she urges, "[I]n ev'ry offered joy / indulge your senses, and your soul employ."[3]

The intriguing aspect of Byron's claim to the Armida/Rinaldo parallel is the way he reversed the gender roles of Tasso's hero and villainess. In reality it was Byron who sought to retreat from the world in Lady Oxford's embrace, exalting Eywood as a sanctuary of sexual pleasure and domestic happiness—the traditional domain of women. Instead of using her charms to unman her prey, Lady Oxford was a Whig Joan of Arc who tried to rouse her indecisive lord to battle with the Tory forces of darkness. This "Armida's Bower," as the poet playfully dubbed Eywood, was no Calypso's isle of forgetfulness but a respite from political responsibility. Lady Oxford knew that her lover was licking the wounds of parliamentary failure and his affair with Caroline Lamb. To his sorrow at selling Newstead was now added worry concerning the buyer's behavior: Clearly regretting his bid, Claughton was using every ruse to delay payment. The Byron who had braved flooded roads to follow Lady Oxford to Eywood was a man besotted, but he was also exhausted and demoralized. She saw their idyll as an opportunity to inspire and rearm him.

Byron recognized the truth of their situation: He knew that his lover was trying to forge a sporadically political poet into a Whig fighter—the role Lady Oxford most certainly would have played publicly, had she been a man. When they parted and Byron retreated from political life, he acknowledged her inspiring role: "Three words and a half smile" from Lady Jane could "recall him to his senatorial duties."[4]

Meanwhile, in Whitehall, Lady Melbourne withdrew into injured silence. It was one matter to intrigue with Byron as éminence grise in his affairs with young women and another to read in his familiar hand that he was now enamored of a woman closer to her own age—that was a blow. Melbourne emerged from her pique only to quiz Byron for insider gossip to which, she assumed, he was now privy. In particular she wanted news of the Princess of Wales's party, that group of radicals led by Sir Francis Burdett and Lady Oxford, who had made of the banished royal wife a rallying point for reform.

Now it was Byron who turned pettish; in reply to a list of questions from Whitehall, he wrote: "I know very little of the P's party & less of her publication (if it be hers) & am not at all in ye secret." He did not mind acknowledging that his "Enchantress" was also his political muse, but he was far from flattered by the assumption that while *he* was in residence, his mistress still kept up with her usual gathering of intelligence whose principal source, as it happened, was Lady Oxford's old lover Burdett. Most displeasing of all to Byron's ego was Lady Melbourne's inference that Lady Oxford's sway over him was so complete that he no longer held opinions independent of hers. The suggestion that he had become Lady Oxford's creature rankled so deeply—as no doubt it was intended to do—that for the first and only time, Byron alluded to his lover's reputation as the *"grande horizontale"* of reform. "M'amie thinks I agree with her in *all* her politics, but she will discover that this is a mistake." As to her role in defending the Princess's innocence, "I look upon it much the same view as I should on Mary Magdalen's vindication of Mrs. Joseph."

Still, he could not resist displaying some evidence of his new insider status. Acknowledging that his "amie" was indeed the Princess of Wales's "little Senate," he revealed that Lady Oxford's advice to her royal intimate had been "to remain quiet & leave all to the P[rincess] C[harlotte]," her daughter.[5]

Byron was aware that Lady Melbourne's silence spoke of her wounded vanity, and he now turned to soothing her pride. The older woman's uncharacteristic display of vulnerability supports Byron's later confession that he had once attempted to gratify her sexually; from his point of view, it had not been a success. But the two exchanged rings, either confirming that their *amitié amoureuse* had moved beyond flirtatious confidences, or indicating an attempt to restore the relationship to one of untroubled friendship. Their sexual encounter seems to have taken place at Middleton when both were guests of Lord and Lady Jersey. Byron now invoked memories of the visit to make a delicately flattering allusion to his friend's allure, writing to her that he found the "wild and beautiful Country" around Eywood "preferable even to Middleton (where the *beauties* certainly did not belong to the *landscape*)." And he closed his letter—written six days after his arrival at Eywood—with the romantic words "Do not quite forget me—for *everywhere* I remember you," followed by an anxious postscript: "Why are you silent?—do you doubt me in the 'bowers of Armida'? I certainly am very much enchanted, but *your spells* will always retain their full force—try them."[6] Lady Melbourne knew better than to take a poet at his word.

Byron's gallantries had a strong element of self-interest: Lady Melbourne scorned would be more than he could manage, especially now. With Caroline under closer family surveillance at Brocket, her present state of wrath exceeded all past eruptions. Her antics veered between theater and talismanic gesture. She had the silver buttons of the Melbourne pages' uniforms inscribed with *"Ne* Crede Byron," adding a negative to the poet's family motto. Then she orchestrated her anger into a sacred drama of revenge. Costuming a band of neighboring little girls in white dresses, she had them dance around a huge bonfire, chanting maledictions she had written for the occasion as they tossed Byron's letters and poems into the flames.* Scandalized, all of London repeated, with relish, descriptions of the event. Byron now took to calling his scourge "little Medea," but he was more frightened than amused at being the public target of her outpourings of grief and rage.

During Byron's stay in Cheltenham, Caroline had bombarded him with letters, and in defiance of Lady Melbourne, he had answered her warmly and with reassuring regularity. Once he decided to follow Lady Oxford to Eywood, however, he reverted to a familiar pattern of behavior: using his new lover to rid himself of the old. Writing to Lady Melbourne, he outlined his strategy: "I mean (entre nous my dear Machiavel) to play off Ly. O[xford] against her, who would have no objection *perchance* but she dreads her scenes and has asked me not to mention that we have met to C[aroline] or that I am going to E[ywood]."[7]

Caroline had learned of Byron's extended visit to Lord and Lady Oxford, but she did not as yet suspect that her old mentor "Aspasia" was the lure. The silence from Herefordshire, however, soon aroused her suspicion and sent her into a frenzy of frustration; every unanswered letter contained a plea for one last meeting. After she had dispatched couriers to Eywood with messages—to no avail—she threatened to appear in person. Reduced to a state of panic, Byron implored Lady Melbourne on November 2: "[O]nly manage *her*—I am *sure* of *every one* else—even *myself*; the person least likely to be depended on."[8]

In her novel *Glenarvon*, Caroline Lamb quotes in full a letter written by the hero to Calantha, his abandoned mistress: "I am no longer your lover," he begins, "and since you oblige me to confess it, by this truly unfeminine persecution,—learn, that I am attached to another; whose name it would of course be dishonorable to mention. I shall ever remember with gratitude the predilection you have shewn in my favor. I shall ever continue as your friend, if your ladyship will permit me so

---

*The sacrificed letters were copies.

to style myself; and as a first proof of my regard, I offer you this advice, correct your vanity, which is ridiculous; exert your absurd caprices upon others; and leave me in peace."9

No copy of the original letter has been found, but Caro claimed that she had reproduced Byron's final dismissal. After a careful reading of the novel, the poet jokingly observed about his portrait, "I did not sit long enough," but he never questioned the letter.10 A certain coarseness and pomposity of expression ring strangely un-Byronic, leading some to question the text's authenticity. This view would have the letter dictated to Byron by Lady Oxford. Only a few weeks later, Byron confirmed his acquiescence in a crude joke they played on Caro. When the heartbroken woman begged for a lock of his hair, he sent her a curl clipped from the head of Lady Oxford instead, crowing to Melbourne that she would never know the difference. But just in case, he fixed the souvenir with Lady Oxford's seal. Caroline, enlightened at last, began aiming her wrath at her successor. The now lovers worried that "little Mania's" threats of revenge would take the form of writing to Lord Oxford, making it awkward for even that most complaisant of husbands to avert his gaze; Byron was especially concerned, as he planned to spend Christmas holidays with the family. But whatever his host knew or suspected, a gentlemanly silence prevailed.

Byron had never felt so "quiet and happy," he told Lady Melbourne, restored to her role of sympathetic conspirator. Byron forgot his diet and grew fat, he told friends. His mistress's lively mind and passionate nature so entranced him that he had not had to "stifle a single yawn" in months of her company. At the same time, they were so perfectly suited, he declared, they "have not even a *difference* to diversify the scene," making their idyll dull to describe.11

Still, no paradise is without its serpent. During the course of his stay, Byron became obsessed with Lady Charlotte, his lover's eleven-year-old daughter. Courting the little girl with gifts, including the keepsakes Caroline Lamb had given him, he was now informed that the donor wanted them returned. Guiltily, Byron resorted to a lie. He could not comply with the request, he told Lady Melbourne, as "the trinkets are travelling (at least most of them) in all parts of England and Wales."12 The presents seem to have been a prelude to seduction. While at Eywood, the poet later confessed to his wife, Lady Oxford had discovered him in the act of sexually forcing himself on her child.13

In his savage exposure of Regency hypocrisies, Byron acknowledged indulging his own taste for young children, beginning, when he was a boy himself, with his patronage of the French procuress in London;

then, more openly, on his Eastern travels. Each of Byron's poetic personae—Childe Harold and the heroes of his Eastern tales—claims a past stained with "a thousand unnamed crimes." In part these allusions are literary devices designed to titillate his largely female readers, but we would be naïve not to read such hints as revenants from Byron's Calvinist childhood. Among "nameless" crimes, the corruption of innocence, the betrayal of trust, the brutalizing of a child—these were the sins Byron knew as both victim and violator. If true, however, his attempt on his lover's daughter raised the ante. Lady Oxford was a particularly loving and protective parent—especially of her little girls. Seducing the child must also be seen as a double act of revenge against mistress and mother.

Then, there was Byron's painful obsession with his own youth. His desire fastened on the very young not because he felt himself sexually inadequate to women or men. Rather, the beauty of the eleven-year-old, as unconscious of her own perfection as a flower, affected him with profound envy and regret. He longed to reclaim this fleeting moment, to become once more the child by possessing her.

Within the next months, the sixth printing of *Childe Harold* sold out. Byron dedicated the seventh edition to Lady Charlotte Harley, rechristened "Ianthe."* In a tribute of five stanzas, the poet sublimates his yearning for the carnal child into a plea that she will act as muse. Her physical presence becomes platonic and thus immutable: "Love's image upon earth without his wing."

In offering his poem to the child, Byron included equivocal homage to her mother:

> And surely she who now so fondly rears
> Thy youth, in thee, thus hourly brightening,
> Beholds the rainbow of thy future years,
> Before whose heavenly hues all sorrow disappears.

---

*Her new name is a telling one: In Greek mythology, Ianthe, a beautiful maiden, falls in love with another girl, Iphis, and her passion is reciprocated. Because of her father's threat to kill any female infant, Iphis had been brought up by her mother as a boy; thus Ianthe supposed that she was enamored of a young man, and the couple were betrothed. The "bridegroom," fearing the moment of truth, constantly delayed the wedding ceremony. Iphis's mother spent twenty-four hours in the temple praying to the goddess Io for help. When she emerged, she found her daughter transformed into a boy, and the marriage took place the following day.

We may wonder whether Byron's consoling message—that Ianthe's radiant womanhood would comfort his forty-year-old mistress's old age—
was a welcome promise. Still, the lines themselves—among the most
beautiful Byron ever wrote—plead that the poet may redeem the man:

> Oh! let that eye, which, wild as the Gazelle's,
> Now brightly bold or beautifully shy,
> Wins as it wanders, dazzles where it dwells,
> Glance o'er this page; nor to my verse deny
> That smile for which my breast might vainly sigh,
> Could I to thee be ever more than friend:
> This much, dear maid, accord; nor question why
> To one so young my strain I would commend,
> But bid me with my wreath one matchless lily blend.[14]

On November 30, Byron left Herefordshire for London. Arriving at
Batt's Hotel on Dover Street, he found thirty-six letters and notes awaiting him, none with welcome news; there were more importunings from
Caroline and reminders of his ever precarious financial situation. In an
effort to economize that was more symbolic than real, he gave up his
horses and dismissed his groom. Lady Oxford had contrived to be in
town then, too, and during their stay, he arranged to have her portrait
painted.

Having returned for Christmas to Eywood, Byron lingered happily
into the new year. On January 4, 1813, he told Lady Melbourne: "We
all go on without any interruptions or disagreeables—very few guests &
no inmates—books music &c. all the amusements. . . . I shall be very
qualmish at the thought of returning to town—it is an accursed abode
for people who wish to be quiet."[15]

His trepidations were well founded; soon enough, the world
impinged on their idyll. Money worries continued to harry him: He
pleaded with Hanson—in vain—to make some arrangement with his
principal creditor among the moneylenders. The Rochdale case dragged
on, and Byron had all but spent the first cash payment for Newstead in
settling his debt to Scrope Davies, paying other bills, and running up
many more. Used to his friend's generosity, Hodgson took this inopportune moment to beg a loan to pay his other debts and thus dispel his
prospective father-in-law's resistance to him as a suitor. Byron simply
did not have the £500 to spare, but it troubled him deeply to refuse. He
temporized with other suggestions and assurances about standing security for Hodgson.

He continued to be harassed by Caro Lamb, whose letters (or so

Byron claimed) included threats on his life. She had also managed to forge his handwriting well enough to fool John Murray, who agreed to release to her a portrait of the poet she had returned earlier, and that Byron had stored with the publisher. Instead, however, she appeared in person at 50 Albemarle Street, Murray's new offices, to seize the picture herself. As she had made off with one portrait, Byron moved to secure the safety of Lady Oxford's miniature. He gave Hobhouse a note for £66, to be delivered personally to the artist in Upper Berkeley Street; he was to pick up the work and, after wrapping the picture in the most anonymous possible package, entrust it to Murray, whom Byron now admonished to release nothing belonging to him without checking with Hobhouse first.

Deferring their own departure from Eywood, the lovers were rewarded by Lord Oxford's decision to precede them to London on January 7. Byron and Lady Oxford were now alone for ten days—if a household of five children can be said to resemble solitude. Finally, on the seventeenth, Lady Oxford, with her family and staff, left Eywood, with Byron traveling separately; their plan was to meet in Ledbury, leaving the children and servants to go on to town without them. While waiting for his mistress to join him in his "sordid inn," Byron wrote to thank Lady Melbourne for suggesting that he avoid traveling with the nursery. As he now acknowledged, there was no detail of his life that did not bear her imprint: "You have been my director & are still," he told her, "for I do not know anything you could not make me do or undo—& m'amie (but this you *wont believe*) has not yet learned the art of *managing* me nor superseded your authority." He had "inadvertently" told this to Lady Oxford herself, so he claimed, "a sentiment which did not meet with the entire approbation of my audience but which I maintained like a Muscovite enamoured of *Despotism.*"16

ONCE IN LONDON, Byron settled into rooms at 4 Bennet Street, St. James's. Now, however, he found his freedom of movement hampered by another constraint: fear of encountering Caroline Lamb. He didn't dare call on "Lady M" with Caro in residence at Melbourne House, or even to accept her mother-in-law's invitation to the theater, lest "little Mania" appear in the family box. Byron's dread of a chance meeting, along with his *volte-face* on another point of contention—he was now willing to have a formally arranged meeting with Caro—aroused all the Spider's suspicions that he was still in love. Lady Melbourne had confided these fears to Lady Bessborough, who, naturally, relayed them to Byron. He was outraged—thereby confirming his confidante's suspicions: "Ly

B[essborough] says *you* fear a renewal—now this is impossible—& that *you* should think so still more incomprehensible."[17] His thralldom to Caroline Lamb was a lingering disease, and no act of will, no love for another, could cure him. The illness had to run its course.

Finally, it was Caroline's most outrageous piece of melodrama that freed him. After a period of silence, when she avoided him publicly, she accepted an invitation to a waltz party at Lady Heathcote's on July 5, knowing that Byron would attend.

In happier times the dance had been her butterfly hour; watching her waltz had so aroused Byron's passion and inflamed his jealousy that he had made her promise never again to abandon herself to its wayward beat.

Now, after supper, as guests drifted toward the ballroom, Caroline passed Byron in a doorway, and she announced her intention to begin the dancing. In Byron's account of the exchange, he replied civilly that "it was better to *waltze* [*sic*] because she danced well—& it would be imputed to *me*—if she did not."[18]

It was his tone—coldness tinged with sarcasm—that seems to have pushed Caroline over the edge. There are many versions of what happened next. The only firsthand account is from Lady Melbourne, who reported with chill concision: "She broke a glass & scratched herself . . . with the broken pieces. Ly O[ssulstone] and Ly H[eathcote] screamed instead of taking it from her, and I had just left off holding her for 2 minutes—she had a pair of scissors in her hand when I went up, with which she was wounding herself but not deeply." Deeply enough, however, to cover herself with blood and faint several times, before she was carried home by her mother-in-law.

Byron claimed to have known nothing of what had taken place until he left the party at 5:00 a.m.—an incredible statement, given the screams and general melee. Writing to Lady Melbourne the next day, however, he owned, at least, to his negligence in the affair. He admitted that, in fact, he had spoken to Caroline before supper "when she said & did even then a foolish thing. . . . She took hold of my hand as I passed & pressed it against some sharp instrument—& said—'I mean to use this'—I answered—against me I presume—& passed on."[19]

What emerges from Byron's account of their exchange, of Caroline's reaction and his misinterpretation, is the picture of a man whose real fear was of any further scandal. Claiming ignorance of Caro's state of mind and her behavior, however, was not enough to get him off the hook. Lady Melbourne herself taxed him with callous disregard for Caroline's overwrought state; after her threat, compassion alone urged his return to her side.

On the defensive now, Byron turned self-pitying and sarcastic: "If I am to be hunted with hysterics where ever I go & whatever I do—I think she is not the only person to be pitied—I should have returned to her after her *doorway whisper*—but I could not with any kind of politeness leave Ly. Rancliffe to drown herself in wine & water or be suffocated in a jelly-dish—without a spoon or a hand to help her—besides—if there was & I foresaw there would be something ridiculous—surely I was better absent than present."[20]

Caroline herself claimed the stabbing had been an accident—caused by others rushing at her to seize a knife brandished in play. Whatever the truth, all the newspapers and scandal sheets reported the event, blaming whichever of the two parties suited them. But socially, the disgrace attached, as always, to the woman. Lady Caroline Lamb's exclusion from the world that was her birthright began that evening. Still, the melodrama accomplished what she had hoped. Fearing an encore, perhaps, Byron cautiously resumed communication; they wrote to one another and even met occasionally. But not in sight of the Spider.

WITH MELBOURNE HOUSE off-limits, Byron was the more firmly enclosed by Lady Oxford's circle. Accompanied by his lover, he was now counted among the regular guests of the Princess of Wales at Kensington Palace. Since they had met two years before, Byron had become a great favorite of the Princess, while her lack of pretension and bawdy humor (made more amusing by her German accent and malapropisms) charmed the poet. She recognized, moreover, that Byron's mood swings made his behavior unpredictable, but she didn't hesitate to tease him by insisting that he present only his famously charming self at her gatherings: "He is quite anoder man when he is *wid* people he like, and who like him, than he is *wid* others who do not please him so well. I always tell him there are two Lord Byrons, and when I invite him, I say, I ask the agreeable Lord, not the disagreeable one."[21]

Increasingly, strains were showing in the relations between Byron and his "Enchantress." As the Princess herself had occasion to remark: "Lady Oxford, poor soul, is more in love this time than she ever has been before. She was with me the other evening and Lord Byron was so cross to her (his Lordship not being in a good mood) that she was crying in the ante-room. Only imagine if anyone but myself had discovered the fair *Niobe* in tears! What a good story it would have made about the town the next day, for who could have kept such an anecdote secret?"[22]

Byron had worried that their idyll would not survive the strains of London. Now his fears seemed about to be fulfilled. He was said to suspect that Lady Oxford was again involved with Francis Burdett. With her frankness in these matters, she may have told him as much, or confessed her interest in someone else. Later, Byron would only confirm that he had been replaced by another. In "A Song" he struggled with the double blow inflicted by her honesty and faithlessness:

> Thou art not false, but thou art fickle,
>   To those thyself so fondly sought;
> The tears that thou hast forc'd to trickle
>   Are doubly bitter from that thought:
>
>   . . . .
>
> The wholly false the heart despises,
>   And spurns deceiver and deceit;
> But she who not a thought disguises,
>   Whose love is as sincere as sweet,
> When she can change who lov'd so truly
> It feels what mine has felt so newly[23]

As poetry, "A Song" is slight; still, the verses manage to capture the ways in which Byron's least-known lover, arguably the most sophisticated and brilliant, managed to disqualify him. He had never met a woman who required from him more than sexual fascination and literary celebrity. Lady Oxford's "fickleness," as he knew, was evidence that he had disappointed her. Certainly, her attempts to "recall him to his senatorial duties . . . in the cause of weakness" had, for the present, failed. Byron would give one more speech in Parliament, a rambling address on the right of petition, delivered in June 1813.

Through the uncertain English spring, his relations with Lady Oxford waxed and waned. In March she proudly announced to Lord Holland that she had had Charlotte's portrait as "Ianthe" engraved for the frontispiece of the new edition of *Childe Harold*, to be published in June. True to form, Byron claimed that they had "broken off," but he then spent April at Eywood, and he still spoke of accompanying the Harleys to Sicily in the early summer. In the middle of his stay he hinted to Lady Melbourne that Lady Oxford was pregnant with his child. Either this proved to be a false alarm, or the pregnancy was terminated. The "event," as Byron called it, was never mentioned again.

IN LATE MARCH, just before setting off for Eywood, Byron completed a long poem that he had been working on since November. Initially, he had planned the stanzas, a verse narrative set in the eastern Mediterranean, as a continuation of *Childe Harold*. Almost immediately, however, the new work claimed an identity of its own. After a half life in the form of ten stanzas without a subject, called "Il Diavolo Inamorato," a first draft of *The Giaour* was completed on March 12. Adding about 100 lines to his original 344, Byron sent the poem off to Murray, asking the publisher to run off fifteen copies for private publication. From this modest beginning, his "snake of a poem" grew, "lengthening its rattles every month."²⁴ The first public edition appeared in early June, and although the early print runs were small, each one sold out rapidly. By December 1813 *The Giaour*, now a serpent of 1,034 lines, had sold out seven editions. (There would be fourteen by 1815, amounting to slightly under twelve thousand copies.)

"*Giaour*," the poem's unpronounceable title, is an insult directed by Turks at non-Muslims, especially Christians, whose meaning embraces both "infidel" and "cur." In Byron's tale, set in the late seventeeth century, the Giaour is a mysterious young Venetian noble pitted in a life-and-death struggle against Hassan, a Muslim ruler, for the love of Leila, the most ravishing slave of his harem. The narrative drew on Byron's own experience in the East, both literary and personal. For the first, he used the gruesome tale of sixteen-year-old Phrosyne, the tragic victim of Jannina. Accused of stealing the affections of Ali Pasha's son, she was said to have been first raped by her accuser's father-in-law, then sewn into a sack and, along with her maidservants, thrown into Lake Pametis. But the poet also pressed into service his own dramatic encounter on the road from Athens to Piraeus, where he met the executioners of a young slave about to be drowned for similar alleged infidelity. Byron, we recall, claimed to have rescued the victim, helping to spirit her, in the dead of night, to Thebes and safety.

In *The Giaour*, Byron's technique is cinematic. For his principal narrator he proposes a Turkish storyteller, one of the bards who were a fixture of both court and coffeehouse until the twentieth century. Assuming the voices of supposed eyewitnesses, the speaker unreels his bloody tale in reverse: Leila's escape from the palace to join the Giaour, her apprehension and drowning by the ruler Hassan, her lover's vengeance, and the Pasha's gory end. These dramatic events, however, function as background to a larger tragedy. As the agent of Leila's death and murderer of her rightful master, the Giaour is haunted by his crimes. He has taken Holy Orders, but there is no peace for him in penitence. Like Hamlet, he is accused by visions of his two victims: Leila, a reminder of love betrayed, and the bloody, severed arm of Hassan, his brave adversary. Destroying both lover and enemy and bereft of human ties, the Giaour is cast into a void of guilt and madness.

Byron's belief in fatality broods over the poem, rescuing the work

from suffocation by stock images, the silver-sheathed daggers and flashing eyes of boilerplate Orientalism. Read as autobiography, his bleak
vision speaks to the impossibility of happiness, the perversion of men's
and women's highest impulse—love. In one of the poet's most famous
stanzas, the Giaour's infernal choice between suicide or slow death is
compared to the agony of a trapped insect:

> So do the dark in soul expire,
> Or live like Scorpion girt by fire;
> So writhes the mind Remorse hath riven,
> Unfit for earth, undoom'd for heaven,
> Darkness above, despair beneath,
> Around it flame, within it death![25]

No one was more astonished by the poem's success than the poet,
and its popularity inspired a series of offspring, each one more enthusiastically received than the last. First, the timing was perfect. Regency
England's passion for all things Eastern and "exotic" continued
unabated. Along with offering opulence of decor and costume, the East
invited the fantasy that it was a region where the passions held sway,
untrammeled by Christian repression. Unlike monogamous marriage,
the image of the harem—of boys as well as girls—promised every sexual
gratification, including the pasha's right to toss any faithless female to
her death. In place of Christian forgiveness, hatred and vengeance were
the accepted moral order.

Besides his own childhood love of Eastern tales, along with works
of history and travel, Byron drew on literary models closer to home,
beginning with his idol Beckford's novel *Vathek* and even the despised
laureate Southey's *Curse of Kehama*. Soon enough he had his own imitators, among them his friend Tom Moore, who entered the lists with
"Lalla Rookh."

Byron's eager readers, however, also revealed themselves to be an
audience thirsty for more autobiographical detail about the poet, whose
reputation was kept alive by Caroline Lamb's public histrionics.
Publication of *The Giaour* offered more intimate outpourings from the
poet as suffering lover, his heart laid bare. Many were the female readers who thrilled to the declaration:

> If changing cheek, and scorching vein—
> Lips taught to writhe, but not complain—
> If bursting heart, and madd'ning brain—
> And daring deed, and vengeful steel—

And all that I have felt—and feel—
Betoken love—that love was mine,
And shewn by many a bitter sign.

. . . .

Give me the pleasure with the pain,
So would I live and love again.[26]

Byron's pessimism about the reception of the new work and the trouble he took with revisions suggest his awareness that the poem was an experiment. He was trying to craft a new form, one that could contain the intimate lyric within a dramatic narrative framework. That he succeeded is the triumph of *The Giaour*. Working on several levels, this poem and the "Oriental Tales," which followed, reached as wide a readership as the poetry (and later the novels) of Walter Scott, John Murray's other best-selling author. Byron's new audience now embraced younger readers, along with an intelligentsia educated in moral allegory and Miltonic combat between good and evil.

PASSION HAD COOLED on both sides, but still Byron could not let go of his "Enchantress." In early June he was juggling three separate plans for going abroad, with three different companions: with the Harleys to Sardinia; with Augusta to Sicily; and with Lord Sligo to return to cruising the isles of Greece. While deferring his decision for as long as possible, Byron went on a shopping spree for the Greek journey, which combined the requirements of an ambassadorial mission and a military invasion. On July 14 he bought an entire set of new luggage, including a mahogany dressing case lined with velvet and fitted with silver bottles, and a portable writing desk of heavy wood, with a secret drawer. After refurbishing the scarlet staff uniform from his earlier grand tour with "Very rich Gold Epaulettes" for £33, he added several "Tartan" costumes, along with an Indian saber and four swords "incised with his coronet and Cypher." He wrote to Lady Melbourne of "hiring doctors, painters, and two or three stray Greeks," along with a Mameluke from Napoleon's guard. "These I am measuring for uniforms, shoes and inexpressibles without number."

The next day, July 15, his order at Byrant's Military Warehouse in Ludgate Hill included camp tables and chairs, two four-poster bedsteads with all the required bedding, and three more without posts; four pairs of fitted canteens, one pair containing articles of silver, the other plate and metalware. In leatherware there were five saddles and eight trunks; there were buckets for horses, and other pails. Further necessities included a nest of camp kettles with a stove and an expensive hammock to sleep in at sea. In the last two weeks of July he visited two different gunsmiths, amassing an arsenal of rifles, pistols, powder flasks, carbines, ramrods, bullet molds, cartridges, balls, gunpowder, and a magazine for storing it. Then, on July 24, he ordered from the Golden Spectacles, a firm on Sackville Street specializing in what were then known as "philosophical instruments," six portable three-foot telescopes, the same number of sliding gilt "astronomic operas," two silver hunting spring compasses, and, on approval, a sextant in a mahogany case. The bills for his two-week spree added a further £800 to his debts, but this sum was soon increased by a purchase of £3,000 worth of circular notes and two purchases of doubloons at nearly £300.[27]

As time drew near for the Harleys to sail, it was decided that Byron would not accompany them on the journey out; whether this was his choice or theirs is unclear. Now that he was faced with her imminent loss, Byron's attachment to Lady Oxford flared up again. They managed to spend a weekend together at Salthill near Maidenhead, after which Byron escorted his lover back to her family at Portsmouth, where they were to board ship. The new plan seems to have been that Byron, traveling separately, would join them later that summer. Then everything blew up. Lady Oxford either showed a letter to her husband, or Lord Oxford intercepted it, one in which, Byron recalled, "I most committed myself."[28] Defiantly, she declared her intention to continue the relationship and to spend as much time with the poet as he could spare. But the couple sailed off in a golden haze of mutual forgiveness and reconciliation, leaving a bitter lover behind.

Once she was gone, Byron felt desolate, more "Carolinish," than he could ever have anticipated, he wrote to his usual confidante. He would never see his "unrepentant Magdalen" again, nor would he ever again risk loving so dazzling and demanding a woman.

CHAPTER 22

"That Perverse Passion"

N THE SHORTEST of notice, Byron's sister, Augusta, arrived in London on June 26.

No woman could have provided a more consoling contrast to Lady Oxford's rationalized infidelities. Loyally, Augusta struggled with marriage to a husband who appeared at home only long enough to provide her with a new baby; the rest of Colonel Leigh's time was passed in racier company, as he spent Augusta's small income and ran up gambling debts. Her flight from her home at Six Mile Bottom near Newmarket was impelled by dread of the bailiffs' imminent descent. She had come to London to ask her brother for help.

Byron was overjoyed at the prospect of seeing his sister—without her family. He swept his calendar clear and informed hostesses that Augusta should be included in his invitations. He wrote to Lady Melbourne for a "She voucher" to Almacks, the exclusive subscription dance "club," entrée to which was the most coveted in London. He brought her to a dinner given by the rich and socially ambitious wife of the great chemist Sir Humphry Davy in honor of the visiting literary lioness Madame de Staël. Augusta charmed the *salonistes* of the intelligentsia, along with the belles and gorgons of Almacks. With a lover's secret pride, Byron watched his shy, unfashionably dressed sister conquer London's social steeps. "I think our being together before 3d. people will be a new *sensation* to *both*," he had written on the eve of her arrival.[1] He rejoiced to see her blossom in the warmth of a carefree holiday and, not least, to observe that she was properly impressed by those now vying to receive her famous brother.

But he also wanted her to himself. He believed in their blood tie as a mystical bond of flesh and spirit. With Augusta he felt the freedom

and ease that came from being wordlessly understood, along with the
tension of a desire so powerful that when Byron was still a schoolboy,
Catherine Byron had felt it her duty to keep them apart.

Byron would later celebrate Augusta's sexual attraction in the person of Dudu, the plump harem slave who shares her bed with his hero
Don Juan, disguised as "Juanna." Dudu is a "kind of sleepy Venus"; her
body, with its "few angles,"

> Looked more adapted to be put to bed,
> Being somewhat large and languishing and lazy,
> Yet of a beauty that would drive you crazy.[2]

In Hayter's drawing of Augusta (the only likeness of her that survives)
we see the inspiration for Dudu's "Attic forehead and her Phidian
nose," along with the slave girl's sensual, "half-shut eyes." Pregnant or
nursing a baby during the entire period of their intimacy, Augusta
embodied the appeal of fecund womanliness while she also provided
flattering assurance to Byron that he had been the first man to awaken
her sexually:

> She looked (this simile's quite new) just cut
>   From marble, like Pygmalion's statue waking,
> The Mortal and the Marble still at strife,
> And timidly expanding into life.[3]

From the first days of her visit, Byron's tone, in speaking of Augusta,
breathed the child's idyllic sense of safety: "My sister is in town, which
is a great comfort—for, never having been much together, we are naturally more attached to each other," he wrote to Tom Moore.[4] Natural in
their own eyes but, soon enough, unnatural in the eyes of the world.

Their elders were all dead. Grown-ups themselves now, they could
play at being children, innocent of sin. Exploring the childhood intimacies they had missed earlier, they became lovers. Never had seduction
been so easy, Byron later boasted to Lady Melbourne. What few objections Augusta had feebly expressed, he claimed, were easily overcome.

Of Augusta's feelings about Byron, as brother and sister became
lovers, we know very little. The record consists largely of others'
impressions—as prejudicial as they are contradictory. She has been
accused of "moral idiotcy,"[5] deemed a "half wit,"[6] and "amoral as a
rabbit"[7]—in other words, a sinner too stupid to know what she was
doing. But she has also been portrayed as the reverse: a manipulator,
exploiting Byron's passion to extract from him large sums of money.

Indeed, within a year he would make her two gifts totaling £3,000—an enormous sum he could ill afford.

Her fondness for baby talk has confirmed the view of Augusta as simpleminded. Even Byron would become irritated by her "damned crinkum-crankum," as he later called it.[8] Given her isolation for months on end, however, in a house with only young children and rural servants for company, it's hardly surprising that Augusta's speech and even her writing should echo with sounds of the nursery.

Still, a woman who claims the dispensation of childish speech is also absolving herself of adult responsibility. As a faithful communicant of the Church of England, Augusta could have been in no doubt as to the gravity of incest—as both sin and crime. Her reversion to infantile speech suggests an escape from knowledge, a way of doing and not knowing.

What we do know about her is that she adored Byron and could always make him feel happy and secure. With her he could be a child again, restored to that most longed-for and regretted paradise. With her natural gaiety, his "Guss" or "Goose" could always tease him out of affectation or sulkiness. She would do anything for him and with him.

Soon they felt the impossibility of being alone together in London. Augusta was staying with her friend the Hon. Theresa Villiers on Upper Berkeley Street, and they could scarcely expect privacy there. Too many sharp eyes and wagging tongues could observe her visiting Byron's rooms in St. James's, an area crossed daily by everyone in the fashionable world. On August 1 Byron accompanied Augusta at least as far as Newmarket, and possibly home to Six Mile Bottom; if he did not stay at the Leighs' house, he may have lodged in the town. In either case, they returned from Newmarket together, arriving in London by August 5. Meanwhile, on August 2, Byron had canceled his passage on the *Boyne*, bound for the Mediterranean. On August 5, the day of his return to London with Augusta, Byron wrote to Lady Melbourne with news that shocked even that most unshockable of worldlings: "My sister who is going abroad with me is now in town where she returned with me from Newmarket—under the existing circumstances of her lord's embarassments [*sic*] she could not well do otherwise—& she appears to have still less reluctance at leaving this country than even myself."[9]

He had persuaded Augusta to abandon husband and children and England for him. For the orphaned poor relation, terrified of disapproval, to have agreed to such a move is evidence of passion more eloquent than trunkfuls of love letters. Trusting to a future as exiled criminal with her mercurial brother, she was prepared to burn all her bridges.

Augusta Leigh's Commonplace Book, which she kept from 1805 until 1848, contains the conventional collection of moral aphorisms, religious homilies, and other scraps from her readings, along with her transcriptions of several of Byron's poems. One entry, however, stands out. Unlike the others, it is not bracketed in quotation marks and bears the unmistakable sound of Augusta's breathless voice: "In early Life there is a moment—perhaps of all the enchantments of Love, it is the one which is never renewed—when passion, unacknowledged to ourselves, imparts greater delight than any after-stage of that ever progressive sentiment. We neither wish nor expect—A new joy has risen like the sun upon our lives; and we rejoice in the radiance of the morning, without adverting to the moon & twilight that is to follow."[10]

Augusta's "ever progressive sentiment" had become, for Byron, the prison of obsession. He took to compulsively discussing their affair. Discretion rarely entered into his calculations, but in this case, the risk of confiding, in almost everyone, seems a plea for punishment. His uncertainty about their future together—more immediately, whether she would actually go away with him and, for that matter, whether he really wanted her (and possibly one of her children) to become his responsibility—Byron allayed all these anxieties by announcing their vague plans as established fact. To gossipy Tom Moore he confided: "I am, at this moment, in a far more serious, and entirely new scrape than any of the last twelvemonths—and that is saying a good deal."[11] He followed this schoolboy boast with a full confession of his affair with his sister. Their plans were delayed, he explained, only by reports of the plague raging throughout the Mediterranean and by Augusta's insistence on taking one of her little daughters with her. "Ly Oxford sickened me of *every body's* children," he told his confidant, either forgetting or remembering too well his infatuation with eleven-year-old Charlotte Harley. As for people traveling with children, "If they want them, can't they get them on the Spot?"[12]

By the end of August, both lovers were wavering. Before taking this irrevocable step, Augusta needed more reassurance than Byron could provide. But just at this crucial moment, he was less importunate than he had been earlier. To placate Lady Melbourne, who had fearfully invoked the scandal he was about to unleash, Byron promised restraint; he would not rush off to see Augusta in the next weeks, but instead would force himself to remain in London, reflecting soberly on the danger of their situation.

Away from Augusta, his obsession fed on itself. While she was immured with family and unpaid bills at home, he was frantic with frustration. He left London for Six Mile Bottom, arriving about September 12. Yet after a night and a day of discussion, nothing had been decided. Perhaps because his arguments were less eloquent, Augusta was losing courage. On September 13, in a grim humor, Byron set off for Cambridge, where he promptly went on an epic drunk with Scrope Davies. Between eight and eleven that night, they polished off six bottles of his host's burgundy and claret, which left Scrope "very unwell & me rather feverish," Byron wrote to Augusta. He arrived back in London at three in the morning on the fifteenth, only to decide to leave again that night—either for James Wedderburn Webster's at Aston Hall or for Newstead, whose buyer had delayed payment. In a state of nervous agitation, waiting for Augusta's final decision, he wondered uncertainly where to go next, "nor does it much matter—as you perhaps care more on the subject than I do," he wrote to her.

He made an effort to be discreet about the logistics of her flight—should she agree to go with him: "When my departure is arranged—& I can get this long-evaded passage—you will be able to tell me whether I can expect a visit or not—I can come for or meet you as you think best."13 But Augusta had retreated, unable finally to leave her family for Byron's wild dream of a life together.

In his "feverish and restless state" Byron decided against Newstead's gloom in favor of the distractions of Aston Hall, where a lively group of young married couples like his hosts, with a sprinkling of bachelors and unattached female relations, had been invited for the Doncaster races. At first sight the ladies present appeared to form a "society of happy wives and unfortunate maidens," he noted.14 It was soon apparent, however, that his hostess, Lady Frances Webster, did not fall into the first category. His earlier London impression of the young bride already bored by her husband was now confirmed by domestic tensions at Aston Hall.

CHARMED as he was by Lady Frances, he was too full of Augusta to be distracted. He knew that Lady Melbourne would be grieved by the obstinacy of his dangerous attachment, and he assured her that his failure to find a replacement did not stem from lack of will: "I have tried & hardly too to vanquish my demon—but to very little purpose," he confessed, "for a resource that seldom failed me before—did in this instance—I mean *transferring* my regards to another. . . . I willingly would but the feeling that [it] was an effort spoiled all again."15

This was the irreplaceable joy of Augusta. She demanded no effort, asked nothing of him but to be himself. She seemed incapable of jealousy; it was impossible to imagine her making a scene. More comforting still, she held no higher expectations of him; with Augusta he felt no

need to live up to Childe Harold or Sir Francis Burdett. Now, surrounded by strangers, he missed her terribly.

At his request, Lady Frances invited Mrs. Leigh to Aston Hall. But
Augusta was in the queasy first months of another pregnancy, and she
declined. She may, in fact, have suspected her condition when she
changed her mind about going abroad. Byron does not mention
Augusta's pregnancy until well into the new year, although they surely
had discussed the possibility that the child might be his. Though she had
good reason for declining the invitation, Byron felt her regrets as rejection. Augusta had withdrawn into her maternal role, and for the time
being, this excluded him. He retaliated by refusing to write, leaving
unanswered several anxious letters from Six Mile Bottom.

Sexually available now, Byron applied himself to cheering the
unhappy wife near at hand. After his months at Eywood, he was skilled
in exploiting the erotic possibilities of the country house visit: the mix
of leisure, boredom, and opportunity. His hostess was too depressed for
flirtation, so, skipping the prelude, he moved from sympathy to shared
confidences to the minuet of seduction.

He tried to live up to Lady Melbourne's expectations of him as
sexual strategist, sending her bulletins of each maneuver in his campaign. She beamed approval on his quarry; Lady Frances (now given the
code name "Ph" in their letters) was, in his confidante's practiced opinion, the best possible antidote to Augusta. At Aston Hall the atmosphere became more sexually charged with each passing day: hands
brushed, notes were exchanged at billiard and dining table. They would
find themselves alone, only to have the husband appear unexpectedly.
Tensions mounted; sensing a new suspiciousness in his host, Byron took
pains to appear indifferent to his hostess. When she accompanied other
guests on excursions, Byron remained behind, working on additions to
The Giaour. He went back to London—only to extract a return invitation from the Websters.

What began as distraction now took on the trappings of a full-scale
drama. And Byron was no longer play-acting the roles of impresario
and leading man. Warmed by his attention, Lady Frances's impassive
beauty melted to reveal a passionate nature. She poured out her heart to
him. She had yielded to a miserable marriage to escape the cruelties of
her own family (an account confirmed, Byron noted, by one of Lady
Frances's brothers). Now, for the first time, she was in love, and so, once
again, was Byron.

For the first time, he believed the sincerity of a woman who said
"No" from scruple and not coquetry. Through the month of October,
Byron shuttled between London and Aston Hall. With each stay, he and

Lady Frances moved closer to becoming lovers; they talked of going off together: "With her I am ready & willing to fly to the 'Green earth's end.'. . . *We* are in despair," he wrote to "Ly M."[16] Ultimately, the virtuous wife placed the decision in his hands; she would do as Byron wanted, even if she should be tormented by guilt for the rest of her life. To his own surprise, Byron found himself moved by her humility and frightened by this example of moral seriousness. This was a diversion that had gotten out of hand—for both of them. He decided, in his words, to "spare" Lady Frances, leaving her to a clear conscience and a loveless marriage. Disappointed yet again—and yet again, relieved—Byron had repeated his now-familiar cycle: pursuit, persuasion, ending in passive withdrawal: "I have left everything to her," he proclaimed. "She wavered—& escaped—perhaps so have I."[17]

Now that his quarry had been spared, Byron missed her; he felt depressed by reflecting on might-have-beens. He wrote to Augusta, summarily put off at the height of his interlude with Lady Frances, assuring her that he was not the least angry with her: "My silence has merely arisen from several circumstances which I cannot now detail."[18] In case Augusta failed to conjecture these for herself, Byron soon confessed, naming her failure to join him at Aston Hall as the cause of his dalliance.

On November 1 Byron began work on a new poem. Writing, as he said, "to dispel reflection during *inaction*,"[19] he completed a first draft of *The Bride of Abydos* in one week. Subtitled *A Turkish Tale* and dedicated to Lord Holland, *Bride* begins with an evocation of that mythic East constructed by Byron, where the lushness of nature mirrors the extremes of human emotions:

> Know ye the land where the cypress and myrtle
>   Are emblems of deeds that are done in their clime,
> Where the rage of the vulture—the love of the turtle—
>   Now melt into sorrow—now madden to crime?[20]

The exotic setting, the Asian side of the Hellespont, and the verse form served as distancing devices, enabling him to write of sexual obsession without being lured into the realism of prose. "I began a comedy and burnt it because the scene ran into *reality*; a novel for the same reason," he wrote on November 17, in the journal he had begun three days earlier. "In rhyme I can keep more away from facts; but the thought always runs through, through . . . yes, yes, through."[21]

He might disguise the "facts" of his own case in divans and turbans; the thought was not so easily veiled. The new poem told the story of

Zuleika, adored daughter of the despot Giaffir. From childhood, her dearest friend and companion has been her brother Selim, whose poetic sensibilities have made him a victim of their father's contempt. Within a day, Zuleika learns, their innocent idyll will end. Giaffir has promised her in marriage to his ally, another aging pasha, thus joining their two empires. Stricken, Selim summons Zuleika to a secret meeting by the shore; there he reveals that they are not brother and sister, but first cousins. His father had been slain by Giaffir, a victim of fratricidal jealousy. Selim further reveals that he is no effeminate courtier but the clandestine leader of a pirate band, preparing to conquer the despot's evil empire. The poem's promise of a happy ending—the forbidden love of brother and sister redeemed by the truth of their blameless blood ties—ends in tragedy. Discovered by Giaffir, Selim's pirate forces engage his uncle's troops in battle. On the sands of Sestos (the point from which Byron had swum the Hellespont), Selim looks back for a glimpse of his beloved in her tower; the delay caused by this unguarded glance proves fatal, and he dies from an enemy arrow. Seeing his lifeless body in the water and realizing that she has been the cause of his death, Zuleika succumbs to a mortal seizure.

Originally Byron had intended Selim and Zuleika to be biological brother and sister, thus allowing the poet to work out his crime along with its punishment. Then he changed his mind, deciding that, in the second canto, his lovers should be revealed as first cousins. He explained his revision in cultural terms, as a bow to the mores of the times: He was "*two centuries* at least too late," he said. The incest theme "is not adapted for this age, at least this country, though the finest works of the Greeks, one of Schiller's and Alfieri's in modern times, besides several of our *old* (and best) dramatists, have been grounded on incidents of a similar cast."

But his real reasons were personal. He knew that inferences about his relationship with Augusta would be drawn from his tale. Artistically, however, he was never happy with the change. He had "altered" the premise of the poem "and in so doing have weakened the whole, by interrupting the train of thought; and in composition I do not think *second* thoughts are the best, though *second* expressions may improve the first ideas."[22] His compromise, moreover, did not defuse the moral minefield of the poem: Throughout the first canto establishing their attachment, Zuleika and Selim believe themselves to be brother and sister; their love, silent and guilty, is based on this belief. Revelation of their innocent connection, moreover, by encouraging the sexual expression of their love, leads to the deaths of both.

Zuleika's provocative sexuality summons the poet's vivid memories of the passionate Augusta: It is Zuleika's voice we hear while she makes love to Selim:

> Thy cheek, thine eyes, thy lips to kiss,
> Like this—and this—no more then this,
> For, Alla! sure thy lips are flame,
>   What fever in thy veins is flushing?
> My own have nearly caught the same,
>   At least I feel my cheek too blushing.[23]

Critics were shocked by the aggressively "unfeminine" expression of a woman's sexual desire. Selim's merest hint to his love that he is not what he appears to be "has a singular effect on the virgin Zuleika," the *Anti-Jacobin* noted pruriently, "for it induces her to make the strongest love to Selim, to proceed to a kind of practical illustration of her passion, and to use language, which would be indecent even in the mouth of her lover—for know, good reader, Selim was not her brother!"[24]

Now, alone in London, Byron succumbed to the sense of abandonment he had come to dread. A man who always had to have an available "object of attachment," he now found himself "pondering on the miseries of separation: Oh how seldom we see those we love! yet we live ages in moments, *when met.*"[25]

He now resumed writing to Annabella Milbanke and his letters to her grew in length. He was flattering and playful in his allusions to her other suitors, respectfully admiring when addressing the issues of her religious faith, and selectively confessional in describing his own bleak spirits and efforts to overcome his moods.

Realizing this to be her second and probably last chance to encourage Byron to renew his suit, Annabella's letters danced around her concern to make known her present availability. Taken together, their exchange gleams with the parry and thrust, advance and retreat of an epistolary courtship.

Annabella now read the poet for clues to the man. She scanned the fifth edition of *The Giaour*, just published, paying close attention to expressions of the hero's intimate feelings: "The description of love almost makes *me* in love," she told Lady Melbourne. "Certainly, he excels in the language of passion."[26]

She was beside herself with delight, then, to read in Byron's letter to her of November 10, "I have been scribbling another poem. . . . Turkish as before—for I can't empty my head of the East—and horrible enough—though not quite so sombre as ye Giaour (that unpronounceable name) and for the sake of intelligibility it is *not* a fragment—the scene is on the Hellespont—a favorite sejour of mine—and if you will accept it I will send you a copy."

After inquiring when she would be in town, Byron teased: "You won't take *fright* when we meet will you? & imagine that I am about to add to your thousand and one pretendants? I have taken exquisite care to prevent the possibility of that," he added—a broad hint that he was paying court to another. Then, casting the serious young woman in the role of a femme fatale, he noted rumors of another acquaintance of his "added to your list of unacceptables—and I am sorry for him—as I know that he has talent—& his pedigree ensures him wit and good humour.*[27]

Annabella, herself, was not interested in making the best marriage; she had firmly decided she wanted only Byron.

"Pray let me have your new composition," she replied eagerly to his offer of a copy of *Bride*. "I have received more pleasure from your poetry than from all the Q.e.d.'s in Euclid." To Byron's query of when she expected next to be in town, she offered a note of encouragement: "I look forward to meeting you next spring in London as one of the most agreeable incidents which my residence there can produce. *I* shall not be distressed if the design to captivate should be imputed to *me*."[28]

She was crushed, then, to read Byron's reply to her overture by return post on November 29. Since his first youthful love for his neighbor Mary Chaworth, he wrote, he had found that his mature " 'ideal'— the being to whom I would commit the whole happiness of my future life—the *only* woman to whom I ever seriously pretended as a wife— had disposed of her heart already."[29] Annabella's anguish at having led Byron to believe that she was in love with another now made her literally ill.

On December 26 she wrote to Byron a wan letter expressing her pleasure that he had not gone to Holland with friends, as she had heard. The Milbankes had planned on a trip to town before spring, but it was postponed—on her account—indefinitely: "Though at present recovered from a severe illness, I remain more unequal than before to the labours of a London life."[30]

---

*Annabella's latest reject was Stratford Canning, whom Byron had met when he was first secretary at the embassy in Constantinople. Another was George Eden, a future viceroy of India.

Byron's own energies were free for literary and social activity: "Now for a *plunge*—high life and low life," he confided to his journal on November 23.[31] He kept up with Jackson's Pugilistic Club, receiving his "professor" at home and dining out with the current champion of England, Thomas Crib. At Lady Holland's table, he noted, was still to be found the most reliable mix of brilliance and breeding, established figures and newcomers. He was a guest in the Hollands' box at Drury Lane and reciprocated by inviting them to Covent Garden, where he had rented a box for the season from Lord Salisbury. He even suffered the rarefied salons of the Berry sisters and Miss Lydia White, "blue-stockings" who redeemed their intellectual accomplishments by success as hostesses; the star of their circle was Lady Charlemont, "the Kashmeer Butterfly of the Blues," Byron called her, sighing that her head seemed "to possess all that sculpture could require for its ideal."[32] His raptures notwithstanding, Byron was never sexually drawn to the "swans" who glided through Regency society; he would have agreed with his contemporary Stendhal that "beautiful women are for men with no imagination."

Like an intermittent fever, the yearning to escape England would come and go. Now, with another new friend, the witty parliamentarian Richard "Conversation" Sharpe, he planned a trip to Holland to witness with his own eyes the triumph of the tiny country that had just succeeded in throwing off the French yoke: "Today, great news—the Dutch have taken Holland," he noted in his journal, betting "two to one on the new dynasty! . . . God speed the little republic!" From the point of view of mores he would have preferred the East, but "no matter,—the bluff burghers, puffing freedom out of their short tobacco pipes, might be worth seeing," he wrote. As it was, with England about to preside over the restoration of the Bourbons in France, Byron's belief in the possibility of more enlightened government had withered: "I don't know what liberty means, never having seen it," he noted bitterly.[33]

Disillusionment was further fueled by the downfall of his onetime idol Napoleon. Since Harrow, when he had physically defended a bust of Bonaparte, "he has been a 'hero de roman' of mine—on the Continent; I don't want him here," added Byron honestly. Now his hero had turned tail, abandoning the Grande Armée to save his own skin. "I am sure when I fought for his bust at school, I did not think he would run away from himself."[34]

Breaking faith with oneself—that was the one fixed sin in Byron's otherwise shifting theology. In these last months of the year, painful evidence of his own bad faith was contributing to his gloom. W. J. Baldwin, incarcerated for debt in King's Bench Prison, had written a series of pathetic letters to Byron, detailing the miserable condition of prisoners and asking the poet to present a petition on his behalf in Parliament. Byron refused.

In his letter to Baldwin of November 14 he made his excuses in a reply stuttering with inconsistencies: "Upon the principle itself—the question at issue on the *confinement* of debtors—as far as regards the rights of humanity and the social compact—my mind is full made up— but the minor grievances—the various though I doubt not—well grounded subjects of complaint which I conjecture will form a consid- erable portion of the petition—I have not had leisure to examine—nor opportunity to collect."

Then, almost involuntarily, the truth emerged: "If I were indifferent to the interests of others—or confident in my own powers I should hold a different language."[35]

"*Aut Caesar aut nihil*"—Either Caesar or nothing—Byron had con- fided to his journal. He could not face returning to the arena where he had failed, three times, to be taken seriously as a contender. "I have spo- ken thrice—but I doubt my ever becoming an orator."[36] Along with the stage fright that translated into a rhetorical stiffness, there was another, more debilitating obstacle to his public career: For Byron, the company he kept was more crucial than the issue he defended. In his last parlia- mentary stand, speaking on behalf of Major Cartwright and the right to petition, Byron's only ally had been "Citizen" Stanhope, the peer whose ineffectual radical speechifying had made him something of a laughing- stock. "Stanhope and I stood against the whole house and mouthed it valiantly," Byron recalled, "and had some fun and a little abuse for our opposition." But then, echoing Richard III, he confessed: " 'I am not in the vein' for this business.' "

He suffered agonies of self-reproach for this final failure of both political principle and human sympathy. He compared himself to the novelist Lawrence Sterne, who by his own admission had "preferred whining over 'a dead ass to relieving a living mother'—villain— hypocrite—slave—sycophant! but *I* am no better." His collapse of will now made him yearn for the inspiring passion of his "tutelar genius. . . . Had [Lady Oxford] been here, she would have *made* me do it," he mourned. "*There* is a woman, who, amid all her fascination, always urged a man to usefulness or glory."[37]

But his "Aspasia" was gone, and Byron retreated—definitively— from the English political scene. He assuaged his conscience by a sweep- ing dismissal of all the "mummeries" of Parliament, the hopelessness of any faith in progress, of either men or nations. "I have simplified my politics into an utter detestation of all existing governments. . . . The first moment of an universal republic would convert me into an advocate for single and uncontradicted despotism. The fact is, riches are power, and poverty is slavery all over the earth, and one sort of establishment is no better, nor worse for a *people* than another."[38]

Ultimately, however, all his expressions of pessimism circled back to feelings of personal failure. "I shall never be any thing or rather always be nothing. The most I can hope is, that some will say 'He might, perhaps, if he would.' "[39]

In this bleak mood of self-hatred, poetry—whether his own or that of his contemporaries—seemed the poorest substitute for his ideal of worth: to be one of the "first men," a Washington or an Aristides. "No one should be a rhymer who could do anything better," he would always insist.[40]

Enthusiastic readings of *The Bride of Abydos* on the eve of publication by Gifford, Hodgson, the Hollands, Canning, and Murray did little to cheer him. On the basis of the success of *The Giaour*, Murray had made him the handsome offer of 1,000 guineas for a new two-volume edition, to include *The Giaour*, *The Bride*, and half a dozen short poems. Although he confessed to having been "strongly tempted, merely for the *say* of it,"[41] Byron turned the publisher down, suggesting that they defer discussion of money until Easter of the following year. Pessimistic about the reception of the new work, he was unwilling to have Murray risk a poor investment, and for the same reason he resisted its publication as a separate volume, preferring that his *Bride* should "steal quietly into the world" hidden in the new edition of his first Oriental tale, when "if liked we can throw off some copies for the purchasers of former *Giaours*, and if not, I can omit it in any future publication. What think you?"[42] he asked Murray.

His own mixed feelings about the new poem made him protective of its first public appearance in a way he had never been before. On the one hand, he was proud of the authenticity of his Oriental tales, comparing his own "palpable" firsthand experience in the Levant with that of writers who took all their local color from others: "It is my story and my *East*," he told Holland. At the same time, he saw the steady sales and seven editions of *The Giaour* as evidence that he was pandering to a mass audience (a view seconded by many critics since). The poem's success "certainly did not raise my opinion of the public taste." He thought the meter used in both works evoked poetry of inferior literary quality, and he was still more dismissive of *The Bride* because of the speed with which it had been written: "The whole . . . cost me *four nights*—and you may easily suppose that I can have no great esteem for lines that can be strung as fast as minutes."[43]

This elaborately defensive posture was an attempt to deflect criticism of a work for which he had complex and intense feelings, starting with the belief that it was the only complete poem he had yet written: "*The Bride* such as it is, is my first *entire* composition of any length (except satire & be d[amn]d to it). For the *G[iaou]r* is but a string of passages—and *C[hil]d[e] Ha[rol]d* is—and I rather think always will be unconcluded."[44]

Composed in a week of emotional turbulence, *The Bride* was entwined with memories of Augusta. Publicly, he might dismiss the speed of its creation; to his journal he confided that those four nights of writing "to distract my thoughts from *****" had been crucial to his sanity: "Had I not done something at that time I must have gone mad, by eating my own heart—bitter diet."[45] To Annabella, at the end of this stormy November, he stated clearly his belief in the saving power of poetry as "the lava of the imagination whose eruption prevents an earthquake."[46] But it is also true that in writing *The Bride of Abydos*, Byron danced on the edge of the volcano. The poem's theme of incest, barely disguised, played a dangerous variation on his need to tell and not tell. He both wanted and dreaded the poem to be understood for what it was: a love song to his sister.

On November 22, he gave Murray a list of ten persons to receive the "earliest copies" of the poem, with a card "from ye *Author*." Most of these—Hodgson, Gifford, Hookham Frere, Stratford Canning, and the dedicatee, Lord Holland—had read proofs and had been consulted on the question of separate or merged publication. One copy, however, was to go to Lady Caroline Lamb (at Brocket Hall), with whom he had cautiously resumed correspondence, and another to Lady Melbourne in Whitehall. While the volume was on its way, Byron dropped a few coy hints to his confidante of what the new poem was really about: "It will for some *reasons interest you* more than anybody—these I leave for you to discover. . . . You know me better than most people—and are the only person who can trace & I want to see whether you think my *writings* are *me* or not." In the same letter he told "Lady M" what she most dreaded to hear: He was more in love with Augusta than ever; neither absence, the distractions of London, nor attempts to defuse his obsession in poetry had succeeded.

"I am afraid that that perverse passion was my deepest after all," he wrote.[47]

Augusta no longer tried to discourage him. In refusing to go abroad with Byron, she had exhausted her frail powers of will, and she now abandoned herself to the feelings that overwhelmed her. By November 29 she had received from Byron her copy of *The Bride*, and without commenting on the poem directly, she replied in verse:

> *Partager tous vos sentimens*
> *Ne voir que par vos yeux*
> *N'agir que par vos conseils, ne*
> *Vivre que pour vous, voilà mes*
> *voeux, mes projets, & le seul*
> *destin qui peut me rendre*
> *heureuse.* *

With these lines, Augusta enclosed a curl of her hair—chestnut with glints of gold—tied with white silk. On the outside of the small folded packet of paper Byron scrawled these words, followed by a cross:

> La Chevelure of
> the *one* whom I
> most loved +48

The cross of two equal branches now became their emblem. Byron and Augusta used the mathematical symbol for the joining of two parts to signify sexual consummation.†49 He made a note in his journal to have a seal made for each of them with their "device."

Two weeks later, Augusta arrived in London. They could no longer be apart. A single entry in Byron's journal for December 14, 15, and 16 notes: "Much done, but nothing to record. It is quite enough to set down my thoughts—my actions will rarely bear retrospection."50 On the eighteenth, Byron attended Covent Garden, possibly with Augusta, where he saw the popular comedy *Love in a Village* by Isaac Bickersteth. Byron's only recorded thoughts about the evening were reflections on the number of whores, including several mother-and-daughter pairs, in the neighboring boxes. "It was as if the house had

---

*To share all of your feelings / see only through your eyes / act only upon your counsel / live only for you / these are my only / wishes and goal and the only / fate that can bring me happiness.

†This was not Byron's invention. He would have known the notorious publication by his friend Payne Knight, *Account of the Worship of Priapus*, privately printed by the Society of Dilettanti, which suggested that the sign "was a symbol of the organs of generation." Knight had also been a reputed lover of Lady Oxford.

been divided between your public and your *understood* courtesans; the only difference between the "Intriguantes" and the "regular mercenaries," Byron noted, was that the first might enter "Carleton [*sic*] and any *other house*," the second were "limited to the opera and b[awdy] house."[51] The bitterness of his remarks points to what he does not say. Were he and his sister to acknowledge their relationship, every house would be closed to her; she would sink to the social level of a common whore and criminal.

After seeing Augusta back to Mrs. Villiers's house in Piccadilly, Byron returned to his rooms in nearby St. James's, writing until late morning. December 17 and 18 were spent on two sonnets. Both titled "To Ginevra," together they closed his attachment to Lady Frances Webster. The first poem's labored conceit contrasts the young woman's physical resemblance to Guido Reni's *Repentant Magdalen* (her "wan lustre" of "sorrow's softness charm'd from its despair") with her moral blamelessness ("Except that *thou* has nothing to repent"). The second sonnet is even less successful; exalting chastity did not inspire Byron, and he knew it: "I never wrote but one sonnet before . . . as an exercise—and I will never write another. They are the most puling, petrifying, stupidly platonic compositions."[52]

Accompanying Augusta back to Cambridgeshire, he brought with him the beginnings of a new poem, begun on December 18. When he returned to London on December 27, he had completed a first draft of *The Corsair*, the third of his Oriental tales; he had written nearly two hundred lines a day at Six Mile Bottom. His nocturnal writing habits were untroubled by domesticity at close quarters: besides him and Augusta, now five months pregnant, the small house contained three young children from five years to eighteen months old, and several servants.

In his dedication to Tom Moore, Byron acknowledged to his friend and fellow poet that *The Corsair* was the most autobiographical of his poems. "If I have deviated into the gloomy vanity of 'drawing from self,' the pictures are probably like, since they are unfavourable, and if not, those who know me are undeceived."[53] The setting for his new "devil of a long story" is a "pirate's isle peopled with my own creatures."[54] The isle itself is one in the Greek archipelago that Byron recalled with both longing and sorrow at its political bondage, while the creatures in question, a man and two women, dispose themselves in a characteristic Byronic triangle.

Conrad, the corsair, is the pirate as intellectual. He may be feared as an outlaw, but his real authority derives from "The power of Thought— the Magic of the Mind!" and his "glance of fire" is the only heroic aspect in a physical form that otherwise boasts "little to admire." The poem is haunted by two women—Medora, Conrad's blonde betrothed, and Gulnare, the dark slave favorite of the ruler Seyd—who provide an operatic study in contrasts.* Waiting passively in her tower, Medora's only role is to die of a broken heart when Conrad, captured and imprisoned by the Seyd, fails to return. Passion's slave as well as her master's, Gulnare is the most violent of Byron's sexually avid heroines. Carried to safety by Conrad when he sacks the pasha's seraglio, she falls helplessly in love with her liberator, murdering her master to free the pirate. Together the women mirror Conrad's divided self: "He thought on her afar, his lonely bride / He turned and saw Gulnare the homicide."

Turmoil—sexual, emotional, political—is the subject of *The Corsair*, and Byron introduces the poem with lines from his favorite poet, Tasso: "*I suoi pensieri in lui dormir non ponno,* 'Within him his thoughts cannot sleep.' " Every conflict that ever gnawed at Byron now found passionate expression:

> There is a war, a chaos of the mind,
> When all its elements convulsed—combined—
> Lie dark and jarring with perturbed force,
> And gnashing with impenitent Remorse.[55]

Freed from the "petrifying stupidly platonic" sonnet form, Byron charged his heroic couplets with combat between this same platonic love and devouring lust; his sexual thralldom to Augusta tainted by guilt; the intense duet of desire, heightened by renunciation, that drew him to Lady Frances. (In an early version, Medora had been called Francesca.) The poet might be a prisoner of paradox and indecision, but his poem shines with a moral certainty wrested from suffering:

> Things light or lovely in their acted time,
> But now to stern reflection each a crime;
> The withering sense of evil unrevealed,
> Not cankering less because the more concealed—
> All, in a word, from which all eyes must start,
> That opening sepulchre—the naked heart.[56]

---

*Verdi's opera *Il Corsaro* was based on this work, one of the composer's favorite among Byron's poems. For greater dramatic intensity—providing the opportunity of a stirring duet—Verdi took the considerable liberty of having the two women meet following the Corsair's death.

Love alone, as violence or sacrifice, is redemptive: Conrad's capacity to feel and inspire love exalts him to heroic stature, assuring his immortality—and that of the most famous of Byron's last lines:

> He left a Corsair's name to other times,
> Linked with one virtue, and a thousand crimes.[57]

Politically, however, *The Corsair* throbs with hatred. By casting his hero in the anarchic role of outlaw, Byron has defined the perspective of the poem. The only moral response to the corruption of "legitimate" government—Regency England or post-Napoleonic France—lies with the individual who defines his own morality, be it the pirate as criminal or the slave who murders her tyrant master. Although sexually repelled by Gulnare as murderess, Conrad concedes (against received opinion that women killers were desexed by their act) that she transcended her guilt to retain a heroic femininity: "Extreme in love or hate, in good or ill, / The worst of crimes had left her woman still!" Byron's own sense of futility—the frustration of the impulse to do good—defines the corsair's tragedy: "Doomed by his very virtues for a dupe / He cursed those virtues as the cause of ill."

NEW YEAR'S DAY found Byron back in London. He had entrusted to Lord Holland the final copy of the poem intended for the printer, and he now instructed Murray to pick up the manuscript from Holland, making sure that Gifford received it that same night—January 2—as he counted on the critic to correct his punctuation. The patient publisher accepted these orders in good grace, just as he did his author's revisions, additions, and corrections. He expressed concern, however, about Byron's dedication to Tom Moore, praising his fellow poet as a great Irish patriot. Murray cited his fear that the label was a dangerous one, but Byron suspected the publisher, as a "damned Tory," was only interested in protecting "Self," he told Moore.[58] While poet and publisher were negotiating this politically sensitive issue, Murray was outraged to learn—only now—that Byron had made a gift of the copyright of *The Corsair* to Dallas, with express permission to publish it with any bookseller he pleased. As Byron knew, Dallas had fallen out with Murray, and his publisher saw this as a deliberate insult, tantamount to taking the poem away from him. Calling Byron's behavior "an act of consummate cruelty," he demanded to know how the poet was able "without motive, or object, & merely from caprice, to place me at the mercy of one, whom your Lordship told me, but a few days ago, would *never* forgive me."[59] Byron tried to make light of this apparent perfidy, due, most probably, to distraction. But he knew that he had behaved badly, and he promptly summoned Dallas to arrange matters. *The Corsair* remained with Murray.

Reparations were also in order to Lady Melbourne. Knowing full well her disapproval of his "perverse passion," Byron had neither written to nor called on his old confidante, declining even to attend her Twelfth Night banquet. Now she made known her suspicion—whose source may have been Caroline Lamb—that it was Augusta who had forbidden him to visit Whitehall. Byron also suspected Caro of having spread word that Augusta was separated from her husband and had stayed with Byron during her visit to London in December. Looking to "Lady M" to quash both rumors, and to divert her thoughts from Augusta, he tossed her a "confidence"—if a small one: Mary Ann Chaworth Musters, "my old love of all loves," had twice written to him. Now separated from her philandering fox hunter, she was ill and unhappy and longed to see Byron again. Clearly not tempted by the prospect of such a "melancholy interview," he nonetheless sought his confidante's advice, more to reestablish their good relations than because he required her counsel. At the same time, he disabused her of hope that Mary Ann Chaworth could distract him from Augusta: "It is impossible I should now feel anything beyond friendship for her or any *one* else in present circumstances—and the kind of feeling which has lately absorbed me has a mixture of the *terrible* which renders all other—even passion (*pour les autres*) insipid to a degree. . . ." As to his relations with Lady Frances, "I have quite resigned my pretensions in that quarter and every other."[60]

While Byron was staying at Six Mile Bottom, he had made plans with Augusta to visit Newstead. She had never seen the abbey, and he wanted them to be together at the place that meant more to him than any other. Newstead's sale gave a new urgency to their plans, which waited only for Augusta's recovery from a bout of illness.

IT WAS a January famous for freezing temperatures. In London the Thames was solid ice, covered by the tents and sideshows of the "Frost Fair," held, since the seventeenth century, during years of record cold. The roads in and out of the city were nearly impassable, banked with snow on both sides and rutted with the slippery tracks of those vehicles that managed to move. In one of these, a public coach without springs, a determined Augusta, six months pregnant, arrived in London on January 16; the next day, installed in Byron's roomy coach, they set out for Newstead on the only real honeymoon he would ever know.

CHAPTER 23

"The Hand That Kindles Cannot
Quench the Flame"

NCE LONDON was left behind, whiteness enveloped the travelers. In places the Great North Road disappeared in snowdrifts. Then the coach inched along or came to a complete halt. Snug in the thickly upholstered interior, the lovers were alone and invisible. There, or in the firelit room of a coaching inn, their pleasure in each other was enhanced by the drawn-out journey and the anticipation of arrival.

At the abbey, Augusta became part of Byron's world of feudal fantasy. The family portraits in the long gallery were, after all, her forebears, too. Old Joe Murray made sure that fires blazed in the Great Hall; in Byron's apartments, the opulent red and gold carpets and hangings (still, for the most part, unpaid for) glowed invitingly.

On January 22 Byron celebrated his birthday: "*Six* and *twenty* complete this day—a very pretty age if it would only last," he wrote to John Murray, adding cheerfully, "Our coals are excellent—our fireplaces large—my cellar full—and my head empty—and I have not yet recovered my joy at leaving London."[1]

Birthdays usually triggered depression, and the contrast between Byron's contentment now, snowbound with Augusta, and his gloomy year's-end thoughts, alone in London only weeks earlier, testifies to the power of her presence.

"At five-and-twenty, when the better part of life is over, one should be *something*," he had complained to his journal, "and what am I? nothing but five-and-twenty—and the odd months."[2]

Snow continued to fall, offering a continued excuse to delay their departure. His sister's advanced pregnancy, Byron explained to Murray, made further travel under present conditions out of the question. Their stay lengthened to almost a month, and for Augusta these weeks would be her happiest memory in a life of griefs and burdens. Twenty years later and a decade after Byron's death, she revisited Newstead, elaborately restored by its new owner. Byron's presence was everywhere still. Writing to a cousin, she excused her allusion to "our dear Abbey. . . . I say *our*—impossible to me to feel it is not *indisputably* connected with *our* Place. There is one comfort to life as pursued through present [pain] I prefer to live it *con amore.* . . . I retreat in memories so very dear to me. . . . I could not divest myself of being still a *child of the Abbey* and I saw his lost image *everywhere.*" As much as Byron loved the gray stone buildings, he was still more attached to the surrounding park, its lakes and trees; it was "particularly passing out of doors" that Augusta recalled her brother, or enjoying "his apartments looking on the lake . . . the dock and little Terrace walk near it—shaded by dark trees."[3] She does not trouble with propriety, detailing her familiarity with Byron's bedroom (now the present owner's, she explains) and his dressing room, where, during Augusta's visit, the poet had seen a ghost.

The last two days of their stay brought a visitor, Thomas Claughton, the young lawyer who had made the winning bid for the abbey, only to have second thoughts, meanwhile finding problems with every clause in the contract—even his right to the contents of Byron's cellar. With Hanson as mediator, delay was exponentially increased. Claughton's visit, however, proved so amicable that Byron felt reassured. Confident that all terms of the sale would be honored, he was able, before they left Newstead on February 6, to allay Augusta's anxiety about money. He could now discharge her husband's debts while also setting aside funds for her and the children that the profligate Colonel Leigh could not get his hands on. The previous fall, he had also changed his will: His estate was to be divided equally between George Anson Byron, his cousin and heir to the title, and his sister.

Welcome as these provisions were, Byron's most cherished legacy to Augusta was her memories of Newstead, "where if I could but live & die, it would seem to me I'd be only too happy."[4]

BYRON'S BUOYANT spirits at the end of their stay were not due solely to his unexpected rapport with Newstead's new owner, or even the restoring effects of more than three weeks of greater happiness than he had ever known. Before they left, he had a letter from Murray, dated February 3, with astounding news of *The Corsair*: "I sold on the day of publication, a thing perfectly unprecedented, 10,000 copies—and I suppose Thirty people who were purchasers (strangers) called to tell the people in the Shop how much they had been delighted and satisfied," the publisher reported jubilantly.5

Disdain as he did the mass appeal of his poems as a sign of artistic failure, no author could fail to be pleased at setting a sales record—and for poetry, a record that stands unbroken still. Replying to Murray's expression of regret that he was not in London to celebrate with him, Byron wrote: "I thank you for wishing me in town—but I think one's success is most savoured at a distance—& I enjoy my solitary self importance—in an agreeable sulky way of my own."6

Well publicized by the triumphant Murray, the phenomenon of *The Corsair*—best-seller in a single day—also roused Byron's enemies to action. Included in the same volume, among other occasional verse, was "Lines to a Lady Weeping," the savage, short philippic on the Prince Regent's betrayal of his Whig friends. When he had written it two years earlier, sending it to the *Morning Chronicle*, Byron had tacitly acknowledged the poem's provocative malice by insisting on anonymous publication. Emboldened by success, he now included the piece in this latest edition of his work. Neither the poet nor his publisher, however, predicted the explosive counterattack orchestrated by the Tory press. Arriving in London after an exhausting three-day journey from Newstead, held up by heavy rains and flooded roads, Byron now found himself vilified in print with a savagery he had never before experienced. The *Courier* recalled the earlier appearance of the "vile and anonymous stuff" in the *Morning Chronicle* two years before as "impudent doggrels [*sic*]."7 The Tory journals of opinion echoed the war cries of the daily press with their next issues. The *Anti-Jacobin* now came at Byron on another count: As a peer and "hereditary councillor of the Crown" he had abused his rank in a "scandalous reflection on an exalted personage; and a calumny on the nation." Criticism of the monarch was not merely libel but also treason; the poet was of that traitorous lot who "sees his native country, the pride of Britons, and the envy of the world; and he labours to degrade it in the eyes of all." In a rhetorical finale, the reviewer demanded, "Is it not natural to conclude from these circumstances that a conduct so perverse and unnatural, must spring from disordered imagination and a depraved heart?"

If lèse-majesté and treason were not enough, the *Anti-Jacobin* tossed in evidence of Byron's hypocrisy and greed. Unearthing a verse from *English Bards* in which the poet had mocked Sir Walter Scott for "yield[ing his muse]" for "half a crown a line" to Murray (now the publisher of both authors), his critic now sneered that "this magnanimous young Lord has actually sold his word" and in the process "pocketted [*sic*] a whole crown a line."[8] This last volley called into question Byron's social status: Gentlemen did not write for money. As he had made a gift of *The Corsair*'s copyright—worth £525—to Dallas, the accusation was untrue. Byron now wrote to his kinsman, hinting broadly that he should set the record straight. Hoping for similar favors to come, Dallas had no choice but to come to his benefactor's defense in print.

A Tory himself, Murray was appalled at what he clearly saw as cries for blood. Without discussing the matter with Byron, he quietly withdrew the offending lines from the later run of the second and from the third edition of *The Corsair*, deciding to bury the poem at the end of a new illustrated edition of *Childe Harold*, now in preparation. After some "second and third thoughts" on the matter Byron insisted that the lines should be reinstated in the next printing. If anything, the intensity of the attacks on him strengthened his resolve; to withdraw the offending poem "looks like shrinking and shuffling," he told Murray.[9] Receiving no reply, he wrote in high dudgeon on February 12: "You have played the Devil by that injudicious *suppression*—which you did totally without my consent—some of the papers have said exactly what might be expected—now I *do not* & *will not* be supposed to shrink—although myself & every thing belonging to me were to perish with my memory."[10]

The newspapers continued to savage him, their assaults turning more gleefully personal. Before he had even arrived back in London, Byron saw that the *Morning Post* "has found out that I am a sort of R[ichard] 3d deformed in mind & *body*—the *last* piece of information is not very new to a man who passed five years at a public school," he wrote to Murray, with weary irony.[11] One accusation, that he was the Devil himself ("*boiteux*, I presume," Byron added), he suspected to be a "female's conjecture," which says more about his own fear of women than it does about his demonizing critic. His retort was a lewd classical allusion; if he and his accuser were ever to meet, he would convince her that a deformed male was superior to the devil in sexual attributes; according to an Amazon queen quoted in a Greek fragment, "The lame animal covers best."

Despite the cool he affected with most of the world, the "abuse against me in all directions . . . vehement, unceasing, loud"—had affected him, he wrote to Moore, confessing, "My friends desire me not to be in a passion, and like Sir Fretful, I assure them that I am 'quite calm, but I am nevertheless in a fury.' "[12]

Returning to Bennet Street, he found, among the mountains of mail awaiting him, a letter from Annabella. With Lady Melbourne, he had cackled over her niece's pious hair-splitting and moral attitudinizing. To his journal, however, Byron's thoughts about Annabella were admiring to the point of worship: "She is a very superior woman, and very little spoiled, which is strange in an heiress—a girl of twenty—a peeress that is to be—in her own right—an only child and a *savante* who has always had her own way. She is a poetess—a mathematician—a metaphysician, and yet withal, very kind, generous, and gentle, with very little pretension. Any other head would be turned with half her acquisitions, and a tenth of her advantages."[13]

He found himself puzzled by her guilty feelings and tortuous confessions: Had she led him on? Did she or did she not care for another? He tried, nonetheless, to reassure her: "You never did—never for an instant—trifle with me or amuse me with what is called encouragement—a thing by the bye—which men are continually supposing they receive without sufficient grounds."[14]

Byron was not the only one to be perplexed; it was becoming evident to Annabella that the contents of her letters to Bennet Street seemed known in Whitehall. But she never suspected Byron as the source of the leak. Instead, she warned her mother to tell Lady Melbourne nothing of her confidences, only that she had her parents' permission to write to her new suitor. She was sufficiently uneasy, however, about the friendship between the older woman and the poet to cautiously try to sound out Byron's "opinion" of her aunt.

Critical of other friends, Byron was unwaveringly loyal to his confidante, and he readily confessed himself to Annabella as incapable of impartial judgment of Lady Melbourne, starting with his "indebtedness to her for my acquaintance with yourself." Beyond her aunt's superior talents, she was "a *supreme* woman—& her heart I know to be of the kindest—in the best sense of the word. Her defects I could never perceive—as her society makes me forget them & everything else for the time.—I do love that woman (*filially* or *fraternally*) better than any being on earth."[15]

More than most, Byron demanded not merely to be loved, but to be loved best, and with possible competition from her daughter Emily, he might reasonably believe himself to be the *only* human being whom "Ly M" cared for. He repaid this privileged state with complete devotion and trust. She might destroy others; she would always defend and protect him.

Another trusted friend, Hobhouse, was back in London after eight months of travel on the Continent, just in time to greet Byron on his return from Newstead. In the emotional upheavals of the past year, Byron had felt his absence keenly. Now, over many late nights and empty bottles, they caught up at leisure. Hobhouse's sexual experience, however, had progressed no further than shamefaced transactions with Athenian whores; Byron felt unable to confide to such a moral innocent the agonies of his affair with Augusta. Naïve though he might be, Hobhouse was nonetheless an attentive and intelligent audience. After many hours of listening to Byron, he compared his impressions with those of Douglas Kinnaird, his recent traveling companion and a man of the world. Although less privy to their mutual friend's confidences, Kinnaird, as it turned out, harbored the same suspicions as Hobhouse about the cause of Byron's agitated state—too "terrible" to be named.

Then, in early March, Byron was party to a bizarre scandal with strange foreshadowings of the future. Out of the blue, John Hanson asked him to give away his older daughter, Mary Ann, now twenty-four, in marriage to the Earl of Portsmouth, a forty-seven-year-old widower. The timing of the request was in itself odd: the day before the ceremony, at St. Stephen's, Bloomsbury, was to take place, on March 8.

As a schoolboy staying with the Hansons, Byron had had an ugly encounter with Portsmouth; on that occasion the older peer, with no provocation whatsoever, had viciously attacked him, pulling his ears. Byron had struck back with such ferocity that the two had to be forcibly separated. What Byron did not know—or so he later claimed—was that Portsmouth had since his own childhood been infamous for acts of sadism toward women, children, servants, and animals—whoever was powerless enough to have no recourse against him. Variously ascribed to eccentricity, mental retardation, or lunacy, his behavior, but for his rank, would have surely had led to his being committed long before. As Hanson was a trustee of Portsmouth's estate, appointed by the family to prevent the weak-minded Earl from wasting its assets, the lawyer could have been in little doubt about his future son-in-law's liabilities.

Evidence shows that the bridegroom had no idea that he was participating in a marriage ceremony—his own: He had arrived at the Hansons' on the morning of the wedding, unkempt and in filthy clothes, to be hustled into an appropriate costume and off to church. Mrs. Hanson did not attend the ceremony; rumored to be brokenhearted, she died a week later.

Byron acknowledged that he and the bride had enjoyed a mild flirtation; while a schoolboy, he had himself promised to make her a peeress, her younger brother reported. In another account, however, Byron later confessed that he had seduced her, and that while escorting the bride down the aisle, he had diverted her with lewd reminders of her sexual initiation. This version has been questioned—but Mary Ann's role in colluding with her father to trap the insane peer into marriage is a matter of public record.*[16] The marriage was annulled in 1822 at the behest of her husband's family.

In the wake of the scandal and the annulment, Mary Ann disappeared without a trace, leaving three children (one of them named Byron); her father was a ruined man.

When informed a decade later of the aftermath of the wedding, Byron was strangely defensive: "I saw nothing particular in the marriage," he told Hobhouse. "Of course, I could not know the preliminaries, except from what he [Hanson] said, not having been present at the wooing, nor after it. . . . I regret very much that I was present at the prologue to the happy state of horse whipping . . . etc. etc.," he wrote, altering his role from key participant to guest "but I could not foresee that a man was to turn out mad who had gone about the world for years as competent to vote and walk at large; nor did he seem to me more insane than any other person going to be married."[17]

Meanwhile, Byron continued his epistolary courtship of Annabella. "You do not know how much I wish to see you," he wrote on March 15, "for there are so many things *said* in a moment—but tedious on the tablets." He had recently had repeated to him a report that she had refused him " 'a *second* time'. . . *I* care not how often it is repeated—it would plague me more to hear that I was *accepted* by anybody else than rejected by you."[18]

Those who claim that Byron never cared for Annabella, that his was a cold-blooded effort to find a wife, have dismissed his declarations to her as the gallantries required of a gentleman who addressed a marriageable young woman. Byron's journal entries for these same weeks, however, provide crucial evidence that he meant exactly what he wrote: "A letter from *Bella* which I answered," he wrote on the same day— March 15. "I shall be in love with her again, if I don't take care."[19]

For the present, he confirmed his bachelor status by moving into Albany House in Piccadilly, the most stylish new address in London for gentlemen about town. By a curious coincidence, the large brick mansion, separated from the thoroughfare by a courtyard, had been built for Lord and Lady Melbourne shortly after their marriage. "So you are settled in Albany," she wrote to him, "where most of my happiest days were passed!—whilst I lived in that house no misfortune reached me &

---

*In the sensational evidence that emerged in annulment proceedings brought by the Earl's brother in 1822, Mary Ann, aided by her sister Laura and by her lover, held the Earl prisoner and in total isolation, torturing him with a sadism equal to his own.

I should not have disliked to be an appendage to ye lease," adding, "Every despairing and distressing event of my life has happened since I lived in Whitehall." She had not spent much time in the rooms that now constituted his ground-floor apartment, but she well remembered their "pleasant and useful furnishings"; she thought he would have liked two pictures that hung in what was now his sitting room: a view of Constantinople against a particularly beautiful sky, and a depiction of Joseph fleeing from Potiphar's wife, "this last offering—of which I do not mean to say you seem'd in need—but there can be no disadvantage in having a good example before your eyes."[20]

Byron's rooms are still today the most desirable of Albany "sets," as they came to be known. His sitting room, where he wrote and received friends, soars two floors in height; three arched windows reaching from floor to ceiling look out onto the garden. A vaulted wine cellar on the floor below tells us a good deal about his social calendar; he drank at home and dined out.

By April 2, the day when Lady Melbourne's pointed warning had reached Albany, Byron, leaving his belongings half unpacked, was installed at Six Mile Bottom. Colonel Leigh had gone off to Yorkshire, and Byron had promptly obeyed Augusta's summons. He was to have joined Hobhouse and Scrope Davies for a party in Cambridge on the fifth, but once he and Augusta were together, he found it impossible to leave, although the mayhem of her disorganized household was hardly the idyll of Newstead in January. It was a time to be helpful rather than amorous; Augusta was within weeks of giving birth. The three children adored him—especially his favorite, the eldest, Georgiana—and he was an indulgent and amusing companion to them. Without other distractions, he abandoned his diet. Despite no noticeable weight gain, he felt out of condition, and on his return to town on April 8, he went back to sparring regularly with Jackson; Byron's physical complaints soon disappeared. His mind, too, he recorded in his journal, was "much relieved" by repaying Scrope Davies £4,800 owed him—"a debt of some standing," Byron noted with some understatement, it being five years overdue.[21]

After his few days of freedom with Augusta, the London social round seemed emptier than ever: "Last night, *party* at Landsdowne House. To-night, *party* at Lady Charlotte Greville—deplorable waste of time.... Nothing imparted—nothing acquired—talking without ideas— if anything like *thought* in my mind, it was not on the subjects on which we were gabbling.... Tomorrow—there is Lady Heathcote's shall I go? yes—to punish myself for not having a pursuit."[22] But in fact, he went out most evenings, and not only to punish himself for not writing; he went out of loneliness, boredom, depression, or in the hope of an encounter, with a beautiful woman, a savant, or a wit—anything to take him from himself, as he said writing poetry did. He was perfectly capable of spending four nights and days without seeing a living soul—but he would then make up for it, abandoning that same self to any diversion that offered. Dutifully, sometimes even with pleasure, he scrutinized the eligible young women: At Lady Heathcote's he was taken with the Marquess of Stafford's daughter, Lady Charlotte Leveson-Gower. With Lady Charlotte, however, there was a problem: Lord Carlisle was her uncle by marriage, and although Augusta—among others—had sought to mollify Byron, he remained mulishly determined never to forgive his guardian and kinsman for refusing to ease his entry into the House of Lords. Especially now that his parliamentary hopes had been blasted, Byron seemed to need this grudge more than ever.

Dissipating his energy on the social round neither distracted him from Augusta nor compensated for his failure to work: "I must set about some employment soon: my heart begins to eat *itself* again," he wrote desperately at the end of March.[23]

A week later, on April 9, he learned that Napoleon had abdicated at Fontainebleau three days before. No other world event could have aroused Byron to such a pitch of feeling: "I mark this day," he wrote momentously in his journal.[24]

His first reaction was compassion: "My poor little pagod . . . pushed off his pedestal; the thieves are in Paris." But he immediately qualified his pity: "It is his own fault." Comparing his fallen idol to rulers who had departed with some shreds of glory intact—Scylla, Diocletian, the Sultan Murad IV, Charles V—Byron rated Napoleon "worst of all." It was not the Emperor's defeat but his self-serving dishonesty that earned his contempt: "What! Wait till they were in his capital, and then talk of his readiness to give up what is already gone! the 'Isle of Elba' to retire to!" Still, the poet who styled himself "the Napoleon of Rhyme" would not find it easy to rid himself of a complicated mix of feelings about his former hero, who since Byron's boyhood had seduced him with a powerful sense of identity. "I am utterly bewildered and confounded," he conceded.[25]

This time the immediate drama of history roused him into poetry: "Today I have boxed one hour—written an Ode to Napoleon Buonaparte—copied it—eaten six biscuits—drunk one bottle of soda water," he recorded the next night in the shorthand style that signaled a burst of energy and high spirits.[26]

The *Ode to Napoleon Buonaparte* is the first of Byron's efforts to explore the meaning of the man who cast the largest shadow over nineteenth-century Europe and Byron's own generation. The staccato verses riddle the fallen despot with ironies, like shot: "The Desolator desolate! / The Victor overthrown! / The Arbiter of other's fate / A Suppliant for his own!"[27] But there is also a gloating tone to his images of the humiliated ruler that reveals a sense of personal betrayal. Napoleon's defeat, the downfall of the individual as superman, struck at Byron's own Promethean strivings: "Nor till thy fall could mortals guess / Ambition's less than littleness!"[28]

Excited by a poem of such topicality from the best-selling poet of the hour, Murray was in a fever to publish the *Ode* as soon as the type could be set. He needed only a few more verses, he told his author, to avoid the stamp tax imposed on pamphlets of a single sheet. But after insisting that the fourth edition of *The Corsair* include his earlier poem attacking the Prince Regent under his own name, Byron now wanted his *Ode* on the downfall of England's archenemy published anonymously. The only explanation was his reluctance to give comfort to the Tory establishment by appearing to make common cause with them in demonizing the "Corsican ogre." In any case, he coyly informed Murray, "you may *say* openly as you like that it is mine."[29]

Hobhouse, meanwhile, still more obsessed with the fallen Emperor than Byron, had decided to go to Paris to witness whatever he could of the tumultuous events following one upon another. Over a bibulous dinner at the Cocoa Tree Club, Byron agreed to accompany him. But the next morning's mail brought word from Claughton that he was unable to make the £5,000 payment due on the Newstead mortgage, and Byron wrote to Hobhouse regretting that "business and other concerns" obliged him to cancel his travel plans.

Principal among the other concerns was Augusta's approaching confinement. Two days later, on April 15, she was delivered of a daughter, christened Elizabeth Medora; the baby's second name was the same as *The Corsair*'s heroine, Conrad's lover, fianceé, or wife—Byron had left their official relationship unclear. This was "their" poem. He had arrived at Six Mile Bottom with a rough draft, and in Augusta's presence he had written and revised, returning to London with the finished work.

Evidence more persuasive than the poem's place of authorship or the baby's name points to Byron's paternity. In response to Lady Melbourne's attempts to warn him of the consequences of his liaison— could Byron still believe the risk he ran was "worth while?"—he had replied: "Oh! but it is 'worth while'—I can't tell you why—and it is *not* an '*Ape*' and if it is—that must be my fault."[30]

These lines have been subject to more analysis than any others he wrote, including his poetry. Alluding to the folk belief that the child of incest will be an ape,* his announcement of the infant's normalcy has been taken to mean that his paternity had not been exposed.

Flippant assurance that their sin did not stand revealed would not, as Byron knew, suffice to allay Lady Melbourne's fears. He needed her approbation, moreover, not only as a friend, but also, if he was to pursue his courtship of Annabella, as a prospective aunt. Thus, immediately after this oblique confession, he turned penitent, promising, "I will positively reform—you must however allow—that it is utterly impossible I can ever be half as well liked elsewhere—and I have been trying all my life to make some one love me. . . . But positively she & I will grow good."[32]

With her parents' approval, Annabella had invited Byron to Seaham, and he was torn between accepting or returning to Six Mile Bottom and Augusta. As though to symbolize his conflict, he bought a parrot and a macaw—the first denizens of what would become a large and loudly quarrelsome menagerie of birds, animals, and reptiles. He now retreated into his spacious new Albany quarters, emerging only to maintain his physique: "I have got up my books; and I box and fence daily; and go out very little," he wrote to Moore.[33]

Then, out of the blue, he announced his intention to stop writing. With no explanation, he sent Murray a draft to cover the reversion of his copyrights to the author, releasing the publisher from his earlier offer (to have been settled in Easter 1814) to pay Byron £1,000 for *The Giaour* and *The Bride*. He further noted: "I expect and request—that the advertisements be withdrawn—and the remaining copies of *all* be destroyed,"[34] with the exception of two copies of each poem that the publisher would be allowed to keep for himself. Other than admitting to "caprice," he felt no obligation to explain his motive, he told Murray in his most high-handed tone. To Moore, however, he was more forthcoming: "No more rhyme for—or rather, *from* me. . . . I have had my day, and there's an end." Then, as though reciting his own eulogy, he observed, "My great comfort is, that the temporary celebrity I have wrung from the world has been in the very teeth of all opinions and

---

*Seen as a degenerate human form, the ape became a medieval symbol of the Fall of Man, illustrating the "biological degradation that results from defiance of a divine or quasi-divine injunction,"[31] of which incest was a prime example. Sexual transgression and its consequences, however, were traditionally sins of the female. As Byron often alluded to the association of lameness with the devil, his remark that if the child was an ape, it had been his fault is a double allusion to his paternity.

prejudices. I have flattered no ruling powers: I have never concealed a single thought that tempted me. They can't say I have trucked to the times, nor to popular topics . . . and whatever I have gained has been at the expenditure of as much personal favour as possible; for I do believe never was a bard more unpopular *Quod homo* than myself."

This was the irony that would shape the rest of his life. Public opinion was turning Byron the man into a pariah, even as Byron the poet established, only to surpass, his own new records of success. In the same weeks that he had suddenly decided to write no more, he was informed of a pirated Irish edition of his juvenile satire *English Bards and Scotch Reviewers*, and was astonished by news of his popularity in America. Recently, a verse attack on him had been submitted to Murray, who showed him the piece, titled "Anti-Byron." Then "that fool of a publisher," as Byron called him, loyally rejected it. A shrewd publicist, Byron recognized that such an attack constituted the best proof of his place at the storm center of literary celebrity.

"I never felt myself important, till I saw and heard of my being such a little Voltaire as to induce such a production," he crowed to Moore.[35] His vow of silence, however, was not to last; a few days later, he rescinded his orders to Murray as peremptorily as he had issued them.

He was no closer to resolving his most pressing personal dilemma: Should he accept Annabella's invitation to Seaham? He tried teasing Lady Melbourne into making his decision for him, but she refused to rise to the bait. Byron had told her of his fear that gossip would make him look ridiculous: a twice-rejected suitor traveling the length of England to plead his case. Lady M replied: "Nonsense . . . you go there in perfect liberty to behave like a friend—or disclose yourself as a lover." Then, revealing her own version of a happy ending, she predicted, "I don't think *you will fall* in love with her—that you may think her a proper person to marry is just possible."[36]

Already, Byron played with the possibilities of a future relationship between Annabella and Augusta—"*Your* A. and *my* A" he called them,[37] for he had begun sending both women's letters in one packet to Whitehall. To this mischievous fantasy, Lady M replied suavely that Annabella "will understandably make a friend (a female one) of any person you may point out & *all friends* is very much to be wished."[38]

As though Byron didn't have troubles enough, Caroline Lamb now reappeared for an operatic last act. The evidence of his relations with both "A"s floating around Melbourne House had the effect of lighting a match to her jealousy. No corner was safe from her snooping, Lady

Melbourne complained, but given the Spider's fondness for torturing her daughter-in-law, it is unlikely that Caro had to force open any drawers. During these spring weeks, Byron himself welcomed Caroline occasionally to his Albany chambers. To Lady Melbourne he denied any renewal of their sexual relations. Caro's version—that in a tender spirit of farewell, they were briefly lovers again—is in keeping with the self-dramatizing duet that was their affair. At the very least, her account of what Byron told her in the course of her visits to Albany points to a privileged intimacy: He apparently made full confession of his sexual relations with John Edleston, his seduction of his young page Robert Rushton, and his present affair with Augusta. In one of her last known letters to Byron, she begged: "Tell your sister to try & not dislike me. I am very unworthy of her and I know it & feel it but as I may not love you nor see you, let her not judge me harshly. . . . Tell her I feel my faults my crime sooner—but try & make her forgive me, if you can, for I love that Augusta with my heart because she is yours and is dear to you."[39]

Lady Melbourne could no longer pretend to such indulgence. Augusta had become a rival, more feared and hated than Caroline had ever been. Besides thwarting her marriage plans for Byron and Annabella, she was leading her beloved friend to ruin and probably exile. It was not to be tolerated, and with rare open savagery, she wrote to Byron, laying all the blame for his "terrible" situation on his sister.

Stricken, Byron tried to make amends. He knew he had betrayed Augusta, delivering her to Lady M and to Caro in the form of her most self-incriminating words. He was also aware that reading only one side of their exchange necessarily diminished his own role in their affair. Guiltily, he now sprang to Augusta's defense: "You—or rather I have done my A—much injustice," he told Lady Melbourne. "It must be some selfish stupidity of mine in telling my own story—but really and truly—as I hope mercy & happiness for her—by that God who made me for my own Misery—& not much for the good of others—she was not to blame—one thousandth part in comparison—she was not aware of her own peril—till it was too late—and I can only account for her subsequent 'abandon'* by an observation that I think is not unjust—that women are more attached than men—if they are treated with anything like fairness or tenderness."[40]

Impossibly, he determined to protect Augusta and their love while

---

*It is unclear whether Byron is quoting Augusta or Lady Melbourne, as no letter from either woman using the word "abandon" has survived.

promising Lady Melbourne that he would try—with all his will—to end their affair. He only insisted that she acknowledge Augusta's moral superiority, "excepting our one *tremendous* fault. I know her to be in point of temper and goodness of heart almost unequalled; now grant me this, that she is in truth a very loveable woman and I will try and not love her any longer." As proof of her goodness, she wanted only the best for him, wholeheartedly endorsing his match with Annabella; "as long as *la Tante* approves" had been his sister's only—and typically deferential—qualification. Confronted by the generosity of Augusta's love, revealed on every page of her artless letters, even the Spider succumbed to feelings of "melancholy," she wrote.

"It is indeed a very triste and extraordinary business," Byron replied, "& what is to become of us I know not."[41]

In these same weeks of early May, he received a request from Tom Moore asking for some verses he could set to music and sing. Sending his friend a poem he called "an experiment," Byron noted that the five stanzas* "cost me something more than trouble."[42] Most probably the lines were too painful for Moore's drawing room audiences. They were never published in Byron's lifetime.

> I speak not—I trace not—I breathe not thy name.
> There is grief in the sound—there were guilt in the fame;
> . . . .
> We repent—we abjure—we will break from our chain;
> We must part—we must fly to—unite it again.
>
> Oh! thine be the gladness and mine be the guilt,
> Forgive me adored one—forsake if thou wilt;
> But the heart which I bear shall expire undebased,
> And man shall not break it—whatever thou may'st.[43]

Struggling to express his pain through poetry, Byron triumphed over deadly inertia. He began work on a new poem, *Lara*, a sequel to *The Corsair*. Conrad, now rechristened Lord Lara, has abandoned piracy in the Mediterranean to return to his ancestral castle in an unidentified land. He is accompanied only by his devoted page, Kaled, later revealed as Gulnare, former favorite of Pasha Seyd. Forgiven by Conrad/Lara

---

*These were enclosed in a letter to Moore dated May 4, 1814, and later called "Stanzas for Music." The poem was not published until 1827–1829.

for murdering her master to set him free, Kaled/Gulnare is now a slave by choice.

On several levels *Lara* represents both continuity and resolution. Politically, Byron's depiction of the carnage of battle extends the anti-war canvas begun in *Childe Harold*. No contemporary "war poet" has gone further in deromanticizing death on the battlefield:

> That panting thirst which scorches in the breath
> Of those that die the soldier's fiery death,
> In vain impels the burning mouth to crave
> One drop—the last—to cool it for the grave.[44]

At the same time, this last and longest of Byron's Oriental tales kills off its generic hero—his death in battle constituting the poem's crescendo of dramatic narrative. Lara, the mysterious and feared leader of men, is then revealed as a suffering prisoner of his own grieving conscience; dying, he experiences self-awareness as the ultimate futility:

> Chain'd to excess, the slave of each extreme,
> How woke he from the wildness of that dream?
> Alas! he told not—but he did awake
> To curse the wither'd heart that would not break.[45]

Like other Byronic heroes, Lara is tormented by a guilty secret. Awakened from night terrors, he is heard to whisper: "*That* must not be known." Kaled, too, deprived of reason before joining her master in death, dies with "Her tale untold—her truth too dearly prov'd."

In an early version, *Lara,* unlike *Childe Harold* and other Oriental tales, came with a key to its hero's guilty secret. Byron subsequently suppressed the poem's original twenty-four opening lines, which offered a valedictory hymn to Augusta:

> When she is gone—the loved—the lost—the one
> Whose smile hath gladdened though perchance undone—
> Whose name too dearly cherished to impart
> Dies on the lip but trembles in the heart.

The final couplet of the omitted prelude begins with Byron's usual salutation in his letters to Augusta, "Oh best and dearest."

> Meantime the tale I weave must mournful be—
> As absence to the heart that lives on thee.[46]

On May 24 Elizabeth Medora Leigh, not quite six weeks old, was christened at home in Six Mile Bottom. There is no evidence that Byron was present at the ceremony, and it seems likely that declining to attend his niece's christening had been another of Lady Melbourne's counsels.

By June Byron was trying—yet again—to rid himself of an importunate Caroline Lamb. She had taken to appearing in his rooms uninvited and at all hours. Entering in his absence, she rummaged through his belongings, just as she had done when their affair ended more than a year before. Knowing that he had no one but himself to blame for this only added to Byron's fury. He became convinced that his obsession with Augusta was a mocking reflection of Caro's crazed pursuit of him: "I am as mad as C., on a different topic and in a different way; for I never break out in scenes, but am not a whit more in my senses," he told Lady Melbourne.[47]

Seeing his own irrationality exposed in another's behavior sent him into paroxysms of rage and fear: "She may hunt me down—it is the power of any mad or bad woman to do so by any man. . . . Torment me she may; how am I to bar myself from her! I am already almost a prisoner; she has no shame, no feeling, no one estimable or redeeming quality."

In his panic he now talked wildly of flight as the only alternative, nor would he flee alone, he threatened: "My first object in such a dilemma would be to take [Augusta] with me," he told Lady Melbourne.[48]

His confidante had done everything she could; Byron was no longer reachable by reason, she decided. "I cannot reproach myself with having omitted anything in my power to prevent the mischief and calamity that must happen," she wrote to him on June 10, adding that whatever forgiveness there might be for their crime in this world, there was no salvation in the next.[49]

"I would rather lose a hundred souls than be bound to C," Byron replied. He did, however, try to reassure her on another issue: Did he intend to marry her niece while remaining his sister's lover?

"If I pursued and succeeded in that quarter," he declared, "of course I must give up all other pursuits—and the fact is that my wife if she had common sense would have more power over me—than any other whatsoever—for my heart always alights on the nearest *perch*."[50]

The heart as a caged bird, restricted and dependent—the imagery of these lines contrasts his own helplessness vis-à-vis the power that a woman would gain over him *if* she had the skill to manipulate and the desire to dominate. Unerringly, he had fixed on the one young woman who possessed neither.

CHAPTER 24

"A Wife Is My Salvation"

HE SUMMER of the Sovereigns" Byron called it, and eight years later, in 1822, he wrote to Moore from Italy: "Do you recollect, in the year of revelry 1814, the pleasantest parties and balls all over London?"[1]

Exile and nostalgia had by then softened his very mixed feelings during the weeks when the brilliance that illumined the city—processions, masques, fireworks—celebrated the British victory over Napoleon and the Bourbon restoration. Besides Louis XVIII himself, June also brought to London Czar Alexander of Russia; the King of Prussia; Prince Metternich, the chess master of the Congress of Vienna; and the military hero Blücher, along with platoons of bemedaled and bejeweled generals, ministers, and their consorts.

On July 3, Byron set out for Six Mile Bottom. He had not seen Augusta since the week before the baby was born, and this was his first glimpse of Elizabeth Medora; first called Libby, she seems to have assumed her Byronic second name just after her godfather's visit. He stayed only a few days, but before leaving, Byron and Augusta made plans to spend the rest of the month together with her children at the seaside. Then he was off to join Hobhouse, Scrope Davies, and Douglas Kinnaird in Cambridge. Emptying many bottles of claret, they weighed the possibility of Hobhouse's winning the constituency's parliamentary seat.

Returning to town on July 7, Byron was greeted by the unwelcome news that Claughton had defaulted on the Newstead purchase—definitively, this time, "and so all my hopes and worldly projects and prospects are gone to the devil," Byron wrote to Moore. A meeting was scheduled for the following day, when Byron, Hanson, and the unhappy

Claughton (who had nervously inquired whether the poet was going to greet him "with temper") would discuss what could be salvaged from the agreement and the one payment already received. Byron agonized between two impoverishing possibilities: "The question is this—I shall either have the estate back, which is as good as ruin, or I shall go on with him dawdling, which is rather worse."[2]

A less painful matter to be decided, in consultation with Murray, was the form in which *Lara*, his latest doomed hero, would make his appearance in print. Once again Byron shrank from the idea of a separate volume, but this time there was no possibility of slipping the new poem unobtrusively into an edition of other verse. An alternative under discussion was the publication of *Lara* and Samuel Rogers's new work, *Jacqueline*, in one volume. For the next weeks, the marriage and divorce of "Jacky" and "Larry," as Byron dubbed the off again, on again merger, was subject to many changes of mind, before they finally appeared in company together on August 5.

One decision, at least, came easily. Hastings, on the Sussex coast, was Byron's choice for a seaside vacation, and he now asked Francis Hodgson, already installed there to be near his new fiancée, to find him a suitable house. Cost was no object, only "it must be good and tolerably large—as Mrs. Leigh—her 4 children—& three maids will be there also—besides my own valet & footman," he instructed Hodgson.[3] His coachman and horses would be boarded out, as would one of the two cooks he would hire locally (they would need another to live in). With the size of the household and numbers of young children—"all fine but damnable squallers"—he further implored Hodgson to "let my bedroom be some way from the *Nursery* or children's apartments and let the Women be near together and as far from me as possible."[4] Along with putting as much distance between himself, "the Women," and noise, Byron was also ensuring that when alone with Augusta, they would have as much privacy as possible.

Within days, Hodgson had found a house for the month, and on July 20, Byron set out from London in a convoy of coaches carrying Augusta and her household, with his cousin and heir Captain George Byron, arriving in Hastings late the same day.

A square Queen Anne building with a dozen bedrooms, Hastings House proved the ideal retreat. And if Newstead in January had been a honeymoon, Hastings in summer was a family vacation. Enveloped by Augusta's love and among children, servants, and friends, Byron relaxed into the sense of domestic well-being he always craved and could never take for granted; here he was father and child, husband, lover, and host. Then there was the pure happiness of water, his element; the moment he was near the sea, he began to thrive. In his expansiveness, he gave up dieting—he ate and drank with gusto. The unaccustomed indulgence of food was offset by exercise: He swam for at least an hour every morning and did much walking, the steep roads doubly strenuous with his limp: "I have drunk two bottles of Claret—and I have hobbled two miles *up* hill—and stumbled as many down hill," he wrote happily to Hobhouse.[5]

Hodgson's chatter about his wedding plans and the declaration of a recently married friend from Harrow and Trinity, Harry Erskine, also summering in Hastings, that he was the "happiest of men" reminded Byron of his own impasse with Annabella. The rhythm of their correspondence can only be characterized as occurring by fits and starts; on Byron's side, pages were covered with excuses: why he had failed to reply immediately to her last, why he was obliged to delay his answer to Sir Ralph's invitation; or else by attempts to clarify "misunderstandings," to explain his "*ambiguous* expression" and Annabella's "perplexity."[6] This was met by mounting frustration from Seaham. Annabella offered, "If I am in any respect mysterious to you, if you desire any explanation of past or present, you will believe that I shall give it most willingly," and she implored, "Above all, do not conceal anything from reluctance to give me pain."[7]

Meanwhile, Byron and Augusta went over the arguments for and against marriage with Annabella. Neither was in any doubt that if Byron proposed this time, he would be accepted. And marry he must; this was no longer an issue. Whatever misgivings Augusta harbored about Miss Milbanke's cerebral, excessively rational cast of mind—a perspective gained from books, not life—her own candidate, Lady Charlotte Leveson-Gower, was not a strong alternative. This time, however, he could hardly have exaggerated the tragicomedy of his situation: Attempting to carry on a courtship while savoring perfect happiness with his real family was more than Byron could bear, and it fell to Augusta to keep him at the task.

One night, trying to write and failing utterly, he gave vent to his frustration: "I got in a passion with an ink bottle, which I flung out of the window . . . with a vengeance," he told Moore, "and what then? why, next morning I was horrified by seeing that it had struck and split [sic] upon, the petticoat of Euterpe's graven image in the garden, and grimed her as if it were on purpose." He added archly, "only think of my distress—and the epigrams that might be engendered upon the Muse and her misadventure."[8] More symbolically, in staining the lead statue he had blackened the muse of music, a divinity associated with joy and pleasure. The holiday was over.

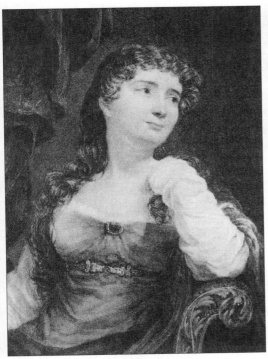

During her second London season in 1812, Annabella Milbanke sat for this portrait by Sir George Hayter, who wanted her to wear her hair down in the careful disarray of curls favored by Regency belles. Annabella refused, saying it was not "in the nature of my character."

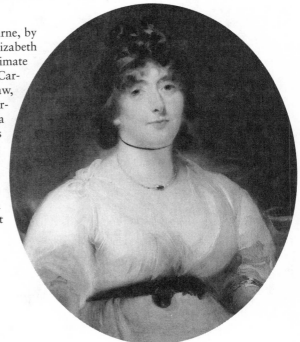

A portrait of Lady Melbourne, by Sir Thomas Phillips. Née Elizabeth Milbanke, Byron's intimate friend and confidante was Caroline Lamb's mother-in-law, and, upon the poet's marriage to her niece Annabella Milbanke, she became his aunt as well. Known as "the Spider" for her malice and stealthy mischief-making, it was said of her that she could never see a happy marriage without trying to destroy it.

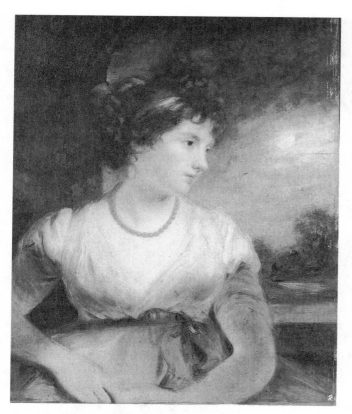

A portrait of Jane Elizabeth, Countess of Oxford, by John Hoppner. The free-thinking daughter of a vicar, she never allowed marriage to stand in the way of her many affairs. In 1813, Byron spent long passionate weeks at Eywood, Lord and Lady Oxford's country house.

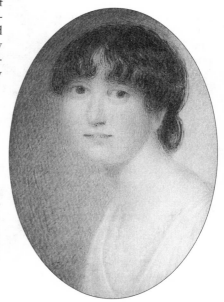

This portrait of Annabella Milbanke, Lady Byron, by an unknown artist, emphasizes her round face and apple cheeks, making it clear why Byron, in the few happy days of their marriage, called his wife "Pippin," shortened to "Pip."

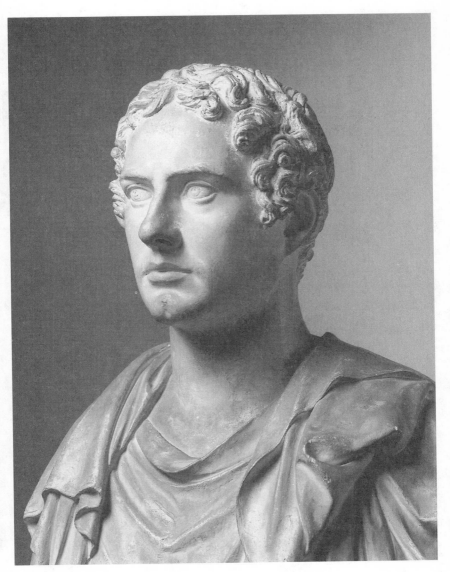

Byron, by Bertel Thorvaldsen. Hobhouse arranged for Byron to sit for the eminent Danish sculptor Bertel Thorvaldsen during the poet's visit to Rome in 1817. By all accounts, the two did not get on; Byron felt that the Dane was insufficiently impressed with his rank and importance, while the sculptor found Byron's romantic view of himself artificial: "He was, above all things, so desirous of looking unhappy," the artist observed.

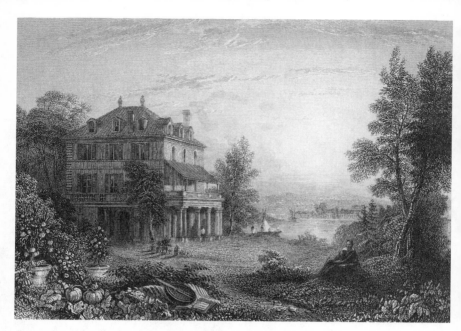

Byron rented Villa Diodati in the hills above Lake Geneva in June 1817 and stayed there for four months, during which time the Shelleys and Claire Clairmont, pregnant with Byron's child, installed themselves nearby.

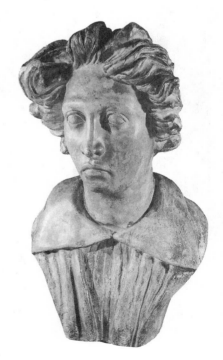

A wooden bust of Percy Bysshe Shelley attributed to Marianne, Leigh Hunt's wife.

This portrait of Claire Clairmont, age twenty-one, is the only surviving likeness of the young woman who "pressed" her love upon Byron just before his flight from England, and who lived to suffer from, if not to regret, her obsession with him.

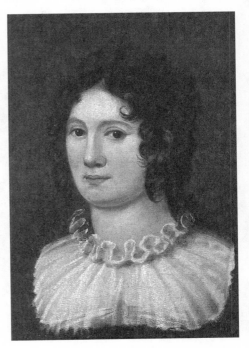

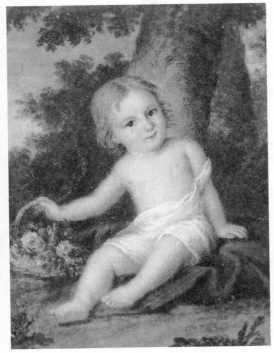

A portrait of Allegra, Byron's "little illegitimate," as he called his daughter by Claire Clairmont.

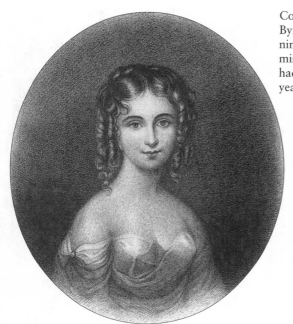

Countess Teresa Guiccioli was Byron's "last attachment." Aged nineteen when she became his mistress in Venice in 1819, she had been married for little over a year.

In September 1821, the four-year-old Allegra wrote to her father, asking him to take her to the local fair. Byron never replied and moved to Pisa at the end of October without visiting the child, who died the following April.

Caro il mio Pappa

Essendo tempo di Fiera desidererei tanto una visita del mio Pappa, che ho molte voglie da levarmi, non vorrà compiacere la sua Allegrina che l'ho ama tanto?

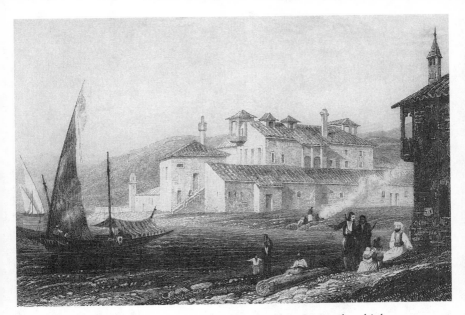

Along with primitive living conditions, low-lying Missolonghi became a malarial swamp in the spring rains that began soon after Byron's arrival. On the far right can be seen the open ground floor of Byron's rented house, which served as a barracks for soldiers and supplies.

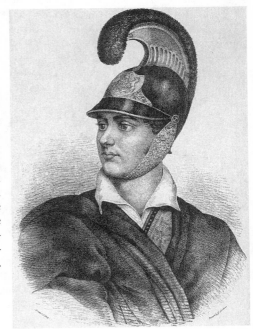

Byron is shown here wearing one of the three helmets he designed for himself, Count Pietro Gamba, and Edward John Trelawny during the Greek campaign. As the grandest, Byron's featured an escutcheon above the visor engraved with his family motto "Crede Byron." When Trelawny made fun of the "toy soldier" headgear, Byron, embarrassed, returned them all to their boxes.

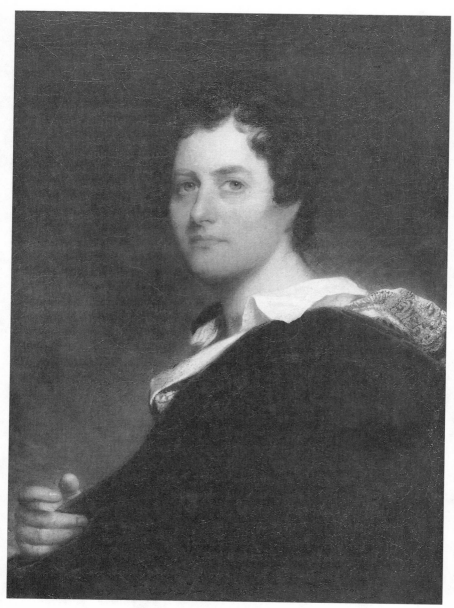

The American painter William Edward West arrived in Leghorn at the end of June 1822 where Byron, installed with the Countess Guiccioli in a villa in the hills of Montenero, had agreed to sit for a portrait. Like Thorvaldsen, West found the poet "a bad sitter": he either chattered incessantly or "when he was silent . . . assumed a countenance that did not belong to him." When the Countess appeared, Byron relaxed into naturalness, making this one of the great portraits of the poet.

On the evening of August 9 he was back in London, where a letter from Annabella was waiting for him. She was now determined to be as truthful about her feelings as convention and her own fears allowed: "Instead of fancying you likely to conceive my regard greater than it is, I have invariably observed that you did not understand how great it was." Then, groping for some means of finding out what Byron felt for her, she reverted to her usual moral sidestep: "My doubt then is—and I ask a solution—whether you are in *any* danger of that attachment to me which might interfere with your peace of mind."[9]

Accustomed by this time to Annabella's circuitous style, Byron went straight to the point of her letter: "I will answer your question as openly as I can.—I did—do,—and always shall love you."[10]

Now it was Annabella's turn to retreat. Once again, her intelligence and moral overreaching silenced the feelings she had just managed to express. She could not escape from the uncomfortable truth that must emerge from a "comparative view of your character and my own—that they are ill-adapted to each other," she told the man she loved. "Not believe me, that I depreciate your capacity for the domestic virtues," she conceded. "Nevertheless, you do not appear to be the person whom *I* ought to select as my guide, my support, my example on earth, with a view still to Immortality."[11]

This is Annabella at her most unfortunate—honest to a fault, priggish, and exalted with spiritual pride. But the tragic dimension of her remarks is that they happen to have been true. In the end, she allowed her better judgment to be overruled by love.

Reading this latest from Seaham, Byron was furious. Had she coaxed him out on a limb, only to reject him a third time?

"Very well, now we can talk of something else," he replied coldly, "though I do not think an intimacy which does not extend beyond a few letters and still fewer interviews in the course of a year could be particularly injurious to either party. . . . It is perhaps as well that even that should end,"[12] he wrote on August 16.

He had been back in London for five days. One of his first errands was to send a peace offering—four brace of grouse—to Lady Melbourne. They had not corresponded during his three weeks in Hastings. Then, on August 20, he heard finally that Claughton had agreed to an indemnity of £25,000, with the abbey to revert to Byron's possession. The next day he left for Newstead, taking Augusta and the children with him.

The languor of late summer had settled on the woods and meadows, and Augusta and Byron yielded to a pastoral illusion of endless time, where "future plans might remain," she declared, "in a glorious state of uncertainty." As one day drifted into another, it was Augusta, once again, who nudged him back to the real world of choice and action—however painful. Stoically, she urged him to move forward with his plans to marry, arguing, as Byron later told Lady Melbourne, that he must do it for both their sakes, "because it was the only chance of redemption for *two* persons."[13]

In contrast to his earlier letter to Annabella, where he had declared, "I did—do" etc., Byron's remarks now are cautious, even legalistic: "A few weeks ago you asked me a question—which I answered—I have now one to propose—to which if improper—I need not add that your declining to reply to it will be sufficient reproof—It is this—are the 'objections'—to which you alluded—insuperable?—or is there any line or change of conduct which could possibly remove them?"

In his reassurance to Annabella—that she need not see her answer as a commitment—Byron was also reassuring himself: "I neither wish you to promise or pledge yourself to anything—but merely to learn a *possibility* which would not leave you the less a free agent." And he concluded his letter with a melancholy truth, mercifully lost on her: "It is not without a struggle that I address you once more on this sentiment," he wrote. Indeed, the struggle appeared to have exhausted him, for he ended wearily: "With the rest of my sentiments you are already acquainted—if I do not repeat them it is to avoid—or at least not increase you[r] displeasure."[14]

Determined to see the matter settled, Augusta professed to be delighted: "Well, this is a very pretty letter; it is a pity it should not go. I never read a prettier one."

"Then it *shall* go," he replied.

However, according to Moore's recollections of a passage in Byron's destroyed memoirs, his friend had still wavered: "He put the letter into his desk—took it out again before post hour—& she (Augusta) made the observation 'It is a very well written letter.' Upon which, he determined it should go—rang the bell, sealed it with the greatest haste, & dispatched it, as if anxious to deprive himself of the power of retracting."[15]

A man who could write offering himself as husband to an innocent young woman, while cohabiting with his sister and lover, would have to be captive to cynicism or denial. Byron was neither. He was fearfully—even morbidly—aware of every implication of what he was about to do, weighing the salvation he hoped—for himself and Augusta—against the retribution he feared. And he loved Annabella. Better than anyone, he knew that mailing the letter would set in motion the inexorable elements of tragedy.

Until the answer arrived, Byron's "agitation was excessive," Augusta later reported to Annabella. "He used to sit upon the steps before Newstead watching for the post two or three days before [her] letter came,"[16] convinced, he told Augusta, Tom Moore, and Hobhouse, that he would be refused a third time. Whether this was wishful thinking or a defense against rejection, Byron himself probably could not have said. On September 15, five days after his letter had gone off to Seaham, he wrote elliptically to Moore, "To-morrow, I shall know whether a circumstance of importance enough to change many of my plans will occur or not. If it does not, I am off for Italy next month and London, in the mean time, next week."[17]

On September 17, in the late afternoon, Byron and Augusta were having dinner with a guest, the local apothecary,* when they were interrupted by the gardener, who excitedly produced a gold ring. It was Catherine Byron's wedding band, lost many years before and now unearthed beneath her bedroom window. A moment later, the mail arrived with Annabella's letter. Seeing her looping hand, Byron declared: "If it contains a consent, I will be married with this ring." But he turned so pale as he handed the open letter to Augusta that she thought he would faint.[18]

Annabella described herself as "almost too agitated to write," but in fact she now expressed herself more freely than ever before. Emerging from her protective thicket of wordiness, she told Byron: "It would be absurd to suppress anything. I am and have long been pledged to myself to make your happiness my first object in life. *If I can* make you happy, I have no other consideration. I will *trust* to you for all I should look up to—all I can love. The fear of not realizing your expectations is the only one I now feel. Convince me—it is all I wish—that my affection may supply that [which] is wanting in my character to form your happiness. This is a moment of joy which I have too much despaired of ever experiencing. I *dared* not believe it possible."[19]

Byron's response gives their exchange the soaring completeness of a Mozart duet. "Your letter has given me a new existence," he began and, taking up Annabella's theme, apologized that, in his present state, he, too, was "scarcely collected" enough to write "rationally": "I have ever regarded you as one of the first of human beings—not merely from my

---

*As we know from Keats's education, the apothecary received the same training as a surgeon and was often expected to prescribe for patients without the intervention of a physician. Byron's health problems and, earlier, those of his mother, would have given him occasion to cultivate this local medical expert.

own observation but that of others—as one whom it was as difficult *not* to love, as scarcely possible to deserve." But he is honest in what he does not say: Never does he claim a passionate or even romantic attraction to Annabella; he loves and values her moral qualities, trusting in these, together with her love, to change him: "I know your worth, & revere your virtues as I love yourself," he told her. "It *is* in your power to render me happy—you have made me so already." Like all lovers, he joyfully compares his earlier luckless state to his present happiness. He was "on the point of leaving England without hope without fear— almost without feeling," he wrote, when her acceptance transformed his life.[20]

Announcing the news to Lady Melbourne, however, required some fence-mending. While she knew he was with Augusta, his confidante had pointedly refused to write—not even to thank him for his propitiatory offering of grouse. Now, disposing of his bulletin in the first sentence—"Miss Milbanke has accepted me"—Byron turned immediately to restoring Lady M's goodwill. "May I hope for your consent too?" he asked. "Without it I should be unhappy . . . & with it I shall have nothing to require except your good wishes now—and your friendship always." On another front he delicately confirmed an earlier promise; that of forsaking all other "pursuits" should his courtship of Annabella succeed: "In course I mean to reform most thoroughly & become 'a good man and true' in all the various senses of these respective & respectable appellations," he promised; "seriously—I will endeavour to make your niece happy not by 'my deserts but what I will deserve.' "[21] Quoting Richard III (however inaccurately*) was not perhaps the best augury for the fulfillment of his good intentions.

That same day, the mail brought another note from Annabella, enclosing one from her father to Byron. "Her happiness is the point nearest our hearts," Sir Ralph wrote, "and I trust she will find it in the esteem and affection you bestow upon her, and which I will venture to say she merits." He concluded, "Whenever you favour us with a visit, you will be most cordially received by me and her Mother as one dear to us for her sake."[22]

His visit to Seaham was a crucial seal to the betrothal. Thus far their courtship had been almost entirely conducted by letter; they had barely seen one another, even socially. Only a prince and princess of distant countries, moving toward an arranged marriage, could have had less occasion to test the idea of the other against the reality. Byron's

---

*"Plead what I will be not what I have been," *Richard III,* act IV, scene 4.

extended stay with his fiancée and her family would be the first occasion when he and Annabella had ever spent time alone together.

Anxiously, he continued to procrastinate. But in asking Annabella's indulgence for the delay, he confessed to fear at the prospect of the visit, "which I wish so much—and yet I feel more tremblingly alive to that meeting than I quite like to own to myself."[23]

Writing to Annabella for the third time in three days, Byron now voluntarily raised the issue of greatest concern to her: religion. "Though you have not lately pressed it—I am sure you feel anxious on my behalf," he noted, hoping she would be reassured "when I tell you that I am so convinced of its importance in fixing the principles that I could never have had perfect confidence in any woman who was slightly impressed with its truth." With this remark Byron endorsed a cultural assumption as old as Christianity itself: the importance of a woman's religious conviction as evidence both of her own virtue and purity, and of her privileged role as heavenly intercessor on behalf of sinful man. Confessing himself "bewildered by the variety of tenets" of orthodox belief, he insisted that his blasphemous reputation was owed to those who, unlike Annabella, would rather "condemn than convert" him. Without denying that "my own impressions are by no means settled," he promised only an open mind: "I will read what books you please—hear what arguments you please—and in leaving the choice to your judgment—let it be proof that my confidence in your understanding & your virtues is equal. You shall be 'my Guide—Philosopher and Friend,' "* he assured Annabella, "my whole heart is yours—and if possible let me make it not unworthy of her to whom it is bound & from whom but one event can divide it."[24]

If Byron had been dragging his feet in setting out for Seaham, he was now given a fresh excuse for delay by Hanson's more than usually dilatory behavior. The all-important marriage settlement, a complicated legal document involving the bride's dowry along with both parties' property, titles, annuities, and bequests, required the lawyer's immediate attention. Not unreasonably, Byron had hoped to have the matter settled, or at least in its final draft, before heading north as bridegroom-elect. Hanson's habitual inertia had been exacerbated by the far less pleasant tasks devolving on his daughter's recent marriage to the Earl of Portsmouth and the legal steps already undertaken by her husband's family that would eventually see the union annulled.

---

*Byron had used this same quotation from Pope earlier to eulogize "Citizen" Matthews, whose influence may be said to have been very different from what he hoped of his future wife.

Well into October, Byron asked, pleaded, then stormed at Hanson—
in vain—to attend to his affairs. He wrote to Annabella, sometimes
twice a day, in terms ever more tender, and whatever his own qualms
about the visit, his letters reflect growing frustration with this external
obstacle to his departure. Even as he confessed to Lady Melbourne that
he felt "very odd" about the Seaham trip, he took pains to point out
that his discomfort had to do with *"it—not her,"* explaining further that
"it was nothing but shyness and a hatred of Strangers which I never
could conquer."[25] And he wrote again to Annabella; he could not go to
sleep without "conversing" with her once more. Since he had yielded to
his "feelings," he told her, "you have never left me for a moment—you
never shall—you never can."[26]

As Byron's letters to Annabella became more passionate, they moved
toward greater intimacy and toward the edge of confession. For the first
time he sounds an ominous theme that would reverberate throughout
their marriage: Had she only accepted him sooner, she could have prevented the affair with Augusta and his descent into hell.

However deep Annabella's faith and thorough her knowledge of
theology, she could never understand the burning reality of sin as suffering, endured each day by Byron the skeptic. For him, a sense of his
own unworthiness, along with feelings of irreparable loss, warred with
the hope that Annabella could still save him: "I yet wish to be good—
with you I cannot but be happy—but I never shall be what I would have
been," he wrote, asking, "Forgive my weaknesses—love what you can
of me & mine—and I will be—I am whatever you please to make me."[27]

More than a love letter, this was a prayer.

HANSON, meanwhile, insisted that Byron should come to see him at his
son-in-law's estate in Hampshire to discuss Newstead and the Rochdale
legacy in light of the marriage settlement. This Byron politely refused to
do. Worse than the inconvenience of adding another journey to the one
he was having trouble enough planning, he was also unwell, still suffering the "complaint I brought on 3 years ago by the use or Abuse of
Acids," the diuretics he took to stay thin.[28]

He laid out to Annabella, with as much clarity as he could, his financial standing: the value, actual and potential, of real assets; the
Rochdale lands and collieries; and Newstead, including rents and outstanding debts. With three favorable verdicts on his Rochdale title challenged on a technicality and Newstead awaiting a new purchaser, both
his principal and his earnings were still tied up. Annabella, as it happened, was in a similar position, enjoying great expectations but little in

the way of immediate disposable income. From her childless uncle Lord Wentworth she stood to inherit considerable property, along with the title Baroness Noel, but most of the income she should have received at this time from her father's estates had been swallowed up by Sir Ralph's expenses from "electioneering," Byron told Hanson confidentially, and thus "her present portion will not be considerable."[29] Where Annabella's fortune was concerned, however, Byron was sincere in his profession of disinterestedness; had he wanted a "golden dolly," other heiresses had far more to recommend them.

Meanwhile, the official announcement of their engagement had appeared in the Durham newspapers and had been reprinted by the *London Morning Chronicle*, only to be followed by a denial. Byron was outraged and wrote immediately to the editor, James Perry: "*Who* instructed you to contradict this?" he demanded, adding, "I suspect mischief (and consequently a woman) to be your authority."[30] The object of his suspicion was Caroline Lamb; as he explained to Annabella, this would only be the latest in a series of her "monkey-tiger tricks," and he recounted her forgery of his handwriting to extract his portrait from the unsuspecting Murray. Once more, Byron's vulnerability to Caro's claims drove him into a fury of self-righteousness: "You cannot conceive what persecution I have undergone from the same quarter—nor the pains I have taken to save that person from herself."[31] He was deeply ashamed, then, to learn that the false informant had not been Caro after all, who, as he was shortly forced to admit, had been "quiet and rational enough" on hearing of his engagement. He still needed Caro as his evil *anima*, just as he needed Annabella as his savior.

In Seaham, meanwhile, each day that Byron's arrival was deferred exacerbated family tension. Annabella now had to defend her fiancé and reassure her parents while trying to calm her own mounting anxiety. Her Uncle Wentworth had come—and gone. Having planned his visit to meet his niece's intended, he had, finally, been obliged to return to London. Lady Milbanke had now taken to her bed, but not before apparently complaining to her sister-in-law, Lady Melbourne, about Byron's failure to appear. Lady Melbourne decided to blame Augusta for the delay. Once again, Byron leaped to his sister's defense, assuring the Spider that "+ never threw any obstacles in the way—on the contrary she has been more urgent than even you that I should go to S[eaham], and wished me to set out from N[ewstead] instead of London."[32] As proof he was pleased to inform Lady M that his sister had, in fact, written to Annabella on October 1.

Augusta's letter to Annabella—the first of hundreds—is a marvel of dangerous truths wafted like blown kisses: "I am afraid I have no better excuse to offer for this *self-introduction* than that of feeling unable to reconcile myself to the idea of being *quite* a *stranger* to one whom I hope *soon* to call *my sister*, and one—may I be allowd [*sic*] to add—whom I already love as such." At the same time, Augusta made it clear that she is Byron's intimate, even his voice, expressing his gratitude (and her own) for "the blessing bestowed upon him in the possession of esteem and affection such as yours, for which I justly consider him (as he does himself) the most fortunate of human Beings." And she conveyed her "deservedly dear" brother's own regret at being "provokingly detained in Town by business, & unable to fix a day for his departure."[33]

Annabella was too grateful for the reassuring sisterly words to question the writer's privileged role. From the outset, she welcomed Augusta as intermediary and even surrogate for her brother, writing to Byron on October 3 that, failing to hear from him, she had "received some compensation in a letter from your Sister—*mine*—so cordially kind that I cannot say how much I thank her."[34] Annabella's dependence on Augusta as guide and intercessor was established.

Byron was rightly appreciative of Augusta's efforts, and his next letter to Annabella included a burst of praise for his sister as "the least selfish & gentlest creature in being, & more attached to me than any one in existence can be." On the same day, he defended her—more sharply than ever before—to Lady Melbourne: "You don't know what a being she is—her only error has been my fault entirely, & for this I can plead no excuse—except passion—which is none."[35]

Further, he offered another defense besides "the law's delay" for his procrastination. Experienced only in seducing servant girls or compliant married women, he did not trust himself to obey the proprieties that permitted a betrothed couple to be alone together before marriage but forbade any physical intimacy. "Without being more impatient than other people," he told Lady M, "you must allow that it is rather a trying situation to be placed near, and with one's intended, and still to be limited to intentions only."[36]

In fact, Byron had run out of excuses except to plead the paralysis of depression. "I am horribly low spirited,"[37] he wrote to Lady Melbourne. He entirely turned over to Augusta the task of writing to Annabella, and in her artlessly artful style, she reported on her brother to the anxious fiancée: "He writes me word that he hopes *very* soon to see you. It is most provoking that his departure to Seaham should have hitherto met with so many impediments."[38]

Annabella was not only reassured, she was completely won over by

Augusta's "confiding good nature," and she answered the chatty letters from Six Mile Bottom "as comfortably as if we *had* been sisters."[39] She invited Augusta to accompany Byron to Seaham, hoping that her acceptance might galvanize him into an appearance. Citing the demands of motherhood, Augusta declined: "I am a *Nurse* to my baby, Governess to my eldest Girl, & something between both to my two intermediate Babes." Pleading indulgence for her brother, Augusta could not resist reminding Annabella, once again, that she had been authorized as go-between; "I am sure you will be amused at his having expressed a wish that *I* would endeavour to describe *his* portion of this fatal shyness to you, & a great many other of what he terms the peculiarities of his disposition."[40] A "great many," perhaps, but not all.

By the end of October, a month and a half after Annabella's acceptance of his proposal, Byron still claimed that he was waiting for Hanson to precede him to Seaham, where the Milbankes' lawyer, William Hoar, was waiting to negotiate the marriage settlement. Annabella was overwhelmed by the strain of reassuring her parents and keeping up her own sagging spirits. She now wrote to Byron a plea for help that was also a reproach: "It is odd that my task should be to pacify the old ones, and teach *them* patience. They are growing quite ungovernable," she wrote with wan humor, "and I must have your assistance to manage them," adding, "O for tomorrow's post! I walk to meet it every day, and sit in the blacksmith's cottage till it arrives."[41]

To this last poignant note, Byron replied promptly on October 25 to say that Hanson, claiming illness, had offered to send his son Charles in his place—a proposal that Byron angrily rejected. Finally, however, he agreed to set out for Seaham in four days, with or without his lawyer; he would even forgo plans to stop at Newstead and Newmarket on the way.

Now he wrote a fierce letter to Hanson: "What to say to them I know not—after the delays already—they will merely look upon your illness as a new excuse—and perhaps of mine . . . but in short—this marriage will be broken off—& if so—whether intentional or accidental—I can't help it—but by God—I can never look upon anyone again as my friend who has even been the innocent cause of destroying my happiness."[42]

Although Byron's projection of the blame for his broken engagement on Hanson—not himself—as the culprit has elements of wish fulfillment, there is no doubt that in Byron's mind, the lawyer was the cause of his delayed visit, not an excuse. The unsettled status of both Newstead and Rochdale, along with his generally uncertain fortunes, had given the proper marriage settlement a symbolic significance for him that went far beyond any concerns of the Milbankes. Pride—individual and family—along with murkier issues of manhood and property were all involved, and his apparent powerlessness to arrange matters in a timely fashion was causing him distress as acute as the anxiety felt at Seaham.

He confided his wretchedness to Augusta, who, taking the cue, wrote at once to Annabella, conveying her brother's "evident agitation and lowness of spirits," his "distress and perplexity at Hanson's inaction." Augusta could not have been plainer: Byron feared that his own excuses would not be believed and "wishes *me* to write . . . to account for the strange delay on his part." She apologized for "tormenting" Annabella with her letters, but Byron was "most anxious that you should attribute his prolonged absence to no cause but the true one."[43]

On Saturday, October 29, Byron left London for Seaham. He did not, however, go directly, as he had earlier promised, but went instead to Six Mile Bottom. "Augusta wishes me so much to pass that way that I shall make 'mine inn' at her abode for a short time and thence to our Papa's,"[44] he told Annabella in his airiest manner. While there he learned that Colonel Leigh was not happy to hear of the impending marriage; knowing that Augusta was to be Byron's heiress, he didn't "like any chance of my wife's being in his way,"[45] Byron wrote to Lady M.

He admitted to "proceeding very slowly" toward his final destination, spending Sunday night at the inn near Wansford. At last, on November 2, Byron arrived at Seaham Manor, the Milbankes' house on the coast in County Durham. He had been expected two days before, and this latest delay, attended by so much anticipation, had taken its toll. The spontaneous welcome he would have received earlier had turned into strained formality. Sir Ralph did his good-humored best, with oft-told jokes and stories; as for his future mother-in-law, "I don't like Lady Milbanke at all," Byron declared to Lady M, adding sourly, "She seems to be every thing here."[46] Under the circumstances, the first encounter of Byron and Annabella since their engagement could hardly have been less auspicious.

"A's meeting & mine made a kind of scene—though there was no acting or even speaking—but the pantomime was very expressive,"[47] Byron reported to Whitehall two days later. Following a brief welcome by her parents, Annabella recalled, it was agreed that she should receive her fiancé alone. She found Byron in the drawing room, standing to one side of the mantelpiece. He did not come forward to greet her, but kissed her extended hand. Both were too overcome with shyness to speak.

Finally, Byron broke the silence, only to murmur, "It is a long time since we have met." Annabella was hardly able to reply.

"I felt overpowered by the situation," she later remembered; excusing herself, she summoned her parents to join them. Byron's discomfort now erupted into nervous chatter; he talked of Kean's latest performance "with an animation of manner that seemed to proceed from agitated spirits." He inquired at what time the household assembled in the morning, and on being told "ten o'clock," hosts and guest then retired.

Rising early, Annabella went to the library, hoping that "a lover's feelings might anticipate the hour."[48] But when Byron had not yet appeared by noon, a headache drove her out of doors for a solitary walk.

Distrust was in the air, and defenses were up. Annabella was struck dumb, and Byron retreated into the shyness that caused him to dread strangers. His wordy "Princess of Parallelograms" he now found "inscrutable," he told Lady Melbourne. "She seems to have more feeling than we imagined—but is the most *silent* woman I ever encountered—which perplexes me extremely. . . . I like them to talk, because then they *think* less—much cogitation will not be in my favour."

Already he had assumed the posture of a wary adversary sizing up his opponent's vulnerability: "If the conversation is to be all on one side—I fear committing myself—& those who only listen—must have their thoughts so much about them—as to seize any weak point at once." The atmosphere of negotiation was intensified by the arrival—finally—of both lawyers: Hanson from London and William Hoar from Durham, who were hard at work on the settlement papers. "I presume the parchment once scribbled, I shall become Lord Annabella," he told Lady M.

After all the delay, the burden fell upon the "laggard lover" to be lovable. Byron, however, required certainty—the certainty of being loved and admired, but above all, managed: "I can't yet tell whether we are to be happy or not. . . . I fear she won't govern me—& if she don't it will not do at all,"[49] he announced to Lady M. It was clear to whom Annabella was being compared—and not to her advantage.

His unworldly twenty-three-year-old fiancée would never develop any skill in managing him, but after four days of being "much together," Byron felt able to report that "Annabella and I go on extremely well," and he seemed to be understating the dramatic change in emotional climate that had taken place when he wrote: "It would not be difficult to prove that we appear much attached & I hope permanently so."

As their shyness dissolved, Byron was reminded of all that had drawn him to Annabella. He now discovered, to his mixed delight and fear, a sexuality ripe for release—"I think not only her feelings and affections—but her *passions* stronger than we supposed," he told Lady Melbourne, adding, in deference to the required innocence of his fiancée: "She herself cannot be aware of this—nor could I[,] except from a habit of attending minutely in such cases to their slightest indications & of course I don't let her participate in the discovery, in which, after all, I may be mistaken."

He went on happily about plans for their "Moon" to be divided between Halnaby, a country house of the Milbankes' in Yorkshire, and Farleigh, Hanson's borrowed estate in Hampshire, suggesting that friendly feelings were restored between lawyer and client.

His bride's financial prospects were brighter than Byron had supposed: Besides a certain £20,000, her Uncle Wentworth now declared Annabella by will to be his heiress, going over to Durham expressly to inform Hoar of his intent. Byron took a prudently fatalistic view of the good news: "*I* wish to trust as little as possible to expectations," he wrote to Lady M, "though even *hers* seem very sanguine—if realized it will all be very well—& if not—should she herself continue what I firmly believe her—I could bear—indeed I could hardly regret any posthumous disappointments—unless I thought that she suffered from her connection with me."[50] Once again, he confirmed that in marrying Annabella, he was marrying for love, and was concerned about money only insofar as it should affect his wife.

Even in the gray November weather, Seaham Manor, sitting on the cliffs overlooking the North Sea, was a place to please Byron. Annabella showed him her favorite walks, one to a curious outcrop called The Featherbed. At high tide its farthest rocks became a tiny island where Byron liked to stand, marooned, waving to those on shore.

Within a week of his arrival, the beginnings of intimacy and trust had frayed. Frightened by Byron's ardor, fearful and guilty about her own sexual response, Annabella retreated, summoning a verbal barrier against a loss of control. "Her disposition is the very reverse of *our* imaginings," Byron sulked to Lady M. "She is overrun with fine feelings—scruples about herself and *her* disposition (I suppose in fact she means mine). . . . I hear of nothing but 'feeling' from morning till night."

Conflict was making Annabella ill—"once every 3 days with I know not what." She would then recover, only to fall sick again. She had even "made one *scene*—not altogether out of C[aroline]'s style, it did me no good,"[51] Byron noted ominously. He professed to find the cause of the explosion too trifling to detail, but for the reserved Annabella to lose control and succumb to an emotional outburst upon slight provocation is hardly in character. During these same days, Annabella recalled, she and her fiancé had a conversation about her sister-in-law-to-be: "Byron spoke of her with an air of sorrowful tenderness. . . . He told me . . . that no one would ever possess so much of his confidence and affection as Augusta." Annabella claimed she "felt an instant's pain perceptible only to myself."[52] In the cruel stab of that moment, unacceptable jealousy was displaced into symptoms of illness, or a scene whose cause appeared too "trifling" for either to recall.

Every time Byron came close to apprehending what might have gone wrong—or to seeing that, like him, his young fiancée needed reassurance—he backed away. He found it most strange, he told Lady Melbourne, that Annabella responded to petting and affection; "the eloquence of *action*," as he put it, "succeeds very well.

"In fact and entre nous it is really amusing—she is like a child in that respect—and quite *caressable* into kindness and good humour—though I don't think her temper *bad* at any time—but very *self*-tormenting—and anxious—and romantic"—the very opposite of Augusta, with her teasing laughter, who could manage him, it seemed, by instinct.

"Do you know I have great doubts . . . if this will be a marriage now," he wrote to his confidante on November 13, "but if there is a break—it shall be *her* doing not mine."[53] It was at Annabella's urging that he left Seaham on the sixteenth.

Three days later, he was at Six Mile Bottom.

AWAY FROM the tensions at Seaham and soothed by the happy familiarity of Augusta and her brood, Byron's pessimism lifted and he wrote to Annabella with the loving impatience proper to a fiancé separated from his beloved.

"Don't scold *yourself* any more," he said, replying to her apologies for the troubled side she had shown during his visit. Addressing her as "My Heart," he was, he assured Annabella, "as happy as Hope can make me—and as gay as Love will allow me to be till we meet."[54]

He remained at Six Mile Bottom for a week; from there, he visited Cambridge several times, spending the day on November 19, followed by an overnight stay on the twenty-second and twenty-third, when, joining Hobhouse, Hodgson, and "our cousin" George Lamb, he reported to Annabella, he went to the Senate House to cast his vote in favor of his friend William Clarke's candidacy for the Chair of Medicine. Clarke lost, but to Byron's surprised delight, the assembled fellows, on recognizing the poet, burst into spontaneous applause.

Returning to Six Mile Bottom to say good-bye to Augusta, Byron
left for London on November 24. When Annabella's uncle, Lord
Wentworth, called, he succumbed to "a fit of the Shys" and was "not at
home,"[55] but within days he got up the courage to return the visit.

Now it was Annabella's turn to have second thoughts. Demoralized
by the delays and the disastrous visit, and further worried by alternating currents of tenderness and irritability in Byron's letters, she offered
him several opportunities to honorably withdraw.

"We have gone on too long with the magnanimity-s [sic] that might
keep us at a distance forever," she wrote on December 16, "and if you
won't, I must take the responsibility of speaking plain. . . . Don't let me
marry you against your will." On the following day, she elaborated further her fear that Byron was feeling trapped: "I have one request to
make from *myself*. If you conceive or feel there is *any* cause which can
render you dissatisfied, or less satisfied with your intended return next
week—that you will prefer it to all I have said in favor of that measure.
Your letters leave something for conjecture," she remarked pointedly.
And in a postscript she asked again: "Are you less confident than you
were in the happiness of our marriage?"[56]

Written after five weeks of pleading with Byron to set a date for his
return to Seaham, the sincerity of Annabella's offer to release him from
the engagement has been treated with skepticism. In the happiest of
circumstances, however, doubts surface as the time approaches for
exchanging vows. Now, each delay on Byron's part drove Annabella's
doubts closer to despair. Her offer, moreover, is entirely in character:
She would be more humiliated by the knowledge that the man she loved
had married her against his will than by a broken engagement.

Avoiding answers to her questions, Byron placed the onus for any
change of heart entirely on Annabella. He ridiculed her concerns: " 'any
cause'? and 'less confident'? a pretty pair of queries—I do not see any
good purpose to which questions of this kind are to lead—nor can they
be answered otherwise than by time and events."[57] But in fact,
Annabella's willingness to ask painful questions and to live with the
answers frightened him. His own doubts, he decided, could only be
silenced by settling the matter as quickly as possible. The first visit to
Seaham had convinced him that his next journey north must be as bridegroom, and he now urged Annabella: "If we meet let it be to marry—
had I remained at S[eaham] it had probably been over by this time," he
remarked ungallantly. [W]ith regard to our being under the same roof
and *not* married—I think past experience has shown us the awkwardness of that situation—I can conceive nothing about purgatory more

uncomfortable." And he informed her that Hobhouse would accompany him "for if we don't marry I should not like a 2nd journey back quite alone."[58]

On December 24, the two friends set out from London. But they separated at Chesterford, Hobhouse going to Cambridge and Byron proceeding to Six Mile Bottom, where he spent Christmas with the Leighs. The colonel was ill, and between his demands on his wife and the freezing temperature, which kept the children indoors, there was little opportunity to be alone with Augusta on this, Byron's last visit before his marriage. Now his sense of purpose ebbed and he sank into melancholy. All of Augusta's arts of persuasion were needed to point him, on the morning of Boxing Day, toward Cambridge and the north.

"Never was lover less in haste," Hobhouse noted in his journal that night.[59] In their slow progress to Wansford that evening and to Newark the following day, Hobhouse recalled that Byron "owned that he felt 'a considerable repugnance in marrying before his pecuniary affairs were arranged,' that he was not in love with Annabella and that he had tried to persuade her to postpone the marriage, but she had overruled him." This last was patently untrue, but he did not want to forfeit Hobby's sympathy or undermine his own pride by admitting that Annabella had offered to end the engagement. On their last evening in Newark, Byron described feeling "indifference, almost aversion" toward his fiancée.

They appeared at Seaham Hall on Friday, December 30, at eight o'clock in the evening. After the six days that had elapsed between their departure from London and their arrival, nerves were on edge. Byron was shown directly to his room, and when Annabella heard him emerge, she ran upstairs to meet him and, throwing her arms around his neck, burst into tears. Lady Milbanke was "so much agitated" that she had retreated to her room.

By the next day, however, a celebratory atmosphere had taken over. On Saturday morning, December 31, the papers were signed to the accompaniment of jokes and laughter, and by dinnertime at six o'clock, Sir Ralph was in such good form that Hobhouse wrote down his better stories.

HOBHOUSE WAS immensely impressed by Annabella. He liked the frank and unaffected way she took his hand on meeting him on the night of their arrival: "Very sensible and quiet" was the way he described her, and although he had found her far from pretty when they met, there was something about her looks that grew on him: "She gains by inspection," he allowed, even to "inspiring an interest which it is easy to mistake for love." There was no mistaking her love for Byron, however. And he was struck by the disparity between the way Byron had claimed to feel about her on their journey north and his manner toward her now. "Byron loves her personally, when present, as it is easy for those used to such indications to observe."

Well before ten o'clock on Monday, January 2, the day of the wedding, Hobhouse, dressed even to his white gloves, went to awaken Byron but found him fully clothed. They greeted the others, excepting the bride, who had not yet appeared. Then Byron and Hobhouse together walked upstairs to the drawing room. In an alcove formed by a large bay window and separated from the rest of the room by a proscenium arch, kneeling cushions had been placed for the bridal pair ("hard as though filled with peach stones," Byron recalled). Two clergymen officiated: the Rev. Richard Wallis, vicar of Seaham, and the Rev. Thomas Noel, vicar of Kirkby Mallory, who, as Lord Wentworth's illegitimate son, was also the bride's cousin. Annabella was attended by her former governess, Mrs. Clermont. The bride wore a simple white muslin gown, lace-trimmed only at the hem, and a short matching jacket called a curricle—"very plain indeed, with nothing on her head," Hobhouse reported. In her responses she was "firm as a rock." It was Byron who stumbled as he repeated, "I, George Gordon," and when he came to the line "With all my worldly goods I thee endow," he looked over at Hobhouse "with a faint smile."

At eleven o'clock the ceremony was over. Wallis shook Annabella's hand first, followed by Hobhouse, who then embraced Byron. Lady Milbanke kissed her son-in-law. After signing the register with Hobhouse and Wallis as witnesses, Annabella quickly left the room, her eyes full of tears. She had, Hobhouse observed, "compleated her conquest—her innocent conquest." To his best man Byron appeared "calm and as usual."

When she reappeared, Annabella was wearing her going-away outfit, a gray satin pelisse* trimmed with a narrow band of white fur worn over the wedding dress. Discreetly, Hobhouse placed his wedding gift to the bride, a set of Byron's complete works bound in yellow morocco, in the carriage. Handing in the new Lady Byron, he wished her many years of happiness.

"If I am not happy, it will be my own fault," she said.

---

*The pelisse, a thin cloak, still survives in the Museum of Costume in Bath. Its size suggests that Annabella could have been no taller than five feet, three inches and slight.

Through the window, Byron grasped his friend's hand; he was still holding tight as the carriage pulled away.

At Six Mile Bottom, Augusta's tension mounted through the morning. At eleven o'clock, the hour when she knew the vows were to be exchanged in Seaham, her surge of feelings, she said, "were as the sea trembles when the earth quakes."[60]

CHAPTER 25

"It Is But the Effervescence of Despair"

*A*s soon as we got into the carriage, his countenance changed to gloom and defiance," Annabella recalled fourteen months after the wedding day.[1]

When their coach passed through Durham and the "joy bells" pealed in their honor, Byron began singing and ranting: By refusing his offer of marriage two years earlier, Annabella had doomed him to nameless tragedy; he had only married her now "to outwit" her and exact his revenge. He then reviled her mother, retailing unflattering instances of her behavior as reported by Lady Melbourne, bemoaned Annabella's meager dowry, and expressed impatience for her relations to die so she could inherit. Worse than these accusations was Byron's "relentless pitying," Annabella recalled, when his regrets were all *for her*: that she had not married a better man.

Even if we concede a certain gothic exaggeration of Byron's behavior by his shocked wife ("Now that I've got you in my power, I can make you feel it,"[2] she recalled him saying), other evidence, including his own, points to his suffering a severe panic attack immediately after the ceremony. The finality of the step he had taken, the physical and emotional claustrophobia of finding himself alone at close quarters with a wife he scarcely knew, triggered a hysterical reaction. Byron's own recollection is the most telling: He always insisted that Mrs. Clermont, Annabella's governess, had "stuck" herself between them in the cramped carriage[3]—a memory disputed by Hobhouse and everyone else who saw them off.

At Halnaby the grounds were covered by deep snow, but the Milbanke servants and tenants, many of whom had known Annabella from birth, were waiting outside to greet the newlyweds. As she emerged from the carriage, the new Lady Byron made a very different impression on two witnesses: The old butler recalled Annabella coming up the steps alone, "with a countenance and frame agonized and list-less with evident horror and despair."⁴ But the maid who had accompa-nied them remembered her mistress as "buoyant and cheerful as a bride should be."⁵ There was no disagreement, however, about Byron's strange behavior. He did not hand his wife from the carriage but "jumped out . . . and walked away."⁶

Byron lashed out at Annabella as the cause of his despair. "It's too late now," "it's done," "it cannot be undone"—these were his blasting words, constantly repeated, from the first day, "and continually, in the first week of our marriage," she recalled. He told her he was more "accursed" in marrying than in any other act of his life, adding, "I am a villain—I could convince you of it in three words."⁷

He harped on the issue of taint. Describing incidences of derange-ment among the Gordons and Byrons—the probable suicide of his grandfather and father, along with a case of arson in the family—he taunted her for writing, in a "Character" of the man she would marry, sent two years earlier to her Aunt Melbourne, that family insanity would be the only disqualifying factor in a future husband. (Thus he also revealed that Lady M had shown him Annabella's letters but not that he had reciprocated in kind.)

As though the required act of sexual possession must be gotten over and done with, he "*had* Lady Byron on the sofa before dinner," he reported in his memoirs.⁸ That same night, Annabella recalled, he inquired "with an appearance of aversion, if I meant to sleep in the same bed with him, said that he hated sleeping with any woman, but that I might do as I chose."⁹ She chose to remain with him. But Annabella omitted the only recorded incident of their wedding night. Samuel Rogers remembered from reading Byron's destroyed memoirs that the poet, startled out of his sleep and seeing the crimson bedcurtains illu-mined by flickering candlelight in the room, screamed, "Good God, I am surely in hell."¹⁰

It was the next morning that Annabella felt "perhaps the deadliest chill that ever fell on my heart." Meeting her in the library, Byron coldly repeated his litany of remorse, now blaming his wife for her failure to avert the tragedy of their marriage. The "desolation of that first day" would be burned into her memory forever.

Terrified by this barrage of abuse, isolated with the naked misery of the man she married, Annabella turned to the one person who both loved and, more urgently, understood Byron and who, she had good reason to believe, was kindly disposed toward her, too. Beginning on their honeymoon, Annabella's reliance on Augusta is the most tangled chapter of the Byron marriage. From the first, the wife both knew and did not know about the relations of brother and sister, but it would soon become clear that the more Annabella knew, the more attached to her rival she became.

"Two or three days after my marriage, suspicions had indeed, crossed my brain, if transient as lightning, not less blasting," she wrote. The first flash was occasioned by her reading of Dryden's *Don Sebastian*, with its theme of an incestuous union of brother and sister ignorant of their parentage. At her mention of the subject, Byron flew into a fury of "terror and rage," demanding to know "where Annabella had heard of this, and seizing a dagger, which he kept on display along with loaded pistols, he rushed off to lock himself in his bedroom."[11]

This literary source of revelation was preceded by a letter from Augusta herself to Byron, which arrived at Halnaby on that first desolate day. Byron took special pleasure in reading the salutation aloud to Annabella, "Dearest, first and best of human beings." "There, what do you think of that?" he demanded. The letter unleashed all of Byron's longing for Augusta, for he was now "continually lamenting her absence, saying no one loved him as she did—no one understood how to make him happy but her."

The next day, January 4, Annabella wrote to invite Augusta to Halnaby. She included in her letter a list of questions, the most important being whether her new sister-in-law would be her "ONLY *friend*."[12] Four days later, she received Augusta's regrets: "Poor Gussey" was unable to get away, she explained, referring to herself in the third person; Annabella was now included in the baby talk that characterized Augusta's discourse with Byron, and she added, "B will tell you what a *helpless* person I am which you will think somewhat excusable considering *my* YOUNG FAMILY." Chattering away in her girlish style sprinkled with nursery French, she thanked Annabella for being "such a superexcellent Sister," reminding her, at the same time, of the privileged place she held in her brother's affections:

"I am only afraid you have adopted B's spoiling system, for you must have discovered that I am thoroughly his *enfant gâté*," she wrote and promised, "Oh yes, I will indeed be your ONLY friend."[13]

If proof is needed of the young wife's despairing loneliness, the stark evidence is here: two days after her wedding, she beseeched a woman she had never met to be her only friend, and despite early suspicions of Augusta's relations with Byron—suspicions fanned by her husband— invited her to join them on their honeymoon.

Tact, more than family claims, kept Augusta at home. In every sense, however, she was with the newlyweds in spirit. Too desperate to be discreet, Annabella wrote to Six Mile Bottom with plentiful hints of the troubles at Halnaby; these letters are lost, but Augusta's replies— lighthearted and rambling as they sound—address the younger woman's perplexity with much skill, praising her perfect understanding and encouraging her confidence in handling her gloomy brother. Buried in all the admiring phrases, however, was Augusta's wise counsel for managing the man she knew far better than his wife did. One must make light of Byron's ravings—tease him, spoil him, scold him, jolly him, but never appear to take "the Magician" seriously, she cautioned. Nothing in Annabella's character, however, could have enabled her to follow this advice. She could never emulate the easy-going, giggling "Goose"; she could only co-opt her.

Byron knew he had suffered an acute attack of depression. With clinical precision, he reported to Hobhouse that "on his wedding night, he had been seized with a fit of melancholy, and had left his bed, and that the oppression had lasted during the first week of his residence with Lady Byron at Halnaby."[14] He spared his friend further details, however. Annabella spares us nothing. Byron did not merely leave their bed, but also, seizing the loaded pistols he always kept nearby while he slept, threatened suicide, rushing to lock himself in his own chamber or to pace the gallery that ran the length of the house. One night, when he returned to Annabella after one of these scenes, she laid her head against his chest.

"You should have a softer pillow than my heart," he told her.

"I wonder which will break first, yours or mine," she said.*[15]

Then, slowly, his rage subsided, yielding, in Annabella's words, to "a sort of *unrelenting pity* which has so often made me feel the hopelessness of my situation more than his most unkind and insulting expressions."

Still, the black ice of depression had melted. Emerging from the nightmare of their first week together, Byron was prepared to behave as though it had never happened. In her relief, Annabella was happy to blame his violent anguish on worries about money, on Newstead remaining unsold, and on a dreadful cold. She had been quick to notice that

---

*Annabella left several versions of this first week of marriage; one may have been written at the behest of her lawyers, or for Byron's "camp" when he threatened to resist a separation. This has weighed against her veracity. On the other hand, her accounts vary only slightly, and they all agree in substance with reports of Byron's behavior in other depressive episodes—as noted by Hobhouse, Augusta, and George Anson Byron.

Byron's obsession with his lameness took the form of circling around the physical fact, with dark allusions to its symbolic meaning: He was a "fallen angel," cursed by the mark of Cain. He had never really moved beyond the fearful "Dinna speak of it" of his Aberdeen childhood. With tact and perseverance, Annabella now engaged him to talk directly about his deformed foot—a triumph of love and trust with which she is rarely credited.

Gradually they settled into the placid rhythm of domestic routine. On January 7 he wrote to Lady Melbourne that "Bell and I go on extremely well so far without any other company than our own selves as yet."[16] And to Tom Moore he reported, "She don't ever bore me"— from Byron, the highest accolade of all.[17] With its good library, Halnaby was "just the spot for a Moon. . . . I have great hopes this match will turn out well—I have found nothing as yet that I could wish changed for the better—but Time does wonders—so I won't be too hasty in my happiness."[18] To Moore, who had begged for news of the newlyweds, Byron was waggish; professing reluctance to "profane the chaste mysteries of Hymen," he allowed, "I like Bell as well as you do (or did, you villain!) Bessy—and that is (or was) saying a great deal."[19]

Together in the library at Halnaby, Byron read or wrote, while Annabella, using her best copperplate script, took on the task of copyist. Byron now assigned to her a project that, in a real sense, she had also inspired. The previous October he had told her about a young Jewish composer and musician, Isaac Nathan, who had written to Byron asking to set some of his verses to airs of his own composition. Nathan was Douglas Kinnaird's protégé, and after appealing to Byron's sympathies for oppressed peoples, Kinnaird moved to more strategic flattery: Nathan had "already set to a very beautiful piece of composition those six lines in *Lara* beginning with 'Night Wanes'—The music is in Handel's style, & I am very much mistaken if all the musical world do not 'ere long mouth your lines after their usual fashions."[20]

Byron agreed and promptly set to work on the new poems. In great excitement, he wrote to Annabella about the authenticity of Nathan's musical setting: His words would be accompanied by the "*real old undisputed Hebrew melodies*," he told her, "which are beautiful & to which David & the prophets actually sang the 'songs of Zion.' " He had already written "nine or ten [poems] on the sacred model—partly from Job &c. & partly my own imagination. . . . It is odd enough that this should fall to my lot, who have been abused as 'an inf.del.' Augusta says 'they will call you a *Jew* next.' "[21] But it was not really odd at all. Byron defined himself as a romantic in his intellectual enthusiasm for folkloric archaeology; he was always fascinated by surviving evidence of ancient popular culture, whether the chants of Suliote sailors or "real undisputed 'songs of Zion.' " He felt particularly inspired by "remains" that gave voice to despised or forgotten peoples. Providing texts for sacred music, however, was also a tribute to Annabella's faith. By this act of collaboration he proved he was not an infidel; if not yet a Christian in her own orthodox image, with his homage to the Old Testament he had started on the road to salvation.

That fall of 1814 he had heard Isaac Nathan sing his airs, including the song set to lines from *Lara*. This was the first occasion he had listened to a young musician singing for him since hearing John Edleston's silvery voice, and he could not have helped but recall the purity of that love in this time of lost innocence. Like the "Thyrza" cycle, *Hebrew Melodies* is also a memorial to that earlier singer and his songs. Several of the poems make no claim to biblical association. Trying to provide Nathan with a context for the three stanzas of "Oh! Snatched Away in Beauty's Bloom,"* Byron explained, "She is no more, and perhaps the only vestige of her existence is the feeling I sometimes fondly indulge."[22] This suggests the transposition of gender that he used for the poems inspired by Edleston. In others, the lamentations of King Saul or the grieving for lost Israel, he appears to mourn another, more personal loss but one that is consoled by hope of a reunion in eternity where love stays unchanged:

> If that high world, which lies beyond
> Our own, surviving Love endears;
> If there the cherish'd heart be fond,
> The eye the same, except in tears—
> How welcome those untrodden spheres![23]

The shadow of Augusta, too, is among the memories that crowd *Hebrew Melodies*. Before putting aside the work for his wedding journey to Seaham, Byron had given Nathan a poem for the collection that he later asked the composer to suppress: This was the "Stanzas for Music," beginning "I speak not, I trace not, I breathe not thy Name." Nathan, naturally, respected the request.†

---

*Nathan's first collection of *Hebrew Melodies*, for example, begins with Byron's best-known lyric, "She Walks in Beauty like the Night," inspired by the vision of his beautiful cousin Lady Anne Wilmot wearing a black mourning gown covered in spangles.

†It was first published after Byron's death in a revised edition of *Hebrew Melodies* (1827–1829).

"Herod's Lament for Mariamne" was a poem that Annabella found especially moving—a "mad song," like one given by Shakespeare to Ophelia or Lear. Byron's afflicted singer is the King of the Jews, who, in "phrensy's jealous raving," has had his blameless wife murdered for infidelity. Crazed by remorse, he ends his lament

> And mine's the guilt, and mine the hell,
>   This bosom's desolation dooming;
> And I have earn'd those tortures well,
>   Which unconsumed are still consuming![24]

One day at Halnaby, Byron saw Annabella writing to Augusta; she was about to enclose a copy of "Mariamne" when he stopped her, saying he objected to sending any of his "gloomy compositions"[25] to Six Mile Bottom.

Friends and family received lighthearted letters from both the newly-weds. Together they wrote to "Aunt" Melbourne, who pointedly addressed her reply to Annabella alone, leaving several letters from Byron unanswered. Instead, she charged Annabella with a message for her husband, concluding, "If you are not too modest, or too shy you may add that *he* has drawn a prize—& that I *believe* you have too, only I make that reservation, as I never speak so confidently of a man as I do of a woman."[26] Byron was only too aware of how justified was Lady M's qualified confidence in him, and his ironic reply has an anxious undertone: "I cannot sufficiently admire your cautious style since I became chicken-pecked, but I love thee, ma Tante, and therefore forgive your doubts *implied* but not expressed, which will last—till the next scrape I get into, and then we shall wax confidential again, and I shall have good advice."[27]

No advice would avail, as they both knew. Neither his rising spirits nor a fruitful collaboration with "Bell" could still his longing for Augusta. He tried to persuade Annabella to remain at Halnaby or to return alone to Seaham while he visited Six Mile Bottom, en route to finding a house for them in London. Annabella, however, would have none of this plan. Aunt Melbourne would be happy to house-hunt for them while they visited Augusta or Seaham—together. Byron yielded, resigning himself to playing the uxorious husband and attentive son-in-law.

THEIR THREE WEEKS at Seaham were happier than either could have anticipated. Exchanging the snows of Yorkshire for the milder climate of the coast gave Byron the freedom of the cliffs and beaches. Exuberantly, Annabella described their outings to Augusta; her "Werther" had reverted to being a "wild mirthful boy when climbing the rugged rocks and defying me to follow him in scrambling."[28] Indoors he threw himself into parlor games or played drafts with Sir Ralph; one evening, in a wild after-dinner romp of tag, he snatched the wig from Lady Milbanke's head. As company, Byron was "delightful and *at home*" in Seaham, Annabella told her sister-in-law. Augusta tried to rejoice with them. "You cannot be more delighted than I am," she wrote, "on learning that *Owls* can frolic sometimes, & that B can play the fool," but she could hardly help feeling excluded.[29]

Byron had written to Augusta only once since Halnaby; it was humiliating to read Annabella's apologies for his silence: "As for B he is certainly very *lazy*—but don't Scold him for it."[30] But Augusta was hurt enough to succumb to both malice and self-pity: "Poor dear B! He must have So many occupations, *walking*, *dining*, playing at Drafts with 'Mama' &c. &c. &c. & no time to scribble to 'Guss.' I am vain enough to think he does not forget her—& so—never mind."[31]

If Augusta suffered at having been forgotten for parlor games, she had a more severe test to come: Within a week of their arrival at Seaham, she was privy to Annabella's confidences about rapturous love-making. As Byron had suspected during his first visit, she proved an eager acolyte and passionate lover; gleefully, she reported that not even menstruation dampened Byron's ardor. To her "ONLY friend" she wondered whether her husband might not be shocked by her tireless enthusiasm for sex. Augusta's reply was restrained: "I am glad B's spirits do not decrease with THE *Moon*. I rather suspect he rejoices at the discovery of your 'ruling passion' for mischief in private."[32]

Writing late one night, Byron threw water on the fire in his dressing room; asleep in the adjoining bedroom, Annabella was awakened by the sounds of choking; he barely made it to bed when he complained of feeling faint and unable to breathe. He began raving deliriously that he was dying of his old Patras fever, and loudly swore he felt no remorse for his sins. Annabella got him to a chair, where he fell unconscious, overcome by the carbon monoxide fumes from the sea coal: "If Bell had not in the nick of time postponed old Nick for the present and sluiced me with Eau de Cologne and all sorts of waters besides, you might now have been repairing your latest suit of black to look like new for your loving nephew," he wrote to Aunt Melbourne. He saw this close call as an argument "in favor of matrimony for had I been single—the lack of aid would have left me suffocated."[33]

From the many weeks she had spent with Byron—at Six Mile Bottom, Newstead, and Hastings—Augusta was convinced that his drinking had caused the accident. While they were at Halnaby, Annabella had written that Byron was in the habit of begging brandy from her toilet case: "Dearest Annabella don't allow him to play the fool any more in this way," Augusta now chided, "& do hide YOUR *Brandy Bottle.*"[34]

Kept indoors by bad weather, husband and wife played *bouts-rimés*, a word game in which each participant supplies a line of verse that must rhyme with the last word of the previous player's contribution. As played at Seaham, the harmless parlor game turned into Truth or Dare, and Byron decided to send several of their best verses to Augusta. Annabella proposed making crosses in the margin to distinguish her lines from Byron's; at this suggestion, "he turned pale—and entreated me not, for I should 'frighten her to death,' " she recalled. In the examples she saved, Annabella italicized her offerings:

> *The Lord defend us from a Honey Moon*
> "Our cares commence our comforts end so soon," Byron countered.[35]

Augusta could bear no more of hearing about Seaham. She wanted Byron back, and after claiming to have looked around Newmarket in vain to find a suitable "castle" for the newlyweds to rent when they visited Six Mile Bottom, she insisted that they stay with her. Colonel Leigh was away, and she would gladly give up the master bedroom to her guests. On March 9, after a frenzy of packing, they left Seaham for Six Mile Bottom. The "treacle moon"[36]—Byron's phrase—was over.

Byron persisted in believing that Annabella's consent two years earlier would have prevented his affair with his sister; it seems more probable that a few months more of marriage—without Augusta, without the sexually charged memories of Six Mile Bottom, without the sight of eleven-month-old Medora—might have averted catastrophe. In little more than two months together they had endured greater trials, extremes of feeling, despair and hope, distance and intimacy than most couples in a decade; Annabella, not yet twenty-three, had experienced greater cruelty and violence in the nine weeks of her marriage than in her entire lifetime; she had proved herself and her love. Byron emerged from depression now into a state of childlike dependency: "He was not content if I was away from him except on the *black days* when he would shut himself up in frenzied gloom," Annabella recalled.[37] She could not have known that the more he needed her, the greater his terror and rage.

The journey south began as an ominous reprise of their wedding trip to Halnaby. He fixed angrily on his mother-in-law's parting words, confiding her daughter to his protection. "What did she mean by that?"

Byron demanded. "Are you not more fit to take care of yourself than I am to take care of you?" But Annabella was learning to ignore Byron's provocative remarks. Assuming a cheerfulness she was far from feeling, she soothed him to the point that at Wandsford, their last night alone together, he turned tenderly affectionate: "You married me to make me happy, didn't you?" And to her loving assent he replied: "Well, then, you *do* make me happy."[38]

With their arrival at Six Mile Bottom the fragile chance of happiness together ended. Leaving Annabella in the coach, Byron rushed ahead, "to prepare Guss," he told his wife. But Augusta was not downstairs to greet them. He then became visibly distraught, a state he attributed to mail awaiting him about Newstead. Finally, their hostess appeared. After her effusive letters, her manner, "timid and guarded," surprised Annabella. She shook hands stiffly with her sister-in-law and embraced her brother. Knowing how long it had been since Byron and Augusta had seen each other, Annabella tactfully withdrew. By the time she returned, she claimed, she had become an object of "aversion" to her husband and was treated as such. From that first evening, and every night thereafter for the next fifteen days, she was sent upstairs early; sometimes by hints, sometimes by grossly insulting behavior: "We can amuse ourselves without you, my *charmer*" was one signal. If she defied him by remaining, Annabella feared she would only break into tears, which, she tells us, she would have "regretted on A's account, believing as I did in her tender heartedness."[39]

A few days later, two gold brooches, identical but for the initials of Byron and Augusta, arrived from London. Each displayed a lock of the other's hair along with three incised crosses—their sign for sexual consummation. Both wore the jewel visibly displayed.

Byron was now drinking heavily. Augusta stayed up with him late into the night; unable to sleep, Annabella listened to their laughter from her bedroom above. When he finally did retire, he left the conjugal bed at dawn to rejoin his sister.

"He never spent a moment with me that could be avoided, & even got up early in the morning (contrary to his general habit) to leave me and to go to her." Their ardent sexual connection of only weeks before ended—with the exception of a few days when his sister was unavailable. Unlike Annabella, Augusta did not welcome sexual intimacy during her menstrual periods, and Byron did not scruple to taunt her for her inhibitions in Annabella's presence: "So you wouldn't Guss . . ."[40] he would say, alluding slyly to the night before.

Playing the two women off against each other had forged a bond between them, arousing his furious suspicions: They were in league

against him and he would humiliate them—together. Threatening to
"work" them both well,[41] he lay down on the sofa, ordering both of
them to take turns embracing him, while he compared them in the
grossest language.

He had not been mistaken. Currents flared between the two women
that excluded him; in the force field of desire, the sexual compass was
swinging wildly. Annabella seems always to have been drawn to
women; among Byron's attractions was his androgyny. Her intense
erotic yearnings now shifted from brother to sister: Appropriating
Augusta, she might also repossess her husband.

Pity joined with desire deflected violent impulses: "There have been
moments when I could have plunged a dagger into her heart but she
never saw them," Annabella confessed.[42] Otherwise, she exalted Augusta
as a fellow victim, "trampled upon" and submitting to Byron in order to
spare her.

"A— was most kindly anxious about me, and when I turned from his
barbarity to her affectionate care, could I have repaid it with the ingratitude of believing her actually his accomplice? I said—'it is impossible—
there is internal evidence it cannot be—I will not visit his sins upon
her—I will spare her feelings'—& I loved her better, as is natural,
because I sacrificed something of my selfish passions to these wishes."[43]

Augusta's role in these forbidden games is, as always, ambiguous.
Against mounting evidence that Augusta was an accessory to Byron's
treatment of her, Annabella continued to believe in her sister-in-law as
a loving ally and to act protectively toward her. There is no reason to
doubt that Augusta, fearful by nature, was frightened by Byron's violence; she herself had warned Annabella about his behavior when drinking. Decorous and reserved, she could only have been appalled by his
coarse revelations about their relationship: his remarks about her
"inflammable constitution,"[44] his humiliation of Annabella, and his
sexually familiar manner with her. Still, what we know about her control over Byron, her skillful "management" of his moods, and also
about the ways in which fear flays desire cast doubt on Augusta's role
as meek instrument of Byron's savagery. There is, moreover, ample evidence of the sister's collaboration in assuring the young wife that she
was unloved; at Byron's request, Augusta immediately produced and
read aloud letters from him, written during his courtship, that dispar-
aged Annabella, declaring his need to marry for money and detailing his
relations with other women. Among Augusta's "recitations," according
to Annabella, was the first verse of the "Stanzas for Music," during
which Byron mockingly asked his wife to guess to whom they were written. On one of their walks together, Augusta's notion of comforting

the younger woman was to confirm her fear that Byron had never cared for her; only the most "persevering" love on her part, joined with the power of "habit" over her husband, would allow them to live happily together.

Yet despite these scenes, enacted with Annabella as captive audience, despite the gold emblems of their passion, the laughter late into the night, and Byron's disappearance at dawn, Annabella insisted that Augusta was blameless. "She submitted to his affection, but never appeared gratified by it."[45]

The day after they had left Seaham, a letter had arrived from Lady Melbourne announcing the results of her house-hunting. She had just taken 13 Piccadilly Terrace for the Byrons, a large red brick mansion overlooking Green Park, and the property of the Duchess of Devonshire. "I am rather in a fright at what I have done," Lady Melbourne had written to Annabella.[46] As well she might be. The rent was exorbitant: £700 per annum, her niece's entire yearly income.

Lady Melbourne's news had reached them just after they arrived at Six Mile Bottom. Now, on the eve of their departure, arrived word that Augusta had been appointed a lady-in-waiting to Queen Charlotte. This unexpected sinecure provided apartments in Flag Court, St. James's Palace. As she would need to come to London to see about furnishing her rooms, Byron eagerly proposed that she stay with them.

Cautiously, Augusta deferred her decision. Whether or not she was playing a double game for the two weeks of the Byrons' stay—acting as Annabella's protective friend while remaining her brother's eager lover—the strain of long nights and intense engagement with two other people's anguish had left her exhausted. When Annabella spoke of going, Augusta, she observed drily, "evidently did not wish to detain us."[47] Before they reached London, however, Annabella wrote, seconding Byron's invitation; now Augusta accepted, planning to arrive ten days after they had moved into their new home.

"It was hopeless to keep them apart," Annabella wrote. "It was not hopeless, in my opinion, to keep them innocent."[48]

Away from Six Mile Bottom, Byron was freed from the obsessional grip of his attachment to Augusta. Without her his heart could "alight on the nearest perch"—in this case, his wife. In the ten days between their departure and Augusta's arrival in London he was "kinder" to her, Annabella recalled, than he had ever been—or ever would be again.

Hobhouse visited 13 Piccadilly Terrace the day after the newlyweds moved into their first home, and soon the claims of London life offered escape from the relentless intimacies of Halnaby, Seaham, and Six Mile Bottom. Aristocratic marriages were designed, after all, to keep unruly passions outside the conjugal relationship. The *ton* was in a fever to see Lord Byron domesticated by his clever young bride, and the newlyweds were lionized. They dined with Samuel Whitbread, an M.P. and heir to the brewing fortune, and visited Holland House. Their hostess was all "aimabilité," Annabella reported to her mother, "handling me as carefully as if I were a hedgehog."[49] Lady Milbanke grieved that she would be unable to see her daughter shine at a grand reception "in your *white Sattin* with lace." Now that he was married, Byron bid fair to become a watchword for the attentive husband: He hovered over Annabella's chair, laughing and talking with her alone.

While still at Six Mile Bottom, Annabella had shown "some symptoms which look a little gestatory," Byron had written to Moore. Once in London, confirmation of her pregnancy would also account for a burst of solicitude from the father-to-be. Byron described himself to Moore as "not particularly anxious" for a child,[50] contrasting his own feelings with the wild enthusiasm of the Milbankes and Lord Wentworth. Neither his financial circumstances—no immediate income and £30,000 of debt—nor abandonment by his own father argued for confidence about his new role. To other friends, however, he referred fondly to his "heir."

Meanwhile, the rewards of the literary life were proving less equivocal than family responsibilities. Not least for Byron, secure now in his success, was the power to help other poets he admired. To a letter from Samuel Taylor Coleridge, seeking aid in finding a publisher for his recent poems, Byron was warmly forthcoming. Assuring the older poet of the pleasure he would feel in complying with his request, he added, "I trust you do not permit yourself to be depressed by the temporary partiality of what is called 'the public' for the favourites of the moment; all experience is against the permanency of such impressions. You must have lived to see many of these pass away," he told the forty-two-year-old Coleridge, "and will survive many more—I mean personally, for *poetically*, I would not insult you by a comparison." Two years earlier, Byron had been instrumental in arranging for Coleridge's tragedy *Remorse* to be performed at Drury Lane, and he took this occasion to encourage the poet, suffering from poverty, depression, and addiction, to have another try at writing for the theater. Both men knew, however, that Byron's helpfulness, now and earlier, could not wipe the slate clean of youthful cruelty; in *English Bards and Scotch Reviewers*, the satire with which Byron, swinging wildly in all directions, had entered the literary scene, he had lampooned the author of *The Ancient Mariner* for a recent work, "To a Young Ass." So he was all the happier to make fur-

ther amends, explaining gracefully of *English Bards* that "it has been a
thorn in my side ever since; most particularly, as almost all the persons
animadverted upon became subsequently my acquaintances, and some
of them my friends."51 The next year, 1816, Murray, at Byron's urging,
published Coleridge's "Christabel," "Kubla Khan," and other poems in
a single volume.

On April 7, at Murray's, Byron for the first time met the poet (and
later, novelist) he admired above all others, Sir Walter Scott. In the symmetry of their success, the two best-selling authors hit it off instantly;
soon they were meeting at Murray's for several hours every day.
Another bond between the older and the younger man went unmen-
tioned. John Murray's teenage son recalled seeing Byron and Scott, both
lame, limping down the stairs at 50 Albemarle Street together.

AT 13 PICCADILLY TERRACE, where Lady Byron was organizing
the new household, a fragile harmony was about to shatter. On
April 12, the day of Augusta's expected arrival, Byron became so distraught that he left the house, returning only after their guest, accompanied by her eight-year-old daughter, Georgiana, had appeared. Such
was his state of "black agitation," Annabella recalled, that he could not
even greet his sister civilly. Moments later, however, he succumbed once
again to her spell; that same evening, in Augusta's presence, he warned
his wife: "You were a fool to let her come—You will find it will make a
good deal of difference to you *in all ways.*"52 Passive and menacing at
the same time, Byron never denied that he had invited Augusta; like an
undisciplined child, reduced to terror and rage by the absence of limits,
he lashed out at Annabella for her failure to overrule him and to take
command of his life.

Now, like a recurring nightmare, the scenario of Six Mile Bottom
was replayed. If she had suffered then, Annabella's advancing pregnancy now made her more vulnerable and caused Augusta's "Baby
Byron" to feel more abandoned. His manner was recalled by Annabella
as "most savage" and his treatment of her as characterized by "hatred
and loathing." Only days after Augusta moved in with them, Annabella
learned that her Uncle Wentworth was mortally ill: She hurried to the
dying man's bedside in his London house, remaining until her mother
arrived three days later from Seaham, in time only for her brother's
death on April 17.

While Annabella was feeling her uncle's "death bed scene as a relief
from the horrors of an incestuous home," Byron wrote tenderly and
solicitously, urging her to return:

Dearest—Now your mother is come I won't have you worried any longer—more particularly in your present situation which is rendered very precarious by what you have already gone through. Pray—come home.

ever thine
B[53]

This brief note has attracted very diverse interpretation. It has been used to discredit Annabella's accounts of Byron's behavior by revealing him as a loving and concerned husband. Yet others have seen Augusta's hand guiding her brother's pen, in the vague hope, perhaps, that if he began to sound like a fond husband, he would behave like one. In light of Byron's increasingly erratic behavior toward both women—with violent mood swings within shorter and shorter periods of time—his note, primed by Annabella's absence, may simply reveal his state of mind at the moment of writing, in this case, the often noted reflex of the abusive husband's firing off loving messages as soon as his wife has moved beyond his power. There would be other instances of this same behavior.

Lord Wentworth's death at least promised to alleviate Byron's financial worries. The peer's estate proved more substantial than was supposed, with Lady Milbanke and Annabella as principal heirs. (To inherit, the Milbankes, and later Lord and Lady Byron, agreed to assume the Noel family name, so that their family names became Noel Milbanke and Noel Byron.) Annabella, meanwhile, had moved closer to inheriting her uncle's entire estate; more immediately, it seemed that her parents would at last be able to help their only child.

Days after Lord Wentworth's death, Byron wrote several letters relative to his wife's eventual inheritance: He wanted a correction made by newspapers that had failed to mention Lady Byron's portion of the estate, and he wrote excitedly to Lady Melbourne and Tom Moore, providing details of the will.

Ugly as it appears to us, the image of Byron hovering over Annabella's inheritance reflects at this point desperation, not greed.* If Lady Melbourne had believed that the imposing Piccadilly Terrace

---

*Before the passage of the Married Women's Property Acts in the 1870s, brides' dowries were "all but advertised in the press," and a man's expectations that his fortunes would improve with marriage to a woman of means was a matter of law. A husband owned everything belonging to his wife, including what she might inherit, except such property as was specifically secured by trust in her name.

house would reassure Byron's creditors and buy him more time—the kindest interpretation of her folly—she was proved wrong. Nor did Byron's eagerness to see his wife's name published as one of Lord Wentworth's principal legatees work to his advantage. News of his marriage to an heiress brought creditors swarming; moneylenders—from as far back as Byron's minority—reappeared to claim principal long owed, plus many times these sums in interest.

Byron now began brooding about the probability of an execution on his property: the sale of all his possessions to repay debts. He would be forced to sell what he cared about most: his library. Dreading the bailiff's descent, living in the same house with his wife and sister (who was also his lover), his life was sliding into a dark replay of that of the father he had hardly known, Mad Jack Byron.

With increasing bitterness, Byron now blamed his father-in-law for his worsening money troubles. He had received nothing of the £20,000 owed him by the marriage settlement. Sir Ralph, however, had severe cash problems of his own. Litigation was delaying the settlement of Lord Wentworth's will. Furthermore, the end of the Napoleonic Wars and England's shift to a peacetime economy had created financial crisis and depression: High prices, unemployment, and poor crops were imposing hardships on all but the very rich. The failure of banks in Durham and Sunderland thwarted the Noels' efforts to raise mortgages on their property to help their daughter; they had even approached Lord Melbourne about a loan.

Patiently, Augusta defended Sir Ralph, pointing to his own difficulties and unavailing efforts to help the newlyweds. Byron would not hear her, refusing to receive or call on his in-laws, who had come to London in April. He would not even join them, Annabella recalled, in celebrating her twenty-third birthday on May 22.

Annabella has been portrayed as an indulged only child, shielded from concerns about money, incomprehending of her husband's financial straits, and unsympathetic to his despair over the consequences. Her letters, however, disprove this view. Unlike Byron, the "spoiled child" had few personal extravagances, and as time ran out she would soon call on bankers and lawyers herself in efforts to raise money.

Meanwhile, Augusta showed no signs of leaving Piccadilly Terrace, and it may have been the threat of a permanent ménage à trois that now caused the scales to fall from Annabella's eyes. She no longer saw in Augusta a mediator or fellow victim deserving of her protective attentions. The "ONLY friend" was now a full-fledged rival, and this revelation, with its sense of betrayal, seems to have cooled her own attachment, emotional and erotic, to her seductive sister-in-law.

At Six Mile Bottom, in the evening Annabella had been sent away and humiliated. On leaving, she had been able to rationalize the behavior of the others, suppressing memories of the visit like a bad dream. Now, pregnant and banished upstairs in her own home, she paced the floor, driven "almost mad" by the sounds of the two below. Byron was sexually engaged with both women, but it was Annabella who suffered the torments of uncertainty. Would her husband finally come to bed with her or remain with Augusta?

"I used to lay awake watching for that footstep by which my hopes and fears were decided," she recalled; "it was always expressive of the mood that had the ascendancy. It was either the stride of passion which seemed to print its traces on the ground with terrific energy or it was the irregular pace of animal spirits, rousing . . . 'flashes of merriment' and then he would laugh with Augusta as he came up the staircase."[54]

One night, when the two remained downstairs later than usual, the sounds of Annabella walking back and forth in the library above were so disturbing that Byron dispatched Augusta upstairs to quiet her. Out of pride, this time the wife managed to conceal her "agony of tears . . . but the thought of the dagger lying in the next room . . . crossed my mind—I wished it in her heart." For the moment she allowed herself to be soothed by Augusta's "voice of kindness," but as Annabella recognized, she was only deflecting dangerous impulses of murderous rage: "To prevent myself from indulging the passion of Revenge, I was obliged in that tumultuous state of mind to substitute another—that of Romantic forgiveness."[55]

Augusta still tried to intercede when Byron's behavior to his wife was intolerably abusive—and Annabella scrupulously records each of her attempts to mediate his rage. But it was apparent that Augusta's very presence exacerbated the misery of Piccadilly Terrace. In the middle of June, Annabella asked her sister-in-law to leave, and on the twenty-fifth, after a stay of two months, Augusta returned to Six Mile Bottom. Her departure, Annabella hoped, would cure Byron's "black agitation" and heal their failing marriage. There was only the briefest remission for both.

CHAPTER 26

"Woe Without Name, or Hope, or End"

ONLY DAYS after Augusta's departure, an American visitor called at 13 Piccadilly Terrace. George Ticknor, twenty-three, was a Boston Brahmin who had recently rejected the practice of law and was on his way to study classics at the University of Göttingen.* He came prepared to worship Lord Byron, whose verses had thrilled the reading public in America as they had in England. Somewhat to his own surprise, however, he found himself smitten by Lady Byron. Annabella was "pretty, not beautiful," but her "ingenuousness" enhanced her other attributes: "Rich in intellectual endowments, [she] is a mathematician, possesses common accomplishments in an uncommon degree, and adds to all this a sweet temper." Lady Byron "did not talk at all for display" but "revealed considerable knowledge—of America, France, Greece, with something of her husband's visit there—and spoke of all with a justness and light good humor." This is the Annabella who claimed as admirers the most brilliant young men of her London seasons, not the humorless prig and pedant of later portraits.

Like many of those who met the poet after reading his poems, Ticknor was astonished to find Lord Byron "in everything . . . un-like the characters of his own *Childe Harold & Giaour*," making it hard for the visitor to believe what he had heard about his host, "either of his

---

*Combining the grand tour with formal studies, the well-connected young scholar made it a point to meet as many cultural celebrities as possible. Besides Byron, these included in England, Scott, Wordsworth, Southey, Sir Humphry Davy, and Mrs. Edgeworth; on the Continent, Goethe, von Humboldt, and Madame de Staël, among others.

early follies or his present eccentricities." Along with Byron's "gentle" manners and his "natural and unaffected character," Ticknor, after another visit, noted, "Of his own works he talks with modesty, and of those of his rivals, or rather contemporaries, with justice, generosity, and discriminating praise." He was especially struck by Lord Byron's "affectionate manner" toward his wife, and his observations carry an almost prophetic poignancy: As Annabella was leaving the house for her waiting carriage one morning, he noted that "her husband followed her to the door, and shook hands with her, as if he were not to see her for a month."[1]

Mr. Ticknor could not know how privileged he had been to be received twice at home, followed by an evening as Byron's guest in his box at Drury Lane, together with Lady Byron and her parents. There were few visitors to Piccadilly Terrace, and his hosts accepted fewer invitations. Byron told Moore that because of Annabella's pregnancy he preferred to keep her very quiet, but this certainly did not accord with her own wishes at the time or her recollections thereafter.

Unhappy couples seem to run to extremes of social behavior; either they avoid being alone together by means of a frenzied calendar of engagements, or they disappear into isolation *à deux*. After a brief moment of harmony following Augusta's return home, Byron seems to have retreated into the reclusiveness of depression, demanding that Annabella suffer, without sharing, his solitude. On their rare appearances together in public they seemed less like fond lovers than shackled prisoners, leading Hobhouse to note the "fear of some friends that his Lordship confined himself too much with Lady Byron and that occasional separation—for they were never seen apart—might be more conducive to their comfort." With his characteristic literal-mindedness, the good Hobby later expressed astonishment at reading that Byron had complained of "being shut up in a dark London street," when in fact, as Hobhouse noted in his diary, "Piccadilly Terrace looked out upon the Green Park."[2]

Byron now found welcome relief from the claustrophobia of marriage, from missing Augusta, from worries about bailiffs. In May, through the offices of Douglas Kinnaird, he had been asked to join the Sub-Management Committee of Drury Lane Theatre. Now, at the end of one season and with another to be planned, he plunged himself into the unfamiliar business of running a large, financially troubled repertory company.

Byron's passion for the theater went back to his taste of stardom in amateur theatricals at Southwell, followed by the triumph of Harrow Speech Day, when he had declaimed Lear's speech to the storm. His letters and journals bear lavish testimony to his lifelong love of plays and players—towering above them all the legendary Kean in his Shakespearean roles—but also the glamour and excitement of first nights, even the malicious fun of deriding bad plays and worse performances. He could recite much of Shakespeare; he knew the great Jacobean dramatists almost as well, and he and Hobhouse used quotations from their favorite Restoration comedies as tag lines to running jokes. Now he made it his business to become familiar with every detail of his new responsibilities: He read through stacks of plays already submitted and, finding most of them "trash," as he told Moore, set about coaxing works of literary quality from Coleridge and others. Almost immediately he involved himself in casting decisions and in arbitrating other disputes about hiring and firing and even ticket pricing. New to committee work, he soon learned that there were more prima donnas among his fellow managers than ever appeared onstage, the most unmanageable being his irascible friend and sponsor Douglas Kinnaird. Byron's exuberant accounts of his associates—politics, tantrums, and tragedies (on July 6 Whitbread committed suicide by cutting his throat in his house on Dover Street)—all suggest a sense of release from his own worries. Drury Lane's Green Room was his escape from the "dark London street" of domestic life.

Annabella felt her exclusion from Byron's absorbing new life keenly, and she expressed her feelings of neglect by referring to him ironically as "the Manager." In her loneliness, she invited Lady Melbourne (to whom she had been decidedly "not at home" a few weeks earlier) to join her in Byron's box for a performance of *Othello*: "As the Manager is always trotting about behind the Scenes, I should not much like to be alone, unless I had an amant to interrupt my solitude," she wrote to her mother.[3] Her wan little joke seems an allusion to Byron's reported taunt before he disappeared into the backstage world of Drury Lane; informing her of "his profligate intentions in regard to the actresses," he announced: "I am looking out to see who will suit me best."[4] It was far from an idle threat.

The theater also filled the vacuum of a poetically fallow period, when, as Byron told Wedderburn Webster in early September, "I am writing nothing—nor even dreaming of repeating that folly."[5]

Then, on July 29, the day after the disastrous auction of Newstead and Rochdale, he signed his new—and final—will. Once the £60,000 of Lady Byron's marriage settlement was paid, the remainder of his estate was to be left to Augusta and her children. Since the honeymoon, Byron had periodically announced this intended change to Annabella as a taunting reminder of her diminished place in his affections, but she refused to take the new bequests in that spirit, seeing them instead as a generous but reasonable redistribution of his future assets based on his sister's greater need. Now, as though to confirm this view of Augusta's finances, the Leighs' situation was revealed to be as precarious as Byron's own. A relative's will, in which the colonel and his mother were heirs, was suddenly contested, while Charles himself—"that very helpless gentleman," as Byron called him—proved incapable of taking the few necessary steps to secure the military pension to which he was entitled, leaving to his wife the task of pursuing officialdom on his behalf. After trying to find a lawyer to help, Byron left for Six Mile Bottom.

Since Augusta's departure in June, Annabella had suffered feelings of remorse compounded by loneliness. Now their correspondence resumed, on the same sisterly note as before. Outdoing one another in unselfishness, Annabella professed her happiness that Byron was going to Six Mile Bottom to sort out their finances, while Augusta responded with regret that he was making the trip; she feared Charles might succeed in "prying" money from her brother who was himself on the verge of ruin. Annabella was particularly touched by this last evidence of Augusta's "disinterestedness," she told her. She would have been less moved had she known that it would be Augusta herself who did the prying, accepting at least three payments from Byron amounting to more than £720 over the next months.

As soon as her husband left London, Annabella explored every possibility of raising money. She visited Hanson herself and made inquiries of acquaintances with business connections, such as Colonel Doyle, husband of her friend Selina. She became knowledgeable about different types of mortgages, the problems of raising money on entailed estates, and the question of tenants' leases at Newstead.

From Epping, Byron wrote to Annabella, asking her to send on to him at Augusta's by the next coach "*two phials labelled drops* which Fletcher had forgotten to pack," signing himself "ever most lovingly thine B (not *Frac.*)"[6] to let her know that he had gotten over what she called his "Fractious" mood. In fact, he had been in such a rage when he left, Ann Fletcher recalled, that "Lady Byron was under the impression that she would never see him again and that he was going abroad."[7]

Writing to her mother on September 4, her relief is more palpable still: "B comes back today, and Augusta writes that he has been very disconsolate without me. I am marvelous happy at the expiration of my Widowhood."[8]

When she later came to describe Byron's behavior in the days before he left for Six Mile Bottom, there are no more indulgent nursery words, like "fractious" or "naughty." He had been "ferocious," she recalled, demanding a bed apart, only to keep her up at night with his harangues, alternately "cold and sneering" or "half in jest, begging her forgiveness." The house, after he left it, she wrote, "seemed to be inhabited only by remembrances of his Misery."[9]

FOR THE FIVE days of Byron's visit, Augusta loyally kept Annabella abreast of his moods and humors. More than anyone else, she was concerned about drinking as the cause of his violent behavior, and she used her influence to try to reduce Byron's alcohol consumption. Whether or not her arguments for temperance were the real cause of his irritation, for the first time he sounded critical of Augusta, starting with her distracted housekeeping: "Goose left a mousetrap in the apartment allotted to me the consequence of which is that from the very convenient place of its application, I have nearly lost a toe," he complained to Annabella, and there is a certain accusing tone in his report on the young Leighs. "All the children here look shockingly—quite *green*."*[10] His return home confirmed the undercurrent of the letter; Annabella found him "most kind towards me, but offended with her."[11] After four days of affectionate behavior toward his wife, he changed abruptly, she reported, speaking to her and about Augusta with equally "vindictive" feelings—and equal guilt: One day, when he and Annabella were driving in the carriage, he interrupted their conversation to tell her, "I shall break your heart and A's after all," as if it were a destiny he was doomed to fulfill.[12]

Before the Noels left London in early August for Kirkby Mallory, their Leicestershire estate, Lady Noel had offered Byron the use of Seaham, newly painted and refurbished, for Annabella's confinement and as long thereafter as they might like to stay. But their situation vis-à-vis the creditors had convinced Byron that any suspicion that he was leaving town "for a permanency" would end the present period of grace (now extended to early November), bringing the bailiffs before their promised hour. However reasonable his fears on this score, it was also true, as Annabella later recorded, that Byron had refused even to accompany her to Seaham. She was fearful of traveling alone, and still more ashamed to reveal to her parents her husband's refusal to attend the birth of their child. Having made her decision to stay in London, she

---

*In a period when high infant mortality was the norm and surviving childhood diseases, something of a miracle, Byron tended to blame parents for unhealthy children, related, perhaps, to faulting his mother for his deformity.

set about finding a doctor, asking her mother and Augusta to attend her as well.

Still, a threshold had been crossed. Annabella was now a wife, not a daughter. Her husband's griefs and burdens were hers—along with his triumphs—if he would allow her to share them. She now wrote proudly to her mother of Byron's faithful discharge of his Drury Lane responsibilities, when a short time earlier she had derided these same duties. In a stormy meeting "where I fancy he acquired great credit by the propriety and temperance of his conduct,"[13] Byron, with his fellow committee members, had accepted Kinnaird's angry resignation; he then gave the others, Annabella reported, his "honourable" assurance of continuing efforts on behalf of the troubled theater.

Her new approval of Byron's Drury Lane duties also reflects his worsening despair about their finances and Annabella's relief that diversion was to be found anywhere. The Noels had done everything within their power to raise money: They had sold several farms on their Seaham estates and with the help of five separate attorneys were trying to use Lord Melbourne's loan of £6,000 as collateral in a complicated mortgage scheme. Time was the problem; neither lawyers, banks, nor purchasers could be hurried. The Seaham buyer, a Colonel Dalbiac, had refused to pay until a writ was served on him; the period of grace was running out.

"The execution and Col. D's payment will run a race," Annabella wrote desperately to her mother on September 11, "and it would be a sad thing if the latter were to lose it by a few days. For positively, the Execution cannot be suspended beyond the 6th of Nover. . . . Do you know of any means by which a week could be gained?" she asked.

As for their possessions, Byron's library was Annabella's only concern: "I should very much lament the seizure of the books. I believe the sum is now £1,600"—pitiably small, it seems. "When B— has any hope of avoiding this last extremity, he is quite a different man," Annabella wrote, "for he feels it dreadfully, and distracts himself with the idea of Bailiffs in the House at the same time with the Midwife."[14]

His symbolic sense of loss and negation, as a man and a poet, heir to a proud literary patrimony, conflated with fears of his displacement by the child to come: The midwife and the bailiff had become one in their power to diminish and deny him.

Drury Lane provided diversion, but only poetry could help restore his sense of control over chaos. After a long hiatus, he eased into the routine of writing by taking up a poem begun several years earlier. *The Siege of Corinth* is set against the background of the Ottoman assault on the Venetian-occupied Greek city in 1715. Its attraction to

Byron now was the theme of betrayal: his hero, banished by false witness, becomes the archetype of moral outcast, a traitor to his country. Denounced anonymously, Lanciotto, once the warrior pride of Venice, has become "Alp the renegade," his native republic now only "the memory of a thousand wrongs." On the eve of siege, Francesca, Alp's beloved from his earlier life and the daughter of Corinth's embattled governor, appears before him. She implores him to repent and embrace the Cross once more. Unknown to him, she has died that very night; it is her ghost who pleads for them both: "Wring the black drop from thy heart, / And tomorrow unites us no more to part." Like Annabella, Francesca appears inhuman and inaccessible; like his wife, she is destroyed by Alp's betrayal of faith, equated with the betrayal of love. "I will get to heaven by the hem of your garments," Byron had told Annabella, seeing her loving expression in answer to a particularly cruel remark.[15] His surrogate definitively rejects heavenly forgiveness for revenge.

Byron had completed a final draft of another poem. The last of his Oriental tales, *Parisina* is also the clearest exposition of the incest theme he had yet attempted, and the most dramatically exciting. Set in medieval Ferrara, the poem reworks a historical incident of crime and punishment: For loving his stepmother, Parisina, Hugo, the ruler's bastard son, is executed, while his mistress, forced to watch him die, goes mad with grief.* By choosing a documented event instancing the Phaedra topos of a wife's passion for her stepson, Byron avoided the anxiety—and risk—entailed in writing about the relations of brother and sister. Shifting the blame from the male to the female temptress, Byron stacks the cards against the errant wife by assigning her a double betrayal. Fresh from an assignation with her lover, Parisina indicts him by talking in her sleep:

> And Hugo is gone to his lonely bed,
> To covet there another's bride;
> But she must lay her conscious head
> A husband's trusting heart beside.
>
> .   .   .   .
>
> And mutters she in her unrest
> A name she dare not breathe by day,
> And clasps her Lord unto the breast
> Which pants for one away.[16]

---

*The historical Este ruler, Nicholas II, had both lovers beheaded.

On November 2, Annabella, now in her eighth month of pregnancy, finished copying *The Siege*, and possibly *Parisina* as well, for the printer. At the same time that she was transforming Byron's galloping lines with their crossings-out and additions into her elegant, clear script, she was also writing in her own voice, with the urgent task of putting down on paper her attempts to understand her husband. After ten months of life together, in the storm center of his blackest moods and, not infrequently, their victim, she was now more sympathetic, loving, and generous toward Byron than she had ever been—or would ever be again.*

His early Calvinism, she saw clearly, was the source of both his "irritation" toward religion and the "gloom and despair" that "discoloured his views of Divine Government here, and Judgment hereafter." But she accepted that with all his "vague ideas of Virtue," he fulfilled its duties from "the instinctive goodness of his heart." Without ever using the word, she grasped the Promethean tragedy of Byron's moral ambitions: His imagination was "too exalted—and when he cannot do good on the vast scale which it presents, he does not descend to perceive the lesser opportunities of common existence." Her husband's best self had been brutalized by betrayal (especially *"romantic"*), and she mourned his belief that the disinterested impulses of his heart could be repaid only with disappointment. A few days later, she wrote to Augusta in the same vein, but more personally; one of her "greatest fears for B" and his "greatest misfortune" was that "habitual *passion for excitement*," always found in "ardent temperaments."

With perception stripped of pride, she saw in Byron the fatal workings of an existential boredom, what Baudelaire would diagnose as "spleen" and Byron himself called the "craving void" within him. In Annabella's view, it was this "Ennui of a monotonous existence that drives the best hearted people . . . to the most dangerous paths, and makes them often seem to act from bad motives when in fact they are only flying from internal suffering by an external stimulus. The love of Tormenting arises chiefly from this Source."[17]

ENNUI WAS a disease whose cause, in Byron's case, lay somewhere in the vexed relations between mind and body; his "vitiated stomach," hostage to his habits of excess, starving and drinking, was aggravated

---

*In her later, embittered state of mind, she titled these thoughts "Reflections on Lord B's character written under delusive feelings in its favor." It should be pointed out here that Annabella's recollections of these months, along with those of the other participants and/or observers, may have been colored by subsequent events.

by precisely those efforts to escape his mental prison. "For that reason I so much dread B's entering those pursuits of Fashion, whose votaries are always victims of this misery," she wrote to Augusta. "At the same time, I would have his mind diverted from itself by every possible means that would not lead to an accession of the Disease, even if it meant courting Lady M[elbourne]'s Society for him, or anything in the world to arrest its *fatal* course." She begged her "dear, dear A" to "give me every opinion of yours on this & don't mistrust your own judgment." Annabella had exhausted every resource; she saw catastrophe looming: "I know in what it must end if it encrease—and with such apprehensions will you wonder if I am sometimes almost heart broken before my time."[18]

In the next two months, Byron acted out her darkest predictions. On November 8, the event he had most dreaded came to pass: The bailiff arrived at the house to oversee the "executions" or sale of all their possessions for debt. Incredibly, Byron tried to keep up the pretense that Annabella had no idea why this gentleman was there; pride had moved him beyond reason. Acknowledging her uselessness, Annabella yearned for a "man friend of common sense . . . to laugh B out of his excessive horror on this subject, which he seems to regard as if no mortal had ever experienced anything so shocking," she wrote to Augusta.

Now both wife and sister had become one woman in his mind, and the single architect of his ruin: "He loves us or hates us together," Annabella wrote to her double.[19]

To Hobhouse, Byron confessed that he felt driven "half-mad" by financial embarrassments, adding that "he should think lightly of them *were he not married*" but that these same worries "doubled with a wife."[20] His anguish did nothing to soften his stance against accepting money—under any guise—from his publisher. Quite the reverse: Exacerbated pride made him the more adamant. Hearing that Byron was forced to sell his library because of debt, Murray sent him a check for £1,500 with the promise of more in a few weeks, accompanied by the offer to sell the copyrights he owned for the poet's benefit. On November 14—six days after the arrival of the bailiff—Byron returned the check, "not accepted—but certainly not unhonoured" he wrote to Murray graciously, and he added the proud untruth that "the circumstances which induce me to part with my books though sufficiently—are not *immediately* pressing."[21] (Six weeks later, he again returned a draft from Murray for 1,000 guineas for the copyrights of *Parisina* and *The Siege of Corinth*, insisting that the sum was "much more than the two poems could possibly be worth.")[22] Annabella's fair copy of *Parisina* had allayed Murray's fears about the content: "What you hinted to me and wrote had alarmed me," he told Byron, "and I should not have read it aloud to my wife if my eye had not traced the delicate hand that transcribed it."[23] It was as though his "violent" male text had been emasculated by Annabella's virtue, in the form of her "feminine" penmanship, and Byron now warned the publisher, "You must not trust to that—for my copyist would write out anything I desired in all the ignorance of innocence."[24] His insistence on Annabella's "ignorance" and "innocence" even after his efforts to include her in his own incestuous scenario suggests that he took Murray's fatuous remark as an accusation to be guiltily denied.

He had certainly made good on an earlier threat to his wife's innocence, taking a mistress from among the actresses at Drury Lane. Susan Boyce was barely more than an extra in the company. Undoubtedly pretty, if not talented, she was also angry, ambitious, and jealous; her letters to Byron bristle with accounts of backstage catfights because another actress had received unfair preferment or had insulted her. ("I was attacked last night in a most cruel manner by Mrs. Scott who by the way was *much elevated*—I don't know whether it was the smell or taste of gin—one it was for certain. She was most disgusting in her manner. My situation was truly pitiable.")[25]

When they first became lovers, in late October or early November, Boyce was living with her six-year-old son and her sister near the Foundling Hospital in Coram Fields. Then she took a room in New Ormonde Street, nearer the theater, where Byron could visit whenever he liked—not often enough, she found. As her plaintive letters reveal, Boyce waited up on several occasions when Byron neither appeared as promised nor made any excuses. In fact, he was too demoralized to do more than go through the motions of a love affair. He had never had any real feelings for Boyce; now, depressed and drinking heavily, his sexual performance was, at best, perfunctory. When Boyce began asking him for money, he found the perfect excuse to get rid of her.

This cheerless dalliance with a marginal actress would hardly merit a footnote in Byron's life but for the way he used her. He reported—or invented—details of their relations to torture Annabella and, soon, to humiliate Augusta as well. He came to Annabella's bed directly from visiting Susan (or so he said), and he compared his very pregnant wife's swollen body to the "unrespectable" allure of his lover. He forbade Annabella to use his box at the theater, warning that he was likely to tryst there with Miss Boyce. He provided an inventory of the jewels he had given to his mistress and threatened to bring her home to his own bed. Finally he ordered Annabella to relay all of this to Augusta.

There is childish pathos as well as irony to Byron's exhibitionism: the flogging of his tepid affair with poor Susan Boyce to convince

Annabella and Augusta that he was a monster worthy of the Marquis de Sade—his literary discovery of these months. Actually, the "sins" of halfhearted sexual activity outside Piccadilly Terrace soon paled in light of the crazed behavior within.

With Annabella weeks away from giving birth, Byron's brandy intake increased. Augusta was summoned in advance of her scheduled visit for the lying-in. When she arrived on November 15 she was horrified by what she found: servants in a state of terror and Annabella cowering in her room. Periodically Byron would work himself up to "paroxysms" during which (he later confessed to Hobhouse and Scrope Davies) he may have been "bereaved of reason." From raving that he hoped Annabella and the baby would die, he moved to rampages of physical violence, smashing furniture and valuables and firing pistols in his room (just below his wife's). Augusta had never seen Byron in such a state before, and she quickly despaired of managing him alone. She sent for Captain George Byron.

Lady Noel had arrived in London on November 16, the day after Augusta, but she promptly succumbed to various ailments, keeping to her rooms at Mivart's Hotel. Her absence was the one source of relief; if her mother ever learned what was going on at Piccadilly Terrace, Annabella believed it would destroy her, and she had been dreading the charade of happy anticipation.

As Annabella's time approached, Byron spiraled further toward disintegration. He was rarely home, unless to appear late at night, drunk and threatening. Augusta now asked Mrs. Clermont to stay with them, explaining (in the ex-governess's account) that Byron "appeared to feel the greatest hatred towards his Wife and the unborn Child"[26] and reiterating what others had heard him say: that he hoped they would both die. All those now staying in the house agreed that Lord and Lady Byron were never to be together without a third person present, and there seems to have been an informal arrangement to ensure that someone was with Annabella at all times.

In this waking nightmare, the superhuman task of running the household fell to Augusta; hers was the harrowing responsibility of protecting Annabella while attempting to soothe Byron and keep him from drink, verbal and physical abuse of his wife, or self-inflicted injury, as he had also begun threatening suicide. Reasoning with him was futile—not because he was irrationally unaware of what he was doing but because he knew only too well. When Augusta pointed out to him that he was destroying himself along with those whose happiness he was bound to consider, he replied: "I am determined to fling Misery around me & upon all those with whom I am concerned."[27]

Annabella paid tribute to her sister-in-law's courage, along with her devotion: "To defend me from his threatened violence & cruelty, she seemed to acquire a fortitude inconsistent with her timid nature."[28] Even if guilt played a part in Augusta's heroism, her triumph in preventing a bloodbath could only have succeeded through the love and trust she inspired in all concerned. We need not wonder why Byron adored her.

On December 9, the day before the baby was born, Annabella, with Augusta's encouragment, consulted with a family friend, Samuel Heywood, sergeant-at-law, on the advisability of leaving the house for the delivery. Either on his advice, or following her own counsel, she decided that the risk of her parents' discovering that she had left home for the lying-in was too great, and she remained at Piccadilly Terrace. Byron, however, seems to have got wind of this plan and taken it very ill; with labor already beginning, he berated Annabella savagely, and "with the strongest expressions of aversion and disgust" demanded to know "whether she chose to live with him anymore."[29] Then he left for the theater.

The next day, Sunday, December 10, at 1:00 p.m., Annabella gave birth to a girl, Augusta Ada, named for her godmother. She would be called Ada, however, a name her father claimed had entered the family in the reign of King John. On being shown his healthy infant daughter, Byron supposedly said, "Oh! What an implement of torture I have acquired in you!"[30]

The days just before Annabella's confinement, Byron's behavior, for the first time, called into question his sanity. Although he spoke constantly to Hobhouse and others of going abroad, in his own mind, the condition of his "Liberty" was getting rid of Annabella; either she and the child would live with her parents indefinitely, or they would divorce, or—he would destroy her.

According to sworn testimony given by Ann Rood Fletcher, Annabella's maid and the wife of Byron's valet,* just after the baby was born, Byron would "lock himself into Lady Byron's room, scream and shout at her." Mrs. Fletcher heard him "walk about the room violently as if in a state of just anger," she recalled in a telling phrase, after which "he remained in the room for an hour; leaving it in a great rage & slamming the door violently after him."

Then comes testimony by both Fletchers so horrific as to be

---

*Ann Rood and Fletcher were married in the second week of January 1816, but as her testimony was given at that time in the name of Fletcher, that is the form used.

shrouded—still—in shame and secrecy. Entering the room immediately after Byron left, Mrs. Fletcher found her mistress "in a very great state of alarm & agitation; saying that he had attempted to push . . . ." Here the word "push" had been crossed out by another hand, and the phrase substituted "to persuade her to go to bed with him." To continue with Ann Fletcher's testimony, "This happened three times within a fortnight of Lady Byron's confinement." On the fourth occasion of Byron's attempted rape of his wife, Mrs. Fletcher herself came upon them locked in physical struggle and called for help. From this point on, Mrs. Fletcher, "with the view of preventing Lord B from entering her Ladyship's room by surprise . . . used to keep the doors, which led into her ladyship's chamber locked."[31]

More than the firing of pistols, or even Byron's ravings that he wished his wife and child dead, these incidents of attempted rape help to explain the terror and peculiar paralysis of the household, caught between the horror of the act and the deference accorded a man's power—particularly a nobleman's power—over his wife, female relations, and servants.

Over his own life Byron felt he had no control whatsoever. If he saw his infant daughter as an instrument of torture, then he accepted the role of Annabella's executioner. It is hardly a coincidence that he became virtually obsessed in these weeks by the writings of the Marquis de Sade* and he threatened "to carry the ideas into execution;"[32] the "Divine Marquis," as other acolytes baptised him, provided Byron with a user's guide down the mine shaft of evil: More important than the crimes, de Sade's writings offered a manual for moral suicide.

Like the Marquis, who, when accused, denied everything, Byron insisted on his innocence. No martyr to ideology, he had shown with his flight from Edleston that he would not risk transgressive behavior known beyond the private realm, and he was shrewdly legalistic about the distinction between punishable and nonpunishable offenses committed in his domestic life: In the course of an angry exchange with Annabella in her room on January 3 that reduced her to tears he announced, "A woman has no right to complain if her husband does not beat or confine her—and you will *remember* that I have neither *beaten* nor *confined* you. I have never done an act that would bring me under the law—at least on this side of the Water."[33]

---

*He ordered a reluctant Augusta to send to Carlin's Library for de Sade's works, but when the books did not arrive, he asked his old fencing master, Henry Angelo, to fetch them in person.

What Annabella most feared was that Byron would claim his legal right to take their child from her, either leaving England with Ada or giving the infant to Augusta to raise. He had threatened both, and Augusta now sought Mrs. Clermont's advice as to what her reply should be if Byron proposed placing the child with her.

After their altercation on January 3, Byron did not visit Annabella or the baby. Then, on January 6, she received from him the following note: "When you are disposed to leave London—it would be convenient that a day should be fixed—& (if possible) not a very remote one for that purpose.—Of my opinion upon that subject—you are sufficiently in possession—& of the circumstances which have led to it—as also—to my plans—or rather—intentions—for the future.—When in the country I will write to you more fully—as Lady Noel has asked you to Kirkby— there you can be for the present—unless you prefer Seaham.—As the dismissal of the present establishment is of importance to me—the sooner you can fix on the day the better—though of course your convenience & inclination shall first be consulted.—The child will of course accompany you—there is a more easy and safer carriage than the chariot—(unless you prefer it) which I mentioned before—on that you can do as you please."[34]

There was no signature.

Annabella was shocked. Whatever alternatives to the Piccadilly establishment had been discussed during their stormy interchange a few days before, nothing prepared her for Byron's note (delivered by Augusta) ordering her coldly from her own house with a four-week-old infant. Mrs. Clermont was with her when she read his words and recalled that "she cryed & said although I expected it I cannot help feeling *this—to think* I have lived to be hated by my husband." She wrote to him the next day with one sentence, saying, "I shall obey your wishes, and fix the earliest day that circumstances will admit for leaving London."[35]

Before leaving, however, she sought professional opinion on Byron's mental state. Probably her motives in doing so were mixed: If he were declared of unsound mind, his chances of securing paternal rights to their child were diminished. And she had ample reason for believing him to have been delusional, from his behavior toward her to his threats of suicide. Both Augusta and George Byron, moreover, were even more strongly convinced of his madness. There was also Byron's own conviction of his fatal predisposition to crime, leading to acts beyond his control and suggesting what we would now call paranoid episodes. "The principal insane ideas are—that he *must* be wicked—is foredoomed to evil—and compelled by some irresistible power to follow this destiny, doing violence all the time to his feelings," Annabella now wrote in a memo to Dr. Baillie, who had treated Byron's foot in his Harrow days.

The dilemma for her, she told Baillie, was the evidence that her presence triggered what she elsewhere called his "seizures": "Undoubtedly I am more than anyone the subject of his irritation, because he deems himself (as he has said) a villain for marrying me on account of former circumstances—adding that the more I love him, & the better I am, the more accursed he is."

This observation also allowed Annabella to recast her dismissal as an "experiment" into which she willingly entered: "I am convinced that my removal will compose him for a time—and I wish to defer any attempt at restraint till its effects are seen," she noted coolly.[36] Annabella also called on Hanson, visiting the lawyer at home. According to Hobhouse—the only source for this interview—Hanson was horrified by her apprehensions. The lawyer's inaction may have contributed to Byron's breakdown, but he would never be so disloyal to his client as to acknowledge so much as a worrisome symptom—hardly surprising, given his recent cover-up of the insanity of his son-in-law, Lord Portsmouth. "Mr. Hanson *actually thought it possible*," Hobhouse commented, "her Ladyship might have a design of *resorting to personal restraint*," and Hobhouse, too, explained away the behavior she now described, including threats of suicide, as "eccentricities" observed in Byron since childhood.[37]

George Byron had moved out shortly after the birth, but on January 13 he called at Piccadilly Terrace to see the baby. While Annabella and Augusta received the visitor in the drawing room, Byron entered in a state of towering rage. He left moments later, holding a terrified Annabella in his grip. Augusta recalled, "The expression of his countenance was so shocking when he took her from the room where we were that George and I were in terror till he returned and stood listening in expectation that something dreadful was about to take place."[38] That it did not was due only to Annabella's managing to flee upstairs to her quarters. Until then, she said, "I never apprehended *immediate* danger to my life."[39]

It was the decisive encounter. Early on the morning of Monday, January 15, without waking her sleeping husband, Annabella and the baby, accompanied by a maid, left Piccadilly Terrace for the freezing trip north. Byron would never see his wife or their child again.

CHAPTER 27

"Fare Thee Well!"

𝓘N THE LATE afternoon of January 16, while Annabella and the baby were on their way to Leicestershire, Augusta, "in an agony of nerves," waited for a visit from Dr. LeMann. Byron complained of "languor and of feeling ill," she reported to her sister-in-law, adding that he had asked after her. She had replied reassuringly and "spoke as you desired *lightly* of your feelings," she told Annabella.[1]

Thus, on the night after her departure from London, Annabella set herself to the task of composing a letter "as may accord with the medical advice I have received for Lord B—, and with the wishes of those relations who concurred in deeming it necessary. I therefore wrote cheerfully & kindly, without taking any notice of what might revive diseased associations," she recalled.[2] In fact, she managed two letters: The first, written that same night, gave news of the travelers, with pleas to "remember my medical prayers & injunctions"; teasing Byron with one of his own self-deprecating phrases, she urged: "Don't give yourself up to the abominable trade of versifying—nor to Brandy—nor to any thing or any body that is not *lawful & right*." Playfully, she asked him to send word of his "obedience" to her at Kirkby, closing with "Ada's love to you and mine." Once they arrived, she wrote again, a cozy letter, brimming with domestic trivia and expressions of affection. Addressing her husband as "Dearest Duck," she reported on their safe arrival, told him how much both her parents "long[ed] to have the family party completed," and promised privacy for all his needs: "Such a W.C.! and such a *sitting*-room or *sulking*-room all to yourself. If I were not always looking about for B," she wrote wistfully, "I should be a great deal better already for country air. *Miss* finds her provisions increased & fattens thereon." And she sent "love to the good goose, [Augusta] & every body's love to you both from hence." It was signed,

> Ever thy most loving
> Pippin . . . Pip—ip[3]

With this second endearing letter, in particular, Annabella may be said to have succeeded too well; it would be used to discredit all her subsequent accounts of their year-long marriage. From any point of view, this letter is problematic. While she had been instructed about the tone to take in writing to Byron, it is still hard to accept her tender teasing as a tranquilizer fabricated to doctor's orders. More plausibly, the letter points to her own feelings of security and relief; from the safety of her childhood home, she could reveal how much she still loved her husband and wanted desperately to believe that his cruelty and rejection were caused by disordered spirits. In this construction, too, his behavior could not be taken personally: "To avenge disease on its victim would be as inhuman as disgraceful," she now wrote to her friend Selina Doyle.[4]

Disappointingly, then, Dr. LeMann's initial consultation proved inconclusive. Appearing confused at first, Byron had soon talked "openly, rationally and good humouredly, *always avoiding ye main point*" (presumably his violent behavior prior to Annabella's departure).[5] LeMann had prescribed calomel, or mercurous chloride, an all-purpose remedy given for ailments as various as kidney and bowel complaints and syphilis.

Her bags packed, Augusta had planned to return immediately with Georgiana to Six Mile Bottom; the little girl had been ill during their entire London visit, and a peevish Colonel Leigh reported that all the children at home had bad colds. LeMann, however, now enjoined Augusta to delay her departure. His patient's condition perplexed him; Byron complained of feeling worse and begged the doctor to return the next day. Indeed, he looked dreadful, Augusta wrote, in what would now become daily bulletins to Annabella. His complaints included pains in his hip—on the same side as the lame foot; other pains in his loins the doctor ascribed to a liver ailment, while palsylike tremors and memory lapses gave LeMann cause to believe that he may even have suffered a mild stroke. One eye appeared much smaller than the other, and Augusta remarked on periodic swelling of his entire face.

To divert him, a theater party was organized with Augusta, George

Byron, and Scrope Davies. Although the play was a comedy,* Byron was moved to tears. Otherwise, he stayed up drinking with Hobhouse all night, every night. Augusta was helpless to stop him; with Hobhouse as drunk as Byron, it fell to her, kept up until the small hours of the morning, to get rid of their guest and assist her brother, staggering and falling on his face, upstairs to bed. Both women were united in their hatred of Hobhouse. Annabella believed that from motives of jealous spite, he was actively conspiring in Byron's ruin, while the normally charitable Augusta now confessed to wishing Hobby dead!

From the outset, Annabella had suffered doubts about leaving Byron and Augusta together when it would be known all over London that she had gone. Now she wondered why she should meekly accept the doctor's word that Augusta must stay. Through the intermediary of George Byron she informed LeMann—and in no uncertain terms—that her husband must be persuaded to join her at Kirkby Mallory for his health, further asking George to convey her views to Augusta and Hanson. If George is to be believed, the doctor just as strongly advised against this move. He preferred to convince Byron indirectly, prescribing, for example, more vigorous exercise—like long rides—than the city could provide. By this means, he was sure, Byron would decide on going to Kirkby as his own idea. But the doctor was mistaken.

As long as he could keep Augusta with him at Piccadilly Terrace, Byron had no real intention of going to the country. When the beleaguered Colonel Leigh now threatened to come to London and take his wife home, Byron craftily insisted he must stay with them. The colonel backed down. As Augusta ingenuously explained to Annabella: "He (sposo)† has been seized with such a comical fright of B. following me if I go home that he now entreats me to stay."[6]

More than a little malice snakes through Augusta's daily bulletins to Kirkby. On the one hand, she reported that Annabella was "mentioned by him with great kindness"; she noted how often Byron read her letters and relayed tender messages from the patient himself: "Tell her as I told Murray that she is the only woman I could have lived 6 months with." She passed along Byron's pleas of "laziness" as his only reasons for not writing and for failing (as he told LeMann) to go to the country sooner. But Augusta also conveyed disquieting news of Byron's pursuit of two sisters, the Misses Cooke, both ingenues at Drury Lane, where

---

*It is not clear on which night they attended, but the entire week's programme at Drury Lane featured comedies.

†Husband.

his advances to the young players were already the cause of gossip. Worse, he was writing to Frances Webster in Paris and talked of going to see her. Mrs. Clermont, too, weighed in with reports from Piccadilly Terrace. She confirmed Augusta's account of Byron's infatuation with one of the Cooke sisters, adding that he had also spoken of marrying the charming heiress Miss Margaret Mercer Elphinstone "if he could rid himself of his present connection."[7]

Meanwhile, LeMann moved closer to the view that Byron suffered from physical illness alone; his concern about his patient's excessive and continuous drinking suggests that he had come to attribute the irrational and violent behavior, the shakes, memory loss, the spells of weeping, and grandiosity (Byron had taken to comparing himself to Napoleon), to nightly binges of brandy.

Annabella was devastated. According to her own logic, she had no choice now but to see Byron's behavior in moral terms: She had been the victim, not of a man so far disordered in mind and spirit that he must be forgiven all responsibility for his words and actions, but of a monster of knowing and unrepentant depravity.

Events now moved forward with an inexorable rhythm of their own. A few days after her daughter's arrival at Kirkby, Lady Noel asked for news of Piccadilly Terrace. By way of reply, Annabella showed her a letter from Selina Doyle, confidante and friend of both mother and daughter. To her horror, Lady Noel read the phrases "ill-treatment" and "outrages committed one after the other" and demanded to know their meaning. Annabella broke down, describing to both her parents the nightmare of her marriage and confinement—with one significant omission: She did not, it seems, raise the issue of incest. What she did confess, however, was quite enough to determine Lady Noel upon going to London immediately to seek legal advice on a separation; the outraged father had already decided that his daughter would never set foot under Byron's roof again.

Before Lady Noel left Kirkby on January 20, 1816, she had arranged an interview with a rising young lawyer, Stephen Lushington, taking with her, for purposes of the meeting, a memo from Annabella documenting the grievances of her marriage of twelve months and one week.

Lushington was not the only lawyer, however, or even the most distinguished to be consulted by the Noels. In addition, they retained Sir Samuel Romilly, fifty-nine, a barrister in Chancery and old family friend. Acknowledged to be one of the most brilliant jurists of the period, Romilly was a Whig M.P., king's counsel, and a tireless advocate of reform. Unhappily, the burdens of political activism combined with a busy practice caused a bizarre professional lapse on the jurist's part.

Within months of being retained by the Noels, he absentmindedly agreed to represent Byron in the separation proceedings. For this the poet demonized Romilly in letters and even verse as a monster of perfidy, plotting to destroy him.

Before bowing out of this embarrassment of clients, Romilly urged that Sir Ralph Noel deliver to Lord Byron a letter that he, the lawyer, would dictate, proposing, first, a quiet separation, and, second, that Annabella must neither write to nor speak with Byron "on any account." With her assent to the latter proposal, the strong-willed young woman effectively yielded control of her life to her family and their appointed surrogates. The machinery to end her marriage had been set in motion; from now on, how she felt about the man she still loved became irrelevant.

Annabella's only purchase on autonomy was to outdo her advisers. She became more outraged and accusing, more unforgiving and vengeful, than any of them. If Byron had truly set out to corrupt his wife, he succeeded beyond his wildest dreams. He had turned her heart to stone.

As THE MOST documented and dissected marriage in literary history, the twelve months that Byron and Annabella lived together have, in the intervening 182 years, attracted an army of analysts, biographers, mostly, but also other commentators, starting with Harriet Beecher Stowe and the journalist Harriet Martineau, all of whom added their own particular biases to the historical record. To complicate further the tangled yarn of Byron's brief marriage, Annabella Milbanke Noel, as Lady Byron, devoted most of the remainder of her long life to accumulating evidence of her "Annus Terribilis": She conducted interviews, took depositions, had letters copied, and provided two detailed "Narratives" and several shorter summaries of her version of events.

In history's judgment, the ugliness of her enterprise—legalistic, self-justifying, and, finally, obsessive—has served to indict Annabella herself. If she has not been found guilty of outright falsehood, she has been accused of distorting the record through her selective memory, desire for revenge, and obtuse reading of Byron's behavior.

At the outset, Annabella's reason for building her case was to assure the custody of her baby. By law, the children of a marriage belonged to the father. Byron could have taken their infant daughter anywhere he chose, or given her to any surrogate parent or institution; the mother would have had no further right even to see her child again. (Annabella's fears were not unfounded; Byron threatened to do just that, and within five years he would separate another woman from their child, with devastating consequences.) The only card she held was evidence against her estranged husband so criminally damaging if made public that its possession alone would effectively deter any claim of paternal rights.

To the end of his life, Byron denied—totally and categorically—Annabella's account of events, along with the reports of every other contemporary who had taken her side and contributed to her vast archive. Unhappily for him, many of those who "cooperated" with Annabella were close to Byron. Among those witnesses who either publicly or privately confirmed Annabella's words were George Anson Byron, the poet's cousin and heir to the title; his valet Fletcher; Fletcher's wife, Ann, then employed as Annabella's maid; John Cam Hobhouse; and finally, most damaging of all, Augusta herself.

Still, one voice rises above the others. Victim, witness, defender, prosecutor, and judge, surviving most of the other participants in the drama, Annabella, Lady Byron, had the last word. She now informed Lady Noel in London: "I being in a sound state of mind & body do give my authority for such measures as may be necessary to effect a separation—of the propriety of which none of my advisors seem to doubt. I therefore no longer consider this person as connected with me, or as the subject of consideration in any way but that of business."[8] The style of her statement—that of a last will and testament—is also an epitaph.

On January 29, a letter from Sir Ralph to Lord Byron was delivered to Piccadilly Terrace. Respectful and moderate in tone, it left specific charges vague, a key strategy crafted by Lushington. After noting politely that "circumstances have Come to my knowledge which Convince me, that with your opinions, it cannot tend to your happiness to continue to live with Lady Byron," Sir Ralph moved to the issue, stating that he was "yet more forcibly convinced that her return to you after her dismissal from your house and the treatment she experienced whilst in it is not consistent with her comfort, or, I regret to add, personal safety."* And he proposed "that a *professional friend* should be fixed on by you, to Confer with a person of the same description appointed by me, that they may discuss and Settle such terms of Separation as may be mutually approved."[9]

Byron, however, did not see his father-in-law's proposal of a separation for several days. Guessing the contents, Augusta intercepted the letter and returned it—unopened—not to the writer, but to Annabella at Kirkby.

---

*On being shown a draft, Annabella demanded the deletion of this last phrase as too accusatory, risking the possibility of tipping their hand prematurely.

Augusta knew how such interference would be viewed, and she was prepared to defend herself: "For once in my life I have ventured to act according to my own judgment," she wrote to Annabella. Seeing two people she loved torn apart—less by their own will than through decisions made by others—she had taken this risk to buy time. "I only wish *a few days delay*, & that you would hear all that I have to say before you send the enclosed." It was, she contended, "of the VERY *utmost* consequence for *you* & *your child* (for you must believe *that* to be my first consideration) that you should *pause.*"[10]

Guilt, too, played a part in Augusta's attempts to save the marriage. For the moment, the issue of incest had been pushed to the background—but she could scarcely doubt that the passionate attachment of brother and sister, along with her constant and competing presence, had helped doom the marriage.

The next day she wrote to Annabella again, giving her letter to George Byron, newly engaged and house-hunting nearby, to deliver to Kirkby. This time she offered a new argument for delaying any action: the certainty that Byron would retaliate.

"I am very strongly of opinion *revenge* will be uppermost & this from my late observations," she warned her sister-in-law. "What revenge could he take so effectual as depriving you of the child & *who* could prevent him?"[11]

On this issue, Annabella hardly needed to be frightened further. But the effect of the warning was quite the reverse of what Augusta had hoped. Fear made her more rigid; the greater her terror that Byron would take their child, the more completely she was prepared to place her interests in the hands of powerful protectors.

Now, like automata, the figures in the Byron marriage moved backward, forward, and around in circles toward dissolving the union. At times, though, it seems that the defining behavior of all three principals was inconsistency. Byron, Annabella, and Augusta were each torn by warring emotions: revenge and regret, hatred and forgiveness, jealousy and guilt. Husband and wife were further buffeted by opposing needs: the dictates of the heart and a desire to save face. But when Byron eventually received his father-in-law's letter on February 2, he felt nothing but shocked disbelief. Too distraught to confront Annabella directly, he delegated Augusta to put the question to her: Had she agreed to her father's proposal to end the marriage?

On that same day, Byron replied to Sir Ralph. He began by denying everything, from his "dismissal" of his wife from their house, to any "ill treatment" she had received at his hands. In the same letter, however, Byron undermined his denial by a long and garbled defense of actions he claimed never to have committed: Whatever he *had* done was excused by "distress without—& disease within," including financial embarrassments, physical illness, and "morbid irritability of temper." Lady Byron, he now informed her father, was such a paragon as to render any abuse of her an impossibility (surely, one of the most unpersuasive lines of defense ever advanced).

"And now Sir—not for your satisfaction—for I owe you none—but for my own—& in justice to Lady Byron—it is my duty to say that there is no part of her conduct—character—temper—talents—or disposition—which could in my opinion have been changed for the better—neither in word nor deed—nor (as far as thought can be dived into) thought—can I bring to recollection a fault on her part—& hardly even a failing—She has ever appeared to me one of the most amiable of beings—& nearer to perfection than I had conceived could belong to humanity in its present existence." Finally he came to his point: His rights as a husband superseded those of Annabella's father. "Your daughter is my wife:—she is the mother of my child—& until I have express sanction of your proceedings—I shall take leave to doubt the propriety of your interference." [12]

Annabella's sanction was as prompt as it was terse; replying on the same day, February 3, to Augusta's long, agonized letter, she declared: "You are desired by your brother to ask if my father has acted with my concurrence in proposing a separation. He has." [13]

Before Byron had read her reply (sent first to Lushington for vetting), he had gathered courage to write to her directly. He could give no answer to her father's letter "without being acquainted with your own thoughts and wishes—& from *yourself*: to vague & general charges & exaggerated statements from others I can give no reply:—it is to *you* that I look—& with *you* that I can communicate on the subject." But his tone of perplexity moves swiftly to one of implied threat. Using the very words of Augusta's warning, he promised, "I shall eventually abide by your decision—but I request you most earnestly to weigh well the probable consequences—& to pause before you pronounce." [14]

Hearing nothing from Kirkby by February 5, Byron wrote again to Annabella. Gone was the hauteur of innocent victim he had assumed with Sir Ralph; he now struck a pleading note: "The whole of my errors—or what harsher name you choose to give them—you know—but I loved you—& will not part with you without your *own* most express & *expressed* refusal to return or to receive me." And he concluded gallantly: "Only say the word—that you are still mine in your heart—and 'Kate!—I will buckler thee against a million.' " [15]

Byron's quote from *The Taming of the Shrew* could not have been less apt; it was no million against whom his Kate had required protection, but only one: her husband. Still, the letter produced its intended effect; at Kirkby, Ann Fletcher reported having come upon her mistress rolling around on the floor of her bedroom, sobbing in a "paroxysm of grief" over the promise she had made to her parents to separate.*16

As though on cue, from Piccadilly Terrace George Byron and Augusta now reported that Byron, reconciled to a separation, planned to go abroad as soon as matters were settled. Whether her vanity was piqued that he would give her up so easily or from more generous motives—relief that her refusal to return would not lead Byron to suicidal despair—Annabella was now fixed again in her determination to end the marriage. That same day, she answered Byron's letter.

"You know what I have suffered, and would have sacrificed to avoid this extremity," she told him, using the same word as Hobhouse. She had come to this decision only after "reviewing the misery I have experienced almost without interval from the day of my marriage." Then, in one of her acute flashes of insight into Byron's character—and rare accusations—she wrote: "It is unhappily your disposition to consider what you *have* as worthless—what you have *lost* as invaluable. But remember that you declared yourself *most miserable* when I was yours."17

Before receiving this first direct communication from Annabella since the separation proceedings had begun, Byron fired off another letter to Sir Ralph. Summoning "exhibit A" in his defense, the two fond letters from his wife, with their pet names and private jokes, Byron took the offensive: As Lady Byron had left London without a hint of her present intentions, "I am therefore reduced to the melancholy alternative of either believing her capable of a duplicity—very foreign to my opinion of her character—or that she has lately sunk under influence . . . however respected & respectable heretofore—not recognized in her vows at the Altar." After this swipe at the parental role in her decision, Byron, for the first time, attacked Annabella's own motives: She could only have left "with a view to escape from my shattered fortunes."18

On February 7 Murray brought out *Parisina* and *The Siege of Corinth* in one volume, as he had originally planned. In Byron's distraught state, however, the occasion passed unremarked. Besides, the

---

*Ann Fletcher's evenhanded testimony—earlier, she had testified to Byron's attempts to rape his wife; now she confirmed Annabella's despair at being trapped into separating against her will—argue for her honesty.

poet and the publisher were estranged by another quarrel. After refusing Murray's generous offer to redeem his library, Byron changed his mind. He would accept the £1,500—but not for himself; through the intermediary of Samuel Rogers, Byron now informed Murray, he wished half the money to be given to William Godwin, social philosopher (soon to be Shelley's father-in-law), and the rest divided between two needy poets: Coleridge and Charles Robert Maturin.* Murray was outraged: Why should he, who worked hard for every shilling, be instructed by a millionaire like Rogers to change an act of personal generosity into one of literary philanthropy? Byron had no choice but to back away from his princely gesture.

At the moment, he was too distracted by his own affairs to let other matters claim his attention for long. Launching another appeal to Kirkby, on February 8 he told Annabella, "All I can say seems useless—and all I could say might be no less availing—yet I still cling to the wreck of my hopes—before they sink forever." He then tried summoning intimate memories of their marriage: "Were you then *never* happy with me?" he asked Annabella. "Did you never at any time or times express yourself so?" and in an unmistakable allusion to the sexual pleasure they had once found with each other, he demanded, "Have no marks of affection—of the warmest & most reciprocal attachment passed between us? Will you see me," he begged simply, "when & where you please—in whose presence you please:—the interview shall pledge you to nothing—& I will say & do nothing to agitate either," he promised. "It is torture to correspond thus."[19]

Ending the week of silence that followed withholding Sir Ralph's letter, Augusta now seconded Byron's plea: "He writes today to ask you to see him—*pause* ere you refuse *for God's Sake*." She knew what Annabella was suffering, but her brother's condition was worse; she feared "the most serious consequences from the manner in which *he* has taken this *sad* business to heart."[20]

But Annabella was unmoved. Designating Mrs. Clermont as her proxy to meet with Byron if he so wished, she enclosed his letter to the ex-governess, remarking that it was written "evidently from Self-delusion not Deception." She was still less charitable in her covering note to Lushington: "Such confidence in guilt," she wrote.[21]

---

*Maturin's tragedy, *Bertram,* was produced at Drury Lane in 1816 on the recommendation of Byron and Scott. The author of the popular gothic novel *Melmoth the Wanderer*, Maturin is more memorably the great-uncle of Oscar Wilde.

To Hobhouse, however, Byron exhibited no such confidence. On the same day as he had written to Annabella, hoping to quicken her fonder memories, he told his friend: "It is all in vain—& all over. She has written two letters—one to Mrs. L[eigh] & since—a second to me—quite decisive of her determination on the subject."[22]

His mood alternated between resigned misery and angry obstinacy. "They" would not be allowed to take his wife away, subjecting him to public humiliation. Annabella now anticipated correctly that the separation process would be neither swift nor easy. Both sides dug in for the fight ahead. Lady Noel extracted from Annabella the revelation that Byron had confessed to sexual relations with both Caroline Lamb *and* Lady Melbourne—the latter demanded by "the old lady" herself. Further, Byron had even showed Annabella letters from "the Spider" urging that he "subdue" her niece if he wanted the marriage to succeed. Lady Noel had always detested her sister-in-law; crowing with triumph, she sent testimony of these "horrors" in their daughter's own hand to Sir Ralph in London. Caro herself now weighed in with Byron's confidences to *her* about his homosexual conquests—Kinnaird relayed this latest bombshell from Whitehall to Hobhouse, who could not even bring himself to write the dreaded word in his diary; he used a long dash—broadened at the end—to signify pederasty. Caro would have more to add on this subject shortly. In the way of skilled divorce lawyers, Lushington proved a thorough researcher. He discovered that Susan Boyce, Byron's discarded lover from Drury Lane, was reputedly infected with syphilis. Endangering a wife's health with a venereal infection, if acquired since the marriage, pushed adultery into the more serious charge of physical cruelty.

ON FEBRUARY 21 the legal chapter of the drama opened. Together, Stephen Lushington, representing Lady Byron, and John Hanson, on behalf of his client, called on Sir Ralph Noel at Mivart's Hotel. They had never met, but Hanson's name was notorious in the courts, where he was known as both incompetent and dishonest. At the least, Hanson was no match for the skill and intellect of the younger man. Playing directly into his opponent's hands, Hanson began by admitting that "he knew from Lord Byron himself that his conduct had been blameable . . . but could not yet make up his mind to advise him to own himself guilty which he would do by acceding to the separation unless there were stronger reasons than he was acquainted with."

To this, Lushington (not without irony, we may assume) replied, "I would advise that you, Mr. Hanson, should question Lord B. himself."

He had tried, was Hanson's answer, "but that Lord Bs [*sic*] memory was very treacherous."

"I think you will get from him sufficient to satisfy your mind," Lushington assured him.

Hanson then attempted, he told Byron, "to press for specific facts which the other declined giving."[23] The only case he made with any eloquence was to plead his client's agitation and depressed state, with a view of buying time. Seeing no disadvantage, Lushington and Sir Ralph agreed to wait.

There was one point, however, on which both parties were in tacit agreement: Of the two possible ways to end a marriage, the only sane expedient was a private legal separation. The alternative, divorce, subjected litigants to a nightmare of overlapping jurisdictions. In Regency England, divorce involved the Ecclesiastical Court, or Doctors' Commons, and required an Act of Parliament (never obtainable by women), and if a father's automatic custody was challenged, the case was also referred to Chancery. The time and money required for this, as well as increasing numbers of couples seeking such relief from the beginning of the nineteenth century onward, created a popular alternative among the better-off classes: "private separation," defined as an "agreement to part, negotiated between two spouses and embodied in a deed of separation, drawn up by a conveyancer."*[24]

In principle, the private separation was the avenue least fraught with delay, expense, and—of crucial importance to both Byron and Annabella—publicity: Then as now, divorces, especially those among the aristocracy, with all of their juicy details, were the favorite topic of scandal sheets. But this was a relative matter; failing an immediate agreement between the spouses as to the cause of separation, the same issues—accusations, proof, money, child custody—had to be arbitrated as would arise in the more tortuous divorce case, and the same Byzantine rules of evidence obtained: Neither spouse was allowed to testify; evidence was in the form of written depositions submitted by witnesses in advance of their questioning. In practice, then, it fell to the aggrieved partner to marshal the material evidence—inevitably, from servants or other intimates of the household—each accusation requiring two corroborating witnesses. In the mountains of print devoted to the Byron separation, this aspect of the law is never mentioned, and of course it puts Annabella's much-maligned evidence gathering in a very different light.

---

*A lawyer specializing in property and/or title settlements.

Private separations had nothing in common with present-day "no-fault" divorce; they were granted on the same narrow grounds as divorce itself, namely, adultery or life-threatening cruelty. Marital rape did not qualify. Other statutory crimes, such as sodomy (including heterosexual anal intercourse) and incest, could be grounds for separation *provided* the behavior had taken place during the marriage and had not been condoned by the spouse. With Augusta still living at Piccadilly Terrace, the issue of condonement would become a loaded one.

Meanwhile, gossip had gathered force in the wake of Lady Byron's departure. Some rumors were invented; Byron was supposed to be the lover of a beautiful Irish actress and star of Drury Lane, Mrs. Mardyn—a player he had barely met. Broadsheets were circulated that showed them prancing about together in the Green Room. Mardyn's career capsized overnight, while Byron was so edgy about further scandal that he refused to set foot in the theater. Indeed, he rarely left his room, and not least among the reasons why Augusta and Byron's male friends now lobbied frantically for reconciliation was fear that his mounting feelings of persecution would lead to permanent derangement.

On February 12, shortly before the lawyers met, Hobhouse had visited Piccadilly Terrace, intending to warn his friend about fresh calumnies making the rounds and how he should deal with such lies. Instead, what he heard shocked him into a complete reversal on the issue of reconciliation. Coming into the house, he met Augusta and George Byron "and from them I learnt what I fear is the real truth that Byron has been guilty of very great tyranny—menaces—furies—neglects, and even real injuries—such as telling his wife he was *living with another woman*—& actually *in fact* turning her out of the house." To this behavior they had added "locking doors, showing pistols, pouring reproaches on her in bed—everything he seems, to believe them, to have been guilty of!" The upright Hobhouse was further appalled by the way his informants excused this abuse of his wife—"and they acquit him—how? by saying he is mad or by LeMann's blaming Byron's behaviour on a torpid liver!" Contrary to what Byron had told him earlier, Annabella's departure, Hobhouse now realized, could have come as no surprise. "George Byron suspected she would leave him & told him so, a month before she went," he noted in his diary.

Shocking as these revelations were, they paled before the wounding evidence that Byron had lied to him; the loyal Hobhouse was devastated: "I found it difficult to account for his wishing to deceive me," he confided stiffly to his diary.

Unflinchingly, he confronted his friend with what he had heard "on the street" without giving away his other sources: "I now thought it my duty to tell Byron I had changed my opinion and to tell him so without informing my informants." From Lady Melbourne Byron had already heard that he was accused of cruelty, drunkenness, and infidelity—all of which he had consistently denied. Now, under Hobhouse's questioning, he broke down: "I got him to own much of what I had been told in the morning," Hobhouse noted grimly in his journal, "he was dreadfully agitated—said he was ruined & would blow his brains out.

"Alas! What a mess," Hobhouse stated. He had already moved beyond hurt feelings. All loyalty once more, he pondered how to protect Byron's reputation from further damage, even if it meant lying himself.

"I'm going to work openly to [disprove] everything," he promised his journal. "The thing must not come before the public." Like Augusta, he took Byron's threats of suicide seriously. "I never knock at his door without expecting to hear some fatal intelligence, yet he flashes up sometimes in his fits & is the same man as before—could his wife but know, she must surely relent."[25]

Surrounded by those dedicated to reopening every wound, Annabella was beyond relenting. On February 15 Byron had made one of his last appeals and the first to acknowledge the injuries he had inflicted. After a feeble effort to regain the high road of the "wronged" husband ("How far your conduct is reconcileable [*sic*] to your duties & affections as a wife and a mother—must be a matter for your own reflections") he dropped the mask, mourning the wreck he had made of their marriage: "The trial has not been very long—a year—I grant you—of distress—distemper—and misfortune—but these fall chiefly on me—& bitter as the recollection is to me of what I have felt—it is much more so to have made you a partaker in my desolation."

Still, he complained to Annabella that he was ignorant of the charges to be brought against him; he had twice been refused information by Sir Ralph and the lawyers. He had spent the last weeks "in suspense—in humiliation—in obloquy—exposed to the most black & blighting calumnies of every kind"; in the sweep of his own rhetoric, he blotted from memory the guilt he had confessed to Hobhouse, but the profound sadness of this letter surges from a deeper truth: It was too late for love to heal them.

"And now—Bell—dearest Bell . . . whether you are restored to or torn from me—I can only say in the truth of affliction—& without hope—motive—or end in again saying what I have lately but vainly repeated—that I love you: bad or good—mad or rational—

miserable or content—I love you—& shall do to the dregs of my memory & existence."[26]

"He knows he has injured me too deeply ever to forgive me,"[27] Annabella said.

All communiqués arriving from the Byron "camp" were now turned over to Lushington, who could observe the success of his strategy: A husband "terrified" of public opinion, in an agony of "suspense" over the charges to be brought against him, was his best weapon in what was otherwise a weak case.

For their part, Byron's advisers now agreed that reconciliation was the only way of saving the poet from a pariah status certain to destroy him, and to this end they were perfectly willing to sacrifice Annabella. Hobhouse, as he had promised, was ready to perjure himself on every count, while Augusta, torn between devotion to her brother and her dearest "Sis," attempted, as she often did, to " 'run with the hares and hunt with the hounds.' "[28] To Francis Hodgson, Byron's friend who had recently become a confidant of Augusta, she conceded that "B deceives himself and deceives others," declaring of Annabella that "I CAN *not* urge her to return & expose herself to a repetition of all I have witnessed—& heard of."[29] But when Augusta wrote to Annabella, it was clear that Byron alone was to be considered: "Supposing even that nothing is LEGALLY proved against him which can procure you this separation, what will the *world think!* won't his character be blasted forever! He is convinced of this, & I am convinced not only will his reputation be sacrificed to this exposure but *his* LIFE."

Lest Annabella fail to share her spirit of self-sacrifice, Augusta invoked the bogeyman of Byron's seizure of Ada, warning, "There is one thing, my dearest A., you should be prepared for (if worse don't occur) which is about the Child. He seems determined to have it, & I understand the Law wd allow it to him when a year old. I see in short such a *host of evils* in perspective & not ye least of all what your feelings would be if *any one* was the consequence of your separating from him."

Threats about the baby only served to persuade Lady Noel to engage armed guards at Kirkby against the danger of kidnapping and to convince Annabella that she should hurry to London to meet with Lushington and plan their strategy further. Another reason for the trip: She had evidence for the lawyer that she was unwilling to put into writing. Then, on February 17, as she was preparing for the journey, she received a hysterical communiqué from Augusta with news of "reports abroad of a nature *too horrible to repeat.*" George Byron had already informed both Hobhouse and Byron himself of this latest and worst scandal:

"Every other sinks into nothing before this MOST horrid one," Augusta wrote. If one recalls the terror of exposure that had caused Byron's break with John Edleston, his reaction to the new rumors leaves no doubt that these concerned homosexual practices: Now he was "in an agony," Augusta reported, telling Annabella: "Even to have such a thing *said* is utter destruction & ruin to a man from which he never can recover." Once again, Augusta, seconded by an imploring letter from Hodgson, pleaded for reconciliation: "I do think in my heart, dearest A," she wrote, "that *your return* might be the *saving & reclaiming* of him."[30]

On February 21—the same day he had met with the lawyers—Sir Ralph was notified by Hanson of Byron's definitive refusal of any separation, and on the next day, Annabella arrived to join her father at Mivart's Hotel. At her request, Lushington called on her that same evening. She now produced her own bombshell: a brief of incestuous relations between Byron and his sister. Initially, Lushington was too shocked to take her accusations seriously. As a lawyer, moreover, he took the view that by airing such suspicions, she would appear to be motivated by malice. In any case, since she was disbarred as a wife from giving evidence, her charge would be impossible to prove. He advised Annabella to stay narrowly with the accusation of "brutally indecent conduct and language."

Within the week, however, Lushington changed his mind. Rumors of incest were all over London. Those closest to Augusta now feared for her reputation and appointment at court: Her stepmother, the dowager Duchess of Leeds, pleaded with her to leave Piccadilly Terrace immediately. Lushington now advised his client that all communications between her and Augusta cease. To her singular credit, Annabella refused; she saw Augusta several times while she was in London and continued writing to her. To avoid being compromised by their ongoing relations, however, Lushington insisted that his client protect herself. To this end, he drew up a statement, signed by Annabella, documenting her suspicions of incest, along with her reasons for continuing to see Augusta, so that "if circumstances should compel Lady Byron to prefer the charge, she should be at full liberty to do so without being prejudiced by her present conduct." Annabella remained adamant on another point. "The charge" would be preferred on one contingency only: If Byron succeeded in gaining legal custody of Ada and placed her in the care of "Mrs. L[eigh]."[31]

With this document in hand, together with Byron's letter refusing any private separation agreement, Annabella was impatient to begin legal proceedings. Knowing how deeply his client, too, dreaded having the miseries of her marriage aired in court, Lushington had one more card to play. Like Byron, the young lawyer was a friend and sometime protégé of Lord Holland, and he now engaged the kindly peer to act as mediator with a final separation proposal: On March 2, Holland called on Byron with a draft proposal suggesting that if Byron would agree to separation, Annabella was prepared to give up £500 of her present income, with one half of the Noel reversion to follow.

This was the lawyer's only tactical error. Assaulted in his pride as a man who could be "bought," Byron was outraged. Among the four pleading letters he wrote to Annabella in the two weeks between his official refusal and March 4, his only angry words concerned this piece of the proposal, and he seemed genuinely shocked to learn that Annabella claimed its authorship: "It appeared to me to be a kind of appeal to the supposed mercenary feelings of the person to whom it was made,"[32] he wrote to her, forgetting, of course, that he had railed furiously against Sir Ralph's failure to come forth with the marriage settlement or other financial help.

Hurling accusations and counteraccusations, recalling injury upon injury, Byron and Annabella, together, with their chorus of "advisers," enacted that sad progress from husband and wife to mortal enemies. Of his father-in-law's hopes for an "amicable separation" Byron sneered, "Which means I suppose something the same as a hostile alliance."[33] For the rest, his final letters to Annabella have the wan and weary sound of an exhausted animal at bay: Addressing her for the last time as "Dearest Pip," he begged, "I wish you would make it up—for I am dreadfully sick of all this. . . . If you will—I am ready to make any penitential speech or speeches you please—& will be very good & tractable for the rest of my days—& very sorry for all that have [sic] gone before."[34]

The flippant tone (for which he apologized in his next letter) was coldly received: "He endeavors to make a joke of the whole business. . . . I didn't answer," Annabella reported to her father. Learning that Byron had rejected the proposal brokered by Lord Holland, she announced, "Well—nothing but war remains."[35]

Meanwhile, Lushington, with the help of Sir Samuel Romilly, quietly instituted the procedures required to make Ada a ward of Chancery— a fact of which Byron would remain in ignorance until the following year.

On March 5, Augusta visited Annabella at Mivart's Hotel. It was a dramatic interview: The two women had not seen each other since the freezing dawn, nearly two months earlier, when Annabella and her baby had left Piccadilly Terrace for the last time. Now Augusta felt a visceral shock at the sight that greeted her: "I can never describe Ly B's appearance to you," she wrote to Francis Hodgson that night, "but by comparing it . . . to that of a Being of another world. She is positively reduced to a Skeleton—pale as *ashes*—a deep hollow tone of voice & a *calm* in her manner quite supernatural. She received *me* kindly, but that really appeared the only SURVIVING *feeling*—all else was *death like* calm. *I* can never forget it—never!"

But she also saw in the shattered young woman a steeliness that awed the will-o'-the-wisp Augusta. "I see & am convinced she will not be Shaken. What then is left but for B to consent to [an] amicable arrangement?" As she predicted, however, "There are many who will persuade him to the contrary."[36]

Byron himself had become convinced, Augusta told Annabella, that Mrs. Clermont was the evil genius behind the plot to deprive him of his wife, poisoning her mind against him, then holding her to the promise of separation. Without mentioning the former governess by name, Augusta made clear, as Annabella recalled, that "the impression of my being unduly influenced, prevails very strongly with everyone in Lord B's house—and the accusation of a Conspiracy is to be adduced."

Indeed, the next day found Byron, Hobhouse, and Hanson at Doctors' Commons, where they met with three advocates of that court to determine the advisability of a legal counterattack: either one that would make good on Byron's threat (conveyed by Hobhouse to Sir Ralph) of "suing *people* for conspiracy to detain his wife," or by bringing suit for the restitution of his conjugal rights, which, if successful, would compel Lady Byron's return. Byron left the chambers while Hobhouse described the accusations to be brought against his friend. On the basis of what they heard (and probably what they suspected would yet emerge), the jurists advised Byron not to "cite,"[37] although they conceded that he had a "defendant's case."

Three days later, on March 9, Robert Wilmot* rushed to Piccadilly Terrace, where, drawing Hobhouse aside, he informed him of yet another unnamed allegation to be raised by Lady Byron, urging that "it must not come into court." Since incest and homosexual practices were already the common currency of gossip, Annabella's unplayed card was clearly something else—something Byron had been unwilling to include even in his recent full confession to Hobhouse.

With the statutory grounds for separation on the table, so to speak, the behavior or act in question was clearly of another order—possibly

---

*Byron's first cousin, but one of Lady Byron's advisers.

"morally repugnant," as opposed to criminal.[38] Byron's repeated attempts to rape Annabella during the weeks just before and after the birth would fall into this category. Another much-debated theory has proposed heterosexual sodomy within the marriage—either anal coition or what the criminal statute delicately referred to as the "mutual caress"—the act so unnatural it could only be whispered, never written.

Heterosexual sodomy, whether practiced by wedded couples or others, was judged, like pederasty and incest, both a sin and "a Crime *Inter Christianos non nominandum*"[39]—not to be named among Christians. Therein lay its power.

Byron's unnamed crime proved the decisive factor in keeping him out of court. "Both parties were anxious to keep the secret," a legal historian recently concluded, "but in the end Lord Byron was more anxious."[40] The only hand left for him to play now was obstructionist. He agreed, before witnesses, to a draft agreement drawn up by Hobhouse, only to change his mind and claim he had been misunderstood. Hobhouse himself insisted that Byron honor his promise. When he refused, Hobby provided an excuse in the guise of a new demand: a "rider" in the form of a statement of disavowal from Lady Byron, denying the two criminal charges of incest and homosexual practice.* Finally, when Byron was ready to sign a formal statement of terms to a separation, he balked at a clause concerning the financial settlement; this would have bound him to future arbitration determining an equitable distribution of property that would otherwise have come to him. Horrified, Augusta blamed Hanson, who, she complained, "would not hear . . . of B. pledging himself *legally* to do what was judged right by *Arbitrators* respecting a division of the Kirkby property." Aware that Byron had already reneged on his promise to accept a separation if this reflected Annabella's expressed decision, Augusta now feared that his refusal to sign this last agreement would be "injurious to B . . . for it appears to me wishing to give him an *opportunity* of acting *dishonourably* by breaking his word!"[41]

The impasse was resolved by submitting the matter for arbitration to the Solicitor General, who decided in favor of Lady Byron, and on March 17 a preliminary separation agreement was signed by Byron and Annabella.

---

*When the statement of disavowal was accepted by the Byron camp, no one noticed that Annabella only disclaimed having made such accusations herself; she never denied that the behavior or acts in question had taken place.

Near emotional collapse and in the last six weeks of pregnancy, Augusta had moved from Piccadilly Terrace to her apartment in St. James's Palace the day before. Quarreling furiously among themselves and with the poet, the rest of Byron's advisers now dispersed. After the frenzy of negotiations, of meetings and messengers, drafts and revisions, Byron suddenly found himself alone. On March 18, he completed and sent to Annabella the first draft of a poem mourning the end of their marriage.

A wail of self-pity and sentimental moralizing, "Fare Thee Well!" hardly ranks among Byron's most distinguished poems. As a cri de coeur, however, it breathes an immediacy that is the essence of romanticism; until recently, ink blots on the verso of the manuscript sheets have been taken for tear stains. In another sense, however, the poem reveals Byron's bad faith; it is a self-portrait of the poet as martyr, ever turning the other cheek:

> Fare thee well! and if for ever—
>   Still for ever, fare *thee well*—
> Even though unforgiving, never
>   'Gainst thee shall my heart rebel.—

A recent critic observed, "What the poet declared that his heart would never do, it had been doing all along; rebelling and seeking to inflict wound for wound."[42]

> Though my many faults defaced me,
>   Could no other arm be found
> Than the one which once embraced me,
>   To inflict a cureless wound!

Anticipating the lachrymose Victorian taste of the future, Byron's lines on his baby daughter seem to cry out for a painting depicting Annabella, with little Ada pointing to an empty paternal armchair:

> And when thou wouldst solace gather—
>   When our child's first accents flow—
> Wilt thou teach her to say—"Father!"
>   Though his care she must forego?
> When her little hands shall press thee—
>   When her lip to thine is prest—

> Think of him whose prayer shall bless thee—
> Think of him thy love had bless'd.[43]

As an attempt to soften Lady Byron to reconciliation, the poem failed. Other readers, however, were much moved, including Madame de Staël, who claimed that any wife reading its appeal must rush back into her husband's arms.

With good reason, Byron did not favor Annabella with a draft of the sequel to "Fare Thee Well!" Titled "A Sketch from Private Life," it was at the same time a venomous attack on Mary Anne Clermont, Annabella's ex-governess, and a canonization of her charge. Whatever Mrs. Clermont's actual influence may have been in pressing for separation, Byron's polemic—like his demonization of Lord Elgin—turns nastily personal, taking aim at every aspect of the enemy: her class, appearance, character. "Born in the garret, in the kitchen bred," she had wormed her way into Lady Noel's service, where "With eye unmoved, and forehead unabash'd, / She dines from off the plate she lately wash'd."

What makes the poem so psychologically revealing, however, is the way Byron uses his vilification of Clermont to exalt Annabella; only a saint could have escaped contamination by this malign caretaker:

> Foil'd was perversion by that youthful mind,
> Which Flattery fooled not—Baseness could not blind,
> Deceit infect not—near Contagion soil—
> Indulgence weaken—nor Example spoil

Humble despite her gifts of Beauty and Genius; uncorrupted by Fortune, Pride, or Passion, Annabella's tragedy (and Byron's) is that her blameless Virtue cannot conceive—and thus cannot pardon—the faults of lesser mortals:

> Serenely purest of her sex that live,
> But wanting one sweet weakness—to forgive.[44]

Along with demonstrating the "fantastic unreality of the marriage,"[45] privileging his wife's role in its dissolution also exempted Byron from responsibility. His—their—loss is due entirely to the machinations of other forces bent on disuniting them.

If the elegiac "Fare Thee Well!" softened public opinion in Byron's favor, the ferocity of "A Sketch" had the reverse effect. Byron had broken a code: No aristocrat or gentleman savaged a servant and a female

in print. On learning of its imminent publication in *The Champion*, a
Whig newspaper,* Annabella noted scornfully that it was "blackguard
beyond belief,"[46] and she correctly foresaw that its appearance would
deal further blows to the poet's battered reputation.

In the politics of separation, pain and loss become weapons in the
battle for public opinion. During the month between the informal agreement by both parties on the terms of the agreement and the signing
of the final papers on April 21, Byron and Annabella, abetted by an
expanding cast of meddling allies (some of whose alliances shifted in the
course of their involvement), indulged in some of their ugliest behavior.

Under cover of darkness, Annabella crept off for a clandestine meeting with Caroline Lamb at the house of "Caro George," where she
learned details of Byron's boasts that he had "corrupted" his page,
Robert Rushton, along with three Harrow classmates, and seduced his
sister; Caroline also produced intimate letters from Augusta to Byron,
given her by her erstwhile lover. Annabella now informed Lushington
that she had changed her mind about Augusta's probable innocence into
"*absolute* conviction of her guilt," deciding that it would be "unwise"
for their relations to continue at present.[47] Convinced that Annabella
accused him of speaking ill of her to all London, Byron set about collecting letters from all his friends, swearing that no unkind word about
his wife had ever passed his lips. These he delivered to Mivart's Hotel,
but when he had no reply, he accused Sir Ralph of withholding the
packet and threatened to refuse to sign the separation papers. Annabella
now panicked at what she feared would be the first of endless excuses
to renege on his agreement and flee abroad. In the hope of dissuading
Byron from further foolishness, Hobhouse moved into Piccadilly
Terrace on April 3, where he was repaid in drunken quarrels with his
host and other "fracas" among Byron's friends Kinnaird, Scrope Davies,
and Robert Wilmot. Duels were threatened. After all this, Hobhouse
might well have been relieved to learn that Byron had found a temporary distraction with a pretty young woman.

---

*Both poems were privately printed by Murray in editions of fifty copies each and
circulated "among friends and foes" on April 8. One of the foes, however, was
apparently on Byron's own mailing list: Henry Brougham, lawyer, literary critic, and
political intriguer, who, while ostensibly acting as mediator in the Byron separation,
was in fact operating on behalf of Lady Byron. Brougham arranged to have both
poems published in *The Champion* a week later, with a devastating commentary.
For this episode as new evidence of the Whig role in vilifying the poet, see note 42
for this chapter.

Jane, or Clara or Claire Clairmont, as she now called herself, was
only seventeen when, at the end of March 1816, she first laid siege to
the poet with a battery of letters, whose transparent excuse was the need
for career advice. But she was no ordinary starstruck teenager. The stepdaughter of William Godwin, author of *An Enquiry Concerning Political Justice*, Clairmont was also the stepsister of Mary Wollstonecraft
Godwin, whose brilliant mother, author of *Vindication of the Rights of
Women*, had died days after her birth. To the consternation of the
Godwins, sixteen-year-old Mary had run off with Percy Bysshe Shelley,
then twenty-three, after the poet had abandoned his first wife and their
two children. With a constant need to appropriate others' lives, Claire
insinuated herself into the new ménage, now consisting of Shelley, the
pregnant Mary, and their infant son. For the time being, Claire's designs
of prying Shelley from Mary were frustrated; she could not compete
with her beautiful and accomplished stepsister. The conquest of a more
famous, more aristocratic, best-selling poet was just the triumph Claire
fantasized.

But when Byron finally allowed the dark-eyed buxom girl to call on
him, his disappointment was palpable: "One thing I am afraid of—you
rather dislike me & may therefore be prejudiced on the wrong side," she
wrote airily after her visit.[48] It took more than dislike, however, to discourage Claire. In answer to Byron's skepticism that this importunate
young person could be a member of Shelley's chosen family,* Claire was
ready with living proof: On another visit to Piccadilly Terrace, she managed to produce Mary Godwin, long an admirer of Byron's poetry,
along with several of Shelley's letters. The visit appears to have been a
success, and Claire now bombarded Byron with passionate daily communiqués. He need only accept "that which it has long been the
passionate wish of my heart to offer you,"† and she would take care
of everything else, including arrangements for their first tryst, at a
country inn. Byron seems to have objected to the meeting place, but his
resistance was worn down. In the melancholy of packing up his life,

---

*As early as June 1814, according to Thomas Moore, Shelley had sent the older
poet a copy of *Queen Mab*. An accompanying letter was lost, but according to
Moore, "Lord Byron was known to have expressed warm admiration of the opening lines of the poem." Claire also assumed Byron had read Shelley's *Alastor*, published with other poems in March 1816. And we know, from Byron's expressed
desire to help the ever-needy Godwin, that he admired the radical philosopher and
would have been been curious to meet his stepdaughter and the daughter of Mary
Wollstonecraft.

†This phrase has been variously assumed to mean Claire's virginity, or a child.

erotic diversion with an adoring seventeen-year-old was, finally, not unwelcome.

On April 14 Hobhouse tactfully vacated the house so Byron and Augusta could be alone to say their good-byes. Her fifth child would be born within weeks and she was on her way home, while Byron waited only for the final separation papers before leaving England. It was a terrible parting. Overwhelmed by the certainty that they would never see each other again, both were in agony. Augusta might have controlled her own grief but for the sight of Byron, who wept uncontrollably. Her farewell gift to him was a Bible; it was with him at his death.

He had written a tribute to the sustaining power of her love, but in the end, he could not bear the thought of her reading the lines while he was still in England:

> Then let the ties of baffled love
> Be broken—thine will never break.[49]

When she was gone, he wrote to Annabella the most bitter words he would ever address to her: "I have just parted from Augusta—almost the last being you had left me to part with—& the only unshattered tie of my existence—wherever I may go—& I am going far—you & I can never meet again in this world—nor in the next. . . . If any accident occurs to me—be kind to *her*.—if she is then nothing—to her children." And he reminded Annabella that although he had changed his will, leaving everything to his sister and her children, he had not done this "in prejudice to you, for we had not then differed,"* but because he knew that Annabella and their child were already provided for "by other & better means. . . .

"I say therefore, be kind to her & hers—for never has she acted or spoken otherwise towards you—she has ever been your friend— this may seem valueless to one who has now so many,"[50] he concluded. He enclosed a ring for his daughter with the request that news of her should be sent to him through Augusta.

Then on Sunday, April 21, at three-thirty, Hanson brought the deed of separation. "I deliver this as Mrs. Clermont's act and deed,"[51] Byron said as he signed the papers. Two days later, the poet, accompanied by

---

*Annabella, however, recalled that during their honeymoon at Halnaby, Byron had threatened angrily to change his will in Augusta's favor, even demanding that she instruct Mr. Hoar, the Milbanke family lawyer, to draw up a new one.

Scrope Davies, set off at dawn for Dover in a splendid new coach. A replica of Napoleon's, it had just been delivered by Baxter, the leading London coach builder, at a cost of £500. They were followed by Hobhouse traveling in Scrope Davies's chaise, along with a young doctor, John William Polidori, engaged by Byron to serve as his personal physician. No sooner had they left Piccadilly than the bailiffs came and seized everything, even his "birds & squirrel," Byron noted bitterly.[52] The books had already gone, sold at auction on April 8.

He embarked on Thursday, the twenty-fifth, with "a rough sea and contrary wind," Hobhouse reported, who, running to the end of the wooden pier, watched his friend waving to him from on board "until I could not distinguish him any longer."[53]

Byron would never see England, his wife, daughter, or sister again. He had cast off ties of love, enmity, and debt, along with the sanctions of the responsible and respectable. Traveling light, he embraced the mobility of the exile. Buoyant with freedom, his poetry would soar.

PART THREE

Exile into Hero

CHAPTER 28

The Year Without a Summer

ATCHING THE packet cast off and
cut through the busy harbor to the open sea, Byron felt both the levity
of flight and the deadweight of loss. His family and possessions gone, he
had never traveled lighter. He had been hounded out of England, but in
spite of himself, the lure of the unknown worked its charm:

> I depart,
> Whither I know not; but the hour's gone by,
> When Albion's lessening shores could grieve or glad mine eye.[1]

Recalling his earlier self also served to remind Byron of his literary
double, Childe Harold, and the poem that had vaulted him to fame and
adulation.

> In my youth's summer I did sing of One,
> The wandering outlaw of his own dark mind.[2]

Now, in the sixteen hours of the rough Channel crossing, between bouts
of seasickness, he felt moved to "seize the theme then but begun" seven
years before. In the interval, the young poet's posture of adolescent
brooding had given way to the pain of a man "Wrung with the wounds
which kill not, but ne'er heal."[3]

Canto I had opened, conventionally enough, with an invocation to
the muse and to Greece herself: "Oh, thou! in Hellas deem'd of heav'nly
birth."[4] The new third canto of *Childe Harold* began with a cry of intimate and intense loss: "Ada! sole daughter of my house and heart."[5]
He disembarked with the first three stanzas written. Mobility had given

him access to feelings impacted for too long—an augury of productive months ahead.

Ostend, with its Flemish tidiness and well-kept inn, was a happy surprise, and the promise of creature comforts released a surge of sexual energy: "As soon as he reached his room," noted the shocked Dr. Polidori, "Lord Byron fell like a thunderbolt upon the chambermaid."6 When they toured Antwerp and Ghent, however, Byron was repelled by Rubens's similarly carnal appreciation of women: "They have all red gowns and red shoulders—to say nothing of necks—of which they are more liberal than charming. . . . I suppose it must be Art—for—I'll swear—'tis not Nature," he wrote to Augusta. But he complained about Flemish nature, too, finding in the landscape "a perpetuity of plain & an eternity of *pavement*."7 Overloaded with china, silver, books, and bedding, the imperial carriage kept breaking down. Instead of making straight for the Rhine as planned, they were forced to detour to Brussels for repairs. While waiting there, Byron called on his mother's kinsman Pryse Lockhart Gordon. The two had not seen each other since Byron's Harrow days, when Gordon had taken his young cousin riding in Hyde Park, where he had noted with amusement the boy's fiercely competitive streak, which did not rule out a little cheating to win a race. Now he was delighted to act as cicerone to the noted poet. Polidori hired a chaise and they drove to Waterloo, where Byron struggled to reconcile the scenes of carnage fixed in his imagination with the prospect of peaceful fields returning to farmland:

> As the ground was before, thus let it be;—
> How that red rain hath made the harvest grow!8

Had it not been for the "importunity of boys and the glitter of buttons in the hands, there would be no sign of war," Polidori noted.9 Along with buttons, Byron acquired other souvenirs prized by visitors to battlefields: swords and military decorations and cockades, which in the interests of mobility, he had their host dispatch to Murray in London. After this brief visit, Byron and Polidori returned the next day by carriage. This time, they rode over the site on "Cossac" horses, which Byron insisted had been abandoned by their departed Russian riders. Galloping from the field, he burst into a Romaic war song.

After more than two weeks on the road together, it was apparent that in John William Polidori, Byron had chosen the wrong traveling companion as well as physician. Son of an Italian father and an English mother, the darkly handsome Polidori had been something of a prodigy himself: Two years earlier, aged nineteen, he had been the youngest recorded graduate in medicine at Edinburgh, with a much-praised thesis on somnambulism. Unfortunately, he also harbored literary ambitions. The younger man was all ego and no self-esteem: jealous, childish, vain, thin-skinned, and with a total lack of humor (the latter guaranteed to bring out Byron's mean streak). In one of his frequent outbursts he later demanded to know just what his employer could do—aside from writing poetry—that he, Polidori, could not do just as well. "First . . . I can hit with a pistol the keyhole of that door," Byron retorted. "Secondly, I can swim across that river to yonder point—and thirdly, I can give you a d——d good thrashing."[10]

Polidori was also of frail constitution, and among the ironies of this his first engagement as a physician was that he was constantly sick: From the moment they left Dover, he suffered from intestinal problems, dizziness, and fainting spells. With his own recent illness, Byron was sympathetic to the young doctor's recurrent ailments and patient with the delays to his travel plans. It was Polidori's emotional volatility (discerned at the outset by Hobhouse, who had warned Byron against him) that would be the cause of grief to both.

As they crossed into the kingdom of Prussia, the flatness of the Flemish landscape yielded to the dramatic contrasts of the Rhine valley. Here Byron found more congenial vistas of broad water flowing between "banks whose beauty would endure forever"; on both sides of the river, white-walled towns alternated with orchards and vineyards, ascending at intervals into rocky hills crowned by the ruins of medieval towers. Making their way along the western bank of the Rhine, they crossed the river several times, most memorably at Koblenz, where they admired the remains of the fortress of Ehrenbreitstein. Farther along, Byron gazed somberly on the monuments to Generals Hoche and Marceau, the stones "defaced" by time, with the help of a restored monarchy in a hurry to forget the Napoleonic presence. Fallen in battle at ages twenty-seven and twenty-nine, respectively, the two heroes were another reminder of the flower of Europe's youth, whether in Waterloo's unmarked graves or commemorated by cenotaphs, sacrificed to limitless ambition and "King-making Victory." At Mannheim they were obliged to cross again, since without French passports they could not enter the territory of Strasbourg. In the event, Byron had "no desire to view a degraded country and oppressed peoples," he said.[11] Still, with his love/hate fascination for Napoleon, it is surprising that he never set foot on French soil.

Since disembarking at Ostend with the first three stanzas, Byron

continued working on the new canto, writing late at night on whatever
odd sheets of paper were at hand. With the growing distance of time
and space, he tried to make sense of the debacle of his marriage. In his
own disgrace and exile he found melancholy parallels to the fallen
Emperor, to whom he had once compared himself in heroic terms. Pride,
ambition, but above all, the restless discontent for which there was no
peace, were the same "fever at the core / Fatal to him who bears, to all
who ever bore."[12] Carried by "the madmen who have made men mad /
By their contagion," the disease claimed

> Conquerors and Kings,
> Founders of sects and systems, to whom add
> Sophists, Bards, Statesmen, all unquiet things
> Which stir too strongly the soul's secret springs,
> And are themselves the fools, to those they fool.[13]

Polidori's inadequacies intensified Byron's longing for Augusta.
Deprived as he was of her loving presence and wordless understanding,
the beauty of all he saw felt muted. Her image blotted out the scenes
before his eyes, and he now interrupted the flow of stanzas with a lyric
tribute known by its first line, "The castled crag of Drachenfels." Each
of its four verses ends with a rhymed couplet lamenting an earthly
paradise less perfect without her: "But one thing want these banks
of Rhine / Thy gentle hand to clasp in mine!" He sent the poem to
Augusta, enclosing some lilies:

> Though long before thy hand they touch,
> I know that they must withered be,
> But yet reject them not as such;
> For I have cherish'd them as dear,
> Because they yet may meet thine eye,
> And guide thy soul to mine even here.[14]

One night, half a century after these lines were written, Henry James
was on his way to visit Byron's grandson, the Earl of Lovelace, who had
promised to show him the poet's letters to Augusta. The novelist had
long been fascinated by the scandal of Byron's incestuous passion,
and with the recent death of his own sister, he was meditating a "tale"
based on "two lives, two beings, and *one* experience." The story,
as James envisioned it, "would contain the idea of some unspeakable
intensity of feeling, of tenderness, of sacred compunction" but would
omit "the nefarious—abnormal—character" of the Byron-Leigh rela-

tion. We may be tempted to smile at James's own "sacred compunction": What is left, after all, from Byron's self-described "perverse passion" for Augusta without its driving element of the sexually forbidden? As the Drachenfels lyric makes plain, however, the novelist's reading goes to the heart of the tragedy: A lost Eden, impermissible in its perfection, their union offered "the image of a deep participating devotion" from whose loss the "brother suffers . . . is carried along by fate . . . and the sister understands, perceives, shares with every pulse of her being. He has to tell her nothing—she *knows*; it's identity of sensation, of vibration."*15

Miraculously, his Rhine journey enveloped Byron in a beneficent sense of peace; in place of the "double joy" Augusta's presence would have given, solitude had opened him to nature's forgiving beauty:

> Thine is a scene alike where souls united
> Or lonely Contemplation thus might stray;
> And could the ceaseless vultures cease to prey
> On self-condemning bosoms, it were here,16

Crossing into Switzerland at Basel, they visited nearby Morat, where, in 1476, the Swiss forces had defeated Charles the Bold. Here Byron indulged his gothic fascination for bones—death cleansed by history—taking from the remains of an ossuary "the leg and wing of a Burgundian,"17 he wrote gleefully to Hobhouse. At Avenches, the Roman Aventicum, his imagination fixed on the legend of Julia Alpinula, a first-century priestess who, according to an anthology of classical epitaphs owned by the poet, had died on her father's corpse when she had been unable to save him from execution by the Roman conqueror.† Female sacrifice, in the form of death, always particularly stirred Byron, and Julia's martyrdom reminded him of his sister's self-less love and the wordless communion of blood. Earlier, in "To [Augusta]," he exalted the devotion of his sister, protective of him while heedless of her own danger:

---

*James never wrote his "tale" of a brother and sister's love. Instead, his fascination with the Byron legend seized on the shadowy figure of the aged Claire Clairmont, still living with her niece in Florence when the novelist, unaware of their existence, visited that city. Transposed to Venice, the imagined transaction of a romantic poet's surviving mistress with his would-be biographer became *The Aspern Papers*.

†Both the noble Julia's deed and the inscription honoring her appear to have been an earlier fiction passing as history.

> The winds might rend—the skies might pour,
>   But there thou wert—and still wouldst be
> Devoted in the stormiest hour
>   To shed thy weeping leaves o'er me.[18]

Now the last lap of their journey seemed endless. Arriving at the outskirts of Geneva at about midnight on May 23, they made straight for the fashionable Hôtel de l'Angleterre in the suburb of Secheron; the location exempted visitors from the city's curfew, and the host, M. Dejean, enjoyed a four-star reputation for taking good care of his well-off English guests. Byron was so exhausted that in the register, where travelers were required by law to provide vital statistics, he wrote after *Age*: "One Hundred." (The hotelier was not amused; he awakened Byron half an hour later for a correction.)

Someone else besides the management had marked Byron's arrival. Ten days earlier, Claire Clairmont and the Shelley party had taken the cheapest rooms on the top floor of the hotel. Since then, she had been waiting ever more anxiously; fearing that Byron might have deliberately misled her as to his destination, she had even taken to foraging through poste restante at Geneva, where she was reassured to see a letter addressed to Dr. Polidori.

She knew that Byron was indifferent to her; if her drowned corpse were to float past his window, she teased, his only comment would be *"Tiens!"* Still, she hoped for pity if not love: Might not her misery move him to exclaim, " 'Poor thing'?" she had written before he had left London, ending her letter with the lovelorn wail that Byron had come to dread: "Pray write, I shall die if you don't write."[19]

Whether he wrote or not, Claire was determined to follow him. Conveniently for her purposes, Shelley, too, had been anxious to leave England as soon—and as secretly—as possible. He had lost a suit in Chancery to pry more funds from his family; Mary's father, William Godwin, was flaying his sense of guilt by constant importunings for money that he had earlier promised, and the poet believed himself to be under constant surveillance for his irregular household, consisting now of Mary, their infant son William, and Claire. With worrisome symptoms of consumption, Shelley had thought of moving from the outskirts of London to distant Cumberland or Scotland, but Claire seems to have decided for all of them in favor of Switzerland.* From Paris, she wrote

---

*It has been conjectured that Byron's plan to spend the summer in Geneva was the deciding factor for the Shelleys, but there is no evidence that supports this view.

to Byron crowing at the prospect of their reunion. Shrewdly, she sought to allay his fears of sexual entrapment, declaring, "I had ten times rather be your male friend than your mistress."20 This was also a neatly executed gesture of face-saving, as Byron was deaf to all pleas to take her abroad with him as his official companion; if she insisted on following him, Claire acknowledged, he had warned her not to come "without protection." Now, she reported triumphantly, she was Shelley's responsibility, but, given her chaperon's philosophy of sexual sharing, she was also free to love where she pleased. Aware of Byron's distaste for free-thinking women, however, Claire also entreated him to address her under the name "Madame Clairville,"21 a bid for the married woman's respectability.

Thus far her determination had triumphed over Byron's passivity, boredom, and even dislike. She had seduced him and, as she now hinted, was probably pregnant with his child. He might come to care for her, after all. If this failed to work, she dangled her stepsister as a more alluring alternative, one that also promised the fallback position for Claire of having Shelley to herself. "You will I suppose wish to see Mary who talks, & looks at you with admiration," she wrote to Byron; "you will I dare say fall in love with her; she is very handsome and very aimiable [*sic*] & you will no doubt be blest in your attachment. If it should be so I will redouble my attentions to please her; I will do everything she tells me whether it be good or bad for I would not stand low in the affections of the person so beyond blest as to be beloved of you."22

If we need wonder why Byron moved from indifference and mild antipathy to implacable loathing of Claire, this letter provides crucial evidence: The hysterical professions of love, the hectoring reproaches, the masochistic offer of servitude to a hated rival—every sentence could have been written by Caroline Lamb. Byron himself signals the demonic character he attributed to both women; they were the only lovers he called "little fiend." Now, in the quiet following his arrival at the hotel, Claire left Byron an adoring note of welcome, directing him to reply "under cover to Shelley, for I do not wish to appear either in [love?] or curious."23

She heard nothing from Byron all the next day—Sunday—and in the early hours of Monday morning, she left him a note aquiver with righteous indignation, as though Byron had entreated her to make the eight-

---

What seems likelier is that Claire's determination to waylay her reluctant lover inspired her to make a persuasive case for Switzerland and that Shelley, feeling harassed and ill, was relieved to have the decision made for him.

hundred-mile journey, only to ignore her once she arrived. "I have been in this weary hotel this fortnight & it seems so unkind, so cruel of you to treat me with such marked indifference," she scolded. She then instructed him to "go straight to the top of the house this evening at ½ past seven & I will infallibly be on the landing place & shew you the room. Pray do not ask any servants to conduct you as they might take you to Shelley which would be very awkward."[24] (Just how awkward Byron would realize shortly when he learned that Claire had most probably been Shelley's lover, a role she would resume during the more troubled periods of his union with Mary.)

By the time the Shelley party descended late on Monday morning, Byron had already left the hotel for Geneva and a meeting with his banker. Scion of an eminent banking family, Charles Hentsch, then only twenty-six, was a charming young man with literary aspirations. Proud of his new client, an English lord and celebrated poet, he introduced Byron to the *salons* of a city famously closed to foreigners. Hentsch was helpful in a myriad of other ways, beginning with Byron's first concern: finding a suitable house. The hotel was expensive and filled with a procession of visiting compatriots for whom Byron's notoriety made him an unexpected tourist attraction; the most shameless would soon avail themselves of telescopes to observe him from across the lake.

Accompanied by Hentsch, he looked at several properties, including a villa owned by Madame de Staël; exiled by Napoleon, she had not yet returned to her château in the lakeside village of Coppet. Of the available houses, the only one that appealed to Byron was a villa in the still-rustic suburb of Cologny, about two miles from Geneva. Situated on a ridge above vineyards with views across the lake, the house was owned by a M. Diodati, member of a distinguished Geneva family of civil servants.* To Byron's disappointment, he learned that the house had been rented to other English visitors for three years. Accompanied by Polidori, he now sailed back across the lake.

Claire, meanwhile, was determined that Byron would avoid her no longer, and she made certain that Shelley's morning stroll brought them to the small, pebbly beach below the hotel just as Byron, in his newly

---

*Two centuries earlier, another branch of the Diodatis had immigrated to England, where a descendant had been the school fellow and friend of the young John Milton. It's still assumed—wrongly—that Milton stayed at the Villa Diodati when he visited Geneva in 1638, thus giving the house a double literary pedigree. In fact, when Milton came to Switzerland to mourn his friend's death, he stayed with the Diodatis in town; the villa in Cologny had not yet been built.

rented boat, was approaching the shore. As an elderly lady, she would recall how both Mary and Shelley, seeing the two men across the water, mistook the darker young doctor for the poet. Byron would not have have been pleased. He scrambled onto land and limped toward the little group. The famous first meeting of the two poets began awkwardly. To begin with, there was the embarrassment of Claire's eager presence. Then, both Byron and Shelley suffered acutely from "the Shys." Shelley's high seriousness made no concession to clubbable chat, so Byron promptly invited the younger poet to dine with him that evening. Polidori was allowed to join them, and he noted in his diary his impressions of their guest:* "Dined, P[ercy] S[helley], the author of *Queen Mab* came; bashful, shy, consumptive; twenty-six; separated from his wife; keeps the two daughters of Godwin who practise his theories: one L[ord] B[yron]'s."25 The doctor had most of his facts wrong: Shelley was not yet twenty-four, nor was he consumptive (although he believed he was), and Claire was not Godwin's daughter. His final remark, however, is significant: Either Byron had told him earlier that Claire was his mistress, or the conversation between the two poets that evening turned to an intimate discussion of both their relations with the problematic young woman.

Within days, the little group was inseparable; followed by the curious stares of other guests, they took meals together, along with walks, and expeditions on the lake. Shelley's funds, however, were fast dwindling, and he felt pressed to move from their expensive hotel. His house-hunting proved easier than Byron's, and on June 1 Shelley moved his family into a simple box of a two-story villa, known locally as the *compagne Chappuis*, across the lake in the hamlet of Montalègre. Besides being affordable, the house had its own small harbor and was large enough to accommodate Shelley, Claire, Mary, six-month-old William, and a new member of the household, the baby's Swiss nurse, Elise Duvillard. Then, only days later, Byron learned that the Villa Diodati was available. After two weeks in Switzerland, the rent— prorated at 25 louis a month—sounded less prohibitive, while the location now seemed predestined: An eight-minute walk down a narrow path through vineyards led to the doorway of Shelley's cottage and the lake. On June 10, accompanied by Polidori and the servants Robert Rushton and Fletcher, Byron moved into the villa, claiming for himself

---

*Murray had paid Polidori £500 to keep a journal of his travels with Byron; it's not clear whether Byron knew of this arrangement.

the narrow room on the southern side of the house; from his balcony he enjoyed splendid views across the lake to terraced vineyards folding into the Jura's silhouetted hills.

In the mornings and through the heat of noon, the Byron and Shelley households kept to themselves, convening in the late afternoon for excursions on the lake. They often remained on the water through the long, balmy evenings while the boat moved idly with the soft breeze, seldom returning before 10:00 p.m. Sailing so delighted all of them that Byron and Shelley decided to share the cost of buying a more seaworthy boat, ordering from Bordeaux an English-made skiff with two sails, whose deeper keel promised greater safety in the sudden squalls that whipped the lake's waters into a rough sea.

Shelley had never learned to swim, and he remained in the boat with the two women while Byron rediscovered his favorite sport. His speed and stamina in the water amazed the others, who were accustomed to his halting gait on land, and they were still more admiring when, in the high spirits always inspired by his natural element, Byron later burst into an Albanian war chant. Either to commemorate his solo or to mimick local pronunciation of his initials, L(ord) B(yron) "el be," Mary and Claire began calling him "Albé."

On the tranquil water, tensions were building. Now that Byron had found in Shelley a companion who shared his interests, Polidori felt more than ever that he was odd man out. For his own reasons, Shelley conceived a violent dislike for the young doctor and, as the two poets drew closer, they persecuted the thin-skinned "PollyDolly" with a savagery that seemed to replay all the torments they had suffered at Eton and Harrow. Promising to keep secret Polidori's confession of unrequited love for a young Genevan lady, Byron promptly betrayed his confidence and, worse, mocked the youth's lovelorn state in his presence to the assembled company. Another day, while the young doctor was paddling awkwardly about in the water near the boat, Byron proposed that they let him go under to test the adage that drowning men grasp at straws. A born victim, Polidori rose to the bait every time. Blaming Shelley for having turned Byron against him, he returned the younger poet's hostility in full and challenged his enemy to a duel. Byron promptly interceded in the matter, which ended there, but his own behavior toward his traveling physician veered between cruelty and guilty overcompensation; he tried to mollify the unhappy young man by paying 15 Napoleons toward the price of a watch that, as it turned out, was not to Polidori's taste. When Byron teasingly dared Polidori to jump from a wall and to prove his gallantry by escorting Mary up the rain-slicked path to the villa, Polidori slipped, severely spraining his ankle. Byron was stricken, carrying the doctor up to the house, tenderly laying him on a sofa—even fetching pillows for his head. However, the group chose that same evening to dismiss a play the doctor had written and read aloud earlier. "All agreed it was worth nothing," he confided miserably to his diary.[26]

Polidori's only happy relationship within the circle was with Mary, now in her sunniest mood, enjoying her little boy, the house, and the glorious weather. Polidori gave her Italian lessons, and she was delighted to add Tasso to her prodigious reading schedule; but despite his romantic yearnings, Mary viewed the twenty-one-year-old, three years her senior, as a younger brother. Finally, the physician earned Shelley's gratitude by taking little William, called "Willmouse," to be vaccinated against smallpox, for which the poet gave him a seal with a gold chain.

As for Claire, Byron had given her a wide berth when they were all lodged at the hotel. Soon after moving into the Diodati, however, he weakened, allowing her once more into his bed. He now put both Claire and Mary to work fair-copying the disparate leaves of *Childe Harold*'s new canto, still flowing from his pen; in Claire's physical presence, Byron felt those "intermittences"—Stendhal's word for alternating flashes of desire and disgust—that had characterized his feelings for Caroline Lamb. Shelley, too, experienced Claire as an electrical charge of opposites: She is his

> Comet beautiful and fierce,
> Who drew the heart of this frail Universe
> Towards thine own; till, wrecked in that convulsion,
> Alternating attaction and repulsion
> Thine went astray and that was rent in twain.[27]

Moved to confess to Augusta, Byron justified his infidelity by his sister's abandonment of him; as that most vulnerable of God's creatures, a lonely, love-starved male, "What could I do?—a foolish girl—in spite of all I could say or do—would come after me—or rather went before me—for I found her here. . . . I could not exactly play the Stoic with a woman—who had scrambled eight hundred miles to unphilosophize me." To be sure, a long fast had rendered him particularly susceptible to her sexual bounty; having been "regaled of late with so many 'two courses and a *desert*' (Alas!) of aversion . . . I was fain to take a little love (if pressed particularly) by way of novelty."[28]

But in resuming their sexual relations, Byron had encouraged her hopes at the worst possible moment. As soon as she told him—with certainty—that she was pregnant with his child, his distaste froze into fear. Claire now had a claim on him, and she would use it.

Interviewed late in her life, Claire advanced another reason for Byron's hatred. In their last weeks at Diodati, she recalled, he had told the group of his affair with Augusta, even claiming to be the father of two of her children. His subsequent cruelty toward her, Claire believed, was based on what she knew. At the least, his indiscretions were another reason to fear her.

SUDDENLY the weather changed; the unseasonably warm spring turned cold, and they were driven indoors by incessant rains that hid the mountains in fog. At one end of the long drawing room at the Diodati, the little group huddled around the fire, turning toward the high windows when a flash of lightning illuminated the sky and churning water.

The year 1816—when Byron's world turned to ashes—witnessed one of the worst global disasters in recorded history. One year earlier, the eruption of Mount Tomboro, in what is now Indonesia, had unleashed a vast quantity of fine volcanic dust into the atmosphere. Circling the earth in the high stratosphere, the dust reflected sunlight back into space. As though under a biblical curse, the earth literally darkened; temperatures dropped; throughout western Europe and North America crops failed and cattle died. Weakened by the Napoleonic Wars, the sagging economy and frayed food chain led to widespread hunger and social unrest.[29]

The personal disaster of Byron's life and its blighting losses—wife, child, sister, possessions, and reputation—appear as a microcosm of that catastrophe, supplying a cosmic dimension to his famous metaphor of poetry as "lava of the imagination."[30] With its images of a blasted natural world emptied of living creatures, Byron's poem "Darkness," written in these weeks, is his contribution to the literature of Apocalypse and one of the great examples of English blank verse:

> I had a dream, which was not all a dream.
> The bright sun was extinguish'd, and the stars
> Did wander darkling in the eternal space,
> Rayless, and pathless, and the icy earth
> Swung blind and blackening in the moonless air.

Starving, all creatures have become predators or their victims:

> The wild birds shriek'd,
> And, terrified, did flutter on the ground,
> And flap their useless wings; the wildest brutes
> Came tame and tremulous; and vipers crawl'd
> And twined themselves among the multitude,
> Hissing, but stingless—they were slain for food:
>
> . . . .
>
>   no love was left;
> All earth was but one thought—and that was death,
> Immediate and inglorious; and the pang
> Of famine fed upon all entrails—men
> Died, and their bones were tombless as their flesh;

By an altar, desecrated for "unholy usage,"

> [Two survivors] beheld
> Each other's aspects—saw, and shriek'd, and died—
> Even of their mutual hideousness they died.[31]

In the literature of horror, the "hideousness" of a monster created in a laboratory far eclipsed Byron's neglected poem. Ten days after he had completed "Darkness," a tale told by Mary Shelley became the most famous literary consequence of the Diodati gatherings, giving its name to these same months: "the Frankenstein summer."

The Shelley party had taken to dining up the hill with Byron, but after eating and talking until late, the torrential rains made the descent too dangerous, and the visitors now stayed the night. Conversation continued; while Mary and Claire listened silently in the darkness, the two poets discussed and argued. Since his school days, Shelley had been given to scientific tinkering, and the talk soon turned to the great question, inspired by recent experiments of Dr. Erasmus Darwin, grandfather of the evolutionist, that seemed to array the promise of science against religious doctrine: Could human life be created in the laboratory? One widely publicized experiment had explored the further possibilities of spontaneous generation, as a strand of spaghetti was observed to have "moved" in an airtight glass case.

From science, the discussion drifted to the supernatural; Byron had come upon a rare collection of German horror stories translated into French under the title *Fantasmagoriana*, and the group now took turns reading aloud from these spine-tingling tales. Then, at about midnight on June 18, after some "ghostly" talk, Byron recited from Coleridge's still-unpublished poem *Christabel*. The verse he chose described a scene where the female serpent, or *Lamia*, invited into the innocent Christabel's bedchamber disguised as a beautiful princess, undresses before her victim, revealing her monstrous form:

> Her silken robe and inner vest
> Dropt to her feet, and in full view
> Behold her bosom and half her side—
> Hideous, deformed and pale of hue—

In the silence that followed, Polidori recalled "Shelley suddenly shrieking and putting his hands to his head ran out of the room with a candle." The others remained, shocked into a kind of paralysis. Only the doctor moved quickly: "Threw water in his face and after gave him ether," he noted briskly. To the young physician, Shelley then revealed his hallucination: "He was looking at Mrs. S[helley] and suddenly thought of a woman he had heard of who had eyes instead of nipples."[32] Taken together with Christabel's waking nightmare of a ravaged female body, Shelley's vision appears as both dreadful prophecy and accusation: Six months later, Harriet Westbrook Shelley, his abandoned wife and mother of his two young children, was found floating in the Serpentine, the narrow artificial lake in Hyde Park; a suicide, she had been missing for almost five weeks, and was judged to have "lain in the Water for some days."[33] The dead woman was also pregnant, the child possibly Shelley's.

Byron was not ready to give up these exciting entertainments, however disturbing to Shelley; feeling, perhaps, that homemade horror stories would be less alarming, he now suggested that each of them in turn write a ghost story, to be read aloud. Shelley, understandably, made only a fainthearted stab, with a tale based on a childhood experience, while Polidori's confused narrative confirmed the group's earlier opinion of his literary talents. Byron himself produced a sketchy version of a plot involving the supernatural (later appended to his narrative poem *Mazeppa*), but as he showed no interest in developing the story as prose fiction, Polidori, adding gore and gothic bric-a-brac, published it in pamphlet form, three years later, as *The Vampyre*.*

Only Mary's effort ripened into novel form in the next year. Since

---

*An indication of his complicated appropriation of Byron was Polidori's insistence that the author appear as "Anonymous" while telling everyone that the work came directly from Byron's pen.

then, *Frankenstein or The Modern Prometheus* has cast its spell over readers of every generation and has been reborn in every medium since the author's first telling while the storm raged outside Diodati's rattling windows. Both Frankenstein and his monster, she recalled, came to her in a vision: "I saw the pale student of unhallowed arts kneeling beside the thing he had put together."[34] She drew the novel's settings, including scenes on Lake Geneva, from her own life and travels, but the tale's interlaced motifs reflect Byron's current preoccupations, starting with the subtitle; in the next weeks, Byron would complete his poem "Prometheus," with its theme of a catastrophe unleashed by defiance of divine law. An early version of *Frankenstein* flirts with incest in the blood ties of Victor and his bride, while the monstrous creation endures all the sufferings of Byron's pariah-heroes: thwarted sexuality, blood guilt, isolation, and exile. Together, Victor Frankenstein and his creature mirror the Byronic double: the poet and his avenging fate.

Evoking Alpine majesty as "palaces of nature," Mary quoted directly from Canto III of *Childe Harold*, the work she had been copying when her vision came to her. In a letter to her half sister Fanny Imlay, she described their nocturnal return across the lake "when, as we approach the shore, we are saluted by the delightful scent of flowers and new mown grass, and the chirp of the grasshoppers, and the song of the evening birds."[35]

The identical odors and sounds rise from Byron's new canto, evoking the same experience of landfall:

> and drawing near
> There breathes a living fragrance from the shore,
>   Of flowers yet fresh with childhood; on the ear
>   Drops the light drip of the suspended oar,
> Or chirps the grasshopper one good-night carol more.[36]

Did Mary appropriate from Byron's draft of Canto III, which she was copying, or could she have read her letter aloud with the poet present, who then borrowed her images?

On Saturday, June 22, Byron and Shelley set sail for a tour of Lake Geneva (or Lake Leman, as Byron preferred to call it) and the villages on the shore. He was delighted to be rid of the importunate Claire and the temperamental doctor. For both poets, the next eight days together were filled with the leisurely exchange of ideas and experience that is the coin of intimacy.

They spent hours on the water comparing their early years. Rebellious sons, both were "gentlemen" with the same reference points of privilege: Eton and Harrow, Oxford and Cambridge. They had come of age denouncing their country's betrayals, both political and personal: England's abdication of social justice at home and support of restored monarchy abroad. Now each suffered the sense of being hounded into exile by enemies using the excuse of their private lives to rid a reactionary society of dangerous critics.

But there were also barriers between the two that would never disappear: Lord Byron, *seigneur* of Diodati, never allowed Shelley to forget the distance that separated a peer of the realm from a mere scion of landed gentry.* This, together with Byron's best-selling poetry and fame (following him even to Geneva), acted as constant reminders to Shelley, whose two published poems had met with indifference or ridicule, of the chasm between success and failure. At the same time, as an admirer of his poetry, the radical Shelley was shocked to learn of Byron's deeply conventional attitudes—toward sex, women, established religion. Accepting as though by divine right the privileges of class and gender, Byron had no desire to abolish existing institutions, like marriage or the church. His new friend, Shelley now realized, was an eighteenth-century libertine who wanted to break laws, not change them. Striking down tyranny was the duty of free men; working toward a new world order was the labor of lunatics.

"Lord Byron," Shelley wrote to his friend the writer Thomas Love Peacock, "is an exceedingly interesting person and as such is it not to be regretted that he is slave to the vilest and most vulgar prejudices, and as mad as the winds."[37]

By "prejudices" Shelley also had in mind Byron's distaste for his own utopian belief in salvation through communal love. But in fact, Byron's rejection of progressive views—whether on the rights of women, or the end of marriage—stemmed from pessimism, not prejudice; he would never accept Shelley's faith that changing (or abolishing) laws or institutions made men and women happier or better. Byron was, as he said of himself, the "careful pilot of my proper woe." But this was true of all suffering humanity. In Byron's cosmos the individual struggles against the forces of darkness—alone.

Still, along with spirited disagreement, the two poets established areas of profound affinity, of which the lake tour itself was an expression. Both recent converts to the cult of Rousseau, their sailing trip was first and foremost a literary pilgrimage and a chance to tread hallowed ground. Each found reflections of himself in the Swiss philosopher,

---

*Sir Timothy Shelley of Field Place, Sussex, was the poet's father.

whose own turbulent life was a tissue of conflict and contradiction: his social criticism and persecution mania; the moral somersaults and nagging guilt with which he justified abandoning his children. Although Rousseau was born in Geneva, Byron took the liberty (one of which Jean Jacques would have approved) of providing him with a pastoral birthplace:

> Here the self-torturing sophist, wild Rousseau,
> The apostle of affliction, he who threw
> Enchantment over passion, and from woe
> Wrung overwhelming eloquence, first drew
> The breath which made him wretched.[38]

Before leaving Diodati, Byron had carefully prepared an itinerary that would take them to all the places mentioned in his new favorite among Rousseau's works, *Julie, ou la Nouvelle Héloïse*. A novel in the form of love letters written at a fever pitch of passion, Rousseau's rambling text validated crucial areas of each poet's behavior and beliefs. Contrasting the corrupt society of cities to the ennobling natural settings of Lake Leman, Rousseau exalted the virtues of bucolic life while allowing his hero, Saint-Preux, tutor to the lovely Julie, to be less than virtuous, seducing and impregnating his aristocratic young pupil. Following Julie's arranged marriage to a friend of her father, however, all is forgiven. The new husband invites his wife's former lover to live with them and their two children in the château of Clarens. This paradise of a Shelleyan ménage à trois is short-lived. A martyr to maternal love,* Julie dies of pleurisy, the consequence of rescuing her children from drowning in the waters of the lake!

For the literary tourists, the heart of the pilgrimage was the village of Clarens, where their obliging landlady pointed to the view from their window of the famous *"bosquet de Julie,"* the grove where Rousseau's heroine rushed to read her lover's letters. Unaware that the setting had been invented, Byron raged that the monks who owned the land had despoiled the sacred wood for timber. But the poets also explored other sites mentioned in the novel, inadvertently reenacting one of the lovers' misadventures. A sudden squall near the rocks between St. Gingolph

---

*Sexually compliant, fecund, and maternal, Julie bears a striking resemblance to Augusta; at the outset, her innocent relations with Saint-Preux have so much of brother and sister that when their love turns to passion, Julie herself describes them as "incestuous."

and Meillerie sent high waves over their open boat, smashing the rudder, and they came close to capsizing "precisely in the spot where Julie and her lover were nearly overset, and St. Preux was tempted to plunge with her into the Lake,"[39] Shelley reported proudly. Byron was a strong swimmer, and as they were close to shore, he was confident he could easily make it to safety with Shelley, who was unable to swim, in tow. In Tom Moore's version of the event,* Shelley "positively refused" to be saved, and "seating himself quietly upon a locker, and grasping the rings at each end firmly in his hands, declared his determination to go down in that position, without a struggle."[40] Shelley himself insisted that seated side by side, he and Byron had both assumed this fatalistic position. Six years later, however, Shelley would reenact this same refusal to be saved—with fatal consequences. This time the wind blew them safely to shore, where Shelley, once again, felt diminished by evidence of Byron's superiority: "I knew that my companion would have attempted to save me, and I was overcome with humiliation."[41]

Deepening the wounds of inadequacy was his inability to write anything during their journey other than letters and journal jottings, while Byron managed to convert most of what he saw and felt, including many of their conversations, into poetry. He continued adding to the third canto of *Childe Harold*, whose new stanzas bore evidence that Shelley's arguments about poetry—if not the perfectability of men and women in the real world—were gaining ground. His companion, Byron recalled, had dosed him with Wordsworth "even to nausea."[42] Swallowing the medicine, Byron tried to be cured. Dazed by his losses, he was open, as never before, to the older poet's healing message. In a benevolent natural world we find confirmation of human love, starting with our earliest ideal of "Maternal Nature," the source of masculine strength:

> By the blue rushing of the arrowy Rhone,
> Or the pure bosom of its nursing lake,
> Which feeds it as a mother . . .[43]

In contrast to "the wild world I dwelt in," the lake, as female principle, teacher, and, significantly, sister, has restored him to nature: ". . . once I loved / Torn ocean's roar, but thy soft murmuring / Sounds sweet as if a sister's voice reproved."[44] Moving close to a Wordsworthian pastiche, Byron wondered

---

*Moore's information was based on interviews with Mary Shelley, who, if anything, exaggerated her husband's heroic qualities.

> Are not the mountains, waves, and skies, a part
> Of me and of my soul, as I of them?[45]

In a reborn state of pantheistic ecstasy, he found his own "intimations of immortality": "Spurning the clay-cold bonds which round our being cling,"[46] he envisioned "bodiless thought" soaring beyond things seen. Wordsworth himself saw an appropriator, not a convert, in Byron's stanzas, accusing the younger poet of "poaching on my manor." Indeed, Byron succeeded in displacing his poetic forebear in lines that have come to stand for all human experience of oneness with nature:

> Then stirs the feeling infinite, so felt
> In solitude, where we are *least* alone."[47]

If Shelley felt reassured by the skeptic's conversion to a Wordsworthian faith in nature as love, he was disappointed by Byron's worship at two other literary shrines. Gathering acacia leaves from Gibbon's neglected garden, Byron paid homage to "The Lord of Irony . . . sapping a solemn creed with solemn sneer," and at Ferney he commemorated Voltaire, whose protean talents "Breathed most in ridicule . . . now to o'erthrow a fool and now to shake a throne." Shelley disapproved of both: Despite their common enemies, these "gigantic minds" had been led astray—like Byron himself—into a cynical rejection of human community and of love's redemptive power.

Both poets were stirred by a visit to the Château de Chillon, whose dungeons revealed floors striated by the chains dragged by centuries of prisoners and a sluice gate for death by drowning; a blackened beam that had anchored the executioner's rope still swung overhead. Byron especially was drawn to their guide's story of the Swiss patriot François Bonivard, incarcerated in the 1530s by the Duke of Savoy. After a dramatic tour, the travelers spent two storm-drenched days in the Hôtel de l'Ancre in Ouchy, below Lausanne, where, in a room facing the gray, rain-pitted lake, Byron meditated on the meaning of Bonivard's survival: Was he an example for the ages, a hero whose spirit emerged triumphant from his trials, or did loss and solitary suffering leave him a husk of a man, fit only to embrace his isolation? "My very chains and I grew friends, / So much a long communion tends / To make us what we are."[48] In either reading, Bonivard is a measure of Byron's increasing skill at creating characters both heroic and psychologically complex, while the poem's popularity testifies to its grim relevance today when political prisoners—missing, tortured, and languishing in jails—are not romantic figures but accusing witnesses.

They returned on June 30, and two weeks later the Shelley party set off for an excursion to Chamonix. Claire was frantic to see Byron before they left: "We go in two days—are you satisfied?" she wrote in her habitual tone of reproach and self-pity. Seeking to disabuse her of false hopes, Mary and Shelley gently conveyed (as they were clearly meant to) news of her banishment from Diodati. Clutching at the straw of usefulness, she begged to be allowed to finish copying *The Prisoner of Chillon*: "If you trust it down here I will take the *greatest* possible care of it; & finish it in an hour or two. Remember how very short a time I have to teize [*sic*] you & that you will soon be left to your dear bought freedom. . . ." Desolation submerged her efforts to sound light-hearted: "Shall I never see you again? Not once again?" she asked. "Pray send me an answer directly—I cannot wait."[49] But Byron did not answer her directly—then or ever again.

As it happened, Shelley and Mary delayed their departure for another five days. Because Claire was accompanying them, Byron declined to join the excursion. Shelley was keenly disappointed; he had looked forward to continuing the discussions begun on their lake tour. Now, the marvels they saw, the Mer de Glace and the glittering white claw of Mont Blanc at close range, made him regret Byron's absence all the more, and he wrote from their inn near Chamonix asking his friend to reconsider. But Byron was enjoying his freedom and privacy. Echoing Mary, who deeply resented her stepsister's intrusion into their household and, more important, her claims on Shelley, Byron, too, might have defined happiness as *absentia Clariae*. Now, without anyone to challenge his radical views, Shelley had to be satisfied with writing "Atheist" in Greek after his signature in the registers of mountain inns.

Alone at Diodati, memories crowded Byron's solitude. "The Dream" evokes the boy he was, hopelessly in love with Mary Chaworth: "I saw two beings in the hues of youth / Standing upon a hill." Their two lives, like the blasted cosmos of "Darkness," would wither into living death: Her marriage a mockery, Mary had retreated to mental illness, becoming "Queen of a fantastic realm"; in his banishment and loss, the poet felt himself "a mark for blight and desolation." His friend and onetime idol, Sheridan, had died in London on July 7, and Douglas Kinnaird, on behalf of the Drury Lane management, had asked Byron for a commemorative poem to be recited from the stage. The circumstances of the playwright's last days—he died in the most squalid poverty, with bailiffs camped downstairs—were horrifying. Byron's "Monody on the Death of Sheridan," however, remains a strangely impersonal Wordsworthian effort: Either the public commission froze him—not for the first time— or his friend's terrible end struck too close to home. The best he could muster, then, was a tepid meditation on the persecution of great men. In compensation, Byron tried to exert some influence on the choice of actress to recite his lines—without success.

Earlier in July, Shelley, a brilliant classicist, had translated Aeschylus' *Prometheus Bound* aloud for Byron, who now recast this favorite subject with autobiographical fervor in his own poem "Prometheus":

> Thou art a symbol and a sign
> To Mortals of their fate and force;
> Like thee, Man is in part divine,
> A troubled stream from a pure source.[50]

Unlike the stoical Bonivard, Prometheus offers a reminder that men are also gods, with power to transcend human suffering. Of his own sufferings, the most bitter, still, was separation from his sister. Now, in "Stanzas to Augusta," dated July 24, Byron reached once again for a Promethean image to describe his triumph over affliction:

> Though the rock of my last hope is shiver'd,
>   And its fragments are sunk in the wave,
> Though I feel that my soul is deliver'd
>   To pain—it shall not be its slave.[51]

Within the next weeks, he pushed further: In a more intimate tribute to "My Sister—my sweet Sister" he tried—vainly—to apply Shelleyan lessons in the consolations of nature as human love:

> I feel almost at times as I have felt
>   In happy childhood—trees and flowers and brooks
> . . . .
> Come as of yore upon me—and can melt
>   My heart with recognition of their looks—
> And even at moments I could think I see
> Some living things to love—but none like thee.[52]

By way of diversion, a happy surprise awaited Byron at Coppet, where the return of the chatelaine, Madame de Staël, occasioned a flurry of invitations. On home ground, the argumentative "Mrs. Stale" revealed herself an incomparable hostess and mother figure to Byron, who now pronounced her "the best creature in the world." Several times a week, setting out in midafternoon, he sailed directly across the lake to arrive in time for dinner at Coppet. With one exception—an

Englishwoman who fainted with horror upon hearing his name announced—Byron found a welcoming circle of genial spirits: He was charmed by de Staël's "secret" husband, M. de Rocca, a handsome officer some three decades his wife's junior. He was admiring of her beautiful daughter, the Duchesse de Broglie, and was both awed and irritated by the children's ex-tutor and resident scholar, the German critic, philologist, and poet A. W. Schlegel.

Shelley and the two women returned on July 26, and on the next day, Byron relented, allowing Claire to join the others at Diodati. Then, on August 2, Shelley and Claire were asked to call—alone. The specific exclusion of Mary suggests that they met to discuss the future of Claire's baby. It was at this time, Claire later recalled, that Byron agreed the child would remain with one parent until age seven; if that parent were Byron, Claire would be allowed to visit under the guise of an aunt "without injury to anyone's reputation." At the same time, Byron made it quite clear to Claire that she would never be permitted to be part of his household.

Questions still linger about whether Byron or Shelley was the child's father; Shelley seems to have earlier acknowledged to Byron that he and Claire had been lovers, but after some calculation Byron decided to believe Claire and recognize the child as his.* To his friend Douglas Kinnaird he wrote, "Is the brat mine? I have reason to think so, for I know as much as one can know such a thing—that she had not lived with S[helley] during the time of our acquaintance—that she had a good deal of that same with me."[53] In the next years, he would point to the resemblance, in both appearance and temperament, of his "little illegitimate" to her Byron forebears.

On August 14, the first guests arrived from England. "Monk" Lewis, writer of gothic best-sellers and heir to a West Indian fortune, appeared with a retinue of colorfully costumed Jamaican servants. Earlier, Byron had found him a "good man, a clever man, but a bore."[54] Now, however, Lewis redeemed himself by reading aloud one evening from Goethe's *Faust*, translating freely as he went along. A week and a half later brought the long-deferred visit from Hobhouse, accompanied by Scrope Davies. With the reunion of the three old friends, their boisterous reminiscences, and private jokes, Shelley felt superfluous; it was

---

*Shelley's new will, drawn up at this time, has suggested that he was none too confident of Byron's willingness to provide for the child. Thus, besides £6,000 he left to Claire outright, he added another £6,000 for "such other person as the said Mary Jane Clairmont should name (if she should be pleased to name one)," interpreted as a discreet reference to her illegitimate child. During Shelley's lifetime, Claire herself would remain his responsibility.

time for him to leave. He and Hobhouse joined forces in urging Byron to dismiss Polidori, but otherwise Shelley made so little impression on Hobhouse that he is barely mentioned in his voluminous diaries. On August 28, while Mary and Claire were packing, Byron and Shelley had a last sail together, followed by a long talk while seated on the sea wall of the little harbor. Before they parted, Shelley was entrusted with the red leather quarto volume containing the printer's copies of the poems Byron had written since embarking at Dover, to be delivered to Murray in London. The contents were among his finest poetry: Canto III of *Childe Harold*, "Darkness," "Prometheus," *Prisoner of Chillon*, "The Dream," "Monody on the Death of Sheridan," and "Stanzas to Augusta." On the morning of August 29 the Shelley household left for Geneva, and that same day, Byron, Hobhouse, and Scrope Davies set off for Chamonix and Mont Blanc. Staying at inns where the Shelley party had lodged, Byron protectively inked out the word "Atheist" after his friend's name in every register but one—the most eloquent evidence, perhaps, of the difference between the two men. Neither the frozen waves of the Mer de Glace nor Mont Blanc's beckoning summit inspired written comment from Byron; his only mention of the excursion was to alert Augusta to the souvenirs he was sending home with Scrope Davies: crystal from the local caverns, fashioned into jewelry for her, and toys for her children and for Ada. Three days later they were back at Diodati, where Scrope Davies was preparing to leave for England, taking with him Robert Rushton, Augusta's crystals, and another set of the manuscript poems* Byron had given to Shelley.

Then, on September 17, Byron and Hobhouse left for a tour of the Bernese Alps. In his letters and especially in the Alpine journal he began keeping for Augusta, Byron's record of his daily adventures takes on the flavor of those of other, earlier visitors to this icy world; he chronicles mountain passes and vales traversed, glaciers and waterfalls admired, peaks sighted. Alpine travel brings out statistical record-keeping: Byron reported on time spent on mule, horseback, or walking, how many feet below the summit of the Wengernalp or the Jungfrau they halted. Although his longest walk was only about an hour and a half,[55] when we recall his limp and the thin mountain air, the

---

*For reasons unknown, Scrope Davies never delivered to Murray his copy of Byron's manuscript nor several poems entrusted to him by Shelley. They remained in a locked trunk deposited in Kinnaird's bank, Ransome and Moreland, which became part of Barclay's Bank in the late nineteenth century. The cache was only discovered in 1976.

poet's stamina and grit appear heroic. Approaching the summit of the Dent de Jaman, "The chill of the wind & snow made me giddy but I scrambled on & upwards—H[obhouse] went to the highest *pinnacle*— I did not."[56] Descending the icy trails, crevasses plunging darkly on either side, was the most dangerous; on one trip alone, their guide had fallen three times. "I fell a laughing & tumbled too—the descent luckily soft though steep & slippery." To avoid the risk of falling rocks, their guide advised quickening the pace "like most good advice impracticable," Byron observed, the trail being so rough that "neither mules, nor mankind—nor horses—can make any violent progress." Their rewards were those sudden panoramic views that have stopped the hearts of all visitors since the first tourists ventured to these parts in the early eighteenth century. Two miles from the Wengernalp on the Kleine Scheidegg pass they saw the Eiger and Jungfrau peaks loom to their east. The lunar expanse of glaciers seen in the crystalline night air tempted Byron to still riskier excursions. Arriving at Grindelwald after a long day, they "dined, mounted again, & rode to the higher (upper) glacier. . . . Starlight, beautiful, but a devil of a path!" He was so transported by the vision of the Staubbach Falls that he made two visits, one at night, the second on the following day at 7:00 a.m.: the nine-hundred-foot torrent "in shape curving over the rock—like the *tail* of a white horse streaming in the wind" inspired him to poetry based on precise observation: "It is neither mist, nor water but a something between both—its immense height . . . gives it a wave—a curve—a spreading here—a condensation there—wonderful—indescribable."

Surrounded by inhuman grandeur, Byron found relief in evidence of human activity: a shepherd playing on his reed pipe sent him back to Rousseau, romanticizing Alpine dwellers as privileged survivors of an Old Testament state of nature, before the Fall. Like Rousseau, Byron preferred to see purity rather than misery in these peasants, whose conditions of near starvation reduced them to hunting scarce chamois at dangerous heights or scraping crystals from cavern walls to sell to tourists. He observed unmistakable symptoms of blight (most probably the effects of the freezing summer): "Passed *whole woods of withered pines—all withered*—trunks stripped and barkless—done by a single winter. . . . Their appearance," he wrote to Augusta, "reminded me of me & my family." He did not relate the blasted topography to the scrawny goats and goiterous children he and Shelley had noticed on their tour. Then, as though on cue, whom should they meet but another whose life had been changed—and not for the happier—by Byron: The forlorn Polidori was wandering these same mountains, alone but for the company of his sick dog. Having spent the last of his wages, he was crossing the Alps on foot to Italy, where he hoped to find refuge with relatives.

Sublime nature had diverted Byron without consoling him. Before setting out on this last Alpine tour, he had written to Augusta of his despair. Seeking to rationalize his losses, he now shifted between human fault and external fatality—an evil star—which drove him to lay waste to his own life. In the new canto of *Childe Harold*, Byron had proposed an ideal of sublimation:

> 'Tis to create, and in creating live
> A being more intense, that we endow
> With form our fancy . . .[57]

He needed a new form and a new persona to express a desolation whose source was in his stars, in himself, and in a female nemesis. *Manfred*, the title and subject of his new work, is the first of a series of dramatic dialogues, plays that—defensively, perhaps—the poet claimed were not intended to be performed, and which he later called "mental theatre."[58]

With debts to, among others, Hamlet, Macbeth, Faust, and Byron's own Giaour, Count Manfred, standing on the edge of an Alpine precipice, considers suicide. Dissuaded from self-destruction by the simple humanity of a chamois hunter, Manfred is less ambiguous in his guilt than his Shakesperean prototype. Instead of Oedipally inspired murder, he has destroyed—and been destroyed by—incest. Byron's hero evokes the twinn'd lovers' resemblance:

> She was like me in lineaments—her eyes,
> Her hair, her features, all, to the very tone
> Even of her voice, they said were like to mine.[59]

In the tower that looms above the Alpine setting of the drama, Manfred had killed his sister, Astarte, by mingling their blood in a forbidden act: "When we were in our youth, and had one heart, / And loved each other as we should not love. . . . My wrongs were all on those I should have cherished— / But my embrace was fatal."[60]

Manfred's wrongs against "those I should have cherished" took more than a single victim. Another woman interposes her presence, merging now with the silent, unforgiving phantom of his sister, Astarte, one who "had the same lone thoughts and wanderings,"

> The quest of hidden knowledge, and a mind
> To comprehend the universe.

Unbidden, the Princess of Parallelograms, the brilliant student of God's design and Euclid's, Annabella has claimed her place. Now a coven of spirits and nemeses interrogate Manfred about his crime and confession:

> "I loved her, and destroy'd her!"
> "With thy hand?" one asks.

His reply:

> "Not with my hand, but heart—which broke her heart—
> It gazed on mine, and withered."[61]

"He has injured me too deeply ever to forgive me," Annabella had predicted. Writing to Augusta, Byron was not merely unforgiving; he wanted blood: "She has destroyed your brother," he wrote of his wife, "but woe unto her—the wretchedness she has brought upon the man to whom she has been everything evil . . . will flow back into its fountain."[62] In the first scene of *Manfred*, Byron had inserted an "Incantation" (recycled from a discarded "Witch Drama" begun years before). To these lines he now added a curse on Annabella:

> By thy cold breast and serpent smile,
> By thy unfathom'd gulfs of guile,
> By that most seeming virtuous eye,
> By thy shut soul's hypocrisy;
> By the perfection of thine art
> Which pass'd for human thine own heart;
>
> . . . .
>
> I call upon thee! and compel
> Thyself to be thy proper Hell![63]

During his honeymoon visit to Six Mile Bottom he had boasted of "working" both women well; in the nightmare months at Piccadilly Terrace he had struck out at sister and wife:

> If I had never lived, that which I love
> Had still been living; had I never loved,
> That which I love would still be beautiful—
> Happy and giving happiness. What is she?
> What is she now?—a sufferer for my sins.[64]

The two women, fused by the poet's bitterness and guilt, had become one.

CHAPTER 29

Lord Byron, *Inglese*

*I*N ENGLAND, the two sufferers withdrew into the isolation of their separate mourning, hiding from the world and from each other.

Augusta had taken leave from her duties at St. James's Palace, returning home to await the birth of her fifth child and second son, Frederick George, on May 9. The Leighs' financial situation was desperate. The colonel had been passed over for any royal sinecure, and Augusta could find no buyer for Six Mile Bottom. In Byron's absence, she felt far more exposed to scandal, and she was pained and worried by Annabella's continuing silence, which Annabella herself had called a temporary edict, to last only until the separation papers had been signed.

At Kirkby Mallory, Annabella retreated into melancholy. The curtain had come down on the public drama. Now, without husband, home, or social position, she feared becoming, in the words of another estranged wife, one of the "sick and hunted deer of the herd."[1] Writing of his own grief, Byron spoke for Annabella, too:

> It is not in the storm nor in the strife
> We feel benumb'd, and wish to be no more,
> But in the after-silence on the shore,
> When all is lost, except a little life.[2]

She hardly ate, complaining of sleeplessness and violent headaches. She took no interest in her child; Ada was a reminder of all she had lost, and her parents' distress—rage toward Byron and fear for their daughter—depressed her further.

Beyond any doubt now, she was convinced of the *fact* of incest between Byron and Augusta. Worse than Augusta's continued protestation of innocence, however, was fresh evidence that she had betrayed Annabella's love and unselfish efforts to protect her from scandal. From London she heard reports that Augusta had publicly criticized Annabella's supporters and—despite all she had witnessed at Piccadilly Terrace—had pronounced her sister-in-law "unforgiving," even defending Byron as the injured party. On June 3, Annabella wrote, explaining her silence, "You have not disguised your resentment against those who have befriended me and have countenanced the arts which have been employed to injure me. Can I then longer believe those professions of affection and even of exclusive zeal for *my* welfare?"[3]

Augusta replied with pained astonishment: "I have uniformly considered you and consulted your happiness before and above any thing in this world," she insisted, before admitting that the importance of Annabella's friendship to her had little to do with personal feelings: "I have been assured that the tide of public opinion has been so turned against my Brother that the least appearance of coolness on your part towards me would injure me most seriously—& am therefore for the sake of my children compelled to accept from your compassion the 'limited intercourse' which is all you can grant to one whom you pronounce no longer worthy of your esteem or affection."[4]

Distracted by her own despair, Annabella might well have let matters rest. A new confidante, however, would not countenance such spiritual laxity. Theresa—or "Thérèse," as she preferred to be called—Villiers, an old friend of Augusta's, saw a new and powerful role for herself: She would orchestrate the Christian drama of Augusta's fall, redemption, and salvation. To this end, Mrs. Villiers now convinced Annabella that she owed her errant sister more than turning the other cheek. Together they must work to purify Augusta's soul. Once she had made full confession of her sins, Augusta would purge her brother from her thoughts, her affections, her life—and the penitent would be restored to God.

Still, Annabella wavered; her conscience was troubled by past collusion and her own complicated feelings about Augusta: "I have sometimes thought that a tacit understanding existed between us," she told Mrs. Villiers.[5]

KIRKBY MALLORY had become unbearable, and on June 8, Annabella, taking the baby and three servants, left for a small rented house in Lowestoft on the Suffolk coast. Besides the sea air, she was revived by a new friendship that must have seemed preordained. The Reverend

John William Cunningham, whose family lived nearby, had been vicar of Harrow since 1811, where he would have learned much about the school's notorious graduate. Dr. Cunningham, a best-selling author of religious texts, was also a leading light of the Clapham sect, the circle of well-off and well-connected reformers whose evangelical fervor provided a more emotionally expressive community within the established church and a socially preferable alternative to lower-class "chapel" congregations of Methodists and Baptists. Instead of returning to her parents' home, Annabella followed her seaside stay with a visit to Dr. Cunningham at Harrow. Until now her Christianity had been cool and intellectual, driven by her interest in theology. At this low point, however, she embraced the evangelicals' message with missionary fervor.* Once, she had harbored hopes of leading Byron back to orthodox belief; now, her born-again faith made wresting Augusta from his baleful influence a Christian duty.

Her resolve strengthened, Annabella, with Mrs. Villiers, now embarked on a campaign of enlightenment; letters flew back and forth debating the finer points of strategy: How much of what they knew should they reveal to Augusta and when? What must the sinner do to be forgiven and saved? In fact, they need not have troubled with subtle analyses: Augusta required no Grand Inquisitor. As soon as Annabella came to London on August 31, Augusta made full and detailed confession to both her "Guardian Angel," as she now took to calling her "dearest Sis," and to Mrs. Villiers. The latter now provided Augusta with plentiful proof of Byron's earlier betrayal of her to two other women: Caroline Lamb and the latter's mother-in-law, Lady Melbourne. This evidence of Byron's perfidy produced the desired effect. Demoralized and humiliated, Augusta swore, "I shall never write to him again!" But her confessors mistrusted such swift conversion. Then Augusta hit on a retaliatory strike of her own: She offered to show Annabella all of Byron's letters.

Not for the first time, the weak had outmaneuvered the strong. Augusta's revenge was double-edged: Byron had no idea that every word he wrote to his beloved sister would be read by Annabella; while the sinner, abject and contrite, was well aware that each letter offered

---

*Annabella's evangelical conversion at this time has been largely overlooked. Her new faith enabled her to sublimate personal motives of revenge into a missionary project but also explains her later involvement in the antislavery movement and education of the poor, principle reform goals of William Wilberforce, leader of the Clapham sect.

up to Annabella was a poisoned arrow straight to the wife's heart. "She has shown me of her own accord *his* letters to her—having only suppressed them because of the bitterness towards me," Annabella wrote to Mrs. Villiers. "They are <u>absolute love letters</u>"—Annabella's underlining slash of those three words is a cry of pain—"and she wants to know how she can stop them!"⁶

Without mentioning her confession, Augusta wrote to Byron, hoping to discover what, in fact, he had told Caroline Lamb and to forestall, if possible, further indiscretions on his part. Byron sensed that he stood accused, and his reply manages at the same time to sound apology, denial, and reassurance: "Your confidential letter is safe and all the others. This one has cut me to the heart because I have made you uneasy. Still, I think all these apprehensions—very groundless. Who can care for such a wretch as C[arolin]e or believe such a seventy times convicted liar? and in the next place, whatever she may suppose or assert—I never 'committed' any one to her but *myself*. . . . Really this is starting at shadows." And he implored her "do not be uneasy—and do not 'hate yourself' if you hate either let it be *me*—but do not—it would kill me; we are the last persons in the world who ought—or could cease to love one another."⁷ And before his initial, he signed with their cross.

In a postscript, he addressed another concern raised by Augusta: He had sent her his latest verses, titled "Stanzas to ******." Unknown to Byron, of course, she had shown the poem, along with his letter, to Annabella, and both women agreed that it should not be published. He followed the *Stanzas*, with the as yet untitled "Epistle to Augusta," whose declaration "There yet are two things in my destiny / A world to roam through—and a home with thee"⁸ would have made bitter reading for the censor. Byron instructed Murray that Mrs. Leigh must have the "option" to decide whether the poems should be published; after much dithering and discussion with Annabella, Augusta allowed only the "Stanzas" to appear.*

As far as Byron knew, Annabella had shown only "kindness" to his sister, and in late August his own angry feelings toward her softened. On one of his regular visits to Coppet, Madame de Staël showed him a newspaper account of Lady Byron's recent illness, and his distress con-

---

*Initially, Augusta refused to allow publication of either poem. She then changed her mind, and "Stanzas to ******" was published with *The Prisoner of Chillon and Other Poems*, which appeared in December 1816. Byron's draft of the more intimate and damning "Epistle to Augusta," included in the red leather folio delivered by Shelley to John Murray was first printed in Tom Moore's biography of Byron, published in 1830, six years after the poet's death.

firmed his hostess's suspicions that Byron still loved his wife. Meanwhile, de Staël's London informants gave her to understand that Annabella's failing health was caused by grief over the separation. Fired by romantic visions of a passionate reconciliation, de Staël now offered her services to Byron as mediator. His reply was encouraging: "To say that I am merely *sorry* to hear of Lady B's illness is to say nothing—but she has herself deprived me of the right to express more. The separation may have been *my* fault—but it was *her* choice.—I tried all means to prevent—and would do as much & more to end it,—a word would do so—but it does not rest with me to pronounce it.—You asked me if I thought that Lady B was attached to me—to that I can only answer that I love her."[9] He had started writing a satire of the marriage, which he now destroyed; instead, he began another poem, which opened floodgates of tenderness:

> And thou wert sad—yet I was not with thee;
> And thou wert sick, and yet I was not near;
> Methought that joy and health alone could be
> Where I was not—and pain and sorrow here![10]

Self-protective as always, he expressed pessimism; de Staël's efforts, he feared, would be "unavailing." When Annabella's reply was made known (through an intermediary), it was ambiguous. She had read too many passionate letters to Augusta from Diodati: "Lord Byron is well aware that my determination *ought not* to be changed,"[11] she said.

After its elegiac beginning, "Lines on Hearing That Lady Byron Was Ill" abruptly shifts course, mounting a surprise attack, including a curse more savage—because more personal—than the "Incantation" in *Manfred*:

> Thy Nights are banish'd from the realms of sleep!—
> Yes! they may flatter thee, but thou shall feel
> A hollow agony which will not heal,
> For thou art pillow'd on a curse too deep;
> Thou hast sown in my sorrow, and must reap
> The bitter harvest in a woe as real![12]

With its echoes of "Fare Thee Well!" and "A Sketch from Private Life" (Byron's attack on Mrs. Clermont), the new poem confirms what he had written to Augusta of his deadened spirits. The brute fact of Annabella's leaving him was more painful now than when he had fled England. Byron saw the sympathy that continued to flow in her direction as

evidence that she had manipulated the official version of their failed
marriage into a morality play, in which he was cast as Cynical Vice brutalizing Innocent Virtue. Now his pride suffered a final assault in her
refusal of reconciliation:

> I have had many foes, but none like thee;
> For 'gainst the rest myself I could defend,
> And be avenged, or turn them into friend;
> But thou in safe implacability
> Hadst nought to dread—in thy own weakness shielded,
> And in my love, which hath but too much yielded,
>
> . . . .
>
> And thus upon the World's trust in thy truth—
> And the wild fame of my ungovern'd youth
> On things that were not, and on things that are
> Even upon such a basis hast thou built
> A monument, whose cement hath been guilt!
> The moral Clytemnestra of thy lord[13]

A poet always has the last word; the merely eccentric Princess of
Parallelograms has turned monstrous; his inspired thrust of "moral
Clytemnestra" has such a classical ring of truth that few have ever questioned the aptness of comparing Annabella to the tragic adulteress who
murders her faithless husband and his concubine. Casting Annabella as
implacable avenger, however, made it easy for Byron to assign malign
motives to her every impulse. Upon learning that she planned to spend
the winter on the Continent with Ada,* he fired off a volley of furious
letters to Augusta, Hanson, and finally to Annabella herself, aimed at
preventing his child from leaving England. Citing Ada's age, health,
comfort, and the unstable state of postwar Europe, he went so far as to
threaten legal action if she were taken abroad. It's curious that as he
himself planned to remain on the Continent indefinitely, he never envisioned Lady Byron's trip as an opportunity to see his daughter, which
suggests that he fabricated the whole issue in an attempt to reopen the
case. Meanwhile, unbeknownst to Byron, Ada had been made a ward of
Chancery; he had no further legal power over his child.

Finally, the summer brought literary evidence of the bruised passions he had left behind. In July Madame de Staël lent Byron her
copy of Caroline Lamb's two-volume novel of madness and mayhem,

---

*The indirect source of the report was Lady Melbourne.

Glenarvon, published in May 1816. Her Byronic hero stalks through his thousand crimes—which include infanticide, poisoning, blackmail, seduction, and abandonment; his one virtue is being irresistible. Lest anyone fail to grasp Lord Glenarvon's close resemblance to his real-life model, the author made good use of her lover's cruelest letter, written from Eywood under Lady Oxford's supervision.

Byron took a lofty position of amused detachment, but as a writer whose most brilliant satire was still to come, he took close measure of Caro's devastating portrait of Regency society.[14]

The Melbournes were not amused. Emerging from the languor of his first forty years, William Lamb was on the verge of launching himself politically; this was no time for him to be ridiculed as a cynical, complaisant husband, or to have the female powers behind the Whig oligarchy portrayed as a freak show. However, *Glenarvon* gave the Melbournes the opportunity they were looking for; entering in evidence the author's self-portrait as an adulterous wife, they had Caroline declared insane. Then, on the very morning that William Lamb was to sign the divorce papers, the fond husband was found in his rooms with Caro on his lap, feeding him bits of bread and butter.

ON THE LAKE OF GENEVA, golden days of Indian summer followed the cold and rain. But the visitors had been warned: A brief autumn would be followed suddenly by the icy Alpine winter. Byron made plans to start for Italy while the Simplon pass was still easy to travel. He sent the boat—sails and oars intact, but otherwise somewhat the worse for hard use—to his banker, Hentsch, to dispose of as he could.

Before leaving, he dined several times at Coppet, which his "particularly kind and friendly" hostess had made a second home.[15] His final meal there was, he noted sadly, a "family dinner"; Madame de Staël was leaving shortly for Paris, and there was a melancholy sense that her charmed circle was disbanding. Then, on October 5, Byron and Hobhouse, accompanied by Fletcher, Berger, the Swiss servant hired in England, and their new guide and driver, Angelo Springhetti, set out along the southern side of the lake, toward the Rhône valley and Napoleon's Simplon route to Milan.

Once again Byron was forced to admire the imperial genius; the paved road unfurled as smoothly, Hobhouse noted approvingly, as though they rode through an English park. Switchbacking around mountains or carving a narrow ledge above ravines, Napoleon's engineers, like the Emperor himself in his glory days, brooked no obstacles. The party cleared customs at the hamlet of Iselle, and on October 10, 1816, Byron entered Italy.

Descending into Lombardy, they crossed Lake Maggiore to the Borromean Islands, which Byron pronounced "too artificial." Italian inns gave Hobhouse the chance to mourn Swiss cleanliness and honesty; reports of local bandits convinced the travelers that Springhetti should sleep in their imposing coach, pistols at the ready. Finally, the flat horizon of the Lombard plain was broken by the spires of Milan's cathedral.

Arriving in the city, they forgot the squalor of their hotel in the hospitality of the Marchese Di Breme, an ecclesiastic, man of letters, and administrator under Napoleon whom Byron had met at Coppet. At the family's Palazzo Roma Byron found himself at the heart of Italian romanticism: Here he was introduced to the liberal circle of aristocrats, polemecists, and poets chafing under Austrian occupation, while waiting to aid the stirrings of revolt aleady under way in the south. He was most impressed by Silvio Pellico, writer and supporter of the revolutionary cells called Carbonari.

Gatherings at the Palazzo Roma were discreetly political; Milan's social, cultural, and even sexual life revolved around La Scala, the splendid theater where Byron promptly arranged to take a box for the duration of his stay. From here he could observe the *mores*—earlier remarked in Seville—according to which girls from the ruling families were married directly from the convent, it being understood that, immediately thereafter, they were free to pursue love where they found it. News of Byron's arrival excited a parade of beautiful young noblewomen who lingered about his box, in the foyer, and even outside the theater after the performance, hoping that the glamorous poet and *Pari d'Inghilterra* would request an introduction. But between Claire Clairmont's lesson in the dangers of casual encounters and worry about Augusta's silence, he was happy to forgo sexual conquest for the less complicated pleasures of masculine company.

Among his new acquaintances was another visitor to Milan. Henri Beyle was a young French diplomat recently demobilized as *intendant,* or requisitions officer, of Napoleon's army. Regaling Byron with stories about the Emperor, embroidered and possibly invented, he rehearsed his vocation: He would later write novels under the pen name Stendhal. Physically unprepossessing, with his chubby raccoon cheeks and pursy little mouth, Beyle was mesmerized by Byron's beauty—especially by the haunting gaze of the poet's gray eyes. Eight years later, when trying to envisage the form a great painter would give to genius, Byron's sublime head reappeared before him.

The two writers fell into the habit of spending part of each evening together. When talking about poetry and drama, the Frenchman found Byron a delight, pouring forth ideas, theories, prejudices, and passions in a brilliant cataract of words. Then Byron was visibly transported, Beyle recalled, shedding the cold and guarded manner he often assumed—that of a nobleman fending off an importunate beggar. Ordinary social situations, however, showed him at his least attractive and revealed Byron's vanity and childish fear of appearing ridiculous. Worst of all, the poet was guilty of that form of hypocrisy that Beyle—using the English word—called cant: Byron would say anything, no matter how compromising to his real beliefs, for a word of praise from his listeners.

Dutifully, Byron accompanied his French guide to the Brera Gallery, where he admired one painting out of a thousand, he told Augusta. His happiest discovery was in the Ambrosiana Library, where he was enthralled to find an exchange of love letters between Lucrezia Borgia and Cardinal Bembo; he rhapsodized about a lock of her fine gold hair preserved among the manuscripts, along with the startling coincidence that Lucrezia had signed letters to her lover with the same cross used by Byron and Augusta. The library would not allow the letters to be copied, so Byron swiped a strand of Lucrezia's hair as a souvenir. He was similarly unable to resist a naughty joke to Augusta, comparing her to the notorious Lucrezia: Hadn't they both kept sexual passion all in the family while appearing model matrons to the world? "After all she ended with being Duchess of Ferrara, and an excellent mother & wife also; so good as to be quite an example."[16] Another reader of Byron's letter was not amused by jokes about incest; Annabella now warned Augusta—a little late in the day, perhaps—that she must discourage her brother's levity as leading to wantonness.

On the day after their arrival, Polidori appeared at their hotel. He not only had survived his Alps crossing but even, so it appeared, had prospered. In the several weeks he had spent in Milan before Byron and Hobhouse arrived, the doctor had attached himself to Lord and Lady Jersey as their traveling physician and had been taken up by the same circle of liberal intelligentsia who now welcomed Byron. Polidori bore his former employer no ill will, and he now brought a quartet of young Greek admirers to call on Byron; one of them had come from Paris especially to meet him. Between revived memories of Turkish rule in Greece and daily evidence of life under Austrian occupation, Byron's political sympathies, pushed from his mind during months of personal turmoil, now returned. And soon enough, thanks to Polidori's impulsiveness, he found himself face to face with the swaggering power of military law.

On the evening of October 29, Byron reported, he was "quietly staring at the Ballet from the Cavalier di Brema's box,"[17] along with other guests, including M. Beyle, when they were interrupted by Silvio Pellico, who informed them that, after an altercation with an Austrian officer in the pit, Polidori had been seized by the authorities. Following Pellico from the theater, Byron and the others now found "the man of medicine begirt with grenadiers—arrested by the guard—conveyed into the guardroom—where there was much swearing in several languages." The Marchese Di Breme shrewdly suggested that only those gentlemen with titles remain in the guardhouse to defend their hotheaded young friend. Duly impressed by the prisoner's noble connections, the presiding officer allowed him to leave, Lord Byron's card functioning as bail bond to guarantee his appearance on the following day. But at the hearing, Polidori was ordered to leave Milan for Florence within twenty-four hours.

Byron, worried that when reports of the doctor's arrest and banishment reached England he, too, would be implicated, wrote detailed accounts of the case to both Murray and Augusta. To his sister, especially, his self-exculpatory remarks have a hysterical edge: "*I* had nothing to do with his squabble—& was not even present—though—when he sent for me—I tried of course to get him out of it—as well as Mr. Hobhouse—who tried also for him—but to no purpose. I tell you all this because in England—by some kind of mistake—his squabbles may be set down to me—and now (if this should be the case) you have it in your power to contradict it." *18

His fears—unheroic and unguarded—expose another painful truth: For Byron, England was the only court of judgment that counted; English opinion of him—as a poet and a man, a public or private citizen—would always remain the real measure of his worth.

MORE THAN a month had passed since he had heard from Augusta; once more he was the abandoned child, and for the first time he addressed her angrily: "You are not to suppose that your letters do not arrive—all the assertions of the post being impeded—are (I believe) false—and the faults of their non-arrival are in those who write—(or rather do not write) not in the conveyance. I have hitherto written to you very regularly,—indeed perhaps rather too often—but I now tell you that I will not write again at all—if I wait so long for my answers,"

---

*Four days later, on November 6, he wrote to Augusta from Verona, repeating his earlier account of the Polidori arrest, concerned still that in England "someone or other will probably transfer his adventures to me," again urging Augusta to "contradict any such report," and this time giving the names of witnesses who could "corroborate" his role in the affair.

he warned. As evidence of the mail's reliability (along with that of his other correspondents), he noted having received "no less than three letters from one person—all dated from within *this month* Octr." He tried to sound less petulant—without success: "I mention all this—not from any wish to plague you but because my [unfortunate] circumstances perhaps make me feel more keenly anything which looks like neglect—and as among my many faults towards you—*that*—at least—has not been one."[19]

Before Byron could mail this cry of distress, however, he received a letter from Augusta, dated October 12. Although its receipt "revived" him somewhat, what he read was more disturbing than his sister's earlier silence. His announced plans for visiting England in the spring had clearly thrown Augusta into a panic, and she was still negotiating with Annabella as to what her response should be. To Byron she now hinted at the possibility that she would not see him. He was mystified but also defiant: "I really do not & cannot understand all the mysteries & alarms in your letters & more particularly in the last. All I know is— that no human power short of destruction—shall prevent me seeing you when—where—& how—I may please—according to time & circumstance . . . anything which is to divide us would drive me quite out of my senses."[20]

Without knowing the circumstances behind Augusta's withdrawal, his own feelings of persecution pointed to his wife: "Miss Milbanke appears in all respects to have been formed for my destruction," he wrote, insisting, with more feeling than honesty, "I have thus far—as you know—regarded her without feelings of personal bitterness . . . but if directly or indirectly—but why do I say this? You know she is the cause of all—whether intentionally or not is little to the purpose." And returning to the painful issue at hand, he wrote: "You surely do not mean to say that if I come to England in Spring, that you and I shall not meet? If so, I will never return to it."

His suspicion that Annabella was behind Augusta's behavior added fuel to his festering obsession: "Either this must end or I must end—but I repeat it again & again—*that Woman* has destroyed me."[21] But in his next letter to Augusta he enclosed another plea to Lady Byron for a reconciliation. "You will not relieve me—you will not even believe me— but I loved—and love you most entirely," he wrote to the woman he had just accused of destroying him. "Had I trusted you—as I had almost resolved soon after our marriage—all would have been better—perhaps well—However I am paying the penalty of my evils—and eating my heart—Do not write to me—do not destroy whatever slender or remote hope I may still cling to—but believe me when I protest to you with the most sincere & solemn truth to you and before God—that if there were a means of becoming reunited to you I would embrace it—and that I am very wretched."[22]

BYRON'S THREE WEEKS in Milan had exposed him to the reality of post-Napoleonic Italy under Austrian rule. He had observed the political spectrum of conquerors, collaborators, and dissenters that would define this carvery of kingdoms, principalities, and papal states for the next twenty years: He had encountered revolutionary Carbonari, moderate republicans, ultrareactionary Sanfedistas, bureaucrats, and spies (of all camps), along with those, like the well-known poet he had just met, Vincenzo Monti, who changed affiliation with every shifting political wind. Milan's underground of romantic radicals already looked to the future. On November 3, Byron and Hobhouse set off for Venice— and the past.

Traveling light for a change, they rode in Hobhouse's chaise, sending the guide Springhetti ahead with servants and baggage in Byron's two heavy coaches. At Verona they paid their respects to the Roman amphitheater—"Wonderful—beats even Greece,"[23] wrote Byron. All he had suffered of lost love drew him to the dubious monument touted to English visitors as "Juliet's Tomb." Taking legend on faith, Byron the romantic was further persuaded by the autumnal season, the setting, and the object itself: "a plain, open and partly decayed sarcophagus, with withered leaves in it, in a wild and desolate conventual garden, once a cemetery, now ruined to the very graves . . . blighted as their love."[24] Or his own. Pocketing granite chips from the official tomb of Shakespeare's thirteen-year-old martyr to passion, family, and politics, Byron sent the relics to Augusta and his nieces, with the request to forward pieces of the same to Ada (not yet a year old) and her mother.

Although he had plunged into sightseeing with renewed zest, Byron complained to his "Goose" about "flying rheumatism" from the rainy Lombard autumn; more worrisome, he noted symptoms recurring from his illness at Piccadilly Terrace, "casual giddiness and faintness."[25] Finally, on November 10, another day of pouring rain, they arrived in Mestre, the mainland port of departure for Venice. Mestre is dismal in the best of weather, but Byron's spirits were undampened by zero visibility; his own excitement conjured from the fog "the greenest island of my imagination," illuminated now by proximity and anticipation.[26]

Leaving the horses and carriages at the inn, Byron, like Ruskin, found "the black knot of gondolas in the canal of Mestre more beautiful to me than a sunrise full of clouds of scarlet and gold."[27] Enclosed in their own gondola slicing through the choppy lagoon, Byron supplied images, stored from his earliest readings, of the enchanted city that awaited him:

> I lov'd her from my boyhood—she to me
> Was as a fairy city of the heart,
> Rising like water-columns from the sea,
> Of joy the sojourn, and of wealth the mart;
> And Otway, Radcliffe, Schiller, Shakspeare's [*sic*] art,
> Had stamp'd her image in me, and even so,
> Although I found her thus, we did not part,
> Perchance even dearer in her day of woe,
> Than when she was a boast, a marvel, and a show.[28]

Parting the curtains of the gondola cabin, they were welcomed by the lights of palazzi looming above them. Their destination was another hostelry favored by English travelers: the Hôtel de la Grande Bretagne, near the Rialto. It was a palace whose former glory as a private residence, Hobhouse noted sadly, was apparent in the splendid grand staircase rising from the landing on the Grand Canal, and their vast rooms, hung with the faded silks and tapestries of better times.

Venice's "days of woe" had started long before she yielded to Napoleon in 1797, and during the twenty years that followed, conditions worsened as the Emperor drained the region of manpower and money. By the time the Austrians took possession in 1814, two years before Byron's arrival, Venice had deteriorated further. The new rulers found the city "stripped of ornaments and treasure, her harbour filled with sand, her Arsenal deserted, her manufactures annihilated, her palaces crumbling piecemeal into the canals and filling them with the debris; her ships rotting at the stocks and quays."[29] The city's population had shrunk by a quarter (from 130,000 to 100,000), while her pauper list numbered 54,000, and the charitable institutions on which she had prided herself were utterly bankrupt. At the same time, the Lombardo-Venetian kingdom, though embracing only a seventh of the inhabitants of the Austrian Empire, furnished a quarter of her taxes— 65 percent of Venetian revenues flowed back to Vienna. Press and tongue were fettered, and the entire city swarmed with troops and spies.

Like many another tourist, Byron found the ravaged face of decay romantic. Venice, like one of her twenty thousand whores, offered herself up to him with a beauty made more seductive by symptoms of disease. Byron gleefully seized on the gondola, sliding in and out of her dark canals, as the city's phallic emblem, providing sexual transport in funerary guise:

It glides along the water looking blackly,
Just like a coffin clapt in a canoe,
Where none can make out what you say or do.

And up and down the long canals they go,
    And under the Rialto shoot along,
By night and day, all paces, swift or slow,
    And round the theatres, a sable throng,
They wait in their dusk livery of woe,
    But not to them do woeful things belong,
For sometimes they contain a deal of fun,
Like mourning coaches when the funeral's done.[30]

In the space of four days Byron had engaged his own gondola, sta-
bled his horses on the Lido, found a commodious apartment, and fallen
in "fathomless love."[31] Marianna Segati, the object of his passion, was
twenty-two, the wife of his landlord, mother of a young daughter, and
conveniently domiciled in the apartment below his own. The shop of
Signor Segati, a cloth merchant, was on the ground floor of the house at
1673 Calle della Piscina, just off the Frezzaria, the thoroughfare flank-
ing the porticos of San Marco. The sign for his establishment, *al cervo*—
"at the sign of the stag"—featured a pair of antlers, soon to be the subject of rude jokes. These, apparently, caused the merchant little anguish.
The cuckolded husband, Marianna reassured Byron, had an official mistress of his own; he could be counted on to leave the lovers to their own
happy devices.

Seizing his favorite image of female desirability, Byron told Moore,
Murray, and all of his other correspondents, that Marianna was "in
her appearance altogether like an antelope." Small and slight, with
dark, glossy curls, she had the "large black oriental eyes, with that
peculiar expression in them which is rare seen among *Europeans*—
even the Italians—and which many of the Turkish women give themselves by tingeing the eyelid—an art not known out of that country, I
believe. This expression she has *naturally*."[32] Marianna was available
for lovemaking whenever Byron wanted her, and her deep flush, he suggests, was due to a continuous state of arousal. She was also a diva in
another sense, being "a mighty and admirable singer."[33] "But her great
merit," Byron allowed, "is finding out mine—there is nothing so
amiable as discernment."[34]

Byron at Casa Segati, visiting his mistress who also happened to be
his landlady, seems a world away from Byron climbing the stairs at
Melbourne House to find Caro Lamb in her boudoir, or romping with

Lady Oxford and her children at Eywood, or crowded with Augusta and her brood at Six Mile Bottom. The configuration and the need, however, were the same: He was drawn to women who provided him with a family setting and role—however subversive—within it. As the most complaisant in this series of obliging husbands, Segati promised no titillating fear of discovery or jealous scenes; he left that to his wife, as Byron now discovered.

One night, when the Segatis were, exceptionally, out together, Byron received an unsigned note "intimating a wish on the part of the writer to meet me, either in a gondola or at the island of San Lazzaro or at a third rendez-vous,"[35] Byron related to Moore. Prudently, the poet declined the places proposed, suggesting instead that he would "either be at home at ten *alone*, or be at the *ridotto* at midnight, where the writer might meet me masked." Promptly at the hour mentioned, "the door of my apartment opened, and in walked a well looking and (for an Italian) *bionda* girl of about nineteen, who informed me that she was married to the brother of my *amorosa* and wished to have some conversation with me." Only a few minutes later, however, "in marches to my great astonishment, Marianna Segati," and despite the apparently decorous nature of the visit she had just interrupted, his mistress, "after making a most polite curtsey to her sister-in-law and to me, without a single word seizes her said sister-in-law by the hair, and bestows upon her some sixteen slaps, which would have made your ear ache only to hear their echo. I need not describe the screaming which ensued," he reported. After the visitor's flight, Marianna's rage turned to hysteria; she "fairly went into fits in my arms, and in spite of reasoning, eau de Cologne, half a pint of water, and God knows what other waters beside, continued so till past midnight." Still trying to calm his beloved, "in comes—who? why, Signor Segati, her lord and husband." Finding his wife "fainting upon the sofa . . . pale as ashes, without sense or motion, his first Question was 'What is all this?' " Byron's more than vague reply—that "the explanation was the easiest thing in the world"— easily satisfied M. Segati's honor. Or as Byron explained to Moore: "Jealousy is not the order of the day in Venice, and daggers are out of fashion."

With his first Venetian mistress, Byron now found himself cast in a new role of *cicisebeo* or *cavaliere servente*, the wife's acknowledged companion and lover in a culture where marriage was understood not as a sacrament but as social convenience. It was originally an aristocratic arrangement, but the unique mobility of Venice allowed a middle-class wife like Marianna Segati the same rewards as a *zentildonna*. For his part, the lover occupied a position in an officially sanctioned triangle; far from undermining the conjugal relationship as a rival, he was encouraged to become the husband's intimate friend as well.

This was all a bit too "civilized" for Byron; he felt morally adrift in such an absence of hypocrisy. As for his landlord, the social distance between Lord Byron and the "Merchant of Venice" (as he jokingly dubbed the shopkeeper) was too great for friendship. More important for Byron, he could not compromise his need for freedom, social and sexual. He might be in love with his black-eyed songstress, but their idyll was confined to the Casa Segati. He wanted no official consort on his arm to foreclose the chance adventures that Venice offered so lavishly—beyond any other place he had ever lived.

He rode on the Lido and subscribed to the season's offerings at the Fenice and San Benedetto theaters, the two most consistently brilliant of eight flourishing companies. He saw less of Hobhouse and avoided other English, whether traveling or resident; gradually he was falling out of touch with news from home. Nor was he any more attracted by what he saw of the Venetian aristocracy; the men had become foppish caricatures through sheer inanition, and the ladies—unlike their counterparts lower on the social ladder—Byron pronounced "ugly as vertue."[36] They were best experienced masked at the *ridotto* when no lady's status was an obstacle to mutual pleasure.

The *ridotto* had begun as elegant rooms for gaming, usually annexed to theaters and, unlike London's gambling hells, open to both men and women. Masks were the only requirement for admission, disguising gender along with individual identity. Here, the loss of a fortune at the faro table was softened by the unlucky gambler's Harlequin disguise; soon other, less public rooms were added when it appeared that certain noblewomen, after losing all their money, were compelled to sell their favors for the price of returning to play. The *ridotto* lured as many of those addicted to chance couplings with strangers as those transfixed by the roll of the dice. Byron had no interest in gambling, but after midnight, when the theaters closed, he disappeared behind the anonymity of his mask to join the other faceless figures prowling the crowded rooms.

When he craved the stimulus of ideas, discussion, or news from the Continent, he could count on the *conversazione* at the Countess Albrizzi's. Of Greek origin, Isabella Teotocchi Albrizzi had been known in her prime as the "Madame de Staël of Venice." ("As though one weren't enough," Hobhouse had groaned.) Now her salon was among two survivors among many such gatherings that had flourished in the last days of the Venetian Republic. Some guests found these receptions stiff affairs; Byron, however, was delighted by the un-English custom of serving rum punch instead of ices. At the Albrizzis, Byron met artists, writers, and amateurs, including any foreign visitors of distinction. Although political discussion was officially banned by their hostess, Byron could still hear the latest Milanese news from Silvio Pellico and learn about the situation in Greece from Countess Albrizzi's compatriots. Here, too, he met one of his few living idols in the plastic arts, the great Venetian sculptor Antonio Canova,* whose marble bust of Helen of Troy, a gift to their hostess, Byron extolled—clumsily—as "the most perfectly beautiful of human conceptions—and far beyond my ideas of human execution."[37] The poet used the chiseled marble to elaborate a Platonic ideal of beauty, which the visual arts alone were able to express:

> Beyond Imagination's power—
>   Beyond the Bard's defeated art,
> With Immortality her dower—
>   Behold the *Helen* of the *heart*![38]

Byron's Italian had become effortlessly fluent (if never grammatically correct), and he picked up the Venetian dialect in the Segati household. Finding it "necessary to twist my mind around some severer study,"[39] he decided to learn Armenian. Every day he was rowed out to the Armenian monastery on the island of San Lazzaro, two miles across the lagoon from the Lido, where he received lessons from the learned Father Aucher in both the spoken and written languages, as well as instruction in the rich cultural history of the people. The monastery had seventy or so friars, and was also a missionary school with forty pupils. While tackling the thirty-eight characters of the Armenian alphabet, Byron enjoyed escaping the feminized world of Venice. The friars made much of their handsome and noble guest; he was given a paneled study with sweeping views of the lagoon and free run of the library with its illuminated manuscripts and early printed books, and of the gardens, where he wandered the tree-shaded walks alone with his thoughts. The sight of youthful seminarians, trying to repress high spirits for priestly decorum, inevitably brought back happy memories of his stay in the Capuchin convent in Athens. As the friars would not accept money for

---

*On seeing the Elgin marbles exhibited in London in 1815, Canova defended their removal from the Parthenon, becoming an eloquent advocate of their purchase by Parliament. It seems unlikely that Byron was aware of the sculptor's position on this issue.

his retreat into monastic study and peace, he offered to collaborate with Father Aucher on an English-Armenian grammar, and eventually paid for its publication.

He was writing nothing at the moment, but last summer's burst of productivity was now in London bookstores. Within twelve days of one another, Murray brought out two volumes: on November 18, Canto III of *Childe Harold*, followed by *The Prisoner of Chillon and Other Poems* on December 5. With Douglas Kinnaird acting as his agent and business manager, Byron's dealings with his publisher now took a very different turn. Murray had offered 1,500 guineas for both collections; Kinnaird demanded £2,000 and he won. Byron had begun to take a professional view of his work and its market value, a change that marked a seismic shift in his attitude toward money generally. The profligate young noble was becoming a prudent steward of his fortunes—earned and unearned. He wanted to pay his English debts once and for all; he began to look carefully at expenses and—unimaginable for the younger Byron—to contemplate with pleasure the accumulation of capital.

In line with his new interest in profit, he took a more expedient view of the publication process—not with the happiest results. He had always gone over proof sheets himself, revising, correcting, hectoring Murray about printer's mistakes. Now he was only too glad to delegate the responsibility of seeing a work through the press to Shelley, to Gifford, or to whoever could be induced to take on the painstaking task. At the end of August, when he had entrusted the red leather folio containing fair copies of the summer's work to Shelley, Byron had given the younger poet to understand that he should introduce himself to Murray as the designated editor; he had told Shelley that he was writing to the publisher to confirm this arrangement. Byron's letter to Albemarle Street, however, seems almost deliberately unspecific; as for Canto III, he hoped that Gifford would be "kind enough to read it over; I know not well to whom to consign the correction of the proofs." He proposed Moore "(if in town) . . . If not—Mr. S[helley] will take it upon himself,—and in any case—he is authorized to act for me in treating with you &c.&c. on the subject."[40]

Murray was unhappy with the radical tone of some of Byron's notes to Canto III of *Childe Harold*, and together with Gifford decided to soften or eliminate the anti-Bourbon, anti-British comments. Knowing that such revisions would never be permitted by Shelley (whose own work they firmly rejected), they decided that he should be quietly eased out of any editorial role. Relaying Gifford's extravagant praise of the poem to Byron, Murray shrewdly counted on flattery to help his author forget any earlier commitment. Puzzled and hurt, Shelley wrote to

Byron on November 20, noting that the publisher had refused his request to send him the proof sheets and adding delicately, "My situation with respect to Murray, claiming a duty to which I was not entitled, had some degree of awkwardness in it."[41] But if he received any explanation or apology, it has not survived.*

There is no question, however, that Byron ignored another, more poignant plea from Shelley; would he please enclose a "kind message" for Claire in his next letter to them. Shelley had decided that Claire should be housed separately until her baby was born; too much scandal already surrounded their household. Lonely, depressed, and resentful, Claire had become obsessed with Byron's refusal to write to her and, in the way of the rejected and desperate, behaved in a manner guaranteed to justify his loathing. She criticized his friend Kinnaird, taunted him about Augusta's silence, and coarsely reminded him that he had once been "so fond" of her "*chose.*"† In one sixteen-page screed she flirted, scolded, begged, and threatened suicide. "Write me a nice letter," she continued, "& tell me that you *like* me that you will be very pleased to have a little baby of which you will take great care." As though this presumption was not enough to set Byron's teeth grinding, Claire now let fly at the Shelleys: "Nothing makes me so angry as when M[ary] & S[helley] tell me not to expect to hear from you. They seem to know well enough how little you care for me & their hateful remarks are the most cruel of all! How proud I should be of a letter to disappoint their impertinent conjectures!"[42] When Byron's letter arrived, with no message of any kind, it was clear to her that they had been right. Three weeks later, on January 12, Claire gave birth to a daughter. In late April, after months of silence from Italy, Shelley wrote to Byron for the second time, asking, "And now, what are your plans with respect to the little girl?"[43] The baby was called Alba, meaning "dawn," an echo, too, of Albé, their pet name for Byron, and throughout her short life she would be hostage to his anger and fear.

---

*There is a missing letter from Byron to the Shelleys dated, according to Claire, October 26. This is the letter that ended her hopes of hearing from him. In it Byron may also have addressed Murray's replacement of Shelley with Gifford as editor.

†Her "thing," most certainly a sexual reference.

CHAPTER 30

Roman Spring

YRON HAD been well aware of the imminent arrival of Claire's "new Baby B,"[1] even if news of the birth—so he claimed—kept missing him until spring. Forced to relinquish his legitimate rights of father and husband, he had no impulse to celebrate the arrival of an illegitimate child, especially when the mother would be sure to take advantage of any hint of tender feelings.

England now seemed farther away than ever. When letters weren't lost or delayed, they took three weeks to arrive. Unwelcome news, however, could be counted on to travel faster. From several friends, Byron learned of a recently published forgery of poems attributed to him, one of which bore the painfully intimate title "To my Daughter on the Morning of her Birth"; the forger clearly hoped to exploit the poet's recent notoriety, going so far as to advertise the work in the newspapers. Byron left it to Murray and Kinnaird to pursue the matter as they thought best. Despite Sir Samuel Romilly's recent role as Annabella's counsel in the separation proceedings—a lapse of judgment that earned him the poet's lifelong hatred—Byron had never dismissed him, and the barrister now moved for an injunction "on the part of the Noble Plaintiff to restrain the Defendant from publishing a spurious edition of his Works." The injunction was granted. Through Shelley and others Byron now also learned of a nasty swipe at him in a notice of Coleridge's new poem *Christabel* in the *Edinburgh Review*. In the advertisement for the poem, Byron had called it "wild and singularly original and beautiful," regarding which the reviewer noted: "Some of [Lord Byron's] latest publications dispose us to distrust his authority."[2]

The silence from England was worse. Just after Christmas, Byron complained to Murray, "This is my sixth or seventh letter since summer and Switzerland," without either acknowledgment or reply.[3] He wanted news of *The Prisoner of Chillon* and Canto III of *Childe Harold*. When he did hear from the publisher, it was merely to be informed that the poems were out and that Murray felt "in good spirits" about them. Byron wanted more specific word of their success; now he began worrying over his earlier nonchalant attitude toward choice of editor and correction of proofs: "I wonder if he has published them *as sent*," he wrote to Kinnaird about Murray. "If he has made alterations or omissions—I shall not pardon him. I suspect him as a *Tory*—of softening my M.S.—if he *has*—by the Ass of Balaam! He shall endure my indignation."[4]

Anxiously, he wrote twice to Augusta to learn whether she had received his new "po's"[5]—use of her baby talk a sign of his longing to reach her emotionally. When, finally, he received an evasive letter merely acknowledging their arrival, Byron wrote again, prodding her for a reaction. Their love and the agony of separation had, after all, been the inspiration for continuing *Childe Harold*, his longest and most important work to date.

"I am certain in my mind that this Canto is the *best* which I have ever written; there is a depth of thought in it throughout and a strength of repressed passion which you must feel before you find; but it requires reading more than once, because it is in part *metaphysical*, and of a kind of metaphysics which not everybody will understand. I never thought that it would be *popular* & I should not think well of it if it were but those for whom it is intended will like it." He even tried to draft Augusta into checking the published version against her manuscript copy to see where Murray had censored by omission, charging her particularly to attend to cuts the publisher might have made from "his notions about *family* considerations."[6] But poor Augusta was the last reader to demand the restoration of verses criticial of the Noels or of Annabella. And she was horrified—or so she told Annabella—by Byron's reminder that the Drachenfels lyric was addressed to her.

FINALLY, at the end of January, he had reassuring word of Tom Moore's enthusiasm. Responding with becoming modesty, he wrote, "I tremble for the 'magnificence' you attribute to the new Childe Harold, I am glad you like it; its a fine indistinct piece of poetical desolation, and my favourite. I was half mad during the time of its composition, between metaphysics, mountains, lakes, love unextinguishable, thoughts inutterable and the nightmare of my own delinquencies. I should, many a good day, have blown my brains out, but for the recollection that it would have given pleasure to my mother in law."[7]

Meanwhile, Byron's favorite work, along with its companion volume of shorter poems, had appeared to resounding success: On publication, booksellers had taken seven thousand copies of each, and their optimism was justified. The important reviews all weighed in approvingly, and while Augusta may have been too frightened to express—or even to hold—an opinion about Canto III, her "spiritual adviser" Lady Byron was admiring, despite herself: "He is the absolute monarch of words," Annabella wrote to her friend Lady Barnard, "and uses them, as Bonaparte did lives, for conquest. . . . His allusions to me in Childe Harold are cruel and cold, but with such a semblance as to make *me* appear so, and to attract all sympathy to himself. . . . It is not my duty to give way to hopeless and wholly unrequited affection; but so long as I live, my chief struggle will probably be not to remember him too kindly."[8]

WHILE SILENCE seemed to have enveloped his connections at home, in Venice Byron was swept into the frenzy that was Carnival. There was no celebration anywhere in Christendom to rival the orgy of merry-making, of "fiddling—masqing—singing and t'other thing,"[9] as Byron waggishly wrote to Kinnaird, that gathered force until, by the middle of January, every Venetian from beggar to marchesa seemed possessed by the urge to pleasure. Theaters competed for the best talent in Italy and on the Continent in drama, opera, ballet, and music; determined to miss nothing, Byron had taken a box at the Fenice for the entire season. Out of doors, day and night, in every piazza, *calle*, and *sottoportico*, tumblers, singers, and troupes of commedia dell'arte players exhibited their talents. St. Mark's Square was reserved for feats of strength and danger; the end of the festivities on February 18 was marked by the death-defying *volo*, when, high above the *piazzetta*, an acrobat slid down a rope that stretched from the top of the Campanile to the lagoon.

Performers and audience alike were garbed in fantastic costumes, from lovelorn Harlequin's motley to monster disguises; even the traditional domino, worn by men and women and consisting of a black or white mask with a Punchinello nose, attached to a hood and crowned with a tricorne, suggested a race of hybrid creatures.

Every night, gorgeously attired and jeweled guests alighted from gondolas at the landing steps of palazzi whose windows blazed with lights, where foreign embassies and those great Venetian families who could still afford such display vied in playing host at masked balls and sumptuous suppers, while the *ridotto* and its more inclusive crowd of revelers threw themselves into the games of chance and conquest they had come to play. Traditionally, Carnival was the time to change lovers, and each erotic encounter increased the promise of pleasures never before experienced and provided the excuse to explore every possibility. Byron gives us a tantalizing glimpse of his companion of one evening; removing her mask, he found a blonde, blue-eyed creature "insatiate of love."

In Venice, Byron, too, had become insatiate; he felt renewed by sex. Night seeped into day, writing and lovemaking merged: "There's a whore on my right / For I rhyme best at Night / When a C——t is tied close to *my* Inkstand,"[10] he wrote to Murray. From these nocturnal olympiads he returned to the Casa Segati and Marianna, whose skills at reviving her lover's flagging energies should not be underestimated as the source of her power: "Never a twenty-four hours—without giving from one to three (and occasionally an extra or so) pretty unequivocal proofs of mutual good contentment," he assured the publisher.[11] Despite his ardor, Marianna found her Anglo-Saxon lover more cerebral than she could have wished. Byron made the mistake of reading to her a particularly clever analysis of the "awful notions of constancy" held by Venetians: Within marriage, sexual fidelity was seen as risible; a pair of adulterous *amorosi*, however, known to be faithful to one another for years, was exalted as the highest form of morality. His own astute mistress saw that the poet's sense of protective irony would soon subvert his passion: "If you loved me thoroughly, you would not make so many fine reflections, which are only good *forbirsi i scarpi*—to clean shoes with,"[12] she scolded. But during the seventeen months of her sovereignty over him, Marianna cut her lover considerable slack—as long as he did not exercise this freedom with her relations. "She plagues me less than any woman I ever met," he wrote to Hobhouse,[13] in Rome since early December. Marianna's only other restriction concerned travel: She herself had never been farther than Milan, and she was terrified of his leaving Venice without her. For his part, Byron wanted to join Hobhouse in Rome as soon as the Eternal City was no longer "pestilent of English—a parcel of staring boobies, who go about gaping and wishing to be at once cheap and magnificent. A man is a fool who travels now in France or Italy, till this tribe of wretches is swept home again," he told Moore.[14] He was planning his visit to fall between the end of Holy Week—ever a magnet for tourists—and the onset of the Roman malarial fevers of late spring. He did not want to take Marianna with him, professing to believe that she should not leave her child; but to Hobhouse, who had heard rumors that he would be accompanied by la Segati, he wrote to reassure that dependable misogynist, "How could you suppose that I would take any (carnal) baggage with me? do you suppose me quite out of my senses?—I had enough of that in Switzerland."[15] The truth was, however, that he continued to agonize over whether he could bear to leave her. So he remained in Venice.

On February 18 the Venetian revels came to an end. Byron celebrated at a masked ball at the Fenice, the last of "three or four up all nights," he reported to Kinnaird.[16] On this final night of Carnival, the pit was boarded over so that players and audience, including "all the Vice & Vertue" of the city, mingled freely.[17] Then the frenzy was over and it was Lent. Byron had done no writing since leaving Switzerland, but he was meditating a poem, his first with a Venetian theme. Visiting the Doge's Palace, he had seen the portrait of the disgraced Doge Marino Faliero, his likeness painted out with a black veil, and had been shown the Giant's Staircase, where Faliero was decapitated for treason in 1355. Byron now asked Murray for historical materials in English on the traitor; Venetian chroniclers, he felt, had been muzzled by fear. "I mean to write a tragedy upon the subject."[18] He wrote *Marino Faliero* four years later, but, just as the fortress of Chillon had worked on his imagination, in Venice the poet's muse would emerge not as a living nymph or a fallen hero, but as the city itself, haunted by history.

The Lent season also coincided with Byron's birthday. Although he had just turned twenty-nine, "yet I find 'the sword wearing out the scabbard,'" he told Moore, and in the same letter he recast the hackneyed line into one of his most beautiful lyrics:

> So we'll go no more a roving
> So late into the night,
> Though the heart be still as loving,
> And the moon be still as bright.
>
> For the sword outwears its sheath,
> And the soul wears out the breast,
> And the heart must pause to breathe,
> And Love itself have rest.
>
> Though the night was made for loving,
> And the day returns too soon,
> Yet we'll go no more a roving
> By the light of the moon.[19]

His usual birthday gloom deepened by exhaustion and a sense of waste, he saw himself redeemed in a heroic future when he would move beyond the making of poems toward acts of greatness yet unknown: "If I live ten years longer, you will see, however, that it is not over with me," he told Moore. "I don't mean in literature, for that is nothing; and it may seem odd to say, but I do not think it my vocation. But you will see that I will do something or other—the times and fortunes permitting—that, 'like the cosmogony, or creation of the world, will puzzle the philosophers of all ages.' " Having indulged in this burst of grandiose prophecy, he was brought down by a less happy premonition.

"But I doubt whether my constitution will hold out. I have, at intervals, exercised it most devilishly."[20] A few days later, at the very beginning of March, he knew he was really sick, not with the "low vulgar Typhus" that was "decimating Venice" that month, but with a "sharp gentlemanly fever," he joked to Hobhouse.[21] The lower-class epidemic generally proved fatal, but Byron's case of the malarial sickness that commonly attacked visitors was nonetheless persistent and debilitating. By the middle of the month, his symptoms had worsened: "half delirium, burning skin, thirst, hot headache, horrible pulsation and no sleep."[22] He spent the last two weeks of the month in bed, where Marianna's nursing, a diet of barley water, and, so he claimed, the refusal to see a physician finally restored him, much weakened, to something like a living state. As an inducement to his recovery, his mistress even gave him permission to visit Rome without her. But the fever still came and went—though less fierce than before—leaving him more indecisive than usual.

Just before succumbing to illness, Byron had learned of the successful suit in Chancery brought by the Noels the previous spring "on a financial technicality," Byron claimed, "to deprive me of my paternal right over my child."[23] He was especially grieved, he wrote to Annabella on March 5, "that our daughter is to be the entail of our disunion—the inheritor of our bitterness." And echoing the curse on his wife that reverberates through the first act of *Manfred*—more frightening because more real than all the witches and nameless crimes—he now warned: "If you think to reconcile yourself to yourself—by accumulating harshness against me—you are again mistaken—you are not happy nor even tranquil—nor will you ever be so. . . . Time and Nemesis will do that which I would not—even were it in my power remote or immediate. . . . You will smile at this piece of prophecy—do so but recollect it."[24]

Three weeks later, in the throes of fever, he wrote to Augusta in a frenzy of self-righteous wrath. He wanted her to convey his full fury to Annabella, so he decided to forget that he had already written to his wife on this same subject. "I have been too ill to write to Lady Byron myself," he told his sister, "but I desire you to repeat what I have said and say.—I have forgiven everything up to this—but this I never will forgive. . . . I curse her from the bottom of my heart—& in the bitterness of my soul—& I only hope that she may one day feel what she has made me suffer. . . . Ten thousand curses be upon her and her father and mother's family now & forever."[25] To Hanson he declared, "I am determined to *reclaim* the child to myself—as the natural guardian," and charged the lawyer to "get *this* Chancery *Bill*—answer it—& proceed upon it." And he asked for Hanson's "best advice—how & in what manner to assume the care & personal charge of my daughter."[26] But as soon as his fever and wrath had cooled down, he realized that given the Noels' determination, Hanson's torpor, and his own unsettled—and most undomestic—life, he was in no position to pursue the custody of a young child. For Byron, his legitimate daughter's only reality would be as an object of contention: "Some day or other," he predicted melodramatically, "Ada will become my Orestes & Electra too, both in one."[27]

More immediately, while he was trying to muster the energy to make plans, Dr. Polidori reappeared on his way home to England in the company of the young Lord Guilford and his widowed stepmother. Sounding like Hamlet's gravedigger, Byron joked to Moore that the physician "had no more patients because his patients are no more."[28] "In short, he seems to have had no luck unless he had any with Lady W[estmoreland]'s Clitoris—which is supposed to be of the longest,"[29] he reported to Hobhouse. Byron had advised the doctor "to marry if only to fill in the gap which he has already made in the population." The physician's previous patient, Lord Guilford, had died of an inflammation of the bowels, and Byron now mused with a certain ghoulish fascination on the fate of his organs: "They took them out and sent them (on account of their discrepancies) separately from the carcass, to England," he reported. "Conceive a man going one way, and his intestines another, and his immortal soul a third! was there ever such a distribution?"[30] A prophetic question, indeed. And he returned to worrying the age-old puzzle of enduring spirit and decaying flesh: "One certainly has a soul; but how it came to allow itself to be enclosed in such a body is more than I can imagine."[31]

Thus far Byron had avoided sightseeing in Venice; now, however, he allowed himself to be swept along by Polidori and the Guilfords to see the Palazzo Manfrin and its great picture collection. Reversing the cliché of our own century, Byron had earlier reminded Murray, "You must recollect . . . that I know nothing of painting—& that I detest it—unless it reminds me of something I have seen or think it possible to see."[32] But one painting in the Manfrin collection was of particular interest to him.

Called *Giorgione* at the time, the composition of three half-length figures was believed to depict the artist's family:*

> 'Tis but a portrait of his son and wife,
> And self; but *such* a woman! love in life!
>
> Love in full life and length, not love ideal,
>   No, nor ideal beauty, that fine name,
> But something better still, so very real,
>
> . . . .
>   That the sweet model must have been the same;
> The face recals some face, as 'twere with pain,
> You once have seen, but ne'er will see again.[33]

Most revealing about these lines is the way Byron gradually subverts his own distinction between the real and the ideal. Initially, the lady in the painting moves him just because she appears to be "so very real"—his stanzas are a love song to the physicality of Venetian women, their expressive sensual beauty. Significantly, the figure that he exalts as "love in life" is also a wife and mother, a "sweet model" whose maternal love is also a model of sweetness. No sooner do we "see" this earthly embodiment of "love in life," however, than she vanishes: unobtainable "ideal beauty," after all. From provider of sustaining love and tenderness, she has become a disappearing star:

> Whose course we know not, nor shall know
> Like the lost Pleiad, seen no more below.[34]

It was a year since Byron had last seen Augusta. Her letters, infrequent and troubled, seemed addressed to a stranger. To reawaken her memories of his physical presence, Byron now sat for two miniatures by Prepiani, a then fashionable but now forgotten Venetian portraitist of the period. Before the era of the photograph, the miniature as portable keepsake was the closest that painting came to the intimacy of a snapshot.

---

*The specific painting in the Manfrin collection described by Byron has long been the subject of dispute. Giorgione's *Tempesta*, now in the Accademia, Venice, with its three mysterious figures in a landscape, was once believed to be the picture in question. It's now generally accepted that Byron's "Giorgione," depicting a young woman, youth, and older man, is a work by a follower of Titian. Purchased by the Duke of Northumberland, it hangs in Alnwick Castle.

Byron's commission included one close-up and one half-length pose. Polidori was to deliver the portraits to Murray on his return, and Byron now wrote to the publisher, asking him to have "Mr. Love, the jeweler, set them in plain gold, with my arms complete, and 'Painted by Prepiani—Venice 1817'—on the back." Before delivering the miniatures to Mrs. Leigh, however, Murray was to arrange for the fashionable London portraitist, Holmes, to make a copy of each, these to be held at Albemarle Street until his return. And while he was at it, would Murray please be sure and send him "*Waite's tooth powder—red—a quantity— Calcined Magnesia,* of the best quality . . . & by the Lord! do it," he told his publisher.[35]

With characteristic generosity toward his friends—even when they were fellow poets—Byron now cheered Moore on the publication of his narrative poem "Lalla Rookh." Begun in 1812, more than a year before Byron had begun *The Giaour*, Moore's Oriental tale had been more than five years in the writing, probably slowed in part by his friend's brilliant success in this same genre. Byron attempted to soothe Moore's last-minute fears—among these, that the heroine's name did not fall trippingly from the tongue: "I like a tough title,"[36] Byron wrote, observing that the " *'Giaour'* has never been pronounced to this day." He empathized with his friend's every worry about the new work, noting to Murray, "I feel as anxious for Moore as I could do for myself . . . and I would not have him succeed otherwise than splendidly—which I trust he will do."[37] When Byron received his copy, however, he could not bring himself to read it for some time; he lacked the necessary concentration, he told Moore, suggesting more competitive feelings than he could acknowledge toward a friend.

Finally, on April 17, Byron set off for Rome via Ferrara and Bologna. Besides Fletcher, he took his saddle horses and a live souvenir of Switzerland, a dog named Mutz, whose enterprise in native habitat, where he had opened doors on request, had yielded to cringing cowardice abroad; his master was disgusted to see him terrified en route by a mere pig.

Thanks to his new travel regime of rising before dawn, Byron managed to do Florence in a day, seeing the treasures of both the Uffizi and the Pitti Palace: "I went to the two galleries—from which one returns drunk with beauty," he reported to Hobhouse. In the Uffizi, "What struck me most were the mistress of Raphael a portrait—the mistress of Titian a portrait—a Venus of Titian in the Medici gallery—*the* Venus," and in the Pitti Palace, another portrait believed to be of Titian's mistress, and a marble Venus by Canova. For the rest, he dutifully reeled off guidebook lists of the principal Hellenistic and Hadrianic masterpieces, while expressing active loathing for the large population of powerful Florentines ornately entombed in the Medici Chapel, "fine frippery in great slabs of various expensive stones—to commemorate fifty rotten and forgotten carcasses." In Santa Croce, he was no more admiring of monuments to genius, calling the tombs of Machiavelli, Michelangelo, Galileo, even Alfieri—a writer and patriot he revered, commemmorated by his idol Canova—"much illustrious nothing"; it was all "heavy" and "overloaded," and he complained and sighed for the chaste Georgian funerary style, wondering "what is necessary but a bust and a name?—and perhaps a date? . . . All your Allegory and eulogy is infernal."[38] Leaving Padua, he made a detour to Arquà to visit two houses where Petrarch had once lived, finding both "rather ragged" and only "somewhat poetical." Still, crumbling or faded, the material remains of a great artist's life and work were more thrilling than any marble masterpiece erected to his fame.

Crossing the "winding Po" to arrive in Ferrara, Byron visited the dungeons of the fourteenth-century Este castle, where his incestuous lovers Hugo and Parisina had been beheaded, and in the Palazzo Paradiso, he found to his delight that "all [Tasso's] Gerusalemme, all Guarini's . . . original Pastor Fido . . . letters of Titian to Ariosto & Tasso's correspondence about his dirty shirts—are all duly displayed," he reported to Hobhouse.[39] Even this was eclipsed by the drama of seeing the cell where Tasso had been confined for madness; like Bonivard's dungeon at Chillon, the suffocating little room with one barred window in the bowels of the Sant'Anna hospital spoke to Byron's own feelings of persecution and exile. In *The Lament of Tasso* Byron now imagined a poet to represent the artist sacrificed to the arrogance of power. Despotism cannot tolerate the threat of genius. Tasso's crime was his assumption of freedom: He had dared to adore a noblewoman, Eleonora d'Este, sister of his patron and ruler Alfonzo II. In Byron's new poem the signifying "sister" functions like a shuttle, drawing his own tragedy through the weave of Tasso's travails: The captive poet mourns the completion of the poem he has just brought forth, his unjust imprisonment, his torment by the sounds and sights of the insane, and, throughout, the silence of his beloved.

A more remote figure than Manfred's vengeful sister, Astarte, Tasso's Leonora evokes memories of both Annabella and Augusta. Indifferent to his love, Tasso's princess is "a crystal-girded shrine / Worshipped at holy distance,"[40] a saintly figure unwilling to "save" him and, like that other devout Princess of Parallelograms, a cause of his sufferings. As the Ice Queen recedes, however, she is replaced by a sexualized Leonora, whose model is unmistakable; introducing her, Byron evokes the opening lines of his first poem to Augusta: "I told it not, I breathed it not."* In contrast to Tasso's earlier worshipful stance toward the rejecting Leonora, this love "Hath been the sin which shuts me from mankind"; Byron has transformed his poet's haughty muse to recall a mutual and consuming obsession:

> The wretched are the faithful; 'tis their fate
> To have all feeling save the one decay,
> And every passion into one dilate,
> As rapid rivers into oceans pour;
> But ours is fathomless, and hath no shore.[41]

The Lament of Tasso has been seen as a turning point in Byron's life and work. Earlier, he had cast himself in the heroic mold of men of action: the "grand Napoleon of the realms of rhyme,"[42] exiled like his disgraced idol, persecuted like the patriot Bonivard, sacrificed like the anonymous young warriors of Marathon or Waterloo. Now, in identifying with the madness of poets, not kings or conquerors, Byron, according to a recent critic, "fully commits himself to a life as artist,"[43] freed from the prison of self by the act of creation. Composed in a single day in Bologna, *The Lament of Tasso*, written at white heat, seems to confirm itself a manifesto. Revising and copying the 247 lines immediately, he sent the manuscript to Murray on April 22 or 23.

Unburdened of the poem and his imprisoned surrogate, Byron arrived in Rome on April 29, free to be a tourist. For a change he did not try to avoid his compatriots, renting rooms on the first floor of 66 Piazza di Spagna, the quarter where all the English stayed. From his balcony he could see Bernini's *Barcaccia* fountain and the Spanish Steps, flanked by the house where, five years later, Keats would pass his final days.

One of his first excursions confirmed that he was still the bogeyman of right-thinking Englishwomen. As he and Hobhouse emerged onto the roof of St. Peter's, they encountered friends of the Milbankes', Lady Liddell and her party. When the poet was identified to her, the lady, "horror-struck," ordered her daughter to keep her eyes down, stating with a hiss, "Don't look at him, he is dangerous to look at."[44]

Hobhouse had spent the previous five months in the Eternal City,

---

*"Stanzas for Music," written for Augusta in the spring of 1814, begins, "I speak not—I trace not—I breathe not thy name."

preparing for the role of ideal cicerone; he had studied every source and scrutinized every inscription and monument that could be fitted into his strenuous schedule. Byron had sensibly taken his saddle horses with him, which gave him far greater mobility than a hired carriage in navigating Rome's steep hills and far-flung archaeological sites. "I was hardly off my horse's back the whole time—except in poring over churches & antiquities," he told Kinnaird.[45] They explored the Forum, where excavations recently undertaken by Napoleon's short-lived Republic had recovered much of imperial Rome from the rubble of centuries. With Hobhouse holding forth learnedly on Roman emperors and Christian martyrs, recent scholarship, topography, and mythology, Byron paid homage to all the masterworks, from the Sistine Chapel to the Apollo Belvedere. Rome reduced Byron to that dazed state familiar to all visitors: "There must be a sense or two more than we have as mortals—which I suppose the Devil has—(or t'other) for where there is much to be grasped we are always at a loss—and yet feel that we ought to have a higher and more extended comprehension," he told Murray.[46] Sifted and distilled, his impressions of Rome became a meditation on the individual's engagement with history that would shape the fourth and final canto of *Childe Harold*.

In the next weeks, though, he returned in memory to September in the Alps, revising the third act of *Manfred*; he had never solved the problem of dramatically disposing of his hero, and Gifford had tactfully seconded the poet's own dissatisfaction with the weak conclusion. Byron was pleased with the new version he sent to Murray on May 5, noting that he had "rewritten the greater part—& returned what is not altered in the *proof* you sent me."[47] Once again, despite his repeated outrage over mistakes in the published work, he declined to be bothered with checking the text himself: "You will find I think some good poetry in this new act here & there—& if so print it—without sending me further proofs—*under Mr. G[ifford]'s correction*." He decided to consider *The Lament of Tasso*, sent to Murray earlier from Florence, and *Manfred* as a package, declaring to the publisher: "For the *two—it* & the drama—you will disburse to me (via Kinnaird) *Six* hundred guineas." Anticipating Murray's objection that he was foisting upon him a minor poem with his first theater piece, Byron now insisted on the equal importance of both and he further informed the publisher, "I won't take less than three hundred g[uinea]s for anything—the two together will make *you* a larger publication than the 'Siege & Parisina' so you may think yourself let off very easy."[48] Now, having seen to his finances, the poet returned to absorbing Rome.

He explored the Campagna, that mysterious area around the city whose flatness is interrupted only by sections of broken aqueduct leading nowhere and isolated clusters of ruins. He visited the glacier lakes nestled in the Alban Hills and the resort of Tivoli at the foot of the Sabine Hills, with its vast and romantic ruins of Hadrian's villa. He made stops at Ariccia and Frascati, along with two trips to the high cascade of Terni, to see the falls both from the top and from below. But neither nature nor, still less, art, however, could match for Byron the high drama of public execution, Roman style.

On May 19, the day before his return to Venice, he and Hobhouse joined the crush of Romans in the Piazza del Popolo to watch the beheading of three men convicted of robbery and murder. Five years before, Bryon had rented a room with a view of Newgate Prison yard to observe the hanging of the man who had killed the Prime Minister, Perceval. Byron's excited anticipation of that first execution had been fused with the erotic seesaw of his feelings for Caroline Lamb, and he had defended himself from the horror of the hanging by laconic "gallows humor" in which he conflated the insane assassin and his crazily importunate mistress: The dead man "launched into eternity" and his lover "launched into the country" on the same day had been his only comment on the gruesome proceedings. Now, with the help of opera glasses, he recorded in telegraphic style and unsparing detail, in a letter to Murray, the combination of theatrical spectacle and religious ritual that accompanied the Roman sentence, death by decapitation: "the ceremony—including the *masqued* priests—the half naked executioners—the bandaged criminals—the black Christ & his banner—the scaffold—the soldiery—the slow procession—& the quick rattle and heavy fall of the axe—the splash of the blood—& the ghastliness of the exposed heads."

With the release of suppressed memories of the Newgate execution, Byron became a connoisseur, comparing the "more impressive" scene he had just witnessed to "the vulgar and ungentlemanly dirty 'new drop'* and dog-like agony of infliction upon the sufferers of the English sentence." However, this particular performance of the executioner "Maestro Titta," a famous local figure, did not bear out Byron's insistence on the privileged Roman way of death, dependent, as it clearly

---

*Introduced in the 1780s as a wonder of science in the service of more humane executions, the "new drop" outside Newgate Prison consisted of a movable platform on top of the stationary gibbet. When the signal was given, the executioner pressed a lever, at which point the upper platform was supposed to fall instantly beneath the feet of the hanged man, assuring a quick and painless death. In practice, however, the gears often stuck, leaving the prisoner dangling in agony.

was, on the "cooperation" of the condemned. "Two of these men—behaved calmly enough—but the first of the three died with great terror and reluctance—which was very horrible—he would not lie down—then his neck was too large for the aperture—and the priest was obliged to drown his exclamations by still louder exhortations—the head was off before the eye could trace the blow—but from an attempt to draw back the head—notwithstanding it was held forward by the hair—the first head was cut off close to the ears—the other two were taken off more cleanly." At this point, Byron himself seems to retreat from his earlier comparison of humane Italy to the "agony of infliction" imposed at Newgate. The Roman method, he now notes cautiously, is merely "better than the Oriental way—& (I should think) than the axe of our ancestors. The pain seems little—& yet the effect to the spectator—& the preparation to the spectator—is very striking and chilling." Politically, Byron's account was an attempt to disparage British cruelty and hypocrisy. On the personal level, however, the process of watching and recording what he saw represented a moral coming of age. By transforming the voyeuristic into the vicarious experiencing of his own death, Byron as an artist had, paradoxically, moved from aesthetizing the event as ceremony (the black-robed priests and half-naked executioners) to testing his own courage and manhood by imaginatively assuming its terrors. "The first [execution] turned me quite hot and thirsty—& made me shake so that I could hardly hold the opera glass (I was close—but *was determined to see—as one should see everything once—with attention*) the second and third (which shows how dreadfully soon things grow indifferent) I am ashamed to say had no effect on me—as a horror—though I would have saved them if I could."[49]

Unexpectedly, the Roman execution also came to serve as a kind of moral barometer for Byron, registering a worrisome hardening of his emotional arteries. In the course of three violent deaths, he had shed the pity and terror of a witness to tragedy, assuming the role of mere spectator. "I once was quick in feeling—that is o'er / my scars are callous," mourns Byron's Tasso, and we cannot doubt that the poet spoke of himself. When he and Hobhouse later parted ways, the latter recalled his friend's saying that "once he had been a man of a great deal of feeling but that it had been absorbed."[50]

Shortly before they separated, Hobhouse persuaded Byron to sit for a marble bust by Bertel Thorvaldsen, a prominent Danish sculptor working in Rome. Initially, Byron resisted the project; he disliked the idea of being "immortalized in marble while still alive," an aversion that seems related to his worries about creeping death-in-life, his mobile form being frozen into the static posture of the safely dead. In his view, a likeness in stone was entirely different from painted portraits, which, since his student days, he had freely commissioned as gifts for friends and lovers: "Everybody sits for their picture," he mused later to his journal, "but a bust looks like putting up pretentions to permanency."[51] Nonetheless, he agreed, appearing at Thorvaldsen's studio for at least two sittings. By all accounts, sculptor and sitter did not get on.

"He placed himself just opposite me," Thorvaldsen recalled, "and began immediately to assume quite another countenance to what was customary to him." After telling Byron to "sit still," the sculptor further admonished, "but you must not make these faces."

"It is my expression," Byron protested.

"Indeed!" the sculptor replied. Then, giving up all hopes of a relaxed and "natural" sitter, Thorvaldsen "made him as I wished, and everybody said when I was finished that I had hit the likeness." Others differed—and still do—about the resemblance, but Byron's reaction to the clay model (he never saw the marble) was unequivocal: "It does not resemble me at all," he told Thorvaldsen.

"He was, above all things, so desirous of looking extremely unhappy," the sculptor explained mischievously.[52]

Byron was now outraged by Hobhouse's plan to wreathe the brow of his marble likeness with gold laurel leaves. Modesty was not the reason for his objection, but a yearning for immortality so intense that failure must be grotesque; the verdict of posterity could turn any such crown into a bad joke, "a most awkward assumption and anticipation of that which may never come to pass,"* he explained. "I won't have my head garnished like a Xmas pie with Holly—or a Cod's head and Fennel—or whatever the damned weed they strew around it—I wonder you should want me to be such a mountebank."[53] His irritability suggests his own sense of waste; he had squandered too much of his energies in the role of conqueror—in drawing rooms and bedrooms, whether garbed in the black frock coat he had made so fashionable, in scarlet staff uniform, or as pirate pasha, dagger at his belt. But his testiness was also a symptom of the depression that was always lying in wait, suggesting that the expression of melancholy found risible by the sculptor had not been a pose after all.

On May 20, the day after the execution, Byron left for Venice. He

---

*All of Hobhouse's efforts to have his friend commemorated posthumously with a public effigy were rebuffed until, finally, in 1829, Thorwaldsen, now an admirer of the poet who had fought for Greek independence, generously offered to make a new marble; it was installed in the Wren Library of Trinity College, Cambridge, in 1845.

was "wretched" without Marianna, he confessed to Murray. His need and longing for a beloved woman at least were feelings that had not gone dead. But he also missed being part of life at the Casa Segati. Days of cultural tourism in Rome reminded him that he was not only a foreigner, but also, as he believed, a man "hounded" from his own country. His emotional ties to England were dissolving—a source of both relief and anguish. Intimacy with Augusta was the worst casualty of exile. In a letter to her, written from Florence, he sounded a note of pained formality, new to them both: "I shall be glad to hear from or of you & of your children—& mine by the way." Informing her of the birth of his daughter, he confessed, "I am a little puzzled how to dispose of this new production (which is two or three months old though I did not receive the accounts till at Rome)." By July, however, he was still too puzzled to answer Shelley's query—his third—as to Byron's plans for the child. To Augusta, Byron had one proposal for the little girl's upbringing: "[I] shall probably send for and place it in a Venetian convent—to become a good Catholic—& (it may be) a *Nun*—being a character somewhat wanted in our family." Venetian convents being a byword for licentiousness, this was meant as a naughty joke. Future nun or courtesan, his awakened interest in "Alba" reflected Byron's certainty that he would lose his only other child and, turning serious, he reminded Augusta that "in case of the eternal war and alienation which I foresee about my legitimate daughter—Ada—it may be well to have something to repose a hope upon—I must love something in my old age—& probably circumstances will render this poor little creature a greater (& perhaps my only) comfort than any offspring from that misguided & artificial woman who bears and disgraces my name."[54]

Back in Venice, Byron found that he had returned to the suffocating heat of late June, and he promptly joined the seasonal flight of all well-off Venetians known as *la villeggiatura*, a few months of reclaiming rustic roots and seeking cooler temperatures in a mainland farmhouse or, as Byron preferred, a villa on the Brenta River. He rented a long, boxy house facing the canal at La Mira, near Fusina, where he was immediately joined by a rapturous Marianna. There, on June 26, by a running brook in the cool of leafy shade trees, Byron began writing the fourth and final canto of *Childe Harold*. With its last canto, Byron emerged from the shadow of the artist as pariah; he was ready, in Shelley's famous decree, to be anointed "poet legislator of the world."

The final chapter of Byron's song of innocence, begun eight years earlier on his Eastern travels, was now tempered by experience. Tragedy no longer meant the gothic secrets of an invented past or a mask

borrowed from a martyred Renaissance bard, but his own crimes and
their punishment:

> The thorns which I have reaped are of the tree
> I planted,—they have torn me,—and I bleed:
> I should have known what fruit would spring from such a seed.[55]

Disposing of his alter ego, the "Childe" of his title, Byron the poet-
narrator (if not the man) came out in the open. His pilgrim was a
seeker; he wanted answers to his questions about the random horrors of
history, he wanted revenge on his enemies, and, not least, he wanted a
place in the pantheon of immortal poets.

A self-contained quest, the fourth Canto traces, in the most literal
sense, this pilgrim's progress. As he sets out from his villa on the "purple
Brenta" across the lagoon from Venice, the brilliant sunset fading to
"porpoise grey" reminds him of the death of youth. He will end his
journey near Rome, where, standing above the sea, recalling the joyful
swims of boyhood, the poet nears rebirth. Byron dedicated the last
canto of this, "the longest, the most thoughtful and comprehensive" of
his works, now in its "complete or at least concluded state," to
Hobhouse, and "in so doing, I recur from fiction to truth." A friend
"often tried and never found wanting," Hobhouse, his travel companion for the first stage of his pilgrimage, has also been witness to the
rivening sorrow of his life: The date of his dedication—January 2,
1817—Byron reminds him, is "the anniversary of the most unfortunate
day of my past existence,"[56] the marriage whose ending in disgrace and
exile is still a throbbing wound.

In Canto III he had sought balm for pain in nature's immanent love.
Now, Byron staked his claim to the other great theme of romanticism:
the ruins of empire as a text of human folly. Leaving a decayed Venice
with her "crumbling palaces" and "songless gondoliers," he introduces
another motif, sounding a roll call of artists whose inventions ensure
that the dead republic lives in memory. From Shakespeare's Shylock on,
fictive Venetians remind us

> The beings of the mind are not of clay;
> Essentially immortal, they create
> And multiply in us a brighter ray
> And more beloved existence.[57]

Once, he had thought of challenging these larger-than-life characters with
his own: "I saw or dreamed of such,—but let them go— / They came

like truth, and disappeared like dreams."[58] Exile, with its feared loss of a mother tongue, had undermined his faith in the enduring life of his art:

> I twine
> My hopes of being remembered in my line
> With my land's language.[59]

Miraculously, on his journey from Venice to Rome, the poet's fractured spirit begins to heal. Restored to consciousness as an artist, he rejoins the community of creators: "To the mind / Which is itself, no changes bring surprise."[60] His way stations are shrines to literary immortals: Petrarch at Arquà, Tasso in Ferrara, Dante, banished from "ungrateful Florence" to Ravenna, Boccaccio—even Horace, the bane of his schoolboy youth. But nowhere is Italy's "fatal gift of beauty" more seductive, Byron insists, than in the antique sculpture that has survived to affirm the triumph of genius.

Byron seems always to have exaggerated his famous antipathy to art. As impassioned an amateur as Stendhal, accompanying the poet on several visits to the Brera Gallery in Milan, was struck by his eloquence, enthusiasm, and discernment. His professed dislike of the plastic arts may owe more to insecurity: Fear of making the "wrong" judgment lurks below his stated horror of echoing the received rapture of the herd. Until he redefined the Elgin marbles as masterpieces to make a political point, Byron felt easier mouthing the opinions of provincial collectors, dubbing the Parthenon frieze "Phidian freaks" rather than forming his own judgment.

Now that his pilgrimage from Venice to Rome was to include his own "imaginary museum," Byron found a guide who expressed his own amazed discovery of the civilization of Italy and its art. In the form of lyrical letters, Abbé Charles Dupaty,* a follower of Rousseau, provided a tour of Italian cities through the four-star masterpieces to be found on every tourist's itinerary. Beginning with the Medici Venus in the Uffizi, Byron never deviated from the abbé's "A" list, often borrowing his ideas and sometimes his phrases as well. Exhorting us to "contemplate that divine face!" Dupaty asks, "Does not luxurious pleasure breathe in every feature—as every leaf of a rose exhales the delicious perfume of the flower?"[61] Byron gives to the senses of smell and sight the durability of marble:

---

*Byron used the English translation, *Travels Through Italy in a Series of Letters Written in the Year 1785 by the Abbé Dupaty*, London, 1788.

There, too, the Goddess loves in stone, and fills
The air around with beauty; we inhale
The ambrosial aspect, which, beheld, instils
Part of its immortality.[62]

"How does the eye lose itself in a labryinthe [*sic*] of beauties?" his guide
marvels of the Venus. Taking this same trope of sight confused by
perfection, Byron uses a quick series of dynamic images to convey the
visual impact of the marble: From staggering inebriates, we, the viewers,
become slaves who no longer need shackles to imprison us.

We gaze and turn away, and know not where,
Dazzled and drunk with beauty, till the heart
Reels with its fullness; there—for ever there—
Chain'd to the chariot of triumphal Art,
We stand as captives, and would not depart.[63]

When it came to Rome, Byron could look to a rich poetic tradition
of meditations on ruins; English aristocrats returned from the grand
tour so enamored of the melancholy charm of overgrown marble fragments that in the parks of their grand new houses they built their own
versions of Byron's "steps of broken thrones and temples." Here,
too, however, the poet's guidebook provided him with a lesson plan
more moral than aesthetic: "Others may bring home from Rome paintings, marbles, medals and productions of natural history; as for me,"
promised Abbé Dupaty, "I will bring back feelings, sentiments and
ideas: and above all, those ideas sentiments and feelings which arise in
the mind and in the heart, at the foot of antique columns, on the top of
triumphal arches, in the depths of ruined tombs, and on the mossy
banks of fountains."[64]

At the same time, the reminder of so much past splendor reduced to
rubble made Byron's own desolated state—"a ruin amidst ruins"—easier
to bear: "Come and see," he invites us,

The cypress, hear the owl, and plod your way
O'er steps of broken thrones and temples, Ye!
Whose agonies are evils of a day—
A world is at our feet as fragile as our clay.[65]

Robbed of his possessions, of his good name, without wife, daughter,
sister, he feels at one with the city, repeatedly sacked and pillaged

through recorded time: "The Niobe of nations! there she stands, / Childless and crownless, in her voiceless woe."[66]

Rome as a grieving mother, her children slain by "The Goth, the Christian, Time, War, Flood and Fire"—this figure of mourning required a landscape of leveled human constructs reclaimed by nature, with only here and there a familiar monument. Recalling the blasted setting of "Darkness," in Byron's Rome,

> Temple and tower went down, nor left a site:—
> Chaos of ruins! who shall trace the void,
> O'er the dim fragments cast a lunar light,
> And say, "here was, or is," where all is doubly night?[67]

In fact, the void had recently been traced and much of Byron's "marble wilderness" explored.[68] To sustain his preferred Romantic view of Rome as "the desert, where we steer / Stumbling o'er recollections,"[69] the poet had to ignore the accumulated evidence of eight years of archaeology and scholarship.*

Undertaken first by Napoleonic decree, then by the Vatican (the latter project, moreover, under the direction of Byron's revered Canova), excavations had cleared major sections of the Forum and Capitoline Hill. Still, against the neoclassical impulse of historical recovery, energetically bringing to light layers of antiquity,[70] Byron clung to a Romantic image of Rome as the "city of night," a Piranesi-like setting of toppled overgrown columns and broken arches. If anything, Napoleon's campaign to excavate Rome, restoring the city to its original glory as second capital of his republic, was another indictment of his fallen idol: "The fool of false dominion—and a kind / Of bastard Caesar, following him of old / With steps unequal."[71]

Trapped in an endless cycle that begins with conquest and subjugation, men "plod in sluggish misery . . . / Bequeathing their hereditary rage / To the new race of inborn slaves." Yet even as he condemns the turn of the wheel to retaliation and revenge, Byron utters a curse on

---

*Initially, Byron and Hobhouse collaborated on historical notes intended to bridge the gap between the poet's "buried" Rome and evidence recovered by recent archaeology and scholarship. Hobhouse's extended prose commentary, however, ultimately required a separate volume, published by Murray as *Historical Illustrations to the Fourth Canto of Childe Harold* in 1818. His mind-numbing details about every site, saint, and emperor manage to justify Byron's disdain for fact; indeed, the poet freely made fun of Hobhouse's guide.

those who caused his own sufferings—thus perpetuating the eternal
dynamic of hatred. Obsessed by the idea that the agents of his pain—
Annabella, her family, his enemies in England, all the "reptile crew"—
have gotten away with their crimes against him, he calls on "Great
Nemesis" to revenge him with that most Christian of maledictions:
"That curse shall be Forgiveness." He follows with an unforgiving list
of rhetorical questions enumerating all the wrongs inflicted upon him as
he demands:

> Have I not suffered things to be forgiven?
> Have I not had my brain seared, my heart riven,
> Hope sapp'd, name blighted, Life's life lied away?
> And only not to desperation driven,
> Because not altogether of such clay
> As rots into the souls of those whom I survey.[72]

From his initial identity with the artist as outcast, a man of sorrows survived only by his works, the poet now moves to claim the revenge of
genius:

> My mind may lose its force, my blood its fire,
> And my frame perish even in conquering pain,
> But there is that within me which shall tire
> Torture and Time, and breathe when I expire;
> Something unearthly, which they deem not of,
> Like the remembered tone of a mute lyre,
> Shall on their softened spirits sink, and move
> In hearts all rocky now the late remorse of love.[73]

Within Rome, the route of Byron's pilgrimage moves back and forth
between sites of futility and monuments of hope. Seated by the tomb of
Cecilia Metella, now a vacant tower on the Appian Way, he experiences
a sense of renewed possibility—the dead Roman matron's mysterious
blessing:

> Yet could I seat me by this ivied stone
> Till I had bodied forth the heated mind
> Forms from the floating wreck which Ruin leaves behind.[74]

In contrast, the fountain of Egeria, consecrated to the nymph beloved of
Numa, first lawgiver of Rome, stands in idyllic woodland beauty to

mock other mortals with its cruel promise, like the naiad forever out of reach on Keats's Grecian urn:

> Oh Love! no habitant of earth thou art—
> An unseen seraph, we believe in thee,
> A faith whose martyrs are the broken heart,

Egeria embodies the poet's most despairing revelation: She is a creature born of human yearning:

> The mind hath made thee, as it peopled heaven,
> Even with its own desiring phantasy,
> . . . .
> Of its own beauty is the mind diseased,
> And fevers into false creation.
> . . . .
> Where are the charms and virtues which we dare
> Conceive in boyhood and pursue as men,
> The unreach'd Paradise of our despair[75]

Unexpectedly, this taunting muse, too, points the way to a rebirth of hope. Failed by the "immedicable soul, with heart-aches ever new," the source of renewal lies in the rational faculty of consciousness:

> Yet let us ponder boldly—'tis a base
> Abandonment of reason to resign
> Our right of thought—our last and only place
> Of refuge; this, at least, shall still be mine.[76]

The poet's full revelation of the powers of mind to illumine and create emerges, paradoxically, at Christendom's principal spiritual shrine, St. Peter's, where Byron commands us:

> Enter: its grandeur overwhelms thee not;
> And why? it is not lessened; but thy mind,
> Expanded by the genius of the spot,
> Has grown colossal.[77]

Our intelligence can only apprehend such splendors in piecemeal fashion, but this process mirrors the artist's act of creation, moving from the part to the whole, from fragment to totality, "Till, growing with its growth, we thus dilate / Our spirits to the size of that they contemplate."[78]

Leaving Rome, the poet makes his way to the sea, his natural element. "We have had our reward—and it is here." Along the way, he still nursed regrets. The glacial stillness of Lake Nemi recalls the venom of his enemies: Its surface "calm as cherished hate," while his "pleasure in the pathless woods" and "rapture on the lonely shore" arouse memories of Augusta, his sister soul:

> Oh! that the Desert were my dwelling place,
> With one fair spirit for my minister,
> That I might all forget the human race,
> And, hating no one, love but only her!

Still, the bond of larger human sympathy has been restored. He grieves with his compatriots at the death in childbirth of Princess Charlotte and her infant son. Now, with the power of art and mind revealed to him, with feelings of love and pity unfrozen, his final rebirth is supplied by nature.

> Ye Elements!—in whose ennobling stir
> I feel myself exalted.

His pilgrimage at an end, the poet allows himself the reward of hope. From the summer contentment of his villa at La Mira, Byron could count his trip to Rome, along with the rich and great conclusion to *Childe Harold* it inspired, as fulfilling a prophecy contained within the poem itself:

> So shall a better spring less bitter fruit bring forth.[79]

CHAPTER 31

"Vile Assignations, and Adulterous Beds"

WO DAYS after he arrived back in Venice, Byron was once again chivying Douglas Kinnaird to get rid of Newstead Abbey and the Rochdale estate "at any price." But his sense of urgency was not due to any pressing need for money. Rather, he wanted all ties with England severed: "If I could or can expatriate myself altogether, I would and will," he wrote to his friend and banker on May 30, 1817.[1]

Augusta's hold over him had become an irritant, the more so as the woman he loved seemed to have vaporized. To Byron's probing letters, her replies (as orchestrated by Annabella) were infrequent, distant, and evasive. On his side, puzzlement now soured to impatience: She was no longer "Dearest and best beloved" or even "Dearest Sis" but merely "Dearest Augusta." He complained that her letters to him were "full of woes—as usual—megrims & mysteries—but my sympathies remain in suspense—for—for the life of me I can't make out whether your disorder is a broken heart or the ear-ache—or whether it is *you* that have been ill or the children—or what your melancholy—& mysterious apprehensions tend to—or refer to—whether to Caroline Lamb's novels—Mrs. Clermont's evidence—Lady Byron's magnanimity—or any other piece of imposture." And with singular obtuseness, he added, "I should think—all that could affect *you* must have been over long ago."[2]

But it was not long ago for Augusta. On June 16, *Manfred* was published. Safely removed from any reverberations set off by the poem's theme of incest, Byron gleefully inquired of Augusta whether the poem had caused a "pucker."[3] It had. The lead paragraph of one review revived the scandal of the poet's relations with his sister. Expressing shock that Byron would press into poetic service "vice of the most horrid and appalling form," the reviewer allowed himself to hope "for the sake of manhood and morality, that the rumour is incorrect which has identified his inmost feelings with the subject before us."[4]

Byron himself was still fulminating over Annabella's failure to provide assurance—in terms satisfactory to him—that she had no plans for taking Ada abroad and he threatened to reopen the whole case: "They are not aware that if I please I can dissolve the separation—which is not a legal act," he wrote to Augusta. "I shall therefore not only take all proper & legal steps—but the former correspondence shall be published—& the whole business from the beginning investigated in all the points of which it is susceptible." And he claimed to have "already given the proper instructions to the proper persons—to prepare for the steps above mentioned."* In his postscript, however, he now directed his anger at Augusta, saying "that it would be much better at once to explain your mysteries—than to go on with this obscure hinting mode of writing.—What do you mean?—What is there known? or can be known? which *you* & *I* do not know much better?" Among Augusta's hints was one clear enough to trouble Byron's conscience and arouse all of his defensive venom: the accusation that he had hidden certain actions from her—an unmistakable allusion to what he had told Caroline and Lady Melbourne: "What concealment can you have from me? *I* never shrank—& it was on your account principally that I gave way at all—for I thought that they would endeavor to drag you into it."[5] So now it was all Augusta's fault: His refusal to go to trial, seen as a tacit admission of all his crimes, had all been with a view to protecting his sister. This second, mean-spirited letter to Augusta was written on June 19, five days after Byron was installed at La Mira. His bad conscience soothed by taking the offensive, he was now free to enjoy his new surroundings; indeed, Byron's *villeggiatura*, a summer holiday for Venetians, would last for six months, and in this peaceful suburban setting he experienced the most liberating and productive transformation of his life, coming to see exile as destiny—if not freely chosen, than embraced as his star.

He came to know his neighbors; many were Jews who were not allowed to own property in Venice itself. His nearest was a Jewish doctor with three unmarried daughters, one of whom would give her name, Allegra, to Byron's "little illegitimate," Claire's daughter. While she stayed with Byron, Marianna Segati boarded her little girl with this same family, which also was host to Hobhouse in late July. Throughout

---

*There is no surviving evidence that Byron took any such steps.

the month Byron worked on Canto IV of *Childe Harold*. On July 1 he had written to Murray about the addition, complete with a "tease" of its famous opening lines:

> I stood in Venice, on the Bridge of Sighs;
> A palace and a prison on each hand.[6]

"There—there is a brick of your new Babel & now Sirrah, what say you to the sample. . . . I have no idea yet of the probable length or calibre of ye canto—or what it will be good for—but I mean to be as mercenary as possible," he warned his publisher.[7]

When Hobhouse arrived from Naples, he and his host set to work on the notes to Canto IV. Hobhouse later inflated his contribution to the poem itself, insisting that his role in jogging Byron's memory about Roman sites they had visited together and supplying details of their history elevated their conversations to the level of collaboration. And on the evidence of his copious published notes, Hobhouse's knowledge and curiosity did expand Byron's imaginative and moral reading of these monuments, suggesting to the poet new avenues among the ruins they had explored together.

Hobhouse found Byron in high spirits, "well, and merry, and happy, more charming every day,"[8] and in this mood he required company. Another houseguest, "Monk" Lewis, joined them far too often to suit Hobhouse, who found the writer of gothic tales an egotistical bore. But there was also a visit from George Ticknor, the young American who had spent several evenings with Byron and Annabella in the first weeks of their marriage. Now the observant Bostonian was struck by the contrast between his host and his friend. Hobby was planning to stand for Parliament when he returned to England, and talk turned to his plans to visit the Americas with Byron should he lose the election: "Hobhouse," Ticknor recalled, "who is a true politician, talked only of seeing a people whose character and institutions are still in the freshness of youth; while Lord Byron, who has nothing of this but the prejudices and passions of a partisan, was evidently thinking only of seeing our Indians and our forests; of standing in the spray of Niagara; even of climbing the Andes, and ascending the Orinoco. They are now in all respects so different that I hardly think they will ever undertake the expedition."[9] Nor would they—separately or together.

There were also invitations from neighbors; in a singular gesture of friendship from the normally closed Jewish community, Byron and Hobhouse were among the guests at the "circumcision of a sucking Shylock." Byron found the ceremony "very moving" he told Murray, but decided to spare him the gory details, beyond the surgical observation that he had now seen "three men's heads and a child's foreskin cut off in Italy."[10]

As a good host, Byron tried to provide his inhibited friend Hobhouse with sexual adventure. On horseback, they cruised the beach at Dolo* looking for "assignations," Hobhouse reported, and found two young women who were there for the same purpose. Margarita Cogni, the taller of the two, promptly attached herself to Byron; as a married woman, she was free to do as she liked. With his habitual bad luck, Hobhouse was left her unmarried cousin, required by her unwedded state to be less yielding.

The twenty-two-year-old wife of a consumptive unemployed baker, Margarita had heard of Lord Byron's reputation for charity—his generosity being notably directed toward young women in need. And she now saucily accosted him with this demand: "Why do not you who relieve others—think of us also?" Thinking to flatter her (and perhaps to test whether this was strictly business), Byron replied silkily, *"Cara— tu sei troppo bella e giovane per aver' bisogno del' soccorso mio."†* To which she retorted, "If you saw my hut and my food you would not say so." More serious negotiations followed a few nights later. As clever as she was earthy, Margarita knew that a simple transaction of sex for money would reduce her in his lordship's eyes to the coin of a night's pickup, so she "made some bother—at the propositions," claiming she needed time to think them over.[11] Now it was Byron's sexual ego that was on the line: Even if she was a whore, he did not like the idea that she was selling herself to him out of *need*, and his efforts to untangle lust, romance, and commerce reduced him to the kind of double talk that could only have left Margarita secure in the knowledge that *la sua excellenza*, his lordship, was already besotted with her.

"I told her," Byron recalled, "if you really are in want I will relieve you without any conditions whatever—and you may make love with me or no just as you please—*that* shall make no difference—but if you are not in absolute necessity—this is naturally a rendezvous—and I presumed that you understood this—when you made the appointment."

Now the redoubtable Margarita yielded, but not before she had introduced the erotic charge of danger into the transaction. Although "all married women did it," she allowed, she wanted Byron to know

---

*Contemporary descriptions of the Lido make it clear that, aside from fishermen, beaches were frequented only by prostitutes, full-time or occasional.

†"Sweetheart—you're much too young and beautiful to need any help from me."

that her husband was "ferocious—and would do her a mischief" should he discover them. Pride on both sides satisfied, passion followed. The tempestuous Fornarina, as Byron called her in reference to the baker who sat for Raphael, with her dark skin, velvety black eyes, streaming raven hair, and "certain other qualities which need not be mentioned,"[12] was a force of nature, an Amazon with a body "fit to breed gladiators from," Byron observed.[13] But he was still more appreciative that this same body had all the inviting firmness of youth: "She was two and twenty years old—and never having had children—had not spoilt her figure—nor *anything else*," Byron told Murray, "which is I assure you—a great desideration in a hot climate where they grow relaxed and doughy and *flumpity* in a short time after breeding."

Local gossips were prompt to inform la Segati of Byron's destination when she heard the sound of his horses neighing "late into the night" as he galloped off to Dolo and his new lover.[14] Unwisely, Marianna, goaded by troublemaking friends in the vicinity, confronted her rival. Dramas—the more terrifying and threatening the better—were meat and drink to la Fornarina; teeth bared and muscular arm upraised, Margarita took on the enemy. Throwing back her *fazziolo*, the white head covering worn by Venetian working women, she said with a snarl, "*You* are not his wife: *I* am *not* his *wife*—*you* are his *donna*—and I am his *donna*—*your* husband is a cuckold—and mine is another; for the rest, what *right* have you to reproach me? If he prefers what is mine—to what is yours—is it my fault? If you wish to secure him—tie him to your petticoat string—but do not think to speak to me without a reply because you happen to be richer than I am." Marianna recognized that her days as Byron's official *amica* were numbered. Her sorrow may, however, have been assuaged by the evidence that, in contrast to the faithfulness that Byron had shown in the first months of their affair, her rival's claim would never be exclusive. Indeed, Byron's description of himself at this period as only "somewhat promiscuous" would appear, for a change, to have been a modest understatement.[15] As his thirtieth birthday loomed, he was driven by a new sexual urgency.

When Murray wrote to him asking how he should reply to Dr. Polidori's submission of an unreadable tragedy, Byron whipped off some stanzas in the form of a mock rejection letter that notes, in passing, Lord Byron's disappointing recent work:

> So altered since last year his pen is—
> I think he's lost his wits at Venice—
> Or drained his brains away as Stallion
> To some dark-eyed and warm Italian.[16]

If the verses lulled Murray into believing that the poet's sexual appetites diverted him from money matters, he was brought up short by the next letter. Here Byron rapped out his terms for the work in progress: "You offer 1,500 guineas for the new canto—I won't take it," he announced. "I ask 2,500 guineas for it—which you will either give or not as you think proper." Even from Venice, Byron kept a weather eye, down to the last shilling, on what his peers were earning, and he made sure his publisher did as well by him: "If Mr. Moore is to have three thousand for Lallah [Rookh] &c.—if M. Campbell is to have three thousand for his prose on poetry—I don't mean to disparage these gentlemen or their labours—but I ask the aforesaid price for mine.—You will tell me that their productions are considerably *longer*—very true—& when they shorten them—I will lengthen mine, and ask less."17

Meanwhile, before his civilized relationship with Marianna was ended, the lovers received, on August 29, a friendly visit from Signor Segati, on his way to see *his* mistress nearby. He arrived with a delicious piece of gossip then making the rounds. Hobhouse recorded the tale as follows.

A Turk recently arrived in Venice took rooms in a well-known inn, then asked for a private interview with his landlady. Laura was a buxom Venetian widow "of a certain age" whose husband had been lost at sea many years before and had long been replaced by an aristocratic lover. Once they were alone, the Turk began to grill his hostess about her late spouse; in particular, the visitor wanted to know whether the missing man had any distinguishing physical marks by which he could be recognized: Yes, said the widow, he had a scar on his shoulder. "Something like this, said the Turk, pulling down his robe, I am your husband—I have been to Turkey—I have made a large fortune and I make you three offers—either to quit your amoroso and come with me—or to stay with your amoroso or to accept a pension and live alone." But here M. Segati, in the tradition of Scheherazade, left his audience in suspense, noting that the lady had not yet given her reply. Marianna, however, gave her answer immediately: "I'm sure I would not leave my amoroso for any husband," she said, looking at Byron. Such shameless sexual frankness left Hobhouse indignant: "This is too gross even for me," he confided to his diary.18

The incident inspired Byron's most radical and original poem. With *Beppo: A Venetian Story*, Childe Harold goes native, shedding his romantic gloom and guilt, his bitterness and regret for the past, to become, finally—Lord Byron. His new narrator, "a broken Dandy lately on his travels," offers himself as guide to the real Venice, a nocturnal hive of music, laughter, and lovemaking:

The moment night with dusky mantle covers
　　The skies (and the more duskily the better),
The time less liked by husbands than by lovers
　　Begins, and prudery flings aside her fetter;
And gaiety on restless tiptoe hovers,
　　Giggling with all the gallants who beset her;
And there are songs and quavers, roaring, humming,
Guitars, and every other sort of strumming.[19]

No more brooding count or lord with a bloodstained past, Byron's new hero "Beppo" (short for Guiseppe, or Joe), that Everyman of all languages, is resolutely middle class, a seaborne traveling salesman; his disappearance leaves his pleasure-loving wife, Laura, widowed by default. Just as she finds consolation with a dilettante noble, so her husband finds his way home, and on this "found object" of a tale Byron hangs his poem.

Like a stroll through Venice itself, *Beppo*'s progress takes place by means of endless detours and switchbacks, ducking through *calle*, under *sottoportici*, and over bridges, all to map sex as comedy, marriage as convenience, and concludes with no corpses but amiable accommodation by all. Created from the same raw material as Byron's Oriental tales—pirates, abductions, sexual rivalry, bereft bride, and a husband's inopportune return—the cup of poison is now a soufflé, for as Byron had earlier observed, daggers and duels were long since out of fashion. But Segati's anecdote, along with some of Byron's recent readings, had also given him a plot perfectly suited to musings on his own life: on passion and marriage and money; faithful lovers and good-humored cuckolds, on English climate, character, and cant, compared to Venice's sunny skies, where Eros smiles on all. In Shakespeare's Venice, sex was a serious matter; where passion struck, bloodshed was sure to follow:

Vile assignations, and adulterous beds,
Elopements, broken vows, and hearts, and heads[20]

Since that benighted time, however, good sense has come to prevail; passions are muted, and the marriage bond is no longer an impediment to faithful love—elsewhere.

This question lingers: Was Byron setting the cheerful amorality of Venice, standing for the "world," against the England of repressive hypocrisy? Of erosion of liberty in public life and "damage and divorce" in the private realm? Or does each culture simply represent

another form of corruption—two mirrors of individual despair? In subverting any answers, Byron's new style, heard for the first time in *Beppo*,
speaks to us in the wary ironies of modernism. Amused and disabused,
all-knowing and all-accepting, that "nameless broken Dandy" is a casualty of both systems. In Byron's inspired choice of the rolling ottava
rima, with its bullet shot of a last line, he found the perfect vehicle for
the traveler with nothing to declare:

> I fear I have a little turn for satire,
>   And yet methinks the older that one grows
> Inclines us more to laugh than scold, though laughter
> Leaves us so doubly serious shortly after.[21]

Like Byron's other transitional poem, *The Lament of Tasso*, *Beppo*
came together quickly. He wrote his first "Venetian Story" in two days,
October 9 and 10, and two days later he announced to Murray, "I have
since written a poem (of 84 octave Stanzas) humorous." To his astonishment, recent reviews had attacked *Manfred* for lack of originality, citing the poet's unacknowledged debt to Marlowe's *Dr. Faustus*. Claiming
he had never read the Elizabethan drama, Byron now bent over backward to forestall similar criticisms: In his first mention of the poem by
name to Murray, he described *Beppo* as having been written "in or after
the excellent manner of Mr. Whistlecraft (whom I take to be Frere)";*[22]
a few weeks later, he was still worried enough by the plagiarism issue to
repeat his insistence that *Beppo* was indeed a pastiche: "Mr. Whistlecraft has no greater admirer than myself—I have written a story in 89
stanzas—in imitation of him," he told Murray.[23] He also tried to forestall criticism of *Beppo* as proof of its author's immorality. Reviewers
had exhumed the scandal of his personal life to discuss *Manfred*'s theme
of incest. With *Beppo* he would appear to exalt adultery at the expense
of marriage, and, in passing, to have ridiculed every feature of English
life, including the weather:

---

*John Hookham Frere, diplomat and man of letters, used the pseudonym
Whistlecraft for his recently published pastiche of Arthurian legends. The brothers
Whistlecraft, the putative authors, were introduced as saddlemakers, a parody of
the current vogue for self-taught poets from the laboring classes. Byron had just
read the witty verses, brought to Venice by the Kinnaird brothers, and he became an
instant fan of this "sire of half serious rhyme." Whistlecraft, in turn, borrowed
heavily from *Le Novelle Galante*, by the Abbé Casti, an eighteenth-century collection of loosely linked tales of playful eroticism in the style of Boccaccio. In a real
sense, then, *Beppo* is a pastiche of pastiches, transformed by genius.

Our standing army, and disbanded seamen,
    Poor's rate, Reform, my own, the nation's debt,
Our little riots just to show we are free men,
    Our trifling bankruptcies in the Gazette,
Our cloudy climate, and our chilly women,
    All these I can forgive, and those forget,
And greatly venerate our recent glories,
And wish they were not owing to the Tories.[24]

With his conflicting impulses to protect and expose himself, Byron insisted, on the one hand, that the publisher make all such changes as the author wanted, but *not* such as Murray might deem prudent. Among the latter were several swipes at a minor poet and dramatist, William Sotheby, who Byron believed—wrongly, as it turned out—had written to him both insultingly and anonymously. Even when he realized he had been mistaken, he insisted that his lines should stand, telling Murray that *Beppo* "is not to be published in a garbled or mutilated state."[25]

At the same time, he tried to soften the risks posed by the new work. He offered to throw it in with *Childe Harold* Canto IV (thus letting Murray have it for nothing) and, as a further measure of his apprehension, demanded that *Beppo* be published anonymously.*[26]

Byron's concern about the poem's subversive content displaced his awareness of its radical style. If anything, he was too ready to credit his supple new idiom—its fizz of conversational intimacy, linguistic play (puns, tortured rhyme, in-jokes, and slang), buffoonery, and stinging social satire—to his skills as a pasticheur. To be sure, he had found his raw materials in Italian models and in the skilled use made of the "medley style" in English by Frere. What Byron did was to modulate these elements to his own voice and moral view that life was tragic but not serious. For the moment, however, he was only able to explain his restless exploration of new form by dissatisfaction with the limited choices presently available, and in particular, with romanticism as a simplistic way of seeing and of making sense of life: "With regard to poetry in general," he wrote to Murray, "I am convinced, the more I

---

*Beppo was published on or before February 24, 1818. As Byron was uncertain of the date when Murray planned to issue the poem, he only sent the corrected proofs to London on February 25, and he continued to make changes and add stanzas to the first four editions that appeared before April; there more were to follow before the end of the year. All were published anonymously, but the identity of the author was an open secret.

think of it—that . . . *all* of us—Scott, Southey, Wordsworth—Moore—
Campbell—I—are in the wrong—one as much as another—that we
are all upon a wrong revolutionary poetical system—or systems—not
worth a damn in itself . . . and that the present & next generations will
finally be of this opinion." The measure of poetry's decline in his own
time was all too apparent in any reading of the "classic" he had always
loved best: "I took Moore's poem's and my own & some others—
& went over them side by side with Pope's—and I was really astonished
(I ought not to have been so) and mortified—at the ineffable distance
in point of sense—harmony—effect—and even *Imagination* Passion—
& *Invention*—between the little Queen Anne's Man—& us of the lower
Empire." Pope's clear advantage in the last three elements, especially—
the battle cry of romanticism—was particularly damning. "If I had to
begin again," Byron now claimed, "I would model myself accordingly."[27] But he had already tried Pope as a model, in *English Bards*, as
well as in his nasty (and still unpublished) attack on Lord Elgin, *The
Curse of Minerva*. He could not go back either to Pope or to the clichés
of romanticism. Instead, he had invented a poetic language so uniquely
his that he could not yet see his own creation.

BYRON'S COMPLETION of *Beppo* marked the end of his idyllic *villeggiatura* at La Mira. On November 13 he returned to Venice and to
the awkward role of continuing as the Segatis' tenant in the Calle della
Piscina while looking for suitable lodgings of his own. In the meantime
he rented a casino, a uniquely Venetian solution to escaping the stifling
formality of aristocratic life and the few restrictions that marriage still
placed on husbands and wives. Located mostly in the San Marco quarter, casinos could be small, free-standing structures* or a suite of rooms
in a larger house. Furnished with charm and elegance "in the French
style," this pied-à-terre provided a cozy getaway for rich Venetians
where they could entertain informally and, most important, make assignations away from the prying eyes of servants, innkeepers, or, in Byron's
case, other lovers; even food and drink appeared discreetly, by dumb-
waiter. In the course of his Venetian stay, Byron is known to have rented
two casinos, one of them in Santa Maria Zobenigo (now Santa Maria
del Giglio), the square flanked by the Gritti Palace; another possibly on
the Guidecca, the strip of land between the city and the open lagoon.

. . .

---

*These seem to have been constructed of wood, explaining why almost none have
survived.

ON DECEMBER 10, Byron received word that Newstead Abbey had been sold. The new owner, Colonel Thomas Wildman, a wealthy retired officer and Harrow classmate of Byron's, paid the asking price—£94,500, the same figure the defaulted former purchaser was to have paid. Byron was relieved, but like all answered prayers, the sale had its somber side, underlining the reality that he had no home nor even a fixed residence. Then, at the beginning of 1818, he heard from Shelley, who was anxious to make arrangements for little Alba to join her father. Together with other problems caused by their complicated household, the baby's paternity was becoming an issue. Shelley's earlier hope of leaving England for Italy and delivering the child himself had been thwarted by legal delays, and he now pressed Byron to designate an agent to accompany the one-year-old from London to Venice. The need to find a suitable residence thus took on new urgency, since, as he explained to Kinnaird, "I shall acknowledge & breed her myself—giving her the name of *Biron* (to distinguish her from little Legitimacy)—and mean to christen her Allegra."[28] He entered into negotiations with the owner to lease the Gritti Palace, conveniently adjacent to his casino, but just as he thought they had come to an agreement, matters stalled. Once again it was Carnival, when all of Venice abandoned thoughts of business.

Byron, too, had cleared his head of work. On January 8 Hobhouse had left for England, carrying with him the manuscript of Canto IV of *Childe Harold*; in little more than a week Byron would send his fair copy of *Beppo* to the publisher, whose impatience for the new works Byron celebrated in teasing couplets:

> My dear Mr. Murray,
> You're in a damned hurry
>   To set up this ultimate Canto,
> But (if they don't rob us)
> You'll see Mr. Hobhouse
>   Will bring it safe in his portmanteau—[29]

Also in this first month of the new year, Byron changed his *conversazione*, forsaking the drawing room of the Albrizzi for the salon of her rival, Countess Marina Querini Benzoni—a defection that caused ripples in the small town that was Venice. Byron called la Benzoni "the Venetian Lady Melbourne"; at sixty-one she was the same age as his old confidante when they had first met. La Benzoni's sexual spell seems to have been more durable, however; Venetian gossip held that the poet was one of her many younger lovers. It was also rumored that her half brother was the father of her son; for Byron, this would have given her the added attraction of a shared fatality. Like Madame de Staël, she was soon inviting him to intimate family dinners, where he was treated as an honored second son.

La Benzoni exemplified all that Byron found most appealing in Venetian society, starting with her singular absence of snobbery; she welcomed the fierce Margarita with the same warmth as she would a marchesa. In her later years, love for her fellow Venetians was equaled only by her passion for food. She never set forth from her palazzo, it was said, without a freshly cooked slice of polenta tucked into her ample bosom; wisps of steam issuing from her cleavage identified the occupant of her gondola to all passersby on the canal. "Here comes *el fumeto*—the Steaming Lady," the gondoliers would announce.[30]

At her *conversazione*, the old and the learned mingled with the young and the beautiful. On Byron's first visit, at the end of January, he reported meeting the "prettiest girl I ever saw half Greek Half French a foreigner from Padua for the Carnival."[31] He did not mention (or barely noticed) another pretty young woman, eighteen-year-old Countess Teresa Gamba Ghiselli Guiccioli of Ravenna, visiting Venice on her wedding trip with her husband, Count Alessandro Guiccioli, aged fifty-seven. Less the predator than usual, Byron confessed himself "in the estrum & agonies of a new intrigue," this with the "insatiate" unknown woman with the fair hair and blue eyes who managed—even unmasked—to retain her mystery.[32] He didn't mention his momentous thirtieth birthday—upon him within weeks—except to note obliquely to Murray: "I shall make what I can of the remainder of my youth—& confess—that like Augustus—I would rather die *standing*."[33]

Byron expected to pay for his pleasures if money was needed or expected by a woman he wanted; sometimes his largesse, well known to all of Venice, might extend to the young and pretty without sex included in the bargain. At the same time, despite his own beauty and magnetism that few could resist, he was still pathetically proud when a desirable partner offered herself to him gratis, and he unfailingly recorded these encounters. His lame foot—especially in Venice's watery thoroughfares—might hardly be noticed by others; in his own mirror, he always saw a man with a limp. Discovering that he had been "clapt" by one Elena da Mosta, "gentildonna,"* he described his infection as the

---

*Da Mosta may have been a noblewoman, as Byron mantained, but the "da" of her surname was no proof thereof; since the sixteenth century, this form was freely adopted by the more successful courtesans.

"first case of gonhorrhea I have not paid for," and he still reported proudly that "she positively refused money or presents from me."[34] With the end of Carnival came Byron's final break with Marianna. She did not, however, prove as unmercenary. Knowing the end was near, she pawned diamonds that Byron had given her and for which he had reputedly paid £500. Her lover promptly redeemed them for the express purpose, it would seem, of exposing her venality. But why should she have been sentimental when it was clear that her days were numbered? From Padua, where she went to see a doctor about stomach spasms, she wrote to Byron, begging to see him when she returned; she hoped that they could remain friends. There is no evidence that Byron ever replied. Temporarily, at least, he had tired of domesticity—even Venetian style. He soon joked that in place of the Segati household, his "whore hold has been much extended since the Masquing began and closed,"[35] and to Kinnaird he noted, "I have broke my old liaison with la Segati—& have taken a dozen in stead."[36] A few months later, the dozen had increased exponentially.

Scheduling the visitors to his casino required care. He took pains to avoid an encounter between his current favorite, the strapping, dark-skinned "Fornarina" with another woman of similar proportions, that could unleash a possible battle of the Amazons. For the rest, however, simultaneous partners were even preferred. One of his boon companions during these months, Cavaliere Angelo Mengaldo, a retired Napoleonic officer and man-about-town, professed himself shocked by the frenzied pace of activity to which he was privy; even to his journal, he censored his description by switching into French, referring elliptically to Byron's " *'orrible système*," the term suggesting a certain mechanical nature to the proceedings.[37] Other friends were less discreet. His "reward" for sharing his pleasures with Lord Lauderdale, Byron noted sourly, was reports that the elderly peer had been spreading scurrilous stories about his "pieces" all over London. Byron's defiant response was to fuel further gossip; he boasted of the record number of his couplings along with his taste for women who were related to one another: sisters or mothers and daughters.

"Which 'piece' does he mean?" he sneered in a joint letter to Hobhouse and Kinnaird. "Since last year I have run the Gauntlet; is it the Tarruscelli—the Da Mosti—the Spineda—the Lotti—the Rizzato—the Eleanora—the Carlotta—the Giulietta." Farther down the list come "the Glettenheimer—& her sister—the Luigia & her mother . . . the Tentora and her sister—*cum multis aliis*—some of them are Countesses—& some of them are cobblers' wives—some noble—some middling—some low—& all whores—which does the damned old

'Ladro—& porco fottuto'* mean? I have had them all & thrice as many to boot since 1817."38

Signed letters to Byron from some of the women who figure in this list—seventeen, including Marianna Segati, along with others, the more poignant in their anonymity—have recently come to light.39 These include notes from correspondents he had never met but who had seen him once and been struck by his beauty, or who had heard of *milordo*'s wealth, generosity, and possibly sexual prowess. Others were written by the transient "pieces" of an hour's amusement; they beg for money, another meeting, a word in return, or, most touching, merely to be remembered. There is a note from the younger woman in a mother-daughter assignation (possibly the same pair he mentioned); she reminded the poet that her mother was to have arranged their next rendezvous, but since she had failed, she had taken matters in hand herself. Only one voice rises above the pleadings of cast-aside mistresses or brief, anonymous encounters and she was, significantly, an opera singer.

"The prettiest Bacchante in the World and a piece to perish *in*" was how Byron described Arpalice Taruscelli. He had cause to preen himself on his new conquest; her most recent protector, an Austrian colonel, had been so infatuated with his diva that he had refused to introduce her to Lord Kinnaird, older brother of Byron's friend Douglas, when the Kinnairds visited Venice in late summer. A week after their first meeting in May, Byron could boast that he had "fucked her twice a day for the last six" everywhere, including one midnight assignation at Arpalice's milliner! But he took pains to reassure Hobhouse that his feelings were not engaged: "With regard to . . . the Madcap above mentioned—recollect there is no *liaison* only *fuff-fuff* and passades—& fair fucking."40 For her part, Arpalice wrote witty, playful letters, often to arrange trysts and, in the Mozartian style befitting a soprano, her notes were carried to her lover by her maid and the answers returned by Byron's gondolier. Initially Arpalice had the good sense to deflect Byron's mocking humor, his refusal to play the lovesick cavalier, with persiflage: She threatened to make him a "present of a little sermon for the many insolent remarks made to me yesterday morning . . . but I let you know now so that you will not be frightened, that the sermon will be very brief."41 This would be followed, he could be sure, by a delicious form of forgiveness. Her engagements often took her away from Venice;

---

*Thief and filthy bugger.

then she had more difficulty taming her jealousy, and her usual light tone in dealing with the infidelities Byron rarely troubled to hide turns coarse: "Tell me something, Baby! how many baker-girls, how many little seamstresses, how much mischief have you made in the last two days? Already I seem to read your black crimes on your handsome face. Poor Arpalice! but poor Giorgio, if I find out about them upon my return!"[42]

Byron could not resist taking his turn with Countess Spineda (also inscribed in his Venetian catalogue), the legacy of a compatriot returned to England. When Taruscelli found out, she attacked her rival, sending anonymous letters to that lady's official protector and provoking stormy quarrels with her own Austrian officer, still on the scene, and with Byron himself. He had had enough. "She's gone to Padua by the blessing of the Gods," he reported to Murray.[43] When she returned, he refused to answer her letters—now tearful and imploring. Only when it became clear that a resigned Taruscelli had transferred her affections to another (probably a principal tenor with whom she performed) did Byron feel safe enough to shift to friendly relations. Byron's final engagement with his diva was to offer both singers introductions to friends in England. The introduction to Douglas Kinnaird was accompanied by the sexual "references" that were the coin of Byron's more intimate friendships: He prided himself on his generosity with cast-off lovers:* *"Try her,"* he urged his friend, "you will find her a good one to go—and she is—or was uncommonly *firm* of *flesh* a *rarity* in Italian & Southern women after twenty—she is also sufficiently expert in all the motions—like the rest of her countrywomen."[44]

AT THE END of April, Byron learned of Lady Melbourne's death. He had known for some time of her declining health, but their friendship had languished following the separation, and his response to the news was perfunctory; after trotting out his well-used encomium to "the best & kindest & ablest female I ever knew," he concluded briskly

---

*Kinnaird had recently ended his long-standing relations with a charming singer, Maria Keppel, who had lived with him for nine years, during which time she served as his official hostess and was much admired by his friends, especially Byron. An irascible man of violent temper, Kinnaird, claiming to have discovered that he was not the father of their little son, threw Mrs. Keppel out of their house on Clarges Street, and sending the boy to board in Hackney, threatened the mother that if she ever tried to visit her child without his express permission, she would never see her son again.

to Murray, "—there is one link the less between England & myself—Now to business."*[45] He appeared to have been far more affected by the death of Madame de Staël the previous July. From dismissing the writer as an overbearing bluestocking, he had come to cherish her as a real friend.

In their different ways, both older women had allowed Byron to prolong his boyhood, encouraging him to play ideal lover, son, protégé. Now, for the first time, he was to take on that most adult responsibility: raising a child. The Shelleys had arrived in Milan with their two children, together with Claire and eighteen-month-old Alba, who had been christened Clara Allegra, the new name chosen by Byron, just before the group left London on March 11.

Shelley was uneasy with Claire's decision to give up her child to a man who loathed the mother, and when he read Byron's latest letter (lost along with others written to Shelley at this period), his worst fears seemed to be confirmed: "You write as if from the instant of its departure all future intercourse were to cease between Clare [sic] and her child," Shelley wrote. "This I cannot think you ought to have expected, or even to have desired." Giving voice to Claire's suffering, he pointed out, "What assurance have I of the tenderness of the father for his child, if he treats the feelings of the mother with so little consideration."[46] To reassure Claire and to make the painful transition easier, Shelley proposed that Byron join them in a villa he planned to rent on the shore of Lake Como. Then, instead of sending an agent and stranger to take Allegra to Venice, he could bring his daughter back with him. Byron's reply was all reassurance. He had been misunderstood; he had no wish to separate mother and child irrevocably; but neither was he able to leave Venice at this time.[47]

To Hobhouse, however, Byron confided his real suspicions: They were using Allegra as a decoy to trap him into renewed intimacy with Claire. "Shelley has got to Milan with the bastard & it's mother—but won't send the shild [sic]—unless I will go & see the mother—I have sent a messenger for the Shild."†[48]

———

*Her children were outraged when, on the day after her death, Hobhouse (most likely acting on Byron's instructions) appeared at Melbourne House and without a word of condolence, asked that Byron's letters to their mother be turned over to him immediately.

†Byron's messenger was Francis Merryweather, a dealer in alabaster vases and, illegally, in wine and tobacco. Byron subsequently hired Merryweather to perform secretarial and accounting chores but later brought suit against his fellow expatriate for cheating him.

Shelley was was deeply insulted by Byron's offer to reimburse him for the baby's expenses during the time she had been living with them. He and Mary loved Allegra as if she were one of their own children, and the money in question was "trifling."

"Perhaps you will be kind enough not to place me in so degrading a situation as to estimate a matter of this kind," he wrote sharply.[49] Before the messenger arrived from Venice, he tried to persuade Claire that there was still time to change her mind; this was the second of his "Sybilline volumes," as he later called his forebodings of disaster to come. But she held firm in the belief that in giving up her child, she was providing Allegra with a life of privilege, and on May 2 the little girl, accompanied by the Shelleys' Swiss nurse, Elise, arrived in Venice. Her father was at once struck by her resemblance to him: "My bastard came three days ago—very like—healthy—noisy—& capricious," Byron reported to Hobhouse of the eighteen-month-old.[50]

In preparation for this new role as head of his own household, he took a three-year lease on one of three adjoining seventeenth-century palaces known collectively as the Palazzo Mocenigo and situated on the Grand Canal just above the Rialto Bridge. Byron's residence, called the Palazzo Nuovo, is the most elegant of the trio, the only one with tall, arched windows on the *piano nobile* (the main floor) and a stone balcony overlooking the water from the vast drawing room. Entering the palace from the street, however, was a gloomy affair. The visitor crossed a luxuriant garden courtyard to plunge into the darkness of a dank, cobblestoned ground floor, whose feeling of being a forgotten thoroughfare was reinforced by ranks of Byron's coaches gathering dust in the shadows.

Byron himself was delighted with his new home, its splendid situation, grand scale, and furnishings (including linen) provided by the noble and ancient family whose many Mocenigo doges stared down from the walls, and he was perfectly willing to overpay, the rent being £200 a year. Still, satisfying Byron's requirements in the way of comforts and staff took time; the new establishment would not be ready for a month. In the meantime, having barely been inspected by the papa she had never seen before, Allegra was whisked off with her nurse to stay with Byron's friends, British consul Richard Belgrave Hoppner and his Swiss wife, recent parents of a baby son.

Finally, in early June, Byron moved into his new lodgings—the closest he had come to replicating Newstead Abbey's crumbling grandeur. The highest and coldest floor was given over to the servants—fourteen in number. Fletcher, as inept and allergic to foreigners as ever, was in command of the household, which now included a menagerie. Among the carriages on the ground floor were deposited cages and baskets from which issued the cries, cackles, barkings, and meows of the resident felines and a ferocious mastiff, along with a fox, a wolf, smaller dogs, fowl, and birds. Attrition did little to make this unpeaceable kingdom sound less like a jungle; as Byron confessed, even "the elopement of one cat, the decease of two monkeys and a crow by indigestion" left a "flourishing and somewhat obstreperous establishment."[51]

Allegra captivated everyone. In Venice, as throughout Italy, strangers melted in the presence of an adorable *bambina*, and even Byron was won over by the credit she reflected on her father, reporting proudly that "she is counted a very fine child—much admired in the gardens & on the Piazza—and greatly caressed by the Venetians from the Governatrice downwards."[52] Allegra inspired his first letter in months to her godmother: "She is very pretty—remarkably intelligent," he wrote to the baby-loving Augusta, "but what is more remarkable—much more like Lady Byron than her mother—so much so as to stupefy the learned Fletcher—and astonish me—is it not odd? I suppose she must also resemble her sister Ada," he added wistfully of the daughter he had not seen since infancy. "She has very blue eyes—that singular forehead—fair curly hair—and a devil of a spirit—but that is Papa's."[53] To summon fond feelings for his daughter, he had to write Claire out of the genetic picture; more astonishing, however, is to find his nemesis, Lady Byron, in her place.

In the heat of the Venetian summer, Byron now yielded to his Aquarian self: He triumphed in two swimming contests. In a race from the Lido to the Riva della Schiavone he bested Consul Hoppner; the *cavaliere* Mengaldo, his sometime companion of casino revels; and Alexander Scott, another well-off young English resident of Venice. Mengaldo, who boasted that he had swum the Berezina River under gunfire in Napoleon's Russian campaign, made it halfway to the Riva; Mengaldo and Scott, Byron crowed, were exhausted and vomiting water as they were helped into their boats. In a return match, he and Scott beat Mengaldo "hollow—leaving him breathless and five hundred yards behind hand before we got from Lido to the entrance of the Grand Canal," Byron reported to Hobhouse. Scott had to be hauled out at the Rialto, leaving Byron to make it alone to the end of the canal directly across from Mestre, reckoned at about four and a half miles: "staying in half an hour &—I know not what distance more than the other two—& swimming easy . . . I was in the sea from half past 4—till a quarter past 8—without touching or resting." Throwing in some sexual braggadocio with his other statistics, he added, "I could not be much fatigued having had a *piece* in the forenoon—& taking another in the evening at ten of the Clock."*⁵⁴

With all of his athletic triumphs, aquatic and sexual, Byron's most remarkable feat of the summer was still poetry. On July 10 he wrote to Murray, "I have completed an Ode on Venice; and have two stories— one serious & one ludicrous (à la Beppo) not yet finished and in no hurry to be so."⁵⁵ The "Ode" suggests discarded descriptions of the city from Canto IV and *Beppo*; the serious tale is *Mazeppa*.

Like *The Giaour*, *Mazeppa* is a tale within a tale, whose narrator is also the hero. A Cossack prince, Mazeppa hopes to soothe his commander, the Swedish King Charles XII, on the eve of battle, by recalling his own earlier triumph over death. For loving the wife of his ruler, Count Palatine, Mazeppa, then a young page, had been lashed naked to a wild horse. In their frenzied ride though forest and river, pursued by wolves and birds of prey, the youth learns that self-mastery lies in acceptance of pain, not in struggle. His exhausted horse lying dead beneath him, Mazeppa is rescued by a Turkish princess: Doomed to a violent death, the page is spared by the lesson of passivity to become prince of the Turks.

On one level, *Mazeppa* is an allegory of good and bad government. Inspired by Voltaire's study of Charles XII, Byron plays off the Napoleonic king—rigid and power-driven—against the supple heroism of his vassal; passing the test of self-rule, Mazeppa is fit to rule others. Byron's own lessons in stoicism, learned since the separation, are part of his story. From the punishment that, Mazeppa recalls,

> Sent me forth to the wilderness,
> Bound, naked, bleeding, and alone,
> To pass the desert to a throne,—

His rescue and present high estate have taught him hope:

> What mortal his own doom may guess?—
> Let none despond, let none despair!⁵⁶

---

*Despite evidence suggesting that his physical exertions were largely horizontal, Byron constantly begged his friends in England to send him "corn plasters" two dozen at a time—"recollect they are light and may come in letters." Strenuous walking could not have been the cause of his pain; his gondolier waited at the Mocenigo landing. It seems likely that the poet succumbed to elegant Venetian boots that were unforgiving to his feet—especially the misshapen one.

In addition, Byron was allowing a "ludicrous" story to germinate, one "not yet finished—& in no hurry to be so," and it would be five years before the last stanzas of the still uncompleted poem were finished. Begun in this championship summer, *Don Juan* stands as Byron's claim to genius.

Among other works started in July, in defiance of the season's torpor, were his memoirs. Within a few weeks Byron alerted Murray that "about 20 *sheets* of *long* & a few of letter paper—are already written of 'the Life' & I think of going through with it. We will see what sort of stuff it is & decide accordingly."[58] That confused decision would be his most divisive legacy.

Despite the productive summer, he felt a nagging sense of impasse. "I have several things begun—verse and prose—but none in much forwardness." Typically, Byron professed indifference if not actual disdain toward critics, even when they confined themselves to attacking what he *had* written. In his present uncertainty he needed the reaction of reviewers to show him what he *should* write. "If you would tell me exactly . . . the state of the reception of our late publications & the feeling upon them—without consulting any delicacies," he urged Murray, "I should know how and in what manner to proceed." And he confessed to a kind of vacuum where once there had been a plenitude of inspiration, to the collapse of grand ambitions into mere desire for success: "I once wrote from the fullness of my mind—and the love of fame (not as an *end* but as a *means* to obtain that influence over men's minds—which is power in itself & in its consequences) and now from habit—& from avarice—so that the effect may probably be as different as the inspiration."[59] His sense of diminished power mirrored his state of mind; but he was prescient enough to foresee the results only as "different." Just as he predicted, when he read the reviews praising *Beppo*, his confidence resurged and he returned with zest to the new work: "I have finished the First Canto (a long one, of about 180 octaves) of a poem in the style and manner of 'Beppo' encouraged by the good success of the same. It is called 'Don Juan,' and it is meant to be a little quietly facetious upon everything," he told Moore. "But I doubt whether it is not—at least—as far as it has yet gone—too free for these very modest times."[60] In England, certainly, the times were becoming ever less free, but in a Venice empty of Venetians and somnolent in the summer heat, the poet was released from doubt.

For his own *villeggiatura* he had leased from Hoppner the consul's villa, I Capuccini, in the Euganean Hills near Este, a picturesquely situated residence built on the ruins of a Capuchin monastery, with the crumbling Medici palace on the opposite cliff. But events now conspired to ensure that, having visited the house briefly in spring before accepting Hoppner's offer, he never set foot there again.

THE SHELLEY household, meanwhile, had found the Lake Como villa disappointing and proceeded to Bagni di Lucca (despite its popularity with English tourists), a hilly spa on the Serchio River, where they found a most satisfactory house with garden and view. Claire, however, was becoming increasingly anxious about Allegra. Letters from Elise made it clear that the Palazzo Mocenigo was no place for a child. When the nursemaid reported the goings-on there to the consul's wife and fellow Swiss, Mrs. Hoppner, that lady persuaded Byron to let her take Allegra and her caretaker to the consulate. Claire, however, now fixed on the idea of going to Venice to confront Byron as a delinquent father. As Shelley plainly saw, this plan was a recipe for disaster; at the very least, it ensured that Claire would never see her child again. Thus he decided to accompany her in the hope of dissuading the distraught woman from this imprudence; Shelley's own motives in making the trip were mixed and certainly included the desire to be alone with Claire, his "Comet, beautiful and fierce." Writing to Mary en route, he subtracted several days from the leisurely seven he and Claire spent on the road together. He also announced a new plan: Claire was to remain in Padua, while Shelley, alone with Byron, took up the subject of Allegra and the child's reunion with her mother. But in fact, Claire and Shelley saw Venice for the first time together, on a starry midnight from the recesses of a gondola. The next day, Shelley remained discreetly in a boat below the consular residence while Claire visited Mrs. Hoppner and was joyfully reunited with her little daughter. Mother of a young child, the consul's wife was as sympathetic to Claire as she was disapproving of Lord Byron, and she now filled Claire's ears with all the local gossip of his lordship's depravity. She also made sure to inform Claire, Shelley wrote to Mary, that "Byron often expresses his extreme horror of her arrival, & the necessity which it would impose on him of instantly quitting Venice." Mrs. Hoppner's solution was "that Claire being here should be concealed"—advice that was to have disastrous consequences.[61]

When Shelley joined the group at the Hoppners', he found Allegra "so grown you would hardly know her—she is pale and has lost a good deal of her liveliness, but is as beautiful as ever but more mild."[62] What Shelley was describing to Mary is the listless affect of the abandoned child.

Tactfully allowing time for his lordship to rise, make his toilette, and dismiss any embarrassing companions of the night before, Shelley appeared unannounced at the Palazzo Mocenigo at three o'clock that Sunday afternoon, August 23. To his surprise, he found Byron delighted by his unexpected visit. Expansive with the pleasure of their reunion, his host was generous and conciliatory about Allegra and her mother. Shelley, however, had led Byron to believe that both Claire and Mary were in Padua; he was also aware from Elise's letters that despite his lordship's own libertine way of life, he took a dim view of the sexual sharing he suspected governed the Shelley household. Now, when Byron suggested that Shelley take Allegra to Padua to join her mother and Mary, offering them his villa at Este for the month and even suggesting that Claire might keep her child if she so decided, Shelley panicked. His part in concealing Claire at the Hoppners' and the fact that they were traveling alone together (and Byron's reaction if he found out) would sabotage the very reunion he had come to Venice to mediate. Shelley now decided that Mary must make good on the lies that everyone else had been telling. He instructed her to pack up the house at Bagni di Lucca at once, and make the five-day journey with the two children, meeting him at Byron's villa in Este. He and Mary would then join Byron in Venice.

Unknown to Shelley, one-year-old Clara had been suffering from fever and dysentery before Mary set out in the heat of August. He and his family convened at I Cappuccini on September 6, but on the thirteenth Shelley wrote to Byron to say that the child had been "dangerously ill" for a week, "so am detained an anxious prisoner here," thwarted in his plans to return to Venice.[68] Although the baby failed to improve, Shelley was far more concerned with Claire's intestinal troubles and accompanied her to the doctor in Padua on Tuesday, September 22; when they missed "the Medico" on that day, he decided to go on to Venice alone. He sent Claire back to Este, instructing Mary to escort her to her next appointment with the doctor early on Thursday morning, "a thing to be accomplished only by setting out at $\frac{1}{2}$ past three in the morning," he told his wife. He might meet them in Padua, but in case he should decide to remain in Venice, he would send word how she and the children were to find him there.

"Am I not like a wild swan to be gone so suddenly?" he asked coyly.[64]

In the event, he was at Padua when his family arrived, Mary frantic, as the weakened Clara had begun showing signs of convulsions. Her condition worsened on the gondola crossing from Fusina and as soon as they landed in Venice, Shelley rushed to find Byron's physician, the noted Dr. Aglietti. But the doctor was out, and shortly after Shelley's return to the inn little Clara died in her mother's arms. Mary was devastated; added to the horror of the baby's death was evidence, stark and accusing, that it need not have happened. Her child had been sacrificed to Claire's demands and Shelley's egoism.

Like the needle of a compass, the magnetic force directing all their actions swung back to Byron. Shelley and Claire's distrust of his paternal custody had driven them to Venice. Then Byron's unexpected offer of his Este villa had forced Shelley to produce Mary at Padua. Finally, it had been Byron's seductive invitation that, superseding any needs of wife and child, had unleashed the final act of the tragedy.

After the burial on Friday, Byron, together with the Hoppners, did their best to distract the grieving parents with tours of Venice, but Mary, "reduced to a kind of despair," Shelley wrote to Claire, would not be comforted.[65] They returned early in the week to Este, Mary carrying the manuscript of *Mazeppa* with her; in the hope that work might distract her from sorrow, Byron had tactfully solicited her editorial judgment and elegant hand for the printer's copy of the poem. When they arrived, they mourned with Claire and watched the games of three-year-old William and Allegra, soon to be parted again from her mother.

But a few weeks later, Shelley and Mary were back in Venice; there was too much painful intimacy in the villa at Este. Byron now arranged for the cavaliere Mengaldo, a great admirer of *Frankenstein*, to escort its author to operas and comedies, while he and Shelley rode on the Lido; other evenings Shelley escaped again to join Byron at the Mocenigo, where they talked into the early morning.

With alternating surges of envy, admiration, and disgust, Shelley listened as Byron described his night prowls through Venice, which on at least one occasion seems to have included him. In Byron's company, everything he heard or saw offended the fastidious Shelley, beginning with his host's taste for Italian women, "the most contemptible of all who exist under the moon; the most ignorant the most disgusting, the most bigoted, the most filthy. Countesses smell so of garlick that an ordinary Englishman cannot approach them."[66] But when he stopped holding his nose, Shelley was also dismayed by his friend's exploitation of poverty: "He allows fathers & mothers to bargain with him for their daughters, & tho this is common enough in Italy, yet for an Englishman to encourage such sickening vice is a melancholy thing." He hinted, too, that Byron had reverted to homosexual practice. "He associates with wretches who seem almost to have lost the gait & phisiognomy[*sic*] of man & who do not scruple to avow practices which are not only not named but I believe seldom even conceived in England."[67] Puritanical and provincial, Shelley was sincerely shocked (as no doubt Byron intended he should be) with evidence of his friend's corruption. But along with disapproval went a strong dose of jealousy; Byron flaunted his promiscuity, but when it came to work, he exercised the discipline of a monk. Shelley was honest enough to admit, moreover, that not even a dissolute life, leading inevitably to nihilistic disgust, could diminish Byron's genius: "Heartily and deeply discontented with himself & contemplating in the distorting mirror of his own thoughts, the nature & the destiny of man, what can he behold but objects of contempt & despair? But that he is a great poet, I think the address to the Ocean* proves."[68] During these last weeks of October, Byron read to his visitor Canto I of *Don Juan*, "a thing in the style of Beppo, but infinitely better," Shelley reported.[69]

This time, however, neither Byron's brilliance nor his own complicated feelings of rivalry silenced Shelley, as they had on Lake Geneva; instead, Byron's quicksilver conversation and challenging arguments spurred him to new efforts; in his friend's "great palace . . . his wit / and subtle talk would cheer the winter night / And make me know myself." Leaving Mary behind, Shelley returned alone to Este to write "the first of his masterworks."[70] Set in Venice, *Julian and Maddalo* is a tribute both to the deepening personal intimacy of the two poets and the chasm of belief between them. Their philosophical and emotional polarities became the poem's subject, the dynamic of their arguments following the physical movement of the narrative. From their opening gallop along the Lido, Julian, the idealistic young Englishman, radical and utopian in his faith, challenges his double, Lord Byron, Italianized as Count Maddalo. At first both young men are as buoyant as their prancing horses:

> I rode one evening with Count Maddalo
> Upon the bank of land which breaks the flow
> Of Adria towards Venice
>
> . . . .
>
> So, as we rode we talked; and the swift thought,
> Winging itself with laughter, lingered not,
> But flew from brain to brain,—such glee was ours.
> Charged with light memories of remembered hours,
> None slow enough for sadness

On returning to the city, however, their thoughts turn "forlorn"— dangerous, even—moving to Promethean questioning of the divine order:

---

*Stanzas 179–84 of Canto IV, *Childe Harold's Pilgrimage*.

> Concerning God, free will and destiny
> Of all that earth has been or yet may be,
> All that vain men imagine or believe

As narrator, Shelley/Julian seizes the moral advantage: His faith in the perfectibility of man is based on unselfish love, while Count Maddalo's belief—that human weakness foils the most "irrefutable" arguments for individual happiness—is merely (in his adversary's view) a defense of Maddalo's own arrogant amorality. From Shelley's own conflicts about his friend, Byron emerges as a superman dazzled by his own genius:

> The sense that he was greater than his kind
> Had struck, methinks, his eagle spirit blind
> By gazing on its own exceeding light.[71]

CHAPTER 32

An Uncommon Hero

READING Byron's letters from Venice, his friends at home heard the exuberant voice of a young man restored to health and sanity. But those who saw the poet at the end of the year 1818 came away with a very different impression. In November Byron received a delegation of visitors from England: John Hanson, his son Newton, and a Mr. Townsend, a clerk representing Colonel Wildman, the new owner of Newstead Abbey.

The Hansons found the poet nervous and irritable. He harped on three packages containing books left by Murray at the lawyers' offices. Refusing to carry a "waggon load" of the poet's library across the Alps, Hanson had brought only one box (the lightest), and this contained only the corn plasters, toothbrushes, toothpowder, and severel kaleidoscopes. Byron's annoyance turned to rage when one of the instruments came apart in his hand and he was cut by pieces of glass while trying to force the two sections back together. Newton Hanson, who had last glimpsed him in the glamour of his "years of fame," was appalled by the man he now saw.

"Lord Byron could not have been more than thirty," he recalled, "but he looked forty. His face had become pale, bloated and sallow. He had grown very fat, his shoulders broad and round, and the knuckles of his hands were lost in fat."[1] He chewed his nails constantly and to compensate for a prematurely receding hairline, he had let his hair grow long, adding to the impression of neglect.

When the papers transferring the Newstead title were duly signed, Hanson turned to his real object in making the journey himself: He had come, according to his son, to persuade Byron to attempt a reconciliation with Annabella. Remarkably, the lawyer's efforts were not dismissed out of hand. It was only when a jubilant Byron rushed to Hanson's hotel with news of Sir Samuel Romilly's suicide that the lawyer abandoned the role of marriage counselor: Romilly had taken his life in despair over his wife's recent death. "How strange it is that one man will die for the loss of his partner, while another would die if they were compelled to live together," Byron remarked.[2] In death as in life, he was still Romilly's double—and victim; once again, the politically engaged barrister and loving husband accused the poet who had fled family and country. Now Byron crowed over the suicide's revealed weakness of character, raving to—of all people—Annabella: "This Man little thought when he was lacerating my heart according to law—while he was poisoning my life at it's sources—aiding and abetting in the blighting—branding—and Exile that was to be the result of his Counsels in their *indirect effects*—that in less than thirty-six moons—in the pride of his triumph as the highest Candidate for the representation of the Sister-City of the mightiest of Capitals—in the fullness of his professional Career—in the greenness of a healthy old age—in the radiance of Fame—and the Complacency of self-earned Riches—that a domestic Affliction would lay him in the Earth—with the meanest of Malefactors—in a Cross road with the Stake in his body—if the Verdict of Insanity did not redeem his ashes from the sentence of the Laws he had lived by interpreting or misinterpreting, and died in Violating. . . . Perhaps previous to his Annihilation he felt a portion of what he contributed his legal mite to make me feel,—but I have lived, lived to see him a Sexagenary Suicide—It was not in vain that I invoked Nemesis in the Midnight of Rome from the Awfullest of her Ruins.—Fare you well."[3]

Angrier still than his "Curse of Forgiveness," was this *danse macabre* on Romilly's grave. If Byron did in fact send the letter,* a "Verdict of Insanity" might more reasonably have been pronounced upon the writer by Annabella; it would only confirm all that she herself had experienced.

"Fidgetting" until the Hansons took the hint and hastened their departure, Byron was no less cranky when they left. He suspected Hanson of padding a bill that Kinnaird had just received and asked Kinnaird to insist on an itemized accounting; when Kinnaird then suggested that the lawyer might have falsified papers relating to the

---

*The letter survives in draft in the archives of John Murray. It is not among the large collection of the poet's letters to Lady Byron in the Lovelace Byron archive, suggesting that it may not have been sent.

Newstead sale for his own interests, Byron blew up: Why had not Kinnaird, his financial manager, voiced this suspicion earlier, before he had signed all the documents? Angered by his friends' failure to protect his interests in England, he was now harassed by domestic turmoil in his new home.

In late August, the tempestuous Margarita left her husband and moved into the Palazzo Mocenigo. Byron claimed that she arrived uninvited but, as he admitted, his "indolence" made him no match for this force of nature. At the outset he had little cause to regret his passivity; the Fornarina soon made herself indispensable. Belowstairs, she established a reign of terror, boxing ears and cracking heads. Much as he valued his tranquillity, Byron suffered the screams and howls because his new housekeeper ended the thievery assumed by Venetian servants as part of their salary from foreigners, and thereby reduced his household bills to less than half of what they had been. Childless herself, Margarita adored Allegra, whose nurse had just given notice. Pleading harassment by the menservants, Elise rejoined the Shelleys when they left for Naples in late October. (In fact, the young woman had been seduced by Shelley's domestic, Paolo Foggi, and wanted to rejoin her lover.)

Still, no evidence of devotion to his household could have enthralled Byron as much as Magarita's passionate abandon: to sex, laughter—even hatred: "For if I began in a rage she always finished by making me laugh, with some Venetian pantaloonery or other—and the Gypsy knew this well enough—as well as her other powers of persuasion—and exerted them with the usual tact and success of all She-things—high and low—they are all alike for that," he told Murray. Losing his temper with her for once, Byron called her *vacca*—cow. Without missing a beat, she curtsied prettily and replied: *"Vacca* sua, *'cellenza,"* "*Your* cow, your excellency."

All too soon, however, the Fornarina was undone by her fantasies and so crazed by jealousy that she lost all her native good sense. Encouraged by the kindly attentions of la Benzoni, she yearned to sweep through the great world on Byron's arm, thus destroying the charm of her otherness: "In her fazziolo—the dress of the lower orders—she looked beautiful," Byron explained, "but alas! she longed for a hat and feathers and all I could say or do (and I said much) could not prevent this travestie. I put the first into the fire—but I got tired of burning them before she did of buying them." Having won the battle of the feathers, Margarita moved to the next round: "Then she would have her gowns with a *tail*—like a lady forsooth," Byron jeered, but since her pronunciation of the Venetian word for "train," *cua,* sounded like a less publicly exhibited female attribute, Byron collapsed into laughter, "and she dragged this diabolical tail after her every where."

Soon, however, Margarita began beating any young woman in the house she could lay her hands on. She took to intercepting Byron's mail; unable to read, she studied the shapes of the letters to see if they yielded the gender of the writer. Earlier, Byron's rages had been able to quell hers; now even for him she became "quite ungovernable." Ordered to leave, she departed with threats of revenge, to return the next day while Byron was at dinner. Shades of Caroline Lamb, she had broken a glass door that led from the great hall to the staircase, and marching straight to the table where Byron sat, snatched the knife from his hand. Fletcher disarmed her, and he and the other servants were ordered to conduct her home. She went quietly, but a short time later, the men returned with great commotion. She had thrown herself into the canal. Unable to swim, she may have counted on being rescued and her remorseful lover's allowing her back. Byron, however, was unyielding: "She made many attempts to return, but no more violent ones."

Still, our final image of her is the most beautiful of all of Byron's portraits of women, fictional or real. One afternoon, despite gathering storm clouds, Byron insisted that his gondoliers take him to the Lido; heading straight into a squall on their return, the gondola barely made it back through the churning waters of the lagoon. When they arrived at nightfall, Byron recalled, Margarita was waiting: "I found her on the open steps of the Mocenigo palace on the Grand Canal—with her great black eyes flashing through her tears and the long dark hair which was streaming drenched with rain over her brows & breast;—she was perfectly exposed to the storm—and the wind blowing her hair & dress about her tall thin figure—and the lightning flashing round her—with the waves rolling at her feet—made her look like Medea alighted from her chariot or the Sybil of the tempest that was rolling around her." Her joy and relief, "like a tigress over her recovered cubs," expressed itself in cursing Byron roundly before rushing into the house to swear at the boatmen for exposing him to the storm!

Only the refusal of any gondolier to put out into the lagoon had prevented her from searching for her lover, the servants told Byron. Then, collapsing into despair, she "sate down on the steps in all the thickest of the Squall—and would neither be removed nor comforted."

That her behavior on this occasion exhibited "sufficient regard for me" Byron modestly acknowledged, and being susceptible always to dramatic proofs of love, he put up with the destructive jealousy and her "demolition of head dresses and handkerchiefs"[4] belonging to other women whom Byron paraded through the palace. Since he also had a casino at his disposal, we may find a whiff of cruelty in bringing partners home for sexual assignations. Margarita's fierce possessiveness needed small encouragement; at the Cavalchina, the masked ball celebrating the last night of Carnival, the "Pythoness,"[5] as Byron now also called his lover, sprang at a Madame Contarini, tearing the mask from her face "for no other reason but because she happened to be leaning on my arm," he noted innocently. When Byron objected, on the grounds that her victim was a lady, Margarita, furious, retorted, "So what! I am a Venetian!"[6]

However exciting, these dramas were exhausting him—and his purse: "I have quite given up Concubinage," he told his banker wearily when at last the defeated Fornarina was delivered back to her husband. Lust—Shakespeare's "expense of spirit in a waste of shame"—was costly in every sense. He calculated to Kinnaird and Hobhouse that since living abroad, he had spent half of his income on women—over £5,000.* He now instructed Kinnaird:

"Whatever Brain-money—you get in my account from Murray—pray remit me—I will never consent to pay away what I *earn*—that is *mine*—& what I get by my brains—I will spend on my b[alloc]ks—as long as I have a tester or a testicle remaining. . . . My balance—also—my balance—& a copyright—I have another Canto—too—ready—& then there will be my half year in June†—recollect—*I* care for nothing but 'monies.' "[7]

Less than a decade separated the young man who loftily refused to take any payment for his copyrights and the poet who, sounding like any inky Grub Street scribbler, announced that he cared only for "monies" to spend on his "b——ks."

It was sobering, now, for Byron to learn that Hobhouse's answer to the passage of time was to finally grasp the nettle of a career decision. As it happened, Romilly's death left a parliamentary vacancy for Westminister, and Hobby's friends all urged him to stand. Any feelings of regret or envy Byron may have harbored for his own failed political

---

*Initially, Margarita's husband, the failed baker, had lodged several complaints to the police, citing his lordship for carrying off his wife. Byron's retort to the constabulary—that he was welcome to come and take her back at any time—may have called his bluff, or Byron's payments to his "housekeeper" were used to compensate the bereft husband for his loss.

†The time when mortgage installments and other income from Lady Byron's estate were due.

ambitions were sublimated into enthusiastic support for the candidate: "Now is your time—& remember that in your very *Start* you have overtaken all whom you thought before you—above all, don't *diffide* in yourself," he urged his friend, who was all too prone to paralyzing self-doubt "& don't be afraid of your own talents—I tell you as I have told others—that you think too humbly of them—you have already shown yourself fit for very great things."[8]

With no great conviction other than a hope of increasing his "Brain-money," Byron had sent Canto I of his new poem to Murray in late December. At the head of the 222 stanzas was a dedication announcing that *Don Juan*, earlier described by the poet as a "little quietly facetious about everything," was, in fact, an attack dog in verse.[9]

The luckless dedicatee of the new work was the poet laureate Robert Southey, whom Byron had first met in 1813. The son of a shopkeeper, the precociously talented Southey had risen to become the social peer and toast of the Reform Whig aristocracy. The two poets' earlier encounter had been a wary mutual sizing up. Byron always felt disadvantaged by a splendid figure of a man, and he was forced to acknowledge that the tall and handsome Southey, fourteen years his senior, was also "the best looking bard I have seen for some time," he wrote to Moore. "To have that poet's head and shoulders, I would almost have written his Sapphics. He is certainly a prepossessing person to look on, and a man of talent, and all that, and—*there* is his eulogy,"[10] he joked. (Southey's grudging encomium to the younger poet was characteristically self-righteous: "I saw a man whom in voice, manner, and countenance, I liked very much more than either his character or his writings had given me reason to expect," he wrote to his wife.)[11]

Six years later, Byron had cast Southey as a watchword for a careerist devoid of poetic ability or personal merit; a political turncoat and boot-licking opportunist who stood for the worst of romantic mannerisms:

> Bob Southey! You're a poet—poet Laureate,
>   And representative of all the race;
> Although 'tis true you turn'd out a Tory at
>   Last,—yours has lately been a common case:—
>   .   .   .   .
> You, Bob! are rather insolent, you know,
>   At being disappointed in your wish
> To supersede all warblers here below,
>   And be the only Blackbird in the dish;
> And then you overstrain yourself, or so,

>   And tumble downward like the flying fish
>   Gasping on deck, because you soar too high, Bob,
>   And fall, for lack of moisture, quite adry, Bob![12]

Reading these last lines three stanzas into the dedication, Byron's publisher, along with all his friends, were aghast. A "dry Bob" was slang for "dry humping." The poet had been away from England too long if he believed that he or Murray could get away with publishing a frontal attack on the cultural establishment that included obscenity rarely if ever seen on the printed page.

What had turned Byron's guarded admiration for the man and even his "talent" into pure hatred waiting for an opportunity to strike? In November Byron had alerted Hobhouse that he was sending the first canto to him, in care of Murray, along with its dedication to "Bob Southey—bitter as necessary . . . I will tell you why.—The Son of a Bitch on his return from Switzerland two years ago—said that Shelley and I 'had formed a League of Incest and practiced our precepts with &c'— he lied like a rascal—for they *were not Sisters—one* being Godwin's daughter by Mary Wollstonecraft—and the other the daughter of the present Mrs. G[odwin] by a *former* husband. . . . He lied in another sense—for there was no promiscuous intercourse—my commerce being limited to the carnal knowledge of the Miss C[lairmont]." But with his old friend, Byron could be honest; he had taken his revenge, clothing a vendetta in the robes of high-minded polemic: "The Attack contains no allusion to the cause—but—some good verses—and all political & poetical."[13] Not that Byron was underhanded; he even asked Murray to alert the victim to what was in store for him.

While they were still stunned by the attack on the poet laureate, Byron's friends, reading further in the dedication, found that the poet had turned his guns on a still more powerful figure, Robert Stewart, Lord Castlereagh, former Lieutenant Governor of Ireland, now Foreign Secretary, whose brief at the Congress of Vienna had been to secure the restoration of monarchy throughout Europe. Comparing Southey the sycophant to *sublime* Milton the lifelong "tyrant-hater," Byron asks, "Would *he* adore a sultan? *he* obey / The intellectual eunuch Castlereagh?" Thereafter, the minister, "emasculated to the marrow," is referred to only with the neuter pronoun:

>   Cold-blooded, smooth-faced, placid miscreant!
>   Dabbling its sleek young hands in Erin's gore,
>   And thus for wider carnage taught to pant,

> Transferr'd to gorge upon a sister-shore,
> The vulgarest tool that tyranny could want[14]

Byron was outraged by his friends' fearful pleadings to omit the dedication, or at least to cut the obscene and libelous content. From the freedom of Italy, he accused them of becoming a "cursed puritanical committee." Protracted negotiations followed: whether to keep the offending passages but publish the stanzas anonymously, or cut two "dry Bobs" and leave the "eunuch Castlereagh" to stand; defiant, Byron considered a private printing of fifty copies. When the first two cantos were published in July 1819, neither author nor publisher was mentioned on the title page. Even then, the dedication was suppressed, appearing in print only after the poet's death.

With its outrageous gibes, the dedication looked back to the provocations of the younger Byron—the "great Hater." But times had changed: Threatened by libel laws, the freewheeling, provocative writers of the Regency had lost their nerve. Byron's friends at home scrutinized the early cantos of *Don Juan* with the eyes of censors, unaware that they were reading an overture to what Shelley was alone in recognizing as the "greatest long poem in English since *Paradise Lost.*"[15] Byron himself preferred to be tentative; these first cantos were an "experiment,"[16] a new play on old "materials": high romance and epic thrills, threaded with episodes from the drama of his own life, interleaved with history unfolding on a world stage, and all told in the intimate, conversational style of everyday life. Indeed, his epigraph from Horace announced the object of his experiment: *Difficile est proprie communia dicere*—"It is hard to speak of ordinary things in the right way."

In a real sense, every poem Byron had written, from his first schoolboy verses to *Beppo*, had been an apprenticeship for *Don Juan*. He reread the classics he had hated at Harrow, studying Horace's conversational style and accounts of epic warfare on sea and land in Virgil and Homer; he had long since assimilated his beloved Augustans, Pope and Dryden, counting himself their heir. Touchstones of his own efforts, these disabused forebears, dismissed by his contemporaries, now became another measure of the Romantics' presumption. Moreover, since living in Italy, he had delighted ever more in her writers who shared his own debunking impulse, subverting the classics in works whose hyphenated genre—mock-heroic, serio-comic—bore witness to their double game: turning epic, tragedy, and romance on their heads. With *Beppo* he had tested the waters, but with a model boat. For all its slyly drawn parallels with another tight little island, his Venetian tale was still insular, even miniaturized. That vessel was too small to convey his vision of a moral Ice Age that was paralyzing Europe; from the French Revolution through the present Restoration, Byron saw an inexorable retreat from the flood tide of freedom, back to absolute power and its absolute corruption. And England's role in this betrayal, he came to feel, must be exposed. More and more, his own life seemed a tracing of the blighted hopes, rejection, and loss of oppressed peoples everywhere. While his enemies—the enemies of liberty: Southey, Words-worth, and Coleridge—flourished, rewarded for bad poetry and politi-cal expediency, he had been cast out of his own country, deprived of wife, child, sister, and reputation.

The *War and Peace* of English poetry, *Don Juan* manages to contain all this and more: an epic sweep that moves from Spain, to the East, and to Russia before ending in England, but also the constant deflation of its own large ambitions. At the same time that Byron's broad canvas foretells the scope of the great nineteenth-century novels, the poet's own sensibilities echo the picaresque eighteenth-century novels of his early reading, Smollett and Fielding, with their bawdy humor and sly inver-sions of vice and virtue. Unlike these prose narratives, however, *Don Juan* has no beginning, middle, or end. It draws us in, not to learn "what happens next" but to hear what this seductive, confidential, teas-ing voice is going to tell us.

Cautiously, Byron emphasized the provisional nature of his new work. In answer to Murray's query about the nature of the beast—beyond the two cantos Byron had just completed—Byron replied, "You ask me for the plan of Donny Johnny: I *have* no plan—I *had* no plan; but I had or have materials. . . . If it don't take, I will leave it off where it is, with all due respect to the Public. . . . Why, Man, the Soul of such writing is its license; at least the *liberty* of that license, if one likes."[17] As always, we hear the pull and tug of Byron's conflict: between the defi-ant patrician demanding the "*liberty* of license" and the fearful poet promising that "if it don't take," he would stop with these first cantos. Byron kept on writing *Don Juan* for five years, despite the fact that what was published did not "take," either with critics or the public. Even his adoring new mistress begged him to abandon the poem (he resumed work in secret, so as not to pain her). But he also put it aside to write other major poetry, including his verse dramas. Ultimately the two cantos became seventeen. The last remained unfinished, "stopped" only by the poet's death.

Among *Don Juan*'s enthralled readers was Virginia Woolf, but as a writer she also studied the poem for the secret of its fascination. "It is the most readable poem of its length ever written, I suppose: a quality which it owes in part to . . . its method," she decided. "This method is a discovery in itself. It's what one has looked for in vain—an elastic shape which will hold whatever you choose to put into it. . . . He could say whatever came into his head. He wasn't committed to be poetical; and thus escaped his evil genius of the false romantic and imaginative."[18]

How Byron evades the demons of romanticism is a measure of his own genius and a matter of two inspired inventions. There is first his narrator, "a plain man and in a single station," who, alas, aspires to the title of "epic poet."

> I want a hero: an uncommon want,
>   When every year and month sends forth a new one,
> Till after cloying the gazettes with cant,
>   The age discovers he is not the true one;
> Of such as these I should not care to vaunt,
>   I'll therefore take our ancient friend Don Juan,
> We all have seen him in the pantomime
> Sent to the devil somewhat ere his time.[19]

After a mock-epic enumeration of generals, admirals, and emperors classical and modern, our aspiring Homer must concede:

> Brave men were living before Agamemnon
>   And since, exceeding valorous and sage,
> A good deal like him too, though quite the same none;
>   But then they shone not on the poet's page,
> And so have been forgotten:—I condemn none,
>   But can't find any in the present age
> Fit for my poem (that is, for my new one);
> So, as I said, I'll take my friend Don Juan.

With supreme confidence, our narrator promises to improve on the classics; following Horace, "most epic poets plunge in 'medias res,' " leaving the hero to tell the reader "what went before":

> That is the usual method, but not mine—
>   My way is to begin at the beginning;
> The regularity of my design
>   Forbids all wandering as the worst of sinning.[20]

As deficient in epic genius as in self-knowledge, our narrator's voice—
the voice of a reliable friend of the family—is his dispensation. He has
a tale to tell, and if we bear with his style of free association, with
its digressions, conversational asides, scraps of remembered reading,
and opinions on every topic, he will get there. We even forgive his occasional meddling in his subjects' lives:

> I loathe that low vice curiosity,
>   But if there's any thing in which I shine
> 'Tis in arranging all my friends' affairs.
>   Not having, of my own, domestic cares.[21]

For, as we soon learn, the protagonist of his tale could use some protective intervention. Deconstructing the figure of sinister seducer, Byron's
"Donny Johnny" is a proto-hero so innocent, unformed, and passive that
his very name becomes a running joke. This Don Juan is no Casanova,
he's Candide. Even the pronunciation of his name is enlisted to keep the
reader off balance: "Ju-an" rhymes—appropriately—with "new one."

A young noble of Seville, Juan at sixteen is a pious mama's boy, dedicated to heaven by a mother from hell. Donna Inez is "a learned lady,
famed / For every branch of every science known." She had, however, a
specialty:

> Her favourite science was the mathematical,
>   Her noblest virtue was her magnanimity,
> Her wit (she sometimes tried at wit) was Attic all,
>   Her serious sayings darken'd to sublimity;
> In short, in all things she was fairly what I call
>   A prodigy . . .[22]

His parents' unhappy union announces *Don Juan* as vividly autobiographical. Does Donna Inez begin to seem familiar? Her creator has a
few more hints as to his model:

> Some women use their tongues—she look'd a lecture,
>   Each eye a sermon, and her brow a homily,
> An all-in-all—sufficient self-director,
>   Like the lamented late Sir Samuel Romilly[23]

Predictably, the marriage of this "walking calculation . . . perfect
past all parallel" to Don José, "a mortal of the careless kind," was
doomed. All too soon, "Don José, like a lineal son of Eve / Went pluck-

ing various fruit without her leave." There is no doubt, however, where the poet stands on his hero's mismatched parents. In a couplet that some have taken as irrefutable proof of Byron's genius, he urges:

> But—Oh! ye lords of ladies intellectual,
> Inform us truly, have they not hen-peck'd you all?[24]

But here the poet's antic heights of rhyme were laid low by bitter memories still smoldering:

> For Inez call'd some druggists and physicians,
>   And tried to prove her loving lord was *mad*,
> But as he had some lucid intermissions,
>   She next decided he was only *bad*;
>
> . . . .
>
> She kept a journal, where his faults were noted,
>   And open'd certain trunks of books and letters,
> All which might, if occasion served, be quoted;
>   And then she had all Seville for abettors,
> Besides her good old grandmother (who doted);
>   The hearers of her case became repeaters
> Then advocates, inquisitors, and judges,
> Some for amusement, others for old grudges.
>
> . . . .
>
>   Calmly she heard each calumny that rose,
> And saw *his* agonies with such sublimity,
> That all the world exclaim'd "What magnanimity!"[25]

Snuffling over the fate of Don José, the martyred husband, Byron's satirical edge sagged to self-pity:

> It was a trying moment that which found him
> Standing alone beside his desolate hearth,
>   Where all his household gods lay shiver'd round him;
> No choice was left his feelings or his pride
> Save death or Doctors' Commons—so he died.[26]

After hounding Juan's father to his death, Donna Inez takes up the business of educating her son into asexual purity, separating him from his peers and shielding him from any reading that "hints continuation of the species." This last requires even censorship of the household prayer book, and is our first hint of Mama's pious hypocrisy:

The Missal, too (it was a family Missal)
    Was ornamented in a sort of way
Which ancient mass-books often are, and this all
    Kinds of grotesques illumined; and how they,
Who saw those figures on the margin kiss all,
    Could turn their optics to the text and pray
Is more than I know—but Don Juan's mother
Kept this herself, and gave her son another.[27]

Such fanatically maintained innocence is set up for a fall; Juan, unchaperoned, is permitted the company of Donna Julia, "married, charming,
chaste, and twenty-three," and his mother's dear friend. Another bond
united the ladies: Don Alfonso, Julia's husband of twice her age.

Some people whisper (but, no doubt, they lie,
    For malice still imputes some private end)
That Inez had, ere Don Alfonso's marriage,
    Forgot with him her very prudent carriage.[28]

If Annabella was the principal inspiration for Donna Inez,* the shade of
Catherine Byron also lurks in a dragon mother's humiliating passion for
the dancing master. Juan's ignorance and Julia's arrogance ("She now
determined that a virtuous woman / Should rather face and overcome
temptation") turn the hero's first epic adventure into bedroom farce. At
the approach of the jealous husband, the stripling is hidden at the foot
of his mistress's bed. When Don Alfonso returns for another look, however, a pair of large shoes gives the lovers away: Juan is forced to flee
half naked, but a worse fate awaits the errant wife.

    Byron never scanted the disparate punishments suffered by men and
women for sexual misconduct: Donna Inez merely arranges a convenient
grand tour for her son ("To mend his former morals, or get new.").
Julia, divorced and disgraced, is banished to a convent. Her sin lay in
getting caught. Here, the pathos of her circumstances and her acceptance of suffering elevate the frisky matron to tragic heroine. Byron's
new skills in the serio-comic genre enabled him to shift from satirizing
Julia's self-delusion to speaking movingly in her voice. Some three weeks
after he sent the first printer's copy of Canto I to Murray, the poet added
six new stanzas in the form of a letter sent by Juan's grieving mistress,

---

*His savage caricature of Annabella as Donna Inez added further to the arguments
of Byron's friends against the publication of *Don Juan*.

incarcerated in a nunnery, to her young lover about to embark on the high seas. The restrained verse is a stately portrait of a mourning queen:

> I loved, I love you, for that love have lost
>   State, station, heaven, mankind's, my own esteem,
> And yet can not regret what it hath cost,
>   So dear is still the memory of that dream;
> Yet, if I name my guilt, 'tis not to boast,
>   None can deem harshlier of me than I deem:
> I trace this scrawl because I cannot rest—
> I've nothing to reproach, nor to request.

It is Donna Julia to whom the poet gives his most famous lines on love:

> Man's love is of his life a thing apart,
>   'Tis woman's whole existence; man may range
> The court, camp, church, the vessel, and the mart,
>   Sword, gown, gain, glory, offer in exchange
> Pride, fame, ambition, to fill up his heart,
>   And few there are whom these can not estrange;
> Man has all these resources, we but one,
>   To love again, and be again undone.[29]

Leaving Julia as she seals her letter, with Juan on his way to Cadiz to board his boat, Byron returns to his narrator. But the gossipy storyteller has been changed by his tale: He now lusts for literary success, which enables his creator to set him up as straw man. This first installment, our narrator assures us, is only a market test and, raiding Byron's letter to Murray, he confides:

> This was Don Juan's earliest scrape; but whether
>   I shall proceed with his adventures is
> Dependent on the public altogether;
>
> .   .   .   .
>
> And if their approbation we experience
> Perhaps they'll have some more about a year hence.[30]

Unlike the poet with his planless plan, his surrogate will doggedly stick to the recipe for successful epic: "Divided in twelve books; each book containing, / With love, and war, a heavy gale at sea, / A list of ships, and captains, and kings reigning." Further:

> I've got new mythological machinery,
> And very handsome supernatural scenery.[31]

If legitimate efforts to please the public do not suffice, the ambitious maker of epics will stoop to others:

> For fear some prudish readers should grow skittish,
> I've bribed my grandmother's review—the British.[32]

Having had his fun with this "plain gentleman" of poetical pretensions, Byron's high spirits subside into melancholy reflection; as a work in progress, *Don Juan* pulsates to the artist's emotional polarities. Like Donna Julia's in her grief, his mood "trembled as magnetic needles do." With its accelerating transitions, Canto I announces the poet as quick-change artist, whisking on and off his masks of comedy and tragedy.

> No more—no more—Oh! never more on me
>   The freshness of the heart can fall like dew,
> Which out of all the lovely things we see
>   Extracts emotions beautiful and new,
>
>   . . . .
>
> No more—no more—Oh! never more, my heart,
>   Canst thou be my sole world, my universe!
> Once all in all, but now a thing apart,
>   Thou canst not be my blessing or my curse:
> The illusion's gone for ever, and thou art
>   Insensible, I trust, but none the worse,
> And in thy stead I've got a deal of judgment,
> Though heaven knows how it ever found a lodgement.[33]

At thirty, feeling the approach of middle age, when common sense prevails over passion, Byron returned through sixteen-year-old Juan to the rule of heart over head. In Canto II the tearful youth watches from his ship as his native land disappears from view. Now, however, his creator refuses to sympathize:

> I'd weep, but mine is not a weeping Muse,
>   And such light griefs are not a thing to die on;
> Young men should travel, if but to amuse
>   Themselves; and the next time their servants tie on
> Behind their carriages their new portmanteau,
> Perhaps it may be lined with this my canto.[34]

Disabused himself of belief in eternal love, the poet is no longer inclined to leave this belief for his hero. As he clutches Donna Julia's letter, Juan's vows of deathless passion yield to near-death sufferings of sea-sickness:

> "Sooner shall heaven kiss earth"—(here he fell sicker)
> "Oh, Julia! what is every other woe?—
> (For God's sake let me have a glass of liquor,
> Pedro, Battista, help me down below.)
> Julia, my love!—(you rascal, Pedro, quicker)—
> Oh Julia! (this curst vessel pitches so)—
> Beloved Julia, hear me still beseeching!"
> (Here he grew inarticulate with reaching.)[35]

Torturing his rhymes along with Juan's digestive tract, Byron gives fair warning of the moral theme of the new canto: materialism, or how the body's imperatives drive out all higher feelings. A hero who vomits his lovesickness away is nothing compared to the horrors to come.

Bound for Leghorn, Juan's ship, the ill-named *Trinidada*, runs into a gale. Her rudder smashed, her stern torn, water pours through every opening. Then, just as the pumps have almost succeeded in drying her, "A squall came on, and while some guns broke loose / A gust—which all descriptive power transcends— / Laid with one blast the ship on her beam ends." Discipline breaks down, and the crew, in terror of death, threatens a riot to get at the supply of rum. For the first time, Juan shows his heroic mettle, guarding the caskroom with a pair of pistols:

> "Give us more grog," they cried, "for it will be
> All one an hour hence." Juan answer'd, "No!
> 'Tis true that death awaits both you and me,
> But let us die like men, not sink below
> Like brutes" . . .

Setting a moral example allows no exceptions; reversing their roles, Juan repulses his preceptor: "And even Pedrillo, his most reverend tutor, / Was for some rum a disappointed suitor."[36] His natural heroism is instinctive—like the animal appetites of his fellows.

From his avid reading of shipwreck lore, including the memoirs of his grandfather "Foulweather Jack," Byron found his materials, first-hand descriptions of the physical and emotional horrors of death at sea, and of the differing ways men meet catastrophe:

> Some lash'd them in their hammocks, some put on
>   Their best clothes, as if going to a fair;
> Some cursed the day on which they saw the sun,
>   And gnash'd their teeth, and howling, tore their hair;
> And others went on as they had begun,
>   Getting the boats out, being well aware
> That a tight boat will live in a rough sea,
> Unless with breakers close beneath her lee.[37]

The longboat and a cutter were all the lifesaving craft that could be stored; together they held fewer than half of the two hundred passengers and crew. As to provisions, "Two casks of biscuit, and a keg of butter, / Were all that could be thrown into the cutter."

The *Trinidada* sinks, "going down head foremost" with some left aboard:

> Then some leap'd overboard with dreadful yell,
>   As eager to anticipate their grave;
> And the sea yawn'd around her like a hell,
>   And down she suck'd with her the whirling wave,
> Like one who grapples with his enemy,
> And strives to strangle him before he die.

Byron's final image of the disaster is the most dreadful, that of drowning men, scattered and alone in their last moments of struggle. The ocean has swallowed the ship, "then all was hush'd,"

> Save the wild wind and the remorseless dash
> Of billows; but at intervals there gush'd,
>   Accompanied with a convulsive splash,
> A solitary shriek, the bubbling cry
> Of some strong swimmer in his agony.[38]

In the high waves following the storm, the "poor little cutter" with its nine passengers goes under. Watching it sink, the thirty sailors crowded into the longboat "grieved for those who perish'd with the cutter, / And also for the biscuit casks and butter."[39]

No two lines Byron would ever write unleashed more censure than the psychological reality expressed in this jaunty couplet. In a culture whose Christianity, however nominal, was supposed to keep the baser instincts at bay, to describe men reduced to their animal appetites and,

worse, to accept this cheerfully as a fact of life was blasphemy. His critics felt too accused by Byron's materialist assumptions to see that his
laughter was based on a common humanity: Faced with starvation, we
should all mourn the "biscuit casks and butter" as much as our lost
shipmates. Now, calm seas, blue skies, and sleep lull the survivors into
optimism, leading them to consume the small hoard of provisions all at
once. There follow four days under a blazing sun without food or drink.
Don Juan's dog, his father's old spaniel, is killed and divided among the
ravenous men. At first his owner refuses to partake of his pet. Then
hunger overcomes his scruple and he divides a forepaw with Pedrillo.
Slowly and ominously, Byron prepares us for the inevitable:

> They lay like carcases; and hope was none,
>   Save in the breeze that came not; savagely
> They glared upon each other—all was done,
>   Water, and wine, and food,—and you might see
> The longings of the cannibal arise
> (Although they spoke not) in their wolfish eyes.[40]

In these first cantos alone, *Don Juan* is stamped as the masterpiece of
Byron's maturity. His narrative skills achieve pace and polish worlds
beyond the earlier "tales." In terms of psychological penetration, no
work had come close to the authority of his insights and the force of
their expression, all within the formal constraints of ottava rima; thus
the process by which the unthinkable thrust its way into the consciousness of the starving men:

> At length one whisper'd his companion, who
>   Whisper'd another, and thus it went round,
> And then into a hoarser murmur grew,
>   An ominous, and wild, and desperate sound,
> And when his comrade's thought each sufferer knew,
>   'Twas but his own, suppress'd till now, he found:
> And out they spoke of lots for flesh and blood,
> And who should die to be his fellow's food.
>
> . . . .
>
> The lots were made, and mark'd, and mix'd, and handed,
>   In silent horror, and their distribution
> Lull'd even the savage hunger which demanded,
>   Like the Promethean vulture, this pollution;
> None in particular had sought or plann'd it,

'Twas nature gnaw'd them to this resolution,
By which none were permitted to be neuter—
And the lot fell on Juan's luckless tutor.[41]

Creeping back into the final couplet, Byron's waggish rhyme signals
the horrors to come as more gruesome details are displaced—and
emphasized—by means of the jingle. Offered first choice in lieu of fee,
the thirsty ship's surgeon prefers to drink the tutor's blood, after which

Part was divided, part thrown in the sea,
    And such things as the entrails and the brains
Regaled two sharks, who follow'd o'er the billow—
The sailors ate the rest of poor Pedrillo.[42]

At the same time that Byron the behaviorist allows that extreme situations level human beings to animal needs, Byron the Calvinist metes
punishment and salvation to individuals according to their Christian
example: Juan and a few others abstain from feasting on human flesh
(" 'Twas not to be expected that he should, / Even in extremity of their
disaster, / Dine with them on his pastor and his master"). Those who
feast on their fellow man

Went raging mad— Lord! how they did blaspheme!
And foam and roll, with strange convulsions rack'd,
    Drinking salt-water like a mountain-stream,
Tearing, and grinning, howling, screeching, swearing,
And, with hyaena laughter, died despairing.[43]

Others, however, are preserved by a stoical resignation to human loss.
Of two fathers among the crew, the one who, on learning of his son's
death, says, "Heaven's will be done! / I can do nothing," and watches
the boy "thrown Into the deep without a tear or groan,"[44] lives. The
emotionally connected father, cradling his dying boy in his arms, cannot
survive the blow; as his son's body is cast overboard, "he himself sunk
down all dumb and shivering, / And gave no sign of life, save his limbs
quivering."[45] Byron's remark on Ada's birth, "Oh what an implement of
Torture I've acquired," echoes in his chilling moral here: The distant,
self-protective parent survives.

When land is finally sighted, Juan alone is able to swim to shore; the
poet's own proficiency has saved his hero's life. Byron's pride in the
mythic feat of *his* youth compels him to remind the reader that although

the lad "Had often turn'd the art to some account," he has yet to surpass his creator:

> A better swimmer you could scarce see ever,
>   He could, perhaps, have pass'd the Hellespont,
> As once (a feat on which ourselves we prided)
>   Leander, Mr. Ekenhead, and I did.[46]

Juan's reward for his heroic sufferings is idyllic love on a tropical isle. Like his predecessor Mazeppa, he awakens from his near-death experience in the arms of a beautiful young woman. Haidée is a pirate princess and only daughter of Lambro, a "sea attorney" whose Cycladic stronghold becomes the paradise of the two lovers. Fearful that her father would sell him into slavery, Haidée hides the handsome shipwrecked youth in the cave to which she first carried his lifeless and naked body. Once again, Juan finds himself a happily passive prisoner of love. Emerging only in darkness, when

> They fear'd no eyes nor ears on that lone beach,
>   They felt no terrors from the night, they were
> All in all to each other: though their speech
>   Was broken words, they *thought* a language there,—[47]

Theirs is the dream of union without words; unable to understand each other's language, the lovers avoid the civilized traps of lies and misunderstandings. Haidée, moreover, embodies a Byronic ideal of woman before the Fall. Transparent with truth, innocent of fear, expectation, or demand, she lives only in the present:

> Haidée spoke not of scruples, ask'd no vows,
>   Nor offer'd any; she had never heard
> Of plight and promises to be a spouse,
>   Of perils by a loving maid incurr'd;
> She was all which pure ignorance allows,
>   And flew to her young mate like a young bird;
> And, never having dreamt of falsehood, she
> Had not one word to say of constancy.[48]

Still, Byron recognized Haidée as fantasy; a child-woman, she has nothing to do with her real-life counterparts whose social and sexual constraints he elsewhere acknowledged as their "she condition." No feminist writer of any century has equaled Byron's bleak mapping of women's lives as shrunken possibility; as one who had both exploited and suffered from their dependence, he had reason to know:

> Alas! the love of women! it is known
>   To be a lovely and a fearful thing;
> For all of theirs upon that die is thrown,
>   And if 'tis lost, life hath no more to bring
> To them but mockeries of the past alone,
>   And their revenge is as the tiger's spring,
> Deadly, and quick, and crushing; yet, as real
> Torture is theirs, what they inflict they feel.
>
> They are right; for man, to man so oft unjust,
>   Is always so to women; one sole bond
> Awaits them, treachery is all their trust;
>   Taught to conceal, their bursting hearts despond
> Over their idol, till some wealthier lust
>   Buys them in marriage—and what rests beyond?
> A thankless husband, next a faithless lover,
> Then dressing, nursing, praying, and all's over.
>
> Some take a lover, some take drams or prayers,
>   Some mind their household, others dissipation,
> Some run away, and but exchange their cares,
>   Losing the advantage of a virtuous station;
> Few changes e'er can better their affairs,
>   Theirs being an unnatural situation,
> From the dull palace to the dirty hovel:
> Some play the devil, others write a novel.[49]

What then was he to do with a sexualized Haidée, cast out from the purity of paradise? He had also to decide on the fate of his candid youth Don Juan, who, having forgotten one woman, was poised to become a man and forget another—and another. For the time being, however, Byron leaves his young lovers in limbo. Reflections on his own volatile feelings, however, moved him to mourn male inconstancy. Promiscuity, beyond tormenting women, also proved debilitating to men: "Whereas if one sole lady pleased for ever / How pleasant for the heart, as well as liver!"[50]

His final bilious remarks on ending Canto II point to the intestinal problems Byron had suffered since the beginning of the year, probably the effect of Carnival—his third now. He had been able to keep nothing in his stomach, he told Hobhouse, nor was his illness remedied by his friends' response to the new work. Now that both cantos had been received and passed around, the question of publication—unadulterated, emasculated, or not at all—was at a stalemate. Byron could understand Murray's fears, but he was repelled by the cowardice of his friends, and he complained to the publisher, "If they had told me the poetry was bad—I would have acquiesced—but they say the contrary—& then talk to me about morality—the first time I ever heard the word from any body who was not a rascal that used it for a purpose. I maintain that it is the most moral of poems—but if people won't discover the moral that is their fault—not mine."[51]

In this state of disgust, Byron appeared at la Benzoni's *conversazione* on the evening of April 2 or 3. There he saw the young countess he had met the year before, then newly wedded to her middle-aged and twice-widowed bridegroom. On this occasion Teresa Guiccioli had not wanted to extend the evening beyond the theater; she was in mourning for three deaths in the past year, those of her mother, older sister, and her own four-day-old infant son. But her husband had insisted on going to Benzoni's, promising that they would stay for only a few minutes. Byron had hardly noticed the shy young bride twelve months earlier; now he could not tear himself from her side. Teresa, too, was instantly besotted and the few minutes she had reluctantly agreed to spend at the Benzoni's became hours. Before they separated that night, Byron asked Teresa to see him alone the next day. In a strange document in the form of a later written confession to her husband, she recalled her response: "I was so imprudent as to agree, on the condition that he would respect my honour," she claimed. "He promised and we settled on the hour after dinner in which you [Count Guiccioli] took your rest." At the appointed time an elderly gondolier appeared with a note and took her to Byron's gondola, where he was waiting; then "together we went to a casino of his. I was strong enough to resist at that first encounter but was so imprudent as to repeat it the next day, when my strength gave way—for B. was not a man to confine himself to sentiment. And the first step taken there was no further obstacle in the following days."

Not that she placed any in their way. As she further confessed to her husband, "I felt attracted to him by an irresistible force."[52] This would have scarcely distinguished her from hundreds of others. At nineteen, however, Teresa had a will and energy equal to her romantic nature. She had already determined that Byron would be hers, and she was fully prepared to stake her claim to the world.

Announcing to Hobhouse a few days later that he was "damnably in love,"[53] Byron expressed his misgivings in the face of Teresa's disdain for propriety, even as he confirmed her conquest. On the night they met, the "pretty fair-haired Girl last year out of convent horrified a correct company . . . by calling out to me '*Mio* Byron' in an audible key during a dead Silence of pause in the other prattlers." Teresa's indiscretion was the smallest proof of her confidence. Before Byron's gondolier spirited her to his casino the next day, she had already announced her terms: "One of her preliminaries is that I must never leave Italy," he told Hobhouse. "I have no desire to leave it—but I should not like to be frittered down into a regular cicisbeo. What shall I do? I am in love— and tired of promiscuous concubinage—& have now an opportunity of settling for life."[54] The question was only rhetorical; in his own mind the decision had been made. Before the spring was over, he would write to Teresa, "Every thing depends on you—my life—my honour—my love. . . . To love you is my crossing of the Rubicon & has already decided my Fate."[55]

CHAPTER 33

"A Stranger Loves a Lady of the Land"

EFORE THE YEAR was out, Byron would indeed "fritter down into a regular cicisbeo." Not, however, before putting up a struggle. He was no match, though, for the purposeful young woman who loved him—not too well, like all the others, but wisely. Her immediate sexual acquiescence followed by a public proclamation of their intimacy gave him pause, but only for a moment. Soon Teresa's unavailability in other ways lent her the mystery and provided the intrigue Byron required in romantic love.

Indeed, Countess Guiccioli remains a mysterious and contradictory figure: a romantic realist, shrewd more than intelligent, innocent and amoral, affected and feeling, worldly and provincial. Her biographer called her Byron's "last attachment."[1] In a crucial way, however, she was also his first, if by attachment we mean a devotion and loyalty that outlasted *l'amour fou*. For the first time, Byron felt—and acted on—a love that included concern for his lover that extended to her entire family, embraced as his own. Although she often bored and irritated him, Teresa's love for "*mio* Byron" was unwavering, and the poet, older now, was able to value her constancy. For the next five years he came as close as he would ever come to conjugal affection based on habit and trust. He would never have been an ideal husband, but at intervals with Teresa we glimpse Byron in something like a happy marriage.

TERESA GAMBA GHISELLI GUICCIOLI was the second daughter and one of seven children of a liberal nobleman, descendant of an ancient Romagnola family. Count Ruggero Gamba's progressive views included pride in the well-read Teresa, who, he said, "had been born with a book in her hand."[2] When her convent school proved to be more concerned with piety than learning, he allowed her to be instructed with her brothers by their tutor, before she and her sister were sent to the Santa Chiara convent in Faenza. Founded under Napoleon, the school provided an education exceptional for upper-class girls at that time, emphasizing the classics as well as French and Italian literature.* But for a land-poor noble, the reality of marrying off five daughters made lengthy studies for the older ones impractical. Thus, at sixteen, Teresa was summoned home from her beloved Santa Chiara to find a husband. A year later, with no likelier suitors, she was produced for the inspection of Count Alessandro Guiccioli, rich, propertied, and forty years her senior.

Years later, Teresa recalled the evening when, accompanied by her maternal uncle, her future husband appeared. She was brought into the *salone* and requested to stand stock still while the prospective fiancé circled around her slowly, examining the attributes of the young woman being offered as his wife.

Teresa was small—some said too small for her large bust—proportions that would cause Byron's friends to describe her as "dumpy." Everyone who saw her, however, praised her glowing skin, bright blue eyes, and luxuriant red-gold hair, worn lose in ringlets that tumbled to her shoulders; in contrast to the black-eyed beauties about whom Byron rhapsodized, she enjoyed the fair northern Italian coloring closest to the English rose. But it was Teresa's Latin vivacity that attracted as much as her appearance; when she laughed (as she did often), her pretty mouth revealed little white teeth like perfectly matched pearls.

Pleased by what he saw, as well as by the Gamba Ghiselli connections, reaching to the Vatican and as far as the Congress of Vienna, the Count agreed to overlook the bride's meager dowry. Of Teresa's family, only her father objected to the match, and he was overruled by his wife and in-laws. Nor did the bride-to-be protest, although she would have had paternal support in her objections. The Count was a rich and powerful man. Her sisters and friends chattered enviously about the best box at the opera, along with the coach and six horses she would soon enjoy. These would surely compensate for the bridegroom's age and certain unpleasant rumors that persisted about his past.

In Venice, Byron had heard about the Count's reputation, one worthy of a Borgia. The stories only added to the Countess's romantic aura,

---

*It was closed in the period of reaction that followed Napoleon's retreat, when Romagna became a papal state.

justifying her infidelity and conferring a chivalrous burnish on Byron's easy conquest. It was whispered that Guiccioli had murdered two wives; the first, a widowed noblewoman of property, had been banished to the country, where she died—just after making a new will in her husband's favor. Her successor had already borne him seven children before he married her to legitimize an heir. On the night of her death, the Count was attending the opera. Not murder but shady business dealings landed Guiccioli in jail in Rome's Castel Sant'Angelo; his accuser had strong ties to the papacy, but these did not prevent him from being killed in the street by an unknown assassin shortly after Guiccioli's release. Beyond the bloody acts ascribed to him, the Count was obsessed with power and money. Both rapacious and miserly, he reportedly refused to visit a certain corner of his property from a horror of seeing its boundaries. To her humiliation, his bride soon learned that she would be denied the prerogative of every wife: managing the household accounts.

More sinister still, the Count was whispered to be a man of violent sensuality. His grandson later described him as "skilled in seduction,"[3] and Byron's continued jealousy of Alessandro Guiccioli seems an acknowledgment that his power over his wife was more than legal and social; Teresa's sexual thralldom to her husband would remain a dark counterpoint to her intimacy with Byron.

As physically passionate as their affair was from the beginning, Byron's attraction to Teresa was another chapter in his romance with patents of nobility. In Byron's imagination his "lady of the land" was a universe away from the Venetian *zentildonne*, promiscuous and mercenary, "all of them whores." Although the Gambas had a palazzo in Ravenna, Teresa and her seven brothers and sisters had grown up on the family's country estate; her ties to the land—as opposed to that "Sea Sodom," as Byron now called Venice—and her strict convent schooling beginning at age five gave to the nineteen-year-old, sold into marriage, the purity of a princess imprisoned in a tower.

Nonetheless, before the Guicciolis left Venice on April 12 or 13, Byron and Teresa managed four days of ardent lovemaking. But the Count may have had his suspicions; he had, after all, looked properly "embarrassed," Byron noted, at the Benzoni's when he clearly heard his wife claim her lover publicly as "*mio* Byron," and he was not the sort of man to forget a humiliation or to forgive one. Most probably he was kept informed through spies, since he advanced the day of their departure with strange suddenness; how else to explain Teresa's rushing through the opera house during a performance of Rossini's *Otello*, to look for Byron and tell him the sad news? They were still together when the Count arrived at the theater to escort his wife back to their lodgings, at which time he suavely invited Byron to visit them in Ravenna. Two days later, on the evening they were to leave, Byron was the last to pay a farewell call on husband and wife, even handing a mournful Teresa into the gondola. He felt no less desolate as he watched her disappear across the starlit lagoon toward the mainland.

During their rendezvous in his casino, they, too, had talked of plans for Byron to come to Ravenna. His usual agonies of indecision now intensified; there were so many questions and uncertainties surrounding such a move. Where and when could they see each other—alone? Then again, to come and to stay would, indeed, be to give his assent to that risible role of *cicisbeo*, which he had renounced when he ended relations with Marianna Segati. In leaving Venice at Teresa's summons, he would effectively burn his bridges and, worse, open himself to public ridicule should he be dismissed: "If She should plant me—and I should make a 'fiasco' never could I show my face on the Piazza," he worried to Hobhouse.[5] He even bemoaned his Countess's financial independence, or rather, her dependence on another man with greater wealth than his own. But he also missed her terribly. Written in Italian, his first surviving letter to Teresa was as extravagantly romantic in bemoaning his lovelorn state as any young girl's fantasy. "You, who are my only and last love, who are my only joy, the delight of my life—you who are my only hope—you who were—at least for a moment—all mine—you have gone away—and I remain here alone and desolate."[6]

His distress was further compounded by difficulties in communication. Anticipating the danger of letters being intercepted, Teresa had stationed her former governess and confidante, Fanny Silvestrini, to remain in Venice as a drop: Teresa's letters to Byron were enclosed in ones addressed to Fanny, while her lover's, dispatched under cover by Silvestrini, would be sent to another accomplice, Padre Spinelli, a former priest living in Ravenna. Yet Byron received no news from Teresa. Following such double precautions, what could have gone wrong? Everything, as it happens.

First, the Guicciolis did not proceed directly to Ravenna, but stopped at a new property of the Count's, Cà Zen, at the mouth of the Po River. Teresa, however, had failed to provide Byron with the address. But there was a more serious reason for the interruption in her flow of love letters. Three months pregnant when she and Byron became lovers, she had suffered a miscarriage—or the effects of a self-induced abortion—at Pomposa, on the way to the isolated estate. Byron had been aware of his mistress's condition at the outset of their relations: "I can't tell whether I was the involuntary cause of the miscarriage but certes I was not the father of the foetus for She was three months advanced before our first Passade," he told Lord Kinnaird, Douglas's older brother.[7] Byron was unaware, however, that Teresa's affair with him was not, as she had led him to believe, "her first outbreak since Marriage."[8] Six months after her wedding and in the trimester of a first pregnancy, the young Countess, visiting her grandparents in Pesaro, had taken a lover.

A former officer who called himself a poet, Count Cristoforo Ferri appears, sexually at least, to have had much in common with Count Guiccioli: "a licentious brazen satyr . . . not a count, but a peasant, not a gentleman but a horse driver."[9] Unknown to her biographer or to Byron's, the existence of Teresa's first lover, the brutish Count Ferri, says much about her attraction to violent men and, more than that, reveals the artfully contrived persona she knew to be crucial in capturing her romantic puritan. Playing Guinevere to Byron's Arthur, she made sure he saw her as a sleeping beauty awakened by him into love.

With erotic experience gained from a husband and lover, practiced in all the strategies of deceit (Fanny Silvestrini and Padre Spinelli had been used as go-betweens in her first affair), Teresa was well rehearsed for the grand passion of her life. To these Mozartian "seconds" in their affair, the lovers now added a third go-between: another former priest, Lega Zambelli, was employed by Count Guiccioli, but he shortly defected to Byron's household in Venice, where he would become the poet's trusted secretary and majordomo. (He was also Fanny's lover and the father of her child.) Inevitably, then, all of this mediation merely added to human error. Letters were delayed, crossed, or simply failed to arrive.

"My love. What is the matter . . . that you do not write to me? Perhaps you have also not received my Letters?" Teresa wrote on April 18, "but that is not possible, since I already sent you two, one dated the twelfth of this month, and the other the fifteenth and this is the third.—Have you not had the opportunity? But that cannot be lacking when one is truly in love. . . . Ah! my happiness! If you could imagine a thousandth part of the joy that one of your Letters would have given me, and of the pain that your silence causes me instead, I am sure that you would be seized with such pity for me that you would loathe yourself and call yourself cruel!"[10]

Taking his cue from his beloved, Byron's own epistolary style— direct, intimate, and muscular—became feminized and ornamental; he even adopted Teresa's sign-off: *tua amica e amante in eterno* (your friend and lover for eternity). He now reassured her: "Your dearest letter came today and gave me my first moment of happiness since your departure. Perhaps if I loved you less it would not cost me so much to express my thoughts, but now I have to overcome the double difficulty of expressing an unbearable suffering in a language foreign to me. Forgive my mistakes, the more barbarous my style, the more it will resemble my Fate away from you. . . . Love me—not as I love you—for that would make you too unhappy, love me not as I deserve, for that would be too little—but as your Heart commands." And his postscript edges close to a parody of the public scribe's formulas: "How much happier than I is this letter, which in a few days will be in your hands—and perhaps may even be brought to your lips. With such a hope I am kissing it before it goes. Goodby—my soul."11

Besides serving as post office, Fanny Silvestrini also played the role of confidante and even cupid. During the periods she spent in Venice when the lovers were separated, she was fervent in reassuring Teresa of Byron's solitary existence and lavish with advice, along with reminders of her own indispensable role. Increasingly she took to speaking for both principals, interpreting silences, smoothing over quarrels and "misunderstandings." "Do not attribute his silence to coldness of sentiment, for God's sake, no, . . ." Fanny pleaded. "Be well assured he lives like a Hermit; he not only never leaves his House but not even his Room and he receives no one, except sometimes people with whom he may still have some business."12

In telling Teresa what she wanted to hear while inflating her own importance in the affair, Fanny glossed over an awkward truth; her occasional visits to the Mocenigo scarcely constituted round-the-clock surveillance. While Byron was assuring his convalescent mistress, "When you do not get news from me—believe that I am dead rather than unfaithful or ungrateful,"13 he was not only very much alive but also was athletically seeking consolation elsewhere. Reactivating a romance begun a year earlier, when he had been put off by too many chaperons, Byron now paid a midnight call on a certain Angelina, the eighteen-year-old daughter of a noble family whose palazzo was conveniently nearby.

Who knows what might have become of his vows of eternal love for Countess Guiccioli had it not been for Angelina's pressing need to find a husband. Not for the first—or last—time, Byron was discomfited by the lack of hypocrisy of Italian women: "She proposed me to divorce my mathematical wife," he noted to Murray, "and I told her that in England we can't divorce except for *female* infidelity—'and pray' (said she, 'how do you know what she may have been doing these last three years?' I answered *that* I could not tell, but that the status of

Cuckholdom [*sic*] was not quite so flourishing in Great Britain as with us here. 'But'—she said—'can't you get rid of her?' "[14]

As opposed to the artlessly practical Angelina, his married mistress worried him by her vague and highly impractical plans—"not to any purpose," he complained—about how they should meet. Teresa's insistence on public display of passion, moreover, triggered memories of another histrionic love: "She is a sort of an Italian Caroline Lamb, except that She is much prettier, and not so savage.—But she has the same red-hot head—and the same noble dis*dain* of public opinion. . . . To be sure they may go much further here with impunity—as her husband's rank ensured their reception at all societies including the Court."[15] The Count, however, was no William Lamb or even Beppo. Byron had regaled his friends with the rumor that Guiccioli had gotten away with three murders already, and Hobhouse, for one, did not see this as any laughing matter; he was genuinely concerned that, should his friend follow his illicit love to Ravenna, he would be in real danger.

A jealous and violent husband and Teresa's ill-conceived plans for their reunion, along with the lingering effects of her miscarriage—or abortion—provided ample excuse for delaying his departure. Byron waited until May 15 even to reply to Teresa's formal invitation to Ravenna, issued more than a month earlier. As he hovered on the brink of this momentous step, his thoughts turned to Augusta. Irritated by her evasions, he had lapsed into silence but he had not stopped thinking of her. Once again, she was "My dearest Love," and he apologized, "I have been negligent in not writing, but what can I say[?] Three years' absence—& the total change of scene and habit make such a difference—that we now have nothing in common but our affections & our relationship." This was scarcely "nothing," and he went on to confess, "I have never ceased nor can cease to feel for a moment that perfect & boundless attachment which bound & binds me to you—which renders me utterly incapable of *real* love for any other human being— what could they be to me after *you*[?] My own XXXX we may have been very wrong—but I repent of nothing except that cursed marriage— & your refusing to continue to love me as you had loved me—I can neither forget nor *quite forgive* for that precious piece of reformation—but I can never be other than I have been—and whenever I love anything it is because it reminds me in some way or other of yourself." (Passing along this letter, as she had all of Byron's others, to Annabella, Augusta remarked, "He is surely to be considered a Maniac.")[16]

Finally, on June 1, Byron set off toward Bologna, where he was to await further instructions from the still-convalescent Teresa. Traveling across the flat Veneto toward Ferrara, Byron felt the exalted sensations of love and longing crystallize in lines he had meditated since his lover's arrival at Cà Zen. "To the Po. June 2nd 1819" is one of Byron's most beautiful love lyrics. In the sadness of Teresa's departure from Venice, the poet consoled himself by imagining his beloved as a princess in a book of hours, walking below her castle on the banks of the long river that has come to stand for Italy itself. But the Po is also their lifeline to each other, flowing from its source in the Alps to the Adriatic:

> The current I behold will sweep beneath
>   Her palace walls, and murmur at her feet,
> Her eyes will look on thee, when she shall breathe
>   The twilight air unchained from Summer's heat.
> She will look on thee,—I have looked on thee
>   Full of that thought, and from this moment ne'er
> Thy waters could I name, hear named, or see
>   Without the inseparable Sigh for her.

Connected by the river and by the poet's deep feeling for Teresa's country, they are separated only by the forces of human agency:

> . . . the distractions of a various lot,
> Ah! various as the climates of our birth!

Preordained by an affinity in nature, his attachment still leaves him vulnerable to sufferings he had thought were behind him:

> A Stranger loves a lady of the land,
>   Born far beyond the Mountains, but his blood
> Is all meridian, as if never fanned
>   By the bleak wind that chills the Polar flood.
> My heart is all meridian, were it not
>   I had not suffered now, nor should I be—
> Despite of tortures ne'er to be forgot—
>   The Slave again, Oh Love! at least of thee!
> 'Tis vain to struggle, I have struggled long
>   To love again no more as once I loved.
> Oh! Time! why leave this earliest Passion strong?
>   To tear a heart which pants to be unmoved?[17]

His final conceit revealed more truth than poetry and inverts the conventional trope of the panting heart, as his own pursues an ideal of indifference. Far from achieving the self-mastery he had exalted in *Mazeppa*, Byron was only too aware of his powerless state—of which this journey was grotesque proof. He had packed up the Palazzo Mocenigo at a married woman's bidding, his fate and even his destination unclear. Teresa was pulling all the strings, and her adoring lover was now feeling angry and manipulated. Thus, on the very date he signed his great love lyric—June 2—we find Byron complaining to Hoppner from Padua: "I am proceeding in no very good humour—for La G[uiccioli]'s instructions are rather calculated to produce an éclat—and perhaps a scene—than any decent iniquity. I had a letter from her on Monday which merely repeated the directions she had given me before with the addition of something about her own house.—Now to cuckold a Papal Count, who like Candide—had already been 'the death of two men, one of whom was a priest'* in his own house is rather too much for my modesty." Within a year Byron would do precisely that. Meanwhile, he vented his anger in crude remarks about Teresa's availability—all the uglier as Hoppner, gossip and scandalmonger that he was, had disapproved of the Countess from the beginning. "The Charmer forgets that a man may be whistled any where *before*," Byron declared, "but that *after*—a Journey in an Italian June is a Conscription—and therefore she should have been less liberal in Venice—or less exigent at Ravenna."[18] But it was too late. His Countess had whistled for him *"after,"* and he still found himself slogging across half of Italy to see her again.

Once more, Byron's ambivalence played out in detours; proceeding via Padua, he stopped to revisit Ferrara, where he was particularly charmed by the epitaphs in the Certosa cemetery. He planned to appropriate one humbly brief prayer, *Implora pace,* for his own tombstone, he told Murray, insisting further that his remains should not be "pickled" and sent home.[19] In Bologna he was assaulted by still worse heat; "settled like a Sausage—and shall be broiled like one if this weather continues," he told Hoppner. There was no word from Teresa. Earlier he had assured Hoppner that if he did not find instructions from his mistress, he would return to Venice. But on the next day, he added to the still-unposted letter, "I am just setting off for Ravenna—June 8th, 1819—I changed my mind this morning and decided to go on."[20]

Greeted by silence once more, he had no choice on his arrival but to stick to Teresa's operatic scenario of meeting at the theater. But she was not there. In her place, there first appeared Count Giuseppe Alborghetti—

---

*Byron seems to have scrambled the number and gender of the Count's alleged victims.

a nobleman of considerable importance in the province for whom Byron had left a letter of introduction—who informed the visitor that the Countess was at death's door. This discreet courtier was shocked by the young English lord's open expression of grief. But soon Count Guiccioli joined them with less dire news of his wife's illness, silkily conveying her regrets that she could not be with them. Count Alessandro was in his element: He had added a famous poet, a peer of England and Teresa's lover, to the numbers of those squirming in his power. The next day the Count arrived in his grand coach at the door of Byron's dingy little hotel, the inaptly named Albergo Imperiale, to personally accompany his guest to the Palazzo Guiccioli.

Husband and lover now flanked the sick woman's bedside, and this unstable mix of drama, pathos, and farce, along with a shifting dynamic of power, would characterize the relations of the three for the next four years. At the same time, the stage was set for what would be the final chapter in Byron's history of triangular passions. To complicate matters further, the three principals—Alessandro, Teresa, Byron—did not constitute an isolated trio. By following his lover to Ravenna, Byron had also become part of a chorus consisting of the large Gamba and Guiccioli families, and his fate, for better and worse, would be inextricably bound with theirs.

Now, however, it was Teresa's symptoms that frightened him; when the effects of her miscarriage subsided, she had begun coughing blood, especially alarming as there was a high incidence of consumption in the Gamba family. Then her gynecological problems reappeared. Byron vowed to remain until she recovered—or failed to—and he wrote to Alexander Scott, the least disapproving of his Venetian friends, to send the smaller carriage he had left behind, together with coachman and saddle horses, as far as Bologna, explaining, "The G[uiccioli] has been very ill—still in bed but better—I have seen her—and *she* is as usual—I am in love with her."[21]

To acknowledge his feelings to a male friend without irony or mockery of the beloved was rare for Byron and reveals both the intensity of his attachment and his lack of distraction. He was a stranger in a strange city, and his isolation was exacerbated by ennui, by the sweltering heat and stuffy little rooms. He could only see Teresa surrounded by friends, family, and servants; even so, he visited the Palazzo Guiccioli—sometimes twice a day—and wrote to her as often. "I have no life now except in you,"[22] he told her after his first visit, escorted by the impassively courteous Alessandro. And his dependency depressed him further.

Ravenna in 1819 was a rundown backwater of a town, scarcely a place to raise the spirits. A reluctant tourist in the best of times, Byron resisted the polite efforts of Teresa's friends and family to show him the sights: "I have tried to distract myself with this farce of visiting antiquities," he wrote to Teresa. "It seems quite intolerably tedious—but at the moment everything else is equally displeasing." He had looked forward to seeing Dante's tomb and certain manuscripts in the library, only to find he reviewed them "with an indifference made pardonable by the state of my heart."[23] In his hotel room at night, he succumbed to fits of weeping and irrational anxiety: Count Gamba, Teresa's father, looked at him "with suspicion," he said. "Passion makes me fear everything and everyone," he told his mistress. "If I lose you, what will become of me?"[24]

In his desperate state, he conceived that desperate measures were the only solution. Four days after his arrival in Ravenna, he wrote again to Teresa, proposing that they run off together. "Tell me what I am to do?" he pleaded. "Remain here?—Or return to Bologna. If trouble arises there is only one adequate remedy, that is, go away together—and for this a great Love is necessary—and some courage. Have you enough?" he demanded before replying to his own question: "I can already anticipate your answer. It will be long and divinely written—but it will end in a negative."[25]

Teresa defended her "great Love" for the poet, while making it clear that running off together was out of the question; she saw no reason why she should not enjoy the social position of Countess Guiccioli while indulging the passion of her life with her *gran poete.* Still, Teresa recognized that a refusal based on these considerations would appear cynical and amoral to her English lover, and she would be diminished in his eyes. Thus she reached for the role of virtuous wife, pleading the horror of wounding her husband.

Byron saw through this hypocrisy, noting sardonically that her sudden concern for the Count's feelings "has come a little late—for the greatest injury to —— was already done in Venice." Then, to avert his own loss of face, he agreed with Teresa: "To go away would be the height of imprudence—a thing only to be done if we were discovered—in case you were obliged to abandon *one* of us two. But forgive me if I say (now that we are speaking of morals) that the greatest injury is in the deception, not the desertion of a man who is already in the condition of a great number of husbands."[26]

There would be hundreds of such exchanges between them in the next years; some represented real grievances, or the age-old anxiety of all lovers about who loves whom more. For her part, Teresa played shrewdly on Byron's need to be kept guessing. Piqued by doubt and occasional suspicion, his passion could be kept at its *estro,* its most intense heat. More troubling now, however, was her accusation that Byron had been responsible for her miscarriage:* "You tell me that I, and not *riding*, have done you so much harm—this means that the cause of the 'illness' was a fault of mine. This is the first time that you have said this to me—and being a rather serious accusation—and seriously made— I should like to have some explanation."[27] Here we have reason to believe that Teresa was, finally, honest with her lover. Whether he was the "cause" of a miscarriage or a self-induced abortion, neither was unflattering to his masculinity; the first suggested that the violence of their lovemaking had injured the fetus, and the second points to Teresa's fear that a pregnancy brought to term in October would have kept them apart.[28]

Accident or no, Byron rose to the seriousness of the event. He began exploring the possibility of marrying Teresa; ignorant of the relations between the two women he had left behind him, he asked Augusta to sound out Lady Byron on her willingness to divorce him, and failing that possibility, to look into ecclesiastical law in Scotland, where divorced spouses were free to remarry.[29] In a burst of optimism, he wrote to Murray that they would soon set to "repair"[30] the termination of one pregnancy with another. None of these hopes, however, came to fruition.

In the meantime, Teresa's symptoms of consumption continued—"a perpetual cough and intermittent fever."[31] Byron had sent to Venice for Peruvian bark—a source of quinine—for the fever, but it had not helped. Frantic, he now summoned the famed Dr. Aglietti, offering to pay all his expenses for the trip from Venice to Ravenna to examine Teresa. Not only did the physician set out immediately, he also refused to accept a fee. Prescribed leeches and a special diet, the patient began to improve. The Guicciolis were impressed—as much by the deference shown to His Lordship as by the doctor's skills.

Now the lovers could be alone together, restoring Byron's own equilibrium. They walked and rode in the famous *pineta*, the pine forest that separated Ravenna from the sea, and resumed the passionate sexual encounters joyfully recalled from those first days in Venice. Their transports took place in the Palazzo Guiccioli, under Alessandro's nose. "By the aid of a Priest—a Chambermaid—a young Negro-boy and a female friend," Byron crowed. It fell to Teresa to organize the cast of extras in this carefully staged drama.

---

*To compound the murkiness surrounding this episode, *abortire,* the word Byron originally wrote, can refer to either miscarriage or abortion. Teresa later crossed it out, writing *"male"* (illness) in its place.

"She manages very well," Byron boasted of his mistress to Hoppner, "though the local[e] is inconvenient—(no *bolts* and be d——d to them) and we run great risks—(were it not at sleeping hours—after dinner) and *no* place—but the great Saloon of his own palace—so that if I come away with the Stiletto in my gizzard some fine afternoon—I shall not be astonished." Here, too, was Byron's revenge on Alessandro's greater wealth and power, along with his maddeningly mysterious behavior: "I can't make him out at all,"[32] Byron complained of the visits and drives with the Count along the Corso. On display in the Count's coach and six, Byron felt like "Whittington and his Cat"[33] paraded by the Lord Mayor of London. But elsewhere—and more accurately—he cast his landlord as the "Chat" while he was the mouse in this strange game. At the same time, he recognized that both of them were manipulated by Teresa. "The fact appears to be that he is completely *governed* by her—for that matter—so am I."[34]

Surveillance, however, was not the Count's only motive in befriending his wife's lover. With the departure of Napoleon, Romagna had become a papal state. Continuing the shady business dealings that had landed him earlier in the Castel Sant'Angelo, Alessandro had reason to fear trouble from the Vatican. Diplomatic immunity could solve all his problems, and he now asked for Byron's help in securing a British vice-consulship—an honorific title, with no salary or perks, but affording, so he hoped, His Majesty's protection from prosecution. For his part, Byron now jumped at the chance to do Alessandro a large favor; the Count would be in his debt, while providing him with a welcome opportunity for one-upmanship in the display of his political connections. He wrote first to Hoppner, assuring him that the applicant "*rich & independent*" wanted no emolument or power from the office, but simply immunity as a British officeholder "since he does not trust to the arbitrary proceedings on this side the Po,"[35] Byron noted vaguely. When Hoppner's efforts came to nothing, he then appealed to Murray, loftily suggesting that the publisher apply to his highly placed Tory friends in the government: Croker, First Lord of the Admiralty; Canning, the Foreign Secretary; "or my old schoolfellow Peel."[36] In the event, Murray could—or would—do nothing, and the matter ended there.

Byron's sense of vulnerability—the fear and fawning that characterized his relations with the Count—was a consequence of his outrageous behavior toward the husband, bribing his servants to stand watch while he made love to his wife in his own house. If it is always true in adulterous relationships that there are at least three people in bed, then Byron and Teresa came close to turning psychological truth into physical reality; the Count's proximity, the real possibility of the "Chat" awakening early—as he once did—from his nap, also piqued their sexual rapture. *"Think,"* my love, of *those* moments," Byron recalled to Teresa early in August, "delicious—dangerous—but *happy*, in every sense—not only for the pleasure, more than ecstatic, that you gave me, but for the danger (to which you were exposed) that we fortunately escaped. The Hall! Those rooms! The open doors! The servants so curious and so near—Ferdinando*—the Visitors!"[37]

Byron the jaded libertine needed a gallery of viewers—real or imagined—to intensify pleasure; Byron the puritan hoped for discovery and punishment. In the Palazzo Guiccioli, both desires might be gratified.

Meanwhile, Byron's confidences about Teresa's "exigent" love-making (echoing his boyhood boasts of exhaustion caused by too much sex) aroused more than envy in the heart of less lucky male friends. In Venice both Hoppner and Scott were indignant at losing Byron to love in Ravenna, and there ensued much prurient clucking about the unworthiness of his mistress. Hoppner especially, with his stiff-necked Swiss wife, gave proof of the most venomous jealousy. Under the guise of trying to protect his friend, he took aim at the weakest points of Byron's ego: sexual vanity, fear of ridicule, and, at the deepest level, his lifelong terror of abandonment. Hinting of scandal too lurid to relate in writing, Hoppner insisted that Teresa had ensnared Byron only to display her conquest; once she was sure of him, he would be dropped for the next lover. Even as Byron recognized the *"bile"* that prompted the consul's letter—his "gratuitous—bilious—officious—intermeddling," the poisoned arrows went straight to the mark, undermining his fragile confidence in himself, in Teresa, in the possibility of love itself.

"What does H[oppner] mean by *'when she is sure of me'? how 'sure'?"* he demanded to Scott, "when a man has been for some time in the habit of *keying* a female—methinks it is his own fault if the 'being left in the lurch' greatly incommodes him—because the woman can never forget that she has been 'under his paunch'—and unless he is a sighing swain . . . accounts at parting are at least equal." Already he meditated his revenge: "—if the lady takes another caprice? Ebbene? can't we match her in that too think you & then let her boast of 'betraying &c.'[?]" Byron's misogyny, always smoldering, was at the flash point; without waiting to hear the substance of the Venetian gossip, Byron confronted Teresa with his translation of Hoppner's letter while

---

*The Count's adolescent son by his second wife.

dismissing her defense in advance: "You may imagine her answer—" he sneered to Scott, "of course She would be at no loss for that—none of them are." But he also quoted Teresa's offer to elope with him, " 'then instead of being at my mercy—I shall be at yours,' "[38] she had said. Perhaps she did propose such a step at this time; if so, Byron failed to note that earlier he had begged *her* to run off with him but that she had declined. It would not be the last time he would reverse their positions on this issue to others.

Contretemps crackled through the July heat: accusations and counteraccusations, sulks and reconciliations, not all of it unwelcome. Different in so many respects, the lovers shared a strong taste for intrigue and complications. Teresa had been quick to recognize that Byron bored was far more dangerous to her than Byron angry. It was time for a change of scene. The Countess's restored health now permitted their long-deferred visit to Bologna; first, however, the Guicciolis planned to visit another of the Count's properties in Forlì. Byron declined Alessandro's invitation to join them there or to stay with them at their Bologna residence, preferring an inn. Shortly after the three convened on August 12, they went to the theater to see Alfieri's play *Mirra*, based on a tale in Ovid's *Metamorphoses*. In this tragedy of incestuous love, Mirra, daughter of Venus, becomes the mother of Adonis by her own father and, on discovering this truth, kills herself. Byron had read Alfieri and other works on the same theme, but he was unprepared for the shock of seeing their dreadful fate presented by live actors on a stage. The last two acts "threw me into convulsions," he told Murray, adding, "I do not mean by that word—a lady's hysterics—but the agony of reluctant tears."[39] Two weeks later, Byron had still not recovered from the emotional assault of the play, his distress compounded by his lover's absence; the Count and Countess were off to inspect yet another estate.

Before she left Bologna Teresa had given Byron the keys to the Palazzo Savioli, and wandering her apartments there or seated in the still heat of the garden, "under a purple canopy of grapes,"[40] he pondered the restricted choices of *serventissimo*: He could come when called, or remain behind and mope. Writing to Hobhouse, he complained of being "so nervous that I cry for nothing—at least today I burst into tears all alone by myself over a cistern of Gold fishes—which are not pathetic animals."[41] Like caged birds, however, these decorative creatures, swimming around in circles, are mirrors of domestic captivity, whether of animals, women, or *cavalieri serventi*.

In Teresa's sitting room he found her open copy of *Corinne*, Madame de Staël's homage to Italian women: He took the volume, bound in violet plush with a clasp,* outdoors, and after rereading parts, inscribed this famous tribute to his "lady of the land": "My dearest Teresa—I have read this book in your garden—my Love—you were absent or I could not have read it.—It is a favorite book of yours—and the writer was a friend of mine. You will not understand these English words—and *others* will not understand them—which is the reason I have not scribbled them in Italian—but you will recognize the handwriting of him who passionately loved you—and you will divine that over a book which was yours—he could only think of love. In *that word* beautiful in all languages—but most so in yours—*Amor* mio—is comprized my existence here and hereafter . . . to *what* purpose—you will decide—my destiny rests with you—& you are a woman [nineteen?]† years of age—and two years out of a Convent—I wish you had staid there with all my heart—or at least that I had never met you in your married state—but all this is too late."[42]

"Alone and unhappy," as he now now described himself,[43] Byron sent to Venice for Allegra, demanding that she be delivered "instantly."[44] Her father's sudden impatience to have his daughter with him was only the latest round in the alternating cycles of neglect and attention to which the child was victim. Although Byron was profuse in his thanks to Mrs. Hoppner for taking care of the little girl, he now discovered that she and her husband had been shockingly irresponsible caretakers. In fact, the consul's wife disliked Allegra—which she freely admitted to everyone—and without informing Byron, she had farmed out the child to three different families in as many months. Byron had delivered her to the Hoppners along with a nursemaid; that person had disappeared and was not replaced. When Allegra arrived in Bologna early in September, Byron was startled to discover that his daughter knew not a word of English or even correct Italian; from being only in the company of servants, she spoke nothing but Venetian: "Bon dí Papa," she greeted him. But he was amused by the "very droll," precocious three-year-old, who still "has a good deal of the Byron," he reported to Augusta. "Can't articulate the letter *r* at all—frowns and pouts quite in our way—blue eyes—light hair growing *darker* daily—and a dimple in the chin—a scowl on the brow—white skin—sweet

---

*Still in Ravenna, at the Biblioteca Classense.

†Teresa later decided that she would cut a more romantic figure for posterity by subtracting two years from her age as given in Byron's inscription, so she scratched out the original "nineteen," writing "seventeen" above.

voice—and a particular liking of Music—and of her own way in every thing—is not that B. all over?"[45]

WHEN THE Guicciolis returned to Bologna, Alessandro repeated his invitations: Byron must stay with them. But once again he declined. As it happened, the Count had another favor to ask. Could his lordship manage to lend him the equivalent of £1,000? Eager to compensate for his failed efforts to obtain a vice-consulship for the Count, Byron agreed. When his Venetian bankers expressed doubts about the Count's probity, however, he rescinded his pledge. Guiccioli now blamed Teresa for her lover's change of mind, and she reacted to the ugly scenes that followed with a recurrence of her old symptoms. Byron urged a consultation in Venice with Dr. Aglietti. Since the Count's pressing need for cash compelled his immediate return to Ravenna, he allowed Byron to accompany Teresa on this medical mission.

The lovers set off for the Veneto in a daze of happiness; for appearances, Teresa, accompanied by her maid and a manservant, rode in the Count's coach and six. Sending Allegra and the servants ahead, Byron traveled in his own splendid carriage, being reunited with Teresa at each stop on the three-day journey. Before reaching Padua, they made a pilgrimage both sentimental and literary. Byron wanted to show his "Laura" Petrarch's house and tomb in Arquà. The road that climbed the Euganean Hills became too steep and narrow for the large coaches, so the lovers dismounted and made the last part of the trip on foot, walking past vineyards and pomegranate trees. Byron had signed the guest book on his earlier visit, but now, on leaving, they inscribed their names together.

He fantasized aloud about emigrating together to South America. Some time ago, he had read that the Venezuelan government was offering land to those willing to develop the country. With the dream of every settler in the New World, he saw himself recouping his losses and healing the fractures of his life: "I am not yet thirty-two years of age—I might still be a decent citizen and found a *house* and a family—as good or better than the former," he wrote wistfully to Hobhouse. Byron had chosen the southern part of the hemisphere, he explained, because "The Anglo-Americans are a little too coarse for me—and their climate too cold." But there was a political dimension to his romance: With its recent liberation from Spain, he saw South America as an Italy free of Austrian oppression and puppet kings. "There is no freedom in Europe—that's certain," he declared, adding, "It is besides a worn-out portion of the globe."[46]

As he traveled with Teresa, the Venezuelan project now began to seem a plausible plan; in Padua they discussed heading not across the lagoon to Venice, but to France, and from there, to America; as his beloved became persuaded, however, Byron drew back: "We were very near going off together, but as I had more prudence—and more experience—and know that the time would come when both might repent—I paused—& prevailed on her to pause also," he told Kinnaird.[47] The dream of a new beginning did not include a naïve, romantic, and married twenty-year-old.

In Padua they were also reminded that the freedom of an adulterous wife had its limits; at their inn, the long-widowed Countess Benzoni and *her* longtime *cavaliere servente*, Count Rangone, appeared at breakfast. Sexual jealousy or envy of youth may have played its part, but the usually tolerant Benzoni bristled with disapproval. Public appearances or private trysts at home were one matter; no married lady, however, could be seen racketing around the country alone with her lover! More scandal would now buzz around them in Venice, adding to the gossip already circulating about Teresa. Byron had maintained his rental of La Mira, and after one night there, they settled into the Palazzo Mocenigo to await Teresa's examination by Dr. Aglietti. She had now openly broken her promise to her husband—to stay at the lodgings he had arranged for her. The doctor's visit, however, gave them fresh cause for rejoicing; as Teresa jubilantly reported to her husband, Aglietti prescribed a change of air to complete the patient's recovery: A trip to Lakes Como and Garda was his recommendation. Alessandro once again gave permission for Byron to accompany his wife, and the lovers returned to La Mira and the privacy of the Villa Foscarini.

Their month-long idyll echoed with memories of Byron's Newstead honeymoon with Augusta. Even the contrasting seasons—the blizzard five years earlier and the final burst of summer in late September in the Veneto—formed parentheses of past and present. La Mira's *giardino all'Inglese*, with its miniature waterways and bridges, recalled Newstead's model fort and lake. But it was the two women—passionate and innocent as children, teasing, giggling (Teresa had "our laugh"[48] he told Augusta)—who, alone in Byron's life, released him into self-forgetful joy. Teresa's chatter, in the language he so loved, had become the sounds of life, so necessary to him that he begged her not to stop talking even while he wrote. He bought her a piano so she could play and sing to him, and, in lieu of singing duets, he read to her from his work in progress, an English translation of Pulci's *Il Morgante Maggiore*, the wicked mock epic whose medley of high and low styles had inspired *Beppo* and *Don Juan*. He had also begun writing Canto III of "the *Don*"; not, however, with much enthusiasm.

On July 19, the first two cantos had been published anonymously—to crashing silence. There was no word from England on sales or reviews; indeed, Byron had not even received a copy of the volume. Nonetheless, Murray continued nagging him to cut and soften; he wanted the next edition to bear the name of poet and publisher, in which event far more caution would be required. With no word about the reception of "Donny Johnny" from any of his friends or his publisher, Byron could only assume the worst. For a change, however, his own faith in the power and originality of the work was unshakable: "I hear nothing of *Don Juan* but in two letters from Murray," he wrote to Hobhouse from Bologna, "the first very tremulous—the second in better spirits. . . . Of the fate of the 'pome' I am quite uncertain, and [do] not anticipate much brilliancy from your silence. But I do not care," he insisted, "I am . . . sure . . . that I never wrote better—and I wish you all better taste."[49] In defending the work, he is never defensive. Exuding a playful and tolerant confidence, he teased Murray, "You are right—Gifford is right—Crabbe is right—Hobhouse is right—you are all right—and I am all wrong—but do pray let me have that pleasure—Cut me up root and branch—quarter me in the Quarterly . . . make—if you will—a spectacle to men and angels—but don't ask me to alter for I can't."[50] He twitted Kinnaird for turning censor: "As to 'Don Juan'—confess—confess you dog—and be candid—that it is the sublime of *that there* sort of writing—it may be bawdy—but is it not good English—it may be profligate—but is it not *life*, is it not *the thing*?—Could any man have written it—who has not lived in the world? and tooled in a post-chaise? in a hackney coach? in a Gondola? against a Wall? in a court carriage? in a vis-à-vis?—on a table?—and under it?"[51]

With no one in England celebrating with him, Byron was all the more delighted to have Tom Moore's visit; after a stopover at La Mira, when he was presented to Teresa, Byron installed his friend at the Palazzo Mocenigo. He now had an excuse to scamper into town, with "all the glee of a schoolboy on holiday," Teresa observed indulgently, to show Moore the sights.[52] It may be that his mistress's chatter, her adoration and little vanities, even her unlimited appetite for the "one thing" that interested them both above all else had begun to pall. Now, when he wrote of his South American project to friends, he spoke of going only with Allegra; there was no further mention of Teresa.

Count Guiccioli had set the end of September as the date for his visit to Venice to collect his wife, but it was now early October and the husband had not yet appeared. In Byron's concern, however, we hear a twitch of impatience.

Knowing that the lovers could not "receive" or "be received" in

Venetian society, Hoppner inquired cattily at the end of October, how they passed the long evenings at La Mira, to which Byron replied, with more honesty than chivalry, that it was a "devil of a question." With a mistress as with a wife, he admitted, the evenings were "surely . . . longer than the nights," adding that the Count was expected in a week, when "I am requested to consign his wife to him, which shall be done—with all her linen."[53] Alessandro's fit of decisiveness was soon explained by an unhappy letter from Teresa's father, Count Gamba. Until now this most indulgent parent had been disposed to put the best face on his daughter's friendship with the aristocratic English poet; like Countess Benzoni, however, he was horrified to learn of their trip from Bologna to Venice alone and, worse, to hear that Teresa was living openly with Byron at La Mira. Ending all pretense of respectable *serventissimo*, a scandalous affair of the heart would blacken her good name and that of the Gambas and of her husband as well. While he himself trusted that Byron was merely "protecting" his daughter, "no doubt in a manner honorable and worthy," society would take a very different view of "this most seductive young man" with whom she traveled.[54]

Still, Alessandro temporized and confined himself to writing a grumpy letter withdrawing his earlier permission to allow the lovers to travel to the lakes and pointedly failing to include greetings to Byron. It was impossible, however, to shame Teresa. Promptly seizing the offensive, she roundly scolded her husband for his unworthy suspicions, for endangering her health by forcing the cancellation of her projected trip, and for his want of courtesy toward the kindest and most solicitous of companions. Alone with Byron, however, she wept like a child for the withdrawal of the promised "treat"; sensing her lover's restlessness, she had looked forward all the more to their trip. But in his next letter, Alessandro informed Teresa of his imminent arrival in Venice—on November 1—where, for the sake of appearances, he planned to stay with them at Palazzo Mocenigo!

The wronged husband was now on the warpath. He arrived with a lengthy "paper of rules," as Byron described this alarming document, consisting of "regulations—of hours and conduct and morals."[55] This humiliating guide attempted to establish the Count's authority over every moment of his wife's existence, waking and sleeping: from expenditures and daily schedule to dispensing judgment on manners and attitude ("Let her not be too conceited or impatient."). The real object of the Count's conjugal rulebook, however, was to end her intimacy with Byron. Should she feel tempted to give preference over her husband to "anyone else . . . let her at once bring such a relation to an end, and not trust herself; otherwise she will be forever condemned in the opinion of a husband, and of a wise Society."[56]

The Countess dealt summarily with this absurd memorandum; in mocking style, she retorted with a few clauses of her own, the first "to get up whenever I like" and ending with two nonnegotiable demands: "a horse with everything necessary for riding" followed by the right *"to receive, without discrimination, any visitor who may come."*[57]

Furious quarrels between husband and wife now echoed through the rooms of Palazzo Mocenigo. Enraged by the fiasco of his "marriage contract," Guiccioli countered with the classic ultimatum: him or me.

All other things being equal, there would have been no doubt about Teresa's choice—"the lover generally having the preference," Byron observed.[58] But things were not equal. This time Byron's triangulated affair was also a three-way battle of wills: Alessandro's determination to be rid of his wife's lover; Byron's desire to have Teresa to himself without the moral indignity of *serventissimo*; and the Countess's sublime insistence on maintaining the rights of every other Italian lady of her class.

Byron reacted to the tense stalemate by taking to his bed with a malarial fever, including sweats, vomiting, and periods of delirium. In despair, Teresa now alternated angry scenes with her husband with tearful vigils, beside Fletcher, at Byron's bedside. Barely had his rival recovered, however, than the Count was ready with his trump card. He himself had been prepared to accept his wife's lover, he told Byron. His father-in-law, however, no longer trusting Teresa as to the platonic nature of their love, had implored Alessandro to end the affair. Appealing privately to Byron as a man of honor, the Count pointed out the disgrace that his continued relations with the Countess would bring on the Gamba family; in particular, he shrewdly underscored the cruel fate the lovers' selfishness would inflict on Teresa's five innocent sisters, dooming them to lives of spinsterhood. If his lordship's character was as noble as his title, he would persuade the Countess to return with her husband to Ravenna—alone.

It may be that Byron was not altogether unhappy with the role "honor" now demanded of him. His innate passivity and indecision always encouraged the stronger will to prevail. And in this case, the alternative to letting Teresa go was not that alluring. Alone in Bologna, at a moment when he had missed his lover most, he had confided to Hobhouse: "I feel and I feel it bitterly—that a man should not consume his life at the side and on the bosom—of a woman—and a stranger—that even the recompense and it is much—is not enough—and that this Cicisbean existence is to be condemned—But I have neither the strength of mind to break my chain, or the insensibility which would deaden its weight." Now he summoned all his eloquence to convince a weeping Teresa that they had no choice: She must return to her family and the duties of a wife and daughter.[59] Sensitive to her fears that his failure to appear with her in Ravenna would fuel gossip that she had been "planted" for another woman, he reassured her that his plan of returning to England would forestall any such rumors.

Even bowed by grief, Teresa was a tough negotiator: Byron conceded that he persuaded her only "with the greatest difficulty to return with her husband to Ravenna—not absolutely denying—that I might come there again—else she refused to go."[60] Finally, on the tenth of November, Teresa, accompanied by the Count, left Venice and Byron for the second time.

Alone, weakened by fever and scenes, Byron turned on the city he had loved with all the bitterness of a lover betrayed. He was sick of Venice, an "oyster with no pearl," sick of being cheated and gossiped about by Venetians and by those English who called themselves his friends. He wanted nothing further to do with Hoppner, Scott, and the insinuating Fanny Silvestrini. He now saw a host of reasons why he should—no, he must—return to England. He nursed a fantasy of challenging Henry Brougham to a duel; the lawyer and literary critic had replaced the dead Romilly as the architect of all his woes. There was Hanson's incomprehensible statement of his finances; following the receipt of the purchase money from the Newstead sale, the lawyer had paid debts outstanding of £28,162 to creditors Byron claimed he had never heard of; then there was the matter of Rochdale, still unsold. He wanted to discuss investments with Kinnaird, including the delicate issue of those shares where his interests and Annabella's were joined forever. Then he must weigh future plans with Murray. The first two cantos of *Don Juan* were already appearing in pirated editions; the publisher wanted to obtain a copyright, which meant that in subsequent printings, the author's name would appear on the title page. Byron feared abandoning his anonymity; the authorities had used Shelley's atheistical and immoral poetry to deny him custody of the two children of his first marriage. Legal proceedings against the poem could deprive him of all rights to Ada; seeing his only legitimate child was another timely reason for a visit. He planned to bring Allegra with him and look into English schools for her. And then there was Augusta. If a reunion could not restore what they had been to each other, a meeting must at least dispel the "megrims & mysteries" of her letters.[61]

But another crisis demanded his attention, keeping him in Venice. Allegra fell ill with the same malarial fever from which he had barely recovered. It was uncertain when she could travel, especially now, in the worst of winter. There was no knowing when they could expect to see him, he told his friends.

In the lowest of spirits, he refused to go out, declining an overture from la Benzoni, who also expressed concern about Allegrina—a great favorite of the Countess. Waiting by the "feverish pillow of a sick infant,"[62] Byron found no cheer in reading the first review of Cantos I and II, only now arriving from England. In Edinburgh, *Blackwood's Magazine* tore into the poet's private life as the poisoned source for his infernal work, "a filthy and impious poem" whose "offences . . . speak the wilful [*sic*] and determined spite of an unrepenting, unsoftened, smiling, sarcastic, joyous sinner—for such diabolical, such slavish vice, there can be neither pity nor pardon." The poet, "this miserable man, having exhausted every species of sensual gratification—having drained the cup of sin even to its bitterest dregs, were resolved to shew us that he is no longer a human being, even in his frailties; but a cool unconcerned fiend." Among the sins denounced was the poet's satire of Lady Byron as Donna Inez; recalling with inaccurate relish the circumstances of the separation, the reviewer intoned, "To offend the love of such a woman was wrong—but it might be forgiven; to desert her was unmanly—but he might have returned and wiped forever from her eyes the tears of her desertion;—but to injure and to desert, then to turn back and wound her widowed privacy with unhallowed strains of cold-blooded mockery—was brutally, fiendishly, inexpiably mean."[63]

Other critics harped on the malign future influence of *Don Juan* as a "manual of profligacy," a guide of "calm and deliberate design to palliate and recommend the crime of adultery, to work up the passions of the young to its commissions, and to afford them the most practical hints for its consummation." Self-censorship in the form of boycott was the only solution: "The good sense, and the good feeling of the English nation must and will banish it from their houses. We should have the worst opinion indeed of any man, upon whose family table this volume were to lie exposed."[64] Even a sophisticated reviewer who saw the brilliance and originality of the poem succumbed nonetheless to worries about the poet as a teacher of vice: "Every one knows and has felt . . . that Lord Byron is a powerful and impressive writer—perhaps the most powerful and impressive of his age. He is one of those who seem born to stamp a character on the times in which they live." Pointing out that this particular author "stands identified in an unusual manner with the characters which he draws," the reviewer concluded that he is "amenable, beyond the ordinary limits of a poet's responsibility, for the sentiments which he permits them to express." Then, having established his case for the moral burden of Byron's poetry, he comes in for the kill. Precisely because of its genius, "*Don Juan* is by far the most offensive of all Lord Byron's performances . . . and the indecency which stained his lighter productions, are here embodied into the compactness of a system. . . .

"The work cannot perish; for it has in it, full and overflowing, the elements of intellectual vigor, and bears upon it the stamp of surpassing power." As for the poet bent on his self-destructive course, the critic could only wonder, "Is it for such a man as this, stupendous in actual performance, and boundless in anticipated achievement, to cast all his honours in the dust, and, from the cherished and chosen poet of a mighty people, to become the lewd minstrel of a brothel?"[65]

To Byron, reading these denunciations one after the other, it was clear that *Don Juan* had rendered him more reviled by his countrymen than all the worst sins of which he had been convicted by the press and public opinion on leaving England. But he was also aware, and had been for some time now, that seismic shifts were taking place in the society he had left behind only five years before—the most crucial being in the words of a modern critic, "that the power of the Regency aristocracy to set the social tone for Britain had been broken. The moralistic middle class is on the march toward Victorianism."[66]

"*Cant* is so much stronger than *Cunt*"[67] was Byron's explanation for the spirit of proto-Pecksniffery abroad in the land. But the virulence of attacks on him aroused all his old fears and hostilities. After the Peterloo Massacre of that August, when His Majesty's troops had charged a peaceful political meeting in a field outside Manchester, killing or wounding only women and children, repressive measures had been quickly enacted to prevent popular outrage from exploding into revolt. Perhaps he should return to England just to help foment the revolution that surely must come to Britain as it promised to do elsewhere, he later wrote to Hobhouse, only half in jest.[68]

In the next weeks, he felt his solitude as never before. He read Teresa's letters, filled with expressions of "dark grief"—Fanny's description—mingled with accusations of how little he loved her. She was wrong, he assured her, "You are and will be always my first thought—but at this moment I am in a terrible state of not knowing what to decide; I am afraid on the one hand to compromise you forever by my return to Ravenna . . . and on the other—of losing you—and myself—and all that I have known or tasted of happiness, by not seeing you ever again.—I beg you—I implore you to be calm—and to believe that I cannot cease loving you as long as I live."[69]

Then he proposed for a second time that they elope. Teresa had refused him once in June. Fearful of being rejected again, he made his offer through Fanny. Byron had come to dislike her, but in the three weeks since Teresa's departure he relied on her even more as interpreter of his thoughts and feelings in a language most reassuring to his mistress. Writing regularly to her "Teresina," she reported on her lover's health, his changing travel plans, and, most important, his undiminished love—all in letters that Byron vetted and approved. Now, in an elaborately self-protective stratagem, Byron promoted Fanny to negotiator: "He charges me . . . to write to you today the following things which I took from his mouth word for word last evening," she informed Teresa on November 30. "If you absolutely cannot live without him, if this causes you unhappiness, if he is necessary for your existence, choose a place to meet, see each other, come to an agreement, and then, if need be, never separate again. He will sacrifice his journey to London, where he is headed, he will live with you in whatever Country suits you both, but he absolutely does not want to come to Ravenna; he wants you to be with either one or the other."[70] Unlike her lover, a confident Teresa staked everything on this last gamble. She would not elope.

By early December Allegra was well enough to travel, and Byron made his plans to leave for England. He wrote Teresa a last wrenching farewell, but in giving his first forwarding address in Calais and the name of the Venetian servant, "Valeriano," who would accompany him, he may have hoped that the note, underlining the reality of his departure, would induce her to change her mind.[71] But she remained adamant, and on December 9 Fanny described Byron, standing on the steps of the Mocenigo, dressed for travel "gloves in his hands, with his *bonnet*, and even with his little Cane"; the servants had gone ahead, the chests were in the gondolas, everything was packed except for his guns, which Fletcher was still trying to find. "Then, in a fit of irritation, this time, perhaps, impelled by his reluctance to leave," Fanny wrote, "he declared that if all was not ready when the one-o'clock bell struck from the *Campanile*, he would not go that day."[72]

He did not leave then—or ever—for England.

Once more, Count Gamba was the force countering Byron's passivity. He now wrote to say that his daughter's grief was accompanied by a recurrence of her old symptoms: She was feverish, coughing, and spitting blood. She may have been shamming or exaggerating. Emotional turmoil, however, has been known to aggravate symptoms of consumption. She was sick enough to frighten her father, who now begged Byron to return to his daughter; Count Guiccioli, he assured him, was entirely in accord with his request. If Byron were to come back to Ravenna, he would enjoy the most complete freedom—including that of the Palazzo Guiccioli, whose second floor would be at his disposal.

In the space of a month, another crucial decision had been made for him. Still unable to act on his own, Byron delegated Fanny to deliver the happy news to Ravenna. His letter to Teresa followed: "Love has won," he told her. "I have not been able to find enough resolution to leave the country where you are. . . . I believed that the best course, both for your peace and for that of your family, was for me to leave, and to go *very far away*. . . . But you have decided that I am to return to Ravenna. I shall return—and do—and *be*—what you want. I cannot say more."[73]

He left Venice for the last time on December 21, and on Christmas Eve he was at Teresa's side once more.

CHAPTER 34

Don Juan Domesticated

*I*N RAVENNA the snow was more than a foot deep, making a mockery of Byron's blood affinity with "meridianal" Italy as the home of his beloved. Nor were his feelings for Teresa at that *estro* of fiery emotion that renders reason useless and claims love as eternal. While he could not yet point to the cause, and still less, the time and the place of their parting, he recognized that *an* end there would be:

> Could love for ever
> Run like a river
> And Time's Endeavor
>   Be tried in vain
> No other Pleasure
> With this could measure
> And like a Treasure
>   We'd hug the chain.
> But since our sighing
> Ends not in dying
> And formed for flying
>   Love plumes his wing,
> Then for this reason
>   Let's love a Season
> But let that Season be only *Spring.*—

He had written these lines when, still weak from fever, he was trying to persuade Teresa to leave Venice without him. The couplets sound a bittersweet lament for the impermanence of passion, and for the next year the question of whose affections were the more perdurable would become the subject of constant and querulous dispute.

Meanwhile, he threw himself into the role playing required by the intricate "rules and decorum" of *serventissimo*. A New Year's Eve party given by Teresa's uncle, Marchese Cavalli, was Byron's opening night, and his debut was warmly received. Teresa now had living proof that she had not been "planted," and she made the most of it: "The G's object appeared to be to parade her foreign lover as much as possible, and faith, if she seemed to glory in the Scandal, it was not for me to be ashamed of it," Byron crowed to Murray. "Nobody seemed surprised;—all the women, on the contrary, were, as it were, delighted with the excellent example. The Vice Legate* and all the other Vices, were as polite as could be;—and I who had acted on the reserve, was fairly obliged to take the lady under my arm, and look as much like a Cicisbeo as I could on so short a notice."[1]

His new role, he decided, also required him to fall in love with Ravenna. With a fervor that even Teresa found excessive (*"Il voyait tout en beau"*† she noted tenderly), he compared the city favorably to Venice on the basis of this holiday party "where there were between two and three hundred of the best company I have seen in Italy—more beauty, more youth and more diamonds than have been seen these fifty years in the Sea-Sodom—I never saw such a difference between two places of the same latitude."[2]

When the diamonds were put away, however, the routine social life of the provinces returned to its round of familiar faces and events: assemblies and *conversazione*; gossip and gambling for small sums. Byron's elation at a surprise visit from an old Cambridge friend, William Bankes—amateur archaeologist and collector of *objets de vertu* and often of less virtuous youths—hints of unexpected relief. Byron swept the visitor off to the opera, followed by a lottery. As to his own performance, he reported to Hoppner, "I am drilling very hard to learn how to double a Shawl, and should succeed to admiration—if I did not always double it the wrong side out—and then I sometimes confuse and bring away two—so as to put all the Serventi out besides keeping their *Servite* in the cold"—a play on the words *cavaliere servente* and *servite*, an order of mendicant monks.[3]

---

*The vice-legate, Count Giuseppe Alborghetti, the second-highest-ranking Vatican emissary (the first being the cardinal), had already gone out of his way to befriend Byron.

†He saw everything through rose-colored glasses.

Humor and especially irony were foreign to Teresa, and therefore suspect; she knew them as weapons used by rational men against romantic women. In Byron's case she saw clearly that his mockery was a defense against the emotional dependency he feared as feminine. "Lord Byron began to play his role [of *cavaliere servente*] with pleasure, indeed, but not without laughing at it a little," she observed. "One would almost have thought that he was a little ashamed—that in showing himself kind he was making an avowal of weakness and being deficient in that virility of soul which he admired so much. . . . This was a great fault of Lord Byron's."[4] What Teresa viewed as fear of "kindness" was her lover's dwindling self-respect and his dread of appearing ridiculous.

Indeed, within weeks, the rose-colored glasses were gone; on every front, Byron's return to Ravenna was souring.

Still camped in the Albergo Imperiale, he had now added Allegra, the animals, and servants to his suite. The Count reiterated his offer (first made in Bologna) of the spacious second floor of the two-story Palazzo Guiccioli. Byron equivocated; in what was clearly a power play, he demanded the dismissal of a servant, also named Teresa. Claiming that she was a spy as well as the Count's mistress, he would not live in the palazzo, he told *his* Teresa mulishly, as long as this creature was employed there. But he managed to find fault with every other available lodging in town, including at least one that his lover had approved for him. So at the beginning of February, accompanied by Allegra, the monkeys, dogs, cats, and birds, Byron settled into his new quarters in the palazzo.

While the move solved his immediate housing problem, the new ménage à trois created a host of others. The Palazzo Guiccioli, with its central plan and single staircase, had more space than privacy; Byron and the Count, his manner increasingly hostile, passed each other several times daily. The dangerous lovemaking of the year before, when Byron was a visitor, had been passion as high drama; the lover as lodger, slinking downstairs to remove locks that the husband-landlord promptly replaced, was sex as bedroom farce. A strange domestic symmetry evolved. The servants chose sides and duties: surveillance, spying, lookout, courier; Byron and Teresa enlisted one and Count Guiccioli the other of two black pages, both dressed in opulent "blackamoor" costumes with pistols and daggers at their belts. Surviving notes passed between the lovers—often scrawled on scraps of paper—reveal that the difficulties of scheduling meetings increased when the caller became a tenant. But this also may reflect a change in Alessandro's attitude. With no hope of further loans or other favors from Byron, the husband was using his presence to build a case against the lovers should such be needed.

Now, when the cat was away the mice were watched at all times. There was no escaping out of doors either; through late January and February, more snow was followed by rain; mountain streams over-flowed, bridges collapsed, city squares were flooded; Byron's horses stayed in their stables, as riding was out of the question.

Ravenna was also too small for a pair of important noblemen to avoid each other. So, besides living in the same house and sleeping with the same woman, Count Guiccioli and his distinguished foreign tenant found themselves on the same opera and theater committees. Quarrels over precedence and money displaced sexual rivalry. Byron had advanced funds for a benefit purse to lure the popular diva Giuditta Pasta to give a concert in Ravenna; his fellow committee member Alessandro refused to give him a receipt, Byron fumed. Other transac-tions suggest that Byron was in turn setting up the avaricious husband. When his light carriage overturned, crashing into a ravine, Byron com-missioned Alessandro to buy him another from Florence, after which he claimed the Count had cheated him. With Teresa he staged small rebel-lions, refusing to stand near her chair while she played cards or, some-what more serious, fondling her best friend.[5]

Behind the petty contretemps, the petulance and sulks, was the pain of sharing Teresa sexually; she had never refused conjugal privileges to her husband, nor did she trouble to disguise evidence of their physical intimacy in Byron's presence; it may be that with Alessandro's current dark mood, she made a point of being more affectionate than usual. What Byron saw rendered what he could not see more excruciating to his imagination. In his jealousy he seems to have reversed the roles of husband and lover; *he* is the one with the right to expect more decorous behavior: "The familiarities of that man may be innocent—but decent they are not."[6] He attacked Teresa's deviousness, her glibness in deflect-ing suspicion—traits he now gloomily assigned to the society that had formed her. The "sincerity" she lacked, he decided, "unfortunately can-not exist in the present condition of Italian morals."[7] The country he had once loved unconditionally, whose culture he had exalted as liber-ating and honest, has become the cynical corrupter of innocence. We are a long way from *Beppo*.

In his mounting disillusion, he now saw Teresa's posturings, her childishness, her triviality as though for the first time. Sir Humphry Davy had passed through Ravenna, but Teresa's only interest in the great scientist was to nag Byron to ask whether he knew of any recipe for darkening her eyebrows so the color would not come off. Without being the least stupid, Teresa was relentlessly frivolous. On the last day of 1819, when he had been in Ravenna for only a week, Byron had written to Annabella "that I think of you is but too obvious," telling her also that only three hours earlier, the "principal person" in his new life had said to him, "You are thinking of your wife." When Byron, startled, had asked Teresa why she believed this, the answer was "because you are so serious—and she is the woman whom I believe *tu ami piu ed ami sempre*"—whom you will always love most.[8]

In three years of living in Italy among Italians, he had never felt as much a foreigner. What irony now to receive from Murray a request that he write a "volume of manners" on his adopted country. He was living the paradox of the expatriate—the sense that the familiar was receding, becoming ever more mysterious, more alien. His very success in role playing guaranteed melancholy. Then, as he was trying to formulate answers to his own question—what precisely was he doing here?—he learned that Hobhouse was in Newgate Prison. Following his parliamentary defeat, he had attacked a fellow Whig for denouncing the reformers in the party. In an anonymous pamphlet, Hobhouse had demanded, "What prevents the people from walking down to the House, and pulling out the members by the ears, locking up the doors and flinging the key into the Thames?" The author answered, "Protection by the Horseguards," adding that only force permits "those who have got the tax-power [to] keep it, and hang those who resist."[9] The pamphlet was voted a breach of privilege on December 11. To spare the printer from going to jail, Hobhouse promptly acknowledged authorship, and he was found guilty of contempt. On December 14, 1819, he was arrested and confined to Newgate Prison, where he remained until February 28, 1820.

Byron's reaction to this news has been the subject of much puzzled apology. He was unable to muster the most perfunctory words of sympathy or support for his oldest friend, and his response to Hobhouse's imprisonment can be summed up quite simply: "Serves him right." Hobby was lucky merely to be jailed instead of landing in the pillory, he wrote to Murray. "I was really glad to hear it was for libel instead of larceny—for though impossible in his own person he might have been taken up by mistake for another at a meeting."

His outrage, so Byron claimed, was directed at the lowlife radicals and rabble rousers, lately Hobhouse's political bedfellows. "I am out of all patience to see my friends sacrifice themselves for a pack of blackguards—who disgust one with their Cause—although I have always been a friend to and a Voter for reform." And to Murray's sympathetic Tory ears he added, "If we must have a tyrant—let him at least be a gentleman who has been bred to the business, and let us fall by the axe and not by the butcher's cleaver."[10]

But there was more to his jeering than fear of the rabble. It was a measure of his bad conscience that Byron had not written to Hobhouse himself since the latter's incarceration in December. He had ignored a shaming letter from Newgate in which his friend noted, "The scoundrels left me here without a word during a seven weeks' adjournment. . . . and would leave me here until the Day of Judgment if they could—I have been cursedly ill and have had so many visitors & so many letters to read & write & such a pother about me that I have not had time to feel myself in prison. All my friends have been most kind."[11] Except one.

Byron knew he had some explaining to do, and he did it badly: "I have paused thus long in replying to your letter not knowing well in what terms to write—because though I approve of the object—yet with the exception of Burdett and Doug. K. and one or two others—I dislike the companions of your labours as much as the place to which they have brought you." As he was well aware, though, snobbish remarks about "blackguards" were beside the point. Honor was due—indeed, long overdue—Hobby for his courage and principles; at the very least, sympathy for his present predicament. The best Byron could manage, however, was grudging approval that ended in more scolding: "I admire your Gallantry and think you could not do otherwise *having* written the pamphlet—but why lend yourself to Hunt and Cobbett—and the bones of Tom Paine? . . . You used to be thought a prudent man—at least by me whom you favored with so much good counsel—but methinks you are waxed somewhat rash at least in politics."[12] Byron's letter was written on March 3, four days after his friend was released from prison. But Byron had not done yet.

Fearful, conventional Hobby, terrified by disapproval, by sex, by saying or doing the wrong thing, had become the Whig firebrand and martyr to freedom. In losing his first parliamentary election he had won something much grander: the laurels that Byron should have had. Brooding on this injustice from the *singerie*, that monkey house of the Palazzo Guiccioli—where it was hard to know at any given moment who was making a monkey of whom—Byron took revenge on his best friend in a lampoon:

> How came you in Hob's pound to cool
> My boy Hobbie O?

Because I bade the people pull
The House into the Lobby O.

. . . .

You hate the house—why canvass, then?
My boy Hobbie O?
Because I would reform the den
As member for the Mobby O.[13]

Byron sent the lines on March 23 to Murray, who circulated them widely before they were published in the *Morning Post* on April 15.

This was the first Hobhouse saw of the lampoon, and he was shocked and wounded—as much by its underhanded distribution as by the contents: "Oh you shabby fellow—so you strike a man when he is down do you? I do not think, however, that you intended your filthy ballad to be read to the reading room at number fifty [Murray's Albemarle Street offices] nor to find its way into the *Morning Post* before I saw it myself." Generously, Hobby decided that their friendship was more important than this piece of nastiness, and in this spirit he threw into the fire "a more serious remonstrance with you."[14] He soon had his revenge. On the strength of his heroic stand, he won in the next general election the parliamentary seat he had lost earlier. Byron's verses "did not find me in prison where I ought to have been in order to give them due effect either with me or the public, but were by a curious coincidence actually dated on the very day on which I was returned for Westminister, the twenty fifth of March."[15]

With this victory, Hobhouse joined Douglas Kinnaird, newly returned M.P. for Bishop's Gate, Shropshire. The young "genteel reformers" were assuming positions of influence, while the man who could have been their spearhead in the House of Lords waited out the wet Romagna spring. He and Teresa fought, made up, made love, listening for unfriendly footsteps. History was passing him by at home, but in Ravenna at least, he was viewed as a political subversive. Reports on his every action filtered from the Palazzo Guiccioli through the corridors of the Vatican itself; letters passed to him from the cardinal's own mailbag by Count Alborghetti assured Byron that he was an enemy of both church and state. Otherwise, writing promised the only refuge from the entropy of provincial life.

Visiting the city in 1874, Henry James marveled that—la Guiccioli's charms notwithstanding—Byron could have endured living in Ravenna for the better part of two years. He had stood it "only by the help of taking a great deal of disinterested pleasure in his own genius," James concluded.[16] Following the reviews of the first cantos of *Don Juan*, however, Byron's pleasure and confidence in the genius of the poem—if not the poet—had seeped away. He had been working on Cantos III and IV since September of the previous year at La Mira, and he was clear about the damage wrought by the attacks: "I have not yet sent off the Cantos," he wrote to Murray, "and have some doubts whether they ought to be published—for they have not the Spirit of the first—the outcry has not frightened but it has *hurt* me—and I have not written 'con amore' this time." "Decent" and "dull" was the way he characterized these stanzas, and confirming his doubts about them, he decided to cut Canto III in two, "because it was too long," assuring Murray that this decision was not made in view of charging him double "but merely to suppress some tediousness in the aspect of the thing."[17]

Tedium as the death of love, however, is a central theme of these stanzas, and insofar as this part of the poem coincides with a damping of his passion for Teresa and his immobilizing role as resident *servente*, Byron's view of the work has more to do with life than art.

> Oh, Love! what is it in this world of ours
> Which makes it fatal to be loved?[18]

is the question asked at the start of Canto III, and Juan's love for Haidée indeed destroys her, thus liberating the hero for further adventures. The poet's task, then, is to bring their story to an end. Thus, before the lovers are discovered by the enraged "piratical papa" who banishes Juan to a slave ship, causing his daughter (along with her unborn child) to die of grief, Byron, with frequent allusions to his own circumstances, anatomizes the decline and fall of an idyll. He begins, significantly, with men's disillusion on learning of women's sexual appetites. In an unmistakable reference to female genitalia as evidence of promiscuity, he notes:

> In her first passion woman loves her lover,
> In all the others all she loves is love,*
> Which grows a habit she can ne'er get over,
> And fits her loosely—like an easy glove[19]

But there is also the inevitability of boredom, of deadly sameness—a peculiarly masculine response to a complex of emotions:

---

*We may wonder whether Byron did not extract from Teresa the confession that he was not her first lover.

> Men grow ashamed of being so very fond;
> They sometimes also get a little tired
> (But that, of course, is rare) and then despond:
> The same things cannot always be admired.[20]

Beginning in perfect innocence, Byron's young lovers are at one with nature and instinct, but soon even the natural passion of these children of nature, corrupted by luxury and idleness, becomes unnatural. When Lambro is rumored to be lost at sea, his daughter barely mourns him; she has turned her father's island stronghold into a Cythera of sensual pleasure. The centerpiece of Canto III is a banquet of opulent Oriental splendor; the austere Lambro's fortune—based on action and daring—is wasted by Haidée on feasting, wine, music, and dancing. Entertainment is provided by a degenerate poet, a witty composite of Southey, Wordsworth, and Byron himself, declaiming the author's most famous lyric:

> The isles of Greece, the isles of Greece!
> Where burning Sappho loved and sung

Mourning the poet he might have been, the bard opportunely blames the decadent times, enemy to art and heroism; in present-day Greece as in certain other isles, "the hero's harp," like "the lover's lute," has been silenced.

> And where are they? and where are thou,
> My country?[21]

But there is no one to answer him. Drunken servants and guests carouse, while Haidee and her lover, drugged by passion, loll, oblivious, on silken divans in their tent:

> 'Twas wonderful how things went on improving,
> While she had not one hour to spare from loving.[22]

This is the scene that greets Lambro-as-Odysseus, upon his return home.

Now his separation of the lovers, fatal to his daughter, turns their island paradise into a ruin. Where love is concerned, however, this act of paternal revenge becomes a mercy—literally a coup de grâce. Killed by habit, by loss of illusion, by feeding on itself, by the betrayal of duty and other affections, denatured by lust and luxury, love is doomed long before lovers die.

By the end of Canto IV, Juan finds himself in a slave ship anchored below the seraglio walls of Constantinople, where he and his fellow prisoners are to be sold in the slave market. Haidée, like poor Donna Julia, is soon forgotten, banished to a romantic past; her lover's immediate fate rests on the block, where he is chained together with "Georgians, Russians, and Circassians / Bought up for different purposes and passions," none of them his own. Juan's future will be to act as a passive agent of powerful women's desires, his strings pulled by a fictional Sultana and a real Empress, Catherine the Great. When their attention turns elsewhere, he is an underrehearsed actor, stumbling onto the stage of history.

Before unloosing his Candide to wander battlefields and boudoirs, Byron tried, in these same cantos, to bridge his own sense of isolation with hope; through poetry, he reaches beyond the ephemeral, the "summer of a dormouse" that is human life.

> But words are things, and a small drop of ink,
>   Falling like dew upon a thought, produces
> That which makes thousands, perhaps millions, think;
>   'Tis strange, the shortest letter which man uses
> Instead of speech, may form a lasting link
>   Of ages; to what straits old Time reduces
> Frail man, when paper—even a rag like this,
> Survives himself, his tomb, and all that's his.[23]

Leaving *Don Juan*, Byron's new purchase on poetry as a noble tradition took the form, first, of tribute. *The Prophecy of Dante* was his gesture of homage to both Teresa ("my own bright Beatrice") and the great poet. He now claimed to Murray that the four cantos were "the best thing I ever wrote if it be not *unintelligible*."[24] Certainly his sense of identity with his subject was more immediate than in the earlier *Lament of Tasso*. Banished from Florence to die in Ravenna, Dante, like Byron, was

> An exile, saddest of all prisoners,
>   Who has the whole world for a dungeon strong,
> Seas, mountains, and the horizon's verge for bars,
>   Which shut him from the sole small spot of earth
>   Where—whatsoe'er his fate—he still were hers,
> His country's.[25]

Anxiety had led him to disparage the new cantos of *Don Juan*, but he was enormously—and justifiably—proud of his translations: earlier from his beloved Pulci, now from Dante himself. He chose the famous stanzas on "Fanny da Rimini" from the fifth canto of the *Inferno*, he told Murray in his covering letter, cuing the publisher about the technical triumph he had pulled off: "Enclosed you will find *line for line* in *third rhyme* [*terza rima*] of which your British Blackguard reader as yet understands nothing."²⁶ He wanted it published alongside the original and together with the *Prophecy*—one of his more assertive bids for a place in the pantheon. His choice of stanzas from *The Divine Comedy*, moreover, touched dramatically on his own life. In the famous episode, Francesca and Paulo, her lover, tutor and brother-in-law, are discovered together and killed by her husband—in Ravenna.

Luckily for Teresa, Count Guiccioli no longer thought he could get away with murdering his wife—at least not one as socially prominent as his present Countess. On the morning of April 2, Teresa rose to find that Alessandro earlier had broken into her writing desk, and, as her distraught note to Byron reported, he had read, one by one, all the letters that were locked inside. Once again, the question of a separation from her husband was raised—this time by a panic-stricken Teresa, who wanted reassurance. Byron's response was to repeat his earlier threat: In the event of a crisis, honor required him to leave Ravenna to save her marriage. Between her husband's increasing ill humor—his "strangeness," as she said—and her lover's threat of abandoning her, the frantic Teresa now developed a severe case of erysipelas; covered with rashes, her face and body burned and itched.

This affliction on top of all the others seems to have led Byron to repent of his egoism. Teresa, frightened and sick, reawakened a tenderness that had fallen victim to mutual power plays. Petty grievances were forgotten in the face of real danger; the shadows of Alessandro and his spying servants loomed everywhere. Byron now teasingly assured Teresa that lovemaking would not affect her illness, which "seems to me only *skin deep*—when shall we see each other—tomorrow?"²⁷ And through April, the beleaguered lovers drew closer than they had ever been. Teresa's skin cleared, and spring brought enchantment to Byron's favorite late-afternoon rides in the *pineta*. His confidence rebounded, and he was encouraged to begin a new work in an untried genre.

Marino Faliero, the first of Byron's two Venetian plays, is, unlike *Manfred*, a well-documented historical drama about the Doge who turned traitor to the Venetian Republic. Byron was explicit about the fascination this larger-than-life betrayal held for him; soon after he arrived in Venice he had visited the Doges' Palace and seen the black veil painted over Faliero's likeness. While there, he had imagined the traitor's execution taking place on the Giants' Staircase. Only days later he had written to Murray asking for contemporary accounts of Faliero's downfall: "an old man—jealous—and conspiring against the state of which he was the actual reigning Chief—the last circumstance makes it the most remarkable—& only fact of the kind in all history of all nations."[28] But his first drama set in Venice offered further homage to Teresa; it was there they had met and fallen in love. "It was written by your side," he reminded her, "and in moments assuredly more tragic for me as a man than as a writer—because *you* were in distress and danger."[29] To Murray, however, he boasted roguishly, "I never wrote or copied *an entire Scene of that play* without being obliged to *break off—to break* a commandment, to obey a woman's and to forget God's."[30]

One evening in the middle of May, the Count returned home and surprised the lovers "*quasi* in the fact,"* Byron reported to Murray (unwisely, since, as he was well aware, his letters were scrutinized by Vatican spies), "and what is worse, . . . she did not *deny* it."[31]

Demanding to see Byron immediately, the Count admitted that the visits he had once allowed, he was no longer prepared to tolerate. Deferring to the husband's age and the fact that it was his house, Byron (according to Teresa's memoirs) made no argument but retired to his apartments upstairs. Alone with his wife, however, Alessandro dropped all pretense of dignity, and made such violent scenes that Teresa feared for her safety. The next day, apparently, she sent for her father, and, after telling him everything, declared it impossible for her to continue living with her husband and begged to be allowed to return to her familial home.

WHY THE COUNT chose this moment to indulge his "fit of discovery"—as Byron dubbed the scene—is a question whose answer points to the changing political climate of Ravenna through the spring of 1820.

By May, the normal paranoia of the papal satraps was justified by real threat of civil unrest. Spreading from Sicily and Calabria, a military

---

*In her "Vie de Byron," Teresa insisted that the Count burst in on an innocent tête-à-tête, but this would be one of a number of instances in which she sanitized their affair into a platonic romantic friendship.

uprising against the monarchy was brewing in Naples, and before it fizzled into farce in July, hope had ignited radical activity throughout Italy, but especially in the Romagna, chafing under the excesses of absolutism. New secret societies throughout the province joined with established Carbonari—literally, charcoal burners—who, adding recruits from all classes, now stepped up their activities, as did those charged with infiltrating their lodges and reporting on their activities.

Since the French occupation, Count Guiccioli had been playing both sides of the fence. But now an ambitious young prelate, Father Marini, courted the Count as a means to an elusive end: ridding Ravenna of Lord Byron. For all the suspicion about his subversive influence, Byron had as yet done nothing for which he could be exiled. Further, he was a peer of England, a monarchy pledged to shore up Italy's own Bourbons. Playing on Alessandro's pride and vanity, his new clerical friend hinted at the *bruta figura* the Count was making, usurped in his own house. The high rent Guiccioli was extracting from his tenant (in lieu of the loan refused) was no longer enough to buy his complicity. Humiliation had tempered greed. This seems to have been the answer to Byron's puzzled reaction to the Count's turnaround: "He has known—or ought to have known all these things for many months—there is a mystery here that I do not understand, and prefer not to understand. Is it only now that he knows of your infidelity," he wrote to Teresa. "What can he have thought—that we are made of stone—or that I am *more* or *less* a man?"

Once more, Byron proposed that the only "remedy" was for him to leave and for Teresa to make things up with her husband, claiming "it is better for you in every way to be with A[lessandro], in six months you will think so too—and will be assured that I have been your *true* and sacrificed friend." When she objected, Byron's anger flared and he insisted that if "they"—Teresa, her husband, and her father—had not manipulated him into doing what he had never wanted to do, which was to come back to Ravenna, none of this would have happened: "You accuse me—I do not deserve it—and you know it," and he reminded her that "the time for deciding was in Venice" where "you will remember how, and how much, I implored you not to force me to return. Behold the consequences!"

He had done all he could to regularize their relations—without success. Lady Byron had not even responded to his feelers about a divorce. But he now repeated the pledge he had given Teresa in Venice: "If the matter ends with your separation from him (which I do not wish—though—on the other hand it would not surprise me) we shall make our decision—and I shall do all that should be done under the circumstances."[32] The words of a gentleman, certainly, but hardly those of a passionate lover.

Again, Count Gamba proved to be the wild card. Expected by both husband and lover to urge a reconciliation, he did the reverse. Whatever he now heard from his daughter about her marriage persuaded him that Teresa could no longer live with Alessandro as his wife, and he became a fervent advocate of a Guiccioli separation, even challenging his son-in-law to a duel. Despite his well-known Carbonari sympathies, Count Gamba enjoyed the highest Vatican connections: His late wife's parents had been married by the present Pope himself, Pius VII, then Bishop of Imola, and he had personally blessed Teresa when she was a schoolgirl. Thus the husband's efforts to keep his wife and to get rid of her lover were doomed; not even the witness of eighteen servants, attesting to the Count's exemplary treatment of his spouse, availed. On reading her father's petition that the Countess should be granted a decree of separation, His Holiness is supposed to have replied, "Such a request, made by Count Gamba on his daughter's behalf . . . cannot be anything but just."*[33]

As important as the petition itself was, of course, the financial settlement—the part that pained Count Guiccioli far more than the loss of his wife. The Gambas were asking an annual allowance of 1,200 scudi, to be paid quarterly; the return of the bride's dowry, with interest; and the right to take with her all her personal possessions. Beyond the money, however, the allowance had a crucial symbolic value: It exonerated the wife from any suspicion of guilt. Fearing that the impulsive Teresa might give this up in her desperation to be free, Byron, less romantic, offered reminders that "he [Guiccioli] will do everything possible (according to his nature—and for revenge) not to let you obtain any *allowance*. In this, you must not *give way*—not so much for the thing in itself, but on account of your reputation."[34]

A corner had been turned from which there was no retreating. Byron officially recognized Teresa as his responsibility. And what he could not prevent, he was prepared to accept. "Now I can hesitate no longer. He may abandon you, but I never shall," he pledged.[35] As the price of his

---

*The irate father was taking no chances; at the same time that he addressed his formal petition to the Pope, he wrote to Cardinal Rusconi, the Vatican legate in Ravenna, defending himself aganst Guiccioli's allegations that he had encouraged his daughter's affair with Byron, and accusing his son-in-law of attempting to "prostitute, sell and disgrace my daughter." Someone—Teresa herself is the likeliest suspect—tried to erase this phrase in the document, preserved among her papers.

new obligations, however, he was prompt in claiming new rights. Byron stood ready to help his mistress financially during what promised to be protracted negotiations with both the Vatican and her husband. In return, however, he would no longer share her with Alessandro. "I cannot be patient where money matters are involved," Byron declared, "—especially with *him*. I would make any sacrifice for you—but in that case I want you *to myself*—entirely and now—all these things belittle me in my own opinion."

Suspecting more strongly than ever that Teresa had not submitted to her husband's embraces through fear or duty alone, he announced, in the most insulting terms, that he had the power to test her and would use it: "If after suffering the insult of his requiring separate rooms . . . you go back to yielding to his false blandishments and dotardly caresses, it is you who will be to blame, and your weakness of character will be more confirmed than ever. However do what suits you," he told her coldly, "as long as I know it for my own guidance."36

In this state of tension, husband, wife, and lover waited out the resolution of the crisis. After two months, on July 12, the news arrived: The decree was granted. "The Pope has pronounced *their separation*," Byron wrote jubilantly to Moore.37 The agreement did not, however, give any imprimatur to adulterous cohabitation, but stipulated that the Countess was permitted only to leave her husband's house "to return to the House of your Father . . . so that you may live there in such a laudable manner as befits a respectable and noble Lady separated from her Husband."38 Count Gamba warned that as soon as Alessandro learned that the papal decree would cost him money, he would do everything in his power to prevent his wife's departure. Thus, on July 14 her father instructed Teresa to pack stealthily and to meet him the next day on the road to Filetto, his estate about fifteen miles west of Ravenna. Indeed, Guiccioli had ordered that no horse or carriage was to leave his stable. Closing the door of the Palazzo Guiccioli for the last time, Teresa slipped into a waiting rented livery for the first lap of the journey to her childhood home.

Predictably, the Count now ordered his wife's lover, the cause of all his troubles, to leave his house. Giving no explanation, Byron refused. For his own purposes, Guiccioli decided not to make an issue of this astonishing behavior; he planned to fight the papal decree, and having the servants continue to spy on his tenant, on the watch for any illegal visits by the Countess, might provide his best evidence for a counter-petition. Thus, for the next year, husband and lover—perhaps less the odd couple than they might appear—coexisted in an uneasy entente, the master of the house outnumbered and certainly drowned out by the Byron camp of cats, dogs, birds, monkeys, and not least noisome, Allegra, her tendency to tantrums unleashed without the attentions of Teresa, her beloved "Mammina."

While his mistress pined and worried—about her lover's certain assassination in the pine woods by the Count's thugs, about his infrequent and less than passionate letters—Byron, freed from sexual intrigue and feminine demands, returned to poetry and politics. On the very day when Teresa set out for the country, he polished the final draft of *Marino Faliero*. He had finished the play in the months of greatest tension. "I have put my soul into this tragedy,"[39] he now told Murray.

The most political of Byron's works, the story of the Doge who betrays the republic of which he is the steward, along with his own class, explores the poet's conflict about revolutionary action against the state. What is or should be the role of the patrician in bringing about the downfall of a corrupt government? When, if ever, is treason justified? Marino Faliero's beautiful young wife has been insulted; her fidelity, along with his honor, has been impugned, and the criminal has received the lightest of sentences. Thus, outraged pride and dreams of revenge drive the Doge to make common cause with the rabble in conspiring against the republic. Allusions to Byron's marriage, destroyed by powerful enemies in the ruling class, flicker through the traitor Faliero's decision:

> Farewell the past! I died to all that had been,
> Or rather they to me: no friends, no kindness,
> No privacy of life—all were cut off:
>
> . . . .
>
> I had one only fount of quiet left,
> And *that* they poison'd! My pure household gods
> Were shiver'd on my hearth, and o'er their shrine
> Sate grinning Ribaldry and sneering Scorn.[40]

Faliero's gradual contamination, less by the act of treason than by association with the mob, throws further light on the feelings behind Byron's mockery of Hobhouse's radical activities. When Israel Bertuccio, leader of the conspiracy, tells Faliero, "I am no spy, and neither are we traitors," the Doge within moments realizes that by joining the plot, he has forfeited his patrician status:

> *We—We!*—no matter—you have earn'd the right
> To talk of *us*.[41]

Ultimately, Faliero transcends class identity and dies a proud instrument of justice. Corrupt and degenerate despots, his fellow Doges had sold the Venice of their heroic forebears to latter-day Huns and a new Attila (among Byron's many references to the Napoleonic and Austrian hegemonies). Before the executioner's ax falls, Faliero curses his city. History has swept him beyond revenge to a prophet's martyrdom.

IN RAVENNA'S stunning July heat Byron was happy to forgo the summer season of opera, theater, and social events. Withdrawing into the cool palazzo, he continued to write with intense concentration, and with few other distractions, he focused on his daughter with a concern he did not often display. Highly susceptible to heat, Allegra reacted to her first Ravenna summer by succumbing to another malarial illness, and Byron, determined to remove the child from the unhealthy city, expended much time and effort finding a house to rent in the countryside, settling finally on the Villa Bacinetti, which had the added advantage of being close to Filetto.

"That blessed villa is being got ready—as quickly as possible on account of the two little girls—Allegra—and *you*," Byron teased Teresa.[42] Soon the sick child was installed under the care of two maids. But she was slow to recover, and during the weeks of her convalescence, her father appeared to be in no hurry to visit either of his two little girls. Thus it was Teresa who now rode over from Filetto to see Allegra, bringing her toys from her own childhood. Allegra in turn entertained her *mammina* with charming renditions of popular songs and devastating imitations of the servants, especially Fletcher, Teresa reported to Byron. He was pleased to hear of the child's improved health, but deplored "that tendency to mockery"—like other traits of Allegra's, so like his own—"which may become a habit very agreeable for others, but which sooner or later brings trouble to those who practice it."[43]

Throughout the spring, Claire had made known her unhappiness with Allegra's situation. Almost two years had passed since she had seen her daughter, and she now accused Byron of reneging on his promise that she could regularly visit the child. She was particularly alarmed to learn of Allegra's removal to Ravenna's notoriously unhealthy climate just at the beginning of the summer heat. Reminding Byron of the child's fevers in Venice, she insisted that "if she be to live at all, she must be guarded from the disorders of an Italian climate." Predictably, Byron refused to reply, merely informing Shelley that "I should prefer hearing from you—as I must decline all correspondence with Claire[,] who merely tries to be as irrational and provoking as she can be—all of which shall not alter my regards to the Child, however much it contributes to confirm my opinion of the mother."[44] Ever the tactful mediator, Shelley tried soothing the Byronic ego while at the same time pleading sympathy for a mother's feelings; then, appealing to Byron's nobler impulses, he reminded him that Claire was "very unhappy & in bad health, & she ought to be treated with as much indulgence as possible." And in his most Shelleyan mode he declared, "The weak & the foolish are in this respect like Kings: they can do no wrong."[45]

Appeals on Claire's behalf only caused Byron's loathing of her to seep into his feelings about Shelley. In May she had all but persuaded Shelley to repeat the Venetian disaster and to descend on Ravenna with her. That plan was averted by lack of funds, but on learning of it, Byron's distrust of Shelley deepened. Then Claire begged Byron to send Allegra to them in Pisa, from where their household was to remove to Bagni di Lucca and its cool mountain air. Without replying directly, he relayed the proposal to Hoppner. Alluding cruelly to the recent death in Rome of the Shelleys' son, little Willmouse, who, like his baby sister, Clara, had died of typhoid or malaria, Byron wrote, "I can only say to Claire—that I so totally disapprove of the mode of Children's treatment in their family—that I should look upon the Child as going into a hospital.—Is it not so? Have they reared *one*?"[46]

Believing the worst of the Shelleys gave Byron more ammunition against Claire, and he encouraged Hoppner's gossip,* reinstating his erstwhile friend, only recently in disfavor, to the role of confidant once more. In his letters to Venice, Byron vented pieties against the whole godless Shelleyan lot: "If Claire thinks she shall ever interfere with the child's morals or education—she mistakes—she never shall—The girl shall be a Christian and a married woman—if possible. As to seeing her—she may see her—under proper restrictions."[47] By which Byron meant, never again.

With Allegra's spiritual and social future assured, and Teresa safe from sexual rivals under the paternal roof, Byron could turn to manly

---

*The Hoppners added another indictment of Shelley as an unfit parent. From Naples they had heard—and busily spread—the rumor that Shelley had fathered a child with Claire and that the baby had been given to a foundling hospital. The facts, such as they are known, are these: Shelley had indeed registered the birth of a daughter, Elena Adelaide Shelley, in Naples in 1819. Boarded with a local family, the baby died seventeen months later. The identity of the mother has been variously assigned to Claire or Elise Foggi, the nursemaid, whose husband, Paolo, promptly proceeded to blackmail the Shelleys. Alternately, the possibility has been raised that the infant, already a foundling, was adopted by Shelley in the failed hope of distracting Mary from the deaths of her own two children.

pursuits and companionship. He rode regularly with an officer friend, Lieutenant Elisei, and pondered tantalizing "leaks" from the Archepiscopal Palace provided by his only other Ravennese associate, Count Guiseppe Alborghetti, who was on the staff of the cardinal legate. Alborghetti had befriended Byron early in his first stay in Ravenna and had made himself useful in myriad ways, largely as a source of classified information—some of it straight from the papal mailbag; thus Byron had received advance notice of the separation decree, of Guiccioli's machinations to have Teresa placed in a convent for breaking the terms of the agreement, of Vatican surveillance of himself, and ultimately (and most dangerous for Alborghetti) of troop movements of the invading Austrian army that would soon suppress the revolutionary uprising. Nonetheless, Byron came to suspect that Alborghetti was playing a double game, feeding him edited information while also reporting on his activities.

In July, days after Teresa left for Filetto, her brother Pietro, seventeen years old, arrived in Ravenna from his studies in Rome. Since the beginning of Byron's affair with Teresa, Count Guiccioli had written letters to his young brother-in-law detailing his ill use by the poet. Expecting to confront the Antichrist upon his arrival home, Pietro instead fell under the Byronic spell and within weeks had become the poet's worshipful disciple and friend. For Byron, the handsome, idealistic boy's appearance in his life came as a reprieve. In these last months, he had come as never before to feel worn out, physically and emotionally. He had become hypersensitive about his age, firing off an irascible letter to Count Guiccioli because he had added a year to Byron's thirty-two in a letter to the Vatican, while fuming over the reference to Hobhouse in an English newspaper as a "young man" when he was a year and a half older than Byron. Now, riding in the *piñeta*, or practicing marksmanship with Pierino, discussing each development in the revolutionary storm rumbling its way north from Naples, Byron could feel as though he was back at Harrow, still a boy himself, with this very un-English young nobleman as acolyte. Overflowing with Latin intensity, fired with unself-conscious and passionate idealism, the young Count Gamba was a creature entirely foreign to Byron's experience. He might tease and patronize the lad to others, telling Teresa, "I Like your little brother very much—he shows character and talent—Big eyebrows! and a stature which he has enriched, I think, at your expense"—his beloved was both short and short-legged. "His head is a little too hot for revolutions—he must not be too rash;" but Byron was really warning himself.[48] The disciple would inspire the master with his instinctive patriotism and spirit of self-sacrifice, together with the physical courage Byron always admired above all: "A very fine, brave fellow (I have seen him put to the proof) and wild about liberty," he later noted.[49] His own fervor was rekindled, and together the two friends discussed how "the very *poetry* of politics"[50] could be forged into action: He had found a blood brother in a holy crusade, the liberation of Italy.

To his English friends, Byron now reported regularly on incidents of local protest escalating into violence. "We are here upon the eve of evolutions and revolutions," he wrote to Murray on July 22; what began as the appearance on Ravenna walls each morning of anti-Bourbon, anti-Austrian graffiti turned into "three assassinations last week here and at Faenza," Byron detailed, "an anti-liberal priest, a factor and a trooper last night.—I heard the pistol shot that brought him down within a short distance of my own door."[51] The presence of an Austrian garrison in Ravenna made the situation still more incendiary, with skirmishes between the military and the populace on the rise. Byron noted that three soldiers had been attacked in July alone.

Behind the scenes, the Gamba men had been keepers of the Carbonari flame since the beginnings of these secret societies under Napoleon. Count Ruggero, Byron realized, had long been a local leader and was joined now by his son and nephew; all three were designated *pecore segnate*, black sheep, and kept under strict police surveillance. Thus Byron's first visit to Filetto, on August 16, marked both a reunion with the joyful Teresa and his initiation into clandestine meetings in the gracious seventeenth-century stone villa at the end of a long avenue of olive trees. The Ravenna Carbonari were divided into three groups: Byron was made chief of the most socially diverse, called the Cacciatori Americani, also known as *Turba*, or the Mob, whose membership included, among others, a blacksmith, an innkeeper, and a merchant, along with adventurers and, no doubt, informers.

Did the irony ever strike him—the horror with which he would have greeted any suggestion in England that he lead a group called "the Mob"? Here, however, the Gambas conferred blue-blooded cachet, and Byron boasted that the " 'Mericani call me the *capo*."[52] It all had the excitement of a game of cowboys and Indians, unlike the Cato Street conspiracy in London, which, he recently learned, had been plotting to assassinate (among others) an old friend of his, Lord Harrowby. What was this strange new word "radical," he asked Hobhouse, which had not even existed in "their" day? As far as Byron could see, the term was synonymous with "butchering."[53] How different were his fellow Carbonari, with their Masonic handshakes and secret passwords.

Other than conferring his own lordly and compelling presence, there is some question about what Byron and his 'Mericani actually did for the cause. According to Teresa, her lover joined with her father as a voice of moderation, dissuading the younger hotheads from poorly planned actions doomed to fail in themselves, and still more dangerous in their failure to the larger movement. But she also described him as irritated by the hours of rhetoric, when he would demand action, not words.

Throughout the sultry summer months, however, Byron himself poured forth a torrent of indiscreet words, writing to Murray, for instance, that "the Italian vespers are fixed for the tenth of Septr,"[54] the date planned for the Carbonari uprising against the Austrians, and also of the lack of unity among the groups and of their efforts to coordinate with associates in Bologna. These letters, as he elsewhere acknowledged, would have been carefully analyzed and compared with other reports by the police. In truth, Byron's dramatic accounts seem to have functioned as a substitute for action. The only enemy now was boredom.

His ennui paled before Teresa's. Until he began discreet visits to Filetto from his official *villeggiatura* at the Villa Bacinetti, he received daily letters from his lover. Despairing over her isolation and Byron's many broken dates for their reunion, she was alternately plaintive, exasperated, or angry to the point of threatening a return to Ravenna. Byron's response was harshly critical, and for the first time his criticism does not stem from personal grievance; he accuses her of larger failings that threaten all of them. How could Teresa not recognize that her insistence on their seeing each other immediately could jeopardize the entire separation decree, along with the safety of her whole family? Then, as though his own lack of urgency to be together was not painful enough, he tactlessly sent her a copy of Benjamin Constant's novel *Adolphe*, the story of a young man grown tired of an importunate mistress whom he finally abandons. Distance and this revelation of Byron's careless cruelty gave Teresa a new objectivity about his flaws, too, and, more startling, the courage to tell him so. When Byron sent her the new French edition of his works, she was appalled by the two poems "A Sketch from Private Life," his attack on Mrs. Clermont, and "Fare Thee Well" ("It gives the impression of a guilty man *asking for pity*," she told him). More positively, his relations with Teresa had moved to a new plane of intimacy; they were now able to be frankly critical without destroying each other.

On October 1, the Neapolitan Parliament opened by declaring war on Austria. Here, then, was an opportunity for Byron to move beyond secret meetings to the real theater of battle. Primed for action, he and his associates were to be frustrated yet again when the Romagnola

Carbonari were dealt a mortal blow: The linchpin of their plans, Bologna, dropped out. Determined to act on his own, Byron now composed a letter to the people of Naples in which he offered not only the lavish sum of 2,000 louis but also "his own services . . . if, as a mere volunteer, his presence were not a burden to whomsoever he might serve under, he would repair to whatever place the Neapolitan Government might point out, there to obey the orders and participate in the dangers of his commanding officer."[55]

Unhappily, his carelessness in dispatching this communiqué thwarted Byron's only chance for military glory in Italy. He entrusted the letter to one Giuseppe Gigante. As a courier Gigante had already failed so spectacularly that others had warned Byron that he was probably a spy. Claiming to have been arrested on his way from Naples by the Austrian police, he had arrived in Ravenna without papers and "almost naked."[56] Along with his letter, Byron had also provided him with clothing and money. Predictably, Gigante was again arrested on his return trip, this time in Pesaro, where, with her connections, Teresa was able to learn that he had swallowed the papers found on his person;* Byron's one documented act as a Carbonaro ended by passing through Gigante's digestive tract.

By November Teresa could bear no more of the lonely and unheated villa, and she returned to her father's house in Ravenna, where she enjoyed apartments of her own, both more luxurious and more private than the rooms where she had received Byron. With her beloved family in the same house, yet with the privileges of a married woman, she was happier than she had ever been. Byron, too, flourished, with the normalcy of their irregular union: Rising, according to his habit, in the early afternoon, he wrote or rode, went shooting with Pierino, or met with such conspirators who were still loyal 'Mericani; in the evenings he went to the Palazzo Gamba, where he visited the family, before retiring with Teresa until late into the night.

HOWEVER TRANQUIL his private life had become, the political situation in Ravenna grew more unstable with each day. Guerrilla warfare was being waged in the streets: militia, police, and mercenaries against Carbonari and enraged citizens. Byron wrote to Kinnaird, pointing out that under such volatile circumstances, ready cash would be crucial: Would he please see about the advisability of Irish mortgages along with Murray's proposed payment for *Marino Faliero*.[57]

---

*Byron's letter survives through a copy found among Teresa's papers.

For the second time he wrote to Annabella, seeking her agreement to transfer their joint investments from the funds (now at an all-time high for selling) into Irish mortgages. Before learning that her trustees refused, he complained of the "harsh" style of her reply; she might have been more "gracious, since communications between us are like 'Dialogues of the Dead.'" But the substance of her letter, he admitted, was generous. Although he had rewritten his will on their honeymoon, making Augusta and her children his beneficiaries, he asked for Annabella's promise that, if he died before her, his portion of the marriage settlement (which would normally revert to his wife) would be given to his sister as well. But when Annabella gave her word, he could not resist a cruel dig: "She & two others were the only things I ever really loved.— I may say it now—for we are no longer young."[58]

His final letters of 1820 concern the disposition of his money and work. He had heard nothing from Murray since early November, and he now wrote, enclosing an additional stanza to Canto V of *Don Juan*, with a note informing the publisher that the rest of the new canto had gone off to Douglas Kinnaird. To Kinnaird, his banker and business manager, Byron suggested for the first time that if no plans for publishing the results of his productive Ravenna spring were forthcoming, he should look into placing his work elsewhere.

As always, the end of the old year and the beginning of the new gave Byron double cause for melancholy; the sense of time running out trickled into his birthday—his thirty-third—on January 22. To Moore he wrote enclosing the latest installment of his memoirs. He reiterated his original request: These should not be published in his lifetime, but with characteristic generosity he directed Moore to look into the possibility of selling them earlier, so that his struggling friend could benefit from the income immediately, "as, with all due regard to your progeny, I prefer you to your grand-children." He went further, giving Moore "discretionary power" to change "a thing or two which is too sincere for the public" and "add what you please from your own knowledge; and *above all, contradict* any thing, if I have *mis*-stated; for my first object is the truth, even at my own expense."[59]

A week into the new year, after a month of ominous calm, rumors and alarms crackled through the Carbonari network: When Pietro spread the word that all conspirators were to be arrested on the night of January 7, Byron promptly offered to hide the suspects in his house. He stayed up all night—but neither arrests nor insurrection took place. The next morning there was a new rumor: The Austrian troops had been put on war pay and were on the march. "They mean to insurrect here and are to honour me with a call. But *onward*, it is now the time to act."[60]

This intelligence, too, proved false. Then, from the Congress of Laibach in Austria, where the monarchs of the Holy Alliance had been summoned to take action against radical demands for constitutional governance, came news of repression to come. "The *Powers* mean to war with the peoples,"[61] Byron reported.

Having volunteered the Palazzo Guiccioli to local leaders for hiding arms and men, Byron now fumed because Pietro had taken him up on his offer. To reinforce the Austrian advance the papal government now cracked down on rebel leaders: A proclamation declared that all persons concealing arms would be liable to arrest; houses had already been searched and men seized; "and what do my friends, the patriots, do two days afterwards? Why, they throw back upon my hands, and into my house, these very arms (without a word of warning previously) with which I had furnished them, at their own request, and at my own peril and expense. . . . I suppose they consider me a depot, to be sacrificed, in case of accidents," he grumbled.[62] He could be inspired by revolutionary rhetoric—his own or others—but he had no desire for martyrdom.

Meanwhile, the insurgents had fixed the date of the uprising for February 15, the day the Austrians were expected to cross the Po. But perhaps this intelligence had been planted, for the enemy, well trained and organized, quickly advanced the date by a week, surprising the Carbonari headquarters in Bologna before they could unite their member groups for any defense. Unopposed, some forty-three thousand Austrian troops swept south toward Naples. The worst blow to the planned uprising, however, did not come from the military: On February 24 the Pope issued a decree warning all good Catholics that participation in the insurgent movement was a blow against the Church and, by implication, against God. Feeling they had been misled (or seizing an excuse to defect), many of the Carbonari—leaders along with rank-and-file volunteers—disappeared. Then, on the Plain of Rieti, seventy-four thousand Neapolitan troops, more than twice the enemy strength and the vanguard of the insurgents, turned and fled from the Austrians with barely a shot fired. Following suit, most deputies of the newly elected constitutional Parliament deserted their posts, and by March 23 the Austrian army occupied Naples. The revolution was over.

Byron's bitterness expressed that of all of his comrades: "The *plan* has missed—the Chiefs are betrayed, military as well as civil—and the Neapolitans not only have *not* moved, but have declared to the P[apal] government, and to the Barbarians, that they know nothing of the matter!!!"[63] But he continued to insist that the "real Italians are *not* to blame—merely the scoundrels at the *Heel of the Boot*—The

Neapolitans have betrayed themselves and all the World, and those who would have given their blood for Italy can now only give her their tears."[64]

He was prepared to do more than weep. He tried to galvanize his fellow insurgents to launch the uprising immediately, advising them to attack in several places at once and throw the Austrian and Vatican forces off guard. Modestly, he offered help in any form—"whatever I can do by money, means or person."[65] For a start, he gave them all the funds he had on hand, 2,500 scudi. But news from outside Ravenna doused his optimism. His associates could not act alone; before they could regroup for battle, they needed agreement from Carbonari groups throughout Romagna. Their former comrades, however, were utterly defeated and ready to disperse. In the north, too, the revolt was crushed without a shot.

Daughter and sister of insurgent leaders, Teresa felt her country's hopelessness more keenly than did Byron. When he came to her for consolation, he found her seated at her harpsichord, too grieved to play: " 'Alas,' she said with the tears in her eyes, " 'the Italians must now return to making operas.' " "I fear," Byron agreed, "*that* and maccaroni [*sic*] are their forte." In tribute to her brave Pierino and "Papa," he reminded her of those "high spirits among them still."[66] As a realist and foreigner, however, Byron accepted that, for the time being, their chapter in the revolution was closed. But he knew that the recent defeat would not be the end; they were part of the future that was gathering force, unstoppable: "The king-times are fast finishing. There will be blood shed like water, and tears like mist; but the peoples will conquer in the end. I shall not live to see it, but I foresee it."[67]

For the present, though, immediate danger loomed. Emboldened by victory, the Vatican determined to rid the papal states of its enemies; reluctant to confront *milordo* directly, the administration confined itself to harassment and arrested Byron's servant Tita Falcieri for carrying arms until, to its embarrassment, it was forced to release him through the intervention of Alborghetti. With arrests multiplying, it was only a matter of time, Byron knew, before direct measures would be taken against them.

One problem rendered more urgent by the crisis was what to do with Allegra. Along with the real danger to her adult caretakers, their tensions were reflected in the child's behavior; she tyrannized everyone belowstairs (the only world over which she had some control), and, to her father's fury, she had learned to lie as barefacedly as any of the maids. Thus, at Teresa's suggestion, it was decided to send her to the

Capuchin convent at Bagnacavallo, fifteen miles from Ravenna. Byron
had wanted her to be educated as a Catholic, and the precocious four-
year-old, having a "learned aversion" to reading,[68] was more than ready
for formal instruction and discipline. She would be several years
younger than any other boarder, but Teresa herself had happily gone off
to board with the nuns at age five, so she certainly did not see this as
inhumane. Doubtful voices were raised about the convent itself; as
unhealthy as Ravenna's climate was known to be, Bagnacavallo, a
low-lying market town in the marshes, was held to be especially insalubrious; the food and cleanliness of the establishment had also been
criticized. With their other concerns, neither Byron nor Teresa visited
the convent beforehand nor even brought the child there on March 1;
her father was satisfied with the good report of his local banker,
Pellegrino Ghigi, whose daughter was also a boarder.

After months of waiting, the blow fell. The Cardinal's office had
finally seen an efficient tactic to dispose of the troublesome foreign
noble: If the Gambas were exiled from Romagna, Teresa's lover must
follow. On the evening of July 10, Pietro Gamba was arrested and
escorted to the border; luckily, Teresa had quickly destroyed all compromising documents before his rooms were searched. Although the
others hoped that age and family responsibilities would spare his father,
Count Ruggero was informed that he, too, was on the list of exiles with
twenty-four hours to leave the state. Since Teresa, by decree, was living
with her father, the Vatican was confident that the Countess would
accompany her father, with her *cavaliere* soon to follow.

Now, however, Teresa suffered a failure of nerves that came close to
a serious breakdown. Overcome with panic, she saw her lover stalked
by the reactionary fanatics of the Sanfedisti, the Vatican police, or their
Austrian henchmen. But she also feared a weakening of his feelings for
her, suspecting (as he had recently written to Augusta) that he was not
"so furiously in love as at first."[69] Paralyzed, she refused to budge, leaving her grieved father to set off alone for Florence.

Alone in the Palazzo Gamba, she tried to enlist Byron's sympathy.
"You will not refuse to become the keeper of my troubles—you who are
their only cause," she pleaded, explaining, "I do not seem to be able to
collect my ideas. . . . My head is all upset—am I losing my mind?"[70]

Predictably, Byron reacted with irritation. This was hysteria, the
feminine reaction to crisis that, along with dependence and need,
brought out his own howling demons. Her abject wretchedness, however, soon won her a brief reprieve; Byron wrote to Count Ruggero a
tactful letter defending Teresa's delay in joining him. At the same time,
he wrote to the Duchess of Devonshire, resident in Rome and with

highly placed Vatican connections, pleading for her intercession on behalf of the Gambas to commute their exile. Finally, Byron persuaded Teresa to leave for Bologna, where he had arranged with her old tutor to escort her to Florence. Before she left, she managed to extract from him the promise that he would not continue *Don Juan*, a work that could only harm his reputation further. He promised—anything, as long as she would leave! But once in Bologna, the distraught woman collapsed again, refusing to go on, and, worse, announcing her return to Ravenna for one more glimpse of her lover. At this point Byron gave way to exasperation: "Your plan of coming back here to see each other for a moment would be real folly—such a proposal really makes me think that you wish to be put in a *convent*—as was threatened," he raged, pointing to the "fatal madness" of her insistence on seeing him just now.[71] Three days later he wrote again, taking another tack: "I hope to hear that you have left for Florence—then I will write to you in detail."[72] Teresa continued her journey.

With the Gambas safely reunited in Tuscany, Byron could now breathe freely. His relief was not unselfish; he had become the *de facto* head of this endearing, impractical, volatile family. He needed a respite, all the more so as responsibility had devolved on him for the crucial decision about where they must move—together. He needed advice—about housing and Allegra and the Gambas. Not from an Italian, he was forced to admit. He wanted to talk to a compatriot who knew Italy, who understood his work, who was a gentleman, a man of "honor" and "truth." There was only one to whom he could speak freely as an equal. He wrote to Shelley, now in Pisa, inviting him for a visit, all expenses to be paid by his host.

"Draw upon me for what you think necessary—I should do so myself upon you without ceremony—if I found it expedient.—Write directly."[73]

CHAPTER 35

Exiles and Serpents

*S*ETTING OFF the day after he received Byron's summons, Shelley arrived exhausted at the Palazzo Guiccioli at ten o'clock on Friday night, August 6. He had not taken Byron up on his offer to pay for the trip, which included an overnight visit with Claire in Leghorn, where she had gone for the sea bathing prescribed for a case of scrofula. Shelley made no mention of this detour to Mary or to Byron, and he had earlier decided that Claire should not learn of his final destination in Ravenna. Many lies were told by the friend Byron called "truth itself."[1] To recoup the expenses, Shelley had saved money on the last stage of the trip by riding for a day and night in an open *calèsse*. Even traveling at a speed of two and a half miles an hour, the flimsy carriage had overturned en route, tossing passenger and driver down a hilly incline.

The invitation from Ravenna had not come as a complete surprise; in late April Byron had written a soothing reply to Shelley's hysterical letter announcing the death of Keats in Rome.[2] In England, doctors had given up on the twenty-two-year-old poet's advanced consumption: As Shelley was aware,* the trip to Italy had been Keats's last hope of recovery, but he now persuaded himself that Keats had died of a burst blood vessel caused by reading the savage attack on "Endymion" in the *Quarterly Review.*

---

*Shelley admired what he viewed as Keats's raw talent and, sympathizing with his poverty and illness, had offered to pay his way to Italy. Keats found both the older poet's criticisms of his poetry and his offer patronizing, and he declined.

Byron was no admirer of Keats. He equated the inwardness of his poetry as a refusal to engage the world, and seizing on images of masturbatory sterility, he dismissed the poet for "frigging his imagination"[3] in *"p-ss a bed"*[4] verse. But then, what could one expect from a "cockneyfying and Suburbing" provincial who had dared to criticize Pope?[5] Now, however, Byron's natural sympathy went out to a fellow poet who had died in such miserable circumstances, and he was gentle in expressing to Shelley his skepticism that a poor review had ever killed anyone. If attacks in print were fatal, who among them would be left alive? Knowing that Shelley was also raging at his own recent—and savage—reception in the same journal, Byron argued that it was living poets who needed each other's support, and he added in a postscript to his letter: "Could not you and I contrive to meet this summer? Could not you take a run *alone*[?]"[6]

Shelley would not have been unhappy at the pointed urging to leave Mary behind: Helped by a new baby, she had emerged from suicidal grief over the deaths of their two children, but in the process she had withdrawn from her husband. Now, in Ravenna, Shelley gratefully settled into Byron's bachelor routine, as he had done in Venice. On the night he arrived, they stayed up talking until dawn; then, while Byron slept and later worked, Shelley read, wrote letters, or explored the town—riding in his host's grand coach, emblazoned with the Byron crest. Toward sunset they rode in the *pineta*, returning about eight o'clock for dinner and more conversation. Installed in great state at the Palazzo Guiccioli with Tita the fiercely devoted ex-gondolier serving as his valet, Shelley accepted Byron's grandiose measure of his Ravenna connections: "Lord B. here has splendid apartments in the palace of his mistress's husband, who is one of the richest men in Italy," he reported to Mary.

Despite the corrupting luxury and curious living arrangements, Shelley found his friend morally and physically restored—indeed, thriving in "a life totally the reverse of that which he had led at Venice," a recovery Shelley attributed entirely to his "permanent sort of liaison" with Countess Guiccioli.[7] In Teresa's absence Byron provided his guest with her letters to him; reading the exile's outpourings of love, suffering, and solicitude from Filetto and now Florence, Shelley discerned the "very amiable woman" who had transformed his friend.[8] But Byron also confronted Shelley with another letter, this one from Hoppner in Venice, relaying horror stories from the dismissed nursemaid Elise Foggi about Shelley's supposed child with Claire, left at the foundling hospital in Naples; further embellishments included physical brutality and insults heaped on Mary by her husband and his mistress.

With this gossip accepted as fact by the Hoppners, Byron hardly needed to second their conclusion: He must never let Claire near Allegra
again!

Reporting the accusations to Mary, Shelley called them "monstrous
& incredible";[9] it is not reassuring, however, to read that he asked his
wife to write to the Hoppners in his defense. Moreover, neither of the
Shelleys' letters—the poet's to Mary nor Mary's long and loyal reply to
the Hoppners*—explicitly denied the substance of the scandal: that
Claire was his lover and that his "Neapolitan ward," as Shelley referred
to the baby, was their child. Alone with Byron, we do not know how—
or even whether—Shelley defended himself against the accusations. But
Byron had gained what he wanted: written proof that a respectable
family like the Hoppners, once sympathetic to Claire, had now decided
that, worse than an unfit mother, she was evil incarnate.

Fearful that Byron might turn against him, too, Shelley now repeated earlier assurances that his generous host was also the most
responsible of fathers. Regarding Byron's decision to place Allegra in
a convent over Claire's furious objections (and his own), Shelley had
written: "I feel more and more strongly the wisdom of your firmness on
this subject; and I applaud it the more because I know how weak I
should have been in your case, and I see most clearly all the evils that
would have sprung from weakness. Allegra's happiness depends upon
your perseverance."[10] To Mary, however, he now wrote with horror of
the poverty of the education chosen for the little girl; not even Byron's
promise to take Allegra with him if he left Italy softened his views on
the child's present situation: "The thing is too improper in itself not to
carry condemnation along with it."[11]

Somehow, Byron always managed to reduce Shelley to the role of
supplicant, waiting on his favor and fearful of giving offense. And
Shelley blamed Byron for his own duplicity, caused by self-hatred and
feelings of powerlessness: "The demon of mistrust & of pride lurks
between two persons in our situation, poisoning the freedom of their
intercourse," he told Mary. "This is a tax and a heavy one which we

---

*This episode is still shrouded in controversy. Shelley asked Mary to send her
defense to Byron, who would forward the letter to the Hoppners, presumably lending added credibility to her case. Because the letter was found among Byron's papers
after his death, it was long assumed that, to avoid exposure at having betrayed
Hoppner's confidence, Byron never sent the letter and was thus guilty of double
treachery. In the 1920s John Murray, a descendant of Byron's publisher, found the
remains of two separate seals on the packet containing the letter, suggesting that the
Hoppners had read and then returned Mary's letter to Byron.

must pay for being human—I think the fault is not on my side; nor is it likely, I being the weaker."[12]

There is no evidence that Byron suspected the feelings of hatred that Shelley harbored toward him. However Byron might disapprove of his friend's beliefs, he trusted in his sincerity above all other men's. He was blind to the way that Shelley's sense of being "the weaker" made frankness an impossibility, and he reported cheerfully to Hoppner that he had received letters "from both Mr. and Mrs. Shelley" approving his plans for Allegra.[13]

As far as Byron knew, then, family matters had been settled before his guest had even arrived, and by the early-morning hours they turned to "politics & literature." Shelley was impressed and more than a little envious of Byron's participation in the historic events of the past months. It was Shelley who had prophesied a new world order, of slaves throwing off the yoke of tyranny—the slaves of England's market economy as well as those under the Turkish heel in Greece—but his own revolution would be confined to personal rebellion against authority. Now he listened raptly to the details of Carbonari activities, and if Byron inflated his own role and its dangers, Shelley was not one to express skepticism.

It was Byron's recent poetry, however, that now plunged Shelley into a spiral of despairing jealousy. A few days after his arrival, his host read aloud from his manuscript copy of Canto V of *Don Juan*.

We know what a wonderful reader Byron was held to be by those lucky enough to have heard him. He could have been a great actor, his friends agreed; like the best players, he used voice, gesture, and psychological understanding to bring his characters to life. In the new unpublished canto, Juan, displayed in all his youthful splendor at the slave mart, catches the eye of the Sultana Gulbeyaz. Ordering her eunuch Baba to purchase the youth, she assumes that imperial desire suffices to command love:

> When, being made her property at last,
> Without more preface, in her blue eyes blending
> Passion and power, a glance on him she cast,
> And merely saying, "Christian, canst thou love?"
> Conceived that phrase was quite enough to move.[14]

Unexpectedly, her question summons images of "Haidée's isle and soft Ionian face," and Juan weeps at the memory: "These words went through his soul like Arab-spears, / So that he spoke not, but burst into tears." Now, the empress of desire, untainted by feeling, is subject to a series of shocks. In Juan, she witnesses a man crying and a subject who spurns her, proclaiming: "Love is for the free!" The Sultana's sentimental education will be to see herself become passion's slave.

Byron's gloss on the theme of a proud woman brought low would be mere homage to an earlier shrew tamed, but the poet has higher stakes. Tender and tearful, the androgynous Juan bends this iron woman, not into abject femininity, but awareness of her own humanity:

> For she felt humbled—and humiliation
> Is sometimes good for people in her station.
>
> . . . .
>
> It teaches them that they are flesh and blood,
>   It also gently hints to them that others,
> Although of clay, are yet not quite of mud.[15]

This was Shelley's subject: the violence that tyranny inflicts on slave and master; the tyranny of gender—and of love. Nor is the yoke of Christian marriage—the evil that drove Shelley to flight—spared. Employing his favorite device of using another culture to ridicule his own, Byron swathes social criticism in sallies of wit. In sunny climes, chastity requires special protection:

> Thus in the East they are extremely strict,
>   And *Wedlock* and a *Padlock* mean the same;
> Excepting only when the former's pick'd
>   It ne'er can be replaced in proper frame;
> Spoilt as a pipe of claret is when prick'd:
>   But then their own Polygamy's to blame;
> Why don't they knead two virtuous souls for life
> Into that moral centaur, man and wife?[16]

To complete his hero's mobility, the canto closes as it had opened, with Juan disguised as a woman. Now, fleeing the scorned Sultana's revenge, Juan is saved by the lascivious gaze of her spouse, the Sultan, by becoming the newest addition to his harem.

SHELLEY WAS stunned by what he heard. His feelings for Byron the man were racked by conflict. He now confronted the brilliance of the poet, along with the bitter reflections that his genius inspired. Canto V confirmed Shelley's earlier sense that *Don Juan* was so "astonishingly fine.—It sets him not above but far above all the poets of the day: every word has the stamp of immortality." But to Mary he could also confide, "I despair of rivalling Lord Byron, as well I may: and there is no other with whom it is worth contending. This canto is in style, but totally, & sustained with incredible ease and power . . . there is not a word which the most rigid assertor of the dignity of human nature could desire to be cancelled; it fulfills in a certain degree what I have long preached of producing something wholly new & relative to the age—and yet surpassingly beautiful."[17] In April Shelley had written an extraordinary letter to Byron, urging him to expand his historical consciousness to create a great work that would interpret their own times to the future; that he knew it was Byron alone who was capable of translating this grand synoptic vision is a measure of Shelley's humility: "Oh, that you would subdue yourself to the great task of building up a poem containing within itself the germs of a permanent relation to the present, and to all succeeding ages!"[18] In the presence of Byron's dazzling power, he must accept the role of tutor to genius, and he now wrote wistfully to Mary, "It may be vanity, but I think I see the trace of my earnest exhortations to him to create something wholly new."[19]

When Byron read aloud on another evening from *Marino Faliero*, however, Shelley felt a certain relief in concluding that the drama was inferior stuff; his own tragedy *The Cenci*, with its Byronic theme of father-daughter incest and murder, had been published the year before, for a change, to generally positive reviews. This was one area where he could stake his claim to greater skill. He faulted Byron's Venetian play for its author's reliance on the desiccated classical "system" he despised.

The two poets had argued before over the principle of a "system of criticism"[20] that Byron—who professed to abhor all "systems"—defended when it suited him. Now their differing views also placed them on opposite sides of a wider debate dividing the entire British literary establishment of writers, poets, critics, and editors. The battle line pitted "classicists," those who, like Byron, had anointed Pope and Dryden standard-bearers of a Golden Age of English letters, against Romantics, psalmists of nature turned panderers to Tory preferments. In Byron's rogues' gallery was the gang of three, Wordsworth, Coleridge, and Southey, followed by that "Tadpole of the Lakes," as Byron dubbed Keats before learning of his death only weeks before.[21]

Shelley, however, recognized Byron's neoclassicism for what it was: a moral club to attack his enemies. In Byron's own writing, it was a given that rules were meant to be broken—especially by Byron. "He affects to patronize a system of criticism fit only for the production of mediocrity," Shelley told Mary, "& although all his fine poems and passages have been produced in defiance of this system: yet I recognize the pernicious effects of it in the Doge of Venice, & it will cramp & limit his future efforts however great they may be unless he gets rid of it."22

Among the unintended "pernicious" consequences of *Marino Faliero* had been a production—unauthorized by the poet—at Drury Lane on April 25, days after its publication. Byron's romance with the theater, his work for the same Drury Lane, and his secret ambition to "best" them all went back a long way, and although he waxed indignant to everyone about this dramatic form of pirating, maintaining that as "mental theatre," none of his plays present or future was "intended" to be performed,23 in the case of *Marino Faliero* it was clear that Byron was waging a defensive action against the drama's poor performance and worse reception. He had read in an Italian newspaper that the production had been "unanimously hissed off the stage."24 Feelings of shame, not the fact of the work's being produced, had led him to protectively repudiate his own debut as a playwright. This view of Byron's "stage fright," a fear of failure as exposure, is confirmed by the poet's jubilant expressions of relief when he learned a few weeks later that his play had not been hissed after all, but had played four performances to mixed reviews before quietly disappearing from the boards.

Although Shelley was exquisitely polite about *Marino Faliero*, Byron would have sensed his lack of enthusiasm; he did not inflict on his guest recitations from three other plays: *Sardanapalus*, his first complete dramatic treatment of a classical subject; a second Venetian drama, *The Two Foscari*; and *Cain* (the last two still in progress). On one level, these are all family tragedies: The family, after all, is the source of original sin, of knowledge as crime; its expulsion from paradise is our eternal legacy of punishment. In *The Two Foscari*, the stoical Doge, placing duty above paternal love, refuses to intervene with the Council of Forty to save his unjustly accused son from exile. For his part, the younger Foscari chooses torture and death over banishment from Venice, figured as a maternal image: "my native earth / Will take me as a mother to her arms."

> I ask no more than a Venetian grave,
> A dungeon, what they will, so it be here.25

Rewriting his own "family romance," Byron imagines Francisco Foscari as being "forced" to sacrifice his son. Unlike Byron's own father, who abandoned his family through weakness, Francisco sacrifices his child on the altar of moral strength.

Calling his hero "almost a comic character," Byron, in *Sardanapalus*, reflects ironically on the family both as failed locus of dynastic power and determinant of sexual identity. Heir of the legendary Assyrian conqueror Nimrod, Sardanapalus is another son abandoned by his father; his mother, Semiramis, however, is a woman warrior who subverts the heroic succession by her unnatural masculinity but also through her incestuous designs on her son. The result is an effeminized leader who has turned his back on conquest for the passive pleasures of the senses. Rejecting bloodshed and violence for the feminine virtues of tenderness and humanity, the degenerate Assyrian ruler wants happiness for his people, not the shared glory of imperial projects. Yet his pacific reign is as much the consequence of the despot's egoism and vanity. In a wonderful scene, Sardanapalus calls for a mirror so he can see to his curls before a rare appearance as a leader of men. Two women love the dandified antihero: Myrrha, his Greek slave and concubine, tries to inspire her lover to heroic self-realization—out of the harem and onto the battlefield—and in her exhortations we hear Lady Oxford "urging a man to glory." In contrast, his rejected wife, Zarina, forgiving all and accepting all, offers a revisionist version of Annabella. With the enemy approaching, Sardanapalus makes his chamber a funeral pyre of his possessions; here he and Myrrha will die together. Before lighting the fire that will consume them, he addresses his "gentle, wrong'd Zarina," reflecting on his failure to value what was most precious when it belonged to him—a strangely familiar accusation:

> . . . if I was not form'd
> To prize a love like thine, a mind like thine,
> Nor doat even on thy beauty—as I've doated
> On lesser charms, for no cause save that such
> Devotion was a duty . . .
> . . . .
> . . . yet hear
> These words, perhaps among my last—that none
> E'er valued more thy virtues, though he knew not
> To profit by them—as the miner lights
> Upon a vein of virgin ore, discovering
> That which avails him nothing.[26]

Five years earlier, on the waters of Lake Geneva, the Shelleys had baptized Byron "Albé." Teasingly, Byron had retaliated, christening Shelley "Shiloh," the name given to the fetus in the false pregnancy announced in 1814 by the sixty-four-year-old evangelical prophetess Joanna Southcott as the Second Coming. It was the perfect name for the poet as a prophet of atheism.[27] But having put the fear of God into Shelley—the fear of losing his friendship—Byron was now prepared to reinstate "Shiloh" as a trusted intimate. He had a favor to ask of him.

When the Gambas' banishment first loomed as a reality, Byron had proposed settling in Switzerland and he had written to Hentsch, his Geneva banker, to find two houses on the lake, opposite Villa Diodati. On reflection, however, Byron regretted the idea: Geneva was horribly expensive and was crawling with English, and he hated the Swiss, he now decided. Unhappily, Pietro Gamba had fixed on Geneva as the ideal haven, and to Byron's irritation, he would not be budged. In vain, he warned the young man that Switzerland was "perhaps the dearest country in Europe for foreigners, its people being the most canny and rascally in the world about all that has to do with money—and deceitfulness—and avarice." Byron further pointed out that the Grand Duchy of Tuscany was "far, far milder than the present government of Geneva—which is now under the yoke of the anti-liberals."[28]

Byron needed Teresa's help to persuade the Gambas to remain in Italy, but as her letters to him from Florence were filled with accusations of his selfishness and neglect, he was in no position to convince her that he had only her family's welfare at heart. Thus he now delegated Shelley to write to Teresa (whom, of course, he had never met) to argue against seeking asylum across the Alps. Shelley took the cue; writing to Teresa in Florence, he described their past sojourn on Lake Geneva as a *via dolorosa* of persecution and suffering, starting with the "calumnies" planted against himself and Byron by both Swiss and English.

In his enthusiastic assumption of Byron's role in convincing Teresa to move to Tuscany Shelley had his own agenda of self-interest. He dreamed of founding an expatriate colony in Pisa, consisting of like-minded writers and radical journalists, along with friends already in residence. Lord Byron's presence would provide the "security & protection" they could not hope to find living on their own in Florence (Mary's preferred city), and would also serve as a magnet to attract others. In the next few weeks, his letters from the Palazzo Guiccioli to Mary and to Leigh Hunt in England reveal Shelley the idealist engaged in ugly plans to exploit Byron—his money, fame, even his title—while expressing distrust of his host and contempt for these same attributes, in particular for his "canker of Aristocracy." Regretfully, he conceded that "the regard of such a man is worth—*some* of the tribute we must pay to the base passions of humanity" in its deference to such distinctions.[29] The centerpiece of Shelley's plan was to bring Hunt and his family to Pisa, where together with Byron they would launch a literary and political journal to be called *The Liberal*. Along with his own contributions of poetry and criticism, Hunt's experience as coeditor with his brother John of the well-established *Examiner* promised all the professional skills needed, while Byron's name, literary popularity, and wealth seemed to be guarantees of success.

Although he waxed eloquent in selling the idea to his host, Shelley's resentment still festered; beyond contributions of poetry, he remained ambivalent about the kind of support he wanted from Byron and he warned Hunt against accepting Byron's offer of money to bring him and his family to Italy, pointing out that "there are men, however excellent, from whom we would never receive an obligation, in the worldly sense of the word."*[30] Innocent of being used—and derided—by his guest Byron was relieved by the decision to settle in Pisa, and he wanted the matter of housing resolved promptly. Feeling obligated by the success of his campaign, Shelley now assumed responsibility for house hunting and moving arrangements. Because he remained in Ravenna (claiming to Mary that Byron refused to let him leave), he directed her to find a suitably magnificent residence, and the Shelleys quickly came to an agreement with the owners of the Palazzo Lanfranchi on the Lung'Arno. A Renaissance building of the local ocher stone with a marble-faced balconied facade, the Lanfranchi boasted a garden and a landing stage on the river. It remained only for Byron to fix the date of his departure.

BEFORE SHELLEY left Ravenna, he visited Allegra at her convent in Bagnacavallo. There was no question, it seemed, of Byron's accompanying him. Bringing gifts of a gold chain and a basket of candy, he found, after some initial shyness, a delighted welcome. Allegra's only other visitors had been Teresa's grandparents, confirming for themselves the miracle that *milordo*'s biological daughter was receiving a Catholic education! Although Shelley found that the robust child had grown pale and delicate in appearance, she seemed otherwise well and happy. The nuns adored her—and along with evidence that discipline and security had done wonders for her self-control, the doting Shelley was relieved to observe that she was still an indulged little princess whose Byronic charm allowed her to break the rules without punishment. Predictably, what distressed Shelley was hearing this formerly free spirit spout the catechism: Besides "Paradise & angels . . . she has a prodigious list of saints—and is always talking of the Bambino. . . . The idea of bringing up so sweet a creature in the midst of such trash till Sixteen!"[31] When

---

*Ultimately, however, Shelley had no choice, but as usual, he obfuscated the issue by borrowing the money himself—more than £250—from Byron to lend to Hunt.

he left, he asked Allegra if she had any commissions; from her mother she wanted a kiss and a gold dress and would he please beg her "Papa & Mammina" to visit her, she asked. The last-named Shelley took to mean Claire. But it seems likelier that by *mammina* the four-year-old meant Teresa, the little stepmother who played with her in the country and in town took her for daily rides in her beautiful coach, and not the mother whom she had not seen for more than two years.

Before he left Ravenna on August 17, Shelley was confident that he had prevailed on Byron to bring Allegra with him to Pisa; anticipating her father's reluctance to have the child live with him with Claire nearby, he had urged Mary to sound out suitable families with whom she could board. By his own admission, Byron was always persuaded by the last person who talked to him, and in this instance it was Teresa's written advice that prevailed; still convinced that her lover would be in danger wherever he lived, she had urged him to leave Allegra in the safety of her convent, and for Byron the most congenial decision was always to do nothing.

Shelley, meanwhile, returned to Pisa via Florence, where he had a letter of introduction from Byron to Teresa. Being disposed to like each other, neither was disappointed. Shelley found all the endearing qualities so evident from Teresa's letters to her lover, while for her part, the poetic young woman recognized in Shelley what she found lacking in her worldly lover; the younger man suggested a sweetness and innocence that, together with his emaciated frame and too-small boy's clothing, gave the impression of a precocious child. Without knowing that Shelley had his own reasons for wanting his friend in Pisa, she felt instinctively that she had found an ally in the cause of prying Byron from Ravenna. Once back in Pisa, where he was about to sign the lease on the Palazzo Lanfranchi, Shelley wrote to Teresa, thanking her for the "confidence with which you have wished to honour me" and promising, "Be assured I shall omit no measure that may hurry the departure of Milord, for I am certain that his happiness, no less than yours, depends on the nearness of her who has been his good Angel, of her who has led him from darkness to light, and who deserves not only his gratitude, but that of everyone who loves him."[32] The unworldly Shelley had nothing to learn in the arts of flattery.

Alone in the city and in the Palazzo Guiccioli, Byron felt the familiar ennui descend like an incubus. Still, he did not want to go. He felt trapped by his own promises and responsibilities. Writing to Moore, he complained, "It is awful work, this love, and prevents all a man's projects of good or glory. I wanted to go to Greece lately (as everything seems up here) with [Teresa's] brother, who is a very fine, brave fellow. . . . But the tears of a woman who has left her husband for a man, and the weakness of one's own heart, are paramount to these projects, and I can hardly indulge them."[33]

This was Byron's first mention of wanting to go to Greece; the idea had been planted by Pietro, and in the time it took to germinate in Byron's own mind, others would take up the cause of Greek independence from Turkey. When the time came, he would not yield again to a woman's tears or even his own doubts.

Alternately peevish and apologetic, his letters to Teresa seize on or invent every excuse for delay: the weather, the horses, the servants, the moving permits (owing to his procrastination, they had expired). Buried in his temporizing, however, was the real reason for his paralysis. Always superstitious, he suffered from a premonition of doom attendant on the move: "I am leaving Ravenna so unwillingly—and so persuaded that my departure can only lead from one evil to a greater one—that I have no heart to write any more," he told Teresa.[34]

Still, he finished *Cain*, which he had begun ten days before Shelley's arrival; he wrote a forgettable satire of that tiresome target, the "learned ladies" he called "The Blues"; and by October 4, he completed another ridiculing the poet laureate's eulogy to George III and his apotheosis. Containing quotes from Southey's own pomposities, *The Vision of Judgment* was Byron's mock-heroic response to Southey's tribute, *A Vision of Judgment,* published the previous spring, in which Southey had pronounced on the mad king's fitness to enter heaven. Byron's devastating satire would cost him his publisher.

NEWS OF BYRON'S departure from Ravenna at the end of October spread sorrow among the poor who had known him or had been helped by his charities.

Since his Venetian residence, the poet had claimed to grow ever more parsimonious; certainly he was now concerned about money in a way he could never have foreseen in the heedless days of youth and debt. "I loves lucre," he joked to English friends, and it was true that his earned income had fallen off, adding to his anxieties. When it came to giving money away, however, he appears to have been more charitable than ever before, and whatever their quixotic character, Byron's bounties to the poor of Ravenna were responsible for two successive petitions to the Cardinal beseeching the prelate to persuade *milordo* to remain.

In the last week of October, twelve *vetturini** dispatched by Shelley from Pisa had come to collect the contents of Byron's apartments in the Palazzo Guiccioli, including his menagerie; he would leave behind, in the care of Pellegrino Ghigi, the banker charged with paying Allegra's bills at the convent, his unwanted animals: the old, the ailing, or those their owner had deemed too depressingly ugly. Even now, wandering the empty rooms, Byron still felt so unwilling to leave, he wrote to Tom Moore, that if his bed had not been stripped of linen, he would have remained cowering under the covers.[35] But on October 29, he mounted the imperial coach and set off toward Pisa, with a planned detour to Florence to meet his old London host, Samuel Rogers.

ON THE ROAD between Imola and Bologna he passed another carriage. Glancing idly at the occupant, what Byron saw gave him a shock of disbelief. It was Lord Clare, his only favorite from school still living, for whom his passionate attachment remained unchanged. They had not met for seven years, yet only weeks before, Byron had written in the journal he kept intermittently in Ravenna: "I never hear the word 'Clare' without a beating of the heart."[36] Of their encounter now he marveled, "This meeting annihilated for a moment all the years between the present time and the days of Harrow."[37]

As they stood together at the side of the road, the current of sympathy between them was still electric: "Clare too was much agitated— more—in *appearance*—than even myself," Byron saw, "for I could feel his heart beat to the fingers' ends unless indeed, it was the pulse of my own which made me think so."[38] Traveling in opposite directions now, they planned to meet again in the spring.

Farther along on his trip Byron's carriage passed the public coach coming from Pisa; its occupants would not have claimed his interest, but one had seen him clearly—and with no less shock. Among the passengers was Claire Clairmont, on her way to Florence and the beginnings of a life looking after other people's children. In March she had heard that Byron had placed Allegra in a convent, breaking the promise he had made at the Diodati that the child would never be separated from one of her parents, and she had written to Byron a wildly accusing letter: The physical conditions of convents were notorious enough; beyond that, the schooling he had chosen for her daughter was responsible for "the state of ignorance & profligacy of Italian women, all pupils of

---

*Drivers with wagons, whose services Byron discovered to be far less expensive than those of the Ravenna carters.

Convents. They are bad wives & most unnatural mothers, licentious & ignorant they are the dishonour & unhappiness of society. . . . This step will procure to you an innumerable addition of enemies & of blame."*[39] It would not be Claire's final letter to Byron, but this glancing encounter on the road was her last glimpse of him.

BYRON ARRIVED in Pisa late in the evening on November 1 to find that the Palazzo Lanfranchi suited him perfectly, lacking only sufficient stables for his eight horses and assorted carriages. The Gambas were happily installed in a small house, Casa Parra, a short distance away on the Lung'Arno. He had not seen Teresa in three months, and the endless delays, transparent excuses, and cranky letters had given her reason to fear he might never appear at all. By way of a peace offering he now produced verses written for her, he said, between Florence and Pisa:

> Oh! Fame!—if I e'er took delight in thy praises—
> 'Twas less for the sake of thy high-sounding phrases
> Than to see the bright eyes of the dear One discover
> She thought that I was not unworthy to love her.
>
> *There* chiefly I sought thee, *there* only I found thee,
> Her Glance was the best of the rays that surround thee.
> When it sparkled o'er aught that was bright in my story,
> I knew it was love, and I felt it was Glory.[40]

With her rudimentary knowledge of English it seems unlikely that Teresa saw any painful discrepancy between such limp "versicles"—as Byron elsewhere dubbed his doggerel—and the glowing tribute of "To the Po" or even the elegiac stanzas of "Could Love for Ever." He was there, and she was overjoyed to see him.

Shelley was scarcely less delighted; his hopes for the magic Pisan circle were all but realized, and on November 4 he paid a morning visit to Byron at the Palazzo Lanfranchi. A few days later Byron returned the call at the sunny top-floor rooms the Shelleys had taken across the Arno.

---

*Byron sent Claire's letter along to Hoppner; but instead of dismissing her accusations along with her morals and those of the Shelley household as he usually did, he uneasily defended Italian women, Allegra's convent, and, not least, his own conduct point by point: "The people may say what they please—I must content myself with not deserving (in this instance) that they should speak ill." On every score, Claire's remarks had made themselves felt.

It was the last occasion at which he would be the guest. Thereafter, Shelley and his community of followers convened, at Byron's bidding, at the Palazzo Lanfranchi.

They were a curious lot, Shelley's nucleus of a utopian community, and initially Byron must have been startled to find himself in such "rackety" company, as a later generation of aristocratic English would have called these renegades from respectable society. With the exception of the Shelleys, those who lived as couples were not married to each other. In an earlier life "Mrs. and Mr. Mason" had been, respectively, Lady Mountcashell and George Tighe, her much younger consort. Edward Ellerker Williams had been a lieutenant serving in India when he fell in love with a fellow officer's beautiful young wife; the best he could make of the scandal was to retire at half pay, settling with Jane Cleveland Johnson in Italy, where his tiny pension could still allow "Mr. and Mrs. Williams" to live pleasantly with two babies. Teresa was especially taken with Williams, a brave and handsome young man not unlike Pierino who regaled her with tales of tiger hunts under the Raj.

Also in attendance was Tom Medwin, Shelley's cousin and boyhood friend. After a lapse of some years Medwin, who harbored poetic yearnings himself, decided to track down the kinsman whose published verse had fired his fantasies of genius running in the family. During a stay in Geneva, he had become friendly with Jane and Edward Williams and readily persuaded them to make the Shelleyan pilgrimage to Pisa, where, in any case, living was much cheaper than in Switzerland. They were joined by John Taaffe, another Geneva acquaintance of the Williamses. The black-sheep son of Irish gentry, Taaffe also harbored literary ambitions; he had toiled for years on an endless and unreadable commentary to Dante.

All these now were eagerly awaiting introductions to Lord Byron. The last member of the group arrived at the end of January, nearly three months after Byron had settled into the Palazzo Lanfranchi. Edward John Trelawny might have leaped from the pages of one of Byron's Oriental tales; "I have met today the personification of my Corsair," the poet told Teresa, adding with an author's inevitable pride, "He sleeps with the poem under his pillow, and all his past adventures and present manners aim at this personification."[41] Trelawny, too, was a black sheep, of an old Cornish landed family and, indeed, looked the very picture of a pirate. A huge, swarthy figure with black, curly hair and beard, flashing black eyes, and dazzling teeth, he was an adventurer who freely invented his own life; in time he would do the same for Byron and the Shelleys. The past that Trelawny was escaping included a short naval career and an equally brief and disastrous marriage to an Italian lady, now dead. A romantic in the true sense, Trelawny sincerely loved all women in his fashion, and they responded to his sympathy; the cool and critical Mary Shelley adored him, but Trelawny would later propose marriage to Claire.

Byron had had enough of solitude in Ravenna, and if Shelley's acolytes were not the companions he would have chosen, he was nonetheless soon disposed to treat them as friends, especially since, to a man, they profusely admired him. In fact, he had little choice. Along with the Gambas, Byron was a political refugee, and his precarious status did not make him a visitor to be lionized; no Tuscan counterpart of Count Alborghetti would seek him out now. Quite the reverse. The earlier Vatican proclamation denouncing the Carbonari had been followed by a papal encyclical threatening those who rose up against their rightful monarchs with excommunication, along with their supporters. It was only a matter of time before the neutral grand duchy of Tuscany fell into line. Still, the company of his compatriots soon offered Byron unexpected pleasures, starting with their common language. Years of speaking only Italian had begun to affect his conversational English—in his own mind at least. He missed the verbal play of his native tongue, the sparring and jokes that lost so much in writing or in translation to Teresa. In the seven hours he had spent with Rogers in Florence and Bologna, he reported with relish, they had "abused everybody in our journey," and he had enjoyed his old host's malicious wit.[42] Moreover, these younger men—all under thirty—were a welcome leaven to Shelley's high seriousness.

To the dazzle of Byron the performer, with his magnetism that drew everyone who met him to hover waiting on his favor, Byron the host added the epicurean pleasures of the best men's club in London. The center of the Pisan circle shifted from Shelley and his dreams for a utopia of high-minded and simple-living spirits to the Palazzo Lanfranchi, with its lavish dinners and undemanding fun.

A new billiard table had been ordered, and shortly after their host arose in the early afternoon, members of the group dropped by, lounging around it as they took their turn with the cue. As soon as he settled in Pisa, Byron had requested permission to practice marksmanship in his garden, but, as he learned, the use of firearms within the city was forbidden. With no pine forest nearby, he rented a pasture from a farmer in Cisanello, a few miles from town. Provided with horses and pistols by Byron, his guests, including Pietro Gamba, would ride out together almost every afternoon and, on arriving at the farm, take turns trying to hit a silver half crown balanced on a forked stick. Shelley and Byron were most closely matched in skill; although Byron's firing hand shook, he usually won.

"Gentlemen only" was the new social order; Byron continued to visit the Gambas and Teresa after dinner, as he had done in Ravenna, but the pleasures that drew the disparate group together excluded ladies. But when Teresa heard reports that the farmer's pretty daughter had recently displayed armloads of costly bracelets, she decided that the shooting expeditions bore watching; thereafter she often rode out in her coach, bringing Mary Shelley and Jane Williams with her. With her usual suppleness, Teresa had gracefully accommodated to the loss of Byron as *cavaliere servente*. Since her return to her father's house in Ravenna, he had slipped into the role of Anglo-Saxon lover, visiting his mistress under cover of darkness, while she must make do with the company of similarly abandoned female companions. From the start, she had taken to the simple and lovely Jane, as she had to Ned Williams, romantically calling the union of two such appealing young people "a real idyll." But Mary Shelley, brilliant and relentlessly self-improving, was an alien creature. Learning of Mary's daily Greek lessons, Teresa teased Byron one day, saying, "I will leave you now, so as not to bore you—and to lose time *which should be given up entirely to the history of Hannibal*. But will you love me more when I know by heart the names of the river Trebbia, of Lake Trasimene, and of Cannae?"[43] Happily, she could be confident of the answer. Byron had never been fond of Mary; he preferred women in conventional roles: playful, pious, or tenderly protective, an unthreatening hybrid of sexualized child and nurturing mother.

Yielding to Teresa's sensibilities, he had given up work on *Don Juan* because she disapproved; on her advice, he had added more love interest to *Sardanapalus*; and shortly, she vetoed plans for the group's first "mixed" entertainment, a performance of *Othello*, with Byron playing Iago and Mary Shelley as Desdemona. Since Teresa knew little English, she would not have been able to participate.

In December Byron began giving dinners for his new friends, and his account books, kept meticulously by Lega Zambelli, reveal these to have been grand occasions; he hired extra staff to help his own eight servants, rented more kitchen equipment and tableware, and laid in cases of the best claret from his Leghorn supplier and quantities of cigars. Abstemious himself since Venice, he lived on green tea; hard, round biscuits like pretzels; and soda water. The contrast in outlay for his own meager diet and the five-course meals offered to his friends is dramatic. Once again, these were stag dinners, which now welcomed a new recruit and old friend of Byron's, Captain John Hay. Another officer forced into retirement by the end of the Napoleonic Wars, Hay was better off than most. Employing his leisure in travel, he was visiting Tuscany principally to hunt in the Maremma, the desolate marshland between Pisa and the sea famous for wild boar. Unlike the regulars of their little circle who took it for granted that Lord Byron should pay for everything, Hay reciprocated with generous gifts of boar and other contributions to his host's table.

As fervently as he had hoped to lure Byron to Pisa, Shelley now suffered the curse of answered prayers. Physically he was thriving: The chronic pains in his side disappeared under Byron's strenuous regime of outdoor activities. Intellectually and spiritually, however, Shelley shriveled in the blaze emanating from the Palazzo Lanfranchi until he found himself unable to write or even read. Then, early in the new year, Byron gave him the new volume containing *The Two Foscari, Sardanapalus,* and *Cain,* published on December 19. To complete the bitterness of the offering, it was apparent to Shelley on reading *Cain* how much his own rejection of orthodox belief had liberated Byron to express, through his characters, a cosmic doubt. With its echoes of Shelley's *Prometheus Unbound* and Milton's *Paradise Lost, Cain* focused on Byron's own greatest obstacle to faith: how to accept a God who defines knowledge and truth as evil and sin. Defying Adam, Byron's Cain declares:

> The snake spoke *truth*: it *was* the tree of knowledge;
> It *was* the tree of life:—knowledge is good,
> And life is good; and how can both be evil?[44]

An agent of entrapment (with all the best lines), Lucifer the fallen angel masterminds Cain's fulfillment of original sin in the murder of his brother. But it is Abel's sinless death that, in Byron's terms, indicts what Freud would call the "moral fallacy" of Christianity. Why should the innocent be sacrificed to save the guilty?

Drenched as it was in heterodoxy and skepticism, it was predictable that *Cain* would give Murray palpitations, and so it did, followed by the publisher's usual pleas to trim or tone down offending lines. In his own defense, Byron cited Milton himself against any outcry of "blasphemy";[45] he then ran for cover under the pretext that any blasphemies came from the mouths of his characters, not their author. But Shelley could only admire—and suffer. "I have lived too long near Lord Byron. The sun has extinguished the glow worm."[46]

Just as Canto III of *Childe Harold* was marked by Shelley's vision of human love illumined by a benevolent nature, *Cain,* Byron's strongest statement of doubt, bore the unmistakable stamp of the atheist's visit to Ravenna and of their conversations far into the night. Only weeks before Shelley had arrived, Byron had denounced him as "crazy against religion & morality."[47] But with *Cain* it seems clear that Byron had been more concerned with disassociating himself from Shelley's public profession of his views and from his role as prophet of the Antichrist, for which he had already been punished. "Shiloh" had been Byron's nickname for his friend—but now he had a new name for Shelley: "the Serpent," a siren voice of forbidden truth.[48]

From having been at the center of the Pisan colony, Shelley now found himself on the margins, merely another member of Byron's audience, a guest at his table and companion on his outings. This, along with his own continuing inability to write, increased his impatience for Leigh Hunt's arrival. Then, he hoped, their three-way collaboration in editing and writing *The Liberal* would restore a balance of achievement and power. But Hunt, his ailing and pregnant wife, and their large family would be detained by stormy seas off Portsmouth for the next months, and Shelley was now obliged to ask Byron for £250 for his friends' living expenses in addition to what he had already advanced for their passage; Shelley found his inability to play the Maecenas (ceding to Byron once again) especially galling, and his bitterness continued to smolder.

Another serpent, too, was casting a beady eye on the group's activities. Since the arrival of *il Capitano Scellyny, Sedicente Ateo** the Buongoverno—the "good government," the inaptly named Tuscan police—had been keeping watch on the small English colony and its leader. As soon as Byron and the Gambas appeared, the foreigners were under constant surveillance. The new arrivals' dangerous status as political exiles placed them in a different category from the others, as signaled by their residence permit of only two months. The principal excuse was fear of Byron's subversive influence on students at the University of Pisa; infamous for his "favour of *all political novelties*," the first report noted, Byron would soon become "the Protector and Centre of all those young fanatics."[49] So innocuous was the routine at the Palazzo Lanfranchi, however—the sociable pleasures of a rich expatriate—that not even a spy within the household, in the person of Byron's cook and Count Guiccioli's former servant, Gaetano Forestieri, could pinpoint any activity that showed *milordo* to be an enemy of the state. But on Sunday, March 24, the patience of the police was rewarded.

What has come to be known as the "Pisan affray" began as an ordi-

---

*Captain Shelley, self-proclaimed atheist.

nary afternoon shooting party at the farm. Returning to town toward
sunset, the riders—Byron, Captain Hay, Taaffe and Shelley, Pietro
Gamba and Trelawny—in high spirits, were strung out in two lines
across the road, while ahead of the men went Teresa in her carriage with
Mary Shelley. Byron's coachman, Vincenzo Papi, was driving, and a servant of the Countess's was mounted behind. Suddenly a dragoon of the
local hussar unit, Stefano Masi, galloped from behind and tried dashing
through the narrow space between Taaffe and the ditch. Apparently he
caused Taaffe's mount to shy and back into Byron's horse. Anxious to
make plain where the blame lay, Taaffe shouted to Byron, "Will we
endure this man's insolence?" Byron rose to the challenge: The dragoon
must not be allowed to get away with such behavior. At this Shelley, no
doubt feeling goaded, called to Byron, "As you please." Then, as a body,
the Englishmen spurred their horses and, galloping past the ladies' carriage in a cloud of dust, surrounded the dragoon at the gate. Insults and
threats were exchanged. Wrongly assuming that the dragoon was an
officer and a gentleman, Byron threw down his card, the formal challenge to a duel. The Italian, however, was merely a sergeant major, and
his furious response to the *maldetto Inglese*, "the damned Englishman,"
was to demand the guards at the gate to arrest all the riders. At this
Byron sneeringly invited them to do so if they would and, waving to the
others to follow him, charged through the Porta della Piazza, heading
for the city.

Now, the shouting match turned into a free-for-all. Before galloping
after Byron, Pietro Gamba lashed Masi with his whip. In the fracas that
followed, Shelley rushed the dragoon who, after knocking the poet from
his horse, wheeled around to deal with Captain Hay by taking a slice of
his nose and forehead with his saber. Taaffe, the cause of the incident,
was nowhere in sight, having stayed behind to rescue and brush his hat.
Seeing only the dazed Trelawny, Sergeant Major Masi, deciding that his
honor was satisfied, trotted away toward Pisa and his garrison.

But on the Lung'Arno, Masi once again encountered Lord Byron;
another angry exchange followed and attracted gawking onlookers.
Byron now decided that matters had gone far enough, and he called off
his servants who had rushed from the Palazzo Lanfranchi to detain
Masi. Entering his house, he found Mary tending Teresa, whose hysteria on returning from the scene had worsened into convulsions. Byron
took both women to the Gamba house and tried reaching Dr. Vacca, his
Pisa physician. Meanwhile, as Masi passed in front of the Palazzo
Lanfranchi, an unidentified member of his lordship's household rushed
down the steps with a rake or pitchfork, and while the dragoon struggled
to get free, a blade was thrust into his side. The wounded man just

managed to make his way through the crowd before falling from his horse and collapsing in a jeweler's shop nearby.

Only when he got back to the Palazzo Lanfranchi did Byron learn of the attack on Masi and worse news: The dragoon was not expected to last the night. To forestall charges being brought against them—very possibly for murder—Byron coolly decided that they must, according to Italian law, "be the first to accuse and not wait to be accused." Accordingly, through the night and next days, he sent each member of the group in turn to the police to give his or her version of the affair. As a noble he retained the right to depose evidence at home.

Byron had no way of knowing that, in this case, protocol would be of no use to him. The Tuscan authorities had been waiting for just such an opportunity to rid the province of the Gambas and their trouble-making English friends. Not even the dragoon's unexpected recovery changed the determination of the Buongoverno to drive the subversives from Pisa.

The next two months, April and May, were taken up by further depositions from those who had been present at the affray, while the Tuscan authorities, as cowardly as the Vatican police in Ravenna had been about confronting *milordo* Byron and the Counts Gamba directly, resorted to their familiar strategy of harrassment through the domestics. They detained and arrested for various periods Teresa's servant Maluchielli, who had acted as a footman behind the coach; also members of Byron's household, including Lega Zambelli and his coachman Vincenzo Papi, who turned out to have been Masi's actual attacker; but they reserved their worst treatment for Tita, the fierce-looking gentle giant beloved by everyone in the group. While in jail they humiliated him by cutting off his beard, and when finally they released him for lack of evidence, it was to banish the innocent man who was accompanied to the Tuscan border under police escort.

During this period Byron kept up a campaign of letter writing to Edward Dawkins, British consul in Florence, seeking his intervention on their behalf. Dawkins, to judge from his concerned but diplomatic replies, was trying to balance his sympathy for Byron and his own suspicions that the Tuscan court, bowing to papal pressure, was using the case to harass a British subject and his Ravennese friends against mounting evidence that the expatriates at the least had made themselves unpopular by their arrogance and at worst were guilty of covering for Masi's assailant.

While the case dragged on, animosities within the group surfaced; solidarity unraveled. The first to break ranks was Teresa, who, suspecting that her servant was being made a scapegoat because Byron could afford to pay for the release of Papi, the real culprit, now accused Taaffe of the attack. Taaffe himself filed a separate deposition, dissociating himself from the others. Morally, if not legally, the Buongoverno had managed to divide and conquer.

ONLY DAYS before the Pisan affray, on March 24, Claire had written to Mary Shelley from Florence, voicing her anxiety about Allegra; she had had no news of her child, and she feared that the little girl was sick. Knowing she could never obtain Byron's permission to visit, Claire had conceived the scheme of kidnapping her daughter from the convent, for which she would need a forged letter from Shelley. The Shelleys quashed this plan firmly, but they now took turns reviling Byron to Claire. Mary expressed complete agreement that Allegra "ought to be taken out of the hands of one as remorseless as he is unprincipled."[50] Unhappily they claimed to be out of pocket after helping Hunt* and furnishing their own apartments; otherwise no sacrifice would be too great "to extricate all belonging to me from the hands of L.B. whose hypocrisy & cruelty rouse one's soul from its depths."[51] To this Shelley added the news that they were looking for a house on the sea for the summer months "*far* from Lord Byron's, although it may be impossible suddenly to put an end to his detested intimacy."[52] Coming from one who continued to accept Byron's hospitality on a daily basis, we may wonder against whom the accusation of hypocrisy might more accurately be brought.

On April 13, Pellegrino Ghigi, the Ravenna banker who had been left in charge of Allegra's expenses at the convent, sent the first of several reports to Pisa that the child had indeed been ill, with a recurrence, in the words of the abbess, of the "light and slow"[53] fevers, the same, apparently, from which she had suffered the previous year. The abbess had been sufficiently worried to bypass the local physician and send instead to Ravenna for Dr. Rasi, who ordered the child to be bled three times. Ghigi, charged as he was with the care of Byron's abandoned animals, was in the habit of sending all his communiqués to Lega Zambelli or to Fletcher, with the understanding that anything of importance (as

---

*In fact, it was Byron who had advanced Hunt all the funds needed for his journey. To his credit, Hunt confronted Shelley for trying to pass off Byron's help as coming from him, and the poet apologized abjectly: "I did wrong in carrying this jealousy of my Lord Byron into his loan to you, or rather to me," he wrote to Hunt, "and you in the superiority of wise and tranquil nature have well corrected and justly reproved me."

opposed to notice of routine expenditures) would be passed on to his lordship.

It is not known whether this first warning of Allegra's sickness reached Byron, but the banker's second report, two days later, was certainly conveyed to her father. Now that the child was declared to be out of danger, Ghigi could be frank: "I assure you that she has been very ill, of a dangerous illness," he wrote, reporting that he had visited the convent himself and found Allegra surrounded by three doctors and all the nuns. "If there is any fault, it is of too much care," he concluded, but aside from the bleeding, it is not clear what, if anything, was being done.

According to Teresa, Byron was "very much agitated" by this account,[54] but not so much so that he entertained the idea of going to see the sick child himself. Instead, he sent a courier to Bagnacavallo to provide him with further details of her condition and ask the nuns to send for Professor Tommasini of Bologna, if need be. But there was no need, for on April 19,* after a "convulsive catarrhal attack,"† Allegra died.

Bravely, Teresa took on the grim task of informing Byron of Allegra's death. But, as she recalled, he knew what had happened before she could utter a word, and she attributed his own refusal to speak of the catastrophe to a father's measureless grief.

Others have judged Byron's reaction to the tragedy very differently: He was as unfeeling about Allegra's death as he had been toward the child in her lifetime. But it is also true for Byron that all deep attachments in his life—especially female—were spoken of lightly, even flippantly; when guilt or loss complicated matters, his reaction became defensive, in all the ugliest expressions of that attitude. Now, innocent of Shelley's real feelings about him and his treatment of Claire and Allegra, he wrote to his fellow poet, so recently a bereaved father himself:

The blow was stunning and unexpected; for I thought the danger over, by the long interval between her stated amelioration and the arrival of the express. But I have borne up against it as best I can,

---

*The date of Allegra's death is variously given as April 19, 20, or even 24. Given the delays attending all news from the convent, the earliest date seems the most probable.

†This last symptom, an inflammation of the lungs, suggests that Allegra's recurrent malarial fever, aggravated by pneumonia, was the cause of death. Typhus has also been suggested, but as this disease, carried by lice, is highly contagious, the absence of other fatalities at the convent makes it an unlikely cause of Allegra's death.

and so far successfully, that I can go about the usual business of life with the same appearance of composure, and even greater. . . . I do not know that I have any thing to reproach in my conduct, and certainly nothing in my feelings and intentions towards the dead. But it is a moment when we are apt to think that, if this or that had been done, such event might have been prevented—though every day and hour shows us that they are the most natural and inevitable. I suppose that Time will do his usual work—Death has done his.[55]

He wanted Allegra's remains sent to England, to be buried at Harrow, in the graveyard where he had dreamed so happily as a boy. The biblical verse that he chose for the marble tablet was not perhaps quite apropos:

I shall go to her, but she shall not return to me*

In the thirteen and a half months that she had been in Bagnacavallo, twelve miles from Ravenna, he had never once gone to her.

One letter survives from Allegra to Byron, written from the convent on ruled paper, in a five-year-old's wobbly best penmanship: *"Caro il mio Pappa,"* she wrote, "it being fair-time, I should like so much a visit from my Papa as I have many wishes to satisfy. Won't you come to please your Allegra who loves you so?"[56]

The letter is dated September 28, 1821. Aware of his imminent departure for Pisa, Mother Superior Fabbri had included a note also urging him to come and see his Allegrina, "where and how she is situated, and let me also add, how much she is loved."

Byron sent both notes to Hoppner in Venice. Across Suor Marianna Fabbri's letter he scrawled: "Apropos of Epistles—I enclose you *two*—one from the Prioress of the Convent—& the other from my daughter her pupil which is sincere enough but not very flattering—for she wants to see me because 'it is the fair'—to get some paternal gingerbread—I suppose."[57]

Byron's words have been read as exposure of an egotism so voracious that he required flattery from a five-year-old. What his note

---

*Samuel 2:12.23. The church warden and some parishioners objected on the grounds of both the poet's notoriety and the illegitimacy of his child. Byron's request for the funeral service to be conducted by Henry Drury was not granted. Allegra was buried at the entrance to Harrow Church.

also reveals is a tragic blindness: He did not see his daughter as a child hoping for a holiday treat. She was another mercenary female interested only in what she could get out of him—gingerbread or gold, it was all the same. As far as is known, neither the mother superior nor Allegra ever received a reply.

Now Byron instructed Ghigi to arrange for a costly embalming process, the body then to be shipped from Leghorn in a wooden coffin encased in lead. Unable to come to Pisa himself, the banker sent two emissaries, one of whom, a priest, was his brother-in-law. They had brought Allegra's body to the port themselves and had come to give Byron an account of the child's last days and to learn the disposition of his wishes in her death. But Byron refused to see them, and they were not even granted admittance to the house before being sent away. Such behavior was unheard of, even for a household in mourning: "I am prepared to believe that Mylord is very sensitive and deeply grieved, but I also recognize that every man has his own self-respect . . . and sorrow must not make one forget his manners towards others."*58 Ghigi wrote. This was far from the worst reproach Byron would hear.

The Shelleys, meanwhile, had rented an unused boathouse at San Terenzo, a hamlet near Lerici on the Bay of Spezia. Convinced of the disaster that would follow if Claire, who had just arrived in Pisa, should hear of Allegra's death while in the same place as Byron, they spirited her off with them to their new quarters. There they debated how they should break the news. But she did not need to be told. Coming upon Mary, Shelley, and the Williamses talking together in hushed tones, she guessed immediately. The horror of the following days was beyond describing, was all that Shelley could say. Although she appeared remarkably restrained, Claire wrote Byron a letter of such savagery that merely guessing at its contents Shelley, ever fearful of offending his lordship, felt moved to apologize for her and even for his own indelicacy in conveying Claire's last requests: She wanted to see the coffin before its journey from Leghorn to England and to have charge of any funeral arrangements beforehand; she wished also for a likeness of Allegra (should Byron have only one, Shelley would undertake to have a copy made) and for a lock of her daughter's hair. Byron sent the keepsakes by the next boat, along with word that Claire should make any funeral arrangements she wished. Shelley managed to dissuade her from

---

*It was also left to Teresa to inform the Shelleys of Allegra's death and to arrange for shipping her remains to England.

the "melancholy" plan of seeing the coffin, and in the end she could not face the prospect of any services for her dead child.

FOUR WEEKS LATER, on May 21, Byron and the Gambas also left Pisa. The past months had exhausted his little family, and the Masi affair was still not settled. With great difficulty Byron had succeeded in obtaining permission for the banished Tita to go to the Shelleys' in Lerici, but Count Ruggero was still in Florence trying to secure the release of Teresa's servant. Byron had rented a villa, Villa Dupuy, in Montenero, a hilly suburb of Leghorn much favored by rich English residents for its sweeping views of the harbor and the Mediterranean beyond. Here they would also have to decide where to settle next, since the Gambas, their official residence permit having expired, were only allowed to stay in Montenero at the pleasure of the Buongoverno, a period of grace likely to be short-lived.

Always restored by the sight of water, Byron had another reason to anticipate the move with pleasure. In early winter he had commissioned a yacht, actually a scaled-down model of an American three-masted schooner. Its construction in the Genoa shipyards, supervised by Trelawny, was carried out by a Captain Daniel Roberts, a retired naval officer skilled in the design and building of boats; Roberts was also building an open sailboat for Shelley. During the crises of the past months, Byron had still managed to confer with Trelawny, who was acting as his agent, on all the luxurious features he wanted for his seagoing villa: "Let the cabin be most sumptuously fitted up, with all kinds of conveniences for provisions, wine, Books, tables, sofas, hooks for pistols, riffles [sic], beautifully painted but not gaudily, what think you of blue & white?"[59] Water closets, alas, proved unfeasible. Byron planned to christen his boat the *Countess Guiccioli*, but, persuaded of the indiscretion of that honor, he decided on the *Bolivar*, a provocative name that, along with the two one-pound cannons on her foredeck (purely decorative and bearing Byron's monogram), was noted by the Tuscan authorities as confirming their suspicions. They therefore refused the schooner a permit to discharge or board passengers in any port along the coast. Trelawny was to deliver Shelley's boat in Lerici in early June, and Byron's at Leghorn later in the month.

On his arrival, Byron was a guest of the American Mediterranean fleet anchored in the bay, a visit that gave his spirits a needed lift. He was received "with all the kindness I could wish and with *more* ceremony than I am fond of" by the squadron commander, Jacob Jones, who gave the poet a tour of his gleaming vessels, including the famous frigate *Constitution*. To complete any author's day, the captain showed him a "very pretty"[60] American edition of his poetry and offered him free passage to the United States, and he was told of another group of Americans who wanted to commission his portrait from the painter William Edward West, then studying in Italy. Further homage from the New World came the following day, their first in Villa Dupuy, when the young historian George Bancroft of Boston called on Byron in Montenero. Having met Goethe, he could report the admiration that the great poet—indeed, the Germans in general—felt for *Don Juan*. This news decided Byron to restore the dedication to Goethe which had been dropped from *Sardanapalus*. But soon after the young American scholar's visit, all the pleasure of their *villeggiatura* quite literally wilted.

By early June Tuscany was in the grip of a fierce heat wave that did not spare its only port city. Byron spent much of his time alone in the darkened *salone*, brooding on the past. For all his forbearance at Allegra's death and his claims of innocence, the demons of guilt now descended: "Let the object of affection be snatched away by death, and how is all the pain ever inflicted upon them avenged!" he told Lady Blessington a few months later. "The same imagination that led us to slight or overlook their sufferings, now that they are forever lost to us, magnifies their estimable qualities. . . . How did I feel this when my daughter, Allegra, died! While she lived, her existence never seemed necessary to my happiness; but no sooner did I lose her, than it appeared to me as if I could not live without her."[61]

Not even the promised visit of Lord Clare cheered him; it was so brief as to leave his host feeling more desolate than ever: "I need hardly say what a melancholy pleasure it was to see him for a *day* only," he told Moore.[62]

Recalling the offer of a passage on the *Constitution*, he began to fantasize once more about the South American scheme, writing to England again for the particulars of land for settlement. He talked so much that the dream began to take on reality—one in which Teresa assumed she would be included. But writing to Tom Moore, Byron was clear that his motive was escape—from his entire present life: "I had, and still have, thoughts of South America, but am fluctuating between it and Greece. I should have gone, long ago, to one of them, but for my liaison with Countess G.i. *She* would be delighted to go too, but I do not choose to expose her to a long voyage, and a residence in an unsettled country."[63]

Then, following weeks of drought, the water supply at the villa gave out entirely; every drop had to be carried by muleback from a spring in the hills, more than an hour's climb away. The added labor exacerbated tensions among the domestics, pitting Teresa's servants against

Byron's. Now, with the Pisan affair still dragging through the court, another fracas—more farce than drama this time—erupted belowstairs at Villa Dupuy. One of Byron's servants flatly refused to go on the exhausting errand for water and "began declaiming," in Teresa's words, "against the rich and the aristocracy, and speaking of equality and fraternity";[64] the other servants rushed to the scene, and their shouting produced Count Pietro, who ordered the man to do as he was told. At this, the rebel apparently drew his knife, grazing his master's arm. The revolution had come home to roost. The most radical of the Gambas had no choice but to aim his pistol at the insurgent member of his own household. There were more screams, bringing to the balcony Lord Byron, who threatened to fire on all of them below. Unfortunately, Fletcher now called the police, thus establishing the Byron-Gamba ménage as a source of constant disruption to peace and order. The Gambas were informed that unless they voluntarily left Tuscany within four days, the order of official banishment would follow immediately.*

In the midst of this, Leigh Hunt appeared with his sick wife and children, all of them exhausted by the sea voyage and stunned by the scene taking place in the great Lord Byron's household. However untimely, Hunt's long-delayed arrival provided an excuse to leave the Villa Dupuy and return to the cool marble rooms of the Palazzo Lanfranchi. By July 3 the elder Hunts and their entire *kraal*, as Byron now sourly called their dirty and unruly brood, were settled on the ground floor of the palazzo, while Byron's bulldog, Moretto, chained and snarling at the head of the stairs, made sure they were kept away from his master on the *piano nobile*.

From the first, relations between the floors were strained. Teresa spoke no English and Marianne Hunt, unlike the charming expatriates in the Shelley circle, refused to learn Italian. Her tongue, however, was so sharp that no language barrier could soften her hostility: She was openly disapproving of their host; first, for his insistence on the deference due his title, then for his absurd expectations about the way children were supposed to behave. She reported to her diary, "It is so painful to be under obligation to a person you cannot esteem! Can anything be more absurd than a peer of the realm—and a *poet* making such a fuss about three or four children disfiguring the walls of a few rooms—The very children would blush for him, fye Lord B—fye!"[65] Mr.

---

*In fact, the order had already been prepared, but the coincidence of its timing led the Gambas and subsequent writers to assume that the Montenero episode provided the excuse for their banishment.

Hunt took his revenge for the slights they had all suffered in a book, *Lord Byron and Some of his Contemporaries*, published after the poet's death.

If no favor goes unpunished, Hunt's complete dependence on Byron's largesse ensured punishment of his patron beyond the grave. Having spent their host's original loan on the voyage and its many delays, the Hunts arrived penniless, expecting Byron to provide not only food and lodgings but even pocket money. How could they not hate him? Any gesture their benefactor made to ease the stark comparison between his wealth and their poverty was perceived as miserly or patronizing. The Hunts criticized everything: their barred street-level rooms, the cheap furniture (actually bought by Shelley), the coquetries of Teresa. Madame Guiccioli, Hunt sneered, "was a kind of buxom parlour-boarder, compressing herself artificially into dignity and elegance, and fancying she walked, in the eyes of the whole world, a heroine by the side of a poet."[66] For her part, Teresa was so revolted by Hunt's vulgarity that she began to entertain the shocking new theory that man was descended from the apes.

To spare Hunt the embarrassment of accepting cash directly from him, Byron advised simply "for whatever money you want apply to Lega—I never have any about me—in pocket for I love it in a *casket* but not in a purse," and he added tactfully, "Pray do not deem this out of the way—for when I have occasion for a sixpence—I send after it to him."[67] But at this, Hunt raged that he was fobbed off on the majordomo and obliged to plead for every coin like a beggar. How different from Shelley and his exalted sense that money (borrowed from Byron, to be sure) existed to be shared with kindred spirits.

From Lucca, safely across the Tuscan border,* Pietro wrote imploring letters to his sister. The Vatican had already canceled her allowance from Count Guiccioli, and now that she and Lord Byron lived openly together, she risked incarceration. They must make their plans to leave Pisa—and quickly.

Then, at midnight on July 13, Teresa and her maid were summoned from the balcony by a carriage at the door. Mary Shelley, "as white as marble," stood there, with Jane Williams at her side.[68]

"*Sapete alcuna di Shelley?*"—Have you any news of Shelley?—she gasped. Five days earlier, Shelley and Williams had sailed the poet's beloved new boat, the *Don Juan*—"fast as a witch,"[69] he had boasted—from Leghorn into one of the worst summer squalls in memory. They

---

*Lucca, now part of Tuscany, was then a separate principality.

had not been seen since. But no one at the Palazzo Lanfranchi knew anything of Shelley or the boat, and the distraught women rushed back into the carriage, riding through the night until they reached Leghorn. The next day a note arrived from Captain Roberts, the builder, asking Byron for the use of his schooner to search the coast. Roberts was pessimistic; he had advised Shelley against his repeated demands for dangerous improvements to the light eighteen-foot open craft with no deck. But when Shelley had seen his little boat at the dock next to Byron's schooner, with her soaring masts, he insisted on more sails and a false prow for greater speed. He was further spurred in his imaginary race by rage over his new boat's name. *Don Juan* had been chosen when she had been jointly owned by Williams, Trelawny, and himself. Deciding to buy the others' shares, he had asked for her to be rechristened *Ariel*. But the original name—of the masterpiece he could never hope to equal—had remained painted on the mainsail, "like a coal barge," Mary had said. And he blamed Byron.

In the next days, Byron joined the search at the mouths of the Arno and Serchio Rivers. It was not until July 18, ten days after their disappearance, that the bodies of Shelley, Williams, and their eighteen-year-old boatboy, Charles Vivian, were washed up, several miles apart, on the beach between Viareggio and Massa. Shelley's face and arms had been eaten away. The corpse was identified by strips of the nankeen jacket and white trousers he had worn. Inside one pocket was the binding of a folded volume of Keats's *Lamia*.

Tuscan and Lucchese quarantine law required that the corpses be buried with lime on the beach where they had been found. Mary, however, had determined that Shelley's remains should lie next to their little son in the Protestant Cemetery in Rome. Now Trelawny took over, prevailing first upon the authorities to permit them to exhume the bodies, cremate the remains, and transport the ashes from the site. The romantic mythmaker was in his element, and he decided that his anti-Christian friend should have a proper pagan ceremony for the cremation. But nearly a month passed before the permits were in order, and it was only on August 14 that the gruesome business could proceed. According to Trelawny's plan, he was to set out from Leghorn on the *Bolivar*, bringing a portable iron furnace that he had had designed and built; two boxes of lead enclosed in oak to contain the ashes were to be delivered to Byron in Pisa. Then Byron, accompanied by Hunt, would drive the eight or nine miles to the site in his carriage. By the time the seaborne contingent found the place, however, it was too late to notify Byron, and the matter had to be put off until the next day.

Byron arrived, barely in time for the grisly proceedings. Williams's body had all but disintegrated, and the remains had to be unearthed with fishhooks. Byron had told Trelawny earlier that he could identify anyone by his or her teeth, and he was now obliged to cross the scorching sands to pronounce on the jawbone. "The moment he saw the teeth he exclaimed 'That is him,' " Trelawny recalled, "and his boot being found and compared with one brought for that purpose identified him beyond a doubt. It was a humbling and loathsome sight . . . a livid mass of shapeless flesh. Lord B. looking at it said, 'Are we all to resemble that? Why, it might be the carcass of a sheep, for all I can see'—and pointing to the black handkerchief—said, 'An old rag retains its form longer than a dead body—what a nauseous and degrading sight.' " But when the fire was lit under the makeshift crematorium, Byron, along with the others, found relief in throwing handfuls of incense, salt, sugar, and wine "to add to the fierceness" of the spiraling flames.[70]

Claiming he wanted to test the power of the waves that had engulfed their friends, Byron stripped and swam out beyond the breakers in the direction from which the bodies had washed on the beach. But this was a way of rationalizing the need to escape in the cold currents from the heat, the smells, and the horror of the still-smoldering remains, with Trelawny rooting around in his incinerating contraption until he found an intact jawbone. About a mile from shore, Byron became terribly sick, but when one of the crew swam out to him, he refused to come in, insisting that he must rid his body of "black bile." The next day, they returned to perform the same rites for Shelley. Once again Byron arrived after the digging had begun—much worse this time, since the poet's remains took longer to find; they were located finally by a spade that struck the skull. Byron asked for it, but the cranium shattered on being moved, in contrast to Shelley's heart, which, refusing to be consumed, took on the status of a sacred relic.

Complimenting Trelawny—not without irony—on his incantation over the pyre, Byron observed, "I knew you were a Pagan, not that you were a Pagan Priest; you do it very well."[71] Hunt was too upset to leave the coach, and Byron, too, could not remain long and watch what was left of Shelley, the flesh a horrible indigo, turn to white-hot ashes. Once again he plunged into the sea, swimming to the *Bolivar* anchored a mile and a half offshore; the pleasure craft he would never use had become a funeral transport, bringing all the grim implements for disposal of the dead.

Finally, the boxes containing the ashes were placed in Byron's coach, in which they all repaired to Viareggio, where, according to Hunt, they dined little and drank too much. As they rumbled through the pine forest toward Pisa, the effects of alcohol, exhaustion, and the fearful sights witnessed erupted in hysterical merriment: "They sang, laughed and shouted," Hunt recalled.[72] Byron now suffered the agonizing consequences of three hours in the water in the blazing midday sun: All the exposed parts of his body were so badly burned he became "one large continuous blister," followed by his "whole skin's coming off." For days he could not lie on his back or side, but by August 27 he could write to Moore that "it is over—and I have got a new skin, and am as glossy as a snake in its new suit."[73] He had survived Shelley, that unlucky Serpent whom he would always believe to have been "the best and least selfish man I ever knew," he told Murray. "I never knew one who was not a beast in comparison."[74]

Beset by ironies, their relations could never have been untroubled—even without Shelley's envy and duplicity; without his insistent virtue and arrogant atheism; without Claire or Allegra; without Byron's success, his wealth and title; without his nostalgia for orthodoxy.

"Certain it is," Shelley wrote, "that Lord Byron has made me bitterly feel the inferiority which the world has presumed to place between us and which subsists nowhere in reality but in our own talents, which are not our own but Nature's—or in our rank, which is not our own but Fortune's."[75] For his part, Byron could never escape the little lame boy living above an Aberdeen perfumer's shop, Shelley's aristocratic courage and moral certainties beyond his means.

CHAPTER 36

The Road to Missolonghi

ITH SHELLEY'S DEATH, the Pisan circle scattered. The men were gone, ending the riding and shooting expeditions, along with the stag dinners. Avoiding the Hunts, Byron and Teresa settled into a conjugal intimacy. Twice a week they visited Shelley's grieving widow and her two-year-old son. Jane Williams was soon to return to England, and Mary, feeling completely abandoned, was thankful for Byron's concern, which included assurances that she should think of him as her banker. He was, she said, "very kind to me."[1] The Countess was pointedly excluded from her gratitude.

Otherwise, Byron withdrew into the cool of the Palazzo Lanfranchi, where Tom Medwin, absent from Pisa since January, "found him sitting in the garden under the shade of some orange trees, with the Countess. They are now always together, and he is become quite domestic. He calls her Piccinina and bestows upon her all the pretty diminutive epithets that are so sweet in Italian. His kindness and attention to the Guiccioli have been invariable," Medwin noted.[2] Small wonder that Mary felt aggrieved and excluded. While she excoriated Byron morally, he had long figured in her romantic and sexual fantasies.[3] Alone now, she may well have hoped that his earlier distant manner would soften to intimacy.

Since their return from Montenero, Byron had also been hard at work; writing provided a refuge from his tenants, but in the terrible weeks between Shelley's disappearance and the cremation, retreat into poetry also kept unwelcome images at bay. More confidant of her power, Teresa gave him permission to continue *Don Juan*, and Byron took up his Adam at the point where, cast from his island paradise, Juan is bound for the slave mart at Constantinople. He celebrated Teresa's indulgence by incorporating her happiest memories of Santa Chiara schooldays—the girls dressed in their brothers' clothes playing at courtship—into Cantos VI and VII. When Juan infiltrates the seraglio disguised as "Juanna," however, he exploits his androgyny less innocently in Dudù's bed. Was Byron also remembering his stay in Greece, when he and Hobhouse, dressed in women's costumes, had danced with local boys? By way of contrast, he also completed the most horrifying episode of the poem and significantly, Juan's first foray into history. Byron intended the Siege of Ismail, with its massacre of innocent civilians, a pendant to the Peninsular slaughter in *Childe Harold*, as a harsher political indictment of the greed and opportunism of war. These stanzas, he told Moore, constituted an attack on "these butchers in large business, your mercenary soldiery . . . it is necessary, in the present clash of philosophy and tyranny, to throw away the scabbard. I know it is against fearful odds; but the battle must be fought; and it will eventually be for the good of mankind, whatever it may be for the individual who risks himself."[4]

He had two more verse dramas ready as well. *Werner: A Tragedy* was "taken entirely," Byron insisted, from a story, "The German's Tale," which he had loved since he was a boy.[5] Its setting, moreover, now gave him a chance to redeem the dedication to Goethe that Murray had dropped from *Sardanapalus*. Byron had begun a version of *Werner* before leaving England, but with the unhappy associations of that period, he had put the work aside. Conversations with Shelley, however, seem to have revived his interest in probing the wounds of hereditary taint, specifically the question of whether a father's one immoral act creates a legacy of guilt. Although the new drama reworks themes in *Manfred* and *Cain*, it reveals how the aging of the author changed his earlier romantic view of rebel youth. Unlike *Lara* or *The Corsair*, *Werner* is no outlaw hero with a titillating criminal past; his son Ulric, however, Byron's new protagonist, moves closer to the villain as a young punk whose future, according to one critic, points to a brown shirt and swastika.[6]

Now, from the Gambas in Lucca came the expected bad news: Political exiles under papal proscription were unwelcome there, too; Genoa appeared to be the last and only refuge left for them in Italy. So at the end of August, Byron prepared to move his household for the fourth time since he had come to Italy five years before.

He had tried persuading the Hunts to remain in Pisa, to no avail. The first issue of *The Liberal* was just coming together; now that Shelley, the project's prime mover, was dead, Hunt had every reason to fear Byron's cooling interest, and he was not going to risk letting his sole means of support out of his sight. Mary was eager to leave Pisa, and she yielded to Byron's advice against returning to England, accepting the Hunts' proposal that she share living quarters with them in Genoa. Going ahead, she found two houses, one with forty-four rooms for the nine children and three adults of the Hunt-Shelley ménage, with a separate residence two miles away for Byron and the Gambas. Byron had increased the number of his dependents, but physically, at least, he would soon be rid of the *kraal* and their hostile, demanding parents.

Then, while he was mired in the moving arrangements, he had word from Hobhouse of his imminent arrival. After the bittersweet reunion with Lord Clare, Byron had become self-protective about the feelings of loss inflicted by such brief reunions, explaining frankly, "These transient glimpses . . . however agreeable they make the moment . . . [are] like a dose of laudanum—and its subsequent languor."[7] He feared, too, that Hobby would find him changed—and not for the better. Early in the year, Byron had commissioned busts of himself and Teresa;* his portrait, resembling a "superannuated Jesuit," he found "dreadful—though my mind misgives me that it is hideously like. If it is—I can not be long for this world—for it overlooks seventy," he had told Murray.[8]

Inflexible as always, Hobhouse remained wedded to his itinerary, arriving on the evening of September 15. He did not report finding Byron looking older, but he was certainly "fatter," he said. Teresa recalled the moment just before their visitor appeared. They were sitting together in the garden. "A soft melancholy was spread over [Byron's] countenance; he recalled to mind the events of his life, and compared them with his present situation, and with that which it might have been if his affection for me had not caused him to remain in Italy." Although Teresa chose to read his sadness as redeemed by love for her, Byron's reaction belies this romantic hope, suggesting, instead, feelings of regret and loss she could never assuage. When the servant announced a Mr. Hobhouse, the poet's somber expression "gave instant place to the liveliest joy; but it was so great that it almost deprived him of strength. A fearful paleness came over his cheeks, and his eyes were filled with tears as he embraced his friend."[9] Hobhouse, however, had grown less sentimental and more stodgy with the passage of time. He took a dim view of all that engaged Byron in Italy, personal and political. He dismissed his Carbonari activity as frivolous and was still more disapproving that his friend and his mistress lived together openly and, with the Gambas' blessing, planned to cohabit in Genoa as well: "This is Italian

---

*The artist was the noted neoclassical sculptor Luigi Bartolini.

morality," he said primly. And when he left on the morning of the twenty-first, Byron felt bereft, just as he himself had foreseen. Trying to lift his spirits with a joke, he told Hobby, "You should never have come or you should never leave."[10] But he did not mention a dark foreboding; he would never see his friend again.

On the eve of another expensive move, his plans uncertain beyond the certainty that Genoa was a way station, Byron's anxiety focused on money. The notes from Kinnaird representing his half year's income still had not arrived, and the pace of his nagging letters to the banker quickened. He pressed him about his Noel inheritance; his insurance on Lady Byron's life; his investments in government funds; finding a buyer for the Rochdale property—that "gulph of Litigation,"[11] as he called it; and, finally, the fee Murray was prepared to pay for the new cantos of *Don Juan*. Byron apologized for having "worked" Kinnaird,[12] who, losing patience, had finally complained about Byron's harangues. By way of excuse, he tried justifying his apparent obsession to accumulate capital: "In short—Doug—the longer I live—the more I perceive that Money (honestly come by) is the Philosopher's Stone."[13]

Finally, on September 29, he set off by land for Genoa. With the inedible part of his menagerie installed in the wagons, he had insisted at the last on bringing his geese: He must have roast goose for Michaelmas, or bad luck would follow for the rest of the year. (In the event, he could never bear to wring the creatures' necks for his feast.) Now, in cages that hung swaying behind his great coach, they embarked on a life as household pets, to waddle cackling after their master in his new home. The master spy assigned to Byron in Pisa submitted his final report on the poet to his Vatican employers. Clearly, his underlings had done some hard listening at keyholes: "Mylord has at length decided to leave for Genoa. It is said he is already tired of his new favorite, the Guiccioli. He has expressed his intention of not remaining in Genoa, but of going to Athens to purchase adoration from the Greeks."[14]

The move required the logistics of a military invasion. Byron, accompanied by his worldly goods, animate and inanimate, made a detour to Lucca, where he met Teresa, Pietro, and Ruggero Gamba; from there they proceeded to Lerici, where they were met by a hired boat for the trip to Sestri; there Byron's coach would be waiting to travel the last lap overland to Genoa.

Arriving at Lerici, they met as planned with Trelawny, who had sailed the *Bolivar* from Leghorn. By way of diversion, the "pirate" now proposed a swimming match; he and Byron would race to the schooner, where, treading water, they would be served a picnic lunch on floating trays. Seized with cramps on the way out, the poet nonetheless made it to the boat, where both swimmers ate and drank plentiful quantities of food and ale. Feeling worse, Byron now had to be helped up the ship's ladder, but after a brief rest in the broiling sun, he insisted on swimming back to shore. For the next four days he was deathly ill, wracked by intestinal spasms "in the worst inn's worst room" at Lerici.[5] Dosed with purgatives and hot compresses, he recovered, and at last their convoy—Trelawny in the *Bolivar*, Byron and Teresa in one boat, and the Hunts in another—crossed the Gulf of Sestri.

Clattering up the steep, high-walled streets of Genoa, above the great palaces in the lower town, they arrived late at night on October 2 at the village of Albaro, just outside the city gates. Once again, Mary had done well in her house hunting. She had found for Byron and the Gambas a seventeenth-century villa, the Casa Saluzzo, square and built of gray stone, whose balconies offered sweeping views of the harbor and the Mediterranean. The rent was £24 a year, and there was ample room for the Gambas and Byron to have separate living quarters.

For the next eleven months Byron retreated into a new and painful kind of isolation. In Venice he had been a principal player in the *ridotto* of fashion and vice. In Ravenna he had slipped into the strangest of triangles, one that was part of the larger geometry of the Guiccioli and Gamba families, sharing with them a wife, a daughter, and political exile. Then, in Pisa, he found himself at the center of Shelley's ragtag circle of expatriates. But in this port city, at the end of the long Italian summer, he felt only exhausted possibilities.

Now that he was rid of the Hunts as tenants, Byron never set foot in the Villa Negroto, their cavernous residence. When Mary came to the Casa Saluzzo, it was only to leave the manuscripts Byron continued giving her to copy. She was never invited socially. Teresa alone continued her visits to Mary, now reduced to once a month. So much for the widow's fantasies. As the weather turned cold, the Negroto's one working fireplace forced her into the Hunts' noisome company merely to keep from freezing. Hunt now had Mary in his power; he took to chastising her for her coldness to Shelley, sternly urging that she must admit her guilt and repent. Despite her pleadings, he refused to relinquish Shelley's heart, which he had taken from the cremation pyre, until shamed by Jane Williams into yielding it to his widow. Humiliated by his dependence on Byron, Hunt consoled himself by victimizing one more powerless than himself.

In her despair, Mary unburdened herself to Byron in long letters damp with self-pity, self-righteousness, and unspoken reproach. His replies were terse and snappish. Yes, he had purchased Shelley's sofa not to deprive her of this shabby relic but to save it from the destructive fingers of the little savages; he would replace it with a new one.[16] Meanwhile, he did his best to be helpful—at arm's length: Along with buying furniture from her, he saw to it that she received the effects from the *Don Juan*, recently raised with all its contents intact, including the £50 Byron had given to Shelley at their last meeting. In his capacity as Shelley's executor, he instructed Charles Hanson, John Hanson's son, to see what he could do to induce Sir Timothy Shelley to pay his late son's allowance to his widow and child. And of course he declined to accept the £2,000 that Shelley bequeathed to him in his will. It was Mary's indecision, the paralysis of depression, that irritated Byron most, probably because he suffered from it himself: She changed her mind "five or six times" about whether she would stay or return to England, he complained. As for Hunt, he was even more exasperating at a distance. His letters to Byron alternated the arch with the arrogant—the latter tone reserved for requests for money: "I will trouble you for another 'cool hundred' of your crowns,"[17] he wrote. There were no invitations from the Casa Saluzzo to him either, but undaunted, Hunt invited himself.

Hunt's behavior was not, however, the only cause of Byron's increasing hostility. From the beginning, his collaboration in *The Liberal* had been reluctant, sustained only by Shelley's diplomacy. Sadly, the two poets' last meeting had ended in angry words, with Byron announcing that he did not want his name to appear on the publication. (At the last, Shelley convinced him to relent.) Now, with the first issue about to appear, published by Leigh Hunt's brother, John, and featuring Byron's incendiary satire, *The Vision of Judgment,* his friends in London raised a chorus of alarm; Kinnaird, Hobhouse, Murray, and especially Moore saw Byron's reputation suffering further assaults from his association with the two radical journalists.* From Genoa, Byron had defended his commitment to Leigh Hunt on the grounds that a pledge, once given, was a matter of honor: "You would not have had me leave him in the street with his family, would you?"[18] he wrote to Moore. But then, when Hunt refused his offer of a return passage to England, revealing his intention that Byron should support him and his family permanently, his patron was stirred from irritation to rage that he admitted often approached "phrenzy."[19] He felt trapped. Everywhere he looked were dependents—the Hunts; Mary Shelley; and the Gambas.

The trouble with generosity is that it is quickly taken for granted;

---

*Hunt was already infamous in London as a sponging sycophant who turned on his benefactors, and he was caricatured as such in the person of Harold Skimpole in Dickens's *Bleak House.*

favors become rights. It did not matter that Byron had given Shelley the last £50 he ever saw, or that Byron continued his support of the Hunts and offered repeatedly to help Mary after Shelley's death. These acts have been overshadowed by the petty fits of economy that now seized him: He fussed over the smallest discrepancies in Lega's household accounts and earned the enmity of Captain Roberts, designer of the *Bolivar*, by refusing to let two crew members keep their uniforms. There is another reason, too, why the Byron of these months has come down to us as a monster of stinginess. To express their own grievances in a high-minded and morally gratifying way, both Mary Shelley and Hunt each resorted to a strategy of accusing Byron of deplorable treatment of the other.

Then, after the appearance of the first issue of *The Liberal* on October 22, his friends' worst fears came to pass: The journal itself was not merely denounced. Byron's contribution, *The Vision of Judgment*, caused the publisher, John Hunt, to be indicted for libel of the King and his royal patrons. In large part this was Murray's fault; when it became clear that he was unwilling to publish the work himself, Byron instructed him to send the manuscript to Hunt. But Murray, despite repeated reminders, had failed to include the all-important appendix to *The Two Foscari*. It was here that Byron, by enumerating Southey's calumnies against *him*—accusations that he and Shelley were joined in a "League of incest," with Byron as leader of a "Satanic School"—had made a strong case that *The Vision* was merely one poet's defense against another's earlier libels. Now, however, Byron offered to return to London to stand trial in Hunt's place. When this proposal was declined, the poet paid all of Hunt's legal expenses connected with the trial.* Strangely, it was not *The Vision* but *Heaven and Earth*, a lifeless attempt to dramatize the Deluge, that proved the coup de grâce in Byron's deteriorating relations with his publisher. Poor Murray had had to run for cover with the appearance of *Cain*. Now the prospect of another Byronic challenge to Scripture along with the three new "outrageously shocking" cantos of *Don Juan* goaded him out of circumspect silence: "My company used to be courted for the pleasure of talking about you—it is totally the reverse now," Murray wrote to Byron accusingly, "and by a re-action, even your former works are considerably

---

*With atypical foresight, Byron added to his will the directive that his estate should continue to pay John Hunt's legal expenses, should these continue after the poet's death. Indeed, the matter was settled only in 1825, more than a year after Byron died.

deteriorated in sales."* Then, in a still nastier swipe, he warned of what could happen to Augusta if Byron persisted in this provocative vein: "My name is connected with your Fame and I beseech you to take care of it even for your sister's sake—for we are in constant alarm but she should be deprived of her situation at Court."[20] Considering Murray's presumption in conflating his good name with Augusta's precarious position, Byron's reply was more than civil: "I shall withdraw from you as a publisher, on every account, even on your own, and I wish you good luck elsewhere."[21] In keeping with the restraint of his letter to Murray, Byron never explicitly expressed regret for the end of their ten-year association, which spanned his entire adult career as a poet. Instead, to friends he counted the ways of Murray's unworthiness: the publisher's cowardice, dishonesty, indiscretion, hypocrisy, and ingratitude. But he could not avoid the bleak reality that another chapter of his life had ended.

THE GENOESE AUTUMN darkened into winter. Rains swelled into storms; there were flash floods. Cataracts of water swept down the narrow road that passed in front of the Casa Saluzzo's iron gates; a neighbor's child drowned. Lightning struck the window where Byron and Teresa watched a thunderstorm over the harbor. Byron felt the electric current crackle through him; Teresa was merely terrified.

Gone was the intimacy of their last days in Pisa, when tragedy had drawn them closer together. Now, in separate apartments in the drafty stone house built as a summer villa, the Gambas and Byron reverted to separate lives. He and Teresa had formally established hours together: short morning strolls in the garden, early evening visits (by invitation only) in his apartments. During the long intervals between, Byron retreated to his study overlooking the dripping lemon trees or rode into town alone to dine with William Hill, the British consul, or with his new banker, the courtly Charles Barry, head of the Genoa office of Webb & Co., whose main branch was in Leghorn. When he was kept late, he would write notes to Teresa to announce his safe return. To fill her time, she now embarked on a course of daily English lessons—the only expense she ever allowed Byron to underwrite. She had been eager to learn her lover's native language from Shelley (a project vetoed by Byron), but her studies now seemed a sign of estrangement. Once it had been Byron's joy to lose himself in *her*

---

*Byron was particularly infuriated by this remark, since Kinnaird had managed to elicit from the crafty publisher that *Cain* had sold close to six thousand copies.

language—the language of love. To avoid losing him now, she would try to fathom his unexpressed thoughts.

He had called his attachment to her a "finisher."[22] But his capacity for intense feeling was finished as well. More than ever, he resisted any emotional demands; when her younger and favorite sister Carolina died of consumption in February at age twenty, Byron did not go to the grieving Teresa, sending instead the most perfunctory of condolence notes: "But she is Happy. . . ."[23]

One visitor from the past roused him to his old spirit of mockery. From Paris, Wedderburn Webster turned up, still estranged from Lady Frances and still entranced by himself as an irresistible rake. Byron was amused to learn from the hotel register that Webster deducted ten years from his age and wore a black wig sprouting flirty curls. He tried and failed to extract repayment of a ten-year-old £1,000 loan he had made to Webster— conscience money for trifling with his wife. But he could not even pry from him the interest on the principal, Byron grumbled.

Then, on the last day of March, a fascinating group arrived in Genoa: "the Gorgeous Lady Blessington," accompanied by her lord, her unmarried sister, Mary Ann Power, and the etiolated dandy Count d'Orsay. The young French aristocrat was said to be Lord Blessington's lover, for whom his wife, rumored to be uninterested in men sexually, served as a beard.

Lady Blessington had long yearned to meet Byron—the reason for their Genoa visit. "I never felt before the same impatient longing to see anyone known to me only by his works. I hope he may not be fat, as Moore described him in Venice, for a *fat poet* is an anomaly in my opinion."[24] Byron was so thin that his out-of-style Venetian clothes hung strangely on him, while his gray-streaked curls, allowed to grow too long behind, in the manner of balding men, added to his derelict appearance. "I saw Lord Byron for the first time," she recorded the next day, "and this first impression disappointed me."

Born Margaret Power, Lady Blessington was the daughter of a drunken Irish farmer who had sold her to a neighbor to pay a gambling debt. At fourteen she had run away and, selling herself with ever greater success, eventually married her longtime protector, Lord Blessington. Like all self-invented aristocrats, Lady Blessington (now Marguerite) was highly sensitive to matters of taste. She was appalled by the vulgarity of the famous bed with its "Crede Byron" escutcheons;* Byron's *gaucherie*

---

*Before she had learned that true style consists of understatement, Lady Blessington's own bed had been the talk of London: It was an enormous silver swan, with every feather molded separately.

she recognized as self-consciousness about his lameness—still, this physical defect alone did not explain the strained chatter, the indiscreet revelations about himself and his intimates, the boasts about Count Guiccioli's ducal connections and six black horses. She had imagined a suffering Childe Harold; in his place she found an anxious *arriviste*: "Were he but sensible," she mourned, "how much the *Lord* is overlooked in the *Poet* he would be less vain of his rank; but as it is this vanity is very prominent, and resembles more the pride of the parvenue [*sic*] than the calm dignity of an ancient aristocrat."[26]

Lady Blessington spent the next eight weeks in Genoa, much of the time with Byron; they rode or walked in the Lomellini gardens; there were dinners at the Casa Saluzzo, reciprocated with invitations to the Albergo della Villa. And in her remarkable memoir *Conversations with Lord Byron* we hear, along with the poet's "very self and voice,"[27] the process of a penetrating listener's change of heart. From disillusion at finding the great Romantic poet a "broken dandy," with his dated Regency slang, she came to see a tragic man isolated in another country and language, utterly alone. Like a prisoner hungry for news of the "outside," he was starved for word of England and stories of *their* London. For Byron, Lady Blessington was a glittering emissary from his own past; with all her wit, charm, and large acquaintance in the great world she was also, like him, an outsider, filled with mockery and yearning. Teresa's jealousy of the visitor notwithstanding, Byron was never in love with Lady Blessington. From the brilliance of Sir Thomas Lawrence's great portrait it is apparent why he never could be. Her knowing gaze promises everything but the kind of love—uncritical and unconditional—that Byron needed from a woman.

Her visit, however, had been opportune in yet another sense. Since Byron's move to Genoa, he had continued work on *Don Juan*, and the last six cantos of the poem, with a seventh left unfinished, have been described as his *Remembrance of Things Past*. He had stopped writing his memoirs; in their place he began a journal that he kept intermittently and whose title, "Detached Thoughts," suggests its randomness. Along with musings on religion and philosophy, the activity of writing sparked a free-associative scroll through his early life, that yielded recollections, anecdotes, and scraps of conversation, beginning with his Aberdeen childhood. Fueled by nostalgia, the most evocative of these entries summon up Byron's conquest of London in his "Years of Fame." This is the raw material of the "English Cantos."

Don Juan, more worldly now, following his exposure to savage warfare and a sexually savage Empress, has become Catherine of Russia's special ambassador to another field of combat: Georgian England.

Miming his creator's mobility, he glides through London palaces and the great country houses of their aristocratic inhabitants. Juan is looking for love, along with a suitable bride, and these two incompatible needs provide the excuse for a montage of Byron's women. With an accompanying cast of minor characters, two women engage in a duel of angels for Juan's soul. Lady Adeline Amundeville, brilliant hostess, restless and unhappy wife, appears a composite of all the worldlings Byron had loved or even admired: "Her heart was vacant, though a splendid mansion"[28] evokes memories of Ladies Melbourne, Oxford, and Holland, and the presence of Lady Blessington. In contrast, the purity of Aurora Raby reveals, like a turning prism, facets of Augusta and Annabella. Physically "infantine," orphaned, and devoutly Catholic, the unworldly Aurora reminds Juan himself of his lost Haidée. Aurora's childlike qualities, however, point to another presence. Allegra, first called Alba, or "Dawn," was symbolically orphaned; her parents' sins were to be redeemed by her Catholic education. Mysterious and incomplete, Aurora, the woman Allegra might have been, hovers over the unfinished *Don Juan*.

WHEN THE Blessingtons left on June 3, Byron was desolate. Their company had given his parched spirits a "sense of refreshment," Tom Moore said.[29] But it was his friendship with Marguerite, woven in their common language, social and psychological, that had restored to him a lost intimacy: "Byron's heart," she had observed, "is running to waste for want of being allowed to expend itself."[30] Yet he expended some of his feelings on this woman, radiant with sympathy; as a measure of his trust, he asked her to prevail on another English visitor, Colonel Montgomery, fervent partisan of Lady Byron, to plead on his behalf for a portrait of Annabella. More important, he confided to her the plans he still dreaded to tell Teresa. He had decided to go to Greece as emissary of the London Greek Committee, to see if, as some now claimed, a series of small victories by the Greek insurgents could become a real revolution.

Well before the Blessingtons' arrival, since the turn of the year 1823, Byron had made no secret of his restiveness. "If we do not go to Greece, I am determined to go somewhere, as I am tired of this place, the shore and all the people on it," he told Captain Roberts, hardly a man privy to his intimate feelings.[31] Two years earlier, in the spring of 1821, the Greek war of independence had broken out, starting in the Peloponnese. That September, in a letter to Murray, Byron had interrupted a discussion of other concerns to ask suddenly: "What thinkest thou of

Greece?"³² On hearing the names of places he had visited, now the sites of victories or defeats, his nostalgia for the Levant quickened. At the same time, the suppression of the Carbonari and his disillusion with the possibility of revolution in Italy only diverted his dream of joining a patriots' revolt: it was not provocation alone that had led him to name his boat the *Bolivar* but admiration for the liberator of the South American colonies. Pietro Gamba recalled that Byron "often felt the want of some other occupation than that of writing, and frequently said that the public must be tired of his compositions, and that he was certainly more so . . . and thus, towards the end of February, 1823, he turned his thoughts towards Greece."³³

In fact, throughout February Byron's letters to friends in England, and to Hobhouse especially, reveal that in his imagination Byron already saw himself there. Fourteen years earlier, in a draft of stanza 73 of *Childe Harold* II, the poet had repeated five times the question: Who was to lead the Greeks out of slavery to freedom? Five times he had scrawled across the page the answer: Byron. Here was his chance to move from the margin to the text of history.

Along with his fellow Reform Whigs, Hobhouse was a political supporter of Greek independence, and without asking Byron, he passed his letters to the London Greek Committee. Less an organization than a loose group of sympathizers, the committee met informally at the Crown and Anchor in Pall Mall. John Bowring, its chairman, wrote to Genoa, expressing gratitude to Byron for his "decision" to represent the committee in the theater of war. At the end of March, after a lengthy silence, Byron received a letter from the committee's roving correspondent Captain Edward Blaquiere, announcing that he and the Greek delegate, Andreas Luriottis, proposed stopping off in Genoa on their way to Greece to outline their goals to him, especially where these concerned money.

Arriving at the Casa Saluzzo on April 7, they had a galvanizing effect on Byron. Blaquiere had written persuasively on the revolution in Spain,* and Byron was impressed by his analysis of the current situation, while Luriottis spoke stirringly of the heroic struggle against terrible odds now beginning in his native land. Byron responded by repeating the offers he had made in writing, adding that he was ready to set out for Greece immediately. Not since the secret Carbonari meetings

---

*The Spanish constitution that emerged from the revolution had been the model for the one submitted by the fleeing Carbonari parliament of Naples to King Ferdinand.

had he felt so energized; heady with talk of campaigns, supplies, and troops, he decided on as early a departure as possible. Now, instead of following up the success of their traveling representatives, the London Greek Committee, in its enthusiastic inefficiency, nearly lost its most famous convert. Believing a false report that Byron had left Genoa for Paris, they sent official expressions of gratitude, along with the notice of his election to the committee, to Calais, and by the time these were rerouted back to Genoa two months had passed, during which time Byron had become so outraged that he talked of withdrawing all offers of help: "I conceive that I have already been grossly ill-treated by the committee."[34] This was the first but by no means the most serious stumble by the London Philhellenes.

By mid-May, however, the feelings of their celebrated recruit had been mollified and Byron was full of plans, firing off letters of instruction, commissions, and suggestions. "My first wish is to go to the Levant in person," Byron assured Blaquiere, "where I might be able to advance, if not the cause, at least the means of obtaining information which the committee might be desirous of acting upon."[35] Sensibly starting with intelligence, he then passed along parts of two firsthand reports of conditions in Greece. A pair of German volunteers, ragged and starving, had landed in Genoa from Marseilles (the European staging area for Greece), where, like all bearers of bad news, they had been treated like pariahs and shunned as deserters. Byron spent many hours listening to their experiences. The accounts he relayed to London, however, were heavily edited. He forwarded their report on such matters as badly needed supplies: a park for field artillery, gunpowder, and medical stores. He entirely omitted, however, descriptions of wholesale slaughter by the Greeks; entire Turkish communities had been massacred by their long-time Greek neighbors. The only hint that the official version of martyred Greece might be largely propaganda was one of the young Germans' "philosophic" remarks, as Byron described it—these were not the Greeks of Themistocles.[36]

Along with most of Europe, Byron was invested in the image of a desperate yet heroic Greece poised on the brink of freedom, her arms outstretched for succor. And he attributed any other view to the amateurism of Sunday soldiers: "The attention of the committee had better be directed to the employment of *officers* of experience than the enrollment of raw British soldiers. . . . It would also be as well," he warned further, "that they should be aware that they are not going to 'rough it on a beefsteak and bottle of port' but that Greece—never of late years, very plentifully stocked for a *Mess*—is at present the country of all sorts of *privations*." Here, however, he did admit that "many *foreign* officers . . . have returned in disgust, imagining either that they were going to make up a party of pleasure, or to enjoy full pay, speedy promotion, and a very moderate degree of duty." He did not fail to address another grievance—"They complain, too, of having been ill-treated by the Government or inhabitants"—only to defend the accused: "Those Greeks I have seen strenuously deny the charge of inhospitality, and declare that they shared their pittance to the last crumb with their foreign volunteers."[37] And he concluded with this modest request: "I beg that the Committee will command me in any and every way. If I am favoured with any instructions, I shall endeavour to obey them to the letter, whether conformable to my own private opinion or not."

Byron had not been in Greece since his grand tour of 1811, and of course he had no way of knowing how foreign volunteers were treated by "the Government" (which, in fact, did not exist) or by the inhabitants; he failed to mention local troops, who, as he would soon learn, were mercenaries or bandits serving under tribal chieftains. As to his plea "Command me,"[38] no words he ever wrote would be more severely tested.

For the moment, all that kept him in Genoa was an "objection of a domestic nature." With his dread of women's scenes, Byron deputized Pietro to break the news gradually to his sister. But the transparent "Liberty boy" was even more eager to leave than his idol, and he had no success at softening the blow: In Teresa's words, "a death sentence would have seemed less terrible." Now, in a reprise of the explosions that preceded her departure from Ravenna, she wept and even pleaded to accompany him; she wrote letters she admitted were "unjust," accusing Byron of sacrificing everything for his "reputation"; one letter, however, ending with a prophecy: "I know that we shall never see each other again."[39]

As irritating as these dramas always were, they had the liberating effects of hardening Byron's heart and allowing him the freedom to plan his departure openly. At first Byron left Pietro to deal with the material arrangements of the voyage. But the lad proved hopeless in any practical matter, unable to complete the smallest assignment. Byron needed a second-in-command, and in mid-June he sent a desperate letter to Trelawny in Florence, pleading, "Why do you not come to me? I want your aid!"[40]

For some months Trelawny, another enthusiast of the Greek adventure, had been away from Genoa, first hunting in the Maremma, then at Rome. There he had purchased a plot in the Protestant

Cemetery, where he planned to be buried next to Shelley, the creation of whose monument he was supervising. He was now in Florence, writing Claire tear-stained, misspelled love letters begging her to marry him. But Claire preferred her memories of the real Byron, however bitter, to Trelawny's imitation, and so he was ready to drown his sorrows in preparations for war.

BYRON'S PLANNING for the expedition revealed his own extremes of the rational and romantic; in 1814, when he was already a seasoned traveler, he had ordered enough military matériel in London for an expeditionary force to the East; the trip had never taken place. Now, taking a more prudent view of expenses, he restricted himself to ordering gunpowder and chartering a boat through Henry Dunn, proprietor of the English store in Leghorn. Byron arranged with his banker Barry to send him 10,000 in Spanish dollars and bills of exchange worth 40,000 dollars more. He asked the eminent Pisan surgeon Dr. Vacca to recommend a young doctor who, for £100, would accompany them as traveling physician.

When it came to outfitting himself and his associates, however, Byron yielded to high romance. To crown scarlet uniforms glittering with gold buttons, frogs, epaulettes, and sashes, Byron designed individual helmets for himself and his "personal staff" of three: for Pietro, a green cloth Uhlan-style shako that sat atop a base of brass and black leather, with the goddess Athena in high relief on the front; for himself and Trelawny, helmets worthy of Homeric heroes, with plumes waving above the Byron crest and motto, "Crede Byron," the whole secured by a wide chin strap that clearly meant business.

When Trelawny finally arrived, he had nothing but criticism of the entire operation: the brig *Hercules*, engaged by Dunn and Captain Roberts, Trelawny pronounced a "collier-built tub, built on the lines of a baby's cradle—she would do anything but go ahead,"[41] and despite his own romantic persona, he found the uniforms and helmets so ridiculous he refused even to try his on. Chastened, Byron canceled the order for the uniforms, and the helmets went back into their pink boxes.

As a portent of things to come, Byron now received conflicting advice about his destination. Blaquiere had written from Zante urging him to proceed there or to another of the Ionian Islands, where he could receive firsthand reports about the situation in Greece; on the mainland, he would be harassed by representatives of the factions now fighting among themselves for control of the government. Blaquiere himself was just now setting out for a fact-finding visit to Tripolitza, capital of the

Peloponnese, and he further advised Byron not to leave Genoa until he could give him information obtained on the scene. Then Byron had a letter from Constantine Mavrocordatos, brother of Prince Alexander Mavrocordatos, the European-educated leader of western Greece, who was holding together a fragile coalition. He exhorted Byron to proceed directly to the most hotly contested point on the coast, a present object of Turkish naval attacks and soon to be the focus of civil strife among the Greeks: "The best place for you to establish yourself would be Missolonghi in Aetolia, a place which would be very well adapted to serve as a base for your purposes, as it is the one point in our dear fatherland which is the most threatened by the enemy, and the weakest and most in need in present circumstances."[42]

As soon as Blaquiere arrived on the mainland, he wrote a series of letters to Byron, each more discouraging than the last: Chaos reigned; conditions were appalling, especially the hygiene; there was not even a bed to be found. Prince Alexander Mavrocordatos was obliged to sleep, wrapped in his greatcoat, on the floor. In a letter dated July 9, he warned that the moment could not be worse for Byron to come to Greece; he should remain in Genoa, postponing his departure "indefinitely." But his letter arrived too late. On July 13 Byron embarked on the *Hercules*, bound for Zante.

The leave-taking was terrible. For days beforehand, Teresa sat numbly weeping on her sofa, while her father prepared to accompany her to Bologna, there to await the commutation of his exile and the beginning of her own. Then, in a final masterstroke of malice, Hunt managed to poison any lingering goodwill between Byron and Mary. In an arrogant letter, he threatened that if Byron was not immediately forthcoming with Mary's fare to England, she would be obliged to ask Trelawny for the money. And he reminded his patron that he "owed"[43] Mary £1,000 as forfeit of an unpaid bet made with Shelley about Lady Noel's death and his share of the estate.

This was exactly the behavior that brought out the worst in Byron; in a fury, he replied to Hunt that he would give Mary any sum she needed, as long as he need never suffer her tedious company again.[44] There were other unkind remarks about both Shelleys, which Hunt read aloud to Mary. Utterly humiliated, she nonetheless wrote to Byron a brief and dignified note explaining why she could not accept his money without his friendship. But Hunt had not finished yet. Stricken with remorse, in the days before he sailed Byron deposited with Barry, in Hunt's name, £30 for Mary's return trip home. After what had happened, this was the most tactful gesture of amends Byron could have made. As he explained to Hunt, he did not want Mary to refuse help because it came from him. Barry later attested that Hunt cashed the note, but the money was never given to Mary.[45]

In the belief that he had remedied matters, Byron, at the last, asked Mary to stay with Teresa. He did not want her to be alone at the time of his departure. Thus, in the still blazing sun of early evening, July 13, the two women watched from Casa Saluzzo's garden as a small boat, far below, took its eight passengers out to the *Hercules*: a silent Byron, Pietro Gamba, Trelawny, the nervous young physician Francesco Bruno, and four servants—Fletcher, Tita Falcieri, and the indispensable Lega Zambelli (Byron's staff); and Trelawny's black American groom (soon to be appropriated by the poet). Of Byron's domestic animals he took only his two dogs, Moretto, and a new addition, Lyon. In the makeshift stables on board, eight horses pawed and snorted nervously; the geese, which had now twice been spared being served for Michaelmas dinner, were left with Barry.

A dark portent, Byron and his fellow passengers had to return to land three times before they weighed anchor for the Ionian Islands. Becalmed that first night, they slept on board; then, disembarking in the morning, he and his friends lounged in the cool of the Lomellini gardens, scene of sprightly exchanges with Lady Blessington. The next day, with still not a breeze stirring, the boat from an American frigate towed the *Hercules* out of the harbor, where she sat on the glassy water all day; "the Pilgrim," Trelawny observed, "sat apart, solemn & sad—he took no notice of anything, nor spoke a word."[46] Then the sultry weather exploded into a squall; the *Hercules* rocked violently, the passengers—particularly Pietro—were seasick, and the horses kicked down their makeshift stalls, obliging the captain to put into Genoa once again for repairs. Byron returned to the Casa Saluzzo and its empty, echoing rooms; he had moved his household so often now that he found nothing had been forgotten. But when Barry moved in a few days later, he discovered in a drawer of Byron's desk a long curl of Teresa's red-gold hair. For Byron there were memories enough without mementos. He had been spared the sight, two days earlier, of Teresa screaming hysterically as she was carried into the coach for Bologna.

Setting sail on July 16, the *Hercules* took five days to reach Leghorn. During their two days there, the superstitious Byron might well have seen these three false starts as a sign to turn back; instead he decided, Pietro recalled, "that a bad beginning was a favorable omen."[47] He could not have felt similarly after meeting with representatives of the Greek refugee colony there: "I find the Greeks here somewhat divided amongst themselves," he wrote to Bowring in London. "What they most seem to want or desire is—Money—Money—Money."[48] Before weighing anchor, the brig took on two more passengers: M. Schilizzi, a relative of Prince Mavrocordatos; and a young Scot, James Hamilton Browne. An outspoken philhellene, Browne claimed to have been dismissed from the British service—determinedly neutral by policy—in the Ionian Islands for his open sympathy for their cause. Browne's counsel would have far-reaching consequence: He advised Byron to change his destination from Zante, the largest of the seven Ionian Islands, to the next in size, Cephalonia. Colonel Charles Napier, the British resident there, was another impassioned philhellene who, despite his obligatory official posture of neutrality, would do everything possible, Browne knew, to facilitate Byron's usefulness to Greece.

An exceptional man by any measure, Napier was a professional soldier and a dedicated administrator with a genius for getting things done; he had devoted his career to bringing progress and prosperity to Cephalonia, in the form of roads and markets and harbor works. More astonishing, he loved his subjects—"worth more than all the other nations put together. I like to see, to hear them; I like their fun, their good humour, their Paddy ways, for they are very like Irishmen." And he attributed all their bad habits to the Venetians—the former rulers of his little isle. "Their wit, their eloquence, their good nature are their own," while Cephalonia itself was "so dear to me that every hour not employed to do her good seems wasted."[49] Even in the paternalistic discourse of colonialism, it is clear that Napier, by his example, would influence the new arrival to hold firm to his faith that the Greeks were worthy of his support—and even his life.

As it happened, the issue of Cephalonia versus Zante was settled when, putting in at the latter, Byron learned that Blaquiere, whom he had arranged to meet for a briefing, had not waited for him; in a rush to be first off the press with his book on the war in Greece, he had gone straight from Athens to London without sending so much as a note of apology. Thus, at sunset on August 2, the *Hercules* navigated the channel between Zante and Cephalonia, and the next morning the captain maneuvered the tub into the little harbor of Argostoli. Their first morning at anchor, boatloads of Albanian Suliotes swarmed over the gunwhales. Byron's romantic memories of this "best and bravest" tribe of warriors decided him to hire the lot—about forty men—as a small personal army. Then, for reasons he left vague in his letters, he changed his mind and sent them home with a month's pay.

Even with Colonel Napier's improvements, Cephalonia was hardly one of the "isles of Greece" to inspire Byron to flights of poetry. Twenty-seven miles long with a spine of barren hills known as the Black

Mountains, the island boasted no picturesque ruins, literary associations, or, for that matter, scenic glories. What it provided was a peaceful setting from which to survey the turbulence ahead. For the next five months, freed from the claims of the past, Byron tried to learn what his role would be in the Greek struggle. He listened and questioned, saw emissaries and self-styled experts, read reports and wrote them. He had taken the unfinished Canto XVII of *Don Juan* with him, but it would remain untouched. He had put his life as a poet behind him.

We have no reason to believe that Byron was ever under any illusion that the Greek war against the Turks was an antinomian duel between good and evil. Rather, the "cause" of Greece was his last chance to realize his heroic dream of a life of action. With the first reports from the mainland, he observed that "the hazard is considerable—and perhaps useless."[50] However many letters he would write—to the Greek leaders and the philhellenes in London, asking modestly how he might be of use—utility was always beside the point. As he told Napier, "Fail or not fail, I can hardly be disappointed—for I believed myself on a fool's errand from the outset."[51]

For the first week, Byron and his companions lived on board ship, refusing Napier's offer to the poet and Pietro Gamba to make the residence their home; he did not want to compromise the official by their activities. Then Byron, accompanied by Pietro and Trelawny, made a six-day trip to Ithaca, directly across the straits. Although the visit was intended "merely for pleasure," he wrote to Teresa,[52] it proved to be Byron's first encounter with the devastation two years of warfare had wreaked on the civilian population. Ithaca was overflowing with Greek refugees—homeless, destitute, and mourning their dead. He gave £250 to the British resident there to distribute for relief while he himself took responsibility for the Chalandritsanos family, a widowed mother with three young daughters; their older brother, fifteen-year-old Loukas, was learning to be a soldier with one of the mountain chieftains.

Trelawny, too, hungered for action, and complaining that Byron had become a "tourist," he took off, accompanied by Hamilton Browne. It did not take the adventurer long to attach himself to the unscrupulous bandit leader of eastern Greece, Odysseus Androutsos, and in no time the would-be corsair was writing letters from Androutsos' headquarters—a vast cave on Mount Parnassus—advising Byron on the bargains to be had in local harems of the youngest girls.

Byron, meanwhile, wanted nothing more than to leave all Eastern bric-a-brac behind him—especially "absurd womankind."[53] On returning to Cephalonia, he took a simple whitewashed farmhouse in the village of Metaxata, a remote seven miles from Argostoli. The vaulted ground floor, intended for stores and livestock, housed the servants, while Byron and Pietro shared rooms above. Now, from the privacy of his lodgings, Byron became part of the predominantly male society of the island—a mixture of garrison life and Harrow, complete with a chaplain in the form of Dr. James Kennedy. Actually the resident physician, Kennedy was a fervent evangelical and desperately wanted to be the instrument of the strayed poet's salvation. At the house of Dr. Muir, the chief health officer of the island, who like Byron, was a confirmed rationalist, the three men argued the existence of the divinity, the value of established religion, the probability of an afterlife, and other articles of faith that Byron continued to ponder for himself.

In less strenuous conversation, Byron enjoyed Napier's wit and knowledge of affairs in the Levant, and for exercise the poet rode or fenced with the resident's aide, Colonel Duffie. Byron's paranoia about his compatriots, which in Italy had become almost obsessional, disappeared. His presence thrilled everyone. He found new friends in Napier and his staff, while the young officers of the garrison, he discovered, knew his poems by heart and treated the author with the deference due a visiting celebrity. Listening to the toasts that ended a mess banquet in his honor, Byron was speechless to the point of tears. To complete his sense of well-being, Loukas Chalandritsanos, learning of his family's rescue by the rich English nobleman, swiftly made his way to Cephalonia, where Byron, charmed by the black-eyed adolescent, took him on as his page. The position had remained vacant since Byron had dispatched Robert Rushton home from Turkey. It was a role that, locally, left no doubts about a boy's sexual availability.

For all its pleasures, however, Cephalonia was no Circean isle. Reports from the mainland were discouraging, confirming Byron's own impressions. Now he decided not to censor the bad news, which he heard that Blaquiere was doing all over London. "I must not conceal from you and the Committee," he wrote to Hobhouse, "that the Greeks appear more in danger from their own divisions than from the attacks of the Enemy.—There is talk of treachery—and all sorts of parties amongst them." Their distrust of foreigners created a host of other problems, along with "a desire of nothing but *money*—all improvements in tactics—they decline—and are not very kind, it is said—to the foreign officers &c. in their service." Such were the reports of others, Byron noted punctiliously. As for his own sense of the Greeks, "certainly I cannot say much for those I have seen here—the Slave is not yet improved by his Saturnalia."[54]

No one analyzed the situation more intelligently—or offered better advice—than Byron in the reports he now gave the committee. He saw clearly that the Greek rejection of professional military leadership they urgently needed to train their undisciplined troops, combined with internal divisions, would cause their defeat, and he proposed the appointment of Colonel Napier as commander of a regular army to be financed by the London philhellenes. Byron had already sounded out the resident, who discreetly made known his interest in "going over"[55] *if* he did not have to resign his present commission. But the London committee was uninterested.

After an attack in September, Missolonghi, on the northern shore of the Gulf of Patras, was under Turkish blockade, and Metaxa, the military governor of the town, became "very pressing" in his pleas to Byron to establish himself in the besieged town.[56] Sensibly, he refused to be drawn into the conflict as yet, sending instead much-needed medical supplies for the wounded. By the end of the month Byron's sources reported that the situation throughout Greece was worsening "with matters in great disorder—No less than three parties—and one conspiracy going on at this moment amongst them—a few steps farther and a civil war may ensue." Of the leaders of the three factions, he had the most confidence in Prince Mavrocordatos; although devious and a flatterer, he was, at least, honest in a culture where corruption at every level was the order of the day. As there were no central government or revenues to pay an army or civil administrators, extortion, from local chieftains down to the lowliest clerk, served as salaries. This presented Byron with problems in directing supplies, the medical and war matériel expected from the committee, "as all Agents of the G[reek] Gov[ernment] are said to *peculate* to the extent of their opportunities," he explained.

After threats on his life by a rival, Mavrocordatos fled to Hydra. Another disaster followed: The heroic Suliote military leader Marco Botzaris was killed in Tripolitza. Reporting to London, Byron tried to sound optimistic: "For all this I do not despair."[57] It was a phrase he would repeat like a mantra.

Solicited on all sides for his own money and for his influence in obtaining more, Byron determined to stand firm against co-option by any party. It was neither indecision nor indolence that kept him in Cephalonia, as many claimed then and since, but the knowledge that to appear on the mainland would be to announce his allegiance to one or the other groups whose deputies now besieged him with letters and visits, each proclaiming why "he was the 'Simon Pure' leader of all Greece," Byron said sourly. "I did not come here to join a faction, but a nation," he declared in the journal he had begun keeping as soon as he arrived. As there was no nation, however, he recognized that "it will require much circumspection [for me] to avoid the character of a partizan."[58]

His efforts to sort truth from lies while maintaining his own neutrality were steadily undermined from all sides. In England, philhellene propaganda, bolstered by the spurious claims of the Greek deputies to London, proclaimed the continuing presence of platoons of seasoned soldiers from the first wave of European volunteers in 1821–1822. The reality was very different. Of the largest group, the German Legion, once numbering in the hundreds, there were now twenty-six left, their comrades killed by the Turkish enemy, Greek hosts, disease, starvation, and suicide. As to other survivors among the students and other idealists who had flocked to the cause, "All the foreigners that I have hitherto met with amongst the Greeks—are going or gone back disgusted," Byron recorded.[59]

To his journal alone he confided the truth in detail about the Suliotes who had been his welcoming committee—truth he was too ashamed to describe to his friends on the London Greek Committee. They were not the brave Suliotes of war chants on the beach. They were mercenaries "not quite united among themselves in anything except raising their demands on me." Unwisely, he confessed, he had acceded to their insistence that they be paid one month in advance, after which "they made various attempts at what I thought were extortion."[60] That was why he had dismissed the lot, offering another month's pay and free passage back to Arcanania just to be rid of them.

This is no simple instance of exploitation; had it been, Byron would not have buried the tale in his journal, but would have relayed the episode to his friends in London with outrage to spare. Humiliation seeps through this private account, along with a certain sense of masochistic collusion that frightened him enough in retrospect to hide the evidence. We see Byron watching himself helplessly as he agreed to one demand after the other until he heard them mocking him. And when he finally sent them away, they were handsomely rewarded. Byron's only reward was a palpable sense of relief: This time he had gotten off lightly, but he would not be so lucky again.

In October, a little more than a month after he had begun it, he stopped keeping the journal. In his last entry, he gave as his reason the distress caused him by Augusta's having "intimated" that Ada was ill.[61] But he had a very different explanation for his friend Dr. Muir. He had stopped keeping the journal, he admitted, because once he started writing in it, he could not help abusing the Greeks.

Still, in this same final entry, Byron indulged his fantasy of leading the Greeks to victory—and not just the Greeks, but also the very group he had just accused of extortion. As it turned out, the Suliote leaders proved more skilled in flattery than their troops had been in holding Byron up for money, being "apparently anxious that I should put myself forward as their chief."[62] For now, Byron's good sense prevailed: There were too many chiefs among them and too much division still; "but if it should appear necessary . . . it might—or may—or so happen—that I could—should—or shall take to me the support of such a body of men," and he calculated that with his actual resources, "I could maintain between five hundred and a thousand for as long as necessary."[63]

Fantasies are not harmless escapes from reality; they are dress rehearsals. And Byron, dreaming on his Metaxata balcony as he looked across Homer's wine-dark Ionian Sea, saw himself across the straits in blockaded Missolonghi. The plumed helmet would not remain in its box for long.

For the moment, however, there was no compelling reason to leave Cephalonia. It was the ideal place to serve an ambassadorial role: He received delegates and wrote reports to the philhellenes on what he had learned. He made the timely discovery that the bankers who were supposed to act as local agents for Barry refused to honor their own corresponding bank's notes and would make him "*pay* interest—for my own monies,"[64] he raged. But this infuriating development led Byron to the last of his invaluable banker friends, Samuel Barff of Zante, who was eager to help with every problem. And the problems would multiply.

Realistically, Byron knew that he was not born to command, to deal with maps, strategy, discipline, or provisions. "If you send out a military man," he urged Hobhouse, "he will have every cooperation from me; or if you send out any other person, I have no objection to act as either his coadjutor, or subordinately, for I have none of these punctilios."[65] By the end of October, however, he appeared to have succumbed to a new voice soliciting his presence on the mainland. A messenger arrived from the Legislative Body, the de facto Greek government—led since the self-exile of Mavrocordatos by Kolokotrones, the most powerful of the "predatory chiefs," as Trelawny described this gang—to escort Byron to their headquarters in Nauplia. According to Pietro Gamba, Byron was prepared to leave with the emissary in early November, when an urgent crisis of money caused him to change his plans.

Busy killing, threatening, or simply trying to discredit one another, the Greek chieftains had delayed sending deputies to London to obtain a crucially needed loan of £800,000; they had, in fact, only just left on this mission. In the meantime, funds were running out, and there was no money to pay the naval squadron—the only hope of breaking the

Turkish blockade. Thus Byron now made a personal loan of £4,000 to the provisional government "to succour Missolonghi,"[66] on the understanding that he would be repaid as soon as they received their money from the London committee. "In the meantime, I stand paymaster," Byron wrote to Kinnaird.[67] Then, in December, Mavrocordatos returned from Hydra to Missolonghi, and he now wrote to Byron in terms of flattery that would prove irresistible; his presence, he told the poet, would "electrify the troops."[68] Taking his cue from the wily leader's rhetoric, Byron now announced to Kinnaird, "I am passing the Rubicon—recollect that for God's sake—and the sake of Greece." He had decided to spare nothing of his resources or himself. "You must let me have all the means & credit of mine that we can master or muster," he instructed the banker, "and that immediately—and I must do my best to the shirt—and to the skin if necessary." The reality of crossing to Greece itself activated an imperial fantasy, and his tone becomes exalted: "If Rochdale sale has been completed I can keep an army *here*, aye, and perhaps command it. . . . Why, man! if we had but 100,000 l sterling in hand, we should now be halfway to the city of Constantine."[69] Instead, on the evening of December 29, Byron and Pietro, traveling in two boats, set off from Argostoli, bound for Missolonghi.

CHAPTER 37

"The Land of Honourable Death Is Here"

ACCOMPANIED by Dr. Bruno, Fletcher, his page Loukas, and the two dogs, Byron set sail on December 29 in a long boat with a shallow draw called a *mistico*. Bringing the horses, supplies, and servants, Pietro was installed in a *bombard*, a larger, slower vessel. They arrived in Zante the next morning and left the same night. Just before dawn, however, their little convoy was intercepted by Turkish warships. In the darkness, Byron's fast boat evaded capture, escaping to anchor unseen in a rocky cove near Dragomestre. Meanwhile, the *bombard* was seized; all her passengers expected to be killed. When their captain was ordered aboard the Turkish brig, Pietro weighted a bag of Byron's incriminating papers with gunshot and dropped it overboard. But the captain of the Greek vessel had saved the life of his Turkish counterpart in a shipwreck; instead of torture there were tearful embraces, and the bombard was taken to Patras and feted by the local pasha before being released. They were the first to arrive in Missolonghi.

Meanwhile, the *mistico* was still moored in her cove. Fearful of capture again, Byron sent to the newly arrived military adviser in Missolonghi, Colonel Leicester Stanhope, for an escort to convey them to their destination by land or canal. It was not on his own account that he was anxious, but "for that of a Greek boy with me, for you know what his fate would be; and I would sooner cut him in pieces and myself too than have him taken out by those barbarians."[1] We may wonder what Stanhope (whom Byron had yet to meet) made of this terrible image of murder and suicide, with its unmistakable declaration of passion. Before Byron received a reply, the boat had sprung a leak, and he sent Loukas upcountry to Missolonghi, along with a local guide, some money, and a letter to Stanhope. Meanwhile, Dr. Bruno had been horrified to overhear Byron promise the boy, who was unable to swim, that if the boat sank, he would carry him to safety on his back.

On his last evening at anchor in the little harbor of Dragomestre, Byron began to feel the effects of five days and nights on deck without bathing or a change of clothes. He decided that the "shortest way to kill the fleas—was to strip and take a swim . . . my bath set all to rights."[2] The next day, Loukas returned with an armed detail in a large rowboat to escort them across the lagoon.

Byron and his party disembarked at Missolonghi on January 4, 1824, where he was greeted with a hero's welcome. There was as full a military and naval salute as the forces could muster: The fleet was especially noisy, as Byron was known to have brought their wages with him. The entire populace of the town, dressed in picturesque costumes, cheered and shouted.

Along with committing himself to pay the squadron, Byron now also "engaged to maintain a certain number of troops—with whom it is probable that I shall have to march—when an expedition now projecting takes place," he told Lord Sydney Osborne, the British administrator in Zante.[3] The expedition to which Byron so mysteriously alluded was a proposed attack on the fortress of Lepanto in which he would lead the Suliotes. If successful, Byron would follow in the legendary footsteps of Don John of Austria, who in 1571 led an allied European armada to victory over the Ottomans at Lepanto. The glorious role dangled before him bears the stamp of Prince Mavrocordatos.

In Missolonghi itself, accommodations were more spartan than imperial. The house allotted to Byron and his staff belonged to M. Kapsalis, primate of Argostoli. Built on ground that sloped down to the muddy shallows of the lagoon, it was a three-story building, with no furnishings to speak of. (Stanhope, who preceded him, had commandeered the only European-style piece of furniture, an Ottoman sofa.) Entering, the visitor would have no reason to doubt that this was a campaign headquarters. The officers of Byron's Suliote corps were camped in the barrackslike ground floor, while his own apartments above, looking out to sea, continued the military theme: All of Byron's considerable arsenal—muskets, pistols, sabers—hung on the unpainted plaster walls. There was a camp bed and divans in the Eastern style.

Pietro Gamba's rooms were across the landing, but they had barely moved in when Teresa's brother, of whom Byron had been so fond, fell precipitously from grace, never to rise again. Through inexperience, credulity—or, perhaps, because he was simply stupid—he had given a Zante merchant carte blanche for a standing order: Byron's commission had called for red cloth for a uniform jacket and some oilcloth to be used as waterproof covering for trunks. Without his authorization, Pietro had added Hessian boots, horsewhips, yards of broadcloth, and notebooks, for which the bill came to £645. "But this is what comes of letting boys play the man," Byron noted in disgust. "All his patriotism diminishes into the desire of a sky blue uniform and be d——d to him—for a coxcomb."[4] The notebooks, however, had been ordered at the behest of another volunteer from the London committee, Julius Millingen, a twenty-four-year-old physician with impressive credentials from Edinburgh, who had lived much in the Mediterranean. His commission in Missolonghi was to establish a clinic for the artillery corps.

Pietro's orders were not the only supplies Byron now found unsuitable to the conduct of war. The London Greek Committee was dominated by followers of Jeremy Bentham, the philosopher whose famous utilitarian principle of good as that which leads to "the greatest happiness of the greatest number" his philhellene disciples now applied quite literally. Colonel Leicester Stanhope, a fanatic Benthamite, had taken this charge as a mission to look beyond the present hostilities with the Turks and to promote the education of the civilian population as the best hope for a constitutional government; to this end, he arrived with a printing press and promptly established and distributed two newspapers—one in Greek, the other in Italian. In response to the urgent need for military supplies, he had sent ahead a quantity of mathematical instruments and a large number of trumpets. Byron was prompt to convey his displeasure to London, writing to Sir John Bowring that "in the present state of Greece . . . the Mathematical instruments are thrown away—none of the Greeks know a problem from a poker—we must conquer first and plan afterwards.—The use of the trumpets too may be doubted—unless Constantinople were Jericho—for the Hellenists have no ear for bugles."[5] As for the newspapers, barely any of the military or civilian population could read, but their editorial content posed more serious problems. Stanhope's most dearly held article of faith was his belief in freedom of the press, and from his editor's pulpit he fired off attacks on all the monarchies of the Holy Alliance. Byron now sounded like the most repressive Tory, arguing for immediate censorship from London. In fact, he had simply become a practical politician; he did not want to risk the loss of any support in Europe for the cause of Greek independence through the taint of radicalism.

The optimism and high hopes he had felt in disembarking were dampening, and by the end of January, Byron already had thoughts of leaving—feelings he determined to resist. "I mean to stick by the Greeks to the last rag of canvas or shirt—and not go sniveling back like all the rest of them up till now nearly—if it can be avoided, that is to say."[6] Mavrocordatos continued to entice him with the prospect of leading an assault on Lepanto, but although Byron was still taken with the project, he now had a far less romantic view of his reasons for going: "As I pay a considerable portion of the Clans—I may as well see what they are likely to do for their money,"[7] he told Bowring. He was sick of inaction and of listening to the utopian ideas of the "typographical Colonel,"[8] as he dubbed Stanhope, "tired of hearing nothing but talk—and Constitutions and Sunday Schools."[9]

FROM THE TIME of Byron's arrival, it had not stopped raining; the streets and alleys in the low-lying marsh turned to rivulets of mud when they were not open sewers. His house, with the water lapping yards away from the open ground floor, was prone to flooding: "If we are not taken off with the sword—we are like to march off with an ague in this mud-basket," he told Charles Hancock, who acted as his banker in Zante, "and to conclude with a very bad pun . . . better *mar*tially—than *marsh*-ally." As for the situation of Missolonghi, "the Dykes of Holland when broken down are the Desarts of Arabia for dryness in comparison."[10] Unknown to nineteenth-century medicine, the mosquitoes that bred in the marshy flats carried the malarial fever that had nearly killed Byron in Patras and had recurred in Venice. Its victims were always vulnerable to relapses, and by February Byron reported feeling "unwell," and both Gamba and Loukas were also ailing. The only cheering event was the arrival of the first emissary from the London committee, who promised technical expertise and action. Captain William Parry, "firemaster,"* had been recruited from Woolwich Arsenal, where he was supposed to have made a specialty of Congreve rockets and other firearms whose use was unknown to the Greeks. Parry's boat, the storeship *Ann*, besides carrying needed supplies, mechanics, and other technical personnel, was also heralded as a "laboratory";[11] until Parry had completed his mission of establishing an arsenal in Missolonghi, the ship was equipped to manufacture the latest weaponry and to serve as a training school for the local troops.

Byron took to Parry immediately; "a fine rough subject" he called the unschooled soldier,[12] whose energy and practical competence were happy contrasts to his own staff: the helpless Pietro; the two inexperienced young doctors; and the pedantic Stanhope, with his lectures on progress and enlightenment. That the others snubbed the firemaster for

---

*The artillery officer in charge of explosives.

his lack of social graces only endeared him more to Byron, who gave him all the help possible, including lodgings in his house, where every evening the two withdrew over brandy and water to talk the night away. Parry pressed his advantage by confirming Byron's prejudices: "He sorely laments the printing and civilizing expenses—and wishes there were not a Sunday School in the world—or *any* school *here* at present save and except always an Academy for Artilleryship."[13] Had there been, the firemaster might have been first to profit by its teachings, for Parry, as it turned out, had never fired a Congreve rocket and knew not much more about other weaponry.

Any disappointment Byron felt in Parry's meager skills was overshadowed by his latest round with the Suliotes. The leaders of the troop now demanded that 150—almost half of their number—be promoted to the rank of officer. The object was, of course, to increase their pay. When Byron angrily refused, they capitulated, offering to regroup into a "personal" corps under his direct command. Feeling that he had no choice, he sourly agreed. This latest episode was simply a replay of the extortionist tactics of the Suliotes who had greeted him in Cephalonia. But this time he would not forgive; the romance was over, and with it, his fantasy of an elite "Byron Brigade"[14] he would lead to glory at Lepanto. To stiffen his resolve, he made a note in his journal, whose dry, official tone—that of a memo—speaks of an effort to anesthetize his pain: "Having tried in vain at every expence—considerable trouble—and some danger to unite the Suliots for the good of Greece—and their own—I have come to the following resolution.—I will have nothing more to do with the Suliotes—they may go to the Turks or—the devil [but] they may cut me into more pieces than they have dissensions among them, sooner than change my resolution."[15]

The same day that Byron wrote this note to himself—Sunday, February 15—he suffered a massive seizure. He was seated on the sofa in Stanhope's apartments, having just finished a glass of cider and cold water, when he started convulsing. Terrified, the two young doctors, Bruno and Millingen, could not decide whether it was "Epileptic—Paralytic—or Apoplectic," Byron later noted with some irony in his journal.[16] In fact, reports of the event do not answer to descriptions of grand mal; he did not foam at the mouth, bite his tongue, or, seemingly, lose his memory, since he was able to recall the pain as so excruciating: "Had it lasted a moment longer must have extinguished my mortality." His features, however, were distorted, and he thrashed around so violently that the combined efforts of Parry and Tita—both strong men—could not subdue him. Leeches were applied to his forehead, but the doctors had gone too near the temporal artery, and it took hours to stop the bleeding. Two days later, "though weakly I feel tolerably convalescent," he reported. But he was understandably frightened and tried to allay his fears by rationally considering all possible causes of the attack. He examined such factors as lack of exercise due to the rain and mud underfoot, along with his alcohol intake: He had been "perhaps not uniformly so temperate as I may generally affirm that I was wont to be." *

What Byron really believed, however, was that the source of the event was emotional. Of those "public matters" that weighed on him, there was the strain of finding himself in the middle of "conflicting parties—politics—and circumstances." Ultimately, it was "private feelings" that had caused the revolt of physical systems: "I have been violently agitated with more than one passion lately," he confessed,[17] one that he had never expected to feel again. The fifteen-year-old Loukas had made it clear, in his artless way, that he cared only for the gold helmets and silver-gilt sabers and money he demanded—and was given—but nothing for the man who gave them. Byron was devastated by this rejection, the more so as he imputed it to age, to the waning of beauty and sexual powers. On his birthday three weeks earlier, on January 22, he stated his loss with terrible finality: "On this day I complete my thirty sixth year."

> 'T is time this heart should be unmoved
> Since others it hath ceased to move,
> Yet though I cannot be beloved
> Still let me love.
>
> My days are in the yellow leaf
> The flowers and fruits of love are gone—
> The worm, the canker and the grief
> Are mine alone.
>
> The fire that on my bosom preys
> Is lone as some Volcanic Isle,
> No torch is kindled at its blaze
> A funeral pile!

Only a death of heroic sacrifice, selfless and for the common good, can redeem individual suffering, the solitude of age and decay:

---

*The only previous mention of a seizure came from George Anson Byron, who had accompanied Byron to the theater during the nightmare days of the marriage and reported an attack during the performance. Byron had been drinking heavily at this time as well.

> The Sword—the Banner—and the Field
> Glory and Greece around us see!
> The Spartan borne upon his shield
> Was not more free!
>
> . . . .
>
> If thou regret'st thy youth, why *live?*
> The Land of honourable Death
> Is here—up to the Field! and give
> Away thy Breath.
>
> Seek out—less often sought than found,
> A Soldier's Grave—for thee the best,
> Then look around and choose thy ground,
> And take thy Rest.[18]

These lines—among Byron's last—follow the final entry in his journal.

Two days later, as though in answer to his prayer, Prince Mavrocordatos wrote to the poet and in flowery French appointed him "commander in chief of western Greece," promising once again that his lordship would lead the combined forces against the Turks at Lepanto. Byron's first order to his Suliote troops, only days after his seizure, was less grandiose: "to parade for service this Morning & march under the orders of the Count Pietro Gamba to their place of destination." But he had added a new rank to his recent commission; the order was signed "Generale Noel Byron."[19]

The Greek deputies had only just arrived in London to discuss the loan. Even should they repay Byron, his £4,000 would be a fraction of what he would eventually give. "I am maintaining the whole machine nearly (in *this* place at least) at our own cost," he told Kinnaird, and he announced his intention to contribute all his earnings, along with the proceeds from the Noel estate and the sale of Rochdale, which at long last seemed imminent. "I must do the thing properly & handsomely," he explained—as befitted a commander-in-chief of Western Greece.[20]

In the next month, every woe seemed unleashed on Missolonghi. While Byron was still recuperating from his attack, a small civil war erupted in town, with skirmishes between civilians and soldiers. Then some Suliote troops, demanding access to the arsenal, killed the Swedish artillery officer who was standing guard. At this, Parry's mechanics left in a body, "not used to shooting and slashing in a domestic quiet way." They had served for two weeks. Following the mechanics' defection, the area was rocked by an earthquake, at which point the entire army "discharged their arms upon the same principles that savages beat drums or howl during an eclipse of the moon," Byron noted drily.[21] This was not a comparison that he would have made a few months earlier. Determined to set an example of humane behavior in the face of barbarism on all sides, he obtained the release of twenty-nine Turkish prisoners, sending them home to Prevesa with letters saying that he hoped the same mercy would be shown to Greek prisoners of the Turks. He did not sound optimistic. At the same time, he adopted a ten-year-old Turkish girl, Hatagee,* "as beautiful as the sun and very lively—you can educate her," he informed Teresa.[22] He made the same offer to Augusta, with an alternative proposal: that Lady Byron should adopt the child as a companion for Ada![23] The poet himself was shaping art into life; in Canto VIII of *Don Juan*, the unwitting hero, fighting on the Russian side in the Siege of Ismail, rescues a little Turkish girl from a pile of corpses and takes her with him to England. But the truth of Byron's poetry was also that of his life, with its isolation and distance from everything he had ever loved. Hatagee was his lost Allegra and Ada, but she was also a projection of Byron's yearning to be part of a family, a circle linking past to present: Teresa, Augusta, Annabella.

Concerned about reports of Byron's seizure, James Kennedy had written several times, and Byron was touched by the doctor's solicitude. "I am not unaware of the precarious state of my health," he replied, "nor am, nor have been deceived on that subject. But it is proper that I remain in Greece, and it were better to die doing something than nothing."[24] This was not just heroics; he felt death approaching.

Stanhope had taken off for Athens, where he joined Trelawny in the unlikely role of convert to the camp of Odysseus Androutsos, chieftain of eastern Greece. Now there arrived in Missolonghi a young philhellene scholar, George Finlay, who was later to write a twelve-volume history of Greece. Finlay was yet another recruit of Androutsos', and he had come to invite Byron to a conference of all the Greek leaders in Salona. Despite Mavrocordatos's distrust, they both agreed to go. But flooding caused the roads and rivers to be impassable, and the conference was delayed. Byron tried to find a happy portent in more water: "The spring is come—I have seen a swallow today," he wrote to Teresa on March 17, "and it was time."[25]

For the first time since he had come to Greece, he worried about money. Byron calculated he had spent more than 30,000 Spanish dollars

---

*Byron's rescue fantasy obliged him to ignore the fact that Hatagee had a loving mother. When he entrusted both of them to the care of Dr. Kennedy and his wife in Cephalonia, they located, and reunited mother and child with, the father of the family.

on the war already, and this did not include "personal" expenses, which he did not enumerate. His Suliotes were the only soldiers to be paid a regular salary—and still they demanded higher wages; he dismissed the troublemakers. Other troops received only rations—inedible at that; there had been three mutinies so far because of rotten bread. Now the provisional government asked him for more money; twice he refused. Suddenly he decided that he wanted his personal loan repaid. Not trusting the Greeks, he advised Kinnaird to have the £4,000 deducted from the London Greek Committee's loan when it came through. He instructed Barry to pursue Lord Blessington, who had bought the *Bolivar* but had not yet paid him. And he asked the banker to sell any remaining effects, "except the best, (i.e., the Green travelling Chariot)."[26]

Soon afterward, a report circulated that there was plague in Missolonghi. It seemed to have been a false alarm, but Byron was sick again, along with others. "I have been very unwell," he wrote to Hobhouse at the end of March, "but am supposed to be better & almost everybody else has been ill too. We have had strange weather & strange incidents, natural, moral, physical, martial and political."[27]

The Turks resumed their blockade as fighting erupted within Missolonghi. The wounding of a local chieftain's son roused 150 of his followers, who seized the fort at the entrance to the harbor. Mavrocordatos was convinced of a plot against them. A group of citizens was about to fire on Byron and his corps as they rode near town. The father-in-law of Byron's landlord, who still lived in the Capsalis house, was arrested for treason.

Finally, on April 9, Byron's spirits lifted. From London he had word that negotiations for the loan were concluding and also that both Ada and Augusta had survived a winter's ill health. Further cheered by a break in the weather, he went out riding with Pietro, but the clear skies did not last. They were caught in a downpour and soaked to the skin. Gamba wanted to get home as soon as possible, and he pressed for galloping back to town. Exhausted, Byron insisted on being rowed, which took much longer. He sat silent and shivering in the stern of the boat. On their return, the chills continued, and he complained of shooting pains. During the night he summoned Dr. Bruno, who gave him medication but urged bleeding, which Byron refused. His confidence in Captain Parry was justified; he was the only member of the household who was properly alarmed by Byron's symptoms, especially his spasmodic and disjointed speech. Recognizing that decent treatment would be impossible in their situation (and having besides no great confidence in the inexperienced young doctors), he argued for the sick man to be moved to Zante, where both the climate and the medical facilities held the promise of recovery. To his own surprise, Byron agreed. As a further measure of Parry's enlightened views, he backed the poet's refusal to be bled.

Over the weekend, Byron's condition deteriorated. He complained of pains in his head, and his fever rose. But by Tuesday the thirteenth, when Parry had completed the arrangements for the move to Zante, the sirocco's driving winds had blown into a hurricane, whipping the waters of the gulf into high waves. No vessel could leave port. In the next days, Byron's digestion was affected; even tea made him violently ill. Supported by Parry, he continued to resist the bleeding urged by the doctors; at one point he flew into a rage, shouting that "the lancet had killed more people than the lance." On the fifteenth, in the course of Parry's usual evening visit, Byron spoke as though he expected to recover; he talked of Greece and what he still hoped to do—"but also of death and of his family," Parry recalled, invoking "My wife! My Ada! My Country! The situation in this place, my removal impossible and perhaps death, all combine to make me sad." He talked about retiring to England with his wife and daughter "for heretofore my life has been like the ocean in a storm." A fantasy in substance, it was also the last time, Parry noted, when Byron sounded "calm and collected for any considerable period"; but it was the calm of coming death.[28]

That night, after spasms of coughing and vomiting, the doctors reappeared with their lancets; they threatened Byron with loss of his sanity if he refused bleeding. This was his deepest dread—always. He finally succumbed and was bled twice then, and again the next day. At that point his fever rose and he became delirious; Tita removed the pistols and sabers Byron always kept near his bed. Tormented by lack of sleep, he agreed to another bleeding, after which he begged the doctors not to torment him further.

Parry continued to be the dying man's only source of comfort. Confined to his sofa by a sprained ankle, Pietro Gamba finally limped across the landing, but when he saw Byron's face, he rushed weeping from the room. In his extreme anxiety, Dr. Bruno became hysterical. The servants were terrified: Speaking French, Greek, Italian, and English, they could not understand one another, and no one was in charge. By Easter morning, news had spread through the town that Byron was dying. Celebrations were silenced. Leeches were applied to his forehead, which was then bound with cold bandages, while he drifted in and out of consciousness. In his lucid moments he knew that nothing more could be done. "Let not my body be hacked, or be sent to England," he begged Millingen. He wanted to be buried where he was: "Lay me in the first corner without pomp or nonsense." It distressed the doctor that he "did not hear him make any, even the smallest mention of religion." In the event, his speech was now unintelligible. He muttered complicated directives to Fletcher, but even the man who had known Byron the longest could not understand him. With his usual good sense, Parry loosened the bandage around his head. It had given him so much pain, Byron wept in gratitude. From incoherent sounds, those gathered around the bed seized words: Augusta—Ada—Kinnaird—Hobhouse; he called out place names and numbers. Then one sentence, as Parry recorded: *"Io lascio qualque cosa di caro nel mondo"*—I leave something dear to the world.[29] What had he left to the world that he deemed most "dear" or "valuable"? His sacrifice on behalf of Greece or his poetry? Or did he mean "someone"?

Through the night they took turns raising his head to ease the breathing, which caused the blood raised by the leeches to stream down his face. The next day, Monday, he remained unconscious. Then, at six-fifteen in the evening, when sunset was heralded by darkening skies and thunder, Byron opened his eyes and closed them. Fletcher knew immediately: "Oh, my God, I fear His Lordship is gone." After checking vital signs, the doctors confirmed it: Lord Byron was dead. It was April 19; two years ago to the day Allegra had died in the convent of Bagnacavallo.

FROM SHOCK, those present—Millingen and Bruno, Tita and Fletcher, Parry and Gamba—deflected grief with efficiency. There were papers to seal, people to notify. At dawn the cannons of Missolonghi that had greeted Byron's arrival fewer than four months earlier fired a farewell salute. Then the body was laid out and duly hacked to pieces for the autopsy, before being sewn up again. In the course of the examination, Byron's liver was found to be diseased, his heart enlarged; but strangest of all, the sutures of the skull had fused together, normally a sign of immense age. There were no lead-lined coffins to be found; the body was placed in a long tin-lined packing case, the internal organs distributed among four earthenware jars. Byron's lungs, according to the receipt drawn up by the undertakers, were deposited "in deference to the repeated representations of the citizens of Missolonghi," in the church of San Spiridione.[31] On an errand for Odysseus near Athens, Trelawny heard the news and rushed to Missolonghi. He had always longed to see and feel Byron's deformed foot, and he arrived just before the cases were sealed. After the state funeral in Missolonghi on April 22, the cases, with holes bored through the wood and tin, were deposited in a large barrel filled with 180 gallons of spirit, and on May 3, this was shipped to Zante. Here, quarrels erupted over Byron's last wishes about his remains: Byron had expressed one view to Millingen, also to Lady Blessington and to Trelawny himself, and had said the opposite to Gamba, Parry, and Fletcher. As much as anything else, dissension was his legacy.

In London, Kinnaird was the first to learn of Byron's death. On the evening of May 13, he received at the bank a diplomatic packet from Zante, addressed to Hobhouse. The envelope contained heartbroken letters from Pietro Gamba and from Fletcher, along with official notification from Lord Sydney Osborne. Kinnaird had these delivered by courier the next morning at eight o'clock to Hobhouse in his rooms at Albany House, where they were read "in an agony of grief."[32] A covering note from Kinnaird pointed out, in a characteristically snappish tone, that as other letters in the same bag must be directed to their recipients, he and Hobhouse were responsible for breaking the news to all London: "Nobody knows it as yet, but it must be known in a few hours, as I cannot take it upon me to keep back the letters . . . from their addressees."[33] They must meet immediately to discuss the management of the business. That same day, Sir Francis Burdett broke the news to Augusta at St. James's Palace. Hobhouse appeared later in the afternoon, bringing the distraught woman a letter from Fletcher. In it the faithful valet told her that since his first seizure, Byron had placed the Bible she had given him at his place at breakfast every morning. Hobhouse persuaded Augusta that this fact—if such it was—should not be known: Byron's behavior could be "mistaken for cowardice or hypocrisy . . . unless his mind was shaken by disease I am convinced he made no superstitious use of it [the Bible]—that is to say I am confident that although he might have a general belief in its contents he was not overcome by any religious terrors."[34] Augusta, Kinnaird, and Burdett agreed; cosmetic embalming must remove every blemish—including any reminder of sins that might bear repentance.

Captain George Byron, who now succeeded to the title, broke the news to Annabella. The next day he reported to Hobhouse and Augusta that he had left Lady Byron "in a distressing state."[35] She asked for accounts of Byron's last moments, which Hobhouse dispatched to her with Captain Byron as courier. But Fletcher was less restrained in his account: When he called on her in July, she walked around the room "sobbing so that her whole frame was shaken," while she begged him repeatedly to try to remember Byron's last words.[36]

By May 17 Hobhouse, representing Byron's executors, had organized the group that convened at John Murray's in Albemarle Street. In the publisher's drawing room, where Byron's ribald letters had so often been read aloud, Hobhouse orchestrated the burning of his friend's memoirs—unread by any of those present except the abject Tom Moore. Hobhouse assumed charge of Byron's posterity. With care, the prodigal would be welcomed home.

Meanwhile, in Zante, the brig *Florida* had arrived on April 21 with the first installment of the English loan to Greece. She left on the second of May, carrying Byron's remains, accompanied by Dr. Bruno, Fletcher, Tita Falcieri, Lega Zambelli, the black groom, and the two dogs. At the last minute it was decided that Pietro Gamba should be refused passage; he was a reminder of his sister's liaison with the poet. Already the sanitizing of Byron was well under way.

Teresa was the last to learn of Byron's death. With the connivance of her relations, the Costa family with whom she stayed in Bologna withheld all mail (including Mary Shelley's condolence letter), along with newspaper accounts of the event. Shortly after June 6, the papal authorities allowed her father, exiled in Ferrara, to come to tell her in person. Teresa had had no word from Missolonghi since Byron's first seizure, and when her father appeared suddenly, she suspected the worst. But Count Ruggero could not bring himself to say the dreaded words. The following day, however, when an old school friend from Santa Chiara arrived at the door, "at a scorching hour of the afternoon," Teresa knew in an instant why she had come.[37]

ON JUNE 29, the *Florida* anchored in the Downs of the Thames Estuary. Six days later, on July 5, Hobhouse accompanied Charles Hanson, his co-executor, to Doctors' Commons to prove Byron's will. He then went to Rochester, to board the *Florida* for the five-hour passage to the London docks. When they arrived, the undertakers came on board to begin the process of emptying the cask of its embalming fluid, prior to transferring the remains to a lead-lined coffin. When this was done, Hobhouse was asked if he wished to see the body. "I believe I should have dropped down dead if I had looked at it," he wrote in his diary.[38] While Byron's Newfoundland lay at his feet, Hobhouse covered the coffin with the ship's flag, mounted on a planed board. Small craft jostled for position around the brig, and a crowd of spectators watched from the banks as Hobhouse accompanied the coffin in the barge that carried it to Palace Yard Stairs. For the next seven days Byron lay in state in the front parlor of Sir Edward Knatchbull's house at 20 Great George Street. Hanson now informed Hobhouse that he was required by law to identify the body. Unable to recognize the face he saw, he lifted the red velvet pall to look at his friend's foot.

Not unexpectedly, the dean of Westminister wrote to Murray refusing his request (made in Hobhouse's name) that Byron be interred in the Abbey. In consultation with Augusta, Hobhouse now decided that Byron should be "buried like a nobleman—since we could not bury him like a poet,"[39] and they fixed Monday, July 12, for the ceremony at the Byron family church in Hucknall Torkard. Throughout the weekend in London, hordes of the curious pressed to be admitted to view the body, but these included "no one of note," a disappointed Hobhouse recalled.[40] Indeed, from the procession that followed the hearse, drawn by black-plumed horses, it could be observed that society stayed away; most of the forty-seven carriages were empty. Where Greece was concerned, the government was still officially neutral. The newspapers rushed to praise the poet's heroic death, but no one connected with the establishment wanted to appear to condone the radicals of the London Greek Committee and their support for the overthrow of government in the East. And there was also the scandal that still clung to the Byron name. It was well known that Augusta Leigh was next of kin and chief mourner. The empty carriages were an empty gesture of respect that carried no risk of guilt by association.

The procession took four days to reach Nottingham by the Leeds Road. Lady Caroline Lamb, out riding for the first time after an illness, claimed she was too weak to be told that it was Byron's body passing below the walls of Brocket Hall; galloping ahead of his wife, William Lamb went to meet the procession at the crossroads. In Nottingham the coffin lay in state for two more days at Blackamoor's Head Inn. Then, at 8:00 a.m. on Friday, July 16, the cortège, with Byron's coronet carried separately, set out for Hucknall Torkard. At St. Mary Magdalene the churchyard and porch were so crowded that it was difficult to maneuver the coffin down the nave, where the first part of the service was read before the altar. Besides Hobhouse the mourners included Hanson, Tom Moore, Douglas Kinnaird, and Francis Burdett. At the last, Augusta did not come; she was represented by her husband, Colonel Leigh. The men followed the coffin to the chancel, where, as the second part of the service was read, the body was lowered into the vault. "Too stunned to lament,"[41] Hobhouse descended to see where the casket had been placed upon that of the late Lord Byron and next to Catherine Byron's coffin, so decayed now that the name on the plate was obliterated.

Near the crypt, on the north wall of the chancel, the poet is commemorated by a marble tablet with the following inscription:

IN THE VAULT BENEATH
WHERE MANY OF HIS ANCESTORS AND HIS MOTHER ARE BURIED,
LIE THE REMAINS OF

GEORGE GORDON NOEL BYRON.

LORD BYRON, OF ROCHDALE
IN THE COUNTY OF LANCASTER,
THE AUTHOR OF CHILDE HAROLD'S PILGRIMAGE.
HE WAS BORN IN LONDON ON THE
22ND OF JANUARY 1788.
HE DIED AT MISSOLONGHI, IN WESTERN GREECE, ON THE
19TH OF APRIL 1824,
ENGAGED IN THE GLORIOUS ATTEMPT TO RESTORE THAT
COUNTRY TO HER ANCIENT FREEDOM AND RENOWN.

HIS SISTER, THE HONORABLE

AUGUSTA MARY LEIGH,

PLACED THIS TABLET TO HIS MEMORY.

Postscript

AUGUSTA LEIGH died in St. James's Palace in 1851, aged sixty-seven, preceding Annabella, Lady Noel Byron, by nine years. To the end of their lives, the two women remained locked in their ambiguous—and shifting—roles of torturer and victim.

With age, each yielded to her worst extreme of character. Despite Byron's generous legacy, Augusta spiraled deeper into debt, borrowing from everyone and selling off every keepsake and scrap of paper from her brother. Fecklessness, the support of her profligate children, or blackmail have all been advanced to explain her constant and desperate need for money.

Annabella embraced her evangelical faith ever more fervently—or fanatically. Her zealotry admitted no equals, only dependents or disciples. Her fierce intelligence and energy were directed toward the education of working-class children, the antislavery cause, and the upbringing of her daughter.

Ada inherited her mother's mathematical gifts, encouraged and nurtured by Lady Byron. Married at nineteen to Ralph King, later Earl of Lovelace, she bore three children in rapid succession but continued to pursue her studies, which now included the friendship and collaboration of the scientist John Crosse and the mathematical genius Charles Babbage. When Babbage invented his Analytical Machine, today still considered the first modern computer, he was instrumental in assuring that Ada's contribution to his work was published in 1843.

Soon after her marriage, her father's legacy emerged in signs of manic depression. She turned to compulsive gambling and, like others of mathematical bent, became obsessed with "beating the system" at the races. She lost huge sums and borrowed more, probably from underworld figures who seem to have subjected her to blackmail. Other unsavory episodes followed: the alleged theft of family jewels, later redeemed by Annabella, and possibly blackmail by Crosse, who had become her lover. When Ada and her husband separated, her life swept toward its tragic end. To ease the pain of mysterious digestive ailments, she became addicted to laudanum, which seems to have produced delusional behavior. But her worsening physical symptoms proved to be far from imaginary. She was diagnosed as suffering from advanced uterine cancer and died a slow and agonized death at the age of thirty-six—the same age at which Byron had died. Her final request—to be buried next to her father in the family vault at Hucknall Torkard—was honored. She had not, after all, been his "implement of torture," but her own.

Afterlife

Byron, thou should'st be living at this hour!
   What would you do, I wonder, if you were?
Britannia's lost prestige and cash and power,
   Her middle classes show some wear and tear,
   We've learned to bomb each other from the air;
I can't imagine what the Duke of Wellington
Would say about the music of Duke Ellington.

                    W. H. Auden, *Letter to Lord Byron*

ITH THIS SUMMONS, written from Iceland on the eve of World War II, the poet of our own Age of Anxiety claims Byron for *us*. Somehow we are not prone to wonder what Wordsworth, Coleridge, or Keats would do if confronted by mass destruction sweetened with the trivia of progress. And certainly Shelley's utopian visions, uninflected by irony, would never tempt anyone to bring him up to date on the latest marvels of modern life. Byron is the one nineteenth-century Romantic who could make sense for us of a century crazier even than his own, where sex and consumerism provide the only consolations:

A world of Aertex underwear for boys,
   Huge plate glass windows, walls absorbing noise,
Where the smoke nuisance is utterly abated
And all the furniture is chromium-plated.[1]

His moral circuitry made similar connections; for him, the devastation of Waterloo and a Duchess's dinner table were not unrelated phenomena. For that matter, Lord Byron, who never let anyone forget his title, was the only one of the major Romantic poets to move in circles where he could have asked the Iron Duke for his opinion of the Duke of Jazz. The sense we have that Byron addresses our own experience begins with his mobility—social, psychological, and sexual. He glided through drawing rooms, plotted with Carbonari, loved men and women. His poetry reflects this peculiarly modern mutability. *Don Juan* speaks to us in a language new to poetry, an idiom of puns and wordplay, tweaked pronunciation, free association, and syncopated rhythm; sometimes Byron can sound like the first rap artist. But there is another facet of the man and poet that vaults him squarely into our own celebrity-driven era: his uneasy relationship to his own success. He manipulated his image with the skill of an army of press agents, playing hide-and-seek with the me/not-me questions raised by his heroes. At the same time he recognized the damage that came from playing Byron; the life kept upstaging the poetry.

Set in motion by the living poet, the monster known as Byronism took on a posthumous life of its own. Even prolonged by scandal, the fame he enjoyed and exploited until it soured was obscurity itself compared to the mythologized Byron that virtually rose from his corpse at Missolonghi.

As soon as news of his death began to spread, the human poet, famous or infamous, was replaced by a cult figure answering to every desire. From Byron's lifetime to the present day, competing voices have invoked the poet as an idol in their own image: hero and martyr of revolutionary struggle, aristocratic aesthete and dandy, transgressive rebel of polymorphous sexuality fueled by forbidden substances and with sulfurous whiffs of the Prince of Darkness swirling about him. These last mutations were recharged by the rock culture's canonization of self-destructive artists hallowed by early death: Elvis and James Dean, while "His Satanic Majesty" Mick Jagger still pays tribute to the sneering, demonic Byron of Victorian nightmare.

Obscured by the freedom fighter, fashion leader, fallen angel, and literary bad boy, Byron the great poet has tended to be forgotten. No twentieth-century biographer has troubled to examine his art, as though the breathless excitement of the life had obscured the work. This was not the case among Byron's contemporaries; his stanzas inspired a creative outpouring in his own and succeeding generations as no other writer's work had done since Shakespeare's: Poets and novelists, composers and painters were fired by the drama of Byron's life and its end, while they translated the poems into every medium.

Most immediately, his death in a country whose cause he had championed proved a bonanza for the fading prestige of the Greek cause. In France, Delacroix's stirring canvas *Greece Expiring on the Ruins of Missolonghi* (1824), while not based on a specific work by Byron, relied on the public's knowledge of his deathplace to make the connection between the poet's sacrifice and the martyrdom of the Greek people. Within a year, Byron's accidental death from malaria in a swampy pesthole of the Peloponnese had been transfigured to become a crucial act of heroism. That his role in the war made no difference to its outcome was forgotten. Three years after his death the British-led naval victory in the Battle of Navarino in 1827 ended Turkish rule over Greece. The fighting dragged on for three more years after that. No matter. Byron as liberator would inspire generations of literary rebels. When the Czar crushed the Decembrist rising in 1825, among the young plotters executed on the same day in St. Petersburg was the poet Ryleyev, who mounted the scaffold with a volume of Byron's poems clutched in his hand.

Relics of the living man acquired sacred properties. From the moment when locks of hair were snipped from the corpse, the organs packed separately, and his belongings docketed for appropriate distribution, any connection with Byron through his possessions acquired an unprecedented mystique. In this particular competition the prizes were borne away by two younger writers who inherited his surviving mistresses. As a means of obtaining access to the Byron-Guiccioli correspondence for a series of newspaper articles, the poet Alphonse de Lamartine became Teresa's lover. His literary claim to Byron's legacy took the form of "completing" his predecessor's first major work with *Dernier Chant du Pèlerinage d'Harold* (1829). Another "pseudo-Byron," Edward George Earle Lytton Bulwer, under the name of Bulwer-Lytton, wrote novels in what has been called the "dandiacal Byronic" style of fiction.[2] His first published work, *Vivian Grey*, written when the author was twenty-one, appeared in 1826, two years after Byron's death. For this fictionalized life of the poet, inspiration and documentation were provided by Bulwer-Lytton's scandalous affair with Lady Caroline Lamb. Soon, however, imagination had to suffice. Before he turned to politics, Benjamin Disraeli's literary aspirations produced a novel, *Venetia*, based on the story of Byron's marriage and separation. In Disraeli's account, however, his Byronic hero dies a Shelleyan death by drowning in the Bay of La Spezia.

Contestants for the crown of Byron's successor included a token woman—one who dressed for the part. "Madame, you will live, and you will be the Lord Byron of France," François René de Chateaubriand, poet and diplomat, wrote with oracular approval to George

Sand on the publication of her novel *Lélia* in 1833. Eight years later she
rejected these laurels and repudiated her debut. The hero of her next
novel, *Horace*, was a satire of Byronic imitation mixed with considerable self-parody: "If I give myself up to love," her hero declares, "I want
it to wound me deeply, to electrify me, to break my heart or to exalt me
to the seventh heaven. . . . What I want is to suffer, to go crazy."[3]

For the Victorians, getting over boyish Byron worship was a rite of
passage to literary respectability. When fifteen-year-old Alfred Tennyson
learned of Byron's death, he rushed, weeping, into the woods behind his
father's rectory to carve his dead hero's name on a limestone rock. In
later years, Alfred, Lord Tennyson, soon to become poet laureate, publicly disavowed Byron the man and poet. He felt morally compelled to
this act of censure, he said, because of his deep aversion to adultery. But
in Haworth parsonage, far from the literary cenacles of London, the
Brontë daughters, Charlotte, Emily, and Anne, pored over their father's
complete edition of Byron's poems, lavishly illustrated with the Finden
brothers' steel engravings. In *Blackwood's* magazine the girls read
reviews that served to warn orthodox readers from certain of the poet's
works. Dutifully, Emily advised a friend that she had better skip *Don
Juan* and *Cain*. Byron and his outcast heroes continued to haunt her
juvenile writings as well as her reading; he would soon emerge from the
moors as Heathcliff in *Wuthering Heights*, more Byronic than the poet
himself.

Provincial aspirants to literary glory used Byron as guide and even
go-between. James Joyce, in the voice of his fictional double Stephen
Daedalus, pronounced him to be the greatest English poet. In *Ulysses*,
Leopold Bloom, hoping to win the fickle Molly away from other
lovers, courts her with a gift volume of Byron's poetry. Another
Dubliner, Oscar Wilde, was an Oxford undergraduate in 1878 when his
submission for the university's Newdigate Poetry Prize was a tribute to
Childe Harold's Pilgrimage. In "Ravenna" he paid homage to Byron as
"a second Antony / Who of the world another Actium made." Privately,
however, Wilde and his friends exalted Byron as a hero of homosexuality, believing that his friendship with Shelley ended when Byron
tried to make love to the younger poet. Whether Wilde had some evidence for this conviction, now lost to us, and how much he knew of
Byron's early and late relations with young men is unknown. More certainly he seized the coded challenge to anxious Victorian masculinity
posed by the "dandiacal" style along with its subversive message:
Sex was politics. In Wilde's best-known prose work, *The Picture of
Dorian Gray*, published in 1891, the "open secret"—known but never

mentioned—of Byron's homosexual experience becomes the unnamed sin that haunts the novel's hero. His painted image that ages and decays is the physical expression of a moral sickness "hidden" by Dorian's eternally boyish looks. To those in the know, *Dorian Gray* was held to have "outed" the poet as a lover of men.[4]

It did not take long for Byron's imitators to become themselves the objects of satire. A novel in verse, Pushkin's *Eugene Onegin*, published in 1832, dissected a romantic generation fatally led astray by the author of *Childe Harold*. When the provincial Tatyana is rejected by Onegin, condemned to Byronic wanderings for killing his friend in a duel, the brokenhearted girl prowls through her beloved's abandoned country house, hoping to find in his library (that "modish bachelor cell") the key to his indifference. Soon enough, in works by "The bard of Juan and the Giaour," she discovers lines marked by the owner that reveal the model for Eugene's behavior. For the first time Tatyana sees that "him for whom, by fate's command,"

> She'd been condemned to feel desire
> That dangerous and sad pariah,
> That work of heaven or of hell
> That angel . . . and proud fiend as well.
> What was he then? an imitation?
> An empty phantom or a joke,
> A Muscovite in Harold's cloak,
> Compendium of affectation,
> A lexicon of words in vogue
> Mere parody and just a rogue?[5]

A century later another great Russian poet clung to Byron's humane rationalism as a talisman of hope through the Stalinist nightmare. In 1945 Isaiah Berlin visited Anna Akhmatova at her apartment in Leningrad. "After a silence she asked me whether I would like to hear her poetry," he recalled, "but before doing this she said that she wished to recite two cantos from Byron's *Don Juan* to me, for they were relevant to what would follow. Even if I had known the poem well," her visitor admitted, "I could not have told which cantos she had chosen, for although she read English, her pronunciation made it impossible to understand more than a word or two. She closed her eyes and spoke the lines from memory, with intense emotion. . . . Then she spoke her own poems."[6]

Moving toward modernism, most poets and novelists increasingly identified with the cool Byron of dandyism, or they satirized those provincial Byronists who, like Eugene Onegin, had swallowed *Childe Harold* whole. Neither music nor painting, however, lend themselves to irony. Romantic artists and composers embraced the poet of the Oriental tales: his outcasts and wanderers, pashas and potentates on their funeral pyres; kidnapped slave girls and doomed lovers dying in battle or expiring from grief. Or seeing the marvels of nature in the Swiss Alps or the antique ruins of Italy, they sought visual equivalents of the poet's mind "expanding to the immensity of what it contemplates." The muse of Verdi and Delacroix and Turner is the Byron of the wide screen.

Anglomania was the fashion for the youthful post-Napoleonic generation of French Romantics of the 1820s, and Byron was their god. One group of painters and poets, calling themselves the "Young Cenacle," tried to transform their meeting place, a working-class Paris café, into Newstead Abbey. One of their number whose father was a surgeon donated a skull, from which they took turns drinking cheap red wine. After a few rounds, the poet Théophile Gautier remembered, they had no trouble imagining themselves as Byron and his friends, carousing in monks' habits that occasionally swung open to reveal the white thighs of the "Paphian girls" their idol had mentioned so tantalizingly in his account of these revels.[7]

Delacroix had been obsessed with Byron and England from earliest youth, and he seems to have been the only one of the poet's French acolytes to read his work in the original. He was even said to resemble the poet physically, and one of his friends, the lithographer Achille Devéria, designed a portrait medal with the profiles of Delacroix and Byron juxtaposed. Delacroix's first sexual experience, at age nineteen, had been with his aunt's English lady's maid, and between visits to the servants' quarters he read aloud from *Childe Harold's Pilgrimage* to his elderly relative.

As a boy Delacroix was torn between painting and poetry, and the many references to Byron in his *Journals*[8] reiterate his belief that, in terms of invention, the poet faced the greater challenge with none of the pleasurable physicality of brush and pigment to release his imagination. Byron remained a lifelong inspiration. When ideas and energy failed him, Delacroix reported, he had only to read the preface to his favorite volume of Byron's poems; then "I felt stirring within me that insatiable desire to create." And he continued to count on the poet as "word painter" to inspire him: "Just remember certain passages from Byron whenever you need to rekindle the flame," he reminded himself. Delacroix painted at least eleven known pictures based on Byron's poems, along with many oil sketches and drawings for the major works. Discovering the poet as a twin soul vindicated his own preoccupations—the lure of the East; the attraction and repulsion of female sexuality; the beauty and freedom of animals; the pathos of oppressed peoples; and, most important for Delacroix, the suffering and rejection that were the artist's fate. In addition to these large themes, Delacroix also found in Byron's art an equivalent of the brilliant painterly detail of which he was master. At work on a scene from *The Giaour*, Delacroix noted in his *Journals*, he became obsessed with Byron's horrifying image of the dead Selim's hand, given a semblance of life as it was tossed back and forth by the shallow waves near shore. Here, however, the painter recognized the dynamic role supplied by the reader's imagination. Rendered by his brush, the hand, he knew, would remain inert. Knowing better than to take his Byron literally, he never used this actual detail in his paintings of *The Giaour*. Indeed, Delacroix's greatest work inspired by the poet, *The Death of Sardanapalus* (1827), was based on a scene Byron left out of his tragedy: In the painter's swirling composition the ruler lies on a divan surrounded by his treasured possessions—slave girls and horses, jewels and precious objects, all about to be consumed by the flames. Delacroix's reminder to himself—"Remember Byron's poetry"—was the key that unlocked a wellspring of subjects and images, from the sublime idea to the vivid detail. Once liberated, he did not need to follow the poet slavishly. Even the paintings or lithographs based on specific scenes in the poems—the fight between Hassan and the Giaour, or the shipwreck in *Don Juan*—are far removed from illustrations; rather, they could be described in terms of *"correspondances,"* the theory of equivalences among differing forms of artistic expression as formulated by another dandiacal poet and admirer of Delacroix, Baudelaire.

The son of a Covent Garden barber and wig maker, Joseph Turner had little but Englishness and genius in common with Byron. But he shared with his favorite poet a tremendous productivity along with the Northerner's transforming sense of discovery in his encounter with the South. In *Childe Harold's Pilgrimage—Italy* (1832), the small human figures on a hilltop posed against the Campagna below remind us of the poet's thrilling descent from the gothic summer of Diodati into the golden plain of Lombardy and his new life. When the painting was exhibited in 1832, Turner attached these lines (with his own small changes):

and now, fair Italy!
Thou art the garden of the world, the home
Of all Art yields, and Nature can decree

Even in thy desert, what is like to thee?
Thy very weeds are beautiful, thy waste
More rich than other climes fertility;
Thy wreck a glory, and thy ruin graced
With an immaculate charm which cannot be defaced.

Turner relied on the Byronic associations of certain subjects to give credibility to his own reflections on history: Affixed to *The Fields of Waterloo* (1818), strewn with the dead and dying, are Byron's lines from Canto III invoking the corpses of both sides, "in one red burial blent."

Without specific reference to the poetry, Turner's Venetian paintings exalt Byron's "fairy city of the heart" as dreamed through the painter's intoxication with light and water. In tribute to the poet's discipline and prodigious labor, Turner went on to produce watercolors for engraved illustrations to the most popular and cheapest editions of Byron's collected works, published serially by Murray for decades following the poet's death.[9]

Inevitably, the grandeur of Byron's vision inspired stage designs—an ironic immortality in the light of his own failed theatrical ambitions. John Martin's famous engravings for Milton's *Paradise Lost* prepared him to translate Byron's metaphysical dramas *Cain* and, Martin's particular favorite, *Manfred* into the spectacular "effects" that Victorian mechanical invention was able to provide for rapt audiences.

No cult expires without a legacy of kitsch. Victorian consumers could dine on scenes from Byron's poems at their own table if they could afford a 119-piece porcelain dinner service produced by the Spode factory and featuring the Finden brothers' engravings for his *Works*. And for a present-day Byron "experience" available to visitors for a few pounds, Newstead Abbey itself has been restored into an all-purpose theme park of England's past. Falling somewhere between Graceland and a generic "stately home," Newstead houses relics of the poet's life, an important collection of related material, along with a Jacobean bedroom and a Victorian nursery. (A professed child-hater, Byron would have found this to be the Abbey's ultimate desecration.) Among authentic artifacts on view are two of the poet's contributions to Byronism, the helmets he designed for himself and his personal staff to impress the Greeks. With this fantasy of military glory, Byron made his bid for immortality as "the grand Napoleon of the realm of rhyme."

The Byronic hero, a doomed aristocrat haunted by dark secrets and forbidden loves, defying the laws of God and man, inspired composers of music in every form: There have been 750 compositions based on Byron's poetry.[10] To the musical generation immediately following the poet's, his writings were sacred text: symphonies, oratorios, and operas, program pieces, and innumerable songs poured forth from composers' pens, giving new life to the poetry. In particular, the drive of Byron's poetic line seemed made for the human voice: There are fifty known operas based on the poetry, eleven of them on *Sardanapalus* alone!

The Assyrian ruler was the subject of Berlioz's winning submission for the Prix de Rome in 1826, eight years before his most famous Byronic tribute, *Harold in Italy*. Like Delacroix, the French composer was thought to resemble the poet physically, and he was proud of being described as "the Byron of music." Admiring a marble group by Canova in St. Peter's, Berlioz thrilled to the thought that Byron, accompanied by Madame Guiccioli, would have stopped before this same work, and he fantasizes being Byron, adored by a mistress like Teresa, "a rare and superior woman by whom he was completely understood and as deeply loved! . . . He was loved! He was a poet! . . . He was free! . . . He was rich! . . . He had it all! And I ground my teeth so loudly that the very walls of the confessional echoed and the souls of the damned must have shuddered."

Without suffering the hopelessness of trying to appropriate Byron's life, other composers seemed to fixate on certain poems. Lizst's oeuvre reveals a "near obsession with Byron's *Mazeppa*," one critic noted; he worked and reworked music based on this story. (The same poem acted as a spur to Victor Hugo, who, two years after Byron's death, tried his hand at the story of the Polish noble and his triumphant stoicism.) In the depths of suicidal depression, Robert Schumann sought a fellow sufferer in one of Byron's heroes: "Never have I devoted myself to such love and outlay of force to any composition as that of *Manfred*," the composer wrote of his stirring overture. His father, a publisher, had been the first to issue Byron's complete works in German, and the younger Schumann himself had worked on the translations. On at least one occasion he gave a reading of the play during which, overcome by emotion, he broke down and wept. Tchaikovsky's labor on this same poem, however, a symphonic work in four movements scored for a large orchestra, caused no despair greater than the ongoing melancholy of his troubled life. More recently, using Tchaikovsky's score, Rudolf Nureyev choreographed a ballet called *Manfred*, based not on the poem but on Byron's life, in which the principal female role is given to Augusta. And Tennessee Williams provided the text for a one-act opera, another

Letter to Lord Byron, which again had as its subject the poet's passion for his sister. The life story also prompted Virgil Thomson's last opera, *Lord Byron,* a work, it must be said, which serves to confirm that Gertrude Stein, not Byron, was destined to be this composer's muse. Not even Byron's most severe detractor in American music entirely escaped his spell. Denouncing the Romantic composers Berlioz, Schumann, and Liszt as victims of "the Byronic fallacy,". Charles Ives took aim at the introspective, narcissistic, antidemocratic character of the Romantic hero. Yet among Ives's songs are two based on Byron texts, one from *Childe Harold* and one from *Manfred.*

Byron's protagonists were not merely brooding outcasts, but more often were possessed of larger purpose. Verdi, for example, quickly seized on themes of social upheaval and political oppression—both awaiting the hero's sacrifice—to provide the conflict in two operas he based on Byron dramas: *Due Foscari* (1844) and *Il Corsaro* (1848), both written during the tumultuous events of the Risorgimento. He had long been enamored of Byron's *Corsair*—"I would not know how to find a subject more beautiful, more passionate and more suited to music," he wrote to its publisher. The relevance of the poem's outlaw hero Conrad (Corrado), who takes to piracy to rid the Aegean Sea of Turkish oppression, would not have been lost on Verdi's northern Italian audience, suffering under the Austrian heel for three decades, and Verdi's own ardent patriotism found its perfect expression in Byron's message of liberation. In the prison scene, when Corrado asks Gulnare why she does not love Seid, she replies: "That barbarian? I am a slave, corsair. Can a slave feel desire for her oppressor? Love can grow only in the hearts of the free." The censors in Modena cut all of these lines before the opera could be performed. Byron's provocative words continued to inflame audiences long after the Risorgimento had rid Italy of the oppressor. Donizetti based operas on *Marino Falieri* and *Parisina.* More ambitious still, the same composer adapted *Heaven and Earth (Il Diluvio universale),* which the poet himself called an oratorio. Both productions proved resounding failures. In our own century, Schoenberg's experience as a refugee from Hitler's Germany conferred a personal dimension to his setting of Byron's *Ode to Napoleon.*

Like the popular anthologies of the poet's most romantic verses sold as "Byron's Beauties," the list of musical settings is swelled by the number of Victorian parlor songs based on his expression of the exaltation and pain of love. Starting with the request of the young composer and musician Isaac Nathan to join the short poems from *Hebrew Melodies* to his own compositions, Byron's lyrics have attracted the greatest number of collaborators: Seventy-three musical settings are recorded for

"She Walks in Beauty" alone, followed by fifty-five arrangements of "There Be None of Beauty's Daughters." Another favorite was the poet's lachrymose "Fare Thee Well," written to his wife when he left England, to which at least one enterprising seller of sheet music appended an imaginary "reply" from Lady Byron.

For the concert hall, composers whose musical invention was enhanced by Byron's stanzas include Schumann, Wolf, Mendelssohn, Mussorgsky, Rimsky-Korsakov, Gounod, and Busoni; in the twentieth century, Hindemith, Carlos Chavez, and Ned Rorem found words to their songs in Byron's poetry.

"Byron's somber genius is the romantic spirit of the nineteenth century," George Sand observed. Our own century hears a voice that moves beyond the monochrome minor key, to play all the parts. In his power to speak to and for us, Byron feels, more than any other poet writing in English, Shakespearean in his range; he can be Richard III or Romeo, Hamlet or Falstaff, or, for that matter, Kate, Rosalind, or Lady Macbeth.

Lived or imagined, every experience and mood was grist for his poetry. By the same token, there is a Byron for everyone. Few poets have spawned such proprietarial commentary: He has been claimed by Labour politicians, queer theorists, and specialists in manic depression; in matters of belief, he has been shown to be atheist, agnostic, and a defender of orthodoxy; a true cosmopolitan and the most English of poets; a misogynist who gave voice to women's "She condition" with a sympathy rarely heard in his own day—or ours.

These are not "different" Byrons, but one man discovering himself as he writes. In the process he speaks to the shifting selves of his readers across time: abandoned children; failed lovers, husbands, and wives; citizens and exiles; skeptical communicants and yearning disbelievers. He spares us no example of life's suffering, including the reminder of its brevity: All we have is the "summer of a dormouse." Then, with laughter, he diverts us from our common fate.

Notes, Bibliography, and Index

Notes

Abbreviations Used in the Notes

BOOKS

BLJ   Marchand, Leslie A., ed. *Byron's Letters and Journals.* 13 vols.
       London and Cambridge, Mass.: Harvard University Press, 1973–94.

CMP   Nicholson, Andrew, ed. *Lord Byron: The Complete Miscellaneous*
       Prose. Oxford: Clarendon Press, 1991.

CPW   McGann, Jerome J., ed. *Lord Byron: The Complete Poetical Works.*
       7 vols. Oxford: Clarendon Press, 1980–93.

RR   Reiman, Donald H., ed. *The Romantics Reviewed.* 8 vols. New York:
       Garland Publishing, 1972.

SC   Cameron, K. N., Donald Reiman, and Doucet D. Fischer, eds. *Shelley*
       and His Circle, 1773–1822, 8 vols. Cambridge, Mass.: Harvard Uni-
       versity Press, 1961–86. Letters and other documents, including new
       materials relating to Teresa Gamba Guiccioli, owned by the Carl H.
       Pforzheimer Library, the New York Public Library. Also, essays by the
       editors and other scholars. Two additional volumes planned.

BYRON'S WORKS

CHP	*Childe Harold's Pilgrimage*	EBSR	*English Bards and Scotch*
DJ	*Don Juan*		*Reviewers*
		FP	*Fugitive Pieces*

PRINCIPAL CORRESPONDENTS

AL	Augusta Leigh	CGB	Catherine Gordon Byron
AM	Annabella Milbanke	CL	Caroline Lamb
AMB	Annabella Milbanke Byron	DK	Douglas Kinnaird
CC	Claire Clairmont	EP	Elizabeth Pigot

Sources listed in the Selected Bibliography (pages 809–812) are referred to by the
author's last name.

JB	Jack Byron	MWS	Mary Wollstonecraft
JCH	John Cam Hobhouse		Shelley
JH	John Hanson	PBS	Percy Bysshe Shelley
JM	John Murray	RCD	Robert Charles Dallas
JNM	Judith Noel Milbanke	SBD	Scrope Berdmore Davies
JP	John Pigot	TGG	Teresa Gamba Guiccioli

CHAPTER 1:   *"Shades of the Dead! Have I Not Heard Your Voices?"*

1. Medwin, I, 189.
2. J. H. Plumb, *England in the Eighteenth Century,* Harmondsworth, U.K.: Penguin, 1950, p. 95.
3. *Regency Portrait Painter: The Life of Sir Thomas Lawrence,* P.R.A., London, 1951, p. 262.
4. B to CGB [May 1–10, 1804?], *BLJ,* I, 49.
5. *DJ,* X, 36, *CPW,* V, 447–48.
6. *The Narrative of the Honorable John Byron (Commodore in a Late Expedition round the World) . . . From the Year 1740, till their arrival in England, 1746 . . . Written by Himself,* London, 1768.
7. George Clinton, *Memoirs of the Life and Writings of Lord Byron,* London, 1827, p. 33.
8. Prothero, VI, 231–32.
9. B to JM, possibly July 7, 1823; *BLJ,* X, 208. In defending his father against accusations of abusing his first wife, Byron makes a curious slip: His mother, he insists, had "too proud a spirit to bear the ill usage of any man," suggesting that Amelia, lacking such backbone, was a likely victim.
10. Mrs. Duff to Alexander Russell, December 10, 1786, quoted in Boyes (2), 23.
11. CGB to Miss Urquhart, November 13, 1786, in Symon, 125.

12. John Leslie to James Watson, Gordon Duff Papers, Aberdeen University, MSS, 932.
13. CGB to James Watson, in Marchand, I, 24.
14. T. Moore (1), I, 183.
15. John Byron to James Watson, January 26, 1788, Pforzheimer Collection MSS.
16. CGB to James Watson, February 22, 1788, Morgan Library MSS, quoted in Boyes, 29.
17. Ibid.
18. Later descriptions of Byron's foot and limp point to the congenital malformation known as club foot, wherein the heel is drawn up and the sole of the foot turns inward. Recent evidence, however, suggests that Byron's deformity resulted from a mild version of spina bifida, a developmental abnormality of the spine that, in this case, caused the right leg to be shorter than the left and the foot to remain in spasm. These symptoms, together with the resulting withered calf muscles, would have caused the limp and explains the sliding or running gait (impossible with a club foot) with which Byron as a young man strove to disguise his lameness. See A. B. Morrison, "Byron's Lameness," *The Byron Journal,* 1975, 24–30.

CHAPTER 2: *"A Verra Takkin' Laddie"*

1. T. Moore (1), I, 13.
2. Ibid., 25.
3. All quotations from the letters of Jack Byron to his sister Frances Leigh are from the Lovelace Byron Papers on deposit in the Bodleian Library, and are cited with the kind permission of the Earl of Lytton. JB to Frances Leigh, Valenciennes, October 15, 1790, Box 161.
4. CGB to Frances Leigh, January 21, 1791, Murray MSS. Also in Symon, 33–34.
5. JB to Frances Leigh, February 4, 1791, Lovelace Byron Papers, Box 161.
6. Prothero, I, ix.
7. JB to Frances Leigh, March 30, 1791, Lovelace Byron Papers.
8. Ibid.
9. CGB to Frances Leigh, May 5, 1791, British Museum, Add. MS. 30137.
10. CGB to Frances Leigh, August 23, 1791, Prothero, V, 232.
11. Ibid.
12. Ibid.
13. "Childish Recollections," *CPW*, I, 165.
14. Lovell, I, 58–60.
15. T. Moore (2), I, 10.
16. Symon, 70.
17. W. Gordon Blaikie, *Harper's Magazine*, June–November 1891.
18. T. Moore (1), I, 15.
19. Blaikie, op. cit.
20. "My Dictionary," May 1, 1821, *BLJ*, VIII, 107–8.
21. Ibid.
22. Ibid.
23. *Bon Record: Records and Reminiscences of Aberdeen Grammar School from the Earliest Times by Many Writers*, ed. H. E. Morland Simpson, Edinburgh, 1906, quoted in Kiriakoula Solomou, *Byron and Greek Poetry*, Athens [1977], 171.
24. "My Dictionary," *BLJ*, VIII, 108.
25. Symon, 70.
26. David Masson, *James Melvin, Rector of the Grammar School of Aberdeeen: A Sketch*, Aberdeen, 1895, quoted in Solomou, op. cit., 32.
27. T. Moore (o), I, 16.
28. Blaikie, quoted in Boyes, 45.
29. T. Moore (?), I, 10.
30. Ibid., 14.
31. Ibid., 38.
32. Ibid., 255n.
33. B to JM, October 9, 1821, *BLJ*, VIII, 238.
34. Byron, "Preface" to *Cain*, *CPW*, VI, 228.
35. John Moore, *Zeluco, Various Views of Human Nature*, London, 1789, I, 3–4, in Marchand, I, 39.
36. "Journal," November 26, 1813, *BLJ*, III, 221–22.
37. Ibid.
38. "Song" (1807 or 1808), *CPW*, I, 47.
39. *Lachin Y Gair*, *CPW*, I, 103–4.
40. T. Moore (o), I, 21.
41. Alexander Crombie to Farquhar, June 8, 1798, in Marchand, I, 45.
42. Hanson narrative, Murray MSS.

CHAPTER 3:   *A Peer's Progress*

1. T. Moore (1), I, 25.
2. See Linda Colley, *Britons: Forging the Nation 1701–1837*, New Haven and London, 1992, 117–22 and passim.
3. *DJ*, X, 18; *CPW*, V, 442.
4. T. Moore (1), I, 24.
5. John Hanson to Farquhar, August 30, 1798, in Willis Pratt, *Byron at Southwell*, Austin, 1948, 2.
6. From a manuscript account written by Hobhouse in 1824, the summer following his friend's death, and titled "Lord Byron," in Marchand, I, 50.
7. *The Trial of William Lord Byron* (no author listed), p. 4, in Marchand, I, 52.
8. Hanson narrative, Murray MSS.
9. Ibid.
10. T. Moore (1), I, 101.
11. B to Mrs. Parker, November 8, 1798, *BLJ*, I, 39.
12. Prothero, I, 7n.
13. "Epigram on an Old Lady Who Had Some Curious Notions Respecting the Soul," *CPW*, I, 1.
14. B to CGB, March 13, 1799, *BLJ*, I, 39–40.
15. T. Moore (3), 416.
16. Hobhouse, op. cit., notes, Marchand, I, 57.
17. John Hanson to GGB, September 1, 1799, Prothero, I, 1n.
18. Hobhouse, op. cit., Marchand, I, 57.
19. "Detached Thoughts," 80, October 15, 1821–May 18, 1822, *BLJ*, IX, 40.
20. JH to CGB, Hanson narrative, Murray MSS.
21. Hanson narrative, Murray MSS.
22. Ibid.
23. Ibid.
24. CGB to Mrs. Duff, April 15, 1799, Pforzheimer Collection MSS.
25. CGB to Lord Carlisle, July 9, 1799, in Boyes (2), 62.
26. Prothero, I, 9n.
27. CGB to Mrs. Duff, in Boyes (2), 62.
28. JH to CGB, Hanson narrative, Murray MSS.
29. B to George Anson Byron, February 24, 1801, *BLJ*, I, 41.
30. *DJ*, II, 87; *CPW*, V, 116.
31. T. Moore (1), I, 29.
32. Hanson narrative, Murray MSS.
33. Byron to JH, November (?) 1799, *BLJ*, I, 40.
34. Hanson narrative, Murray MSS.
35. T. Moore (1), I, 30–32.
36. Ibid.
37. Hobhouse, op. cit.
38. "Detached Thoughts," 79, *BLJ*, IX, 40.
39. T. Moore (1), I, 32.
40. B to George Anson Byron, February 24, 1801, *BLJ*, I, 41.
41. T. Moore (1), I, 33.

CHAPTER 4:   *"A Home, a World, a Paradise to Me"*

1. T. Moore (1), I, 35.
2. Ibid.
3. John Chandos, *Boys Together, English Public Schools, 1800–1864*, London, 1984, 21.
4. J. G. Cotton Minchin, *Old Harrow Days*, London, 1898, 193.
5. Ibid.
6. T. Moore (1), I, 35.
7. Ibid.

8. Hunt, I, 151.

9. T. Moore (1), I, 38.

10. Marchand, I, 67.

11. The Rev. A. G. L'Estrange, *The Literary Life of the Rev. William Harness*, London, 1871, 4.

12. Minchin, op. cit., 192.

13. "Detached Thoughts," 89, October 15, 1821–May 18, 1822, *BLJ*, IX, 43.

14. Ibid., 88, 42.

15. *The Deformed Transformed*, I, *CPW*, VI, 531.

16. "Detached Thoughts," 89, *BLJ*, IX, 43.

17. T. Moore (1), I, 19.

18. CGB to Baillie, September 21, 1801, Hanson narrative, as corrected in Marchand, I, 68.

19. Laurie to CGB, December 7, 1801, Hanson narrative, Murray MSS.

20. T. Moore (1), I, 41.

21. CGB to AL, October 18, 1801, in Pratt, 4–5.

22. CGB to JH, October 25, 1801, Hanson narrative, Murray MSS.

23. Pryse Lockhart Gordon, *Personal Memoirs*, London, H. Colburn and R. Bentley, 1830, II, 321, 332–33.

24. Ibid.

25. Ibid.

26. B to Harness, February 16, 1808, *BLJ*, I, 156.

27. Prothero, V, 338.

28. "On the Death of a Young Woman, Cousin to the Author and Very Dear to Him," *CPW*, I, 125.

29. "Detached Thoughts," 91, *BLJ*, IX, 44.

30. T. Moore (1), I, 44.

31. Chandos, op. cit., 308 ff. These quotations are from the unpublished MSS autobiography of A. J. Symonds (London Library). Symonds's words could not be quoted or even paraphrased until restrictions were lifted on the work in 1977. Symonds was describing the school in 1854, but there is every reason to suppose that what was common practice in Victorian Harrow had begun during the Regency.

32. Dr. Joseph Drury to JH, February 4, 1803, in Prothero, I, 12n.

33. CGB to JH, January 14 and January 16, 1803, Hanson narrative, Murray MSS.

34. Ibid.

35. CGB to JH, February 14, 1803, Hanson narrative, Murray MSS.

36. Owen Mealey to JH, British Library, Egerton MSS, 2613.

37. "Detached Thoughts," 91, *BLJ*, IX, 91.

38. "Childish Recollections," *CPW*, I, 167.

39. B to CGB, May 1, 1803, *BLJ*, I, 41–42.

40. Ibid.

41. CGB to JH, May 10, 1803, Hanson narrative, Murray MSS.

42. Prothero, I, 13n.

43. T. Moore (1), I, 39.

44. B to CGB, June 23, 1803, *BLJ*, I, 43.

45. "Childish Recollections," *CPW*, I, 165.

CHAPTER 5: *"Love, Desperate Love"*

1. CGB to JH, May or June 30, 1804, Hanson narrative.

2. B to AL, March 22, 1804, *BLJ*, I, 44.

3. Quoted in Boyes (3), 20.

4. Boyes (3), 22.

5. T. Moore (1), I, 47.

6. Boyes (3), 27.

7. T. Moore (3), 432.

8. "Detached Thoughts," 65, *BLJ*, I, 34.

9. T. Moore (1), I, 48. For Hobhouse's comment see Marchand, I, 85. I have not been able to locate Hobhouse's annotated copy of Moore, formerly in the possession of Sir Harold Nicolson.

10. B to CGB, September 15 (?), 1803, *BLJ*, I, 43–44.

11. CGB to JH, October 30, 1803, Hanson narrative, Murray MSS.

12. Ibid.

13. The incident of the ring was first mentioned in *The Court Magazine or Belle assemblée*, 1833, published in Jack Musters's lifetime, and is told again in Teresa Guiccioli, *My Recollections of Lord Byron*, new ed., London, 1869.

14. Boyes (3), 33.

15. "The Dream," *CPW*, IV, 24.

16. Mealey to JH, British Library, Egerton MSS, 2612.

17. Ibid.

18. B to AL, March 26, 1804, *BLJ*, I, 46.

19. Hobhouse's annotated copy of Moore's *Letters and Journals of Lord Byron*, in Marchand, I, 80.

20. Grey de Ruthyn to B, [1808], Meyer Davis Collection MSS, University of Pennsylvania.

21. Ibid.

22. CGB to JH, November 17, 1804, Murray MSS, in Boyes (3), 96.

23. Mealey to JH, March 29, 1804, British Library, Egerton MSS, 2612.

24. B to AL, November 2, 1804, *BLJ*, I, 54–55.

25. B to AL, November 11, 1804, *BLJ*, I, 55.

26. Mealey to JH, July 30, 1804, British Library, Egerton MSS, 2612.

27. B to AL, April 9, 1804, *BLJ*, I, 48.

28. T. Moore (1), I, 56.

29. *CPW*, I, McGann note, p. 177.

30. "To D[elawarr]," *CPW*, I, 126.

31. B to CGB, May 1–10, 1804 (?), *BLJ*, I, 49.

32. "Answer to the Foregoing, Address'd to Miss [Pigot]," *CPW*, I, 131. Both Elizabeth Pigot's verse and Byron's reply were published in Byron's first two privately printed volumes, *Fugitive Pieces*.

33. Pratt, 14–15. Elizabeth Pigot tore out the page later in her life—whether in shame, anger, or regret can never be known.

34. Pratt, 16.

35. B to JH, in *Magg's Catalogue*, 801, 1951.

36. B to EP, August 29, 1804, *BLJ*, I, 50.

37. B to AL, October 25, 1804, *BLJ*, I, 52.

38. Ibid.

39. B to CGB, May 1, 1804 (?), *BLJ*, I, 49.

40. B to AL, November 2, 1804, *BLJ*, I, 58.

41. CGB to JH, December 8, 1804, Hanson narrative, Murray MSS.

42. B to AL, April 25, 1805, *BLJ*, I, 67.

43. Hanson narrative, Murray MSS.

44. B to AL, November 11, 1804, *BLJ*, I, 56.

45. B to AL, April 25, 1805, *BLJ*, I, 67.

46. CGB to JH, January 23, 1805, Hanson narrative, Murray MSS.

47. B to AL, January 30, 1805, *BLJ*, I, 61.

48. Hanson narrative, Murray MSS.

49. B to AL, April 23, 1805, *BLJ*, I, 66.

50. B to AL, April 25, 1805; *BLJ*, I, 67.

51. Tattersall to B, n.d., Murray MSS.

52. Ibid.

53. B to AL, June 5, 1805, *BLJ*, I, 68.

54. T. Moore (2), II, 623.

55. "On a Change of Masters, at a Great Public School," *CPW*, I, 132.

56. 143 to AL, July 2, 1805, *BLJ*, I, 69–70.

57. "Detached Thoughts," 72, *BLJ*, IX, 37.
58. B to Charles David Gordon, August 4, 1805, *BLJ*, I, 71.
59. B to AL, August 18, 1805, *BLJ*, I, 74.
60. B to AL, August 10, 1805, *BLJ*, I, 74.
61. CGB to JH, February 2, 1805, Murray MSS, in Boyes (1), 115.
62. T. Moore (1), I, 150.
63. B to AL, August 18, 1805, BLJ, I, 76.
64. B to Charles David Gordon, August 4, 1805, *BLJ*, I, 72.
65. "Detached Thoughts," 34, *BLJ*, III, 24–25.

CHAPTER 6: *"Fickle as Wind, of Inclinations Wild"*

1. B to JM, November 19, 1820, *BLJ*, VII, 230.
2. B to JH, October 26, 1805, *BLJ*, I, 78.
3. Ibid.
4. Ibid.
5. B to JH, November 23, 1805, *BLJ*, I, 81.
6. Ibid.
7. B to AL, November 6, 1805, *BLJ*, I,
8. Ibid.
9. CGB to JH, Murray MSS.
10. B to JH, December 4, 1805, *BLJ*, I, 84.
11. B to JH, November 30, 1805, *BLJ*, I, 82–83.
12. Ibid.
13. Ibid.
14. "Ravenna Journal," January 12, 1821, *BLJ*, VIII, 24.
15. Tattersall to B, September 1805, Murray MSS.
16. Ibid.
17. "Detached Thoughts," 72, *BLJ*, IX, 37–38.
18. B to EP, July 5, 1807, *BLJ*, I, 124.
19. An earlier unnamed attachment seems to have been the son of a Newstead tenant farmer; Byron's poem "To E.—" equates the lad's humble station with superior virtue: "And though unequal in *thy* fate / Since title deck'd my higher birth; Yet envy not this gaudy state, / *Thine* is the pride of modest worth." Dated by Byron 1802, the poem is thought by McGann to have been written to his earlier friend, then later addressed to Edleston, whom he only met in October 1805, thus bearing a double allusion to the gender and class shared by both boys.
20. B to EP, June 30, 1807, *BLJ*, I, 123.
21. "To Thyrza," *CPW*, I, 347.
22. B to EP, July 5, 1807, *BLJ*, I, 124–25.
23. "Harrow Notebook," in *CMP*, 203.
24. "To Thyrza," *CPW*, I, 347.
25. B to EP, June 30, 1807, *BLJ*, I, 124.
26. "When I Hang on Your Bosom," words by M. G. Lewis, music by Michael Kelly, Bodleian MS Percy d. 9, folio 23.
27. "Stanzas to Jessy," *CPW*, I, 209.
28. Edward Long to B, Murray MSS.
29. B to EP, June 30, 1807, *BLJ*, I, 123.
30. "Pignus Amoris," *CPW*, I, 181, "The Cornelian," *CPW*, I, 151.
31. B to AL, December 26, 1805, *BLJ*, I, 36.
32. B to AL, December 27, 1805, *BLJ*, I, 86–87.
33. Marchand, I, 10.
34. B to AL, January 7, 1806, *BLJ*, I, 88.
35. Ibid.
36. Ibid.
37. AL to JH, February 19, 1806, Hanson narrative, Murray MSS.

38. B to CGB, February 26, 1806, *BLJ*, I, 88–89.
39. CGB to JH, March 4, 1806, Hanson narrative.
40. Note to *DJ*, XI, 19; *CPW*, V 747.
41. "The Bowles/Pope Controversy (1821)," Letter to JM (1821), *CMP*, 125.
42. Ibid.
43. "Damaetas," *CPW*, I, 51–52.
44. B to JH, April 10, 1806, *BLJ*, I, 91.
45. Edward Long to B, Murray MSS.
46. CGB to JH, April 24, 1806, Hanson narrative, Murray MSS.
47. B to Henry Angelo, May 16, 1806, *BLJ*, I, 92.
48. B to Mrs. Massingberd, July 8, 1806, *BLJ*, I, 93.

CHAPTER 7: *A Literary Cub*

1. B to Lord Clare, February 6, 1807, *BLJ*, I, 167.
2. CGB to JH [October?], July 25, 1807, British Library, Egerton MSS, 2611.
3. A revised interpretation of Byron's early poetry as an autobiographical project is persuasively argued by Jerome McGann.
4. "Dedication," *FP*, *CPW*, I, 364.
5. "Prefatory note to *FP*," *CPW*, I, 363.
6. "On Leaving Newstead Abbey," *CPW*, I, 35.
7. [Translation from Anacreon] Ode 3, *FP*, *CPW*, I, 74.
8. "To Mary, on Receiving Her Picture," *FP*, *CPW*, I, 50.
9. "The Cornelian," *FP*, *CPW*, I, 151.
10. "Thoughts Suggested by a College Examination," *FP*, *CPW*, I, 93.
11. "On the Death of Mr. Fox," *FP*, *CPW*, I, 42.
12. "To a Lady," *FP*, *CPW*, I, 140.
13. Along with the quote "momentous Eve," from B to JP, August 9, 1806, *BLJ*, I, 94.
14. B to EP, April 10, 1806, *BLJ*, I, 96.
15. Ibid.
16. B to JP, August 10, 1806, *BLJ*, I, 97.
17. "To Mary," *FP*, *CPW*, I, 132–33.
18. T. Moore (1), I, n. 68.
19. "To Mary," *FP*, *CPW*, I, 133.
20. Unpublished letter of Thomas M.
Blagg, author of *Newark as a Publishing Town*, in Marchand, I, 114.
21. "To Mary," *FP*, *CPW*, I, 134.
22. B to JP, August 16, 1806, *BLJ*, I, 97–98.
23. Ibid.
24. Ibid.
25. B to JP, August 18, 1806, *BLJ*, I, 98–99.
26. Long to B, April 1806, Murray MSS.
27. All quotations from Henry Long's diary are from the holograph MSS in the Berg Collection.
28. B to JP, August 26, 1806, *BLJ*, I, 99.
29. JP to EP, with note by B, September 1806, T. Moore (1), I, 63.
30. Ibid.
31. B to EP, [September 18, 1806], *BLJ*, I, 100.
32. T. Moore (1), I, 64.
33. Ibid.
34. Ibid.
35. Ibid., 65.
36. "An Occasional Prologue," *CPW*, I, 41.
37. Richard Cumberland, "The Wheel of Fortune," in Elizabeth Inchbald, ed., *The British Theatre*, London, 1808, XVIII, 110.
38. B to Clare, November 4, 1806, *BLJ*, I, 101.

39. Report of Benjamin Hutchinson, November 19, 1806, Murray MSS, in Boyes (1), 126.
40. B to JH, April 2, 1907, *BLJ*, I, 114.
41. B to Clare, February 6, 1807, *BLJ*, I, 106.
42. Long to B, n.d. (probably November 1807), Murray MSS.
43. "Answer to Some Elegant Verses, Sent by A Friend to the Author, complaining that one of his descriptions was rather too warmly drawn," *CPW*, I, 179–80.
44. B to JP, January 13, 1807, *BLJ*, I, 103.
45. Ibid.
46. "To the Sighing Strephon," *CPW*, I, 150.
47. B to JP, January 13, 1807, *BLJ*, I, 104.
48. JCH in margin of his copy of Moore's *Life*, in Marchand, I, 124.
49. B to Captain Leacroft, January 31, 1807, *BLJ*, 1, 104.
50. B to Thomas Jones, February 14, 1807, *BLJ*, I, 108.
51. Long to B, February 12, 1807, Murray MSS.
52. Long to B, n.d., Murray MSS.
53. B to Long, February 23, 1807, *BLJ*, I, 110.
54. B to JH, April 2, 1807, *BLJ*, I, 113.
55. B to JH, April 19, 1807, *BLJ*, I, 116.
56. B to Long, May 14, 1807, *BLJ*, I, 119.
57. Ibid.
58. B to JP [April 1807], *BLJ*, I, 117.
59. B to JH, June 11, 1807, *BLJ*, I, 121.
60. B to Long, April 16, 1807, *BLJ*, I, 115.
61. Ibid.
62. B to Long and EP, June 29, 1807, *BLJ*, I, 122.

CHAPTER 8: *"Paper Bullets of the Brain"*

1. B to EP, June 30, 1807, *BLJ*, I, 122–23.
2. B to EP, July 5, 1807, *BLJ*, I, 124.
3. B to EP, June 30, 1807, *BLJ*, I, 123.
4. B to EP, July 5, 1807, *BLJ*, I, 124.
5. Ibid.
6. Ibid., 125.
7. Ibid., 125–26.
8. Ibid.
9. EP to B, July 9, 1807, Murray MSS, in Boyes (1), 63.
10. B to William Bankes, March 6, 1807, *BLJ*, I, 110.
11. B to William Bankes, March 1807, *BLJ*, I, 112.
12. B to EP, July 5, 1807, *BLJ*, I, 125.
13. B to EP, July 13, 1807, *BLJ*, I, 126–27.
14. Ibid.
15. AL to JH, February 7, 1807, Murray MSS, in Boyes (2), 130.
16. Lord Carlisle to B, July 8, 1807, Boyes (2), p. 134.
17. AL to JH, July 18, 1807, Murray MSS, in Boyes (2), 133.
18. B to EP, July 13, 1807, *BLJ*, I, 127.
19. B to JH, July 20, 1807, *BLJ*, I, 128.
20. "Monthly Literary Recreations," July 1807, in *RR*, Part B: "Byron and Regency Poets," 5 vols., I, 1656.
21. Ibid.
22. "Stanzas to Jessy," *CPW*, I, 208.
23. B to EP, August 2, 1807, *BLJ*, I, 130–31.
24. Ibid.
25. Ibid.
26. July 13, 1807, *BLJ*, I, 127.

27. B to EP, August 2, 1807, *BLJ*, I, 132.
28. B to EP, August 11, 1807, *BLJ*, I, 132.
29. Ibid.
30. EP to JP (original lost), in T. Moore (1), I, 94n.
31. Byron to the Earl of Clare, August 20, 1807, *BLJ*, I, 134.
32. B to EP, October 26, 1807, *BLJ*, I, 135–36.
33. Ibid.
34. B to John Murray, November 9, 1820, Marchand, I, 131.
35. Ibid.
36. B to EP, October 26, 1807, *BLJ*, I, 136.
37. Ibid.
38. Hewson Clarke, *The Satirist*, I (October 1807), *RR*, I, 2102.
39. Ibid., August 1808, *RR*, I, 2105.
40. B to EP, October 26, 1807; BLJ, I, 136.
41. The new edition of *Hours of Idleness* was published as *Poems Original and Translated*, Newark, J. Ridge, 1808.
42. Murray MSS, in Marchand, I, 138.
43. B to Ridge, November 11, 1807, *BLJ*, I, 137.
44. B to Crosby, December 22, 1807, *BLJ*, I, 141.
45. B to John Becher, February 26, 1808, *BLJ*, I, 157.
46. Henry Brougham, *The Edinburgh Review*, XI (January 1808), *RR*, II, 835.
47. B to John Becher, March 28, 1808, *BLJ*, I, 163.
48. CGB to Becher (or JH), March 13, 1807, *The Atheneum*, December 5, 1885.
49. B to JCH, February 27, 1808, *BLJ*, I, 158–59.
50. Written in Hobhouse's copy of Moore, I, 145, in Marchand, I, 48.
51. B to RCD, January 21, 1808, *BLJ*, I, 148.

CHAPTER 9: *Lord of the Manor*

1. B to JCH, February 1808, *BLJ*, I, 150.
2. B to JM, November 19, 1820, *BLJ*, VII, 231.
3. B to Becher, February 26, 1808, *BLJ*, I, 157.
4. B to JCH, February 27, 1808, *BLJ*, I, 158–59.
5. Ibid.
6. B to JCH, February 29, 1808, *BLJ*, II, 160.
7. B to JCH, March 28, 1808, *BLJ*, II, 160–61.
8. Ibid.
9. B to Becher, March 28, 1808, *BLJ*, II, 163.
10. B to JCH, April 15, *BLJ*, II, 164–65.
11. T. Moore (1), 418–19.
12. T. Moore (1), I, 147.
13. Medwin, I, 74.
14. T. Moore (1), I, 147.
15. *Blackwood's Magazine*, November 1824, quoted in Marchand, I, 157.
16. B to JCH, March 26, 1808, *BLJ*, II, 161.
17. B to AL, April 26, 1808, *BLJ*, II, 165–66.
18. B to Becher, in T. Moore (1), I, 145–46.
19. B to Harness, June 4, 1808, *BLJ*, II, 166.
20. B to Hargreaves Hanson, June 15, 1808, *BLJ*, II, 167.
21. B to Harness, March 18, 1809, *BLJ*, I, 197.
22. Captain Gronow, *Reminiscences*, I, 152–53, in T. Moore (1), I, 147.
23. Ibid.
24. B to Mrs. Massingberd, July 20, 1808, *BLJ*, I, 167.

25. SBD to B, November 1808, in Burnett, 47.
26. *CPW*, I, 216, "Remind Me Not, Remind Me Not," *CPW*, I, 217.
27. T. Moore (1), I, 147–48.
28. B to Jackson, October 4, 1808, *BLJ*, I, 171.
29. John Cowell to B, Murray MSS.
30. Hewson Clarke, *The Satirist*, III (August 1808), no. 9, p. 368, and no. 10, p. 489, in *RR*, V, 2105.
31. B to Clarke, July 3, 1808, *BLJ*, I, 167.
32. Clarke, op. cit., *RR*, 2105.
33. CGB to Birch, [August 1808], Egerton MSS, 2613.
34. CGB to Birch, Egerton MSS, 2613.
35. CGB to JH, December 31, 1807, Egerton MSS, 2611.
36. Lord Grey to B, [July] 1808, Meyer Davis Collection, University of Pennsylvania.
37. B to Lord Grey, August 7, 1808, *BLJ*, I, 168.
38. B to Jackson, October 4, 1808, *BLJ*, I, 171.
39. *The Mirror of Literature*, LXVII, January 24, 1824, in Rosalys Coope, *Lord Byron's Newstead: The Abbey and Its Furnishings During the Poet's Ownership*, Nottingham, n.d., 135. All the following descriptions of Newstead's furnishings are from Coope's invaluable pamphlet, based on her pursuit of auction records, bills, and other contemporary documentation.
40. B to CGB, November 2, 1808, *BLJ*, I, 172.
41. Coope, op. cit., p. 140 ff.
42. B to CGB, October 7, 1808, *BLJ*, I, 171–72.
43. Ibid.

44. Finn and Johnson's bill, Murray MSS, in Marchand, I, 158.
45. B to Hodgson, November 3, 1808, *BLJ*, I, 173.
46. B to Hodgson, November 27, 1808, *BLJ*, I, 178–79.
47. B to Hodgson, November 3, 1808, *BLJ*, I, 173–74.
48. "[Epistle to a Friend, in Answer to Some Lines Exhorting the Author to Be Cheerful, and to 'Banish Care']," *CPW*, I, 345.
49. "[Well! Thou Art Happy]," *CPW*, I, 221–23.
50. "The Farewell to a Lady," *CPW*, I, 226.
51. B to JH, November 18, 1808, *BLJ*, I, 175 ff.
52. B to CGB, November 2, 1808, *BLJ*, I, 179–80.
53. B to AL, November 30, 1808, *BLJ*, I, 179–80.
54. T. Moore (1), I, 119.
55. B to Hodgson, November 18, 1808, *BLJ*, 1, 176.
56. "Inscription on the Monument of a Newfoundland Dog," *CPW*, I, 224–25.
57. B to Hodgson, November 18, 1808, *BLJ*, I, 177.
58. B to the Duke of Portland, November 20, 1808, *BLJ*, I, 177.
59. B to JH, January 10, 1809, *BLJ*, I, 185.
60. B to JCH, January 16, 1809, *BLJ*, I, 187–88.
61. B to JH, January 17, 1809, *BLJ*, I, 189.
62. "To My Son," *CPW*, I, 211.
63. Washington Irving, *Abbotsford and Newstead Abbey*, in Marchand, I, 166n.
64. "To My Son," *CPW*, I, 211.

CHAPTER 10: *The Great Escape*

1. Dallas (2), 10.
2. Ibid., 11, and ff quotes.

3. *EBSR*, *CPW*, I, 230.
4. Dallas (2), 18.

5. B to RCD, January 25, 1809, *BLJ*, I, 189–90.
6. *EBSR*, *CPW*, I, 230, 252, var.
7. Ibid., 252, and in B to RCD, January 25, 1809, *BLJ*, I, 194.
8. *EBSR*, *CPW*, I, 232.
9. Ibid., 231.
10. B to RCD, January 25, 1809, *BLJ*, I, 190.
11. Dallas (2), 17.
12. *EBSR*, *CPW*, I, 252.
13. Dallas (2), 34.
14. Ibid.
15. Ibid., 36.
16. B to JH, January 15, 1809, *BLJ*, I, 186–87.
17. B to JH, February 8, 1809, *BLJ*, I, 192.
18. B to JH, February 8, 1809, *BLJ*, I, 192.
19. B to Hodgson, March 6, 1809, *BLJ*, I, 196.
20. B to Harness, March 18, 1809, *BLJ*, I, 197.
21. B to JH, December 17, 1808, *BLJ*, I, 181.
22. CGB to JH, Prothero, I, 206n.
23. Ibid.
24. B to JH, April 16, 1809, *BLJ*, I, 200–1.
25. John Edleston to B, March 3, 1809, in D. Moore (2), 89, Murray MSS. This crucial letter was unknown until its publication by Mrs. Moore.
26. B to CGB, February 22, 1809, in Marchand, I, 181.
27. B to CGB, May 19, 1809, *BLJ*, I, 203–4.
28. B to JH, April 26, 1809, *BLJ*, I, 202.
29. B to JM, November 19, 1820, Hanson narrative, Murray MSS.
30. Prothero, I, 153–54n.
31. *CHP*, Canto I, stanza 7, *CPW*, II, 10.
32. CGB to JH, April 9, 1809, Egerton MSS, 2612.
33. T. Moore (1), I, 183.
34. B to Hodgson, June 25, 1809, *BLJ*, I, 210.
35. Arthur H. Norway, *Highways and Byways in Devon and Cornwall*, London, 1919, 265.
36. B to Charles Skinner Matthews, June 22, 1809, *BLJ*, I, 206–7.
37. Matthews to B, June 30, 1809, Murray MSS, in Crompton, 129.
38. B to Henry Drury, June 25, 1809, *BLJ*, I, 210–11.
39. B to Edward Ellice, June 25, 1809, *BLJ*, I, 209.
40. B to Hodgson, June 25, 1809, *BLJ*, I, 210–11.
41. B to JH, June 30, 1809, *BLJ*, I, 213.
42. B to Hodgson, June 25, 1809, *BLJ*, I, 210–11.
43. "Lines to Mr. Hodgson," *CPW*, I, 268–70.
44. B to Hodgson, July 16, 1809, *BLJ*, I, 215.
45. *CHP*, I, 16; *CPW*, II, 16.

CHAPTER 11:   *"The Foe, the Victim, and the Fond Ally"*

1. *CHP*, I, 16; *CPW*, II, 16.
2. For an excellent short history of the Peninsular Wars see the last chapters of Arthur Bryan, *Years of Victory*, London, 1945.
3. *CHP*, I, 17, *CPW*, II, 17.
4. *CHP*, I, 17, vs. 228–29 var.; *CPW*, II, 17.
5. Broughton I, 9.
6. S. H. Romilly, *Letters to "Ivy" from the First Earl of Dudley*, London, 1905, in Borst, 11.
7. B to Hodgson, July 16, 1809, *BLJ*, I, 215.
8. John Cam Hobhouse, unpublished

diary, British Library, July 8 [7], 1809–July 16, 1824, in Marchand, I, 186.

9. B to Hodgson, July 16, 1809, *BLJ*, I, 215.

10. Broughton, I, 6.

11. Prothero, II, 86.

12. Borst, 9n.

13. R.H. Gronow, *The Reminiscences and Recollections of Captain Gronow, 1810–1860*. 2 vols. London, 1900. II, 1995–96.

14. Hobhouse, II, 220.

15. *CHP*, II, 19, *CPW*, 17–18.

16. B to CGB, August 11, 1809, *BLJ*, I, 218.

17. James T. Hodgson, *Memoir of the Rev. Francis Hodgson*, London, 1878, I, 63. Moore and Prothero omitted this sentence from their version of Byron's letter, quoted in Borst, 15.

18. *CHP*, I, 22, *CPW*, II, 181.

19. *CHP*, I, 24, vs. 292–96 var., *CPW*, II, 19.

20. B to CGB, August 11, 1809, *BLJ*, I, 219.

21. Broughton, I, 10.

22. B to CGB, August 6, 1809, *BLJ*, I, 216.

23. B to Hodgson, August 6, 1809, *BLJ*, I, 216.

24. B to JH, August 7, 1809, *BLJ*, I, 217.

25. B to CGB, August 11, 1809, *BLJ*, I, 221.

26. Prothero, VI, 381–82.

27. B to CGB, August 11, 1809, *BLJ*, I, 218.

28. B to Hodgson, August 6, 1809, *BLJ*, I, 216.

29. Borst's careful reconstruction of the Byron-Hobhouse itinerary in his first chapter reveals the poet's skillful interweaving of settings seen and imagined in his revisions of *Childe Harold*.

30. Egerton MSS, 2611.

31. Prothero, II, 91.

32. *CHP*, I, 51; *CPW*, II, 28–29.

33. See note 29.

34. *CHP*, I, 38–40; *CPW*, II, 24–25.

35. *CHP*, I, 41; *CPW*, II, 25.

36. Broughton, I, 11.

37. B to CGB, January 28, 1810, BLJ, I, 251.

38. B to JM, April 14, 1817, *BLJ*, V, 213.

39. B to CGB, August 11, 1809, *BLJ*, I, 218.

40. The guide related this incident to another traveler, Dr. Horace H. Furness; its publication is described in Borst, 29.

41. Byron's note no. 584 to *CHP*, I, 56, *CPW*, II, 189.

42. *CHP*, I, 57, *CPW*, II, 30.

43. B to CGB, August 11, 1809, *BLJ*, I, 219.

44. Hobhouse journals, Marchand, I, 190.

45. B to CGB, August 11, 1809, *BLJ*, I, 220.

46. Ibid.

47. *CHP*, I, 68, *CPW*, II, 34.

48. *CHP*, I, 69, *CPW*, II, 34.

49. *CHP*, I, 76–77, *CPW*, II, 36–37.

50. Prothero, II, 552.

51. *CHP*, I, 65, *CPW*, II, 33.

52. *CHP*, I, 66, *CPW*, II, 33.

53. Prothero, II, 88–89.

54. B to CGB, August 11, 1809, *BLJ*, I, 220.

55. Hobhouse diaries, Marchand, I, 192.

56. B to CGB, August 11, 1809, *BLJ*, I, 220.

57. Ibid.

58. ["Song, The Girl of Cadiz"], *CPW*, I, 270–71.

59. B to JH, August 7, 1809, *BLJ*, I, 218.

60. Galt, 57.

61. Ibid., 58.

62. B to CGB, August 15, 1809 [part of letter of August 11), *BLJ*, I, 221.

63. This and following quotes are from Galt, 59 ff.

64. Lytton Strachey, *Characters and Commentaries*, London, 1936, 59, in Galt, xvii.

65. Galt, 65.
66. Ibid.

CHAPTER 12: *"Places Without a Name, and Rivers Not Laid Down in Maps"*

1. Hobhouse diary (July 8, 1809–December 26, 1809), British Library, Add. MS. 56527, September 1, 1809.
2. Galt, 66.
3. Hobhouse diary, British Library.
4. B to CGB, September 5, 1809, *BLJ*, I, 223–24.
5. Ibid.
6. Galt, 66.
7. B to Lady Melbourne, September 15, 1812, *BLJ*, II, 198.
8. "Written in an Album," September 14, 1809, *CPW*, I, 2, 273.
9. "To Florence," *CPW*, I, 274.
10. Ibid.
11. B to Captain Cary, September 18, 1809, *BLJ*, I, 224–25.
12. *CHP*, II, 20, *CPW*, II, 50.
13. Hobhouse, I, 18.
14. *CHP*, II, 39, *CPW*, II, 56.
15. *CHP*, II, 40, *CPW*, II, 57.
16. Hobhouse, I, 19.
17. *CHP*, II, 42, *CPW*, II, 57.
18. Hobhouse, I, 26.
19. Hobhouse diary, September 29, 1809.
20. Hobhouse, I, 26.
21. *CHP*, II, 45, *CPW*, II, 58.
22. Hobhouse, I, 41.
23. Ibid, 43.
24. Ibid, 47.
25. Ibid, 41.
26. Quoted in T. Moore (1), I, 162.
27. *CHP*, II, Poem Section, 9, *CPW*, II, 68.
28. *CHP*, II, Poem Section, 6, *CPW*, II, 67.
29. B to CGB, November 12, 1809, *BLJ*, I, 270.
30. Hobhouse, I, 56–57.
31. Hobhouse diary, October 5, 1809, British Library.

32. B to CGB, November 12, 1809, *BLJ*, I, 226.
33. Prothero, II, 206.
34. Hobhouse diary, October 20, 1809, British Library.
35. B to CGB, November 12, 1809, *BLJ*, I, 231.
36. Borst, 84.
37. Hobhouse diary, October 7, 1809.
38. B to CGB, June 28, 1810, *BLJ*, I, 249–50.
39. Hobhouse, I, 61.
40. Borst, 67.
41. Hobhouse, I, 61.
42. B to CGB, November 12, 1809, *BLJ*, I, 231.
43. *CHP*, II, 53, *CPW*, II, 60.
44. *CHP*, II, 47, *CPW*, II, 59.
45. Hobhouse, I, 79–80.
46. "Sweet Florence," *CPW*, I, 276.
47. B to CGB, November 12, 1809, *BLJ*, I, 228–29.
48. Hobhouse, I, 94.
49. B to CGB, November 12, 1809, *BLJ*, I, 226.
50. Hobhouse, I, 80.
51. Prothero, V, 115.
52. Prothero, I, 308.
53. B to Lady Melbourne, August 23, 1813, *BLJ*, IV, 97.
54. *CHP*, II, 55, *CPW*, II, 61.
55. B to CGB, November 12, 1809, *BLJ*, I, 227.
56. *CHP*, II, 58, *CPW*, II, 62.
57. *CHP*, II, 61, *CPW*, II, 63.
58. *CHP*, II, 61, verses 5545–47 var., *CPW*, II, 63.
59. B to CGB, November 12, 1809, *BLJ*, 227–28.
60. In " 'Narcissus Jilted': Byron, Don Juan and the Biographical Imperative" (in *Historical Studies*

and Literary Criticism, ed. Jerome McGann, Madison, Wis., 1985, 143–79), Cecil Y. Lang proposes that Byron, seduced by Ali Pasha, displaced this event in terms of both gender and genre, to figure as the seduction of Don Juan by the "Man Empress" Catherine the Great.

61. B to CGB, November 12, 1809, *BLJ*, I, 227.
62. *CHP*, II, 62, *CPW*, II, 63.
63. *CHP*, II, 48, *CPW*, II, 59.
64. Hobhouse diary, October 20, 1809.
65. Ibid.
66. B to CGB, November 12, 1809, *BLJ*, I, 231.
67. B to CGB, March 19, 1810, *BLJ*, I, 235.

68. George Finlay, a historian of Greece, claimed to have been the recipient of this confidence from both Byron and Hobhouse, and he comunicated the conversation to Colonel Leicester Stanhope, administrator of the London Greek Committee in Missolonghi; in Stanhope, *Greece in 1823 and 1824 . . .* , 2nd ed., London, Sherwood, Gilbert and Piper, 1824, 526; also in Marchand, I, notes, 22, no. 3.
69. Broughton, I, 19.
70. Preface to *CHP*, *CPW*, II, 4.
71. *CHP*, I, 4, *CPW*, II, 9.
72. *CHP*, I, Poem Section, "To Inez," *CPW*, II, 40.

CHAPTER 13: *Civilization and Its Discontents*

1. B to CGB, November 12, 1809, *BLJ*, I, 229.
2. Broughton, I, 20.
3. "Sweet Florence," *CPW*, I, 278.
4. B to CGB, November 12, 1809, *BLJ*, I, 229.
5. B to CGB, November 12, 1809, *BLJ*, I, 230.
6. *CHP*, II, 73, *CPW*, II, 68. His discovery is discussed in McGann (3), 28.
7. B to CGB, November 12, 1809, *BLJ*, I, 230.
8. B to JH, November 12, 1809, *BLJ*, I, 231.
9. B to JH, November 24, 1809.
10. *CHP*, II, 71, *CPW*, II, 66.
11. *CHP*, II, 72, *CPW*, II, 66.
12. Borst, 83.
13. Hobhouse, I, 175.
14. Ibid.
15. Ibid., 180 ff.
16. *CHP*, I, 60, *CPW*, II, 31.
17. *CHP*, I, 61, *CPW*, II, 32.
18. *CHP*, I, 63, *CPW*, II, 32.
19. Hobhouse, I, 192–93.

20. "Translation of the Famous Greek War Song," *CPW*, I, 331.
21. B's journal, March 20, 1814, *BLJ*, III, 253.
22. Ibid.
23. "Detached Thoughts," *BLJ*, IX, stanza 82, p. 41.
24. Hobhouse, I, 208 ff.
25. Ibid., 216.
26. Ibid., 224.
27. Ibid., 229.
28. Broughton, I, 25.
29. Hobhouse, I, 93.
30. Ibid., 243.
31. Like all writers on this still-vexed question, I am indebted to the learned and lucid account by William St. Clair, *Lord Elgin and the Marbles*, Oxford and New York, 1966, 1983, 1998. In the most recent edition, St. Clair includes evidence of the British Museum's damage to the marbles in the late 1930s, through overzealous cleaning, along with new documentation on the unspecific language of the second *firman*.

32. *EBSR, CPW*, I, 261.
33. *EBSR*, note to line 1027, *CPW*, I, 418.
34. Fani-Maria Tsigakou, *The Rediscovery of Greece*, New Rochelle, New York, 1981, 15.
35. Hobhouse, I, 288n.
36. *CHP*, II, papers referred to by note[to stanza 73], *CPW*, II, 200.
37. *CHP*, II, note to line 101, *CPW*, II, 190.
38. Hobhouse, I, 289.
39. *CHP*, II, 1, *CPW*, II, 44.
40. *CHP*, II, 6, *CPW*, II, 46.
41. *CHP*, II, 1, *CPW*, II, 44.
42. *CHP*, II, 12, *CPW*, II, 48.

43. February 28, 1810, Broughton, I, 27.
44. Hobhouse, I, 281.
45. St. Clair, op. cit., 168.
46. *CHP*, II (suppressed verse on Elgin), *CPW*, II, 48.
47. B to Edward Daniel Clarke, January 19, 1812, *BLJ*, II, 156.
48. *The Curse of Minerva, CPW*, I, 325.
49. Ibid.
50. Ibid.
51. *CHP*, II, 2, *CPW*, II, 44.
52. Edward W. Said, *Orientalism*, New York, 1978, 122 passim.

CHAPTER 14:　*"That Seeming Marble-Heart"*

1. *CHP*, II, 73, *CPW*, II, 68.
2. B to Henry Drury, May 3, 1810, *BLJ*, I, 237.
3. Ibid, 240.
4. Hobhouse diary, January 26, [1810].
5. T. Moore (1), I, 24n.
6. Galt, 117.
7. B to JCH, August 23, 1810, *BLJ*, II, 13.
8. "Song," *CPW*, I, 280.
9. Hobhouse, I, 292.
10. Hobhouse diary, January 10, [1810].
11. *CHP*, II, 87, *CPW*, II, 72–73.
12. Hobhouse diary, March 3, 1810.
13. Hobhouse, I, 399.
14. Galt, 111.
15. *CHP*, II, 85–86, *CPW*, II, 72.
16. *DJ*, III, Poem Section "The Isles of Greece," 16, *CPW*, V, 192.
17. *CHP*, II, 90, *CPW*, II, 73.
18. Note to *CHP*, II, 89.
19. *CHP*, II, 5, *CPW*, II, 45.
20. *CHP*, II, 89, *CPW*, II, 73.
21. Prothero, II, 186–87.
22. *DJ*, III, Poem Section "The Isles of Greece," 3, *CPW*, V, 189.
23. Hobhouse, I, 360.

24. Ibid., 397–98.
25. Hobhouse, II, 64.
26. Hobhouse diary, March 9, 1809.
27. B to CGB, March 19, 1810, *BLJ*, I, 235.
28. "The Dream," *CPW*, IV, 26.
29. Galt, 130–31.
30. "Written at Athens," *CPW*, I, 279.
31. *CHP*, II, 32, *CPW*, II, 54.
32. *CHP*, II, 34, *CPW*, II, 55.
33. *CHP*, II, 35, *CPW*, II, 55.
34. B to Lady Melbourne, September 15, 1812, *BLJ*, II, 199.
35. *CHP*, II, 35, *CPW*, II, 55.
36. Broughton, I, 28.
37. "The Bowles/Pope Controversy" (1821), *CMP*, 131.
38. "Ravenna Journal," January 11, 1821, *BLJ*, VIII, 22.
39. Ibid.
40. Prothero, II, 241.
41. B to Hodgson, July 4, 1810, *BLJ*, I, 253.
42. Hobhouse diary, May 3, 1810, note in Byron's hand and signed May 26, 1810.
43. *DJ*, II, 105 *CPW*, V, 121.
44. Medwin, I, 12.

45. B to Henry Drury, May 3, 1810, *BLJ*, I, 237–40.
46. Ibid.
47. B to Hodgson, May 5, 1810, *BLJ*, I, 240.

CHAPTER 15: *"The Vices in Fashion"*

1. Hobhouse, II, 229–30.
2. Hobhouse diary, May 17, 1810.
3. B to CGB, June 28, 1810, *BLJ*, I, 251.
4. B to Hodgson, July 4, 1810, *BLJ*, I, 254.
5. B to CGB, June 28, 1810, *BLJ*, I, 248.
6. Hobhouse, II, 337.
7. B to CGB, June 28, 1810, *BLJ*, I, 251.
8. B to Henry Drury, June 17, 1810, *BLJ*, I, 245.
9. [Translation of the Nurse's Dole in the *Medea* of Euripides], *CPW*, I, 284.
10. *DJ*, V, 46, CPW, V, 255.
11. Galt, 153.
12. B to Robert Adair, July 4, 1810, *BLJ*, I, 256.
13. *The New Monthly Magazine*, XIX (1827), 147 and 310–11, in Borst, 123, and Marchand, I, 242.
14. *The New Monthly Magazine*, 147–48.
15. Borst, 117n.
16. Ibid., 123.
17. Broughton, I, 32.
18. B to CGB, July 20, 1810, *BLJ*, II, 4.
19. T. Moore (1), I, 192.
20. Marchand, I, 256.
21. "Farewell Petition to J[ohn] C[am] H[obhouse] Esq.," *CPW*, I, 283.
22. B to JM, November 15, 1817, *BLJ*, V, 272.
23. B to JM, August 31, 1820, *BLJ*, VII, 169.
24. B to JCH, July 29, 1810, *BLJ*, II, 5.
25. Ibid.
26. B to CGB, July 20, 1810, *BLJ*, II, 3.
27. B to JCH, July 29, 1810, *BLJ*, II, 6.
28. B to JCH, August 23, 1810, *BLJ*, II, 14.
29. T. Moore (1), I, 183.
30. B to JCH, August 23, 1810, *BLJ*, II, 14.
31. Ibid, 13.
32. B to JCH, July 30, 1810, *BLJ*, II, 7.
33. B to JCH, August 16, 1810, *BLJ*, II, 8.
34. B to JCH, August 23, 1810, *BLJ*, II, 12–13.
35. Ibid., 12.
36. Ibid., 14.
37. B to Hodgson, October 3, 1810, *BLJ*, II, 19.
38. B to Lady Melbourne, September 15, 1812, *BLJ*, II, 198.
39. Ibid.
40. Ibid., 21.
41. C. L. Meryon, *Travels of Lady Hester Stanhope*, London, 1846, I, 36.
42. Ibid.
43. B to JCH, June 19, 1811, *BLJ*, II, 49.
44. B's Journal, December 5, 1813; *BLJ*, III, 230.
45. Lord Sligo to B, October 1811, Murray MSS.
46. B to JCH, August 23, 1810, *BLJ*, II, 13.
47. B to Hodgson, November 14, 1810, *BLJ*, II, 27.
48. *CHP*, II, 76, CPW, II, 69.
49. B's notes to *CHP*, Canto II, stanza 73, *CPW*, II, 202.
50. B to Hodgson, January 20, 1811, *BLJ*, II, 37.
51. SBD to B, n.d; enclosed by Byron

in a letter to JH dated 21
June, Egerton MSS, 2611, in
Burnett, 76.

52. SBD to B [c. June 20, 1809],
Burnett, 77.

53. B to JH, June 30, 1809, *BLJ*, I,
213.

54. SBD to B, July 17, 1810, Burnett,
83.

55. B to JCH, November 26, 1810,
BLJ, II, 28.

56. B to JH, January 18, 1811, *BLJ*, II,
35.

57. B to JH, February 1, 1811, *BLJ*, II,
38–39.

58. B to Hodgson, January 20, 1811,
BLJ, II, 37.

59. *Hints from Horace*, *CPW*, I, 310.

60. *The Curse of Minerva*, *CPW*, I,
320.

61. B to JCH, May 15, 1811, *BLJ*, II,
46.

62. B to JCH, May 15, 1811,
Marchand, I, 270.

63. Murray MSS. Parts are incorrectly
transcribed in Peter Quennell and
George Paston, *"To Lord Byron"*:
Feminine Profiles, New York,
1939, 12–15.

64. B to Lady Melbourne, September
15, 1812, *BLJ*, II, 198–199.

65. ["Four or Five Reasons in Favor of
a Change"], May 22, 1811, *BLJ*,
II, 47.

66. B to JCH, frigate *Volage*, at Sea,
June 19, 1811, *BLJ*, II, 50–51.

CHAPTER 16:   *Childe Harold's Homecoming*

1. B to JCH, July 2, 1811, *BLJ*,
II, 56.

2. B to JCH, July 15, 1811, *BLJ*, II,
60.

3. B to JCH, July 2, 1811, *BLJ*, II, 56.

4. B to RCD, June 28, 1811, *BLJ*, II,
53–54.

5. Dallas (2), I, 65.

6. Ibid.

7. Ibid., 74.

8. Ibid., 76–77.

9. B to JCH, July 23, 1811, *BLJ*, II, 61.

10. B to Miller, July 30, 1811, *BLJ*, II,
63.

11. B to Massingberd, July 16, 1811,
BLJ, II, 60.

12. B to Webster, July 31, 1811, *BLJ*,
II, 64.

13. B to AL, September 2, 1811, *BLJ*,
II, 88.

14. *The Scourge, or Monthly
Expositor of Imposture and Folly*,
I (March 1811), 191–211.

15. B to JCH, July 31, 1811, *BLJ*, II,
65.

16. Ibid. If Byron did, in fact, write to
Elgin, the letter has not survived.

17. Ibid.

18. B to JP, August 2, 1811, *BLJ*, II,
67.

19. Galt, 160.

20. Boyes (2), 174.

21. B to JH, August 4, 1811, *BLJ*, II,
68.

22. Frank McLynn, *Crime and
Punishment in 18th-Century
England*, London, 1989.

23. B to SBD, August 7, 181, *BLJ*, II,
68.

24. *The Cambridge Chronicle and
Journal*, August 9, 1811; a cutting
in a contemporary scrapbook,
Cambridge University Library.

25. B to JCH, August 30, 1811, *BLJ*,
II, 83.

26. B to SBD, August 7, 1811, *BLJ*, II,
68–69; B to JCH, August 10,
1811, *BLJ*, II, 70.

27. JCH to B, Graham (2), 77.

28. B to Bolton, "Directions for the
Contents of a Will to Be Drawn Up
Immediately," August 12, *BLJ*, II,
71, followed by a note on August
16.

29. B to Hodgson, August 22, 1811, *BLJ*, II, 77.
30. B to Bolton, *BLJ*, II, 71–72, 72n.
31. B to RCD, August 25, 1811, *BLJ*, II, 79.
32. B to JCH, August 10, 1811, *BLJ*, II, 70.
33. B to RCD, August 21, 1811, *BLJ*, II, 76.
34. B to JCH, August 10, 1811, *BLJ*, II, 69.
35. B to Hodgson, September 3, 1811, *BLJ*, II, 88–89.
36. B to JM, August 23, 1811, *BLJ*, II, 78.
37. B to RCD, September 17, 1811, *BLJ*, II, 101.
38. B to JM, August 23, 1811, *BLJ*, II, 78.
39. Dallas (2), 102.
40. B to RCD, September 7, 1811, *BLJ*, II, 91.
41. JM to B, September 14, 1811, in Smiles, I, 208.
42. B to JM, September 5, 1811, *BLJ*, II, 90–91.
43. B to AL, August 30, 1811, *BLJ*, II,

84; September 2, 1811, *BLJ*, II, 88.
44. B to Hodgson, September 25, 1811, *BLJ*, II, 105–106.
45. All quotations from Mary Loveday's diaries from Sarah Markham, *A Testimony of Her Times: Based on Penelope Hind's Diaries and Correspondence: 1737–1838*, Wiltshire, 1990, 64, 98 ff.
46. *CHP*, II, 8, *CPW*, II, 46–47.
47. *CHP*, II, 9, *CPW*, II, 47.
48. B to RCD, October 14, 1811, *BLJ*, II, 115–16.
49. *CHP*, II, 95, *CPW*, II, 75.
50. *CHP*, II, 96, *CPW*, II, 75.
51. *CHP*, II, 98, *CPW*, II, 76.
52. "Stanzas," *CPW*, I, 349.
53. B to JCH, October 22, 1811, *BLJ*, II, 117.
54. B to Margaret Pigot, October 28, 1811, *BLJ*, II, 119.
55. B to RCD, October 31, 1811, *BLJ*, II, 121.
56. "Stanzas," *CPW*, I, 349.
57. "To Thyrza," *CPW*, I, 350.

CHAPTER 17: *"Ambition Was My Idol"*

1. Rogers, 231.
2. Dallas (2), I, 129.
3. Wilma Patterson, "Was Byron Anorexic," *World Medecine*, May 15, 1982, 35–38 and Dr. J.H. Baron, "Byron's Appetities, James Joyce's Gut and Melba's Meals and Mesalliances," *BMJ*, 1997; 315:1697–1703.
4. B to JCH, November 17, 1811, *BLJ*, II, 132.
5. Terence de Vere White, *Tom Moore: The Irish Poet*, London, 1977, 24.
6. Ibid., 26.
7. *EBSR*, *CPW*, I, 244.
8. T. Moore (1), I, 230.
9. White, op. cit. 109.
10. B to JCH, November 2, 1811, *BLJ*, II, 123.

11. Hunt's *Tatler*, January 14, 1831.
12. "Detached Thoughts," Prothero, V, 424.
13. B to RCD, October 31, 1811, *BLJ*, II, 122.
14. Smiles, I, 207.
15. D. Moore (2), 195.
16. B to Hodgson, December 8, 1811, *BLJ*, II, 141.
17. B to Harness, December 15, 1811, *BLJ*, II, 149.
18. B to Hodgson, December 8, 1811, *BLJ*, II, 140–41.
19. B to Harness, December 15, 1811, *BLJ*, II, 149.
20. B to Hodgson, December 4, 1811, *BLJ*, II, 136.
21. B to JCH, December 17, 1811, *BLJ*, II, 155.

22. "[Lucietta: A Fragment]," *CPW*, I, 349.
23. B to JCH, December 25, 1811, *BLJ*, II, 115.
24. Susan Vaughan to B, Murray MSS. Parts published in Paston and Quennell, 23–39.
25. B to Susan Vaughan, January 28, 1812, *BLJ*, II, 159.
26. B to Hodgson, January 28, 1812, *BLJ*, II, 159.
27. "La Revanche," *CPW*, III, 1.
28. "On the Quotation," *CPW*, III, 1–2.
29. B to Hodgson, February 16, 1812, *BLJ*, II, 163.
30. "[Again Deceived! Again betrayed!]," *CPW*, III, 3.
31. "Stanzas," *CPW*, III, 4–5.
32. B to Moore, January 29, 1812, *BLJ*, II, 160.
33. T. Moore (1), I, 253.
34. B to Hodgson, February 1, 1812, *BLJ*, II, 160.

35. B to Samuel Rogers, February 4, 1812; *BLJ*, II, 160–161.
36. B to Lord Holland, February 25, 1812, *BLJ*, II, 165.
37. Dallas (2), I, 132.
38. Ibid.
39. Ibid.
40. Peter Virgin, *Sydney Smith*, London, 1994, p. 114.
41. B to Hodgson, March 5, 1812, *BLJ*, II, 167.
42. Henry Richard Vassal, third Lord Holland: *Further Memoirs of the Whig Party, 1807–1821*, New York, 1905, 123.
43. This view is most persuasively argued by Malcolm Kelsall in *Byron's Politics*, Totowa, N.J., 1987.
44. "An Ode to the Framers of the Frame Bill," *CPW*, III, 9.
45. T. Moore (1), I, 258.

CHAPTER 18: *Caro's Waltz*

1. Dallas (2), I, 157.
2. "Stanzas ('If sometimes in the haunts of men')," *CPW*, III, 10.
3. "On a Cornelian Heart Which Was Broken," *CPW*, III, 12.
4. T. Moore (1), I, 357n.
5. Lady Caroline Lamb, *Glenarvon*, London, 1816, 3 vols., I, 75.
6. Ibid., 131.
7. Ibid., 141–42.
8. Lady Morgan (Sydney Owenson), *Lady Morgan's Memoirs*, 2 vols., London, 1882, II, 200.
9. Elizabeth Jenkins, *Lady Caroline Lamb*, Boston, 1932, 61.
10. Medwin, II, 65–66.
11. Marcel Proust, *Remembrance of Things Past*, trans. C. K. Scott Moncrieff and Terence Kilmartin, I, 415.
12. Lady Morgan, op. cit., II, 203.

13. CL to Lady Morgan, n.d.; Pforzheimer Collection. Parts quoted in Elizabeth Jenkins, *Lady Caroline Lamb*, Boston, 1932, 26 ff.
14. David Cecil, *The Young Melbourne*, London, 1939, 64.
15. Ibid.
16. CL to Lady Melbourne, Jenkins, op. cit., 61.
17. Ethel Colburn Mayne, *Byron*, New York, 1924, 151.
18. Cecil, op. cit., 150.
19. Ibid., 95.
20. CL to B, Murray MSS, in Marchand, I, 341.
21. B to Moore, March 25, 1812, *BLJ*, II, 169–170.
22. CL to B, March 27, 1812, Prothero, II, 446.
23. CL to B, Jenkins, 97.
24. Rogers, I, 233.

25. B to CL [April 1812,], *BLJ*, II, 170.
26. Thomas Medwin, *Journal of the Conversations of Lord Byron, with Notices of His Life.* 2 vols. London, 1824, 325.
27. Ibid., 326.
28. From a verse unpublished until after the poet's death.
29. Ibid.
30. B to CL, [April] 1812, *BLJ*, II, 171.
31. CL, Commonplace Book, Panshanger Papers, Hertfordshire Record Office.
32. Jenkins, op. cit., 96; Cecil, op. cit., 156.

CHAPTER 19: *The Spider's Stratagem*

1. *Cobbett's Parliamentary Debates*, XXII (1812), 452–63, in *CMP*, 295.
2. "Lines to a Lady Weeping," *CPW*, III, 10.
3. *CMP*, 34.
4. Hobhouse diary, April 22, 1812.
5. B to CL, May 19, 1812, *BLJ*, II, 177.
6. "[To Caroline Lamb]," *CPW*, III, 13.
7. B to CL, May 19, 1812, *BLJ*, II, 177.
8. B to Lady Melbourne, September 13, 1812, *BLJ*, II, 194.
9. Margot Strickland, *The Byron Women*, New York, 1974, 95.
10. Prothero, II, 452.
11. Lady Melbourne to B, n.d., Murray MSS.
12. Lady Morgan, op. cit., II, 248.
13. Ibid.
14. CL to B, Murray MSS.
15. B to Moore, May 20, 1812, *BLJ*, II, 177.
16. AM to Sir Ralph and Lady Milbanke, March 23, 1812, Lovelace Byron Papers. The following quotes from Annabella Milbanke's letters from London to her parents in Seaham are dated March and April, Boxes 29–34, folios 72–97.
17. B to CL, May 1, 1812, *BLJ*, II, 175.
18. Hobhouse diary July 29, 1912.
19. The entire account is from the Hobhouse diary, July 29, 1812, British Library; also in Marchand, I, 358.
20. B to CL [August 1812]; lithographic facsimile, but accepted by Marchand and others, based on Byron's handwriting.
21. The poem and accompanying letter are in Murray MSS; the enclosure was destroyed early in this century. Communication to the author from Virginia Murray, archivist of the publisher.
22. Jenkins, op. cit., 119.
23. B to Lady Melbourne, [August 14, 1812], *BLJ*, II, 188–89.

CHAPTER 20: *By the Waters of Cheltenham*

1. B to JH, August 23, 1812, *BLJ*, II, 189.
2. B to Lord Holland, September 10, 1812, *BLJ*, II, 192.
3. Francis Jeffrey, *Edinburgh Review*, XIX (February 1812), 466–77.
4. George Ellis, *Quarterly Review*, VII (March 1812), 180–200.
5. *Anti-Jacobin* XLII (August 1812), 343–65.
6. *Satirist*, XI (October 1812), 344–58.
7. B to JM, September 14, 1812, *BLJ*, II, 197.
8. B to Lady Melbourne, September 28, 1812, *BLJ*, II, 216–217.

9. *Waltz, CPW*, III, 24–29.
10. B to Lady Melbourne, September 10, 1812, *BLJ*, II, 192–193.
11. B to Lady Melbourne, September 13, 1812, *BLJ*, II, 194–195.
12. Ibid, 195–196.
13. B to Lady Melbourne, September 15, 1812, *BLJ*, II, 198.
14. B to Lady Melbourne, September 18, 1812, *BLJ*, II, 199.
15. B to Lord Holland, September 10, 1812, *BLJ*, II, 191–192.
16. B to Lord Holland, September 22, 1812, *BLJ*, II, 203–204.
17. "Address, Spoken at the Opening of Drury-lane Theatre Saturday, October 10th, 1812," *CPW*, III, 17.
18. AM to Sir Ralph Milbanke, September 1812. Lovelace Byron Papers.
19. AM to Lady Gosford, October 14, 1812, Lovelace Byron Papers, also in Mayne, 50.
20. AM to Lady Melbourne, n.d., Lovelace Byron Papers, also in Mabell, Countess of Airlie, *In Whig Society*, London, 1921, 138–40.
21. B to Lady Melbourne, October 17, 1812, *BLJ*, II, 226–27.
22. Ibid.
23. B to Lady Melbourne, September 25, 1812, *BLJ*, II, 232.
24. B to Lady Melbourne, October 18, 1812, *BLJ*, II, 231.
25. B to Lady Melbourne, October 20, 1812, *BLJ*, II, 232.
26. B to Lady Melbourne, September 25, 1812, *BLJ*, II, 209.
27. B to Lady Melbourne, September 21, 1812, *BLJ*, II, 203.
28. B to Lady Melbourne, September 25, 1812, *BLJ*, II, 209.
29. Lady Melbourne to B, n.d., Murray MSS.
30. B to Lady Melbourne, September 25, 1812, *BLJ*, II, 208.
31. Lady Melbourne to B, n.d., Murray MSS.
32. Medwin, I, 94.
33. Marchand, I, 352; M. W. Patterson, *Sir Francis Burdett and His Times (1770–1844)*, 2 vol. London, 1931, I, 33.
34. Patterson, op. cit., 97.
35. Medwin, I, 35.
36. Lady Oxford to Lord Holland, Holland House Papers, British Library.
37. B to Lord Holland, September 10, 1812, *BLJ*, II, 192.
38. B to Lady Melbourne, October 24, 1812, *BLJ*, II, 235.

CHAPTER 21:   *In Armida's Bower*

1. B's Journal, November 17, 1813, *BLJ*, III, 210.
2. B to Lady Melbourne, April 5, 1813, *BLJ*, III, 36.
3. Torquato Tasso, *Jerusalem Delivered*, trans. John Hook, London, 2 vols, 1797, I, 16.
4. Journal, December 1, 1813, *BLJ*, III, 229.
5. B to Lady Melbourne, December 27, 1812, *BLJ*, II, 263.
6. B to Lady Melbourne, October 30, 1812, *BLJ*, II, 237–38.
7. B to Lady Melbourne, October 20, 1812, *BLJ*, II, 233.
8. B to Lady Melbourne, November 4, 1812, *BLJ*, II, 239.
9. B to CL, November 1812, *BLJ*, II, 242.
10. B to Moore, in Prothero, III, 642.
11. B to Lady Melbourne, December 31, 1812, *BLJ*, II, 265.
12. B to Lady Melbourne, December 14, 1812, *BLJ*, II, 255.
13. Note by Lady Byron, n.d., Lovelace Byron Papers, Box 131,

folio 89. Her text (written in an agitated hand) reads: "He told me that at the time of his connexion [*sic*] with Lady O. she detected him one day in an attempt upon her daughter, then a child of 13 & was enraged with him to the greatest degree." Lady Charlotte Harley was then eleven years old, not thirteen.

14. Dedication "To Ianthe," *CHP*, *CPW*, II, 7.

15. B to Lady Melbourne, January 4, 1813, *BLJ*, III, 9.

16. B to Lady Melbourne, December 23, 1812, *BLJ*, II, 261.

17. B to Lady Melbourne, January 22, 1813, *BLJ*, III, 16.

18. B to Lady Melbourne, July 6, 1813[b], *BLJ*, III, 72.

19. Ibid.

20. B to Lady Melbourne, July 6, 1813[a], *BLJ*, III, 71.

21. Lady Charlotte Bury (Campbell), *The Diary of a Lady-in-Waiting*, 2 vols., London, 1908, II, 288.

22. Ibid.

23. "A Song ('Thou art not false, but thou art fickle')," *CPW*, III, 105.

24. Prothero, II, 252.

25. *The Giaour*, *CPW*, III, 53–54.

26. *The Giaour*, *CPW*, III, 75.

27. D. Moore (2), 200.

28. B to Lady Melbourne, June 21, 1813, *BLJ*, III, 65.

CHAPTER 22:   *"That Perverse Passion"*

1. B to AL, June 27, 1813, *BLJ*, III, 68.

2. *DJ*, VI, 42, *CPW*, V, 311.

3. Ibid., 43, *CPW*, V, 312.

4. B to Moore, July 8, 1813, *BLJ*, III, 73.

5. AMB to Therese Villiers, May 11, 1852, Lovelace Byron Papers, 49.

6. DK to JCH, December 1829, D. Moore (2), 306.

7. Marchand, I, 404.

8. B to DK, November 19, 1817, *BLJ*, V, 273.

9. B to Lady Melbourne, August 5, 1813, *BLJ*, III, 85.

10. Augusta Leigh's Common-place Book, British Library, Add. MSS, 58802, entries undated.

11. B to Moore, August 22, 1813, *BLJ*, III, 96.

12. B to Lady Melbourne, August 21, 1813, *BLJ*, III, 93.

13. B to AL, September 15, 1813, *BLJ*, III, 114–15.

14. B to Lady Melbourne, September 21, 1813, *BLJ*, III, 116.

15. B to Lady Melbourne, September 28, 1813, *BLJ*, III, 124.

16. B to Lady Melbourne, October 19, 1813[a], *BLJ*, III, 148.

17. B to Lady Melbourne, October 19, 1813[b], *BLJ*, III, 149.

18. B to AL, October 10, 1813, *BLJ*, III, 138.

19. B to Lady Melbourne, November 4, 1813, *BLJ*, III, 157.

20. *The Bride of Abydos*, I, 1, *CPW*, III, 107.

21. Journal, November 17, 1813, *BLJ*, III, 209.

22. B to Galt, December 11, 1813, *BLJ*, III, 196.

23. *The Bride of Abydos*, I, 13, verses 394–99, *CPW*, III, 120.

24. *Anti-Jacobin* XLVI (March 1814), 209–37, in *RR*, Part B, "Byron and Regency Society."

25. B's Journal, November 26, 1813, *BLJ*, III, 223.

26. AM to Lady Melbourne, n.d., Airlie, 161–62.

27. B to AM, November 10, 1813, *BLJ*, III, 160.

28. AM to B, November 27, 1813, Mayne, 73–75.

29. B to AMB, November 29, 1813, *BLJ*, III, 178.

30. AM to B, December 26, 1813, Mayne, 80.

31. B's Journal, Tuesday morning, *BLJ*, III, 217.

32. Prothero, V, Appendix: III 549.

33. B's Journal, November 17 and November 22, 1813, *BLJ*, III, 211–12.

34. B's Journal, November 17, 1813, *BLJ*, III, 210.

35. B to W. J. Baldwin, November 14, 1813, *BLJ*, III, 165.

36. B's Journal, Tuesday morning, *BLJ*, III, 217.

37. B's Journal, December 1, 1813, *BLJ*, III, 229.

38. B's Journal, January 16, 1814, *BLJ*, III, 242.

39. Ibid., Tuesday morning, *BLJ*, III, 218.

40. Ibid., 217.

41. Ibid. 163.

42. B to JM [b], November 12, 1813, *BLJ*, III, 163.

43. B to Lord Holland, November 17, 1813, *BLJ*, III, 168.

44. B to JM, November 29, 1813 [c], *BLJ*, III, 182.

45. Journal, November 16, 1813, *BLJ*, III, 207.

46. B to AM, November 29, 1813, *BLJ*, III, 179.

47. B to Lady Melbourne, November 25, 1813, *BLJ*, III, 174–75.

48. Owned by the Earl of Lytton; in Gunn, 188.

49. John Brewer, *The Cult of Pleasure*, New York, 1997, 270 ff.

50. B's Journal, December 14–16, *BLJ*, III, 239.

51. B's Journal, December 17, 18, *BLJ*, III, 240.

52. Ibid.

53. Dedication to *The Corsair*, *CPW*, III, 149. Also B to Moore, January 2, 1814, *BLJ*, IV, 13.

54. B to Moore, January 6, 1814, *BLJ*, III, 16.

55. *The Corsair*, II, 10, *CPW*, III, 182.

56. Ibid.

57. *The Corsair*, II, 24, *CPW*, III, 214.

58. B to Moore, January 8, 1814, *BLJ*, IV, 18.

59. JM to B, April 30, 1814, Murray MSS.

60. B to Lady Melbourne, January 11, 1814, *BLJ*, IV, 23.

CHAPTER 23:   *"The Hand That Kindles Cannot Quench the Flame"*

1. B to JM, January 22, 1814, *BLJ*, IV, 36.

2. B's Journal, November 14, 1813, *BLJ*, III, 204.

3. AL to Miss Porter, February 11, 1834; MSS. Pforzheimer Collection, "Shelley and His Circle," New York Public Library.

4. Ibid.

5. JM to B, February 3, 1814, Smiles, I, 233.

6. B to JM, February 4, 1814, *BLJ*, IV, 46.

7. *The Courier*, February 1, 1814.

8. *The Anti-Jacobin*, XLVI (March 1814), 2009–2037, Reiman, V, 49.

9. B to JM, February 5, 1814, *BLJ*, IV, 46.

10. AMB, August 10, 1814, *BLJ*, IV, 155.

11. B to JM, February 7, 1814, *BLJ*, IV, 49.

12. B to Moore, February 10, 1814, *BLJ*, IV, 51.

13. B's Journal, Sunday, 28th; Monday, 29th; Tuesday, 30th; *BLJ*, III, 227.

14. B to AM, February 12, 1814, *BLJ*, IV, 55.

15. Ibid., 56.
16. For the best account of the affair see Doris Langley Moore, "The Hanson-Portsmouth Scandal," *The Journal of the Byron Society*, I, 9–24.
17. B to Lady Hardy, M[arc]h 28, 1823, *BLJ*, XI, 128.
18. B to AM, March 15, 1814, *BLJ*, IV, 82–83.
19. B's Journal, March 15, 1814, *BLJ*, III, 251.
20. Lady Melbourne to B, April 1, 1814, Murray MSS.
21. B's Journal, March 28, 1814, *BLJ*, III, 255.
22. B's Journal, March 22, 1814, *BLJ*, III, 154.
23. B's Journal, March 28, 1814, *BLJ*, III, 256.
24. B's Journal, April 9, 1814, *BLJ*, III, 256.
25. Ibid.
26. B's Journal, April 10, 1814, *BLJ*, III, 257.
27. *Ode to Napoleon Buonaparte*, 5, *CPW*, III, 260.
28. *Ode to Napoleon Buonaparte*, 2, *CPW*, III, 260.
29. B to JM, April 11, 1814, *BLJ*, IV, 94.
30. B to Lady Melbourne, April 25, 1814, *BLJ*, IV, 104.
31. H. W. Janson, *Apes and Ape Lore*, London, 1952; Nedeln, Lichenstein, 1976, 30–31.
32. B to Lady Melbourne, April 18, 1814, *BLJ*, IV, 99.

33. B to Moore, April 20, 1814, *BLJ*, IV, 100.
34. B to JM, April 29, 1814, *BLJ*, IV, 107.
35. B to Moore, April 9, 1814, *BLJ*, IV, 92–93.
36. Lady Melbourne to B, April 30, 1814, Murray MSS.
37. B to Lady Melbourne, April 30, 1814, *BLJ*, IV, 110.
38. Lady Melbourne to B, June 10, 1814, *BLJ*, IV, 110.
39. CL to B, Murray MSS. Also in Marchand, I, 457, dated by context, early June 1814.
40. B to Lady Melbourne, April 30, 1814.
41. B to Lady Melbourne, April–May 1814, *BLJ*, IV, 111.
42. B to Moore, May 4, 1814 [b], *BLJ*, IV, 114.
43. "Stanzas for Music" ("I speak not—I trace not—I breathe not thy name"), *CPW*, III, 269.
44. *Lara*, II, 16, *CPW*, III, 249.
45. *Lara*, I, 8, *CPW*, III, 218.
46. "Opening Lines to *Lara*," *CPW*, III, 256–57.
47. B to Lady Melbourne, June 10, 1814, *BLJ*, IV, 123.
48. B to Lady Melbourne, June 26, 1814, *BLJ*, IV, 133.
49. Lady Melbourne to B, n.d., Murray MSS.
50. B to Lady Melbourne, April 30, 1814, *BLJ*, IV, 111.

CHAPTER 24: *"A Wife Is My Salvation"*

1. B to Moore, June 8, 1821, *BLJ*, IX, 170.
2. B to Moore, July 1814, *BLJ*, IV, 139.
3. B to Hodgson, July 8, 1814, *BLJ*, IV, 137–38.
4. B to Hodgson, July 11, 1814, *BLJ*, IV, 140.

5. B to JCH, July 23, 1814, *BLJ*, IV, 144.
6. B to AM, August 1, 1814, *BLJ*, IV, 148–49.
7. AM to B, July 19, 1814, Lovelace Byron Papers, Box 38, folios 61–78, reprinted in Elwin, 200.

Where MSS letters in this collection are reprinted in Lovelace's *Astarte* or Mayne, page references to those works will be given.

8. B to Moore, August 12, 1814, *BLJ*, 4, 156, from Moore, I, 574. Probably Moore's error in transcription for "spilt."

9. AMB to B, August 6, 1814, Elwin, 201.

10. B to AMB, August 10, 1814, *BLJ*, IV, 155.

11. AMB to B, August 13, 1814, Dep. Lovelace Byron, Box 38, in Elwin, 202.

12. B to AM, August 16, 1814, *BLJ*, IV, 158–59.

13. B to Lady Melbourne, October 4, 1814, *BLJ*, IV, 191.

14. B to AM, September 9, 1814, *BLJ*, IV, 169–70.

15. T. Moore (1), I, 581. JCH wrote "No" in margin of his copy.

16. AL to AM, "Narrative Q," Lovelace Byron Papers, Box 130. There are several versions of Lady Byron's recollections of her courtship and marriage, designated as "Narrative Q," "F," "N," "S" by her grandson, the Earl of Lovelace. The earliest, "Q," written fourteen months after the marriage, is closest to the events described.

17. B to Moore, September 15, 1814 [a], *BLJ*, IV, 172.

18. T. Moore (1), I, 582n.

19. AM to B, Marchand, I, 474.

20. B to AM, September 18, 1814, *BLJ*, IV, 173–74.

21. B to Lady Melbourne, September 18, 1814, *BLJ*, IV, 175.

22. Sir Ralph Milbanke [Noel] to B, September 14, 1814; Elwin, 208.

23. B to AM, September 19, 1814, *BLJ*, IV, 176.

24. B to AM, September 20, 1814, *BLJ*, IV, 177.

25. B to Lady Melbourne, Octo-

ber 1, 1814, *BLJ*, IV, 187.

26. B to AM, September 26, 1814 [b], *BLJ*, IV, 183–84.

27. Ibid.

28. B to JH, October 1, 1814, *BLJ*, IV, 189.

29. B to JH, September 28, 1814, *BLJ*, IV, 186.

30. B to James Perry, October 5, 1814, *BLJ*, IV, 192–93.

31. B to AMB, October 5, 1814, *BLJ*, III, 193.

32. B to Lady Melbourne, October 4, 1814, *BLJ*, IV, 191.

33. AL to AM, October 1, 1814, Lovelace Byron Papers, Box 79.

34. AM to B, October 3, 1814, Elwin, 221.

35. B to Lady Melbourne, October 7, 1814 [a], *BLJ*, IV, 198.

36. B to Lady Melbourne, October 12, 1814, *BLJ*, IV, 206.

37. B to Lady Melbourne, October 17, 1814, *BLJ*, IV, 212.

38. Al to AM, October 15, 1814, Elwin, 222.

39. AM to B, October 17, 1814, Elwin, 223. Also Mayne, 465.

40. Al to AM, October 15, 1814, Elwin, 223.

41. AM to B, October 22 and 23, 1814, Elwin, 224–25.

42. B to JH, October 25, 1814, *BLJ*, IV, 225.

43. AL to AM, October 26, 1814, Elwin, 225.

44. B to AM, October 27, 1814, *BLJ*, IV, 226.

45. Ibid.

46. B to Lady Melbourne, November 2, 1814, *BLJ*, IV, 228.

47. B to Lady Melbourne, November 4, 1814, *BLJ*, IV, 228.

48. "Narrative Q"; see n. 16.

49. B to Lady Melbourne, November 14, 1814, *BLJ*, IV, 228–29.

50. B to Lady Melbourne, November 6, 1814, *BLJ*, IV, 229–30.

51. B to Lady Melbourne, November 13, 1814, *BLJ*, IV, 131.
52. "Narrative Q"; see n. 16.
53. B to Lady Melbourne, November 13, 1814.
54. B to AM, November 24, 1814, *BLJ*, IV, 234.
55. B to AM, November 29, 1814, *BLJ*, IV, 236.
56. AM to B, December 20, 1814, Elwin, 225.
57. B to AM, December 22, 1814, *BLJ*, IV, 246.
58. B to AM, December 23, 1814, *BLJ*, IV, 246.
59. This quote and all of the following are from the Hobhouse diary, December 24, 1814–January 2, 1815, Berg Collection.
60. AL to B, quoted by AM in "Narrative Q."

CHAPTER 25: *"It Is but the Effervescence of Despair"*

1. AMB, "Statement T," March 16, 1815, Elwin, 250.
2. AMB, "Statement A," Box 131, fol. 22, Elwin, 251.
3. Medwin, I, 47, refuted by Hobhouse review of Medwin in *Westminster Review*, January 1825.
4. Harriet Martineau, *Biographical Sketches*, 1852–68, 2nd ed., New York, Leypoldt and Holt, 1869, 319.
5. Statement by Jane Minns, 1869, *Newcastle Daily Chronicle*, newscutting quoted in Elwin, 251.
6. Martineau, op. cit.
7. "Narrative Q" and "Statement A," Elwin, 251.
8. Moore, who had read the destroyed memoirs, reported this to Hobhouse. Hobhouse diary, May 15, 1824.
9. "Statement T," March 1816, Box 131, fol. 25, Elwin, 251.
10. Rogers, 236.
11. "Narrative Q," Lovelace Byron Papers, Box 130.
12. AMB to AL, January 4, 1815; lines referring to B's longing for his sister not quoted by Elwin.
13. AL to AM, Box 79, January 4, 1815; Elwin, 254.
14. Hobhouse diary, March 1816.
15. "Narrative Q," Lovelace Byron Papers, Box 130.
16. B to Lady Melbourne, January 7, 1815, *BLJ*, IV, 251–52.
17. B to Moore, January 19, 1814, *BLJ*, IV, 255.
18. B to Lady Melbourne, January 7, 1815; *BLJ*, IV, 251–52.
19. B to Moore, January 19, 1815, *BLJ*, 4, 255.
20. Kinnaird to B, September 15, 1814, Murray MSS, in Thomas L. Ashton, *Byron's Hebrew Melodies*, Austin, Tex., 1972, 14–15.
21. B to AMB, October 20, 1814, *BLJ*, IV, 220.
22. Nathan's recollection of a conversation with B, in Ashton, op. cit., 149n.
23. "If That High World," *CPW*, III, 290.
24. "Herod's Lament for Mariamne," *CPW*, III, 307.
25. "Narrative Q," late 1816, Elwin, 264.
26. Lady Melbourne to AMB, January 8, 1815; Elwin, 259.
27. B to Lady Melbourne, January 22, 1815; *BLJ*, 4, 258.
28. "Unidentified Reminiscences of 1818 and 1842," quoted in Lovelace, "Digest of Lady Byron's Statements and Narratives," in Elwin, 286.
29. AL to AMB, January 26, 1815; Elwin, 275.

30. AMB to AL, February 24, 1815, Elwin, 287.
31. AL to AMB, in "Narrative Q," see Ch. 25, n. 15.
32. AL to AMB, January 21, 1815, Elwin, 275.
33. B to Lady Melbourne, February 6, 1815, *BLJ*, IV, 267–68.
34. AL to AMB, February 10, 1815, Elwin, 281.
35. In AMB's hand, "Bouts-Rimés Nonsense at Seaham," 1815, Elwin, 276.
36. B to Moore, February 2, 1815, *BLJ*, IV, 263.
37. "Narrative Q," "Black days" was Augusta's term for the severe Byron melancholy afflicting both of them periodically, thus confirming that depression was a genetic legacy in the family.
38. "Statement G," Box 131, fols. 68–74, and "Statement H," Box 131, fols. 77–85, Elwin, 292.

39. "Statement G," Elwin, 292.
40. "Statement H," Elwin, 295–96.
41. Ibid., 295.
42. "Statement G," Elwin, 296, n1.
43. "Narrative S," Box 130, fol. 6, Elwin, 296.
44. "Statement H," Elwin, 295.
45. "Narrative S," Elwin, 297.
46. Lady Melbourne to AMB, March 7, 1815, Elwin, 289.
47. "Narrative S," Elwin, 299.
48. Ibid.
49. AMB to JNM, April 2, 1815.
50. B to Moore, March 27, 1815, *BLJ*, IV, 285.
51. B to Coleridge, March 31, 1815, *BLJ*, IV, 286.
52. "Statement G," Elwin, 302.
53. B to AMB, April 13–14, 1815, *BLJ*, IV, 287–88.
54. "Statement K," Box 131, fol. 15, 1816, Elwin, 303.
55. "Statement G," Elwin, 302.

CHAPTER 26:   *"Woe Without Name, or Hope, or End"*

1. George Ticknor, *Life, Letters and Journals of George Ticknor*, 2nd ed., 2 vols., London, Samson Low, Marston, Searle, and Rivington, 1876, I, 50–56.
2. Medwin, I, 274; Hobhouse, *Westminister Review*, see note 3, Chap. 25.
3. AMB to JNM, September 6, 1814.
4. "Statement U," partly dictated to Mrs. Clermont, March 1816, Elwin, 51.
5. B to Webster, September 4, 1815, *BLJ*, IV, 310.
6. B to AMB, August 31, 1815, *BLJ*, IV, 308.
7. Ann Rood Fletcher, "Fletcher Deposition," Lovelace Byron Papers, Box 129, fol. 49.
8. AMB to JNM, September 4, 1815.
9. "Statement G," Elwin, 317.

10. B to AMB, September 1, 1815, *BLJ*, IV, 309.
11. "Narrative Q."
12. "Statement G," Elwin, 318.
13. AMB to JNM, October 31, 1815, Elwin, 320.
14. AMB to JNM, October 11, 1815, Elwin, 320.
15. "Narrative Q."
16. *Parisina*, 5, *CPW*, III, 360.
17. "Reflections on Lord B's Character," November 1, 1815, Elwin, 324.
18. AMB to AL, n.d. [November 8?], first part of letter missing, Elwin, 322.
19. AMB to AL, November 9, 1815, Elwin, 322–32.
20. Hobhouse, "The Byron Separation," Broughton, II, 201–2.

21. B to JM, November 14, 1815, *BLJ*, V, 333.

22. B to JM, January 2, 1816, *BLJ*, IV, 13.

23. Smiles, I, 353–54.

24. B to JM, January 2, 1816, *BLJ*, 5, 13.

25. Susan Boyce to B, Murray MSS, in Paston and Quennell, 179.

26. Mrs. Clermont's statement of January 22, 1816, Elwin, 334.

27. Ibid.

28. "Statement Given to My Mother," Kirkby Mallory, January 18, 1816, Lovelace Byron Papers, Box 129, fol. 7.

29. Ibid.

30. Lady Anna Barnard's narrative, reprinted in Harriet Beecher Stowe, *Lady Byron Vindicated*, 1870, 306.

31. Fletcher deposition, Box 129, fols. 47–55, see n. 7.

32. AL to AMB, January 1816.

33. "Statement given to my mother." Note added, "Statement Z," Elwin, 344.

34. B to AMB, January 6, 1816, *BLJ*, V, 15.

35. Clermont statement, see n. 26.

36. "Statement to Dr. Baillie on Byron's Insanity," January 8, 1816, Lovelace Byron Papers, Box 129, folios 1–6.

37. JCH Account of Lady Byron's interview with JH, Broughton, II, 252–54.

38. Fletcher deposition, Box 129, folios 1–6.

39. "Statement U" (Desultory), March 1816, in part dictated to Mrs. Clermont, Box 131, fols. 87–88, Elwin, 348.

CHAPTER 27:   *"Fare Thee Well!"*

1. AL to AMB, January 15, 1816. The first of a series of twenty-eight letters in the form of daily bulletins from Augusta to Annabella, reporting on Byron's condition and behavior, relaying the advice of others along with her own, Box 79–82.

2. AMB to Mrs. Clermont, January 15, 1816, Elwin, 350.

3. AMB to B, January 15, 1816, Elwin, 351.

4. AMB to Selina Doyle, January 15, 1816, Elwin, 351.

5. AL to AMB, January 15, 1816, Elwin, 352.

6. AL to AMB, January 20, 1816, Elwin, 357.

7. Mrs. Clermont to AMB, January 16, 1816, Elwin, 354.

8. AMB to JNM, January 24, 1816, Elwin, 374.

9. Sir Ralph Noel (Milbanke) to B, January 28, 1816, Elwin, 382.

10. AL to AMB, January 29, 1816, Elwin, 384.

11. AL to AMB, January 30, 1816, Elwin, 384.

12. B to Sir Ralph Noel (Milbanke), February 2, 1816, *BLJ*, V, 20–21.

13. AMB to AL, February 3, 1816, Elwin, 392.

14. B to AMB, February 3, 1816, *BLJ*, V, 21.

15. B to AMB, February 5, 1816, *BLJ*, V, 22.

16. Fletcher deposition, Box 129.

17. AMB to B, February 6, 1816 (misdated by Elwin), Elwin, 397.

18. B to Sir Ralph Noel (Milbanke), February 7, 1816, *BLJ*, V, 23.

19. B to AMB, February 8, 1816, *BLJ*, V, 24–25.

20. AL to AMB, February 8, 1816, Elwin, 398.

21. "Remarks" enclosed by AMB to Mrs. Clermont for transmission to

Lushington, February 13, 1816, Elwin, 400.

22. B to JCH, February 8, 1816, *BLJ*, V, 24.

23. Report of Mrs. Clermont to JNM, February 11, 1816, Elwin, 403.

24. Lawrence Stone, *The Road to Divorce: England 1530–1987*, Oxford, 1990, 158.

25. Hobhouse diary, February 12, 1816, Berg Collection.

26. B to AMB, February 15, 1816, *BLJ*, V, 26–27.

27. Statement dated January 19, 1816, Elwin, 361.

28. D. Moore (2), 215.

29. AL to Hodgson, February 15, 1816, Elwin, 411.

30. AL to AMB, letters of February 12, 13, 15, 17, 1816, Elwin, 412–15.

31. "My principles of conduct in regard to Mrs. Leigh," in John C. Fox, *The Byron Mystery*, London, G. Richards, 1924, 113, and Elwin, 440.

32. B to AMB, March 4, 1816, *BLJ*, V, 41.

33. B to Lord Holland, February 23, 1816, *BLJ*, V, 31.

34. B to AMB, February 26, 1816, *BLJ*, V, 33.

35. AMB to JNM, March 4, 1816, in Elwin, 424.

36. AL to Hodgson, March 5, 1816, Elwin, 428.

37. A brilliant legal analysis of the Byron separation in the context of Sir Stephen Lushington's career is in S. M. Waddams, *Law, Politics and the Church of England*, Cambridge, 1992. Waddams also confirms Hanson's dubious reputation in legal circles.

38. Ibid., 116.

39. Michel Foucault, *History of Sexuality*, I, New York, 1978, 37.

40. Waddams, op. cit., 120.

41. AL to Hodgson, March 14, 1816, Elwin, 439.

42. David V. Erdman, "Fare Thee Well," in *SC*, IV, 638–53.

43. "Fare Thee Well!," *CPW*, III, 380–81.

44. "A Sketch from Private Life," *CPW*, III, 382–83.

45. Erdman, op. cit.

46. AMB to JNM, undated, Elwin 463.

47. Memo from AMB to Lushington, April 1[?], Box 129, folios 76–79.

48. CC to B, [? March or April] 1816, in Stocking (2), I, 29.

49. "To [Augusta]" ("When all around grew drear and dark"), *CPW*, III, 388.

50. B to AMB, April [14], *BLJ*, V, 66.

51. Hobhouse diary, April 21, 1816.

52. Ibid., April 23 and 25, 1816.

53. Ibid.

CHAPTER 28: *The Year Without a Summer*

1. *CHP*, III, 3, *CPW*, II, 77.

2. *CHP*, III, 3, *CPW*, 2, 77.

3. *CHP*, III, 8, vs. 68, *CPW*, II, 79.

4. *CHP*, I, 1, vs. 1, *CPW*, II. 8.

5. *CHP*, III, 1, vs. 2, *CPW*, II, 76.

6. Polidori, 33. Polidori's sister married the poet Dante Gabriel Rossetti, whose son edited his uncle's diaries.

7. B to AL, May 1, 1816, *BLJ*, V, 74.

8. *CHP*, III, 17, *CPW*, II, 82.

9. Polidori, 62.

10. Medwin, II, 64.

11. B to JCH, May 16, 1816, *BLJ*, V, 77.

12. *CHP*, 3, 42, *CPW*, II, 92.

13. *CHP*, III, 43, *CPW*, II, 92.

14. *CHP*, III, Poem Section 3, *CPW*, II, 97.

15. Leon Edel, *Henry James*, New

York and Philadelphia, J.B. Lippin-
cott, 1962, 3 vols., II, 305–6.

16. *CHP*, III, 59, *CPW*, II, 99.
17. B to JCH, May 26, 1816, *BLJ*, 5,
76.
18. "To [Augusta], *CPW*, III, 388.
19. CC to B, April 22, 1816, Stocking
(2), I, 42.
20. CC to B, May 6, 1816, Stocking
(2), I, 43.
21. Ibid.
22. CC to B, May 6, 1816, Stocking
(2), I, 43.
23. CC to B, May 25, 1816, Stocking
(2), I, 46.
24. CC to B, [May 27], 1816, Stocking
(2), I, 47.
25. Polidori, 101.
26. Ibid., 123.
27. P. B. Shelley, "Epipsychidion," in
Thomas Hutchinson, ed., *Shelley:
Poetical Works*, Oxford, 1968,
419–20. Richard Holmes has explored the significance of Claire as
comet in the cosmology of this
poem in *Shelley: The Pursuit*,
London, 1974.
28. B to AL, September 8, 1816, *BLJ*,
V, 92.
29. See Henry Stommel and Elizabeth
Stommel, "The Year Without a
Summer," *Scientific American*, June
1979, vol. 240, no. 6, 176–86.
30. B to AMB, November 29, 1813,
BLJ, III, 129.
31. "Darkness," *CPW*, IV, 40–42.
32. Polidori, 128.
33. N. White, I, 485.
34. *Frankenstein or, the Modern
Prometheus*. [With an Introduction
by "M. S. W"] London, 1831, x–xi.
35. Bennett, I, 34.
36. *CHP*, III, 86, *CPW*, II, 108.
37. PBS to Thomas Love Peacock;
July 17, 1816, in Jones, I, 489.

38. *CHP*, III, 77, *CPW*, II, 105.
39. Jones, I, 486.
40. T. Moore (1), I, 499.
41. Jones, I, 483.
42. Medwin, I, 294.
43. *CHP*, III, 71, *CPW*, II, 103.
44. *CHP*, III, 85, *CPW*, II, 108.
45. *CHP*, III, 75, *CPW*, II, 104.
46. *CHP*, III, 73, *CPW*, II, 104.
47. *CHP*, III, 90, *CPW*, II, 109.
48. *The Prisoner of Chillon*, 14; *CPW*,
IV, 16.
49. CC to B, July 16, 1816, Stocking
(2), I, 52.
50. "Prometheus," *CPW*, IV, 32.
51. "Stanzas to [Augusta]," *CPW*, IV,
34.
52. "[Epistle to Augusta]," *CPW*, IV,
37.
53. B to DK, January 20, 1817, *BLJ*,
V, 162.
54. "Detached Thoughts," October 15,
1821, no. 17, *BLJ*, IX, 18.
55. Professor David Robertson, scholar
and Alpinist, kindly provided me
with his reconstruction of Byron's
expeditions.
56. B to AL. This and the following six
quotations are from Byron's
"Alpine Journal," September
18–29, *BLJ*, 5, 96–105.
57. *Manfred*, II, ii, *CPW*, IV, 74.
58. B to JM, August 23, 1821, *BLJ*,
VIII, 187.
59. *Manfred*, II, ii, 105–107, *CPW*, IV,
74.
60. *Manfred*, II, i, 26–27, *CPW*, IV,
68, 70.
61. *Manfred*, II, ii, *CPW*, IV, 74.
62. B to AL, September 17, 1816, *BLJ*,
V, 95.
63. *Manfred*, I, i, *CPW*, IV, 61.
64. *Manfred*, II, ii, *CPW*, IV, 77.

CHAPTER 29: Lord Byron, *Inglese*

1. Sheridan's granddaughter, Caroline Norton, was divorced by her husband who named William Lamb, then Lord Melbourne, correspondent in Jane Grey Perkins, *The Life of the Hon. Mrs. Norton*, New York, H. Holt 1909, 110.
2. "Lines On Hearing That Lady Byron Was Ill," *CPW*, IV, 44.
3. AMB to AL, June 3, 1816, Gunn, 187.
4. AL to AMB, Gunn, 188.
5. AMB to Mrs. Villiers, June 1816, Lovelace, 60.
6. AMB to Mrs. Villiers, September 1816, Lovelace, 257.
7. B to AL, August 27, 1816, *BLJ*, V, 88.
8. "[Epistle to Augusta]," *CPW*, IV, 35.
9. B to Mme. de Staël, August 24, 1816, *BLJ*, V, 87–88.
10. "Lines On Hearing That Lady Byron Was Ill," *CPW*, IV, 43.
11. Ironically, the intermediary was Lady Romilly, wife of the barrister whom Byron blamed for his griefs. T. Moore (1), II, 34.
12. "Lines On Hearing That Lady Byron Was Ill," *CPW*, IV, 44.
13. Ibid.
14. For an analysis of Byron's debt to *Glenarvon* when he came to write *Don Juan*, see Graham (1).
15. B to AL, October 13, 1816, *BLJ*, V, 114.
16. B to AL, October 15, 1816, *BLJ*, V, 114–15.
17. B to JM, November 1, 1816, *BLJ*, V, 121.
18. B to AL, November 2, 1816, *BLJ*, V, 122.
19. B to AL, October 26, 1816, *BLJ*, V, 118.
20. B to AL, October 28, 1816, *BLJ*, V, 119.

21. Ibid.
22. B to AMB, November 1, 1816, *BLJ*, V, 120.
23. B to Moore, November 6, 1816, from the postscript dated November 7, 1816, *BLJ*, V, 126.
24. Ibid.
25. B to Moore, November 6, 1816, *BLJ*, V, 124.
26. B to Moore, November 17, 1816; *BLJ*, V, 129.
27. Tony Tanner, *Venice Desired*, Cambridge, Mass., 1992, 21.
28. *CHP*, IV, 18, *CPW*, II, 130.
29. B. L. Flagg, *Venice: City of the Sea*, 2 vols., New York, 1853, I, 313.
30. *Beppo*, 19–20; *CPW*, IV, 135.
31. B to JM, November 25, 1816, *BLJ*, V, 133.
32. B to Moore, November 17, 1816, *BLJ*, V, 129–30.
33. B to DK, November 27, 1816, *BLJ*, V, 135.
34. B to JM, November 25, 1816, *BLJ*, V, 133–34.
35. B to Moore, January 28, 1817, *BLJ*, 165–66, for account of entire scene.
36. B to JM, November 25, 1816, *BLJ*, V, 134.
37. B to JM, November 25, 1816, *BLJ*, V, 133.
38. "[On the Bust of Helen by Canova]," *CPW*, IV, 46.
39. B to JM, December 4, 1816, *BLJ*, V, 137.
40. B to JM, August 28, 1816, *BLJ*, V, 90.
41. PBS to B, November 20, 1816, Jones, I, 513.
42. CC to B, October 27–November 19, 1916, Stocking (2), I, 89–92.
43. PBS to B, April 23, 1817, Jones, I, 539.

CHAPTER 30: *Roman Spring*

1. B to AL, December 18, 1816, *BLJ*, V, 141.
2. Review of S. T. Coleridge, "Christabel," *Edinburgh Review*, September 1816, in *RR*, II, 460.
3. B to JM, December 7, 1816, *BLJ*, V, 151.
4. B to DK, January 12, 1817, *BLJ*, V, 159.
5. B to AL, January 13, 1817, *BLJ*, V, 159.
6. Ibid., 159–60.
7. B to Moore, January 28, 1817, *BLJ*, V, 165.
8. Marchand, II, 744–45.
9. B to DK, February 3, 1817, *BLJ*, V, 168.
10. B to JM, January 8, 1818, *BLJ*, VI, 5.
11. Ibid.
12. B to Moore, March 25, 1817, *BLJ*, IV, 189.
13. B to JCH, December 19, 1816, *BLJ*, V, 143.
14. B to Moore, March 25, 1817, *BLJ*, V, 187.
15. B to JCH, April 14, 1817, *BLJ*, V, 214.
16. B to DK, February 24, 1817, *BLJ*, V, 172.
17. B to AL, February [19?], 1817, *BLJ*, V, 171.
18. B to JM, February 25, 1817, *BLJ*, V, 173.
19. B to Moore, February 28, 1817, T. Moore (1), II, 78–80; *CPW*, IV, 109–110.
20. B to Moore, February 28, 1817, *BLJ*, V, 177.
21. B to JCH, March 31, 1817, *BLJ*, V, 197.
22. B to Moore, March 25, 1817, *BLJ*, V, 187.
23. B to AMB, March 5, 1817, *BLJ*, V, 180.
24. Ibid.
25. B to AL, March 25, 1817, *BLJ*, V, 190.
26. B to JH, March 25, 1817, *BLJ*, V, 189.
27. B to JCH, March 31, 1817, *BLJ*, V, 198.
28. B to Moore, April 11, 1817, *BLJ*, V, 210.
29. B to JCH, April 14, 1817, *BLJ*, V, 215.
30. B to Moore, April 11, 1817; *BLJ*, V, 210.
31. Ibid.
32. B to JM, April 14, 1817, *BLJ*, V, 230.
33. *Beppo*, 12–13, *CPW*, IV, 133.
34. Ibid., 14, *CPW*, IV, 133.
35. B to JM, April 26, 1817, *BLJ*, V, 219.
36. B to Moore, March 25, 1817, *BLJ*, V, 186.
37. B to JM, March 25, 1817, *BLJ*, V, 192.
38. B to JM, April 26, 1817, *BLJ*, V, 218.
39. B to JCH, April 22, 1817, *BLJ*, V, 217.
40. *The Lament of Tasso*, 5, *CPW*, IV, 120.
41. *The Lament of Tasso*, 2, *CPW*, IV, 118.
42. *DJ*, XI, 55, *CPW*, V, 482.
43. *SC*, VII, 222.
44. Lovelace, 16–17.
45. B to DK, May 30, 1817, *BLJ*, V, 231.
46. B to JM, May 9, 1817, *BLJ*, V, 221–22.
47. B to JM, May 5, 1817, *BLJ*, V, 219.
48. Ibid.
49. B's entire description of the Roman execution is in his letter to JM, May 30, 1817, *BLJ*, V, 229–30. See also V. A. C. Gatrell, *The Hanging Tree: Execution and the English People, 1760–1868*,

Oxford, Oxford University Press, 1994, 52–53, 249–50.
50. Broughton, II, 90.
51. "Detached Thoughts," *BLJ*, IX, 21.
52. Robert Beevors, "Pretensions to Permanency: Thorvaldsen's Bust and Statue of Byron," *The Byron Journal*, no. 23 (1995), 64–75.
53. B to JCH, June 20, 1817, *BLJ*, V, 243.
54. B to AL, May 27, 1817, *BLJ*, V, 228.
55. *CHP*, IV, 10, *CPW*, II, 127.
56. "Dedication" to *CHP*, IV, *CPW*, II, 121.
57. *CHP*, IV, 5, *CPW*, II, 126.
58. *CHP*, IV, 7, *CPW*, II, 126.
59. *CHP*, IV, 9, *CPW*, II, 127.
60. *CHP*, IV, 8, *CPW*, II, 127.
61. Charles Dupaty, *Travels Through Italy in a Series of Letters Written in the Year 1785 by the Abbé Dupaty*, London, G.G.J. Robinson and J. Robinson, 1788., 55 ff.
62. *CHP*, IV, 49, *CPW*, II, 140.
63. *CHP*, IV, 50, *CPW*, III, 140–41.
64. Dupaty, op. cit.
65. *CHP*, IV, 78, *CPW*, II, 150.
66. *CHP*, IV, 79, *CPW*, II, 150.
67. *CHP*, IV, 80, *CPW*, II, 151.
68. *CHP*, IV, 79, *CPW*, II, 150.
69. *CHP*, IV, 81, *CPW*, II, 151.
70. For the romantic "deconstruction" of rediscovered Rome see Carolyn Springer, *The Marble Wilderness: Ruins and Representation in Italian Romanticism* (1775–1850), Cambridge, U.K., Cambridge University Press, 1987.
71. *CHP*, IV, 90, *CPW*, II, 154.
72. *CHP*, IV, 135, *CPW*, II, 169.
73. *CHP*, IV, 137, *CPW*, II, 170.
74. *CHP*, IV, 104, *CPW*, II, 159.
75. *CHP*, IV, 121–22, *CPW*, II, 164–65.
76. *CHP*, IV, 127, *CPW*, II, 166.
77. *CHP*, IV, 155, *CPW*, II, 176.
78. *CHP*, IV, 158, 183–184, *CPW*, II, 177 and stanzas 176–78.
79. *CHP*, IV, 98, *CPW*, II, 157.

CHAPTER 31: *"Vile Assignations, and Adulterous Beds"*

1. B to DK, May 30, 1817, *BLJ*, V, 230.
2. B to AL, June 3–4, 1817, *BLJ*, V, 231–32.
3. Gunn, 204.
4. *The Day and New Times* in Marchand, II, 699.
5. B to AL, June 19, 1817, *BLJ*, V, 242.
6. *CHP*, IV, 1, *CPW*, II, 124.
7. B to JM, July 1, 1817, *BLJ*, V, 244–45.
8. Broughton, ii.
9. Ticknor, op. cit., I, 165, journal entry of October 20, 1817; see Chap. 26, n. 1.
10. B to JM, August 7, 1817, *BLJ*, V, 255.
11. B to JM, August 1, 1819, *BLJ*, VI, 193.
12. Ibid.
13. B to Moore, March 16, 1818, *BLJ*, VI, 23.
14. B to JM, August 1, 1819.
15. B to JM, August 1, 1819.
16. B to JM, August 21, 1817, *BLJ*, V, 255.
17. B to JM, September 4, 1817, *BLJ*, V, 263.
18. Hobhouse diary, August 29, 1817.
19. *Beppo*, 2, 9–16, *CPW*, IV, 129.
20. *Beppo*, 16, 127–28, *CPW*, IV, 134.
21. *Beppo*, 79, 629–32, *CPW*, IV, 154.
22. B to JM, October 12, 1817, *BLJ*, V, 267.
23. B to JM, October 23, 1817, *BLJ*, V, 269.
24. *Beppo*, 49, *CPW*, IV, 144.

25. B to JM, April 23, 1818, *BLJ*, VI, 35.
26. B to JM, October 23, 1817, *BLJ*, V, 269.
27. B to J, September 15, 1817, *BLJ*, V, 265.
28. B to DK, January 13, 1818, *BLJ*, VI, 7.
29. "[Epistle to Mr. Murray] ('My dear Mr. Murray')," *CPW*, IV, 161.
30. Origo (1), 102.
31. B to JCH, January 23, 1818, *BLJ*, VI, 8.
32. B to JM, January 27, 1818, *BLJ*, VI, 9.
33. Ibid.
34. B to JCH, February 23, 1818, *BLJ*, VI, 14.
35. B to JCH, March 3, 1818, *BLJ*, VI, 19.
36. B to DK, May 27, 1818, *BLJ*, VI, 42.
37. Nazzareno Meneghetti, *Lord Byron a Venezia*, Venezia [1910], 132, and Marchand, II, 767.
38. B to JCH and DK, January 19, 1819, *BLJ*, VI, 92.
39. Now part of the Carl H. Pforzheimer Library, the New York Public Library, and published in the ongoing *Shelley and His Circle*. The letters are discussed by Doucet Devin Fischer in an invaluable essay, " 'Countesses and Cobblers' Wives': Byron's Venetian Mistresses," *SC*, VII, 163–214.
40. B to JCH, May 19, 1818, *BLJ*, VI, 40.
41. Taruscelli to B, n.d., *SC*, VII, 325.
42. Taruscelli to B, June 17, 1818, *SC* VII, 336.
43. B to JM, August 3, 1818, *BLJ*, VI, 62.
44. B to DK, May 31, 1821, *BLJ*, VIII, 129–30.
45. B to JM, April 23, 1818, *BLJ*, VI, 34.
46. PBS to B, April 22, 1818, Holmes, 419.
47. B's letters to Shelley from these weeks have been lost, but the context may be inferred from Shelley's remarks.
48. B to JCH, April 24, 1818, *BLJ*, VI, 37.
49. Ibid.
50. B to JCH, May 5, 1818, *BLJ*, VI, 39.
51. B to AL, June 22, 1821, *BLJ*, VIII, 139.
52. B to JCH, May 27, 1818, *BLJ*, VI, 41.
53. B to AL, August 3, 1818, *BLJ*, VI, 62.
54. B to JCH, June 25, 1818, *BLJ*, VI, 54–55.
55. B to JM, July 10, 1818, *LJ*, VI, 58–59.
56. *Mazeppa*, 20, *CPW*, IV, 199–200.
57. B to JM, July 10, 1818, *BLJ*, VI, 59.
58. B to JM, August 3, 1818, *BLJ*, VI, 62.
59. B to JM, July 17, 1818, *BLJ*, VI, 61.
60. B to Moore, September 19, 1818, *BLJ*, VI, 67–68.
61. PBS to MWS [August 23, 1818], Jones, II, 36.
62. Ibid.
63. PBS to B, September 13, 1818, Jones, II, 38.
64. PBS to MWS [September 22, 1818], Jones, II, 38.
65. PBS to CC [September 25, 1818] Jones, II, 40.
66. PBS to Thomas Love Peacock, December [17 or 18], 1818; Jones, II, 57.
67. Ibid.
68. Ibid.
69. PBS to Peacock, October 8, 1818, Jones, II, 42.
70. Holmes, 449.
71. Hutchinson, op. cit., 190–203; see chap. 28, n. 27.

CHAPTER 32:   *An Uncommon Hero*

1. Newton Hanson's account of the visit, in Prothero, IV, 266–69.
2. Ibid.
3. B to AMB, November 18, 1818, *BLJ*, VI, 80–81. For Sir Samuel Romilly as Byron's Calvinist conscience see Kenneth N. Cameron, *SC*, III, 248–51.
4. B relates the entire story of his affair with la Fornarina to JM in one letter of August 1, 1819, *BLJ*, VI, 192–98.
5. B to Moore, September 19, 1818, *BLJ*, VI, 68.
6. B to JM, August 9, 1819, *BLJ*, VI, 205.
7. B to JCH and DK, January 19, 1819, *BLJ*, VI, 92.
8. B to JCH, January 19, 1819, *BLJ*, VI, 93.
9. B to Moore, September 19, 1818, *BLJ*, VI, 67.
10. B to Moore, September 27, 1813, *BLJ*, III, 122.
11. Letter of September 28, 1813, to Mrs. Southey, in Marchand, I, 412.
12. *DJ*, "Dedication," 1–3, *CPW*, V, 3–4.
13. B to JCH, November 11, 1818; *BLJ*, VI, 76.
14. *DJ*, "Dedication," 11–12, *CPW*, V, 6–7.
15. In Anne Barton, *Byron: Don Juan*, Cambridge, U.K., 1992, 1.
16. B to JM, May 25, 1819; *BLJ*, VI, 139.
17. B to JM, August 12, 1819; *BLJ*, VI, 207–8.
18. Virginia Woolf, in McGann (2), 1976, 10.
19. *DJ*, I, 1, *CPW*, V, 9.
20. *DJ*, I, 5–7, *CPW*, V, 10–11.
21. *DJ*, I, 23, *CPW*, V, 16.
22. *DJ*, I, 12, *CPW*, V, 12.
23. *DJ*, I, 15, *CPW*, V, 13.

24. *DJ*, I, 22, *CPW*, V, 15.
25. *DJ*, I, 27–29, *CPW*, V, 17.
26. *DJ*, I, 36, *CPW*, V, 20.
27. *DJ*, I, 46, *CPW*, V, 23.
28. *DJ*, I, 66, *CPW*, V, 29–30.
29. *DJ*, I, 193–94, *CPW*, V, 70–71.
30. *DJ*, I, 199, *CPW*, V, 72–73.
31. *DJ*, I, 201, *CPW*, V, 73.
32. *DJ*, I, 209, *CPW*, V, 76.
33. *DJ*, I, 214–15, *CPW*, V, 77–78.
34. *DJ*, II, 16, *CPW*, V, 94.
35. *DJ*, II, 20, *CPW*, V, 95.
36. *DJ*, II, 36, *CPW*, V, 100.
37. *DJ*, II, 45, *CPW*, V, 103.
38. *DJ*, II, 53, *CPW*, V, 105.
39. *DJ*, II, 61, *CPW*, V, 108.
40. *DJ*, II, 72, *CPW*, V, 111.
41. *DJ*, II, 73–75, *CPW*, V, 111–12.
42. *DJ*, II, 77, *CPW*, V, 113.
43. *DJ*, II, 79, *CPW*, V, 113.
44. *DJ*, II, 87, *CPW*, V, 116.
45. *DJ*, II, 90, *CPW*, V, 117.
46. *DJ*, II, 105, *CPW*, V, 121.
47. *DJ*, II, 189, *CPW*, V, 148.
48. *DJ*, II, 190, *CPW*, V, 148.
49. *DJ*, II, 199–201, *CPW*, V, 151–52.
50. *DJ*, II, 213, *CPW*, V, 156.
51. B to JM, February 1, 1819, *BLJ*, VI, 99.
52. TGG, "Confession," Origo (2), 140; see Chap. 31, n. 30. Origo believed this document to have been "extracted" from Teresa by Count Guiccioli to "disprove what was being said of him by the Gamba family." She herself refers to the "wretched confession" in a letter of July 30 (MSS in the Carl H. Pforzheimer Library), *SC*, VII, 387.
53. B to DK, April 24, 1819, *BLJ*, VI, 115.
54. B To JCH, April 6, 1819, *BLJ*, VI, 107–8.
55. B to TGG, June 16, 1819, *BLJ*, VI, 160.

CHAPTER 33:   *"A Stranger Loves a Lady of the Land"*

1. Origo (1).
2. Doucet Devin Fischer, "Countess Guiccioli's Byron," *SC*, VII, 378.
3. Origo (2), 24.
4. B to DK, April 24, 1819, *BLJ*, VI, 115.
5. B to JCH, April 6, 1819, *BLJ*, VI, 107.
6. B to TGG, April 22, 1819, *BLJ*, VI, 112.
7. B to DK, May 26, 1819, *BLJ*, VI, 141.
8. B to DK, April 24, 1819, *BLJ*, VI, 115.
9. Fischer, "Countess Guiccioli's Byron," *SC*, VII, 383, n. 20.
10. TGG to B, *SC*, VII, 488.
11. B to TGG, April 22, 1819, *BLJ*, VI, 113.
12. Fanny Silvestrini to TGG, November 25, 1819, *SC*, VII, 548.
13. B to TGG, April 23, 1819, *BLJ*, VI, 113.
14. B to JM, May 18, 1819, *BLJ*, VI, 133.
15. B to DK, April 24, 1819, *BLJ*, VI, 15.
16. B to AL, May 17, 1819, *BLJ*, VI, 129. AL note in Lovelace, 81–83.
17. "To the Po, June 2nd 1819," *CPW*, IV, 212.
18. B to R. B. Hoppner, June 2, 1819, *BLJ*, VI, 144.
19. B to JM, June 7, 1819, *BLJ*, VI, 149.
20. B to Hoppner, June 6, 1819, *BLJ*, VI, 148.
21. B to Alexander Scott, June 10, 1819, *BLJ*, VI, 151.
22. B to TGG, June 11, 1819, *BLJ*, VI, 154.
23. Ibid.
24. B to TGG, June 15, 1819, *BLJ*, VI, 159.
25. B to TGG, June 14, 1819, *BLJ*, VI, 156.
26. Ibid.
27. B to TGG, June 17, 1819, *BLJ*, VI, 161.
28. For a discussion of the abortion/miscarriage question see Fischer, op. cit., *SC*, VII, 390–93.
29. B to AL, July [?], *BLJ*, VI, 171.
30. B to JM, June 29, 1819, *BLJ*, VI, 167.
31. Ibid., 168.
32. B to Hoppner, June 20, 1819, *BLJ*, VI, 164.
33. B to JM, June 29, 1819, *BLJ*, VI, 168.
34. B to Hoppner, June 20, 1819, *BLJ*, VI, 163–64.
35. B to Hoppner, June 22, 1819, *BLJ*, VI, 164.
36. B to JM, August 12, 1819, *BLJ*, VI, 208.
37. B to TGG, August 4, 1819, *BLJ*, VI, 199.
38. B to Scott, July 12, 1819, *BLJ*, VI, 178.
39. B to JM, August 12, 1819, *BLJ*, VI, 206.
40. B to JM, August 24, 1819, *BLJ*, VI, 217.
41. B to JCH, August 23, 1819, *BLJ*, VI, 214.
42. B to TGG, August 23, 1819, *BLJ*, VI, 215–16.
43. B to JM, August 24, 1819, *BLJ*, VI, 217.
44. B to Henry Dorville, August 28, 1819, *BLJ*, VI, 218.
45. B to AL [about September 10, 1819], *BLJ*, VI, 223.
46. B to JCH, October 3, 1819, *BLJ*, VI, 225–27.
47. B to DK, November 16, 1819, *BLJ*, VI, 241.
48. B to AL, July 26, 1819, *BLJ*, VI, 186.
49. B to JCH, August 20, 1819, *BLJ*, VI, 212.
50. B to JM, August 12, 1819, *BLJ*, VI, 206–7.

51. B to DK, October 26, 1818 [1819], *BLJ*, VI, 232.
52. Origo (2), 128.
53. B to Hoppner, October 29, 1819, *BLJ*, VI, 238.
54. Origo (2), 123.
55. B to DK, November 16, 1819, *BLJ*, VI, 241.
56. Origo (2), 135.
57. Ibid.
58. B to DK, November 16, 1819, *BLJ*, VI, 241.
59. B to JCH, August 23, 1819, *BLJ*, VI, 214.
60. B to DK, November 16, 1819, *BLJ*, VI, 241.
61. B to AL, June 3–4, 1817, *BLJ*, V, 231.
62. B to JCH, November 21, 1819 (continued from November 20), *BLJ*, VI, 246.
63. *Blackwood's Edinburgh Magazine*, V (August 1819), 512–18; Reiman, I, 1143–45.
64. *British Critic*, 2nd series, XII (August 1819), 195–205; Reiman, 299–300.
65. *Edinburgh Monthly Review*, II (October 1819), 468–86; Reiman, II, Part B, 799.
66. Reiman, introduction to reviews of *DJ*, I and II, in Reiman, II, Part B, 1166.
67. B to DK, October 26, 1818, *BLJ*, VI, 232.
68. B to JCH, October 12, 1821, *BLJ*, VIII, 240.
69. B to TGG [November] 1819, 25, *BLJ*, VI, 247.
70. Fanny Silvestrini to TGG, November 30, 1819, *SC*, VII, 563.
71. Fischer "Commentary," *SC*, VII, 586.
72. Silvestrini to TGG, December 10, 1819, *SC*, VII, 593.
73. B to TGG, December 10, 1819, *BLJ*, VI, 258–59.

CHAPTER 34: *Don Juan Domesticated*

1. B to R. B. Hoppner, December 3, 1819, *BLJ*, VI, 262.
2. Ibid.
3. B to Hoppner, January 31, 1820, *BLJ*, VII, 28.
4. "La Vie," TGG's unpublished memoir of her life with B; Carl H. Pforzheimer Library, 2nd series, 353; *SC*, VII, 403, n. 78.
5. B admitted to squeezing Geltruda Vicari's thigh, precipitating a scene with Teresa. B to TGG, January 3, 1820, *BLJ*, VII, 1820, 20.
6. Ibid.
7. Ibid.; January 4, 1820, 22.
8. B to AMB, December 31, 1819, *BLJ*, VI, 260–61.
9. JCH, *A Trifling Mistake*, London, 1820, 49–50, in Graham (2), 284.
10. B to JM, February 21, 1820, *BLJ*, VII, 44.
11. Graham, 282.
12. B to JCH, March 3, 1820, *BLJ*, VII, 49.
13. "New Song (How came you in Hob's pound to cool)," *CPW*, IV, 287.
14. JCH to B, April 21, [1820], Graham (2), 290.
15. Hobhouse diary, Berg Collection.
16. Edel, III, 171, see Chap. 28, n. 15.
17. B to JM, February 7, 1820, *BLJ*, VII, 34.
18. *DJ*, III, 2, *CPW*, V, 161.
19. *DJ*, III, 3, *CPW*, V, 161.
20. *DJ*, III, 7, *CPW*, V, 163.
21. *DJ*, III, "Poem Section," V, *CPW*, V, 189.
22. *DJ*, III, 39, *CPW*, V, 173.

23. *DJ*, III, 88, *CPW*, V, 192–93.

24. B to JM, March 23, 1820, *BLJ*, VII, 59.

25. *The Prophecy of Dante*, IV, 11, *CPW*, IV, 238.

26. B to JM, March 20, 1820, *BLJ*, VII, 58.

27. B to TGG [April 1820?], *BLJ*, VII, 67.

28. B to JM, February 25, 1817, *BLJ*, V, 174.

29. B to TGG, January 18, 1821, *BLJ*, VIII, 64.

30. B to JM, September 28, 1820, *BLJ*, VII, 182.

31. B to JM, May 20, 1820, *BLJ*, VII, 102.

32. B to TGG [May 1820?], *BLJ*, VII, 88–91.

33. Origo (2), 171.

34. B to TGG [May 1820?], *BLJ*, VII, 90.

35. B to TGG [June 1820?], *BLJ*, VII, 108.

36. B to TGG [May 1820?], *BLJ*, VII, 92.

37. B to Moore, July 13, 1820, *BLJ*, VII, 125.

38. Origo (2), 188–89.

39. B to JM, August 31, 1820, *BLJ*, VII, 168.

40. *Marino Faliero*, III, ii, *CPW*, IV, 378–79.

41. Ibid., 363.

42. B to TGG, August 7, 1820, *BLJ*, VII, 152.

43. B to TGG, August 30, 1820, *BLJ*, VII, 166.

44. B to PBS, August 25, 1820, *BLJ*, VII, 162.

45. PBS to B, September 17, 1820, Jones, II, 236.

46. B to Hoppner, April 22, 1820, *BLJ*, VII, 80.

47. September 10, 1820, *BLJ*, VI, 174.

48. B to TGG, July 29, 1820, *BLJ*, VII, 146.

49. B to Moore, September 19, 1821, *BLJ*, VIII, 214.

50. "Ravenna Journal," February 18, 1821, *BLJ*, VIII, 47.

51. B to JM, July 22, 1820, *BLJ*, VII, 137.

52. B to JM, September 4, 1821, *BLJ*, VIII, 17.

53. B to JCH, April 22, 1820, *BLJ*, VII, 81. Also discussed in B to JCH, October 12, 1821, *BLJ*, VIII, 240.

54. B to JM [August 25?, 1820], September 14, 1820, *BLJ*, VII, 162.

55. B to "the Neapolitan Insurgents" [October ? 1820], *BLJ*, VII, 187–88.

56. Origo (2), 226.

57. B to DK, October 1, 1820, *BLJ*, VII, 190.

58. B to AMB, December 28, 1820, *BLJ*, VII, 257.

59. B to Moore, January 22, 1821. Also Moore's decision to sell is discussed in B to JCH, November 23, 1821, *BLJ*, IX, 68.

60. "Ravenna Journal," January 9, 1821, *BLJ*, VIII, 20.

61. Ibid., January 13, 1821, *BLJ*, VIII, 26.

62. Ibid., February 16–18, 1821, *BLJ*, VIII, 46–47.

63. Ibid., February 24, 1821, *BLJ*, VIII, 49.

64. "My Dictionary," May 1, 1821, *BLJ*, VIII, 106.

65. "Ravenna Journal," February 24, 1821, *BLJ*, VIII, 49.

66. B to Moore, April 28, 1821, *BLJ*, VIII, 105.

67. "Ravenna Journal," January 13, 1821, *BLJ*, VIII, 26.

68. B to AL, June 22, 1821, *BLJ*, VIII, 139.

69. B to AL, October 5, 1821, *BLJ*, VIII, 234.

70. TGG to B, July 11, 1821; Origo, 257.

71. B to TGG, July 25, 1821, *BLJ*, VIII, 159–60.

72. B to TGG, July 29, 1821
[Postscript], *BLJ*, VIII, 161.

73. B to PBS, July 30–31[?], 1821,
BLJ, VIII, 163.

CHAPTER 35: *Exiles and Serpents*

1. B to DK, June 2, 1821, *BLJ*, VIII,
132.

2. B to PBS, April 26, 1821, *BLJ*,
VIII, 103–4.

3. B to JM, November 9, 1820; *BLJ*,
VII, 225.

4. B to JM, October 12, 1820, *BLJ*,
VII, 200.

5. B to JM, April 26, 1821, *BLJ*, VIII,
102.

6. B to PBS, April 26, 1821, *BLJ*,
VIII, 104.

7. PBS to MWS, August 8, 1821,
Jones, II, 322.

8. PBS to MWS, August 7, 1821,
Jones, II, 318.

9. PBS to MWS, August 7, 1821,
Jones, II, 319.

10. PBS to B, July 16, 1821, Jones, II,
309.

11. August 7, 1821, Jones, II, 317.

12. PBS to MWS, August 8, 1821,
Jones, II, 624.

13. B to Hoppner, May 11, 1821, *BLJ*,
VIII, 112.

14. *DJ*, V, 116, *CPW*, V, 278.

15. *DJ*, V, 137–38, *CPW*, V, 285.

16. *DJ*, V, 158, *CPW*, V, 291.

17. PBS to MWS, August 8, 1821,
Jones, II, 323.

18. PBS to B, April 17, 1821, Jones, II,
28.

19. PBS to MWS, August 8, 1821,
Jones, II, 323.

20. PBS to MWS, August 7, 1821,
Jones, II, 317.

21. An "Observation" not published
during Byron's lifetime. Marchand,
II, 846.

22. PBS to MSW, August 7, 1821,
Jones, II, 317.

23. "Ravenna Journal," January 12, 1981, *BLJ*, VIII, 23.

24. B to Moore, May 14, 1821, *BLJ*,
VIII, 117. See David V. Erdman,
"Byron's Stage Fright: The History
of His Ambition and Fear of
Writing for the Stage," *English
Literary History*, VI, (1939),
219–245.

25. *The Two Foscari*, I, i, 142–45;
CPW, VI, 137.

26. *Sardanapalus*, IV, i, *CPW*, VI, 99.

27. Shelley's notorious undergraduate pamphlet *The Necessity of Atheism* (1811) was the
cause of his expulsion from
Oxford and estrangement from his
family.

28. B to Carlo Gamba, August 9,
1821; *BLJ*, VIII, 1775–76.

29. PBS to MWS, August 15, 1821,
Jones, II, 338.

30. PBS to Leigh Hunt, August 26,
1821, Jones, II, 343.

31. PBS to MWS, August 15, 1821,
Jones, II, 335.

32. PBS to TGG, August 22, 1821,
Jones, II, 340.

33. B to Moore, September 19, 1821,
BLJ, VIII, 214.

34. B to TGG, August [16], 1821,
BLJ, VIII, 183.

35. B to Moore, October 28, 1821,
BLJ, VIII, 250.

36. "Detached Thoughts," October 15,
1821–May 18, 1822, no. 91, *BLJ*,
IX, 44.

37. Ibid., November 5, 1821, #113.

38. Ibid., November 5, 1821, #113,
BLJ, IX, 49.

39. CC to B, March 24, 1821,
Stocking (2), I, 163.

40. "[Stanzas Written on the Road
between Florence and Pisa],"
CPW, VI, 14.

41. Origo (2), 298.
42. B to DK, November 4, 1821, *BLJ*, IX, 56.
43. Origo (2), 299.
44. *Cain*, I, i, 36–38, *CPW*, VI, 233.
45. B to JM, February 8, 1822, *BLJ*, IX, 103.
46. PBS to Horace Smith, c. May 21, 1822, Jones, II, 423.
47. B to Hoppner, September 10, 1820, *BLJ*, VII, 184.
48. B to Moore, December 13[?], 1821, *BLJ*, IX, 81.
49. Origo (2), 302.
50. MWS to CC, March 20, 1822, Jones, II, 397.
51. PBS to CC, March 20, 1822, Jones, II, 398.
52. PBS to CC [added to MWS's letter], March 20, 1822, Jones, II, 399.
53. Reports of Allegra's final illness and death are in letters by Pellegrino Ghigi to Fletcher and Lega Zambelli, in Origo, 310 ff.
54. Ibid.
55. B to PBS, April 23, 1822, *BLJ*, IX, 147–48.
56. Both notes dated September 28, 1821, MSS, J. Pierpont Morgan Library. Also in Origo (1), 64.
57. B to Hoppner, September 28[?], 1821, *BLJ*, VIII, 26.
58. Origo (2), 311.
59. Williams, 149.
60. B to JM, May 26, 1822, *BLJ*, IX, 164.
61. Blessington, 71–72.
62. B to Moore, June 8, 1822, *BLJ*, IX, 170.
63. B to Moore, August 27, 1822, *BLJ*, IX, 198.
64. Origo (2), 317.
65. Marianne Hunt's diary, in Origo (2), 320.
66. Hunt, I, 66–68.
67. B to Hunt, September 15, 1823, *BLJ*, IX, 208.
68. TGG, *Vie*, in Origo (2), 318.
69. F. L. Jones, ed., *Maria Gisborne and Edward E. Williams: Their Journals and Letters*, Norman, University of Oklahoma Press, 1951, 149.
70. The account of exhuming the remains of Shelley and Williams is from Trelawny (2), 133 ff.
71. Trelawny (1), Trelawny to W.M. Rosetti, December 18 [1878], 269–70.
72. Leigh Hunt, *The Autobiography of Leigh Hunt*, 2 vols., Westminster, Archibald, Constable and Co., 1903, in Marchand, III, 1024.
73. B to Moore, August 27, 1822, *BLJ*, IX, 197.
74. B to JM, August 3, 1822, *BLJ*, IX, 190.
75. PBS to Hunt, April 10, 1822, Jones, II, 405.

CHAPTER 36: *The Road to Missolonghi*

1. MWS to Maria Gisborne, August 15, 1822, Jones, *Letters*, I, 144.
2. Medwin, II, 124–25.
3. For MWS's feelings for Byron and their reflection in her own writings see Ernest J. Lovell, Jr., "Byron and Mary Shelley," *Keats-Shelley Memorial Journal*, no. 2 (1953), 35–49.
4. B to Moore, August 8, 1822, *BLJ*, IX, 191.
5. B to JCH, September 27[?] 1821 (postmarked October 16, 1821), *BLJ*, VIII, 224.
6. Joseph, 125–26.

7. B to JCH, September 2, 1822, *BLJ*, IX, 210.

8. B to JM, September 23, 1822, *BLJ*, IX, 213.

9. T. Moore (1), II, 614.

10. Broughton, II, 3–4.

11. B to DK, September 11, 1822, *BLJ*, IX, 206.

12. B to DK, September 18, 1822, *BLJ*, IX, 209.

13. B to DK, September 12, 1822, *BLJ*, IX, 207.

14. Report of Torelli, the master spy assigned to Byron, in Origo, 324.

15. B to JM, October 9, 1822, *BLJ*, X, 12.

16. B to MWS, October 4, 1822, *BLJ*, X, 11.

17. Nicolson, 29.

18. B to Moore, February 20, 1823, *BLJ*, X, 105.

19. Origo (2), 330.

20. JM to B, October 29, 1822, Marchand, III, 1040.

21. B to JM, November 18, 1822, *BLJ*, X, 36.

22. B to AL, October 5, 1821, *BLJ*, VIII, 234.

23. B to TGG, February 15, 1823, *BLJ*, X, 100.

24. Blessington, 42 ff.

25. Ibid.

26. Ibid., 154–55.

27. Lovell.

28. *DJ*, XIV, 85, 674, *CPW*, V, 583.

29. Moore, II, 304.

30. Nicolson, 18.

31. Nicolson, 85.

32. B to JM, September 4, 1821, *BLJ*, VIII, 198.

33. Pietro Gamba, in Nicolson, 73.

34. Nicolson, 76.

35. B to John Bowring, May 12, 1823, *BLJ*, X, 168.

36. B to Bowring, May 21, 1823.

37. B to Bowring, May 12, 1821, *BLJ*, X, 170.

38. Ibid., 168.

39. Gamba, 67.

40. B to Trelawny, June 15, 1823, *BLJ*, X, 199.

41. Trelawny (2), 191.

42. Nicolson, 88.

43. MWS to Jane Williams, July 1823, in D. L. Moore, "Byron, Leigh Hunt and the Shelleys," *Keats-Shelley Memorial Bulletin*, no. 10 (1959), 20–29.

44. Origo (2), 330.

45. T. Moore (2), II, 25.

46. Trelawny (2), 181.

47. Nicolson, 102.

48. B to Bowring, July 24, 1823, *BLJ*, X, 213.

49. Nicolson, 116–17.

50. B to Barry, August 10, 1823, *BLJ*, IX, 16.

51. B to Napier, September 9, 1823, *BLJ*, IX, 20.

52. B to TGG, August 11, 1823, *BLJ*, IX, 18.

53. B to JCH, May 19, 1823, *BLJ*, X, 176.

54. B to JCH, September 11, 1823, *BLJ*, XI, 24.

55. Nicolson, 117.

56. B to JCH, September 11, 1823, *BLJ*, XI, 25.

57. B to JCH, September 27, 1823, *BLJ*, XI, 27.

58. "Journal in Cephalonia," September 28, 1823, *BLJ*, XI, 32.

59. Ibid.

60. Ibid., 31.

61. "Journal in Cephalonia," October 17, 1823, *BLJ*, XI, 33.

62. Ibid.

63. Ibid., 35.

64. B to DK, October 29, 1823, *BLJ*, XI, 58.

65. B to JCH, October 16, 1823, *BLJ*, XI, 50.

66. B to JCH, November 10, 1823, *BLJ*, XI, 60.

67. B to DK, December 23, 1823, *BLJ*, XI, 80.

68. B to JCH, December 27, 1823, *BLJ*, XI, 85.

69. B to DK, December 27, 1823, *BLJ*, XI, 85–86.

CHAPTER 37: *"The Land of Honourable Death Is Here"*

1. B to Stanhope, December 31, 1823, *BLJ*, XI, 87.
2. B to Osborne, January 7, 1824, *BLJ*, XI, 91.
3. Ibid.
4. B to G. Stevens, January 19, 1824, *BLJ*, XI, 97.
5. B to Bowring, December 26, 1823, *BLJ*, XI, 83.
6. B to Stevens, January 19, 1824, *BLJ*, XI, 97.
7. B to Bowring, January 28, 1824, *BLJ*, XI, 102.
8. Leslie Marchand, "Biographical Sketch," *BLJ*, XI, 218.
9. B to Bowring, January 2, 1824.
10. B to Hancock, February 5, 1824, *BLJ*, XI, 107.
11. B to Prince Mavrocordatos, February 5, 1824, *BLJ*, XI, 105.
12. B to Hancock, February 7, 1824, *BLJ*, XI, 108.
13. Ibid.
14. William St. Clair, "The Byron Brigade," in St. Clair (2), 173–84.
15. "Notes on Suliotes," February 15, 1824, *BLJ*, XI, 111–12.
16. "Journal in Cephalonia," February 15, 1824 ("17th" as written by B), *BLJ*, XI, 113.
17. B's description of his attack and its aftermath in "Journal in Cephalonia," February 17, 1924.
18. "On this day I complete my thirty sixth year," January 22 1824, Missolonghi, *CPW*, VII, 79–81.
19. [General Orders to the Suliotes], February 17, 1824, *BLJ*, XI, 115; B's "commission" from
Mavrocordatos is noted by Gamba, 133–34, and Marchand, *BLJ*, XI, 115.
20. B to DK, February 21, 1824, *BLJ*, XI, 117.
21. B to JM, February 25, 1824, *BLJ*, XI, 124.
22. B to TGG, February 11, 1824, *BLJ*, XI, 111.
23. B to AL, February 23, 1824, *BLJ*, XI, 120–21.
24. B to James Kennedy, March 4, 1824, *BLJ*, XI, 126.
25. B to TGG, March 17, 1824, *BLJ*, XI, 137.
26. B to Barry, April 9, 1824, *BLJ*, XI, 153.
27. B to DK, March 30, 1824, *BLJ*, XI, 144.
28. Parry, in Nicolson, 254–56.
29. Ibid., 267.
30. Ibid.
31. Nicolson, 269.
32. Hobhouse diary, May 14, 1824; also in Broughton, III, 35.
33. DK to JCH, May 14, 1824, with MSS diary, British Library.
34. Broughton, III, 38.
35. Ibid., 40.
36. Mayne, in Marchand, III, 1258.
37. Fischer, "Countess Guiccioli's Byron," *SC*, VIII, 454.
38. Hobhouse diary, July 5, 1824; also quoted by Nicolson, 272–74, and Marchand, III, 1255.
39. Hobhouse diary, July 12, 1824.
40. Ibid., July 11, 1824.
41. Ibid., July 16, 1824.

Afterlife

1. W. H. Auden, "Letter to Lord Byron," *Complete Works*, Princeton, 1988, 77–100. Quoted by kind permission of Faber and Faber.

2. "Bulwer-Lytton," George Sampson, *The Concise Cambridge History of English Literature*, 3rd ed., Cambridge, 1975, 641.

3. Angeline Goreau, "The Joy of Suffering," Review of reissue of George Sand, *Horace*, in *New York Times Book Review*, December 3, 1995, 52.

4. Andrew Elfenbein, *Byron and the Victorians*, Cambridge, U.K., Cambridge University Press 1995, 237ff.

5. Alexander Pushkin, *Eugene Onegin*, trans. James E. Falen, Carbondale, Ill., 1990, 177.

6. Sir Isaiah Berlin, "Anna Akhmatova: A Memoir," in *The Complete Poems of Anna Akhmatova*, Boston, 1993, repr. in Berlin. *The Proper Study of Mankind*, New York: Farrar Straus, 1998, 543–44.

7. Théophile Gautier, *Histoire de Romantisme*, Paris, 1877, 203 ff.

8. Delacroix, *Journal* (1822–63), Paris, 1996, passim; George Heard Hamilton, "Eugene Delacroix and Lord Byron," *Gazette des Beaux Arts*, no. 23 (1943). John Bandiera, "Byron Subjects in French Art, 1819–1858," M.A. thesis, New York University Institute of Fine Arts, 1975.

9. David Blayney Brown, *Turner and Byron*, catalogue of the exhibition at the Tate Gallery, London, June 3–September 20, 1992.

10. My discussion of Byron and music has drawn on the following: Alice Levine, "Byron and the Romantic Composer," in *Lord Byron and His Contemporaries: Essays from the Sixth International Byron Seminar*, ed. Charles E. Robinson, Newark, Del., 1982, 178–203; Paul Chancellor, "British Bards and Continental Composers," *The Musical Quarterly*, XLVI, no. 1, January 1960, 1–11; Davd Lawton, "The Corsair Reaches Port," *Opera News* XLVI, no. 20, June 1982, 16, 18, 42; David Ewing Gregson, "The Byron Operas," Ph.D. dissertation, University of California, San Diego, 1979, University Microfilm, 1981.

Selected Bibliography

MANUSCRIPT COLLECTIONS

Archivi di Stati, Venice
Berg Collection of English and American Literature, New York Public Library, Astor, Lenox and Tilden Foundation
Biblioteca Classense, Ravenna
The Lovelace Byron Papers on deposit in the Bodleian Library, Oxford University
Egerton Collection, British Library, London
Gennadius Library, Athens
Greater London Record Office, Hertford
Keats-Shelley Memorial, Rome
Hertfordshire Record Office, Hertford
Meyer Davis Collection, University of Pennsylvania, Philadelphia
J. Pierpont Morgan Library, New York City
John Murray Archives, London
Museo Correr, Venice
Roe-Byron Collection, Newstead Abbey
Carl H. Pforzheimer Collection of "Shelley and His Circle," New York Public Library, Astor, Lenox and Tilden Foundation
Trinity College Library, Cambridge University
Victoria and Albert Museum, London

PUBLISHED SOURCES

I have benefited from recent scholarship on Byron and the Romantics, particularly from new scholarly editions of the poetry, prose, journals, and letters of the poet and his contemporaries (some still in progress).

The first debt of any present-day biographer of Byron is to Leslie Marchand's great three-volume work. Published in 1957, it is still the foundation of any life of the poet.

Ashton, Thomas, L. *Byron's Hebrew Melodies.* Austin: University of Texas Press, 1972.
Barton, Anne. *Don Juan.* Cambridge: Cambridge University Press, 1992.
Bennett, Betty T., ed. *The Letters of Mary Wollstonecraft Shelley.* 3 vols. Baltimore and London: Johns Hopkins University Press, 1980.
Blessington, Lady. *Conversations of Lord Byron.* Ed. Ernest J. Lovell, Jr. Princeton: Princeton University Press, 1969.
Borst, William A. *Lord Byron's First Pilgrimage.* New Haven: Yale University Press, 1948.

Boyes, Megan. *Love Without Wings: A Biography of Elizabeth Pigot.* Derby, 1988.

———.*My Amiable Mamma: A Biography of Mrs. Catherine Gordon Byron.* Derby, 1991.

———. *Queen of a Fantastic Realm: A Biography of Mary Chaworth.* Derby, 1986.

Broughton, Lord [John Cam Hobhouse]. *Recollections of a Long Life.* 6 vols. Ed. Lady Dorchester (his daughter). London: J. Murray, 1909–1911.

Burnett, T. A. J. *The Rise and Fall of a Regency Dandy: The Life and Times of Scrope Berdmore Davies.* Boston: Little, Brown, 1981.

Cameron, Kenneth N., Donald H. Reiman, and Doucet D. Fischer, eds. *Shelley and His Circle: 1773–1822.* Cambridge, Mass: Harvard University Press, 1961–1986. Eight vols of a planned ten. Letters and other documents of the Shelley-Byron circle owned by the Carl H. Pforzheimer Library, including important new material relating to Teresa Gamba Guiccioli, and including essays by the editors and other scholars.

"Catalogue of a Collection of Books, late the Property of a Nobleman." Sale catalogue by Evans of Byron's Library. London: April 5 and 6, 1816.

Christensen, Jerome. *Lord Byron's Strength: Romantic Writing and Commercial Society.* Baltimore: Johns Hopkins University Press, 1993.

Cline, C. L. *Byron, Shelley and Their Pisan Circle.* Cambridge, Mass.: Harvard University Press, 1952.

Clubbe, John. "George Gordon, Lord Byron." In *The English Romantic Poets: A Review of Research and Criticism.* 4th ed. Ed. Frank Jordan. New York: The Modern Language Association of America, 1985.

Cochran, Peter. "Nature's Gentler Errors." *The Byron Journal,* no. 23, 1995.

Colley, Linda. *Britons.* New Haven: Yale University Press, 1992.

Crompton, Louis. *Byron and Greek Love.* Berkeley and Los Angeles: Publisher TK, 1985.

Dallas, R. C. *Correspondence of Lord Byron with a Friend.* Philadelphia: A. Small and H. C. Carey and I. Lea, 1825.

———. *Recollections of the Life of Lord Byron.* Philadelphia: A. Small and H.C. Carey and I. Lea, 1825.

Elfenbein, Andrew. *Byron and the Victorians.* Cambridge: Cambridge University Press, 1995.

Eliot, T. S. "Byron." In *English Romantic Poets: Modern Essays in Criticism.* 2nd ed. Ed. M. H. Abrams. London: Oxford University Press, 1975.

Elwin, Malcolm. *Lord Byron's Wife.* New York: St. Martin's Press, 1962.

Erdman, David V. "Lord Byron and the Genteel Reformers." *Publications of the Modern Language Association of America,* 51 (1941).

Fischer, Doucet Devin. *The Grand Napoleon of the Realms of Rhyme: Byron and History.* Ph.D. dissertation, University of Michigan, Ann Arbor, 1989.

Foot, Michael. *The Politics of Paradise.* New York: Harper & Row, 1988.

Franklin, Caroline. *Byron's Heroines.* London: Oxford University Press, 1992.

Galt, John. *The Life of Lord Byron.* New York: Harper & Brothers, 1830.

Gamba, Count Peter [Pietro]. *A Narrative of Lord Byron's Last Journey to Greece.* Paris: Gagliani, 1825.

Gleckner, Robert J. *Byron and the Ruins of Paradise.* Baltimore: Johns Hopkins Press, 1967.

Graham, Peter. *Don Juan and Regency England.* Charlottesville: University of Virginia Press, 1990.

Graham, Peter W., ed. *Byron's Bulldog: The Letters of J. C. Hobhouse to Lord Byron.* Columbus: Ohio State Universty Press, 1984.

Gunn, Peter. *My Dearest Augusta.* New York: Ateneum, 1968.

Hobhouse, J. C. *A Journey Through Albania and Other Provinces of Turkey.* 2nd ed. 2 vols. London: M. Carey and Son, 1813.

Hollander, John. *Rhyme's Reason: A Guide to English Verse.* New Haven: Yale University Press, 1981.

Holmes, Richard. *Shelley: The Pursuit.* New York: Viking Penguin, 1975.

Hunt, Leigh. *Lord Byron and Some of His Contemporaries.* 2nd ed. 2 vols. London, 1828.

Jones, Frederick L., ed. *The Letters of Percy Bysshe Shelley.* 2 vols. New York: Clarendon Press, 1964.

Joseph, Michael. *Byron the Poet.* London: Gollancz, 1964.

Kelsall, Malcolm. *Byron's Politics.* Totowa, N.J.: Barnes and Noble, 1987.

Lang, Cecil Y. "Narcissus Jilted: Byron, Don Juan, and the Biographical Imperative." In *Historical Studies and Literary Criticism.* Ed. Jerome J. McGann. Madison, Wis.: University of Wisconsin Press, 1985.

Lovelace, Ralph Milbanke. *Astarte: A Fragment of Truth Concerning George Gordon Byron.* New York: Scribners, 1921.

Lovell, Jr., E. J., ed. *His Very Self and Voice: Collected Conversations of Lord Byron.* New York: Macmillan, 1954.

Marchand, Leslie A. *Byron: A Biography.* 3 vols. New York: Alfred A. Knopf, 1957.

————, ed. *Byron's Letters and Journals.* 13 vols., Cambridge, Mass.: Belknap Press of Harvard Unversity Press, 1973–94.

Mayne, Ethel Colburn. *The Life and Letters of Anna Isabella,* Lady Noel Byron. London: Constable, 1929.

McGann, Jerome J. "The Book of Byron and the Book of a World." In *The Beauty of Inflections: Literary Investigations in Historical Method and Theory.* Oxford: Oxford University Press, 1985.

————. *Don Juan in Context.* Chicago: University of Chicago Press, 1976.

————. *Fiery Dust: Byron's Poetic Development.* Chicago: University of Chicago Press, 1968.

————, ed. *Byron: The Complete Poetical Works.* 7 vols. Oxford: Clarendon Press, 1980–93.

Medwin, Thomas. *Journal of the Conversations of Lord Byron.* 2 vols. London: Colburn, 1824.

Moore, Doris Langley. *The Late Lord Byron.* London: J. Murray, 1961.

————. *Lord Byron: Accounts Rendered.* New York: Harper & Row, 1974.

Moore, Thomas. *Letters and Journals of Lord Byron, with Notices of His Life.* 2 vols. Paris: Gagliani, 1829.

————. *Memoirs, Journals and Correspondence.* 8 vols. Ed. the Rt. Hon. Lord John Russell. London: Longman, Brown, Green and Longmans, 1858.

————. *Prose and Verse.* New York: Scribner, Armstrong, 1878.

Nicholson, Andrew. " 'That Suit in Chancery': Two New Byron Letters." *The Byron Journal,* 1998.

————, ed. *Lord Byron: The Complete Miscellaneous Prose.* Oxford: Clarendon University Press, 1991.

Nicolson, Harold. *Byron: The Last Journey.* Boston: Houghton Mifflin, 1924.

Origo, Iris. *A Measure of Love.* New York: Pantheon, 1957.

————. *The Last Attachment*. New York: C. Scribner's Sons, 1949.

Parry, Wlliam. *The Last Days of Lord Byron*. London: H. Colburn, 1825.

Paston, George, and Peter Quennell, eds. *To Lord Byron: Feminine Profiles Based upon Unpublished Letters*. London: John Murray, 1939.

Peach, Annette. "Controlling an Image: Two Venetian Miniatures of Byron." *The Byron Journal*, no. 26, 1998 13–28.

Polidori, John William. *The Diary of John William Polidori*. Ed. William Michael Rossetti. London: Elkin Mathews, 1911.

Pratt, Willis W. *Byron at Southwell*. Austin, Texas: University of Texas Press, 1948. Monograph no. 1.

Prothero, Roland E., ed. *The Works of Lord Byron: A New, Revised and Enlarged Edition, with Illustrations, Letters and Journals*. 6 vols. London: J. Murray, 1922–24.

Reiman, Donald H, ed. *The Romantics Reviewed*. 8 vols. New York: Garland Publishing, 1972.

Reiman, Donald H., and Doucet D. Fischer, eds. *Shelley and His Circle, 1773–1882*. 4 vols. Cambridge, Mass.: Harvard University Press, 1970.

Rogers, Samuel. *Recollections of the Table Talk of Samuel Rogers*. New York: D. Appleton and Company, 1856.

Rutherford, Andrew. *Byron: The Critical Heritage*. New York: Barnes and Noble, 1970.

Said, Edward W. *Orientalism*. New York: Pantheon, 1987.

St. Clair, William. *Lord Elgin and the Marbles*. London: Oxford University Press, 1967, 1983, 1998.

————. *That Greece Might Still Be Free: The Philhellenes in the War of Independence*. London: Oxford University Press, 1972.

————. "The Impact of Byron's Writings: An Evaluative Approach." In *Byron: Augustan and Romantic*. Ed. Andrew Rutherford. New York: St. Martin's Press, 1990.

Smiles, Samuel. *A Publisher and His Friends: Memoir and Correspondence of the Late John Murray*. 2 vols. London: J. Murray, 1881.

Soderholm, Jamès. *Fantasy, Forgery and the Byron Legend*. Lexington: University of Kentucky Press, 1974.

Stocking, Marion Kingston, *The Journals of Claire Clairmont*. Cambridge, Mass.: Harvard University Press, 1968.

————, ed. *The Clairmont Correspondence*. 2 vols. Baltimore and London: Johns Hopkins University Press, 1995.

Tomalin, Claire. *The Life and Death of Mary Wollstonecraft*. New York: Harcourt Brace Jovanovich, 1974.

————. *Shelley and His World*. New York: Scribner, 1980.

Trelawny, Edward John. *The Letters of Edward John Trelawny*. Ed. H. Buxton Forman. London: Oxford University Press, 1910.

————. *Recollections of the Last Days of Shelley and Byron*. London, 1858; reprint, Williamstown, Mass.: Corner House Publishing, 1975.

White, Newman Ivey. *Shelley*. 2 vols. New York: Alfred A. Knopf, 1947.

White, Terence de Vere. *Tom Moore: The Irish Poet*. London: Hamish Hamilton, 1977.

Wolfson, Susan J. " 'Their She Condition': Cross-Dressing and the Politics of Gender in *Don Juan*." *English Literary History*, 54 (Fall 1987).

Acknowledgments

In seven years of research and writing about Byron, my work has been made easier through the help and often the encouragement of the following people. At the New York Public Library, Carl H. Pforzheimer Library, Steven Wagner, Curator, and Doucet Devin Fisher, editor, "Shelley and His Circle" Project; Steven Crook and Philip Milito at the Berg Collection; at the J. Pierpont Morgan Library, William M. Voelkle, Marilyn Palmeri, and Carla Denison; Mark Piel, Librarian of the New York Society Library, and his staff; Clare Hills-Nova at the Institute of Fine Arts—New York University; Dan Traister and Nancy Shawcross at the Van Pelt Library, Meyer Davis Collection, University of Pennsylvania; Peter Accardo at the Houghton Library, Harvard University; Sally Brown, Elizabeth James, and Dr. Christopher Wright at the British Library. I recall with pleasure the many days spent working at John Murray, 50 Albemarle Street; the welcome of the late Jock Murray; the helpfulness of Virginia Murray and of John Murray VIII. My thanks to the Earl of Lytton and to his literary representative Gerald J. Pollinger. I owe my introduction to Melbourne House (now Dover House and the Scottish Office) to Pauline Granger and Peter Powlesland, my introduction to Burgage Manor to the hospitality of the present owner, Geoffrey Bond, Esq., Chairman of the Byron Society, and my introduction to Byron's set in Albany to the Secretary, Dr. Peter Davison, and present owner, D. P. de Laszlo. Others who guided me through the resources of their collections include Pamela Wood at Newstead Abbey; Colin Harris of the Western Manuscript Division, Bodleian Library, Oxford; Alasdair Hawkyard, archivist of Harrow School; Dr. Donatino Domini of the Biblioteca Classense, Ravenna; Bathsheba Apse, former Director, the Keats-Shelley Memorial, and Adele Chatfield-Taylor, President, the American Academy in Rome; Donald M. Nicol, former Director, the Gennadius Library in Athens.

Byron's Aberdeenshire was mapped through the guidance of Katherine and Alisdair McIntyre and Dr. Kiriakoula Solomou; in Ravenna, doors were opened by Claudia Baldazzi Gamberini and Dr. Giuliana Bruni; in Venice, Dr. Rosella Mamoli Zorzi was generous with time and counsel. Others who helped with knowledgeable advice were William Baumol, Heather Chalcroft, Rosalyn Coope, Milton Horowitz, William P. J. Jensen, Ralph Kaminsky, Mary M. Luria, Nicholas Mayhew, Jerome J. McGann, Deda Muraro, Donald Oresman, Ned Polsky, Guido Ruggiero, and Steven Rattazzi. Leslie Breed provided neighborly office space.

For many months spent in London in what Byron would call "Superexcellent" accommodations, I have countless times blessed Holland R. Melson, Jr. Timely diversion was offered by Zamira and Jonathan Benthall, Sally and Christopher Brown, Mick and Margaret Mulvahill Gold, John and Felicity Mallet, and Alessandra and Simon Wilson. Besides the care and talent they lavished on the manuscript, I'm grateful to the following—my editors, agents, and friends—who made working abroad a pleasure: Andrew Franklin; Peter and Eleo Carson; Kate Jones at Penguin UK, where I am also indebted to Gráinne Kelly and Lesley Shaw; Mary Kling; and always, Abner Stein.

At Alfred A. Knopf, my thanks to the publisher and editors, Sonny Mehta and Jordan Pavlin; to Webb Younce, Katherine Hourigan, Carol Devine Carson, and Bette Graber.

Andrew Nicholson brought his vast knowledge of Byron and his editorial judgment to his reading of the manuscript. He saved me from errors and offered valuable criticism and suggestions, most of which I've gratefully followed, except where, as Byron complained of Lady Hester Stanhope, I've shown "a disposition to argufy with him." Peter Cochran generously applied his boundless learning in matters Byronic to a corrective reading of the proofs. It's a pleasure to acknowledge my debt to him here.

At every stage of the work, I have been privileged with exceptional assistance. For special projects, I had the help of John Axcelson, Piero Brunello, Susan Katz, Christine Kelly, Reinhold C. Mueller, and Jennifer Schwartz. The first half of the book benefited from the imaginative and knowledgeable research of Dr. Christopher Fletcher, now at the British Library. For the last four years, I've relied on the myriad skills, the generosity, and the faithfulness of Dr. Corinne Abate.

Through his adolescent surrogate, Tonio Kroger, Thomas Mann declared that the artist must "die to life." With no such exalted dispensation, I've given more time and attention to the lives I've imaginatively inhabited than to those who sustain my own. For their indulgence, I'm grateful to Colin and Rachel Eisler, and to my late mother, Frances Blitzer; to Sallie Bingham, Halcyone Bohen, Frederick Brown, Celia and Henry Eisenberg, Wendy Gimbel, Carole Klein, Phyllis LaFarge, Bruni and Alfred Mayor, and Natalie Schwartzberg.

Index

PERMISSIONS ACKNOWLEDGMENTS

Grateful acknowledgment is made to the following for permission to reprint previously published and unpublished material:

John R. Murray: Excerpted material from the John Murray Archive. Reprinted by permission of John R. Murray.

The New York Public Library: Excerpts of letter from Augusta Leigh to Jane Porter. The Carl H. Pforzheimer Collection of Shelley & His Circle. The New York Public Library. Astor, Lenox and Tilden Foundations. Excerpts from the Henry Long MS diary and excerpts from the J. C. Hobhouse MS diary. Berg Collection of English and American Literature. The New York Public Library. Astor, Lenox and Tilden Foundations. Reprinted by permission of The New York Public Library.

Oxford University Press: Excerpts of poetry from *Lord Byron: The Complete Poetical Works,* Vol. I–VII, edited by Jerome J. McGann, copyright © 1980, 1981, 1986, 1991, 1993 by Oxford University Press. Reprinted by permission of Oxford University Press, Oxford, England.

Laurence Pollinger Limited: Excerpts from The Lovelace Byron Papers. The Bodleian Library. Reprinted by permission of Laurence Pollinger Limited, London, and with kind permission of the Earl of Lytton.

Random House, Inc.: Excerpt from "Letter to Lord Byron," Part II, from *W. H. Auden: Collected Poems* by W. H. Auden, copyright © 1937 by W. H. Auden. Reprinted by permission of Random House, Inc.

Nov. 23d 1814

My Love — While I write this letter
I have desired my very old & kind
friend Mr Hodgson to send you a note
which I will enclose as it contains a
piece of information that will come better from him than me — and yet not
give you less pleasure. — — —
I think of setting off for London tomorrow — where I will write again — I
am quite confused & bewildered here
with the voting & the fuss and the
crowd — to say nothing of yesterday's dinner
& meeting all one's old acquaintance the
consequence of which is that infallible
next-day's headach ever attendant upon

sincere friendship. — Here are Hobhouse and our cousin George Lamb — who called on me — & we have all voted the same way — but they say nevertheless our Man won't win — but have many votes howbeit. — Today I dine with Clarke the traveller — one of the best & goodnatured of souls — and uniformly kind to me. — When we meet I think & hope I shall make you laugh at the scene I went through — or rather which went through me — for I was quite unprepared and am not at the best of times sufficiently master of "the family shyness" to acquit myself otherwise than awkwardly on such an occasion. — — — —

friend Mr Hodgson to send you a note
which I will enclose as it contains a
piece of information that will come bet
=ter from him than me — and yet not
give you less pleasure. — — —
I think of setting off for London to=
=morrow — where I will write again — I
am quite confused & bewildered here
with the voting & the fuss and the
crowd — to say nothing of yesterday's dinner
& meeting all one's old acquaintance the
consequence of which is that infallible
next=day's headach ever attendant upon
sincere friendship. — Here are Hobhouse
and our cousin George Lamb — who called
on me — & we have all voted the
same way — but they say nevertheless
our Man won't win — but have many

votes howbeit. — Today I dine with
Clarke the traveller — one of the best
& goodnatured of souls — and uniformly
kind to me. — When we meet I
think & hope I shall make you
laugh at the scene I went through
or rather which went through me —
for I was quite unprepared and am
not at the best of times sufficiently
master of "the family shyness" to acquit
myself otherwise than awkwardly on such
an occasion. — — — — — —
Well but — sweet — Heart — do write &
love me — and regard me as thine
                    " ever & most —

P.S. Love to parents. — — — —